Street by Street

G000292415

BERKSHIRE

Enlarged areas BRACKNELL, MAIDENHEAD, NEWBURY, READING, SLOUGH, WINDSOR, WOKINGHAM

Plus Camberley, Chertsey, Egham, Frimley, Heathrow Airport, Henley-on-Thames, Marlow, Staines, Tadley, Virginia Water, Yateley

3rd edition August 2008
© Automobile Association Developments Limited 2008

Original edition printed May 2001

Enabled by Ordnance Survey® This product includes map data licensed from Ordnance Survey® with the permission of the Controller of Her Majesty's Stationery Office. © Crown copyright 2008. All rights reserved. Licence number 100021153.

The copyright in all PAF is owned by Royal Mail Group plc.

RoadPilot DRIVING TECHNOLOGY Information on fixed speed camera locations provided by RoadPilot © 2008 RoadPilot® Driving Technology.

Published by AA Publishing (a trading name of Automobile Association Developments Limited, whose registered office is Fanum House, Basing View, Basingstoke, Hampshire RG21 4EA. Registered number 1878835).

Produced by the Mapping Services Department of The Automobile Association. (A03729)

A CIP Catalogue record for this book is available from the British Library.

Printed by Oriental Press in Dubai

Ref: MX57y

Key to map pages	ii–iii
Key to map symbols	iv–1
Map pages - 1:10,000	2–15
Map pages - 1:17,500	16–103
Map pages - 1:25,000	104–151
Index – towns & villages	152
Index – streets	153–176
Index – featured places	176–180
Acknowledgements	180

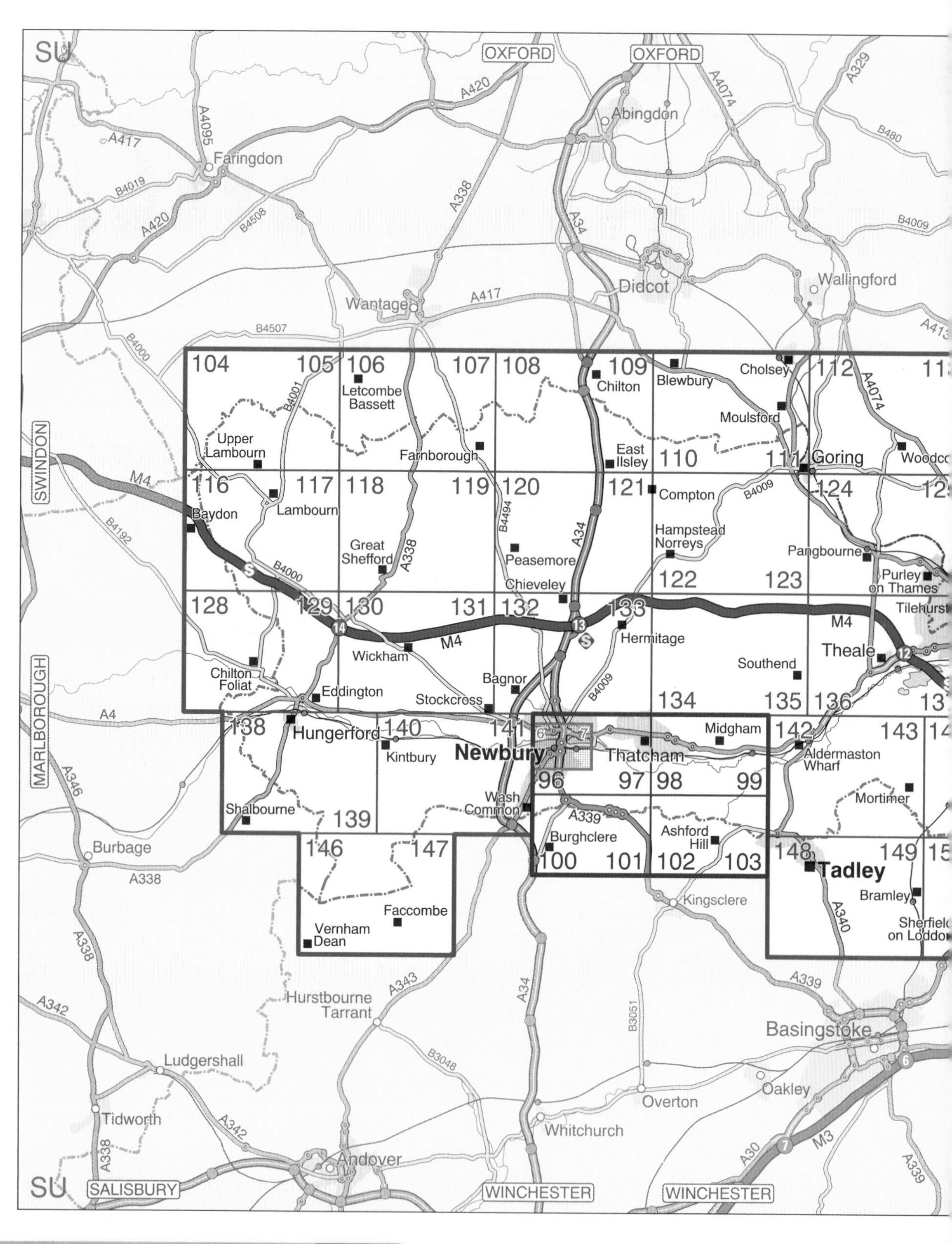

SU
OXFORD
OXFORD
A420
A417
A4095
Faringdon
B4019
A420
B4508
A338
Abingdon
A4074
A329
B480
A34
B4009
Didcot
Wallingford
Wantage
A417
B4507
B4000
SWINDON
M4
B4192
104
105
106
Letcombe Bassett
107
108
109
Chilton
Blewbury
Cholsey
112
A4074
B4001
Upper Lambourn
Farnborough
East Ilsley
110
Moulsford
111
Goring
Woodcote
116
Baydon
117
Lambourn
118
119
120
121
Compton
B4009
124
B4494
A34
Great Shefford
A338
Peasemore
Hampstead Norreys
Pangbourne
B4000
122
123
Purley on Thames
Chieveley
128
129
130
131
132
133
Tilehurst
14
M4
13
Hermitage
M4
Wickham
Theale
12
Chilton Foliat
Bagnor
Southend
Eddington
Stockcross
B4009
134
135
136
MARLBOROUGH
A4
138
Hungerford
140
141
Newbury
Midgham
142
143
Kintbury
Thatcham
Aldermaston Wharf
96
97
98
99
A346
Shalbourne
139
Wash Common
A339
Ashford Hill
Mortimer
Burghclere
146
147
100
101
102
103
148
149
Burbage
Tadley
A338
Kingsclere
Bramley
A340
Sherfield on Loddon
Faccombe
Vernham Dean
A338
A339
A343
A342
Hurstbourne Tarrant
A34
B3051
Basingstoke
B3048
Ludgershall
Oakley
6
Overton
Tidworth
A342
Whitchurch
A30
7
M3
A339
A338
Andover
SU
SALISBURY
WINCHESTER
WINCHESTER

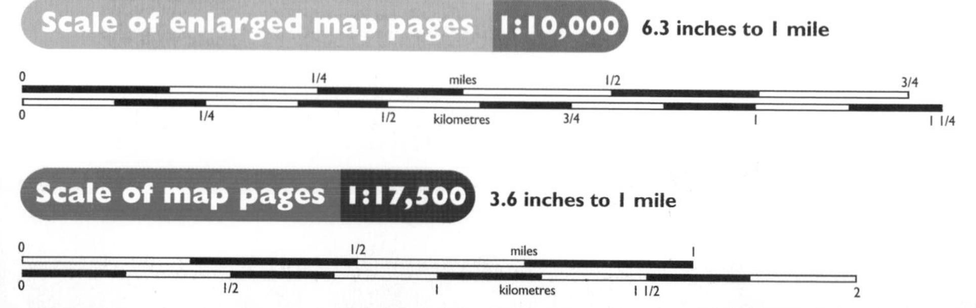

Scale of enlarged map pages 1:10,000
6.3 inches to 1 mile
0
1/4
miles
1/2
3/4
0
1/4
1/2
kilometres
3/4
1
1 1/4
Scale of map pages 1:17,500
3.6 inches to 1 mile
0
1/2
miles
1
0
1/2
1
kilometres
1 1/2
2

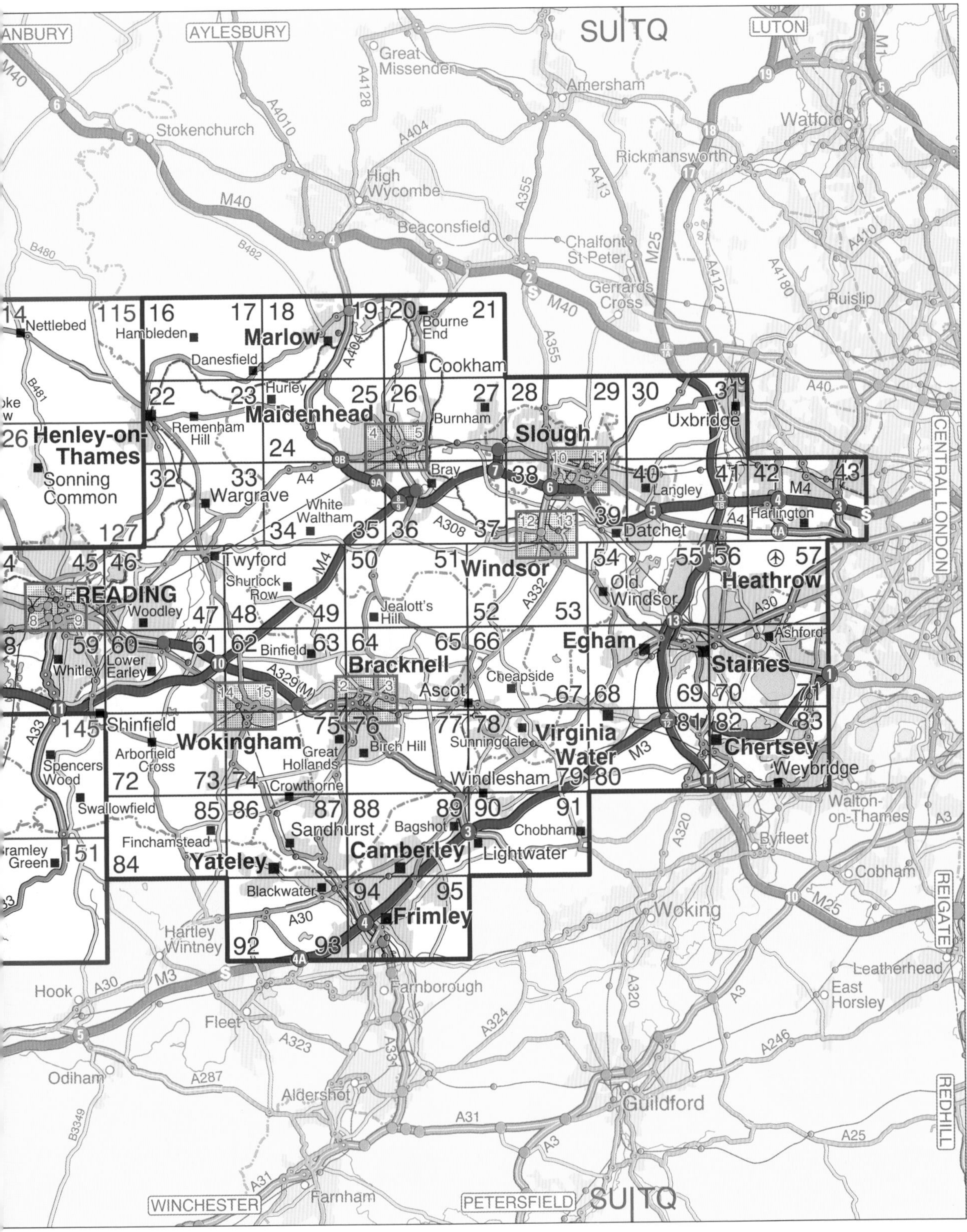

SU TQ
LUTON
ANBURY AYLESBURY

Great Missenden
Amersham
Watford
Stokenchurch
High Wycombe
Rickmansworth
Beaconsfield
Chalfont St-Peter
Gerrards Cross
Ruislip

Nettlebed | 14 | 115 | 16 | 17 | 18 | 19 | 20 | 21
Hambleden
Marlow
Danesfield
Bourne End
Cookham

22 | 23 | 25 | 26 | 27 | 28 | 29 | 30 | 31
Hurley
Maidenhead
Burnham
Slough
Uxbridge
Henley-on-Thames
Remenham Hill
24
Bray
26
32 | 33 | Langley | 40 | 41 | 42 | 43
Sonning Common
Wargrave
A4
White Waltham
Datchet
Harlington
127
34 | 35 | 36 | 37 | 38 | 39

4 | 45 | 46 | 50 | 51 | Windsor | 54 | 55 | 56 | 57
READING
Twyford
Shurlock Row
Old Windsor
Heathrow
Woodley
47 | 48 | 49 | Jealott's Hill | 52 | 53
Ashford
8 | 59 | 60 | 61 | 62 | 63 | 64 | 65 | 66 | Egham | 69 | 70 | 71
Whitley | Lower Earley
Binfield
Bracknell
Cheapside
Staines
11 | 145 | Shinfield | Ascot | 67 | 68 | 81 | 82 | 83
Spencers Wood
Arborfield Cross
14 | 15 | 75 | 76 | 77 | 78 | Virginia Water | 79 | 80 | Chertsey
Wokingham
Great Hollands
Birch Hill
Sunningdale
Weybridge
72 | 73 | 74 | Crowthorne | Windlesham
Swallowfield
85 | 86 | 87 | 88 | 89 | 90 | 91
Finchampstead
Sandhurst
Bagshot
Chobham
ramley Green | 151 | 84 | Yateley | Camberley | Lightwater
Blackwater | 94 | 95
Hartley Wintney | A30 | Frimley
92 | 93

Hook | M3 | Farnborough
Fleet
Odiham | A287 | Aldershot | A31 | Guildford
Farnham
WINCHESTER | PETERSFIELD | SU TQ

Walton-on-Thames
Cobham
Byfleet
Woking
Leatherhead
East Horsley

CENTRAL LONDON
REIGATE
REDHILL

National Grid references are shown on the map frame of Each Page.
Red figures denote the 100 km square and the blue figures the 1km square.

Example, page 6 : St John the Evangelist Infant School **447 166**

The reference can also be written using the National Grid two-letter prefix
shown on this page, where 4 and 1 are replaced by SU to give SU4766

2.5 inches to 1 mile | **Scale of map pages 1:25,000**

0 | 1/2 | miles | 1 | 1 1/2
0 | 1/2 | 1 | kilometres | 1 1/2 | 2

iv

Junction 9	Motorway & junction	⊖	Underground station
Services	Motorway service area	⊖	Light railway & station
	Primary road single/dual carriageway	+++++++++++	Preserved private railway
Services	Primary road service area	*LC*	Level crossing
	A road single/dual carriageway	•—•—•—•—•	Tramway
	B road single/dual carriageway	- - - - - - -	Ferry route
	Other road single/dual carriageway	··················	Airport runway
	Minor/private road, access may be restricted	- · - · - · -	County, administrative boundary
← ←	One-way street	⟁⟁⟁⟁⟁⟁	Mounds
	Pedestrian area	◀151	Page continuation 1:25,000
================	Track or footpath	93	Page continuation 1:17,500
	Road under construction	7	Page continuation to enlarged scale 1:10,000
⊏- - - -⊐	Road tunnel		River/canal, lake
30	Speed camera site (fixed location) with speed limit in mph		Aqueduct, lock, weir
V	Speed camera site (fixed location) with variable speed limit	465 ▲ Winter Hill	Peak (with height in metres)
40	Section of road with two or more fixed camera sites; speed limit in mph or variable		Beach
50⟩→ ←50⟩	Average speed (SPECS™) camera system with speed limit in mph		Woodland
P P+🚌	Parking, Park & Ride		Park
🚌	Bus/coach station	↑ ↑ ↑	Cemetery
	Railway & main railway station		Built-up area
	Railway & minor railway station		

	Industrial/business building		Abbey, cathedral or priory
	Leisure building		Castle
	Retail building		Historic house or building
	Other building	Wakehurst Place NT	National Trust property
	City wall		Museum or art gallery
A&E	Hospital with 24-hour A&E department		Roman antiquity
PO	Post Office		Ancient site, battlefield or monument
	Public library		Industrial interest
i	Tourist Information Centre		Garden
i	Seasonal Tourist Information Centre		Garden Centre Garden Centre Association Member
	Petrol station, 24 hour Major suppliers only		Garden Centre Wyevale Garden Centre
†	Church/chapel		Arboretum
	Public toilet, with facilities for the less able		Farm or animal centre
PH	Public house AA recommended		Zoological or wildlife collection
	Restaurant AA inspected		Bird collection
Madeira Hotel	Hotel AA inspected		Nature reserve
	Theatre or performing arts centre		Aquarium
	Cinema	V	Visitor or heritage centre
	Golf course		Country park
▲	Camping AA inspected		Cave
	Caravan site AA inspected		Windmill
	Camping & caravan site AA inspected		Distillery, brewery or vineyard
	Theme park	•	Other place of interest

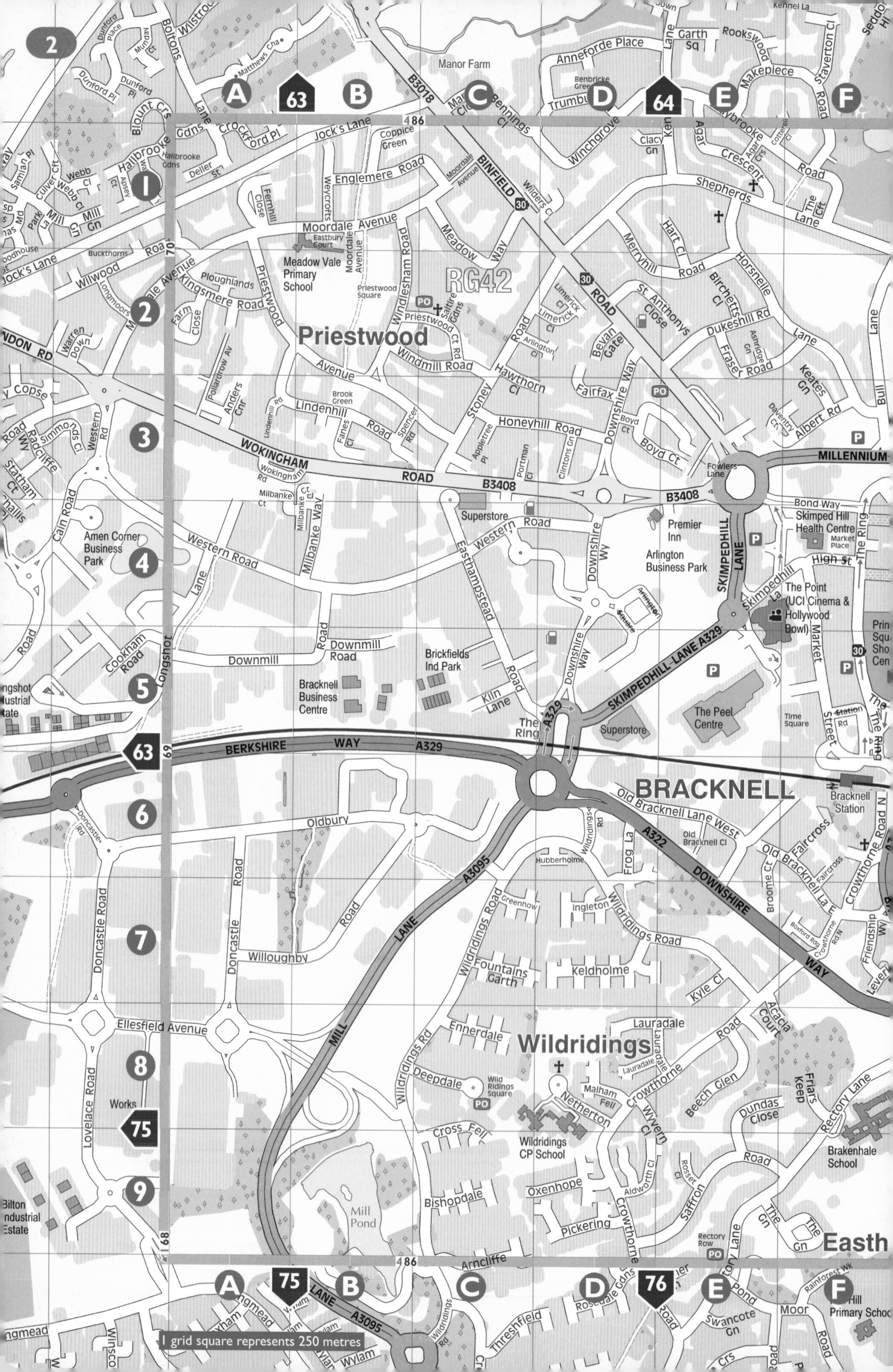
2
63
64
75
76
A
B
C
D
E
F
1
2
3
4
5
6
7
8
9
486
70
69
68
Manor Farm
Anneforde Place
Garth Sq
Rookswood
Makepiece
Staverton Cl
Binfield Road
B3018
Jock's Lane
Crockford Pl
Coppice Green
Englemere Road
Moordale Avenue
Hallbrooke Gdns
Webb Cl
Mill Gn
Wilwood Road
Buckthorns
Meadow Vale Primary School
Eastbury Court
Windlesham Road
Meadow Way
RG42
Priestwood
Priestwood Square
Kingsmere Road
Ploughlands
Farm Close
Windmill Road
Hawthorn Cl
Stoney Road
Honeyhill Road
Lindenhill Road
Brook Green
Fanes Cl
Spencer Rd
Bevan Gate
Fairfax
Downshire Way
Boyd Ct
St Anthonys Close
Merryhill Road
Hart Cl
Horsneile Lane
Birchetts Cl
Dukeshill Rd
Fraser Road
Keates Gn
Albert Rd
Shepherds Lane
Winchgrove
Agar Crescent
Western Road
Wokingham Road
B3408
Millennium
Superstore
Premier Inn
Arlington Business Park
Skimpedhill Lane
Skimped Hill Health Centre
Market Place
High St
The Ring
The Point (UCI Cinema & Hollywood Bowl)
Market Street
Amen Corner Business Park
Cain Road
Radcliffe Wy
Statham Ct
Copse
Easthampstead Road
Milbanke Way
Downmill Road
Cookham Road
Longshot
Brickfields Ind Park
Bracknell Business Centre
Kiln Lane
The Peel Centre
Time Square
Station Rd
Skimpedhill Lane A329
A329
Berkshire Way A329
BRACKNELL
Bracknell Station
Old Bracknell Lane West
Old Bracknell Cl
Old Bracknell La E
A322 Downshire Way
Faircross
Crowthorne Road N
Broome Ct
Friendship Wy
Oldbury
Doncastle Road
Willoughby
Ellesfield Avenue
Lovelace Road
Works
Bilton Industrial Estate
A3095
Mill Lane
Wildridings Road
Wildridings
Hubberholme
Frog La
Greenhow
Ingleton
Fountains Garth
Keldholme
Kyle Cl
Acacia Court
Ennerdale
Lauradale
Deepdale
Wild Ridings Square
PO
Netherton
Malham Fell
Crowthorne Road
Beech Glen
Wyvern Cl
Friars Keep
Rectory Lane
Dundas Close
Brakenhale School
Cross Fell
Wildridings CP School
Oxenhope
Aldworth Cl
Rosset Cl
Saffron Road
Bishopdale
Mill Pond
Pickering
Recktory Row
The Gn
Easth
Arncliffe
Rosedale Gdns
Threshfield
Swancote Gn
Pond
Moor Road
Rainforest Wk
Primary Schoo
Wylam
1 grid square represents 250 metres

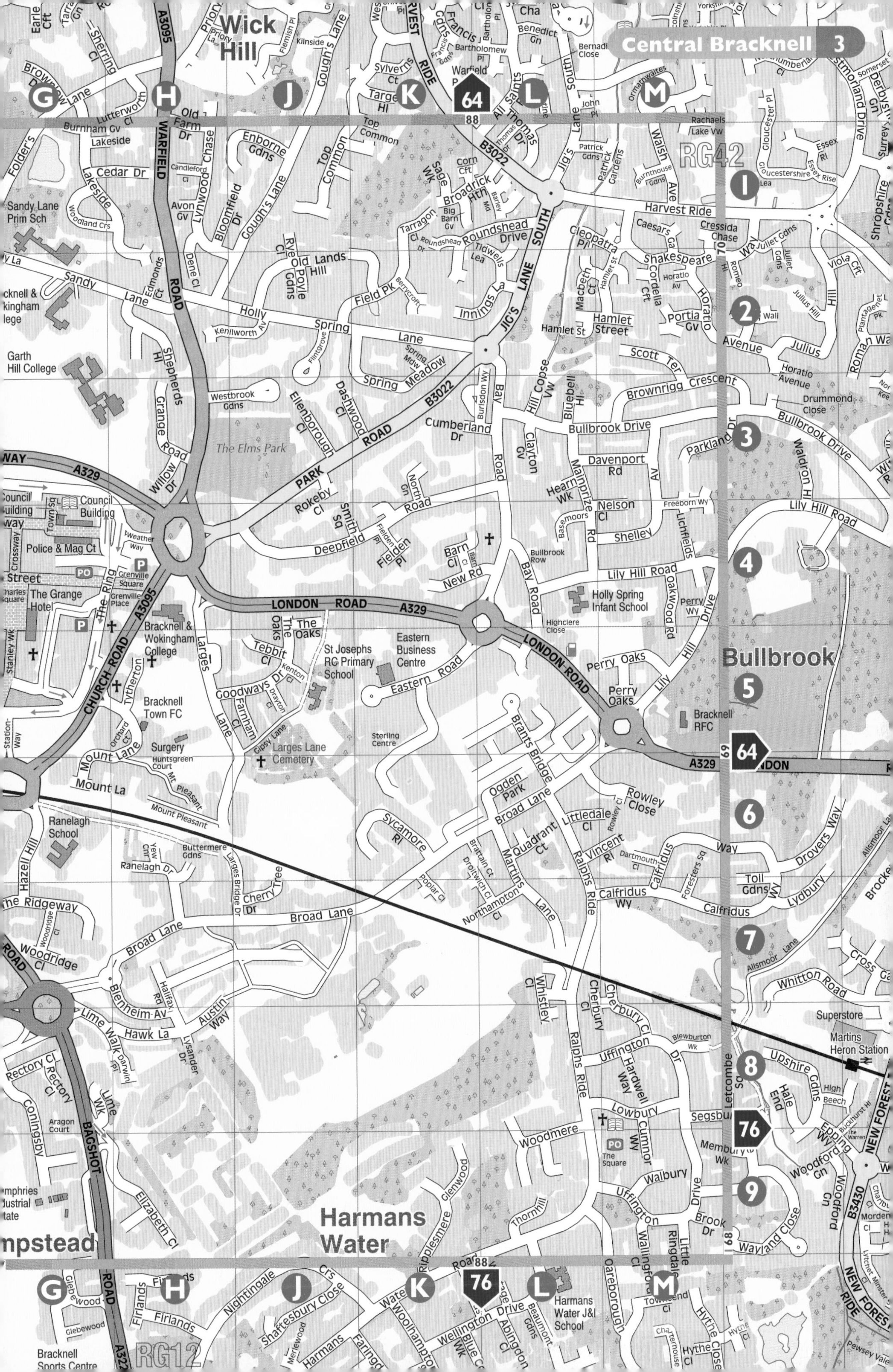
Wick Hill
Bullbrook
Harmans Water
RG42
RG12
The Elms Park
Garth Hill College
Sandy Lane Prim Sch
Bracknell & Wokingham College
Bracknell Town FC
Ranelagh School
Holly Spring Infant School
St Josephs RC Primary School
Eastern Business Centre
Larges Lane Cemetery
Bracknell RFC
Martins Heron Station
Superstore
Harmans Water J&I School
Bracknell Sports Centre
Council Building
Police & Mag Ct
The Grange Hotel
LONDON ROAD
A329
A3095
B3022
PARK ROAD
JIG'S LANE SOUTH
WARFIELD ROAD
CHURCH ROAD
BAGSHOT ROAD
NEW FOREST RIDE
B3430
Harvest Ride
Bullbrook Drive
Lily Hill Road
Broad Lane
Ralphs Ride
Calfridus Wy
Holly Spring Lane
Deepfield Road
Eastern Road
Brownrigg Crescent
Horatio Avenue
Whitton Road
Uffington Dr
Lowbury
Woodmere
Wayland Close
Wellington Drive
Nightingale Crs
Shaftesbury Close
Firlands
Glebewood

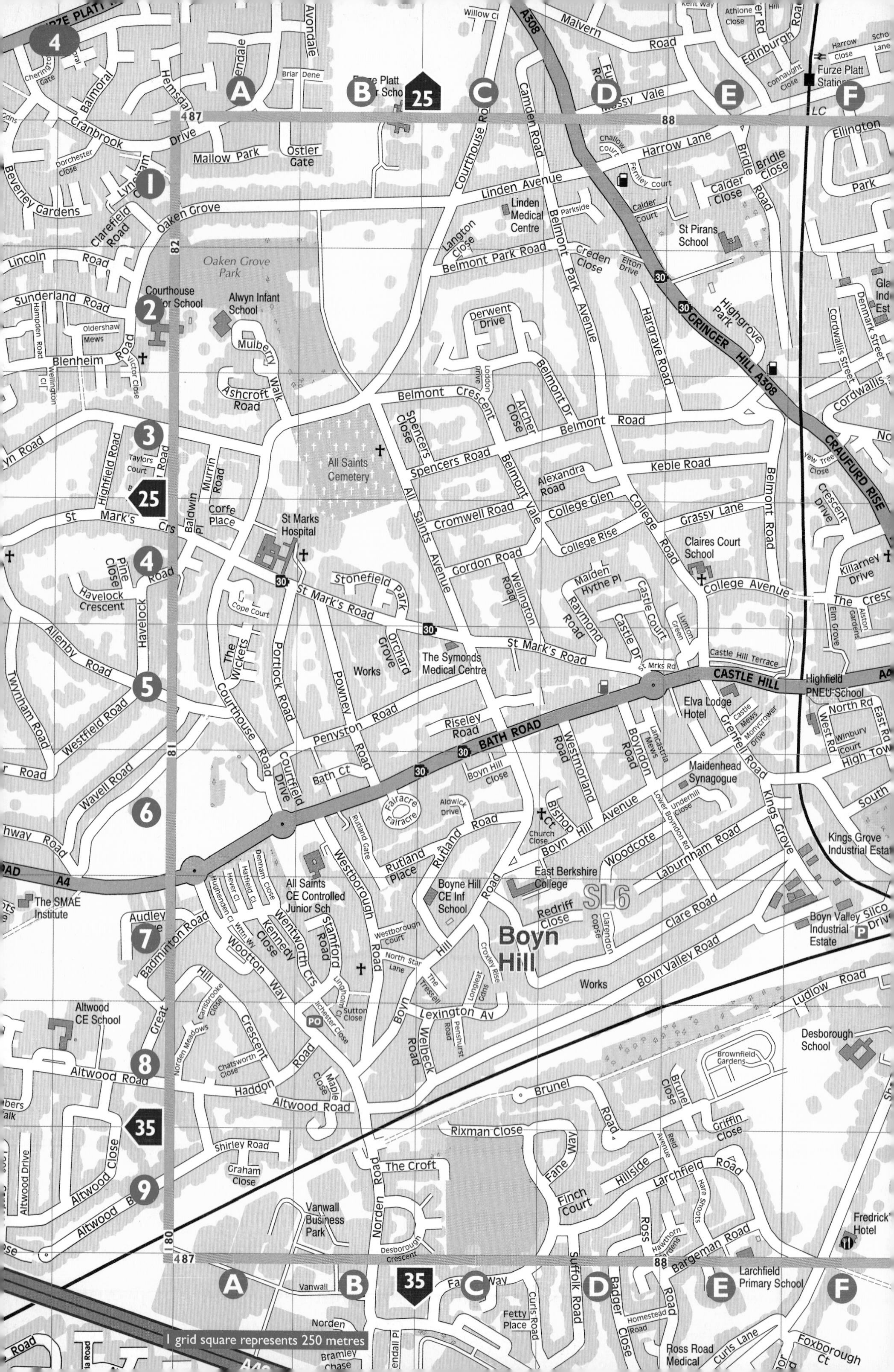

4
25
35
A
B
C
D
E
F
1
2
3
4
5
6
7
8
9
487
88
82
81
80
Furze Platt
Malvern Road
Edinburgh Road
Furze Platt Station
Mossy Vale
Cranbrook Drive
Mallow Park
Ostler Gate
Briar Dene
Courthouse Road
Camden Road
Harrow Lane
Bridle Close
Bridle Road
Ellington Park
Linden Avenue
Linden Medical Centre
Calder Close
Oaken Grove
Oaken Grove Park
Beverley Gardens
Clarefield Road
Lincoln Road
Sunderland Road
Courthouse Junior School
Alwyn Infant School
Oldershaw Mews
Blenheim Road
Victor Close
Mulberry Walk
Ashcroft Road
Belmont Park Road
Belmont Park Avenue
Creden Close
Elton Drive
Hargrave Road
St Pirans School
Highgrove Park
GRINGER HILL A308
Derwent Drive
Belmont Crescent
Belmont Dr
Belmont Road
Archer Close
Spencers Close
Spencers Road
All Saints Cemetery
Keble Road
Alexandra Road
Cromwell Road
College Glen
College Rise
College Road
Grassy Lane
Belmont Road
CRAUFURD RISE
Crescent Drive
Killarney Drive
Cordwallis Street
Denmark Street
Taylors Court
Highfield Road
Murrin Road
Baldwin Pl
Corfe Place
St Mark's Crs
St Marks Hospital
Pine Close
Havelock Road
Havelock Crescent
Allenby Road
Stonefield Park
Gordon Road
Wellington Road
Belmont Vale
All Saints Avenue
Maiden Hythe Pl
Raymond Road
Castle Court
Castle Dr
Claires Court School
College Avenue
St Mark's Road
Cope Court
The Wickets
Portlock Road
Orchard Grove
The Symonds Medical Centre
Works
Pownley Road
CASTLE HILL
Castle Hill Terrace
Highfield PNEU School
Elva Lodge Hotel
Twynham Road
Westfield Road
Courthouse Road
Penyston Road
Riseley Road
BATH ROAD
Westmorland Road
Boyndon Road
Lancastria Mews
Grenfell Road
Maidenhead Synagogue
Kings Grove
North Rd
West Rd
Winbury Court
High Town
Wavell Road
Courtfield Drive
Bath Ct
Fairacre
Boyn Hill Close
Aldwick Drive
Bishop Ct
Boyn Hill Avenue
Lower Boyndon Rd
Underhill Close
Laburnham Road
Woodcote
Kings Grove Industrial Estate
A4
Rutland Gate
Rutland Place
Rutland Road
Church Close
East Berkshire College
The SMAE Institute
Audley
Denham Close
Hatfield Cl
Hever Cl
Hughenden Cl
Wentworth Crs
All Saints CE Controlled Junior Sch
Westborough Road
Boyne Hill CE Inf School
Redriff Close
SL6
Clare Road
Clarendon Copse
Badminton Road
Wootton Way
Kennedy Close
Stamford Road
Westborough Court
North Star Lane
The Tressell
Boyn Hill
Croxley Rise
Boyn Hill
Boyn Valley Road
Boyn Valley Industrial Estate
Silco Drive
Works
Ludlow Road
Altwood CE School
Great Hill Crescent
Carisbrooke Close
Norden Meadows
Sutton Close
Ilchester Close
Lingholm Cl
PO
Longleat Gdns
Lexington Av
Penshurst Road
Welbeck Road
Desborough School
Altwood Road
Chatsworth Close
Haddon Road
Maple Close
Altwood Road
Brunel Road
Brunel Close
Brownfield Gardens
Griffin Close
Rixman Close
Fane Way
Reid Avenue
Altwood Drive
Altwood Close
Shirley Road
Graham Close
Altwood Bailey
The Croft
Norden Road
Vanwall Business Park
Desborough Crescent
Finch Court
Hillside
Larchfield Road
Hare Shoots
Ross Road
Hawthorn Gardens
Bargeman Road
Fredrick Hotel
Larchfield Primary School
Vanwall
Fane Way
Fetty Place
Curls Road
Suffolk Road
Badger Close
Homestead Road
Ross Road Medical
Curls Lane
Foxborough Ct
Norden
Bramley Chase
1 grid square represents 250 metres

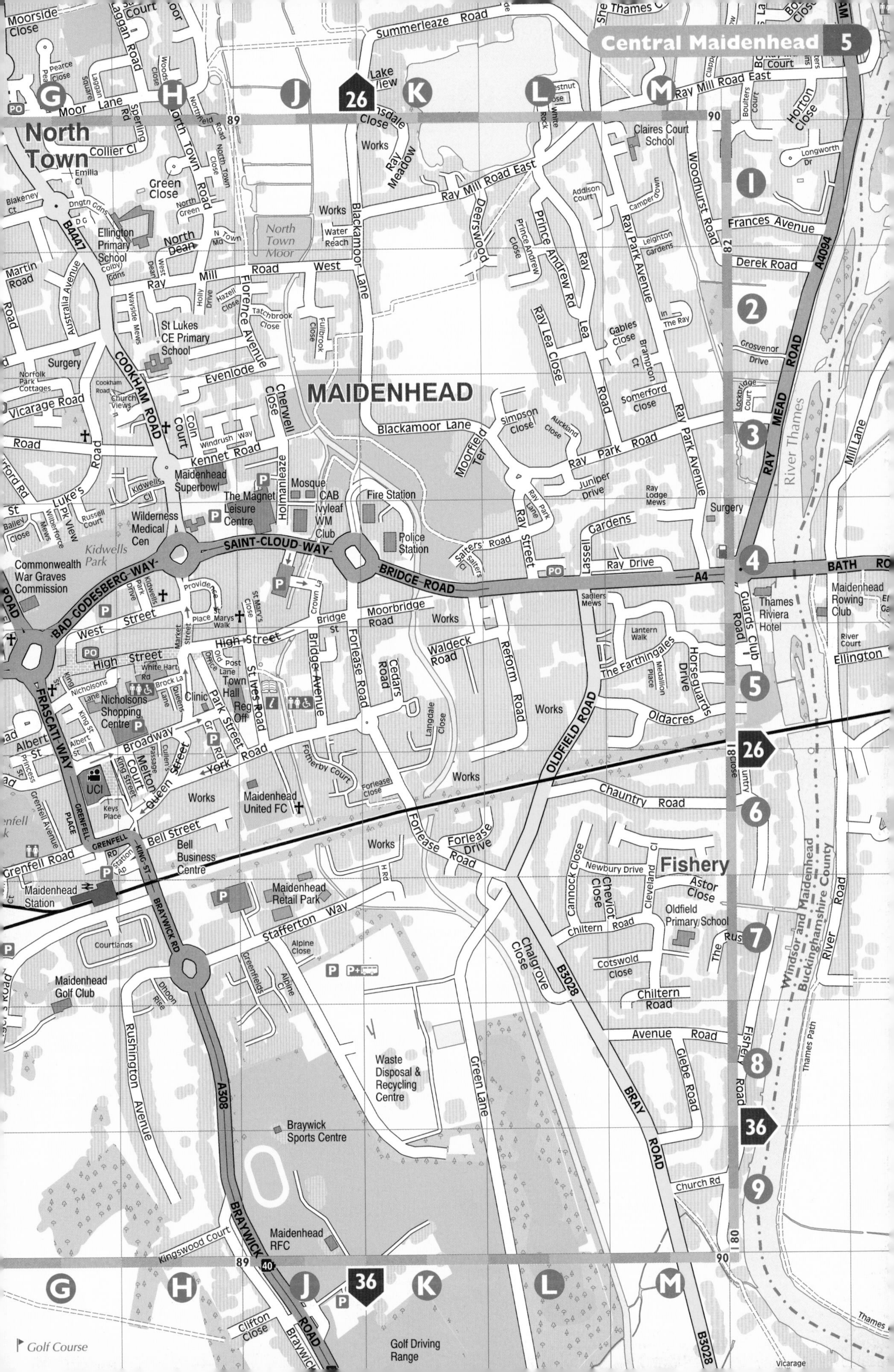
North Town
MAIDENHEAD
Fishery
Moor Lane
North Town Road
Ray Mill Road West
Ray Mill Road East
Blackamoor Lane
Cookham Road
Saint-Cloud-Way
Bridge Road
Bad-Godesberg-Way
Frascati-Way
Oldfield Road
Bray Road
Braywick Road
Ray Mead Road
Ray Park Avenue
Ray Park Road
River Thames
Maidenhead Station
Nicholsons Shopping Centre
Maidenhead Retail Park
Maidenhead Golf Club
Braywick Sports Centre
Maidenhead RFC
Waste Disposal & Recycling Centre
Golf Driving Range
Windsor and Maidenhead
Buckinghamshire County
Thames Path
Golf Course

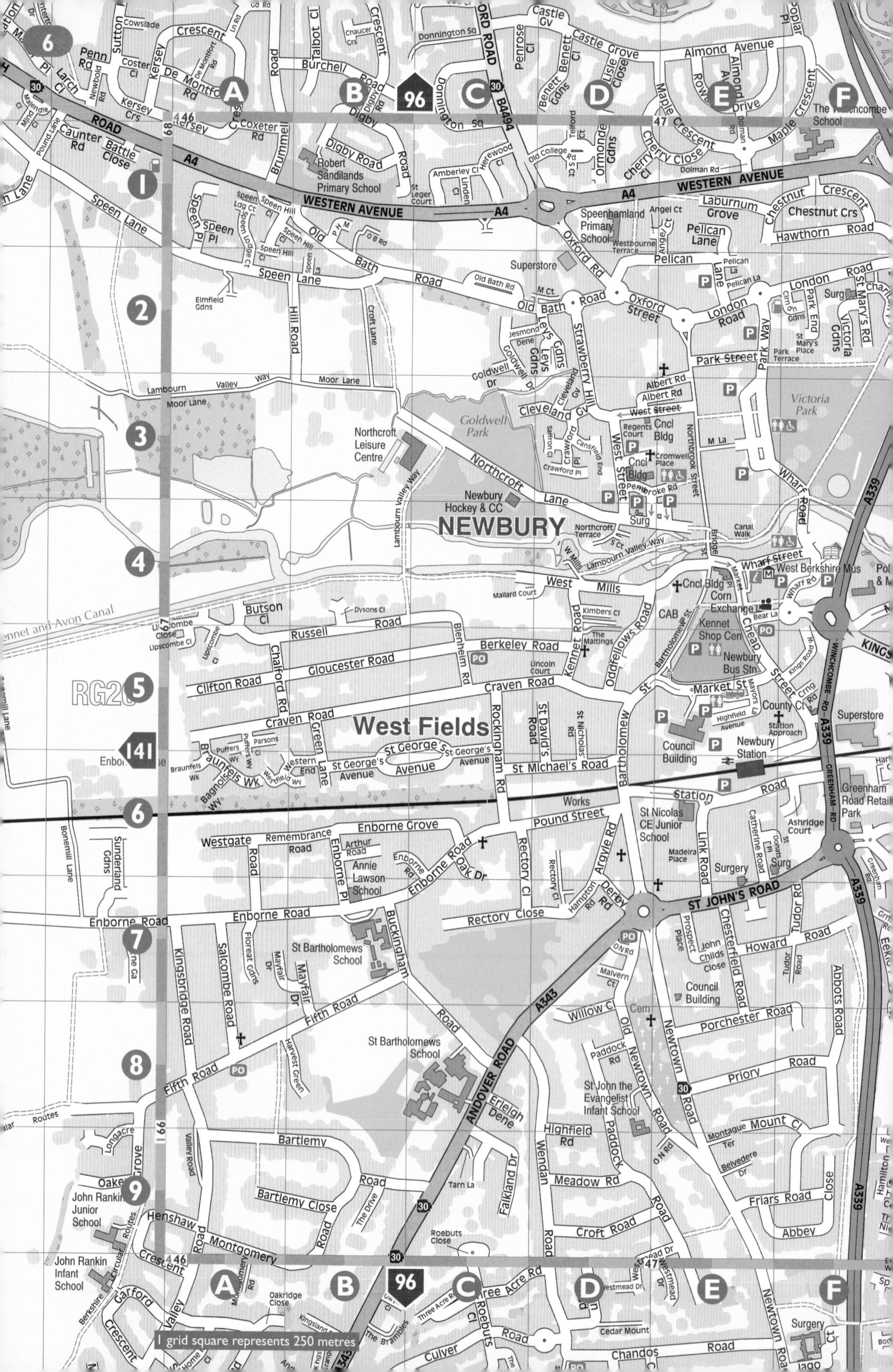

6
96
141
NEWBURY
West Fields
RG20
A
B
C
D
E
F
1
2
3
4
5
6
7
8
9
I grid square represents 250 metres
Western Avenue
Road
A4
B4494
Speen Lane
Bath Road
Old Bath Road
Oxford Road
Oxford Street
London Road
Park Street
Park Way
Pelican Lane
Laburnum Grove
Chestnut Crescent
Chestnut Crs
Hawthorn Road
Almond Avenue
Almond Drive
Maple Crescent
Cherry Close
Castle Grove
Donnington Sq
Digby Road
Burchell Road
Chaucer Crescent
Talbot Cl
Brummell Road
Crescent
De Montfort Rd
Kersey Crescent
Coxeter Rd
Battle Close
Caunter Rd
Penn Rd
Sutton Rd
Larch Cl
Pound Lane
Speen Pl
Speen Hill
Speen Hill Cl
Elmfield Gdns
Hill Road
Croft Lane
Lambourn Valley Way
Moor Lane
Robert Sandilands Primary School
Speenhamland Primary School
Westbourne Terrace
Angel Ct
Superstore
The Winchcombe School
Dolman Rd
Ormonde Gdns
Telford Ct
Old College Rd
Amberley Cl
Herewood Cl
Linden
St Leger Court
Victoria Park
Victoria Gdns
St Mary's Rd
Park End
Park Terrace
St Mary's Place
Wharf Road
Wharf Street
West Berkshire Mus
Canal Walk
Northcroft Leisure Centre
Goldwell Park
Northcroft Lane
Newbury Hockey & CC
Northcroft Terrace
Lambourn Valley Way
Strawberry Hill
Cleveland Gv
Leys Gdns
Jesmond Dene
Goldwell Dr
Saffron Cl
Crawford Pl
Cansfield End
West Street
Albert Rd
Regents Court
Cncl Bldg
Cromwell Place
Pembroke Rd
Northbrook Street
Surg
Bridge St
Market Pl
Cncl Bldg
Corn Exchange
Kennet Shop Cen
Newbury Bus Stn
Market St
Mayors La
Cheap Street
Bear La
CAB
Kings Road W
County Cl
Station Approach
Newbury Station
Council Building
Highfield Avenue
Superstore
Greenham Road Retail Park
Ashridge Court
WINCHCOMBE RD A339
GREENHAM RD
A339
West Mills
Mallard Court
Kimbers Cl
The Maltings
Oddfellows Road
Kennet Road
Bartholomew St
Kennet and Avon Canal
Butson Cl
Dysons Cl
Russell Road
Lipscombe Close
Lipscombe Cl
Berkeley Road
Blenheim Rd
Gloucester Road
Clifton Road
Chalford Rd
Craven Road
Lincoln Court
Green Lane
St George's Avenue
Rockingham Rd
St David's Road
St Nicholas' Rd
St Michael's Road
Bartholomew Street
Puffers Wy
Parsons Cl
Braunfels Wk
Bagnols Wy
Western End
Westfield Wy
Works
Station Road
St Nicolas CE Junior School
Madeira Place
Link Road
Catherine Road
St Donats Pl
Surgery
Pound Street
Argyle Rd
Derby Rd
Hampton Rd
Rectory Cl
Rectory Close
Enborne Grove
Westgate Road
Remembrance Road
Arthur Road
Enborne Pl
Enborne Road
Oak Dr
Annie Lawson School
Sunderland Gdns
Bonemill Lane
St John's Road
Prospect Place
John Childs Close
Chesterfield Road
Howard Road
Tudor Road
Council Building
Abbots Road
Porchester Road
Priory Road
Montague Ter
Mount Cl
Belvedere Dr
Friars Road
Abbey Close
Kingsbridge Road
Salcombe Road
Floreat Gdns
Mayfair Dr
St Bartholomews School
Buckingham Road
Fifth Road
Harvest Green
Andover Road
A343
Erleigh Dene
Willow Cl
Malvern Ct
Cem
Old Newtown Road
Newtown Road
Paddock Rd
St John the Evangelist Infant School
Highfield Rd
Meadow Rd
Wendan Road
Croft Road
Falkland Dr
Tarn La
The Drive
Bartlemy Road
Bartlemy Close
Longacre
Grove
Oaken
Valley Road
Routes
John Rankin Junior School
John Rankin Infant School
Circular Routes
Henshaw Crescent
Montgomery Road
Garford Crescent
Berkshire
Oakridge Close
Roebuts Close
Three Acre Rd
Westmead Dr
Cedar Mount
Chandos Road
Culver Road
The Brambles
Kingsland
Surgery
PO
P
30
46
47
66
67
68

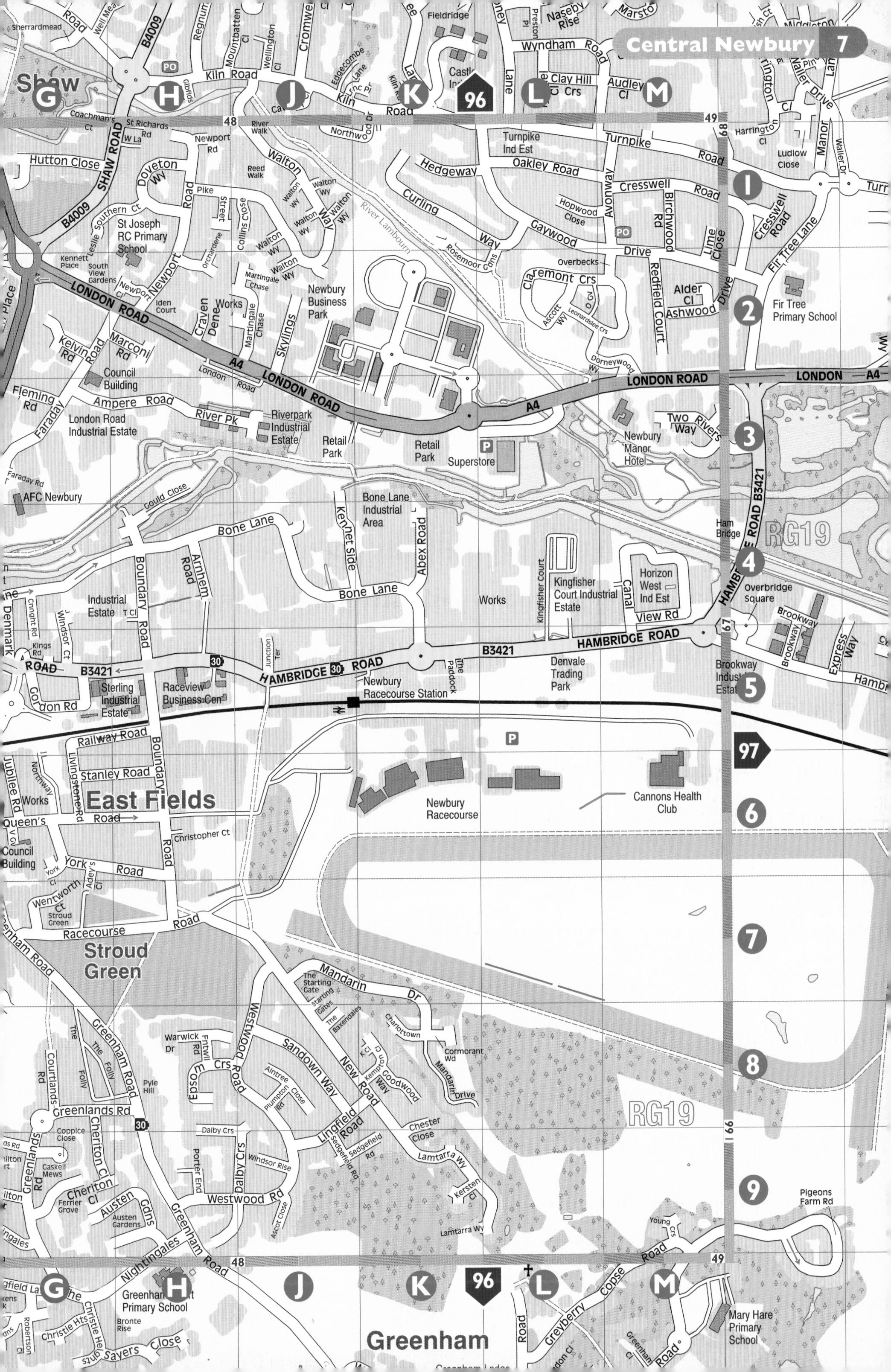
Shaw
Kiln Road
Wyndham Road
Turnpike Road
Oakley Road
Hedgeway
Curling Way
Gaywood Drive
Cresswell Road
Avonway
Birchwood Rd
Redfield Court
Fir Tree Lane
Fir Tree Primary School
SHAW ROAD
B4009
Hutton Close
Doveton Wy
Newport Rd
St Joseph RC Primary School
LONDON ROAD
A4
Newbury Business Park
Walton Way
Craven Dene
Skyllings
Marconi Rd
Kelvin Rd
Council Building
Ampere Road
London Road Industrial Estate
Riverpark Industrial Estate
Retail Park
Superstore
Newbury Manor Hotel
Two Rivers Way
AFC Newbury
Gould Close
Bone Lane
Bone Lane Industrial Area
Kennet Side
Abex Road
Works
Kingfisher Court Industrial Estate
Horizon West Ind Est
Canal View Rd
HAMBRIDGE ROAD
B3421
Ham Bridge
RG19
Overbridge Square
Brookway
Express Way
Boundary Road
Arnhem Road
Industrial Estate
Sterling Industrial Estate
Raceview Business Cen
Newbury Racecourse Station
Denvale Trading Park
Brookway Industrial Estate
Railway Road
Stanley Road
East Fields
Queen's Road
York Road
Racecourse Road
Stroud Green
Newbury Racecourse
Cannons Health Club
Mandarin Dr
Greenham Road
Sandown Way
New Road
Westwood Road
Lingfield Road
Greenlands Rd
Cheriton Cl
Nightingales
Pigeons Farm Rd
Greenham Primary School
Greenham
Mary Hare Primary School
Greyberry Copse Road
96
97
G H J K L M
1 2 3 4 5 6 7 8 9

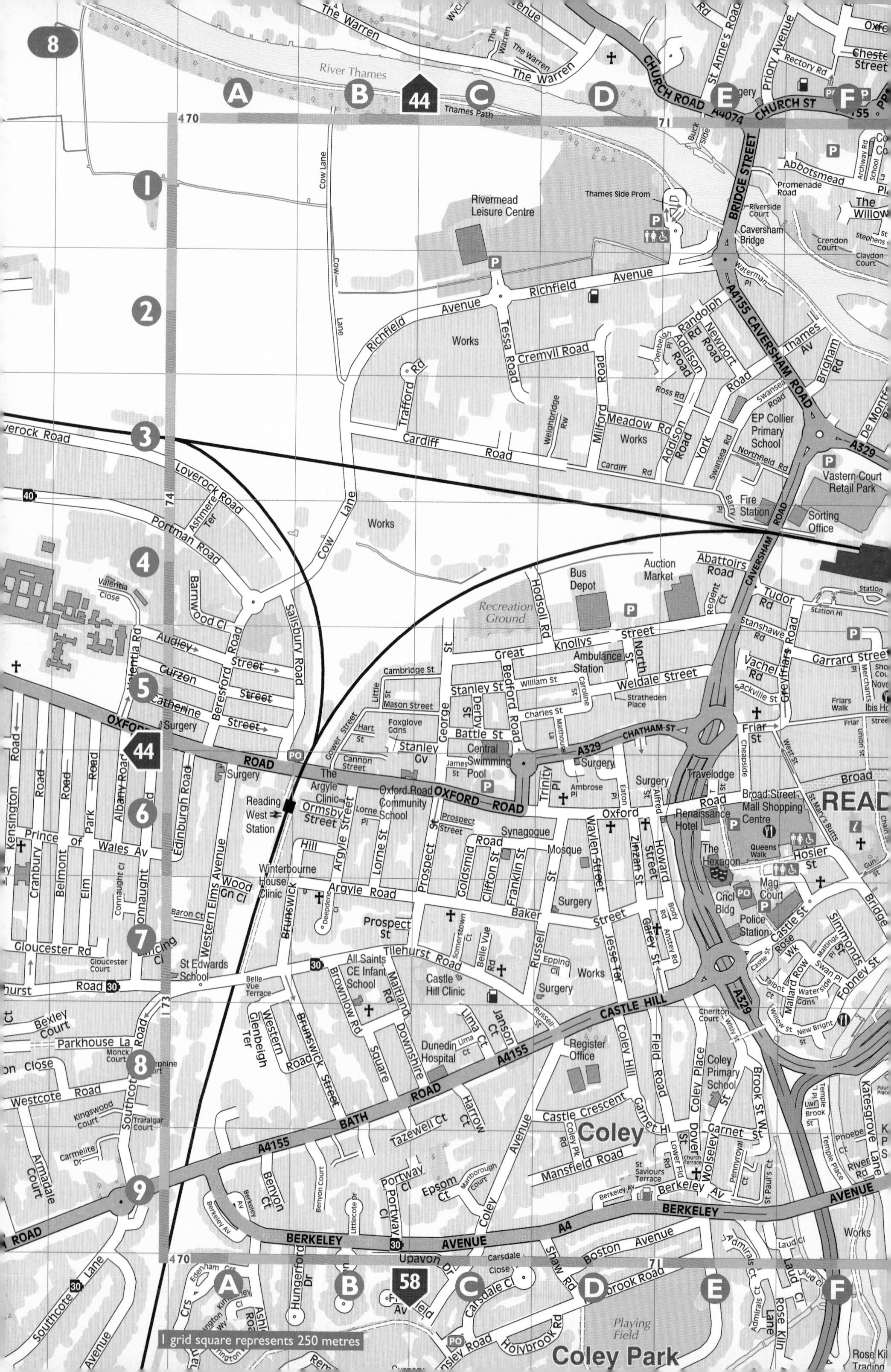

8
44
58
River Thames
The Warren
Thames Path
Church Road
A4074
Church St
St Anne's Road
Priory Avenue
Rectory Rd
Chester Street
Bridge Street
Buck Side
Abbotsmead
Promenade Road
Riverside Court
Caversham Bridge
Crendon Court
Claydon Court
The Willows
Thames Side Prom
Rivermead Leisure Centre
Cow Lane
Richfield Avenue
Tessa Road
Works
Cremyll Road
Trafford Rd
Milford Road
Weighbridge Rw
Randolph Rd
Addison Road
Newport Road
A4155 Caversham Road
Thames Av
Brigham Rd
Ross Rd
Meadow Rd
Cardiff Road
York Road
Swansea Rd
Northfield Rd
EP Collier Primary School
A329
De Montfort
Vastern Court Retail Park
Fire Station
Sorting Office
Barry Pl
Loverock Road
Ashmere Ter
Portman Road
Valentia Close
Barnwood Cl
Salisbury Road
Beresford Road
Audley Street
Curzon Street
Catherine Street
Oxford Road
Surgery
Hodsoll Rd
Bus Depot
Auction Market
Abattoirs Road
Regent Ct
Tudor Rd
Station Hl
Recreation Ground
Great Knollys Street
North St
Ambulance Station
Stanshawe Rd
Vachel Rd
Greyfriars Road
Garrard Street
Cambridge St
Little St
Mason Street
Stanley St
Derby St
Bedford Road
William St
Caroline St
Weldale Street
Stratheden Place
Sackville St
Friars Walk
Charles St
Battle St
Chatham St
Friar St
Gower Street
Hart St
Foxglove Gdns
Stanley Gv
George St
Central Swimming Pool
Cannon Street
The Argyle Clinic
Oxford Road Community School
James St
Reading West Station
Ormsby Street
Lorne Pl
Prospect Street
Trinity Pl
Ambrose Pl
Eaton Pl
Alfred St
Travelodge
Cheapside
West St
Broad Street Mall Shopping Centre
Broad
READ
Renaissance Hotel
St Mary's Butts
Synagogue
Mosque
Waylen Street
Zinzan St
Howard Street
The Hexagon
Queens Walk
Hosier St
Kensington Road
Prince of Wales Av
Cranbury Road
Belmont Road
Elm Road
Park Road
Albany Road
Edinburgh Road
Western Elms Avenue
Wood Gn Cl
Winterbourne House Clinic
Argyle Street
Hill
Lorne St
Argyle Road
Prospect St
Goldsmid Road
Clifton St
Franklin St
Baker Street
Mag Court
Cncl Bldg
Police Station
Castle St
Connaught Cl
Connaught Rd
Baron Ct
Brunswick Hill
Deepdene Cl
Somerstown Ct
Belle Vue Rd
Russell St
Garey St
Anstey Rd
Body Rd
Simmonds St
Rose Wk
Maltings Pl
Swan Pl
Gloucester Rd
Gloucester Court
Lancing Cl
St Edwards School
Belle Vue Terrace
Tilehurst Road
All Saints CE Infant School
Maitland Rd
Brownlow Rd
Castle Hill Clinic
Epping Cl
Jesse Ter
Castle Hill
Mallard Row
Waterside Gdns
Fobney St
Talbot Ct
Willow St
New Bright St
Bexley Court
Parkhouse La
Southcote Road
Monck Court
Glenbeigh Ter
Western Road
Brunswick Street
Downshire Square
Lima Ct
Janson Ct
Dunedin Hospital
Register Office
Coley Hill
Field Road
Cheriton Court
Coley Place
Coley Primary School
Brook St W
Westcote Road
Kingswood Court
Trafalgar Court
Armadale Court
Carmelite Dr
Bath Road
A4155
Tazewell Ct
Harrow Ct
Castle Crescent
Coley Pk Rd
Coley
Garnet Hl
Garnet St
Dover St
Wolseley St
Pennyroyal Ct
St Paul's Ct
Mansfield Road
St Saviours Terrace
Lower Fld
Coley Avenue
Katesgrove Lane
Temple Place
Phoebe Ct
River Rd
Benyon Ct
Benyon Court
Littlecote Dr
Portway Cl
Epsom Ct
Marlborough Court
Berkeley Av
Berkeley Avenue
A4
Laud Cl
Admirals Ct
Boston Avenue
Upavon Dr
Carsdale Close
Carsdale Cl
Shaw Rd
Holybrook Road
Hungerford Dr
Southcote Lane
Avenue
Playing Field
Coley Park
Rose Kiln Lane
1 grid square represents 250 metres

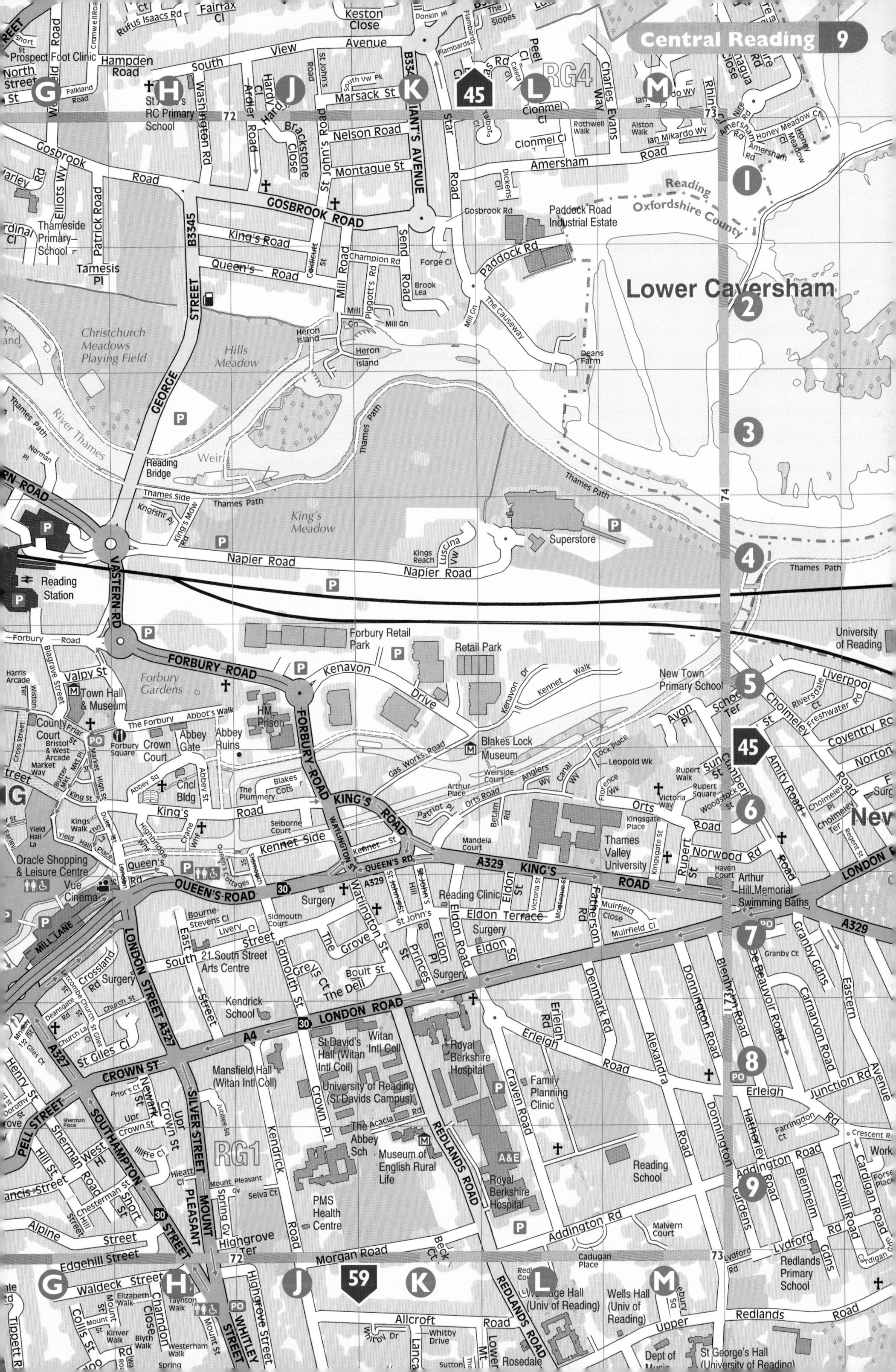

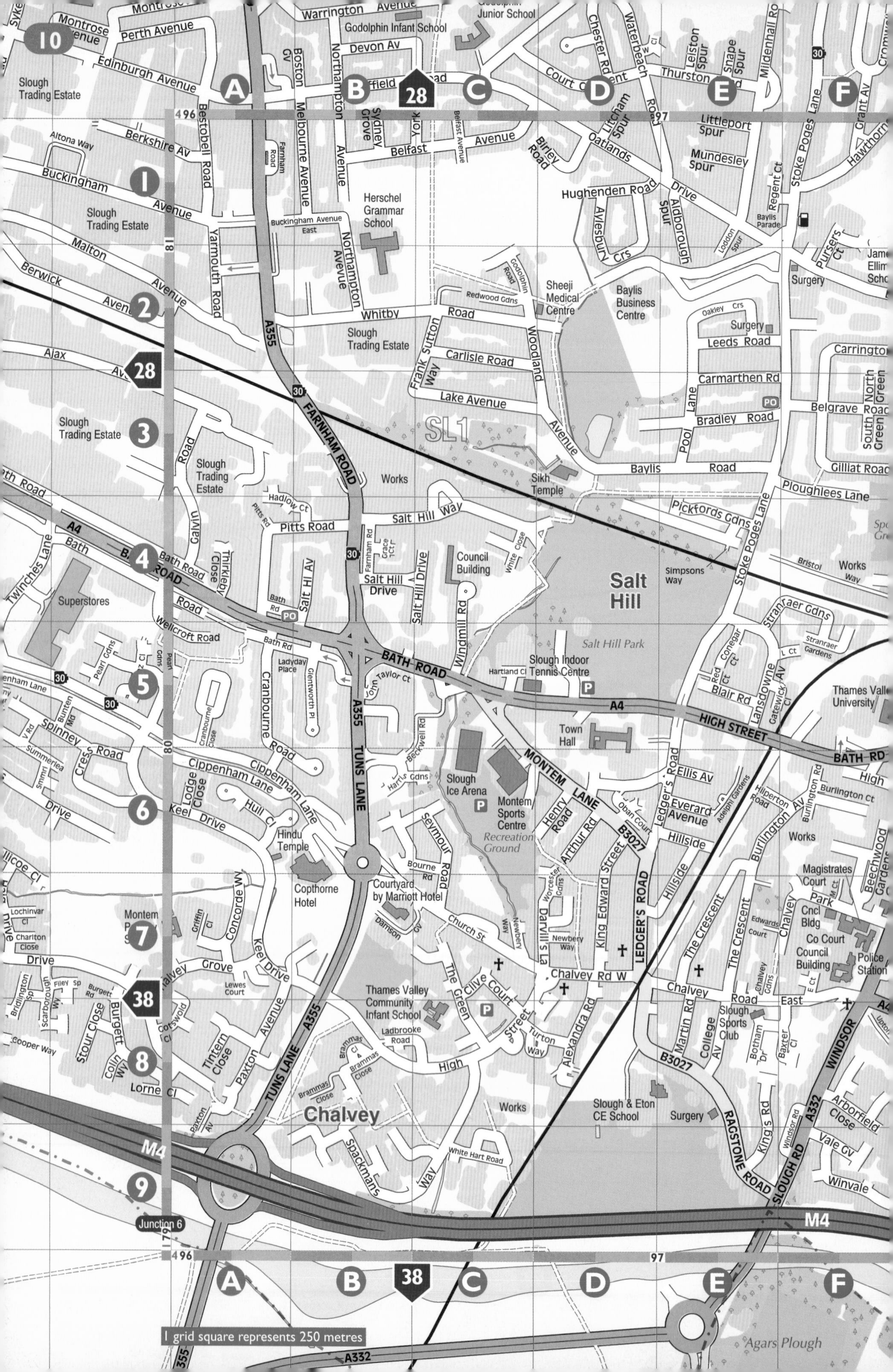

10
28
38
1 grid square represents 250 metres
Junction 6
Slough Trading Estate
Godolphin Infant School
Godolphin Junior School
Herschel Grammar School
Sheeji Medical Centre
Baylis Business Centre
Surgery
Baylis Parade
SL1
Works
Sikh Temple
Council Building
Salt Hill
Salt Hill Park
Slough Indoor Tennis Centre
Town Hall
Thames Valley University
Superstores
Slough Ice Arena
Montem Sports Centre
Recreation Ground
Hindu Temple
Copthorne Hotel
Courtyard by Marriott Hotel
Thames Valley Community Infant School
Chalvey
Slough & Eton CE School
Slough Sports Club
Magistrates Court
Cncl Bldg
Co Court
Council Building
Police Station
Agars Plough
Warrington Avenue
Montrose Avenue
Perth Avenue
Edinburgh Avenue
Devon Av
Boston Gv
Northampton Avenue
Melbourne Avenue
Sydney Grove
York Avenue
Belfast Avenue
Bestobell Road
Farnham Road
Berkshire Av
Altona Way
Buckingham Avenue
Buckingham Avenue East
Yarmouth Road
Malton Avenue
Berwick Avenue
Ajax Avenue
Whitby Road
Frank Sutton Way
Carlisle Road
Lake Avenue
Woodland Avenue
Redwood Gdns
Godolphin Road
Chester Rd
Waterbeach Road
Court Crescent
Leiston Spur
Snape Spur
Thurston Road
Mildenhall Rd
Littleport Spur
Mundesley Spur
Litcham Spur
Birley Road
Oatlands Drive
Hughenden Road
Aylesbury Crs
Spur
Aldborough Spur
Loddon Spur
Regent Ct
Stoke Poges Lane
Grant Av
Hawthorn
Pursers Ct
Oakley Crs
Leeds Road
Carmarthen Rd
Bradley Road
Pool Lane
Baylis Road
Carrington
Belgrave Road
North Green
South Green
Gilliat Road
Ploughlees Lane
Pickfords Gdns
Simpsons Way
Bristol Way
Stranraer Gdns
Stranraer Gardens
Road
Galvin
Hadlow Ct
Pitts Rd
Pitts Road
Salt Hill Way
Salt Hill Drive
Salt Hl Av
Grace Ct
White Close
Windmill Rd
Bath Road
A4
A355
A332
B3027
M4
Twinches Lane
Thirkleby Close
Wellcroft Road
Bath Rd
Ladyday Place
Glentworth Pl
John Taylor Ct
Hartland Cl
Pearl Gdns
Cippenham Lane
Bunten Md
Spinney
Summerlea
Cress Road
Cranbourne Close
Cranbourne Road
Tuns Lane
Beckwell Rd
Harris Gdns
Montem Lane
High Street
Bath Rd
Conegar Ct
Red Ct
Blair Rd
Lansdowne Av
Gatewick Av
Ledger's Road
Ellis Av
Everard Avenue
Adelphi Gardens
Oban Court
Hillside
Hilperton Road
Burlington Road
Burlington Ct
Burlington Av
Beechwood Gardens
Lodge Close
Hull Cl
Keel Drive
Drive
Seymour Road
Bourne Rd
Henry Road
Arthur Rd
King Edward Street
Worcester Gdns
Darvill's La
Newbery Way
Church St
Damson Gv
The Green
Clive Court
Chalvey Rd W
Chalvey Road East
The Crescent
Edwards Court
Chalvey Gdns
Park
E Ct
Windsor Rd
Slough Rd
Lochinvar Cl
Charlton Close
Griffin Cl
Concorde Wy
Chalvey Grove
Lewes Court
Cotswold Cl
Bridlington Sp
Filey Sp
Scarborough Wy
Burgett Rd
Stour Close
Cooper Way
Colin Wy
Tintern Close
Paxton Avenue
Paxton Av
Lorne Cl
Ladbrooke Road
Brammas Cl
Brammas Close
High Street
Turton Way
Alexandra Rd
Martin Rd
College Av
Botham Dr
Baxter Cl
Ragstone Road
King's Rd
Windsor Rd
Arborfield Close
Vale Gv
Winvale
Spackmans Way
White Hart Road

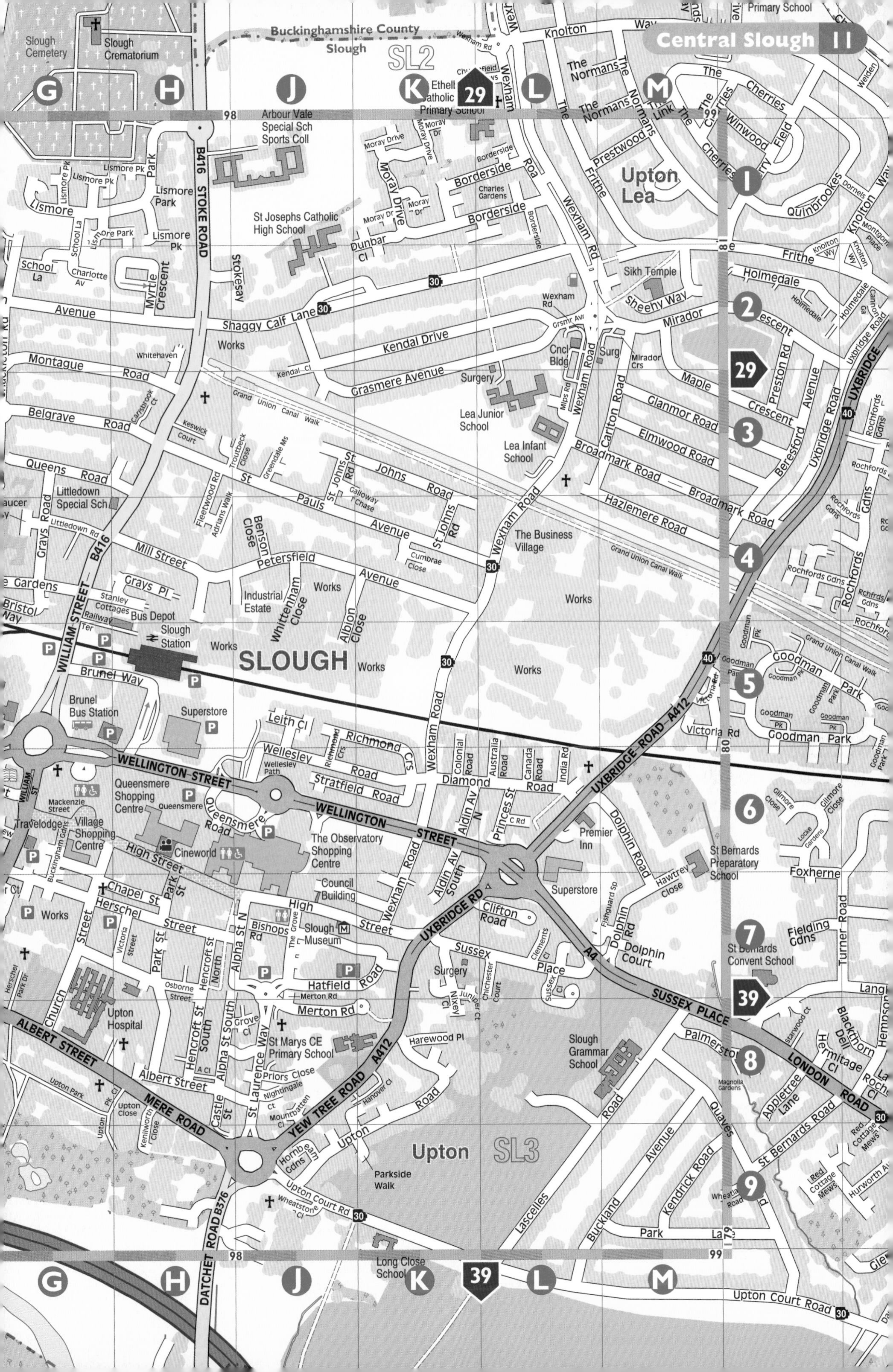
Slough Cemetery
Slough Crematorium
Buckinghamshire County
Slough
SL2
G
H
J
K
L
M
29
98
99
Arbour Vale Special Sch Sports Coll
Ethelbert Catholic Primary School
Knolton Way
The Normans
The Cherries
Winwood
Prestwood
Upton Lea
Frithe
Quinbrookes
B416 STOKE ROAD
Lismore Pk
Lismore Park
Lismore
School La
Charlotte Av
Myrtle Crescent
Stokesay
St Josephs Catholic High School
Moray Drive
Borderside
Charles Gardens
Dunbar Cl
Wexham Rd
Sikh Temple
Sheehy Way
Holmedale
Mirador Crescent
Avenue
Shaggy Calf Lane
Kendal Drive
Kendal Cl
Grasmere Avenue
Surgery
Cncl Bldg
Works
Whitehaven
Montague Road
Belgrave Road
Keswick Court
Troutbeck Close
Grand Union Canal Walk
Lea Junior School
Lea Infant School
Wexham Road
Carlton Road
Maple Crescent
Glanmor Road
Elmwood Road
Broadmark Road
Hazlemere Road
Preston Rd
Beresford Avenue
Uxbridge Road
UXBRIDGE
Rochfords Gdns
Queens Road
St Pauls Avenue
St Johns Road
Littledown Special Sch
Littledown Rd
Fleetwood Rd
Adrians Walk
Benson Close
Galloway Chase
Cumbrae Close
The Business Village
Mill Street
Petersfield Avenue
Grays Pl
Industrial Estate
Whittenham Close
Albion Close
Stanley Cottages
Railway Ter
Bus Depot
Slough Station
SLOUGH
WILLIAM STREET
Goodman Park
Victoria Rd
Brunel Way
Brunel Bus Station
Superstore
Leith Cl
Richmond Crs
Wellesley Road
Wellesley Path
Stratfield Road
Colonial Road
Australia Road
Canada Road
India Rd
Diamond Road
UXBRIDGE ROAD A412
WELLINGTON STREET
Queensmere Shopping Centre
Queensmere Road
Mackenzie Street
Travelodge
Village Shopping Centre
Cineworld
High Street
The Observatory Shopping Centre
Aldin Av North
Aldin Av South
Princes St
Premier Inn
Dolphin Road
Gilmore Close
Locke Gardens
Foxherne
St Bernards Preparatory School
Hawtrey Close
Chapel St
Park St
Herschel Street
Council Building
Slough Museum
Bishops Rd
The Grove
UXBRIDGE RD
Clifton Road
Sussex Place
Dolphin Court
Fielding Gdns
Turner Road
St Bernards Convent School
Victoria Street
Church Street
Osborne Street
Hencroft St North
Hencroft St South
Alpha St North
Alpha St South
Hatfield Road
Merton Rd
Grove Cl
Clements Cl
Sussex Cl
Chichester Court
Upton Hospital
St Marys CE Primary School
Harewood Pl
Slough Grammar School
SUSSEX PLACE
LONDON ROAD
Palmerston
Starwood Ct
Blackthorn Dell
Hermitage Cl
Appletree Lane
Magnolia Gardens
ALBERT STREET
Albert Street
Priors Close
Nightingale Ct
Mountbatten Cl
YEW TREE ROAD A412
MERE ROAD
Castle St
St Laurence Way
Upton Park
Upton Close
Kenilworth Close
Hanover Cl
Hornbeam Gdns
Upton
SL3
Parkside Walk
Quaves
St Bernards Road
Red Cottage Mews
Kendrick Road
Buckland Avenue
Lascelles Road
Park Lane
Upton Court Rd
Wheatstone Cl
DATCHET ROAD B376
Long Close School
Upton Court Road
39
30
40

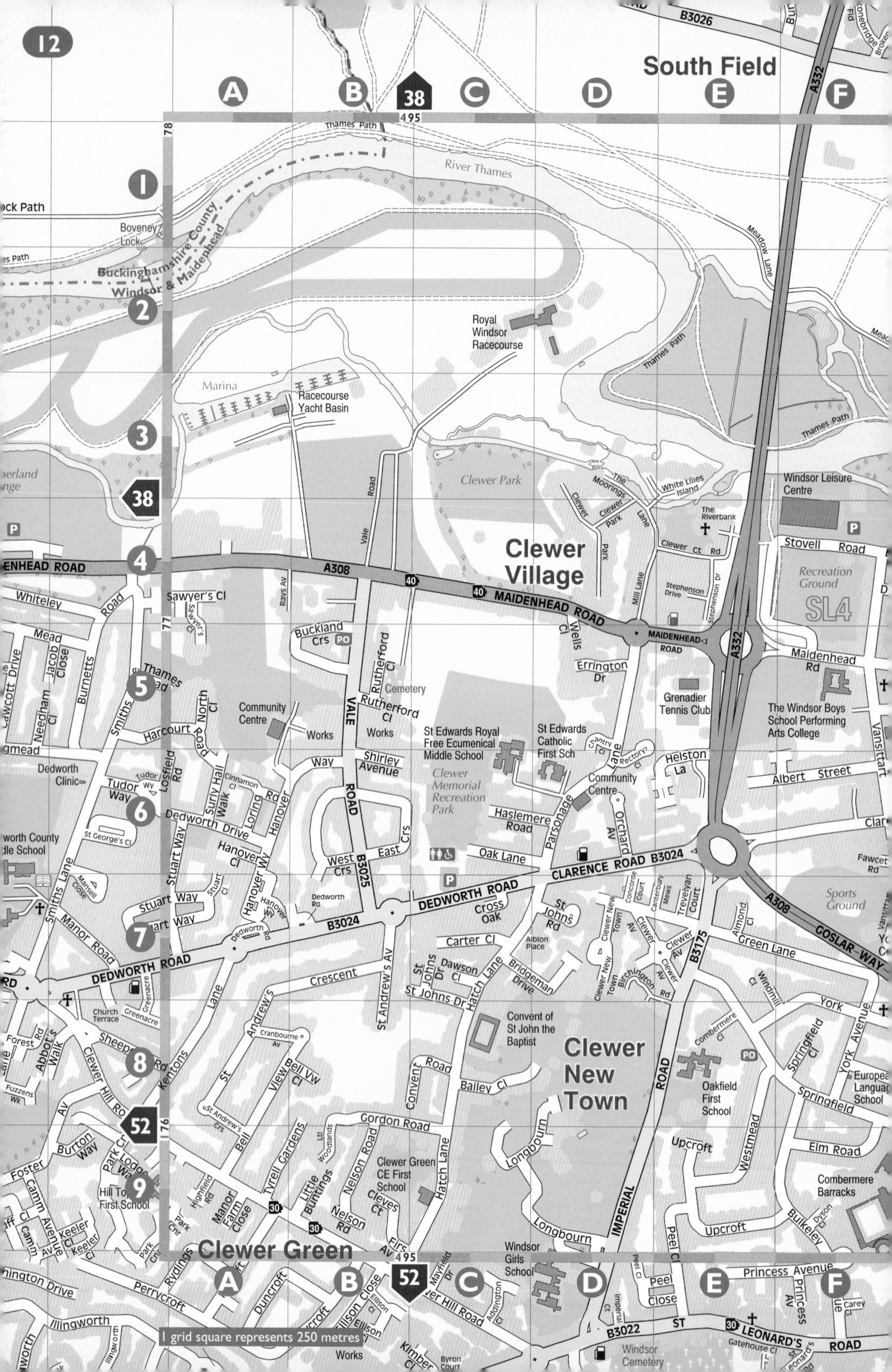
South Field
A
B
38
C
D
E
F
B3026
A332
Thames Path
River Thames
Boveney Lock
Buckinghamshire County
Windsor & Maidenhead
Royal Windsor Racecourse
Marina
Racecourse Yacht Basin
Thames Path
Meadow Lane
Clewer Park
The Moorings
White Lilies Island
Windsor Leisure Centre
The Riverbank
Clewer Village
MAIDENHEAD ROAD
A308
Vale Road
Rays Av
Sawyer's Cl
Whiteley
Mead
Jacob Close
Burnetts
Needham Cl
Thames Road
Smiths Lane
Harcourt Road
North Cl
Buckland Crs
Rutherford Cl
Cemetery
Community Centre
Works
Stovell Road
Recreation Ground
SL4
Clewer Ct Rd
Stephenson Drive
Stephenson Dr
Mill Lane
Wells Cl
Errington Dr
Grenadier Tennis Club
Maidenhead Rd
The Windsor Boys School Performing Arts College
St Edwards Royal Free Ecumenical Middle School
St Edwards Catholic First Sch
Clewer Memorial Recreation Park
Parsonage Lane
Rectory Cl
Helston La
Albert Street
Vansittart
Dedworth Clinic
Tudor Way
Losfield Rd
Surly Hall Walk
Cinnamon Cl
Loring Rd
Hanover Way
Shirley Avenue
VALE ROAD
B3025
Dedworth Drive
St George's Cl
Stuart Way
Hanover Cl
West Crs
East Crs
Haslemere Road
Oak Lane
Orchard Av
Community Centre
CLARENCE ROAD B3024
DEDWORTH ROAD
Cross Oak
St Johns Rd
Albion Place
Carter Cl
Dawson Cl
St Johns Dr
Hatch Lane
Bridgeman Drive
Clewer New Town
Clewer Av
Birchington Rd
Trevelyan Court
Concorde Court
Canterbury Mews
B3175
Almond Cl
Green Lane
Windmill Cl
GOSLAR WAY
Sports Ground
Fawcett Rd
Clarence Road
Manor Road
Mansell Close
Dedworth Rd
Church Terrace
Greenacre
Forest Rd
Abbot's Walk
Sheepcote Rd
Clewer Hill Road
Fuzzens Wk
Kentons Lane
Crescent
St Andrew's Av
Cranbourne Av
St Andrew's Crs
Bell View
Bell Vw Cl
Convent Road
Bailey Cl
Convent of St John the Baptist
Clewer New Town
IMPERIAL ROAD
Combermere Cl
Oakfield First School
Springfield Cl
York Avenue
York
European Language School
Springfield
Elm Road
Combermere Barracks
Upcroft
Westmead
Bulkeley Av
Dyson Cl
Gordon Road
Tyrell Gardens
Little Buntings
Nelson Road
Nelson Rd
Woodlands
Clewer Green CE First School
Cleves Ct
Firs Av
Longbourn
Burton Way
Park Cl
Lodge Way
Foster Av
Camm Avenue
Keeler Cl
Hill Top First School
Highfield Rd
Manor Farm Close
Park Cnr
Rydings
Clewer Green
Windsor Girls School
Peel Cl
Peel Close
Imperial Ct
Princess Avenue
Princess Av
Carey Cl
Perrycroft
Duncroft
Ellison Close
Ellison Cl
Clewer Hill Road
Mayfield Dr
Addington Cl
B3022
ST LEONARD'S ROAD
Gatehouse Cl
Illingworth
1 grid square represents 250 metres
Works
Kimber Cl
Byron Court
Windsor Cemetery
495
76
77
78
52
30
40

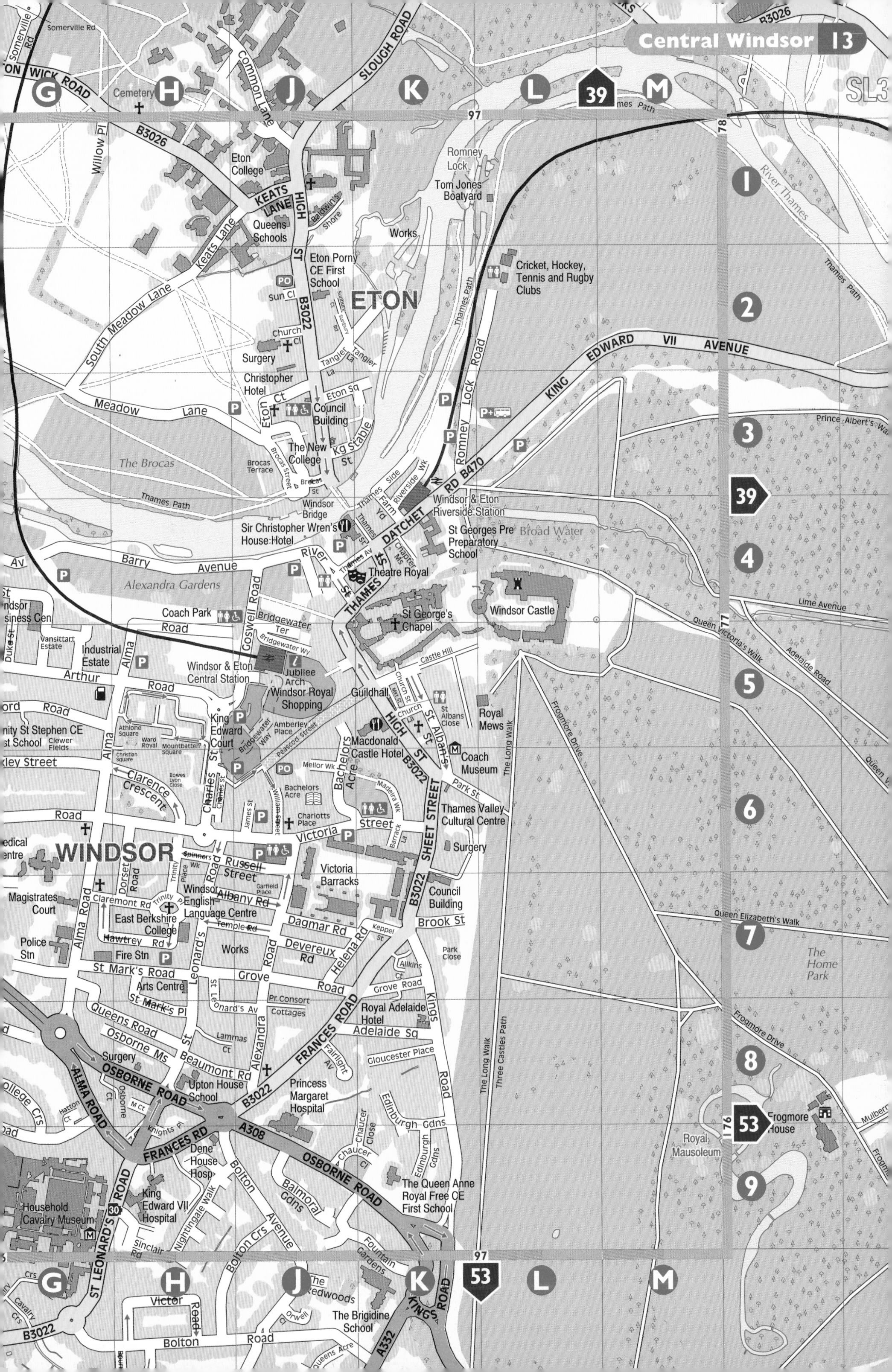

G H J K L **39** M

WON WICK ROAD

Somerville Rd

Willow Pl

Cemetery

B3026

Eton College

KEATS LANE

HIGH ST

Queens Schools

Eton Porny CE First School

PO

Sun Cl

South Meadow Lane

B3022

Church

Cl

Surgery

Christopher Hotel

The New College

Brocas Terrace

Brocas Street

ETON

Works

SLOUGH ROAD

97

Romney Lock

Tom Jones Boatyard

Cricket, Hockey, Tennis and Rugby Clubs

KING EDWARD VII AVENUE

Prince Albert's Walk

River Thames

Thames Path

I

2

3

39

4

5

6

7

8

53

9

Meadow Lane

The Brocas

Thames Path

Eton Ct

Council Building

Kg Stable St

Eton Sq

Tangier La

Tangier

Riverside Wk

Datchet Rd B470

Romney Lock Road

P

P

P+bus

P

P

Windsor & Eton Riverside Station

Broad Water

St Georges Pre Preparatory School

Windsor Castle

Windsor Bridge

Sir Christopher Wren's House Hotel

Barry Avenue

Alexandra Gardens

DATCHET

Thames St

Theatre Royal

St George's Chapel

Castle Hill

Queen Victoria's Walk

Lime Avenue

Adelaide Road

Queen

ndsor usiness Cen

Vansittart Estate

Industrial Estate

Coach Park

Bridgewater Ter

Bridgewater Wy

Windsor & Eton Central Station

Jubilee Arch

Windsor Royal Shopping

Guildhall

Church St

St Albans Close

Royal Mews

The Long Walk

Frogmore Drive

Duke's

Arthur Road

Alma

P

King Edward Court

Bridgewater Walk

PO

Amberley Place

Peascod Street

Macdonald Castle Hotel

HIGH ST B3022

St Alban's

Coach Museum

Park St

Thames Valley Cultural Centre

Surgery

Queen Elizabeth's Walk

The Home Park

ord Road

nity St Stephen CE st School

Clewer Fields

Athlone Square

Ward Royal

Mountbatten Square

Christian Square

Bowes Lyon Close

James St

Charlotts Place

Bachelors Acre

Mellor Wk

Bachelors Acre

Madeira Wk

Victoria

Barrack St

SHEET STREET

Park Close

dical ntre

kley Street

Road

Clarence Crescent

Charles St

Charles St

WINDSOR

Spinners Wk

Russell Street

Trinity Pl

Victoria Barracks

Garfield Place

Council Building

Brook St

Magistrates Court

Police Stn

Dorset Road

Trinity

Claremont Rd

Windsor English Language Centre

Albany Rd

Temple Rd

Dagmar Rd

Keppel St

Allkins Cl

Park Close

East Berkshire College

Hawtrey Rd

Works

Devereux Rd

Helena Road

Grove Road

Grove Road

St Mark's Road

Arts Centre

St Mark's Pl

St Leonard's Av

Pr Consort Cottages

Royal Adelaide Hotel

Kings Road

Three Castles Path

dical

FRANCES ROAD

Lammas

Alexandra

Fairlight

Adelaide Sq

Gloucester Place

The Long Walk

176

Frogmore House

Frogmore Drive

ollege Crs

ALMA ROAD

OSBORNE ROAD

Queens Road

Osborne Ms

Surgery

Beaumont Rd

Upton House School

B3022

Fairlight AV

Princess Margaret Hospital

Edinburgh Gdns

Edinburgh Gdns

Edinburgh Gdns

Royal Mausoleum

Household Cavalry Museum

30

M

King Edward VII Hospital

Dene House Hosp

FRANCES RD

A308

OSBORNE ROAD

Balmoral Gdns

Bolton Road

Chaucer Close

Chaucer

The Queen Anne Royal Free CE First School

Fountain Gardens

Cavalry Crs

B3022

G H J **53** L M

Victor

Victor Road

The Redwoods

KINGS ROAD

97

A332

The Brigidine School

Bolton Road

Queens Acre

Sinclair Rd

Nightingale Walk

Knights Cl

Bolton Crs

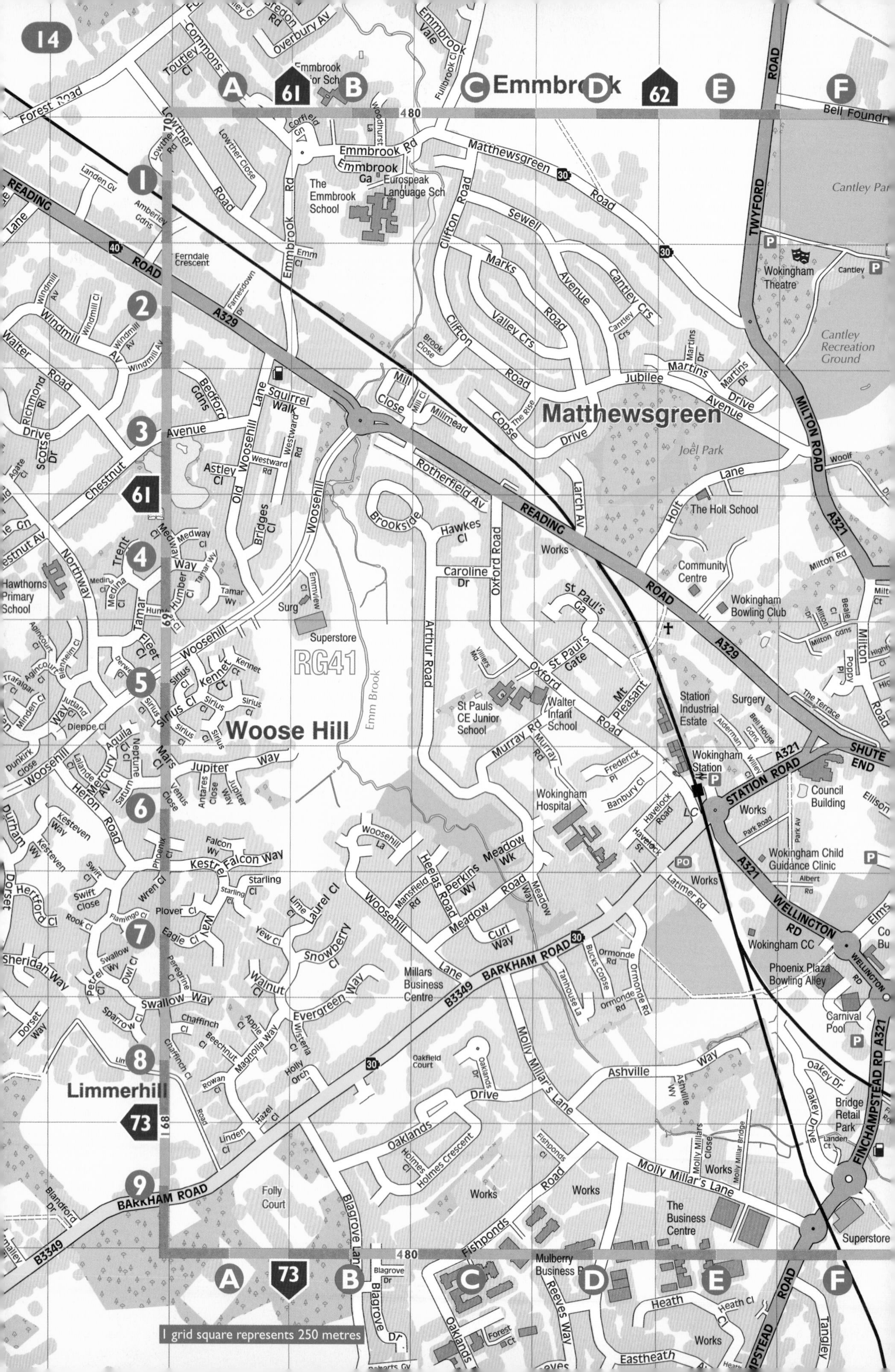
A
B
C
D
E
F
1
2
3
4
5
6
7
8
9
61
62
73
480
Emmbrook
Matthewsgreen
Woose Hill
Limmerhill
RG41
Forest Road
Commons Rd
Toutley Cl
Overbury Av
Emmbrook Vale
Fullbrook Cl
Lowther Road
Lowther Close
Emmbrook Rd
Corfield Gn
Woodhurst La
Emmbrook Ga
The Emmbrook School
Eurospeak Language Sch
Matthewsgreen Road
Clifton Road
Sewell Avenue
Marks Road
Valley Crs
Cantley Crs
Twyford Road
Bell Foundry
Cantley Park
Wokingham Theatre
Cantley Recreation Ground
Reading Road
A329
Landen Gv
Amberley Gdns
Ferndale Crescent
Farnesdown Dr
Emm Cl
Windmill Av
Windmill Cl
Walter Road
Richmond Rl
Scots Dr
Drive
Chestnut Avenue
Bedford Gdns
Old Woosehill Lane
Squirrel Walk
Westward Rd
Astley Cl
Bridges Cl
Mill Close
Mill Cl
Millmead
Brook Close
Copse Drive
The Rise
Jubilee Avenue
Martins Drive
Martins Dr
Joel Park
Milton Road
A321
Woolf
Rotherfield Av
Brookside
Hawkes Cl
Larch Av
Holt Lane
The Holt School
Works
Community Centre
Milton Rd
Wokingham Bowling Club
Caroline Dr
Oxford Road
Arthur Road
St Paul's Ga
St Paul's Gate
Mt. Pleasant
Milton Gdns
Poppy Pl
The Terrace
Station Industrial Estate
Surgery
Alderman Willey Cl
Bell House Gdns
Shute End
Station Road
Wokingham Station
Council Building
Ellison
Northway
Hawthorns Primary School
Medway Cl
Trent
Medina Cl
Tamar Way
Humber Cl
Fleet Cl
Woosehill
Surg
Emmview Cl
Superstore
Emm Brook
Sirius Cl
Kennet Ct
Agincourt
Blenheim Cl
Trafalgar Cl
Minden Cl
Jutland Cl
Dieppe Cl
Dunkirk Close
Aquila Cl
Neptune Cl
Mercury Av
Lalande Cl
Saturn Cl
Mars Cl
Jupiter Way
Venus Close
Antares Close
Villiers Md
St Pauls CE Junior School
Walter Infant School
Murray Rd
Frederick Pl
Banbury Cl
Wokingham Hospital
Havelock Road
Havelock St
Park Road
Park Av
Wokingham Child Guidance Clinic
Albert Rd
Durham Rd
Kesteven Way
Heron Road
Phoenix Cl
Falcon Way
Kestrel Way
Wren Cl
Starling Cl
Woosehill La
Meadow Wk
Heelas Road
Perkins Wy
Mansfield Rd
Meadow Road
Meadow Way
Larimer Rd
Swift Close
Hertford Cl
Rook Cl
Flamingo Cl
Plover Cl
Eagle Cl
Lime Cl
Laurel Cl
Yew Cl
Snowberry Cl
Curl Way
Barkham Road
B3349
Wellington Rd
Wokingham CC
Phoenix Plaza Bowling Alley
Carnival Pool
Sheridan Way
Petrel Cl
Swallow Wy
Owl Cl
Peregrine Cl
Swallow Way
Walnut Cl
Evergreen Way
Millars Business Centre
Bucks Copse
Tanhouse La
Ormonde Rd
Dorset Way
Sparrow Cl
Chaffinch Cl
Beechnut Cl
Apple Cl
Magnolia Way
Wisteria Cl
Molly Millar's Lane
Ashville Way
Oakfield Court
Oaklands Dr
Holly Orch
Rowan Cl
Hazel Cl
Linden Cl
Oaklands Drive
Holmes Cl
Holmes Crescent
Fishponds Cl
Fishponds Road
Molly Millars Close
Molly Millar Bridge
The Business Centre
Oakey Dr
Oakey Drive
Bridge Retail Park
Landen Ct
Finchampstead Rd
Finchampstead Road
Superstore
Blandford Dr
Folly Court
Blagrove Lane
Blagrove Dr
Mulberry Business P
Reeves Way
Heath Cl
Heath
Eastheath
Tangley
Forest Ct
Oaklands
1 grid square represents 250 metres

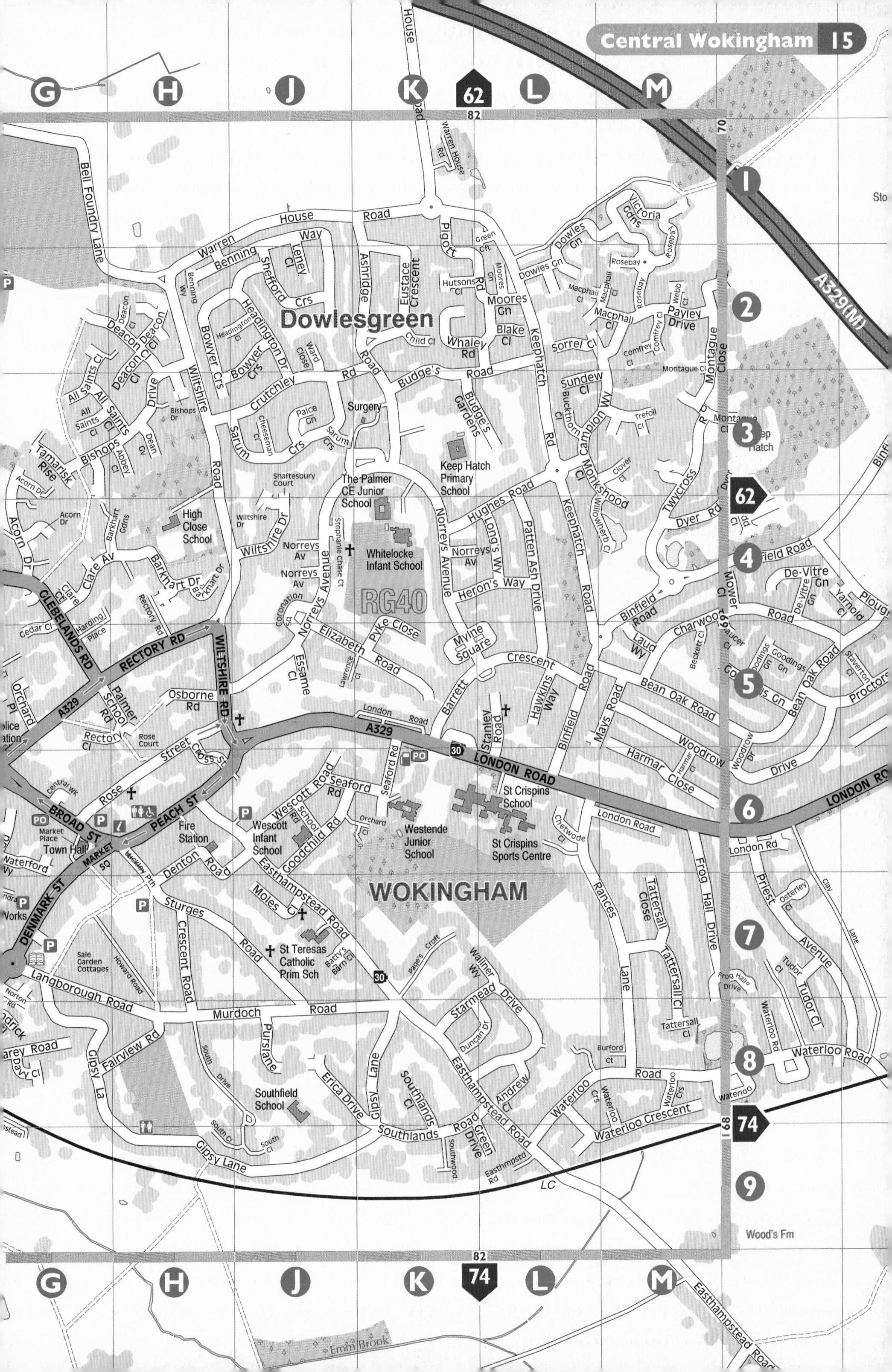

G
H
J
K
L
M
62
82
70
68
74
2
3
4
5
6
7
8
9
A329(M)
House
Warren House Rd
Bell Foundry Lane
Warren House Road
Benning Wy
Benning Way
Leney Cl
Shefford Crs
Ashridge Road
Eustace Crescent
Pigott Rd
Green Cft
Hutsons Cl
Moores Gn
Dowles Gn
Victoria Gdns
Rosebay
Macphail Cl
Webb Ct
Payley Drive
Dowlesgreen
Deacon Cl
Headington Dr
Headington Cl
Bowyer Crs
Ward Close
Child Cl
Whaley Rd
Blake Cl
Keephatch Road
Sorrel Cl
Comfrey Cl
Montague Close
Montague Cl
All Saints Cl
Wiltshire Road
Crutchley Rd
Budge's Road
Budge's Gardens
Sundew Cl
Buckthorn Cl
Campion Wy
Trefoil Cl
Bishops Dr
Cheeseman Cl
Paice Gn
Sarum Crs
Surgery
Dean Gv
Abbey Cl
Bishops Rd
Tamarisk Rise
Acorn Dr
Keep Hatch Primary School
Clover Cl
Monkshood Cl
Twycross Rd
Dyer Rd
Shaftesbury Court
The Palmer CE Junior School
Hughes Road
Willowherb Cl
High Close School
Wiltshire Dr
Barkhart Gdns
Stephanie Chase Ct
Whitelocke Infant School
Norreys Av
Norreys Avenue
Long's Way
Patten Ash Drive
Clare Av
Barkhart Dr
Heron's Way
De-Vitre Gn
Yarnold Cl
Binfield Road
RG40
Coronation Sq
Rectory Rd
Glebelands Rd
Cedar Cl
Harding Place
Rectory Rd
Wiltshire Rd
Elizabeth Road
Pyke Close
Mylne Square
Crescent
Laud Wy
Charwood Rd
Beckett Cl
Goodings Gn
Staverton Cl
Proctors
Lawrence Cl
Essame Cl
Barrett Crescent
Hawkins Way
Mays Road
Bean Oak Road
A329
Orchard Pl
Palmer School Rd
Osborne Rd
London Road
Stanley Road
Woodrow Drive
Woodrow Dr
Harmar Close
Harmar Cl
Rectory Cl
Rose Court
Rose Street
Cross St
Seaford Rd
PO
30
LONDON ROAD
St Crispins School
Central Wk
Broad St
Peach St
Wescott Road
School Rd
Orchard Cl
Westende Junior School
Chetwode Cl
London Rd
Market Place
Town Hall
Fire Station
Wescott Infant School
Goodchild Rd
St Crispins Sports Centre
Waterford Wy
Market Sq
Denton Road
Easthampstead Road
Rances Lane
Tattersall Close
Frog Hall Drive
Priest Avenue
Osterley Cl
Clay Lane
Works
Denmark St
Sturges Road
Moles Cl
WOKINGHAM
Crescent Road
Sale Garden Cottages
Howard Road
St Teresas Catholic Prim Sch
Batty's Barn Cl
Page's Croft
Wallner Wy
Starmead Drive
Tattersall Cl
Tudor Cl
Langborough Road
Norton Rd
Murdoch Road
Duncan Dr
Waterloo Rd
Waterloo Road
Fairview Rd
Purslane
South Drive
Gipsy Lane
Erica Drive
Southlands Cl
Burford Ct
Andrew Cl
Gipsy La
Southfield School
Waterloo Crs
Waterloo Crescent
South Cl
Southlands Road
Green Drive
Southwood
Easthmpstd Rd
LC
Wood's Fm
Emm Brook
Easthampstead Road
Binfield Road

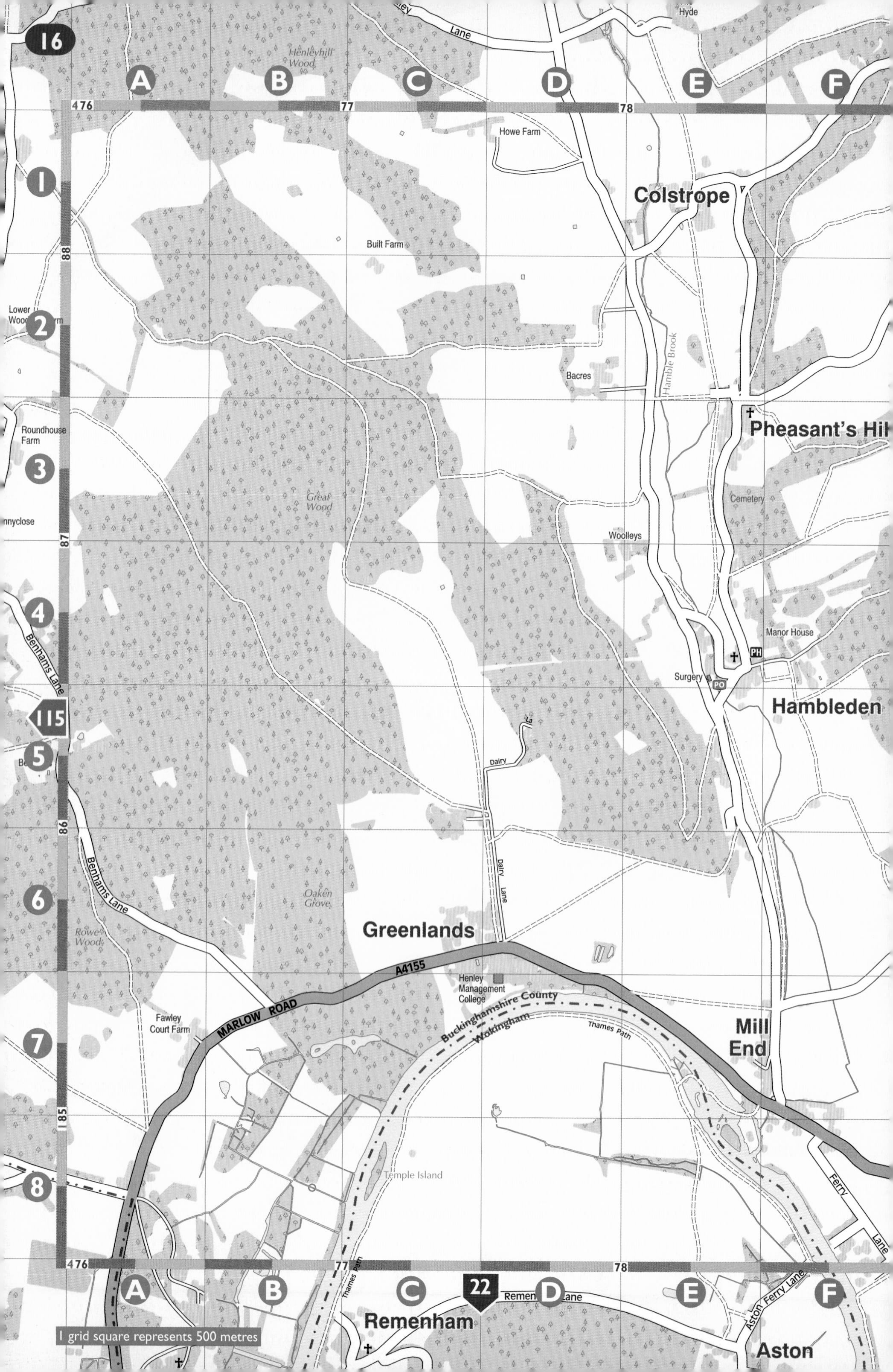

Hyde
Lane
Henleyhill Wood
A
B
C
D
E
F
476
77
78
Howe Farm
1
Colstrope
Built Farm
88
Lower Wood Farm
2
Bacres
Hamble Brook
Roundhouse Farm
Pheasant's Hill
3
Great Wood
Cemetery
nnyclose
87
Woolleys
4
Benhams Lane
Manor House
PH
Surgery
PO
115
Hambleden
5
Dairy La
86
Dairy Lane
Benhams Lane
6
Oaken Grove
Rowe Wood
Greenlands
A4155
Henley Management College
Buckinghamshire County
Wokingham
MARLOW ROAD
Fawley Court Farm
Thames Path
7
Mill End
85
8
Temple Island
Ferry Lane
Thames Path
22
Remenham Lane
Aston Ferry Lane
Remenham
Aston
1 grid square represents 500 metres

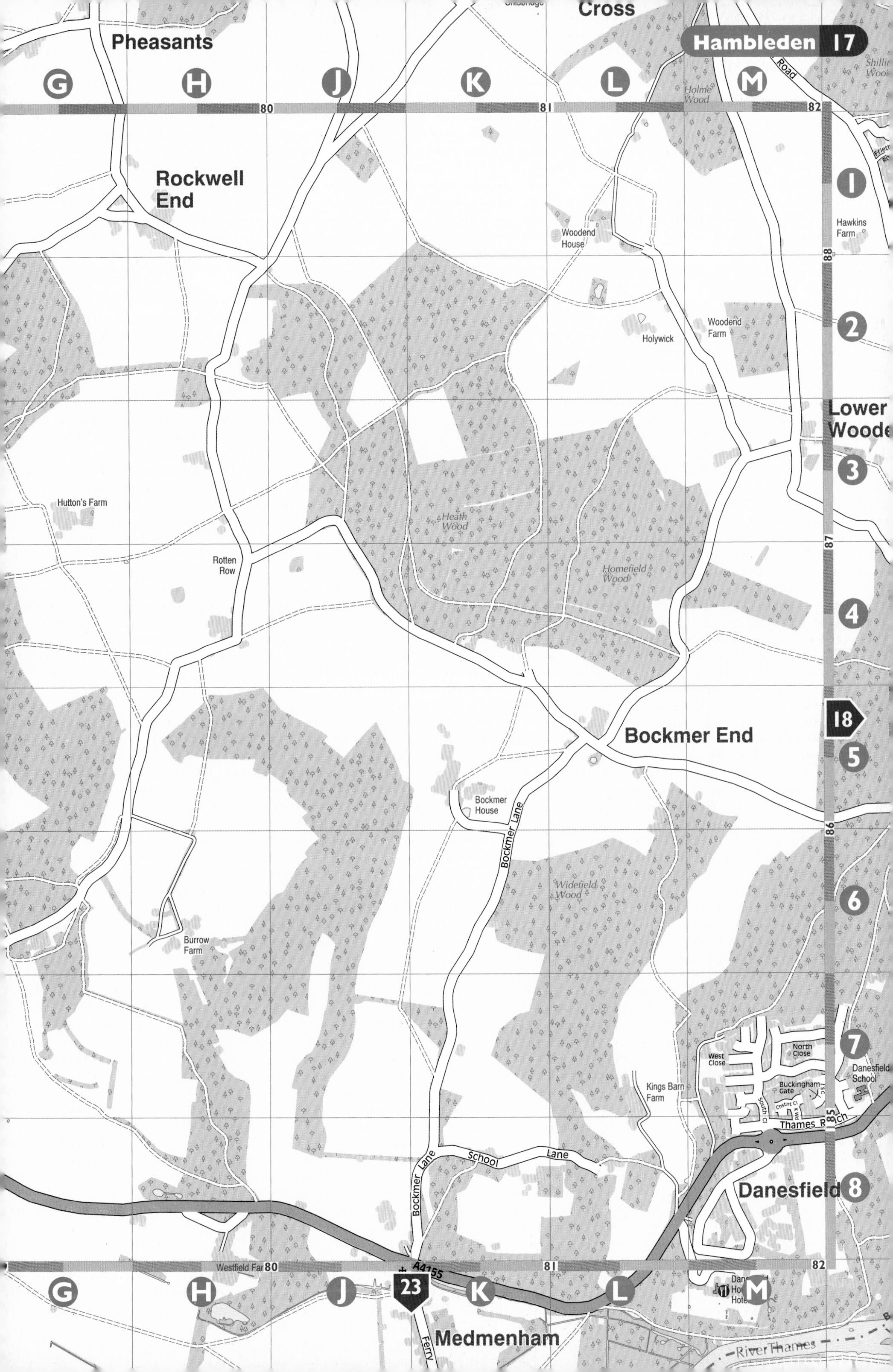
Hambleden 17
Cross
Pheasants
G
H
J
K
L
M
80
81
82
Road
Holme Wood
Rockwell End
Woodend House
Hawkins Farm
88
Woodend Farm
Holywick
Lower Woode
Hutton's Farm
Heath Wood
Rotten Row
87
Homefield Wood
18
Bockmer End
Bockmer House
Bockmer Lane
86
Widefield Wood
Burrow Farm
North Close
West Close
Danesfield School
Kings Barn Farm
Buckingham Gate
South Cl
Thames Reach
85
School Lane
Danesfield
Bockmer Lane
Westfield Far
A4155
23
Medmenham
Ferry
River Thames
1
2
3
4
5
6
7
8

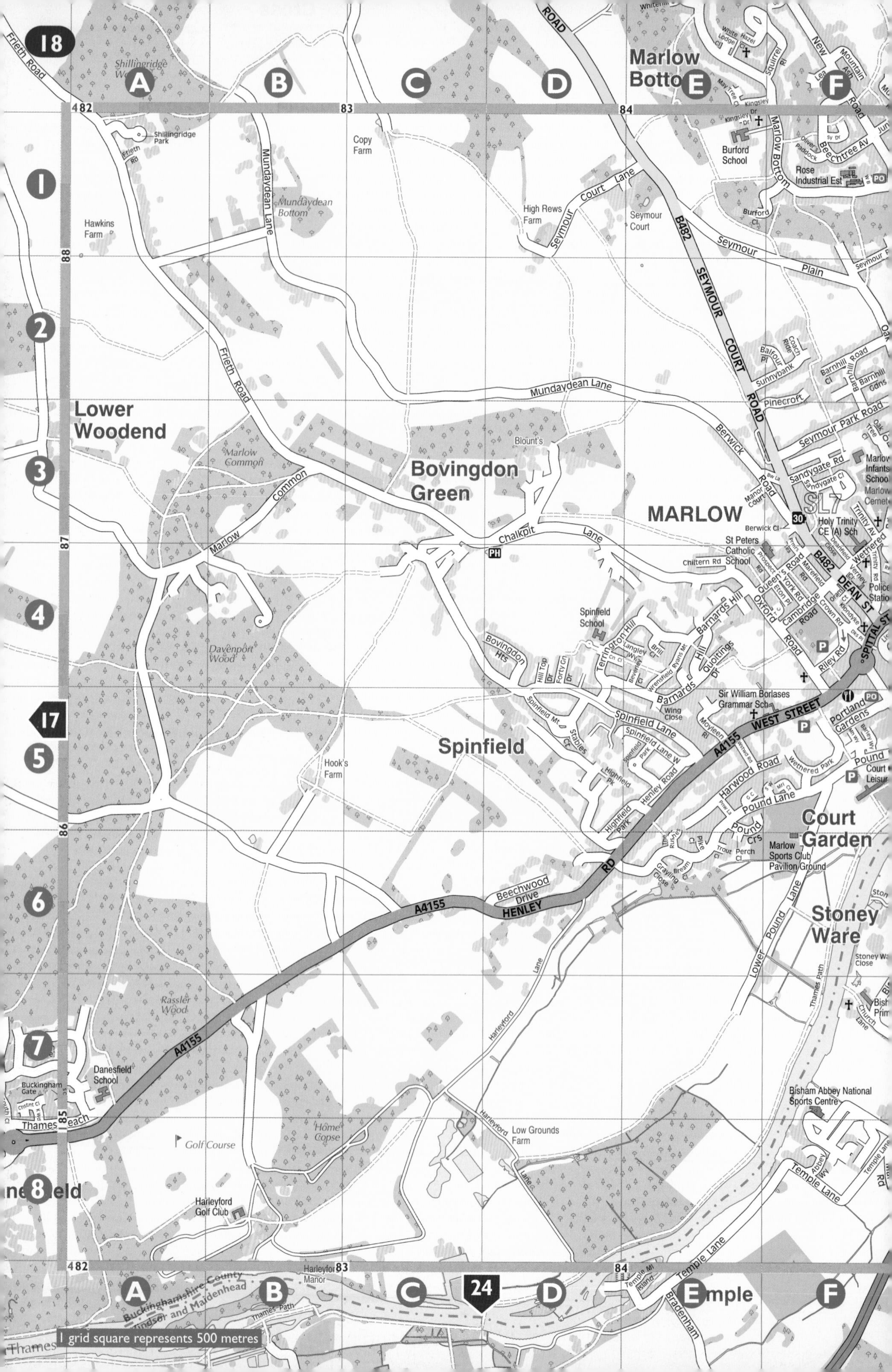

18
17
24
Marlow Bottom
Lower Woodend
Bovingdon Green
MARLOW
Spinfield
Court Garden
Stoney Ware
Shillingridge Wood
Shillingridge Park
Copy Farm
Hawkins Farm
Mundaydean Bottom
Mundaydean Lane
Frieth Road
High Rews Farm
Seymour Court Lane
Seymour Court
B482 SEYMOUR COURT ROAD
Seymour Plain
Burford School
Rose Industrial Est
Marlow Common
Davenport Wood
Blount's
Chalkpit Lane
Spinfield School
St Peters Catholic School
Holy Trinity CE (A) Sch
Sir William Borlases Grammar Sch
A4155 WEST STREET
A4155 HENLEY RD
Hook's Farm
Beechwood Drive
Marlow Sports Club Pavilion Ground
Rassler Wood
Danesfield School
Buckingham Gate
Thames Reach
Golf Course
Home Copse
Harleyford Golf Club
Harleyford Manor
Harleyford Lane
Low Grounds Farm
Bisham Abbey National Sports Centre
Temple Lane
Temple Mill Island
Bradenham
Temple
Thames Path
Lower Pound Lane
Buckinghamshire County
Windsor and Maidenhead
1 grid square represents 500 metres

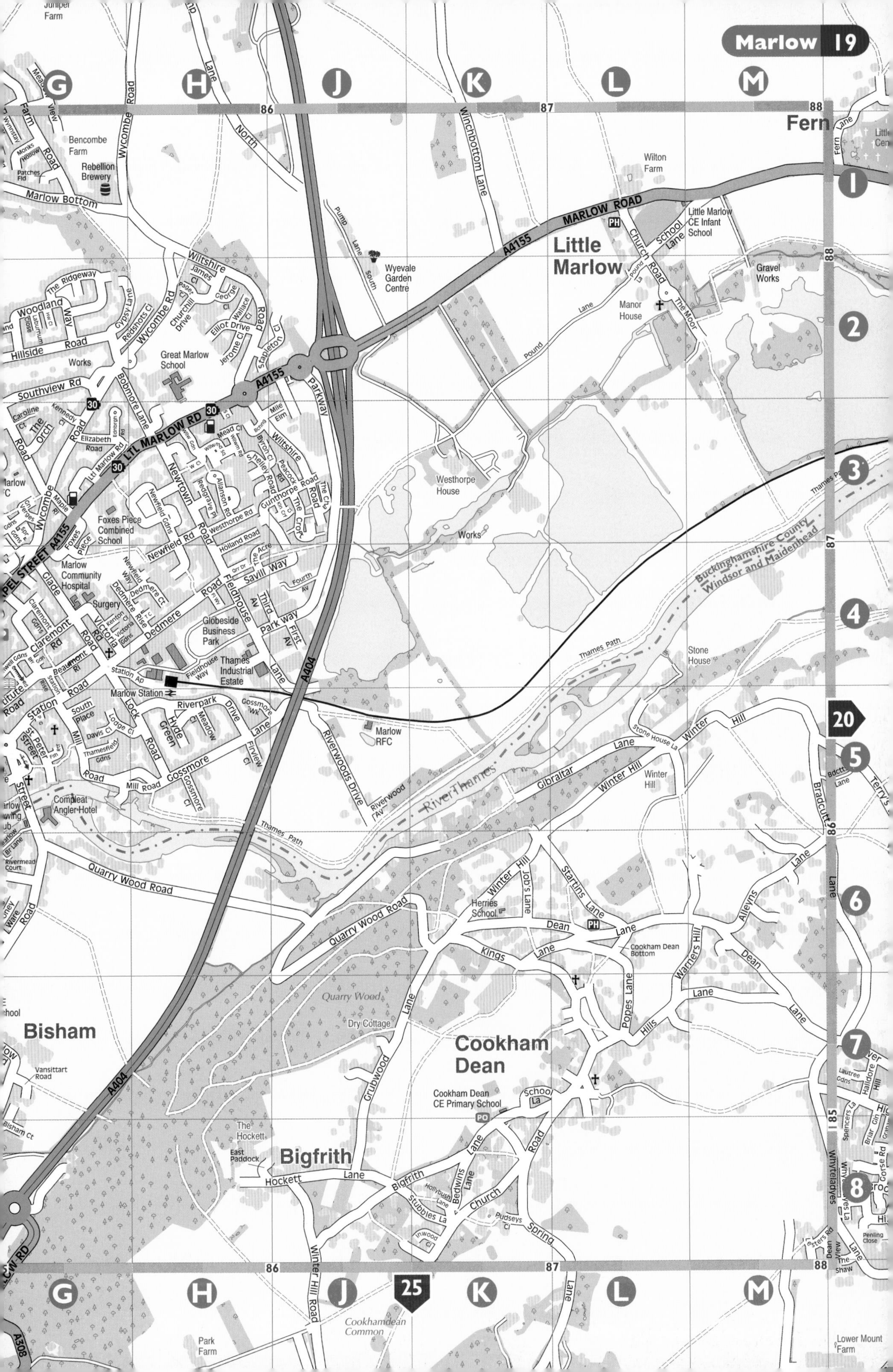
Little Marlow
Cookham Dean
Bisham
Bigfrith
Fern
Marlow Road
A4155
Ltl Marlow Rd
A404
Parkway
Winchbottom Lane
Wilton Farm
Little Marlow CE Infant School
Church Road
School Lane
Pound Lane
Manor House
The Moor
Gravel Works
Wyevale Garden Centre
Pump Lane South
North Lane
Wycombe Road
Bencombe Farm
Rebellion Brewery
Marlow Bottom
Great Marlow School
Wiltshire Road
Woodland Way
Hillside Road
Southview Rd
Bobmore Lane
Westhorpe House
Works
Foxes Piece Combined School
Marlow Community Hospital
Surgery
Newtown Road
Fieldhouse Lane
Globeside Business Park
Thames Industrial Estate
Marlow Station
Station Road
Dedmere Road
Savill Way
Park Way
Riverpark Drive
Gossmore Lane
Marlow RFC
Riverwoods Drive
River Thames
Thames Path
Buckinghamshire County
Windsor and Maidenhead
Stone House
Winter Hill
Gibraltar Lane
Quarry Wood Road
Compleat Angler Hotel
Quarry Wood
Dry Cottage
Herries School
Job's Lane
Startins Lane
Dean Lane
Kings Lane
Cookham Dean Bottom
Popes Lane
Warners Hill
Alleyns Lane
Bradcutts Lane
Cookham Dean CE Primary School
School La
Grubwood Lane
The Hockett
East Paddock
Hockett Lane
Bigfrith Lane
Church Road
Spring Lane
Stubbles La
Whyteladyes Lane
Vansittart Road
Bisham Ct
Winter Hill Road
Cookhamdean Common
Park Farm
Lower Mount Farm
A308
86
87
88
G
H
J
K
L
M
1
2
3
4
5
6
7
8
20
25

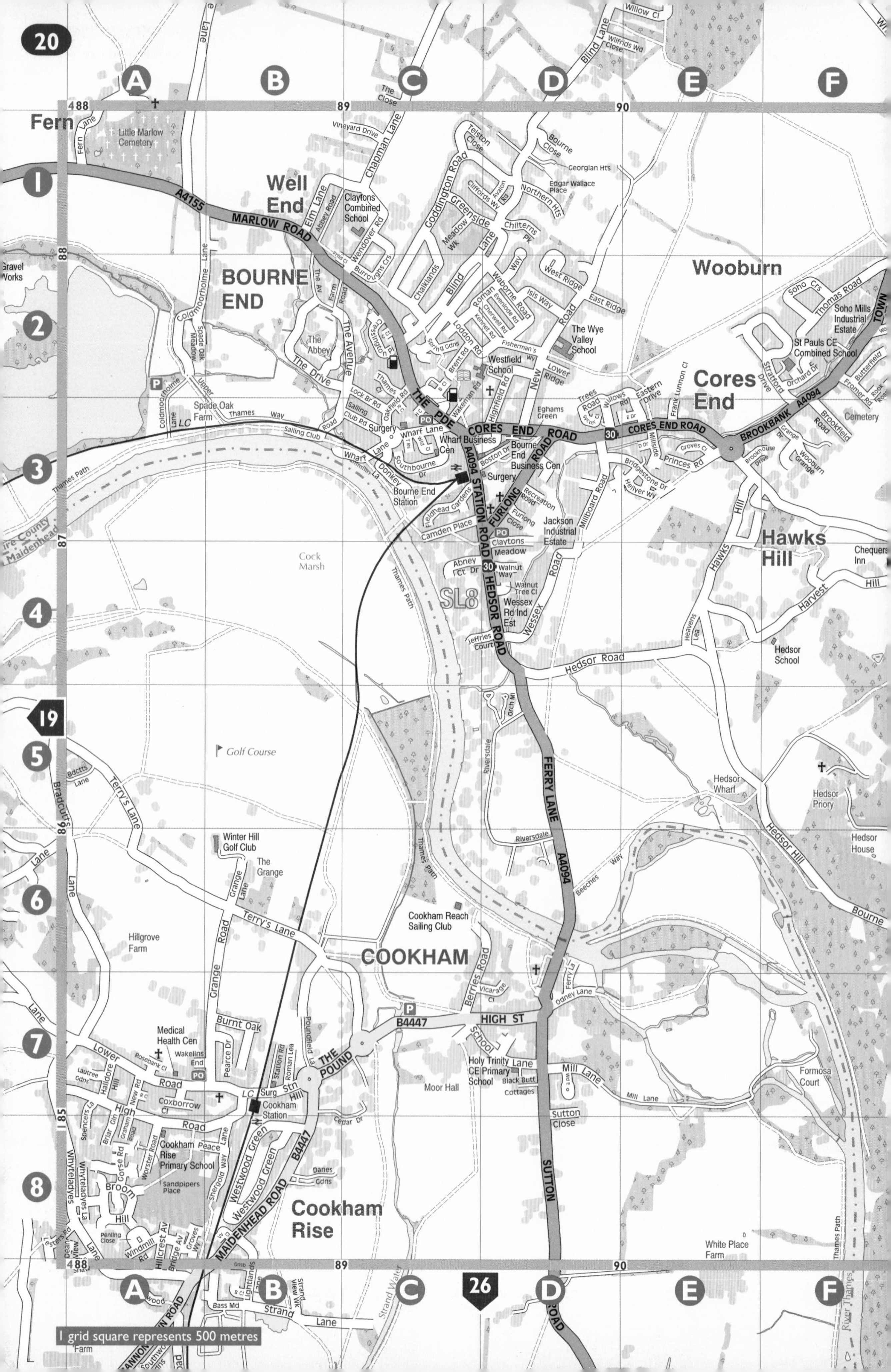
Fern
Little Marlow Cemetery
Well End
BOURNE END
Wooburn
Cores End
Hawks Hill
COOKHAM
Cookham Rise
Cock Marsh
Golf Course
Winter Hill Golf Club
The Grange
Hillgrove Farm
Claytons Combined School
The Wye Valley School
Westfield School
St Pauls CE Combined School
Soho Mills Industrial Estate
Bourne End Station
Bourne End Business Cen
Wharf Business Cen
Jackson Industrial Estate
Wessex Rd Ind Est
Hedsor School
Hedsor Wharf
Hedsor Priory
Hedsor House
Cookham Reach Sailing Club
Holy Trinity CE Primary School
Moor Hall
Cookham Station
Cookham Rise Primary School
Medical Health Cen
White Place Farm
Formosa Court
Spade Oak Farm
Gravel Works
MARLOW ROAD
A4155
CORES END ROAD
BROOKBANK
A4094
STATION ROAD
HEDSOR ROAD
FERRY LANE
SUTTON ROAD
HIGH ST
B4447
MAIDENHEAD ROAD
THE POUND
Thames Path
River Thames
SL8
1 grid square represents 500 metres

19
26

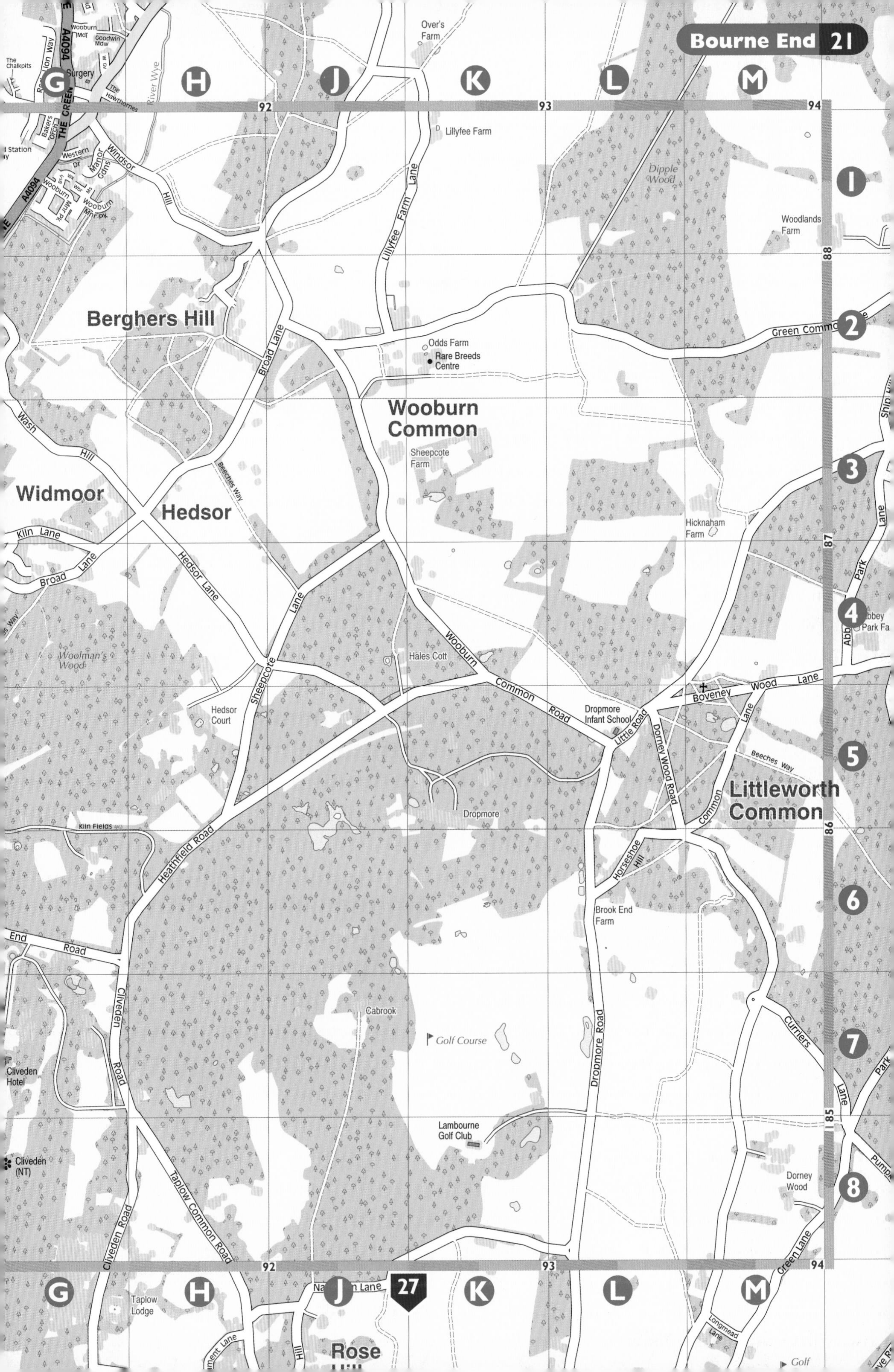

Over's Farm
Lillyfee Farm
Dipple Wood
Woodlands Farm
Berghers Hill
Odds Farm
Rare Breeds Centre
Green Common Lane
Wooburn Common
Sheepcote Farm
Widmoor
Hedsor
Hicknaham Farm
Kiln Lane
Broad Lane
Hedsor Lane
Sheepcote Lane
Woolman's Wood
Hales Cott
Wooburn Common Road
Boveney Wood Lane
Dropmore Infant School
Little Road
Dorney Wood Road
Hedsor Court
Beeches Way
Littleworth Common
Dropmore
Kiln Fields
Heathfield Road
Horseshoe Hill
Brook End Farm
End Road
Cliveden Road
Cabrook
Golf Course
Curriers Lane
Dropmore Road
Cliveden Hotel
Lambourne Golf Club
Cliveden (NT)
Taplow Common Road
Dorney Wood
Green Lane
Taplow Lodge
Longmead Lane
Rose Hill
Wash Hill
Windsor Hill
Broad Lane
Beeches Way
Wooburn Mnr Pk
Western Dr
Manor Gdns
Surgery
The Chalkpits
Station
A4094
THE GREEN
River Wye
The Hawthornes
Wooburn Mdf
Goodwin Mdw
Abbey Park Lane
Park Lane
Common Lane
27
92
93
94
88
87
86
85
G
H
J
K
L
M
1
2
3
4
5
6
7
8

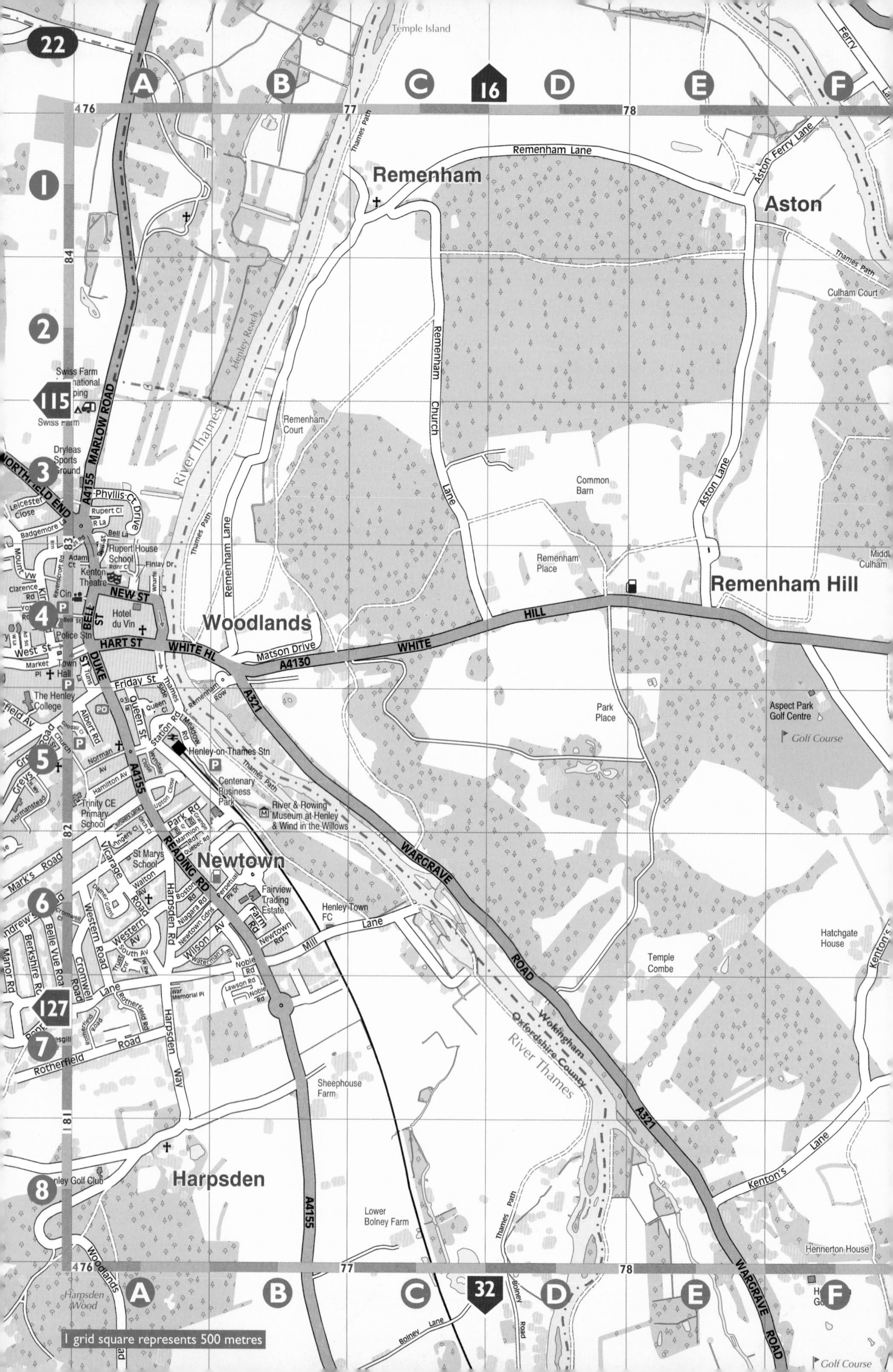

A   B   C   16   D   E   F

476   77   78

I

Temple Island

Remenham

Aston

Thames Path

Culham Court

2

Swiss Farm
International
Camping
115
Swiss Farm

Henley Reach

Remenham
Court

Remenham Church Lane

Common
Barn

Middl
Culham

Dryleas
Sports
Ground

3

NORTHFIELD END

MARLOW ROAD

A4155

Phyllis Ct Drive
Rupert Cl
R La
Bell La
Finlay Dr

Leicester
Close
Badgemore La

83

Rupert House
School

River Thames

Thames Path

Remenham Lane

Remenham
Place

Aston Lane

Remenham Hill

4

Mount
VW
Clarence
Rd
York
Rd
West St
Market
Pl

Adam
Ct

Kenton
Theatre
Cin

Bell St
Police Stn
Town
Hall

Hotel
du Vin

NEW ST

Woodlands

Matson Drive

WHITE HL

HILL

WHITE

A4130

5

field Av
Greys
Road

The Henley
College
PO
Albert Rd
Queen St
Norman
Av
Hamilton Av

Friday St
Queen Cl
Side Rd
Station Rd
Meadow
Remenham
Row

A321

Henley-on-Thames Stn

Thames Path

Park
Place

Aspect Park
Golf Centre
Golf Course

6

Mark's Road
Berkshire Rd
Belle Vue Road

Trinity CE
Primary
School
Vicarage
St Marys
School
Walton
Western Road
South Av
Cromwell Road

Park Rd
Harpsden Rd
Niagara Rd
Newtown Gdns
Wilson AV
Noble
Rd
Mill
Lane

Newtown

Centenary
Business
Park

River & Rowing
Museum at Henley
& Wind in the Willows

Fairview
Trading
Estate
Henley Town
FC

Henley Town
Lane

WARGRAVE

ROAD

Hatchgate
House

Temple
Combe

127

7

Manor Rd
Berkshire Rd
Rotherfield

Lane
Rotherfield Rd
Harpsden Way
War
Memorial Pl
Lawson Rd
Noble
Rd

Wokingham
Oxfordshire County

River Thames

A321

Kenton's Lane

8

Henley Golf Club

Harpsden

A4155

Woodlands

Sheephouse
Farm

Lower
Bolney Farm

Thames Path

Kenton's Lane

Hennerton House

WARGRAVE ROAD

Harpsden
Wood

A   B   C   32   D   E   F

476   77   78

Golf Course

1 grid square represents 500 metres

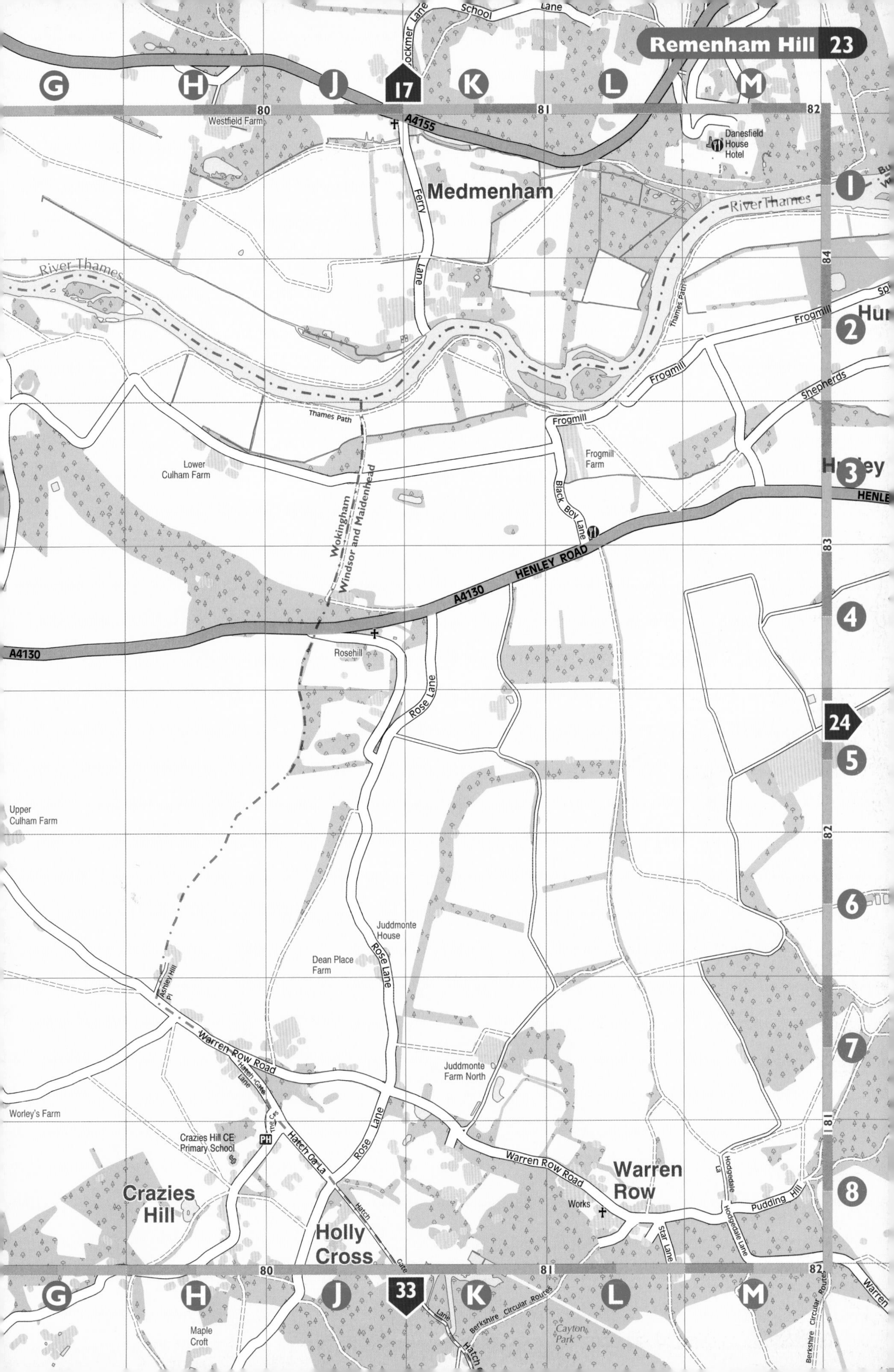

G H J 17 K L M

80 81 82

Medmenham

Westfield Farm

River Thames

Danesfield House Hotel

River Thames

Frogmill Spr

Frogmill

Hur

Frogmill Farm

He ley

HENLE

Black Boy Lane

HENLEY ROAD

A4130

Lower Culham Farm

Thames Path

Wokingham Windsor and Maidenhead

A4130

Rosehill

Rose Lane

24

Upper Culham Farm

Juddmonte House

Rose Lane

Dean Place Farm

Ashley Hill Pl

Worley's Farm

Warren Row Road

Hatch Gate Lane

Juddmonte Farm North

Crazies Hill CE Primary School

PH

Hatch Gate La

Rose Lane

Warren Row Road

Warren Row

Hodgedale La

Pudding Hill

Crazies Hill

Hatch

Works

Gate La

Star Lane

Hodgedale Lane

Maple Croft

Holly Cross

Berkshire Circular Routes

Cayton Park

Warren

Berkshire Circular Routes

G H J 33 K L M

80 81 82

1
2
3
4
5
6
7
8

84

83

82

81

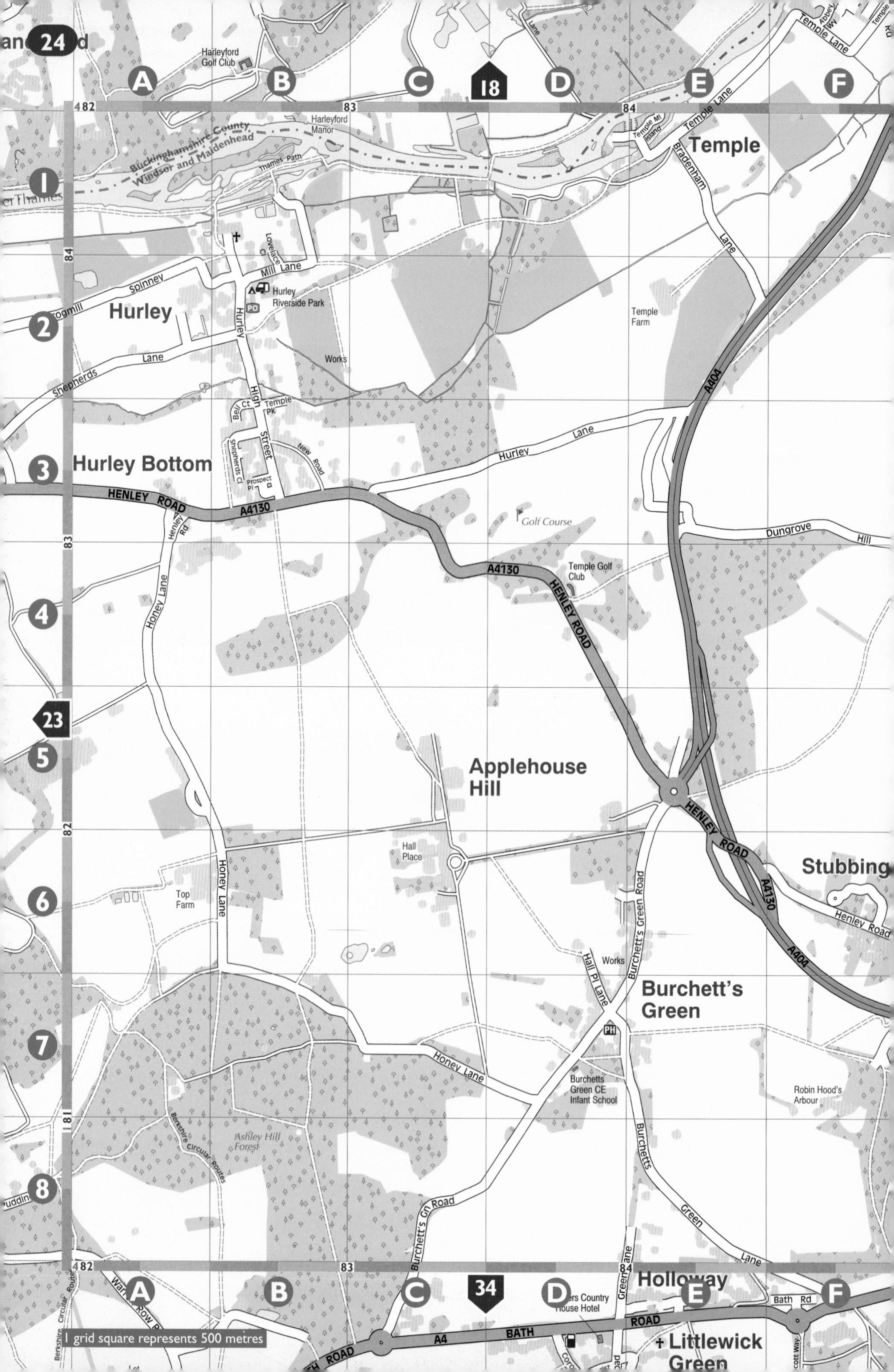
24
18
23
34
A
B
C
D
E
F
1
2
3
4
5
6
7
8
482
83
84
Harleyford Golf Club
Harleyford Manor
Buckinghamshire County
Windsor and Maidenhead
Thames Path
Temple
Temple Lane
Temple Mill Island
Bradenham Lane
Hurley
Mill Lane
Lovelace Cl
Spinney
Hurley Riverside Park
Shepherds Lane
High Street
Works
Temple Farm
A404
Bell Ct
Temple Pk
New Road
Shepherds Cl
Prospect Pl
Hurley Bottom
HENLEY ROAD
A4130
Henley Rd
Hurley Lane
Golf Course
Temple Golf Club
Dungrove Hill
Honey Lane
Applehouse Hill
Hall Place
Stubbings
Henley Road
Top Farm
Burchett's Green Road
Hall Pl Lane
Burchett's Green
Burchetts Green CE Infant School
Robin Hood's Arbour
Ashley Hill Forest
Berkshire Circular Routes
Burchett's Gn Road
Burchetts Green Lane
Holloway
Bath Rd
A4
BATH ROAD
Littlewick Green
1 grid square represents 500 metres

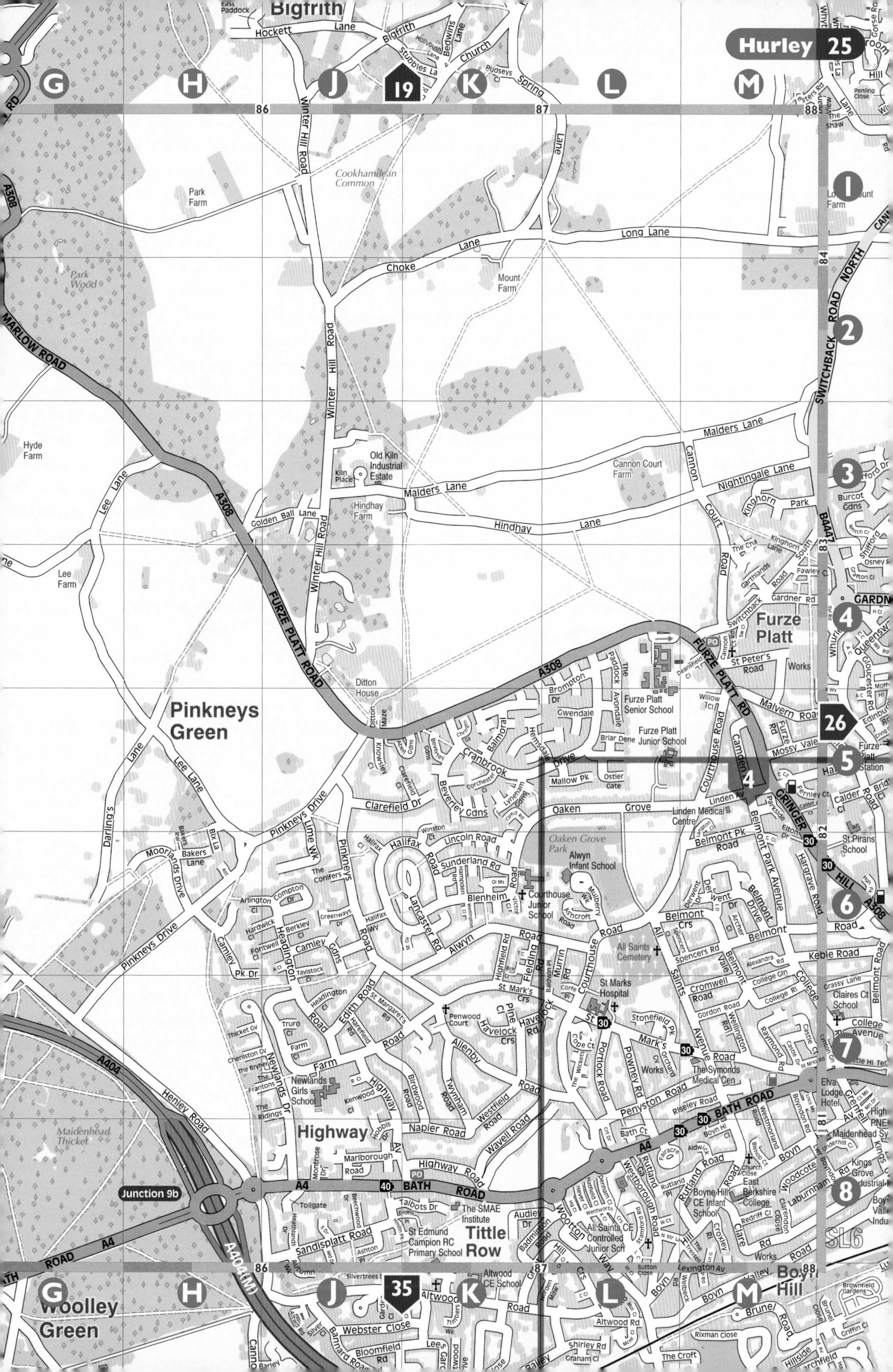
Bigfrith
East Paddock
Hockett Lane
Bigfrith Lane
Bedwins Lane
Hollybush Lane
Stubbles La
Church
Pudseys Cl
Spring
Hurley 25
G
H
J
19
K
L
M
86
87
88
Winter Hill Road
Cookhamdean Common
Park Farm
A308
Lane
Long Lane
Choke Lane
Mount Farm
Park Wood
CANNON COURT
SWITCHBACK ROAD NORTH
84
2
MARLOW ROAD
Hyde Farm
Maiders Lane
Cannon Court Farm
Cannon Court Road
Nightingale Lane
Old Kiln Industrial Estate
Kiln Place
Maiders Lane
3
Burcot Gdns
Kinghorn Park
Hindhay Farm
Hindhay Lane
Golden Ball Lane
Lee Lane
Lee Farm
FURZE PLATT ROAD
B4447
83
Osney Rd
Fawley Cl
Gardner Rd
GARDNER
4
Furze Platt
Switchback Rd South
Garthlands
Kinghorn Lane
St Peter's Road
Works
Queensway
Gloucester Rd
Ditton House
Pinkneys Green
A308
Brompton Dr
Gwendale
The Paddock
Avondale
Furze Platt Senior School
Furze Platt Junior School
Briar Dene
Willow Cl
FURZE PLATT RD
Malvern Road
26
Furze Rd
Mossy Vale
Edinburgh
Furze Platt Station
5
Courthouse Road
Camden Rd
4
GRINGER HILL
Ditton
Maze
Knowsley Cl
Beverley Gdns
Cranbrook
Balmoral
Hemsdale
Drive
Mallow Pk
Ostler Gate
Clarefield Cl
Clarefield Dr
Dorchester Cl
Lyneham Gdns
Pinkneys Drive
Lee Lane
Darling's Lane
Oaken Grove
Linden Av
Linden Medical Centre
Parkside
Fernley Ct
Calder Cl
Bridge Road
82
Elton Dr
30
St Pirans School
Belmont Pk Road
Belmont Park Avenue
Hargrave Road
Lime Wk
Pinkneys Road
Halifax Road
Winston Ct
Lincoln Road
Oaken Grove Park
Alwyn Infant School
Sunderland Rd
Hampden Rd
Blenheim Rd
Courthouse Junior School
Mulberry Wk
Ashcroft Road
Lancaster Rd
The Conifers
Moorlands Drive
Bakers Lane
Blk La
Arlington Cl
Compton Dr
Hardwick Cl
Berkley Cl
Fontwell Cl
Headington Cl
Camley Gdns
Greenways Dr
Halifax Wy
Derwent Dr
Belmont Drive
6
Belmont Crs
Archer Cl
Belmont
Road
Keble Road
All Saints Avenue
All Saints Cemetery
Spencers Rd
Vale
Alexandra Rd
College Gln
College Road
Belmont Road
Grassy Lane
Claires Ct School
College Avenue
Alwyn Road
Highfield Rd
Fielding Rd
Murrin Rd
Courthouse Road
St Marks Hospital
Cromwell Road
College Rl
Camley Pk Dr
Tavistock Cl
Pinkneys Drive
Headington Road
Edith Road
St Margaret's Rd
St Mark's Crs
Pine Cl
Havelock Rd
Havelock Crs
Penwood Court
Baldwin Pl
Corfe Pl
St Mark's Road
Stonefield Pk
Cope Ct
Portlock Road
Powney Rd
Orchard Gv
Works
Gordon Road
Wellington Rd
Raymond Rd
Castle Hill
7
Castle Hl Ter
Thicket Gv
Truro Cl
Farm Cl
Harefield Rd
Allenby Road
The Wickets
The Symonds Medical Cen
Elva Lodge Hotel
Chenilston Gv
The Brynes
The Frantons
The Ridings
Newlands Dr
Farm Road
Newlands Girls School
Kenwood Cl
Highway Road
Birdwood Road
Twynham Road
Westfield Road
Penyston Road
Riseley Road
BATH ROAD
Westmorland Road
Boyndon Rd
Grenfell Av
Maidenhead Sixth Form
Kings Grove Industrial
Highway
Hobbis Dr
Napier Road
Wavell Road
Bath Ct
Boyn Hill
Aldwick
Fairacre
Rutland Road
Boyn Hill Avenue
Woodcote
Laburnham Rd
8
A4
A404
Henley Road
Maidenhead Thicket
Junction 9b
A4
ROAD
Montrose Dr
Marlborough Road
Highway Av
PO
40
BATH ROAD
Tollgate
Beechwood Dr
Talbots Dr
The SMAE Institute
Audley Dr
Badminton Road
Wootton Way
All Saints CE Controlled Junior Sch
Westborough Road
Rutland Pl
Boyne Hill CE Infant School
East Berkshire College
Clarendon Copse
Redriff Cl
Sandisplatt Road
St Edmund Campion RC Primary School
Tittle Row
Heathlands Dr
Ashton
Croxley
Clare Rd
Works
SL6
A404(M)
Autumn Wk
Silvertrees Dr
Altwood CE School
Sutton Close
Lexington Av
Boyn Valley
Boyn Hill
Brownfield Gardens
G
H
J
35
K
L
M
Woolley Green
Altwood
Altwood Rd
Road
Boyn Road
Brunel Road
Griffin Cl
Webster Close
Bloomfield Rd
Silver Cl
Shirley Rd
Graham Cl
Rixman Close
The Croft
Hillside
Barley
Bannard Road
Bailey

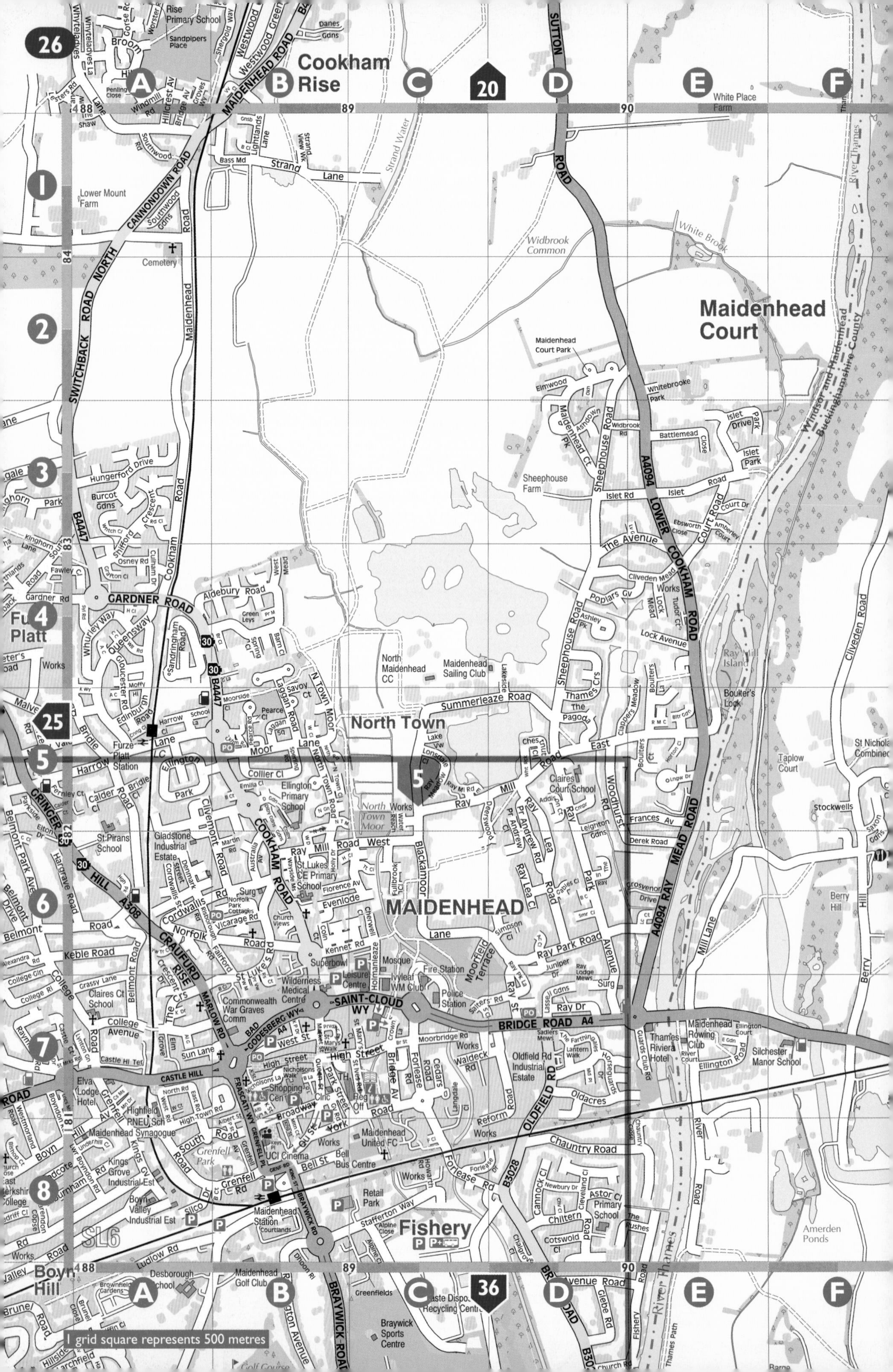

26
Cookham Rise
Rise Primary School
Sandpipers Place
Westwood Green
MAIDENHEAD ROAD
Danes Gdns
Whyteladies Lane
Broom Hill
Penling Close
Windmill Rd
Hillcrest Av
Bridge Av
Groves Wy
Lesters Rd
The Shaw
Southwood
Lightlands Lane
Bass Md
Strand Lane
Strand View Wk
Strand Water
SUTTON ROAD
White Place Farm
Lower Mount Farm
CANNONDOWN ROAD
Southwood Gdns
Cemetery
SWITCHBACK ROAD NORTH
Maidenhead Road
Widbrook Common
White Brook
Maidenhead Court
River Thames
Windsor and Maidenhead
Buckinghamshire County
Maidenhead Court Park
Elmwood
Whitebrooke Park
Widbrook Rd
Battlemead Close
Islet Drive
Islet Park
Sheephouse Farm
Sheephouse Road
Islet Rd
Islet Road
Court Road
Court Dr
Ebsworth Close
Amberley Court
The Avenue
A4094 LOWER COOKHAM ROAD
Hungerford Drive
Burcot Gdns
Park
Shifford Crescent
Kinghorn Lane
B4447
Osney Rd
Cookham Road
Fawley Cl
Gardner Rd
GARDNER ROAD
Aldebury Road
West Mead
Green Leys
Furze Platt
Whurley Way
Queensway
Gloucester Rd
Sandringham Road
Spring Cl
Barn Cl
Clivedon Mead
Poplars Gv
Ashley Pk
Lock Mead
Tudor Ct
Lock Avenue
Ray Mill Island
Boulter's Lock
Clivedon Road
North Maidenhead CC
Maidenhead Sailing Club
Lakeside
Summerleaze Road
Thames Crs
The Pagoda
Clappers Meadow
Boulters La
Works
Edinburgh Road
Moorside
Pearce Cl
Laggan Road
Savoy Ct
N Town Moor
North Town
Harrow Lane
Furze Platt Station
Moor Lane
Lake Vw
Lonsdale Cl
Ray Meadow
Chestnut Cl
East
Boulters Ct
St Nicholas Combined
Taplow Court
Harrow Cl
Calder Cl
Bridle Cl
Ellington Park
Collier Cl
Ellington Primary School
North Town Moor
Ray Mill Rd E
Ray Mill Road
Claires Court School
Woodhurst Rd
Frances Av
Leighton Gdns
Derek Road
Stockwells
Saxon Gdns
GRINGER HILL
St Pirans School
Gladstone Industrial Estate
Clivemont Road
Australia Av
COOKHAM ROAD
Ray Mill Road West
Blackamoor Lane
Deerswood
Pr Andrew Rd
Lea Road
Park Road
Ray Lea Cl
Grosvenor Drive
Berry Hill
Harcrave Road
Belmont Park Ave
Belmont Drive
A308
CRAUFURD RISE
Cordwallis St
Denmark Street
Vicarage Rd
Norfolk Road
St Lukes CE Primary School
Florence Av
Evenlode
Church Views
MAIDENHEAD
Ray Park Road
Moorfield Terrace
Simpson Cl
A4094 RAY MEAD ROAD
Mill Lane
Keble Road
Belmont Road
Grassy Lane
College Avenue
Claires Ct School
St Luke's Rd
Kennet Rd
Superbowl
Holmanleaze
Mosque
Leisure Centre
Fire Station
Juniper Dr
Ray Lodge Mews
Ivyleaf WM Club
Wilderness Medical Centre
Commonwealth War Graves Comm
MARLOW RD
GODESBERG WY
SAINT-CLOUD WY
Police Station
Salters' Rd
Ray St
Ray Dr
BRIDGE ROAD A4
Sadlers Mews
The Farthingales
Lantern Walk
Horseguards Dr
Maidenhead Rowing Club
Thames Riviera Hotel
River Court
Ellington Road
Ellington Court
Silchester Manor School
Castle Hill Ter
Sun Lane
West St
High Street
Moorbridge Rd
Waldeck Rd
Oldfield Rd Industrial Estate
OLDFIELD RD
Guards Club Rd
CASTLE HILL
Elva Lodge Hotel
Highfield PNEU Sch
North Rd
East Rd
High Town Rd
Nicholsons Walk
Shopping Cen
Park Street
Reg Off
Broadway
Forlease Rd
Cedars Road
Reform Road
Oldacres
Maidenhead Synagogue
Kings Grove Industrial Est
Grenfell Park
FRASCATI WY
GRENFELL PL
York Road
Maidenhead United FC
Chauntry Road
UCI Cinema
Bell St
Bell Bus Centre
Forlease Rd
B3028
Grenfell Rd
Boyn Valley Industrial Est
Maidenhead Station
Courtlands
Retail Park
Stafferton Way
Alpine Close
Fishery
Cannock Cl
Newbury Dr
Cleveland Cl
Astor Cl Primary School
Chiltern Road
Cotswold Cl
Chalgrove Cl
The Rushes
River Road
Amerden Ponds
SL6
Ludlow Rd
Boyn Hill
Desborough School
Maidenhead Golf Club
BRAYWICK ROAD
Greenfields
Waste Disposal & Recycling Centre
36
Braywick Sports Centre
Avenue Road
Glebe Rd
Fishery Road
Thames Path
Brunel Road
Hillside
1 grid square represents 500 metres
20
25

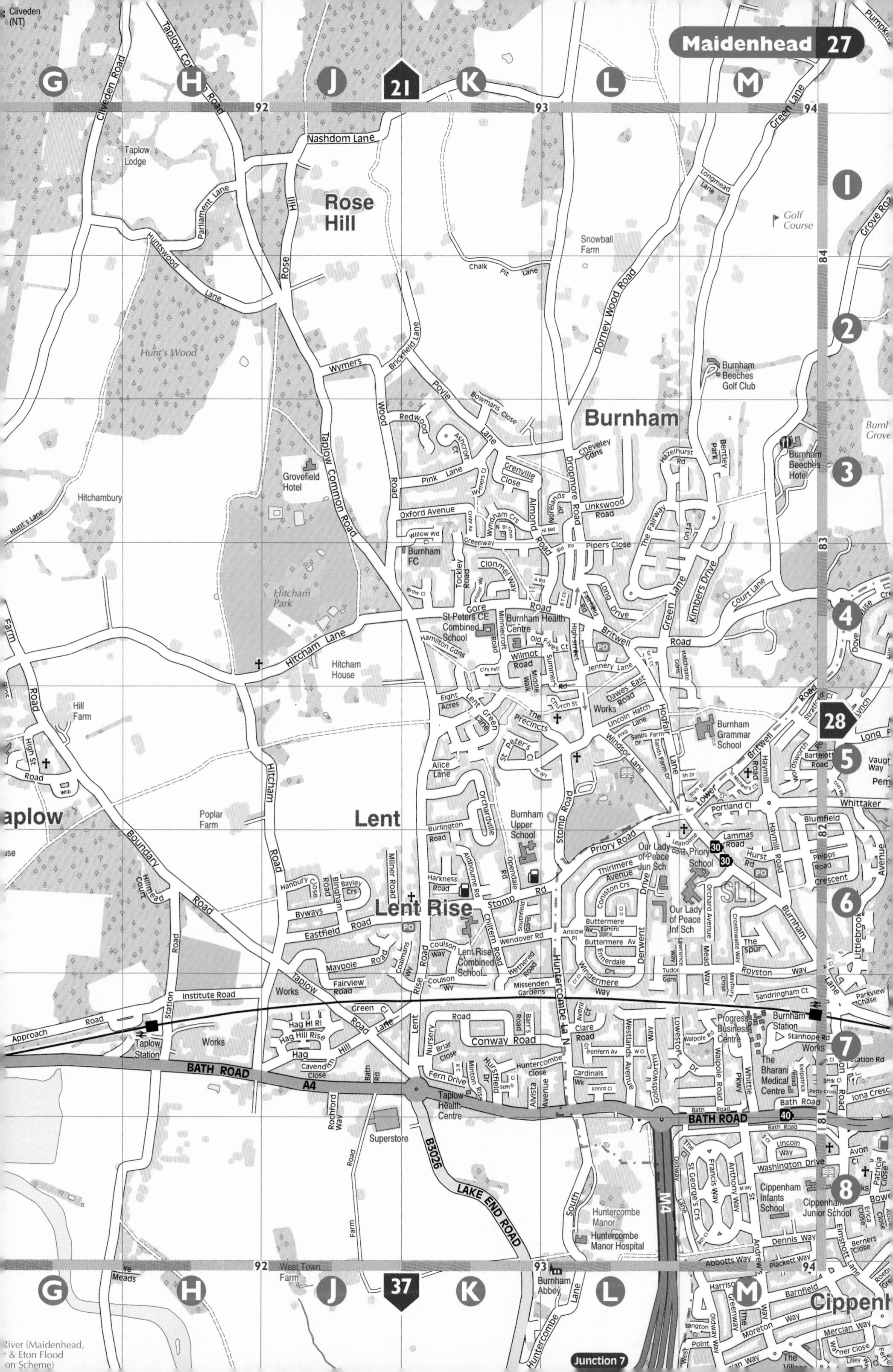
Cliveden (NT)
G
H
J
21
K
L
M
92
93
94
Cliveden Road
Taplow Common Road
Nashdom Lane
Taplow Lodge
Parliament Lane
Rose Hill
Huntswood Lane
Rose Hill
Snowball Farm
Chalk Pit Lane
Dorney Wood Road
Longmead Lane
Golf Course
Green Lane
Grove Road
Hunt's Wood
Wymers
Brickfield Lane
Poyle Lane
Bowmans Close
Burnham Beeches Golf Club
Burnham
Burnham Beeches Hotel
Grovefield Hotel
Hitchambury
Hunt's Lane
Redwood
Ashcroft Ct
Pink Lane
Grenville Close
Cheveley Gdns
Hazelhurst Rd
Bentley Park
Oxford Avenue
Wyndham Crs
Almond Road
Dropmore Road
Linkswood Road
The Fairway
Burnham FC
Greenway
Pipers Close
Kimbers Drive
Court Lane
Hitcham Park
Tockley Road
Clonmel Way
Long Drive
Gore Road
St Peters CE Combined School
Burnham Health Centre
Britwell Road
Hitcham Lane
Hitcham House
Hamilton Gdns
Wilmot Road
Old Fives Ct
Jennery Lane
Dawes East Road
Hatchgate Gdns
Hill Farm
Eight Acres
Lent Green Lane
The Precincts
Church St
Works
Lincoln Hatch Lane
Hogfair Lane
Burnham Grammar School
28
Long
Farm Road
High St
Road
St Peter's Cl
Windsor Lane
Britwell
Haymill Road
Wordsworth Rd
Bartelotts Road
Vaughan Way
Taplow
Poplar Farm
Alice Lane
Stomp Road
Lower
Portland Cl
Whittaker
Lent
Orchardville
Burnham Upper School
Priory Road
Lammas Road
Blumfield
Burlington Road
Boundary Road
Hitcham Road
Hillmead Court
Aldbourne Rd
Milner Road
Our Lady of Peace Jun Sch
Priory School
Hurst Rd
Haymill Road
Phipps Road
Crescent
Avenue
Hanbury Close
Bingham Close
Bayley Crs
Harkness Road
Opendale Rd
Thirlmere Avenue
Coniston Crs
Drive
SL1
6
Lent Rise
Stomp Rd
Byways
Eastfield Road
Chiltern Road
Southfield Gdns
Our Lady of Peace Inf Sch
Orchard Avenue
Crosthwaite Way
Burnham
Littlebrook
Buttermere Av
Buttermere Av
Anslow Pl
Wendover Rd
Derwent
The Spur
Coulson Way
Lent Rise Combined School
Wethered Road
Huntercombe La N
Ennerdale Crs
Lawrence Way
Mead Way
Royston Way
Maypole Road
Fairview Road
Rise Road
Coulson Wy
Missenden Gardens
Windermere Way
Tudor Gdns
Maybury Close
Sandringham Ct
Parkview Chase
Institute Road
Works
Taplow
Green Cl
Barr's Road
Burnham Station
Approach Road
Station Road
Taplow Station
Works
Hag Hill Rise
Hag Hill Lane
Nursery Road
Briar Close
Conway Road
Clare Road
Westlands Avenue
Lowestoft Dr
Progress Business Centre
Stanhope Rd
7
Works
Walpole Road
Whittle Pkwy
The Bharani Medical Centre
Station Rd
Fern Drive
Hurstfield Dr
Minton Rise
Huntercombe Close
Cardinals Wk
BATH ROAD
A4
Cavendish Close
Bath Rd
Taplow Health Centre
Alvista Avenue
Goldsworthy Way
Bath Road
40
BATH ROAD
Iona Cresc
Rochford Way
Superstore
B3026
LAKE END ROAD
Road
Farm
South Lane
Huntercombe Manor
Huntercombe Manor Hospital
M4
Oldway Lane
St George's Crs
Francis Way
Anthony Way
Lincoln Way
Washington Drive
Cippenham Infants School
Cippenham Junior School
8
Avon Cl
Patricia Close
Erica Close
Berners Close
Dennis Way
Plackett Way
Abbotts Way
Andrews Way
Elmshott Lane
Ye Meads
West Town Farm
37
Burnham Abbey
Huntercombe Lane
Greenway
The Moreton Way
Barnfield
Cippenham
Mercian Way
Warner Close
Point
Junction 7
River (Maidenhead, & Eton Flood Scheme)
I
2
3
4
5
82
83
84

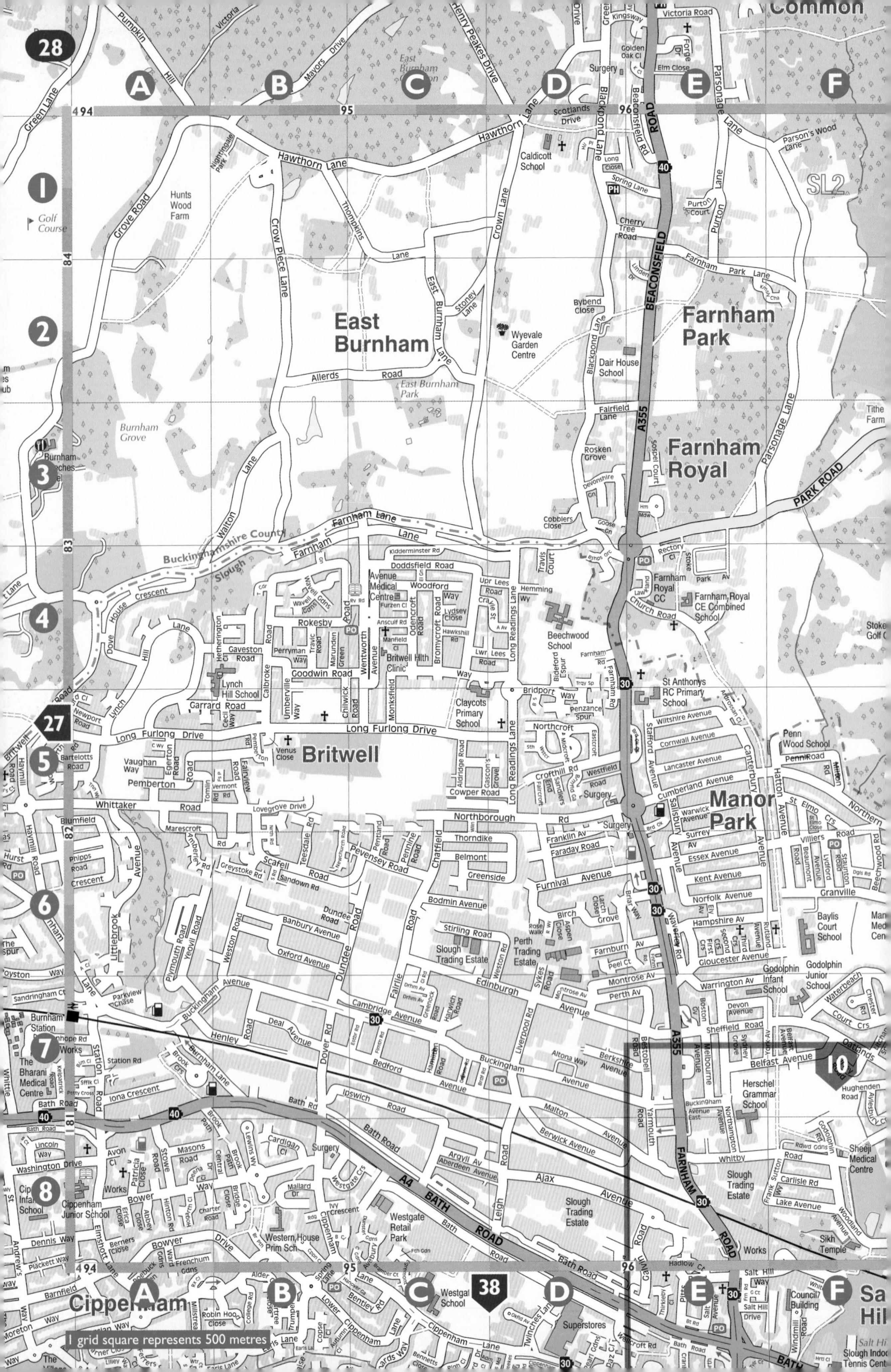
28
A
B
C
D
E
F
Common
Victoria Road
Kingsway
Golden Oak Cl
Forge Dr
Elm Close
Surgery
Parsonage Lane
Pumpkin Hill
Victoria
Mavors Drive
Henry Peakes Drive
East Burnham Common
Green Lane
494
95
96
Scotlands Drive
Blackpond Lane
Beaconsfield Rd
Beaconsfield Road
Parson's Wood Lane
SL2
Hawthorn Lane
Nightingale Park
Caldicott School
Long Close
Spring Lane
PH
40
1
Golf Course
Hunts Wood Farm
Grove Road
Crow Piece Lane
Thompkins Lane
Crown Lane
Purton Court
Purton Lane
Cherry Tree Road
Farnham Park Lane
Linden Dr
84
2
East Burnham
East Burnham Lane
Stoney Lane
Wyevale Garden Centre
Bybend Close
Farnham Park
Dair House School
Allerds Road
East Burnham Park
Burnham Grove
Fairfield Lane
A355
Tithe Farm
Farnham Royal
Rosken Grove
Sospel Court
Parsonage Lane
3
Burnham Beeches Hotel
Walton Lane
Devonshire Gn
PARK ROAD
Cobblers Close
Goose Gn
Farnham Lane
Buckinghamshire County
Slough
83
Kidderminster Rd
Doddsfield Road
Travis Court
Rectory Cl
Stoke Park Av
PO
Avenue Medical Centre
Woodford Way
Upr Lees Road
Hemming Wy
Farnham Royal CC
Farnham Royal CE Combined School
Church Road
Dove House Crescent
Wavell Gdns
Furzen Cl
Lydsey Close
Rokesby
Ansculf Rd
Odencroft Road
Hawkshill Rd
Manfield Cl
Bromycroft Road
4
Lane
Hill
Hetherington Cl
Gaveston Road
Perryman Way
Travic Road
Marunden Green
Britwell Hlth Clinic
Lwr Lees Road
Long Readings Lane
Beechwood School
Stoke Golf C
Goodwin Road
Wentworth Avenue
Way
Bideford Spur
Farnham Rd
Lynch Hill School
Calbroke Road
Umberville Way
Chilwick Road
Monksfield
Claycots Primary School
Bridport Way
St Anthonys RC Primary School
Garrard Road
Penzance Spur
Andrews Cl
Newport Road
Cecil Way
Northcroft
Eastcroft
Wiltshire Avenue
Cornwall Avenue
Penn Wood School
Penn Road
27
Long Furlong Drive
Venus Close
Britwell
Britwell
Aldridge Road
Gascon's Grove
Crofthill Rd
Westfield Road
Lancaster Avenue
Cumberland Avenue
5
Bartelotts Road
Haymill
Vaughan Way
Egerton Road
Tomlin Rd
Vermont Rd
Fairview
Pemberton
Cowper Road
Sandlers End
Surgery
Manor Park
Hatton Avenue
St Elmo Crs
Northern
Whittaker Road
Lovegrove Drive
Northborough Rd
Warwick Avenue
Salisbury Avenue
Blumfield
Marescroft Rd
Amberley Rd
Teesdale Rd
Newchurch Road
Pentland Road
Pennine Road
Chatfield
Thorndike
Franklin Av
Faraday Road
Surrey Av
Villiers Road
82
Haymill Road
Phipps Road
Crescent
Avenue
Greystoke Rd
Scafell Road
Sandown Rd
Pevensey Road
Belmont
Greenside
Furnival Avenue
Essex Avenue
Kent Avenue
Beaumont Road
Lyford Road
Staunton Road
Beechwood Rd
Hurst Rd
PO
6
Bodmin Avenue
Norfolk Avenue
Granville
Dundee Road
Birch Grove
Larch Close
Hampshire Av
Baylis Court School
Littlebrook
Weston Road
Banbury Avenue
Stirling Road
Rose Walk
Aspen Close
Waverley Rd
First Crs
Second Crs
Third Crs
Rutland Avenue
Plymouth Road
Yeovil Road
Oxford Avenue
Dundee Road
Fairlie Road
Slough Trading Estate
Weston Rd
Perth Trading Estate
Farnburn Av
Gloucester Avenue
Godolphin Infant School
Godolphin Junior School
Royston Way
Peel Ct
Sandringham Ct
Parkview Chase
Lane
Buckingham Avenue
Edinburgh Avenue
Sykes Road
Montrose Av
Perth Av
Warrington Av
Waterbeach Road
Chester Rd
Burnham Station
Cambridge Avenue
Henley Road
Deal Avenue
Dover Rd
Liverpool Rd
Devon Avenue
Court Crs
Sheffield Road
Oatlands
7
Station Rd
Station Road
Works
Brook Crs
Burnham Lane
Bedford Avenue
Hamilton Road
Buckingham Avenue
Altona Way
Berkshire Avenue
Bestobell Road
Boston Avenue
Melbourne Avenue
Belfast Avenue
Sydney Grove
10
The Bharani Medical Centre
Iona Crescent
Ipswich Road
Bath Rd
Malton Avenue
Yarmouth Road
Herschel Grammar School
Hughenden Road
Aylesbury Cres
Bath Road
40
81
Bath Road
Brook Path
Lewins Way
Cardigan Cl
Surgery
Bath Road
Berwick Avenue
Buckingham Avenue East
Northampton Avenue
Godolphin Road
Sheeji Medical Centre
Lincoln Way
Avon Cl
Masons Road
Stowe Road
Central Road
Argyll Av
Aberdeen Avenue
Ajax Avenue
Whitby Road
Washington Drive
Patricia Close
Mallard Dr
Westgate Crs
A4 BATH ROAD
Leigh Road
Slough Trading Estate
Frank Sutton Way
Carlisle Rd
8
Cippenham Infant School
Cippenham Junior School
Works
Bower Way
Hinton Rd
Charter Road
Bridge Close
Ivy Crescent
Westgate Retail Park
Slough Trading Estate
FARNHAM ROAD
Lake Avenue
Woodland Avenue
Erica Close
Abbey Close
Dennis Way
Berners Close
Bowyer Drive
Ward Gdns
Frenchum Gdns
Western House Prim Sch
Cippenham Lane
Galvin Road
Works
Sikh Temple
Plackett Way
494
95
96
Hadlow Ct
Salt Hill Way
Salt Hill Drive
Council Building
Barnfield
Cippenham
Robin Hood Close
Bentley Rd
Westgate School
38
Superstores
Windmill Road
Sa Hill
Moreton Way
1 grid square represents 500 metres
Earls Lane
Lower Cippenham Lane
Bennetts
Cippenham Lane
Twinches Lane
Wellcroft Rd
Salt Hill Tennis Centre
Slough Indoor
BATH

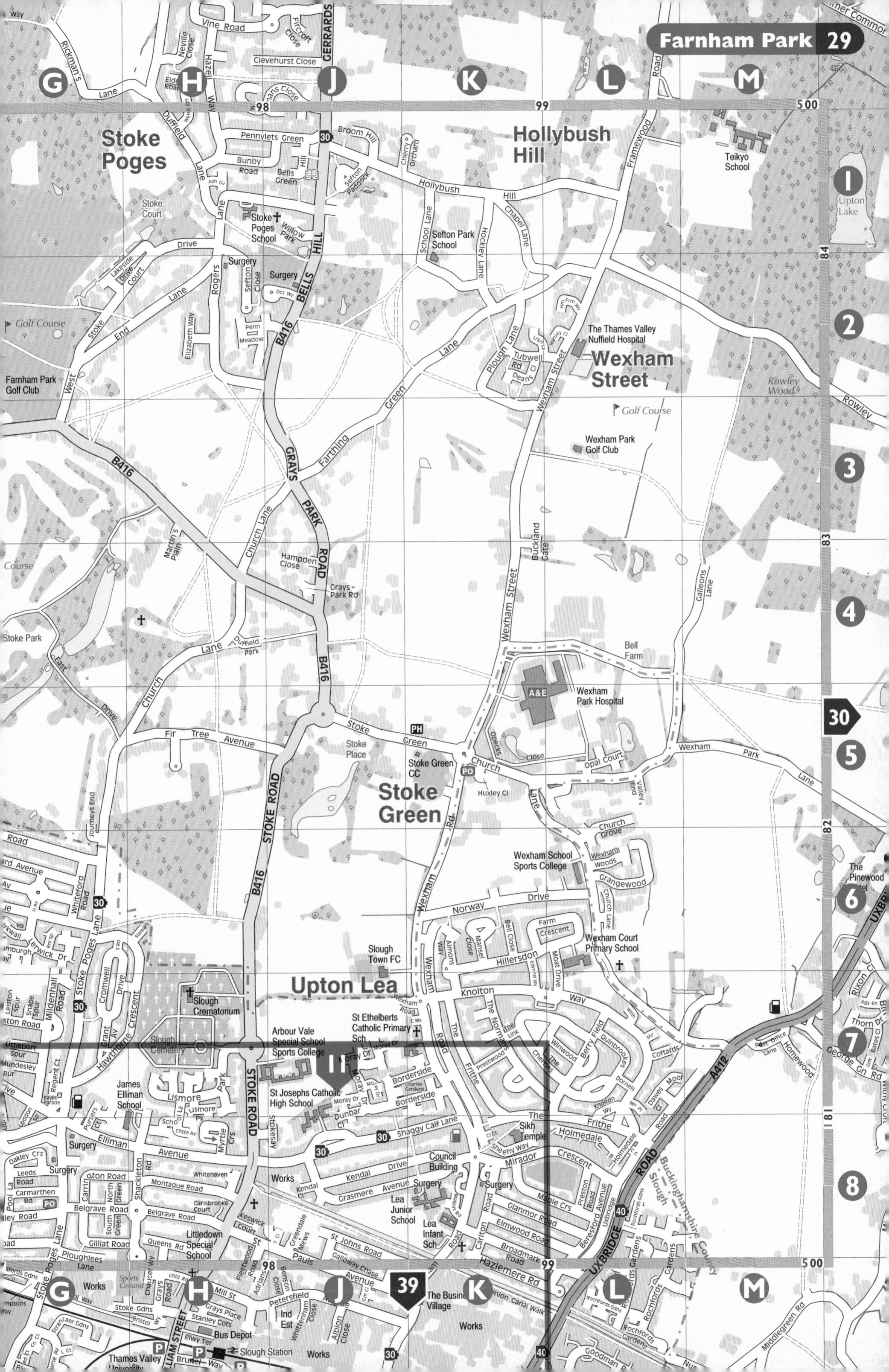
Stoke Poges
Hollybush Hill
Teikyo School
Upton Lake
Sefton Park School
The Thames Valley Nuffield Hospital
Wexham Street
Farnham Park Golf Club
Wexham Park Golf Club
Rowley Wood
Stoke Park
Bell Farm
Wexham Park Hospital
A&E
Stoke Place
Stoke Green CC
Stoke Green
Huxley Cl
Wexham School Sports College
Wexham Court Primary School
Slough Town FC
Upton Lea
Slough Crematorium
Slough Cemetery
Arbour Vale Special School Sports College
St Ethelberts Catholic Primary Sch
St Josephs Catholic High School
James Elliman School
Surgery
Council Building
Lea Junior School
Lea Infant Sch
Littledown Special School
The Sikh Temple
Works
Sports Ground
Bus Depot
Slough Station
Thames Valley University
The Business Village
Ind Est
Buckinghamshire County
Slough
STOKE ROAD
UXBRIDGE ROAD
GERRARDS
BELLS HILL
GRAYS PARK ROAD
B416
A412
30
39
40

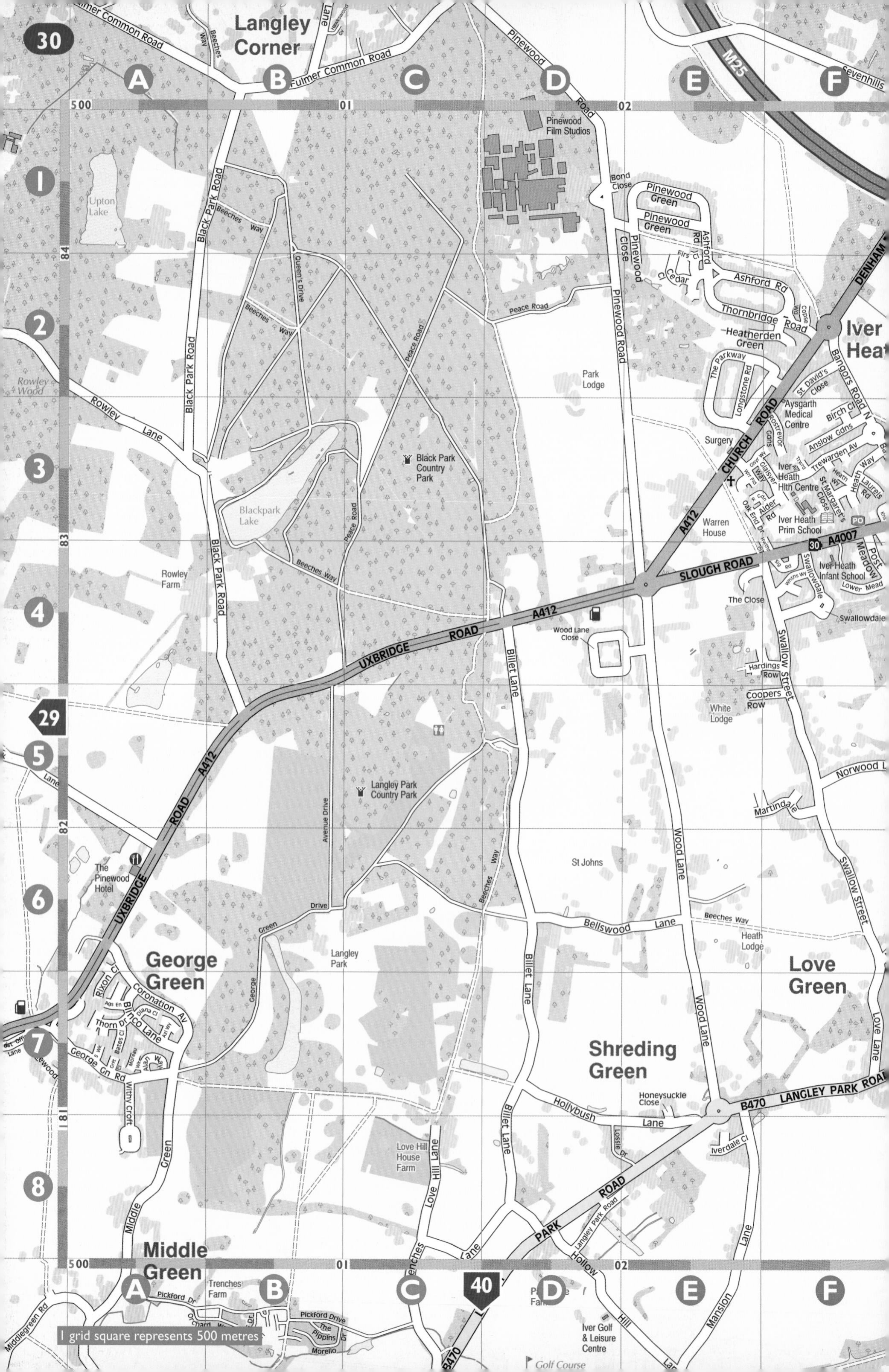
Langley Corner
Fulmer Common Road
Pinewood Road
Pinewood Film Studios
Upton Lake
Black Park Road
Beeches Way
Queen's Drive
Peace Road
Bond Close
Pinewood Green
Pinewood Close
Ashford Rd
Thornbridge Road
Heatherden Green
Iver Heath
Park Lodge
Rowley Wood
Rowley Lane
Black Park Country Park
Blackpark Lake
Aysgarth Medical Centre
Surgery
CHURCH ROAD
A412
Iver Heath Hlth Centre
Iver Heath Prim School
Warren House
SLOUGH ROAD
A4007
Iver Heath Infant School
Rowley Farm
The Close
Swallowdale
UXBRIDGE ROAD
Wood Lane Close
Billet Lane
Hardings Row
Coopers Row
White Lodge
Swallow Street
Langley Park Country Park
Avenue Drive
Norwood Lane
Martindale
The Pinewood Hotel
St Johns
Wood Lane
Bellswood Lane
Beeches Way
Heath Lodge
George Green
Langley Park
Love Green
Coronation Av
Shreding Green
George Gn Rd
Withy Croft
Honeysuckle Close
Hollybush Lane
B470 LANGLEY PARK ROAD
Iverdale Cl
Love Hill House Farm
Love Hill Lane
PARK ROAD
Langley Park Road
Middle Green
Trenches Farm
Pickford Dr
Pickford Drive
The Pippins
Morello
Middlegreen Rd
Hollow Hill Lane
Mansion Lane
Iver Golf & Leisure Centre
Golf Course
1 grid square represents 500 metres

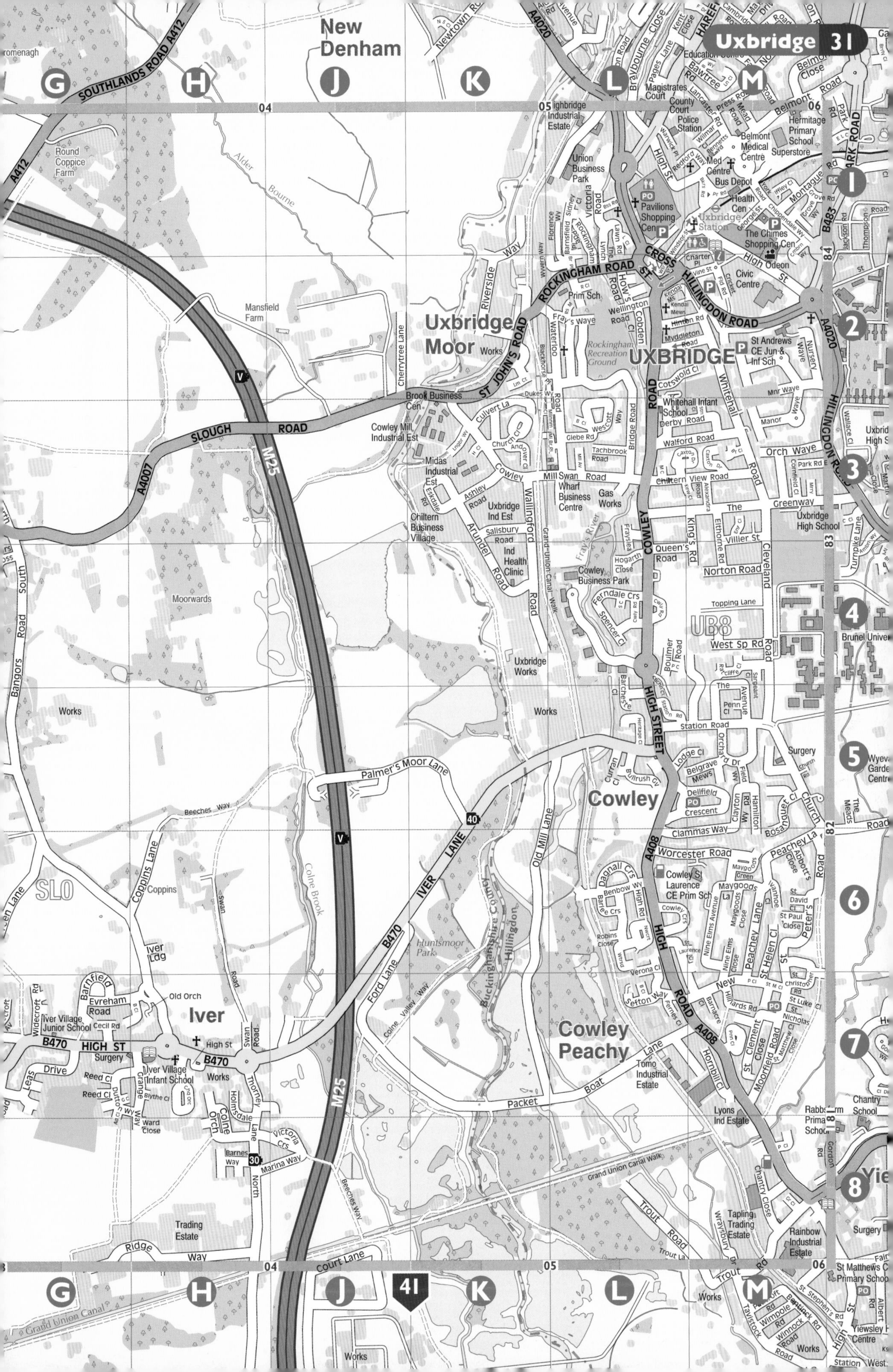
New Denham
Uxbridge Moor
UXBRIDGE
Cowley
Cowley Peachy
Iver
SOUTHLANDS ROAD A412
A412
M25
SLOUGH ROAD
A4007
ST JOHN'S ROAD
ROCKINGHAM ROAD
CROSS ST
HILLINGDON ROAD
A4020
COWLEY ROAD
HIGH STREET
HIGH ROAD
A408
IVER LANE
B470
HIGH ST
Palmer's Moor Lane
Packet Boat Lane
Grand Union Canal Walk
Grand Union Canal
Trout Road
Court Lane
Ridge Way
Round Coppice Farm
Mansfield Farm
Moorwards
Coppins
Iver Ldg
Old Orch
Alder Bourne
Colne Brook
Fray's River
Huntsmoor Park
Rockingham Recreation Ground
Brook Business Cen
Cowley Mill Industrial Est
Midas Industrial Est
Chiltern Business Village
Uxbridge Ind Est
Ind Health Clinic
Swan Wharf Business Centre
Gas Works
Cowley Business Park
Uxbridge Works
Works
Union Business Park
Highbridge Industrial Estate
Magistrates Court
County Court
Police Station
Pavilions Shopping Cen
The Chimes Shopping Cen
Uxbridge Station
Civic Centre
Odeon
Bus Depot
Health Cen
Med Centre
Belmont Medical Centre
Hermitage Primary School
Superstore
St Andrews CE Jun & Inf Sch
Whitehall Infant School
Uxbridge High School
Brunel Univer
Cowley St Laurence CE Prim Sch
Iver Village Junior School
Iver Village Infant School
Surgery
Tomo Industrial Estate
Lyons Ind Estate
Tapling Trading Estate
Rainbow Industrial Estate
Trading Estate
Chantry School
St Matthews C Primary Scho
Yiewsley Centre
Bangors Road South
Coppins Lane
Swan Road
Cherrytree Lane
Riverside Way
Wallingford Road
Arundel Road
Bridge Road
Whitehall Road
Cleveland Road
Norton Road
Station Road
Worcester Road
Clammas Way
Church Road
Peachey Lane
Moorfield Road
Ford Lane
Colne Valley Way
Old Mill Lane
Thorney Lane North
Marina Way
Beeches Way
Leas Drive
Evreham Road
Widecroft Rd
Barnfield
UB8
SL0
G
H
J
K
L
M
1
2
3
4
5
6
7
8
04
05
06
81
82
83
84
30
40
41

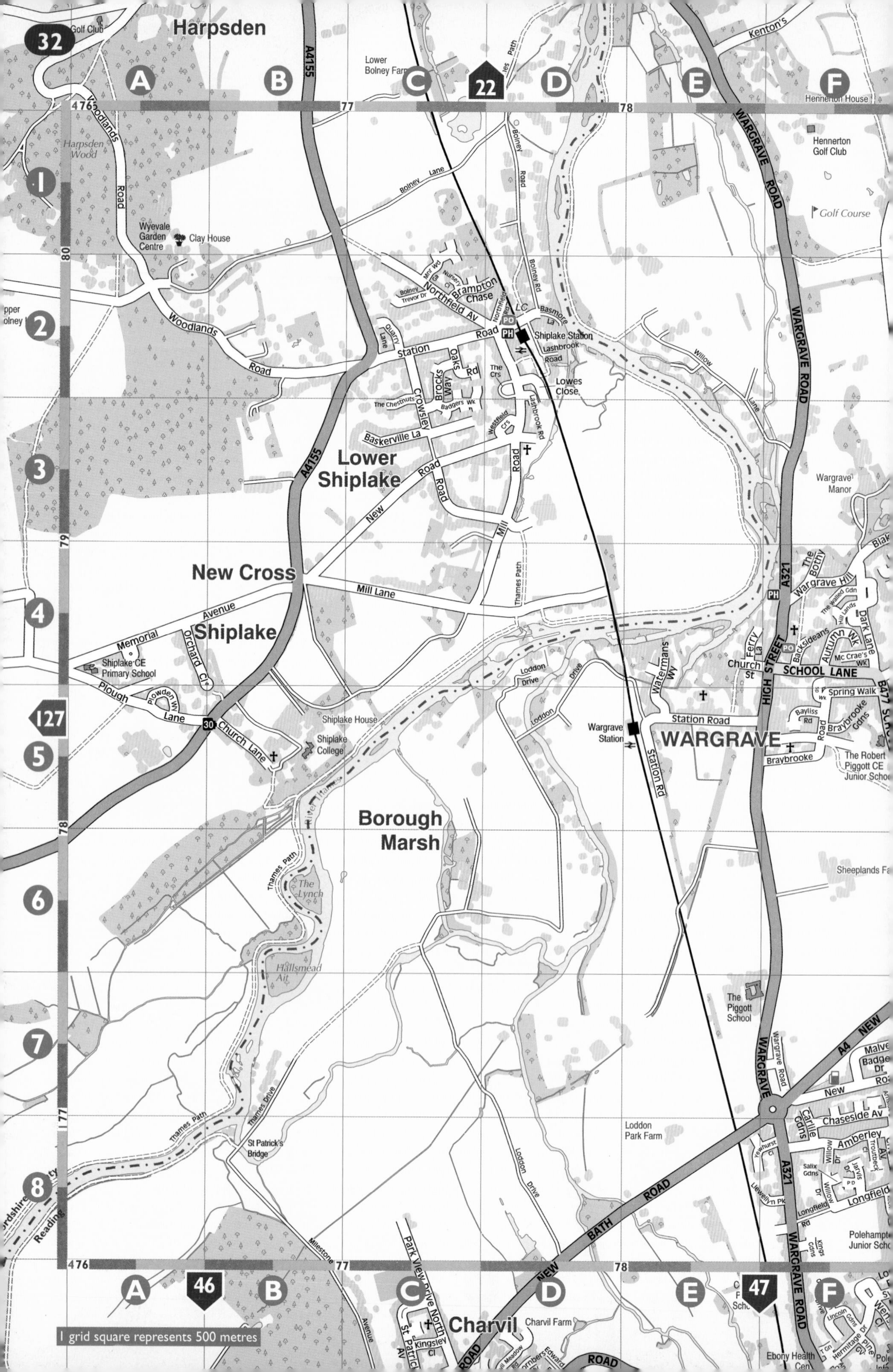

32
Golf Club
Harpsden
A
B
C
D
E
F
22
Lower Bolney Farm
A4155
Kenton's
Henneton House
Woodlands Road
Harpsden Wood
Hennerton Golf Club
Golf Course
Bolney Lane
Bolney Road
WARGRAVE ROAD
Wyevale Garden Centre
Clay House
Brampton Chase
Northfield Av
Bolney Rd
Basmore La
Shiplake Station
Lashbrook Road
Woodlands Road
Station Road
Quarry Lane
Oaks Rd
Brocks Way
The Crs
Lowes Close
Willow Lane
The Chestnuts
Crowsley
Badgers Wk
Westfield Crs
Lashbrook Rd
Baskerville La
Lower Shiplake
New Road
Road
Mill Road
Wargrave Manor
New Cross
Thames Path
Mill Lane
Memorial Avenue
Shiplake
Orchard Cl
Shiplake CE Primary School
Plough Lane
Plowden Wy
127
Church Lane
Shiplake House
Shiplake College
Loddon Drive
Watermans Wy
Wargrave Station
Station Road
Station Rd
WARGRAVE
HIGH STREET
A321
The Bothy
Wargrave Hill
The Walled Gdn
Dark Lane
Backsideans
Autumn Wk
Mc Crae's Wk
Church St
Ferry La
SCHOOL LANE
Spring Walk
Bayliss Rd
Braybrooke Gdns
Braybrooke Road
The Robert Piggott CE Junior School
River Thames
Borough Marsh
Sheeplands Fa
The Lynch
Hallsmead Ait
The Piggott School
Wargrave Road
A4 NEW
New
Chaseside Av
Carlile Gdns
Amberley Av
Loddon Park Farm
Thames Drive
St Patrick's Bridge
Yewhurst Cl
Willow Dr
Salix Gdns
Jarvis Dr
Longfield Rd
Longfield
Llewellyn Pk
NEW BATH ROAD
Loddon Drive
Reading
Milestone Avenue
Polehampton Junior School
Kings Gdns
Park View Drive North
46
47
Charvil
Charvil Farm
St Patrick Av
Kingsley Cl
Ebony Health Cen
ROAD
1 grid square represents 500 metres

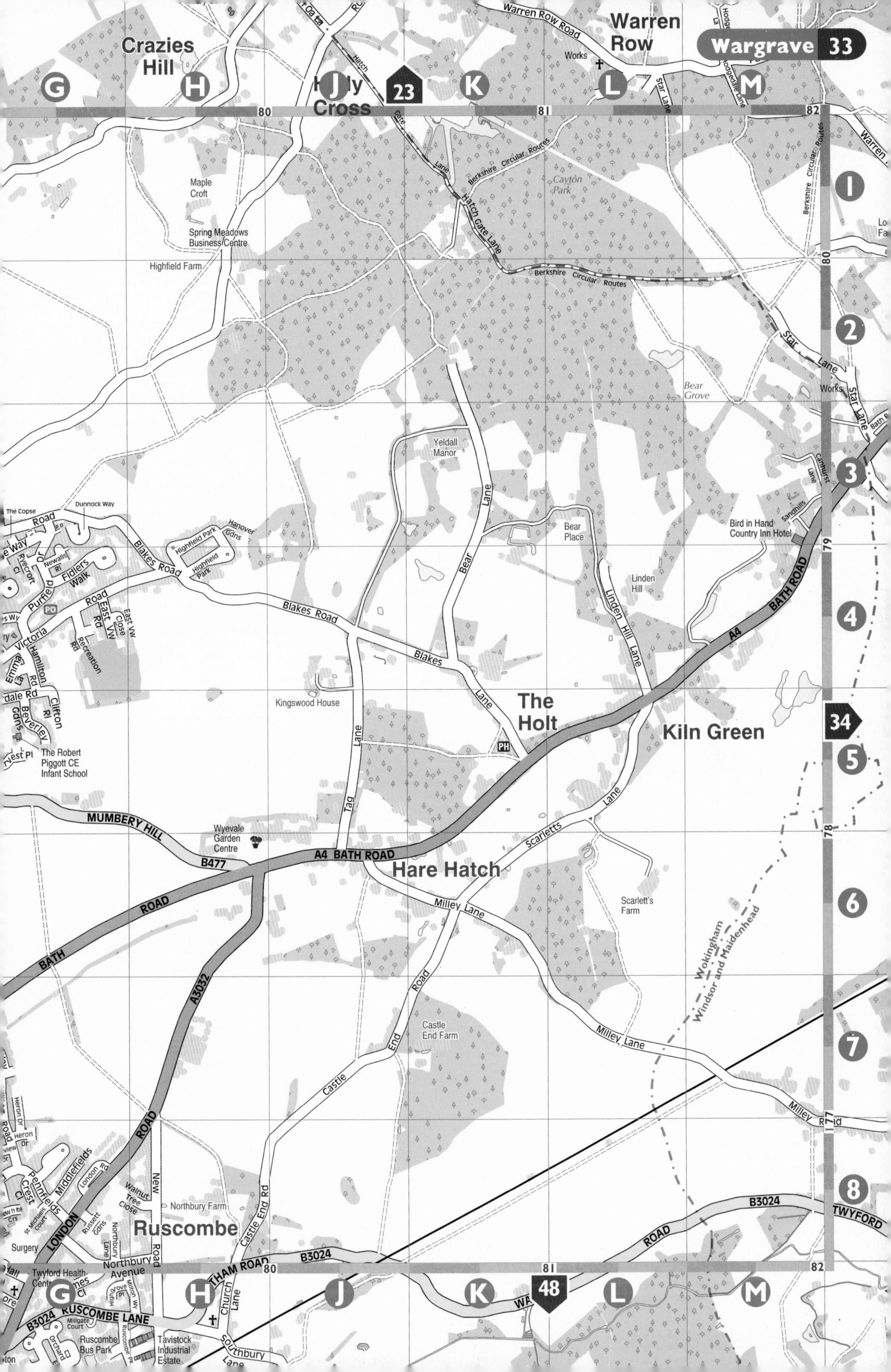
Crazies Hill
Warren Row
Warren Row Road
Holly Cross
Hatch Gate Lane
Berkshire Circular Routes
Cayton Park
Maple Croft
Spring Meadows Business Centre
Highfield Farm
Star Lane
Works
Bear Grove
Yeldall Manor
Bear Lane
Bear Place
Linden Hill
Linden Hill Lane
Bird in Hand Country Inn Hotel
Sandhills
Camhurst Lane
A4 BATH ROAD
Blakes Road
Highfield Park
Hanover Gdns
Dunnock Way
The Copse
Purfield Dr
Fidlers Walk
Victoria Road
East Vw Close
Recreation Rd
Hamilton Rd
Clifton Rl
Beverley Gdns
Kingswood House
The Robert Piggott CE Infant School
The Holt
Kiln Green
Tag Lane
PH
MUMBERY HILL
B477
Wyevale Garden Centre
Hare Hatch
Scarletts Lane
Scarlett's Farm
Milley Lane
Milley Road
Castle End Road
Castle End Farm
Wokingham
Windsor and Maidenhead
A3032
LONDON ROAD
B3024
TWYFORD ROAD
Middlefields
Pennfields
Heron Dr
London Rd
Walnut Tree Close
Russett Gdns
Northbury Farm
New Road
Northbury Lane
Northbury Avenue
Ruscombe
Surgery
Twyford Health Centre
Castle End Rd
Church Lane
RUSCOMBE LANE
Millgate Court
Ruscombe Bus Park
Tavistock Industrial Estate
Southbury Lane
Orchard
G
H
J
K
L
M
1
2
3
4
5
6
7
8
80
81
82
79
78
77
23
34
48

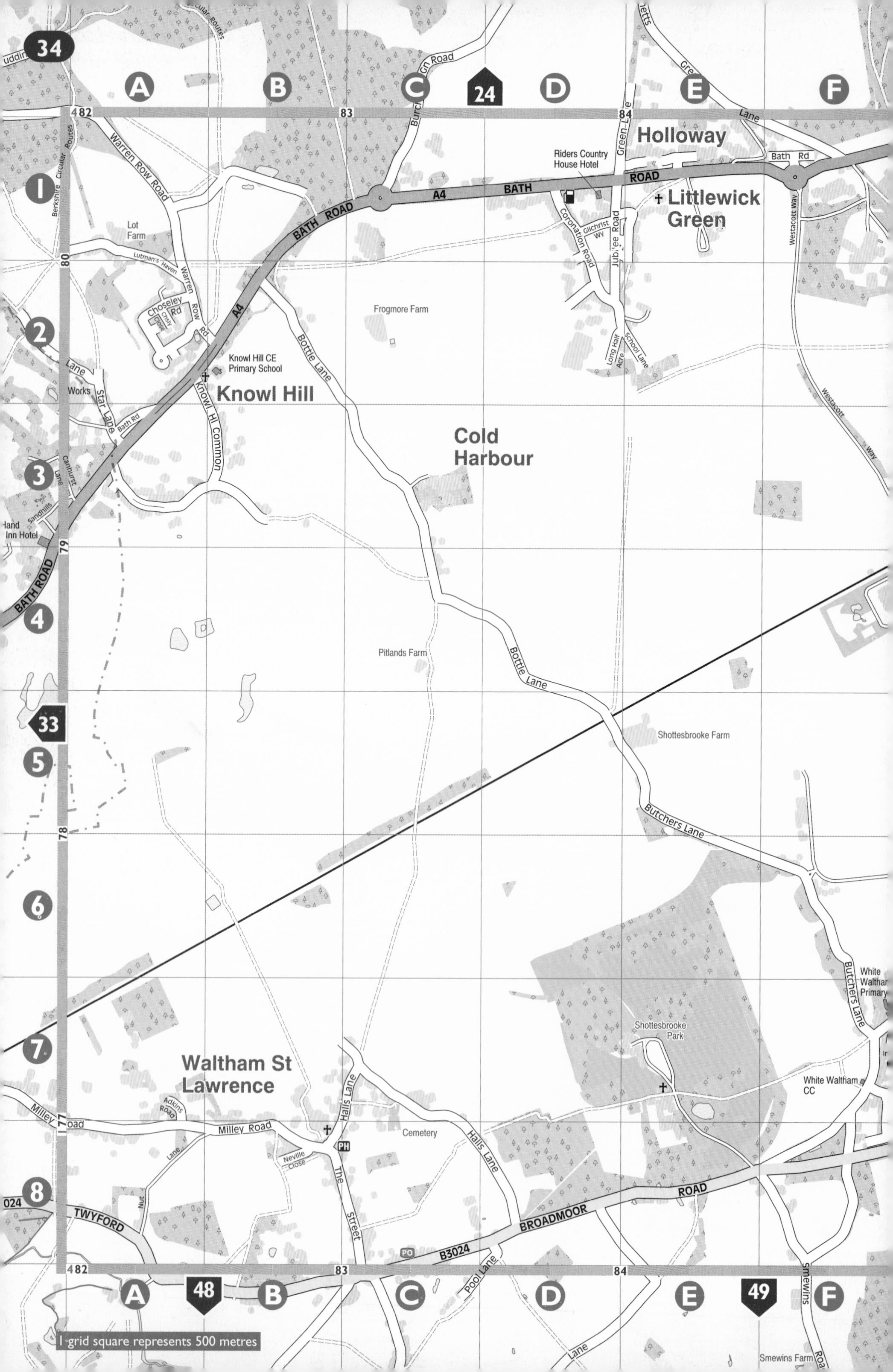
A
B
C
D
E
F
24
1
2
3
4
5
6
7
8
33
48
49
482
83
84
80
79
78
77
Holloway
Riders Country
House Hotel
Littlewick
Green
Bath Rd
BATH ROAD
A4
Warren Row Road
Berkshire Circular Routes
Lot
Farm
Lutman's Haven
Choseley
Rd
Warren
Row
Rd
Works
Star Lane
Bath Rd
Canhurst
Lane
Sandhills
Inn Hotel
Knowl Hill CE
Primary School
Knowl Hill
Knowl Hl Common
Bottle Lane
Frogmore Farm
Coronation Road
Gilchrist
Wy
Jubilee Road
Green Lane
Long Half
Acre
School Lane
Westacott Way
Cold
Harbour
Pitlands Farm
Shottesbrooke Farm
Butchers Lane
Shottesbrooke
Park
White
Waltham
CC
Waltham St
Lawrence
Milley Road
Adkins
Road
Halls Lane
Cemetery
Neville
Close
The Street
Nut Lane
TWYFORD
BROADMOOR
ROAD
B3024
PO
Pool Lane
Smewins
Smewins Farm
1 grid square represents 500 metres

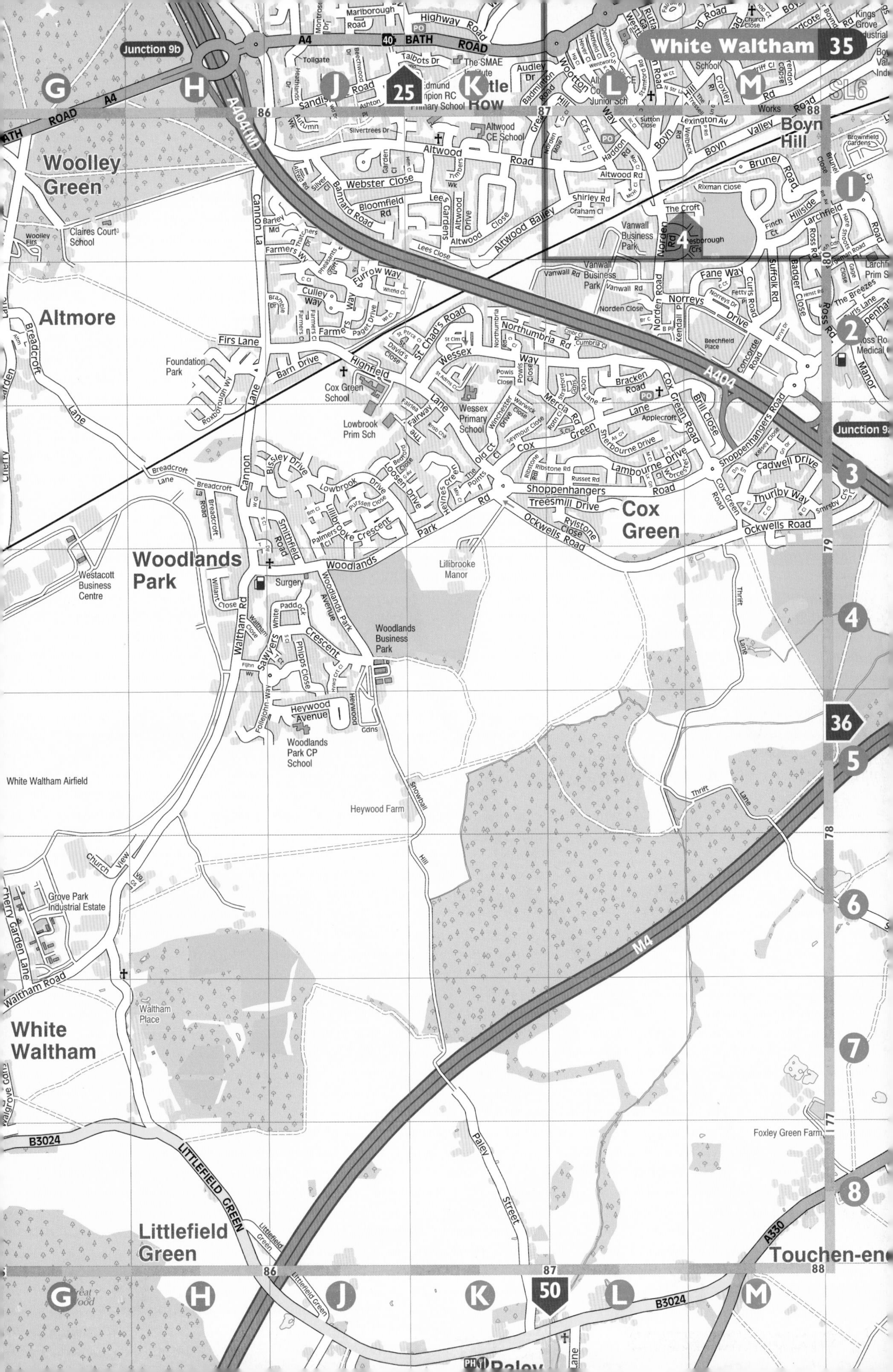
Junction 9b
A4 BATH ROAD
A404(M)
Woolley Green
Woolley Firs
Claires Court School
Altmore
Breadcroft Lane
Firs Lane
Foundation Park
Cannon Lane
Woodlands Park
Westacott Business Centre
Surgery
Woodlands Business Park
Woodlands Park CP School
Heywood Avenue
Lillibrooke Manor
Cox Green School
Lowbrook Prim Sch
Wessex Primary School
Highfield
Shoppenhangers Road
Cox Green
Ockwells Road
Woodlands Park Rd
Cox Green Road
Altwood Road
Altwood CE School
The SMAE Institute
Edmund Campion RC Primary School
Vanwall Business Park
Norreys Drive
Beechfield Place
Boyn Hill
Boyn Valley Road
Junction 9a
A404
White Waltham Airfield
Heywood Farm
Snowball Hill
Thrift Lane
M4
Grove Park Industrial Estate
Church View
Cherry Garden Lane
Waltham Road
White Waltham
Waltham Place
B3024
LITTLEFIELD GREEN
Littlefield Green
Paley Street
Foxley Green Farm
A330
Touchen-end
Great Wood
G H J K L M
1 2 3 4 5 6 7 8
86 87 88
25 36 50

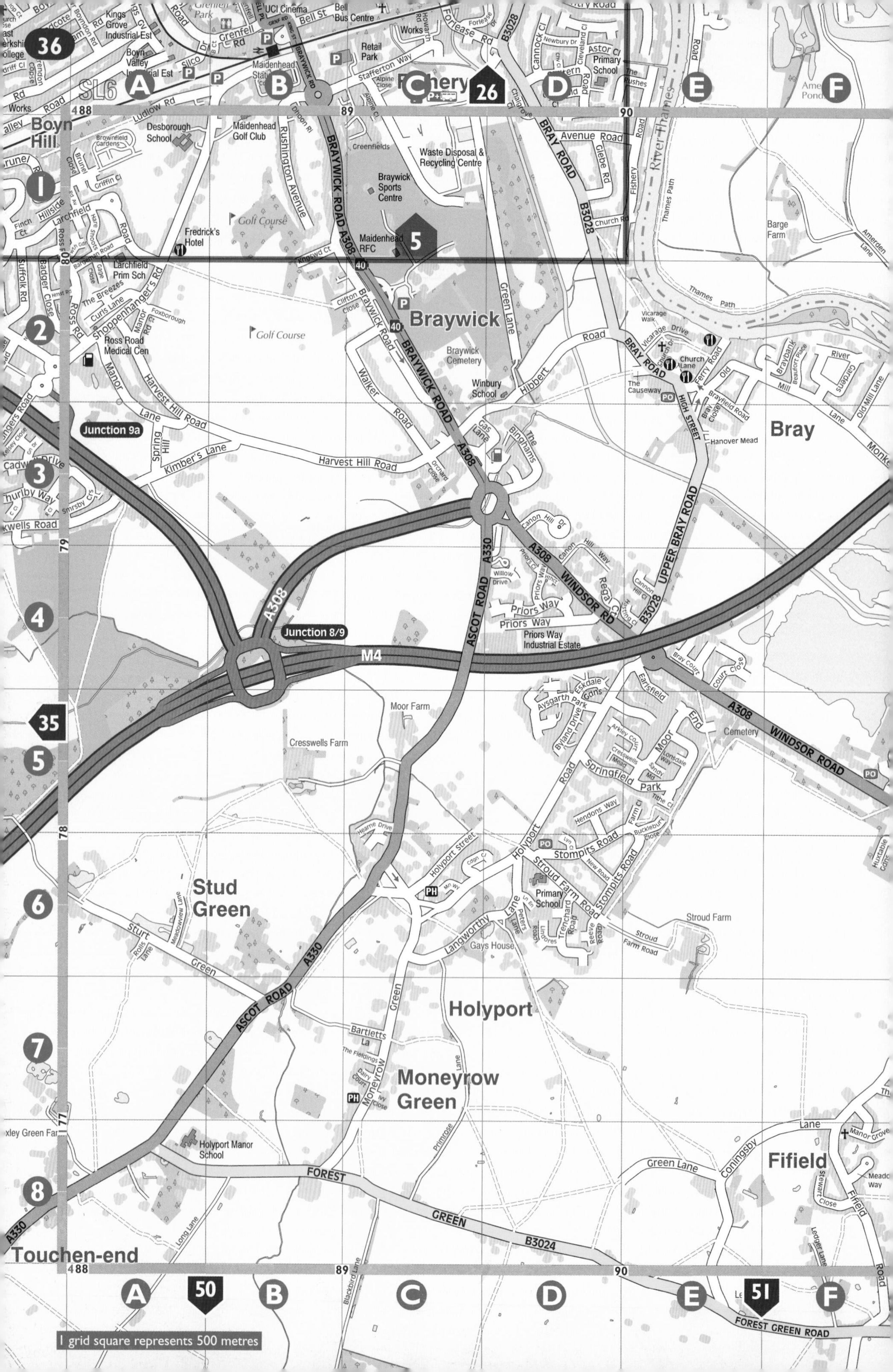

36
26
5
35
50
51
A
B
C
D
E
F
1
2
3
4
5
6
7
8
488
89
90
80
79
78
77
SL6
Boyn Hill
Kings Grove Industrial Est
Boyn Valley Industrial Est
UCI Cinema
Bell St
Bell Bus Centre
Grenfell Rd
Maidenhead Station
Retail Park
Stafferton Way
Works
Forlease Rd
Cannock Cl
Astor Cl
Primary School
The Rushes
Ludlow Rd
Desborough School
Maidenhead Golf Club
Rushington Avenue
Greenfields
Waste Disposal & Recycling Centre
Avenue Road
Braywick Sports Centre
Golf Course
Fredrick's Hotel
Maidenhead RFC
Church Rd
River Thames
Thames Path
Barge Farm
Amerden Lane
Ame Pond
Larchfield Prim Sch
Shoppenhangers Rd
Ross Road Medical Cen
Braywick
Braywick Cemetery
Winbury School
Hibbert Road
Green Lane
Bray Road
B3028
Vicarage Drive
Church Lane
Ferry Road
The Causeway
High Street
Hanover Mead
Brayfield Road
Bray
Mill Lane
River Gardens
Junction 9a
Harvest Hill Road
Kimber's Lane
Spring Hill
Walker Road
Braywick Road
A308
A330
The Binghams
Canon Hill Dr
Windsor Rd
Upper Bray Road
Priors Way
Priors Way Industrial Estate
Junction 8/9
M4
Ascot Road
Moor Farm
Cresswells Farm
Aysgarth Park
Eskdale Gdns
Bray Court
Court Close
Moor End
Springfield Park
Cemetery
Windsor Road
Holyport Street
Holyport Road
Stompits Road
Stroud Farm Road
Primary School
Stroud Farm
Stud Green
Sturt Green
Langworthy Lane
Gays House
Holyport
Bartletts La
Moneyrow Green
Holyport Manor School
Forest Green
B3024
Green Lane
Coningsby Lane
Fifield
Fifield Road
Touchen-end
Blackbird Lane
Forest Green Road
1 grid square represents 500 metres

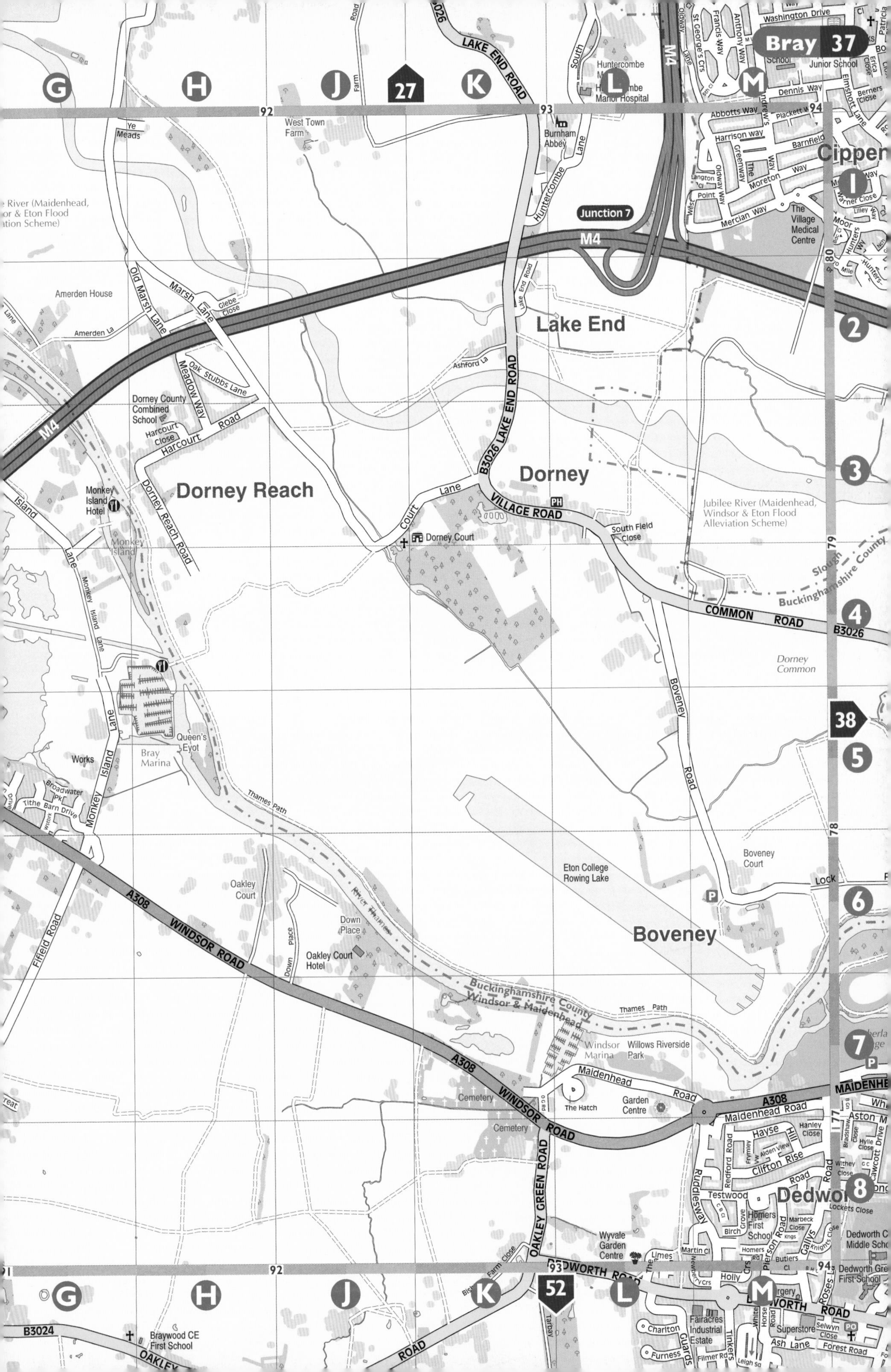

Bray 37
27
38
52
Lake End
Dorney
Dorney Reach
Boveney
Eton College Rowing Lake
Jubilee River (Maidenhead, Windsor & Eton Flood Alleviation Scheme)
Junction 7
M4
LAKE END ROAD
B3026 LAKE END ROAD
VILLAGE ROAD
COMMON ROAD
B3026
Boveney Road
A308 WINDSOR ROAD
OAKLEY GREEN ROAD
DEDWORTH ROAD
Maidenhead Road
Dorney Court
Dorney Common
Burnham Abbey
Huntercombe Lane
West Town Farm
Amerden House
Monkey Island Hotel
Monkey Island
Monkey Island Lane
Dorney County Combined School
Dorney Reach Road
Harcourt Road
Oak Stubbs Lane
Meadow Way
Marsh Lane
Old Marsh Lane
Court Lane
South Field Close
Bray Marina
Queen's Eyot
Thames Path
Oakley Court
Down Place
Oakley Court Hotel
Buckinghamshire County
Windsor & Maidenhead
Windsor Marina
Willows Riverside Park
Cemetery
The Hatch
Garden Centre
Wyvale Garden Centre
Boveney Court
Dedworth
Fifield Road
Tithe Barn Drive
Works
Braywood CE First School
B3024

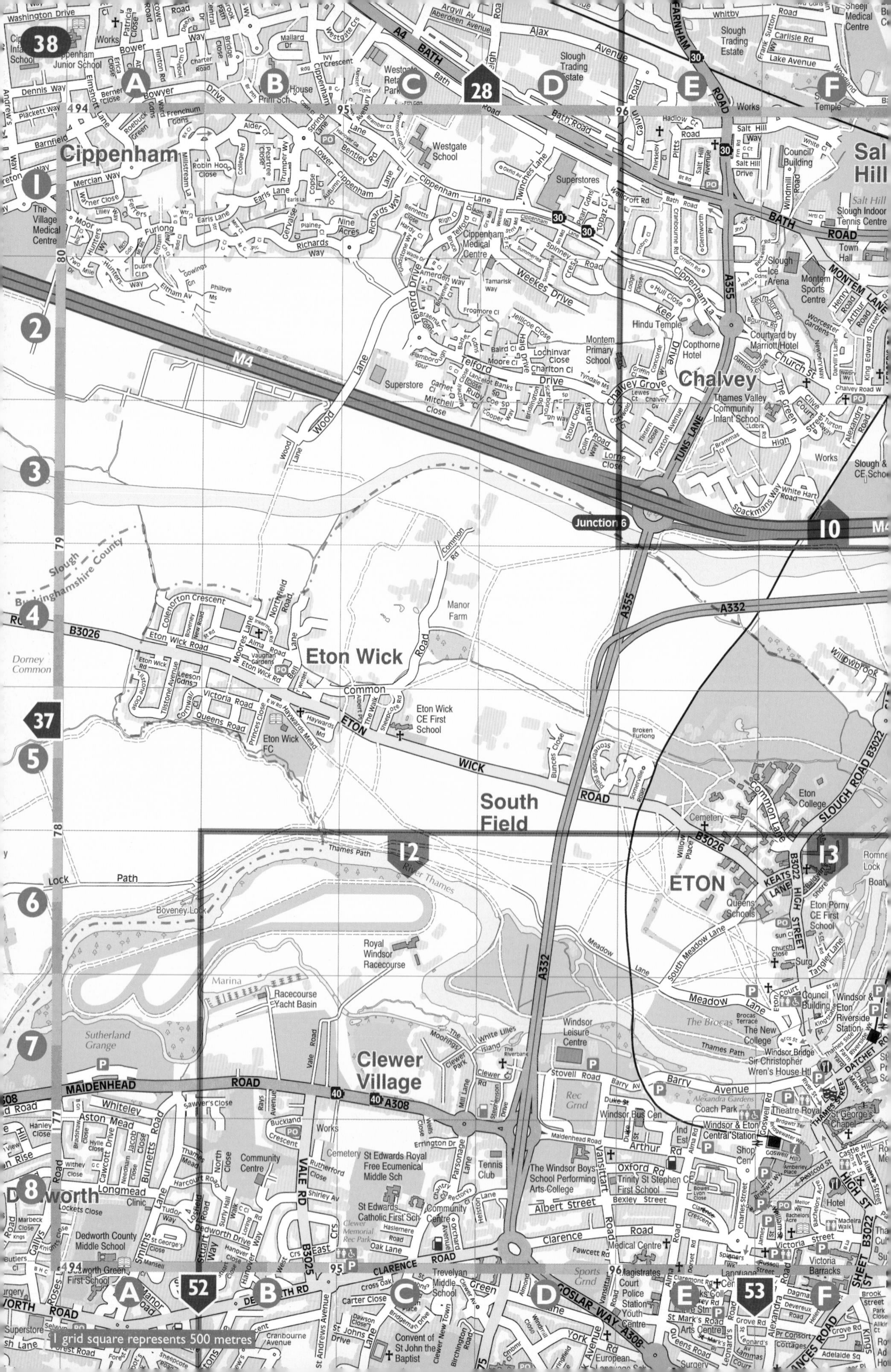

38
Washington Drive
Cippenham Junior School
Bower
Bowyer Drive
Dennis Way
Plackett Way
Barnfield
Cippenham
Mercian Way
Warner Close
Robin Hood Close
Earls Lane
Lower Cippenham Lane
Bentley Rd
Westgate School
Nine Acres
Richards Way
Furlong
Hunters Way
Eltham Av
The Village Medical Centre
Ajax Avenue
Aberdeen Avenue
Argyll Av
A4 BATH ROAD
28
Westgate Retail Park
Slough Trading Estate
Slough Trading Estate
Whitby
Carlisle Rd
Lake Avenue
Medical Centre
FARNHAM ROAD
Works
Temple
Salt Hill
Salt Hill Way
Salt Hill Drive
Council Building
Slough Indoor Tennis Centre
Town Hall
BATH ROAD
MONTEM LANE
Montem Sports Centre
Slough Ice Arena
Windmill Road
Superstores
Cippenham Lane
Telford Drive
Cippenham Medical Centre
Weekes Drive
Spinney
Keel Drive
Hindu Temple
Copthorne Hotel
Courtyard by Marriott Hotel
Church St
Chalvey
Chalvey Grove
Montem Primary School
Lochinvar Close
Charlton Cl
Superstore
Mitchell Close
Thames Valley Community Infant School
High
Works
Slough & CE School
TUNS LANE
A355
Spackmans Way
Junction 6
10
M4
Wood Lane
Burgett Road
Paxton Avenue
Lorne Close
Slough
Buckinghamshire County
Common Rd
Manor Farm
Colenorton Crescent
Northfield Road
Eton Wick Road
B3026
Dorney Common
Eton Wick
Common
Eton Wick CE First School
Victoria Road
Queens Road
Eton Wick FC
ETON WICK ROAD
37
South Field
Broken Furlong
Bunces Close
A332
A355
Willowbrook
SLOUGH ROAD B3022
Eton College
Common Lane
Cemetery
ETON
Queens Schools
KEATS LANE
HIGH STREET
Eton Porny CE First School
South Meadow Lane
Meadow Lane
Romney Lock
12
13
Lock Path
Thames Path
River Thames
Boveney Lock
Royal Windsor Racecourse
Marina
Racecourse Yacht Basin
Sutherland Grange
Clewer Village
White Lilies Island
The Moorings
Windsor Leisure Centre
Stovell Road
Barry Avenue
Alexandra Gardens
Coach Park
Theatre Royal
The Brocas
The New College
Windsor Bridge
Sir Christopher Wren's House Htl
Windsor & Eton Riverside Station
Windsor & Eton Central Station
Windsor Bus Cen
St George's Chapel
Castle Hill
Thames Path
MAIDENHEAD ROAD
A308
40
Whiteley
Aston Mead
Longmead
Dedworth
Dedworth County Middle School
Dedworth Green First School
Clinic
Community Centre
VALE RD
B3025
Works
Cemetery
St Edwards Royal Free Ecumenical Middle Sch
St Edwards Catholic First Sch
Community Centre
Tennis Club
Rec Grnd
The Windsor Boys' School Performing Arts College
Trinity St Stephen CE First School
Oxford Rd
Arthur Rd
Albert Street
Bexley Street
Clarence Road
Medical Centre
Victoria Street
Victoria Barracks
Peascod St
HIGH ST
B3022
Hotel
CLARENCE ROAD
Trevelyan Middle School
Convent of St John the Baptist
Magistrates Court
Police Station
Youth Centre
GOSLAR WAY A308
52
53
Arts Centre
Sports Grnd
1 grid square represents 500 metres
A
B
C
D
E
F
1
2
3
4
5
6
7
8
94
95
96
77
78
79
80

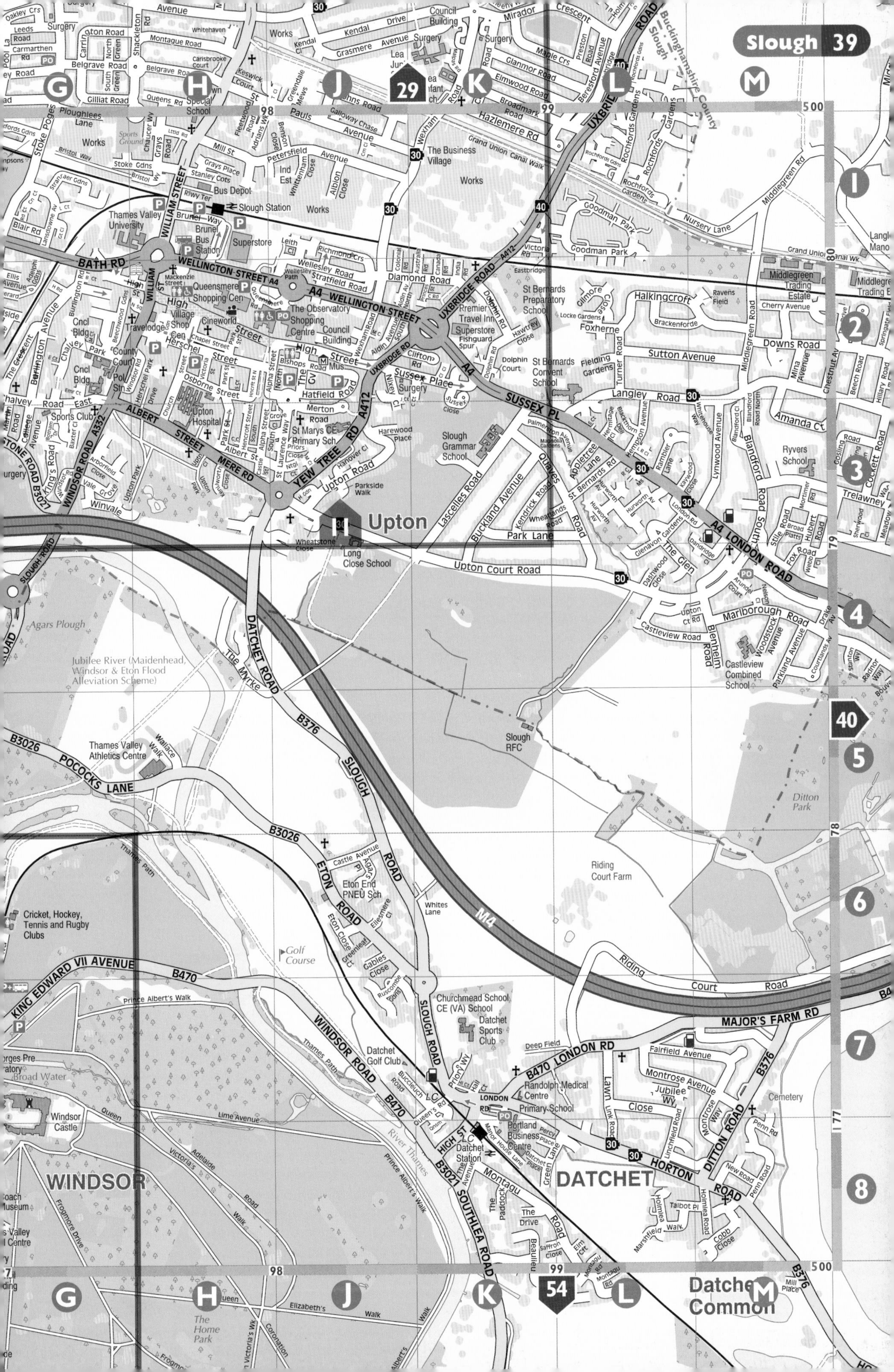
Oakley Crs
Leeds Road
Carmarthen Rd
Surgery
Belgrave Road
Gilliat Road
Carrington Road
Montague Road
Shackleton Rd
Avenue
Works
Kendal Cl
Kendal Drive
Grasmere Avenue
Council Building
Surgery
Lea Jun
Mirador Crescent
Glanmor Road
Elmwood Road
Maple Crs
Preston Road
Beresford Avenue
Broadmark Road
Hazlemere Rd
Buckinghamshire County
Slough
G
H
J
K
L
M
29
30
98
99
500
Ploughlees Lane
Stoke Poges Lane
Works
Sports Ground
Chaucer Wy
Grays Road
Bristol Way
Stoke Gdns
Mill St
Petersfield Avenue
Grays Place
Stanley Cots
Bus Depot
Rlwy Ter
Slough Station
Works
Ind Est
Whittenham Close
Albion Close
St Pauls Avenue
Galloway Chase
Wexham Road
The Business Village
Works
Grand Union Canal Walk
Uxbridge Road
Rochfords Gardens
Nursery Lane
Middlegreen Road
Goodman Park
Thames Valley University
Brunel Way
Brunel Bus Station
Superstore
Leith Cl
Richmond Crs
Wellesley Road
Stratfield Road
Diamond Road
Victoria Rd
Eastbridge
Grand Union Canal Wk
Middlegreen Trading Estate
Langley Manor
Bath Rd
Wellington Street A4
A4 Wellington Street
William Street
High St
Queensmere Shopping Cen
High Village Shop Cen
Cineworld
The Observatory Shopping Centre
Council Building
Travelodge
Herschel Street
Chapel Street
Park St
High Street
Bishops Road
Mus.
Uxbridge Rd
Clifton Rd
Premier Travel Inn
Superstore
Fishguard Spur
Dolphin Rd
Dolphin Court
Hawtrey Close
St Bernards Preparatory School
Gilmore Close
Locke Gardens
Foxherne
Halkingcroft
Brackenforde
Ravens Field
Cherry Avenue
Sutton Avenue
Downs Road
Turner Road
Fielding Gardens
St Bernards Convent School
Langley Road
Mina Avenue
Amanda Ct
Chestnut Av
Beech Road
Hillary Road
Cncl Bldg
Chalvey Park
County Court
Pol Sta
Windsor Rd
Herschel Park Drive
Church Street
Victoria Street
Osborne Street
Upton Hospital
Albert St
Hatfield Road
Sussex Place
Surgery
Sussex Close
Merton Road
St Marys CE Primary Sch.
Harewood Place
Slough Grammar School
Sussex PL
A4 London Road
Palmerston Avenue
Appletree Lane
Hempson Avenue
Rambler Lane
Lynwood Avenue
Blandford Road South
Ryvers School
Cockett Road
Trelawney
Chalvey Road East
Sports Club
Burlington Avenue
The Grove
Albert Street
Mere Rd
Yew Tree Rd
A412
Upton Road
Parkside Walk
Upton Park
Winvale
Vale Grove
Kings Road
Windsor Road A332
Upton
Lascelles Road
Buckland Avenue
Kendrick Road
Wheatlands Road
Park Lane
St Bernards Rd
London Rd
Glenavon Gardens
The Glen
Dashwood Close
Stile Road
Fox Road
Hubert Road
Sherwood Close
Wheatstone Close
Long Close School
Upton Court Road
Slough Road
Agars Plough
Marlborough Road
Castleview Road
Blenheim Road
Castleview Combined School
Woodstock Avenue
Parkland Avenue
Jubilee River (Maidenhead, Windsor & Eton Flood Alleviation Scheme)
The Wyrke
Datchet Road
B376
Slough Road
Slough RFC
40
B3026
Pococks Lane
Thames Valley Athletics Centre
Wallace Walk
Ditton Park
Riding Court Farm
Thames Path
Castle Avenue
Eton Road
Eton End PNEU Sch
Whites Lane
M4
Cricket, Hockey, Tennis and Rugby Clubs
Golf Course
Gables Close
Riding Court Road
King Edward VII Avenue
B470
Prince Albert's Walk
Windsor Road
Churchmead School CE (VA) School
Datchet Sports Club
Major's Farm Rd
Datchet Golf Club
Deep Field
B470 London Rd
Fairfield Avenue
Montrose Avenue
Jubilee Wy
Lawn Close
Randolph Medical Centre
Primary School
Cemetery
Ditton Road
Penn Rd
Broad Water
Windsor Castle
Queen
Lime Avenue
Victoria's
Adelaide Road Walk
Thames Path
River Thames
Portland Business Centre
Datchet Station
High St
Southlea Road
B3027
Montagu Road
The Paddock
The Drive
Datchet
Horton Road
New Road
Talbot Pl
Holmlea Walk
Cobb Close
WINDSOR
Frogmore Drive
Beaulieu Close
Saffron Close
Mill Place
Datchet Common
Queen Elizabeth's Walk
The Home Park
Coronation
54
1
2
3
4
5
6
7
8
77
78
79
80

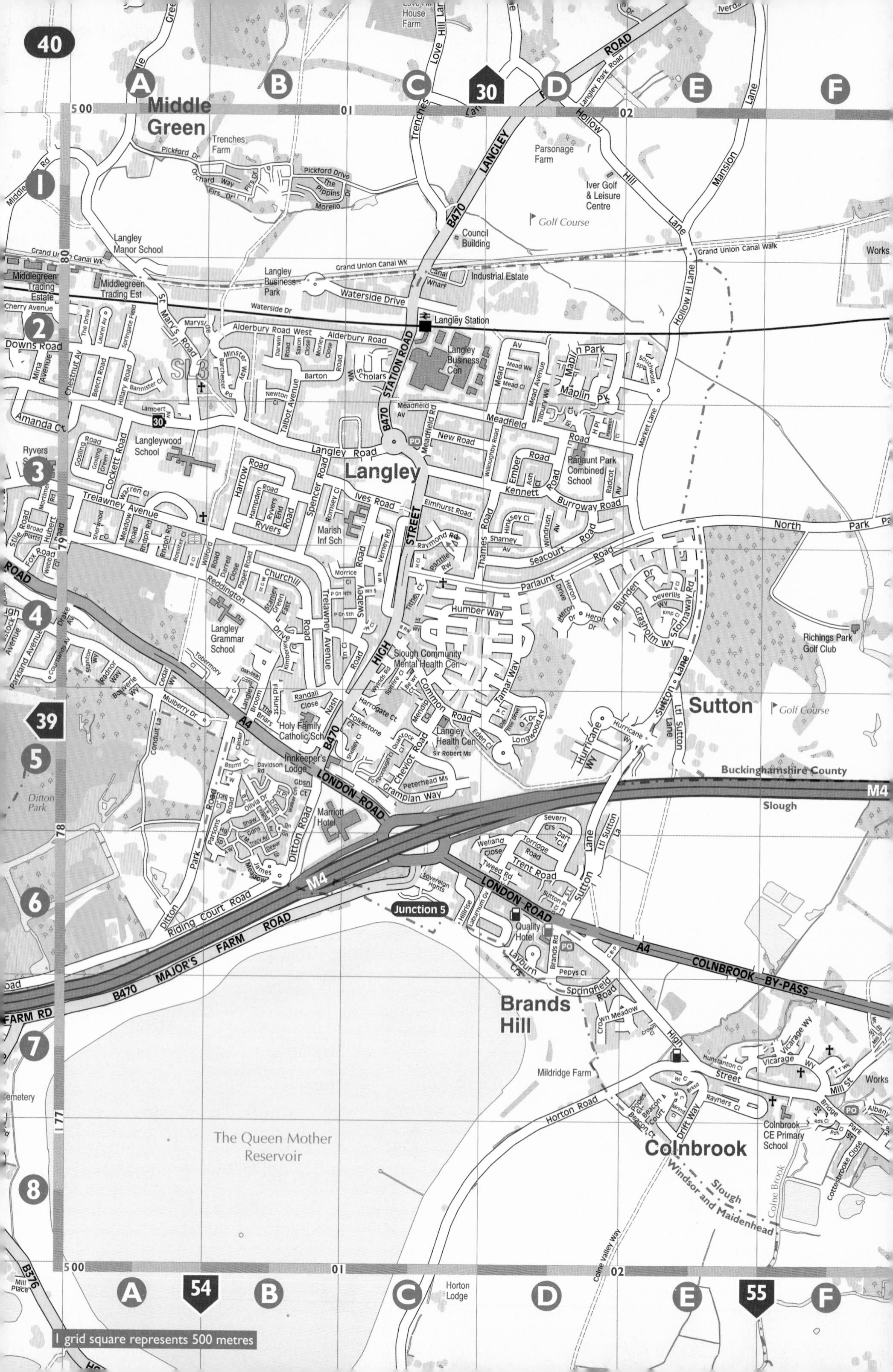
Middle Green
Trenches Farm
Pickford Dr
Pickford Drive
Orchard Way
Firs Dr
The Pippins
Morello Dr
Langley Manor School
Grand Union Canal Wk
Middlegreen Trading Estate
Middlegreen Trading Est
Langley Business Park
Waterside Drive
Waterside Dr
Canal Wharf
Industrial Estate
Council Building
Golf Course
Parsonage Farm
Iver Golf & Leisure Centre
Hollow Hill Lane
Mansion Lane
Langley Park Road
Grand Union Canal Walk
Works
Langley Station
Station Road
Langley Road
Langley Business Cen
Alderbury Road West
Alderbury Road
Cherry Avenue
Downs Road
Mina Avenue
Chestnut Av
Beech Road
Hillary Road
Bannister Cl
Laurel Av
The Drive
Springate Field
Marys Road
Minster Way
Barchester Rd
Darwin Rd
Saxon Cl
Close
Morley Cl
Barton
Scholars Wk
Newton Cl
Talbot Avenue
Amanda Ct
Lambert Av
SL3
Langleywood School
Ryvers
Cockett Road
Gosling Road
Gosling Green
Warren Cl
Trelawney Avenue
Harrow Road
Hampden Road
Ryvers End Road
Ryvers
Spencer Road
Langley
Marish Inf Sch
Romsey Cl
Ives Road
High Street
Elmhurst Road
Meadfield Av
Meadfield Rd
Meadfield
New Road
Mead Av
Mead Wk
Mead Cl
Mead Avenue
Maplin Park
Maplin Pk
Tilbury Wk
Southwold Spur
Market Lane
Willoughby Road
Ember Road
Ash Cl
Kennett Road
Parlaunt Park Combined School
Radcot Av
Burroway Road
Hinksey Cl
Windrush Av
Sharney Av
Thames Road
Seacourt Road
North Park
Raymond Rd
Pantile Rw
Parlaunt Road
Heron Drive
Heron Dr
Blunden Dr
Deverills Wy
Kmp Cl
Grasholm Wy
Stornaway Rd
Richings Park Golf Club
Humber Way
Tamar Way
Longwood Av
Slough Community Mental Health Cen
Common Road
Langley Health Cen
Eden Cl
Sir Robert Ms
Hurricane Wy
Hurricane
Sutton Lane
Ltl Sutton Lane
Sutton
Golf Course
Buckinghamshire County
Slough
M4
Stile Road
Broad Platts
Hubert Road
Mortimer
Sherwood Cl
Meadow Road
Rodney Rd
Ralph Rd
Rossiter Cl
Wilford Road
Darrell Close
Paget Road
Churchill Road
Stanley Green East
Reddington Drive
Fox Road
Webb Cl
Langley Grammar School
Trelawney Avenue
Swabey Road
Morrice Cl
Verney Rd
Tobermory Cl
Kimberley Cl
Randall Close
Nash Road
Holy Family Catholic Sch
Harrogate Ct
Folkestone Ct
Mendip Cl
Quantock Cl
Cheviot Road
Peterhead Ms
Grampian Way
Drake Av
Parkland Avenue
Courtlands Av
Stanton Wy
Radnor Way
Bouverie Wy
Cedar Wy
Mulberry Dr
Oakview Gdns
Langley Broom
The Briars
Eld Hurst
Innkeeper's Lodge
London Road
A4
B470
Davidson Rd
Gbsn Ct
Calder Ct
Conduit La
Olivia Dr
Shaw Gdns
Tracy Av
Dewar Sp
James Meadow
Marriott Hotel
Ditton Road
Ditton Park
Parsons Rd
Ditton Park Road
Riding Court Road
Major's Farm Road
Farm Rd
Sovereign Hghts
Junction 5
Severn Crs
Dart Cl
Welland Close
Torridge Road
Trent Road
Tweed Rd
Sutton Pl
Hillrise
Laburnum Gv
Quality Hotel
Brands Rd
Layburn Crs
Pepys Cl
Springfield Road
Colnbrook By-Pass
Brands Hill
Crown Meadow
Crown Cl
Mildridge Farm
High Street
Hunstanton Cl
Vicarage Wy
Mill St
Works
Horton Road
Pippins Cl
Beacon Ct
Driftway
Rayners Cl
Bridge St
Park St
Colnbrook CE Primary School
Colnbrook
Cottesbrooke Close
Windsor and Maidenhead
Slough
Colne Brook
Colne Valley Way
The Queen Mother Reservoir
Ditton Park
Cemetery
B376
Mill Place
Horton Lodge
A
B
C
D
E
F
1
2
3
4
5
6
7
8
500
01
02
80
79
78
177
30
39
54
55
1 grid square represents 500 metres

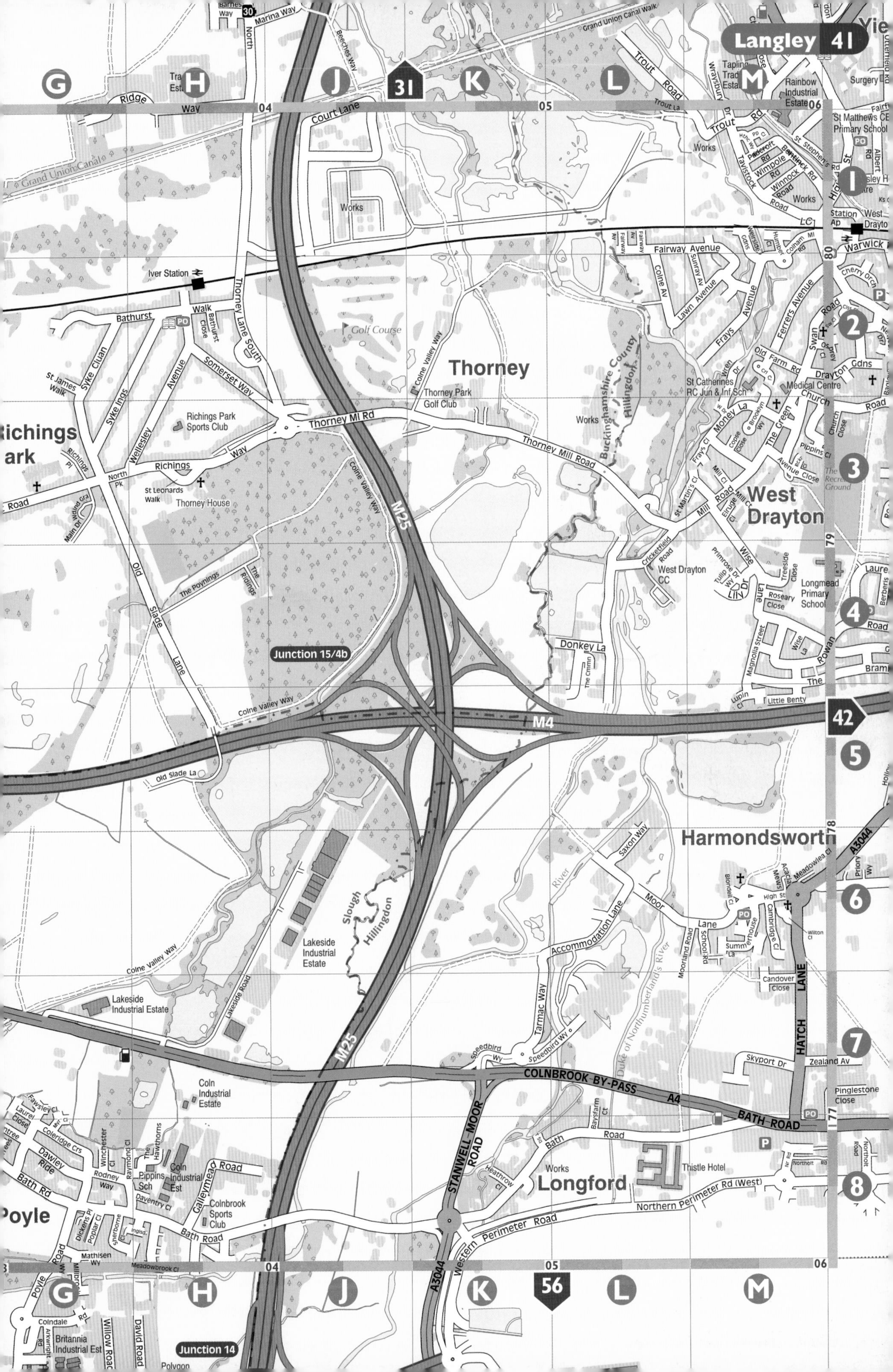

Langley 41
31
42
56
G
H
J
K
L
M
04
05
06
80
79
78
77
2
3
4
5
6
7
8
Thorney
West Drayton
Harmondsworth
Longford
Richings Park
Poyle
Iver Station
Golf Course
Thorney Park Golf Club
Richings Park Sports Club
Thorney House
Junction 15/4b
Junction 14
M25
M4
A4
A3044
COLNBROOK BY-PASS
BATH ROAD
STANWELL MOOR ROAD
HATCH LANE
Grand Union Canal
Grand Union Canal Walk
Ridge Way
Court Lane
Marina Way
Beeches Way
Trout Road
Trout La
Wraysbury Dr
Tapling Trad Esta
Rainbow Industrial Estate
Surgery
St Matthews CE Primary School
Thorney Mill Road
Thorney Ml Rd
Thorney Lane South
Colne Valley Way
Old Slade Lane
Old Slade La
The Poynings
The Ridings
Somerset Way
Bathurst Walk
Syke Cluan
Syke Ings
Wellesley Avenue
St James Walk
Richings Way
St Leonards Walk
North Pk
Fairway Avenue
Colne Av
Lawn Avenue
Frays Avenue
Ferrers Avenue
Old Farm Rd
Drayton Gdns
Church Road
Money La
The Green
Mill Road
Wise Lane
Magnolia Street
Rowan Road
Lupin Cl
Little Benty
Donkey La
Cricketfield Road
West Drayton CC
St Catherines RC Jun & Inf Sch
Medical Centre
Longmead Primary School
Treeside Close
Rosedary Close
Buckinghamshire County
Hillingdon
Slough
Works
Saxon Way
Moor Lane
Accommodation Lane
Tarmac Way
Speedbird Wy
Moorland Road
School Rd
Cambridge Cl
Candover Close
Skyport Dr
Zealand Av
Pinglestone Close
Meadowlea Cl
High St
Lakeside Industrial Estate
Lakeside Road
Coln Industrial Estate
Colnbrook Sports Club
Galleymead Road
Bath Road
Bath Rd
Rodney Way
Winchester Cl
Raymond Cl
Coleridge Crs
Dawley Ride
Poyle Road
Mathisen Wy
Meadowbrook Cl
Britannia Industrial Est
Willow Road
David Road
Colndale Rd
Western Perimeter Road
Northern Perimeter Rd (West)
Thistle Hotel
Baysfarm Ct
Duke of Northumberlands River
Station Ap
Warwick Rd

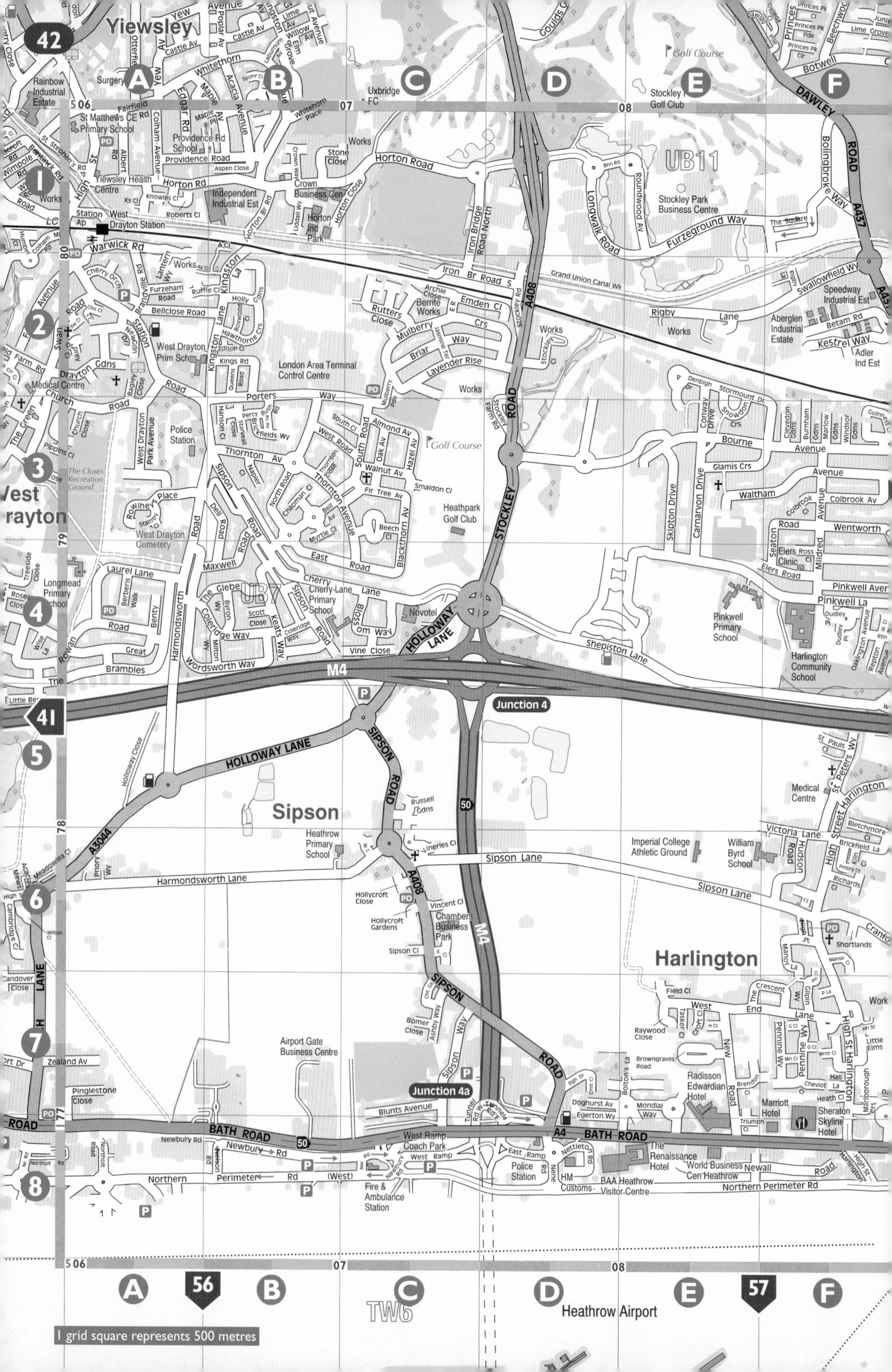

42
Yiewsley
Rainbow Industrial Estate
Surgery
St Matthews CE Primary School
Providence Rd School
Providence Road
Yiewsley Health Centre
Horton Rd
Independent Industrial Est
Uxbridge FC
Works
Stone Close
Horton Road
Crown Business Cen
Horton Close
Horton Ind Park
Iron Bridge Road North
Golf Course
Stockley Park Golf Club
Stockley Park Business Centre
UB11
Longwalk Road
Roundwood Av
Furzeground Way
The Square
Bollingbroke Way
DAWLEY ROAD
A437
Botwell
Princes Pk
Lime Grove
Station Ap
West Drayton Station
Warwick Rd
Works
Furzeham Road
Bellclose Road
Kingston Lane
Iron Br Road S
Grand Union Canal Wk
Stockley Rd
A408
Emden Cl
Rutters Close
Berrite Works
Mulberry Crs
Briar Way
Lavender Rise
Rigby Lane
Works
Swallowfield Wy
Speedway Industrial Est
Aberglen Industrial Estate
Betam Rd
Kestrel Way
Adler Ind Est
West Drayton Prim Sch
Kings Rd
London Area Terminal Control Centre
Swan Road
Drayton Gdns
Medical Centre
Church Road
Station Road
Porters Way
Works
Stockley Farm Rd
Denbigh Dr
Stormount Dr
Conway Drive
Police Station
West Drayton Park Avenue
Thornton Av
Almond Av
South Road
West Road
Walnut Av
Fir Tree Av
Golf Course
Bourne Avenue
Glamis Crs
Waltham Avenue
Colbrook Av
Wentworth
Pippins Cl
The Closes Recreation Ground
West Drayton
Rowlheys Place
West Drayton Cemetery
Sipson Road
Thornton Avenue
Beech Cl
Blackthorn Av
Heathpark Golf Club
STOCKLEY ROAD
Skipton Drive
Carnarvon Drive
Seaton Road
Elers Road
Elers Clinic
Mildred Avenue
Pinkwell Aven
Maxwell Road
East Road
Laurel Lane
Longmead Primary School
UB7
Cherry Lane
Cherry-Lane Primary School
Blossom Way
Novotel
Pinkwell La
Pinkwell Primary School
Harlington Community School
Harmondsworth Road
Scott Close
Coleridge Way
Vine Close
HOLLOWAY LANE
Shepiston Lane
Great Brambles
Wordsworth Way
M4
Junction 4
41
HOLLOWAY LANE
SIPSON ROAD
Sipson
Russell Gdns
Heathrow Primary School
Vineries Cl
Sipson Lane
Imperial College Athletic Ground
William Byrd School
Medical Centre
Victoria Lane
High Street Harlington
A3044
Harmondsworth Lane
Hollycroft Close
Vincent Cl
Chambers Business Park
Hollycroft Gardens
Sipson Cl
Sipson Lane
Shortlands
Harlington
Field Cl
West End Lane
The Crescent
Zealand Av
Pinglestone Close
Airport Gate Business Centre
Bomer Close
Ashby Way
Sipson Way
SIPSON ROAD
Junction 4a
Raywood Close
Browngraves Road
Radisson Edwardian Hotel
Marriott Hotel
Sheraton Skyline Hotel
Blunts Avenue
Doghurst Av
Egerton Wy
Mondial Way
BATH ROAD
A4 BATH ROAD
Newbury Rd
West Ramp Coach Park
West Ramp
East Ramp
Police Station
The Renaissance Hotel
World Business Cen Heathrow
Newall Road
Northern Perimeter Rd (West)
Fire & Ambulance Station
HM Customs
BAA Heathrow Visitor Centre
Northern Perimeter Rd
56
57
TW6
Heathrow Airport
1 grid square represents 500 metres

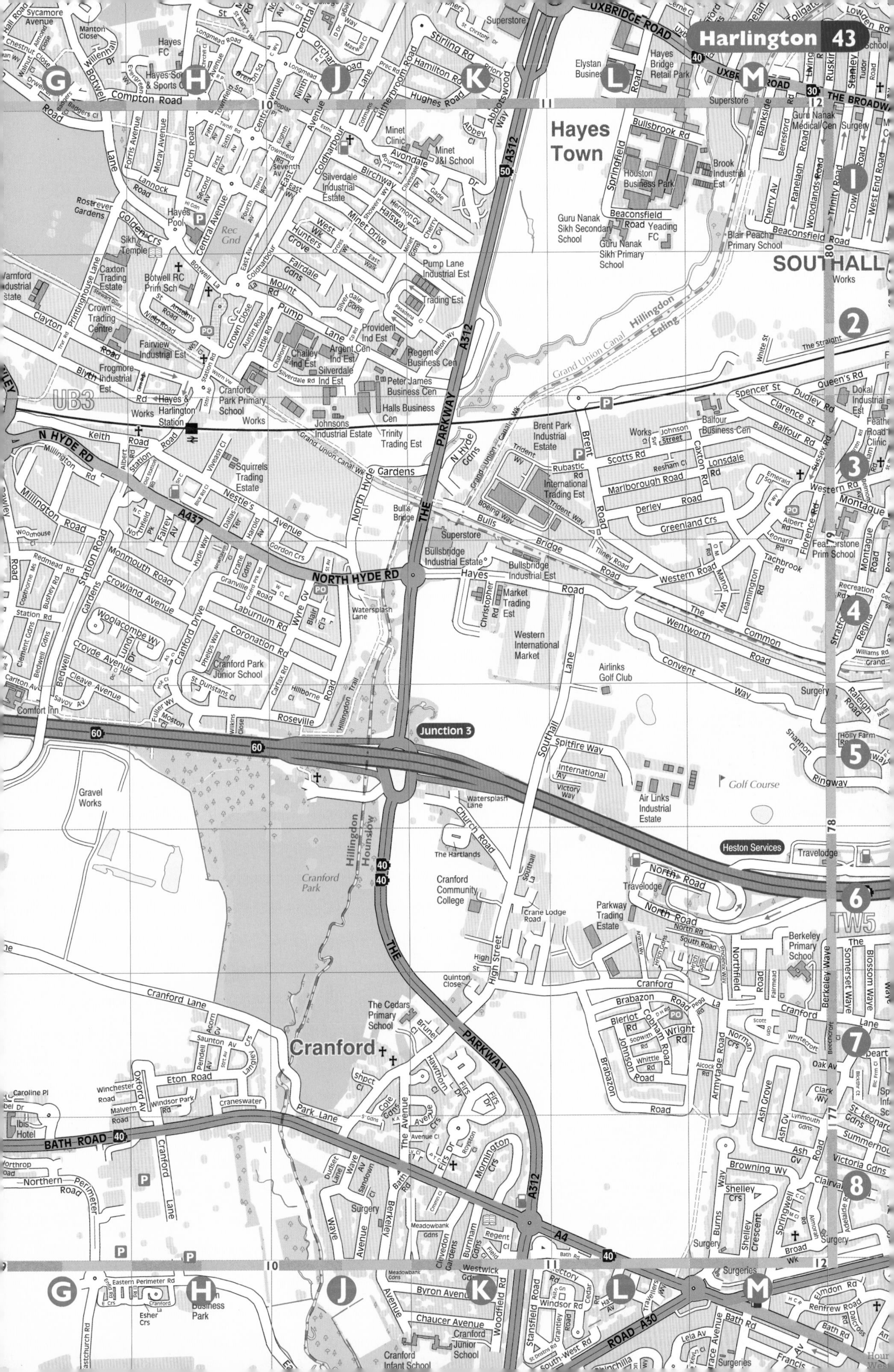
Hayes Town
SOUTHALL
Cranford
UB3
TW5
UXBRIDGE ROAD
THE BROADWAY
Compton Road
Botwell Lane
Church Road
Central Avenue
Coldharbour Lane
Hitherbroom Road
Stirling Rd
Hamilton Rd
Hughes Road
Abbotswood Way
A312
THE PARKWAY
Minet Clinic
Minet J&I School
Avondale Dr
Birchway
Silverdale Industrial Estate
Minet Drive
Halsway
Pump Lane Industrial Est
Trading Est
Pump Lane
Provident Ind Est
Argent Cen
Regent Business Cen
Chailey Ind Est
Silverdale Ind Est
Peter James Business Cen
Halls Business Cen
Johnsons Industrial Estate
Trinity Trading Est
Hayes FC
Hayes Sports Cl
Hayes Pool
Rec Gnd
Sikh Temple
Caxton Trading Estate
Botwell RC Prim Sch
Crown Trading Centre
Fairview Industrial Est
Frogmore Industrial Est
Clayton Road
Blyth Rd
Hayes & Harlington Station
Cranford Park Primary School
Works
Station Road
N HYDE RD
NORTH HYDE RD
A437
Squirrels Trading Estate
Nestle's Avenue
North Hyde Gardens
Bull's Bridge
Superstore
Bullsbridge Industrial Estate
Bullsbridge Industrial Est
Hayes Road
Market Trading Est
Western International Market
Christopher Rd
Grand Union Canal
Hillingdon
Ealing
Elystan Business
Bullsbridge Rd
Springfield Road
Houston Business Park
Brook Industrial Est
Beaconsfield Road
Guru Nanak Sikh Secondary School
Guru Nanak Sikh Primary School
Yeading FC
Blair Peach Primary School
Guru Nanak Medical Cen
Surgery
Brent Park Industrial Estate
Rubastic Rd
International Trading Est
Boeing Way
Bulls Bridge Road
Brent Road
Scotts Rd
Marlborough Road
Derley Road
Greenland Crs
Caxton Rd
Lonsdale Rd
Balfour Business Cen
Spencer St
Clarence St
Balfour Rd
Dudley Rd
Queen's Rd
Dokal Industrial Est
Western Rd
Western Road
Featherstone Prim School
Tachbrook Rd
Leamington Rd
The Common
Wentworth Road
Convent Way
Airlinks Golf Club
Golf Course
Air Links Industrial Estate
Spitfire Way
International Av
Victory Way
Southall Lane
Heston Services
Travelodge
North Road
Parkway Trading Estate
Berkeley Primary School
Cranford Lane
Brabazon Road
Bleriot Rd
Cobham Road
Wright Rd
Johnson Road
Armytage Road
Norman Crs
Northfield Road
Ash Grove
Browning Wy
Shelley Crs
Shelley Crescent
Springwell Rd
Burns Way
Broad Wk
Junction 3
Gravel Works
Cranford Park
Hillingdon Trail
Hillingdon
Hounslow
Watersplash Lane
Church Road
The Hartlands
Cranford Community College
Crane Lodge Road
High Street
Quinton Close
The Cedars Primary School
Park Lane
Eton Road
Windsor Park Rd
Craneswater
Cranford Lane
BATH ROAD
A4
Ibis Hotel
Northern Perimeter Road
Eastern Perimeter Rd
Mornington Crs
Firs Dr
The Avenue
Berkeley Avenue
Bath Rd
Meadowbank Gdns
Clevedon Gardens
Burnham Gdns
Regent Cl
Byron Avenue
Chaucer Avenue
Woodfield Rd
Cranford Junior School
Cranford Infant School
Stansfield Road
Windsor Rd
ROAD A30
Lela Av
Renfrew Road
Elmdon Rd
Surgeries
Monmouth Road
Crowland Avenue
Laburnum Rd
Coronation Rd
Wyre Gv
Cranford Drive
Cranford Park Junior School
St Dunstans Cl
Roseville
Millington Road
Station Road
Woolacombe Wy
Croyde Avenue
Cleave Avenue
Savoy Av
Comfort Inn
Bedwell Gardens
Sycamore Avenue
Manton Close
Willenhall Dr
Rostrever Gardens
Golden Crs
Lannock Road
Printinghouse Lane
Harold Av
Dallas Ter
Fairey Av
Hyde Way
Gordon Crs
Granville Road
Blair Cl
Carfax Rd
Hillborne Cl
Wilkins Close
Moston Cl
Fuller Wy
Sussex Rd
Florence Rd
Montague Rd
Recreation
Williams Rd
Grand
Raleigh Road
Shannon Cl
Holly Farm Rd
Ringway
Oak Av
Clark Wy
Lymouth Gdns
Summerhouse
Victoria Gdns
Clairvale
Adelaide Rd
St Leonards Gdns
Berkeley Wave
The Somerset Waye
Blossom Waye
Cranford Lane
Whytecroft
Sandown
Dudset Lane
Surgery
Winchester Road
Malvern Road
Oxford Av
Caroline Pl
Worthrop Road
Cranford Lane
Esher Crs
Eastchurch Rd
Business Park
Stanley Road
Tudor Rd
Ruskin
Lowlands Rd
Tollgate
Bankside
Beresford
Cherry Av
Ranelagh Road
Woodlands Road
Trinity Road
Town Rd
West End Road
White St
The Straight
Fairdale Gdns
Hunters Grove
West Wk
Mount Rd
Crown Close
Austin Road
Little Rd
Golden Crs
Station Rd
Keith Road
Albert Road
Nield Road
St Anselms Road
Jentink Dr
Johnson Street
Resham Cl
Tilney Road
Trident Wy
Emerald Sq
Leonard Rd
Albert Rd
Manor Wy
Hayes Bridge Retail Park
Superstore
Orchard Road
Longmead Road
Hitherbroom
Prec Rd
Gade Cl
Cherry Gv
Hermon Gv
Woodhouse Cl
Redmead Rd
Bushey Rd
Clement Gdns
Bedwell Gdns
Lundy Dr
Station Rd
Carlton Av
G
H
J
K
L
M
I
2
3
4
5
6
7
8
9
10
11
12
40
50
60
30
77
78
79
80

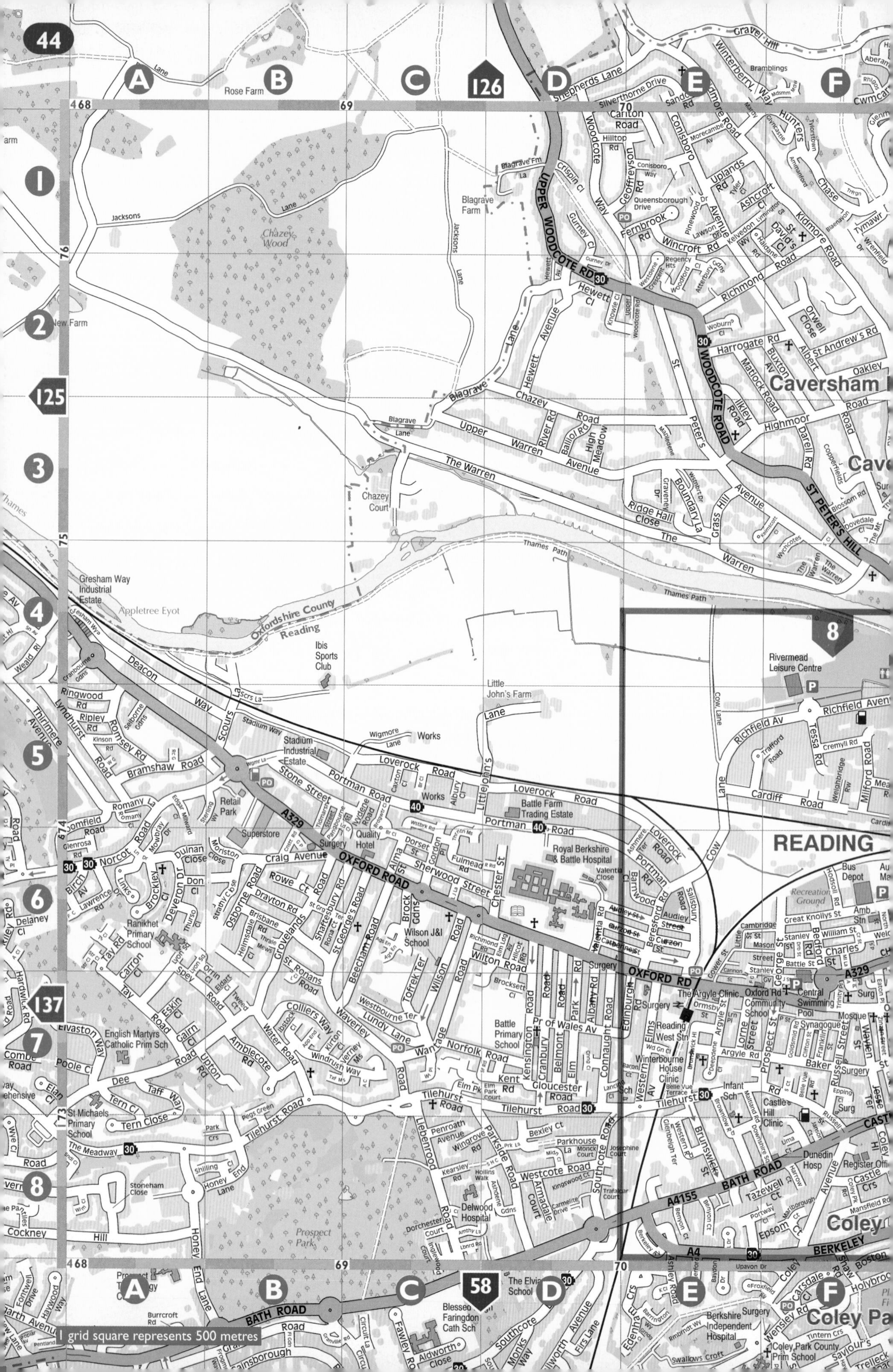
A
B
C
D
E
F
126
125
137
8
58
1
2
3
4
5
6
7
8
468
69
70
76
75
74
173
Rose Farm
Lane
Jacksons
Lane
Chazey Wood
Blagrave Fm La
Blagrave Farm
Jacksons Lane
New Farm
Blagrave Lane
Chazey Court
Thames
Gresham Way Industrial Estate
Appletree Eyot
Oxfordshire County
Reading
Ibis Sports Club
Thames Path
Little John's Farm
Lane
Shepherds Lane
Silverthorne Drive
Gravel Hill
Brambling
Winterberry Way
Carlton Road
Hilltop Rd
Woodcote Way
Crispin Cl
Geoffreyson Rd
Conisboro Way
Queensborough Drive
Fernbrook Rd
Wincroft Rd
Gurney Cl
UPPER WOODCOTE RD
Hewett Cl
Hewett Avenue
Conisboro Avenue
Morecambe Av
Uplands Rd
Ashcroft Cl
Kidmore Road
Richmond Road
Woburn Cl
Harrogate Rd
Buxton Av
Matlock Road
Ilkley Road
Albert Rd
Orwell Close
St Andrew's Rd
Oakley
Caversham
WOODCOTE ROAD
St Peter's Avenue
Chazey Road
Upper Warren Avenue
River Rd
Balliol Rd
High Meadow
The Warren
Highmoor Road
Darell Rd
Ridge Hall Close
Boundary La
Grass Hill
Highmoor
ST PETER'S HILL
Cave
Hunters Chase
Blossom Rd
Deacon Way
Scours Lane
Stadium Way
Stadium Industrial Estate
Wigmore Lane
Works
Loverock Road
Portman Road
Battle Farm Trading Estate
Littlejohn's Lane
Cow Lane
Rivermead Leisure Centre
Richfield Av
Richfield Avenue
Tessa Rd
Cremyll Rd
Milford Road
Cardiff Road
READING
Ringwood Rd
Ripley Rd
Kinson Rd
Romsey Rd
Selborne Gdns
Bramshaw Road
Thirlmere Avenue
Lyndhurst Road
Romany La
Retail Park
Superstore
Stone Street
A329
OXFORD ROAD
Quality Hotel
Works
Surgery
Craig Avenue
Norcot Road
Dulnan Close
Moriston Close
Don Cl
Deveron Dr
Thurso Cl
Brockley Cl
Birch Av
Lawrence Rd
Delaney Cl
Ranikhet Primary School
Tay Rd
Carron Cl
Spey Road
Orrin Cl
Eskin Cl
Cairn Cl
Osborne Road
Drayton Rd
Brisbane Rd
Rowe Ct
Helmsdale Cl
Grovelands Rd
St Ronans Road
Shaftesbury Rd
Beecham Road
St George's Road
Wilson J&I School
Alma St
Dorset St
Sherwood Street
Gordon Pl
Fulmead Rd
Brock Gdns
Tofrek Ter
Wilson Road
Chester St
Royal Berkshire & Battle Hospital
Valentia Close
Audley St
Curzon St
Beresford Rd
Salisbury Road
Richmond Rd
Wilton Road
Brocksett Cl
Battle Primary School
Kensington Road
Cranbury Road
Belmont Rd
Park Rd
Albany Rd
Connaught Road
Edinburgh Rd
Elms Rd
Western Av
OXFORD RD
Surgery
The Argyle Clinic
Reading West Stn
Winterbourne House Clinic
Oxford Rd Community School
Central Swimming Pool
Synagogue
Mosque
Argyle St
Argyle Rd
Lorne Street
Prospect St
Baker St
Russell Street
Waylen St
Surgery
Bus Depot
Recreation Ground
Great Knollys St
William St
Cambridge St
Stanley St
Charles St
Battle St
Bedford Rd
George St
Colliers Way
Windrush Way
Waverley Rd
Westbourne Ter
Lundy Lane
Wantage Road
Norfolk Road
Elm Pk
Kent Rd
Gloucester Road
Tilehurst Road
Elvaston Way
English Martyrs Catholic Prim Sch
Poole Cl
Dee Rd
Taff Way
Tern Cl
Tern Close
Amblecote Rd
Water Road
Upton Rd
St Michaels Primary School
The Meadway
Honey End Lane
Shilling Cl
Stoneham Close
Cockney Hill
Prospect Park
Liebenrood Road
Penroath Avenue
Wingrove Rd
Parkside Road
Kearsley Rd
Hollins Walk
Delwood Hospital
Dorchester Court
Bexley Ct
Parkhouse La
Westcote Road
Armadale Court
Southcote Road
Josephine Court
Trafalgar Court
Western Elms Av
Brunswick St
Castle Hill Clinic
Dunedin Hosp
Register Office
Castle Crs
Tazewell Ct
A4155 BATH ROAD
Epsom Ct
Coley
A4
BERKELEY
Boston
Holybrook
Upavon Dr
Ashley Road
Carsdale
Wensley Rd
Coley Park
Berkshire Independent Hospital
Surgery
Swallows Croft
Tintern Crs
Coley Park County Prim Sch
Saviour's
BATH ROAD
Prospect Technology C
Burrcroft Rd
Fonwell Drive
Haywood Way
Granville Rd
Circuit La
Fawley Rd
Blessed Faringdon Cath Sch
Aldworth Close
Southcote
The Elvian School
Monks Way
Firs Lane
Combe Road
Cockney
Hardwick Rd
Wye Cl
1 grid square represents 500 metres

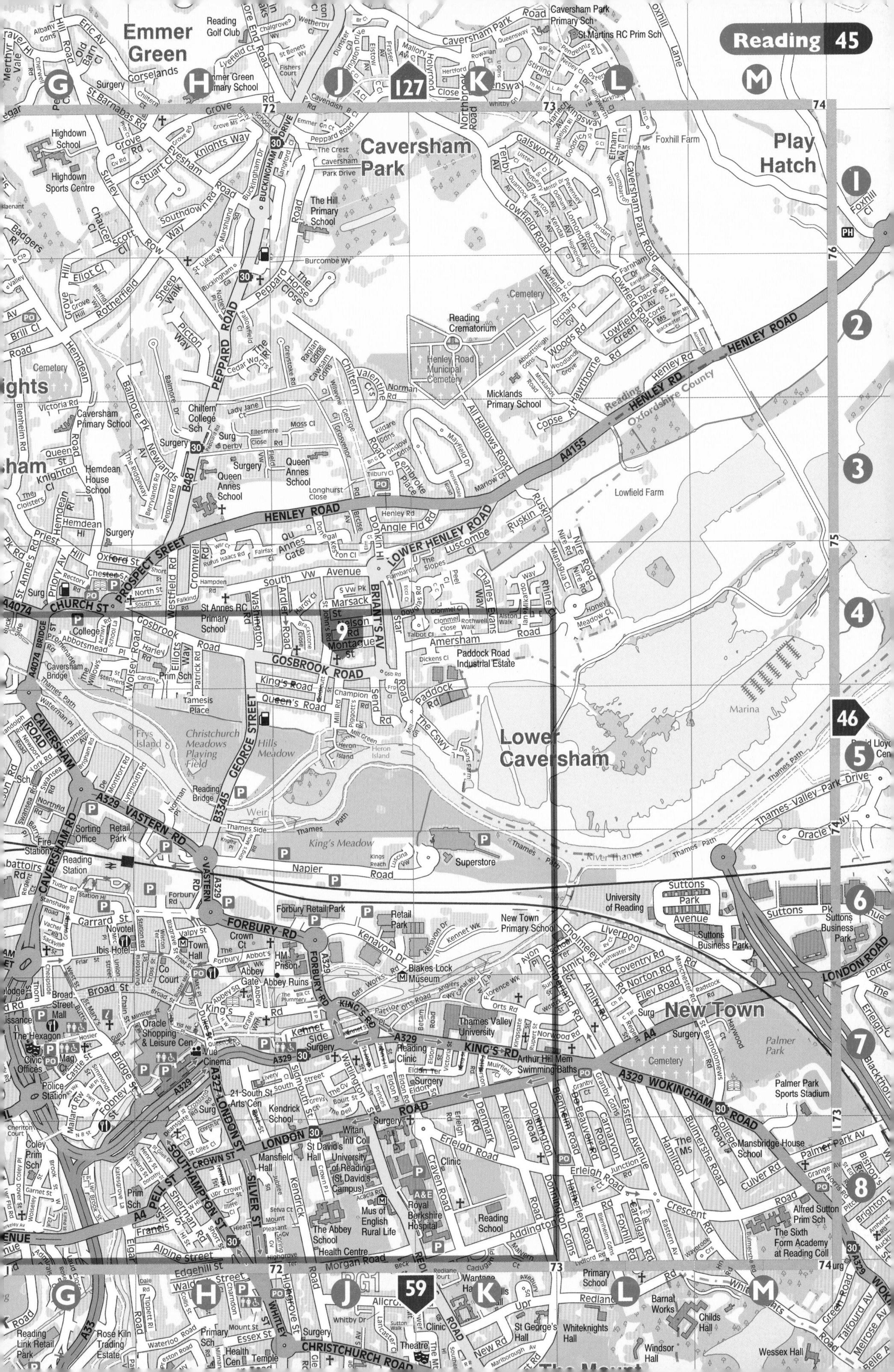
Emmer Green
Caversham Park
Play Hatch
Lower Caversham
New Town
Reading Golf Club
Highdown School
Highdown Sports Centre
The Hill Primary School
Reading Crematorium
Henley Road Municipal Cemetery
Micklands Primary School
Caversham Primary School
Hemdean House School
Queen Annes School
Chiltern College Sch
Lowfield Farm
Foxhill Farm
Marina
Paddock Road Industrial Estate
Christchurch Meadows Playing Field
Frys Island
Hills Meadow
King's Meadow
Superstore
Reading Station
Forbury Retail Park
Retail Park
HM Prison
Abbey Ruins
Blakes Lock Museum
Town Hall
Crown Ct
Oracle Shopping & Leisure Cen
The Hexagon
Civic Offices
Police Station
Broad Street Mall
Thames Valley University
Reading Clinic
Arthur Hill Mem Swimming Baths
University of Reading
New Town Primary School
Suttons Business Park
Palmer Park
Palmer Park Sports Stadium
Mansbridge House School
Alfred Sutton Prim Sch
The Sixth Form Academy at Reading Coll
Royal Berkshire Hospital
Reading School
Mus of English Rural Life
The Abbey School
Kendrick School
Wantage Hall
St George's Hall
Whiteknights Hall
Windsor Hall
Wessex Hall
Childs Hall
Barnat Works
Rose Kiln Trading Estate
Reading Link Retail Park
HENLEY ROAD
LOWER HENLEY ROAD
GOSBROOK ROAD
GEORGE STREET
PEPPARD ROAD
PROSPECT STREET
CHURCH ST
CAVERSHAM ROAD
VASTERN RD
FORBURY RD
KING'S RD
LONDON ROAD
WOKINGHAM ROAD
SOUTHAMPTON ST
SILVER ST
CHRISTCHURCH ROAD
Oxfordshire County
River Thames
Thames Path
A4155
A329
A4
A33
B481
B3345
A4074
127
46
59
RG1

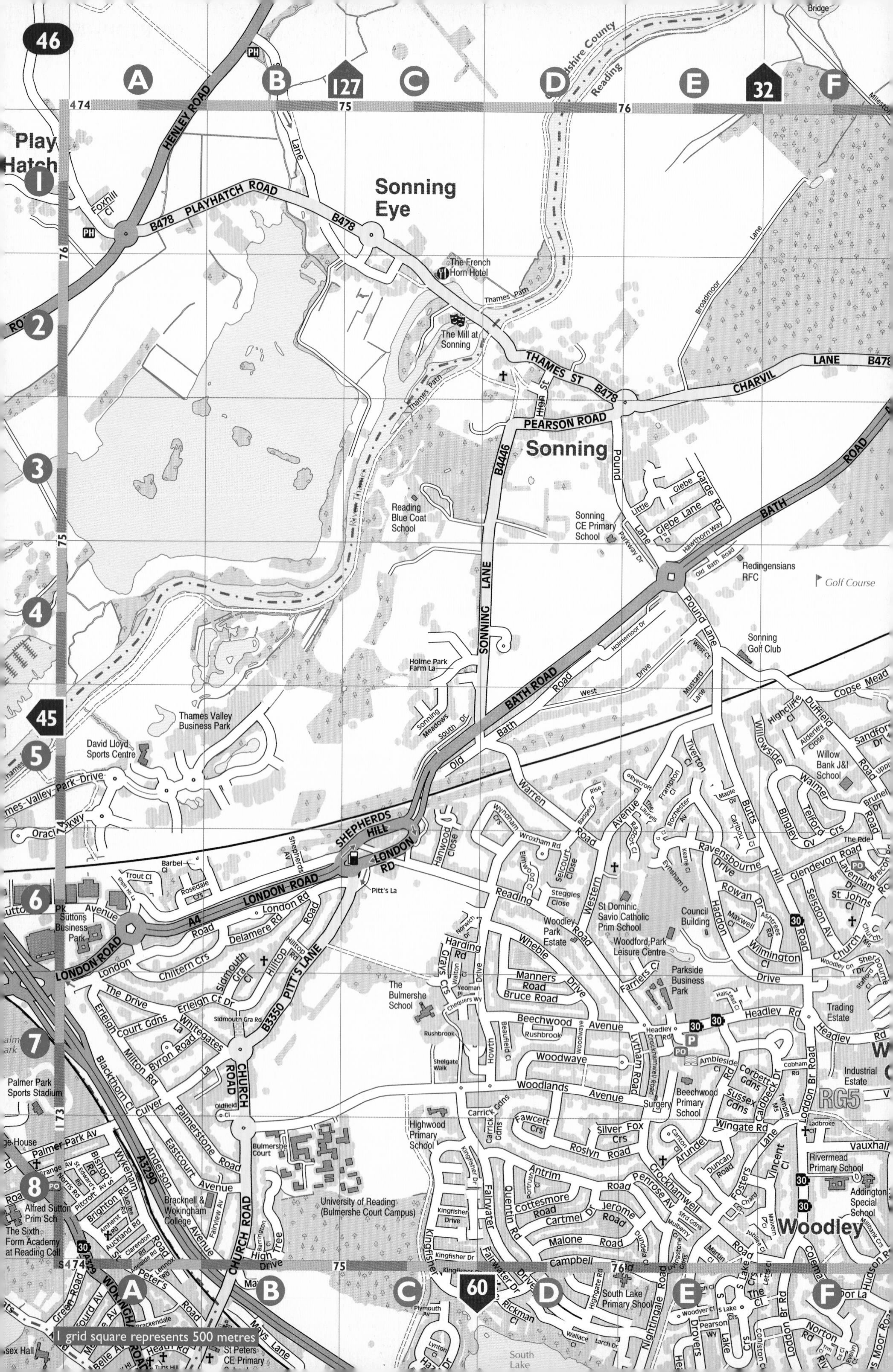
Sonning Eye
Sonning
Woodley
Play Hatch
HENLEY ROAD
PLAYHATCH ROAD
THAMES ST
CHARVIL LANE
PEARSON ROAD
SONNING LANE
BATH ROAD
LONDON ROAD
SHEPHERDS HILL
PITT'S LANE
CHURCH ROAD
WOKINGHAM ROAD
The French Horn Hotel
The Mill at Sonning
Reading Blue Coat School
Sonning CE Primary School
Redingensians RFC
Golf Course
Sonning Golf Club
Thames Valley Business Park
David Lloyd Sports Centre
Suttons Business Park
Willow Bank J&I School
St Dominic Savio Catholic Prim School
Woodford Park Leisure Centre
Council Building
Parkside Business Park
Woodley Park Estate
The Bulmershe School
Trading Estate
Industrial Estate
Beechwood Primary School
Highwood Primary School
University of Reading (Bulmershe Court Campus)
Bracknell & Wokingham College
Palmer Park Sports Stadium
Alfred Sutton Prim Sch
The Sixth Form Academy at Reading Coll
Rivermead Primary School
Addington Special School
South Lake Primary School
St Peters CE Primary
South Lake
RG5
1 grid square represents 500 metres

127 32 45 60

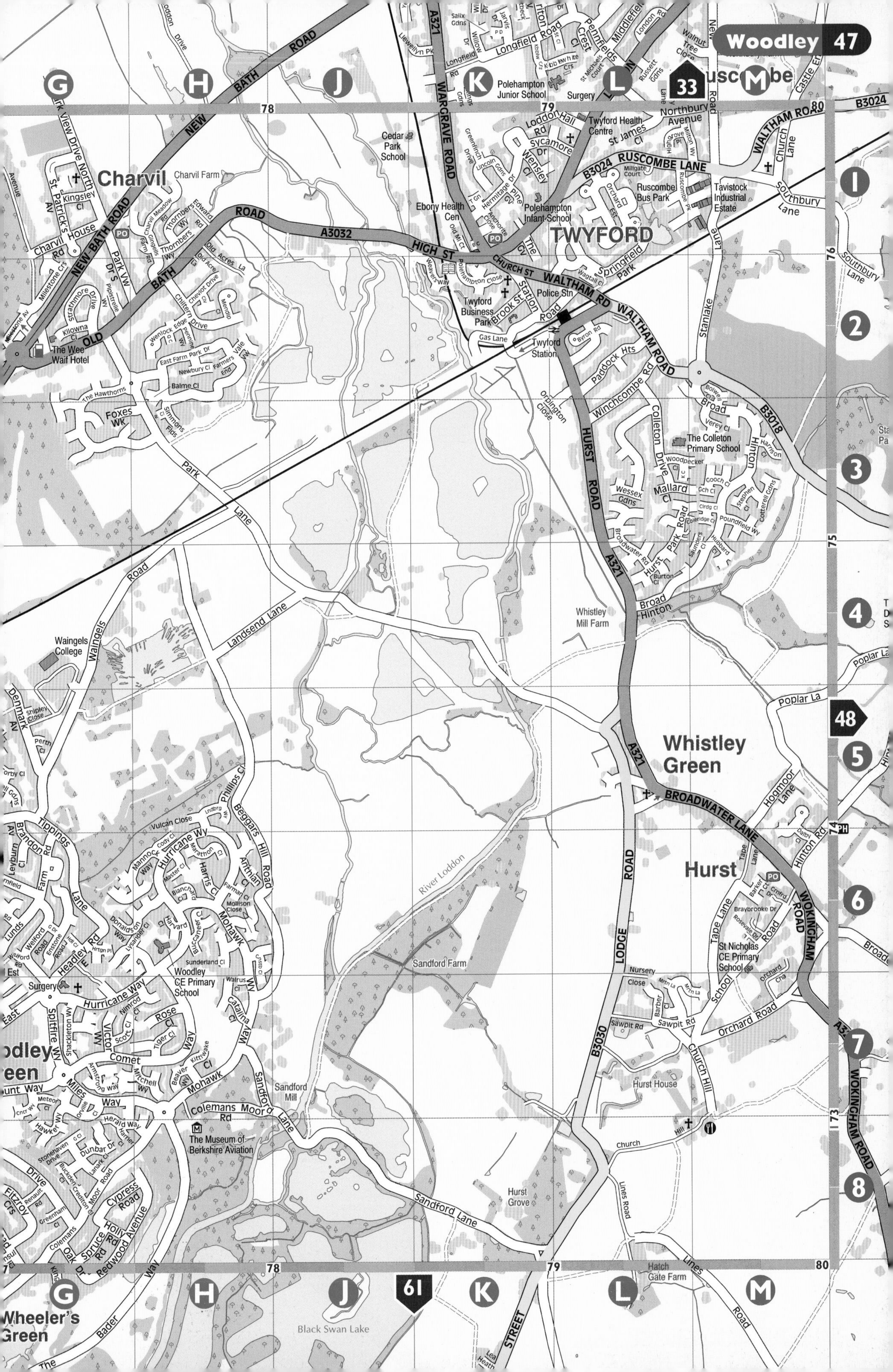
G
H
J
K
L
M
78
79
80
33
Charvil
Charvil Farm
TWYFORD
Whistley Green
Hurst
Woodley Green
Wheeler's Green
NEW BATH ROAD
OLD BATH ROAD
A3032
HIGH ST
CHURCH ST
WALTHAM RD
WALTHAM ROAD
B3024
RUSCOMBE LANE
B3018
A321
WARGRAVE ROAD
HURST ROAD
BROADWATER LANE
WOKINGHAM ROAD
LODGE ROAD
B3030
Cedar Park School
Polehampton Junior School
Polehampton Infant School
Twyford Health Centre
Ebony Health Cen
Surgery
Ruscombe Bus Park
Tavistock Industrial Estate
Police Stn
Twyford Station
Twyford Business Park
Gas Lane
Station Road
The Wee Waif Hotel
Foxes Wk
Park Lane
Waingels Road
Waingels College
Landsend Lane
Whistley Mill Farm
The Colleton Primary School
Colleton Drive
Winchcombe Rd
Paddock Hts
Mallard Cl
Wessex Gdns
Broadwater Rd
Hinton Rd
Poplar La
Hogmoor Lane
Tape Lane
St Nicholas CE Primary School
Orchard Road
Sawpit Rd
Church Hill
Hurst House
Nursery Close
River Loddon
Sandford Farm
Sandford Mill
Sandford Lane
Beggars Hill Road
Hurricane Wy
Hurricane Way
Woodley CE Primary School
Colemans Moor Rd
The Museum of Berkshire Aviation
Mohawk Way
Comet
Miles Way
Spitfire Wy
Cypress Road
Redwood Avenue
Hurst Grove
Lines Road
Hatch Gate Farm
Black Swan Lake
Bader Way
STREET
61
48
1
2
3
4
5
6
7
8
73
74
75
76
Southbury Lane
Stanlake Lane
Northbury Avenue
Loddon Hall Rd
St James Cl
Sycamore Dr
Springfield Park
Twyford
Park Vw

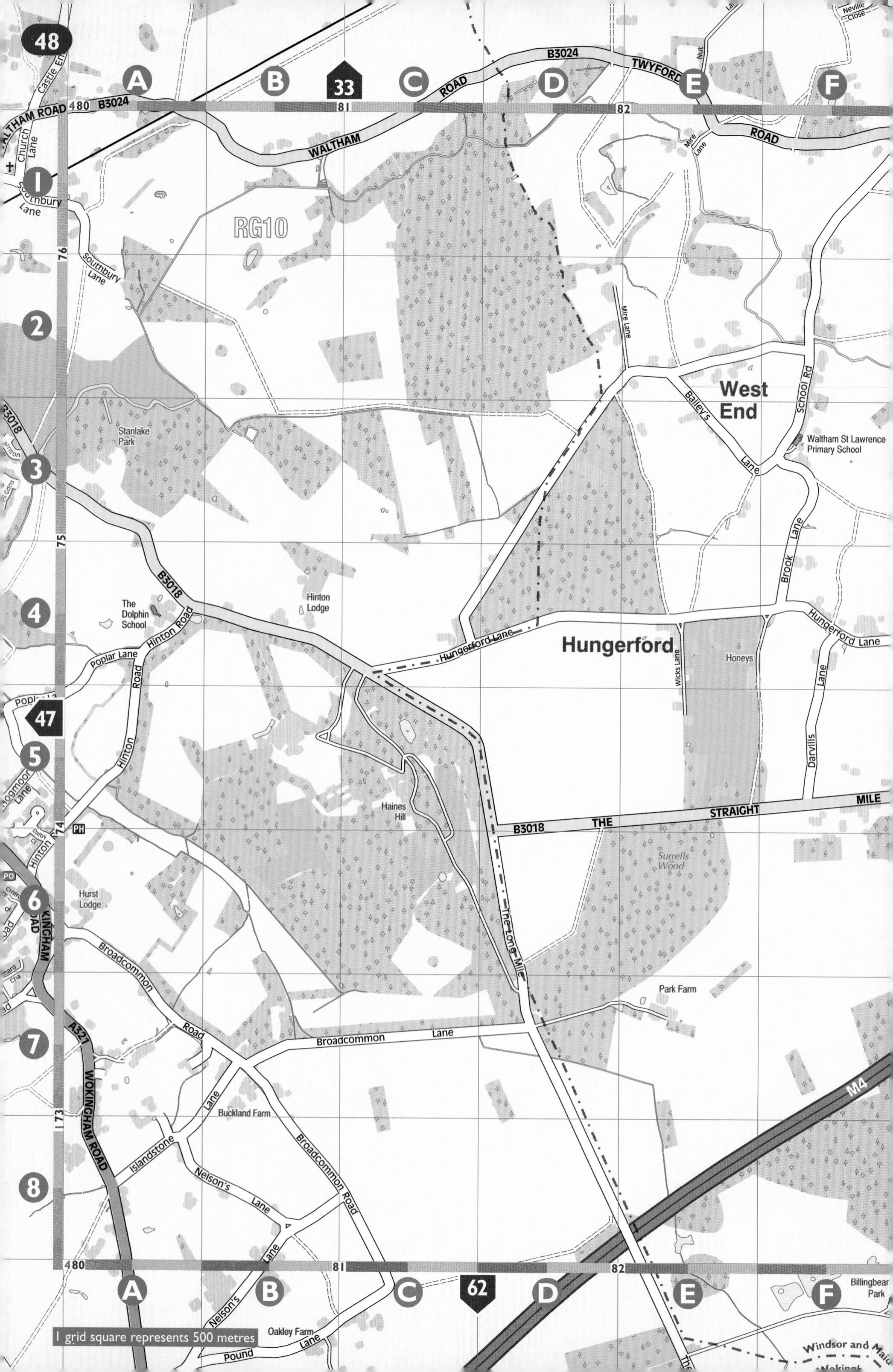

A   B   **33**   C   D   E   F
81
82

WALTHAM ROAD 480   B3024   B3024   TWYFORD
WALTHAM   ROAD
ROAD

Castle End

Church Lane

Southbury Lane

RG10

76

Stanlake Park

B3018

3

75

B3018

Hinton Road

The Dolphin School

Hinton Lodge

4

Poplar Lane

47

Poplar Rd

5

Hogmoor Lane

74

PH

Darvy Clo

6

Hurst Lodge

KINGHAM

Broadcommon Road

A321

7

73

WOKINGHAM ROAD

480

Islandstone

Nelson's Lane

Buckland Farm

Broadcommon Road

8

Nelson's Lane

Oakley Farm Lane

Pound Lane

A   B   81   C   **62**   D   82   E   F

West End

Mire Lane

Bailey's Lane

Waltham St Lawrence Primary School

School Rd

Brook Lane

Hungerford Lane

Hungerford Lane

Honeys

Hungerford

Wicks Lane

Darvills Lane

B3018   THE   STRAIGHT   MILE

Surrells Wood

Haines Hill

The Long Mile

Park Farm

M4

Broadcommon Lane

Billingbear Park

Windsor and Mai

Nut

Neville Close

Lane

I grid square represents 500 metres

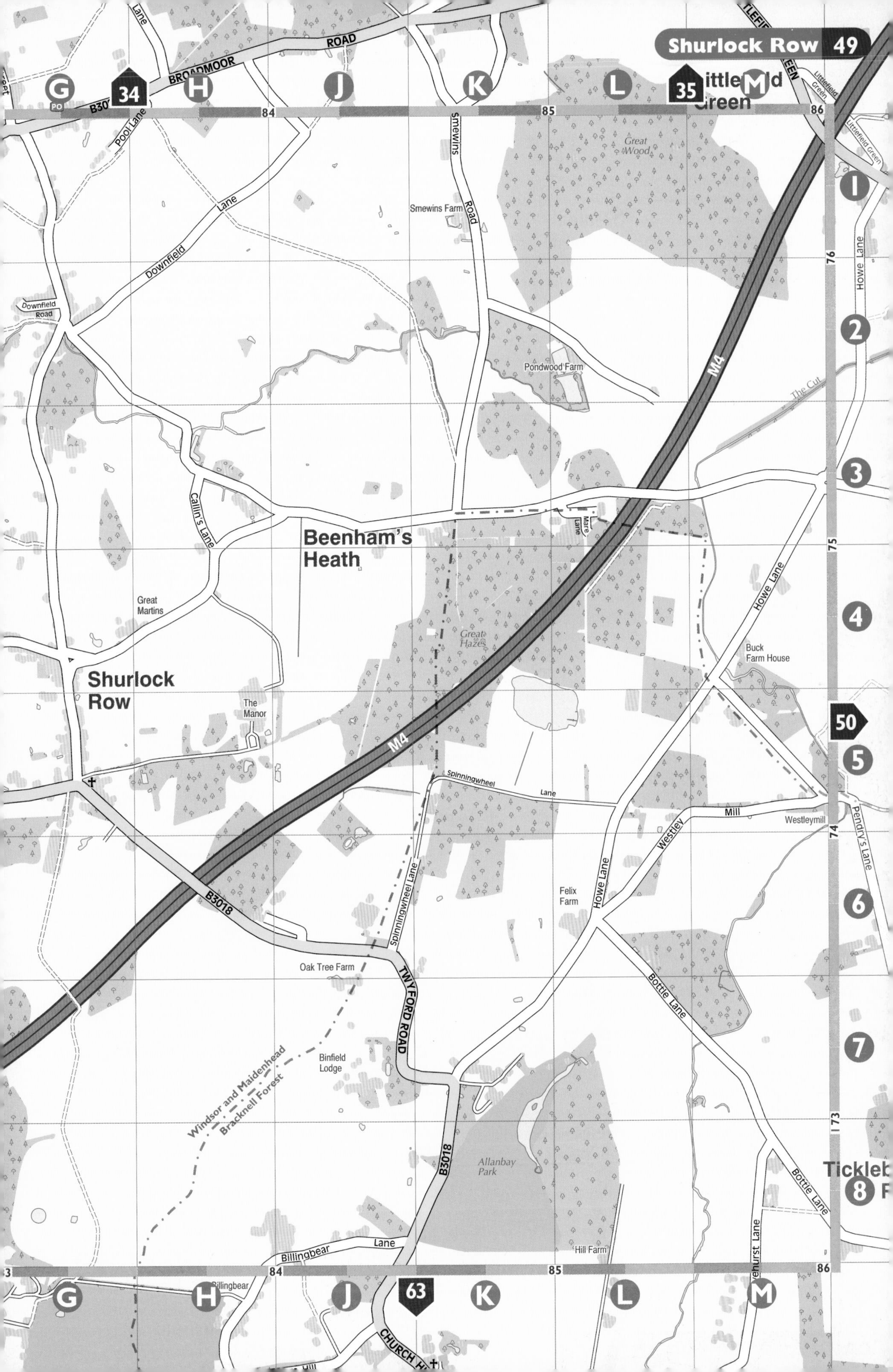
G
H
J
K
L
M
34
35
BROADMOOR
ROAD
B30
Pool Lane
Lane
Littlefield Green
84
85
86
Great Wood
Smewins Road
Smewins Farm
Downfield Lane
Downfield Road
Pondwood Farm
M4
The Cut
Callin's Lane
Beenham's Heath
Mare Lane
Great Martins
Great Hazes
Shurlock Row
The Manor
Buck Farm House
Howe Lane
50
Spinningwheel Lane
Westley Mill
Westleymill
Pendry's Lane
B3018
Felix Farm
Spinningwheel Lane
Oak Tree Farm
TWYFORD ROAD
Bottle Lane
Binfield Lodge
Windsor and Maidenhead
Bracknell Forest
Allanbay Park
Billingbear Lane
Hill Farm
Tickleb
Billingbear
63
CHURCH HILL
76
75
74
73
1
2
3
4
5
6
7
8

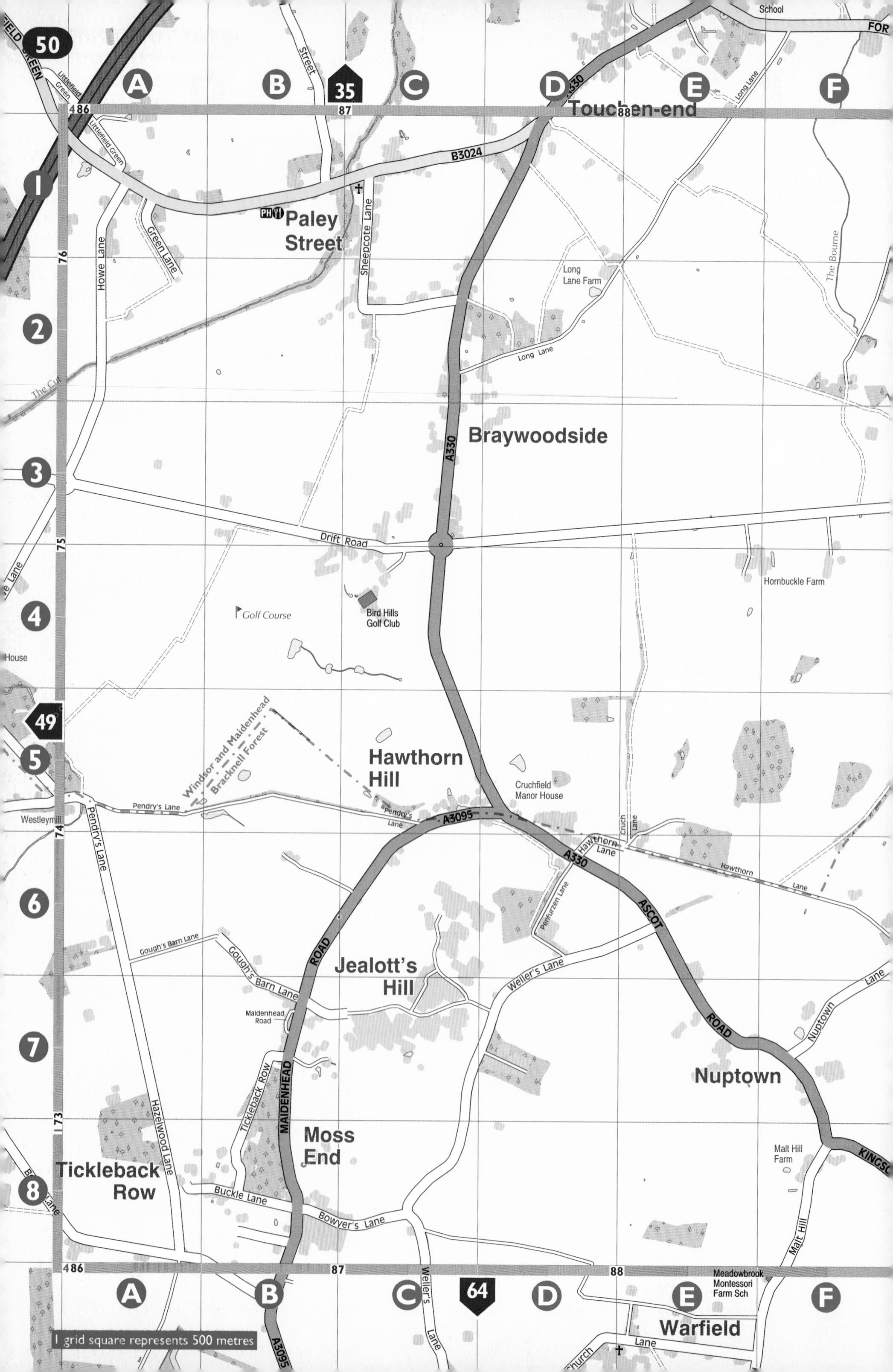

A B 35 C D A330 E F
87
Touchen-end
50
486
76
FOR
School
Littlefield Green
Howe Lane
Green Lane
PH Paley
Street
Sheepcote Lane
B3024
A330
Long Lane Farm
Long Lane
The Bourne
Long Lane
2
The Cut
3
75
Drift Road
A330
Braywoodside
Hornbuckle Farm
Golf Course
Bird Hills
Golf Club
4
House
49
Windsor and Maidenhead
Bracknell Forest
Hawthorn
Hill
Cruchfield
Manor House
5
74
Westleymill
Pendry's Lane
Pendry's Lane
Pendry's
Lane
A3095
A330
Hawthorn Lane
Cruch Lane
Hawthorn Lane
6
ASCOT
Penhurzen Lane
Gough's Barn Lane
Gough's Barn Lane
ROAD
Jealott's
Hill
Weller's Lane
ROAD
Nuptown Lane
7
73
Maidenhead
Road
Nuptown
Hazelwood Lane
Tickleback Row
MAIDENHEAD
Moss
End
Malt Hill
Farm
KINGS
8
Tickleback
Row
Buckle Lane
Bowyer's Lane
Malt Hill Lane
Lane
486
87
64
88
A B C Weller's D E F
Lane
Meadowbrook
Montessori
Farm Sch
Warfield
A3095
Lane
1 grid square represents 500 metres

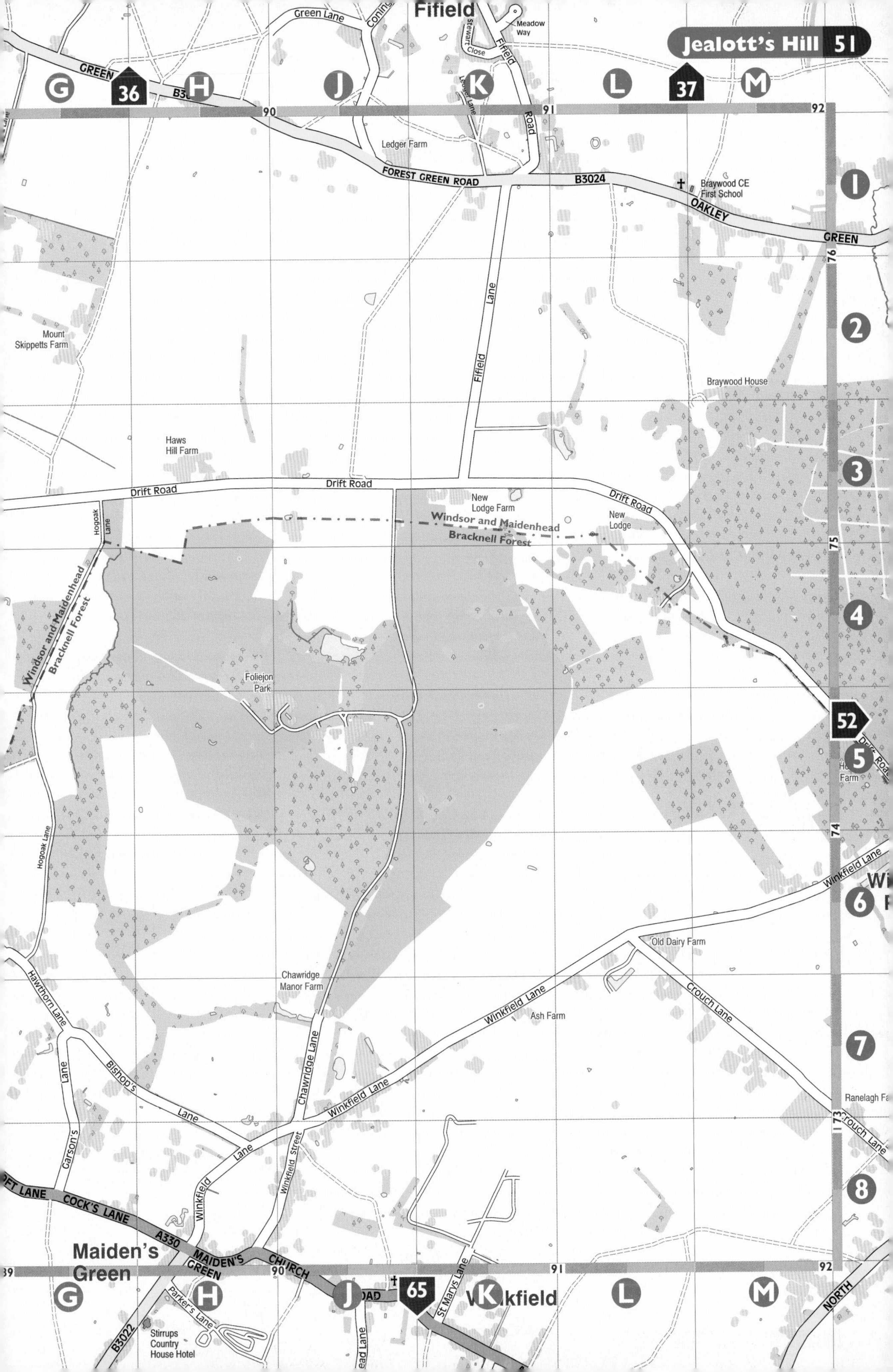
Fifield
Green Lane
Meadow Way
Stewart Close
Fifield Road
GREEN
36
B30
G H J K L M
37
Ledger Farm
FOREST GREEN ROAD
B3024
Braywood CE First School
OAKLEY
GREEN
Mount Skippetts Farm
Fifield Lane
Braywood House
Haws Hill Farm
Drift Road
New Lodge Farm
New Lodge
Windsor and Maidenhead
Bracknell Forest
Hogoak Lane
Foliejon Park
52
Winkfield Lane
Old Dairy Farm
Chawridge Manor Farm
Hawthorn Lane
Crouch Lane
Ash Farm
Bishop's Lane
Chawridge Lane
Ranelagh Fa
Garson's Lane
Winkfield Street
Winkfield Lane
COCK'S LANE
A330
MAIDEN'S GREEN
CHURCH ROAD
Maiden's Green
65
St Marys Lane
Winkfield
Parker's Lane
B3022
Stirrups Country House Hotel
NORTH
1 2 3 4 5 6 7 8
90 91 92
76 75 74 73

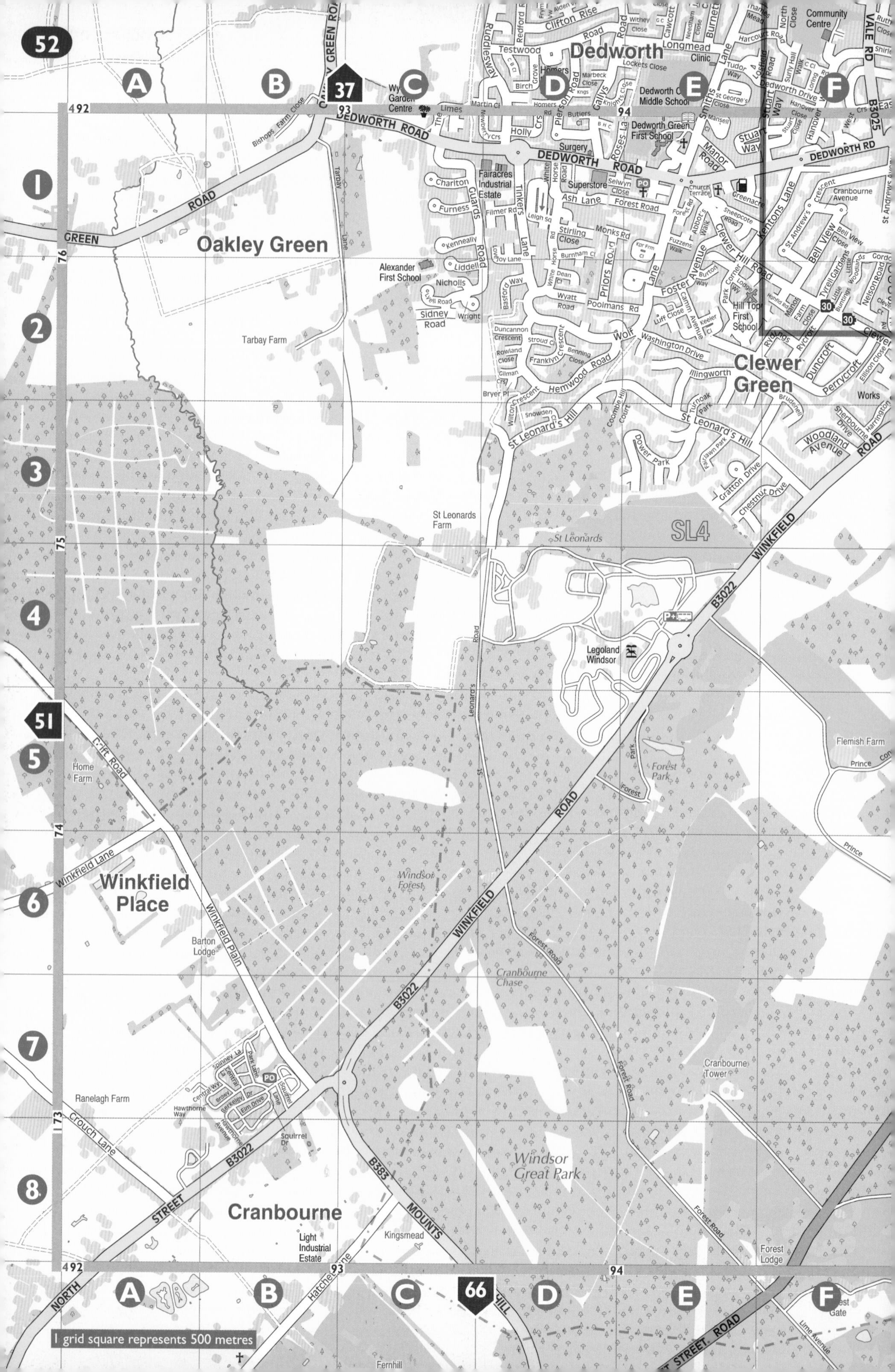

Dedworth
Oakley Green
Clewer Green
Winkfield Place
Cranbourne
Windsor Great Park
Windsor Forest
Legoland Windsor
St Leonards
St Leonards Farm
Tarbay Farm
Alexander First School
Fairacres Industrial Estate
Superstore
Surgery
Dedworth Green First School
Clinic
Community Centre
Hill Top First School
Works
Flemish Farm
Forest Park
Cranbourne Chase
Cranbourne Tower
Forest Lodge
Home Farm
Barton Lodge
Ranelagh Farm
Light Industrial Estate
Kingsmead
Fernhill
DEDWORTH ROAD
DEDWORTH RD
WINKFIELD ROAD
B3022
B3025
B383
MOUNTS HILL
NORTH STREET
Winkfield Plain
Winkfield Lane
Crouch Lane
Forest Road
St Leonard's Hill
St Leonard's Road
Clewer Hill Road
Hemwood Road
Washington Drive
Tarbay Lane
Tinkers Lane
Guards Road
Priors Road
Smiths Lane
Manor Road
Kentons Lane
VALE RD
SL4
37
51
66
30
492
93
94
76
75
74
173
A
B
C
D
E
F
1
2
3
4
5
6
7
8
1 grid square represents 500 metres

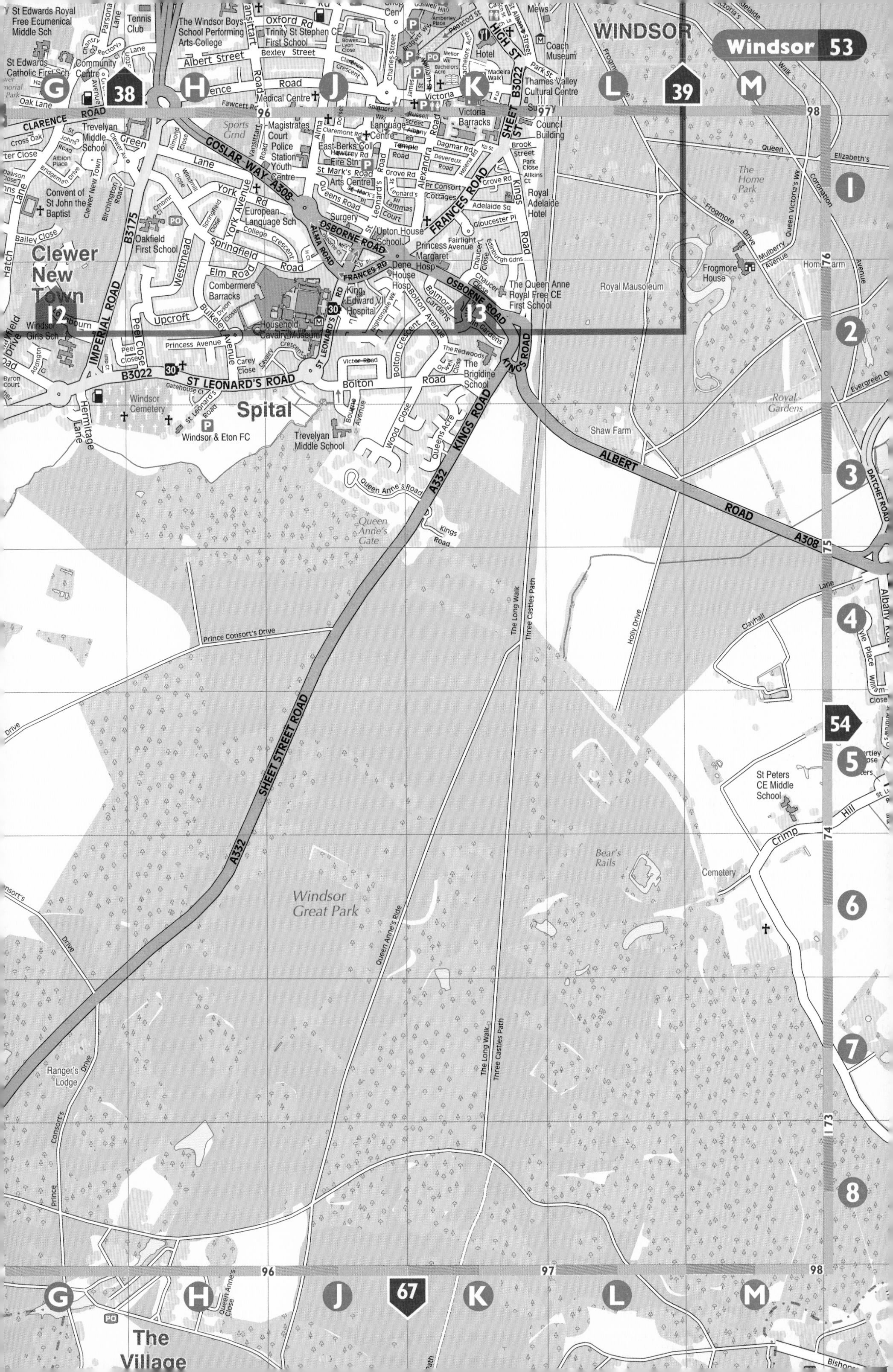
WINDSOR
Clewer New Town
Spital
Windsor Great Park
The Village
The Home Park
Royal Mausoleum
Frogmore House
Shaw Farm
Royal Gardens
Bear's Rails
Cemetery
St Peters CE Middle School
Queen Anne's Gate
Ranger's Lodge
Windsor Cemetery
Windsor & Eton FC
Trevelyan Middle School
Household Cavalry Museum
Combermere Barracks
King Edward VII Hospital
Princess Margaret Hosp
The Queen Anne Royal Free CE First School
Royal Adelaide Hotel
Thames Valley Cultural Centre
Coach Museum
Council Building
Victoria Barracks
Magistrates Court
Police Station
Youth Centre
Oakfield First School
Convent of St John the Baptist
The Brigidine School
European Language Sch
Medical Centre
Trinity St Stephen CE First School
The Windsor Boys School Performing Arts College
St Edwards Royal Free Ecumenical Middle Sch
St Edwards Catholic First Sch
Tennis Club
Community Centre
Windsor Girls Sch
SHEET STREET ROAD
KINGS ROAD
ALBERT ROAD
OSBORNE ROAD
FRANCES ROAD
GOSLAR WAY A308
IMPERIAL ROAD
ST LEONARD'S ROAD
CLARENCE ROAD
DATCHET ROAD
A332
A308
B3022
B3175
The Long Walk
Three Castles Path
Queen Anne's Ride
Prince Consort's Drive
Holly Drive
Crimp Hill
Queen Victoria's Wk
Frogmore Drive
38
39
54
67
12
13
G
H
J
K
L
M
96
97
98
173
74
75
76
1
2
3
4
5
6
7
8

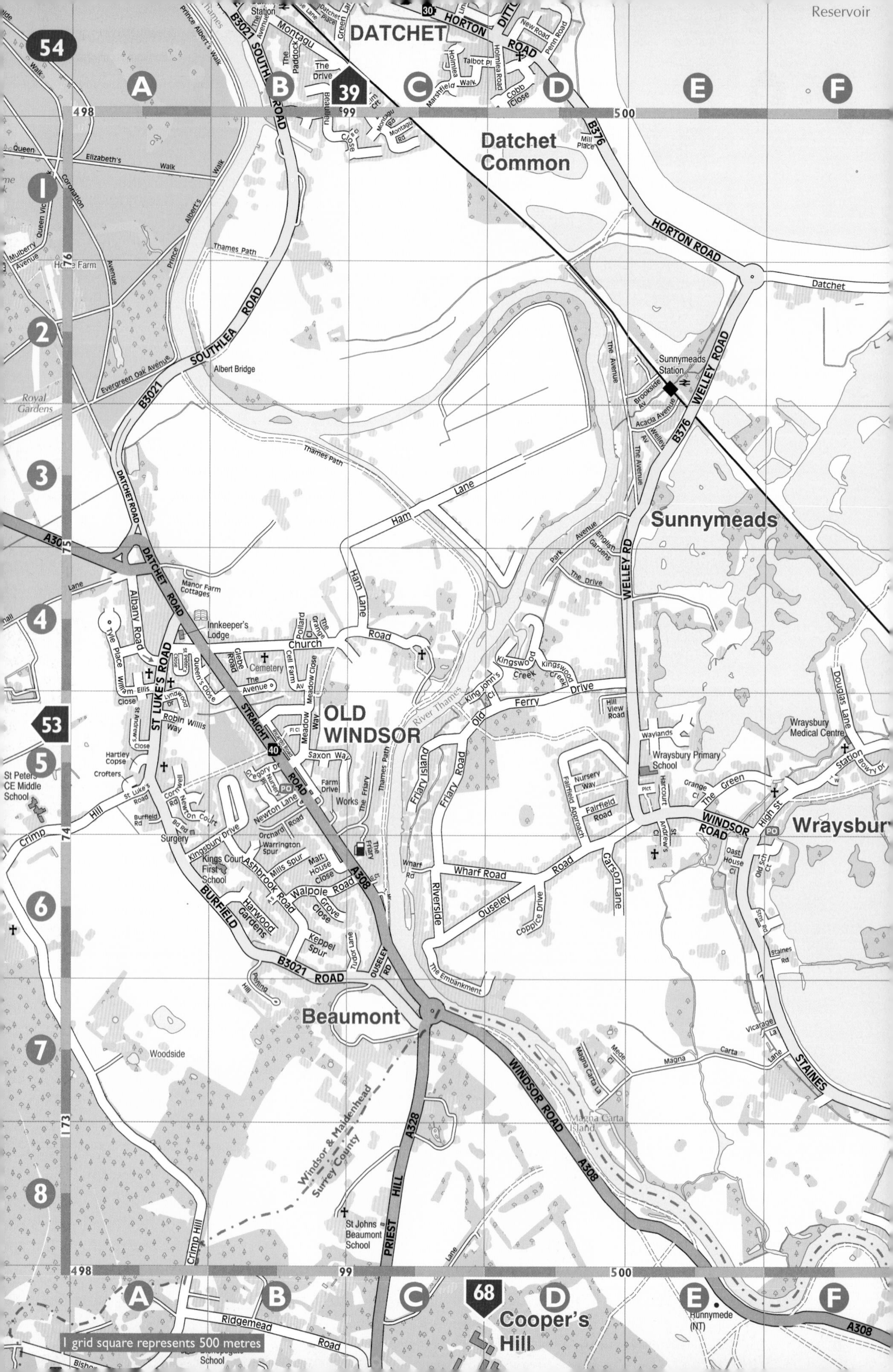
54
53
39
40
68
30
A
B
C
D
E
F
1
2
3
4
5
6
7
8
498
99
500
76
75
74
173
Reservoir
DATCHET
Datchet Common
Sunnymeads
OLD WINDSOR
Wraysbury
Beaumont
Cooper's Hill
Royal Gardens
Home Farm
Queen Elizabeth's Walk
Coronation
Prince Albert's Walk
Albert's Walk
Prince Albert's Avenue
Evergreen Oak Avenue
Albert Bridge
Thames Path
SOUTHLEA ROAD
B3021
DATCHET ROAD
A308
HORTON ROAD
B376
WELLEY ROAD
WELLEY RD
Sunnymeads Station
Datchet
Ham Lane
Ham Lane Road
Church Road
River Thames
Ferry Drive
Innkeeper's Lodge
Manor Farm Cottages
Cemetery
ST LUKE'S ROAD
STRAIGHT ROAD
Robin Willis Way
Wraysbury Primary School
Wraysbury Medical Centre
WINDSOR ROAD
Wharf Road
Ouseley Road
Carson Lane
BURFIELD ROAD
Kings Court First School
Surgery
St Peters CE Middle School
Crimp Hill
Woodside
Magna Carta Lane
Magna Carta Island
WINDSOR ROAD
A328
PRIEST HILL
St Johns Beaumont School
Windsor & Maidenhead
Surrey County
Runnymede (NT)
Ridgemead Road
STAINES
1 grid square represents 500 metres

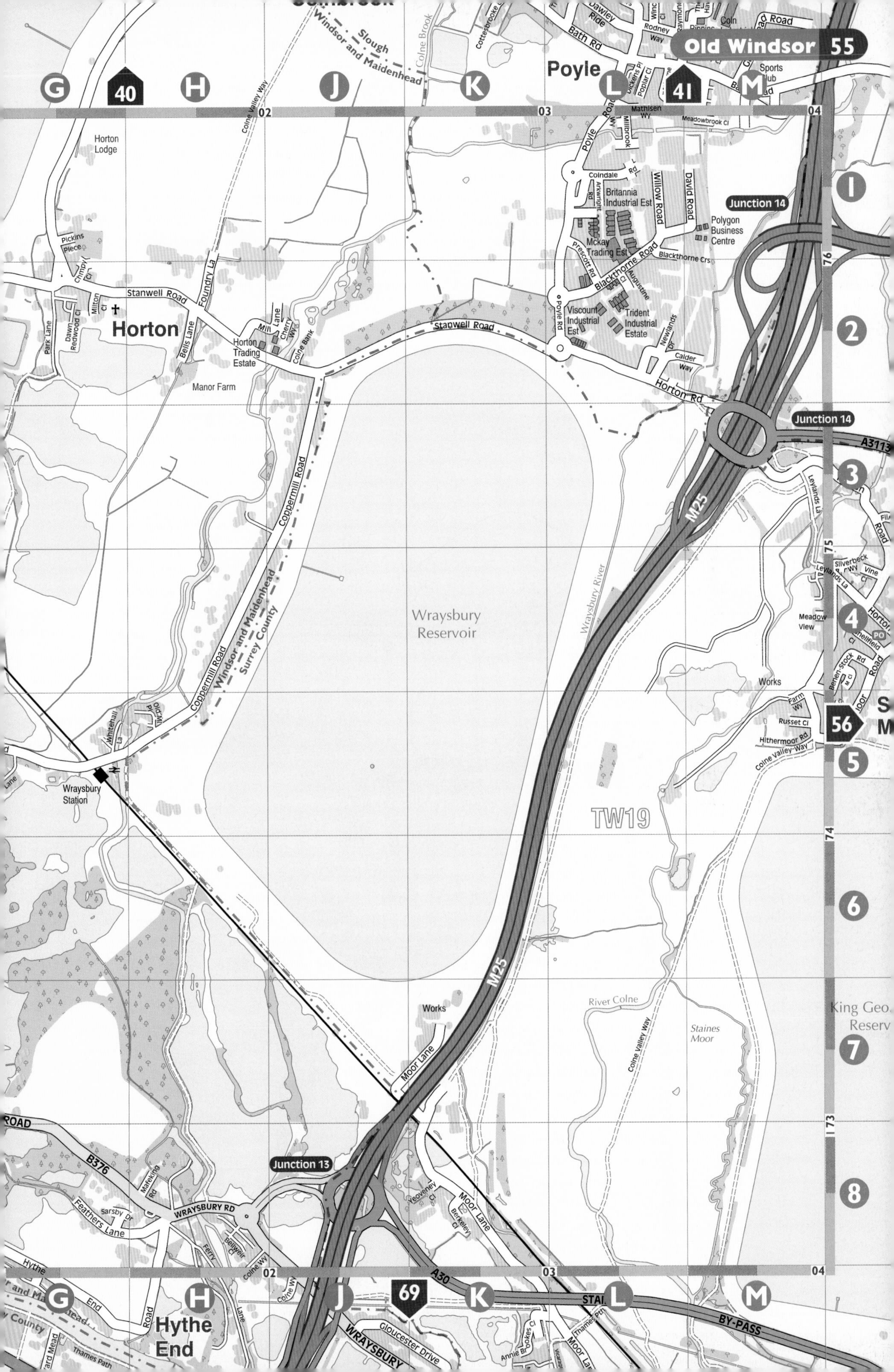
Poyle
Horton
Horton Lodge
Pickins Piece
Stanwell Road
Foundry La
Bells Lane
Park Lane
Dawn Redwood Cl
Milton Cl
Chimpy Cl
Horton Trading Estate
Mill Lane
Cherry Wy
Colne Bank
Manor Farm
Coppermill Road
Windsor and Maidenhead
Surrey County
Slough
Colne Brook
Colne Valley Way
Cottesbrooke
Bath Rd
Dawley Ride
Rodney Way
Dickens Pl
Poplar Cl
Mathisen Wy
Millbrook Wy
Meadowbrook Cl
Poyle Road
Coldale Rd
Arkwright Rd
Britannia Industrial Est
Willow Road
David Road
Polygon Business Centre
Junction 14
Mckay Trading Est
Prescott Rd
Blackthorne Road
Blackthorne Crs
Augustine
Viscount Industrial Est
Trident Industrial Estate
Poyle Rd
Newlands Dr
Calder Way
Horton Rd
Sports Club
A3113
M25
Leylands La
Silverbeck Wy
Vine
Meadow View
Horton
Works
Farm Wy
Russet Cl
Hithermoor Rd
Benen Stock Rd
Colne Valley Way
Wraysbury Reservoir
Wraysbury River
TW19
Wraysbury Station
Whitehall La
Old Mill Pl
River Colne
Staines Moor
King Geo. Reserv
Moor Lane
Junction 13
B376
WRAYSBURY RD
Mafeking Rd
Sarsby Dr
Feathers Lane
Bellweir Cl
Ferry
Colne Wy
Yeoveney Cl
Berkeley Cl
A30
STAINES BY-PASS
Hythe End
Gloucester Drive
WRAYSBURY
Thames Path
Annie Brookes Cl
Thames Pth
Moor La
G H J K L M
40 41 56 69
02 03 04
73 74 75 76
1 2 3 4 5 6 7 8

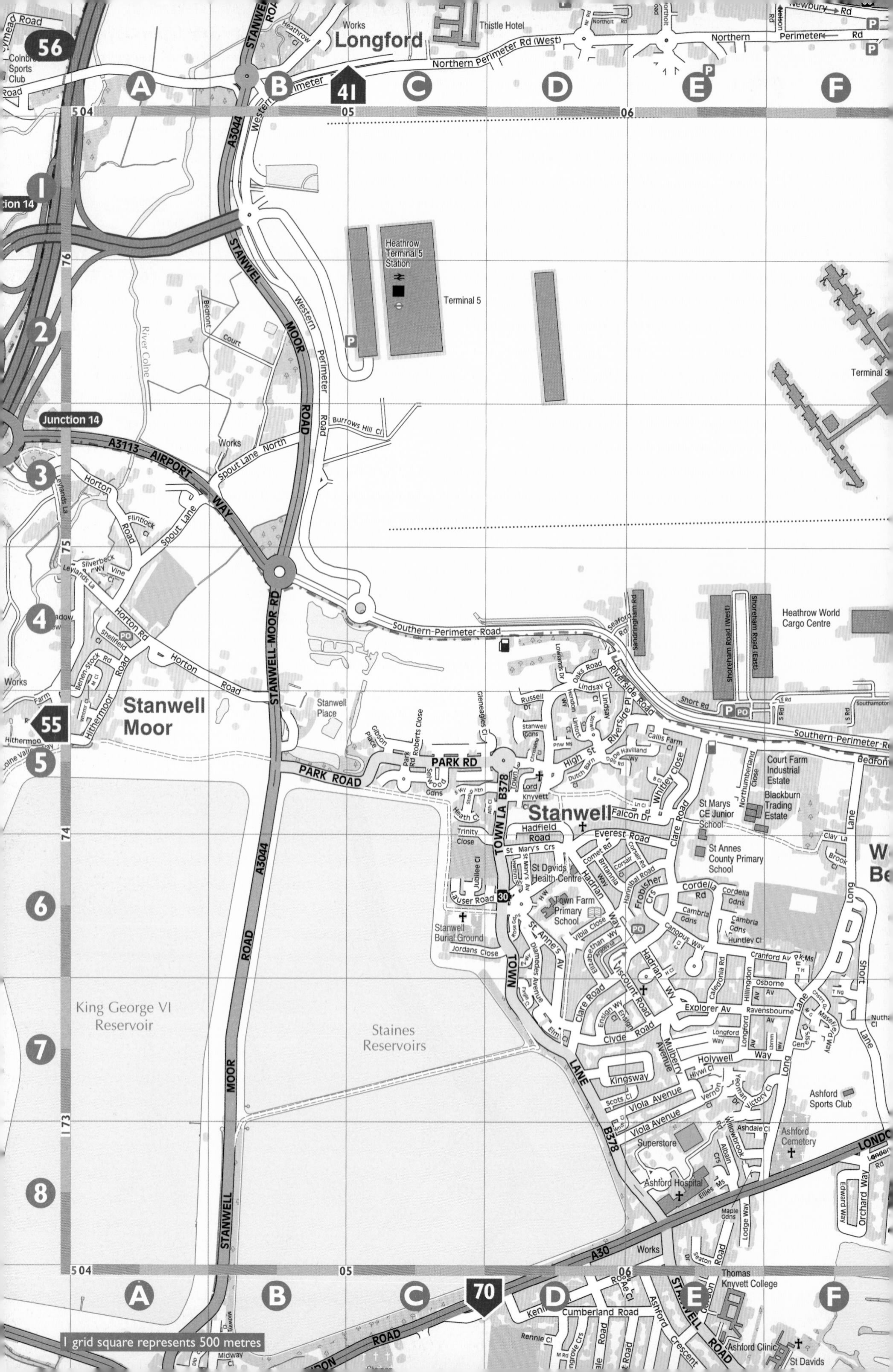

56
Longford
Thistle Hotel
Works
Northern Perimeter Rd (West)
Northern
Perimeter
Rd
Newbury Rd
Western Perimeter
Colnbrook Sports Club
41
A
B
C
D
E
F
504
05
06
1
2
3
4
5
6
7
8
Junction 14
Heathrow Terminal 5 Station
Terminal 5
Terminal 3
STANWELL MOOR ROAD
A3044
Western Perimeter Road
Bedfont Court
River Colne
Burrows Hill Cl
Works
A3113 AIRPORT WAY
Spout Lane North
Spout Lane
Horton Rd
Horton Road
Flintlock Cl
Leylands La
Silverbeck Wy
Vine Cl
Shelfield Cl
Bellen Stock Rd
Hithermoor Road
55
Stanwell Moor
STANWELL-MOOR RD
Southern-Perimeter-Road
Stanwell Place
Heathrow World Cargo Centre
Shoreham Road (West)
Shoreham Road (East)
Sandringham Rd
Riverside Road
Short Rd
PARK ROAD
PARK RD
Gleneagles Cl
Gibson Place
Roberts Close
Court Farm Industrial Estate
Blackburn Trading Estate
Stanwell
TOWN LA B378
High St
Falcon Dr
Hadfield Road
Everest Road
Clare Road
St Marys CE Junior School
St Annes County Primary School
St Davids Health Centre
Town Farm Primary School
Lauser Road
Stanwell Burial Ground
Jordans Close
King George VI Reservoir
Staines Reservoirs
Cordella Rd
Cranford Av
Explorer Av
Holywell Way
Kingsway
Viola Avenue
Mulberry Avenue
Clyde Road
Superstore
Ashford Hospital
Ashford Sports Club
Ashford Cemetery
Long Lane
Short Lane
Works
A30
LONDON ROAD
STANWELL MOOR ROAD
70
Thomas Knyvett College
Cumberland Road
Ashford Crescent
STANWELL ROAD
Ashford Clinic
St Davids
1 grid square represents 500 metres

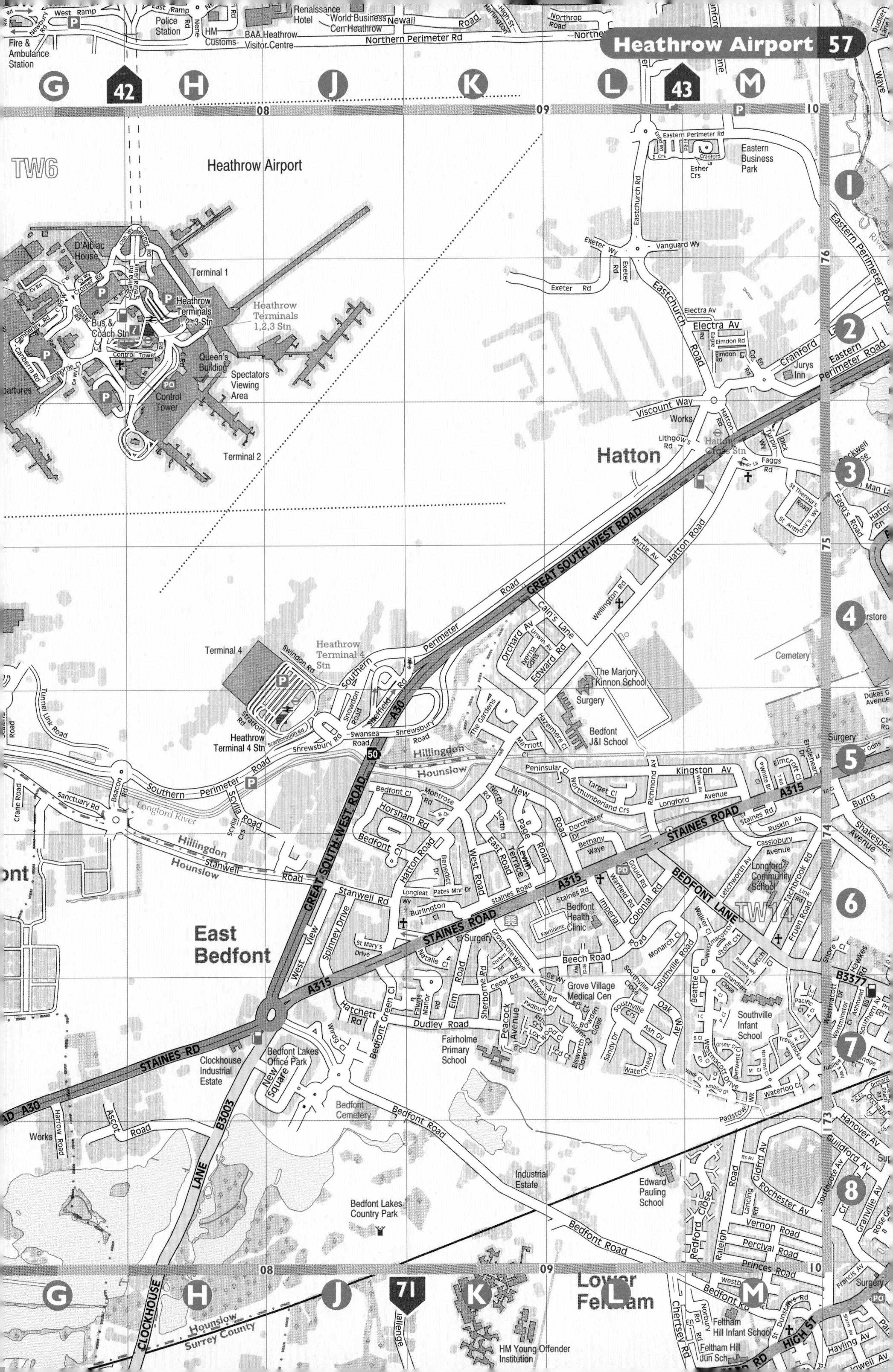
Heathrow Airport
TW6
Terminal 1
Heathrow Terminals 1, 2, 3 Stn
Terminal 2
Terminal 4
Heathrow Terminal 4 Stn
Hatton
East Bedfont
Lower Feltham
Hatton Cross Stn
Eastern Business Park
GREAT SOUTH-WEST ROAD
STAINES ROAD
BEDFONT LANE
Bedfont Lakes Country Park
HM Young Offender Institution
TW14

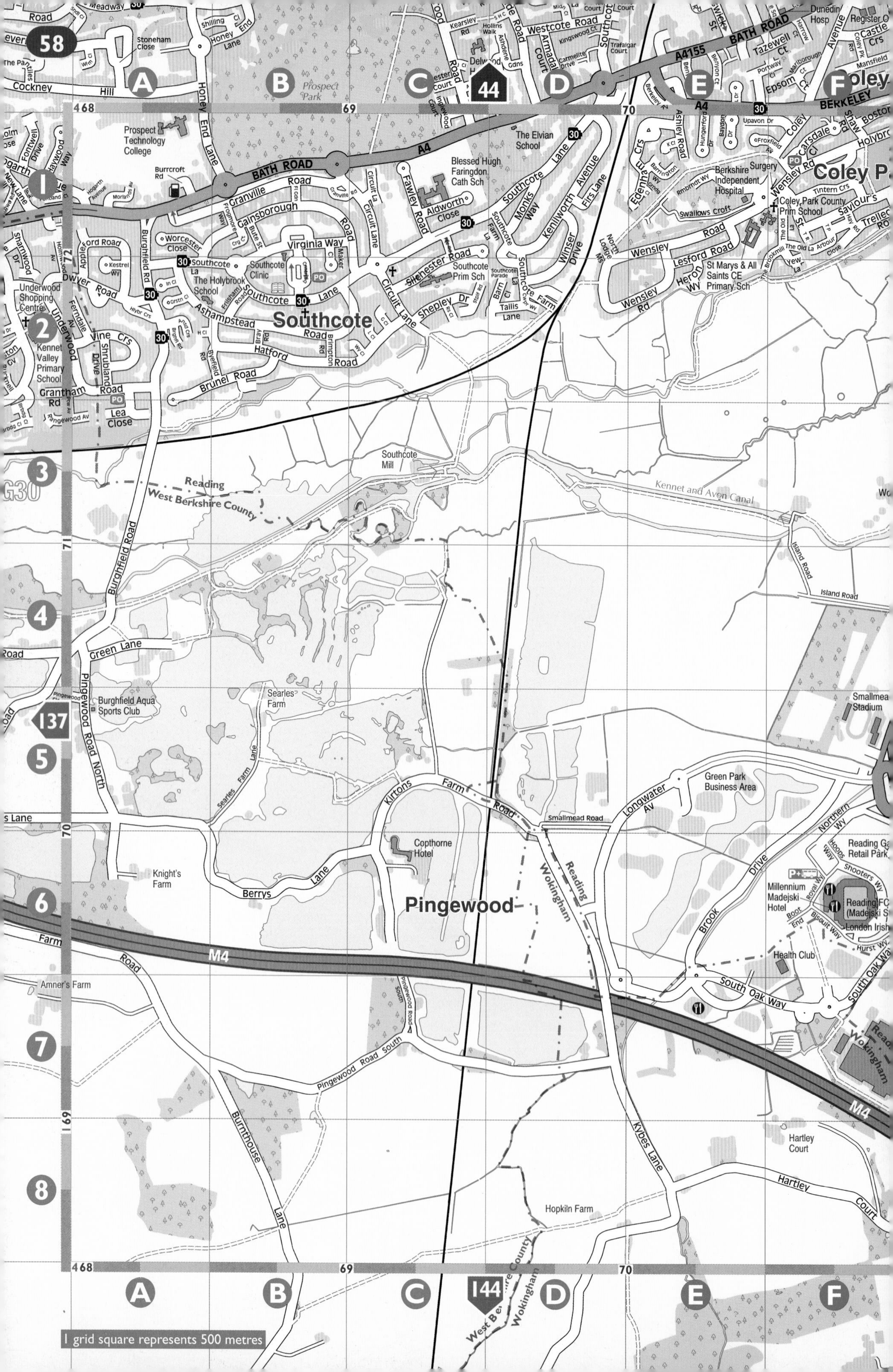

58
44
137
144
A
B
C
D
E
F
1
2
3
4
5
6
7
8
468
69
70
71
72
Cockney Hill
Stoneham Close
Honey End Lane
Prospect Park
Prospect Technology College
Burrcroft Rd
BATH ROAD
A4
A4155
Westcote Road
Armadale Court
Southcote Lane
The Elvian School
Blessed Hugh Faringdon Cath Sch
Fawley Road
Aldworth Close
Circuit Lane
Granville Road
Gainsborough Road
Virginia Way
Worcester Close
Southcote Clinic
The Holybrook School
Southcote Lane
Southcote Road
Silchester Road
Southcote Prim Sch
Southcote
Ashampstead Road
Hatford Road
Brunel Road
Brimpton Road
Shepley Dr
Tallis Lane
Monks Way
Kenilworth Avenue
Firs Lane
Winser Drive
Southcote Farm La
Burghfield Rd
Dwyer Road
Appleford Road
Kestrel Wy
Underwood Shopping Centre
Underwood Road
Ferndale Av
Vine Crs
Shrubland Drive
Kennet Valley Primary School
Grantham Rd
Lea Close
Berkshire Independent Hospital
Swallows Croft
Surgery
Coley Park County Prim School
Wensley Road
Wensley Rd
Lesford Road
Heron Wy
St Marys & All Saints CE Primary Sch
North Lodge Ms
Ashley Road
Tazewell Ct
Epsom Ct
Coley
Coley Park
BERKELEY
Southcote Mill
Reading
West Berkshire County
Kennet and Avon Canal
Island Road
Burghfield Road
Green Lane
Pingewood Road North
Burghfield Aqua Sports Club
Searles Farm
Searles Farm Lane
Kirtons Farm Road
Smallmead Road
Copthorne Hotel
Knight's Farm
Berrys Lane
Pingewood
Reading Wokingham
Longwater Av
Green Park Business Area
Smallmead Stadium
Brook Drive
Northern Wy
Reading Gate Retail Park
Millennium Madejski Hotel
Health Club
South Oak Way
M4
Amner's Farm
Farm Road
Pingewood Road South
Burnthouse Lane
Kybes Lane
Hartley Court
Hopkiln Farm
West Berkshire County
Wokingham
1 grid square represents 500 metres

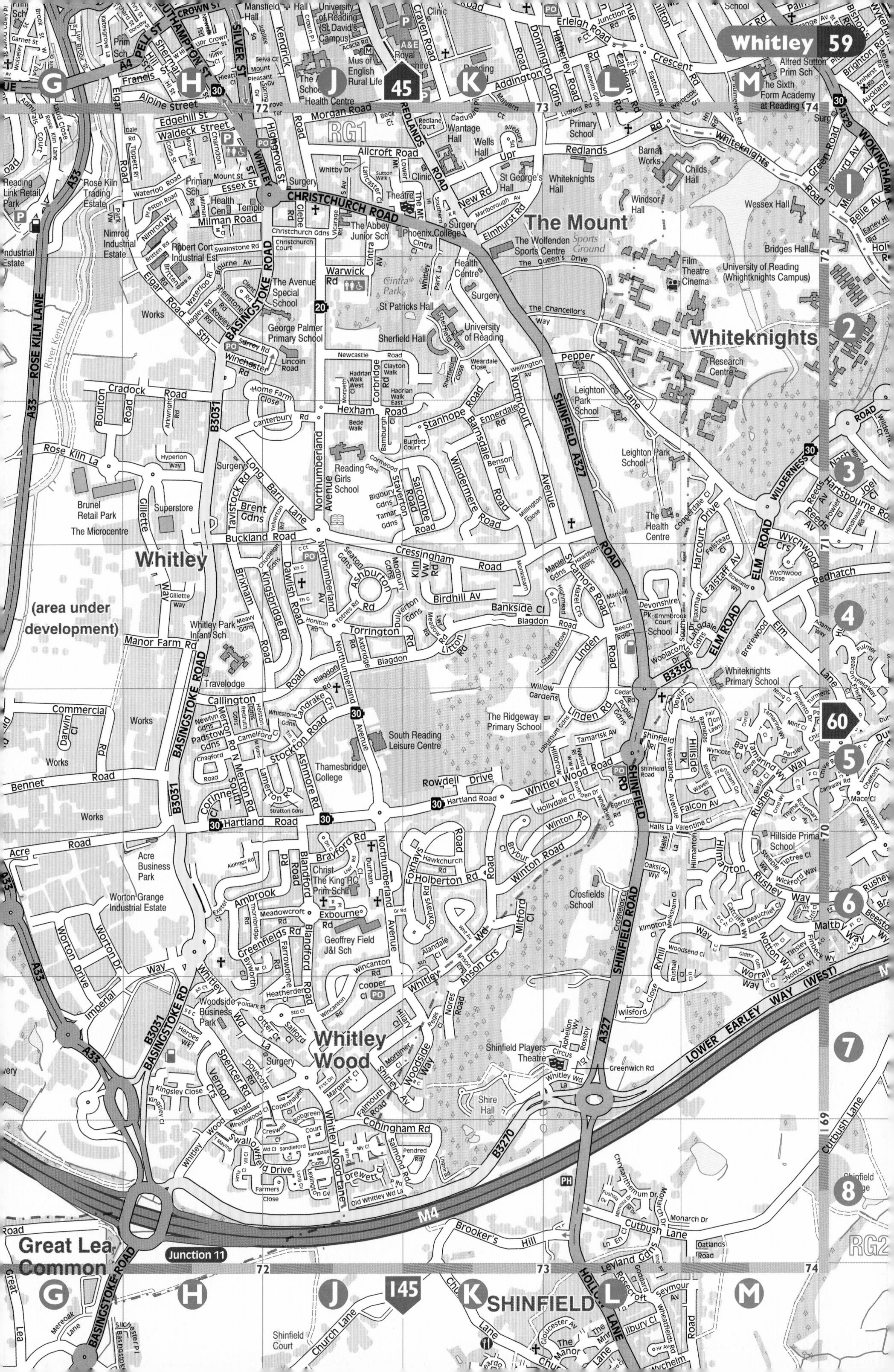

Whitley 59
45
60
145
RG1
RG2
G
H
J
K
L
M
1
2
3
4
5
6
7
8
72
73
74
Junction 11
Whitley
Whitley Wood
The Mount
Whiteknights
Great Lea Common
SHINFIELD
(area under development)
CHRISTCHURCH ROAD
BASINGSTOKE ROAD
SHINFIELD ROAD
LOWER EARLEY WAY (WEST)
ROSE KILN LANE
Northumberland Avenue
Hartland Road
Whitley Wood Road
Cressingham Road
Buckland Road
Long Barn Lane
Bennet Road
Acre Road
Manor Farm Rd
Commercial Rd
Imperial Way
Wortton Drive
Cradock Road
Rose Kiln La
Brunel Retail Park
The Microcentre
Superstore
Works
Travelodge
Acre Business Park
Worton Grange Industrial Estate
Woodside Business Park
Reading Link Retail Park
Rose Kiln Trading Estate
Nimrod Industrial Estate
Robert Cort Industrial Est
Reading Girls School
The Avenue Special School
George Palmer Primary School
Whitley Park Infant Sch
South Reading Leisure Centre
Thamesbridge College
The Ridgeway Primary School
Christ The King RC Prim Sch
Geoffrey Field J&I Sch
Crosfields School
Shinfield Players Theatre
Shire Hall
Whiteknights Primary School
Hillside Primary School
Leighton Park School
University of Reading
University of Reading (Whiteknights Campus)
Film Theatre Cinema
Research Centre
The Wolfenden Sports Centre
Sports Ground
Wessex Hall
Bridges Hall
Childs Hall
Windsor Hall
St Patricks Hall
Sherfield Hall
Whiteknights Hall
St George's Hall
Wells Hall
Wantage Hall
Phoenix College
The Abbey Junior Sch
Royal Berkshire Hospital
Mus of English Rural Life
Alfred Sutton Prim Sch
The Sixth Form Academy at Reading
Primary School
Health Centre
Surgery
Elm Road
Wilderness Road
Redhatch
Rushey Way
Cutbush Lane
Brooker's Hill
Church Lane
Hollow Lane
Whitley Wood Lane
Swallowfield Drive
Redlands Road
Morgan Road
Alpine Street
Southampton St
Silver St
Crown St
Pell St
Wokingham Road

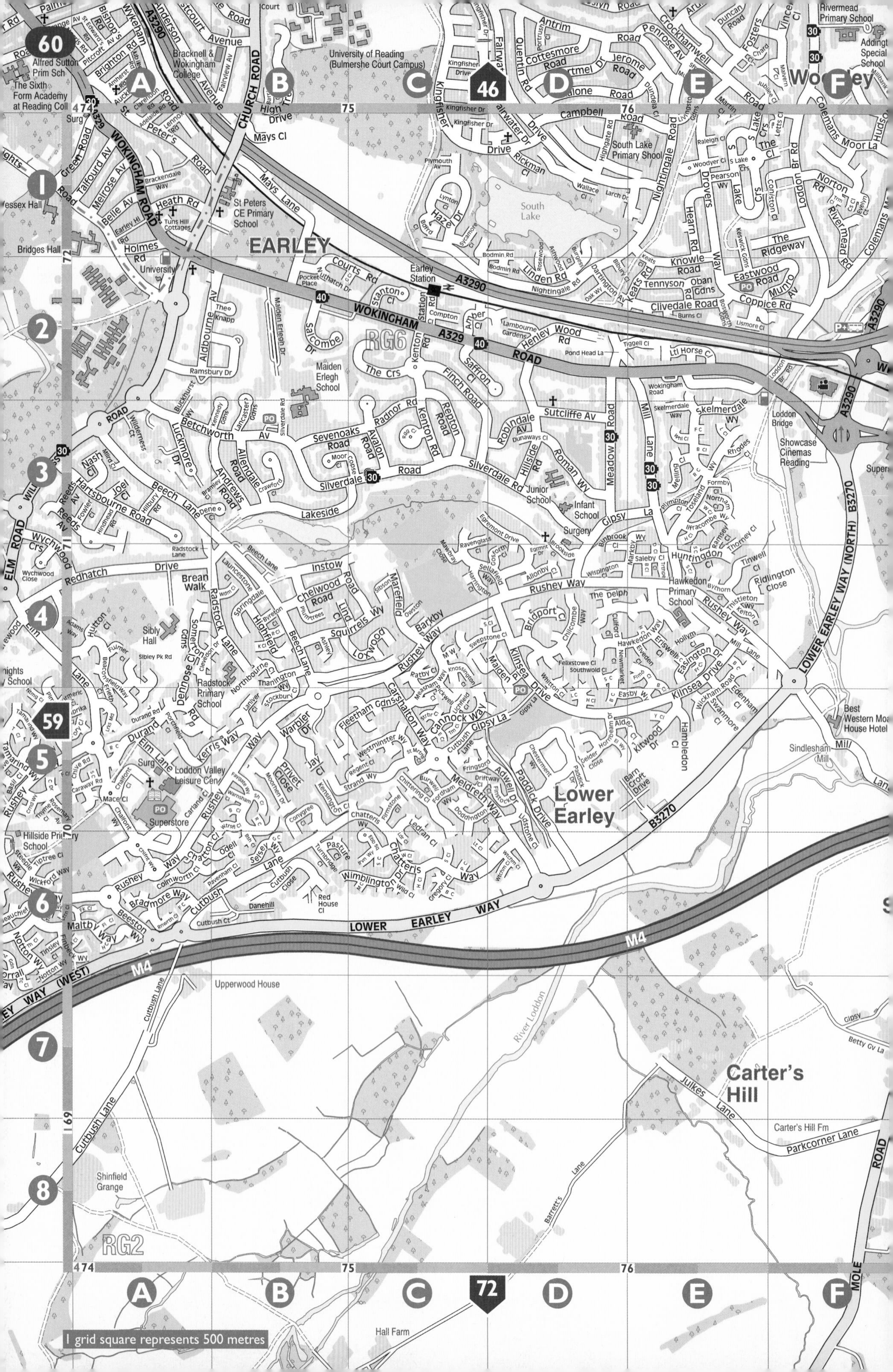

60
46
59
72
A
B
C
D
E
F
1
2
3
4
5
6
7
8
474
75
76
72
71
70
69
EARLEY
RG6
RG2
Lower Earley
Carter's Hill
Woodley
University of Reading (Bulmershe Court Campus)
Bracknell & Wokingham College
Alfred Sutton Prim Sch
The Sixth Form Academy at Reading Coll
Wessex Hall
Bridges Hall
University
St Peters CE Primary School
Earley Station
South Lake
South Lake Primary Shool
Maiden Erlegh School
Junior School
Infant School
Surgery
Hawkedon Primary School
Radstock Primary School
Sibly Hall
Loddon Valley Leisure Cen
Superstore
Hillside Priory School
Loddon Bridge
Showcase Cinemas Reading
Best Western Moat House Hotel
Sindlesham Mill
Rivermead Primary School
Addington Special School
Upperwood House
Shinfield Grange
Carter's Hill Fm
Hall Farm
Red House Cl
River Loddon
WOKINGHAM ROAD
WOKINGHAM A329 ROAD
CHURCH ROAD
LOWER EARLEY WAY
LOWER EARLEY WAY (NORTH) B3270
M4
A3290
A329
B3270
Cutbush Lane
Julkes Lane
Parkcorner Lane
Barrett's Lane
Rushey Way
Silverdale Road
Beech Lane
Redhatch Drive
Kilnsea Drive
Gipsy La
Meadow Road
Mill Lane
Nightingale Road
Drovers Way
Elm Road
Wilderness Road
Mays Lane
1 grid square represents 500 metres

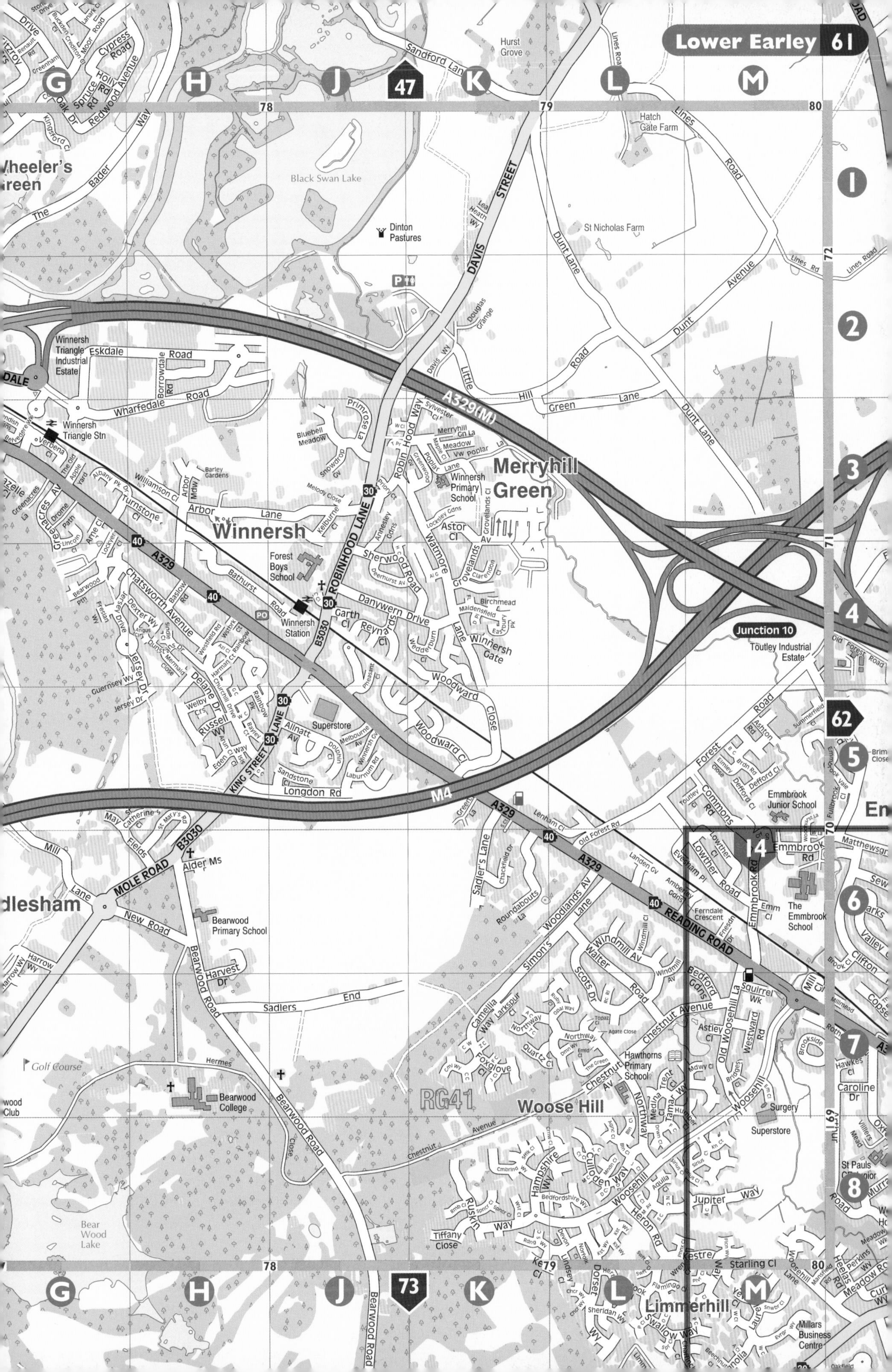
Black Swan Lake
Dinton Pastures
Winnersh
Merryhill Green
Winnersh Triangle Industrial Estate
Winnersh Triangle Stn
Winnersh Station
Forest Boys School
Winnersh Primary School
Superstore
Junction 10
Toutley Industrial Estate
Emmbrook Junior School
The Emmbrook School
Bearwood Primary School
Bearwood College
Hawthorns Primary School
Woose Hill
Limmerhill
Millars Business Centre
Surgery
Hatch Gate Farm
St Nicholas Farm
Hurst Grove
Bear Wood Lake
Golf Course
A329(M)
M4
A329
B3030
READING ROAD
ROBINHOOD LANE
KING STREET LANE
MOLE ROAD
DAVIS STREET
Bearwood Road
Dunt Avenue
Dunt Lane
Lines Road
RG41

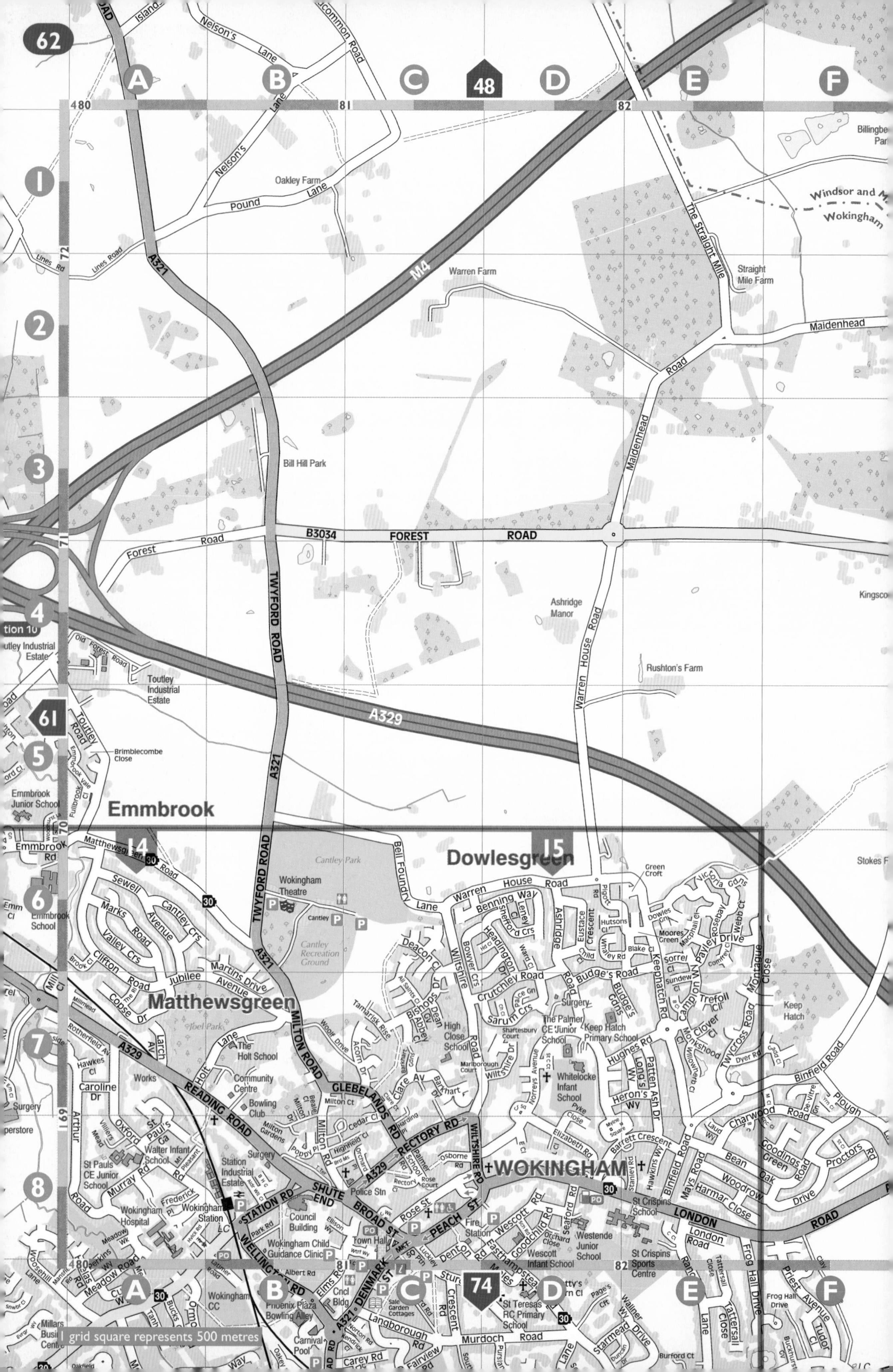

48
Oakley Farm
Nelson's Lane
Pound Lane
Lines Road
A321
M4
Warren Farm
Windsor and Maidenhead
Wokingham
The Straight Mile
Straight Mile Farm
Maidenhead Road
Bill Hill Park
B3034 FOREST ROAD
Forest Road
TWYFORD ROAD
Ashridge Manor
Rushton's Farm
Warren House Road
A329
Toutley Industrial Estate
Bell Foundry Lane
Emmbrook
Dowlesgreen
14
15
Cantley Park
Wokingham Theatre
Cantley Recreation Ground
Matthewsgreen
MILTON ROAD
The Holt School
Community Centre
READING ROAD
WOKINGHAM
Wokingham Station
Council Building
Town Hall
Police Stn
Fire Station
Westende Junior School
St Crispins School
St Crispins Sports Centre
LONDON ROAD
Keep Hatch
Keep Hatch Primary School
Whitelocke Infant School
The Palmer CE Junior School
High Close School
74
St Teresas RC Primary School
Wokingham Hospital
St Pauls CE Junior School
Walter Infant School
Emmbrook Junior School
Emmbrook School
61
Stokes Farm
Kingscote
1 grid square represents 500 metres

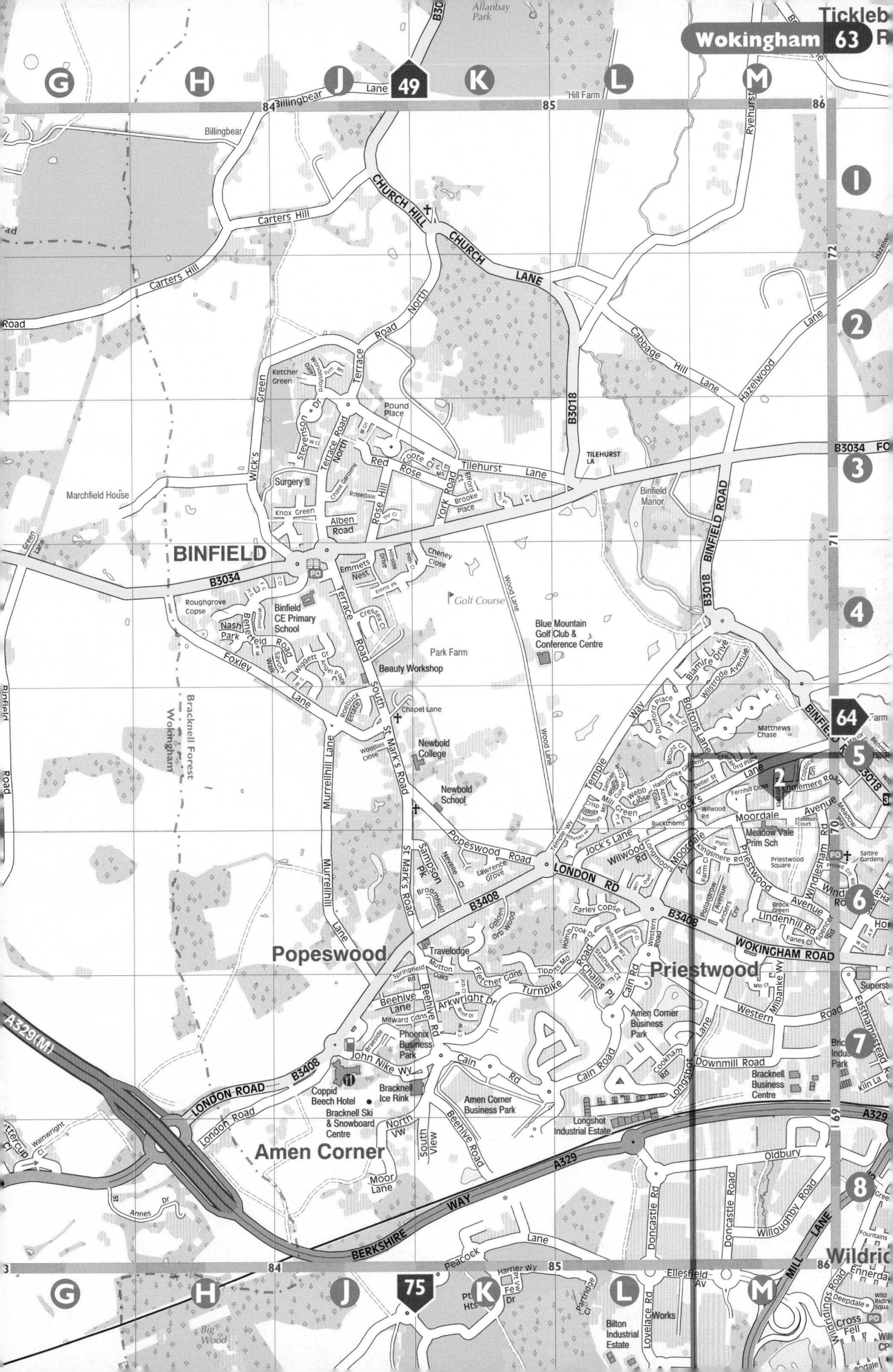

Allanbay Park
Billingbear Lane
Billingbear
Hill Farm
Ryehurst
Carters Hill
Church Hill
Church Lane
Cabbage Hill Lane
Hazelwood Lane
Terrace Road North
Ketcher Green
Stevenson Dr
Wick's Green
Pound Place
Red Rose
Tilehurst Lane
Tilehurst La
York Road
Brooke Place
Rose Hill
Rosedale
Chase Gardens
Surgery
Knox Green
Alben Road
Marchfield House
BINFIELD
B3034
B3018
Binfield Road
Binfield Manor
Emmets Nest
Hillside Drive
Cheney Close
Green Lane
Roughgrove Copse
Binfield CE Primary School
Nash Park
Benetfeld Road
Savory Walk
Wiggett Gr
Angel Place
Foxley Lane
Terrace Road South
Golf Course
Wood Lane
Blue Mountain Golf Club & Conference Centre
Park Farm
Beauty Workshop
Roebuck Estate
Chapel Lane
St Mark's Road
Newbold College
Newbold School
Woodlies Close
Murrellhill Lane
Bracknell Forest
Wokingham
Temple Way
Blamire Drive
Wilstrode Avenue
Dunford Place
Boltons Lane
Matthews Chase
Blount Cres
Jock's Lane
Englemere Road
Fernhill Close
Moordale Avenue
Meadow Vale Prim Sch
Priestwood Square
Eastbury Court
Saltire Gardens
Windlesham Road
Meadow Way
Webb Close
Mill Green
Crisp Gdns
Lammas Ct
Buckthorns
Wilwood Rd
Longmoors
Kingsmere Rd
Popeswood Road
Lawrence Grove
Sampson Pk
Nevelle Cl
Broomfield
London Rd
B3408
Farley Copse
Priestwood Avenue
Lindenhill Rd
Brook Green
Fanes Cl
Spencer Rd
Wokingham Road
Golden Orb Wood
Popeswood
Travelodge
Springfield Rd
Mutton Oaks
Fletcher Gdns
Tippits Md
Turnpike
Challis Pl
Statham Ct
Western Road
Cain Rd
Priestwood
Milbanke Wy
Beehive Lane
Beehive Rd
Arkwright Dr
Milward Gdns
Phoenix Business Park
Amen Corner Business Park
Cain Road
Cookham Rd
Longshot Lane
Downmill Road
Bracknell Business Centre
Easthampstead Road
Kiln La
John Nike Wy
Coppid Beech Hotel
Bracknell Ice Rink
Bracknell Ski & Snowboard Centre
North Vw
South View
Beehive Road
Longshot Industrial Estate
A329(M)
London Road
Wainwright
Amen Corner
Moor Lane
St Annes Dr
A329
Berkshire Way
Oldbury
Doncastle Rd
Doncastle Road
Willoughby Road
Mill Lane
Peacock Lane
Harrier Wy
Partridge Cl
Ellesfield Av
Lovelace Rd
Works
Bilton Industrial Estate
Big Wood
Wildridings Road
Deepdale
Cross Fell
Ennerdale
Fountains
49
64
75
84
85
86

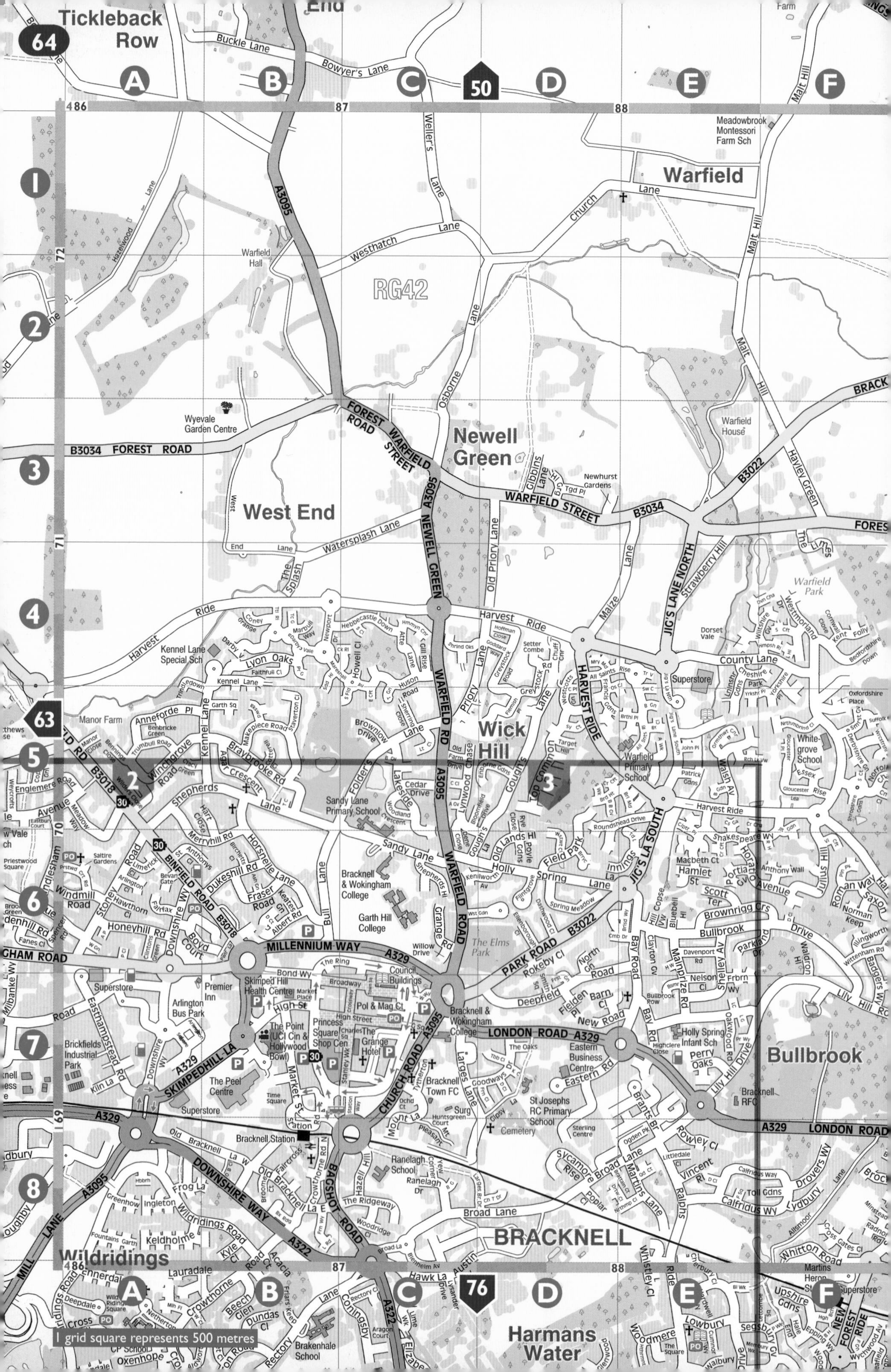
64
Tickleback Row
50
Warfield
RG42
Newell Green
West End
Wick Hill
63
76
BRACKNELL
Bullbrook
Wildridings
Harmans Water
B3034 FOREST ROAD
WARFIELD STREET
A3095
NEWELL GREEN
WARFIELD RD
WARFIELD ROAD
MILLENNIUM WAY
LONDON ROAD A329
CHURCH ROAD
BAGSHOT ROAD
DOWNSHIRE WAY
SKIMPEDHILL LA
BINFIELD ROAD B3018
PARK ROAD B3022
JIG'S LANE NORTH
JIG'S LA SOUTH
HARVEST RIDE
Harvest Ride
Bracknell Station
Bracknell & Wokingham College
Garth Hill College
Sandy Lane Primary School
Warfield Primary School
Whitegrove School
1 grid square represents 500 metres

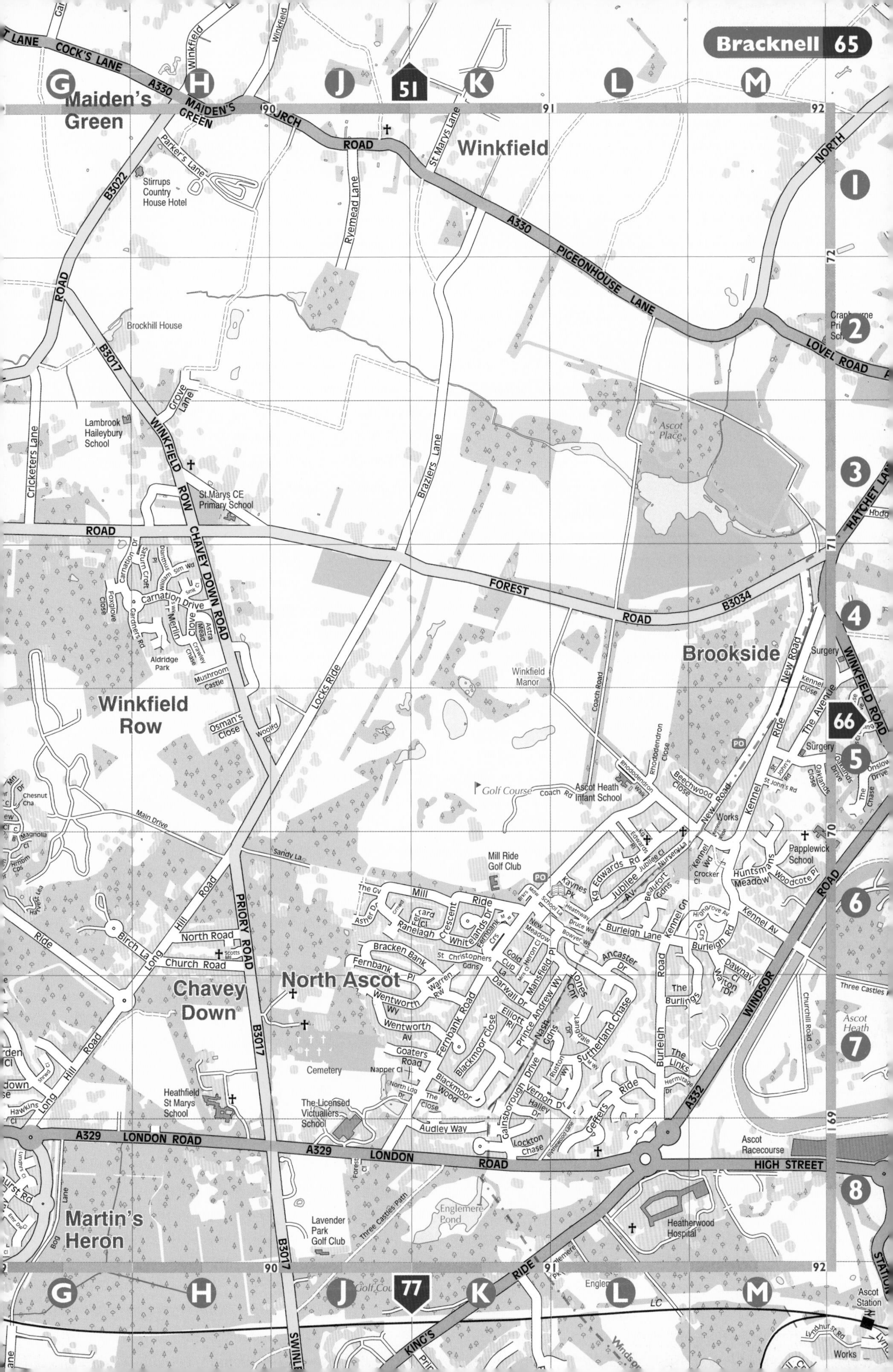
Maiden's Green
Winkfield
Winkfield Row
Brookside
North Ascot
Chavey Down
Martin's Heron
Cock's Lane
Maiden's Green
A330
Church Road
Pigeonhouse Lane
Lovel Road
North Road
B3022
B3017
B3034
A329
A332
Stirrups Country House Hotel
Brockhill House
Lambrook Haileybury School
St.Marys CE Primary School
Forest Road
Chavey Down Road
Winkfield Row
Brazlers Lane
Locks Ride
Ryemead Lane
St Marys Lane
Parker's Lane
Grove Lane
Cricketers Lane
Ascot Place
Winkfield Manor
Coach Road
Golf Course
Ascot Heath Infant School
Mill Ride Golf Club
Main Drive
Sandy La
Priory Road
Long Hill Road
North Road
Church Road
Birch La
Cemetery
Heathfield St Marys School
The Licensed Victuallers School
London Road
High Street
Windsor Road
Winkfield Road
New Road
Kennel Ride
The Avenue
Surgery
Works
Papplewick School
Huntsmans Meadow
Woodcote Pl
Kennel Av
Burleigh Lane
Burleigh Road
Ascot Racecourse
Ascot Heath
Heatherwood Hospital
Englemere Pond
Lavender Park Golf Club
Three Castles Path
King's Ride
Swinley
Ascot Station
Rhododendron Close
Beechwood Close
Mill Ride
Wentworth Wy
Wentworth Av
Fernbank Road
Blackmoor Close
Blackmoor Wood
Prince Andrew Wy
Gainsborough Drive
Sutherland Chase
Audley Way
Lockton Chase
Carnation Drive
Mushroom Castle
Osman's Close
Aldridge Park
Cranbourne Primary School
Hatchet Lane
51
66
77
90
91
92
69
70
71
72

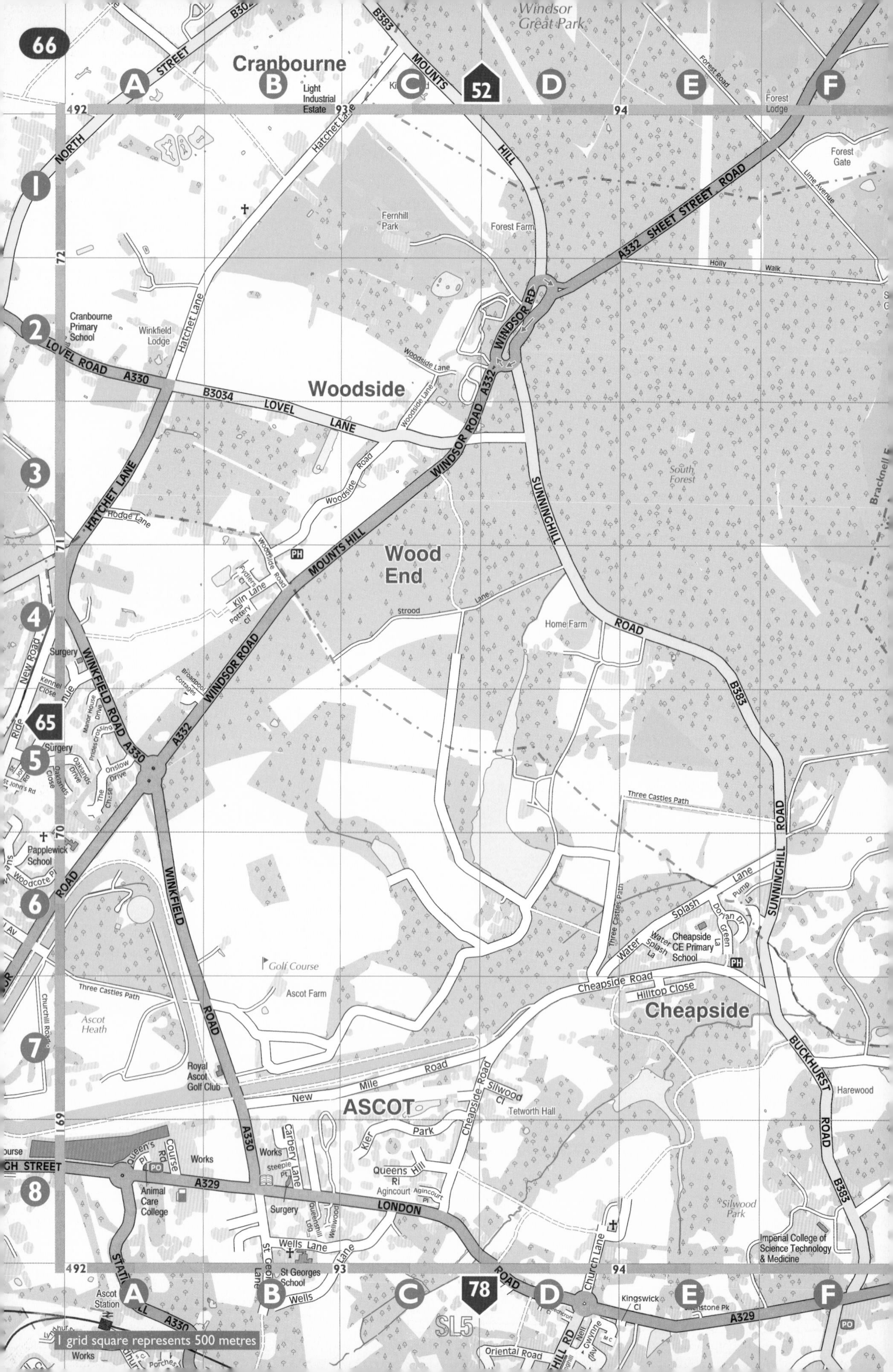
Windsor Great Park
Cranbourne
Light Industrial Estate
52
Forest Lodge
Forest Gate
Fernhill Park
Forest Farm
A332 SHEET STREET ROAD
Holly Walk
Cranbourne Primary School
Winkfield Lodge
LOVEL ROAD A330
B3034 LOVEL LANE
Woodside
WINDSOR ROAD
MOUNTS HILL
South Forest
HATCHET LANE
Hodge Lane
Wood End
SUNNINGHILL ROAD
Strood Lane
Home Farm
WINKFIELD ROAD A330
65
Three Castles Path
Papplewick School
Golf Course
Ascot Farm
Ascot Heath
Cheapside CE Primary School
Cheapside Road
Hilltop Close
Cheapside
BUCKHURST ROAD B383
Royal Ascot Golf Club
New Mile Road
ASCOT
Tetworth Hall
Harewood
Works
Animal Care College
A329 LONDON ROAD
Surgery
Silwood Park
Imperial College of Science Technology & Medicine
Wells Lane
St Georges School
Ascot Station
78
Kingswick Cl
Oriental Road
SL5
1 grid square represents 500 metres

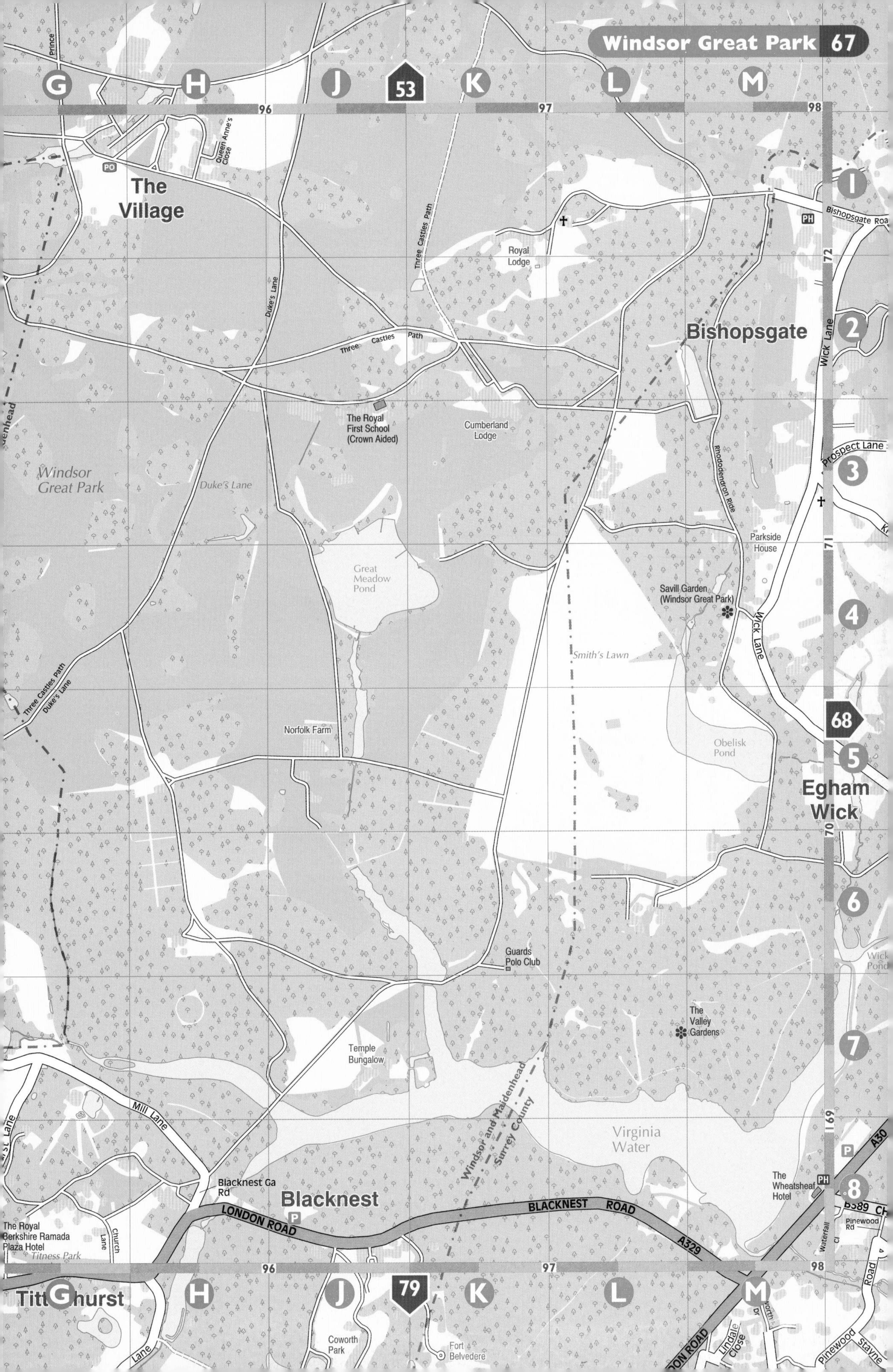

G H J 53 K L M

96 97 98

I
Bishopsgate Roa
PH
Wick Lane 72
Bishopsgate 2
Prospect Lane
3
Parkside House 71
Savill Garden (Windsor Great Park) 4
Wick Lane
68
5
Egham Wick
70
6
Wick Pond
7

PO

The Village

Queen Anne's Close
Duke's Lane

Three Castles Path

Royal Lodge

The Royal First School (Crown Aided)

Cumberland Lodge

Windsor Great Park

Duke's Lane

Great Meadow Pond

Rhododendron Ride

Smith's Lawn

Three Castles Path
Duke's Lane

Norfolk Farm

Obelisk Pond

Guards Polo Club

The Valley Gardens

Temple Bungalow

Mill Lane

Windsor and Maidenhead
Surrey County

Virginia Water

169 A30

P

Blacknest Ga Rd

Blacknest
P

LONDON ROAD

BLACKNEST ROAD

A329

The Wheatsheaf Hotel
PH
8
B389 CH
Pinewood Rd
Waterfall

The Royal Berkshire Ramada Plaza Hotel
Titness Park

Church Lane

G Titthurst H J 79 K L M

Coworth Park

Fort Belvedere

Lane

96 97 98

Lindale Close
Pinewood Road
Stayne

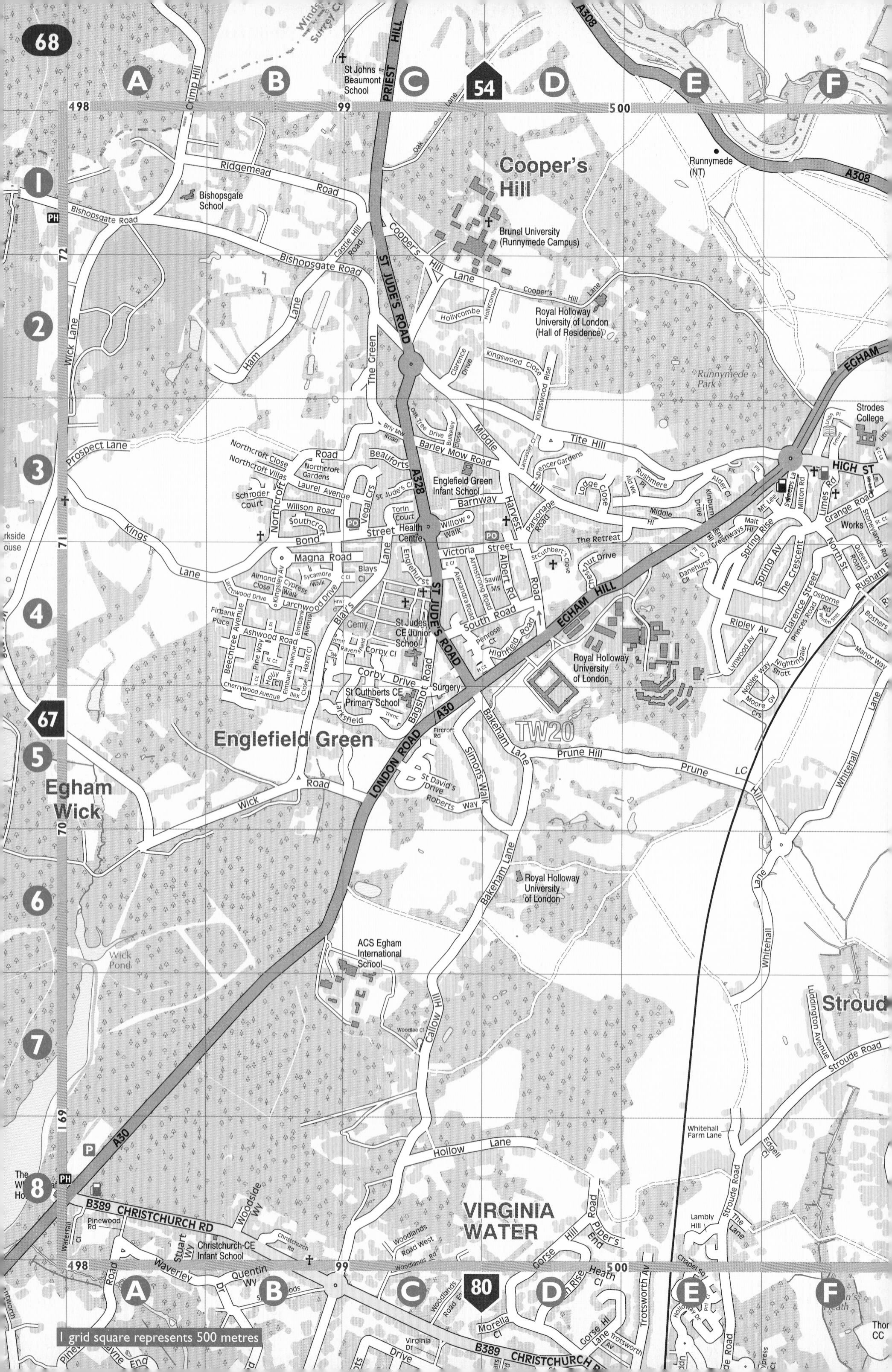
54
80
67
Cooper's Hill
Englefield Green
Egham Wick
VIRGINIA WATER
Stroud
Runnymede (NT)
Runnymede Park
Brunel University (Runnymede Campus)
Royal Holloway University of London (Hall of Residence)
Royal Holloway University of London
Bishopsgate School
St Johns Beaumont School
Englefield Green Infant School
St Judes CE Junior School
St Cuthberts CE Primary School
ACS Egham International School
Christchurch CE Infant School
Strodes College
TW20
Wick Pond
Ridgemead Road
Bishopsgate Road
Wick Lane
Prospect Lane
Kings Lane
Wick Road
Ham Lane
Crimp Hill
Castle Hill Road
PRIEST HILL
ST JUDE'S ROAD
Cooper's Hill Lane
The Green
Middle Hill
Tite Hill
Barley Mow Road
Northcroft Road
Bond Street
Magna Road
Victoria Street
Harvest Road
Parsonage Road
Albert Rd
South Road
Highfield Road
Bagshot Road
Corby Drive
LONDON ROAD
EGHAM HILL
HIGH ST
Bakeham Lane
Prune Hill
Simons Walk
Callow Hill
Hollow Lane
Whitehall Lane
Stroude Road
Luddington Avenue
B389 CHRISTCHURCH RD
Woodside Wy
Gorse Hill Road
Trotsworth Av
A30
A308
A328
1 grid square represents 500 metres

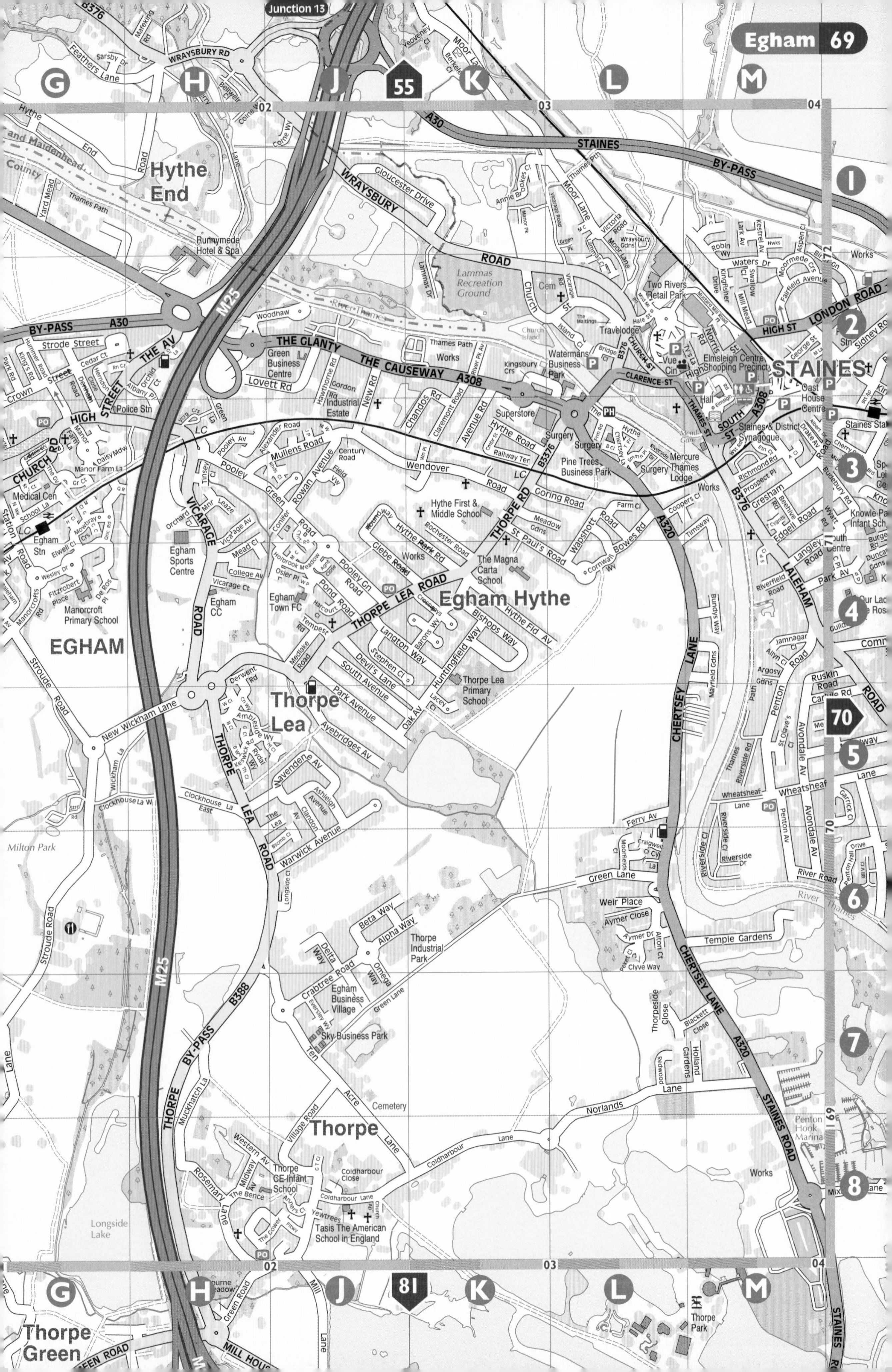
Junction 13
55
70
81
G
H
J
K
L
M
I
2
3
4
5
6
7
8
02
03
04
72
71
70
69
B376
Feathers Lane
Sarsby Dr
Mareking Rd
WRAYSBURY RD
Bellweir
Coine Way
Yeoveney Cl
Berkeley Ct
Moor La
Hythe End
Hythe End
Road
Lane
Thames Path
Yard Mead
County
Runnymede Hotel & Spa
A30
STAINES BY-PASS
WRAYSBURY ROAD
Gloucester Drive
Annie Brookes Cl
Thames Pth
Moor Lane
Vicarage Road
Manor Pk
Green Pk
Victoria Road
Wraysbury Gdns
Lammas Cl
Moor Lane
Lammas Dr
Lammas Recreation Ground
Church
Cem
Vicarage Rd
St
Island Cl
The Maltings
River Thames
Church Island
M25
BY-PASS
A30
Woodhaw
Strode Street
Hummer Road
King's Rd
Cedar Ct
Park Rd
Crown
Street
Road
Denham
Herndon Close
Rn Cr
THE AV
Orchid
Albany Pl
HIGH STREET
Police Stn
Green Business Centre
THE GLANTY
Lovett Rd
THE CAUSEWAY
A308
Hawthorne Rd
Gordon
Industrial Estate
New Rd
Thames Path
Works
Chandos Rd
Claremont Road
River Pk Av
Avenue Rd
Kingsbury Crs
Watermans Business Park
Bridge
B376
CHURCH ST
CLARENCE ST
Superstore
Travelodge
Hale St
Two Rivers Retail Park
Vue Cin
Tyrs La
High
Norris
St
Rd
Kingfisher Drive
Mill Mead
Robin Wy
Lark Av
Kestrel Av
Hwks
Waters Dr
Swallow
Aspen Cl
Moormede Crs
Fairfield Avenue
Birch Gn
Works
HIGH ST
LONDON ROAD
Elmsleigh Centre Shopping Precinct
STAINES
George St
Stn
Sidney Rd
Oast House Centre
Hall
THAMES ST
SOUTH ST
A308
PH
Staines & District Synagogue
Drake Av
Albert Rd
Staines Stn
Cherry
Vicarage Rd
Pooley Av
Alexander Road
Mullens Road
Rowan Avenue
Century Road
Field Vw
Wendover Road
Hythe Road
Railway Ter
B3376
Surgery
Surgery
Pine Trees Business Park
Hythe
Chertsey La
Riverside
Mercure Thames Lodge
Surgery
Meml Gdns
Richmond Rd
Prospect Pl
Gresham Rd
Beehive Rd
Edgell Road
Budebury Rd
Knowle Pa Infant Sch
Works
B376
LC
CHURCH RD
Manor Farm La
Daisy Mdw
Manor Farm
Medical Cen
School La
Station Rd
Egham Stn
Elwell Cl
Mowbray Crs
Wesley Dr
Fitzrobert Place
De Ros Pl
Manorcroft Primary School
Manorcrofts Rd
EGHAM
Pooley
Tinsey Cl
VICARAGE ROAD
Orchard Cl
Mnr Leaze
Vicarage Av
Egham Sports Centre
Mead Cl
College Av
Vicarage Ct
Egham CC
Green
Conifer Cl
Road
Holbrook Meadow
Osler Pl
Pooley Gn Road
Pond Road
Egham Town FC
Harcourt
Tempest Rd
Medlake Road
Hythe First & Middle School
Round Way
Hythe Park Rd
Rochester Road
Glebe Road
Works
THORPE RD
St Paul's Road
Meadow Gdns
Goring Road
Farm Cl
Wapshott Road
Bowes Rd
Cornwall Wy
Coopers Cl
Timsway
A320
The Magna Carta School
THORPE LEA ROAD
Egham Hythe
Hythe Fld Av
Bishops Way
Huntingfield Way
Barons Wy
Langton Way
Stephen Cl
Devil's Lane
South Avenue
Park Avenue
Oak Av
Lacey Cl
Thorpe Lea Primary School
Thorpe Lea
Ayebridges Av
Derwent Rd
Ambleside Wy
Keswick Rd
Rydal Wy
New Wickham Lane
Stroude Road
Wickham La
Clockhouse La W
Clockhouse La East
THORPE LEA ROAD
Wavendene Av
Ashleigh Avenue
Clandon Av
The Lea
Warwick Avenue
Longside Cl
Milton Park
Stroude Road
Lane
M25
Beta Way
Alpha Way
Delta Way
Omega Way
Thorpe Industrial Park
Crabtree Road
Egham Business Village
Eversley Wy
Green Lane
Sky Business Park
B388
THORPE BY-PASS
Muckhatch La
Ten Acre Lane
Cemetery
Village Road
Thorpe
Western Av
Rosemary Lane
Midway Av
The Bence
Thorpe CE Infant School
Coldharbour Close
Coldharbour Lane
Yewtrees
Church
Tasis The American School in England
The Gower
Longside Lake
Norlands Lane
Coldharbour Lane
Ferry Av
Moorfields
Craigwell Cl
Green Lane
Weir Place
Aymer Close
Aymer Dr
Alton Ct
Clyve Way
Temple Gardens
CHERTSEY LANE
A320
Thorpeside Close
Blackett Close
Holland Gardens
Redwood
Lane
STAINES ROAD
Works
Penton Hook Marina
Mixnams Lane
CHERTSEY LANE
Bundys Way
Mayfield Gdns
Thames
Riverside Rd
Path
Riverfield Road
Langley Road
LALEHAM ROAD
Jamnagar Cl
Allyn Cl
Argosy Gdns
Penton Road
Ruskin Road
Carlyle Rd
St Olave's Cl
Avondale Av
Wheatsheaf Lane
Riverside Cl
Riverside Dr
Penton Av
Avondale Av
Garrick Cl
Penton Hall Drive
River Road
River Thames
Thorpe Green
GREEN ROAD
Green Road
MILL HOUSE
Mill
Lane
Thorpe Park
STAINES

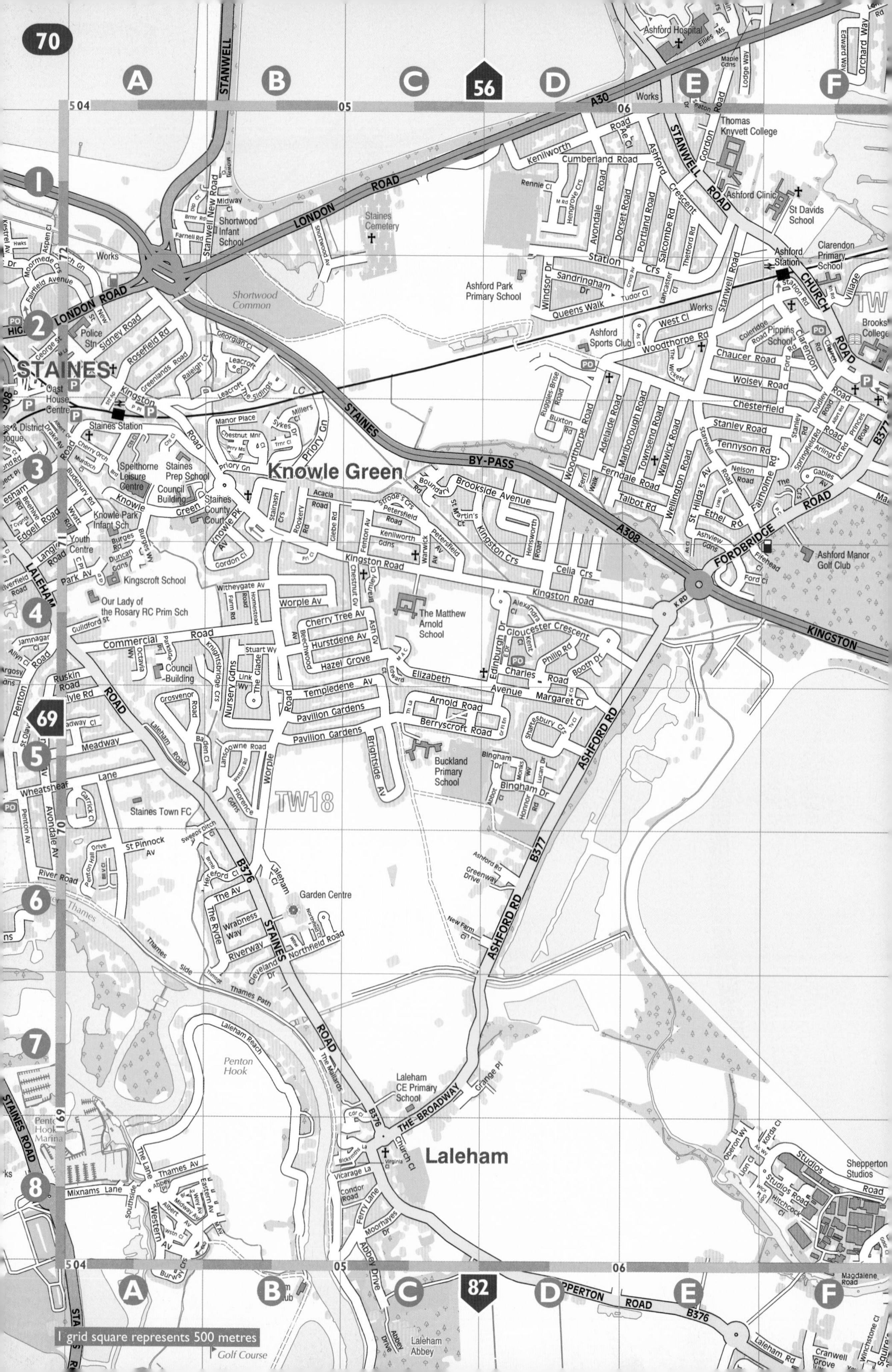

A
B
C
56
D
E
F
504
05
06
1
2
3
4
5
6
7
8
STANWELL
Stanwell New Road
Midway Cl
Shortwood Infant School
Farnell Rd
LONDON ROAD
A30
Staines Cemetery
Shortwood Av
Shortwood Common
Works
Ashford Hospital
Ellies Ms
Maple Gdns
Lodge Way
Edward Way
Orchard Way
Kenilworth
Cumberland Road
Ae Cl
Rennie Cl
Hengrove Crs
Avondale Road
Dorset Road
Portland Road
Salcombe Rd
Thetford Rd
Ashford Crescent
STANWELL ROAD
Gordon Road
Seaton
Thomas Knyvett College
Ashford Clinic
St Davids School
Ashford Station
Clarendon Primary School
CHURCH ROAD
Village
Brooks College
Station Crs
Sandringham Dr
Windsor Dr
Queens Walk
Tudor Cl
Lancaster Cl
Ashford Park Primary School
Stanwell Road
Station Rd
Works
West Cl
Woodthorpe Rd
Ashford Sports Club
PO
Coleridge Road
Pippins School
Clarendon Rd
Ford Rd
Chaucer Road
Wolsey Road
Chesterfield
Dudley Road
Stanley Road
Tennyson Rd
Springfield Road
Arlington Rd
Princes Rd
B377
Nelson Road
Fairholme Rd
Gables Av
Ethel Rd
Ashview Gdns
FORDBRIDGE ROAD
Fifehead Cl
Ford Cl
Ashford Manor Golf Club
KINGSTON
Ruggles-Brise Road
Buxton Rd
Woodthorpe Road
Adelaide Road
Marlborough Road
Townsend Road
Warwick Road
Wellington Road
Stanwell
St Hilda's Av
Fern Walk
Ferndale Road
Talbot Rd
Celia Crs
Kingston Road
A308
STAINES BY-PASS
Brookside Avenue
Boundary Rd
St Martin's Ct
Kingston Crs
Hensworth Road
Knowle Green
Priory Gn
Priory Gn
Millers Ct
Sykes Dr
Manor Place
Chestnut Mnr
Leacroft
Leacroft Cl
The Sidings
Raleigh Ct
Georgian Cl
Greenlands Road
Rosefield Rd
Sidney Road
Kingston Road
Staines Station
LC
STAINES
Oast House Centre
Police Stn
LONDON ROAD
New
George St
HIGH
Moormede Crs
Fairfield Avenue
Aspen Cl
Kestrel Av
Hwks
Works
A308
Staines Prep School
Council Building
Spelthorne Leisure Centre
Staines County Court
Knowle Green
Knowle Pk Av
Gordon Cl
Knowle Park Infant Sch
Youth Centre
Burges Wy
Duncan Gdns
Kingscroft School
Our Lady of the Rosary RC Prim Sch
Park Av
Cherry Orch
Murdoch
Budebury Rd
Wyatt Rd
Edgell Road
Beehive
Langley Road
LALEHAM
Staines & District Synagogue
Stainash Crs
Acacia Road
Rookery Rd
Glebe Rd
Fenton Av
Strode's Crs
Petersfield Road
Kenilworth Gdns
Warwick
Petersfield Av
Kingston Road
Chestnut Gv
Witheygate Av
Farm Rd
Homestead
Worple Av
Cherry Tree Av
Hurstdene Av
Hazel Grove
Beechwood Av
Ash Gv
The Matthew Arnold School
Alexandra Cl
Edinburgh Dr
Gloucester Crescent
Kent
Philip Rd
Booth Dr
Charles Road
Elizabeth Avenue
Margaret Cl
Guildford St
Commercial Road
Octavia Wy
Parkside Pl
Council Building
Knightsbridge Crs
Stuart Wy
Link Wy
The Glade
Nursery Gdns
Templedene Av
Pavilion Gardens
Pavilion Gardens
Worple Road
Arnold Road
Berryscroft Road
Shaftesbury Crs
ASHFORD RD
Jamnagar Cl
Allyn Cl
Argosy
Ruskin Road
Penton Road
69
Meadway
Grosvenor Road
Laleham Road
Baden Cl
Lansdowne Road
Florence Gdns
TW18
Brightside Av
Buckland Primary School
Bingham Dr
Bingham Dr
Monks
Lucan Dr
Abbot Cl
Honnor Rd
Wheatsheaf Lane
Garrick Cl
Avondale Av
Penton Av
Staines Town FC
St Pinnock Av
Penton Hall Drive
River Road
Sweeps Ditch
Hereford Cl
B376
The Av
The Ryde
Wrabness Way
Riverway
STAINES ROAD
Laleham Cl
Garden Centre
Northfield Road
Cleveland Dr
Ashford Rd
Greenway Drive
New Farm Cl
ASHFORD RD
B377
Thames
Thames Side
Thames Path
Laleham Reach
Penton Hook
The Mallards
Laleham CE Primary School
THE BROADWAY
Grange Pl
Laleham
Church Cl
Vicarage La
Condor Road
Ferry Lane
Moorhayes Dr
Abbey Drive
Penton Hook Marina
STAINES ROAD
Thames Av
The Lane
Mixnams Lane
Southside
Western Av
Eastern Av
Albert Av
Midway Av
Burway Crs
Oberon Wy
Korda Cl
Lion Cl
Studios
Shepperton Studios
Studios Road
Hitchcock Cl
Road
Magdalene Road
82
SHEPPERTON ROAD
B376
Laleham Abbey
Abbey Drive
Laleham Rd
Cranwell Grove
Winchstone Cl
Squires
Golf Course
1 grid square represents 500 metres

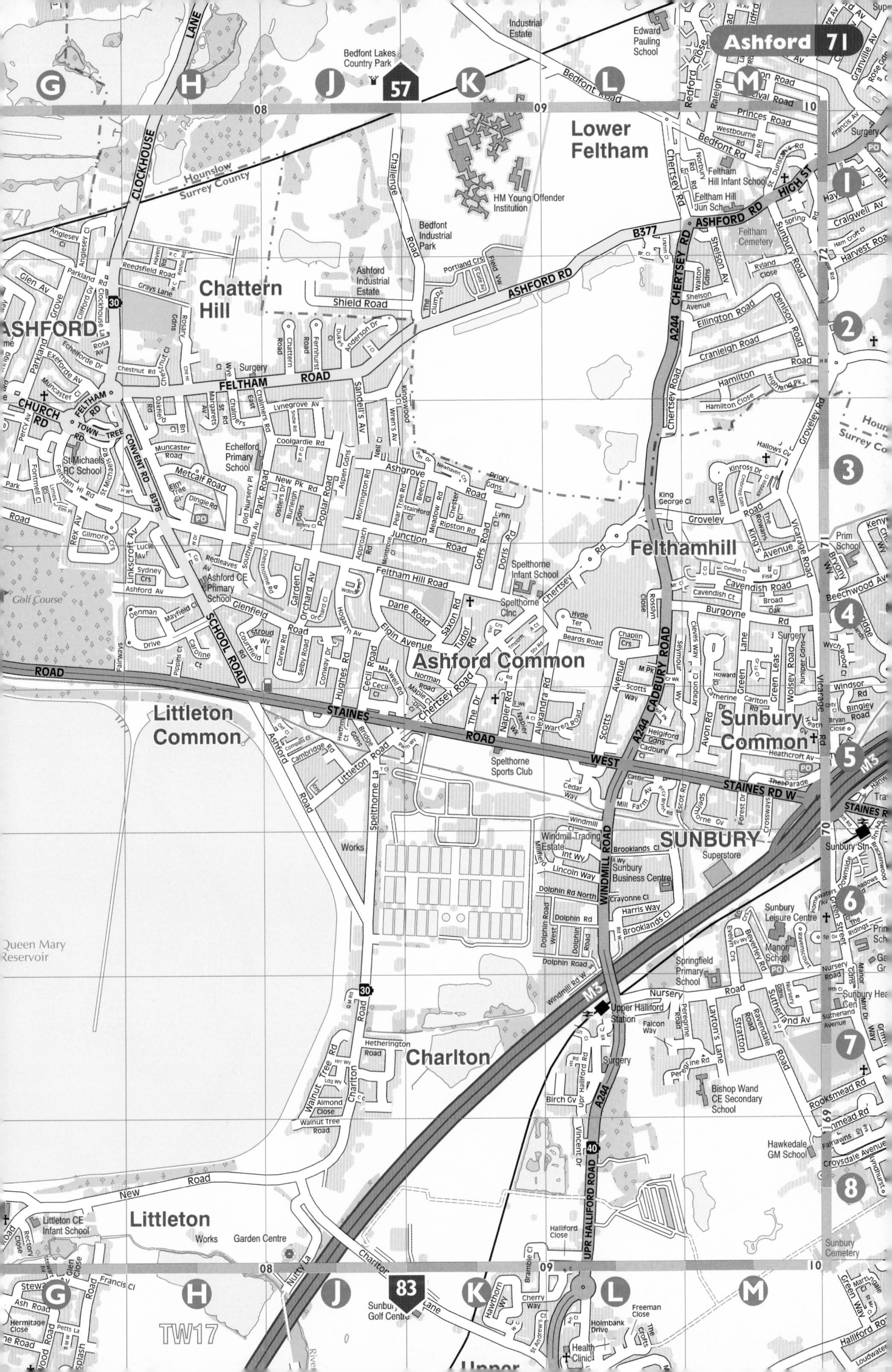
Lower Feltham
Chattern Hill
ASHFORD
Felthamhill
Ashford Common
Littleton Common
Sunbury Common
SUNBURY
Charlton
Littleton
Queen Mary Reservoir
Bedfont Lakes Country Park
Industrial Estate
Edward Pauling School
HM Young Offender Institution
Bedfont Industrial Park
Ashford Industrial Estate
Feltham Hill Infant School
Feltham Hill Jun Sch
Feltham Cemetery
Echelford Primary School
St Michael's RC School
Ashford CE Primary School
Spelthorne Infant School
Spelthorne Sports Club
Windmill Trading Estate
Sunbury Business Centre
Superstore
Sunbury Leisure Centre
Manor School
Springfield Primary School
Upper Halliford Station
Bishop Wand CE Secondary School
Hawkedale GM School
Sunbury Cemetery
Littleton CE Infant School
Garden Centre
Works
Sunbury Golf Centre
Sunbury Stn
Golf Course
Hounslow
Surrey County
CLOCKHOUSE LANE
FELTHAM ROAD
ASHFORD RD
CHERTSEY RD
STAINES ROAD
STAINES ROAD WEST
STAINES RD W
SCHOOL ROAD
CONVENT RD
WINDMILL ROAD
CADBURY ROAD
UPR HALLIFORD ROAD
HIGH ST
Feltham Hill Road
Elgin Avenue
Glenfield Road
Vicarage Road
Groveley Road
New Road
Charlton Lane
M3
A244
B377
B378
TW17
57
83
08
09
10
G
H
J
K
L
M
1
2
3
4
5
6
7
8

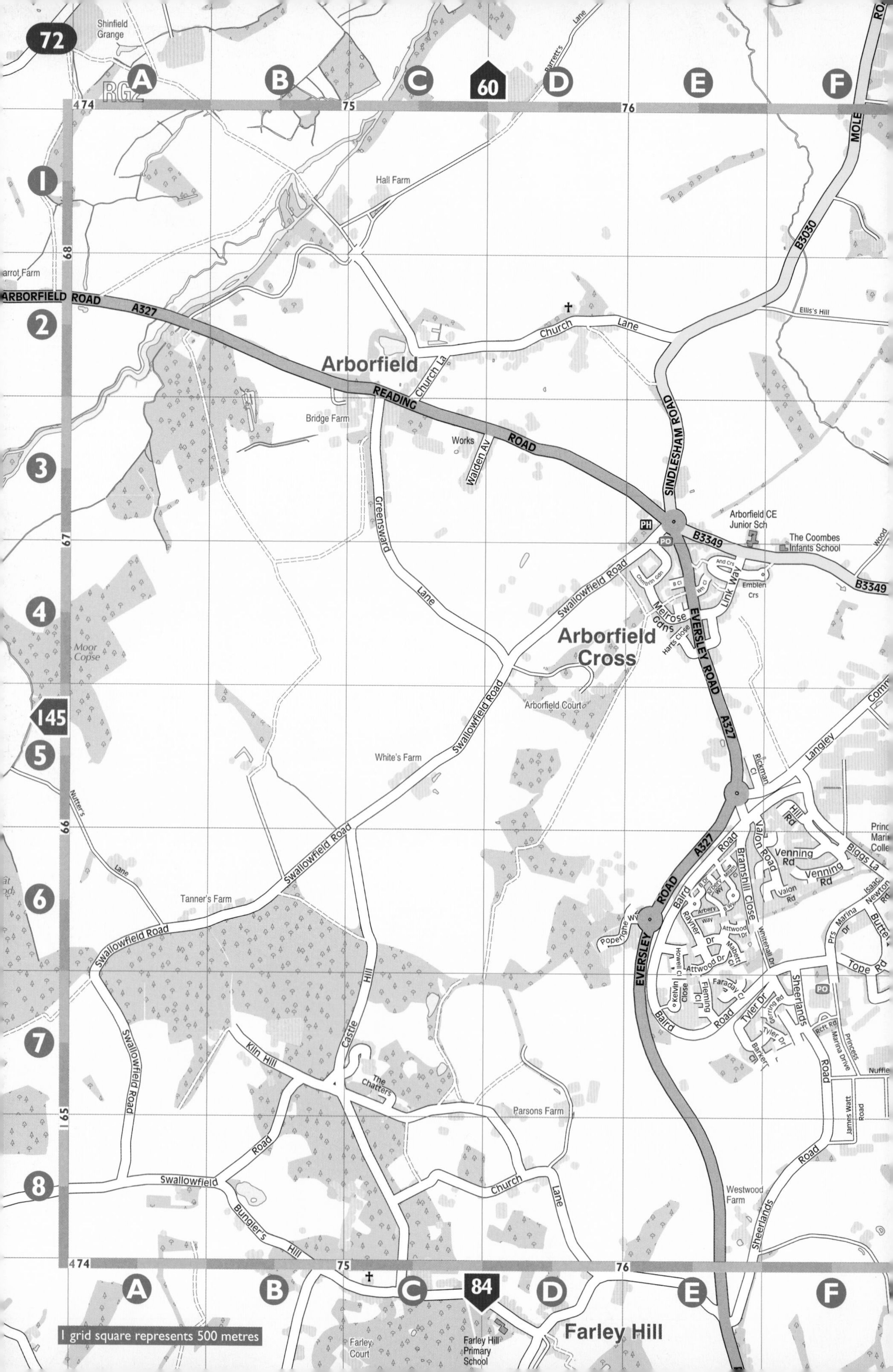

72
Shinfield Grange
A
B
C
60
D
E
F
Barrett's Lane
474
75
76
Hall Farm
1
2
3
4
5
6
7
8
68
67
66
65
Parrot Farm
ARBORFIELD ROAD
A327
Church Lane
Arborfield
Church La
READING ROAD
Bridge Farm
Works
Walden Av
Greensward Lane
SINDLESHAM ROAD
B3030
MOLE
Ellis's Hill
Arborfield CE Junior Sch
The Coombes Infants School
B3349
PH
PO
Swallowfield Road
Link Way
Emblen Crs
Melrose Gdns
Harts Close
EVERSLEY ROAD
Arborfield Cross
Arborfield Court
Moor Copse
145
Nutter's Lane
White's Farm
A327
Rickman Cl
Langley
Hill Rd
Valon Road
Venning Rd
Biggs La
Bramshill Close
Baird Road
Rayner Dr
Arbery Way
Attwood Dr
Mabett Cl
Whitehall Dr
Popeyne Wy
Howell Cl
Kelvin Close
Fleming Cl
Faraday Cl
Tyler Dr
Sheerlands Road
Tope Rd
Marina Dr
Newton
Isaac
Princess Marina Drive
James Watt Road
Barker Cl
Tanner's Farm
Kiln Hill
Castle Hill
The Chatters
Parsons Farm
Church Lane
Swallowfield Road
Bungler's Hill
Westwood Farm
Sheerlands Road
84
Farley Hill
Farley Court
Farley Hill Primary School
1 grid square represents 500 metres

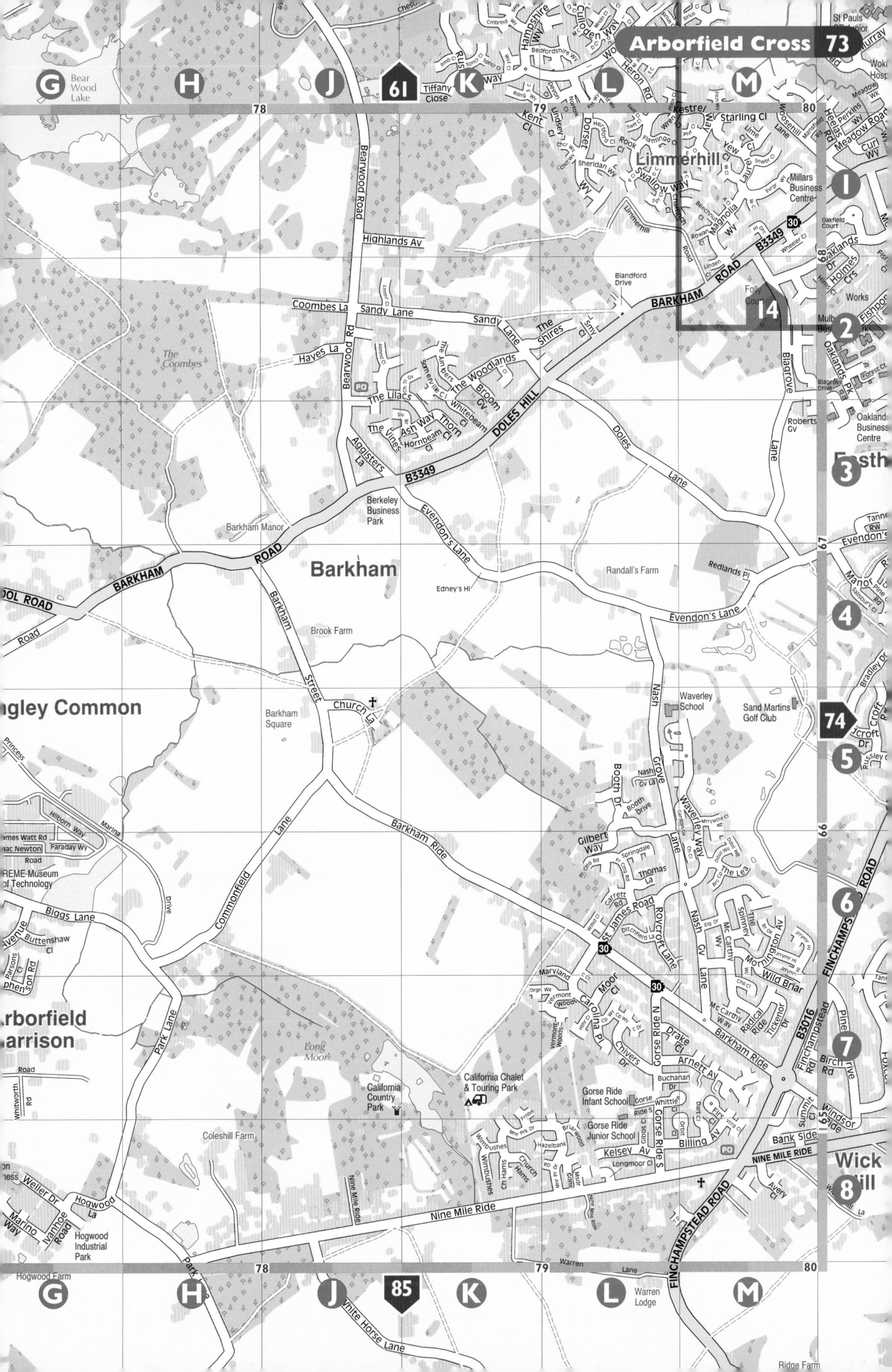

G — Bear Wood Lake
H
J
61 Tiffany Close
K
L
M

78
79
80

I

Limmerhill

Millars Business Centre

Oaklands Dr
Holmes Crs

Works

Blandford Drive

BARKHAM ROAD

Folly Cort

14

Mulberry

Blagrove Drive

Oakland Business Centre

2

Oaklands Pk

Easth

Coombes La
Sandy Lane

Sandy Lane

The Shires

Highlands Av

Bearwood Rd

PO

The Lilacs

The Woodlands
Broom Gr
Whitebeam Cl

DOLES HILL

Doles Lane

Blagrove Lane

Tanne
Evendon's

3

Manor
Salisbur

4

Hayes La

The Vines
Ash Way
Thorn
Hornbeam Cl

Aggister's La

B3349

Berkeley Business Park

Barkham Manor

Barkham

Brook Farm

Evendon's Lane

Edney's Hl

Randall's Farm

Redlands Pl

Evendon's Lane

Bradley Ct

Croft

74

Jcroft Dr

5

BARKHAM ROAD

ngley Common

Barkham Square

Church La

Barkham Street

Nash Grove Lane

Waverley School

Sand Martins Golf Club

Booth Dr
Booth Drive

67

 arborfield arrison

James Watt Rd
Isaac Newton
Faraday Wy

REME Museum of Technology

Hilborn Way
Marina

Biggs Lane
Buttenshaw Cl

ton Rd
stephen

Commonfield Lane

Park Lane

Long Moor

Barkham Ride

Gilbert Way

Springdale
Thomas La

Garrett Rd

St James Road

30

Maryland

Moor Cl

Vermont Woods

Carolina Pl
Chivers La

Waverley Way

Roycroft Lane

The Ley

Mornington Av

Wild Briar

McCarthy Way

Barkham Ride
Tickenor

FINCHAMPSTEAD ROAD

6

B3016

Finchampstead Rd

Pine
Birch Rd

7

99

Whitworth Rd

Coleshill Farm

California Country Park

California Chalet & Touring Park

Gorse Ride Infant School

Gorse Ride N
Drake Cl
Arnett Av

Buchanan Dr

Gorse Ride Junior School

Gorse Ride S

Kelsey Av
Longmoor La

Billing Av

PO

Bank side

NINE MILE RIDE

Windsor

Wick Hill

8

Weller Dr
Marino
Ivanhoe Wy

Hogwood La

Hogwood Industrial Park

Nine Mile Ride

Church Hams

Wimbushes

Nine Mile Ride

Warren

Warren Lodge

FINCHAMPSTEAD ROAD

Ridge Farm

Hogwood Farm

G
H
J
85
K
L
M

78
79
80

White Horse Lane

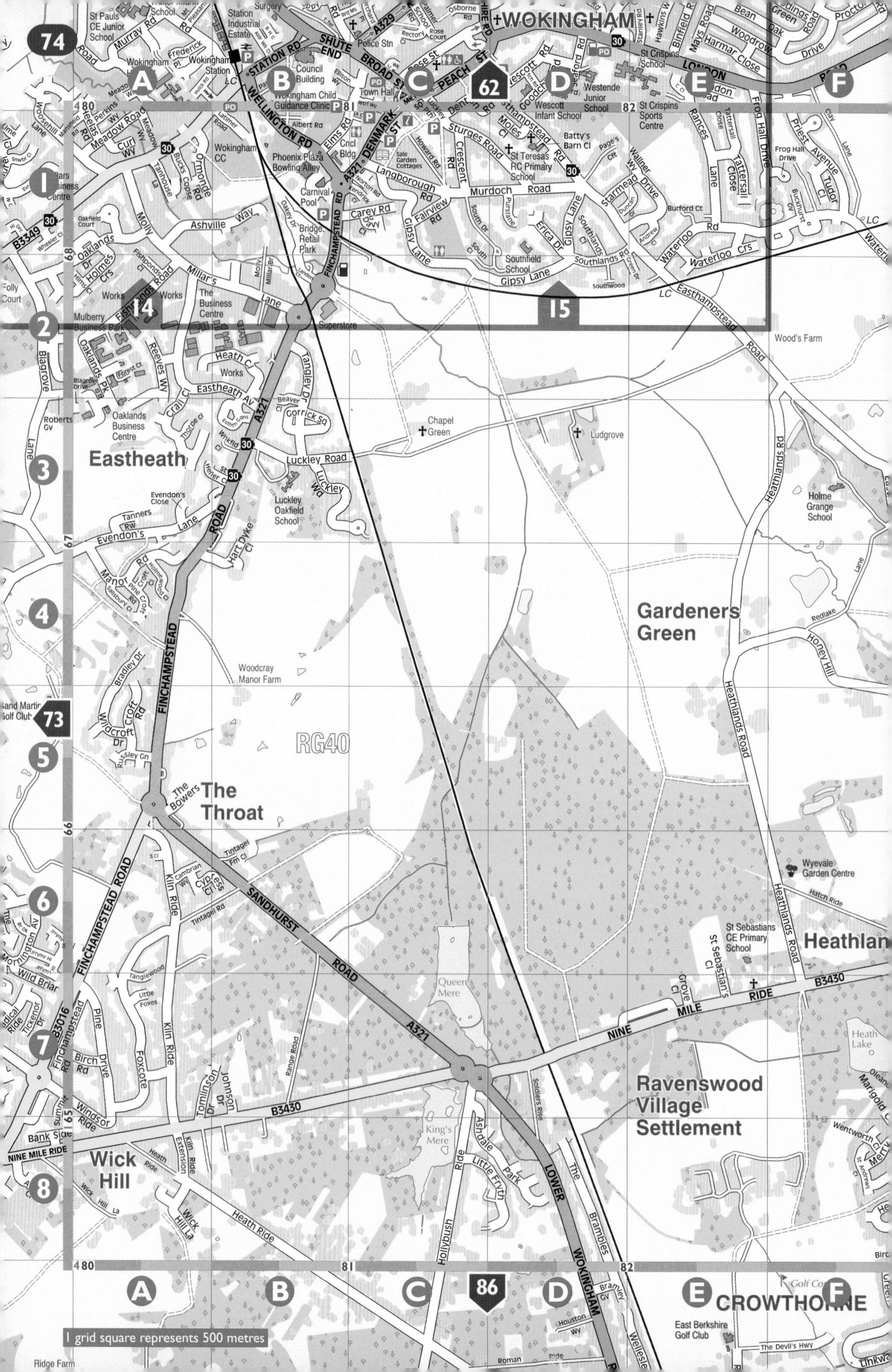

74
WOKINGHAM
62
15
14
73
86
A
B
C
D
E
F
1
2
3
4
5
6
7
8
480
81
82
68
67
66
165
St Pauls CE Junior School
Murray Rd
Frederick Pl
Wokingham Station
Station Industrial Estate
STATION RD
SHUTE END
Council Building
Wokingham Child Guidance Clinic
WELLINGTON RD
Police Stn
Town Hall
BROAD ST
Rose St
PEACH ST
Osborne Rd
A329
Wescott Rd
Goodchild Rd
Westende Junior School
Wescott Infant School
St Crispins School
St Crispins Sports Centre
LONDON ROAD
Woodrow Dr
Harmar Close
Mays Road
Binfield Rd
Bean Oak Rd
Frog Hall Drive
Priest Avenue
Tudor Cl
Clay Lane
Albert Rd
Elms Rd
Cncl Bldg
DENMARK ST
A321
Phoenix Plaza Bowling Alley
Sale Garden Cottages
Sturges Road
Denton Rd
Crescent Rd
Moles Cl
St Teresas RC Primary School
Easthampstead Rd
Batty's Barn Cl
Page's Cft
Walliner Wy
Starmead Drive
Rances Lane
Tattersall Close
Burford Ct
Waterloo Rd
Waterloo Crs
Langborough Rd
Murdoch Road
Carnival Pool
Norton Rd
Carey Rd
Davy Cl
Fairview Rd
Gipsy Lane
Southlands Rd
Southlands Cl
Erica Dr
Southfield School
South Dr
Bridge Retail Park
FINCHAMPSTEAD RD
Oakey Dr
Wokingham CC
Tanhouse La
Bucks Copse
Ormonde Rd
Ashville Way
Molly Millar's Lane
Meadow Road
Curl Wy
Perkins Wy
Woosehill Lane
B3349
Oakfield Court
Oaklands Dr
Holmes Crs
Fishponds Road
Works
The Business Centre
Mulberry Business Park
Superstore
Folly Court
Blagrove Lane
Oaklands Pk
Forest Ct
Reeves Wy
Heath Cl
Eastheath Av
Tangley Dr
Gorrick Sq
Beaver Cl
Oaklands Business Centre
Roberts Gv
Craig Cl
Thorpe Cl
Eastheath
Luckley Road
Luckley Path
Luckley Oakfield School
Chapel Green
Ludgrove
Wood's Farm
Easthampstead Road
Heathlands Rd
Holme Grange School
Evendon's Close
Tanners Rw
Evendon's Lane
ROAD
Hart Dyke Cl
Manor Rd
Pine Croft
Salisbury Cl
Gardeners Green
Redlake Lane
Honey Hill
Woodcray Manor Farm
Bradley Dr
Wildcroft Dr
Croft Rd
Russley Gn
RG40
FINCHAMPSTEAD
Heathlands Road
The Bowers
The Throat
Tintagel Fm Cl
Tintagel Rd
Cambrian Wy
Cypress Cl
Kiln Ride
SANDHURST ROAD
Wyevale Garden Centre
Hatch Ride
St Sebastians CE Primary School
St Sebastian's Cl
Grove Cl
Heathlan
B3430
NINE MILE RIDE
Queen's Mere
Tanglewood
Little Foxes
Pine Drive
Birch Rd
Foxcote
FINCHAMPSTEAD ROAD
Finchampstead Rd
B3016
Wild Briar
Mornington Av
Tickenor Dr
Range Road
Tomlinson Dr
Johnson Dr
Heath Lake
Ravenswood Village Settlement
Marigold
Wentworth Cl
St Andrews
Windsor Ride
Summit Cl
Bank Side
NINE MILE RIDE
Wick Hill
Heath Ride
Kiln Ride Extension
Wick Hill La
Wick Hill La
Heath Ride
King's Mere
Ashdale Park
Little Frith
Hollybush Ride
Soldiers Rise
LOWER WOKINGHAM
The Brambles
Bramley Gv
Houston Wy
Roman Ride
CROWTHORNE
East Berkshire Golf Club
The Devil's Hwy
Ridge Farm
1 grid square represents 500 metres

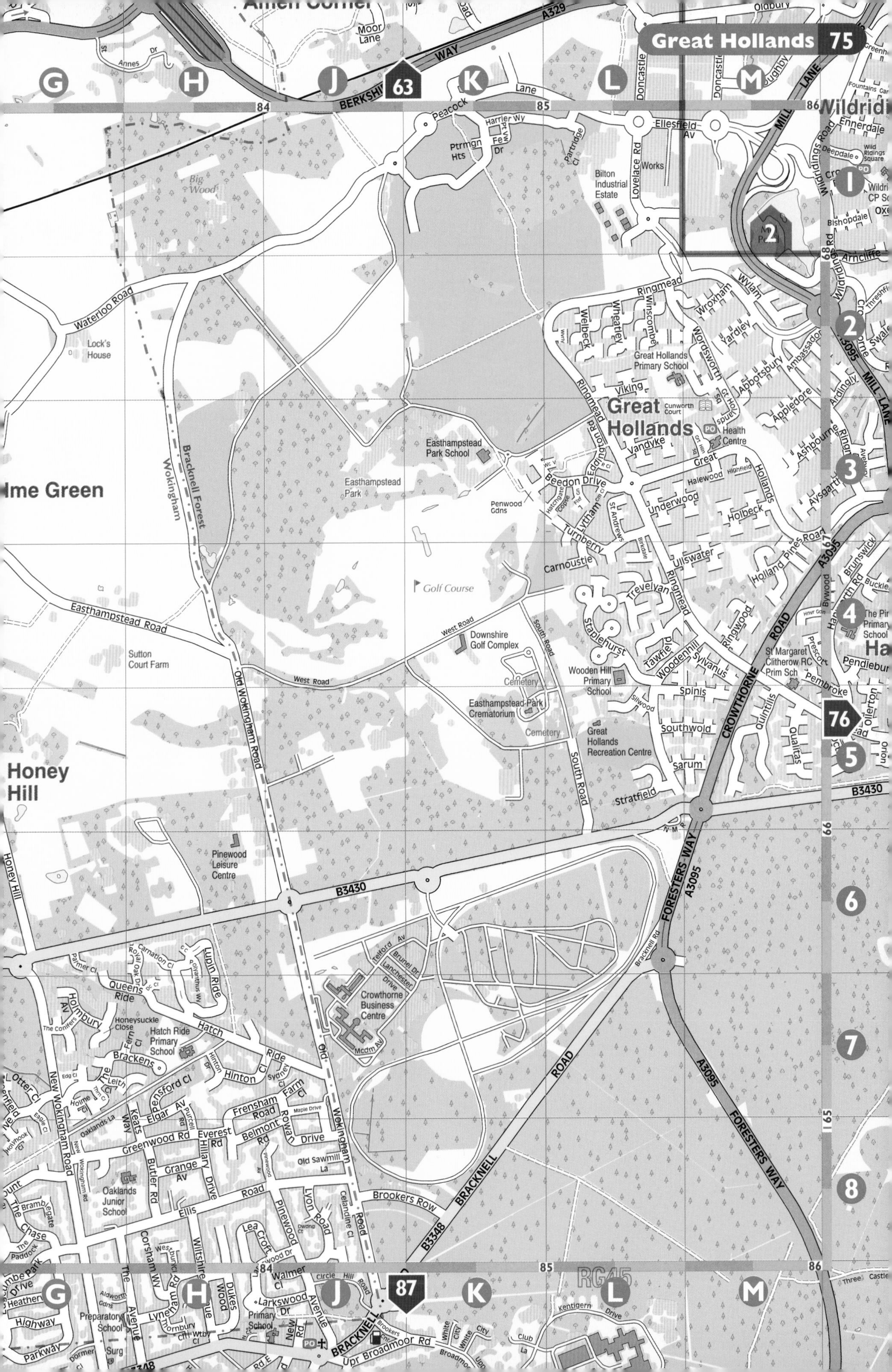
Great Hollands
Ime Green
Honey Hill
Big Wood
Lock's House
Waterloo Road
Easthampstead Road
Sutton Court Farm
Wokingham
Bracknell Forest
Old Wokingham Road
Easthampstead Park School
Easthampstead Park
Golf Course
West Road
Downshire Golf Complex
South Road
Cemetery
Easthampstead Park Crematorium
Great Hollands Recreation Centre
Wooden Hill Primary School
Great Hollands Primary School
Health Centre
Bilton Industrial Estate
Works
Ringmead
Ellesfield Av
Lovelace Rd
Peacock Lane
Berkshire Way
A329
B3430
A3095
Foresters Way
Crowthorne Road
Mill Lane
Holland Pines Road
St Margaret Clitherow RC Prim Sch
Pinewood Leisure Centre
Crowthorne Business Centre
Bracknell Road
B3348
Hatch Ride Primary School
Oaklands Junior School
Preparatory School
Brookers Row
New Wokingham Road
Upr Broadmoor Rd
RG45
Wildridings
63
87
76
84
85
86

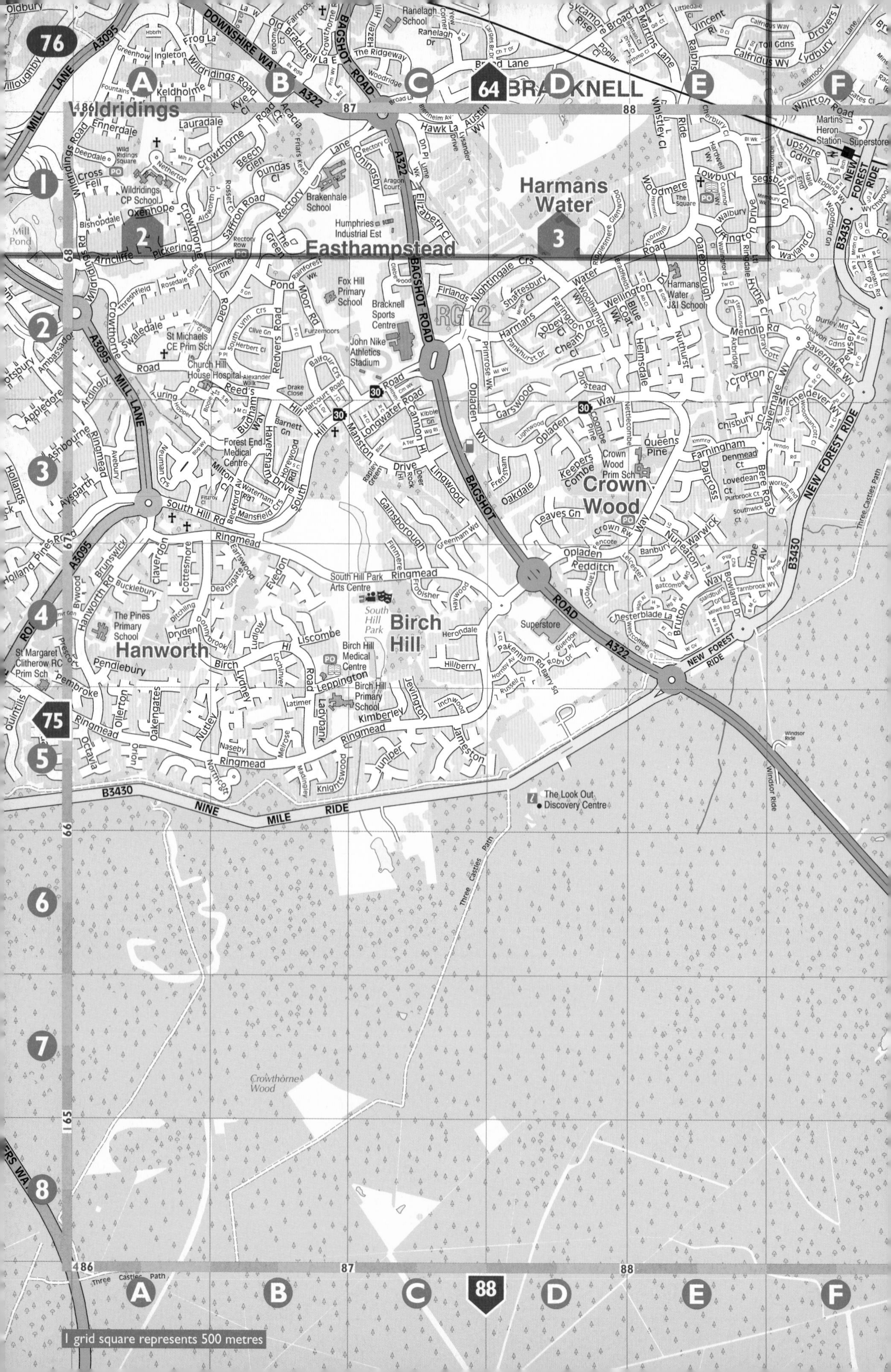

76
64
75
88
BRACKNELL
Wildridings
Easthampstead
Harmans Water
Crown Wood
Birch Hill
Hanworth
RG12
Wildridings CP School
St Michaels CE Prim Sch
Brakenhale School
Humphries Industrial Est
Fox Hill Primary School
Bracknell Sports Centre
John Nike Athletics Stadium
Church Hill House Hospital
Forest End Medical Centre
South Hill Park Arts Centre
South Hill Park
Birch Hill Medical Centre
Birch Hill Primary School
The Pines Primary School
St Margaret Clitherow RC Prim Sch
Crown Wood Prim Sch
Harmans Water J&I School
Superstore
Martins Heron Station
Ranelagh School
The Look Out Discovery Centre
Crowthorne Wood
Mill Pond
Three Castles Path
Windsor Ride
MILL LANE
A3095
A322
BAGSHOT ROAD
DOWNSHIRE WAY
B3430
NINE MILE RIDE
NEW FOREST RIDE
Ringmead
Crowthorne Road
Opladen Way
Nightingale Crs
Harmans Water Road
Wildridings Road
South Hill Rd
Rectory Lane
Pond Moor Rd
Longwater Road
Whitton Road
1 grid square represents 500 metres

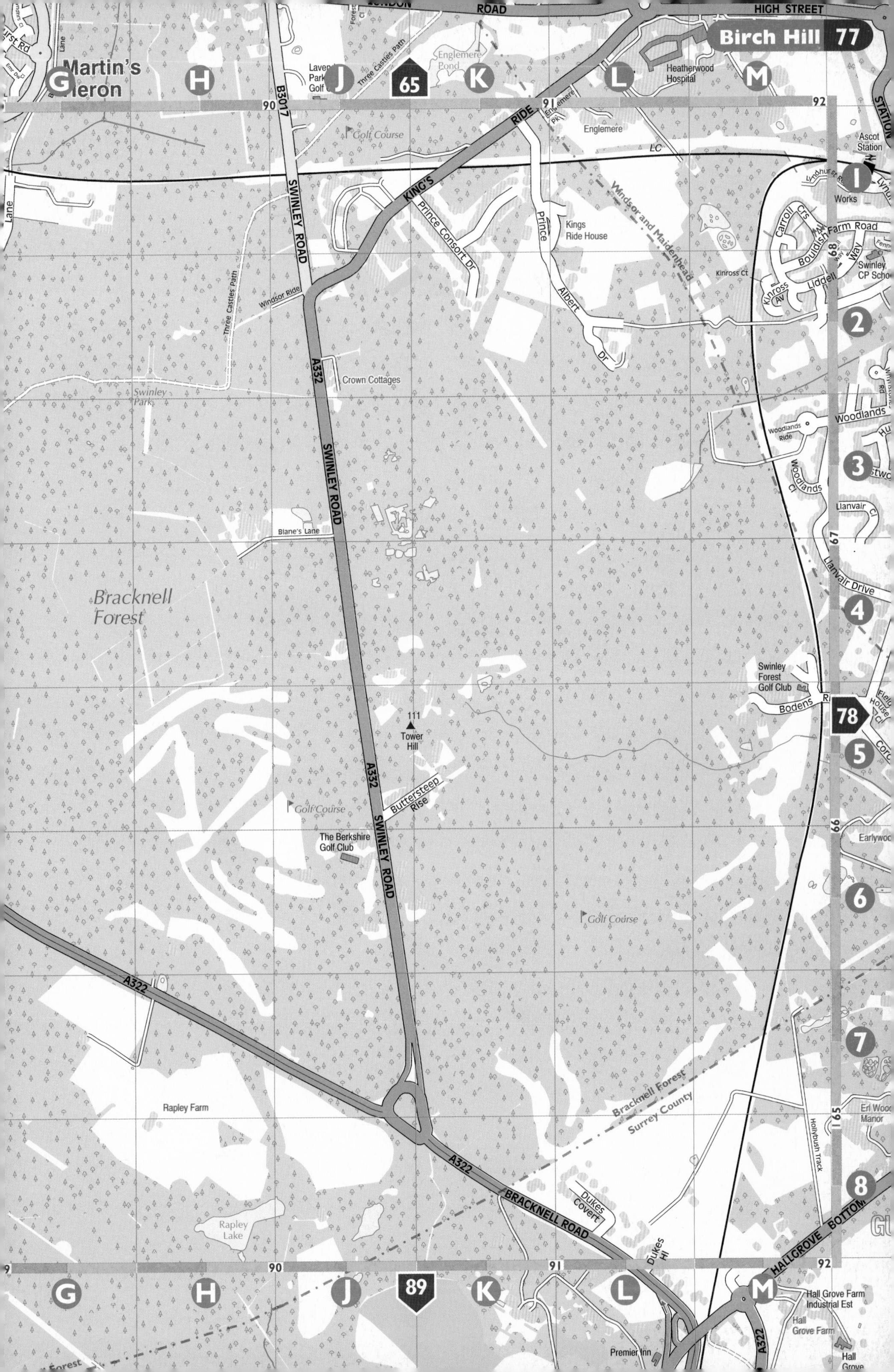

Birch Hill 77
Martin's Heron
ROAD
HIGH STREET
65
Englemere Pond
Heatherwood Hospital
Three Castles Path
B3017
SWINLEY ROAD
Golf Course
KING'S RIDE
Englemere
LC
Ascot Station
Works
Prince Consort Dr
Prince Albert Dr
Kings Ride House
Windsor and Maidenhead
Carroll Crs
Bouldish Farm Road
Liddell Way
Kinross Ct
Kinross Av
Swinley CP School
Windsor Ride
A332
Crown Cottages
Swinley Park
Woodlands
Woodlands Ride
Woodlands Cl
Llanvair Cl
Llanvair Drive
Blane's Lane
Bracknell Forest
Swinley Forest Golf Club
Bodens Ride
78
111
Tower Hill
Buttersteep Rise
Golf Course
The Berkshire Golf Club
Earlywood
A322
Rapley Farm
Bracknell Forest
Surrey County
Hollybush Track
Erl Wood Manor
BRACKNELL ROAD
Dukes Covert
HALLGROVE BOTTOM
Rapley Lake
Dukes Hl
89
Hall Grove Farm Industrial Est
Hall Grove Farm
Premier Inn
G H J K L M
1 2 3 4 5 6 7 8
90 91 92
68 67 66 65

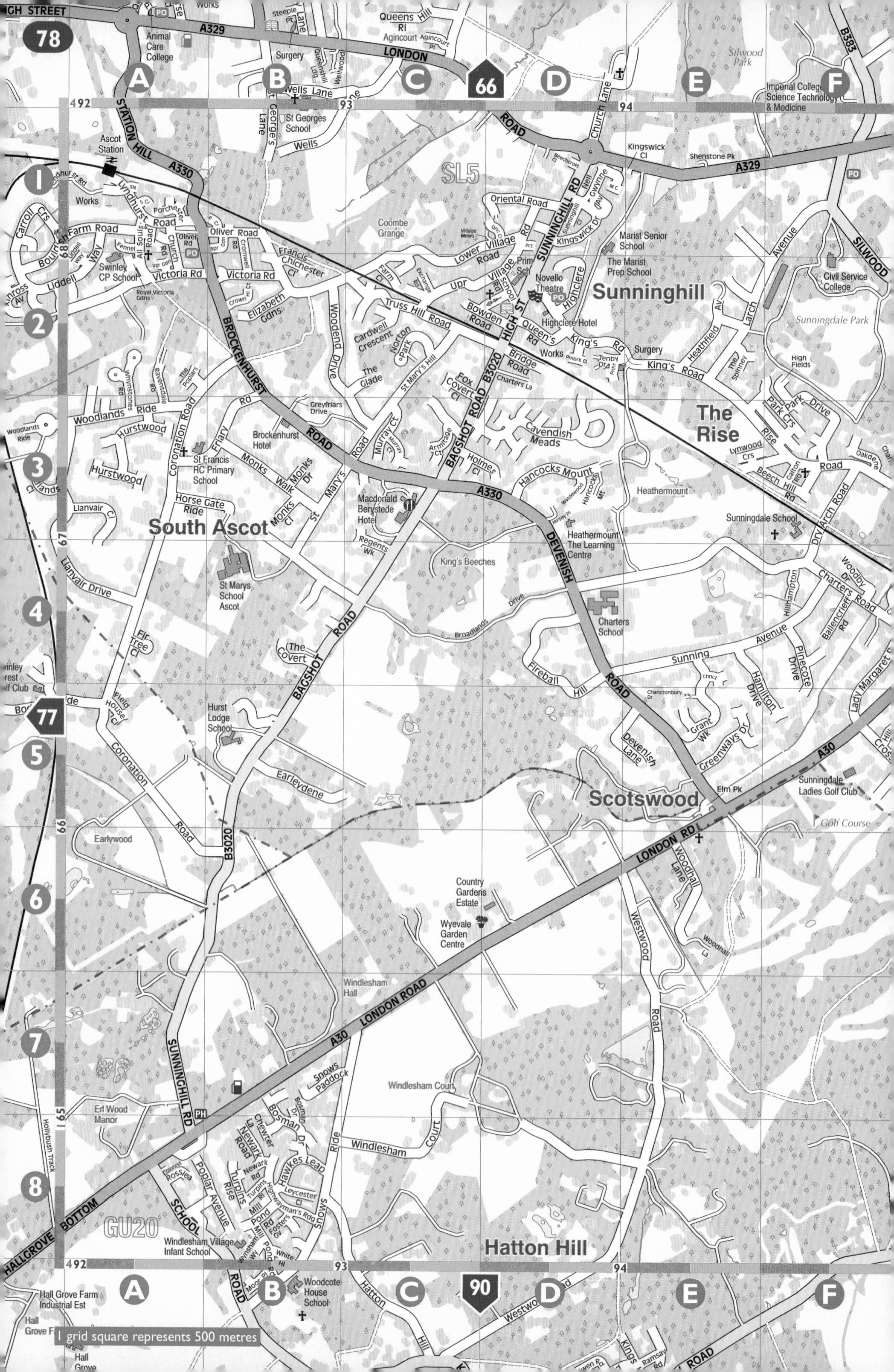

HIGH STREET
A329
LONDON ROAD
Animal Care College
Surgery
Queens Hill Ri
Agincourt
Wells Lane
St George's Lane
St Georges School
Wells
66
Church Lane
Silwood Park
Imperial College Science Technology & Medicine
B383
STATION HILL
A330
Ascot Station
Kingswick Cl
Shenstone Pk
SL5
Works
Lyndhurst Road
Porchester
Oriental Road
SUNNINGHILL RD
Coombe Grange
Carroll Crs
Bouldish Farm Road
Oliver Road
Victoria Rd
Swinley CP School
Liddell Way
Royal Victoria Gdns
Francis Chichester Cl
Lower Village Road
Upr Village Road
Kingswick Dr
Marist Senior School
The Marist Prep School
Sunninghill
Civil Service College
SILWOOD
Sunningdale Park
Novello Theatre
Highclere Hotel
Highclere
Elizabeth Gdns
BROCKENHURST
Woodend Drive
Truss Hill Road
Cardwell Crescent
Norton Park
The Glade
St Mary's Hill
Bowden Road
HIGH ST
Queen's Rd
King's Rd
Surgery
King's Road
Heathfield Av
Larch Avenue
The Spinney
High Fields
Park Drive
Park Crs
The Rise
Bridge Road
Charters La
B3020
Fox Covert Cl
Woodlands Ride
Wynstones Rd
Ravensdale Rd
The Poplars
Coronation Road
Greyfriars Drive
Brockenhurst Hotel
Hurstwood
Friary Rd
Monks Walk
Monks Dr
Murray Ct
Armitage Ct
BAGSHOT ROAD
Cavendish Meads
Holmes Cl
Hancocks Mount
Lynwood Crs
Rise Road
Beech Hill Rd
Oakdene
Heathermount
St Francis RC Primary School
Horse Gate Ride
Llanvair Cl
South Ascot
Monks Cl
St Mary's Road
Macdonald Berystede Hotel
A330
DEVENISH
Heathermount The Learning Centre
Sunningdale School
Dry Arch Road
Regents Wk
King's Beeches
Charters Road
Woodby Dr
Llanvair Drive
St Marys School Ascot
Broadlands Drive
Charters School
Hilhampton
Ballencrieff Rd
Fir Tree Cl
The Covert
Avenue
Pinecote Drive
Sunning Fireball Hill
ROAD
Chanctonbury Dr
Hamilton Drive
Lady Margaret Rd
Field House Cl
Hurst Lodge School
Grant Wk
Greenways Dr
77
Coronation Road
Earleydene
Devenish Lane
A30
Elm Pk
Scotswood
Sunningdale Ladies Golf Club
Golf Course
Earlywood
B3020
LONDON RD
Woodhall Lane
Westwood Road
Country Gardens Estate
Wyevale Garden Centre
Woodhall La
Windlesham Hall
A30 LONDON ROAD
SUNNINGHILL RD
Snows Paddock
Windlesham Court
Erl Wood Manor
Hollybush Track
Bosman Dr
Chewter La
Newark La
Hawkes Leap
Windlesham Court
Leycester Cl
Turpins Rise
Highwayman's Rdg
Mill Pond Rd
Fosters Gv
Poplar Avenue
SCHOOL ROAD
Snows Ride
HALLGROVE BOTTOM
GU20
Windlesham Village Infant School
Hatton Hill
Woodcote House School
90
Westwood Rd
Hall Grove Farm Industrial Est
Hall Grove
1 grid square represents 500 metres

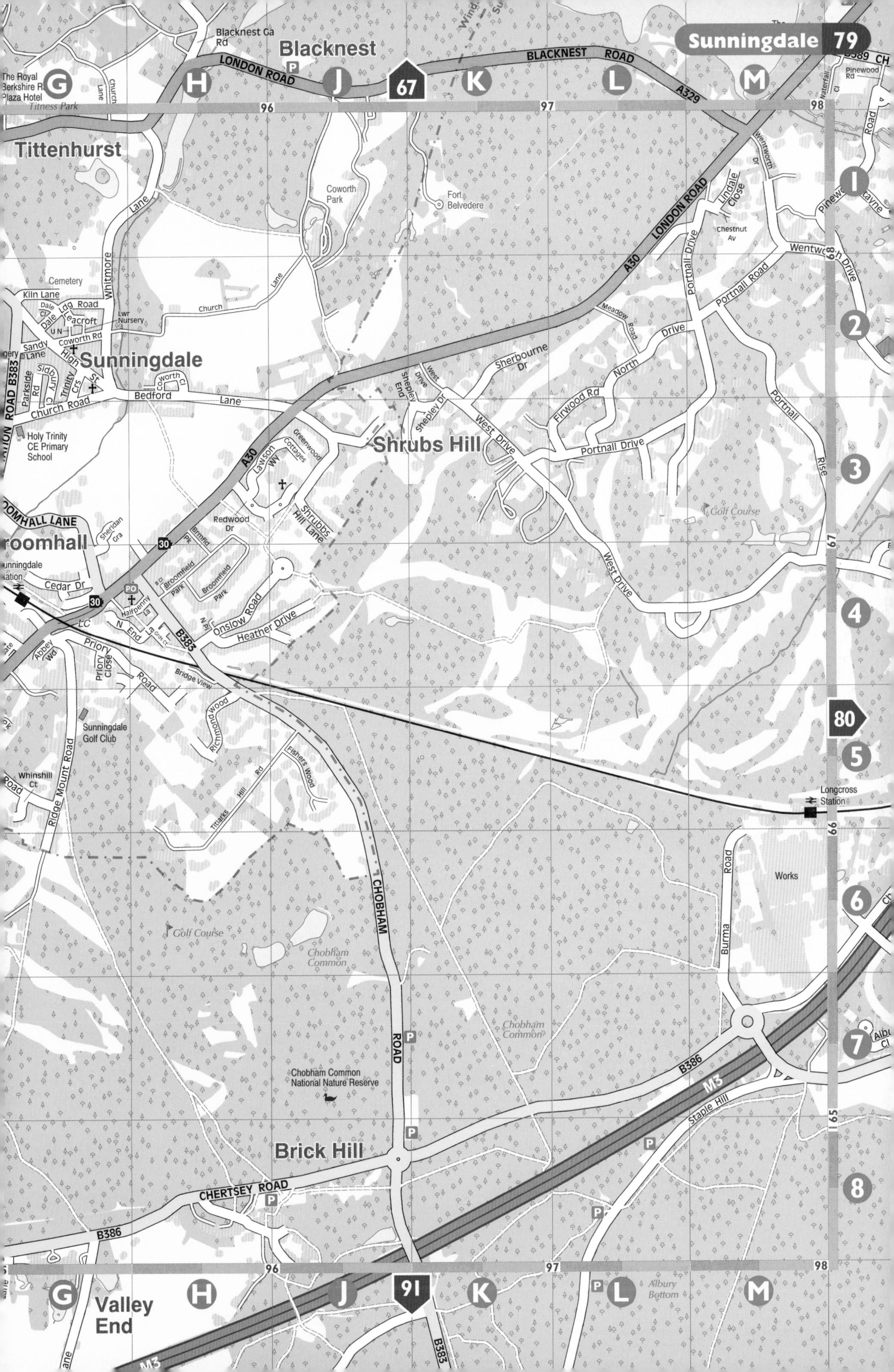

Blacknest

Tittenhurst

LONDON ROAD

BLACKNEST ROAD

A329

Pinewood Rd

The Royal Berkshire R Plaza Hotel

Fitness Park

Coworth Park

Fort Belvedere

LONDON ROAD

A30

Wentworth Dr

Portnall Drive

Lindale Close

Chestnut Av

Wentworth Drive

Pinewood Lane

Whitmore Lane

Cemetery

Church

Lane

Meadow Road

North Drive

Firwood Rd

Portnall Road

Portnall Rise

Kiln Lane
Dale Log Road
Leacroft
Lwr Nursery
Sandy Lane

Coworth Rd

High St

Church

Sherbourne Dr

Sunningdale

Sidny Trinity Crs

Bedford Lane

worth Cl

Shepley End

West Drive

Shepley Dr

Sherbourne Dr

Portnall Drive

West Drive

Golf Course

Holy Trinity CE Primary School

Church Road

Parkside Rd

ION ROAD B383

Shrubs Hill

Lawson Cottages

Greenwood

Redwood Dr

Shrubbs Hill Lane

Portnall Drive

OMHALL LANE

roomhall

Sheridan Gra

A30

A329

67

30

Sunningdale ation

Cedar Dr

PO

Halfpenny La

N End

Broomfield Park

Broomfield Park

Onslow Road

Heather Drive

West Drive

LC

B383

Priory Close

Priory Road

Abbey Wd

Bridge View

Richmond Wood

80

Sunningdale Golf Club

Whinshill Ct

Ridge Mount Road

Fisher's Wood

Tinarts Hill Rd

Longcross Station

66

Golf Course

CHOBHAM

Chobham Common

Burma Road

Works

Chobham Common

B386

M3

Staple Hill

Albt Cl

CHOBHAM ROAD

Chobham Common National Nature Reserve

Brick Hill

CHERTSEY ROAD

B386

M3

B383

Albury Bottom

Valley End

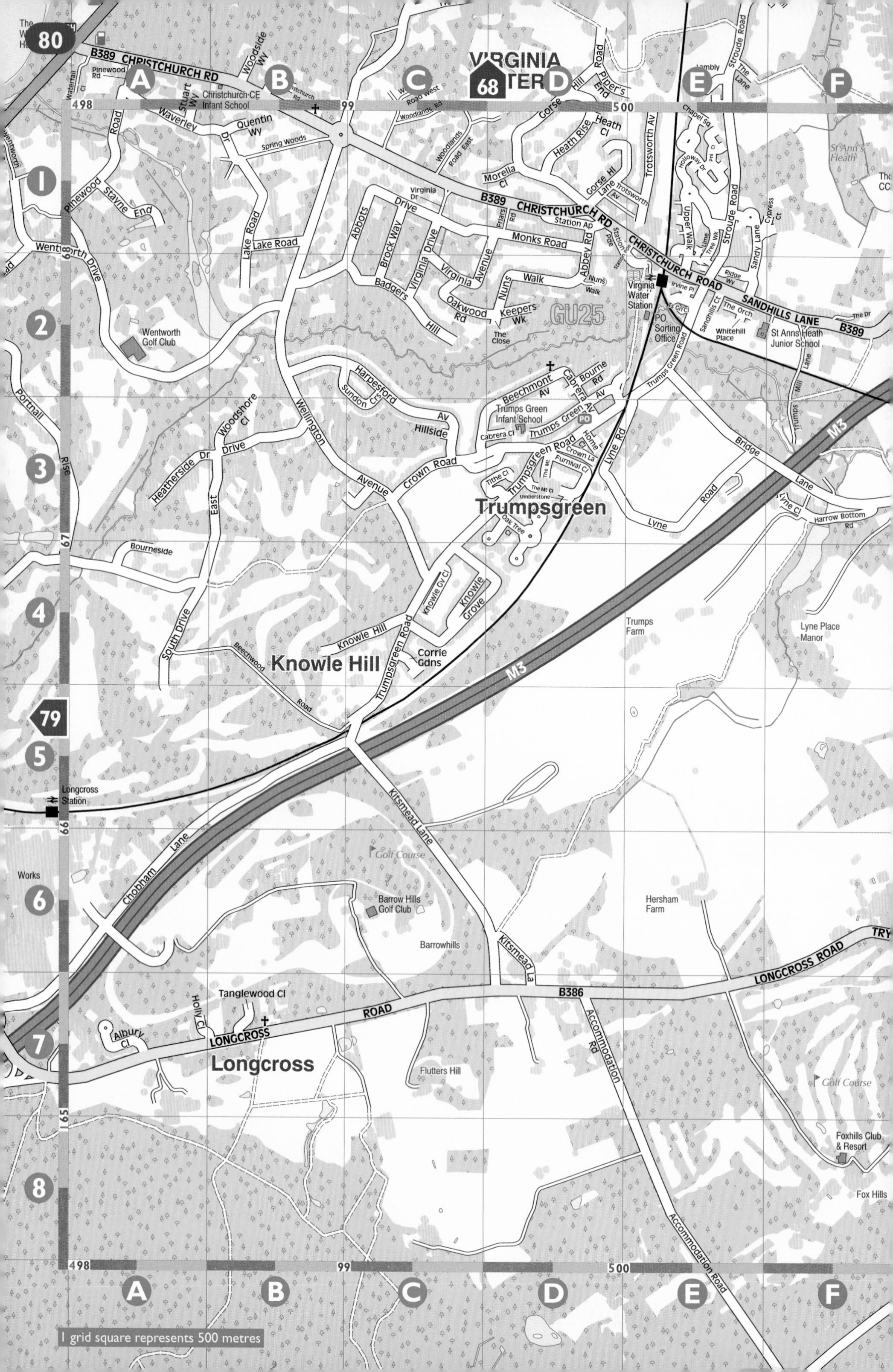

80
68
79
VIRGINIA WATER
B389 CHRISTCHURCH RD
Christchurch CE Infant School
Virginia Water Station
PO Sorting Office
SANDHILLS LANE
St Anns Heath Junior School
St Ann's Heath
GU25
Wentworth Golf Club
Trumps Green Infant School
Trumpsgreen
Knowle Hill
M3
Longcross Station
Trumps Farm
Lyne Place Manor
Golf Course
Barrow Hills Golf Club
Barrowhills
Hersham Farm
Works
LONGCROSS ROAD
B386
Longcross
Flutters Hill
Accommodation Road
Foxhills Club & Resort
Fox Hills
498
99
500
1 grid square represents 500 metres

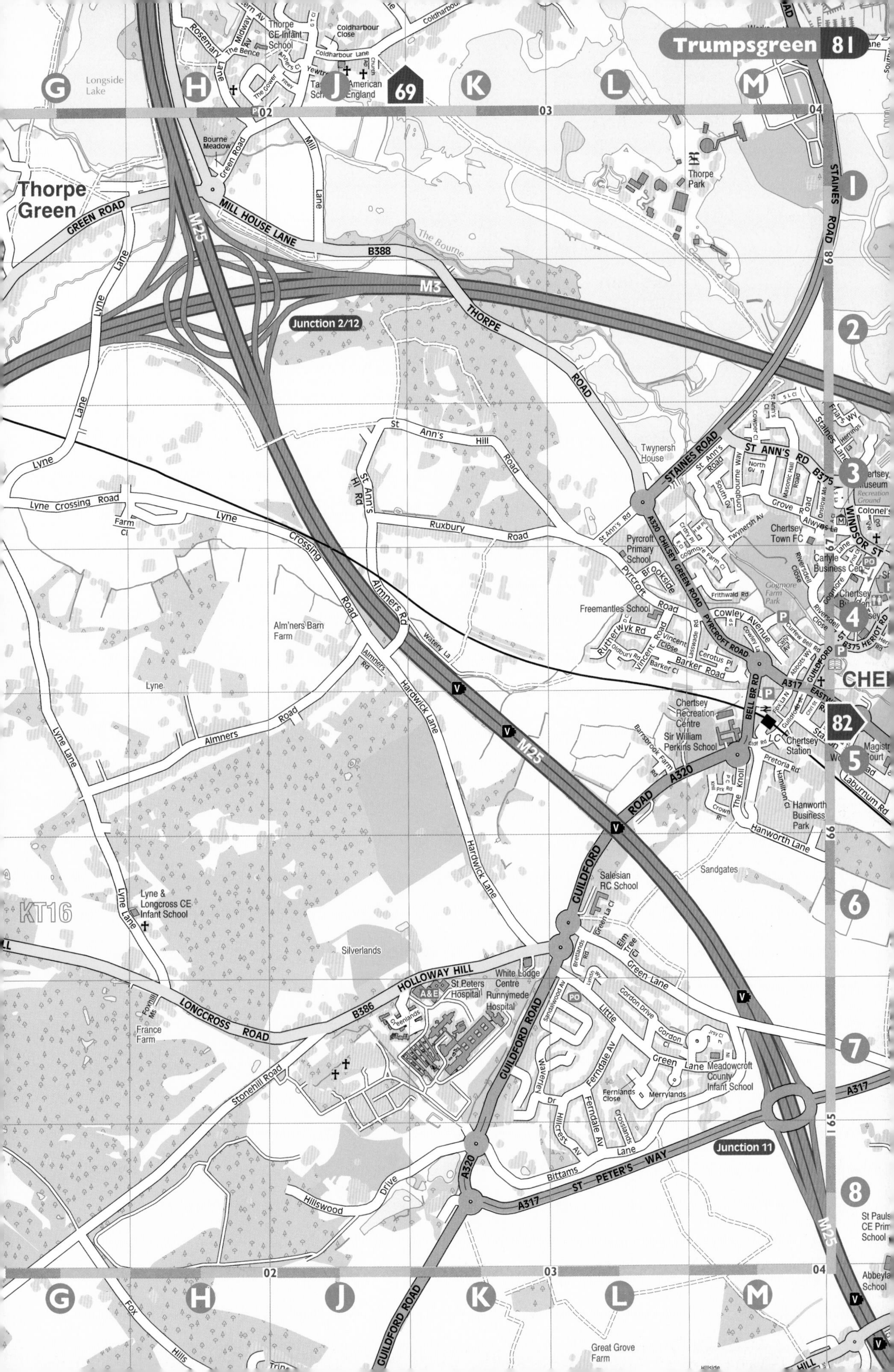
Thorpe Green
Longside Lake
Thorpe CE Infant School
Coldharbour Close
Coldharbour Lane
Bourne Meadow
Green Road
Mill Lane
Mill House Lane
B388
The Bourne
Thorpe Park
Staines Road
M25
M3
Junction 2/12
Thorpe Road
Lyne Lane
Lyne
Lyne Crossing Road
Farm Cl
St Ann's Hill Road
St Ann's Hl Rd
Ruxbury Road
Twynersh House
St Ann's Rd
B375
Chertsey Museum
Chertsey Town FC
Windsor St
Carlyle Business Cen
Pyrcroft Primary School
Chilsey Green Road
A320
Pyrcroft Road
Brookside
Freemantles School
Cowley Avenue
Gogmore Farm Park
Rutherwyk Rd
Vincent Road
Barker Road
Frithwald Rd
Alm'ners Barn Farm
Almners Rd
Almners Road
Watery La
Hardwick Lane
Bell Br Rd
A317
Guildford Rd
Chertsey Recreation Centre
Sir William Perkins School
Chertsey Station
Barrsbrook Farm Rd
The Knoll
Pretoria Rd
Hamilton Cl
Hanworth Business Park
Hanworth Lane
Sandgates
Guildford Road
Salesian RC School
KT16
Lyne & Longcross CE Infant School
Silverlands
Holloway Hill
B386
Longcross Road
St Peters Hospital
White Lodge Centre
Runnymede Hospital
France Farm
Green Lane
Gordon Drive
Little Green Lane
Ferndale Av
Waverley Dr
Sandalwood Av
Meadowcroft County Infant School
Fernlands Close
Merrylands
Crosslands
Hillcrest Av
Stonehill Road
Hillswood Drive
Bittams Lane
St Peter's Way
Junction 11
St Pauls CE Prim School
Abbeylands School
Great Grove Farm
Fox Hills
69
82

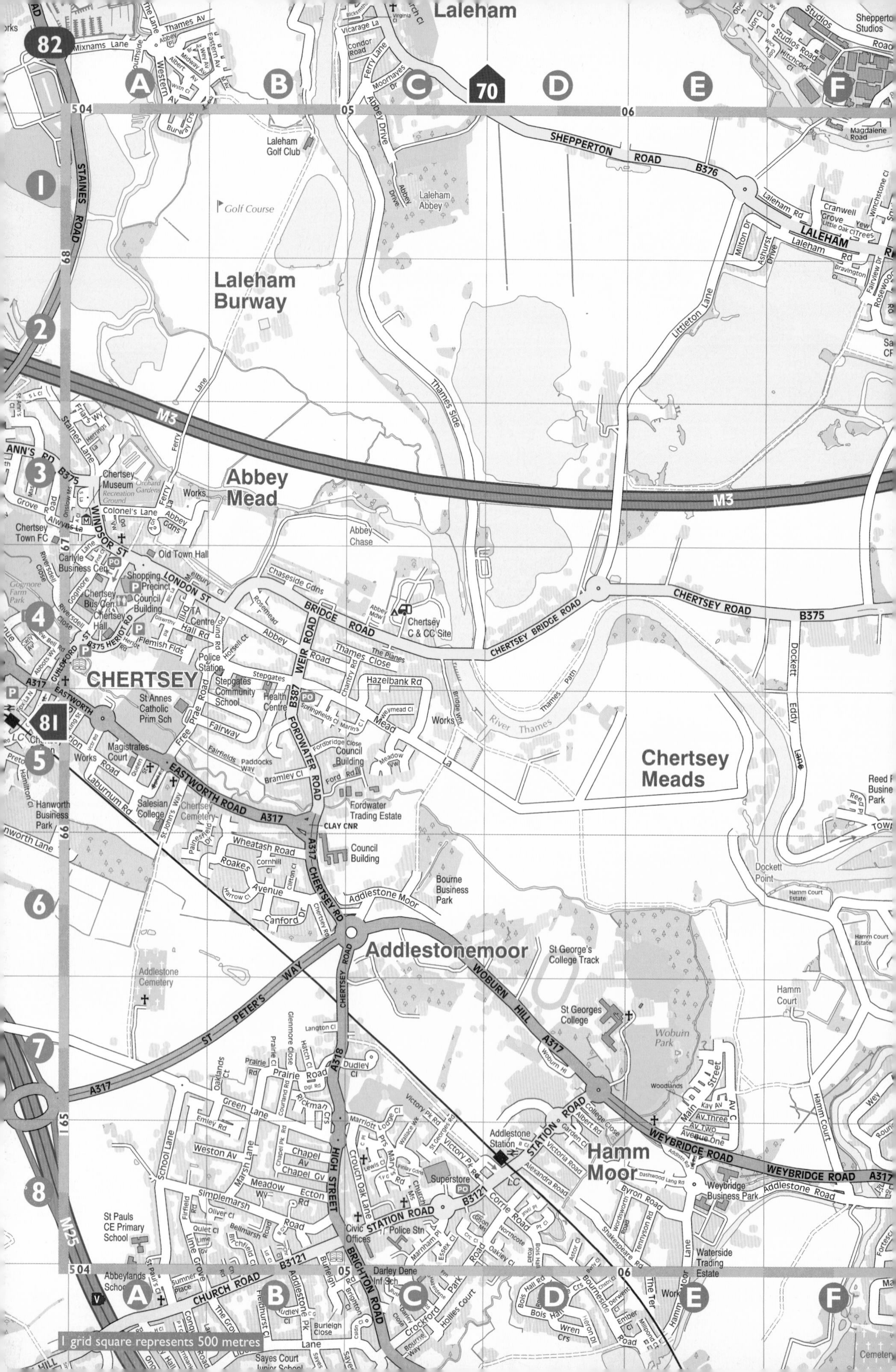

Laleham
82
70
81
A
B
C
D
E
F
Shepperton Studios
504
05
06
Laleham Golf Club
Golf Course
SHEPPERTON ROAD
B376
Laleham Abbey
LALEHAM
Laleham Rd
Laleham Burway
Littleton Lane
STAINES ROAD
M3
Abbey Mead
Chertsey Museum
Recreation Ground
Orchard Gardens
Works
Colonel's Lane
WINDSOR ST
Chertsey Town FC
Old Town Hall
Carlyle Business Cen
Shopping Precinct
LONDON ST
Council Building
Chertsey Bus Cen
Chertsey Hall
TA Centre
Police Station
Abbey Chase
Chaseside Gdns
BRIDGE ROAD
WEIR ROAD
Chertsey C & CC Site
CHERTSEY BRIDGE ROAD
CHERTSEY ROAD
B375
Thames Side
Thames Close
Hazelbank Rd
CHERTSEY
Stepgates Community School
Health Centre
St Annes Catholic Prim Sch
EASTWORTH
Magistrates Court
Works
Fairway
FORDWATER ROAD
Council Building
Fordwater Trading Estate
River Thames
Thames Path
Chertsey Meads
Dockett Eddy Lane
Reed Pl Business Park
Dockett Point
Hamm Court Estate
Hanworth Business Park
Salesian College
Chertsey Cemetery
EASTWORTH ROAD
A317
CLAY CNR
Wheatash Road
Council Building
Roakes Avenue
Canford Dr
Addlestone Moor
Bourne Business Park
Addlestonemoor
St George's College Track
WOBURN HILL
ST PETER'S WAY
Addlestone Cemetery
St Georges College
Woburn Park
Hamm Court
Woodlands
A318
HIGH STREET
Prairie Road
Green Lane
Weston Av
Chapel Av
Meadow
Superstore
Addlestone Station
STATION ROAD
Hamm Moor
WEYBRIDGE ROAD
Weybridge Business Park
Addlestone Road
M25
St Pauls CE Primary School
Simplemarsh Road
Civic Offices
Police Stn
B3121
Waterside Trading Estate
Abbeylands School
CHURCH ROAD
BRIGHTON ROAD
Darley Dene Inf Sch
Bois Hall Rd
Wren Crs
Sayes Court Junior School
Cemetery
1 grid square represents 500 metres

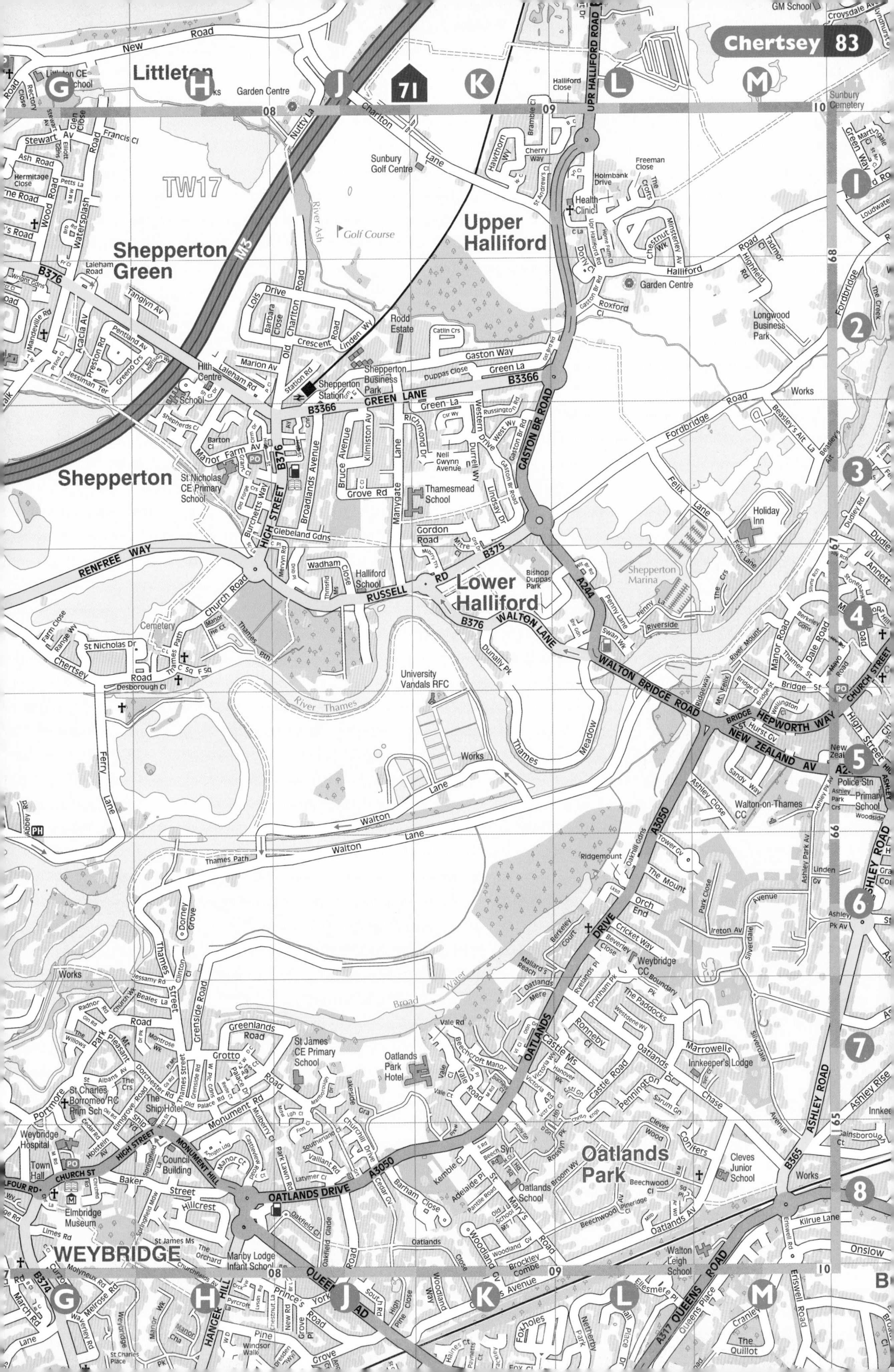
71
Littleton
Shepperton Green
Shepperton
Upper Halliford
Lower Halliford
Oatlands Park
WEYBRIDGE
TW17
M3
River Ash
Golf Course
Sunbury Golf Centre
Rodd Estate
Shepperton Business Park
Shepperton Station
Thamesmead School
St Nicholas CE Primary School
Halliford School
Longwood Business Park
Holiday Inn
Shepperton Marina
University Vandals RFC
River Thames
Broad Water
Walton Lane
Walton Bridge Road
New Zealand Av
Hepworth Way
Church Street
Gaston Br Road
Green Lane
High Street
Renfree Way
Russell Rd
Oatlands Drive
Monument Hill
Queens Road
Ashley Road
Fordbridge Road
Charlton Lane
Halliford Road
Chertsey Road
Ferry Lane
Thames Street
Oatlands Park Hotel
St James CE Primary School
Weybridge Hospital
Elmbridge Museum
Council Building
Town Hall
Manby Lodge Infant School
Oatlands School
Cleves Junior School
Walton Leigh School
Walton-on-Thames CC
Weybridge CC
Police Stn
Sunbury Cemetery
Cemetery
Works
Garden Centre
Health Clinic
Innkeeper's Lodge
B376
B3366
B375
A244
A3050
A317
B365
B374
G H J K L M
1 2 3 4 5 6 7 8
08 09 10
65 66 67 68

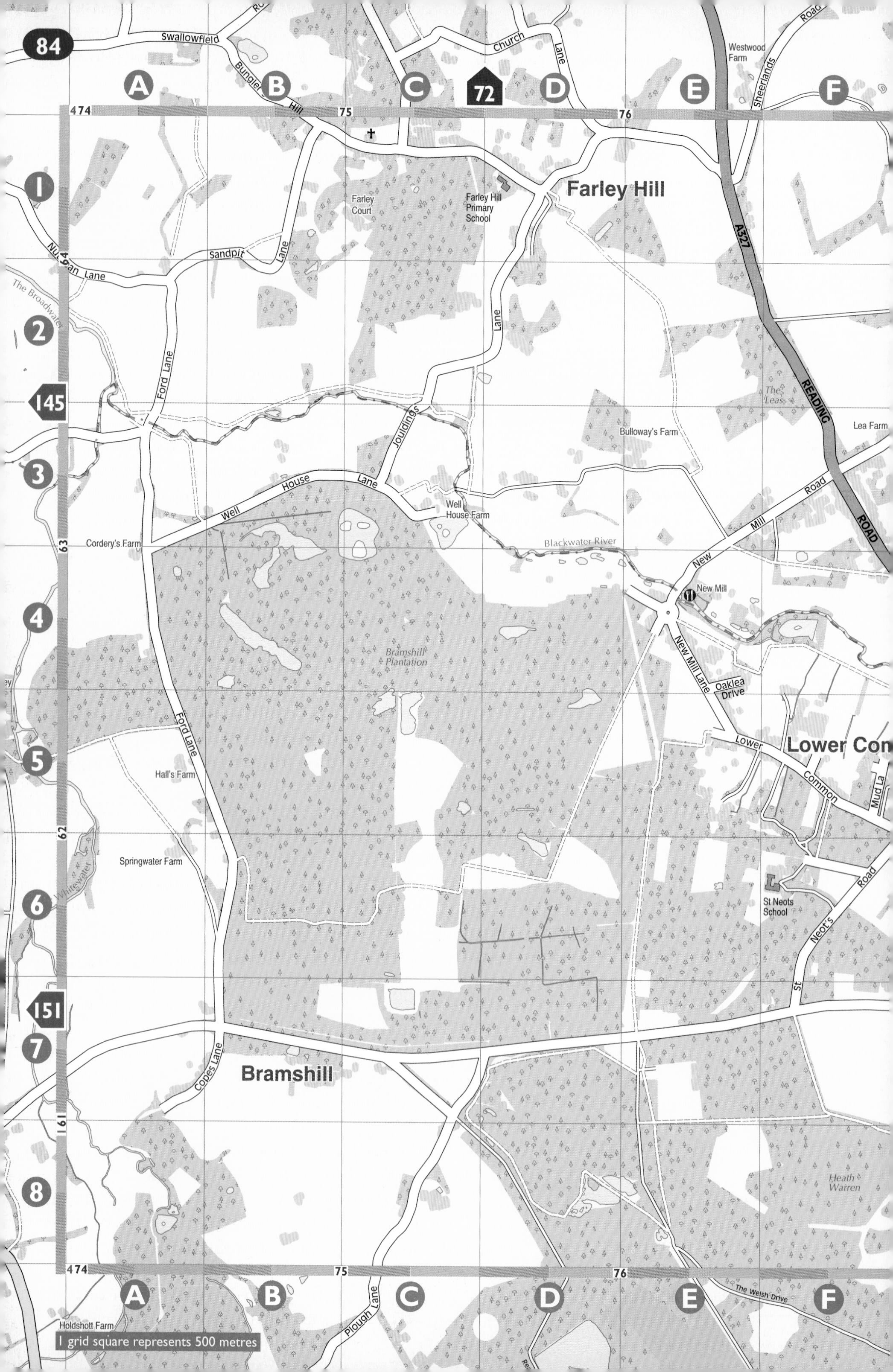

A B C 72 D E F

474 75 76

I Nu-49an Lane The Broadwater Swallowfield Rd Bungler Hill Church Lane Westwood Farm Sheerlands Road

Farley Court Farley Hill Primary School Farley Hill

A327

sandpit Lane Ford Lane READING

2

145 The 'Leas' Lea Farm

3 63 Cordery's Farm Well House Lane Jouldings Bulloway's Farm

Well House Farm Blackwater River New Mill Lane ROAD New Mill Lane

4 New Mill Oaklea Drive

Bramshill Plantation

5 Hall's Farm Ford Lane Lower Lower Con

6 62 Whitewater Springwater Farm St Neots School Mud La Neot's Road

151 161 St

7 Copes Lane Bramshill

8 Holdshott Farm Heath Warren The Welsh Drive

A B Plough Lane C D E F

474 75 76

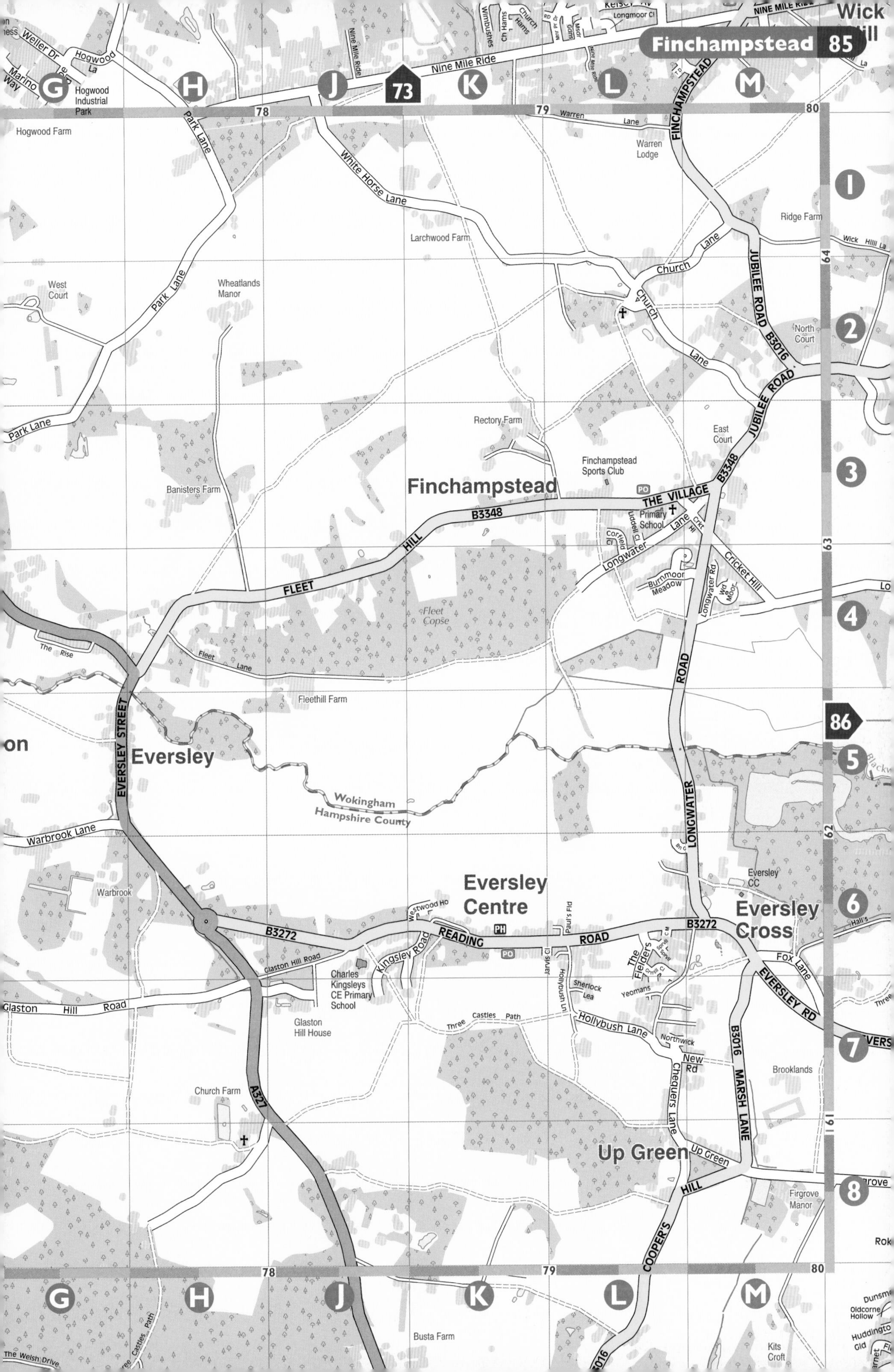

Wick Hill

G H J 73 K L M

Nine Mile Ride

78 79 80

Weller Dr
Marino Way
Hogwood La

Wimbushes
Church Hams
Longmoor Cl

Nine Mile Ride

I

Hogwood Industrial Park

Hogwood Farm

Park Lane

White Horse Lane

Warren Lane

Warren Lodge

Ridge Farm

Wick Hill La

64

2

West Court

Wheatlands Manor

Larchwood Farm

Church Lane

Church Lane

North Court

JUBILEE ROAD B3016

JUBILEE ROAD

Park Lane

Banisters Farm

Rectory Farm

Finchampstead Sports Club

East Court

B3348

3

Finchampstead

FLEET HILL B3348

THE VILLAGE

PO
Primary School
Juddell Cl
Cricket Hill
Longwater Lane
Corfield

Burnmoor Meadow
Wd Moor
Longwater Rd

Cricket Hill

Lo

63

4

The Rise

Fleet Copse

Fleet Lane

Fleethill Farm

LONGWATER ROAD

86

5

Eversley

EVERSLEY STREET

Wokingham
Hampshire County

Blackw

62

Warbrook Lane

Eversley CC

Eversley

6

Warbrook

Eversley Centre

Westwood Ho
Paul's Fld

B3272

Eversley Cross

Hall's

Fox Lane

EVERSLEY RD

Three vers

B3272 READING ROAD

PH
PO

Kingsley Road
Claston Hill Road

Charles Kingsleys CE Primary School

Jarvis Cl
Hollybush Ln
Sherlock Lea

The Fielders
Yeomans

61

7

Glaston Hill Road

Glaston Hill House

Three Castles Path

Hollybush Lane
Northwick
New Rd

Chequers Lane

MARSH LANE B3016

Brooklands

A327

Church Farm

COOPER'S HILL

Up Green

Up Green

Firgrove Manor

grove

8

Glaston Hill Rd

78 79 80

G H J K L M

Busta Farm

Kits Croft

Dunsm
Oldcorne Hollow
Huddingto

Rok

The Welsh Drive
Three Castles Path

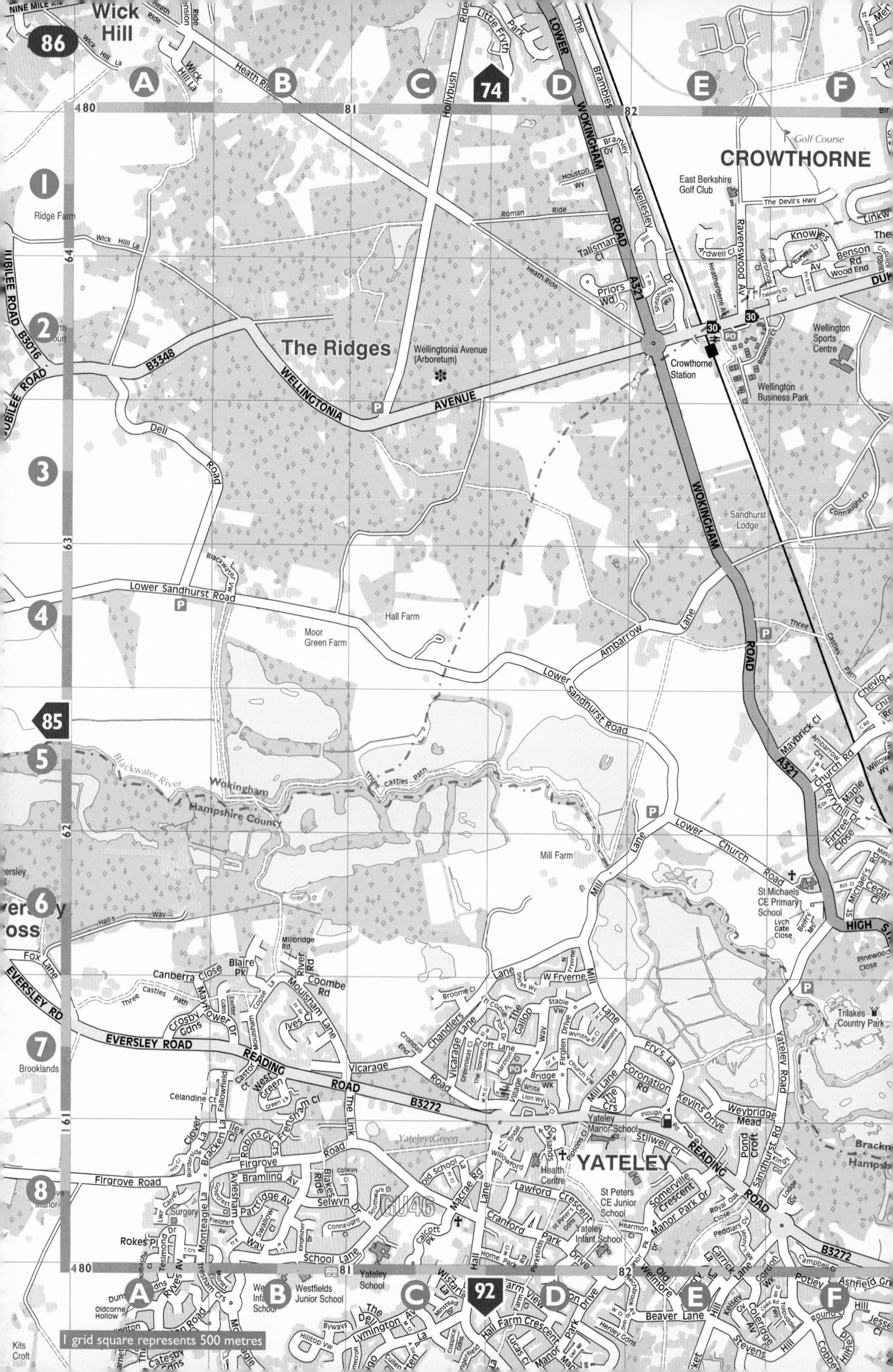

86
Wick Hill
74
85
92
CROWTHORNE
East Berkshire Golf Club
Golf Course
The Ridges
Wellingtonia Avenue (Arboretum)
WELLINGTONIA AVENUE
B3348
Crowthorne Station
Wellington Sports Centre
Wellington Business Park
Sandhurst Lodge
WOKINGHAM ROAD
A321
Ridge Farm
Lower Sandhurst Road
Hall Farm
Moor Green Farm
Blackwater River
Three Castles Path
Wokingham
Hampshire County
Mill Farm
St Michaels CE Primary School
Trilakes Country Park
EVERSLEY ROAD
READING ROAD
B3272
YATELEY
Yateley Manor School
Health Centre
St Peters CE Junior School
Yateley Infant School
Yateley School
Westfields Junior School
Yateley Green
GU46
Brooklands
Firgrove Road
1 grid square represents 500 metres

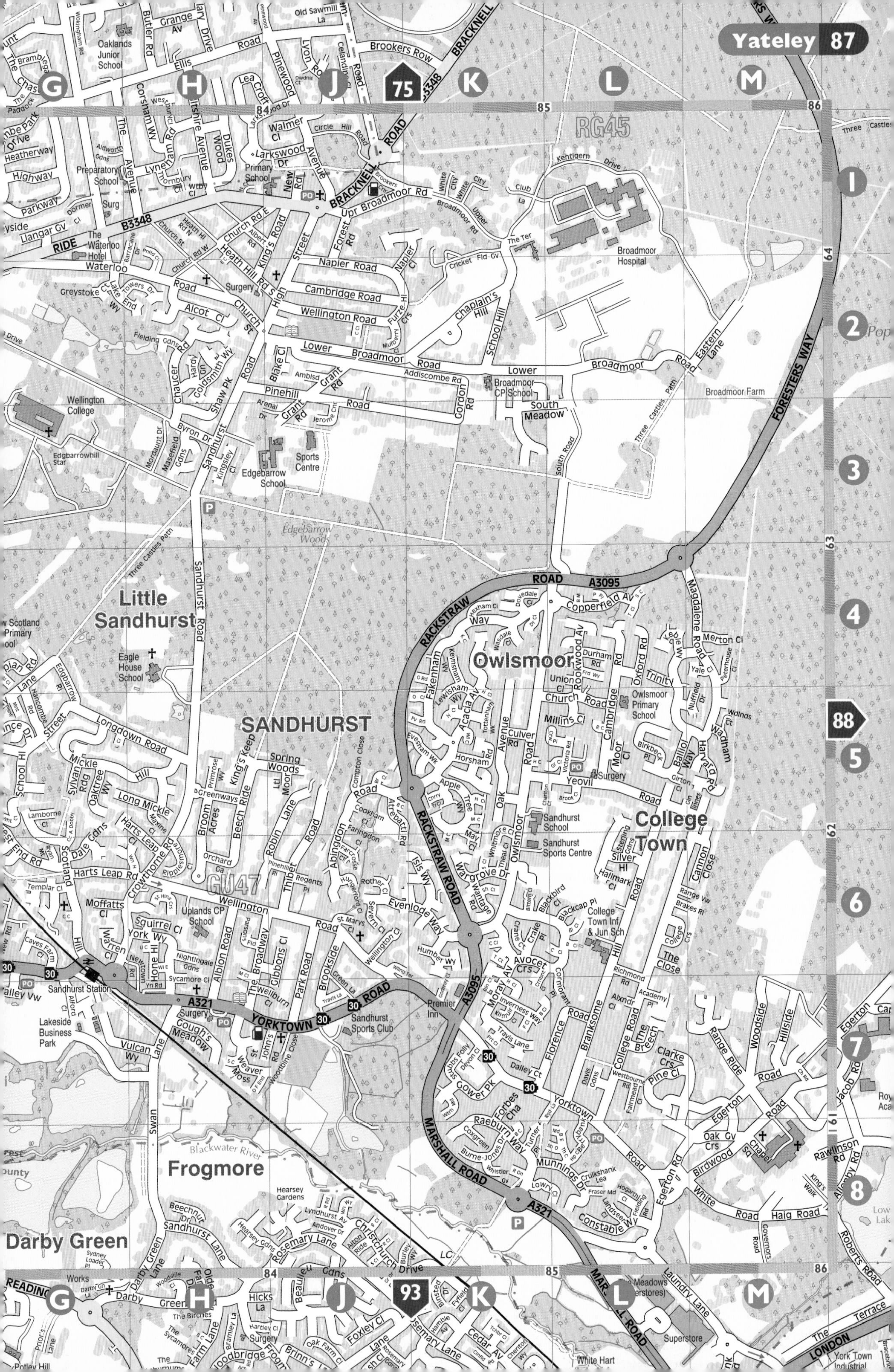

G
H
J
K
L
M
75
84
85
86
RG45
Grange Av
Butler Rd
Oaklands Junior School
Ellis
Road
Corsham Wy
Pinewood
Brookers Row
Old Sawmill La
Lea Croft
Walmer Cl
Circle Hill Road
BRACKNELL ROAD
B3348
Heatherway
Highway
Parkway
Preparatory School
Surg
Dormer Cl
Llangar Gv
Lynwood Av
The Avenue
Dukes Wood
Larkswood Dr
Primary School
New Rd
Avenue
PO
Brookers Cnr
Kentigern Drive
Club La
Upr Broadmoor Rd
White City
Broadmoor Hospital
The Ter
Cricket Fld Gv
RIDE
The Waterloo Hotel
Waterloo Road
Church Rd E
Church Rd W
Heath Hill Rd N
Heath Hill Rd S
King's Road
High Street
Forest Rd
Napier Road
Napier Rd
Cambridge Road
Wellington Road
Furze Hl
Mulberry Crs
Greystoke Ct
Lake End Wy
Towers Dr
Alcot Cl
Church St
Surgery
Chaplain's Hill
School Hill
Fielding Gdns
Hardy Gn
Goldsmith Wy
Chaucer Rd
Lower Broadmoor Road
Lower Broadmoor Road
Eastern Lane
Blake Cl
Grant Rd
Addiscombe Rd
Pinehill Road
Ambisd
Arenal Dr
Jerome Cnr
Gordon Rd
Broadmoor CP School
South Meadow
South Road
Broadmoor Farm
Three Castles Path
FORESTERS WAY
64
63
62
61
1
2
3
4
5
6
7
8
88
Wellington College
Edgbarrowhill Star
Mordaunt Dr
Byron Dr
Masefield Gdns
Shaw Pk
Sandhurst Road
Kingsley Cl
Edgebarrow School
Sports Centre
P
Edgebarrow Woods
ROAD A3095
RACKSTRAW ROAD
Copperfield Av
Dovedale Cl
Hexham Cl
Way
Wasdale Cl
Little Sandhurst
New Scotland Primary School
Eagle House School
Owlsmoor
Fakenham Wy
Keynsham Wy
Lewisham Wy
Acacia Av
Rookwood Av
Durham Rd
Oxford Rd
Union Cl
Church Road
Cambridge Rd
Owlsmoor Primary School
Trinity
Merton Cl
Magdalene Road
Keble Way
Yale Cl
Peterhouse Cl
Nuffield Dr
Wdlnds Ct
SANDHURST
Longdown Road
Edgbarrow Rise
Hancombe Rd
Lane
Street
Spring Woods
King's Keep
Compton Close
Evesham Wk
Tottenham Wk
Horsham Rd
Avenue
Culver Rd
Millins Cl
Victoria Rd
Moor Cl
Birkbeck Pl
Balliol Way
Wadham
Harvard Rd
Girton Cl
Mickle Hill
Sylvan Rdg
Oaktree Wy
Long Mickle
Lamborne Cl
Primrose Wk
Greenways
Broom Acres
Beech Ride
Ltl Moor
Robin Lane
Road
Apple Tree Wy
Oak
Yeovil Road
Surgery
Brook Cl
College Town
Dale Gdns
Harts Leap Rd
Maxine Cl
Crowthorne Rd
Ripplesmere
Orchard Ga
Pinehill Rl
Thibet Road
Regents Pl
Abingdon Road
Cookham Cl
Faringdon Cl
Farcrose Cl
Atrebatti Rd
Isis Wy
RACKSTRAW ROAD
Wargrove Dr
Wantage Rd
May
Whitmore Cl
Owlsmoor Road
Sandhurst School
Sandhurst Sports Centre
Sterling Gdns
Silver Hl
Hallmark Cl
Cannon Close
Range Vw
Brakes Ri
Templar Cl
GU47
Wellington Road
Moffatts Cl
Squirrel Cl
York Wy
Uplands CP School
Nightingale Gdns
Sycamore Cl
Albion Road
The Broadway
Gibbons Cl
Park Road
Brookside
Rother Cl
Evenlode Way
Severn Cl
St Marys Cl
Wellington Cl
Humber Wy
Blackbird Cl
Blackcap Pl
College Town Inf & Jun Sch
Crane Ct
Crake Pl
Avocet Crs
Cormorant Pl
College Crs
The Close
Richmond Rd
Academy Pl
Alxndr Cl
Caves Farm Cl
Warren Cl
Hill
Scotland
Newtown Rd
Home Hl
Yn Rd
Wellburn Cl
Green La
Travis La
Sandhurst Station
Sandhurst Sports Club
Premier Inn
A3095
A321
YORKTOWN ROAD
Surgery
Gough's Meadow
St John's Rd
Woodbine Close
Lakeside Business Park
Vulcan Wy
Lane
Weaver Moss
Moray Av
Inverness Way
Kilmuir Cl
Travis Lane
Florence Road
Branksome Hill Road
College Road
The Breech
Clarke Crs
Pine Cl
Woodside Road
Hillside
Range Ride
Egerton Road
Jacob Rd
Stubbs Folly
Devon Cl
Gower Pk
Dalley Ct
Yorktown Road
Davis Gdns
Westbourne Rd
Fairmead Cl
Egerton
Oak Gv Crs
Birdwood
Chapel Sq
Rawlinson Rd
Forbes Cha
Raeburn Way
Coxgreen
Burne-Jones Dr
Whistler Gv
Turner Pl
Munnings Dr
Lowry Cl
Cruikshank Lea
Fraser Md
Hogarth Cl
Landseer Cl
Constable Wy
Fielding Rd
Egerton Rd
White Road
Haig Road
Governors Road
Roberts Road
Kings Walk
MARSHALL ROAD
A321
Swan
Blackwater River
Frogmore
Hearsey Gardens
Beechnut Dr
Sandhurst Lane
Darby Green
Darby Green Lane
Lyndhurst Av
Andover Dr
Hearsey Gdns
Rosemary Lane
Alton Ride
Christchurch Drive
Burley Wy
LC
Sydney Loader Pl
READING
Works
Darby Green
The Birches
The Sycamores
Farm Lane
Bramley La
Hicks La
Beaulieu Gdns
Hartley Cl
Surgery
93
Foxley Cl
Oak Farm Cl
Rosemary Lane
Hamble Av
Fyfield Cl
Cedar Av
Laundry Lane
Superstore
The Meadows
MARSHALL ROAD
White Hart
London
The Terrace
York Town Industrial
Potley Hill
Prior's Lane

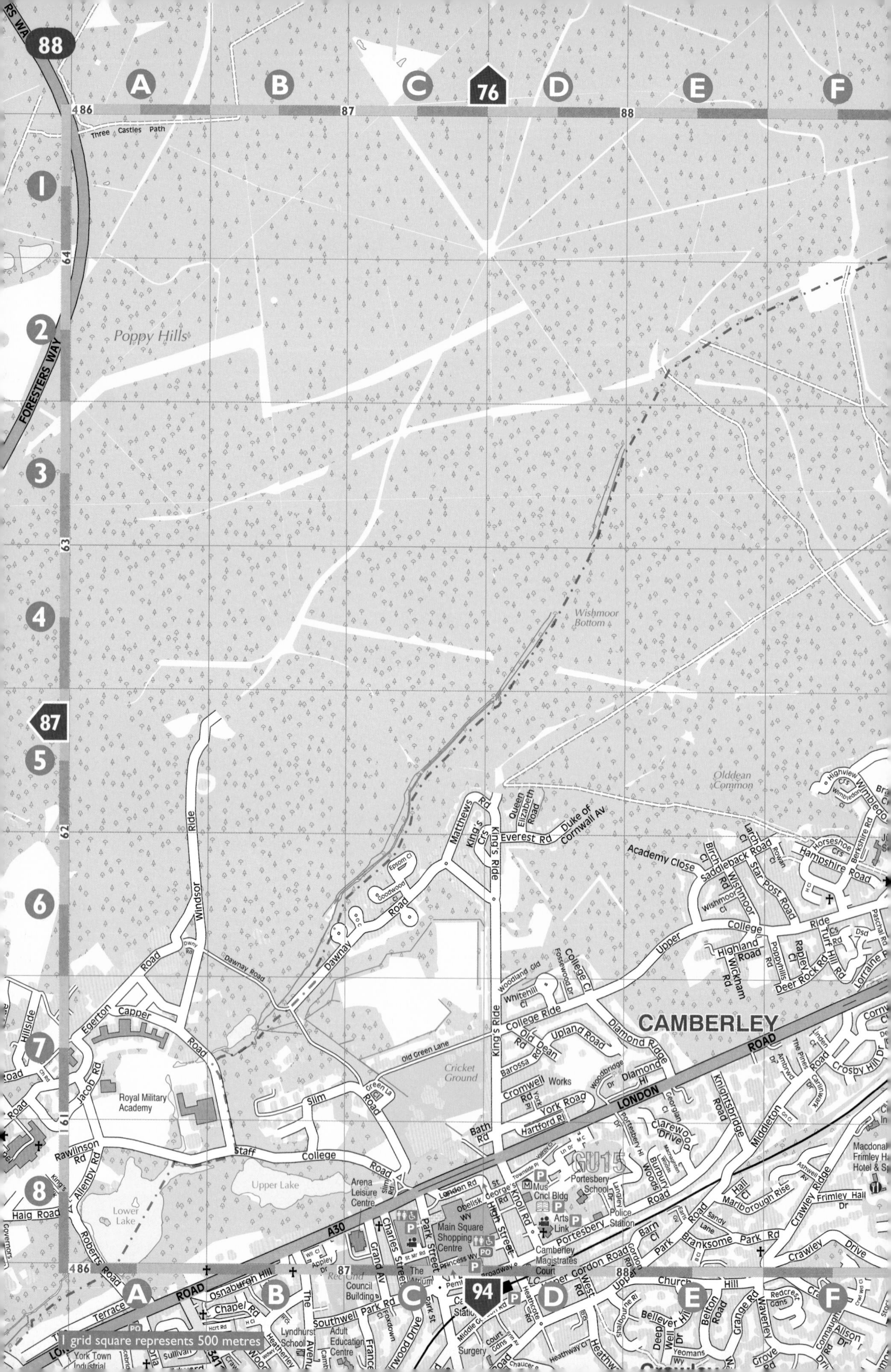

88
76
87
94
Poppy Hills
Wishmoor Bottom
Olddean Common
CAMBERLEY
Royal Military Academy
Upper Lake
Lower Lake
Cricket Ground
Arena Leisure Centre
Main Square Shopping Centre
Portesbery School
Police Station
Camberley Magistrates Court
Council Building
Adult Education Centre
Lyndhurst School
Macdonald Frimley Hall Hotel & Spa
FORESTERS WAY
Three Castles Path
LONDON ROAD
A30
Windsor Ride
Dawnay Road
Egerton Road
Capper Road
Jacob Rd
Rawlinson Rd
Staff College Road
Haig Road
Roberts Road
Old Green Lane
Slim Road
King's Ride
Upper College Ride
College Ride
Diamond Ridge
Knightsbridge Road
Middleton Rd
Crawley Ridge
Crawley Drive
Frimley Hall Dr
Marlborough Rise
Branksome Park Rd
Park Road
Portesbery Rd
Upper Gordon Road
Academy Close
Saddleback Road
Star Post Road
Hampshire Road
Crosby Hill Dr
Everest Rd
Duke of Cornwall Av
Matthews Rd
Park Street
High Street
Charles Street
Grand Av
Osnaburgh Hill
Southwell Park Rd
Church Hill
1 grid square represents 500 metres

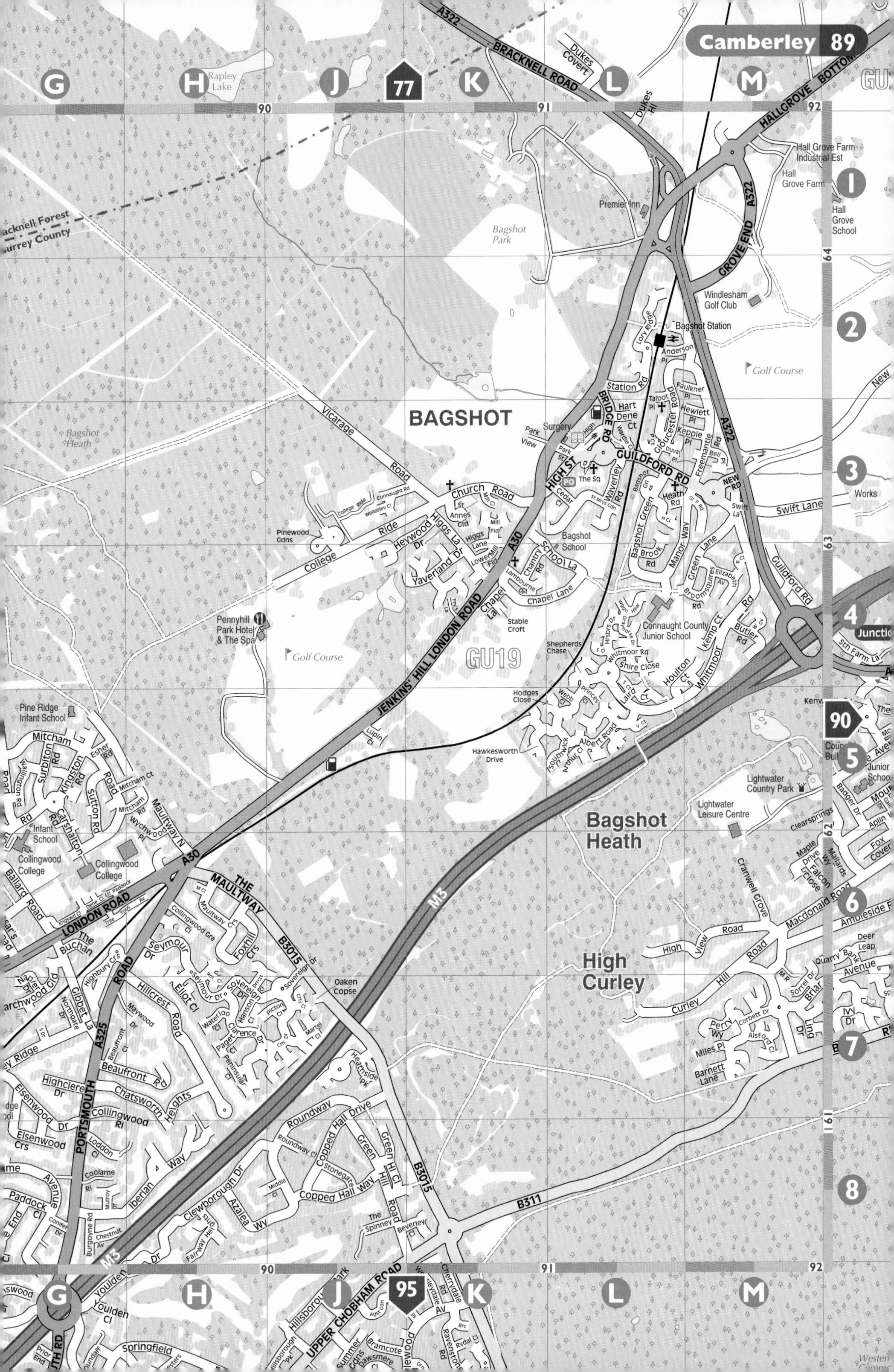

G H J K L M GU

77

Bracknell Forest
Surrey County

Rapley Lake

A322 BRACKNELL ROAD

Dukes Covert

Dukes Hill

HALLGROVE BOTTOM

Hall Grove Farm
Industrial Est

Hall Grove Farm

Hall Grove School

1

Premier Inn

Bagshot Park

GROVE END

A322

Windlesham Golf Club

Bagshot Station

Lory Ridge

Anderson

2

Golf Course

New

BAGSHOT

Vicarage Road

Bagshot Heath

Station Rd

Faulkner Pl

Hewlett Pl

Kepple Pl

Fremantle

Bell Pl

3

NEW RD

Swift Lane

Works

Surgery

Park View

BRIDGE RD

Hart Dene Ct

HIGH ST

The Sq

PO

GUILDFORD RD

Heath Rd

A322

A30

Church Road

Ride

Connaught Rd

Wellesley Cl

College Rise

St Annes Cld

Higgs La

Mill Fld

St Mary's Gdn

Cedar Cl

Waverley Rd

Gloucester Rd

Talbot Rd

Bagshot Rd

Bagshot Green

Brook Rd

Manor Way

Green Lane

Elizabeth Av

Guildford Rd

63

College

Heywood Dr

Higgs Lane

Lowen Fld

Firs

Pinewood Gdns

Yaverland Dr

Chattern

Lambourne

Bagshot School

School La

Broomscales Rd

Kemp Ct

Butler Rd

4

Junctio

Pennyhill Park Hotel & The Spa

Golf Course

JENKINS' HILL LONDON ROAD

A30

Chapel

Chapel Lane

Stable Croft

Shepherds Chase

Whitmoor Rd

Shire Close

Connaught County Junior School

Houlton Ct

Whitmoor

Kenw

5th Farm La

A

90

5

Junior School

Pine Ridge Infant School

Lupin Rd

Hawkesworth Drive

Hodges Close

Webb

Princes

Southwick

Arthur Rd

Albert Road

Clearsprings

Lightwater Country Park

Lightwater Leisure Centre

Badger Dr

Fox Covert

Mitcham Rd

Surbiton Rd

Kingston Rd

Esher Rd

Mitcham Ct

Mauldwyn Ct

Wychwood La

Collingwood Gro

MAULTWAY N

A30

Mitcham Rd

Carshalton Rd

Infant School

Collingwood College

Collingwood College

Ballard Road

THE MAULTWAY

Bagshot Heath

High View Rd

Cranwell Grove

Maple Drive

Hatton Close

Macdonald Rd

Ambleside Rd

Deer Leap

6

Highbury Ct

LONDON ROAD

The Buchan

Seymour Crs

Foxhill

B3015

High Curley Rd

High Curley

Curley

Hill

Perry Wy

Corbett Dr

Alsfo

Ling

Ivy Dr

7

61

archwood Gld

A325

PORTSMOUTH ROAD

Hillcrest Road

Beaufront Rd

Elliot Cl

Seymour Dr

Sovereign Dr

Picton Cl

Clarence Cl

Peninsula

Oaken Copse

Roundway

Martel Cl

Barnett Lane

Miles Pl

Barnett Lane

B

62

Eisenwood Dr

Highclere Dr

Chatsworth

Collingwood Ri

Maywood

Hillsborough

Heathside Pk

Hancock Dr

Roundway Cl

Copped Hall Drive

Green Hill Ct

B3015

B311

8

Eisenwood Crs

Loddon Cl

Coolarne Ri

Iberian Way

Clewborough Dr

Azalea Wy

Middle

Copped Hall Way

Green Hill Rd

Beverley Rd

The Spinney

M3

Paddock

Avenue

Burgoyne Rd

Conifer Ln

Chestnut Ln

Fairway Hgt

Bramcote

Dawsmere

Rydal Cl

Western

G H J K L M

90 91 92

95

UPPER CHOBHAM ROAD

TH RD

Youlden Cl

Youlden Dr

Springfield

Summer Gdns

Hillsborough Pk

Cherrydale Rd

Cherrydale Av

Ravensmore Rd

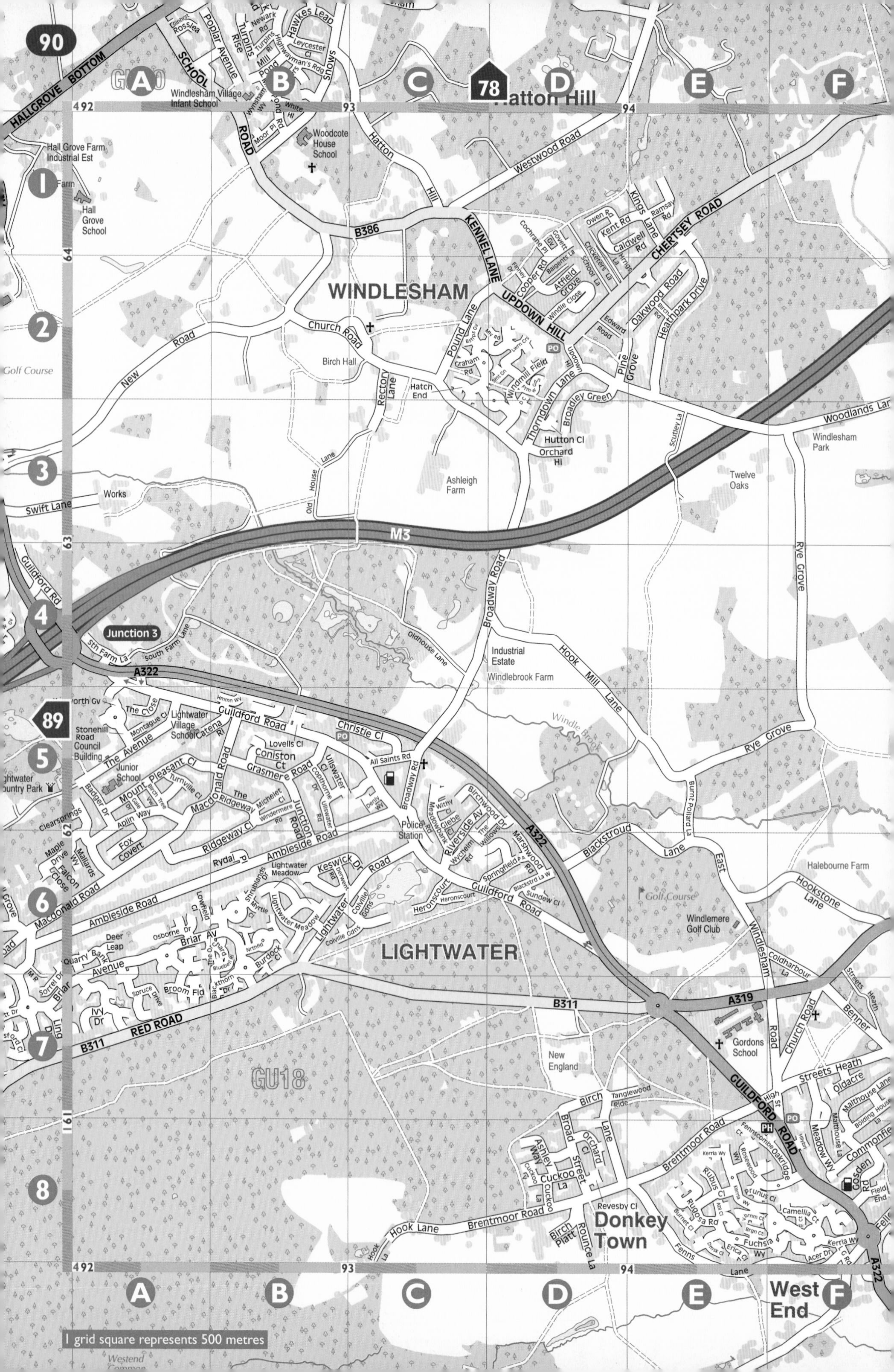

90
78
89
Hatton Hill
WINDLESHAM
LIGHTWATER
Donkey Town
West End
M3
Junction 3
A322
A319
B311
B386
HALLGROVE BOTTOM
SCHOOL ROAD
KENNEL LANE
UPDOWN HILL
CHERTSEY ROAD
RED ROAD
GUILDFORD ROAD
Westwood Road
Church Road
New Road
Broadway Road
Hook Mill Lane
Rye Grove
Guildford Road
Macdonald Road
Ambleside Road
Brentmoor Road
Hook Lane
Windlesham Road
Woodlands Lane
Blackstroud Lane
Hall Grove Farm Industrial Est
Hall Grove School
Woodcote House School
Windlesham Village Infant School
Birch Hall
Hatch End
Ashleigh Farm
Windlesham Park
Twelve Oaks
Industrial Estate
Windlebrook Farm
Lightwater Village School
Junior School
Police Station
Windlemere Golf Club
Halebourne Farm
Gordons School
New England
Golf Course
GU18
1 grid square represents 500 metres

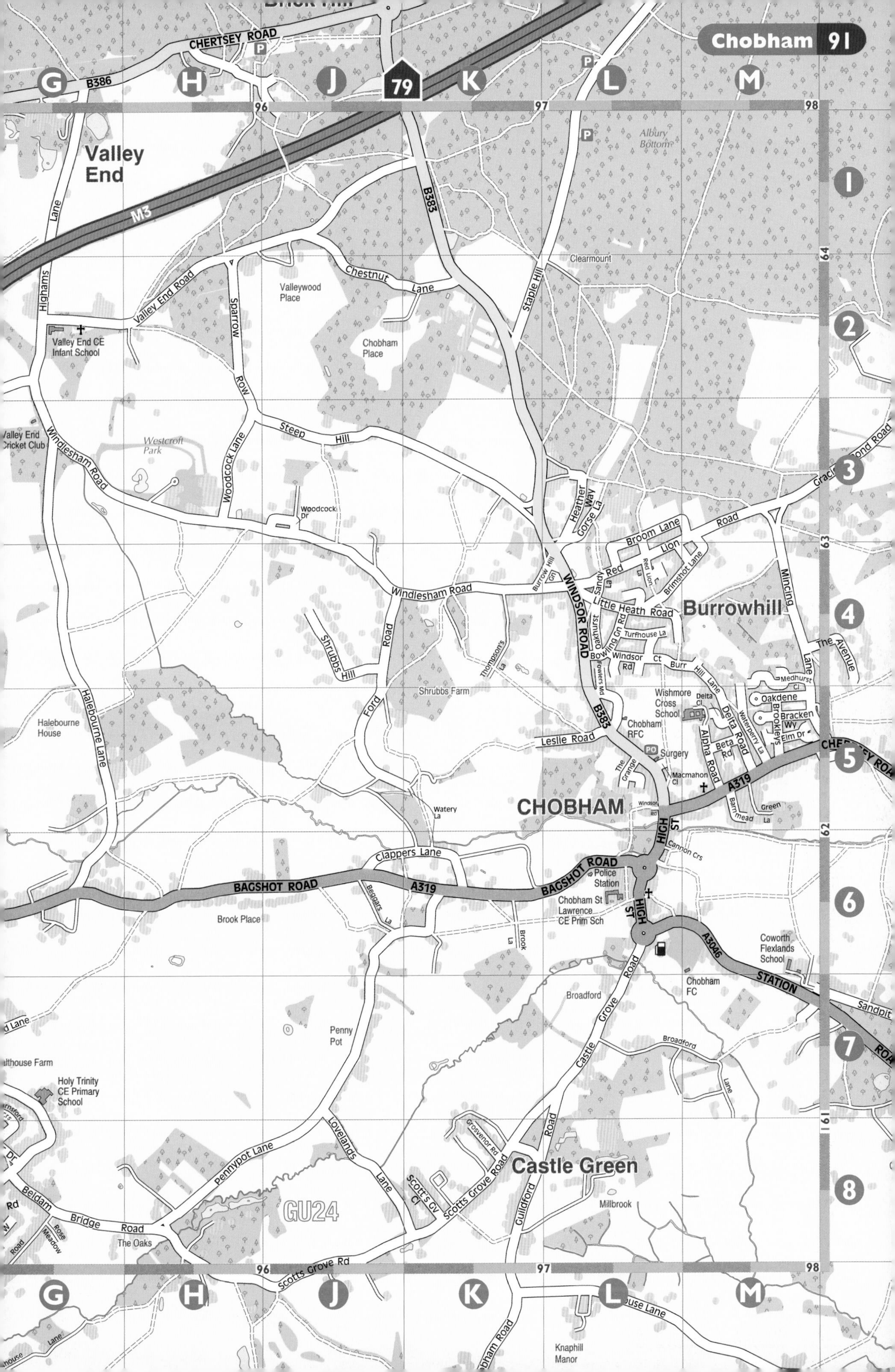
79
CHERTSEY ROAD
B386
M3
B383
Valley End
Highams Lane
Valley End Road
Valley End CE Infant School
Sparrow Row
Chestnut Lane
Valleywood Place
Chobham Place
Staple Hill
Clearmount
Albury Bottom
Steep Hill
Woodcock Lane
Westcroft Park
Valley End Cricket Club
Windlesham Road
Woodcock Dr
Heather Way
Gorse La
Broom Lane
Red Lion
Road
Brimshot Lane
Sandy La
Burrow Hill Gn
WINDSOR ROAD
Little Heath Road
Burrowhill
Mincing Lane
The Avenue
Shrubbs Hill
Ford Road
Thompson's La
Shrubbs Farm
Turfhouse La
Bowling Gn Rd
Windsor Ct
Burr Hill Lane
Fowlers Md
Medhurst Cl
Oakdene
Brookleys
Bracken Wy
Elm Dr
Wishmore Cross School
Delta Cl
Delta Road
Waterperry La
Alpha Road
Beta Rd
Halebourne House
Halebourne Lane
Chobham RFC
Leslie Road
Surgery
The Grange
Macmahon Cl
A319
Barnmead
Green La
CHOBHAM
Watery La
Windsor Rd
HIGH ST
Cannon Crs
Clappers Lane
BAGSHOT ROAD
Police Station
Chobham St Lawrence CE Prim Sch
Brook Place
Beggars La
Brook La
A3046
STATION
ROAD
Coworth Flexlands School
Chobham FC
Castle Grove Road
Broadford
Broadford Lane
Sandpit
Penny Pot
Holy Trinity CE Primary School
Pennypot Lane
Lovelands Lane
Scott's Gv Cl
Scotts Grove Road
Grosvenor Rd
Guildford Road
Castle Green
Millbrook
GU24
Beldam Bridge Road
Rose Meadow
The Oaks
Scotts Grove Rd
Knaphill Manor
G
H
J
K
L
M
96
97
98
64
63
62
61
1
2
3
4
5
6
7
8

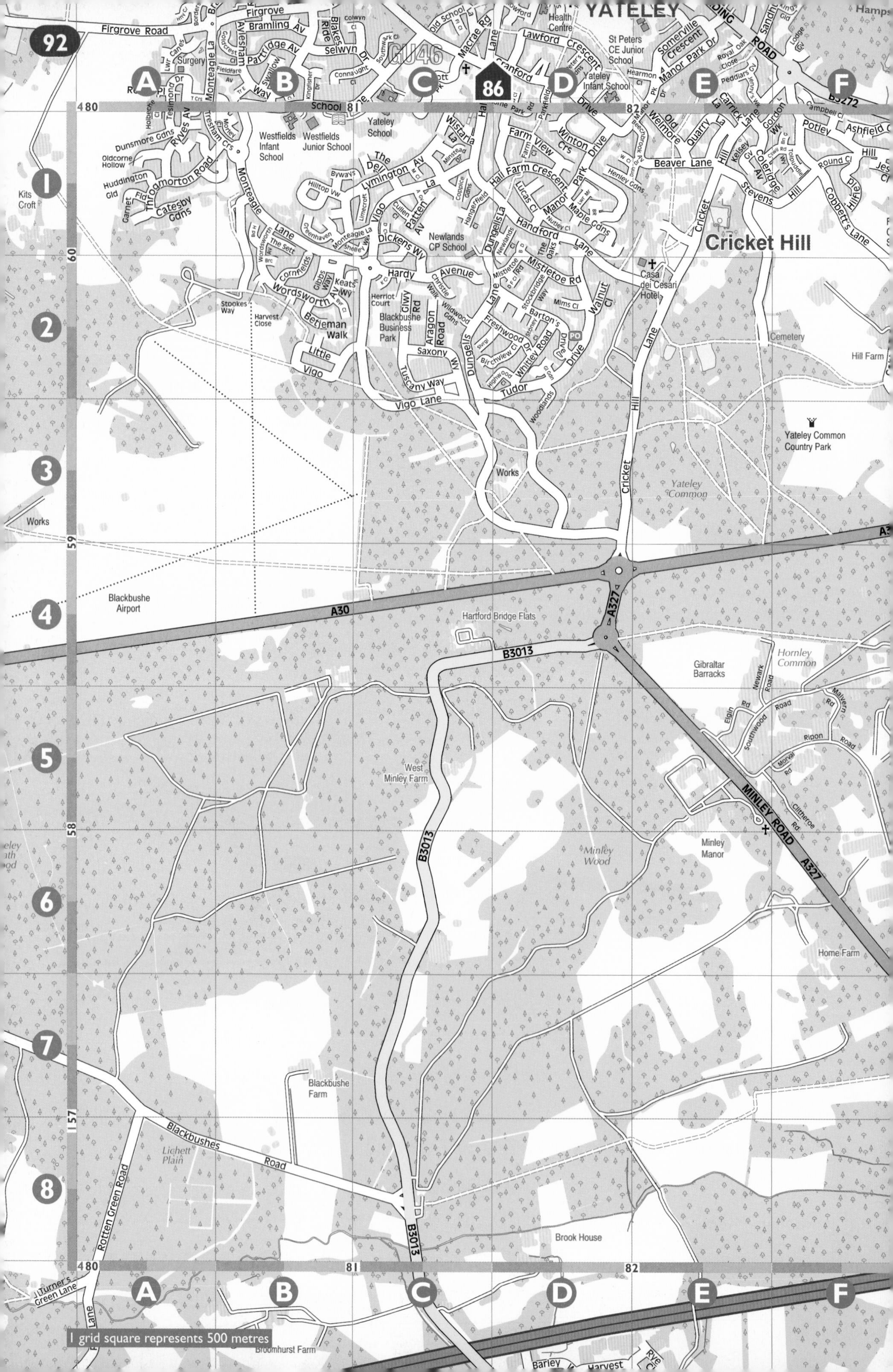

92
86
YATELEY
Cricket Hill
Yateley Common Country Park
Yateley Common
Blackbushe Airport
Hartford Bridge Flats
Gibraltar Barracks
Hornley Common
West Minley Farm
Minley Wood
Minley Manor
Home Farm
Blackbushe Farm
Lichett Plain
Brook House
Broomhurst Farm
Works
Kits Croft
Hill Farm
Cemetery
Westfields Infant School
Westfields Junior School
Yateley School
Newlands CP School
Blackbushe Business Park
Casa dei Cesari Hotel
St Peters CE Junior School
Yateley Infant School
Health Centre
Surgery
Firgrove Road
Blackbushes Road
Rotten Green Road
Vigo Lane
Cricket Hill Lane
Minley Road
A30
A327
B3013
B3272
GU46
1 grid square represents 500 metres

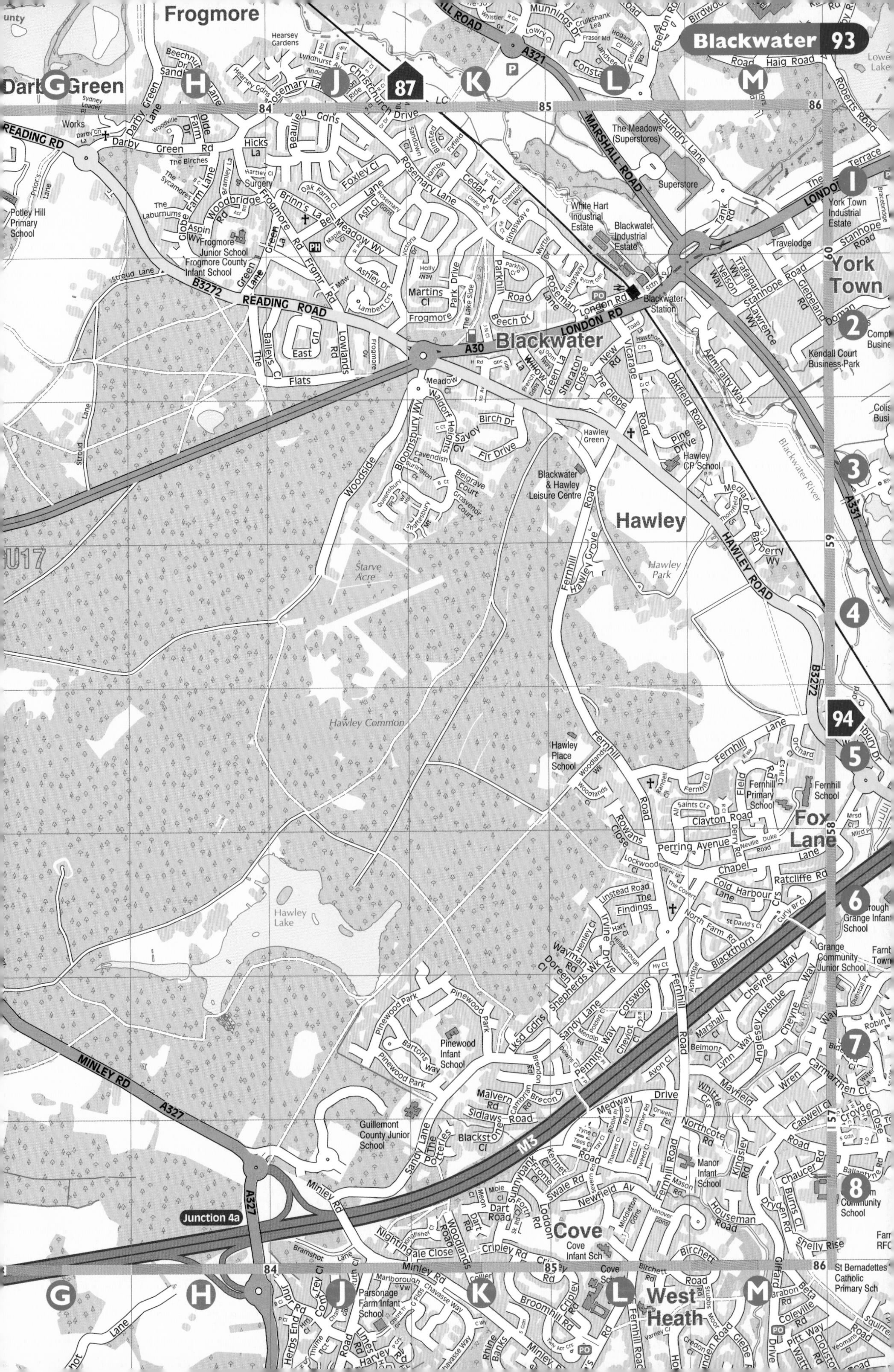

Frogmore
Darby Green
Blackwater
Hawley
York Town
Fox Lane
Cove
West Heath
Hawley Common
Hawley Lake
Starve Acre
Hawley Park
READING RD
READING ROAD
B3272
LONDON RD
A30
MARSHALL ROAD
A321
HAWLEY ROAD
MINLEY RD
A327
M3
Junction 4a
Blackwater Station
The Meadows (Superstores)
Superstore
White Hart Industrial Estate
Blackwater Industrial Estate
York Town Industrial Estate
Kendall Court Business Park
Travelodge
Frogmore Junior School
Frogmore County Infant School
Potley Hill Primary School
Hawley CP School
Blackwater & Hawley Leisure Centre
Hawley Place School
Fernhill Primary School
Fernhill School
Pinewood Infant School
Guillemont County Junior School
Manor Infant School
Cove Infant Sch
Parsonage Farm Infant School
Grange Community Junior School
St Bernadettes Catholic Primary Sch
Blackwater River
Hearsey Gardens
87
94

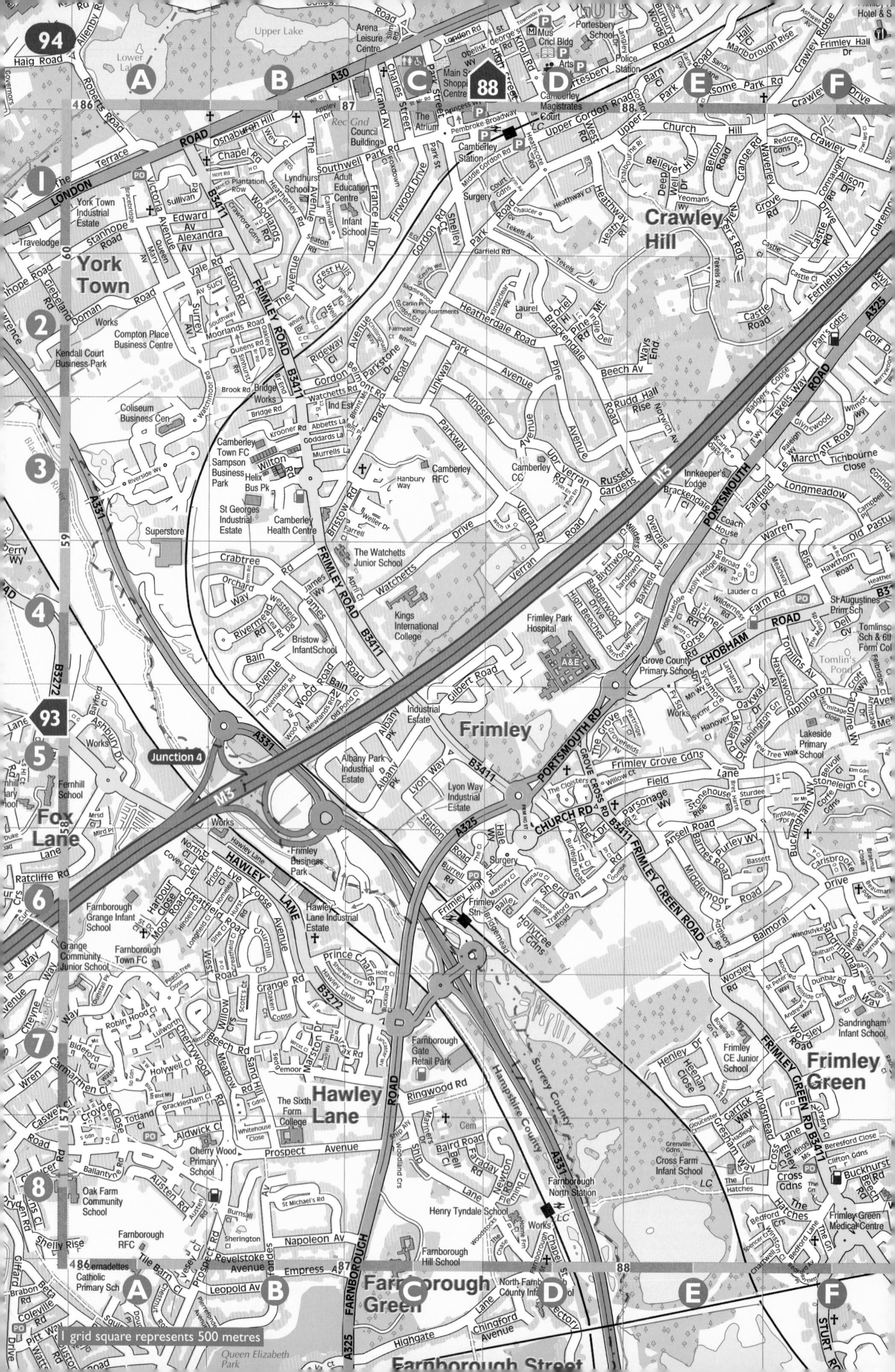

94
93
88
Junction 4
1 grid square represents 500 metres
York Town
Crawley Hill
Frimley
Fox Lane
Hawley Lane
Frimley Green
Farnborough Green
Farnborough Street
Upper Lake
Lower Lake
Arena Leisure Centre
Main Shopping Centre
The Atrium
Council Buildings
Camberley Station
Camberley Magistrates Court
Police Station
Portesbery School
Mus
Cncl Bldg
Arts
Lyndhurst School
Adult Education Centre
Infant School
Surgery
York Town Industrial Estate
Travelodge
Works
Compton Place Business Centre
Kendall Court Business Park
Coliseum Business Cen
Bridge Works
Ind Est
Camberley Town FC
Sampson Business Park
Helix Bus Pk
St Georges Industrial Estate
Camberley Health Centre
Superstore
Camberley RFC
Camberley CC
The Watchetts Junior School
Kings International College
Bristow Infant School
Frimley Park Hospital
A&E
Innkeeper's Lodge
Coach House
Grove County Primary School
St Augustines Prim Sch
Tomlin's Pond
Lakeside Primary School
Industrial Estate
Albany Park Industrial Estate
Lyon Way Industrial Estate
Frimley Business Park
Hawley Lane Industrial Estate
Frimley Stn
Fernhill School
Farnborough Grange Infant School
Grange Community Junior School
Farnborough Town FC
Farnborough Gate Retail Park
The Sixth Form College
Cherry Wood Primary School
Oak Farm Community School
Farnborough RFC
Henry Tyndale School
Farnborough Hill School
Farnborough North Station
Frimley CE Junior School
Cross Farm Infant School
Sandringham Infant School
Frimley Green Medical Centre
North Farnborough County Infant School
Queen Elizabeth Park
Surrey County
Hampshire County
LONDON ROAD
A30
M3
A331
A325
B3411
B3272
FRIMLEY ROAD
PORTSMOUTH ROAD
CHOBHAM ROAD
FRIMLEY GREEN ROAD
HAWLEY LANE
FARNBOROUGH ROAD

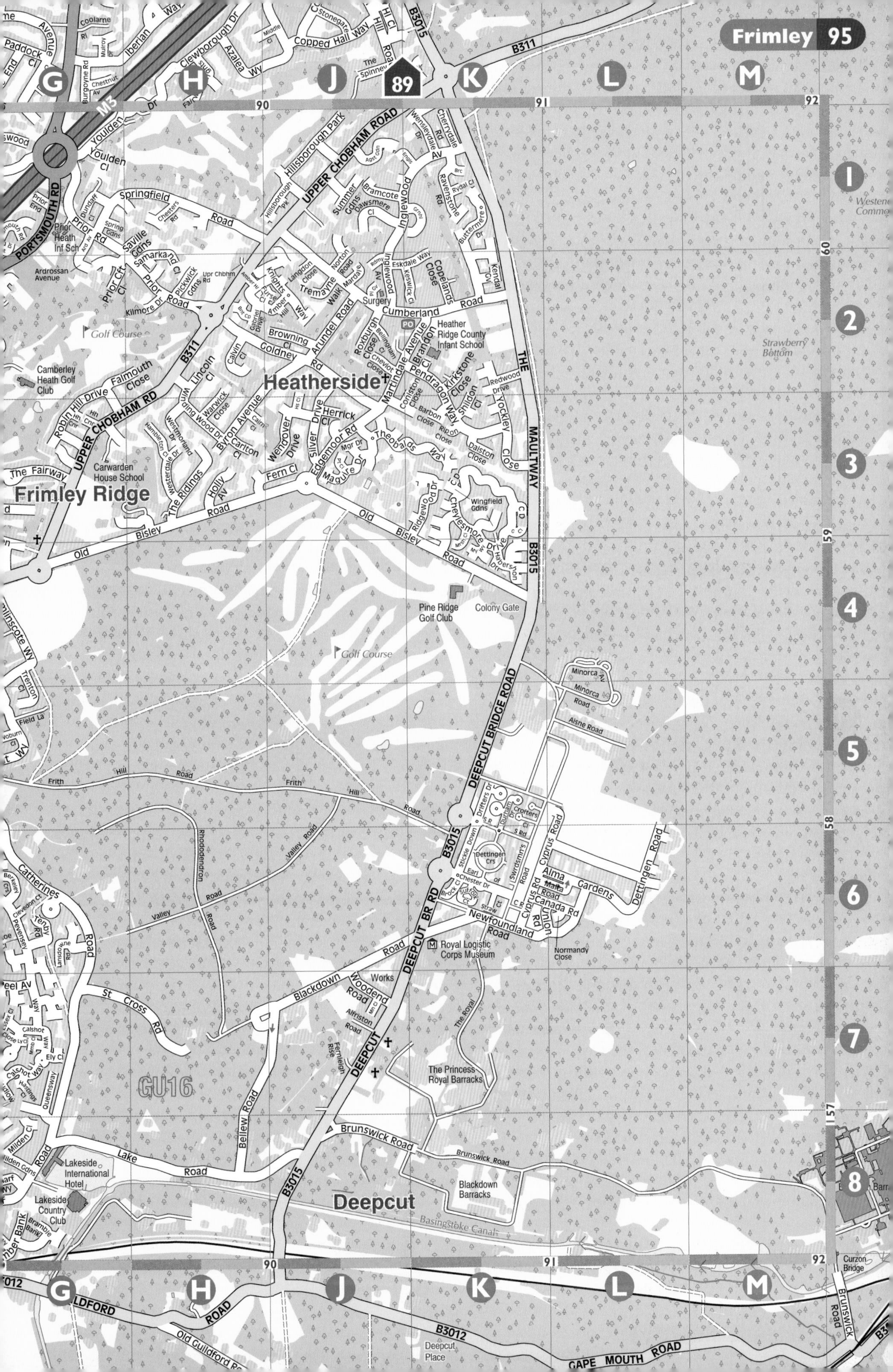

Heatherside
Frimley Ridge
Deepcut
UPPER CHOBHAM ROAD
UPPER CHOBHAM RD
PORTSMOUTH RD
THE MAULTWAY
DEEPCUT BRIDGE ROAD
DEEPCUT BR RD
B3015
B311
B3012
M3
Springfield Road
Prior Road
Old Bisley Road
Cumberland Road
Frith Hill Road
Valley Road
Rhododendron Road
Blackdown Road
Brunswick Road
Lake Road
Newfoundland Road
Dettingen Road
Alma Gardens
Minorca Road
Aisne Road
Bellew Road
St Cross Rd
Catherines Road
Hillsborough Park
Copped Hall Way
Clewborough Dr
Iberian Way
Azalea Wy
Youlden Dr
Youlden Cl
Arundel Road
Goldney Rd
Browning Cl
Martindale Avenue
Pendragon Way
Kilkstone Close
Yockley Close
Byron Avenue
Winding Wood Dr
Lincoln Cl
Falmouth Close
Robin Hill Drive
The Ridings
Holly Av
Fern Cl
Edgemoor Rd
Silver Drive
Wendover Drive
Herrick Cl
Theobalds Way
Tremayne Walk
Inglewood Av
Copelands Close
Kendal Gr
Buttermere Dr
Ravenstone Rd
Cherrydale Rd
Wensleydale Dr
Saville Gdns
Samarkand Cl
Ardrossan Avenue
Heather Ridge County Infant School
Prior Heath Inf Sch
Carwarden House School
Camberley Heath Golf Club
Golf Course
Pine Ridge Golf Club
Colony Gate
Strawberry Bottom
Westend Common
Royal Logistic Corps Museum
Works
The Princess Royal Barracks
Blackdown Barracks
Lakeside International Hotel
Lakeside Country Club
Basingstoke Canal
Curzon Bridge
Deepcut Place
GAPE MOUTH ROAD
Old Guildford Rd
GUILDFORD ROAD
GU16
Surgery
PO
89
G H J K L M
90 91 92
1 2 3 4 5 6 7 8
60 59 58 157

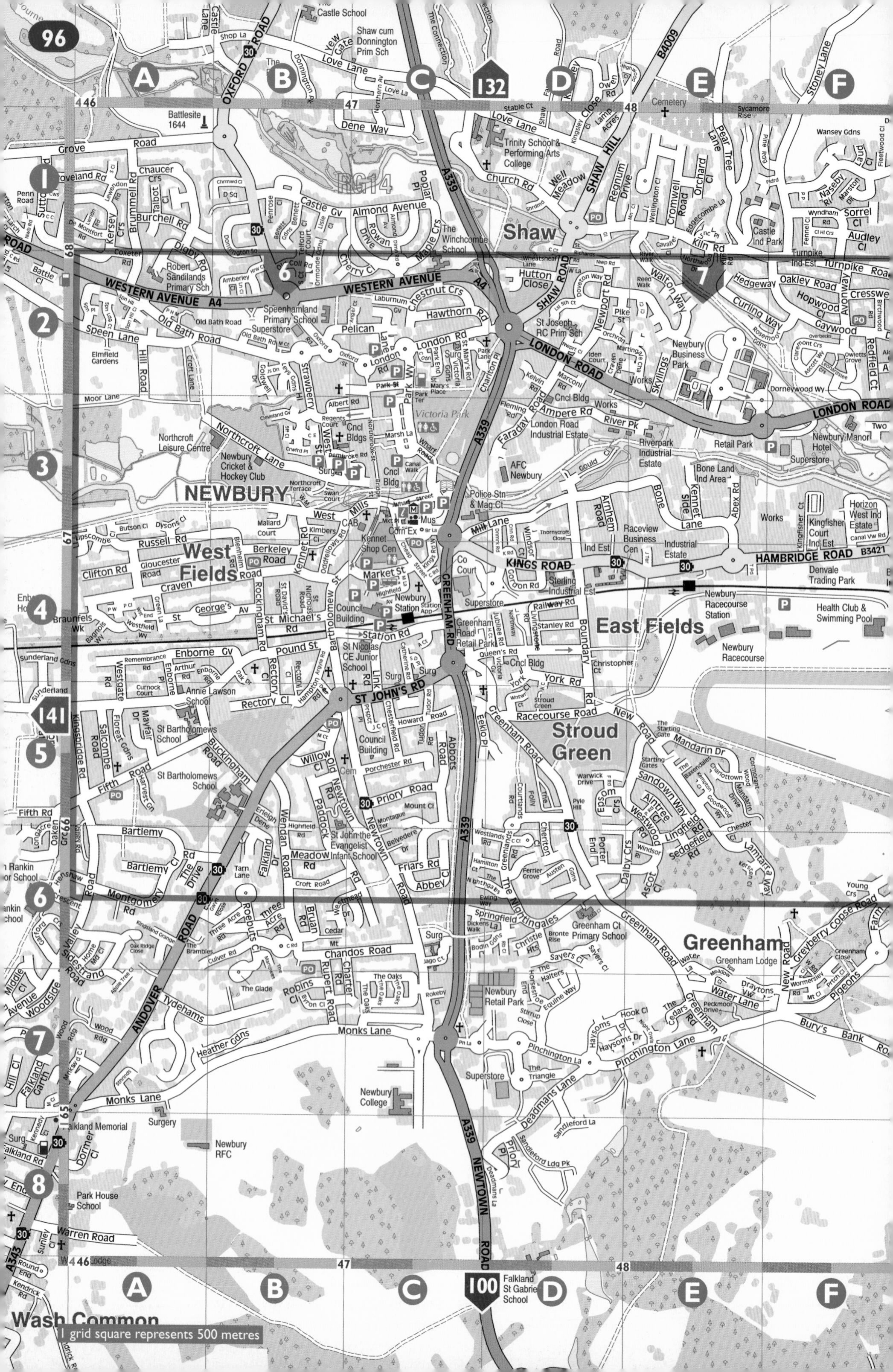

A **B** **C** **D** **E** **F**

RG14

132

NEWBURY

West Fields

Shaw

London Road

East Fields

Stroud Green

Greenham

141

100

Wash Common

1 grid square represents 500 metres

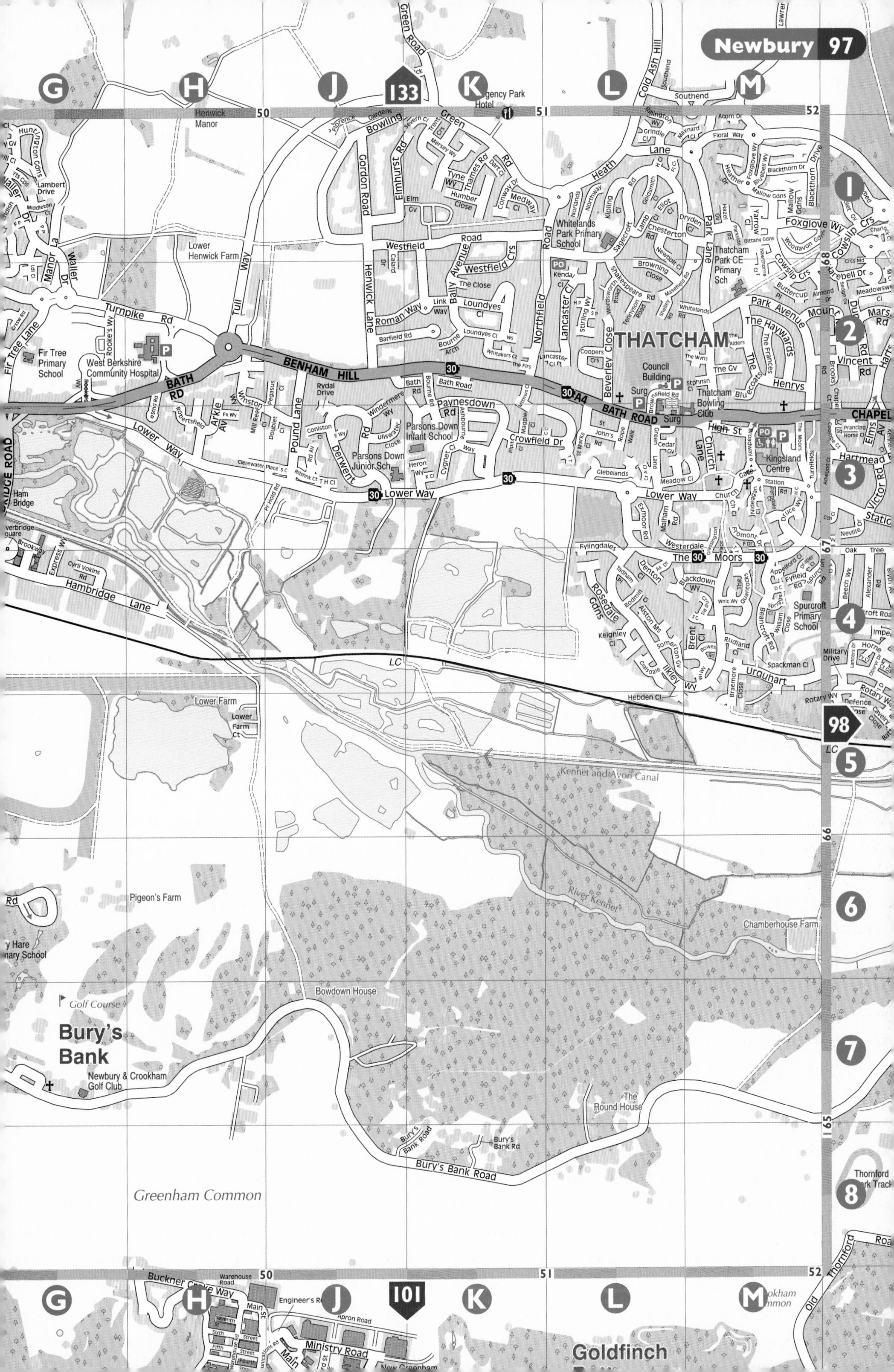

G H J 133 K L M

I

Henwick Manor

Lower Henwick Farm

Fir Tree Primary School

Waller Dr

Manor Dr

Lambert Drive

Middleton

Hungerford Gdns

Turnpike Rd

Rocke's Close

West Berkshire Community Hospital

BATH RD

Lower Way

Ham Bridge

BENHAM HILL

BRIDGE ROAD

Everbridge quare

Brookway

Express Wy

Cyril Vokins Rd

HAMBRIDGE LANE

Tull Way

Henwick Lane

Elmhurst Rd

Gordon Road

Bowling

Green Road

133

Regency Park Hotel

Cold Ash Hill

Southend

Southend

Acorn Dr

Floral Way

Tyne Wy

Thames Rd

Humber Close

Conway Dr

Medway Cl

Mersey Wy

Heath Road

Lane

Maynard Cl

Grindle

Foxglove Wy

Mallow Gdns

Blackthorn Dr

Bluebell Wy

Meadowsweet

Cowslip Crs

Harebell Dr

I

Westfield Road

Westfield Crs

Whitelands Park Primary School

Park Lane

Lamb Cl

Chesterton Rd

Browning Close

Shakespeare Rd

Woodavon Ct

Buttercup

Almond Cl

Park Avenue

Mount

Mars Rd

2

Calard Dr

The Close

Roman Way

Bally Avenue

Loundyes Cl

Link Way

Northfield Road

Lancaster Cl

Kendal

PO

THATCHAM

Council Building

The Haywards

The Frances

The Escorts

Henrys

Vincent Rd

2

Barfield Rd

Bourne Arch

Whitakers Ct

Lancaster Crs

The Firs

Coopers Crs

Beverley Close

Surg

P

Thatcham Bowling Club

The GV

The Alders

CHAPEL

Hartmead

Elms Av

3

Arkle Av

Winston

Pegasus

Pound Lane

Rydal Drive

Bath Rd

Bath Road

30

30 A4

BATH ROAD

High St

St John's Rd

Church Lane

PO

P

Kingsland Centre

Victor Rd

Static

3

Robertsfield

Doublet

Mill Reef

Windermere Wy

Ulleswater

E Wy

Parsons Down Infant School

Paynesdown Rd

Ashbourne

Crowfield Dr

Maple Cl

St Cedars

Meadow Cl

Glebelands

Church

Lower Way

Exmoor Rd

Clerewater Place S C

Coniston Ct

Derwent

Cygnet Cl

Heron

Parsons Down Junior Sch

30

Lower Way

Lower Way

Church

Malham Rd

Fromont

Neville

Oak Tree

4

30

The Moors

30

Rosedale Gdns

Denton Wy

Blackdown Wy

Appleford Cl

Fyfield Rd

Spurcroft Rd

Spurcroft Primary School

Beech Wk

Alexander

Horne

Croft Rd

Impe

4

Keighley

Ilkley

Brent Wy

Braemore Close

Rutland

William

Spackman Cl

Urquhart

Military Drive

Hebden Cl

Rotary Wy

efence

wen

5

LC

98

LC

5

Lower Farm

Lower Farm Ct

Kennet and Avon Canal

6

Pigeon's Farm

River Kennet

Chamberhouse Farm

6

Hare ary School

Rd

Golf Course

Bury's Bank

Bowdown House

The Round House

7

Newbury & Crookham Golf Club

Bury's Bank Rd

Bury's Bank Road

Thornford ark Track

8

Greenham Common

Warehouse Road

Engineer's R

Apron Road

Main

Ministry Road

New Greenham

Mokham ommon

Old Thornford

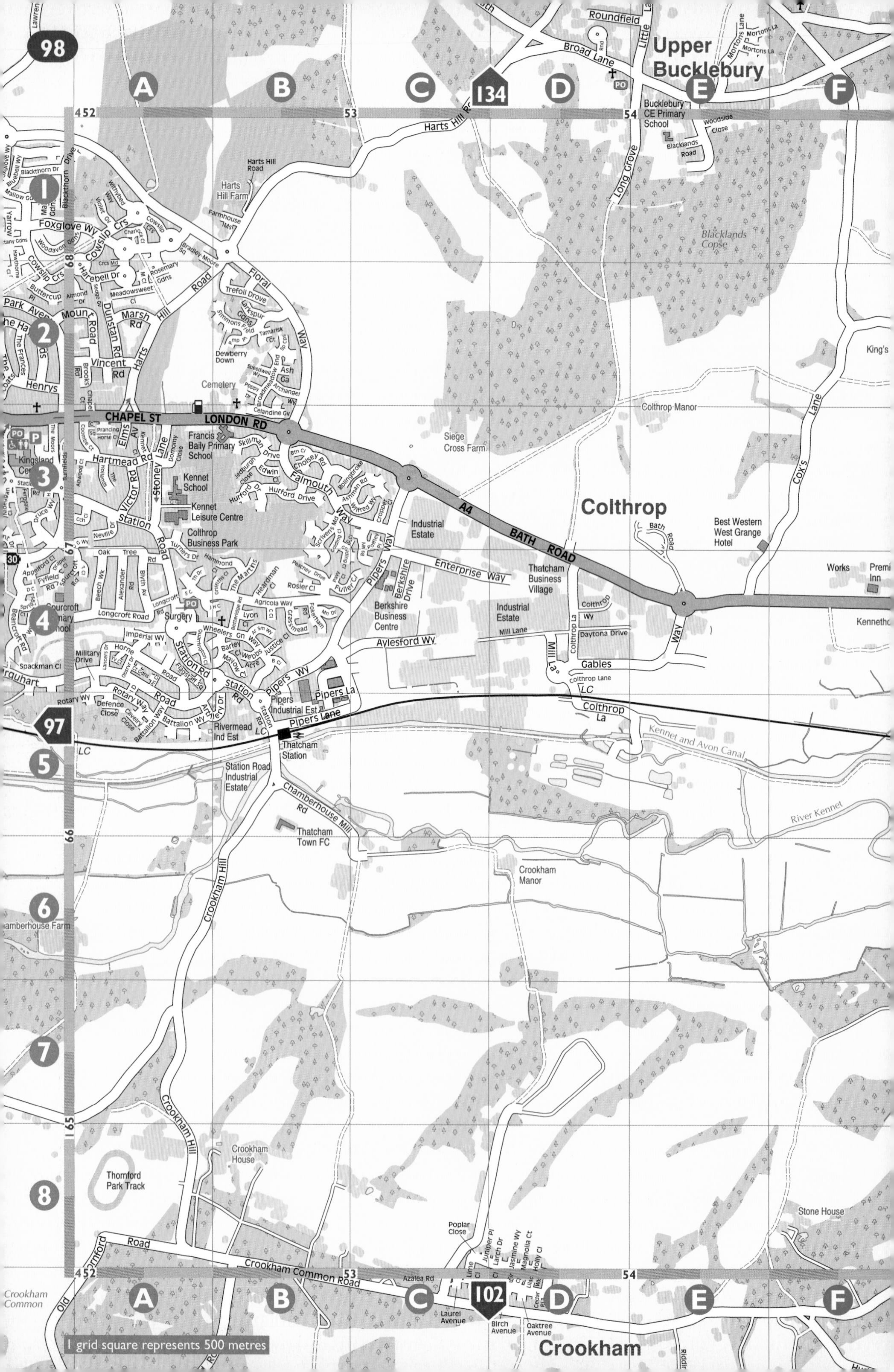
98
A
B
C
134
D
E
F
Upper Bucklebury
Roundfield
Broad Lane
Little La
Mortons Lane
Mortons La
PO
Bucklebury CE Primary School
Woodside Close
Blacklands Road
Harts Hill Rd
Harts Hill Road
Harts Hill Farm
Long Grove
Blacklands Copse
Blackthorn Drive
Foxglove Wy
Cowslip Crs
Harebell Dr
Meadowsweet Cl
Bradley-Moore
Floral Way
Trefoil Drove
Marsh Rd
Mount Road
Dunstan Rd
Harts Hill Road
Park Avenue
Buttercup Pl
The Frances
Vincent Rd
Henrys
Cemetery
Dewberry Down
Broadmeadow End
Ash Ga
Celandine Gv
Colthrop Manor
King's
CHAPEL ST
LONDON RD
Francis Baily Primary School
Kennet School
Kennet Leisure Centre
Colthrop Business Park
Hartmead Rd
Victor Rd
Stoney Lane
Station Road
Kingsland Centre
Falmouth Way
Hurford Drive
Siege Cross Farm
Industrial Estate
A4 BATH ROAD
Colthrop
Best Western West Grange Hotel
Cox's Lane
Works
Premier Inn
Kennetholme
Enterprise Way
Thatcham Business Village
Pipers Way
Berkshire Drive
Berkshire Business Centre
Industrial Estate
Mill Lane
Colthrop La
Daytona Drive
Gables
Mill La
Way
Aylesford Wy
Longcroft Road
Surgery
Oak Tree Rd
Station Rd
Pipers Industrial Est
Pipers La
Pipers Lane
Colthrop Lane
LC
Colthrop La
Rotary Way
Battalion Wy
Artillery Dr
Rivermead Ind Est
Thatcham Station
97
5
LC
Kennet and Avon Canal
Station Road Industrial Estate
Chamberhouse Mill Rd
Thatcham Town FC
River Kennet
Crookham Manor
Crookham Hill
6
Chamberhouse Farm
7
Crookham House
Thornford Park Track
8
Stone House
Poplar Close
Thornford Road
Crookham Common Road
Azalea Rd
102
Crookham Common
Laurel Avenue
Birch Avenue
Oaktree Avenue
Crookham
1 grid square represents 500 metres
452
53
54
68
67
66
165

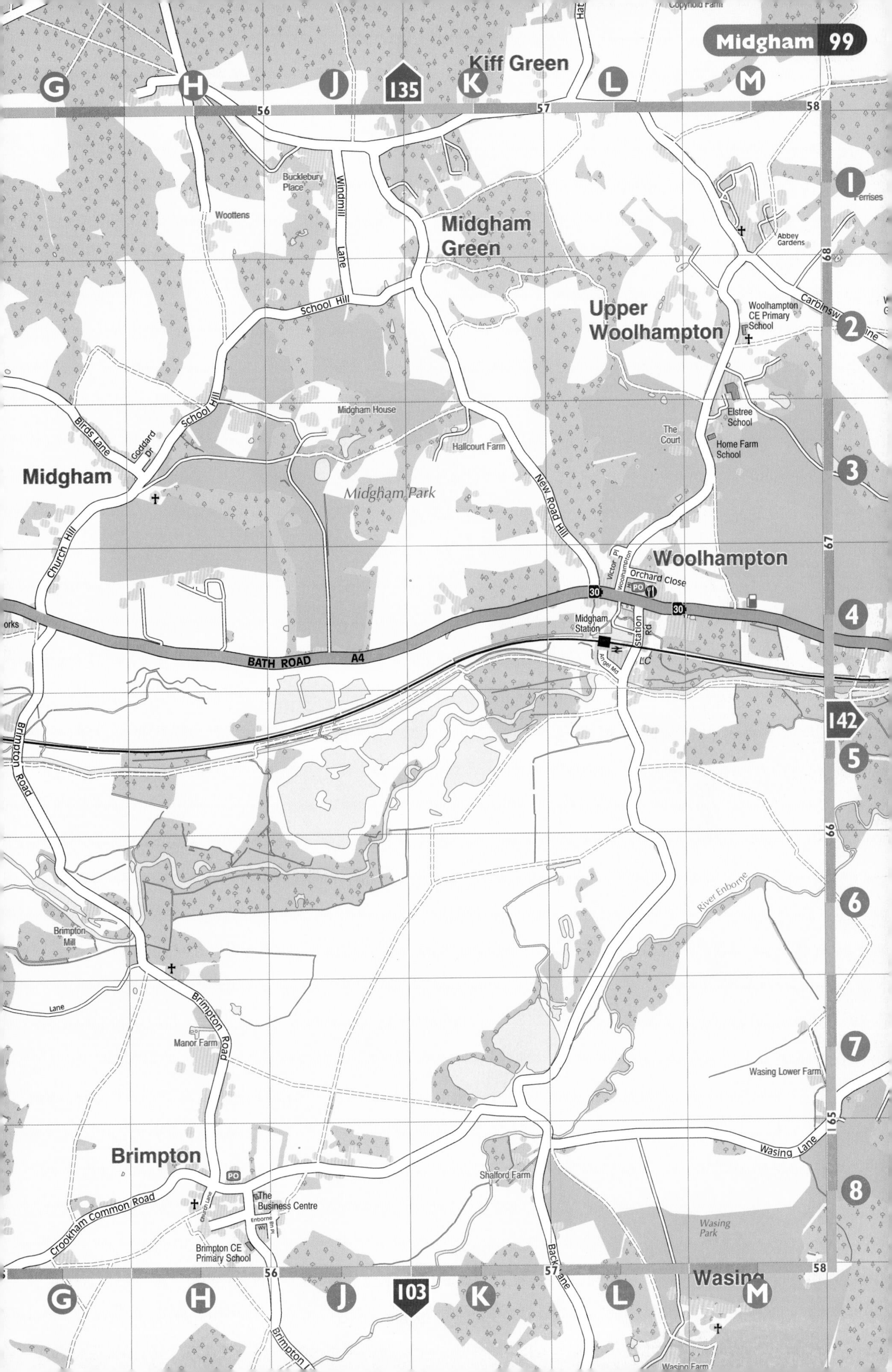

Kiff Green

G   H   J   135   K   L   M

56   57   58

I
Ferrises

2

3

Midgham
Green

Upper
Woolhampton

Woolhampton CE Primary School

Elstree School

The Court

Home Farm School

Abbey Gardens

Carbinsw... Lane

68

Midgham

School Hill

Windmill Lane

Bucklebury Place

Woottens

Birds Lane

Goddard Dr

School Hill

Church Hill

Midgham House

Midgham Park

Hallcourt Farm

New Road Hill

Woolhampton

Victor Pl

Orchard Close

PO

30

30

Midgham Station

Station Rd

Woolhampton

Angel Mead

L/C

4

67

...orks

BATH ROAD   A4

142

5

Brimpton Road

Brimpton Mill

Lane

Brimpton Road

Manor Farm

River Enborne

Wasing Lower Farm

66

6

7

Brimpton

PO

The Business Centre

Church Lane

Shalford Farm

Back Lane

Wasing Lane

Wasing Park

65

8

Crookham Common Road

Enborne W...

Brimpton CE Primary School

Wasing

G   H   J   103   K   L   M

56   57   58

Wasing Farm

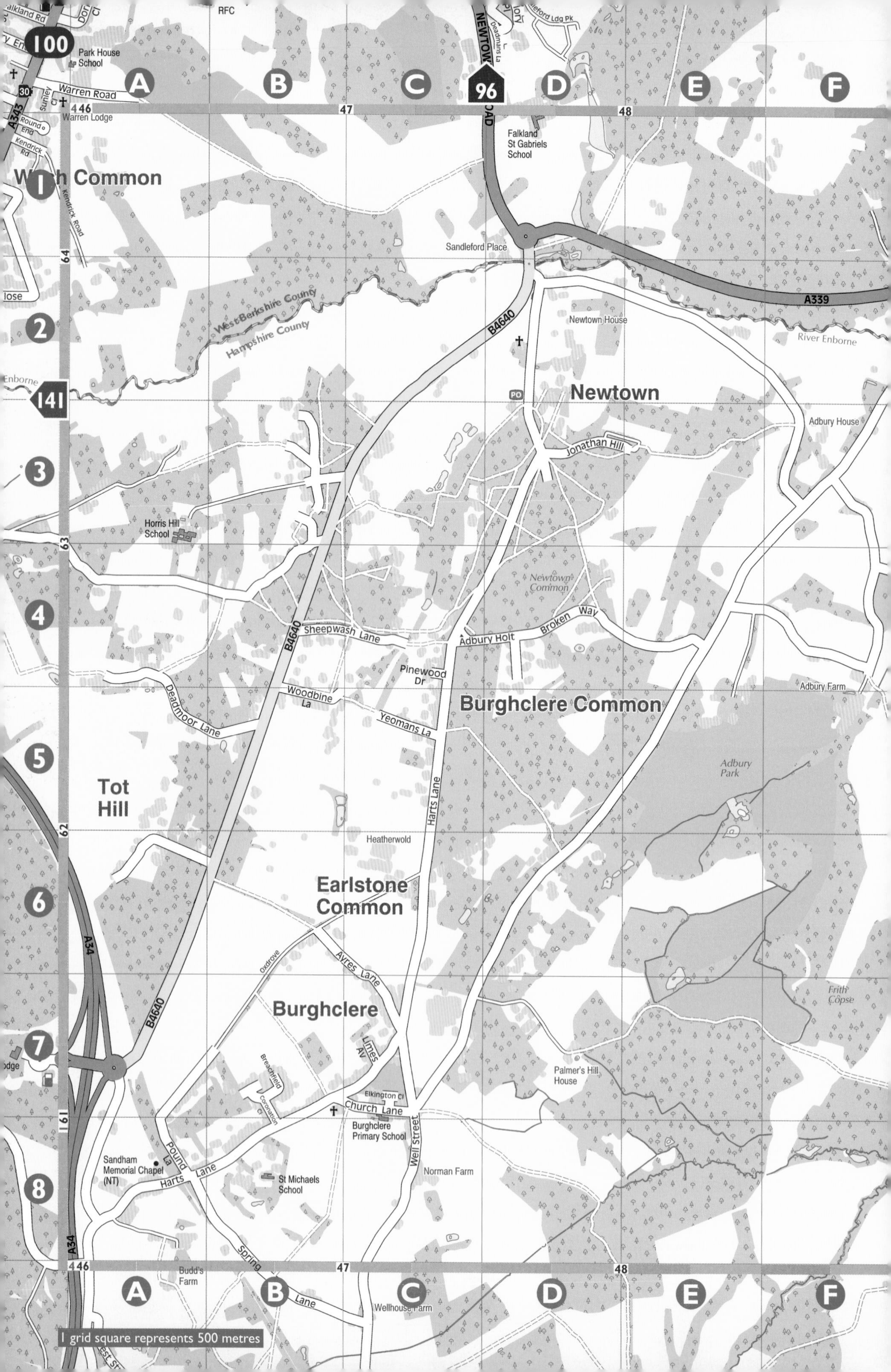

100
96
141
Park House School
Warren Road
Warren Lodge
RFC
Falkland St Gabriels School
Sandleford Place
Woolton Common
Kendrick Road
West Berkshire County
Hampshire County
B4640
A339
A343
A34
Newtown House
River Enborne
Enborne
Newtown
Adbury House
Jonathan Hill
Horris Hill School
Newtown Common
Sheepwash Lane
Adbury Holt
Broken Way
Pinewood Dr
Woodbine La
Yeomans La
Deadmoor Lane
Burghclere Common
Adbury Farm
Adbury Park
Tot Hill
Harts Lane
Heatherwold
Earlstone Common
Ayres Lane
Oxdrove
Burghclere
Limes Av
Frith Copse
Palmer's Hill House
Elkington Cl
Church Lane
Burghclere Primary School
Well Street
Breachfield
Coronation Cl
Sandham Memorial Chapel (NT)
Pound La
Harts Lane
St Michaels School
Norman Farm
Spring Lane
Budd's Farm
Wellhouse Farm
Newtown Road
Deadmans La
A B C D E F
1 2 3 4 5 6 7 8
446 47 48
64 63 62 61
1 grid square represents 500 metres

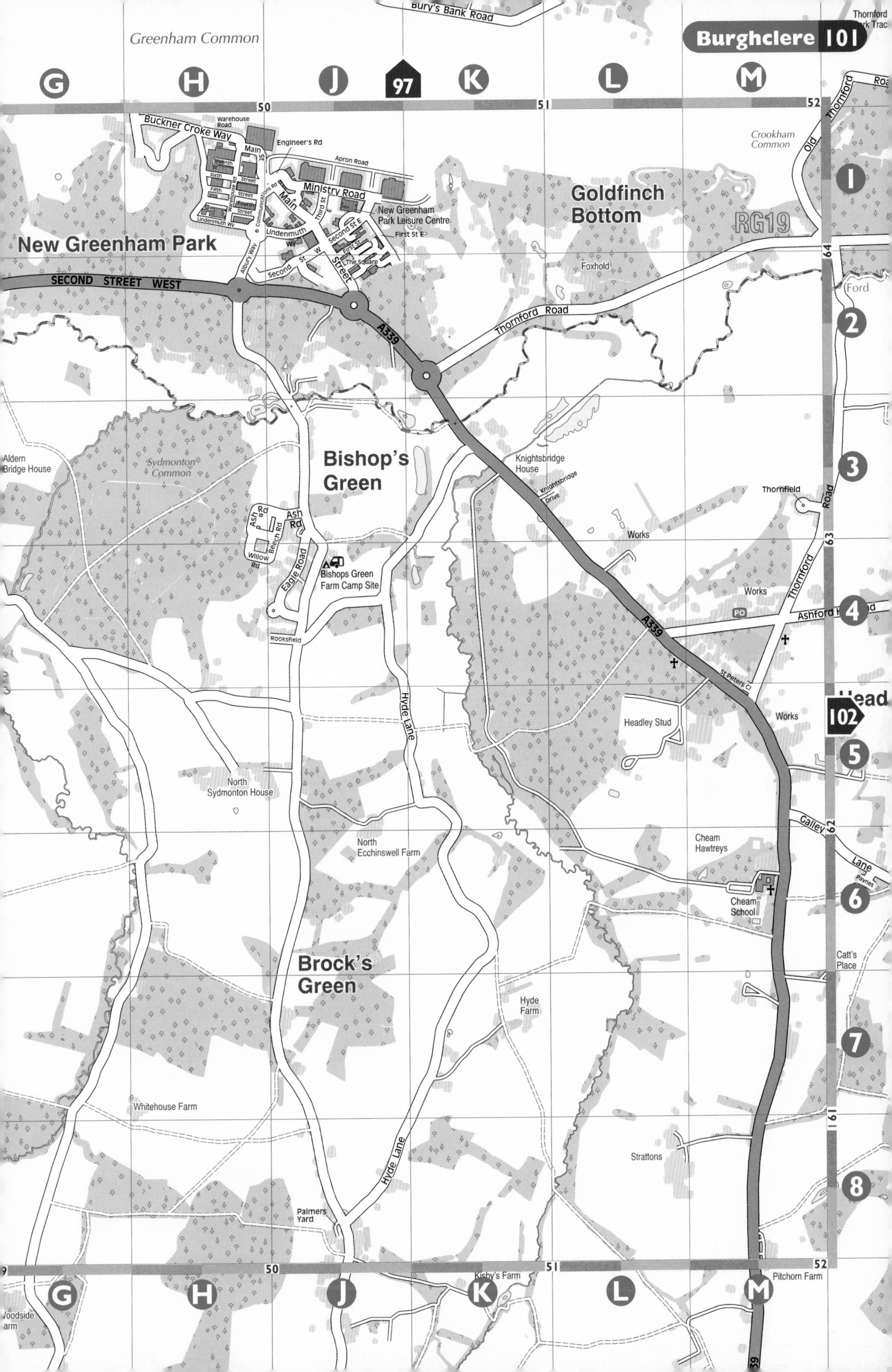

Greenham Common

Bury's Bank Road

Thornford Park Trac

G 50 **H** **J** ▮**97** **K** 51 **L** **M** 52 Old Thornford Road

Buckner Croke Way

Warehouse Road

Main St

Engineer's Rd

Apron Road

Crookham Common

I

Ministry Road

New Greenham Park Leisure Centre

RG19

Goldfinch Bottom

Foxhold

New Greenham Park

Lindenmuth

The Square

First St E

Communications Rd

64

Ford

SECOND STREET WEST

Thornford Road

2

A339

Thornford Road

3

Knightsbridge House

Aldern Bridge House

Sydmonton Common

Knightsbridge Drive

Thornfield

Bishop's Green

Works

63

Ash Rd

Ash Rd

Beech Rd

Works

Willow Rd

Eagle Road

▲ Bishops Green Farm Camp Site

PO

Ashford Hill

4

St Peter's Ct

Rooksfield

✝

A339

Head **102**

Headley Stud

Works

5

North Sydmonton House

Hyde Lane

62

Galley Lane

Paynes

North Ecchinswell Farm

Cheam Hawtreys

6

Cheam School

✝

Catt's Place

Brock's Green

Hyde Farm

7

Whitehouse Farm

61

Strattons

8

Palmers Yard

Woodside Farm

G 50 **H** **J** 51 Kisby's Farm **K** **L** **M** 52 Pitchorn Farm

A339

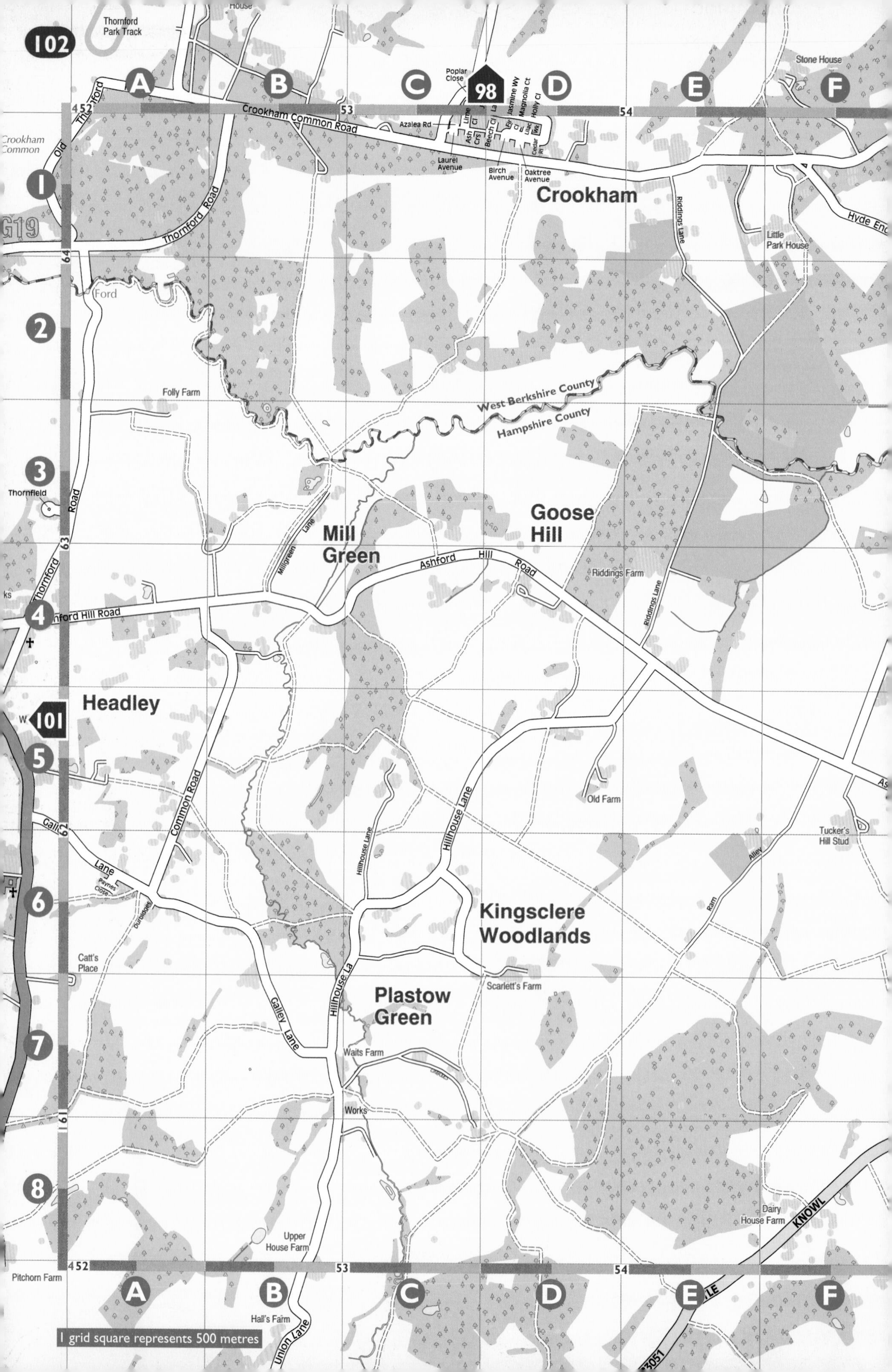

A **B** **C** **D** **E** **F**

4 52 53 54

Thornford Park Track

House

Old Thornford

Crookham Common Road

98

Poplar Close

Jasmine Wy
Magnolia Ct
Holly Cl

Azalea Rd

Lime Cl
Ash Crs
Beech Cl La

Laurel Avenue

Birch Avenue

Oaktree Avenue

Cedar Rd

Crookham

Stone House

Crookham Common

Little Park House

Hyde End

64

1

G19

Ford

Thornford Road

Riddings Lane

2

Folly Farm

Thornford 63 Road

West Berkshire County

Hampshire County

3

Thornfield

Mill Green

Goose Hill

Riddings Farm

Riddings Lane

ks

Ashford Hill Road

Ashford Hill Road

4

Thornford 63

Millgreen Lane

As

Headley

W **101**

Old Farm

Tucker's Hill Stud

5

Common Road

Hillhouse Lane

Hillhouse Lane

Galley 62 Lane

Ram

Alley

6

Payne's Close

Lane

Dukbridge

Catt's Place

Kingsclere Woodlands

Scarlett's Farm

Hillhouse La

Galley Lane

Plastow Green

7

61

Waits Farm

8

Works

Upper House Farm

Dairy House Farm

KNOWL

4 52 53 54

A **B** **C** **D** **E** **F**

Pitchorn Farm

Union Lane

Hall's Farm

LE

B3051

1 grid square represents 500 metres

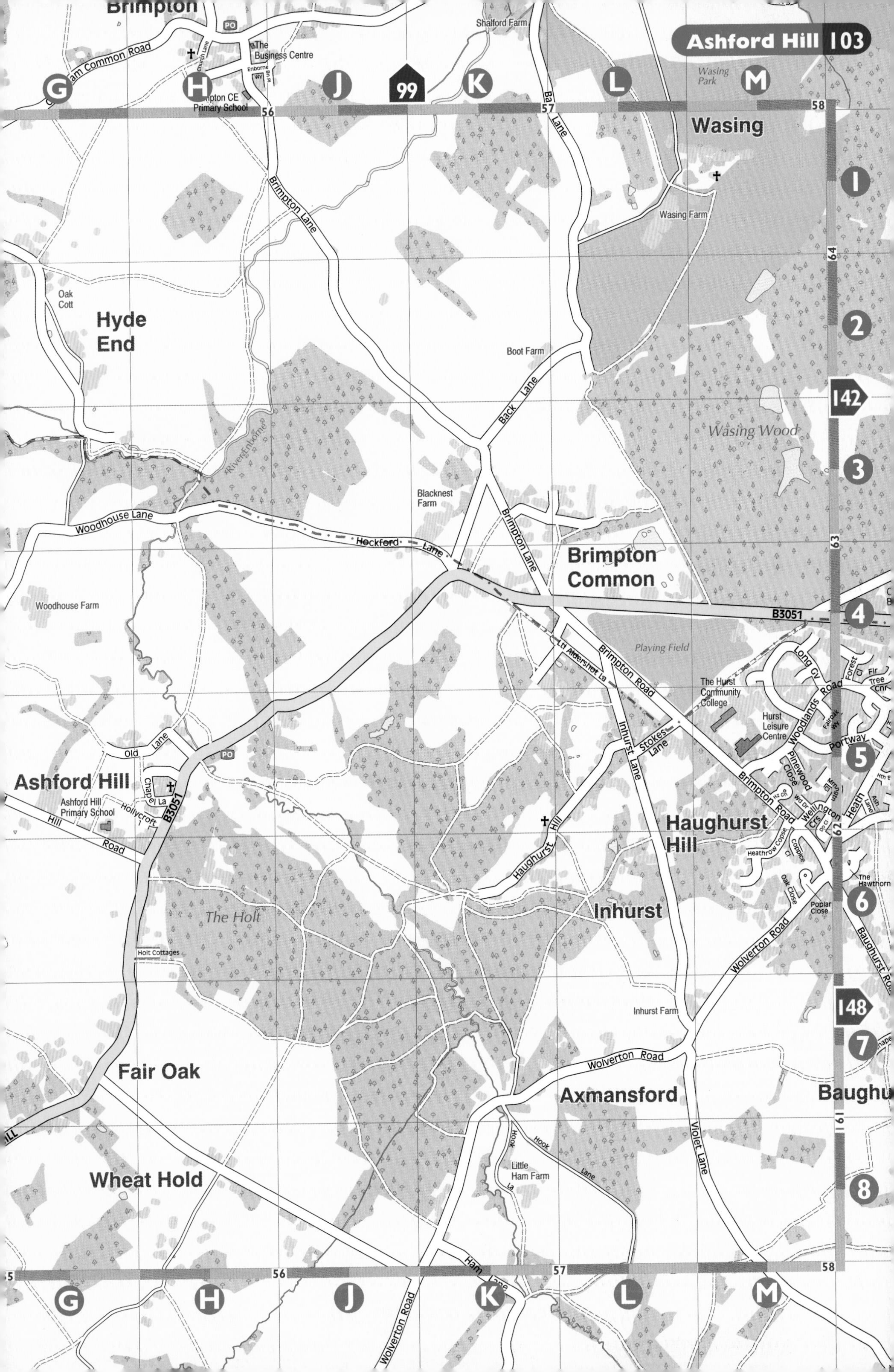

Brimpton

G
Gm Common Road
H
PO
Enborne
The Business Centre
Brimpton CE
Primary School
Church Lane
J
99
K
Ba Lane
L
Wasing Park
M
Shalford Farm
Wasing

56
57
58

Oak Cott

Hyde End

Wasing Farm

I

64

142

Boot Farm

Back Lane

Rivergnborne

2

Wasing Wood

3

Woodhouse Lane

Blacknest Farm

Brimpton Lane

63

Brimpton Common

Hockford Lane

Woodhouse Farm

B3051

4

Playing Field

La Aldershot La

Brimpton Road

The Hurst Community College

Long Gv

Forest

Fir Tree Cnr

Hurst Leisure Centre

Woodlands Road

Foxcoll Wy

5

Old Lane
PO

Pinewood

Welllington Cls

Portway

Ashford Hill

Chapel La

Ashford Hill Primary School

Hollycroft

B3051

Haughurst Hill

62

Heath

Haughurst Hill

Hill Road

Heathrow Copse

Cottage

Inhurst

Oak Close

The Hawthorn

6

The Holt

Inhurst Lane

Stokes Lane

Poplar Close

Baughurst Rd

Holt Cottages

148

Inhurst Farm

7

Fair Oak

Wolverton Road

Axmansford

Violet Lane

Baughu

61

Wheat Hold

Hook La

Little Ham Farm

Hook Lane

Ham Lane

8

55
56
57
58

G
H
J
K
L
M

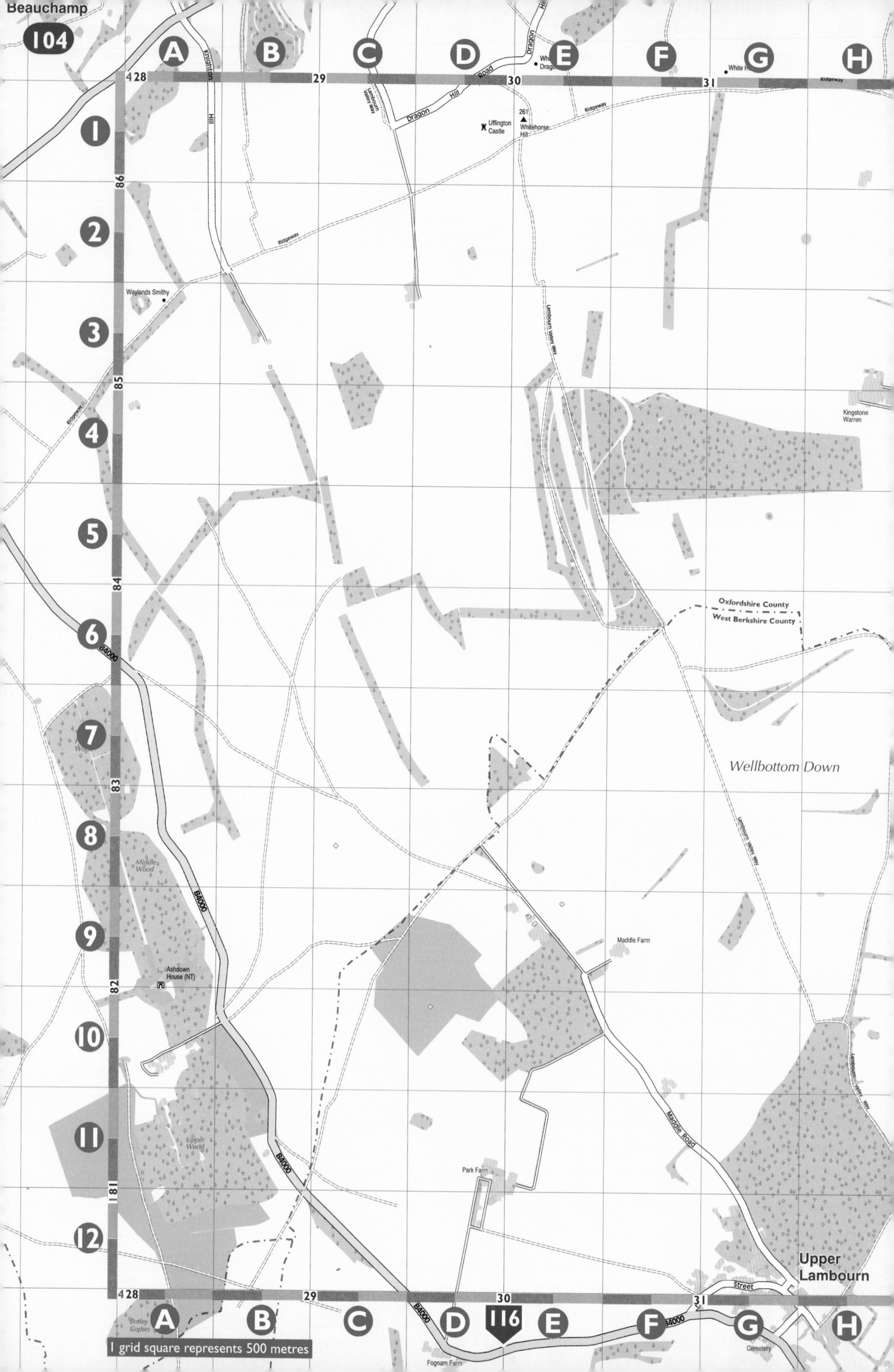

Beauchamp
104
A
B
C
D
E
F
G
H
428
29
30
31
1
2
3
4
5
6
7
8
9
10
11
12
86
85
84
83
82
181
Knighton Hill
Dragon Hill Road
Lambourn Valley Way
Uffington Castle
261
Whitehorse Hill
Ridgeway
White Horse
Waylands Smithy
Kingstone Warren
Oxfordshire County
West Berkshire County
Wellbottom Down
B4000
Middles Wood
Ashdown House (NT)
Upper Wood
Maddle Farm
Maddle Road
Park Farm
Upper Lambourn
Street
116
Botley Copses
Cemetery
Fognam Farm
1 grid square represents 500 metres

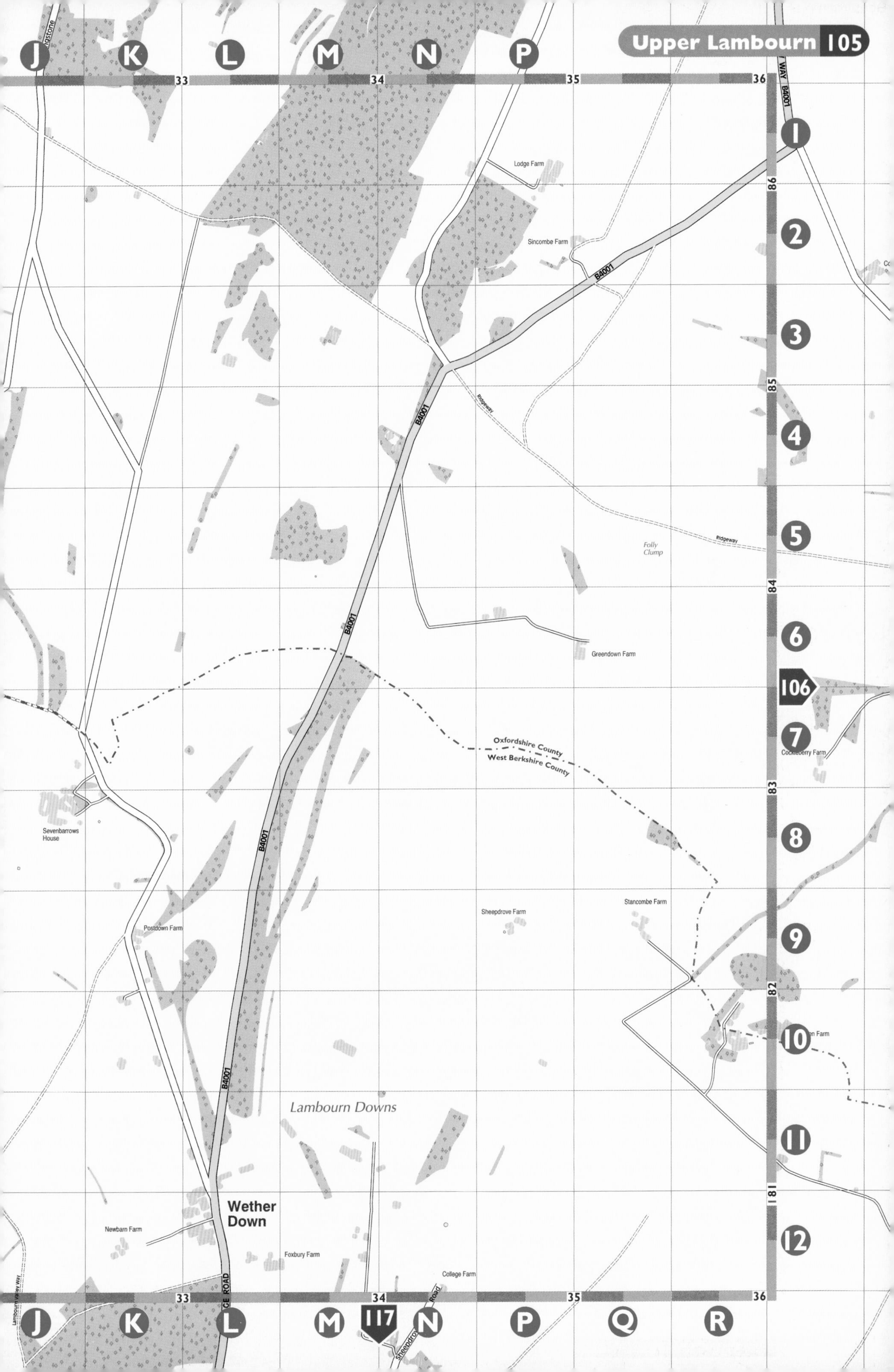

J K L M N P

33 34 35 36

WAY B4001

Lodge Farm

Sincombe Farm

B4001

Rogersett

B4001

Folly
Clump

Ridgeway

Greendown Farm

106

Oxfordshire County
West Berkshire County

Cockleberry Farm

Sevenbarrows
House

Sheepdrove Farm

Stancombe Farm

Postdown Farm

on Farm

Lambourn Downs

Newbarn Farm

Wether
Down

Foxbury Farm

College Farm

J K L M N P Q R

33 34 35 36

Lambourn Valley Way

GE ROAD

B4001

Sheepdrove Road

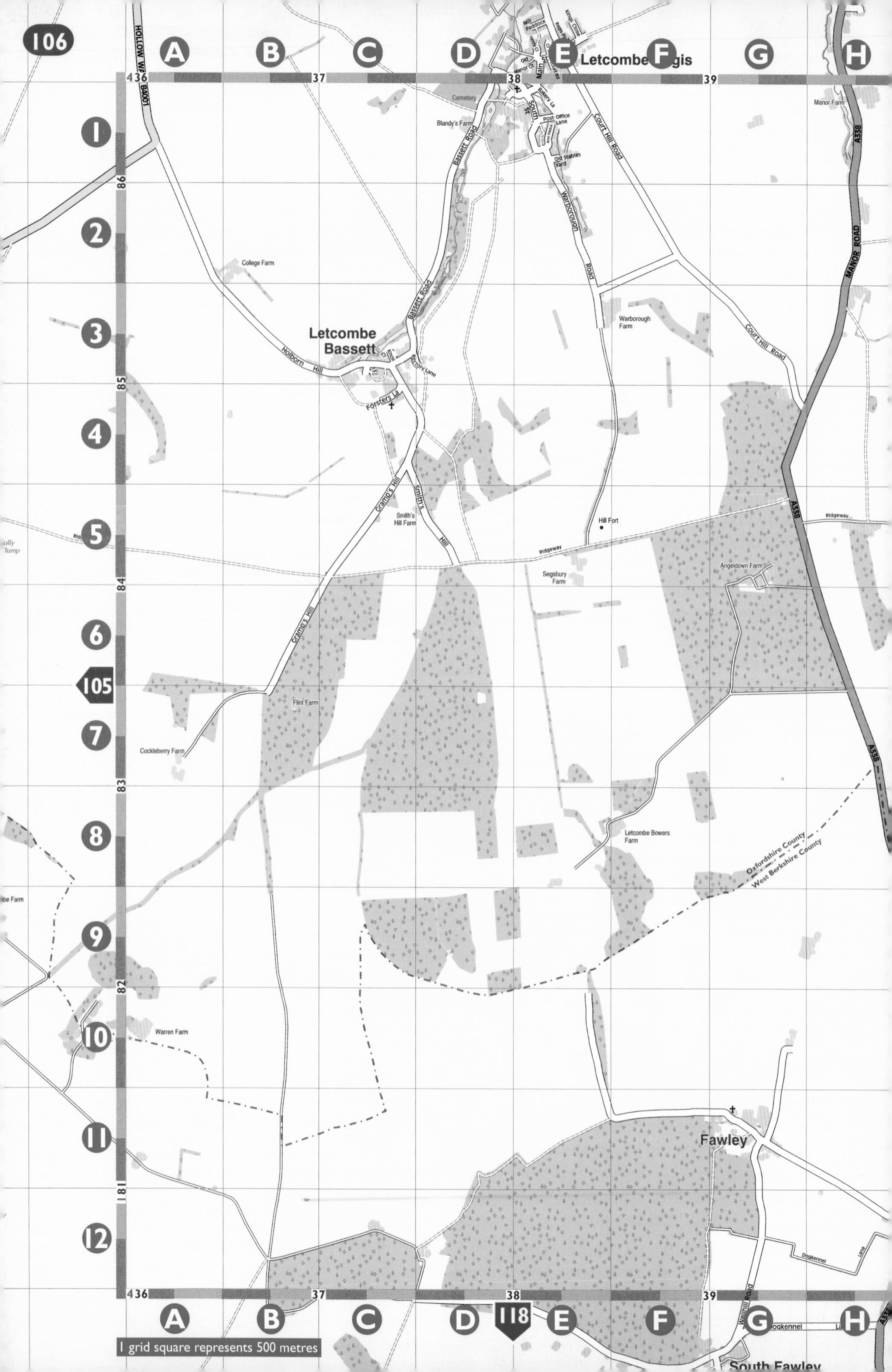

A B C D E Letcombe Regis F G H

436 37 38 39

Manor Farm

1

Hollow Way B4001

86

2

College Farm

Cemetery

Blandy's Farm

Bassett Road

Warborough Road

3

Letcombe Bassett

85

Holborn Hill

Rectory Lane

Warborough Farm

Court Hill Road

Forsters La

4

Granno's Hill

Smith's Hill

Smith's Hill Farm

A338

5

Ridgeway

Hill Fort

Ridgeway

Segsbury Farm

Angeldown Farm

84

6

105

Flint Farm

7

Cockleberry Farm

83

8

Letcombe Bowers Farm

Oxfordshire County

West Berkshire County

9

82

10

Warren Farm

11

81

Fawley

12

436 37 38 39

Woolhill Road

Dogkennel

A B C D 118 E F G H

South Fawley

1 grid square represents 500 metres

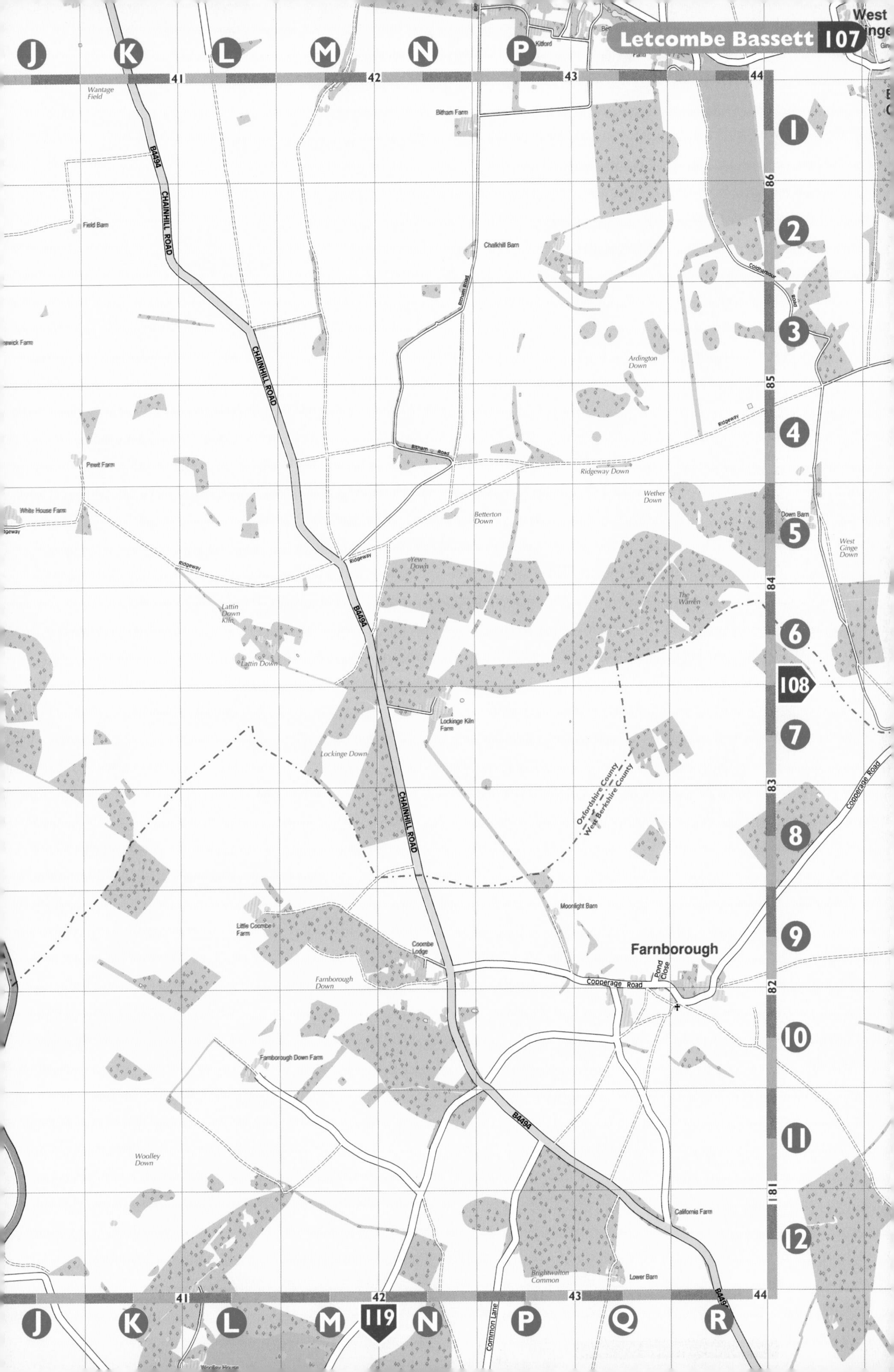

West
inge

J K L M N P

Kidford

West
inge

Wantage
Field

41 42 43 44

Bitham Farm

1

86

CHAINHILL ROAD

B4494

Field Barn

Chalkhill Barn

2

Costhamour
Road

swick Farm

3

85

Ardington
Down

4

Ridgeway

Pewit Farm

Ridgeway Down

Wether
Down

Down Barn

5

White House Farm

Ridgeway

Betterton
Down

West
Ginge
Down

Ridgeway

Lattin
Down
Kiln

Yew
Down

The
Warren

84

6

Lattin Down

B4494

108

Lockinge Kiln
Farm

7

83

Lockinge Down

Oxfordshire County
West Berkshire County

8

Copperage Road

Little Coombe
Farm

Moonlight Barn

Coombe
Lodge

9

Farnborough

82

Farnborough
Down

Pond
Close

Copperage Road

10

Farnborough Down Farms

11

181

Woolley
Down

California Farm

12

Brightwalton
Common

Lower Barn

B4494

41 42 43 44

J K L M 119 N P Q R

Common Lane

Woolley House

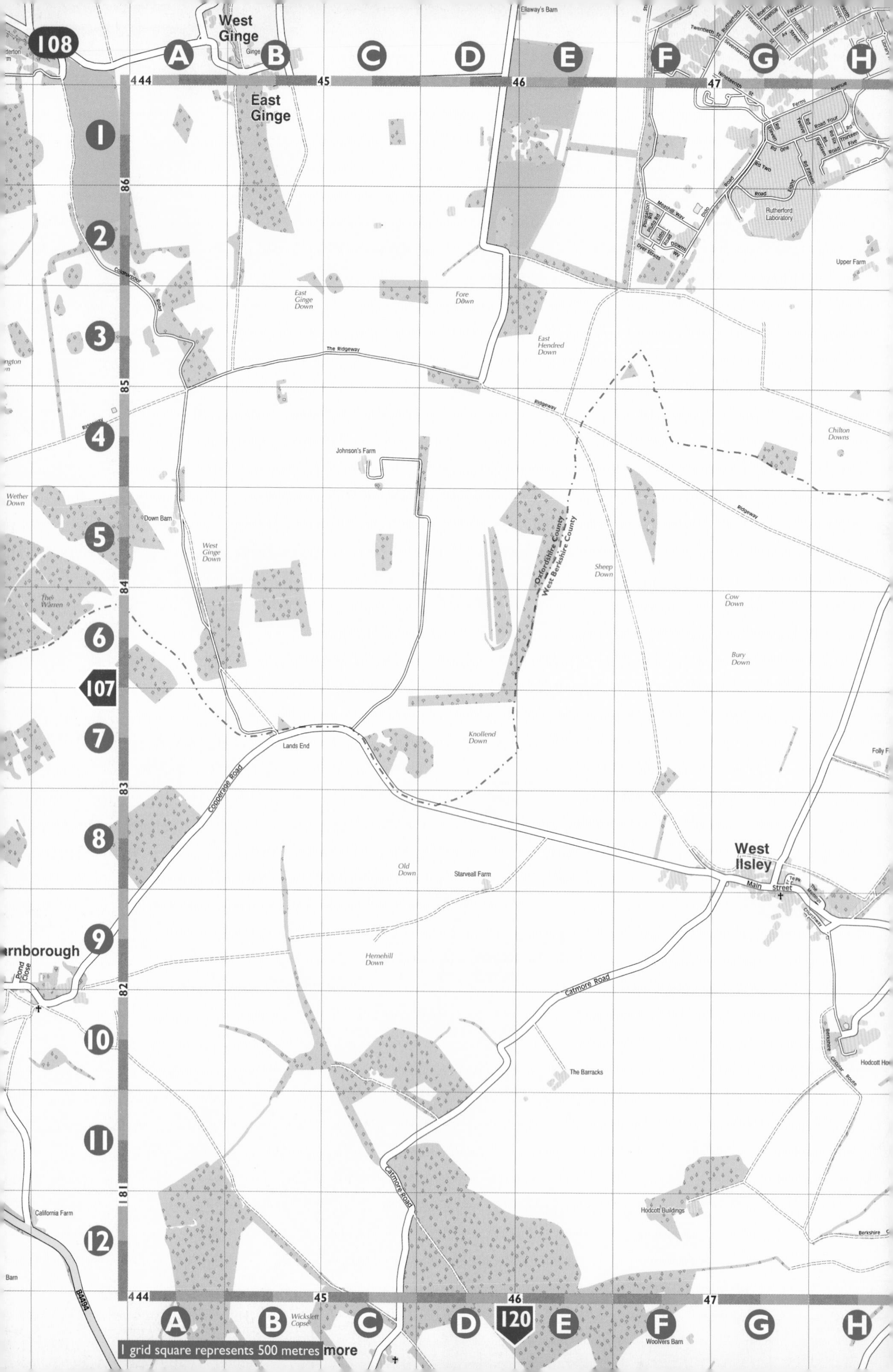

West
Ginge

A   B   C   D   E   F   G   H

4 44   45   46   47

East Ginge

Ellaway's Barn

1

86

Twentieth St

Seventeenth St

Faraday
Av

2

Colouredale Road

East
Ginge
Down

Fore
Down

East
Hendred
Down

Rutherford
Laboratory

Upper Farm

3

85

The Ridgeway

Ridgeway

Chilton
Downs

4

Johnson's Farm

Ridgeway

Wether
Down

Down Barn

5

84

West
Ginge
Down

Oxfordshire County

West Berkshire County

Sheep
Down

Cow
Down

The Warren

6

Bury
Down

7

83

Coppergore Road

Lands End

Knollend
Down

Folly F

8

West
Ilsley

Main   street

9

rnborough

82

Pond
Close

Hernehill
Down

Catmore Road

10

California Farm

The Barracks

Hodcott Hou

11

81

Catmore Road

Hodcott Buildings

Berkshire

12

Barn

B4494

4 44   45   46   47

A   B   C   D   E   F   G   H

Wickslett
Copse

Woolvers Barn

1 grid square represents 500 metres more

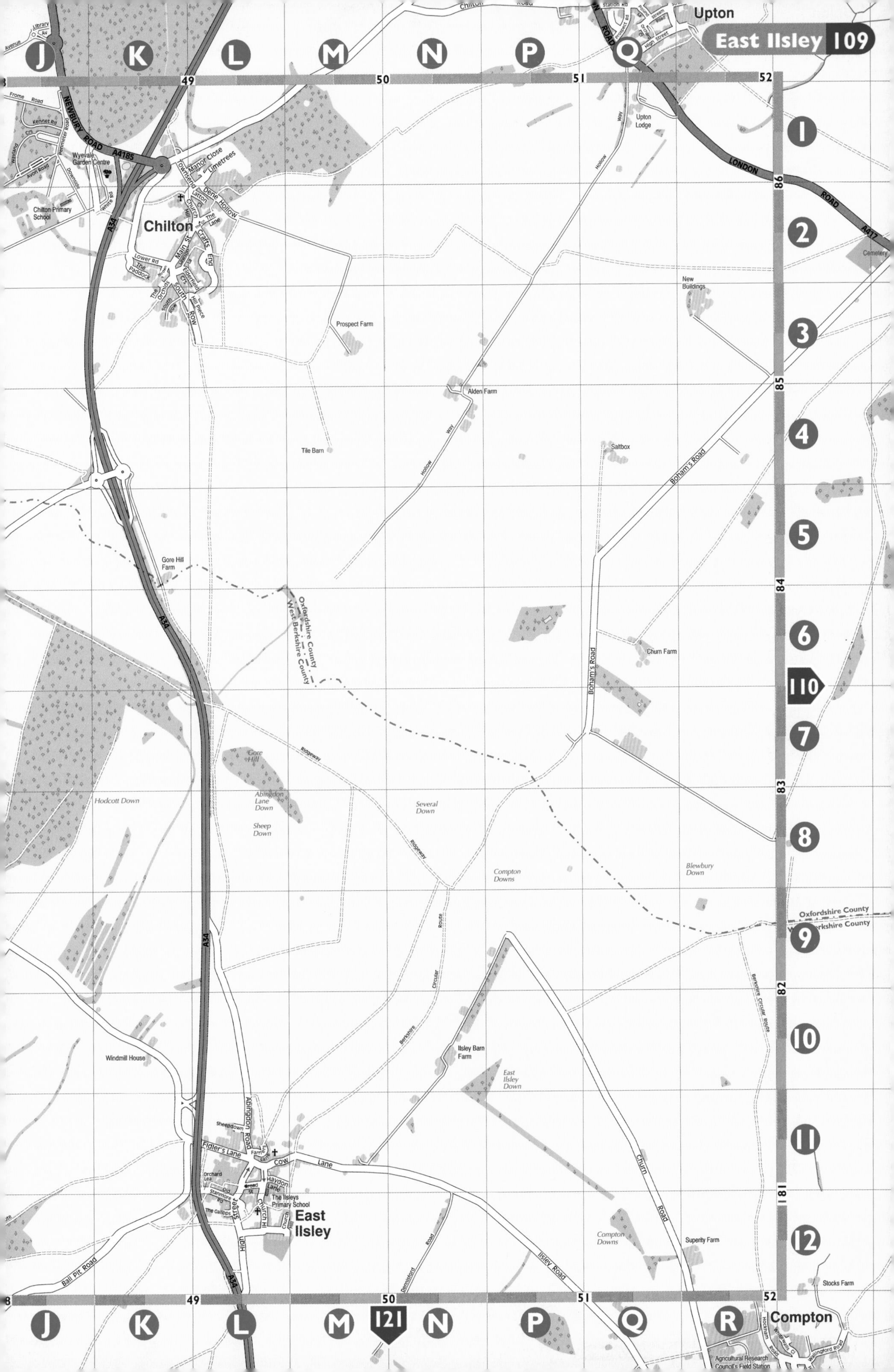
Upton
Chilton
East Ilsley
Compton
NEWBURY ROAD
A4185
A34
LONDON ROAD
A417
Wyevale Garden Centre
Chilton Primary School
Manor Close
Limetrees
Dene Hollow
Upton Lodge
Prospect Farm
New Buildings
Alden Farm
Tile Barn
Saltbox
Hollow Way
Boham's Road
Gore Hill Farm
Oxfordshire County
West Berkshire County
Churn Farm
Ridgeway
Gore Hill
Abingdon Lane Down
Sheep Down
Hodcott Down
Several Down
Compton Downs
Blewbury Down
Berkshire Circular Route
Windmill House
Ilsley Barn Farm
East Ilsley Down
Churn Road
Superity Farm
Stocks Farm
Ilsley Road
Ball Pit Road
Abingdon Road
Fidler's Lane
Cow Lane
Haydon Lane
The Ilsleys Primary School
High Street
Church Hill
Orchard Lea
Cemetery
Agricultural Research Council's Field Station
121
110

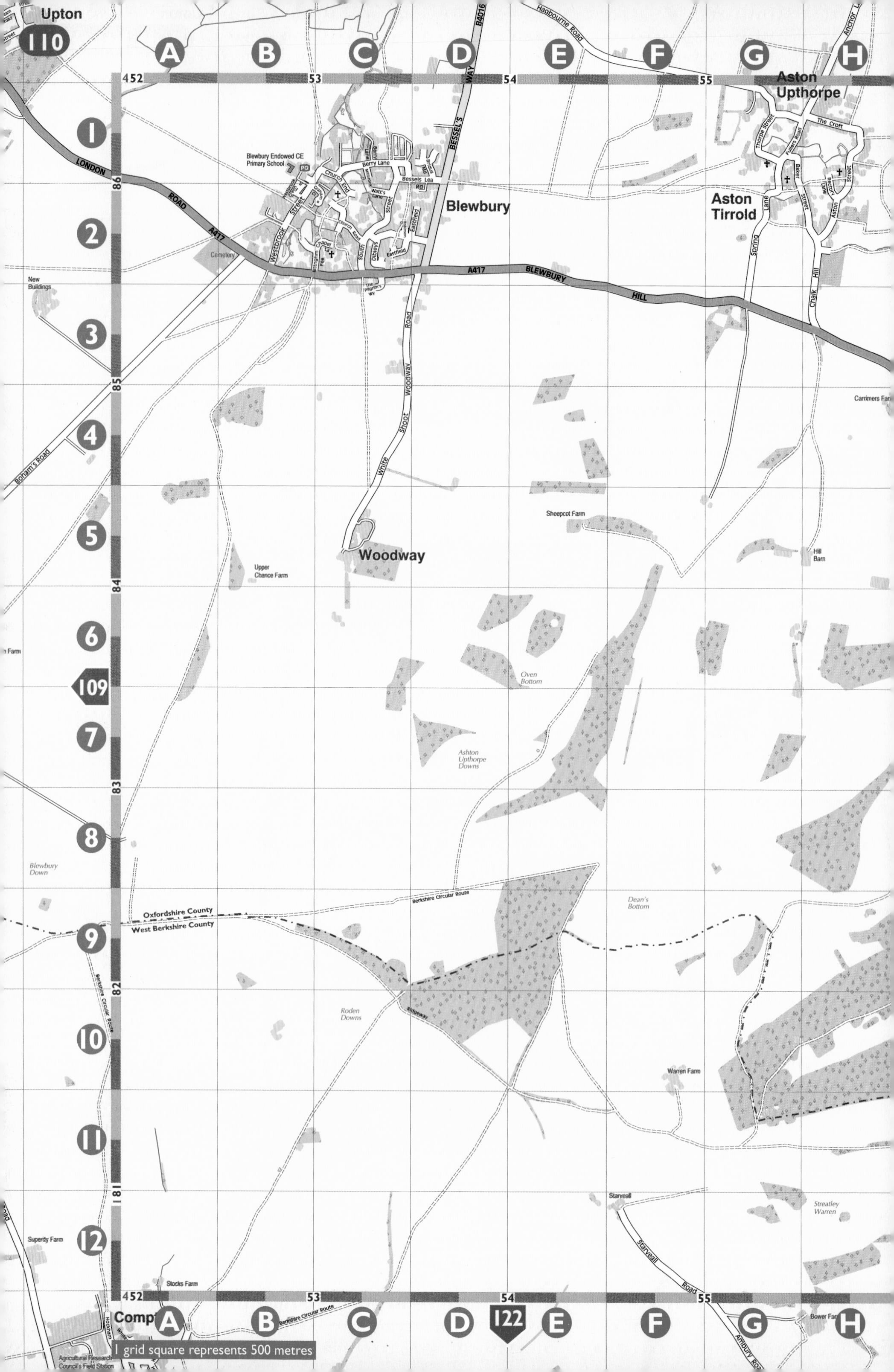
Upton
110
Blewbury
Aston Upthorpe
Aston Tirrold
Woodway
Blewbury Endowed CE Primary School
Cemetery
New Buildings
Upper Chance Farm
Sheepcot Farm
Hill Barn
Carrimers Farm
Oven Bottom
Ashton Upthorpe Downs
Blewbury Down
Oxfordshire County
West Berkshire County
Berkshire Circular Route
Dean's Bottom
Roden Downs
Ridgeway
Warren Farm
Starveall
Starveall Road
Streatley Warren
Superity Farm
Stocks Farm
Bower Farm
Agricultural Research Council's Field Station
Compton
LONDON ROAD
A417
BLEWBURY HILL
B4016
BESSEL'S WAY
Hagbourne Road
Westbrook Street
Church End
Berry Lane
Bessels Lea
Watt's Lane
South Street
Dibleys
Eastfield
Church Road
Chapel Lane
The Pilgrim's Wy
White Shoot
Woodway Road
Boham's Road
Thorpe Street
Fullers Road
The Croft
Baker Street
Aston Street
Spring Lane
Chalk Hill
Ambury Road
Hockham
109
122
1 grid square represents 500 metres

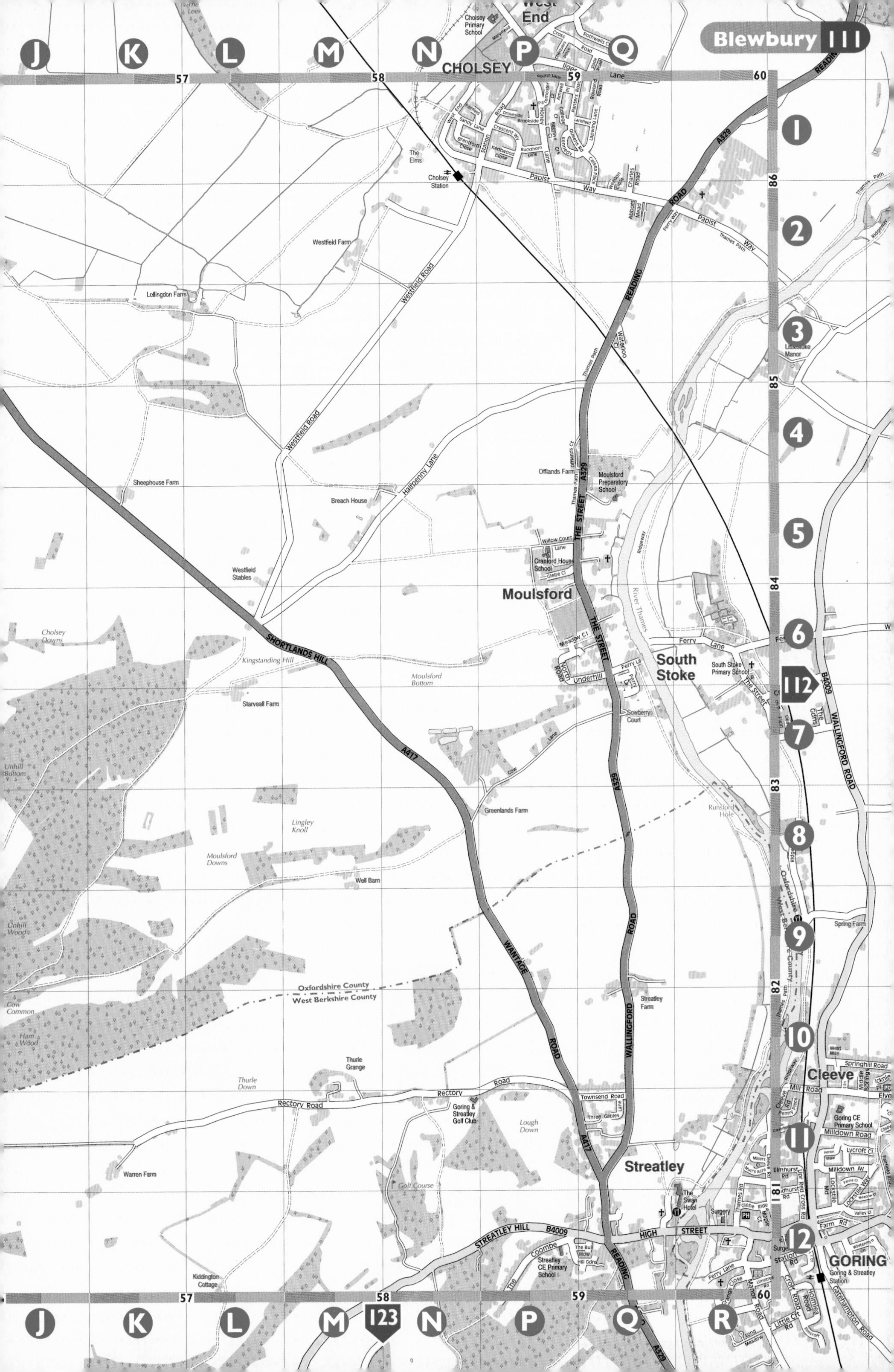
CHOLSEY
West End
Cholsey Primary School
Cholsey Station
The Elms
Papist Way
READING ROAD
A329
Westfield Farm
Westfield Road
Lollingdon Farm
Halfpenny Lane
Sheephouse Farm
Breach House
Westfield Stables
Offlands Farm
Moulsford Preparatory School
Cranford House School
Moulsford
THE STREET
Waterloo Ct
Thames Path
River Thames
Littlestoke Manor
Ferry Lane
South Stoke
South Stoke Primary School
SHORTLANDS HILL
Kingstanding Hill
Cholsey Downs
Moulsford Bottom
Starveall Farm
Underhill
Sowberry Court
Unhill Bottom
A417
Cow Lane
Greenlands Farm
Lingley Knoll
Moulsford Downs
Well Barn
Runsford Hole
Unhill Wood
WANTAGE ROAD
WALLINGFORD ROAD
Spring Farm
Oxfordshire County
West Berkshire County
Cow Common
Ham Wood
Streatley Farm
Thurle Grange
Thurle Down
Rectory Road
Goring & Streatley Golf Club
Lough Down
Townsend Road
Three Gables Lane
Cleeve
Mill Road
Goring CE Primary School
Milldown Road
Warren Farm
Golf Course
Streatley
The Swan Hotel
STREATLEY HILL
B4009
HIGH STREET
Streatley CE Primary School
Kiddington Cottage
GORING
Goring & Streatley Station
Gatehampton Road
Ferry Lane
Manor Road
Station Rd
57
58
59
60
81
82
83
84
85
86
J
K
L
M
N
P
Q
R
112
123

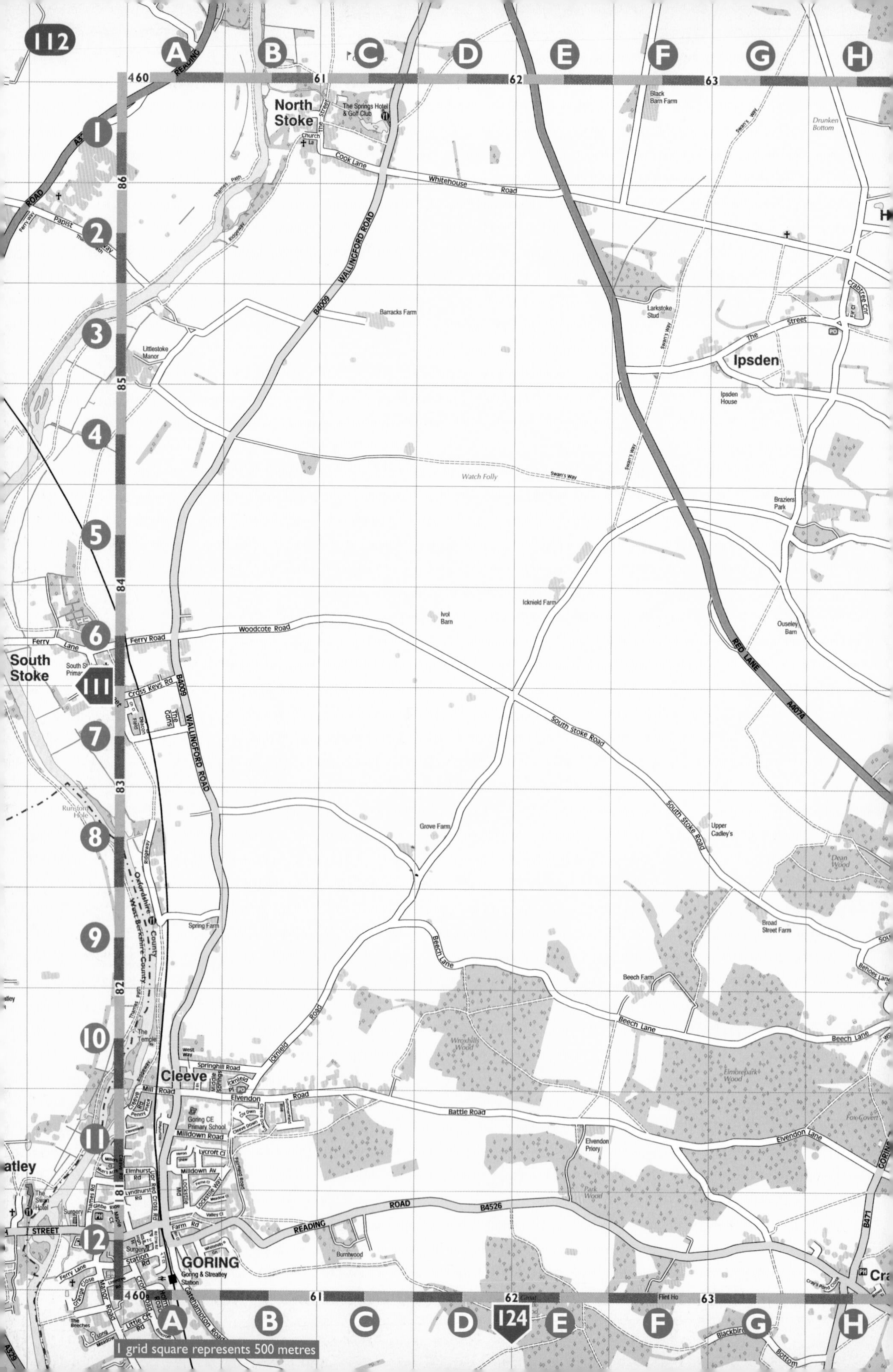
North Stoke
The Springs Hotel & Golf Club
Cook Lane
Whitehouse Road
Black Barn Farm
Swan's Way
Drunken Bottom
WALLINGFORD ROAD
B4009
Barracks Farm
Larkstoke Stud
The Street
Ipsden
Ipsden House
Littlestoke Manor
Watch Folly
Braziers Park
Icknield Farm
Ivol Barn
Woodcote Road
Ferry Road
Ferry Lane
South Stoke
Cross Keys Rd
Ouseley Barn
RED LANE
A4074
South Stoke Road
Upper Cadley's
Grove Farm
Dean Wood
Spring Farm
Broad Street Farm
Beech Lane
Beech Farm
Behoes Lane
Icknield Road
Wroxhills Wood
Elmorepark Wood
Cleeve
Springhill Road
Mill Road
Elvendon Road
Battle Road
Fox Covert
Goring CE Primary School
Milldown Road
Elvendon Priory
Elvendon Lane
Lycroft Cl
Milldown Av
Park Wood
READING ROAD
B4526
B471
Burntwood
GORING
Goring & Streatley Station
The Swan Hotel
STREET
Ferry Lane
Manor Road
Gatehampton Road
Flint Ho
Blackbird Bottom
Runstord Hole
Oxfordshire County
West Berkshire County
Thames Path
Ridgeway
The Temple
1 grid square represents 500 metres

111
124

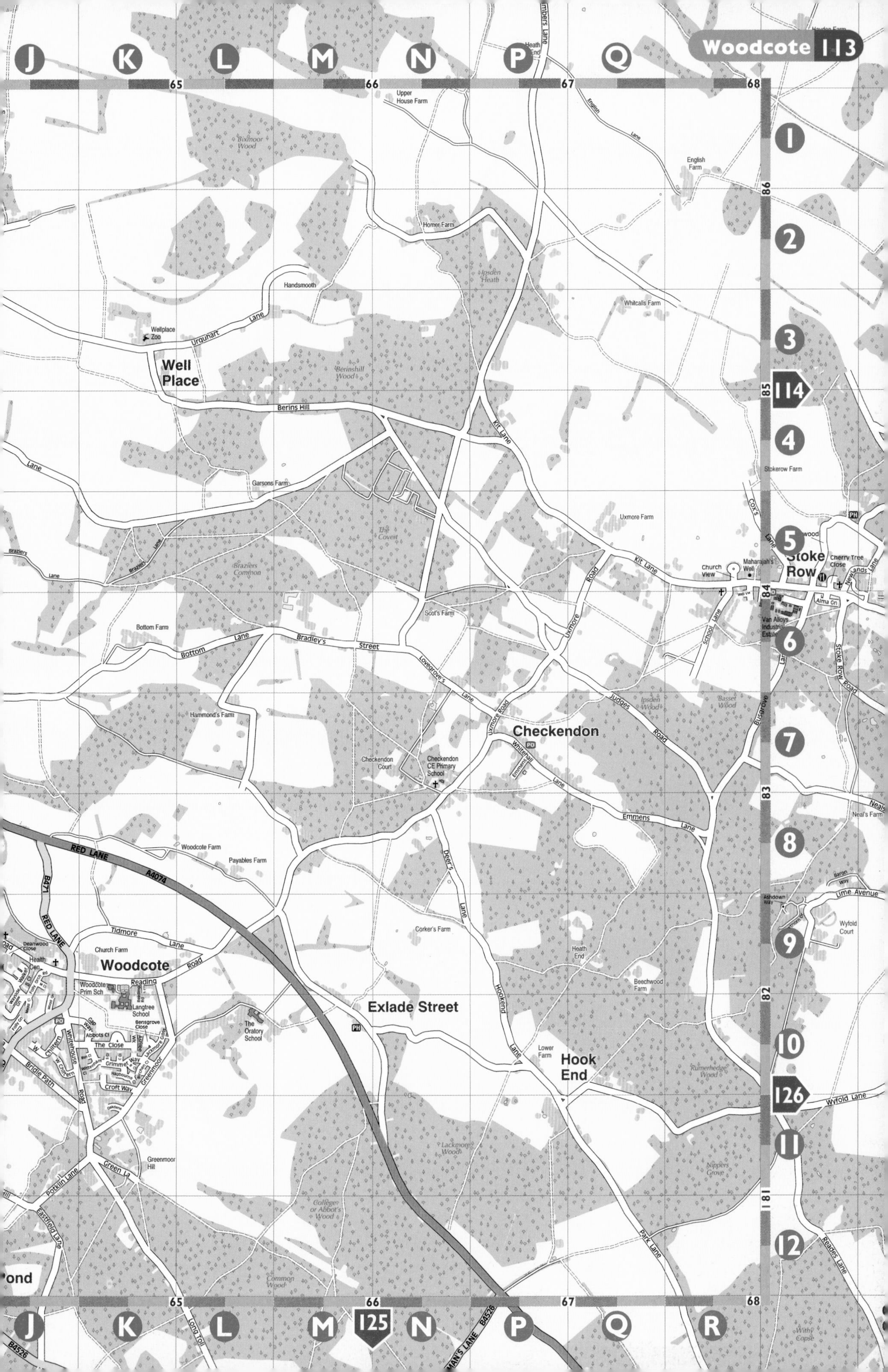
Upper House Farm
Bixmoor Wood
English Lane
English Farm
Homer Farm
Ipsden Heath
Handsmooth
Whitcalls Farm
Wellplace Zoo
Urquhart Lane
Well Place
Berinshill Wood
Berins Hill
Kit Lane
Stokerow Farm
Garsons Farm
The Covert
Uxmore Farm
Braziers Common
Braziers Lane
Kit Lane
Church View
Maharajah's Well
Stoke Row
Cherry Tree Close
Newlands Lane
Alma Gn
Van Alloys Industrial Estate
Scot's Farm
Uxmore Road
School Lane
Bottom Farm
Bottom Lane
Bradley's Street
Lovegrove's Lane
Ipsden Wood
Basset Wood
Stoke Row Road
Judges Road
Busgrove Lane
Hammond's Farm
Checkendon
Whitehall Lane
Emmens Cl
Checkendon Court
Checkendon CE Primary School
Emmens Lane
Neal's Farm
Woodcote Farm
Payables Farm
RED LANE
A4074
B471
Deer's Lane
Baron Way
Ashdown Way
Lime Avenue
Wyfold Court
Tidmore Lane
Corker's Farm
Deanwood Close
Health Cen
Church Farm
Woodcote
Reading Road
Heath End
Beechwood Farm
Woodcote Prim Sch
Langtree School
Bensgrove Close
Exlade Street
The Oratory School
Abbots Cl
The Close
Chiltern
Whitehouse Road
Grimmer Way
Croft Way
Greenmoor
Bridle Path
Hookend Lane
Lower Farm
Hook End
Rumerhedge Wood
Wyfold Lane
Oakdene
Lackmore Wood
Greenmoor Hill
Green La
Potkiln Lane
Nippers Grove
Eastfield Lane
College or Abbot's Wood
Park Lane
Reades Lane
Common Wood
Long Toll
B4526
Withy Copse
J K L M N P Q R
65 66 67 68
86 85 84 83 82 81
114 125 126

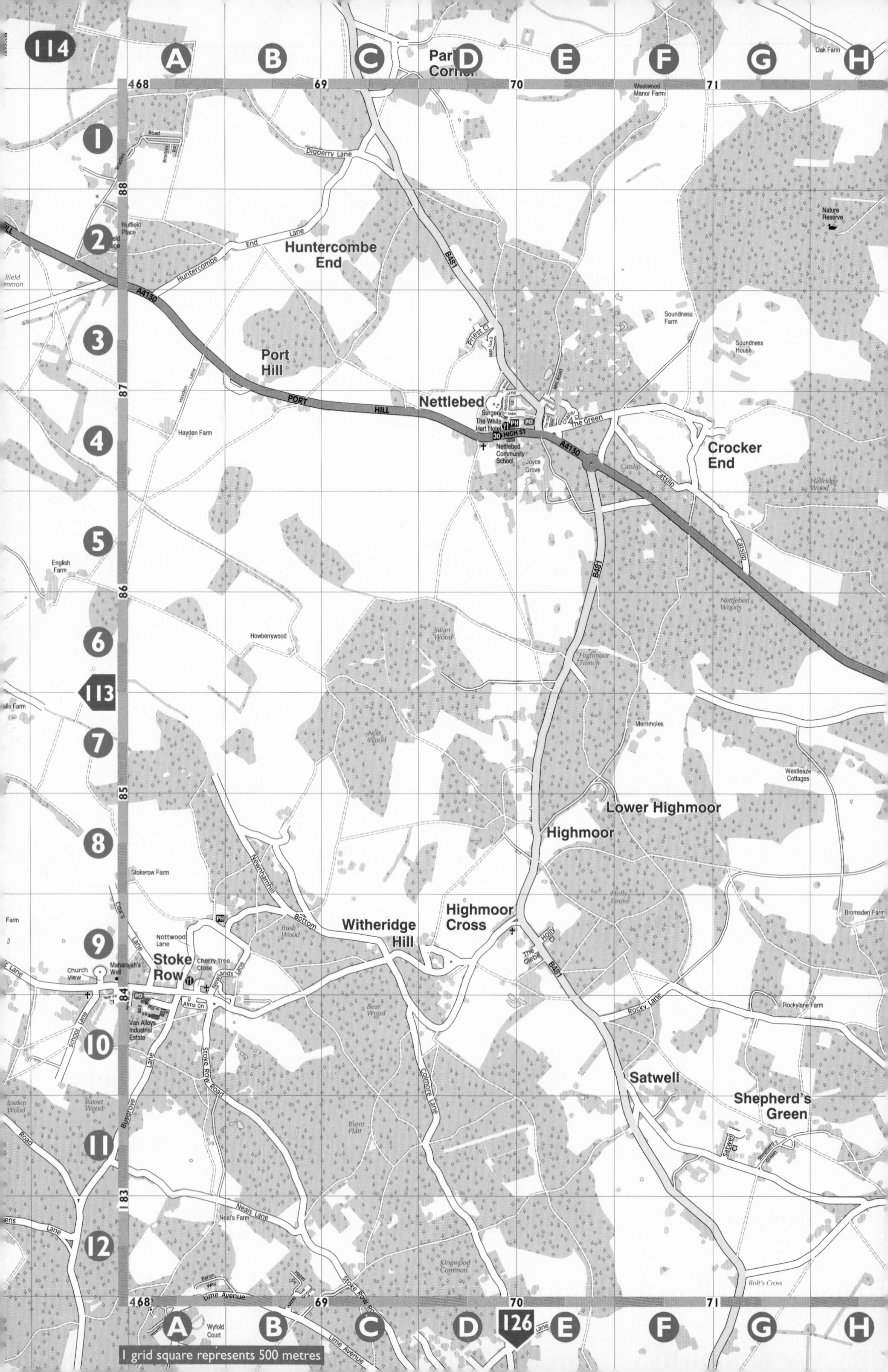

Park Corner
Westwood Manor Farm
Oak Farm
Digberry Lane
Bradley Road
Nuffield Place
Huntercombe End Lane
Huntercombe End
A4130
B481
Port Hill
PORT HILL
Hayden Lane
Hayden Farm
Priest Cl
Nettlebed
Surgery
The White Hart Hotel
HIGH ST
Nettlebed Community School
Joyce Grove
The Green
Crocker End
Catslip
Soundness Farm
Soundness House
Nature Reserve
Halfridge Wood
Nettlebed Woods
English Farm
Howberrywood
Swan Wood
Highmoor Trench
Merrimoles
Nott Wood
Westleaze Cottages
Lower Highmoor
Highmoor
Stokerow Farm
Newnhamhill Bottom
Holly Grove
Bromsden Farm
Witheridge Hill
Highmoor Cross
Bush Wood
Nottwood Lane
Cox's Lane
Stoke Row
Church View
Maharajah's Well
Cherry Tree Close
Newlands Lane
Alma Gn
Holly Cl
The Glebe
Rocky Lane
Rockylane Farm
Bear Wood
School Lane
Van Alloys Industrial Estate
Bushgrove Lane
Stoke Row Road
Colmore Lane
Satwell
Shepherd's Green
Satwell Cl
Basset Wood
Ipsden Wood
Burnt Platt
Neals Lane
Neal's Farm
Kingwood Common
Baron Way
Lime Avenue
Hazel Gr
Bolt's Cross
Wyfold Court
113
126
1 grid square represents 500 metres

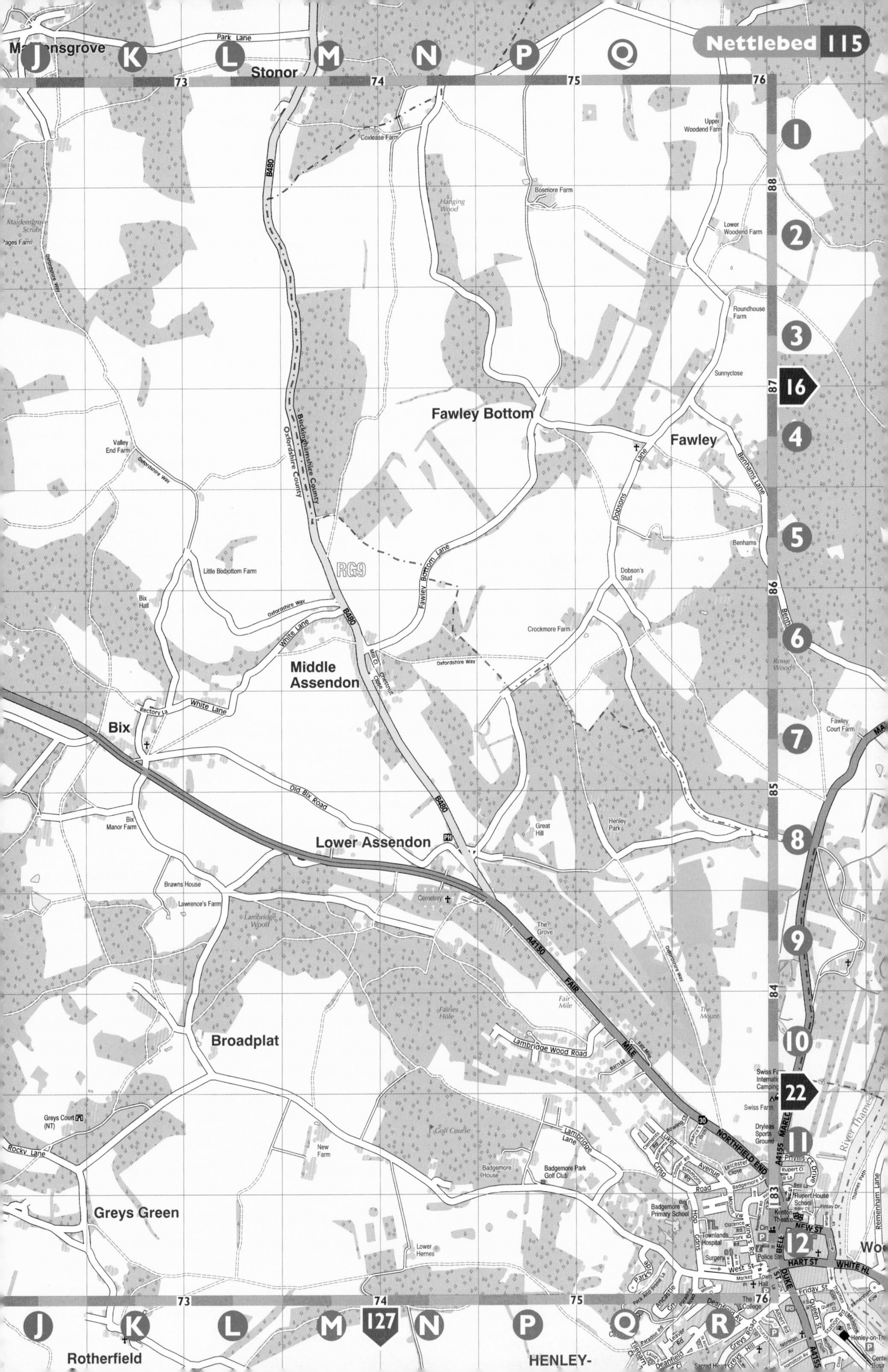

Maidensgrove

Stonor

Park Lane

Coxlease Farm

Upper Woodend Farm

Lower Woodend Farm

Maidengrove Scrub

Pages Farm

Hanging Wood

Bosmore Farm

Roundhouse Farm

Sunnyclose

16

Fawley Bottom

Fawley

Benhams

Dobson's Stud

Valley End Farm

Little Bixbottom Farm

RG9

Fawley Bottom Lane

Oxfordshire Way

Crockmore Farm

Rowe Woods

Bix Hall

Fawley Court Farm

White Lane

B480

Middle Assendon

Oxfordshire Way

Rectory La

White Lane

Bix

Old Bix Road

B480

Great Hill

Henley Park

Lower Assendon

PH

Bix Manor Farm

Brauns House

Lawrence's Farm

Lambridge Wood

Cemetery

The Grove

A4130

Swiss Farm International Camping

22

Broadplat

Fair Mile

Faines Hole

The Mount

Lambridge Wood Road

Golf Course

New Farm

Swiss Farm

Dryleas Sports Ground

Greys Court (NT)

Rocky Lane

Lambridge Lane

Badgemore House

Badgemore Park Golf Club

Badgemore Primary School

Townlands Hospital

Rupert House School

Kenton Theatre

NEW ST

Greys Green

Lower Hernes

HART ST

WHITE HI

12

127

Rotherfield

HENLEY-

J K L M N P Q R

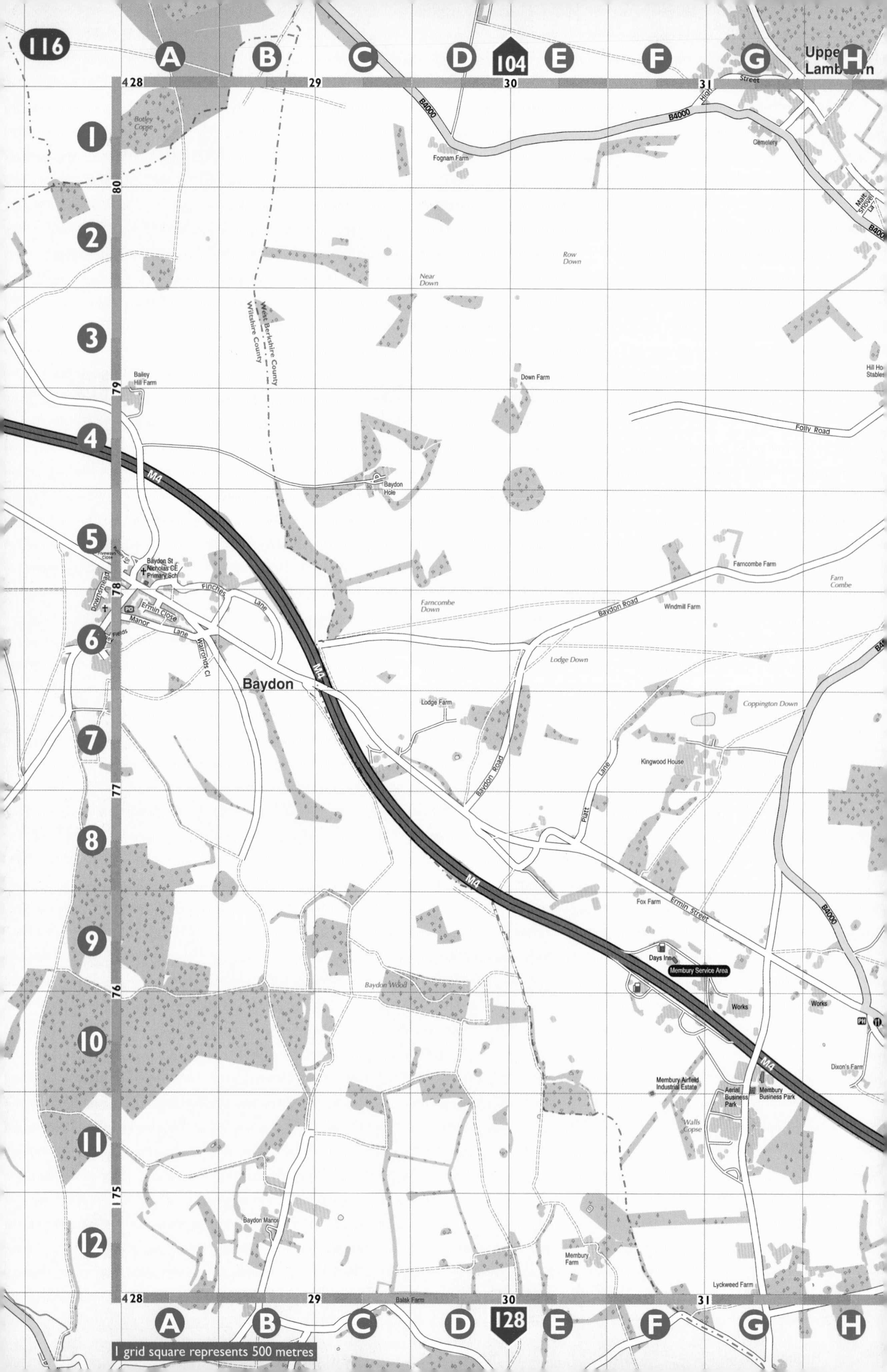
104
128
Botley Copse
Fognam Farm
B4000
High Street
Upper Lambourn
Cemetery
Malt Shovel La
Near Down
Row Down
West Berkshire County
Wiltshire County
Bailey Hill Farm
Down Farm
Hill House Stables
Folly Road
M4
Baydon Hole
Fiveways Close
Baydon St Nicholas CE Primary Sch
Downsmead
Finches Lane
Ermin Close
Manor Lane
Fields
Walronds Cl
Baydon
Farncombe Down
Baydon Road
Farncombe Farm
Windmill Farm
Farn Combe
Lodge Down
Lodge Farm
Coppington Down
Kingwood House
Platt Lane
Fox Farm
Ermin Street
Days Inn
Membury Service Area
Baydon Wood
Works
Dixon's Farm
Membury Airfield Industrial Estate
Aerial Business Park
Membury Business Park
Walls Copse
Baydon Manor
Membury Farm
Lyckweed Farm
Balak Farm
428
29
30
31
80
79
78
77
76
175
1 grid square represents 500 metres

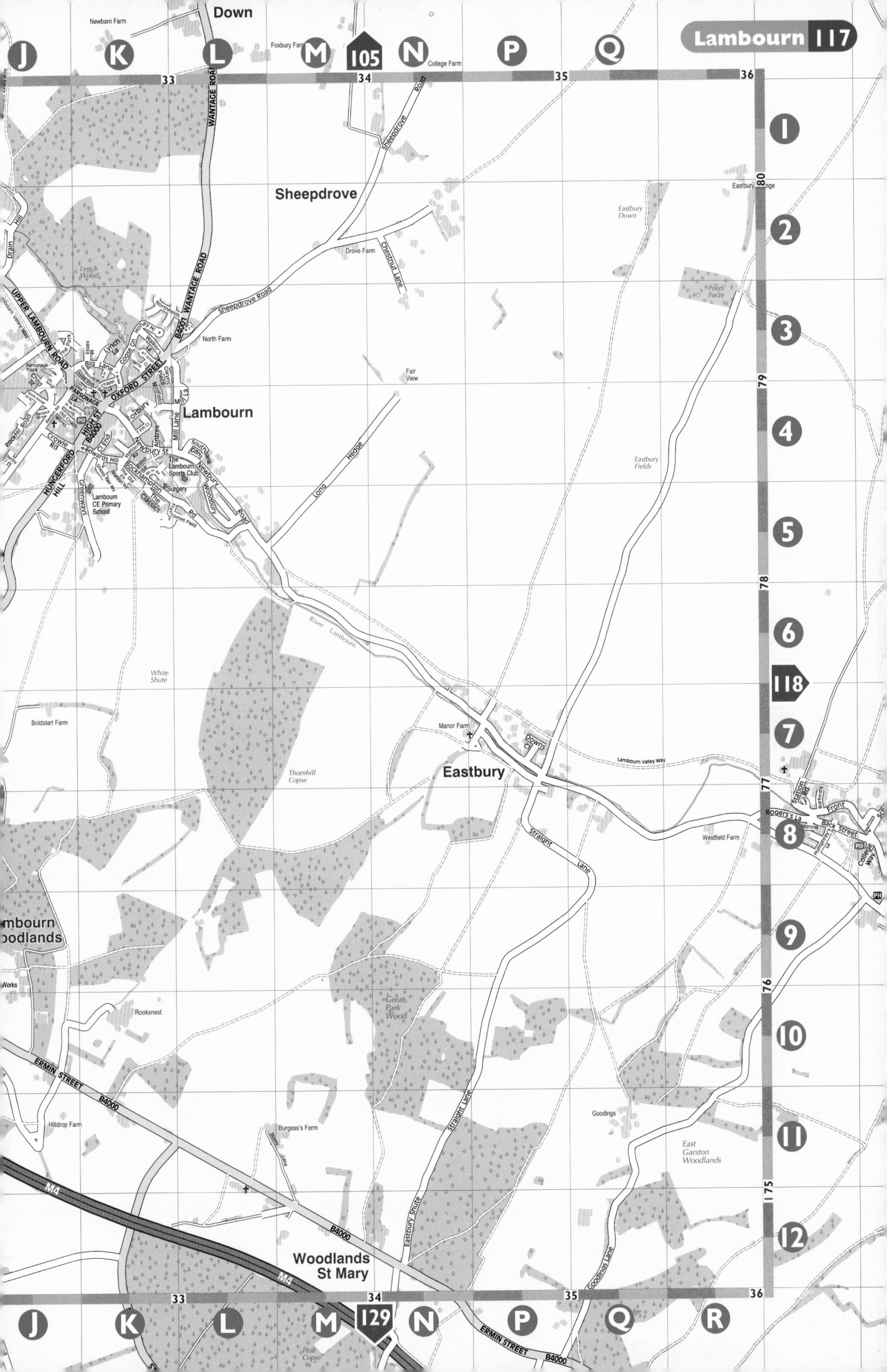
Down
Newbarn Farm
Foxbury Farm
105
College Farm
WANTAGE ROAD
Sheepdrove Road
Sheepdrove
Drove Farm
Chestnut Lane
Eastbury Grange
Eastbury Down
Poors Furze
Lynch Wood
Sheepdrove Road
North Farm
B4001 WANTAGE ROAD
UPPER LAMBOURN ROAD
OXFORD STREET
Lambourn
Fair View
Mill Lane
HIGH ST
B4000
HUNGERFORD HILL
Newbury St
The Lambourn Sports Club
Surgery
Lambourn CE Primary School
Greenways
Newbury Road
Long Hedge
Eastbury Fields
River Lambourn
White Shute
Boldstart Farm
Manor Farm
Downs Cl
Eastbury
Lambourn Valley Way
Thornhill Copse
118
Westfield Farm
Straight Lane
Rogers's La
Back Street
Front
Station Rd
College Way
PO
PH
Lambourn Woodlands
Works
Great Park Wood
Rooksnest
ERMIN STREET
B4000
Hilldrop Farm
Burgess's Farm
Stony Lane
Straight Lane
Goodings
East Garston Woodlands
M4
Eastbury Shute
B4000
Woodlands St Mary
Goodings Lane
129
ERMIN STREET
B4000
Ptolt Copse
J K L M N P Q R
33 34 35 36
1 2 3 4 5 6 7 8 9 10 11 12
80 79 78 77 76 175

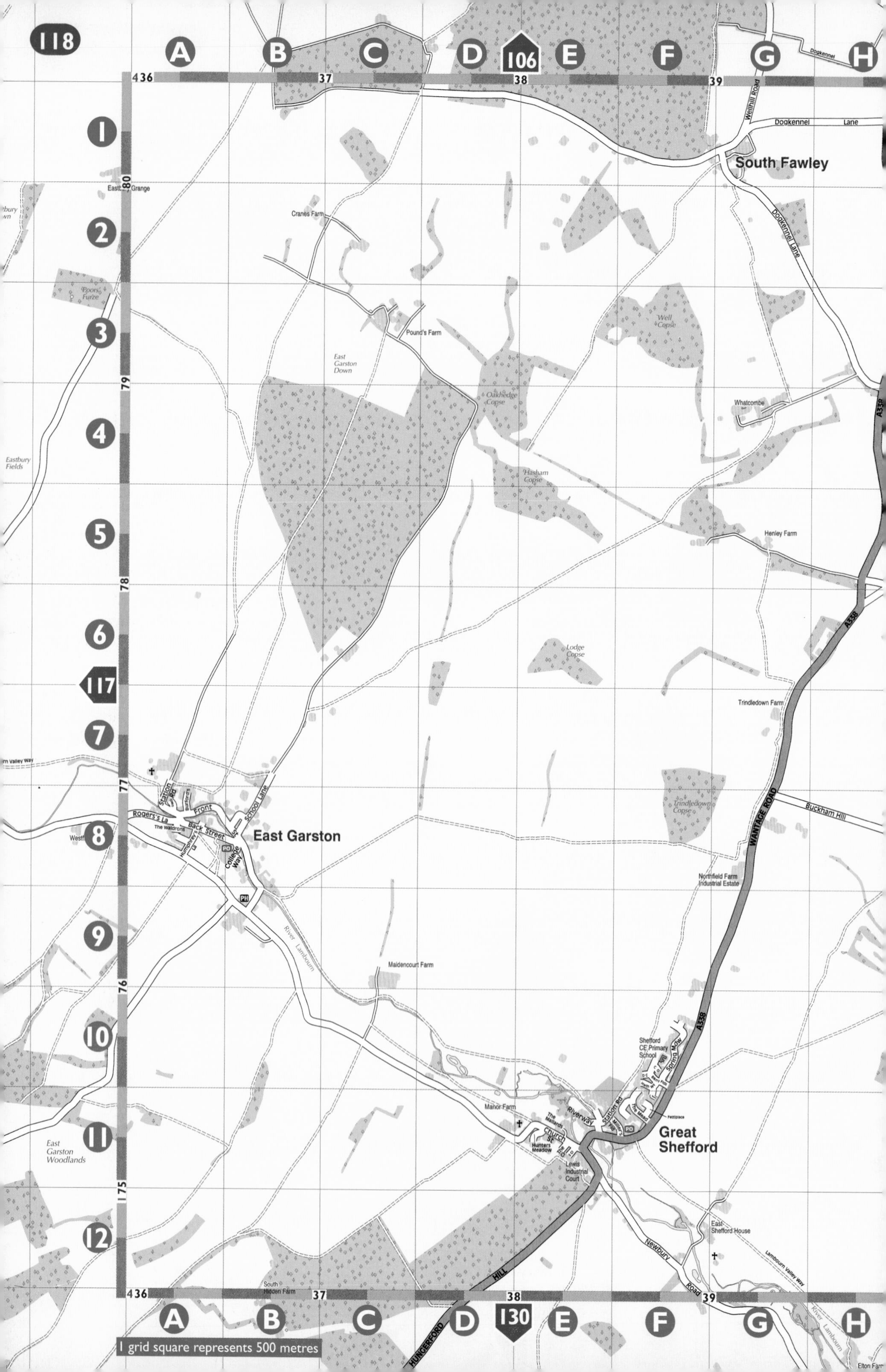

A
B
C
D
106
E
F
G
H
436
37
38
39
1
2
3
4
5
6
117
7
8
9
10
11
12
80
79
78
77
76
175
Dogkennel
Wellhill Road
Dogkennel Lane
South Fawley
Dogkennel Lane
Eastbury Grange
Cranes Farm
Poors' Furze
Pound's Farm
East Garston Down
Well Copse
Oakhedge Copse
Whatcombe
A338
Eastbury Fields
Hasham Copse
Henley Farm
A338
Lodge Copse
Trindledown Farm
Trindledown Copse
Buckham Hill
WANTAGE ROAD
Station Rd
Front
School Lane
Rogers's La
The Waldrons
Back Street
East Garston
College Way
PO
PH
Northfield Farm Industrial Estate
River Lambourn
Maidencourt Farm
Shefford CE Primary School
Spring Mdw
A338
Manor Farm
The Mallards
Riverway
Station Rd
Church St
Hunters Meadow
Great Shefford
Lewis Industrial Court
East Garston Woodlands
East Shefford House
Newbury Road
Lambourn Valley Way
South Hidden Farm
HUNGERFORD HILL
130
River Lambourn
Elton Farm
1 grid square represents 500 metres

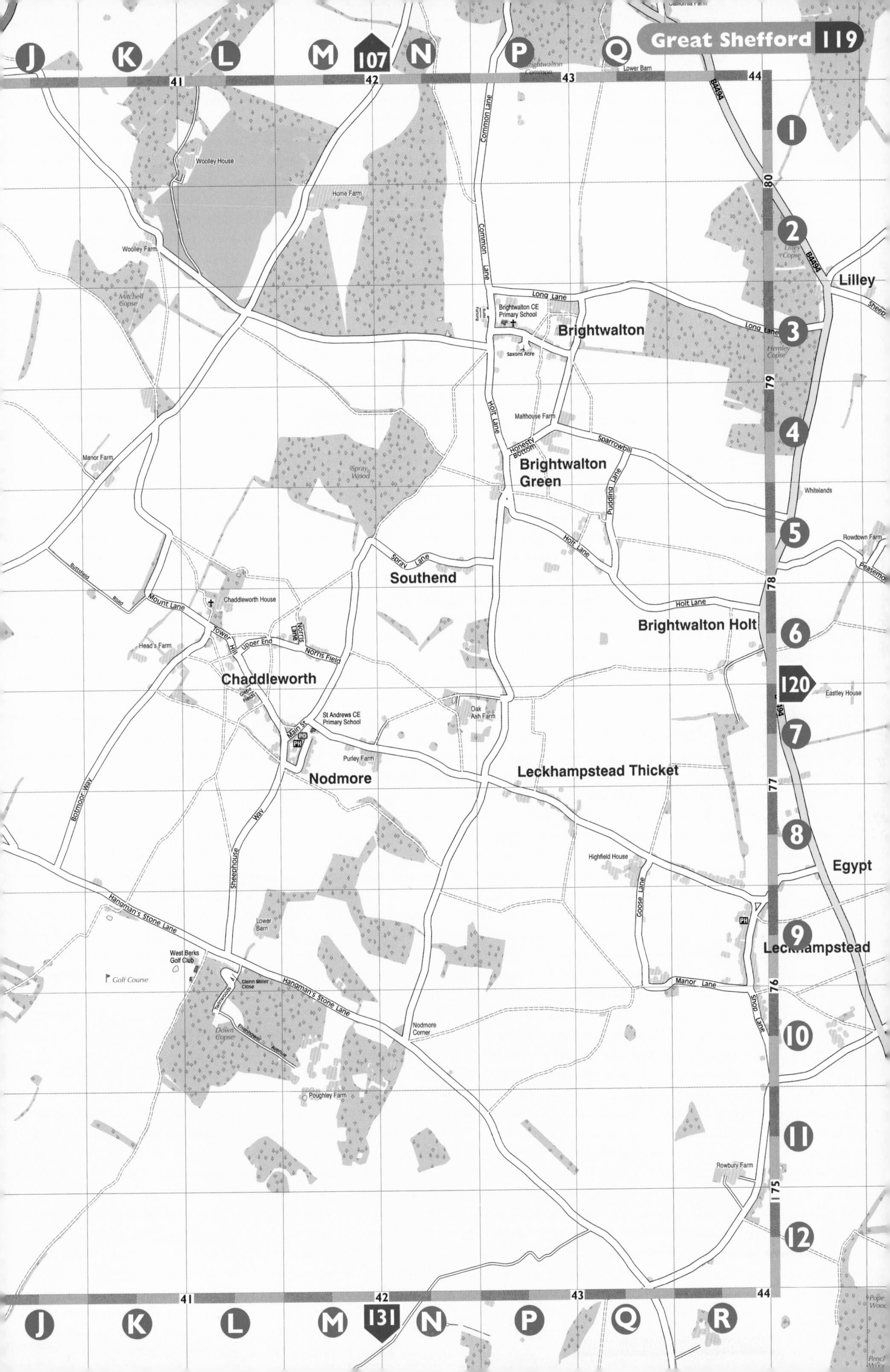

J K L M 107 N P Q

Woolley House

Woolley Farm

Mitchell Copse

Home Farm

Common Lane

Long Lane

Brightwalton CE Primary School

Brightwalton

Saxons Acre

Lower Barn

Lilley

Lilley Copse

Hemley Copse

Manor Farm

Spray Wood

Malthouse Farm

Honeybottom

Sparrowbill

Brightwalton Green

Pudding Lane

Holt Lane

Whitelands

Rowdown Farm

Buttsbull

Mount Lane

Chaddleworth House

Tower Hill

Head's Farm

Upper End

Norris Lane

Norris Field

Southend

Spray Lane

Holt Lane

Holt Lane

Brightwalton Holt

120

Eastley House

Chaddleworth

St Andrews CE Primary School

Main St

PO PH

Oak Ash Farm

Purley Farm

Nodmore

Botmoor Way

Sheephouse Way

Leckhampstead Thicket

Highfield House

Goose Lane

Egypt

PH

Leckhampstead

Hangman's Stone Lane

West Berks Golf Club

Glenn Miller Close

Hangman's Stone Lane

Thornwood

Golf Course

Down Copse

Footprint Avenue

Nodmore Corner

Manor Lane

Shop Lane

Rowbury Farm

Poughley Farm

J K L M 131 N P Q R

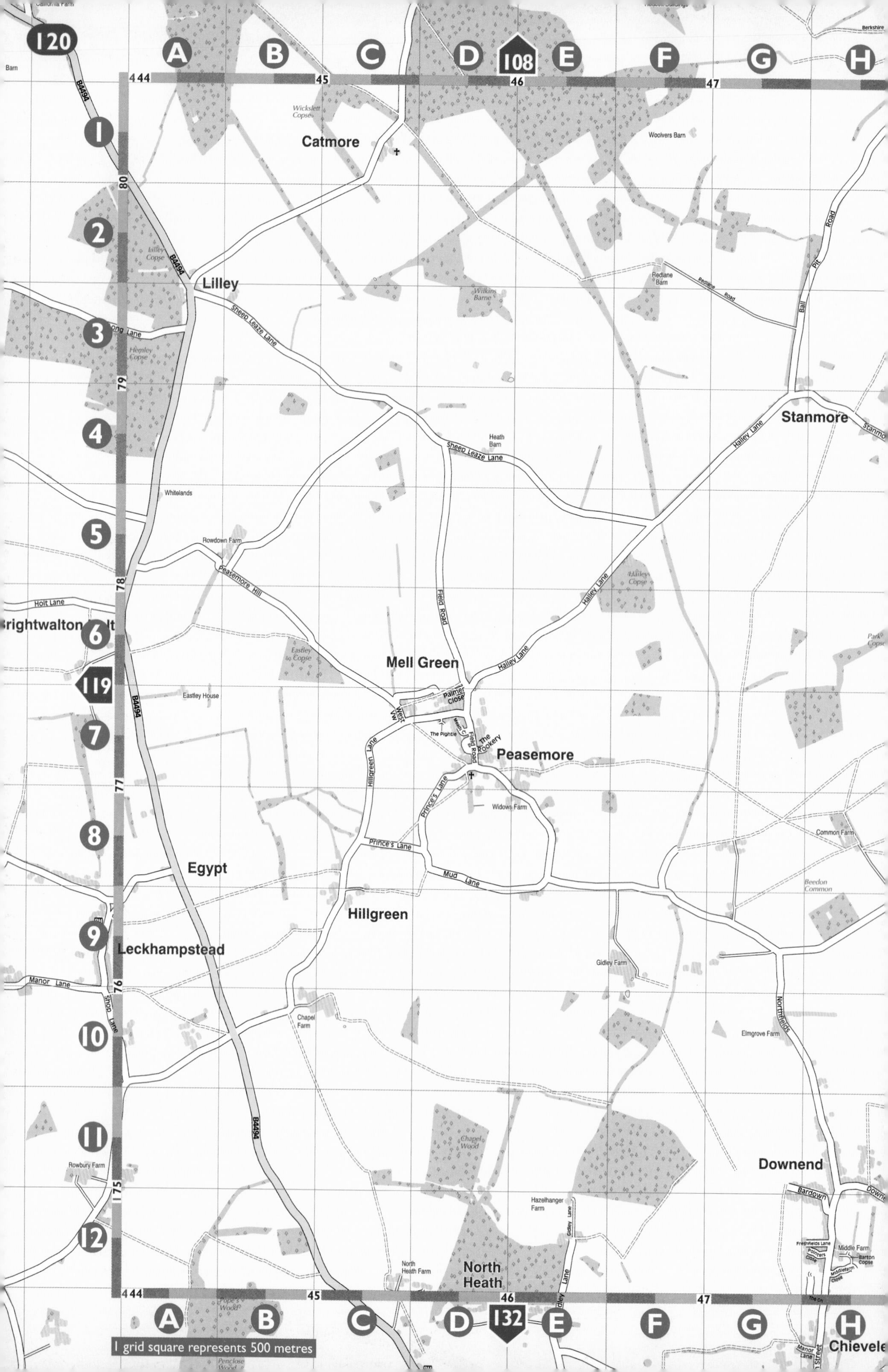
120
108
119
132
A
B
C
D
E
F
G
H
1
2
3
4
5
6
7
8
9
10
11
12
44
45
46
47
80
79
78
77
76
175
B4494
Catmore
Wickslett Copse
Woolvers Barn
Lilley
Lilley Copse
Long Lane
Henley Copse
Sheep Leaze Lane
Redlane Barn
Redlane Road
Wilkins Barne
Ball Pit Road
Stanmore
Halley Lane
Heath Barn
Whitelands
Rowdown Farm
Peasemore Hill
Holt Lane
Brightwalton Holt
Halley Copse
Field Road
Eastley Copse
Mell Green
Palmer Close
West Vw
Eastley House
The Pightle
The Rookery
Peasemore
Hillgreen Lane
Prince's Lane
Widows Farm
Park Copse
Common Farm
Mud Lane
Beedon Common
Egypt
Hillgreen
Leckhampstead
Gidley Farm
Manor Lane
Shop Lane
Chapel Farm
Northfields
Elmgrove Farm
Chapel Wood
Rowbury Farm
Downend
Bardown
Hazelhanger Farm
Gidley Lane
Freshfields Lane
Middle Farm
Barton Copse
Middlefarm Close
North Heath Farm
North Heath
Pope's Wood
Manor Lane
Chieveley
1 grid square represents 500 metres

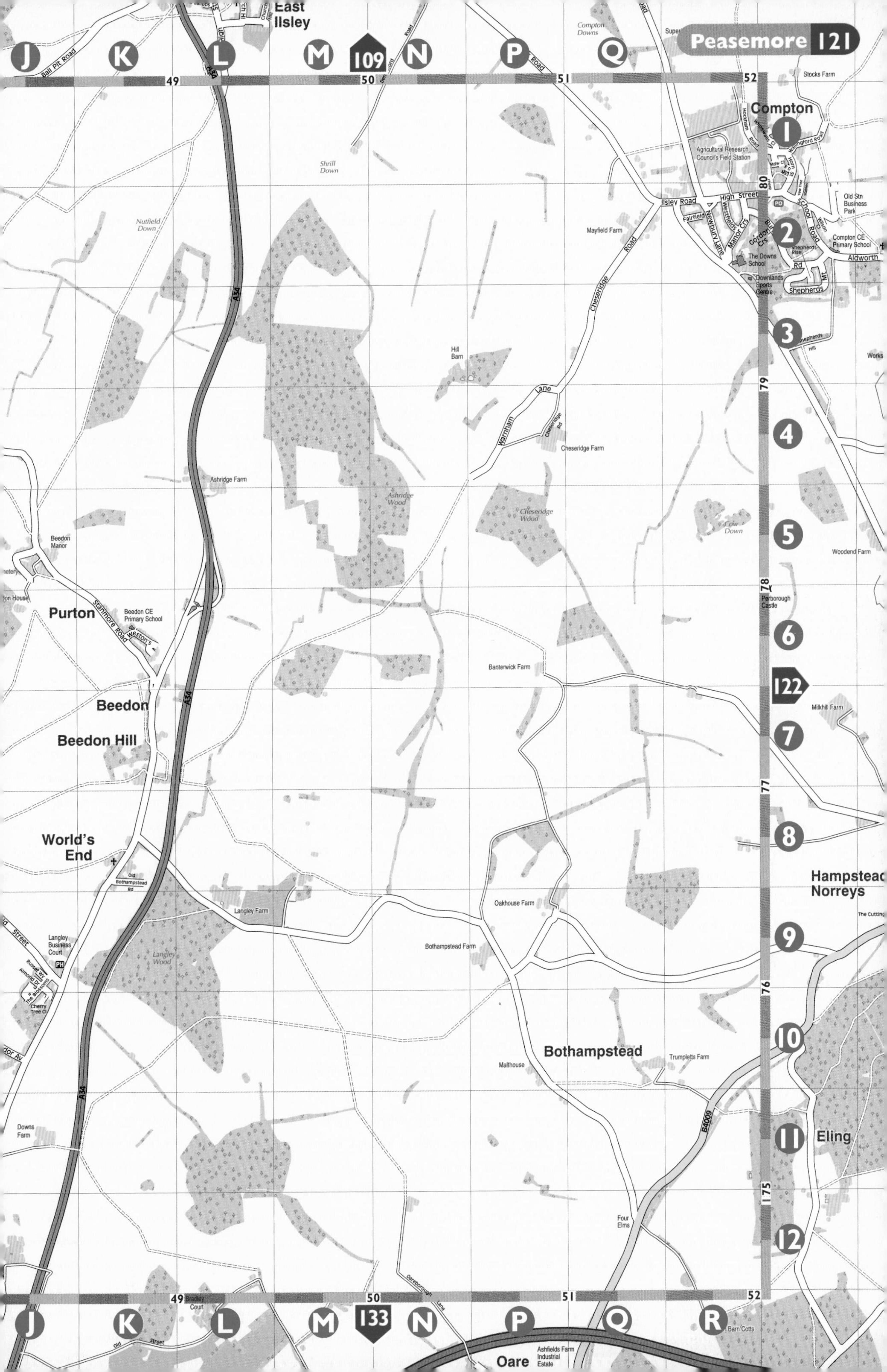

East Ilsley
Compton Downs
Compton
Stocks Farm
Agricultural Research Council's Field Station
Shrill Down
Nutfield Down
Ilsley Road
High Street
Old Stn Business Park
Mayfield Farm
Fairfield
Newbury Lane
Westfields
Manor Crs
Gordon Crs
School Road
Compton CE Primary School
Aldworth
The Downs School
Shepherds Rise
Downlands Sports Centre
Shepherds Hill
Cheseridge Road
Hill Barn
Works
Warnham Lane
Cheseridge Rd
Cheseridge Farm
Ashridge Farm
Ashridge Wood
Cheseridge Wood
Cow Down
Beedon Manor
Woodend Farm
Purton
Beedon CE Primary School
Stanmore Road
Weston's
Perborough Castle
Banterwick Farm
Milkhill Farm
Beedon
Beedon Hill
A34
World's End
Old Bothampstead Rd
Hampstead Norreys
Oakhouse Farm
Langley Farm
The Cutting
Langley Business Court
Bothampstead Farm
Langley Wood
Russet Wy
Almond Dr
The Blossoms
Cherry Tree Cl
Bothampstead
Malthouse
Trumpletts Farm
B4009
Downs Farm
Eling
Four Elms
Bradley Court
Oareborough Lane
Old Street
Barn Cotts
Oare
Ashfields Farm Industrial Estate
J
K
L
M
N
P
Q
R
1
2
3
4
5
6
7
8
9
10
11
12
49
50
51
52
80
79
78
77
76
175

109
122
133

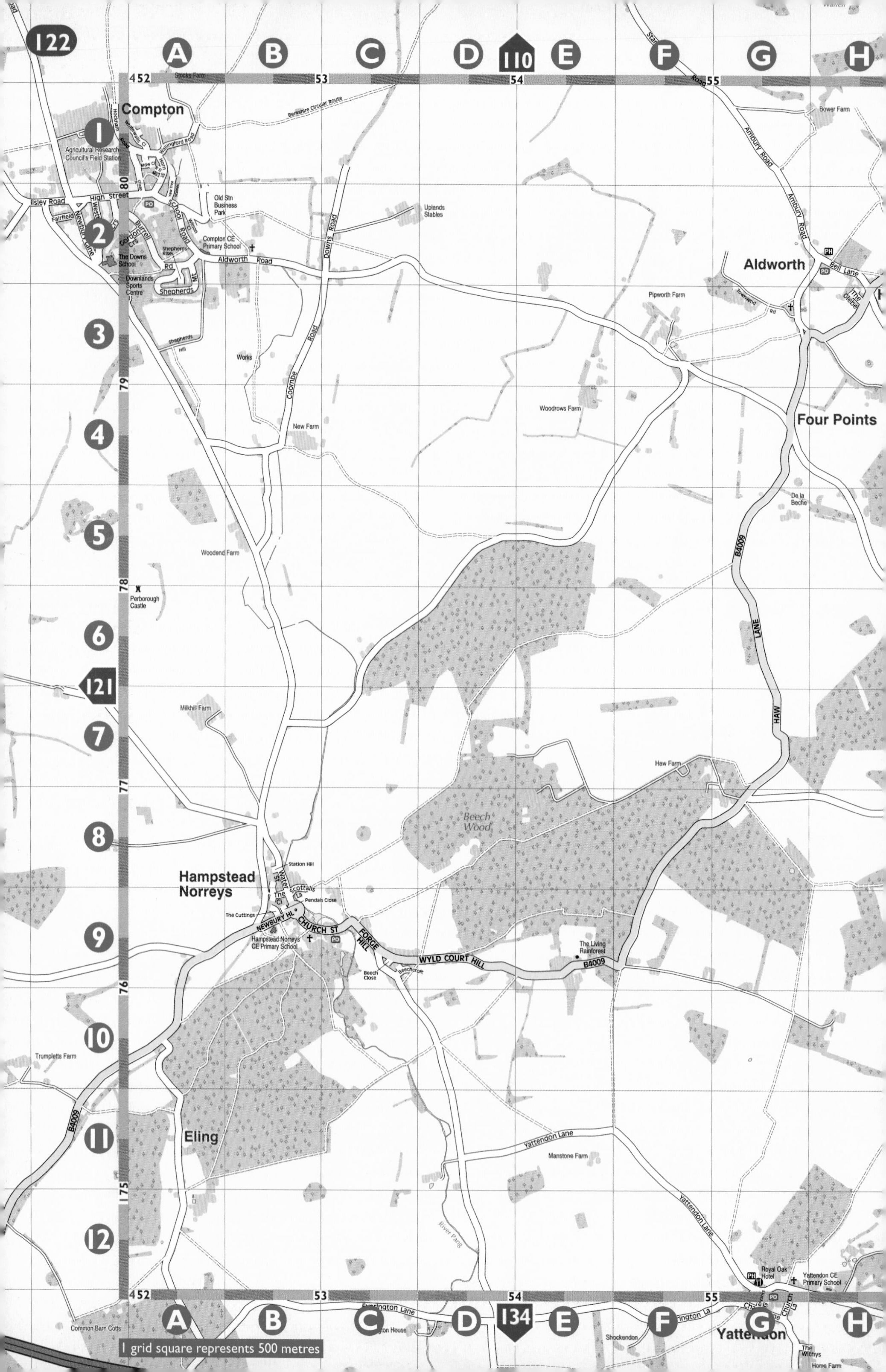

A
B
C
D
E
F
G
H
110
Compton
Agricultural Research Council's Field Station
Hockham Road
Wallingford Road
Ilsley Road
High Street
Fairfield
Newbury Lane
West
Gordon Crs
Burrell Rd
School Road
Old Stn Business Park
Compton CE Primary School
The Downs School
Shepherds Rise
Downlands Sports Centre
Shepherds
Aldworth Road
Shepherds Hill
Berkshire Circular Route
Stocks Farm
Downs Road
Uplands Stables
Works
Coombe Road
New Farm
Ambury Road
Aldworth
Bell Lane
Townsend Rd
The Glebe
Pipworth Farm
Woodrows Farm
Four Points
De la Beche
B4009
Woodend Farm
Perborough Castle
121
Milkhill Farm
HAW LANE
Haw Farm
Beech Wood
Hampstead Norreys
Station Hill
Water St
The Cl
Scottalls La
Pendals Close
The Cuttings
NEWBURY HL
CHURCH ST
FORGE HILL
WYLD COURT HILL
Hampstead Norreys CE Primary School
Beech Close
Beechcroft
The Living Rainforest
B4009
Trumpletts Farm
B4009
Eling
Yattendon Lane
Manstone Farm
River Pang
Yattendon Lane
Royal Oak Hotel
PH
Yattendon CE Primary School
Church La
Everington Lane
Everington House
Shockendon
Everington La
Yattendon
The Withys
Home Farm
Common Barn Cotts
134
452
53
54
55
80
79
78
77
76
175
1
2
3
4
5
6
7
8
9
10
11
12
1 grid square represents 500 metres

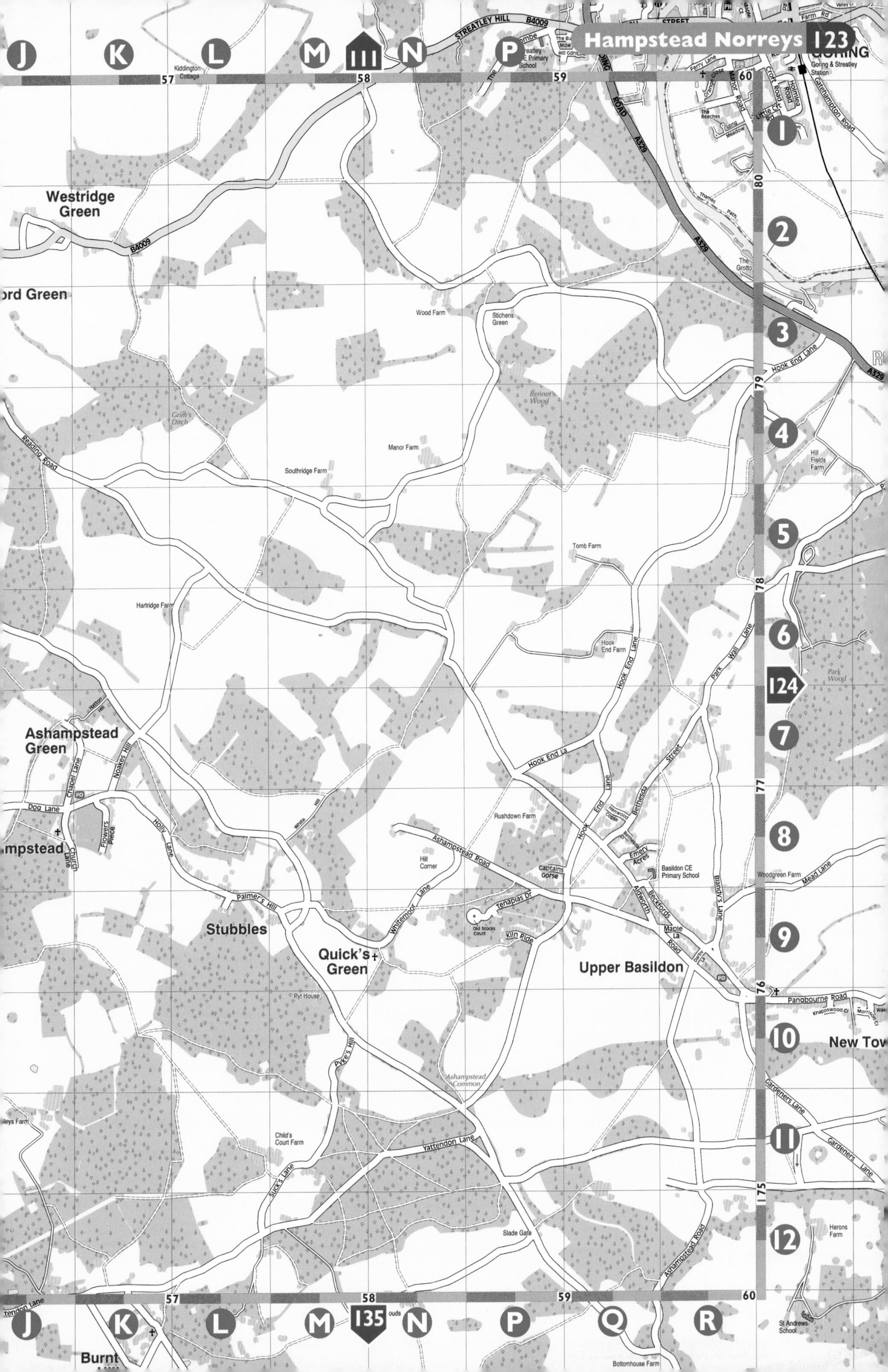
Westridge Green
Ashampstead Green
Stubbles
Quick's Green
Upper Basildon
New Tow
Wood Farm
Stichens Green
Bennet's Wood
Manor Farm
Southridge Farm
Grim's Ditch
Reading Road
Hartridge Farm
Tomb Farm
Hook End Farm
Hook End Lane
Hook End La
Park Wall Lane
Park Wood
Hill Fields Farm
Hook End Lane
Rushdown Farm
Ashampstead Road
Hill Corner
Captains Gorse
Basildon CE Primary School
Woodgreen Farm
Mead Lane
Blandy's Lane
Tenapias Dr
Old Stocks Court
Kiln Ride
Whitemoor Lane
White Hill
Palmer's Hill
Holly Lane
Noakes Hill
Chapel Lane
Dog Lane
Church Lane
Flowers Piece
Pyt House
Pyke's Hill
Ashampstead Common
Child's Court Farm
Yattendon Lane
Suck's Lane
Slade Gate
Gardeners Lane
Pangbourne Road
Herons Farm
St Andrews School
Bottomhouse Farm
Burnt
STREATLEY HILL
B4009
A329
Goring & Streatley Station
Thames Path
The Grotto
Kiddington Cottage
Bethesda Street
Maple La
Road
Aldworth
Beckfords
Emery Acres
Henwood Copse
Manor Road
The Beeches
Long Meadow
124
135

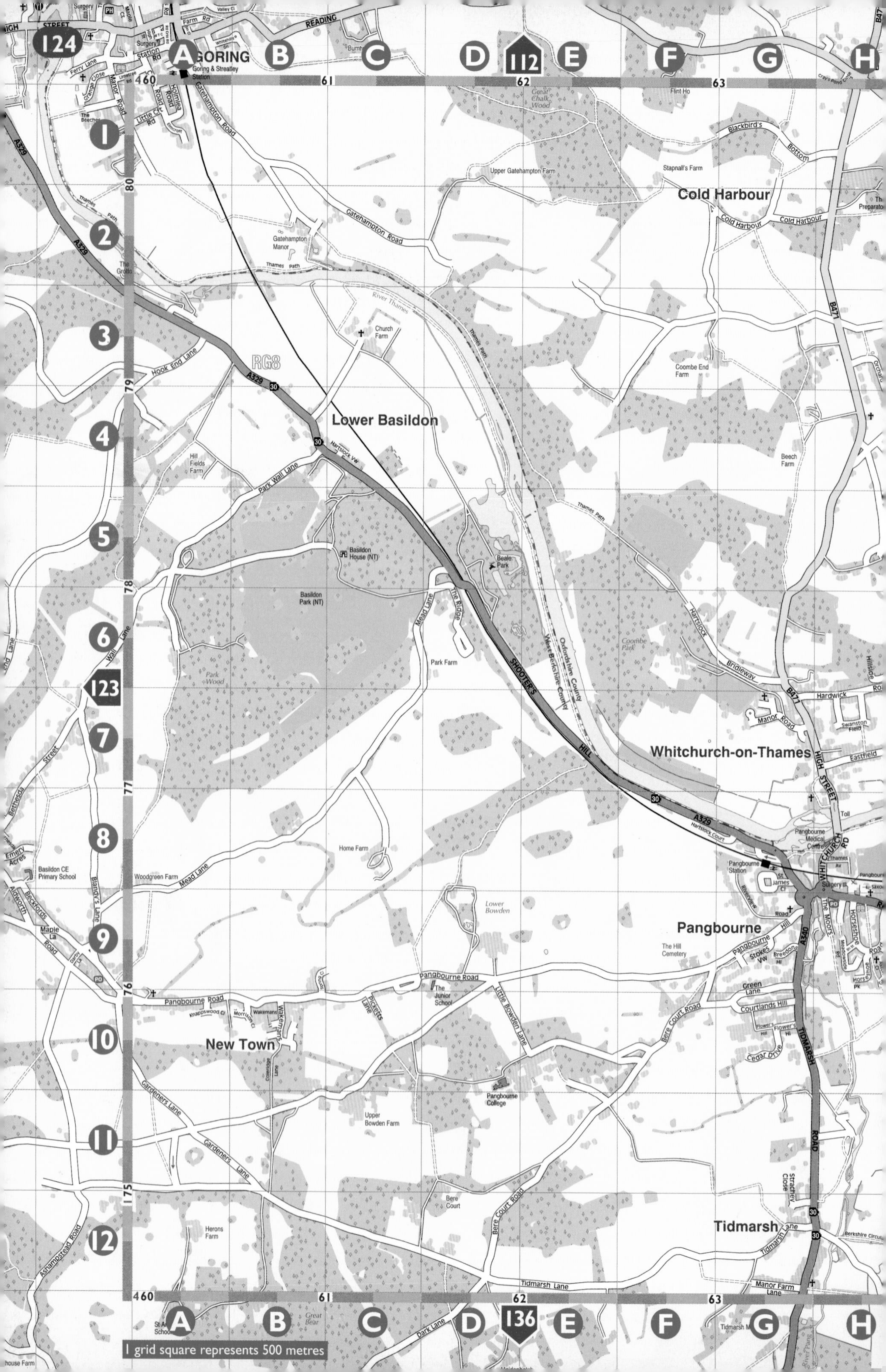

124
112
123
136
GORING
Goring & Streatley Station
Lower Basildon
Basildon House (NT)
Basildon Park (NT)
Park Wood
Beale Park
Church Farm
Gatehampton Manor
Upper Gatehampton Farm
Great Chalk Wood
Cold Harbour
Stapnall's Farm
Coombe End Farm
Beech Farm
Coombe Park
Whitchurch-on-Thames
Pangbourne
Pangbourne Station
Pangbourne Medical Centre
The Hill Cemetery
Park Farm
Home Farm
Lower Bowden
Woodgreen Farm
Basildon CE Primary School
Hill Fields Farm
New Town
The Junior School
Pangbourne College
Upper Bowden Farm
Bere Court
Herons Farm
Tidmarsh
River Thames
Thames Path
Gatehampton Road
Hook End Lane
Park Wall Lane
Mead Lane
Pangbourne Road
Little Bowden Lane
Bere Court Road
Tidmarsh Lane
Gardeners Lane
Ashampstead Road
Blandy's Lane
Bethesda Street
Hartslock Bridleway
Hartslock Court
Hardwick Road
Manor Road
HIGH STREET
WHITCHURCH RD
TIDMARSH ROAD
Courtlands Hill
Green Lane
Cedar Drive
Strachey Close
Manor Farm Lane
Dark Lane
SHOOTER'S HILL
A329
A340
B471
RG8
Oxfordshire County
West Berkshire County
460
61
62
63
175
76
77
78
79
80
I grid square represents 500 metres

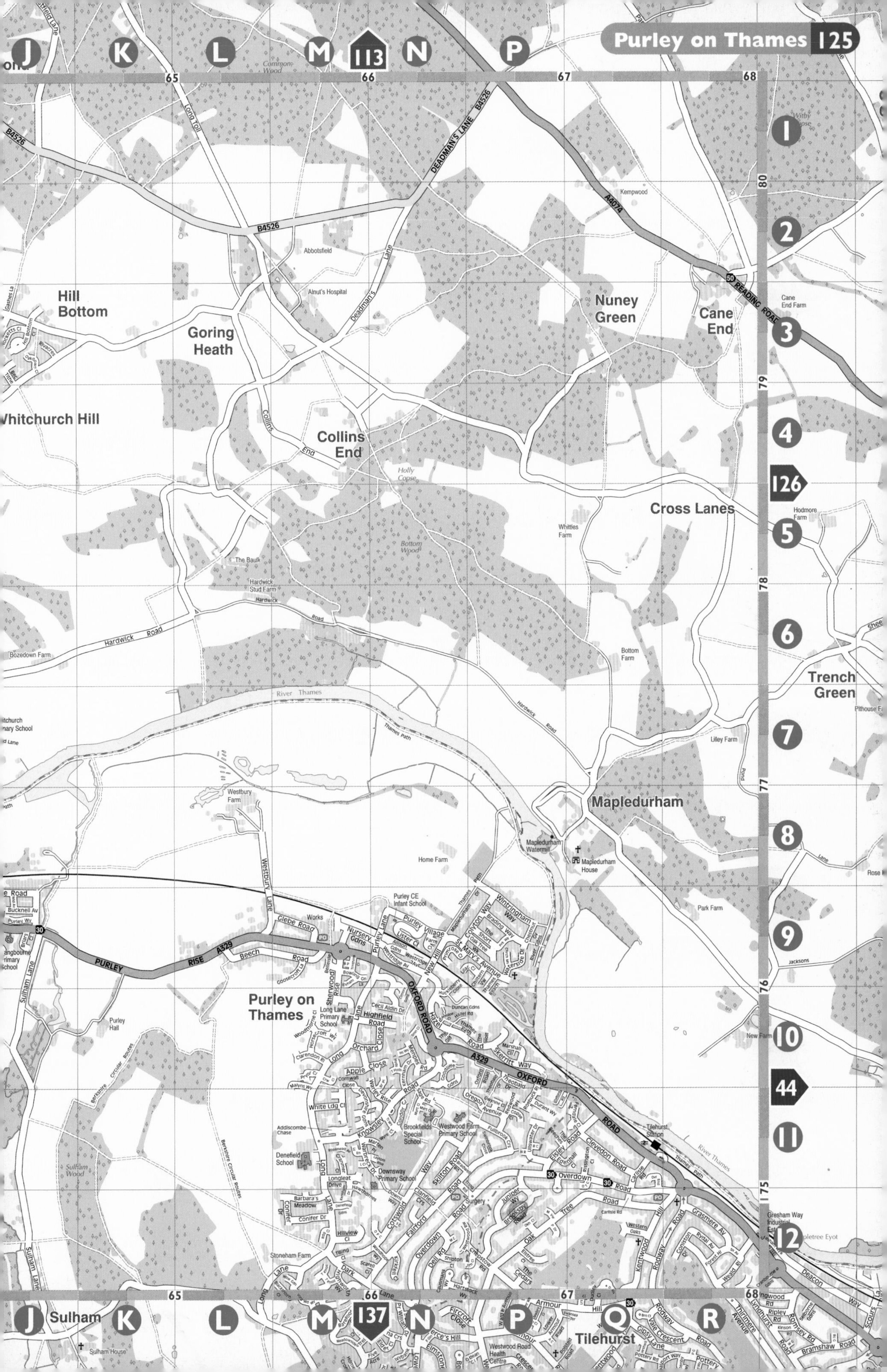
Hill Bottom
Goring Heath
Whitchurch Hill
Collins End
Nuney Green
Cane End
Cross Lanes
Trench Green
Mapledurham
Purley on Thames
Tilehurst
Sulham
B4526
A4074
READING ROAD
DEADMAN'S LANE
Long Toll
Abbotsfield
Alnut's Hospital
Kempwood
Hardwick Road
Bozedown Farm
Hardwick Stud Farm
The Baulk
Bottom Wood
Holly Copse
Whittles Farm
Bottom Farm
Hodmore Farm
Lilley Farm
River Thames
Thames Path
Westbury Farm
Home Farm
Mapledurham Watermill
Mapledurham House
Park Farm
Jacksons
New Farm
PURLEY RISE
A329
OXFORD ROAD
Westbury Lane
Glebe Road
Beech Road
Purley Village
Purley CE Infant School
Long Lane Primary School
Highfield Road
Orchard Close
Purley Hall
Berkshire Circular Routes
Sulham Lane
Sulham Wood
Denefield School
Addiscombe Chase
Brookfields Special School
Westwood Farm Primary School
Downsway Primary School
Overdown Road
Clevedon Road
Tilehurst Station
Gresham Way Industrial Estate
Appletree Eyot
Stoneham Farm
Sulham House
Westwood Road Health Centre
Armour Hill
Gipsy Lane
Vale Crescent
Bramshaw Road
Deacon Way
Scours Lane
113
126
44
137
J K L M N P Q R
65 66 67 68
1 2 3 4 5 6 7 8 9 10 11 12
80 79 78 77 76 175

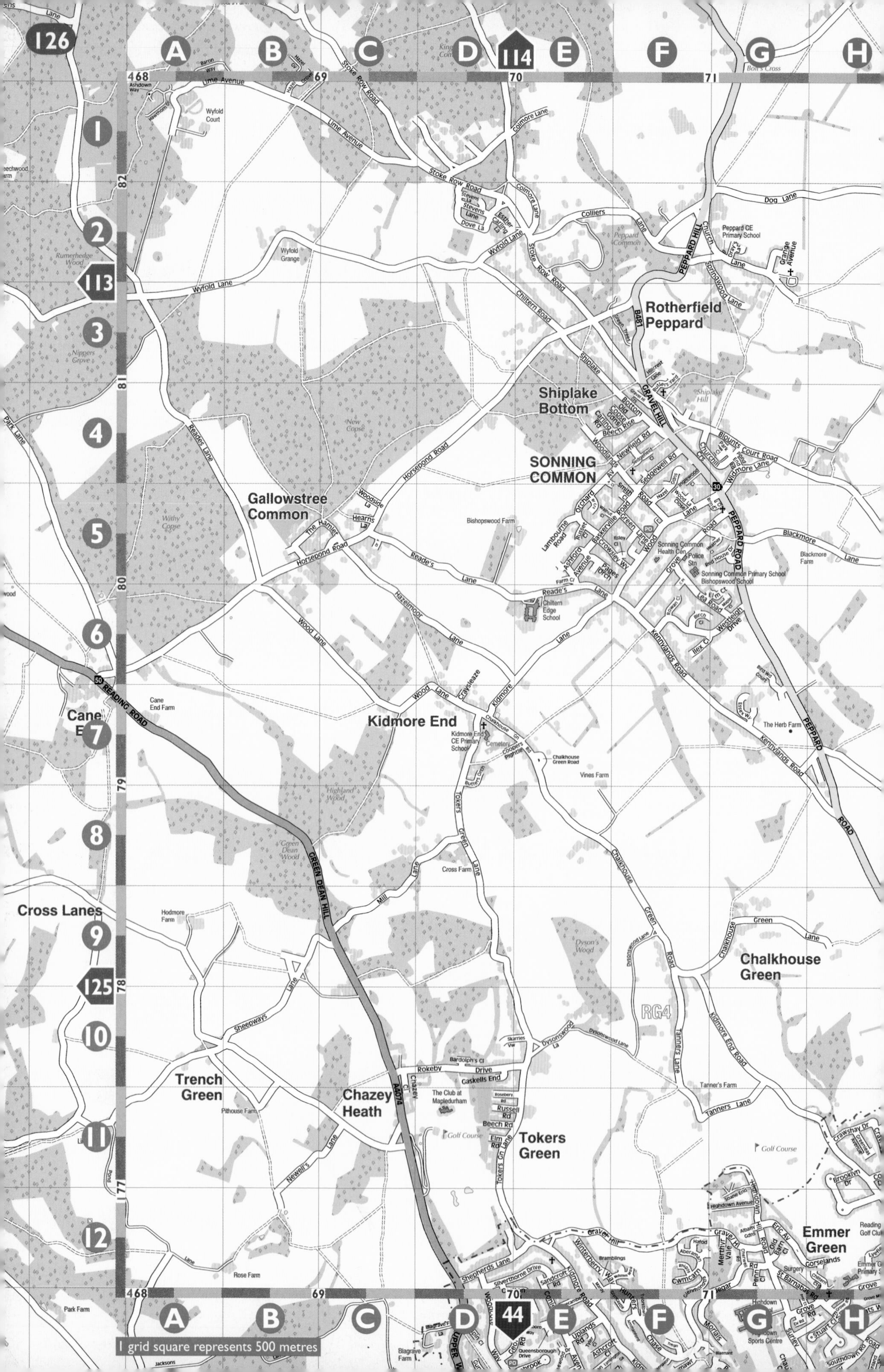

126
114
113
125
44
Rotherfield Peppard
Shiplake Bottom
SONNING COMMON
Gallowstree Common
Kidmore End
Cane End
Cross Lanes
Chalkhouse Green
Trench Green
Chazey Heath
Tokers Green
Emmer Green
Lime Avenue
Stoke Row Road
Colmore Lane
Wyfold Lane
Wyfold Court
Wyfold Grange
Colliers Lane
Dog Lane
Peppard Common
PEPPARD HILL
Peppard CE Primary School
Chiltern Road
Shiplake Bottom
GRAVEL HILL
Blounts Court Road
Widmore Lane
Horsepond Road
Reades Lane
Reade's Lane
Hazelmoor Lane
Wood Lane
Kennylands Road
PEPPARD ROAD
Blackmore Lane
Blackmore Farm
Sonning Common Primary School
Bishopswood School
Bishopswood Farm
Chiltern Edge School
Sonning Common Health Cen
READING ROAD
Cane End Farm
GREEN DEAN HILL
A4074
Kidmore End CE Primary School
Cemetery
Tokers Green Lane
Cross Farm
Mill Lane
Chalkhouse Green Road
Vines Farm
The Herb Farm
Dyson's Wood
Dysonswood Lane
RG4
Kidmore End Road
Tanners Lane
Tanner's Farm
Sheepways Lane
Hodmore Farm
Pithouse Farm
Newell's Lane
The Club at Mapledurham
Golf Course
Rokeby Drive
Gaskells End
Rosebery Rd
Russell Rd
Beech Rd
Elm Rd
Highdown Avenue
Highdown Hill Road
Grave Hill
Shepherds Lane
Silverthorne Drive
Kidmore Road
Rose Farm
Park Farm
Highdown Sports Centre
Reading Golf Club
1 grid square represents 500 metres

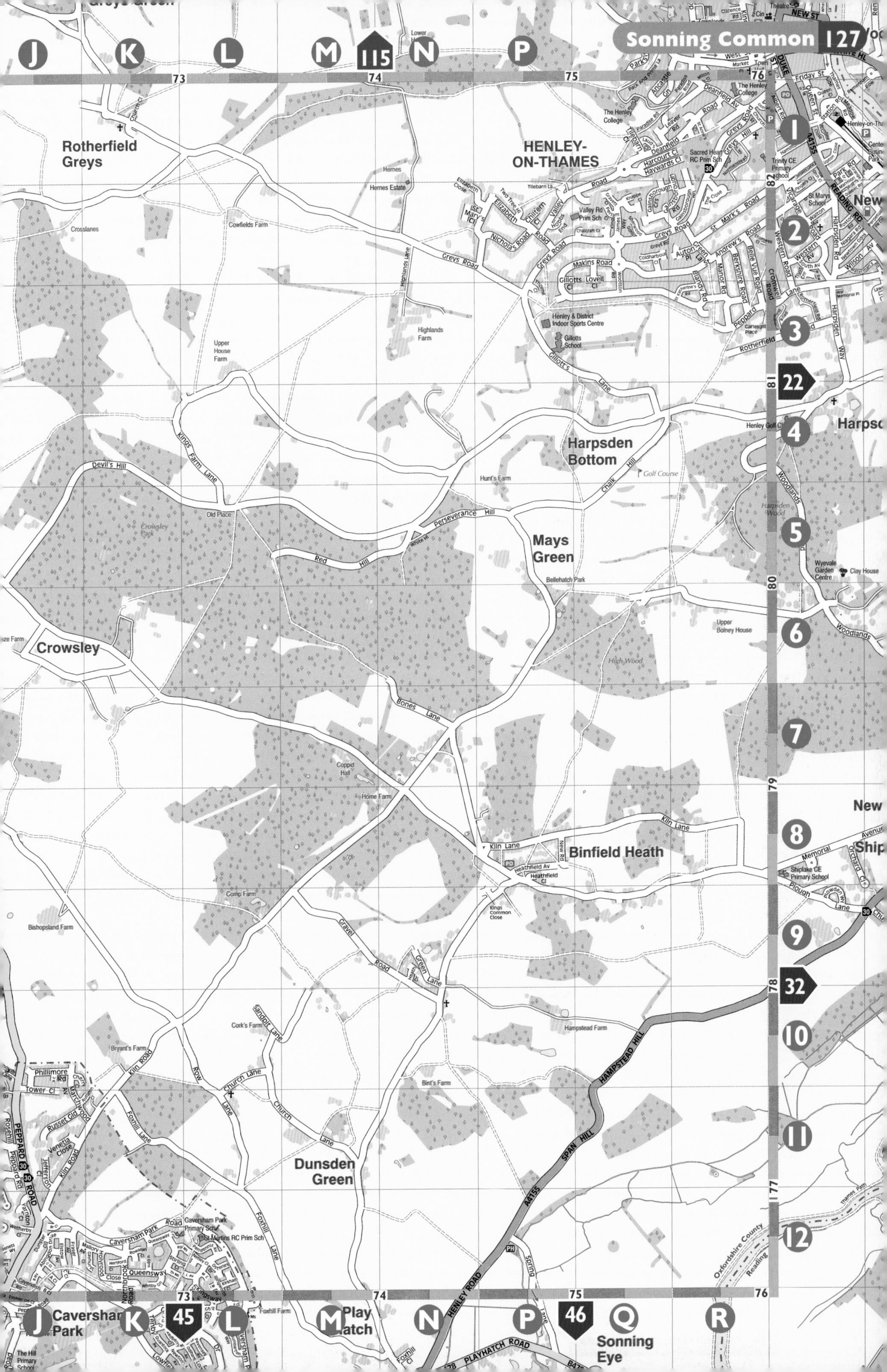
Rotherfield Greys
HENLEY-ON-THAMES
Greys Road
Harpsden Bottom
Mays Green
Crowsley
Devil's Hill
Kings Farm Lane
Perseverance Hill
Red Hill
Bones Lane
Binfield Heath
Kiln Lane
Dunsden Green
Gravel Road
Church Lane
Foxhill Lane
HAMPSTEAD HILL
SPAN HILL
HENLEY ROAD
PLAYHATCH ROAD
Sonning Eye
Caversham Park
Play Hatch
Harpsden Wood
High Wood
Crowsley Park
Upper House Farm
Highlands Farm
Hernes Estate
Cowfields Farm
Crosslanes
Old Place
Hunt's Farm
Golf Course
Bellehatch Park
Upper Bolney House
Coppid Hall
Home Farm
Comp Farm
Bishopsland Farm
Cork's Farm
Bryant's Farm
Bint's Farm
Hampstead Farm
Gillotts School
Henley & District Indoor Sports Centre
Wyevale Garden Centre
Shiplake CE Primary School
Caversham Park Primary Sch
St Martins RC Prim Sch
Oxfordshire County
Reading
115
22
32
45
46

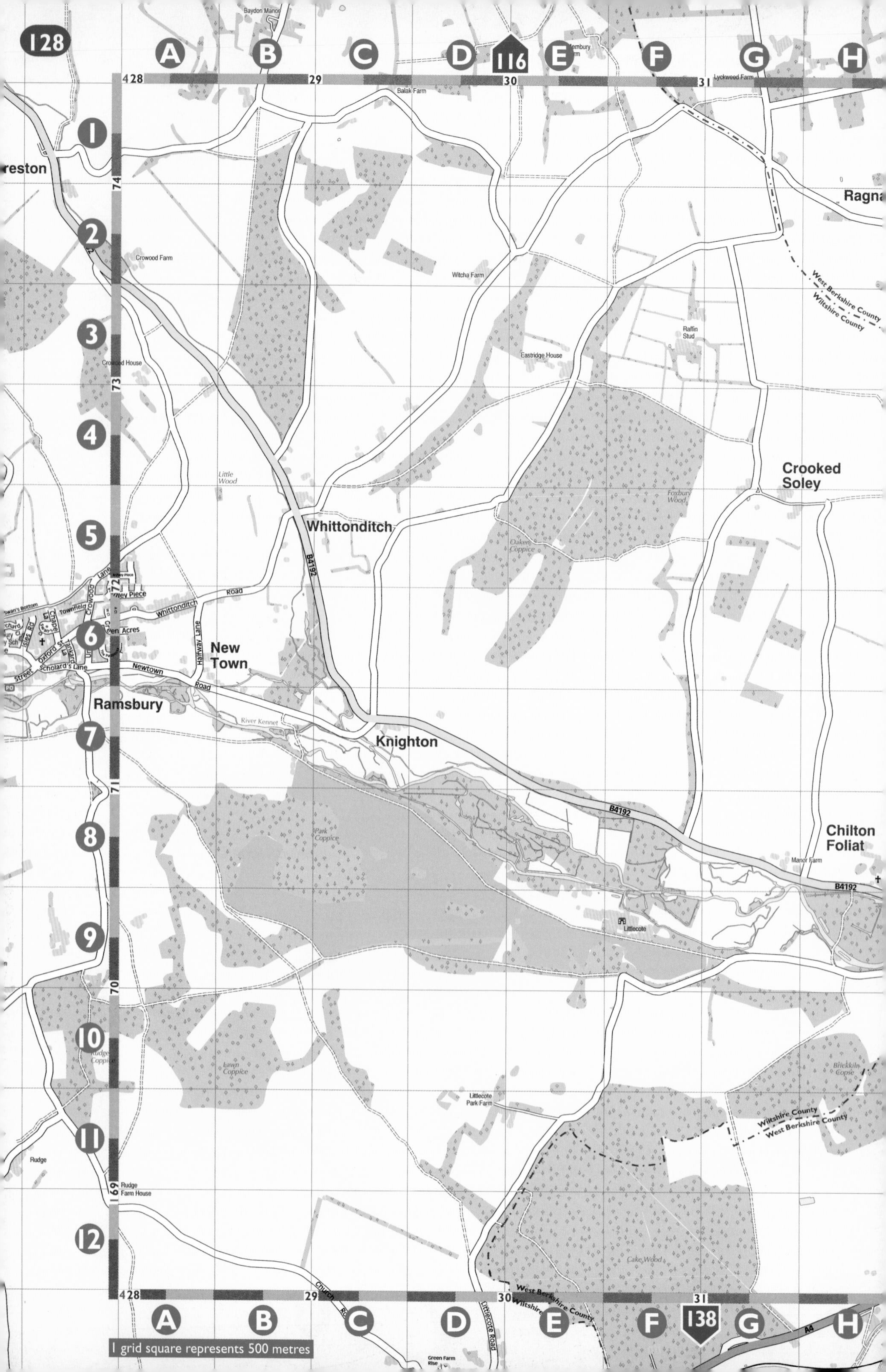

A B C D 116 E F G H

428 29 30 31 Lyckweed Farm

Baydon Manor

1

74

Preston

Balak Farm

Ragna

2

Crowood Farm

Witcha Farm

West Berkshire County
Wiltshire County

3

73

Crowood House

Raffin Stud

Eastridge House

4

Little Wood

Oakers Coppice

Foxbury Wood

Crooked Soley

5

B4192

Whittonditch

Ashley Piece
Townfield Piece
Green Acres

Whittonditch Road

6

New Town

Newtown Road

Halfway Lane

Oxford Rd

Scholard's Lane

Ramsbury

River Kennet

7

711

Knighton

B4192

8

Park Coppice

Chilton Foliat

Manor Farm

B4192

9

70

Littlecote

10

Budge Coppice

Lawn Coppice

Brickkiln Copse

11

Littlecote Park Farm

Wiltshire County
West Berkshire County

69

Rudge

Rudge Farm House

12

West Berkshire County
Wiltshire

Cake Wood

428 29 30 31

A B C D E F 138 G H

Chilton Rd
Littlecote Road
A4

Green Farm Rise

1 grid square represents 500 metres

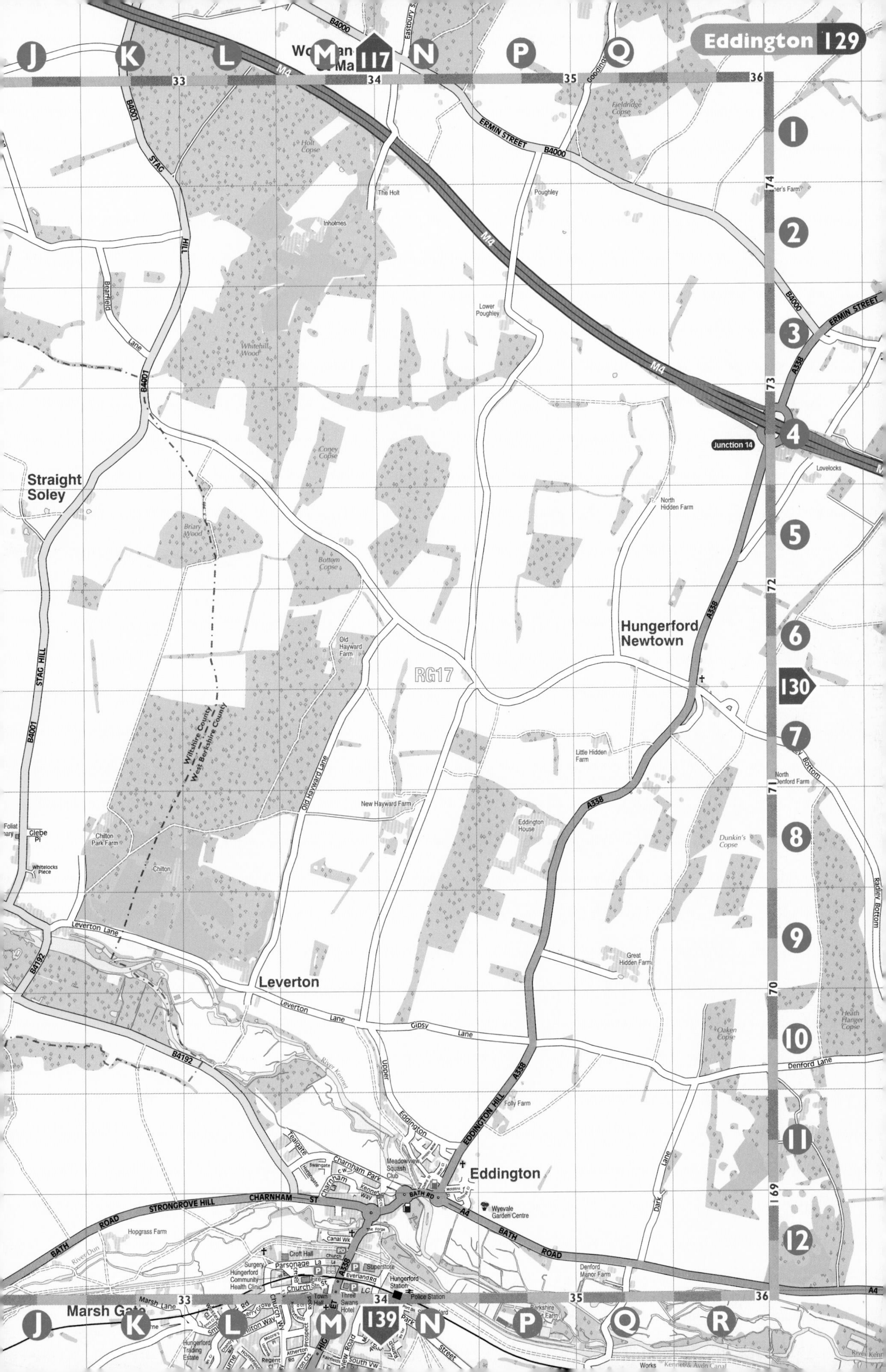

M4
B4000
ERMIN STREET
Fieldridge Copse
Holt Copse
The Holt
Poughley
Inholmes
STAG HILL
B4001
Bearfield Lane
Whitehill Wood
Lower Poughley
Junction 14
A338
Lovelocks
Coney Copse
Straight Soley
North Hidden Farm
Briary Wood
Bottom Copse
Hungerford Newtown
Old Hayward Farm
RG17
Little Hidden Farm
Wiltshire County
West Berkshire County
Old Hayward Lane
North Denford Farm
New Hayward Farm
Eddington House
Dunkin's Copse
Glebe Pl
Chilton Park Farm
Whitelocks Piece
Chilton
Radley Bottom
Leverton Lane
Great Hidden Farm
B4192
Leverton
Gipsy Lane
Oaken Copse
Heath Hanger Copse
Denford Lane
River Kennet
Upper Eddington
EDDINGTON HILL
Folly Farm
Tealgate
Charnham Park
Meadowview Squash Club
Eddington
BATH RD
STRONGROVE HILL
CHARNHAM ST
Wyevale Garden Centre
BATH ROAD
A4
Hopgrass Farm
Canal Wk
Dark Lane
Croft Hall
Parsonage La
Superstore
Everland Rd
Surgery
Hungerford Community Health Clinic
Hungerford Station
Church St
Town Hall
Police Station
Three Swans Hotel
Denford Manor Farm
Berkshire Farm
Marsh Gate
Marsh Lane
Hungerford Trading Estate
Regent
South Vw
Park Street
Works
Kennet & Avon Canal
River Kennet
J K L M N P Q R
33 34 35 36
69 70 71 72 73 74
1 2 3 4 5 6 7 8 9 10 11 12
117 130 139

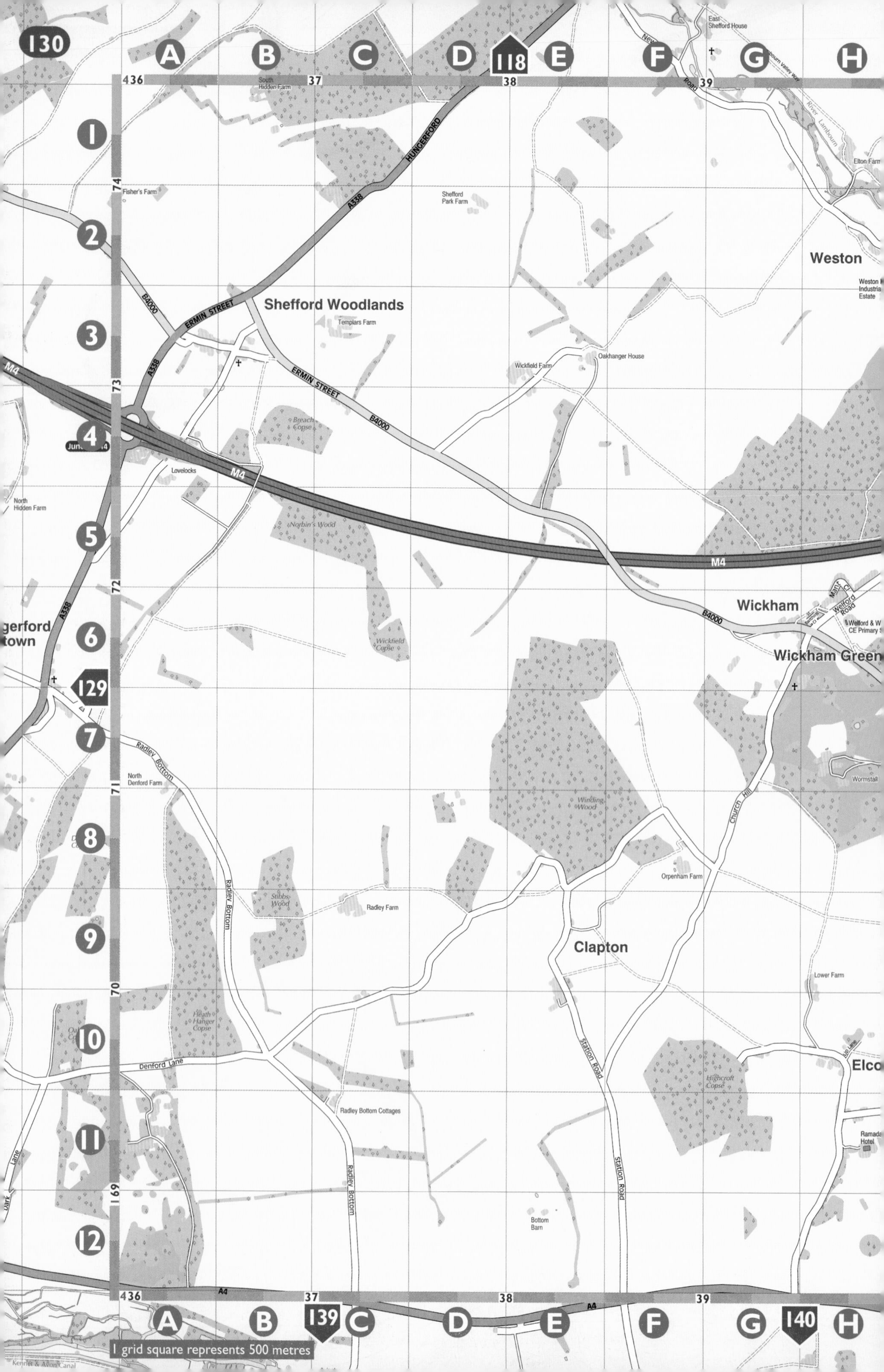

A   B   C   D   E   F   G   H

436   South Hidden Farm   37   38   New   Road   39   East Shefford House

I

Fisher's Farm

Weston

74

2

Weston Industrial Estate

A338   ERMIN STREET   Shefford Park Farm

Elton

Shefford Woodlands

3

Templars Farm   Wickfield Farm   Oakhanger House

ERMIN STREET   B4000

73   †

M4

Junc. 14   Breach Copse

4

M4

Lovelocks   Norbin's Wood   M4

B4000   Wickham

North Hidden Farm

5   Welford & W CE Primary S

72   Wickham Green

gerford town   Wickfield Copse

6   Wormstall

A338   †

129   †

7

Radley Bottom   Winding Wood

North Denford Farm

71

8   Orpenham Farm

Stibbs Wood

9   Clapton   Lower Farm

Radley Bottom   Radley Farm

70

Heath Hanger Copse

10

Denford Lane   Highcroft Copse   Elco

Jarr Lane   11   Ramada Hotel

69   Radley Bottom

Radley Bottom Cottages   Station Road

12

Bottom Barn

436   A4   37   38   A4   39

A   B   139   C   D   E   F   G   140   H

Kennet & Avon Canal

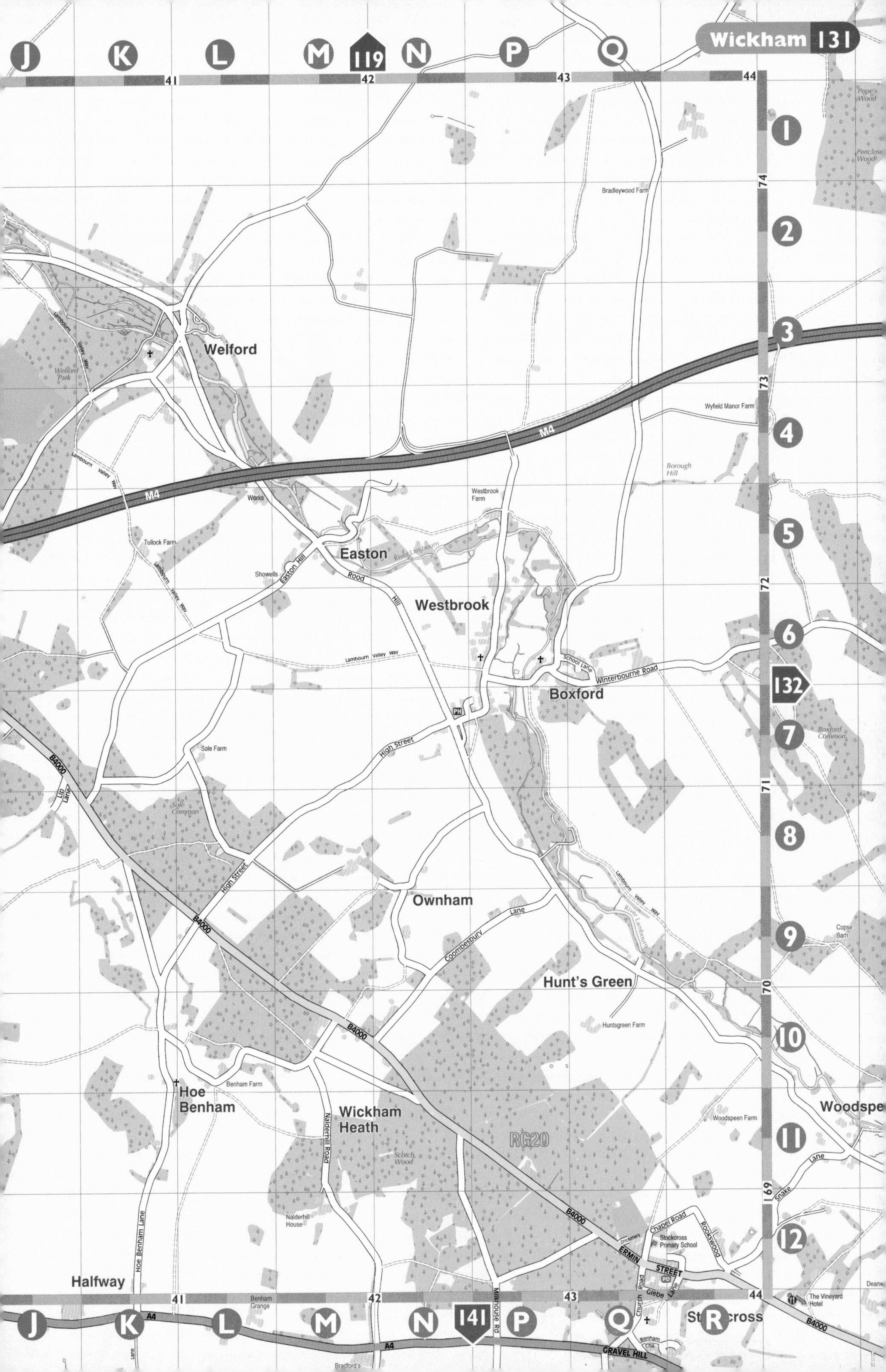
J
K
L
M
119
N
P
Q
Welford
Welford Park
Lambourn Valley Way
M4
Works
Tullock Farm
Showells
Easton Hill
Easton
River Lambourn
Road Hill
Westbrook
Westbrook Farm
Bradleywood Farm
Wyfield Manor Farm
Borough Hill
Pope's Wood
Penclose Wood
Lambourn Valley Way
School Lane
Winterbourne Road
Boxford
132
Boxford Common
High Street
Sole Farm
Sole Common
B4000
Lid Lane
High Street
Ownham
Coombesbury Lane
Hunt's Green
Huntsgreen Farm
Copse Barn
Hoe Benham
Benham Farm
Wickham Heath
Nalderhill Road
Scotch Wood
RG20
Nalderhill House
Woodspeen Farm
Woodspe
Snake Lane
Chapel Road
Rookswood
Stockcross Primary School
ERMIN STREET
Church Road
Glebe Lane
Hoe Benham Lane
Halfway
Benham Grange
Milkhouse Rd
The Vineyard Hotel
Stockcross
A4
GRAVEL HILL
Bradford's
141
R
41
42
43
44
74
73
72
71
70
69
1
2
3
4
5
6
7
8
9
10
11
12

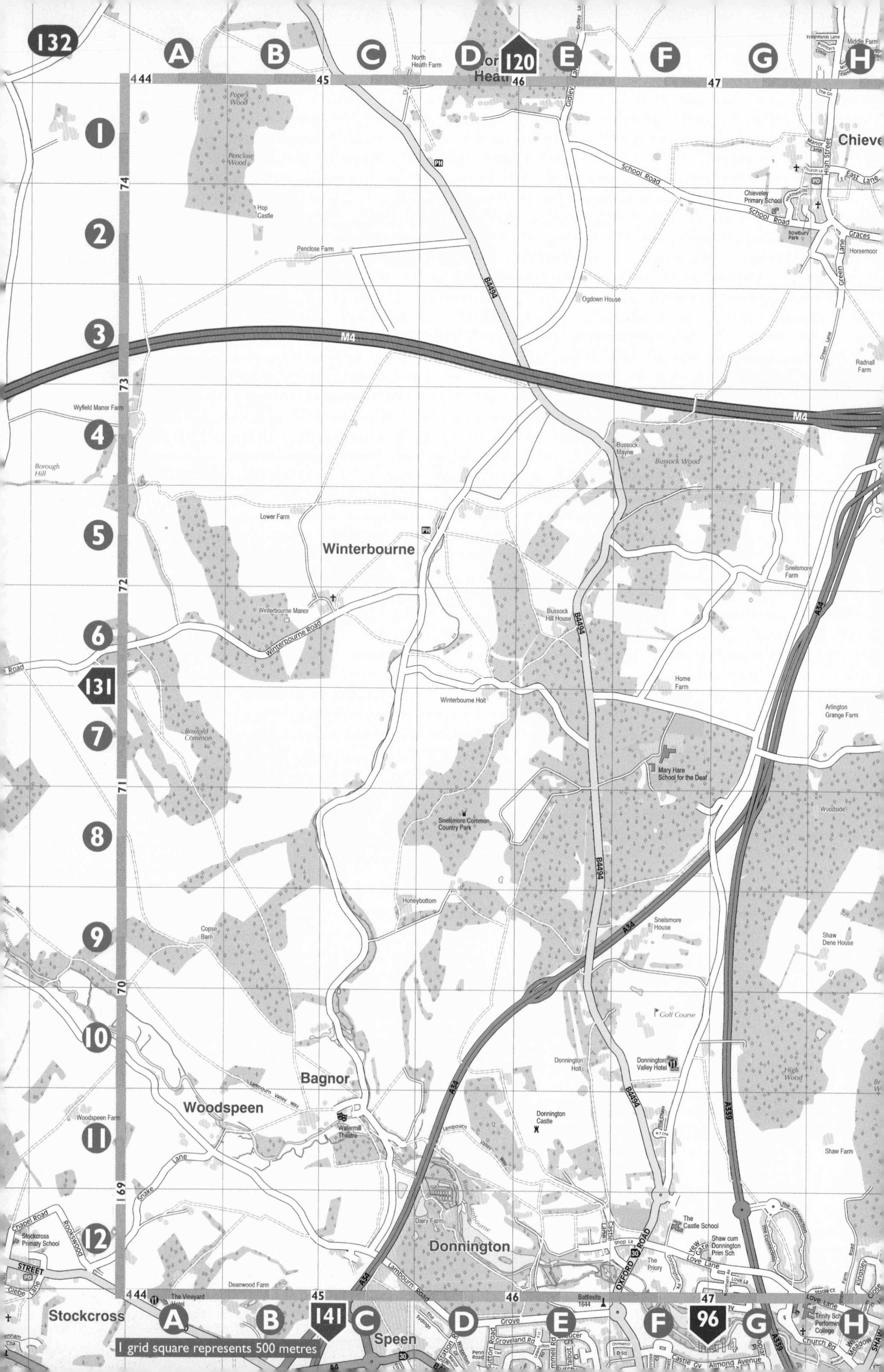

132
A
B
C
D
E
F
G
H
120
North Heath Farm
Heath
Gidley Lane
Freshfields Lane
Middle Farm
Pope's Wood
Penclose Wood
Hop Castle
Penclose Farm
PH
B4494
School Road
Chieveley Primary School
Manor Lane
High Street
Church La
East Lane
Sowbury Park
Green Lane
Graces
Horsemoor
Ogdown House
M4
Radnall Farm
Wyfield Manor Farm
Borough Hill
Bussock Mayne
Bussock Wood
Lower Farm
Winterbourne
Snelsmore Farm
Winterbourne Manor
Winterbourne Road
Bussock Hill House
A34
Home Farm
Winterbourne Holt
Arlington Grange Farm
Boxford Common
Mary Hare School for the Deaf
Woodside
Snelsmore Common Country Park
Honeybottom
Snelsmore House
Shaw Dene House
Copse Barn
Golf Course
Donnington Holt
Donnington Valley Hotel
High Wood
Bagnor
Lambourn Valley Way
Woodspeen
Woodspeen Farm
Watermill Theatre
Donnington Castle
A339
Shaw Farm
Snake Lane
Chapel Road
Rooksnest
Stockcross Primary School
River Lambourn
Dairy Farm
Donnington
The Castle School
Castle Lane
Shop La
Oxford Road
Shaw cum Donnington Prim Sch
The Priory
Love Lane
Street
Glebe Lane
Deanwood Farm
The Vineyard Hotel
Lambourn Road
Battlesite 1644
Stockcross
Speen
Grove
Groveland Rd
Station Rd
Church Rd
Castle Gv
Almond Avenue
Trinity Sch Performing College
Kingsley Close
141
96
1 grid square represents 500 metres

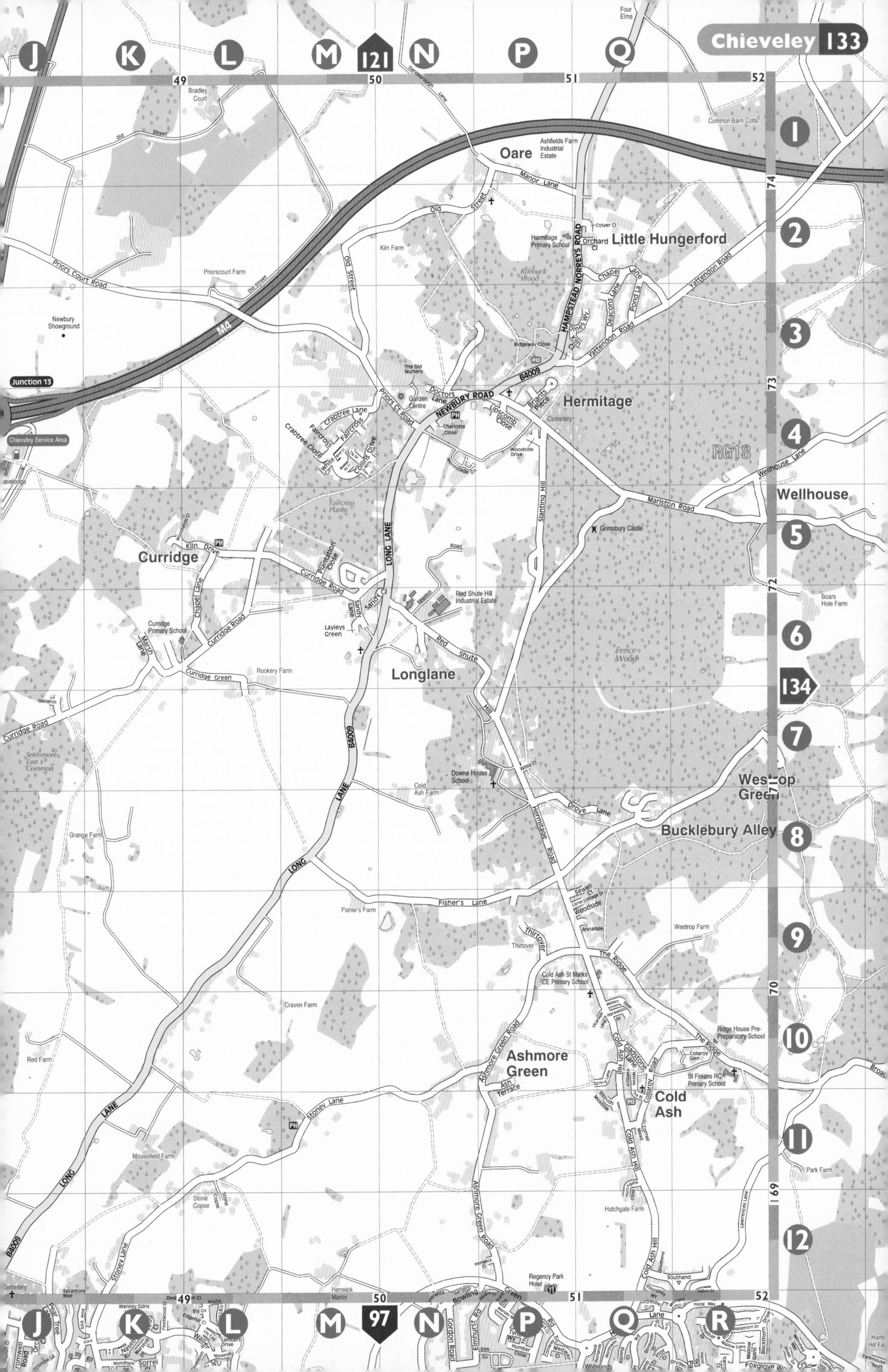

J K L M **121** N P Q

49   50   51   52

J I

Oare

2

Little Hungerford

Hermitage **3**

Garden Centre

NEWBURY ROAD **4**

Wellhouse

5

Curridge

Grimsbury Castle

6

Longlane **134**

7

West?op Green

Bucklebury Alley **8**

9

10

Ashmore Green

Cold Ash

11

12

J K L M **97** N P Q R

49   50   51   52

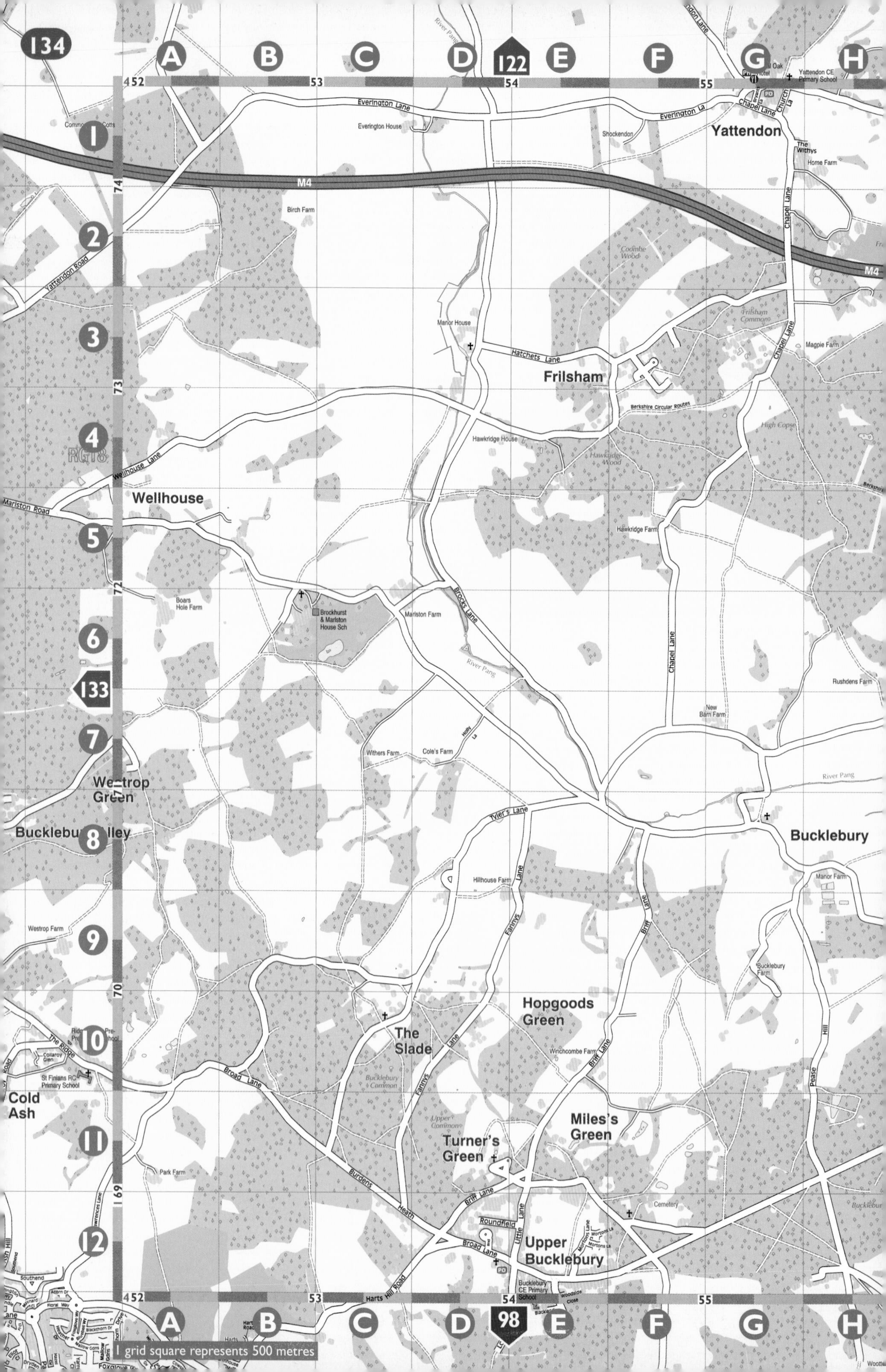

134
A
B
C
D
122
E
F
G
H
452
53
54
55
Everington Lane
Everington House
Shockendon
Everington La
Chapel Lane
Church La
Yattendon
Yattendon CE Primary School
The Withys
Home Farm
M4
Birch Farm
Chapel Lane
Yattendon Road
Coombe Wood
Manor House
Frilsham Common
Hatchets Lane
Magpie Farm
Frilsham
Berkshire Circular Routes
High Copse
Hawkridge House
Hawkridge Wood
Wellhouse Lane
Wellhouse
Marlston Road
Hawkridge Farm
Boars Hole Farm
Brockhurst & Marlston House Sch
Marlston Farm
Brocks Lane
River Pang
Chapel Lane
133
Rushdens Farm
New Barn Farm
Withers Farm
Cole's Farm
Holly La
Westrop Green
River Pang
Tyler's Lane
Bucklebury Alley
Bucklebury
Manor Farm
Hillhouse Farm
Fannys Lane
Briff Lane
Westrop Farm
Bucklebury Farm
Hopgoods Green
The Slade
The Ridge
Collaroy Glen
St Finians RC Primary School
Broad Lane
Bucklebury Common
Winchcombe Farm
Briff Lane
Pease Hill
Cold Ash
Upper Common
Turner's Green
Miles's Green
Park Farm
Burdens Heath
Briff Lane
Cemetery
Roundfield
Little Lane
Mortons Lane
Mortons La
Upper Bucklebury
Broad Lane
Southend
Harts Hill Road
Bucklebury CE Primary School
Woodside Close
98
1 grid square represents 500 metres
1
2
3
4
5
6
7
8
9
10
11
12
74
73
72
71
70
69

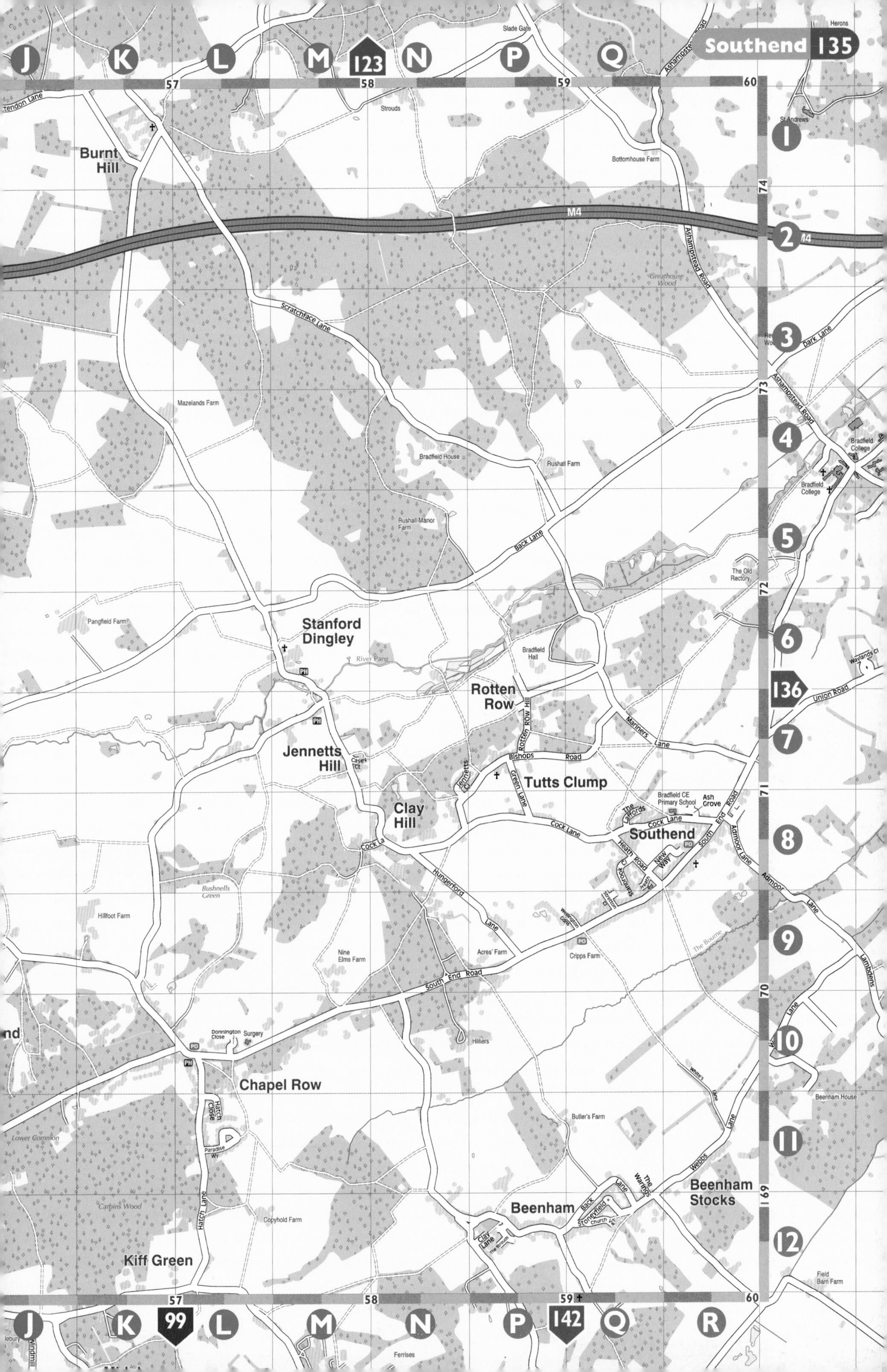
J
K
L
M
123
N
P
Q
57
58
59
60
Burnt Hill
Slade Gate
Strouds
Bottomhouse Farm
Ashampstead Road
M4
Greathouse Wood
Scratchface Lane
Mazelands Farm
Bradfield House
Rushall Farm
Rushall Manor Farm
Back Lane
Dark Lane
Bradfield College
St Andrews
Herons
The Old Rectory
Pangfield Farm
Stanford Dingley
River Pang
Bradfield Hall
Rotten Row
Rotten Row Hill
Waylands Cl
Union Road
136
Mariners Lane
Bishops Road
Jennetts Hill
Casey Ct
Clay Hill
Tutts Clump
Green Lane
Cock Lane
Cock La
Bradfield CE Primary School
Ash Grove
The Lawfords
Southend
South End Road
Admoor Lane
Heath Road
New Way
Sandhurst Cl
Stretton Cl
Hungerford Lane
Bushnells Green
Hillfoot Farm
Nine Elms Farm
Acres' Farm
Cripps Farm
Willington Cotts
The Bourne
Lambdens
South End Road
Donnington Close
Surgery
Hillers
Chapel Row
Hatch Close
Lower Common
Paradise Wy
White's Lane
Beenham House
Butler's Farm
Webbs Lane
The Warings
Back Lane
Beenham Stocks
Stoneyfield
Church La
Beenham
Clay Lane
The Stroude
Carbins Wood
Hatch Lane
Copyhold Farm
Kiff Green
Field Barn Farm
Ferrises
Windmill
99
142
R
1
2
3
4
5
6
7
8
9
10
11
12
74
73
72
71
70
69

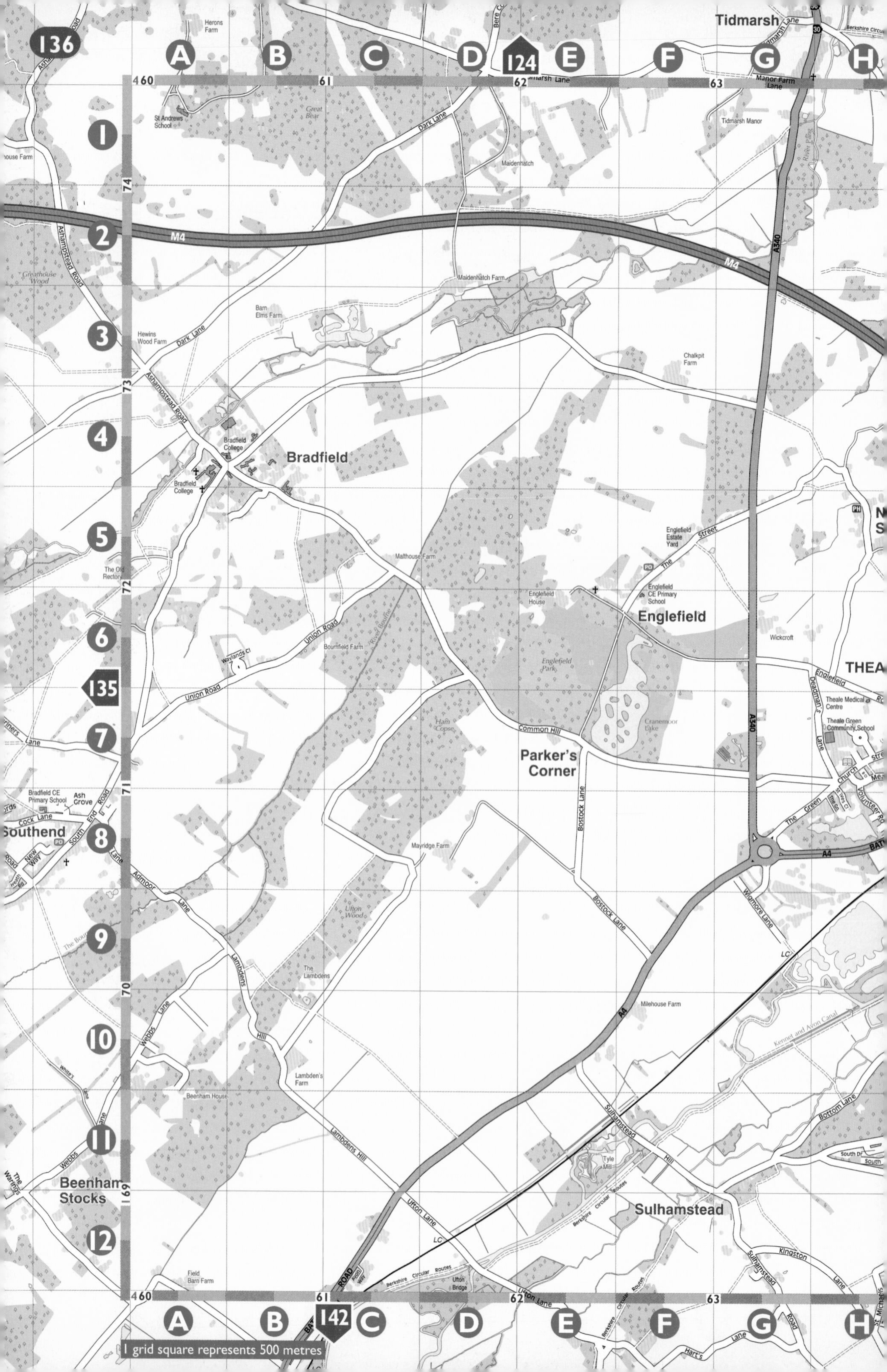

136
124
135
142
A
B
C
D
E
F
G
H
1
2
3
4
5
6
7
8
9
10
11
12
460
61
62
63
74
73
72
71
70
169
Tidmarsh
Herons Farm
Manor Farm Lane
St Andrews School
Great Bear
Dark Lane
Tidmarsh Manor
Maidenhatch
River Pang
M4
A340
Ashampstead Road
Greathouse Wood
Maidenhatch Farm
Barn Elms Farm
Hewins Wood Farm
Chalkpit Farm
Bradfield College
Bradfield
The Old Rectory
Malthouse Farm
Englefield Estate Yard
The Street
Englefield CE Primary School
Englefield House
Englefield
Union Road
Bournfield Farm
Waylands Cl
Wickcroft
Englefield Park
Ham Copse
Common Hill
Cranemoor Lake
Parker's Corner
Theale Medical Centre
Theale Green Community School
Deadman's Lane
Bradfield CE Primary School
Ash Grove
Cock Lane
South End Road
Southend
New Way
Bostock Lane
Mayridge Farm
The Green
Church
A4
Admoor Lane
Ufton Wood
Wigmore Lane
LC
Lambdens
The Lambdens
Milehouse Farm
Kennet and Avon Canal
Webbs Lane
Hill
Lambden's Farm
White's Lane
Beenham House
Sulhamstead Hill
Bottom Lane
Tyle Mill
Lambdens Hill
Beenham Stocks
The Warings
Ufton Lane
Berkshire Circular Routes
Sulhamstead
Kingston Lane
Sulhamstead Road
Field Barn Farm
Ufton Bridge
Hart's Lane
1 grid square represents 500 metres

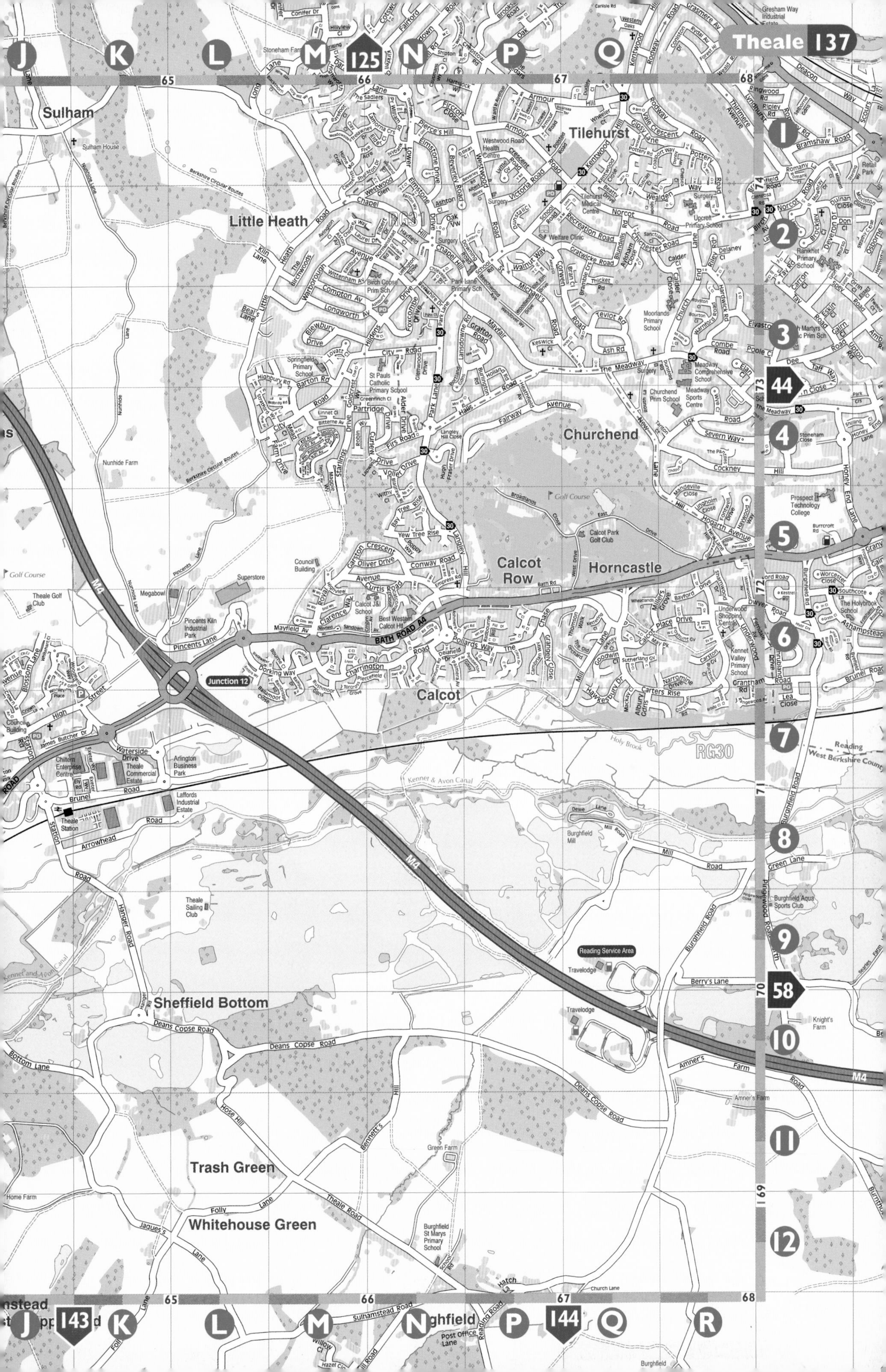

Theale 137
125
44
58
143
144
J
K
L
M
N
P
Q
R
1
2
3
4
5
6
7
8
9
10
11
12
65
66
67
68
74
73
72
71
70
69
Sulham
Sulham House
Little Heath
Tilehurst
Churchend
Calcot Row
Horncastle
Calcot
Sheffield Bottom
Trash Green
Whitehouse Green
Junction 12
M4
BATH ROAD A4
RG30
Holy Brook
Kennet & Avon Canal
Reading
West Berkshire County
Berkshire Circular Routes
Nunhide Farm
Theale Golf Club
Golf Course
Megabowl
Superstore
Pincents Kiln Industrial Park
Pincents Lane
Council Building
Calcot Park Golf Club
Theale Station
Chiltern Enterprise Centre
Theale Commercial Estate
Arlington Business Park
Laffords Industrial Estate
Arrowhead Road
Hanger Road
Theale Sailing Club
Burghfield Mill
Reading Service Area
Travelodge
Burghfield Aqua Sports Club
Knight's Farm
Amner's Farm
Green Farm
Home Farm
Burghfield St Marys Primary School
Deans Copse Road
Bottom Lane
Hose Hill
Folly Lane
Theale Road
Berry's Lane
Mill Road
Green Lane
Burghfield Road
Pingewood Road North
Church Lane
Sulhamstead Road
Post Office Lane
Burghfield
Springfield Primary School
St Pauls Catholic Primary School
Birch Copse Prim Sch
Park Lane Primary Sch
Moorlands Primary School
Meadway Comprehensive School
Meadway Sports Centre
Churchend Prim School
Upcroft Primary School
Ranikhet Primary School
Prospect Technology College
Kennet Valley Primary School
Calcot J&I School
Best Western Calcot Htl
Underwood Shopping Centre
Westwood Road Health Centre
Tilehurst Medical Centre
Welfare Clinic
The Meadway
Norcot Road
City Road
Park Lane
Mayfair
Fairway Avenue
Cockney Hill
Hogarth Avenue
Honey End Lane
Burghfield Rd
Stoneham Farm
Gresham Way Industrial Estate

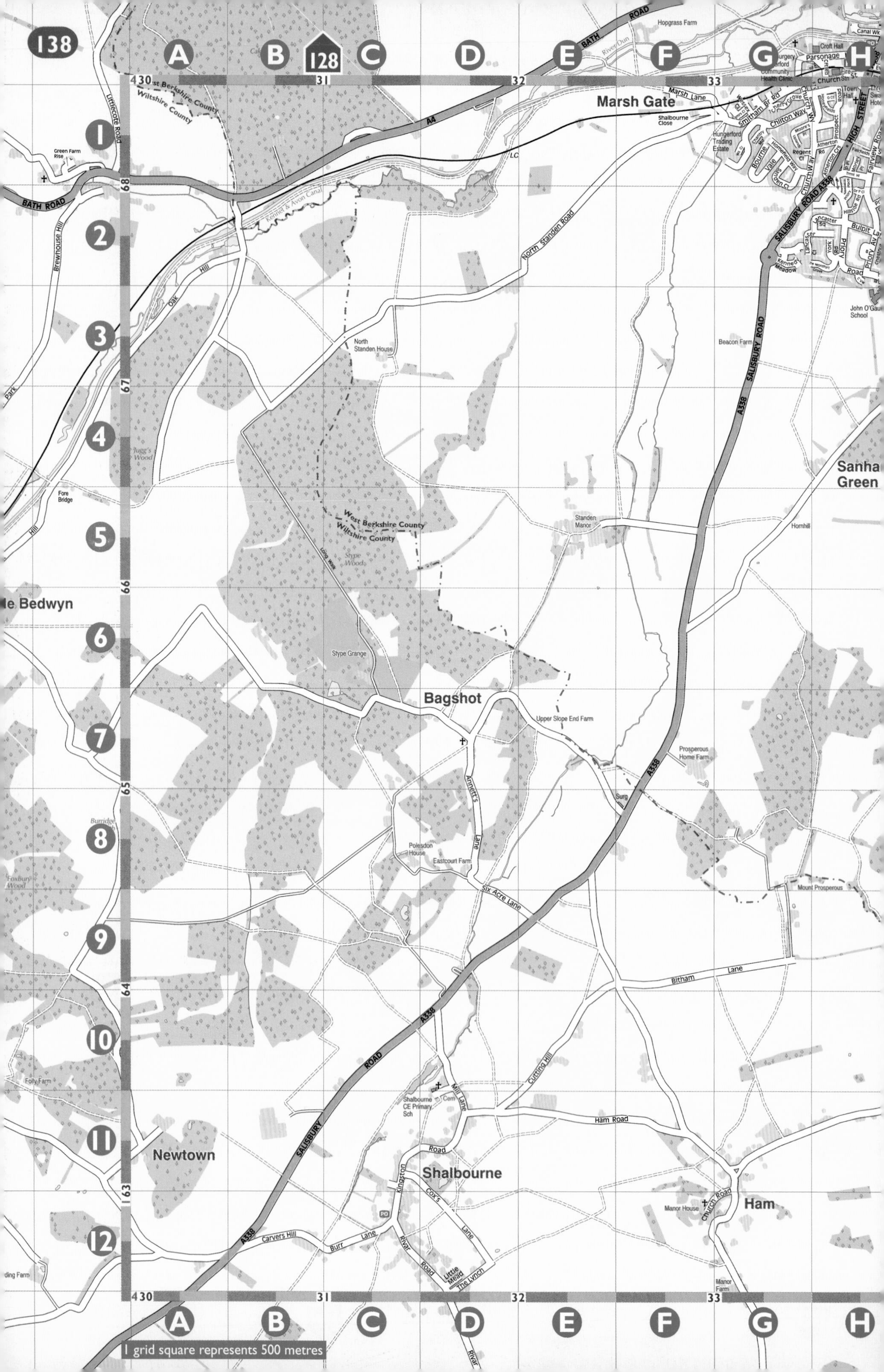

128
Marsh Gate
Hopgrass Farm
Bath Road
A4
Marsh Lane
Shalbourne Close
Hungerford Trading Estate
Kennet & Avon Canal
North Standen Road
North Standen House
West Berkshire County
Wiltshire County
Littlecote Road
Green Farm Rise
Brewhouse Hill
Oak Hill
Jugg's Wood
Fore Bridge
Stype Wood
Long Walk
Stype Grange
Standen Manor
Bagshot
Upper Slope End Farm
Prosperous Home Farm
Beacon Farm
Salisbury Road
A338
Hornhill
Sanha Green
Annett's Lane
Polesdon House
Eastcourt Farm
Six Acre Lane
Mount Prosperous
Bitham Lane
Cutting Hill
Ham Road
Shalbourne CE Primary Sch
Mill Lane
Shalbourne
Kingston Road
Cox's Lane
Rivar Road
Little Mead
The Lynch
Burr Lane
Carvers Hill
Newtown
Burridge
Foxbury Wood
Folly Farm
Ham
Church Road
Manor House
Manor Farm
John O'Gaunt School
High Street
Bulpit Lane
Priory Road
Atherton Road
Regent
Chilton Way
Smitham Br Rd
Croft Hall
Parsonage
Church St
Town Hall
Canal Wk
Bedwyn
1 grid square represents 500 metres

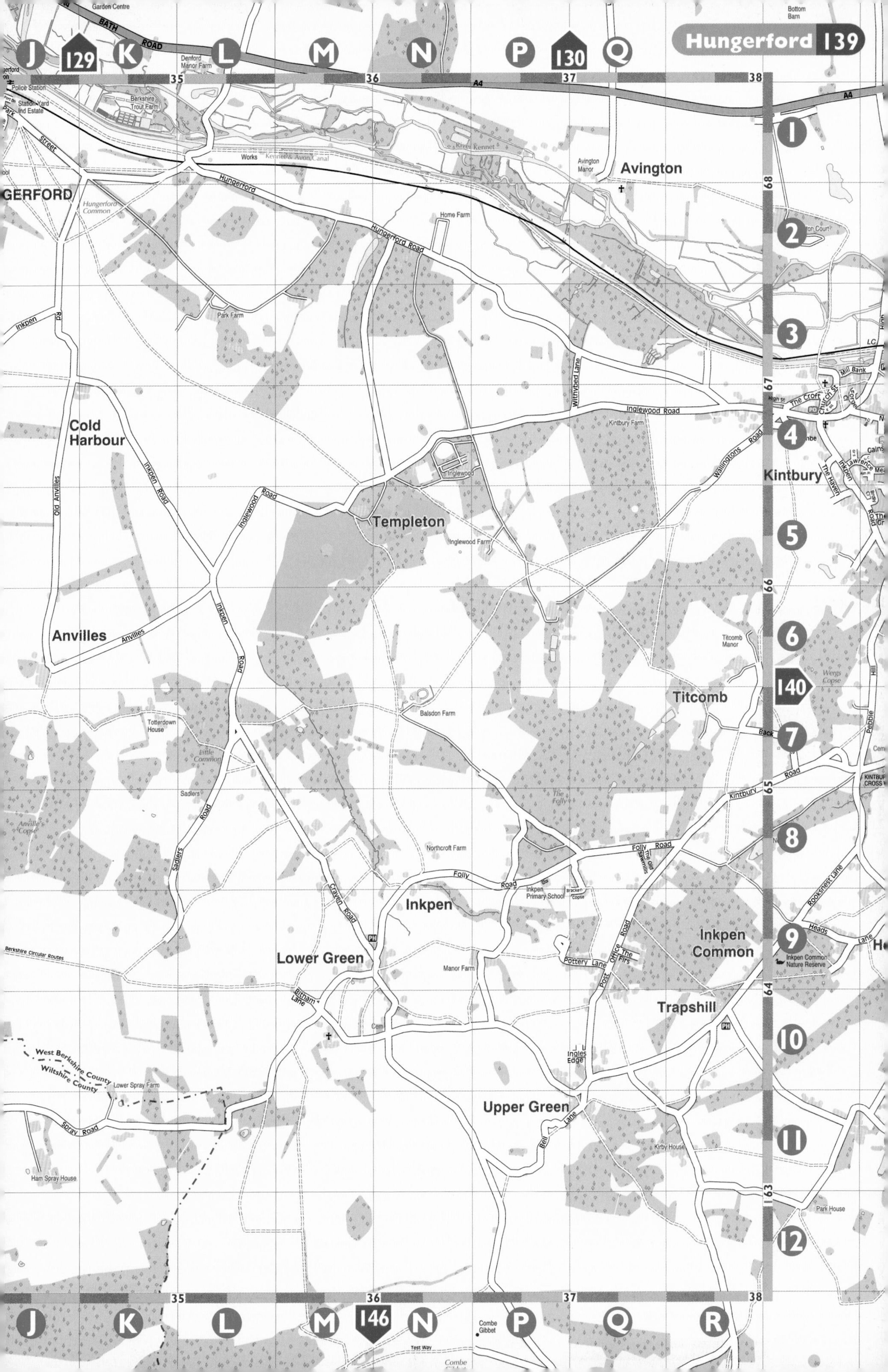

J 129 K L M N P 130 Q

BATH ROAD

Garden Centre

Denford Manor Farm

35 36 A4 37 38

Police Station

Station Yard and Estate

Berkshire Trout Farm

Works Kennet & Avon Canal

River Kennet

Avington Manor

Avington

1

HUNGERFORD

Hungerford Common

Home Farm

Hungerford Road

Park Farm

68

2

Avington Court

3

LC

Mill Bank

High St The Croft

Church St

Withybed Lane

Inglewood Road

Kintbury Farm

67

4

Kintbury

The Haven

Lawrence Mead

Cold Harbour

Old Anvilles

Inkpen Road

Inkpen Road

Inglewood Road

Inglewood

Templeton

Inglewood Farm

Wallingtons Road

Combe

Gains

5

66

Anvilles

Anvilles

Anvilles

Inkpen Road

Titcomb Manor

6

Titcomb

Wergs Copse

140

Pebble Hill

Totterdown House

Little Common

Balsdon Farm

Back Road

7

Kintbury Road

Kintbury Cross

65

Sadlers

Sadlers Road

Anville's Copse

The Folly

Northcroft Farm

Folly Road

The Old Sawmills

8

Rooksnest Lane

Heads Lane

Craven Road

Folly Road

Inkpen Primary School

Bracken Copse

Post Office Road

Inkpen Common

9

Inkpen Common Nature Reserve

64

Lower Green

PH

Manor Farm

Pottery Lane

The Firs

Inkpen

Berkshire Circular Routes

Bitham Lane

Cem

Post Office Road

Trapshill

PH

10

West Berkshire County
Wiltshire County

Lower Spray Farm

Ingles Edge

Bell Lane

Upper Green

Kirby House

11

63

Spray Road

Ham Spray House

Park House

12

J K L M 146 N P Q R

35 36 37 38

Combe Gibbet

Test Way

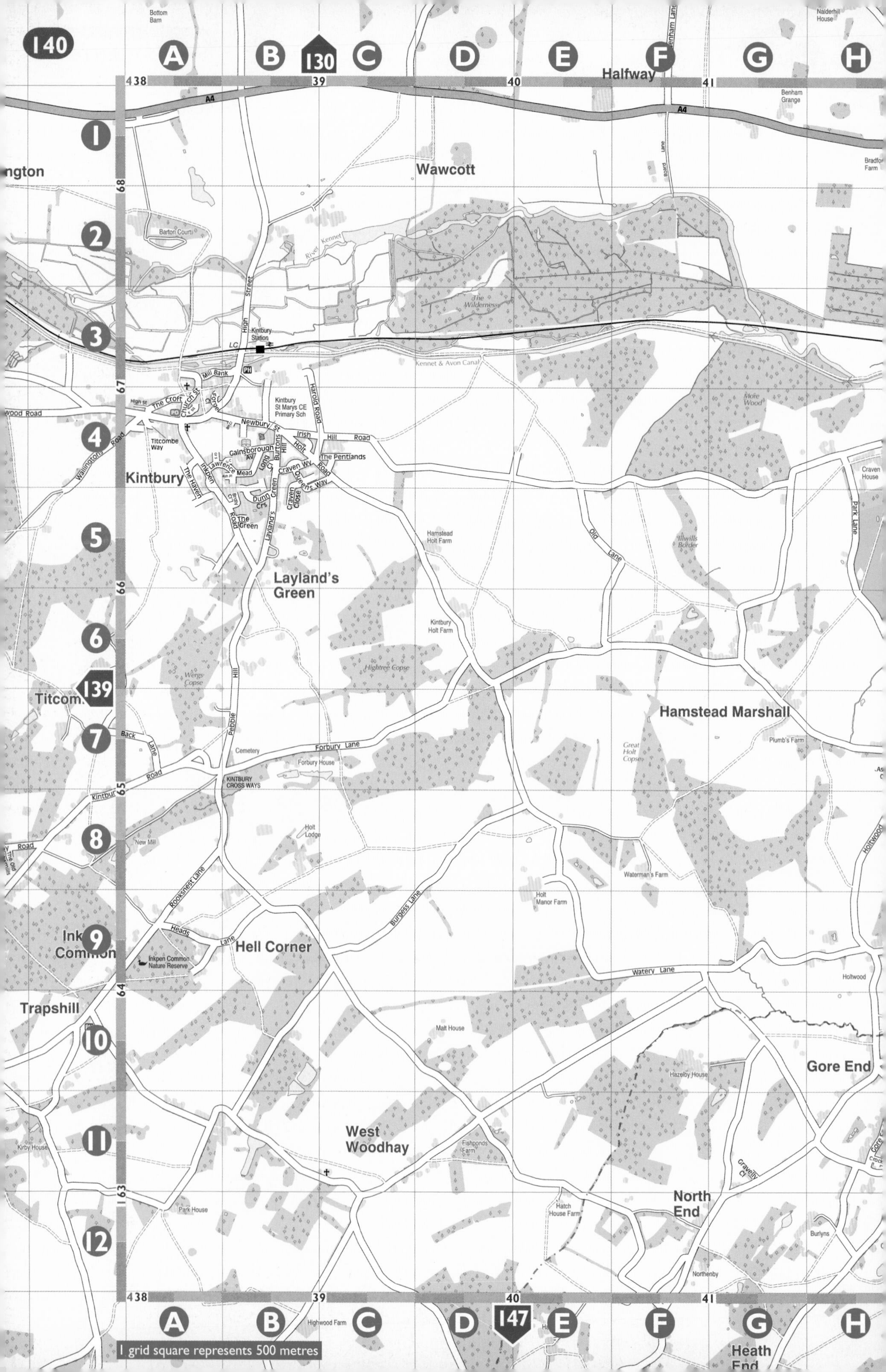
130
139
147
Wawcott
Halfway
Kintbury
Layland's Green
Hamstead Marshall
Hell Corner
Inkpen Common
Trapshill
West Woodhay
North End
Gore End
Heath End
Titcombe
A4
High Street
Kintbury Station
Kennet & Avon Canal
River Kennet
The Wilderness
More Wood
Barton Court
Hamstead Holt Farm
Kintbury Holt Farm
Hightree Copse
Wergs Copse
Forbury Lane
Forbury House
Cemetery
KINTBURY CROSS WAYS
Pebble Hill
Rooksnest Lane
Burgess Lane
Holt Lodge
Holt Manor Farm
Waterman's Farm
Watery Lane
Inkpen Common Nature Reserve
Malt House
Hazelby House
Fishponds Farm
Hatch House Farm
Park House
Northenby
Burlyns
Holtwood
Plumb's Farm
Craven House
Park Lane
Old Lane
Illwills Border
Great Holt Copse
Benham Grange
Benham Lane
Board Lane
Bradford Farm
Nalderhill House
Bottom Barn
Kirby House
New Mill
Highwood Farm
Hill Road
Harold Road
Kintbury St Marys CE Primary Sch
Newbury St
Irish Hill
The Pentlands
Craven Wy
Gainsborough Av
Titcombe Way
The Haven
The Croft
Church St
Mill Bank
Back Lane
Heads Lane
Wallingtons Road
Kintbury Road
Gravelly Cl
1 grid square represents 500 metres

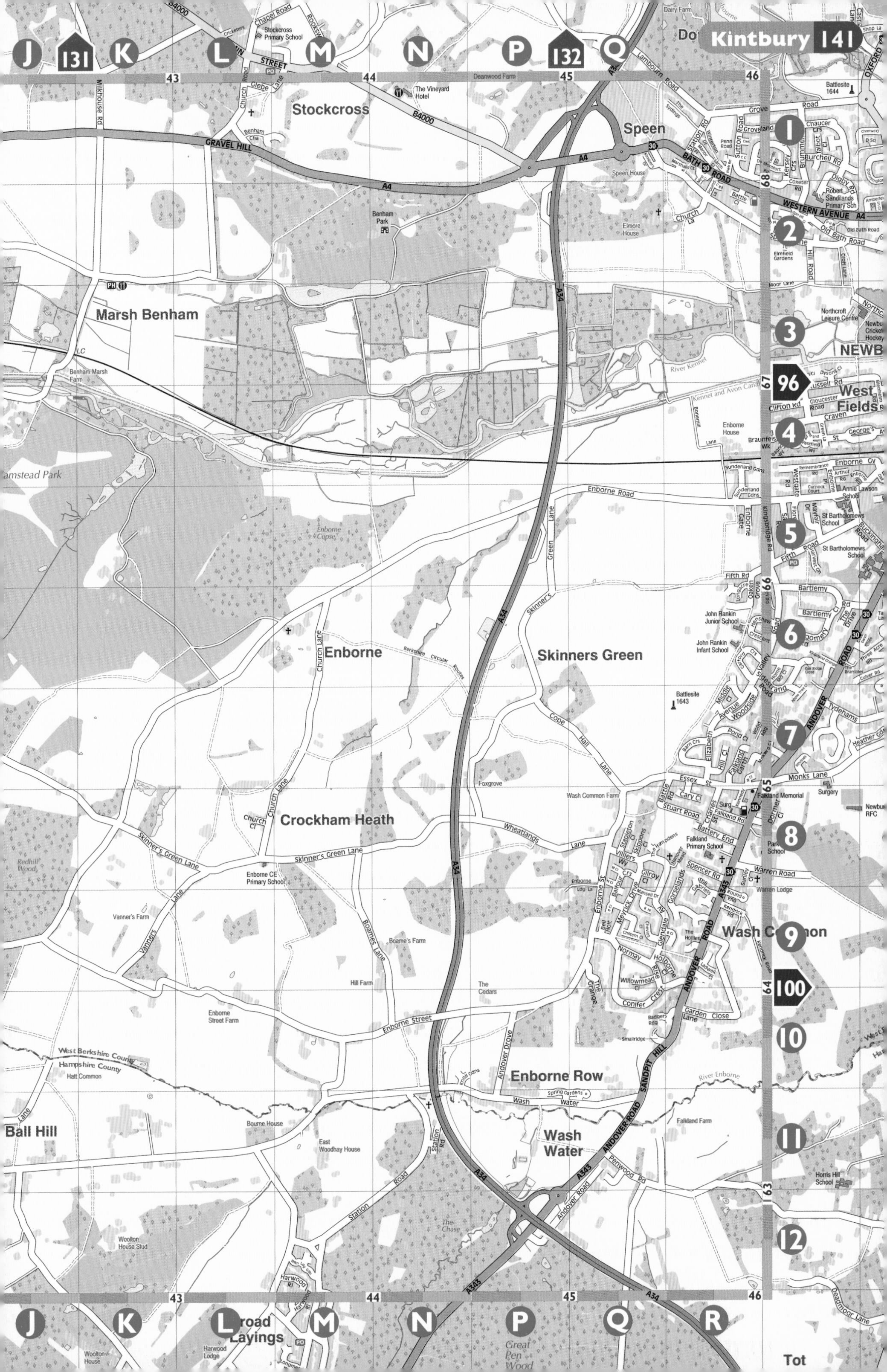
Stockcross
Speen
Marsh Benham
Enborne
Skinners Green
Crockham Heath
Enborne Row
Wash Water
Wash Common
Ball Hill
West Fields
Stockcross Primary School
The Vineyard Hotel
Benham Park
Speen House
Elmore House
Robert Sandilands Primary Sch
Northcroft Leisure Centre
River Kennet
Kennet and Avon Canal
Enborne House
Enborne Road
John Rankin Junior School
John Rankin Infant School
St Bartholomews School
Falkland Primary School
Falkland Memorial
Enborne CE Primary School
Vanner's Farm
Boame's Farm
Hill Farm
The Cedars
Enborne Street Farm
West Berkshire County
Hampshire County
Halt Common
Bourne House
East Woodhay House
Woolton House Stud
Falkland Farm
Horris Hill School
Wash Common Farm
Foxgrove
Battlesite 1643
Battlesite 1644
Skinner's Green Lane
Wheatlands Lane
Enborne Street
Andover Road
Sandpit Hill
Gravel Hill
Western Avenue
Bath Road
River Enborne
Penwood Rd
Station Road
Church Lane
Boames Lane
Green Lane
Cope Hall Lane
Monks Lane
Essex St
Warren Road
Garden Close
Berkshire Circular Routes
Enborne Copse
Redhill Wood
Great Pen Wood
Broad Layings

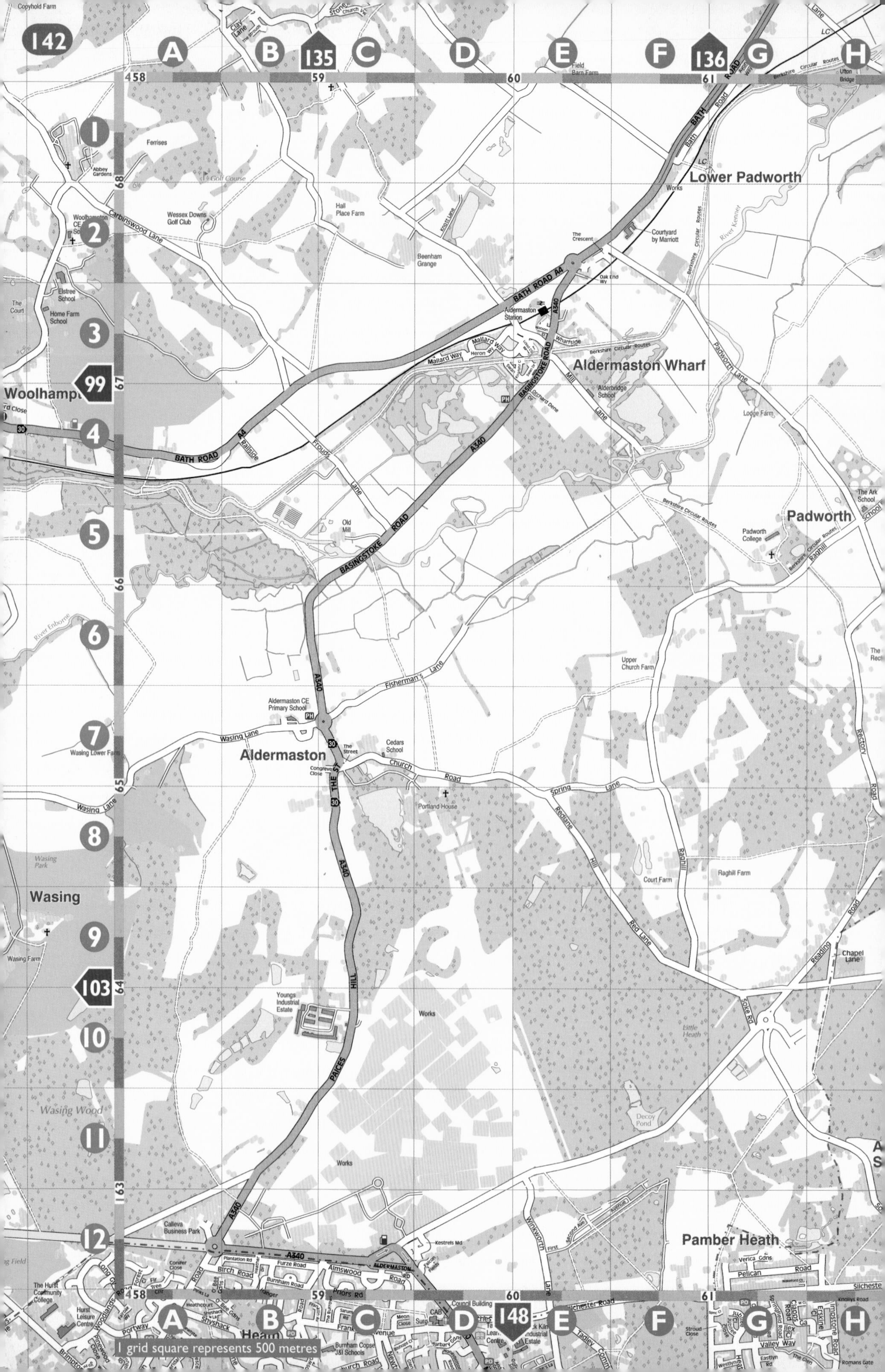

142
A
B
135
C
D
E
F
136
G
H
Lower Padworth
Aldermaston Wharf
Woolhampton
Padworth
Aldermaston
Wasing
Pamber Heath
Ferrises
Abbey Gardens
Golf Course
Wessex Downs Golf Club
Carbinswood Lane
Hall Place Farm
Beenham Grange
Knotts Lane
Field Barn Farm
Works
The Crescent
Courtyard by Marriott
Oak End Wy
Aldermaston Station
Wharfside
Mallard Way
Heron Wy
Berkshire Circular Routes
Alderbridge School
Mill Lane
Orchard Dene Dr
Padworth Lane
Lodge Farm
The Ark School
Padworth College
Raghill
River Kennet
Elstree School
Home Farm School
The Court
BATH ROAD
A4
A340
BASINGSTOKE ROAD
Froud's Lane
Old Mill
River Enborne
Fisherman's Lane
Upper Church Farm
Aldermaston CE Primary School
Wasing Lane
Wasing Lower Farm
The Street
Cedars School
Congreve Close
Church Road
Spring Lane
Portland House
Redlane Hill
Red Lane
Court Farm
Raghill Farm
Wasing Park
Wasing Farm
Rectory Road
Reading Road
Chapel Lane
Soke Rd
Little Heath
Youngs Industrial Estate
PAICES HILL
Works
Decoy Pond
Wasing Wood
Works
Calleva Business Park
Kestrels Md
Winkworth Lane
First Avenue
Second Avenue
Plantation Rd
Birch Road
Furze Road
Burnham Road
Almswood Road
ALDERMASTON ROAD
Priors Rd
Conifer Close
The Hurst Community College
Hurst Leisure Centre
Heathcourt
Portway
Shyshack Lane
Woodlands Road
Silchester Road
Council Building
CAB
Burnham Copse J&I Schools
Industrial Estate
Tadley Common
Stroud Close
Verica Gdns
Pelican Road
Valley Way
Imperial Road
Knollys Road
Romans Gate
148
99
103
458
59
60
61
68
67
66
65
64
163
1
2
3
4
5
6
7
8
9
10
11
12
1 grid square represents 500 metres

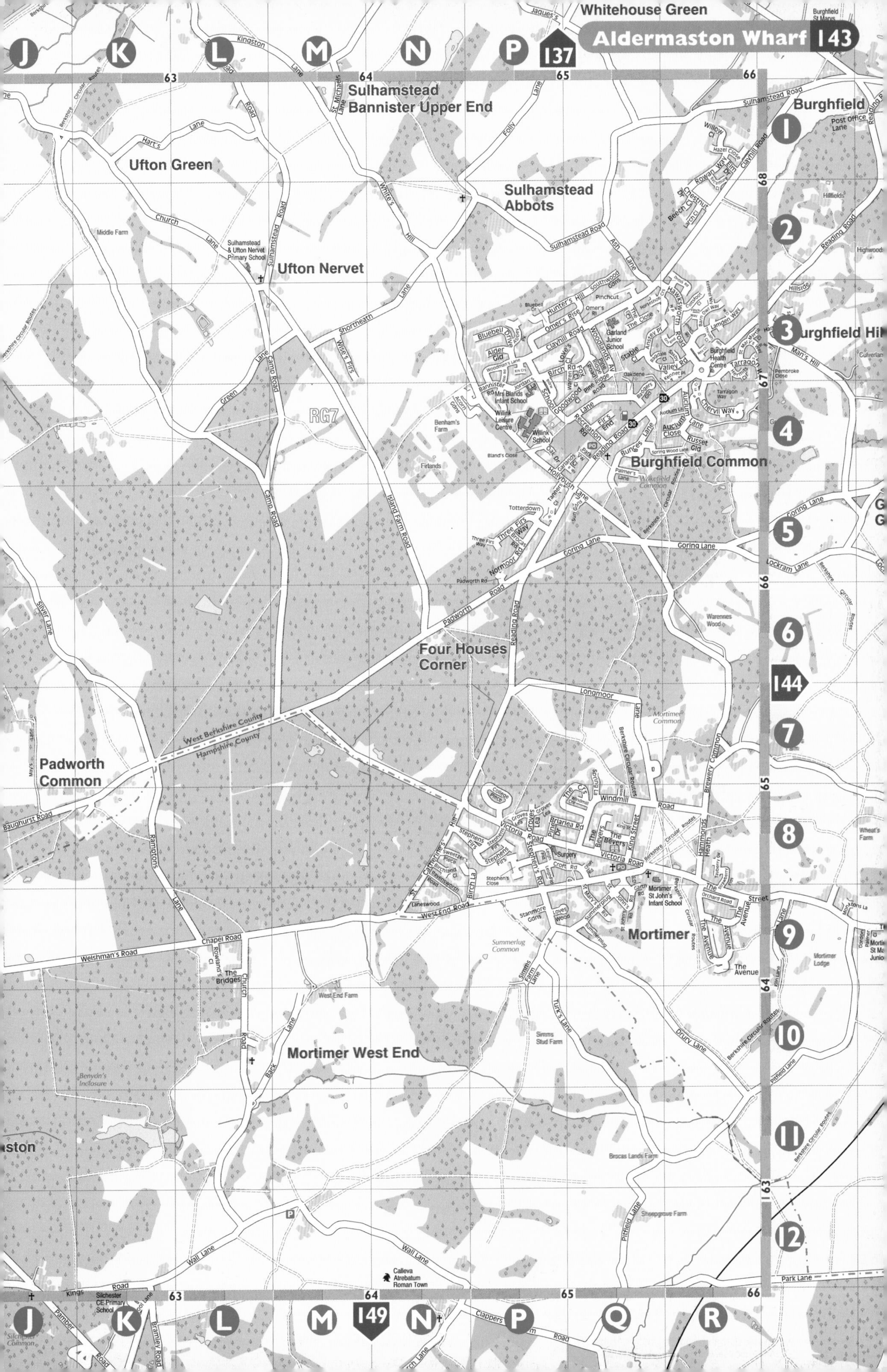

Sulhamstead
Bannister Upper End

Ufton Green

Sulhamstead
Abbots

Ufton Nervet

Burghfield

Burghfield Hill

Burghfield Common

RG7

Four Houses
Corner

Padworth
Common

144

West Berkshire County
Hampshire County

Mortimer

Mortimer West End

Mortimer Common

Summerlug
Common

149

Calleva
Atrebatum
Roman Town

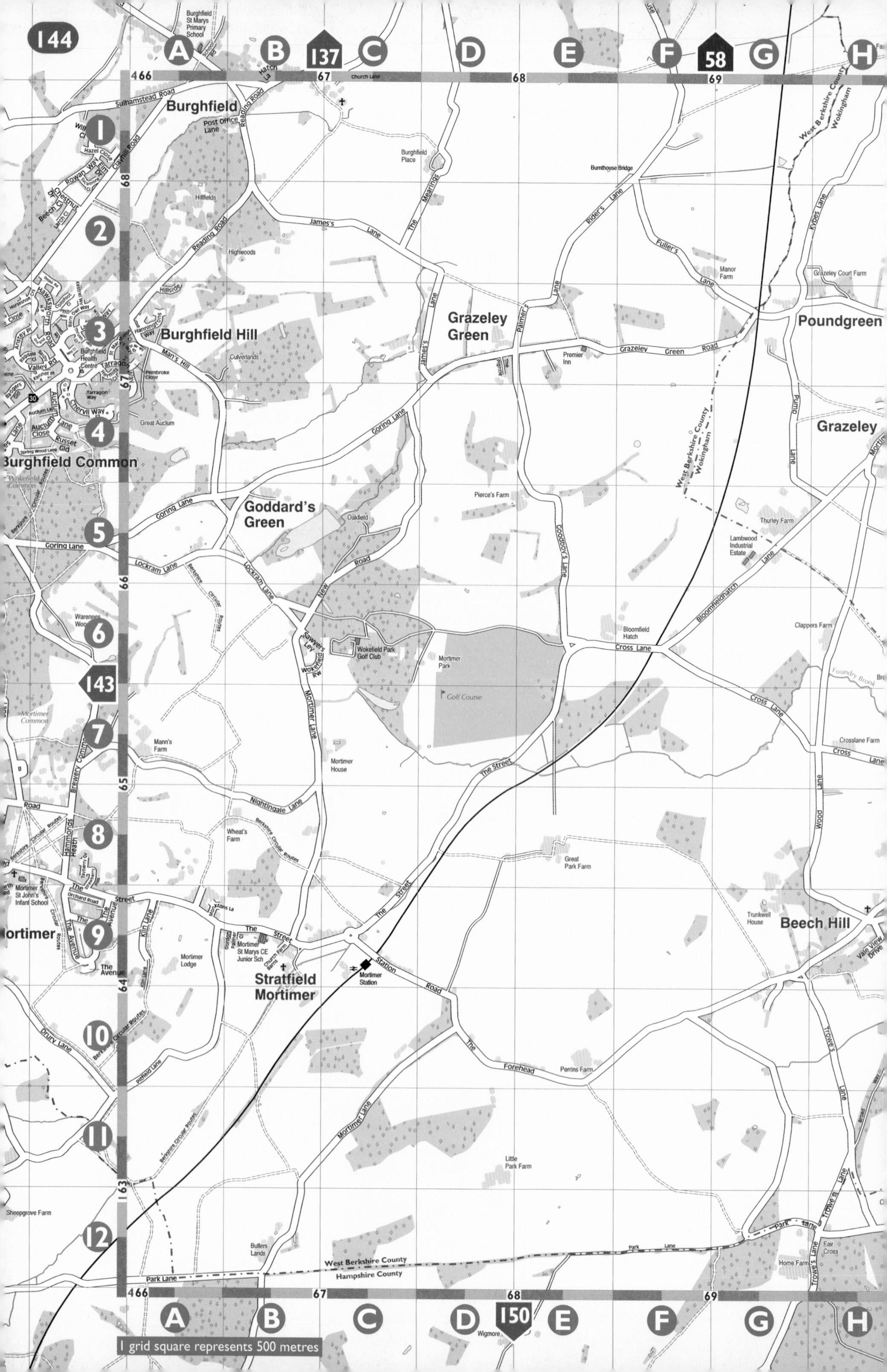
Burghfield
Burghfield Hill
Burghfield Common
Grazeley Green
Goddard's Green
Poundgreen
Grazeley
Stratfield Mortimer
Beech Hill
Mortimer
Burghfield St Marys Primary School
Burghfield Place
Burnthouse Bridge
Hillfields
Highwoods
James's Lane
Manor Farm
Grazeley Court Farm
Culverlands
Premier Inn
Great Auclum
Pierce's Farm
Oakfield
Thurley Farm
Lambwood Industrial Estate
Bloomfield Hatch
Wokefield Park Golf Club
Mortimer Park
Golf Course
Clappers Farm
Mann's Farm
Mortimer House
Crosslane Farm
Wheat's Farm
Great Park Farm
Mortimer St Marys CE Junior Sch
Mortimer Lodge
Mortimer Station
Trunkwell House
Perrins Farm
Little Park Farm
Sheepgrove Farm
Butlers Lands
West Berkshire County
Hampshire County
Home Farm
Fair Cross
Wigmore
Goring Lane
Lockram Lane
Mortimer Lane
Cross Lane
The Street
Station Road
The Forehead
Nightingale Lane
Park Lane
Reading Road
Church Lane
Sulhamstead Road
Grazeley Green Road
Goodboy's Lane
Rider's Lane
Fuller's Lane
Kybes Lane
Pump Lane
Wood Lane
Trowe's Lane
Bloomfieldhatch Lane
Berkshire Circular Routes
137
58
143
150

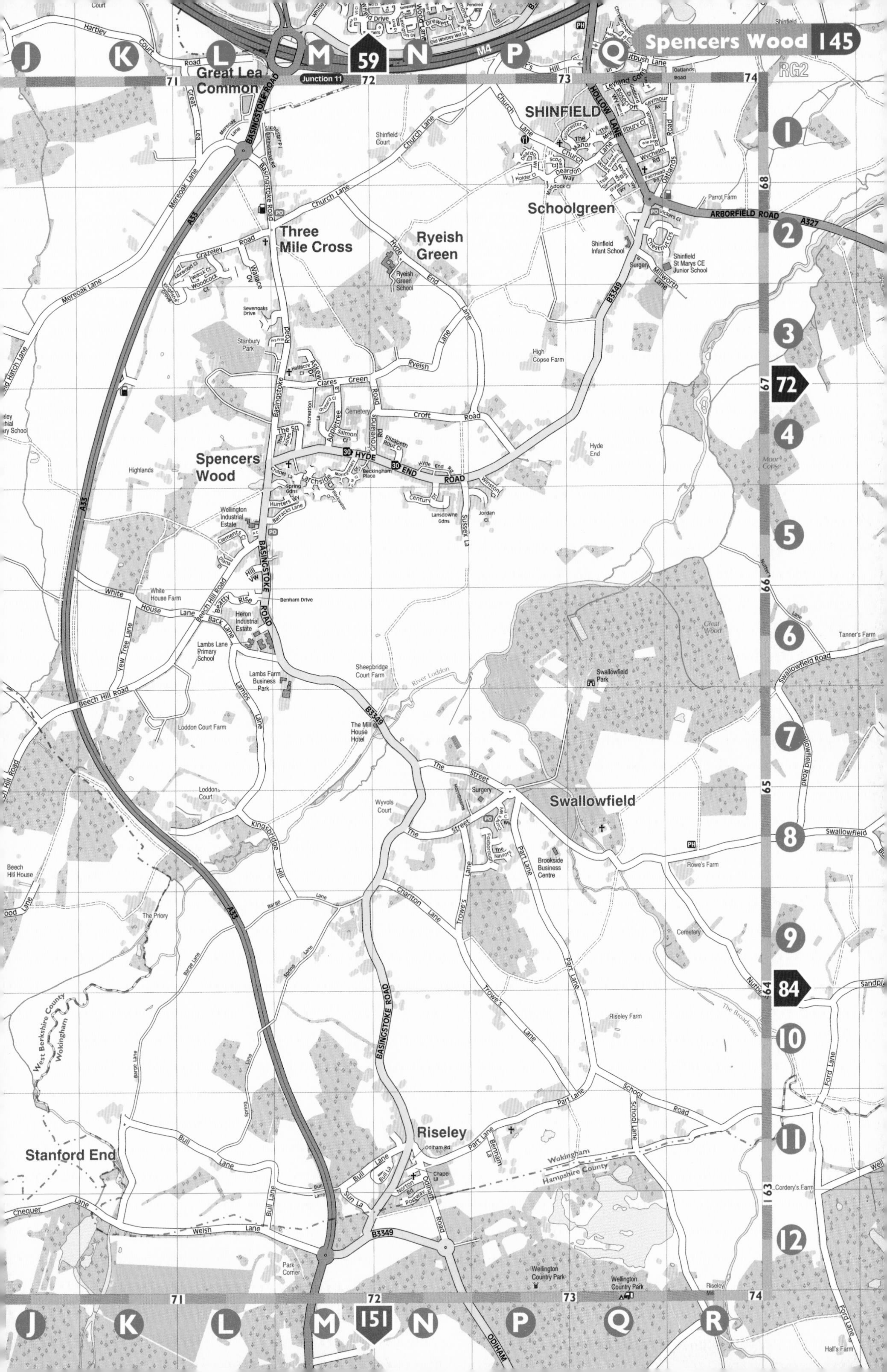

Great Lea Common
Junction 11
SHINFIELD
HOLLOW LANE
BASINGSTOKE ROAD
Three Mile Cross
Ryeish Green
Schoolgreen
ARBORFIELD ROAD
A327
A33
Shinfield Infant School
Shinfield St Marys CE Junior School
Ryeish Green School
B3349
High Copse Farm
Stanbury Park
Spencers Wood
HYDE END ROAD
Hyde End
Moor Copse
Highlands
Wellington Industrial Estate
White House Farm
Benham Drive
Heron Industrial Estate
Lambs Lane Primary School
Lambs Farm Business Park
Sheepbridge Court Farm
River Loddon
Swallowfield Park
Great Wood
Tanner's Farm
Swallowfield Road
Loddon Court Farm
The Mill House Hotel
Loddon Court
Wyvols Court
Swallowfield
Brookside Business Centre
Rowe's Farm
Beech Hill House
The Priory
Charlton Lane
Trowe's Lane
Part Lane
Cemetery
The Broadwater
Riseley Farm
West Berkshire County
Wokingham
Hampshire County
School Road
Riseley
Stanford End
Chequer Lane
Welsh Lane
Bull Lane
Barge Lane
Spring Lane
Park Corner
Wellington Country Park
Riseley Mill
Cordery's Farm
Ford Lane
Hall's Farm
ODIHAM
Mereoak Lane
Beech Hill Road

59 72 84 151

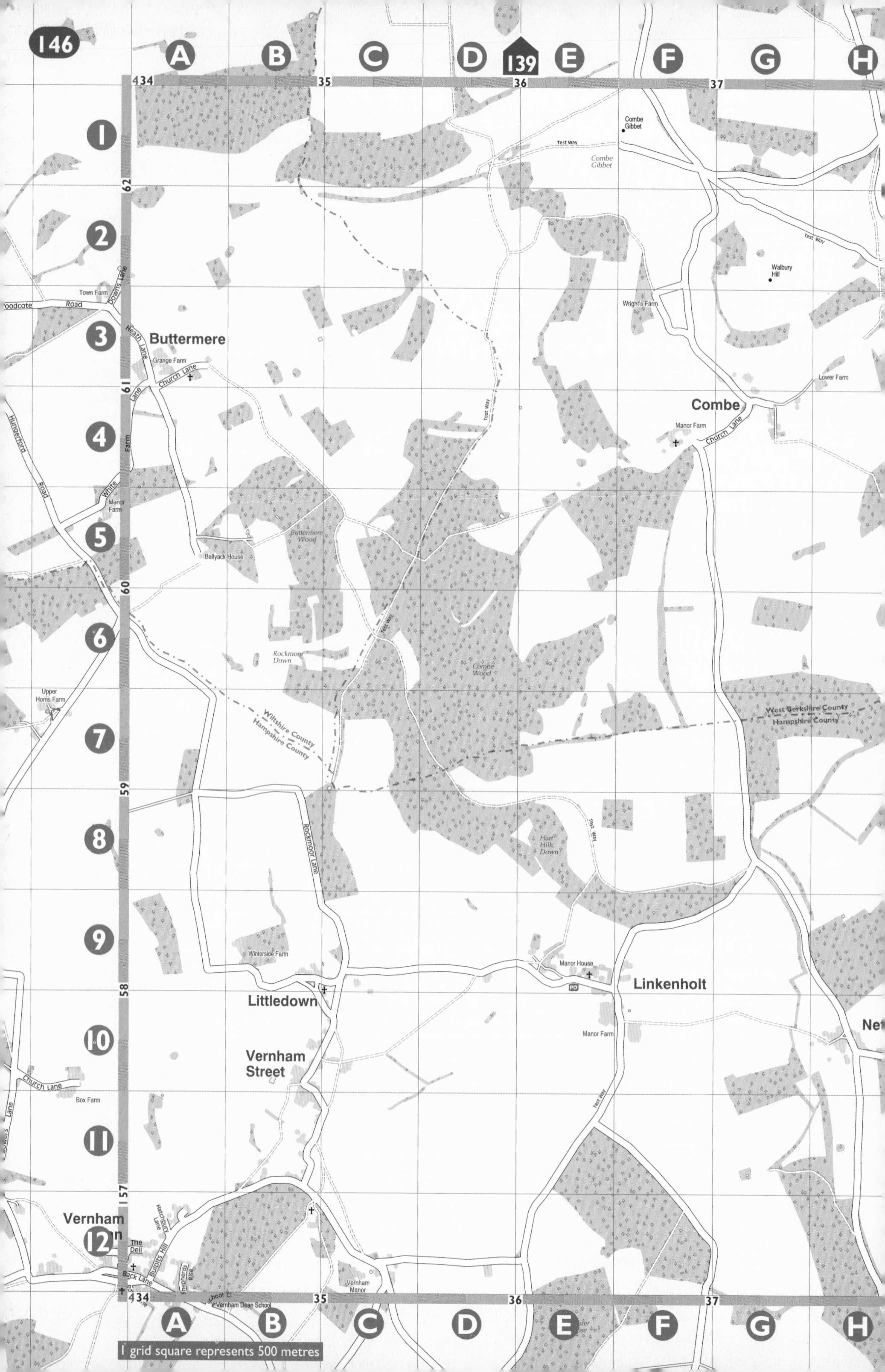

146
139
A
B
C
D
E
F
G
H
434
35
36
37
62
61
60
59
58
157
1
2
3
4
5
6
7
8
9
10
11
12
Combe Gibbet
Test Way
Combe Gibbet
Walbury Hill
Town Farm
Downs Lane
Woodcote Road
Wright's Farm
Buttermere
Heath Lane
Grange Farm
Church Lane
Lower Farm
Combe
Manor Farm
Church Lane
Hungerford Road
Farm Lane
White
Manor Farm
Buttermere Wood
Ballyack House
Rockmoor Down
Combe Wood
Upper Horns Farm
Wiltshire County
Hampshire County
West Berkshire County
Hampshire County
Rockmoor Lane
Hart Hill Down
Winterside Farm
Manor House
PO
Linkenholt
Littledown
Manor Farm
Vernham Street
Church Lane
Box Farm
Hatchgum Lane
The Dell
Back Lane
Bulpits Hill
Shepherds Rise
School Cl
Vernham Dean School
Vernham Manor
1 grid square represents 500 metres

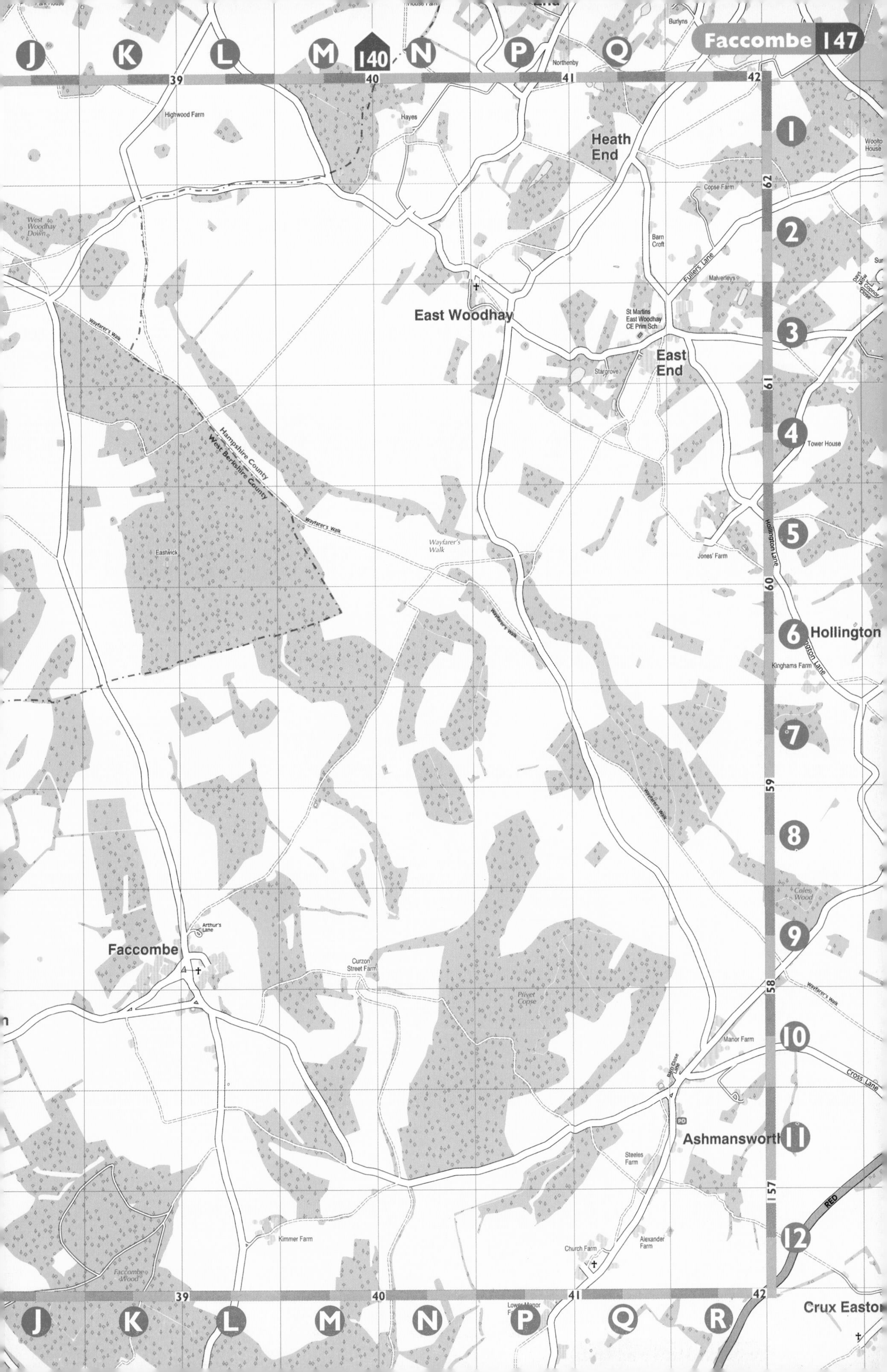

J K L M 140 N P Q

39 40 41 42

1

Highwood Farm Hayes Heath End Woolto House

62

2 Copse Farm

Barn Croft Malverleys

3 East Woodhay St Martins East Woodhay CE Prim Sch East End

Fuller's Lane

Stargrove

4 Tower House

61

West Woodhay Down

Wayfarer's Walk

Hampshire County West Berkshire County

Wayfarer's Walk

5

Hollington Lane

Jones' Farm

Wayfarer's Walk 60

Eastwick Wayfarer's Walk

6 Hollington

Kinghams Farm Curzon Lane

7

59

8 Coles Wood

Arthur's Lane

9

Faccombe

Curzon Street Farm 58 Wayfarer's Walk

Privet Copse

10 Manor Farm

Cross Lane

Bunny House Lane

11 Ashmansworth

Steeles Farm

57

Kimmer Farm RED

12

Faccombes Wood Kimmer Farm Church Farm Alexander Farm

39 40 41 42

Crux Easton

J K L M N P Q R

Lower Manor Farm

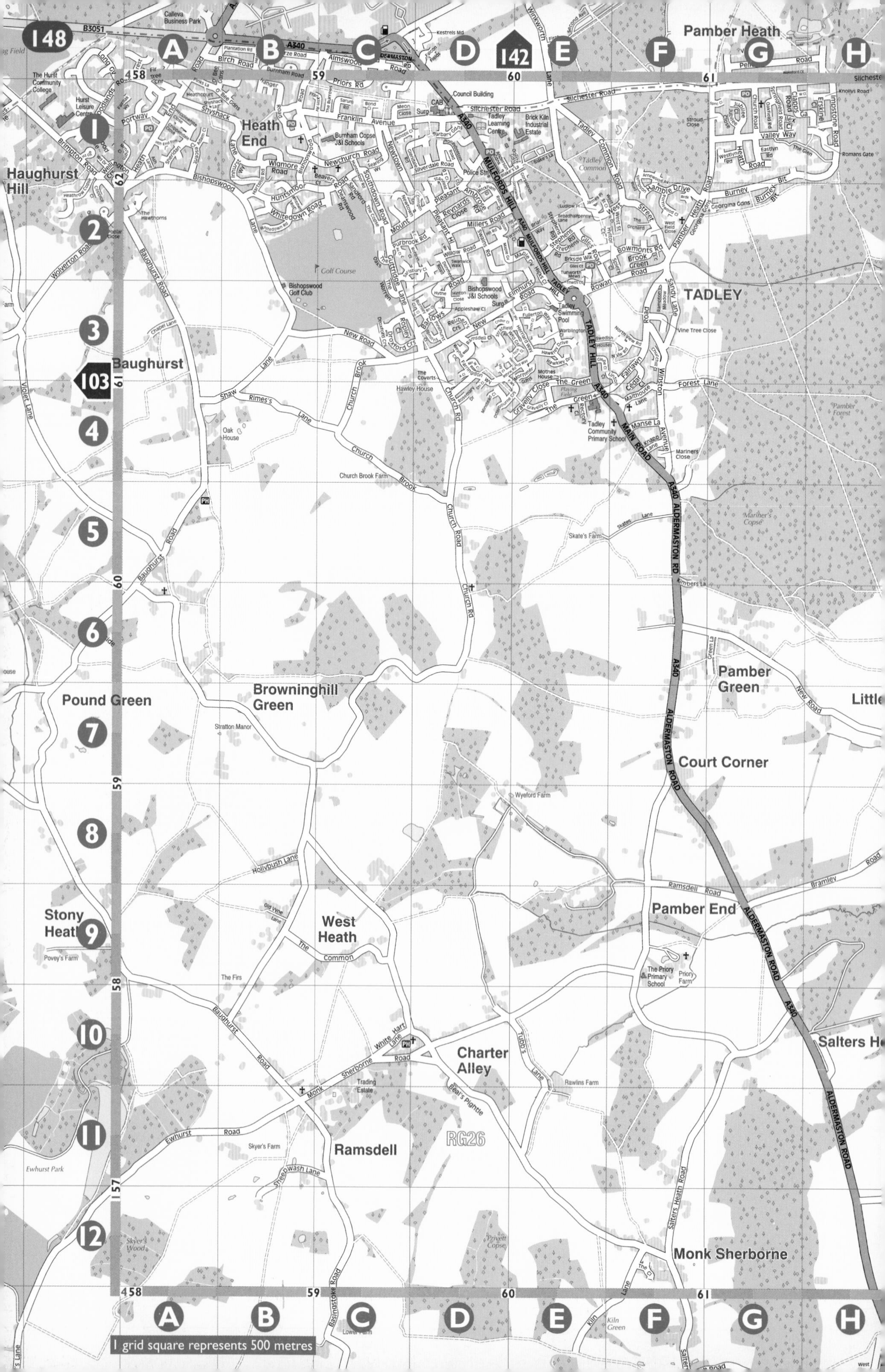

148
142
103
Pamber Heath
Heath End
Haughurst Hill
TADLEY
Baughurst
Pound Green
Browninghill Green
Pamber Green
Court Corner
Stony Heath
West Heath
Pamber End
Charter Alley
Salters Heath
Ramsdell
Monk Sherborne
RG26
A340
Mulfords Hill
Tadley Hill
Main Road
Aldermaston Road
Church Road
Baughurst Road
Bishopswood Lane
Silchester Road
Ramsdell Road
Ewhurst Road
Basingstoke Road
Salters Heath Road
Bishopswood Golf Club
Golf Course
Church Brook Farm
Skate's Farm
Wyeford Farm
Stratton Manor
Rawlins Farm
Skyer's Farm
Povey's Farm
Ewhurst Park
Tadley Community Primary School
The Priory Primary School
Priory Farm
1 grid square represents 500 metres

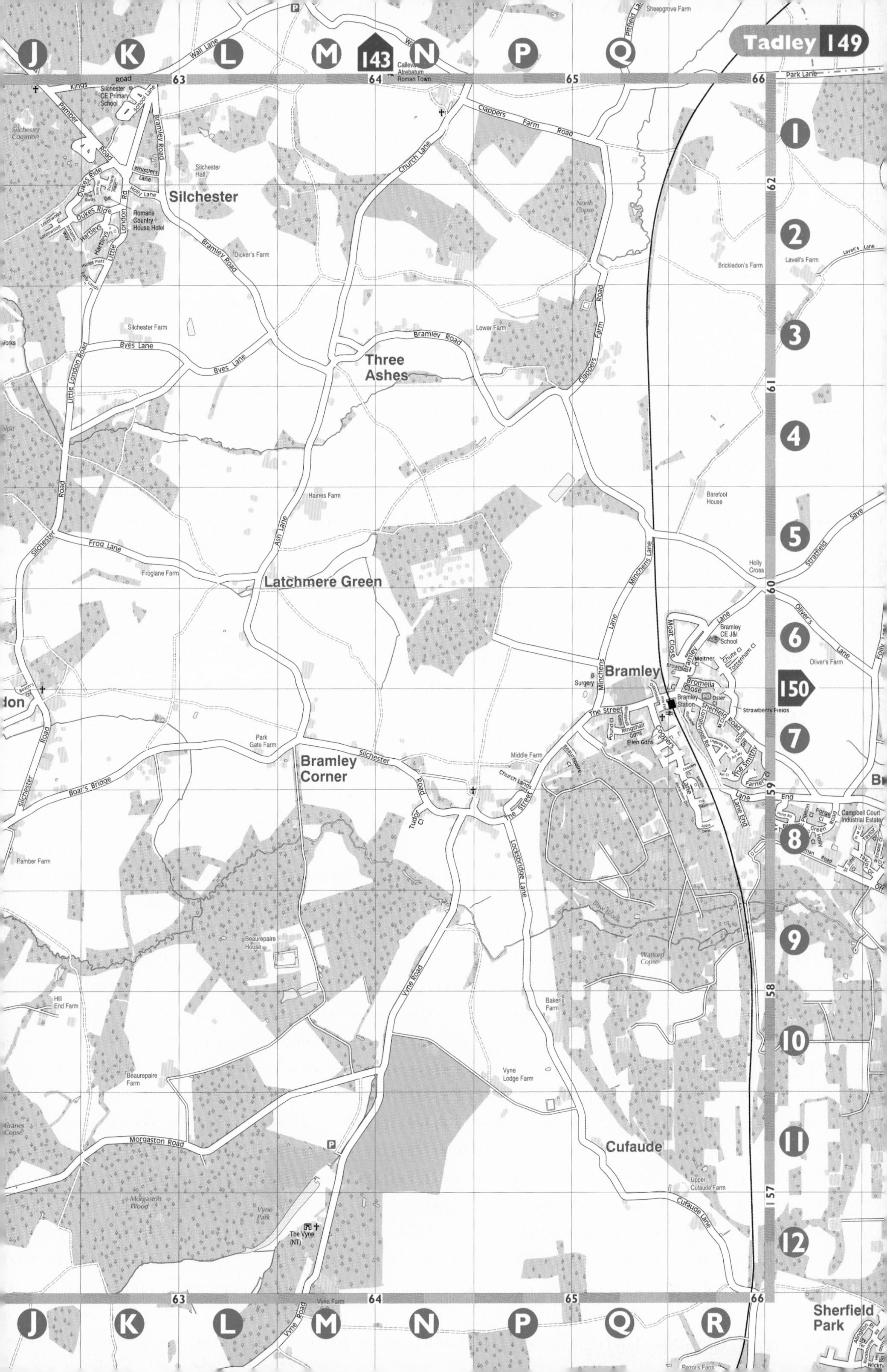

Silchester
Three Ashes
Latchmere Green
Bramley
Bramley Corner
Cufaude
Sherfield Park
Silchester Common
Silchester CE Primary School
Silchester Hall
Romans Country House Hotel
Dicker's Farm
Silchester Farm
Lower Farm
North Copse
Brickledon's Farm
Lavell's Farm
Sheepgrove Farm
Calleva Atrebatum Roman Town
Haines Farm
Froglane Farm
Barefoot House
Holly Cross
Oliver's Farm
Bramley CE J&I School
Bramley Station
Surgery
Strawberry Fields
Park Gate Farm
Middle Farm
Campbell Court Industrial Estate
Pamber Farm
Beaurepaire House
Watford Copse
Baker's Farm
Hill End Farm
Beaurepaire Farm
Vyne Lodge Farm
Cranes Copse
Morgaston Wood
Vyne Park
The Vyne (NT)
Upper Cufaude Farm
Vyne Farm
Bazol's Farm
Kings Road
Wall Lane
Pamber Road
School Lane
Bramley Road
Whistlers Lane
Holly Lane
Dukes Ride
London Rd
Little London Road
Church Lane
Clappers Farm Road
Pitfield Lane
Park Lane
Byes Lane
Frog Lane
Ash Lane
Silchester Road
Boar's Bridge
Minchens Lane
Moat Close
Bromelia Close
Sherfield Road
The Street
Coopers Lane
Lane End
Church Lands
Tudor Cl
Lockbridge Lane
Vyne Road
Morgaston Road
Cufaude Lane
Stratfield Saye
Oliver's Lane
Rowan Road
Forge Cl
Farrier's Cl
The Smithy
Ringshall Gdns
Ellen Gdns
Pound Cl
Beaurepaire Cl
Bow Brook
143
150
63
64
65
66
62
61
60
59
58
57
J K L M N P Q R
1 2 3 4 5 6 7 8 9 10 11 12

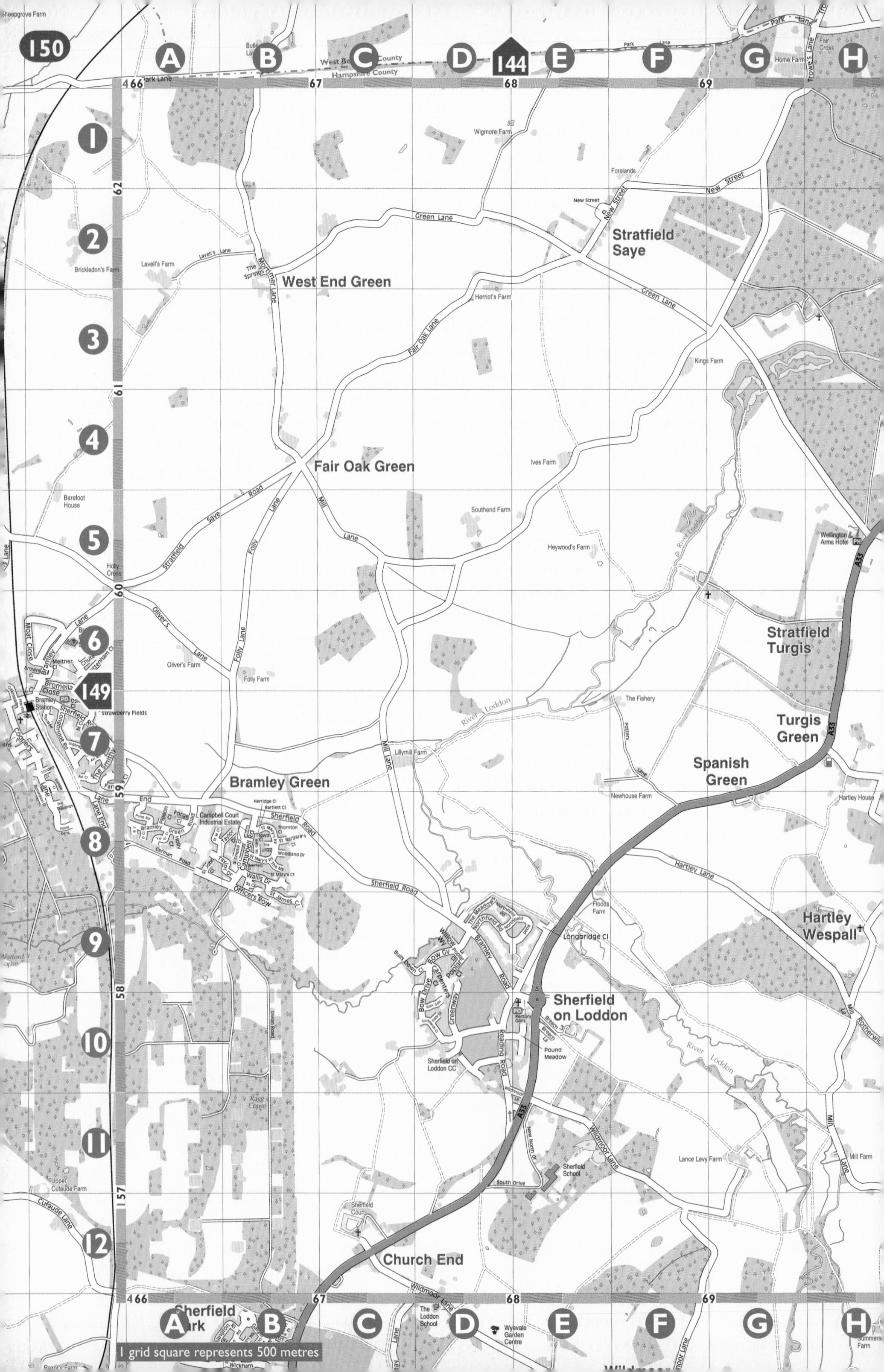
144
149
A B C D E F G H
1 2 3 4 5 6 7 8 9 10 11 12
66 67 68 69
62 61 60 59 58 57
West End Green
Stratfield Saye
Fair Oak Green
Bramley Green
Stratfield Turgis
Turgis Green
Spanish Green
Hartley Wespall
Sherfield on Loddon
Church End
Sherfield Park
Park Lane
Hampshire County
Green Lane
New Street
Mortimer Lane
Fair Oak Lane
Stratfield Saye Road
Mill Lane
Folly Lane
Oliver's Lane
Sherfield Road
Bramley Road
Reading Road
Wildmoor Lane
Hartley Lane
River Loddon
A33
Wigmore Farm
Forelands
Lavell's Farm
Brickledon's Farm
Herriot's Farm
Kings Farm
Ives Farm
Southend Farm
Heywood's Farm
Barefoot House
Holly Cross
Oliver's Farm
Folly Farm
Strawberry Fields
Bramley Station
The Fishery
Lillymill Farm
Newhouse Farm
Hartley House
Floods Farm
Longbridge Cl
Wellington Arms Hotel
Campbell Court Industrial Estate
Sherfield on Loddon CC
Pound Meadow
Sherfield School
South Drive
Lance Levy Farm
Mill Farm
Sherfield Court
The Loddon School
Wyevale Garden Centre
Upper Cufaude Farm
Cufaude Lane
Home Farm
Fair Cross
Trowe's Lane
Sheepgrove Farm
1 grid square represents 500 metres

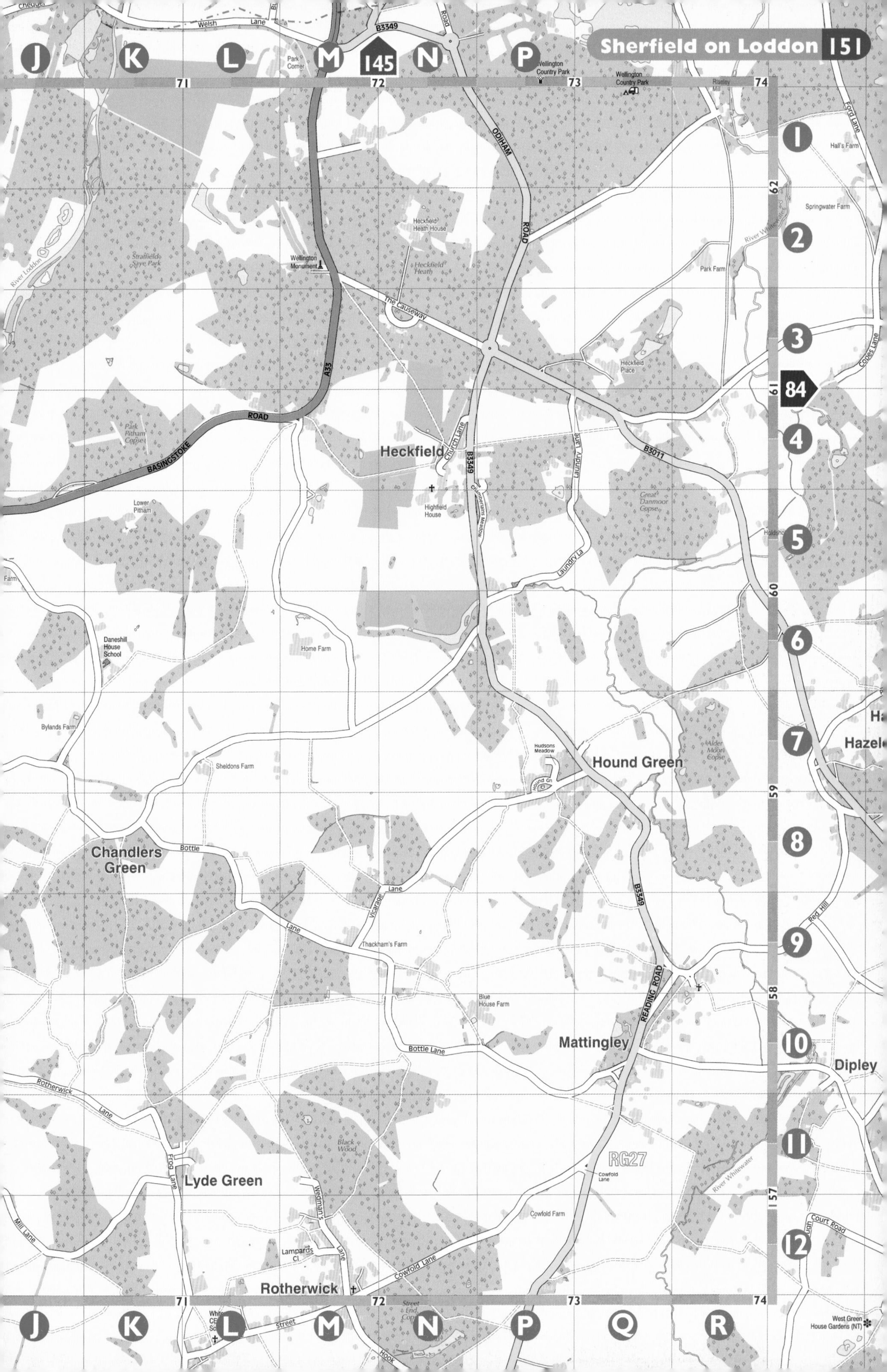
J
K
L
M
145
N
P
71
72
73
74
Welsh Lane
B3349
Park Corner
Wellington Country Park
Riseley Mill
Ford Lane
Hall's Farm
Springwater Farm
River Whitewater
Park Farm
River Loddon
Stratfield Saye Park
Wellington Monument
Heckfield Heath House
Heckfield Heath
ODIHAM ROAD
The Causeway
A33
Heckfield Place
84
Copes Lane
BASINGSTOKE ROAD
Park Pitham Copse
Heckfield
Church Lane
B3349
Laundry Lane
B3011
Great Danmoor Copse
Highfield House
Lower Pitham
Holdshot
Laundry La
Farm
Daneshill House School
Home Farm
Bylands Farm
Sheldons Farm
Hudsons Meadow
Hound Green
Hound Gn
Alder Moor Copse
Hazeley
Chandlers Green
Bottle
Vicarage
Lane
Thackham's Farm
Red Hill
READING ROAD
Blue House Farm
Mattingley
Bottle Lane
Dipley
Rotherwick
Lane
Black Wood
RG27
Cowfold Lane
Frog Lane
Lyde Green
Wedmans Lane
Mill Lane
Cowfold Farm
Court Road
Lampards Cl
Rotherwick
Cowfold Lane
Street
Street End Copse
Hook
Q
R
West Green House Gardens (NT)
1
2
3
4
5
6
7
8
9
10
11
12
62
61
60
59
58
57

- Abbey Mead 82 B3
- Addlestonemoor 82 C6
- Aldermaston 142 B7
- Aldermaston Soke 142 H11
- Aldermaston Wharf 142 E3
- Aldworth 122 G2
- Altmore 35 G2
- Amen Corner 63 H8
- Anvilles 139 J6
- Applehouse Hill 24 C5
- Arborfield 72 B2
- Arborfield Cross 72 D4
- Arborfield Garrison 73 G7
- Ascot 66 C7
- Ashampstead 122 H8
- Ashampstead Green 123 J7
- Ashford 71 G2
- Ashford Common 71 K4
- Ashford Hill 103 G5
- Ashmansworth 147 R11
- Ashmore Green 133 P10
- Aston 22 E1
- Aston Tirrold 110 G2
- Avington 139 Q1
- Axmansford 103 L7
- Bagnor 132 B10
- Bagshot 89 K3
- Bagshot 138 D7
- Bagshot Heath 89 L5
- Ball Hill 141 J11
- Barkham 73 J4
- Baughurst 103 M7
- Baydon 116 B6
- Beaumont 54 B7
- Beech Hill 144 G9
- Beedon 121 K7
- Beedon Hill 121 J7
- Beenham 135 P12
- Beenham's Heath 49 J3
- Beenham Stocks 135 R11
- Berghers Hill 21 G2
- Bigfrith 19 J8
- Binfield 63 H4
- Binfield Heath 127 P8
- Birch Hill 76 C4
- Bisham 19 G7
- Bishopsgate 67 M2
- Bishop's Green 101 J3
- Bix 115 K7
- Blacknest 67 J8
- Blackwater 93 K2
- Blewbury 110 D2
- Bockmer End 17 L5
- Borough Marsh 32 C5
- Bothampstead 121 P10
- Bourne End 20 B2
- Boveney 37 L6
- Bovingdon Green 18 C3
- Boxford 131 P7
- Boyn Hill 4 C7
- Bracknell 2 D6
- Bradfield 136 B4
- Bramley 149 Q6
- Bramley Corner 149 M7
- Bramley Green 150 B7
- Bramshill 84 B7
- Brands Hill 40 D7
- Bray 36 F3
- Bray Wick 36 C2
- Braywoodside 50 C3
- Brick Hill 79 J8
- Brightwalton 119 P3
- Brightwalton Green 119 P4
- Brightwalton Holt 119 Q6
- Brimpton 99 G8
- Brimpton Common 103 L4
- Britwell 28 B5
- Broadplat 115 L10
- Brock's Green 101 J6
- Brookside 65 L4
- Broomhall 78 F4
- Browninghill Green 148 B7
- Bucklebury 134 C8
- Bucklebury Alley 133 Q8
- Bullbrook 64 F7
- Burchett's Green 24 E7
- Burghclere 100 B7
- Burghclere Common 100 C5
- Burghfield 144 A1
- Burghfield Common 143 Q4
- Burghfield Hill 144 A3
- Burnham 27 L3
- Burnt Hill 135 K1
- Burrowhill 91 M4
- Bury's Bank 97 G7
- Buttermere 146 A3
- Calcot 137 N7
- Calcot Row 137 P5
- Camberley 88 E7
- Cane End 125 R3
- Carter's Hill 60 E7
- Castle Green 91 K8
- Catmore 120 B1
- Caversham 44 F3
- Caversham Heights 44 F2
- Caversham Park 45 J1
- Chaddleworth 119 L6
- Chalkhouse Green 126 G9
- Chalvey 10 B8
- Chandlers Green 151 K8
- Chapel Row 135 L10
- Charlton 71 J7
- Charter Alley 148 D10
- Charvil 47 G1
- Chattern Hill 71 H2
- Chavey Down 65 H7
- Chazey Heath 126 C11
- Cheapside 66 E7
- Checkendon 113 P7
- Chertsey 82 A4
- Chertsey Meads 82 E5
- Chieveley 132 H1
- Chilton 109 K2
- Chilton Foliat 128 H8
- Chobham 91 K5
- Churchend 137 Q4
- Church End 150 C12
- Cippenham 37 M1
- Clapton 130 E9
- Clay Hill 135 N8
- Cleeve 112 A10
- Clewer Green 12 A9
- Clewer New Town 12 D8
- Clewer Village 12 C4
- Cold Ash 133 Q11
- Cold Harbour 34 C3
- Cold Harbour 124 F2
- Cold Harbour 139 J4
- Coley 8 D9
- Coley Park 58 F1
- College Town 87 L5
- Collins End 125 M4
- Colnbrook 40 E8
- Colstrope 16 E1
- Colthrop 98 D3
- Combe 146 F4
- Compton 121 R1
- Cookham 20 C6
- Cookham Dean 19 K7
- Cookham Rise 20 B8
- Cooper's Hill 68 D1
- Cores End 20 E2
- Court Corner 148 F7
- Court Garden 18 F5
- Cove 93 L8
- Cowley 31 L5
- Cowley Peachy 31 L7
- Cox Green 35 L3
- Cranbourne 52 B8
- Cranford 43 J7
- Crawley Hill 94 E1
- Cray's Pond 112 H12
- Crazies Hill 23 G8
- Cricket Hill 92 E1
- Crocker End 114 F4
- Crockham Heath 141 M8
- Crooked Soley 128 C4
- Crookham 102 D1
- Cross Lanes 125 Q5
- Crown Wood 76 D3
- Crowsley 127 J6
- Crowthorne 86 E1
- Cufaude 149 Q11
- Curridge 133 K5
- Danesfield 17 M8
- Darby Green 87 G8
- Datchet 39 K8
- Datchet Common 54 C1
- Dedworth 37 M8
- Deepcut 95 J8
- Donkey Town 90 D8
- Donnington 132 D12
- Dorney 37 K3
- Dorney Reach 37 H3
- Dowlesgreen 15 J2
- Downend 120 G11
- Dunsden Green 127 M11
- Earley 60 B1
- Earlstone Common 100 B6
- East Bedfont 57 H6
- East Burnham 28 B2
- Eastbury 117 N7
- East End 147 Q3
- East Fields 7 G6
- East Garston 118 B8
- East Ginge 108 B1
- Easthampstead 2 F9
- Eastheath 74 A3
- East Ilsley 109 M12
- Easton 131 M5
- East Woodhay 147 N3
- Eddington 129 N11
- Egham 69 G4
- Egham Hythe 69 K4
- Egham Wick 67 M5
- Egypt 120 A8
- Elcot 130 H10
- Eling 122 A11
- Emmbrook 62 A5
- Emmer Green 126 G12
- Enborne 141 M6
- Enborne Row 141 P10
- Englefield 136 F6
- Englefield Green 68 B5
- Eton 13 J2
- Eton Wick 38 B4
- Eversley 85 H5
- Eversley Centre 85 K6
- Eversley Cross 85 M6
- Exlade Street 113 M10
- Faccombe 147 K9
- Fair Oak 103 G7
- Fair Oak Green 150 B4
- Farley Hill 84 D1
- Farnborough 107 Q9
- Farnham Park 28 E2
- Farnham Royal 28 E3
- Fawley 106 F11
- Fawley 115 Q4
- Fawley Bottom 115 N4
- Felthamhill 71 L4
- Fern 19 M1
- Fifield 36 F8
- Finchampstead 85 K3
- Fishery 5 M6
- Four Houses Corner 143 N6
- Four Points 122 G4
- Fox Lane 93 M5
- Frilsham 134 E3
- Frimley 94 C5
- Frimley Green 94 F7
- Frimley Ridge 95 G3
- Frogmore 87 H8
- Furze Platt 25 M4
- Gallowstree Common 126 B5
- Gardeners Green 74 E4
- George Green 30 A6
- Goddard's Green 144 B5
- Goldfinch Bottom 101 L1
- Goose Hill 102 D3
- Gore End 140 H10
- Goring 112 A12
- Goring Heath 125 L3
- Grazeley 144 H4
- Grazeley Green 144 D3
- Great Hollands 75 L3
- Great Lea Common 59 G8
- Great Shefford 118 F11
- Greenham 96 E6
- Greenham Common 101 G1
- Greenlands 16 C6
- Greys Green 115 K12
- Hailey 112 H2
- Halfway 131 J12
- Ham 138 G12
- Hambleden 16 F5
- Hamm Moor 82 D8
- Hampstead Norreys 122 A8
- Hamstead Marshall 140 F7
- Hanworth 76 A4
- Hare Hatch 33 J6
- Harlington 42 E6
- Harmans Water 3 J9
- Harmondsworth 41 L6
- Harpsden 22 A8
- Harpsden Bottom 127 P4
- Hartley Wespall 150 G9
- Hatton 57 L3
- Hatton Hill 78 D8
- Haughurst Hill 103 L5
- Hawks Hill 20 E4
- Hawley 93 L3
- Hawley Lane 94 B7
- Hawthorn Hill 50 C5
- Hayes Town 43 L1
- Headley 102 A5
- Heath End 147 Q1
- Heath End 148 B1
- Heatherside 95 H2
- Heathlands 74 F6
- Heckfield 151 N4
- Hedsor 21 H3
- Hell Corner 140 B9
- Henley-on-Thames 127 P1
- Hermitage 133 P4
- High Curley 89 L6
- Highmoor 114 E8
- Highmoor Cross 114 D9
- Highway 25 J8
- Hill Bottom 125 J3
- Hillgreen 120 C9
- Hoe Benham 131 L11
- Holloway 34 E1
- Hollybush Hill 29 K1
- Holly Cross 23 J8
- Holme Green 74 F3
- The Holt 33 K5
- Holyport 36 C7
- Honey Hill 75 G5
- Hook End 113 P10
- Hopgoods Green 134 E10
- Horncastle 137 Q5
- Horton 55 G2
- Hound Green 151 Q7
- Hungerford 48 D4
- Hungerford 138 H2
- Hungerford Green 122 H3
- Hungerford Newtown 129 Q6
- Huntercombe End 114 B2
- Hunt's Green 131 P9
- Hurley 24 A2
- Hurley Bottom 23 M3
- Hurst 47 L6
- Hyde End 103 G2
- Hythe End 69 H1
- Inhurst 103 L6
- Inkpen 139 N9
- Inkpen Common 139 R9
- Ipsden 112 G3
- Iver 31 H7
- Iver Heath 30 F2
- Jealott's Hill 50 B6
- Jennetts Hill 135 M7
- Kidmore End 126 C7
- Kiff Green 135 K12
- Kiln Green 33 L5
- Kingsclere Woodlands 102 C6
- Kintbury 140 A4
- Knighton 128 C7
- Knowle Green 70 B3
- Knowle Hill 80 B4
- Knowl Hill 34 B2
- Lake End 37 K2
- Laleham 70 C8
- Laleham Burway 82 B2
- Lambourn 117 L4
- Lambourn Woodlands 117 J9
- Langley 40 B3
- Langley Common 72 F5
- Latchmere Green 149 L5
- Layland's Green 140 B5
- Leckhampstead 119 R9
- Leckhampstead Thicket 119 P7
- Lent 27 J5
- Lent Rise 27 J6
- Letcombe Bassett 106 B3
- Leverton 129 L9
- Lightwater 90 C6
- Lilley 120 A3
- Limmerhill 73 L1
- Linkenholt 146 F9
- Littledown 146 B10
- Littlefield Green 35 H8
- Little Heath 137 L2
- Little Hungerford 133 Q2
- Little London 148 H7
- Little Marlow 19 L1
- Little Sandhurst 87 G4
- Littleton 71 H8
- Littleton Common 71 H5
- Littlewick Green 34 E1
- Littleworth Common 21 M5
- Longcross 80 B7
- Longford 41 K8
- Longlane 133 N6
- Love Green 30 F6
- Lower Assendon 115 M8
- Lower Basildon 124 B4
- Lower Caversham 9 M2
- Lower Common 84 F5
- Lower Earley 60 D5
- Lower Feltham 71 L1
- Lower Green 139 M9
- Lower Halliford 83 K4
- Lower Highmoor 114 E8
- Lower Padworth 142 F1
- Lower Shiplake 32 B3
- Lower Woodend 18 A3
- Lyde Green 151 L11
- Maidenhead 5 J3
- Maidenhead Court 26 E2
- Maiden's Green 51 G8
- Malpas 136 H4
- Manor Park 28 E5
- Mapledurham 125 Q8
- Marlow 18 E3
- Marsh Benham 141 K3
- Marsh Gate 138 E1
- Martin's Heron 65 G8
- Matthewsgreen 14 D3
- Mattingley 151 P10
- Mays Green 127 P5
- Medmenham 23 K1
- Mell Green 120 C6
- Merryhill Green 61 K3
- Middle Assendon 115 M6
- Middle Green 30 A8
- Midgham 99 G3
- Midgham Green 99 K1
- Miles's Green 134 E11
- Mill End 16 E7
- Mill Green 102 B3
- Moneyrow Green 36 C7
- Monk Sherborne 148 F12
- Mortimer 143 Q9
- Mortimer West End 143 M10
- Moss End 50 B8
- Moulsford 111 P6
- The Mount 59 K1
- Netherton 146 H10
- Nettlebed 114 D4
- Newbury 6 C4
- New Cross 32 A4
- Newell Green 64 C3
- New Town 45 L7
- New Town 124 A10
- New Town 128 A6
- Newtown 22 A6
- Newtown 100 D2
- Newtown 138 A11
- Nodmore 119 M7
- North Ascot 65 J7
- North End 140 F12
- North Heath 120 D12
- North Stoke 112 B1
- North Street 136 H5
- North Town 5 G1
- Nuney Green 125 Q3
- Nuptown 50 E7
- Oakley Green 52 A1
- Oare 133 P1
- Oatlands Park 83 L8
- Old Windsor 54 B5
- Owlsmoor 87 K4
- Ownham 131 N9
- Padworth 142 G5
- Padworth Common 143 J7
- Paley Street 50 B1
- Pamber End 148 F9
- Pamber Green 148 G6
- Pamber Heath 142 F12
- Pangbourne 124 F9
- Parker's Corner 136 E7
- Peasemore 120 D7
- Pheasant's Hill 16 E3
- Pingewood 58 C6
- Pinkneys Green 25 H5
- Plastow Green 102 C7
- Play Hatch 45 M1
- Popeswood 63 H6
- Port Hill 114 B3
- Poundgreen 144 G3
- Poyle 41 G8
- Priestwood 2 B2
- Purley on Thames 125 L10
- Purton 121 J6
- Quick's Green 123 M9
- Ragnal 128 H2
- Ramsdell 148 C11
- Ravenswood Village Settlement 74 E7
- Reading 8 F6
- Remenham 22 C1
- Remenham Hill 22 E4
- Richings Park 41 G3
- The Ridges 86 B2
- Riseley 145 N11
- The Rise 78 E3
- Rockwell End 17 H1
- Rose Hill 27 J1
- Rotherfield Greys 127 J1
- Rotherfield Peppard 126 F3
- Rotherwick 151 L12
- Rotten Row 135 P7
- Ruscombe 33 H8
- Ryeish Green 145 N2
- Salters Heath 148 H10
- Salt Hill 10 D4
- Sandhurst 87 H5
- Sanham Green 138 H4
- Satwell 114 F10
- Schoolgreen 145 P2
- Scotland 134 H10
- Scotswood 78 D5
- Shalbourne 138 D11
- Shaw 96 D1
- Sheepdrove 117 M2
- Sheffield Bottom 137 K10
- Shefford Woodlands 130 B3
- Shepherd's Green 114 G11
- Shepperton 83 G3
- Shepperton Green 83 G1
- Sherfield on Loddon 150 E10
- Shinfield 145 P1
- Shiplake 32 A4
- Shiplake Bottom 126 E4
- Shreding Green 30 D7
- Shrubs Hill 79 J3
- Shurlock Row 49 G4
- Silchester 149 K2
- Sindlesham 60 F6
- Sipson 42 B5
- Skinners Green 141 P6
- The Slade 134 C10
- Slough 11 J5
- Sonning 46 D3
- Sonning Common 126 E4
- Sonning Eye 46 C1
- Southall 43 M2
- South Ascot 78 A3
- Southcote 58 B2
- Southend 119 N5
- Southend 135 Q8
- South Fawley 118 G1
- South Field 38 D5
- South Stoke 111 Q6
- Spanish Green 150 F7
- Speen 141 Q1
- Spencers Wood 145 L4
- Spinfield 18 C5
- Spital 53 H3
- Staines 69 M2
- Stanford Dingley 135 M6
- Stanford End 145 J11
- Stanmore 120 C4
- Stanwell 56 D5
- Stanwell Moor 56 A5
- Stockcross 141 M1
- Stoke Green 29 J5
- Stoke Poges 29 G1
- Stoke Row 114 A9
- Stoney Ware 35 F6
- Straight Soley 129 J4
- Stratfield Mortimer 144 B9
- Stratfield Saye 150 F2
- Stratfield Turgis 150 G6
- Streatley 111 Q11
- Stroude 68 F7
- Stroud Green 7 G7
- Stubbings 24 F6
- Stubbles 123 L9
- Stud Green 36 A6
- Sulham 137 J1
- Sulhamstead 136 F12
- Sulhamstead Abbots 143 P2
- Sulhamstead Bannister Upper End 143 M1
- Sunbury 71 L6
- Sunbury Common 71 M5
- Sunningdale 79 G2
- Sunninghill 78 D2
- Sunnymeads 54 E3
- Sutton 40 E5
- Swallowfield 145 P8
- Taplow 27 G5
- Temple 24 E1
- Templeton 139 M5
- Thatcham 97 L2
- Theale 136 H6
- Thorney 41 K2
- Thorpe 69 J8
- Thorpe Green 81 G1
- Thorpe Lea 69 J5
- Three Ashes 149 M3
- Three Mile Cross 145 M2
- The Throat 74 A5
- Tickleback Row 49 M8
- Tidmarsh 124 F12
- Tilehurst 137 Q1
- Titcomb 139 R7
- Tittenhurst 79 G1
- Tittle Row 25 K8
- Tokers Green 126 E11
- Tot Hill 100 A5
- Touchen-end 35 M8
- Trapshill 139 Q10
- Trash Green 137 L11
- Trench Green 126 A10
- Trumpsgreen 80 C3
- Turgis Green 150 G7
- Turner's Green 134 D11
- Tutts Clump 135 P7
- Twyford 47 L1
- Ufton Green 143 K1
- Ufton Nervet 143 M2
- Up Green 85 L8
- Upper Basildon 123 Q9
- Upper Bucklebury 134 E12
- Upper Green 139 P11
- Upper Halliford 83 K1
- Upper Lambourn 104 H12
- Upper Woolhampton 99 L2
- Upton 11 K9
- Upton Lea 11 M1
- Uxbridge 31 L2
- Uxbridge Moor 31 K2
- Valley End 91 G1
- Vernham Street 146 B10
- The Village 67 H1
- Virginia Water 68 C8
- Waltham St Lawrence 34 A7
- Warfield 64 E1
- Wargrave 32 E5
- Warren Row 23 L8
- Wash Common 141 R9
- Wash Water 141 P11
- Wasing 103 M1
- Wawcott 140 D1
- Welford 131 L3
- Well End 20 B1
- Wellhouse 134 A5
- Well Place 113 K3
- West Bedfont 56 F6
- Westbrook 131 N6
- West Drayton 41 M3
- West End 48 E2
- West End 64 B3
- West End Green 150 B2
- West Fields 6 B5
- West Heath 148 C9
- West Ilsley 108 G8
- Weston 130 H2
- Westridge Green 123 J2
- Westrop Green 133 R7
- West Woodhay 140 C11
- Wether Down 105 L12
- Wexham Street 29 L2
- Weybridge 83 G8
- Wheat Hold 103 G8
- Wheeler's Green 61 G1
- Whistley Green 47 L5
- Whitchurch Hill 125 J4
- Whitchurch-on-Thames 124 F7
- Whitehouse Green 137 L12
- Whiteknights 59 M2
- White Waltham 35 G7
- Whitley 59 H4
- Whitley Wood 59 J7
- Whittonditch 128 B5
- Wickham 130 G6
- Wickham Green 130 G6
- Wickham Heath 131 M11
- Wick Hill 64 C5
- Wick Hill 74 A8
- Widmoor 21 G3
- Wildridings 2 C8
- Windlesham 90 B2
- Windsor 13 G6
- Winkfield 65 K1
- Winkfield Place 52 A6
- Winkfield Row 65 G5
- Winnersh 61 H3
- Winterbourne 132 C5
- Witheridge Hill 114 C9
- Wokingham 15 K7
- Wooburn 20 E2
- Wooburn Common 21 J3
- Woodcote 113 K9
- Wood End 66 C4
- Woodlands 22 A4
- Woodlands Park 35 H4
- Woodlands St Mary 117 M12
- Woodley 46 F8
- Woodley Green 46 F7
- Woodside 66 B2
- Woodspeen 132 A11
- Woodway 110 C5
- Woolhampton 99 L4
- Woolley Green 35 G1
- Woose Hill 14 A5
- World's End 121 J8
- Wraysbury 54 F5
- Yateley 86 D8
- Yattendon 134 G1
- York Town 94 A2

USING THE STREET INDEX

Street names are listed alphabetically. Each street name is followed by its postal town or area locality, the Postcode District, the page number, and the reference to the square in which the name is found.

Standard index entries are shown as follows:

Abattoirs Rd *READ* RG1 **8** E4

Street names and selected addresses not shown on the map due to scale restrictions are shown in the index with an asterisk:

Abbey Cha *CHERT* KT16 * **82** B3

GENERAL ABBREVIATIONS

ACC ACCESS
ALY ALLEY
AP APPROACH
AR ARCADE
ASS ASSOCIATION
AV AVENUE
BCH BEACH
BLDS BUILDINGS
BND BEND
BNK BANK
BR BRIDGE
BRK BROOK
BTM BOTTOM
BUS BUSINESS
BVD BOULEVARD
BY BYPASS
CATH CATHEDRAL
CEM CEMETERY
CEN CENTRE
CFT CROFT
CH CHURCH
CHA CHASE
CHYD CHURCHYARD
CIR CIRCLE
CIRC CIRCUS
CL CLOSE
CLFS CLIFFS
CMP CAMP
CNR CORNER
CO COUNTY
COLL COLLEGE
COM COMMON
COMM COMMISSION
CON CONVENT
COT COTTAGE
COTS COTTAGES
CP CAPE
CPS COPSE
CR CREEK
CREM CREMATORIUM
CRS CRESCENT
CSWY CAUSEWAY
CT COURT
CTRL CENTRAL
CTS COURTS
CTYD COURTYARD
CUTT CUTTINGS
CV COVE
CYN CANYON
DEPT DEPARTMENT
DL DALE
DM DAM
DR DRIVE
DRO DROVE
DRY DRIVEWAY
DWGS DWELLINGS
E EAST
EMB EMBANKMENT
EMBY EMBASSY
ESP ESPLANADE
EST ESTATE
EX EXCHANGE
EXPY EXPRESSWAY
EXT EXTENSION
F/O FLYOVER
FC FOOTBALL CLUB
FK FORK
FLD FIELD
FLDS FIELDS
FLS FALLS
FM FARM
FT FORT
FTS FLATS
FWY FREEWAY
FY FERRY
GA GATE
GAL GALLERY
GDN GARDEN
GDNS GARDENS
GLD GLADE
GLN GLEN
GN GREEN
GND GROUND
GRA GRANGE
GRG GARAGE
GT GREAT
GTWY GATEWAY
GV GROVE
HGR HIGHER
HL HILL
HLS HILLS
HO HOUSE
HOL HOLLOW
HOSP HOSPITAL
HRB HARBOUR
HTH HEATH
HTS HEIGHTS
HVN HAVEN
HWY HIGHWAY
IMP IMPERIAL
IN INLET
IND EST INDUSTRIAL ESTATE
INF INFIRMARY
INFO INFORMATION
INT INTERCHANGE
IS ISLAND
JCT JUNCTION
JTY JETTY
KG KING
KNL KNOLL
L LAKE
LA LANE
LDG LODGE
LGT LIGHT
LK LOCK
LKS LAKES
LNDG LANDING
LTL LITTLE
LWR LOWER
MAG MAGISTRATE
MAN MANSIONS
MD MEAD
MDW MEADOWS
MEM MEMORIAL
MI MILL
MKT MARKET
MKTS MARKETS
ML MALL
MNR MANOR
MS MEWS
MSN MISSION
MT MOUNT
MTN MOUNTAIN
MTS MOUNTAINS
MUS MUSEUM
MWY MOTORWAY
N NORTH
NE NORTH EAST
NW NORTH WEST
O/P OVERPASS
OFF OFFICE
ORCH ORCHARD
OV OVAL
PAL PALACE
PAS PASSAGE
PAV PAVILION
PDE PARADE
PH PUBLIC HOUSE
PK PARK
PKWY PARKWAY
PL PLACE
PLN PLAIN
PLNS PLAINS
PLZ PLAZA
POL POLICE STATION
PR PRINCE
PREC PRECINCT
PREP PREPARATORY
PRIM PRIMARY
PROM PROMENADE
PRS PRINCESS
PRT PORT
PT POINT
PTH PATH
PZ PIAZZA
QD QUADRANT
QU QUEEN
QY QUAY
R RIVER
RBT ROUNDABOUT
RD ROAD
RDG RIDGE
REP REPUBLIC
RES RESERVOIR
RFC RUGBY FOOTBALL CLUB
RI RISE
RP RAMP
RW ROW
S SOUTH
SCH SCHOOL
SE SOUTH EAST
SER SERVICE AREA
SH SHORE
SHOP SHOPPING
SKWY SKYWAY
SMT SUMMIT
SOC SOCIETY
SP SPUR
SPR SPRING
SQ SQUARE
ST STREET
STN STATION
STR STREAM
STRD STRAND
SW SOUTH WEST
TDG TRADING
TER TERRACE
THWY THROUGHWAY
TNL TUNNEL
TOLL TOLLWAY
TPK TURNPIKE
TR TRACK
TRL TRAIL
TWR TOWER
U/P UNDERPASS
UNI UNIVERSITY
UPR UPPER
V VALE
VA VALLEY
VIAD VIADUCT
VIL VILLA
VIS VISTA
VLG VILLAGE
VLS VILLAS
VW VIEW
W WEST
WD WOOD
WHF WHARF
WK WALK
WKS WALKS
WLS WELLS
WY WAY
YD YARD
YHA YOUTH HOSTEL

POSTCODE TOWNS AND AREA ABBREVIATIONS

ADL/WDHM Addlestone/Woodham
ASC Ascot
ASHF Ashford (Surrey)
BAGS Bagshot
BEAC Beaconsfield
BFOR Bracknell Forest/Windlesham
BLKW Blackwater
BNEND Bourne End
BNFD Binfield
BRAK Bracknell
CAV/SC Caversham/Sonning Common
CBLY Camberley
CHERT Chertsey
CHIN Chineham
CHOB/PIR Chobham/Pirbright
CKL/HW Cricklade/Highworth
CWTH Crowthorne
DEN/HRF Denham/Harefield
DID Didcot
DTCH/LGLY Datchet/Langley
EARL Earley
EBED/NFELT East Bedfont/North Feltham
EGH Egham
EWKG Wokingham east
FARN Farnborough
FELT Feltham
FGDN Faringdon
FLEETN Fleet north
FLKWH/TG Flackwell Heath/Tylers Green
FRIM Frimley
GOR/PANG Goring/Pangbourne
HEN Henley-on-Thames
HEST Heston
HGDN/ICK Hillingdon/Ickenham
HSLWW Hounslow west
HTHAIR Heathrow Airport
HTWY Hartley Wintney
HUNG Hungerford/Lambourn
HYS/HAR Hayes/Harlington
IVER Iver
KSCL Kingsclere/Rural Newbury
LTWR Lightwater
MARL Marlborough
MDHD Maidenhead
MLW Marlow
NTHA Thatcham north
NWBY Newbury
NWDGN Norwood Green
RAND Rural Andover
RDGW/BURGH Reading west/Burghfield
READ Reading
SHPTN Shepperton
SHST Sandhurst
SL Slough
SLN Slough north
STA Staines
STHA Thatcham south
STHL Southall
STKPK Stockley Park
STWL/WRAY Stanwell/Wraysbury
SUN Sunbury
TADY Tadley
THLE Theale/Rural Reading
TILE/CALC Tilehurst/Calcot
UX/CGN Uxbridge/Colham Green
VW Virginia Water
WANT Wantage
WAR/TWY Wargrave/Twyford
WDR/YW West Drayton/Yiewsley
WDSR Windsor
WEY Weybridge
WGFD Wallingford
WHIT Whitley/Arborfield
WODY Woodley
WOKN/KNAP Woking north/Knaphill
WOT/HER Walton-on-Thames/Hersham
WWKG Wokingham west
YEAD Yeading
YTLY Yateley

Index - streets

A

Abattoirs Rd *READ* RG1 8 E4
Abbetts La *CBLY* GU15 94 B3
Abbey Cha *CHERT* KT16 * 82 B3
Abbey Cl *BRAK* RG12 76 D2
EWKG RG40 15 H3
HYS/HAR UB3 43 K1
NWBY RG14 6 F9
SL SL1 28 A8
Abbey Ct *CHERT* KT16 * 82 B4
Abbey Dr *STA* TW18 70 C8
Abbey Gdns *CHERT* KT16 82 A3
THLE RG7 99 M1
Abbey Gn *CHERT* KT16 82 A3
Abbey Mdw *CHERT* KT16 82 C4
Abbey Ms *STA* TW18 * 70 C8
Abbey Pk *THLE* RG7 143 P3
Abbey Pl *CHERT* KT16 70 A8
Abbey Rd *BNEND* SL8 20 B1
CHERT KT16 82 B4
SHPTN TW17 83 G5
VW GU25 80 D2
Abbey Sq *READ* RG1 9 H6
Abbey St *READ* RG1 9 H6
The Abbey *BNEND* SL8 * 20 B2
Abbey Wy *MLW* SL7 18 F8
Abbey Wd *ASC* SL5 79 G4
Abbot Cl *STA* TW18 70 D5
Abbotsbury *BRAK* RG12 75 M2
Abbots Cl *GOR/PANG* RG8 113 K10
Abbots Dr *VW* GU25 80 C1
Abbots Md *WGFD* OX10 111 Q2
Abbotsmead Pl *CAV/SC* RG4 8 E1
Abbots Rd *NWBY* RG14 6 F7
THLE RG7 143 P4
Abbot's Wk *READ* RG1 9 H5
WDSR SL4 52 E1
Abbots Wy *CHERT* KT16 81 M4
Abbotswood Wy *HYS/HAR* UB3 43 K1
Abbott's Cl *UX/CGN* UB8 31 M6
Abbottsleigh Gdns *CAV/SC* RG4 45 K2
Abbotts Wy *SL* SL1 37 M1
Abbottswood Cl *TADY* RG26 148 D3
Abelia Cl *CHOB/PIR* GU24 90 E8
Abell Gdns *MDHD* SL6 25 J5
Aberaman *CAV/SC* RG4 126 F12
Aberdeen Av *SL* SL1 28 C8
Aberford Cl
RDGW/BURGH RG30 44 C7
Abex Rd *NWBY* RG14 7 K4
Abingdon Cl *BRAK* RG12 76 E2
Abingdon Dr *CAV/SC* RG4 127 J12
Abingdon Rd *KSCL* RG20 109 L11
SHST GU47 87 J6
Abney Court Dr *BNEND* SL8 20 C4
Aborn Pde *THLE* RG7 * 143 Q8
Abrahams Rd *HEN* RG9 115 Q11
Acacia Av *SHPTN* TW17 83 G2
SHST GU47 87 K5
STWL/WRAY TW19 54 E3
Acacia Ct *BRAK* RG12 2 E7
Acacia Ms *WDR/YW* UB7 41 M6
Acacia Rd *READ* RG1 9 K8
STA TW18 70 B3
Academy Cl *CBLY* GU15 88 E6
Academy Pl *SHST* GU47 87 L7
Accommodation La
WDR/YW UB7 41 L6
Accommodation Rd
CHERT KT16 80 D7
Acer Cl *BNFD* RG42 65 G6
Acer Dr *CHOB/PIR* GU24 90 F8
Ackrells Md *SHST* GU47 86 F5
Acorn Cl *DTCH/LGLY* SL3 40 D5
Acorn Dr *EWKG* RG40 15 G3
NTHA RG18 97 M1
Acorn Gdns *THLE* RG7 143 N4
Acorn Gv *HYS/HAR* UB3 43 H7
Acorn Rd *BLKW* GU17 93 H1
Acre Rd *WHIT* RG2 59 G6
The Acre *MLW* SL7 19 H4
Adam Cl *SL* SL1 38 C1
TADY RG26 148 A1
Adam Ct *HEN* RG9 115 R12
Adams Wy *EARL* RG6 59 M4
Addington Cl *WDSR* SL4 53 G2
Addington Rd *READ* RG1 9 L9
Addiscombe Cha
TILE/CALC RG31 125 M11
Addiscombe Rd *CWTH* RG45 87 J2
Addison Cl *IVER* SL0 31 G8
Addison Ct *MDHD* SL6 5 L1
Addison Rd *FRIM* GU16 94 E6
READ RG1 8 E2
Addlestone Moor
ADL/WDHM KT15 82 C6
Addlestone Rd
ADL/WDHM KT15 82 E8
Adelaide Cl *SL* SL1 38 C2
Adelaide Pl *WEY* KT13 83 K8
Adelaide Rd *ASHF* TW15 70 D3
EARL RG6 60 A1
WDSR SL4 39 H8
Adelaide Sq *WDSR* SL4 13 J8
Adelphi Gdns *SL* SL1 10 E6
Adey's Cl *NWBY* RG14 7 G7
Adkins Rd *WAR/TWY* RG10 34 A7
Admiral Kepple Ct *ASC* SL5 * 65 L5
Admirals Ct *READ* RG1 8 E9
Admiralty Cl *WDR/YW* UB7 42 A2
Admiralty Wy *CBLY* GU15 93 M2
Admoor La *THLE* RG7 135 R8
Adrians Wk *SLN* SL2 11 H4
Adwell Dr *EARL* RG6 60 D5
Adwell Sq *HEN* RG9 115 R12
Adwood Ct *STHA* RG19 98 A3
Aerodrome Wy *HEST* TW5 43 L6
Agar Crs *BNFD* RG42 2 E1
Agars Pl *DTCH/LGLY* SL3 39 J6
Agate Cl *WWKG* RG41 61 L7
Aggisters La *WWKG* RG41 73 J3
Agincourt Cl *WWKG* RG41 61 L8
Agincourt Pl *ASC* SL5 66 C8
Agnes Scott Ct *WEY* KT13 83 H7
Agricola Wy *STHA* RG19 98 B4
Ainsdale Crs
RDGW/BURGH RG30 58 A2
Aintree *HUNG* RG17 117 K4
Aintree Cl *DTCH/LGLY* SL3 41 G8
NWBY RG14 7 J8
Airport Wy *STWL/WRAY* TW19 56 A3
Aisne Rd *FRIM* GU16 95 L5
Ajax Av *SL* SL1 28 D8
Alandale Cl *WHIT* RG2 59 K6
Alan Pl *RDGW/BURGH* RG30 * 58 A1
Alan Wy *DTCH/LGLY* SL3 30 A7
Albain Crs *ASHF* TW15 56 E8
Albany Gdns *CAV/SC* RG4 126 G12
Albany Pk *DTCH/LGLY* SL3 40 F7
FRIM GU16 94 C5
Albany Park Dr *WWKG* RG41 61 G3
Albany Pl *EGH* TW20 69 G2
Albany Rd *RDGW/BURGH* RG30 44 D7
WDSR SL4 13 H7
WDSR SL4 54 A4
Alben Rd *BNFD* RG42 63 J3
Albert Av *CHERT* KT16 70 A8
Albert Br *WDSR* SL4 54 B2
Albert Cl *SL* SL1 11 H8
Albert Dr *STA* TW18 69 M3
Albert Illsley Cl
TILE/CALC RG31 137 P2
Albert Pl *WDSR* SL4 38 C5
Albert Rd *ADL/WDHM* KT15 82 D7
ASHF TW15 70 F3
BAGS GU19 89 L5
BNFD RG42 2 F3
CAV/SC RG4 44 F2
CBLY GU15 * 88 C8
CWTH RG45 87 H1
EGH TW20 68 D4
EWKG RG40 14 F7
HEN RG9 22 A5
HYS/HAR UB3 43 G3
NWBY RG14 6 D3
NWDGN UB2 43 M3
WDR/YW UB7 42 A1
WDSR SL4 53 L3
Albert St *MDHD* SL6 5 G5
SL SL1 11 G8
WDSR SL4 12 E6
Albion Cl *SLN* SL2 11 J5
Albion Pl *WDSR* SL4 12 C7
Albion Rd *SHST* GU47 87 H7
Albion Ter *READ* RG1 * 9 J8
Albury Cl *CHERT* KT16 80 A7
RDGW/BURGH RG30 44 C5
Albury Gdns *TILE/CALC* RG31 137 Q7
Albury Wy *STHA* RG19 101 H2
Alcock Rd *HEST* TW5 43 M7
Alcot Cl *CWTH* RG45 87 H2
Aldborough Sp *SL* SL1 10 E1
Aldbourne Av *EARL* RG6 60 A2
Aldbourne Cl *HUNG* RG17 138 H1
Aldbourne Rd *SL* SL1 27 K6
Aldeburgh Cl *CAV/SC* RG4 127 J10
Aldebury Rd *MDHD* SL6 26 A4
Aldenham Cl *CAV/SC* RG4 127 J12
Aldenham Ter *BRAK* RG12 76 C3
Alden Vw *WDSR* SL4 37 M8
Alderbrook Cl *CWTH* RG45 86 E1
Alderbury Rd *DTCH/LGLY* SL3 40 B2
Alderbury Rd West
DTCH/LGLY SL3 40 B2
Alder Cl *EARL* RG6 60 D5
EGH TW20 68 E3
NWBY RG14 7 M2
SL SL1 38 B1
Alder Dr *TILE/CALC* RG31 137 N4
Alderfield Cl *THLE* RG7 137 K6
Alder Gld *THLE* RG7 143 P3
Alder Gv *YTLY* GU46 92 C1
Alderley Cl *WODY* RG5 46 F5
Alderman Willey Cl
WWKG RG41 14 E5
Aldermaston Rd *TADY* RG26 142 C12
TADY RG26 148 H11
Alder Ms *WWKG* RG41 61 H6
Alderney Gdns *WWKG* RG41 61 K4
Alder Rd *IVER* SL0 30 E3
Alderside Wk *EGH* TW20 68 E3
The Alders *NTHA* RG18 97 M2
Aldin Av North *SL* SL1 11 K6
Aldin Av South *SL* SL1 11 K7
Aldridge Pk *BNFD* RG42 65 H4
Aldridge Rd *SLN* SL2 28 C5
Aldwick Cl *FARN* GU14 94 A8
Aldwick Dr *MDHD* SL6 4 C6
Aldworth Cl *BRAK* RG12 2 D9
RDGW/BURGH RG30 58 C1
Aldworth Gdns *CWTH* RG45 87 G1
Aldworth Rd *GOR/PANG* RG8 123 Q8
KSCL RG20 122 A2
Alexander Cl *SHST* GU47 87 L7
Alexander Rd *EGH* TW20 69 H3
STHA RG19 98 A4
Alexander Wk *BRAK* RG12 76 B2
Alexandra Av *CBLY* GU15 94 A1
Alexandra Cl *ASHF* TW15 71 K5
STA TW18 70 D4
Alexandra Ct *EWKG* RG40 14 F7
Alexandra Rd *ADL/WDHM* KT15 82 D8
ASHF TW15 71 K5
EGH TW20 68 C4
MDHD SL6 4 C3
READ RG1 9 M8
SL SL1 10 D8
UX/CGN UB8 31 M3
WDSR SL4 13 J8
Alexandre Ter *HTWY* RG27 * 150 D9
Alford Cl *RDGW/BURGH* RG30 137 P2
SHST GU47 87 G7
Alfred St *READ* RG1 8 D6
Alfriston Rd *FRIM* GU16 95 J7
Alice La *SL* SL1 27 K5
Alison Cl *THLE* RG7 143 P5
Alison Dr *CBLY* GU15 94 F1
Allanson Rd *MLW* SL7 19 H3
Allcot Cl *EBED/NFELT* TW14 57 M7
Allcroft Rd *READ* RG1 59 J1
Allenby Rd *CBLY* GU15 88 A8
MDHD SL6 25 K7
Allendale Cl *SHST* GU47 87 G4
Allendale Rd *EARL* RG6 60 B3
Allerds Rd *SLN* SL2 28 B2
Alleyns La *MDHD* SL6 19 M6
All Hallows Rd *CAV/SC* RG4 45 K3
Allison Gdns *GOR/PANG* RG8 125 N9
Allkins Ct *WDSR* SL4 13 K7
Allnatt Av *WWKG* RG41 61 J5
Allonby Cl *EARL* RG6 60 D4
All Saints Av *MDHD* SL6 4 B3
All Saints Cl *EWKG* RG40 15 G3
All Saints Ct *READ* RG1 * 8 B8
All Saints Crs *FARN* GU14 93 L5
All Saints Ri *BNFD* RG42 64 D4
All Saints Rd *LTWR* GU18 90 C5
Allsmoor La *BRAK* RG12 64 F8
All Souls' Rd *ASC* SL5 78 A2
Allyn Cl *STA* TW18 69 M4
Alma Gdns *FRIM* GU16 95 K6
Alma Gn *HEN* RG9 114 A10
Alma Rd *WDSR* SL4 13 G6
WDSR SL4 38 B4
Alma St *RDGW/BURGH* RG30 44 C6
Almners Rd *CHERT* KT16 81 H5
Almond Av *NWBY* RG14 96 C1
WDR/YW UB7 42 C3
Almond Cl *EGH* TW20 68 B4
FARN GU14 94 A7
SHPTN TW17 71 J7
WDSR SL4 12 E7
WWKG RG41 73 J2
Almond Dr *CAV/SC* RG4 45 M2
KSCL RG20 121 J9
NTHA RG18 97 M2
Almond Rd *SL* SL1 27 K3
Almons Wy *SLN* SL2 29 K6
Almorah Rd *HEST* TW5 43 M8
Almswood Rd *TADY* RG26 142 C12
Alpha Est *HYS/HAR* UB3 * 43 G2
Alpha Rd *CHOB/PIR* GU24 91 M5
Alpha St North *SL* SL1 11 J7
Alpha St South *SL* SL1 11 H8
Alpha Wy *EGH* TW20 69 J6
Alphington Av *FRIM* GU16 94 F5
Alphington Gn *FRIM* GU16 94 E5
Alphington Rd *WHIT* RG2 59 H6
Alpine Cl *ASC* SL5 * 77 M2
MDHD SL6 5 J7
Alpine St *READ* RG1 9 G9
Alsford Cl *LTWR* GU18 89 M7
Alston Gdns *MDHD* SL6 4 F4
Alston Ms *STHA* RG19 97 L4
Alston Wk *CAV/SC* RG4 9 M1
Altmore *MDHD* SL6 35 G2
Altona Wy *SL* SL1 28 D7
Alton Ct *STA* TW18 69 L6
Alton Ride *BLKW* GU17 87 J8
Altwood Bailey *MDHD* SL6 35 K1
Altwood Cl *MDHD* SL6 35 K1
SL SL1 28 A6
Altwood Dr *MDHD* SL6 35 K1
Altwood Rd *MDHD* SL6 4 A8
Alvista Av *MDHD* SL6 27 K7
Alwyn Rd *MDHD* SL6 25 K6
Alwyns Cl *CHERT* KT16 82 A3
Alwyns La *CHERT* KT16 81 M3
Alyson Ct *MDHD* SL6 * 5 H1
Amanda Ct *DTCH/LGLY* SL3 39 M3
Ambarrow Crs *SHST* GU47 86 F5
Ambarrow La *SHST* GU47 86 D4
Ambassador *BRAK* RG12 75 M2
Amber Cl *EARL* RG6 60 C2
Amber Hl *CBLY* GU15 95 H2
Amberley Cl *NWBY* RG14 6 C1
Amberley Ct *MDHD* SL6 26 E3
Amberley Dr *WAR/TWY* RG10 32 F8
Amberley Gdns *WWKG* RG41 61 L6
Amberley Pl *WDSR* SL4 13 J5
Amberley Rd *SLN* SL2 28 A6
Amberwood Dr *CBLY* GU15 88 F7
Amblecote Rd
RDGW/BURGH RG30 44 B7
Ambleside *CWTH* RG45 87 J2
Ambleside Cl *WODY* RG5 46 E7
Ambleside Dr
EBED/NFELT TW14 57 M7
Ambleside Rd *LTWR* GU18 90 A6
Ambleside Wy *EGH* TW20 69 H5
Ambrook Rd *WHIT* RG2 59 H6
Ambrose Pl *READ* RG1 8 D6
Ambrose Rd *TADY* RG26 148 D2
Ambury Rd *GOR/PANG* RG8 122 G1
Amerden Cl *MDHD* SL6 26 F7
Amerden La *MDHD* SL6 36 F1
Amerden Wy *SL* SL1 38 C2
Amersham Rd *CAV/SC* RG4 9 L1
Amethyst Cl *WWKG* RG41 61 K7
Amethyst La
RDGW/BURGH RG30 44 C8
Amherst Rd *EARL* RG6 46 A8
Amity Rd *READ* RG1 45 L7
Amity St *READ* RG1 45 L7
Ammanford *CAV/SC* RG4 44 F1
Amner's Farm Rd
RDGW/BURGH RG30 137 R10
Ampere Rd *NWBY* RG14 7 G3
Amwell Pl *WGFD* OX10 111 P1
Ancaster Dr *ASC* SL5 65 L6
Ancastle Gn *HEN* RG9 127 Q1
Anchorite Cl *WAR/TWY* RG10 47 K1
Andermans *WDSR* SL4 * 37 M8
Anders Cnr *BNFD* RG42 2 A3
Anderson Av *EARL* RG6 46 A8
Anderson Crs *WHIT* RG2 72 E4
Anderson Dr *ASHF* TW15 71 J2

Anderson Gdns TADY RG26 148 D1
Anderson Pl BAGS GU19 89 L2
Anderson Rd WEY KT13 * 83 K7
Andover Cl EBED/NFELT TW14 57 M7
TILE/CALC RG31 137 P1
UX/CGN UB8 31 K3
Andover Dro KSCL RG20 141 P10
Andover Rd BLKW GU17 87 J8
KSCL RG20 141 Q11
NWBY RG14 6 C8
Andrew Cl EWKG RG40 15 L8
Andrews Cl THLE RG7 137 J7
Andrews Rd EARL RG6 60 B3
Angel Ct NWBY RG14 6 D1
Angel Md THLE RG7 99 L4
Angel Pl BNFD RG42 63 J4
Angle Field Rd CAV/SC RG4 45 J3
Anglers Wy READ RG1 9 L6
Anglesey Av FARN GU14 93 M7
Anglesey Cl ASHF TW15 71 G1
Angus Cl TILE/CALC RG31 137 Q6
WWKG RG41 61 H4
Annadale NTHA RG18 133 Q9
Anne Cl MDHD SL6 26 A4
Anneforde Pl BNFD RG42 64 A5
Anners Cl EGH TW20 69 J8
Annesley Gdns WWKG RG41 61 J3
Annett Cl SHPTN TW17 83 L1
Annett's La HUNG RG17 138 D7
Annie Brookes Cl STA TW18 69 K1
Ansculf Rd SLN SL2 28 C4
Ansell Rd FRIM GU16 94 E6
Anslow Gdns IVER SL0 30 F3
Anslow Pl SL SL1 27 L6
Anson Crs WHIT RG2 59 K6
Anstey Pl THLE RG7 143 Q3
Anstey Rd READ RG1 8 E7
Anston Cl EARL RG6 59 M6
Antares Cl WWKG RG41 14 A6
Anthian Cl WODY RG5 47 H6
Anthony Wall BNFD RG42 64 F6
Anthony Wy SL SL1 27 M8
Antrim Rd WODY RG5 46 D8
Anvil Cl TADY RG26 149 R7
THLE RG7 145 L5
Anvilles HUNG RG17 139 K6
Anvil Paddock WANT OX12 106 E1
Anvil Wy TADY RG26 149 R7
Apex Dr FRIM GU16 94 D5
Apex Plaza READ RG1 * 9 G4
Aphelion Wy WHIT RG2 59 L7
Aplin Wy LTWR GU18 90 A5
Appelford Cl STHA RG19 97 M4
Appleby End
RDGW/BURGH RG30 44 B7
Appleby Gdns
EBED/NFELT TW14 * 57 M7
Apple Cl TILE/CALC RG31 125 M10
WWKG RG41 14 A8
Applecroft MDHD SL6 35 L3
Apple Dene TADY RG26 149 R8
Appledore BRAK RG12 75 M3
Appledore Ms FARN GU14 94 A7
Appleford Rd
RDGW/BURGH RG30 58 A2
Appleshaw Cl TADY RG26 148 D3
Appletree Cl CAV/SC RG4 126 E4
Apple Tree Cl NWBY RG14 96 A7
Appletree La DTCH/LGLY SL3 39 L3
THLE RG7 145 M4
Appletree Pl BNFD RG42 2 C3
Apple Tree Wy SHST GU47 87 K5
Appley Dr CBLY GU15 94 B1
Approach Rd ASHF TW15 71 J4
MDHD SL6 27 G7
April Cl CBLY GU15 94 C4
Apron Rd STHA RG19 101 J1
Apsey Ct BNFD RG42 63 L5
Aquila Cl WWKG RG41 61 L8
Araby Cnr SHPTN TW17 83 J3
Aragon Cl SUN TW16 71 M5
Aragon Ct BRAK RG12 3 G8
Aragon Rd YTLY GU46 92 C2
Arbery Wy WHIT RG2 72 E6
Arborfield Cl SL SL1 10 F8
Arborfield Rd WHIT RG2 145 R2
Arbor La WWKG RG41 61 H3
Arbor Mdw WWKG RG41 61 H3
Arbour Cl READ RG1 58 F1
The Arcade GOR/PANG RG8 * 112 A12
MDHD SL6 * 20 D7
Archangel Wy NTHA RG18 98 B2
Archer Cl MDHD SL6 4 C3
The Arches WDSR SL4 * 13 H5
Archie Cl WDR/YW UB7 42 C2
Archway Rd CAV/SC RG4 8 F1
Arden Cl BRAK RG12 65 G7
Ardesley Wd WEY KT13 83 L8
Ardingly BRAK RG12 76 A3
Ardler Rd CAV/SC RG4 9 J1
Ardrossan Av CBLY GU15 95 G1
Ardrossan Cl SLN SL2 28 E5
Ardwell Cl CWTH RG45 86 E1
Arenal Dr CWTH RG45 87 H3
The Arena STKPK UB11 * 42 E1
Argent Cl EGH TW20 69 J4
Argent Ter SHST GU47 * 87 L6
Argosy Gdns STA TW18 69 M4
Argosy La STWL/WRAY TW19 56 D6
Argyle Rd NWBY RG14 6 D6
READ RG1 8 B7
Argyle St READ RG1 8 B6
Argyll Av SL SL1 28 C8
Arkle Av STHA RG19 97 H3
Arkley Ct MDHD SL6 36 D5
Arkwright Dr BNFD RG42 63 K7
Arkwright Rd DTCH/LGLY SL3 55 L1
WHIT RG2 59 H3
Arlington Cl BNFD RG42 2 A2
MDHD SL6 25 H6
Arlington Ct HYS/HAR UB3 42 F5
Arlington Ldg WEY KT13 83 H8
Arlington Rd ASHF TW15 70 F3
Arlington Sq BRAK RG12 2 D4
Armadale Ct
RDGW/BURGH RG30 44 D8
Armitage Ct ASC SL5 78 C3
Armitage Dr FRIM GU16 94 F5
Armour Hl TILE/CALC RG31 137 P1
Armour Rd TILE/CALC RG31 137 P1
Armour Wk TILE/CALC RG31 137 P1
Armstrong Rd EGH TW20 68 C4
Armstrong Wy WODY RG5 47 G7
Armytage Rd HEST TW5 43 M7
Arncliffe BRAK RG12 76 A2
Arndale Wy EGH TW20 69 G3
Arne Cl WWKG RG41 61 G4
Arnett Av EWKG RG40 73 L7
Arnewood Av TADY RG26 148 F1
Arnhem Rd NWBY RG14 7 H4
Arnold Rd STA TW18 70 C5
Arnside Cl WAR/TWY RG10 32 F7
Arrowhead Rd THLE RG7 137 K8
Arrow Smith Wy STHA RG19 98 A4
Arthur Cl BAGS GU19 89 L5
Arthur Pl READ RG1 9 K6
Arthur Rd NWBY RG14 6 B6
SL SL1 10 D6
WDSR SL4 13 G5
WWKG RG41 14 D4
Arthur's La RAND SP11 147 L9
Arthurstone Birches
BNFD RG42 63 K3
Artillery Dr STHA RG19 98 A5
Artillery Ms
RDGW/BURGH RG30 * 44 D8
Arun Cl WWKG RG41 61 H5
Arundel Cl MDHD SL6 25 J6
Arundel Ct DTCH/LGLY SL3 39 M4
Arundel Rd CBLY GU15 95 J2
UX/CGN UB8 31 K3
WODY RG5 46 E8
Ascot Cl NWBY RG14 7 J9
Ascot Ga ASC SL5 * 66 F5
Ascot Pk ASC SL5 * 65 L8
Ascot Rd BNFD RG42 50 E6
EBED/NFELT TW14 57 G7
MDHD SL6 36 B7
Ascott Wy NWBY RG14 7 L2
Ashampstead Rd
GOR/PANG RG8 123 N8
RDGW/BURGH RG30 58 A2
Ashbourne BRAK RG12 75 M3
Ashbourne Gv MDHD SL6 35 L3
Ashbourne Wy STHA RG19 97 K3
Ashbrook Rd WDSR SL4 54 B6
Ashburton Rd WHIT RG2 59 J4
Ashbury Dr BLKW GU17 94 A5
TILE/CALC RG31 137 N3
Ashby Ct WHIT RG2 59 H7
Ashby Wy WDR/YW UB7 42 C7
Ash Cl BLKW GU17 93 J1
DTCH/LGLY SL3 40 D3
Ashcombe Cl ASHF TW15 70 D1
Ash Crs STHA RG19 102 C1
Ashcroft Cl CAV/SC RG4 44 E1
Ashcroft Ct SL SL1 27 K3
Ashcroft Rd MDHD SL6 4 A3
Ashdale Cl STWL/WRAY TW19 56 E8
Ashdale Pk EWKG RG40 74 C7
Ashdene Cl ASHF TW15 * 71 J5
Ashdene Gdns
RDGW/BURGH RG30 44 D8
Ashdown MDHD SL6 26 D3
Ashdown Cl BRAK RG12 64 F7
Ashdown Wy HEN RG9 126 A1
Asher Dr ASC SL5 65 J6
The Ashes THLE RG7 145 M4
Ashfield Gn YTLY GU46 92 F1
Ashford Av ASHF TW15 71 H4
CAV/SC RG4 126 E5
Ashford Cl ASHF TW15 70 E2
Ashford Crs ASHF TW15 70 E1
Ashford Hill Rd STHA RG19 101 M4
STHA RG19 102 F5
Ashford La WDSR SL4 37 K2
Ashford Rd ASHF TW15 71 J5
FELT TW13 71 K2
IVER SL0 30 E1
STA TW18 70 C6
Ash Ga NTHA RG18 98 B2
Ash Gv EBED/NFELT TW14 57 L7
HEST TW5 43 M8
SLN SL2 29 H1
STA TW18 70 C4
THLE RG7 135 R8
Ashgrove Rd ASHF TW15 71 J3
Ash La TADY RG26 148 A1
TADY RG26 149 M5
THLE RG7 143 Q2
WDSR SL4 52 D1
Ashlee Wk GOR/PANG RG8 113 K10
Ashleigh Av EGH TW20 69 J5
Ashley Cl EARL RG6 60 B4
FRIM GU16 94 F8
WOT/HER KT12 83 L5
Ashley Dr BLKW GU17 93 J2
Ashley Hill Pl WAR/TWY RG10 23 H7
Ashley Pk MDHD SL6 26 D4
Ashley Park Av WOT/HER KT12 83 M5
Ashley Rd UX/CGN UB8 31 K3
WOT/HER KT12 83 M8
Ashley Wy CHOB/PIR GU24 90 D8
Ashman Rd STHA RG19 98 B3
Ashmere Cl TILE/CALC RG31 137 N6
Ashmere Ter
RDGW/BURGH RG30 8 A4
Ashmore Green Rd
NTHA RG18 133 N11
Ashmore Rd WHIT RG2 59 J5
Ashridge FARN GU14 93 M7
Ashridge Ct NWBY RG14 6 F6
Ashridge Gn BNFD RG42 2 E2
Ashridge Rd EWKG RG40 15 K2
Ash Rd KSCL RG20 101 H3
RDGW/BURGH RG30 137 Q3
SHPTN TW17 83 G1
Ash Ter MARL SN8 * 116 A5
NTHA RG18 133 P10
Ashton Cl TILE/CALC RG31 137 N2
Ashton Pl HUNG RG17 140 A4
MDHD SL6 25 J8
Ashton Rd WWKG RG41 61 M5
Ash Tree Gv KSCL RG20 140 H7
Ashtrees Rd WODY RG5 46 F6
Ashurst Cl TADY RG26 148 C2
Ashurst Dr SHPTN TW17 82 E2
Ashurst Pk ASC SL5 * 66 D8
Ashview Cl ASHF TW15 70 E4
Ashview Gdns ASHF TW15 70 E3
Ashville Wy WWKG RG41 14 D8
Ash Wy WWKG RG41 73 K3
Ashwell Av CBLY GU15 88 F8
Ashwood WODY RG5 60 D1
Ashwood Cl TILE/CALC RG31 137 M4
Ashwood Dr NWBY RG14 7 M2
Ashwood Gdns HYS/HAR UB3 43 H4
Ashwood Rd EGH TW20 68 B4
Ashworth Dr STHA RG19 97 L4
Askew Dr THLE RG7 145 M3
Aspen Cl SLN SL2 28 D6
STA TW18 69 M1
WDR/YW UB7 42 B1
Aspen Gdns ASHF TW15 71 J3
Aspin Wy BLKW GU17 93 H1
Astleham Wy SHPTN TW17 70 E8
Astley Cl WWKG RG41 14 A3
Aston Av TILE/CALC RG31 137 M2
Aston Cl GOR/PANG RG8 124 H9
Aston Ferry La HEN RG9 22 E1
Aston La HEN RG9 22 E3
Aston Md WDSR SL4 38 A8
Aston St DID OX11 110 H2
Astor Cl ADL/WDHM KT15 82 D8
MDHD SL6 5 M7
WWKG RG41 61 K3
Astoria Pde ASHF TW15 * 71 G2
Astra Md BNFD RG42 65 H4
Atfield Gv BFOR GU20 90 D2
Atherton Cl
RDGW/BURGH RG30 137 R2
STWL/WRAY TW19 56 D5
Atherton Crs HUNG RG17 138 H1
Atherton Pl HUNG RG17 117 K3
Atherton Rd HUNG RG17 138 H1
Athlone Cl MDHD SL6 26 A5
Athlone Sq WDSR SL4 13 H5
Atrebatti Rd SHST GU47 87 J5
Attebrouche Ct BRAK RG12 76 D4
Atte La BNFD RG42 64 C4
Atterbury Gdns CAV/SC RG4 44 E2
Attwood Dr WHIT RG2 72 E6
Auburn Ct CAV/SC RG4 * 45 G4
Auckland Cl MDHD SL6 5 L3
Auckland Rd EARL RG6 46 A8
Auclum Cl THLE RG7 143 R4
Auclum La THLE RG7 143 Q4
Audley Cl NWBY RG14 96 F1
Audley Dr MDHD SL6 25 K8
Audley St RDGW/BURGH RG30 44 D6
Audley Wy ASC SL5 65 K8
Augur Cl STA TW18 69 M3
August End DTCH/LGLY SL3 30 A7
RDGW/BURGH RG30 44 C6
Augustine Cl DTCH/LGLY SL3 55 L2
Augustine Wk BNFD RG42 64 E5
Augustus Gdns CBLY GU15 95 J1
Austen Gdns NWBY RG14 7 G9
Austen Rd FARN GU14 94 A8
Austin Rd HYS/HAR UB3 43 H2
WODY RG5 46 F8
Austinsgate MDHD SL6 25 H6
Austin Wy BRAK RG12 3 H8
DTCH/LGLY SL3 40 B6
Australia Av MDHD SL6 5 G2
Australia Rd SL SL1 11 L6
Auton Pl HEN RG9 127 R2
Autumn Cl CAV/SC RG4 127 J11
SL SL1 38 B1
Autumn Wk MDHD SL6 25 J8
WAR/TWY RG10 32 F4
Avalon Rd BNEND SL8 20 D1
EARL RG6 60 C3
Avebury BRAK RG12 76 A3
SL SL1 38 C1
Avebury Sq READ RG1 59 K1
Aveley Wk WHIT RG2 * 59 H1
Avenue C ADL/WDHM KT15 82 E7
Avenue Cl HEST TW5 43 K8
WDR/YW UB7 41 M3
Avenue Crs HEST TW5 43 K8
Avenue Dr DTCH/LGLY SL3 30 B6
Avenue Gdns HEST TW5 * 43 J7
Avenue One ADL/WDHM KT15 82 E8
Avenue Rd FELT TW13 71 M1
MDHD SL6 5 M8
STA TW18 69 K3
Avenue Sucy CBLY GU15 94 A2
The Avenue ASC SL5 65 M5
BNEND SL8 20 B2
CBLY GU15 94 B1
CHOB/PIR GU24 91 M4
CWTH RG45 87 G1
DTCH/LGLY SL3 39 K8
EGH TW20 69 H2
HEST TW5 43 J8
LTWR GU18 90 A5
MDHD SL6 26 D4
STA TW18 70 B6
STWL/WRAY TW19 54 D2
THLE RG7 143 R9
UX/CGN UB8 31 M5
WDSR SL4 54 B4
Avenue Three ADL/WDHM KT15 82 E7
Avenue Two ADL/WDHM KT15 82 E8
Averil Ct MDHD SL6 27 L7
Avery Cl EWKG RG40 73 M8
Avington Cl TILE/CALC RG31 137 M2
Avocet Crs SHST GU47 87 K6
Avon Cl FARN GU14 93 L7
SL SL1 28 A8
Avondale MDHD SL6 25 L5
Avondale Av STA TW18 69 M5
Avondale Dr HYS/HAR UB3 43 J1
Avondale Rd ASHF TW15 70 D1
Avon Gv BRAK RG12 3 H1
Avon Pl READ RG1 9 M5
Avon Rd DID OX11 109 J1
SUN TW16 71 M5
Avonway NWBY RG14 7 M1
Avon Wy THLE RG7 136 C12
Axbridge BRAK RG12 76 E2
Axbridge Rd WHIT RG2 59 J4
Ayebridges Av EGH TW20 69 J5
Aylesbury Crs SL SL1 10 D1
Aylesford Wy STHA RG19 98 C4
Aylesham Wy YTLY GU46 86 B8
Aylesworth Av SLN SL2 28 D4
Aylesworth Sp WDSR SL4 54 B6
Aylsham Cl
RDGW/BURGH RG30 137 Q2
Aymer Cl STA TW18 69 L6
Aymer Dr STA TW18 69 L6
Ayres La KSCL RG20 100 B6
Ayrton Senna Rd
TILE/CALC RG31 137 N3
Aysgarth BRAK RG12 75 M3
Aysgarth Pk MDHD SL6 36 D5
Azalea Cl WWKG RG41 61 H4
Azalea Rd STHA RG19 102 C1
Azalea Wy CBLY GU15 89 H8
DTCH/LGLY SL3 30 A7

B

Babbage Wy BRAK RG12 76 A3
Babbington Rd WHIT RG2 * 59 K8
Bachelors Acre WDSR SL4 13 J6
Back Dr CWTH RG45 * 87 H3
Back La HUNG RG17 139 R7
THLE RG7 99 K8
THLE RG7 135 P5
THLE RG7 135 Q12
THLE RG7 143 L10
THLE RG7 145 L6
Backsideans WAR/TWY RG10 32 F4
Back St HUNG RG17 118 A8
Bacon Cl SHST GU47 87 K8
Baden Cl STA TW18 70 A5
Bader Gdns SL SL1 38 C2
The Bader Wy WODY RG5 61 G1
Badgemore La HEN RG9 115 R11
Badger Cl MDHD SL6 35 M2
Badger Dr LTWR GU18 90 A5
WAR/TWY RG10 32 F7
Badgers Cl ASHF TW15 * 70 F3
HYS/HAR UB3 43 G1
Badgers Copse CBLY GU15 94 E3
Badgers Cft THLE RG7 * 143 Q8
Badgers Gld THLE RG7 143 Q4
Badgers Hl VW GU25 80 C2
Badgers Holt YTLY GU46 92 B1
Badgers Rdg NWBY RG14 141 Q10
Badgers Ri CAV/SC RG4 45 G1
WODY RG5 46 D5
Badgers Sett CWTH RG45 86 F1
Badgers Wk HEN RG9 32 C3
Badgers Wy BRAK RG12 64 F6
Badgerwood Dr FRIM GU16 94 D4
Bad Godesberg Wy MDHD SL6 5 G5
Badminton Rd MDHD SL6 25 K8
Bagley Cl WDR/YW UB7 42 A2
Bagnols Wy NWBY RG14 6 A6
Bagshot Gn BAGS GU19 89 L3
Bagshot Rd ASC SL5 78 B5
BRAK RG12 2 F7
CHOB/PIR GU24 91 H6
EGH TW20 68 C5
Baigents La BFOR GU20 90 D2
Bailey Cl FRIM GU16 94 D6
MDHD SL6 5 G4
WDSR SL4 12 C8
Baileys Cl BLKW GU17 93 H2
Bailey's La WAR/TWY RG10 48 E2
Baily Av NTHA RG18 97 K2
Bain Av CBLY GU15 94 B4
Bainbridge Rd TILE/CALC RG31 137 M6
Baird Cl SL SL1 38 D2
Baird Rd FARN GU14 94 C8
WHIT RG2 72 E6
Bakeham La EGH TW20 68 C5
Bakers La MDHD SL6 25 H6
Bakers Orch FLKWH/TG HP10 21 G1
Baker's Rd UX/CGN UB8 31 M1
Bakers Rw MDHD SL6 25 H5
Baker St DID OX11 110 G1
READ RG1 8 C7
WEY KT13 83 G8
Bakery La WANT OX12 106 E1
Baldasarre WAR/TWY RG10 * 49 G5
Baldons Cl GOR/PANG RG8 * 113 K10
Baldwin Pl MDHD SL6 4 A4
Baldwin Rd SL SL1 27 L4
Baldwin's Shore WDSR SL4 13 J1
Balfour Crs BRAK RG12 76 B2
NWBY RG14 141 Q9
Balfour Dr TILE/CALC RG31 137 M6
Balfour Pl MLW SL7 18 E2
Balfour Rd NWDGN UB2 43 M3
WEY KT13 82 F8
Balintore Ct SHST GU47 87 K7
Ballamoor Cl TILE/CALC RG31 137 L6
Ballantyne Rd FARN GU14 94 A8
Ballard Gn WDSR SL4 38 A7
Ballard Rd CBLY GU15 89 G6
Ballencrieff Rd ASC SL5 78 F4
Balliol Rd CAV/SC RG4 44 D3
Balliol Wy SHST GU47 87 L5
Ball Pit Rd KSCL RG20 120 G3
Balme Cl WAR/TWY RG10 47 H2
Balmoral MDHD SL6 25 K5
Balmoral Cl SL SL1 28 A7
Balmoral Dr FRIM GU16 94 E6
Balmoral Gdns WDSR SL4 13 J9
Balmore Dr CAV/SC RG4 45 H2
Balmore Pk CAV/SC RG4 45 G2
Bamburgh Cl WHIT RG2 59 J3
Bamford Pl TILE/CALC RG31 * 137 M6
Banbury BRAK RG12 76 E4
Banbury Av SL SL1 28 B6
Banbury Cl FRIM GU16 94 F7
WWKG RG41 14 D6
Banbury Gdns CAV/SC RG4 45 J3
Bancroft Cl ASHF TW15 * 71 G3
Bancroft Pl TILE/CALC RG31 137 M7
Band La EGH TW20 68 F3
Bangors Cl IVER SL0 31 H7
Bangors Pk IVER SL0 * 31 G5
Bangors Rd North IVER SL0 30 F2
Bangors Rd South IVER SL0 31 G5
Bank Side EWKG RG40 73 M8
Bankside STHL UB1 43 M1
Bankside Cl WHIT RG2 59 K4
Banks Sp SL SL1 38 D2
Bannard Rd MDHD SL6 35 J1
Bannister Cl DTCH/LGLY SL3 40 A2
Bannister Gdns HTWY RG27 85 L6
YTLY GU46 92 F1
Bannister Pl THLE RG7 99 H8
Bannister Rd THLE RG7 143 P4
Banstead Cl SHPTN TW17 83 H2
Barbara's Meadow
TILE/CALC RG31 125 M12
Barbel Cl EARL RG6 46 A6
Barber Cl WAR/TWY RG10 47 L7
Barberry Wy BLKW GU17 93 M3
Barbon Cl CBLY GU15 95 K3
Barbrook Cl TILE/CALC RG31 125 P11
Barchester Cl UX/CGN UB8 31 L4
Barchester Rd DTCH/LGLY SL3 40 B2
Barclay Rd TILE/CALC RG31 137 P6
Barclose Av CAV/SC RG4 45 J3
Bardney Cl MDHD SL6 35 M3
Bardolph's Cl CAV/SC RG4 126 D10
Bardown KSCL RG20 120 G11
Barefoot Cl TILE/CALC RG31 137 M1
Barfield Rd NTHA RG18 97 J2
Barge La THLE RG7 145 K10
Bargeman Rd MDHD SL6 36 A2
Barham Cl WEY KT13 83 J8
Barholm Cl EARL RG6 60 E4
Barkby EARL RG6 60 C4
Barker Cl CHERT KT16 81 L4
WHIT RG2 72 E7
Barker Ct WAR/TWY RG10 47 M6
Barker Rd CHERT KT16 81 L4
Barkers Meadow ASC SL5 65 K6
Barkham Ride EWKG RG40 73 J5
Barkham Rd WWKG RG41 14 C7
Barkham St EWKG RG40 73 J4
Barkhart Dr EWKG RG40 15 H4
Barkhart Gdns EWKG RG40 15 H4
Barkis Md SHST GU47 87 L4
Barkwith Cl EARL RG6 60 E4
Barlee Crs UX/CGN UB8 31 L6
Barley Cl STHA RG19 98 B4
Barley Gdns WWKG RG41 61 H3
Barley Md BNFD RG42 3 L1
MDHD SL6 35 H1
Barley Mow Rd EGH TW20 68 C3
Barley Mow Wy SHPTN TW17 83 G1
Barley Wy MLW SL7 18 F5
Barlows Rd TADY RG26 148 D3
Barnacre Cl UX/CGN UB8 31 M7
Barnard Cl CAV/SC RG4 127 J12
FRIM GU16 94 F6
Barnards Hl MLW SL7 18 E4
Barn Cl ASHF TW15 71 H3
BRAK RG12 3 K4
CBLY GU15 88 E8
HUNG RG17 140 B4
MDHD SL6 26 B4
RDGW/BURGH RG30 58 D2
Barn Close La KSCL RG20 147 R10
Barn Crs NWBY RG14 141 R7
Barn Croft Dr EARL RG6 60 D5
Barn Dr MDHD SL6 35 H1
Barnes Rd FRIM GU16 94 E6
Barnes Wy IVER SL0 31 H8
Barnett Gn BRAK RG12 76 B3
Barnett La LTWR GU18 89 M7
Barnfield IVER SL0 31 G7
SL SL1 37 M1
YTLY GU46 92 D1
Barnfield Cl MDHD SL6 26 B1
Barnhill Cl MLW SL7 18 F2
Barnhill Gdns MLW SL7 18 F2
Barnhill Rd MLW SL7 18 F2
Barn La HEN RG9 115 Q10
Barnmead CHOB/PIR GU24 91 M5
Barn Owl Wy THLE RG7 143 R3
Barnsdale Rd WHIT RG2 59 K3
Barnsfield Pl UX/CGN UB8 31 L1
Barnsford Crs CHOB/PIR GU24 91 G7
Barnway EGH TW20 68 C3
Barnwood Cl
RDGW/BURGH RG30 8 A4
Baronsmead HEN RG9 115 R11
Barons Wy EGH TW20 69 K4
Baron Wy HEN RG9 114 A12
Barossa Rd CBLY GU15 88 D7
Barracane Dr CWTH RG45 87 H2
Barrack La WDSR SL4 13 K6
Barracks La THLE RG7 145 M5
Barrett Crs EWKG RG40 15 K5
Barrett's La WHIT RG2 60 D8
Barrington Cl EARL RG6 46 B8
Barrington Wy READ RG1 58 E1
Barrsbrook Farm Rd
CHERT KT16 81 L5
Barr's Rd MDHD SL6 27 K7
Barry Av WDSR SL4 12 F4
Barry Pl READ RG1 8 E3
Barry Sq BRAK RG12 76 D4
Barry Ter ASHF TW15 * 56 F8
Bartelotts Rd SLN SL2 27 M5
Bartholomew Cl NWBY RG14 * 6 D6
Bartholomew Pl BNFD RG42 64 E5
Bartholomew St NWBY RG14 6 D6
Bartlemy Cl NWBY RG14 6 A9
Bartlemy Rd NWBY RG14 6 A9
Bartlett Cl TADY RG26 150 B8
Bartletts La MDHD SL6 36 C7
Barton Cl SHPTN TW17 83 H3
Barton Copse KSCL RG20 120 H12
Barton Rd DTCH/LGLY SL3 40 B2
TILE/CALC RG31 137 M4
Barton's Dr YTLY GU46 92 D2
Bartons Wy FARN GU14 93 J7
Barwell Cl CWTH RG45 86 F2
Basemoors BRAK RG12 3 L4
Basford Wy WDSR SL4 52 D2
Basil Cl EARL RG6 59 M5
Basingstoke Rd HTWY RG27 151 K4
THLE RG7 142 C5
THLE RG7 142 E4
THLE RG7 145 L1
THLE RG7 145 L5
THLE RG7 145 N10
WHIT RG2 59 H5
WHIT RG2 59 H7
Baskerville La HEN RG9 32 C3
Baskerville Rd CAV/SC RG4 126 E5
Baslow Rd WWKG RG41 61 H4
Basmore La HEN RG9 32 D2
Bassett Cl EARL RG6 60 C6
FRIM GU16 94 E6
Bassett Rd UX/CGN UB8 31 L1
WANT OX12 106 C3
Bass Md MDHD SL6 26 B1
Batcombe Md BRAK RG12 76 E4
Bates Cl DTCH/LGLY SL3 30 A7
Bath Ct MDHD SL6 4 B6
Bath Rd CAV/SC RG4 46 D5
CBLY GU15 88 C8
DTCH/LGLY SL3 41 G8
HSLWW TW4 43 J8
HTHAIR TW6 43 G8
HUNG RG17 129 J12
HUNG RG17 129 P12
HYS/HAR UB3 42 D8
MDHD SL6 4 C5
MDHD SL6 27 H7
MDHD SL6 34 B1
NTHA RG18 97 H2
NWBY RG14 141 R1
RDGW/BURGH RG30 58 B1
READ RG1 8 B9
SL SL1 10 A4
SL SL1 10 F6
SL SL1 27 M7
SL SL1 28 B7
SL SL1 28 C8
STHA RG19 98 D3
THLE RG7 99 H4
THLE RG7 136 H8
THLE RG7 142 E3
TILE/CALC RG31 137 N6
WAR/TWY RG10 33 J6
WAR/TWY RG10 33 M4
WDR/YW UB7 41 K8
Bathurst Cl WDR/YW UB7 41 H2
Bathurst Rd WWKG RG41 61 H4
Bathurst Wk DTCH/LGLY SL3 41 G1
Battalion Wy STHA RG19 98 A5
Battery End NWBY RG14 141 R8
Battle Cl NWBY RG14 141 R2
Battlemead Cl MDHD SL6 26 E3
Battle Rd GOR/PANG RG8 112 D11
NWBY RG14 141 Q8
Battle St READ RG1 8 C5
Batty's Barn Cl EWKG RG40 15 J7
Baughurst Rd TADY RG26 148 A10
THLE RG7 143 J8
The Baxendales NWBY RG14 7 J8
Baxter Cl SL SL1 10 F8
Bay Cl EARL RG6 59 M5
Baydon Dr READ RG1 58 E1
Baydon Rd HUNG RG17 116 D8
Bayfield Av FRIM GU16 94 E4
Bayford Cl BLKW GU17 94 A5
Bayford Dr TILE/CALC RG31 137 R6
Bayley Ct WWKG RG41 61 H5
Bayley Crs SL SL1 27 J6
Baylis Pde SL SL1 10 E1
Baylis Rd SL SL1 10 D3
Bayliss Rd WAR/TWY RG10 32 F5
Bay Rd BRAK RG12 3 L3
Bays Ct TADY RG26 * 148 B1
Baysfarm Ct WDR/YW UB7 41 L8
Bay Tree Ct SL SL1 27 L4
Bay Tree Ri TILE/CALC RG31 137 N5
Beach's Crs TADY RG26 149 J7
Beacon Ct DTCH/LGLY SL3 40 E7
Beacon Rd HTHAIR TW6 57 G5
Beaconsfield Rd SLN SL2 28 E2
STHL UB1 43 M1
YEAD UB4 43 L1
Beaconsfield Wy EARL RG6 60 A4
Beale Cl EWKG RG40 14 F4
Beales Farm Rd HUNG RG17 117 K4
Beales La WEY KT13 83 H7
Beal's La TILE/CALC RG31 137 L3
Beal's Pightle TADY RG26 148 D11
Beancroft Rd STHA RG19 97 M4
Bean Oak Rd EWKG RG40 15 M5
Beards Rd ASHF TW15 71 L4
Bearfield La HUNG RG17 129 K2
Bear La NWBY RG14 6 E4
WAR/TWY RG10 33 K4
Bearwood Pk WWKG RG41 * 61 G4
Bearwood Pth WWKG RG41 61 G4
Bearwood Rd WWKG RG41 61 H6
Beasley's Ait SUN TW16 83 M3
Beasley's Ait La SUN TW16 83 M3
Beattie Cl EBED/NFELT TW14 57 M6
Beatty Dr RDGW/BURGH RG30 137 Q2
Beatty Ri THLE RG7 145 L6
Beauchief Cl EARL RG6 59 M6
Beaufield Cl WODY RG5 46 D7
Beaufort Gdns ASC SL5 65 L6
MLW SL7 19 G4
Beaufort Pl MDHD SL6 36 F2
Beauforts EGH TW20 68 C3
Beaufront Cl CBLY GU15 89 G7
Beaufront Rd CBLY GU15 89 G7
Beaulah Pl WDSR SL4 * 52 B8
Beaulieu Cl BRAK RG12 64 F8
DTCH/LGLY SL3 39 K8
Beaulieu Gdns BLKW GU17 93 J1
Beaumaris Pde FRIM GU16 94 F6
Beaumont Cl MDHD SL6 35 J3
Beaumont Dr ASHF TW15 71 K3

Beaumont Gdns BRAK RG12 76 E2
Beaumont Ri MLW SL7 19 G4
Beaumont Rd SLN SL2 28 F6
WDSR SL4 13 H8
Beaurepaire Cl TADY RG26 149 P7
Beaver Cl WWKG RG41 74 B3
Beaver La YTLY GU46 92 E1
Beavers Cl TADY RG26 148 B1
Beaver Wy WODY RG5 47 H7
Beck Ct READ RG1 9 K9
Beckett Cha DTCH/LGLY SL3 40 B5
Beckett Cl EWKG RG40 15 M5
Beckford Av BRAK RG12 76 B3
Beckford Cl WWKG RG41 61 M5
Beckfords GOR/PANG RG8 123 Q9
Beckingham Pl THLE RG7 145 M4
Beckley Ct GOR/PANG RG8 113 K10
Beckwell Rd SL SL1 10 B6
Bec Tithe GOR/PANG RG8 125 J3
Bede Wk WHIT RG2 59 J3
Bedfont Cl EBED/NFELT TW14 57 J5
Bedfont Ct STWL/WRAY TW19 56 A2
Bedfont Court Est
STWL/WRAY TW19 * 56 B3
Bedfont Green Cl
EBED/NFELT TW14 57 J7
Bedfont La EBED/NFELT TW14 57 L6
Bedfont Rd EBED/NFELT TW14 57 J7
FELT TW13 57 L8
STWL/WRAY TW19 56 F5
Bedford Av SL SL1 28 C7
Bedford Cl MDHD SL6 35 J3
NWBY RG14 141 Q9
Bedford Crs FRIM GU16 94 E8
Bedford Gdns WWKG RG41 14 A3
Bedford La ASC SL5 79 H2
FRIM GU16 94 F8
Bedford Rd READ RG1 8 C5
Bedfordshire Down BNFD RG42 64 F4
Bedfordshire Wy WWKG RG41 61 K8
Bedwell Gdns HYS/HAR UB3 43 G4
Bedwins La MDHD SL6 19 K8
Beecham Rd
RDGW/BURGH RG30 44 C7
Beech Av CBLY GU15 94 D2
Beechbrook Av YTLY GU46 92 D1
Beech Cl ASHF TW15 71 K3
MDHD SL6 25 K6
NTHA RG18 122 C9
RDGW/BURGH RG30 143 R2
STHA RG19 102 D1
TADY RG26 150 A8
WDR/YW UB7 42 C3
Beech Ct MLW SL7 * 19 G4
Beechcroft NTHA RG18 122 C9
Beechcroft Cl ASC SL5 78 D1
Beechcroft Mnr WEY KT13 83 K7
Beech Dr BLKW GU17 93 K2
The Beeches GOR/PANG RG8 123 R1
STA TW18 * 70 A3
TILE/CALC RG31 125 P11
Beeches Wy BNEND SL8 20 D6
DTCH/LGLY SL3 30 B1
FLKWH/TG HP10 21 G4
IVER SL0 31 H5
SL SL1 21 M5
Beechfield Pl MDHD SL6 35 L2
Beech Gln BRAK RG12 2 E8
Beech Gv ADL/WDHM KT15 82 B8
Beech Hill Rd ASC SL5 78 E3
THLE RG7 145 J8
Beechingstoke MLW SL7 19 H3
Beech La EARL RG6 60 A3
GOR/PANG RG8 112 D9
Beechmont Av VW GU25 80 D2
Beechnut Cl WWKG RG41 14 A8
Beechnut Dr BLKW GU17 87 H8
Beech Ride SHST GU47 87 H6
Beech Ri CAV/SC RG4 126 E4
Beech Rd CAV/SC RG4 126 D11
DTCH/LGLY SL3 40 A2
EBED/NFELT TW14 57 L6
FARN GU14 94 B7
FRIM GU16 94 F8
GOR/PANG RG8 125 L9
KSCL RG20 101 J4
WEY KT13 83 K8
WHIT RG2 59 L4
Beech Ter MARL SN8 * 116 A5
Beechtree Av EGH TW20 68 B4
MLW SL7 18 F1
Beech Tree La STA TW18 * 70 B7
Beech Wk STHA RG19 98 A4
Beechwood Av STA TW18 70 B4
TILE/CALC RG31 137 P2
WEY KT13 83 L8
WODY RG5 46 D7
Beechwood Cl ASC SL5 65 L5
GOR/PANG RG8 124 H1
WEY KT13 83 L8
Beechwood Dr MDHD SL6 25 J8
MLW SL7 18 D6
Beechwood Gdns SL SL1 10 F7
Beechwood Mnr WEY KT13 83 L8
Beechwood Rd SLN SL2 28 F6
VW GU25 80 B4
Beedon Dr BRAK RG12 75 K3
Beehive Cl WGFD OX10 111 P1
Beehive La BRAK RG12 63 J7
Beehive Rd BRAK RG12 63 K7
STA TW18 69 M3
Beeson Cl GOR/PANG RG8 113 K10
Beeston Wy EARL RG6 60 A6
Beggars Hill Rd WODY RG5 47 H5
Beggars La CHOB/PIR GU24 91 J6
Behoes La GOR/PANG RG8 112 H9
Beighton Cl EARL RG6 * 59 M6
Beldam Bridge Rd
CHOB/PIR GU24 91 G8
Belfast Av SL SL1 10 B1
Belfry Ms SHST GU47 86 F6
Belgrave Ct BLKW GU17 93 K3
Belgrave Ms UX/CGN UB8 31 M5
Belgrave Pde SL SL1 * 10 E3
Belgrave Rd SL SL1 10 F3
Bell Av WDR/YW UB7 42 B3
Bell Bridge Rd CHERT KT16 81 M5
Bell Cl FARN GU14 94 C8
SLN SL2 29 K6
Bellclose Rd WDR/YW UB7 42 A2
Bell Ct MDHD SL6 24 B3
WAR/TWY RG10 47 K1
Belle Av EARL RG6 60 A1
Belleisle GOR/PANG RG8 125 M9
Bellever Hl CBLY GU15 94 E1
Belle Vue Cl STA TW18 70 A6
Belle Vue Pl SL SL1 * 11 H8
Belle Vue Rd HEN RG9 127 R2
READ RG1 8 C7
Belle Vue Ter READ RG1 8 A7
Bellew Rd FRIM GU16 95 H8
Bell Foundry La EWKG RG40 14 F1
Bell Holt NWBY RG14 141 Q9
Bell House Gdns WWKG RG41 14 E5
Bellingham Cl CBLY GU15 95 J2
Bell La BLKW GU17 93 J1
GOR/PANG RG8 122 H2
HEN RG9 22 A3
HUNG RG17 139 P11
WDSR SL4 38 B4
Bellmarsh Rd ADL/WDHM KT15 82 B8
Bell Pl BAGS GU19 89 M3
Bells Hl SLN SL2 29 J2
Bells Hill Gn SLN SL2 29 J2
Bells La DTCH/LGLY SL3 55 H2
Bell St HEN RG9 115 R12
MDHD SL6 5 H6
Bellswood La IVER SL0 30 M12
Bell Vw WDSR SL4 12 A9
Bell View Cl WDSR SL4 12 A8
Bellweir Cl STWL/WRAY TW19 55 H8
Belmont SLN SL2 28 C6
Belmont Cl FARN GU14 93 M7
Belmont Ct READ RG1 * 8 E5
Belmont Crs MDHD SL6 4 B3
Belmont Dr MDHD SL6 4 C3
Belmont Ms CBLY GU15 94 C3
Belmont Park Av MDHD SL6 4 D1
Belmont Park Rd MDHD SL6 4 C2
Belmont Rd CBLY GU15 94 C2
CWTH RG45 75 H8
MDHD SL6 4 D3
RDGW/BURGH RG30 44 D8
UX/CGN UB8 31 M1
Belmont V MDHD SL6 4 C2
Belstone Ms FARN GU14 94 A7
Belton Rd CBLY GU15 94 E1
Belvedere Ct BLKW GU17 93 K3
Belvedere Dr NWBY RG14 6 E9
Belvedere Wk WWKG RG41 61 G3
Belvoir Cl FRIM GU16 94 F5
Bembridge Ct CWTH RG45 86 E2
Bembridge Pl READ RG1 * 9 J6
Benares Gv HEN RG9 114 A10
Benbow Moorings
UX/CGN UB8 * 31 L6
Benbow Wy UX/CGN UB8 31 L6
Benbricke Gn BNFD RG42 64 A5
The Bence EGH TW20 69 H8
Bencombe Rd MLW SL7 18 F1
Benedict Dr EBED/NFELT TW14 57 K6
Benedict Gn BNFD RG42 64 E5
Benen-Stock Rd
STWL/WRAY TW19 56 A5
Benetfeld Rd BNFD RG42 63 H4
Benett Cl NWBY RG14 96 B1
Benett Gdns NWBY RG14 96 B1
Benham Cha KSCL RG20 141 L1
Benham Dr THLE RG7 145 M6
Benham Hl NTHA RG18 97 J2
Benham La THLE RG7 145 P11
Benhams La HEN RG9 115 R4
Benner La CHOB/PIR GU24 90 F7
Bennet Rd WHIT RG2 59 G5
Bennetsfield Rd STKPK UB11 42 D1
Bennett Ct CBLY GU15 94 C1
Bennetts Cl SL SL1 38 C1
Bennett's Hl
RDGW/BURGH RG30 137 M11
Bennetts La
RDGW/BURGH RG30 * 137 M11
Bennetts Yd UX/CGN UB8 31 M1
Benning Cl WDSR SL4 52 D2
Bennings Cl BNFD RG42 64 A5
Benning Wy EWKG RG40 15 H2
Bensgrove Cl GOR/PANG RG8 113 K10
Benson Cl SLN SL2 11 J4
WHIT RG2 59 K3
Benson Rd CWTH RG45 86 F1
Bentinck Rd WDR/YW UB7 41 M1
Bentley Copse CBLY GU15 95 H2
Bentley Dr WHIT RG2 72 E6
Bentley Pk SL SL1 27 M3
Bentley Rd SL SL1 38 B1
Benyon Ct READ RG1 8 A9
Beomonds Rw CHERT KT16 * 82 A4
Berberis Wk WDR/YW UB7 42 A4
Bere Court Rd GOR/PANG RG8 124 D12
Bere Rd BRAK RG12 76 E3
Beresford Av SLN SL2 29 L8
Beresford Cl FRIM GU16 94 F8
Beresford Rd
RDGW/BURGH RG30 8 A5
STHL UB1 43 M1
Bergenia Ct CHOB/PIR GU24 90 E8
Berins Hl WGFD OX10 113 M4
Berkeley Av HSLWW TW4 43 J8
READ RG1 8 A9
Berkeley Cl STWL/WRAY TW19 55 K8
Berkeley Ct WEY KT13 83 M8
Berkeley Crs FRIM GU16 95 G6
Berkeley Dr WDSR SL4 52 B7
Berkeley Gdns WOT/HER KT12 83 M4
Berkeley Ms MLW SL7 * 19 H4
Berkeley Rd NWBY RG14 6 C5
Berkley Cl MDHD SL6 25 J6
Berkshire Av SL SL1 28 D7
Berkshire Circular Routes
GOR/PANG RG8 124 H12
HUNG RG17 139 J9
KSCL RG20 108 H12
KSCL RG20 141 N6
MDHD SL6 24 A7
NTHA RG18 134 F4
THLE RG7 136 C12
THLE RG7 142 E3
THLE RG7 142 F5
THLE RG7 143 Q5
THLE RG7 143 R8
TILE/CALC RG31 137 L4
WAR/TWY RG10 33 K1
Berkshire Dr STHA RG19 98 C4
TILE/CALC RG31 137 N2
Berkshire Rd CBLY GU15 88 F6
HEN RG9 127 R2
Berkshire Wy BRAK RG12 2 A6
Bernadine Cl BNFD RG42 64 E5
Berners Cl SL SL1 28 A8
Bernersh Cl SHST GU47 87 J5
Berries Rd MDHD SL6 20 C7
Berrybank SHST GU47 87 L8
Berrycroft BRAK RG12 3 K2
Berry Fld SLN SL2 29 L7
Berry Hl MDHD SL6 26 F7
Berrylands Rd CAV/SC RG4 45 H3
Berry La DID OX11 110 C1
Berryscroft Rd STA TW18 70 C5
Berrys La RDGW/BURGH RG30 58 B6
Berry's La RDGW/BURGH RG30 137 R9
Berstead Cl EARL RG6 60 B5
Berwick Av SL SL1 28 D8
Berwick Cl MLW SL7 18 E3
Berwick La MLW SL7 18 F3
Berwick Rd MLW SL7 18 E3
Bessels Lea Rd DID OX11 110 C1
Bessel's Wy DID OX11 110 D1
Bessemer Cl DTCH/LGLY SL3 40 B5
Bestobell Rd SL SL1 28 E7
Beswick Gdns BRAK RG12 64 F6
Betam Rd HYS/HAR UB3 42 F2
READ RG1 9 L6
Beta Rd CHOB/PIR GU24 91 M5
Beta Wy EGH TW20 69 J6
Betchworth Av EARL RG6 60 A3
Bethany Waye
EBED/NFELT TW14 57 L6
Bethesda Cl GOR/PANG RG8 123 Q8
Bethesda St GOR/PANG RG8 123 Q8
Betjeman Ct WDR/YW UB7 * 41 M1
Betjeman Wk YTLY GU46 92 B2
Betteridge Rd STHA RG19 98 B4
Betties Cl UX/CGN UB8 31 L3
Betty Grove La WWKG RG41 60 F7
Bevan Ga BNFD RG42 2 D2
Beverley Cl CBLY GU15 89 J8
MLW SL7 18 E4
NTHA RG18 97 L2
WEY KT13 83 L6
Beverley Gdns MDHD SL6 25 K5
WAR/TWY RG10 33 G5
Beverley Rd SUN TW16 71 M6
TILE/CALC RG31 137 N1
The Bevers THLE RG7 143 Q8
Bexley Ct RDGW/BURGH RG30 44 D8
Bexley St WDSR SL4 12 F6
Bibury Cl WODY RG5 60 D2
Bicknell Rd FRIM GU16 94 E4
Biddles Cl SL SL1 38 A1
Bideford Cl FARN GU14 94 A7
WODY RG5 60 C1
Bideford Sp SLN SL2 28 D4
Big Barn Gv BRAK RG12 3 K1
Bigbury Gdns WHIT RG2 59 J3
Bigfrith La MDHD SL6 19 J8
Biggs La WHIT RG2 72 F6
Big La HUNG RG17 117 K3
Biko Cl UX/CGN UB8 31 L7
Billet La DTCH/LGLY SL3 30 D7
IVER SL0 30 D4
Billing Av EWKG RG40 73 L8
Billingbear La BNFD RG42 49 J8
Billington Wy NTHA RG18 133 Q12
Bilton Wy HYS/HAR UB3 43 K2
Binbrook Cl EARL RG6 60 D4
Binfield Rd BNFD RG42 2 C1
EWKG RG40 15 L6
EWKG RG40 63 G4
Bingham Dr STA TW18 70 D5
Bingham Rd SL SL1 27 J6
The Binghams MDHD SL6 36 D3
Bingley Gv WODY RG5 46 F5
Binsted Dr BLKW GU17 93 K1
Birch Av RDGW/BURGH RG30 44 A6
STHA RG19 102 D1
Birch Cl CAV/SC RG4 126 F6
CBLY GU15 88 E6
IVER SL0 30 F3
Birch Dr BLKW GU17 93 K3
Birchen Cl GOR/PANG RG8 113 K10
The Birches BLKW GU17 93 H1
Birchett Rd FARN GU14 93 L8
Birchetts Cl BNFD RG42 2 E2
Birchfield Cl ADL/WDHM KT15 82 B8
Birchfields CBLY GU15 94 C2
Birch Gn STA TW18 69 M2
Birch Gv SHPTN TW17 71 L7
SLN SL2 28 D6
WDSR SL4 37 M8
Birch Hill Rd BRAK RG12 76 B4
Birchington Rd WDSR SL4 12 D8
Birchland Cl THLE RG7 143 N8
Birch La ASC SL5 65 G6
CHOB/PIR GU24 90 D7
THLE RG7 143 P9
Birchmead WWKG RG41 61 K4
Birch Platt CHOB/PIR GU24 90 D8
Birch Rd BFOR GU20 90 E2
EWKG RG40 74 A7
TADY RG26 142 A12
THLE RG7 143 P5
Birch Side CWTH RG45 74 F8
Birch Tree Vw LTWR GU18 90 A5
Birchview Cl YTLY GU46 92 C2
Birchway HYS/HAR UB3 43 J1
Birchwood Cl CAV/SC RG4 127 J12
Birchwood Dr LTWR GU18 90 C5
Birchwood Rd NWBY RG14 7 M1
The Birchwoods
TILE/CALC RG31 137 M2
Birdhill Av WHIT RG2 59 K4
Bird Ms EWKG RG40 14 F5
Birds La THLE RG7 99 G3
Bird Wood Ct CAV/SC RG4 126 G6
Birdwood Rd CBLY GU15 87 M8
MDHD SL6 25 K7
Birkbeck Pl SHST GU47 87 L5
Birkdale BRAK RG12 75 L3
Birkhall Cl TILE/CALC RG31 137 N5
Birley Rd SL SL1 10 C1
Biscuit Wy WHIT RG2 58 F6
Bisham Ct MLW SL7 19 J5
Bisham Rd MLW SL7 18 F7
Bishop Ct MDHD SL6 4 D6
Bishopdale BRAK RG12 2 C9
Bishop Duppas Pk
SHPTN TW17 83 K4
Bishops Cl TADY RG26 148 C1
Bishops Dr EBED/NFELT TW14 57 K5
EWKG RG40 15 G3
Bishops Farm Cl WDSR SL4 52 B1
Bishopsgate Rd EGH TW20 68 A1
Bishops Gv BFOR GU20 90 C2
Bishop's La BNFD RG42 51 G7
Bishops Orch SLN SL2 28 D6
Bishops Rd EARL RG6 * 46 A8
Bishop's Rd EARL RG6 46 A8
Bishops Rd SL SL1 11 J7
THLE RG7 135 P7
Bishops Wk FLKWH/TG HP10 21 G1
Bishops Wy EGH TW20 69 K4
Bishopswood La TADY RG26 148 A1
Bishopswood Rd TADY RG26 148 B1
Bissley Dr MDHD SL6 35 J3
Bitham La HUNG RG17 138 F9
HUNG RG17 139 M10
Bitham Rd WANT OX12 107 N3
Bittams La CHERT KT16 81 K8
Bittern Cl SHST GU47 87 K6
Bitterne Av TILE/CALC RG31 137 M4
Bix La MDHD SL6 25 H5
Blackamoor La MDHD SL6 5 J1
Blackberry Cl SHPTN TW17 83 L1
THLE RG7 * 143 Q4
Blackbird Cl SHST GU47 87 K6
THLE RG7 * 143 R3
Blackbird La MDHD SL6 51 G1
Blackbird's Bottom
GOR/PANG RG8 124 G1
Black Boy La MDHD SL6 23 L3
Blackbushe Pk YTLY GU46 * 92 C1
Blackbushes Rd FLEETN GU51 92 A8
Black Butt Cots MDHD SL6 20 D7
Blackcap Pl SHST GU47 87 L6
Blackdown Rd FRIM GU16 95 J7
Blackdown Wy STHA RG19 97 L4
Blackett Cl STA TW18 69 L7
Black Horse Cl WDSR SL4 52 D1
Blackhorse Pl UX/CGN UB8 31 K2
Blacklands Rd THLE RG7 98 E1
Blackley Cl EARL RG6 60 E3
Blackmeadows BRAK RG12 76 C4
Blackmoor Cl ASC SL5 65 K7
Blackmoor Wd ASC SL5 65 K7
Blackmore La CAV/SC RG4 126 G5
Blacknest Gate Rd ASC SL5 67 H8
Blacknest Rd ASC SL5 67 K8
Black Park Rd DTCH/LGLY SL3 30 A1
Blackpond La SLN SL2 28 D1
Black Rod Cl HYS/HAR UB3 43 H3
Blacksmith Rw DTCH/LGLY SL3 40 C4
Blacksmiths La CHERT KT16 82 A4
Blacksmith's La STA TW18 70 B8
Blackstone Cl FARN GU14 93 K8
Blackstroud La East
LTWR GU18 90 D6
Blackstroud La West
LTWR GU18 90 D6
Blackthorn Av WDR/YW UB7 42 C4
Blackthorn Cl EARL RG6 46 A7
TILE/CALC RG31 125 M12
Blackthorn Crs FARN GU14 93 M6
Blackthorn Dell DTCH/LGLY SL3 39 L3
Blackthorn Dr LTWR GU18 90 B7
NTHA RG18 97 M1
Blackthorne Crs DTCH/LGLY SL3 55 L1
Blackthorne Rd DTCH/LGLY SL3 55 L2
Blackwater Cl CAV/SC RG4 45 L2
THLE RG7 145 M5
Blackwater Ri TILE/CALC RG31 137 L6
Blackwater Vw EWKG RG40 86 A4
Blaenant CAV/SC RG4 45 G1
Blaenavon CAV/SC RG4 44 F1
Blagdon Cl STHA RG19 96 F7
Blagdon Rd WHIT RG2 59 J4
Blagrave Farm La CAV/SC RG4 44 D1
Blagrave La CAV/SC RG4 44 C3
Blagrave Ri TILE/CALC RG31 137 N4
Blagrave St READ RG1 9 G5
Blagrove Dr WWKG RG41 74 A2
Blagrove La WWKG RG41 14 B9
Blair Cl HYS/HAR UB3 43 J4
Blaire Pk YTLY GU46 86 B6
Blair Rd SL SL1 10 E5
Blake Cl CWTH RG45 87 J2
EWKG RG40 15 L2
Blakeney Ct MDHD SL6 5 G1
Blakeney Flds HUNG RG17 118 F10
Blakes Cots READ RG1 9 J6
Blake's La TADY RG26 148 D1
Blakes La WAR/TWY RG10 33 K4
Blakes Ride YTLY GU46 86 B8
Blakes Rd WAR/TWY RG10 32 F4
Blamire Dr BNFD RG42 63 L4
Blanchard Cl WODY RG5 47 H6
Blandford Cl DTCH/LGLY SL3 39 M3
Blandford Dr WWKG RG41 73 L2
Blandford Rd WHIT RG2 59 J6
Blandford Rd North
DTCH/LGLY SL3 39 M3
Blandford Rd South
DTCH/LGLY SL3 39 M3
Bland's Cl THLE RG7 143 P4
Blandy Rd HEN RG9 127 R2
Blandy's La GOR/PANG RG8 123 R8
Blane's La ASC SL5 77 H4
Blatch's Cl THLE RG7 136 H7
Blays Cl EGH TW20 68 C4
Blay's La EGH TW20 68 B4
Bledlow Cl NWBY RG14 141 R9
Blenheim Av BRAK RG12 3 G7
Blenheim Cl WWKG RG41 61 L8
Blenheim Gdns READ RG1 45 L8
Blenheim Pl READ RG1 * 8 E7
Blenheim Rd CAV/SC RG4 45 G3
DTCH/LGLY SL3 39 M4
MDHD SL6 25 K6
NWBY RG14 6 C4
READ RG1 9 M7
Blenhiem Pl CBLY GU15 94 B3
Bleriot Rd HEST TW5 43 L7
Bletchmore Cl HYS/HAR UB3 42 F5
Blewburton Wk BRAK RG12 3 M8
Blewbury Dr TILE/CALC RG31 137 M3
Blewbury Hl DID OX11 110 E2
Blinco La DTCH/LGLY SL3 30 A7
Blind La BNEND SL8 20 C2
HUNG RG17 117 K4
Blomfield Dl BNFD RG42 63 K7
Blondell Cl WDR/YW UB7 41 M6
Bloomfield Dr BRAK RG12 3 H1
Bloomfieldhatch La THLE RG7 144 F6
Bloomfield Hatch La
THLE RG7 145 J4
Bloomfield Rd MDHD SL6 35 J1
Bloomsbury Wy BLKW GU17 93 J3
Blossom Av THLE RG7 137 J7
Blossom La THLE RG7 137 J7
Blossom Rd CAV/SC RG4 44 F3
The Blossoms KSCL RG20 121 J10
Blossom Wy WDR/YW UB7 42 C4
Blount Crs BNFD RG42 63 L5
Blounts Court Rd CAV/SC RG4 126 G4
Bloxworth Cl BRAK RG12 76 F1
Blue Ball La EGH TW20 68 F3
Bluebell Dr THLE RG7 143 P3
Bluebell Hl BRAK RG12 3 L3
Bluebell Meadow WWKG RG41 61 J3
Bluebell Ri LTWR GU18 90 B6
Bluebell Wy NTHA RG18 97 M1
Bluecoats NTHA RG18 97 M2
Blue Coat Wk BRAK RG12 76 D2
Bluethroat Cl SHST GU47 87 L6
Blumfield Crs SL SL1 27 M5
Blundells Rd
RDGW/BURGH RG30 137 Q2
Blunden Dr DTCH/LGLY SL3 40 D4
Blunts Av WDR/YW UB7 42 C7
Blyth Av STHA RG19 98 A4
Blythe Cl IVER SL0 31 H7
Blythewood La ASC SL5 65 K8
Blyth Rd HYS/HAR UB3 43 G2
Blyth Wk WHIT RG2 * 59 H1
Blythwood Dr FRIM GU16 94 D4
Boadicea Cl SL SL1 38 A1
Boames La KSCL RG20 141 M9
Board La KSCL RG20 140 F1
Boarlands Cl SL SL1 28 B8
Boar's Br TADY RG26 149 J8
Bobgreen Ct WHIT RG2 59 J8
Bobmore La MLW SL7 19 G2
Bockhampton Rd HUNG RG17 117 K4
Bockmer La MLW SL7 17 K6
Bodens Ride ASC SL5 77 M5
Bodin Gdns NWBY RG14 96 C6
Bodmin Av SLN SL2 28 C6
Bodmin Cl STHA RG19 97 L4
Bodmin Rd WODY RG5 60 C1
Body Rd READ RG1 8 E7
Boeing Wy NWDGN UB2 43 K3
Bog La BRAK RG12 76 F2
Boham's Rd DID OX11 109 Q4
Bois Hall Rd ADL/WDHM KT15 82 D8
Bolding House La
CHOB/PIR GU24 90 F8
Boldrewood THLE RG7 143 P3
Boleyn Cl STA TW18 69 L3
Bolingbroke Wy HYS/HAR UB3 42 F1
STHA RG19 98 B3
Bolney La HEN RG9 32 C1
Bolney Rd HEN RG9 32 D1
Bolney Trevor Dr HEN RG9 32 C2
Bolton Av WDSR SL4 13 H9
Bolton Crs WDSR SL4 53 J2
Bolton Rd WDSR SL4 53 J2
Boltons La BNFD RG42 63 L5
Bolton's La HYS/HAR UB3 42 E7
Bolwell Cl WAR/TWY RG10 47 M2
Bomer Cl WDR/YW UB7 42 C7
Bomford Cl NTHA RG18 133 M4
Bond Cl IVER SL0 30 D1
TADY RG26 148 C1
Bond St EGH TW20 68 B4
Bond Wy BRAK RG12 2 F4
Bone La NWBY RG14 7 H4
Bonemill La KSCL RG20 141 R4
Bones La HEN RG9 127 N7
Boole Hts BRAK RG12 76 A3
Boot End WHIT RG2 58 F6
Booth Dr EWKG RG40 73 L5
STA TW18 70 D4
Borderside SLN SL2 11 K1
YTLY GU46 86 A8
Bordon Cl TADY RG26 148 C2
Borrowdale Cl EGH TW20 69 H5
Borrowdale Rd WWKG RG41 61 H2
Bosanquet Cl UX/CGN UB8 31 M6
Boscawen Wy STHA RG19 98 C4
Boscombe Cl EGH TW20 69 J6
Bosham Cl EARL RG6 60 B6
Boshers Gdns EGH TW20 68 F4
Bosman Dr BFOR GU20 78 B7
Bostock La THLE RG7 136 E8
Boston Av READ RG1 58 F1
Boston Dr BNEND SL8 20 D3
Boston Gv SL SL1 28 E7
Boston Rd HEN RG9 22 A6
Bosworth Gdns WODY RG5 60 E2
Botany Cl STHA RG19 98 B3
Botham Dr SL SL1 10 E8
The Bothy WAR/TWY RG10 32 F4
Botmoor Wy KSCL RG20 119 J8
Bottisham Cl EARL RG6 * 60 C6
Bottle La BNFD RG42 49 L7
HTWY RG27 151 K8
MDHD SL6 34 B2
Bottom La GOR/PANG RG8 113 L6
THLE RG7 136 H11
Botwell La HYS/HAR UB3 43 H2
Bouldish Farm Rd ASC SL5 77 M2
Boulmer Rd UX/CGN UB8 31 L4
Boulters Cl SL SL1 38 C2
Boulters Ct MDHD SL6 26 E5
Boulters Gdns MDHD SL6 26 E5
Boulters La MDHD SL6 26 E5
Boulton Rd WHIT RG2 59 G3
Boult St READ RG1 9 J7
Boults Wk WHIT RG2 * 59 H1
Boundary Cl TILE/CALC RG31 137 N4
Boundary La CAV/SC RG4 44 E3
Boundary Pk WEY KT13 83 L7
Boundary Rd ASHF TW15 70 C3
MDHD SL6 27 H6
NWBY RG14 7 H4
Bourn Cl EARL RG6 * 60 C5
Bourne Arch NTHA RG18 97 K2
Bourne Av CHERT KT16 70 A8
HYS/HAR UB3 42 E3
WDSR SL4 53 J3
WHIT RG2 59 H2
Bourne Cl BNEND SL8 20 D1
TILE/CALC RG31 137 M6
Bourne End Rd BNEND SL8 20 F6
MDHD SL6 21 G6
Bourne Meadow EGH TW20 81 H1
Bourne Rd GOR/PANG RG8 125 J9
NTHA RG18 97 K2
SL SL1 10 B6
VW GU25 80 D2
Bourneside VW GU25 80 A4
Bourne-Stevens Cl READ RG1 9 H7
Bourne V HUNG RG17 138 G1
Bourton Cl HYS/HAR UB3 43 J1
RDGW/BURGH RG30 137 R3
Bouverie Wy DTCH/LGLY SL3 40 A5
Boveney Cl SL SL1 38 C2
Boveney New Rd WDSR SL4 38 A4
Boveney Rd WDSR SL4 37 L4
Boveney Wood La SL SL1 21 M5
Bovingdon Hts MLW SL7 18 D4
Bowden Cl EBED/NFELT TW14 57 L7
Bowden Rd ASC SL5 78 C2
Bow Dr HTWY RG27 150 D10
The Bowers EWKG RG40 74 A5
Bower Wy SL SL1 28 A8
Bowes Lyon Cl WDSR SL4 13 H6
Bowes Rd STA TW18 69 L4
STHA RG19 97 M4
Bowfell Cl TILE/CALC RG31 * 125 N12
Bow Gdns HTWY RG27 150 D10
Bow Gv HTWY RG27 150 D9
Bowland Dr BRAK RG12 76 E4
Bowling Ct HEN RG9 115 Q11
Bowling Court Gn FRIM GU16 94 E7
Bowling Green La
GOR/PANG RG8 125 M9
Bowling Green Rd
CHOB/PIR GU24 91 L4
NTHA RG18 97 J1
Bowman Ct CWTH RG45 86 E2
Bowmans Cl SL SL1 27 K2
Bowmonts Rd TADY RG26 148 F2
Bowry Dr STWL/WRAY TW19 54 F5
Bowyer Crs EWKG RG40 15 H2
Bowyer Dr SL SL1 28 A8
Bowyer's La BNFD RG42 50 B8
Bowyer Wk ASC SL5 65 L6
Boxford Rdg BRAK RG12 2 F7
Boxwood Cl WDR/YW UB7 42 B2
Boyd Ct BNFD RG42 2 D3
Boyndon Rd MDHD SL6 4 D5
Boyn Hill Av MDHD SL6 4 D6
Boyn Hill Cl MDHD SL6 4 C6
Boyn Hill Rd MDHD SL6 4 B8
Boyn Valley Rd MDHD SL6 4 D7
Brabazon Rd HEST TW5 43 L7
Bracebridge CBLY GU15 94 A1
Bracken Bank ASC SL5 65 J6
Bracken Cl SUN TW16 * 71 M4
TILE/CALC RG31 * 137 N1
Bracken Copse HUNG RG17 139 P9
Brackendale Cl CBLY GU15 94 E3
Brackendale Rd CBLY GU15 94 D2
Brackendale Wy EARL RG6 60 A1
Brackenforde DTCH/LGLY SL3 39 L2
Bracken La YTLY GU46 86 A8
Bracken Rd MDHD SL6 35 L2
The Brackens ASC SL5 * 65 H8
CWTH RG45 75 G7
Bracken Wy CHOB/PIR GU24 91 M5
THLE RG7 143 Q4
Brackenwood CBLY GU15 95 K1
Bracklesham Cl FARN GU14 94 A7
Bracknell Beeches BRAK RG12 * 3 K4
Bracknell Cl CBLY GU15 88 F5
Bracknell Rd BAGS GU19 77 K8
BNFD RG42 64 F2
CBLY GU15 89 G4
CWTH RG45 87 J1
EWKG RG40 75 L6
Brackstone Cl CAV/SC RG4 9 J1
Bradcutts La MDHD SL6 19 M5
Bradenham La MLW SL7 24 E1
Bradfields BRAK RG12 76 D2
Bradford Rd SL SL1 28 C7
Brading Wy GOR/PANG RG8 125 P9
Bradley Cl HUNG RG17 140 B5
Bradley Dr EWKG RG40 74 A5
Bradley-Moore Sq NTHA RG18 98 A1
Bradley Rd HEN RG9 114 A1
SL SL1 10 E3
Bradley's St GOR/PANG RG8 113 M6
Bradmore Wy EARL RG6 60 A6
Bradshaw Cl WDSR SL4 38 A8
Bradwell Rd TILE/CALC RG31 125 N11
Braemar Cl FRIM GU16 94 F6

Braemar Gdns SL SL1 38 C2
Braemore Cl STHA RG19 97 M5
Braeside BRAK RG12 63 J7
Brakes Ri SHST GU47 87 L6
Bramber Ct SL SL1 38 C1
Bramber Ms CAV/SC RG4 45 L2
Bramble Bank FRIM GU16 95 G8
Bramble Cl SHPTN TW17 83 K1
Bramble Crs
RDGW/BURGH RG30 137 Q3
Brambledown STA TW18 70 B6
Bramble Dr MDHD SL6 35 J2
Bramblegate CWTH RG45 75 G8
The Brambles CWTH RG45 74 D8
NWBY RG14 96 A6
WDR/YW UB7 41 M5
Bramblings CAV/SC RG4 126 E12
Bramcote CBLY GU15 95 J1
Bramdean Cl TADY RG26 148 D3
Bramley Cha MDHD SL6 35 L2
Bramley Cl CHERT KT16 82 B5
EARL RG6 60 A3
MDHD SL6 35 L3
STA TW18 70 C4
Bramley Crs CAV/SC RG4 126 E5
Bramley Green Rd TADY RG26 150 A8
Bramley Gv CWTH RG45 86 D1
Bramley La BLKW GU17 93 H1
TADY RG26 149 R6
Bramley Rd CBLY GU15 94 B4
HTWY RG27 150 D9
TADY RG26 148 H9
THLE RG7 149 L2
Bramling Av YTLY GU46 86 B8
Brammas Cl SL SL1 10 B8
Brampton Cha HEN RG9 32 C2
Brampton Ct MDHD SL6 5 M2
Brampton Ms MLW SL7 * 18 F5
Bramshaw Rd
RDGW/BURGH RG30 44 A5
Bramshill Cl WHIT RG2 72 E6
Bramshot La FARN GU14 93 J8
Bramwell Cl STHA RG19 98 B4
Bran Cl RDGW/BURGH RG30 137 Q2
Brandon Av WODY RG5 47 G5
Brandon Cl CBLY GU15 95 K2
Brands Rd DTCH/LGLY SL3 40 D6
Brandville Rd WDR/YW UB7 42 A2
Brandy Bottom YTLY GU46 * 92 E3
Branksome Cl CBLY GU15 88 E8
Branksome Hill Rd SHST GU47 87 L6
Branksome Park Rd CBLY GU15 88 E8
Brants Br BRAK RG12 3 L5
Brants Cl WHIT RG2 72 E4
Brattain Ct BRAK RG12 3 K6
Braunfels Wk KSCL RG20 141 R4
NWBY RG14 6 A5
Bravington Cl SHPTN TW17 82 F2
Braybank MDHD SL6 36 F2
Braybrooke Dr WAR/TWY RG10 47 M6
Braybrooke Gdns
WAR/TWY RG10 32 F5
Braybrooke Rd BNFD RG42 64 B5
WAR/TWY RG10 32 F5
Bray Cl MDHD SL6 36 E3
Bray Ct MDHD SL6 36 E4
Braye Cl SHST GU47 87 J5
Brayfield Rd MDHD SL6 36 E2
Brayford Rd WHIT RG2 59 J6
Bray Rd MDHD SL6 5 M8
RDGW/BURGH RG30 58 B2
Braywick Rd MDHD SL6 5 H7
Braywood Av EGH TW20 68 F4
Braziers La BNFD RG42 65 K3
GOR/PANG RG8 113 K5
WGFD OX10 113 J5
Breachfield KSCL RG20 100 B7
Breach La HTWY RG27 150 E10
Breach Sq HUNG RG17 * 138 H2
Breadcroft La MDHD SL6 35 G2
Breadcroft Rd MDHD SL6 35 H3
Bream Cl MLW SL7 18 E6
Brean Wk EARL RG6 60 A4
Brecon Cl FARN GU14 93 K7
Brecon Rd WODY RG5 46 F6
Bredon Rd WWKG RG41 61 M5
Bredward Cl SL SL1 27 K4
The Breech SHST GU47 87 L7
Breedons Hl GOR/PANG RG8 124 G9
The Breezes MDHD SL6 36 A2
Bremer Rd STA TW18 70 A1
Brendon Cl HYS/HAR UB3 42 E7
RDGW/BURGH RG30 137 Q1
Brendon Rd FARN GU14 93 K7
Brent Cl STHA RG19 97 M4
Brentford Cl WGFD OX10 111 N1
Brent Gdns WHIT RG2 59 H3
Brentmoor Rd CHOB/PIR GU24 90 C8
Brent Rd BNEND SL8 20 C2
NWDGN UB2 43 L3
Brerewood EARL RG6 59 M4
Bret Harte Rd FRIM GU16 94 E5
Bretlands Rd CHERT KT16 81 L6
Brewery Common THLE RG7 143 R8
Briant's Av CAV/SC RG4 45 J4
Briants Piece NTHA RG18 133 P4
Briar Av LTWR GU18 89 M7
Briar Cl CAV/SC RG4 45 G2
MDHD SL6 27 K7
Briar Dene MDHD SL6 25 L5
Briar Gln MDHD SL6 20 A8
Briarlea Rd THLE RG7 143 P8
Briar Rd SHPTN TW17 82 F2
Briars Cl GOR/PANG RG8 125 J9
The Briars DTCH/LGLY SL3 40 B5
Briar Wy SLN SL2 28 D6
TADY RG26 148 E2
WDR/YW UB7 42 C2
Briarwood EWKG RG40 73 L8
Briarwood Cl FELT TW13 71 L1
Brickfield La HYS/HAR UB3 42 F6
SL SL1 27 J2
Brickfields Wy WDR/YW UB7 42 B3
Bridge Av MDHD SL6 5 J5
MDHD SL6 26 A1
Bridge Cl SL SL1 28 B8
STA TW18 69 L2
WOT/HER KT12 83 M4
Bridge End CBLY GU15 94 B2
Bridge Gdns ASHF TW15 71 J5
Bridge La VW GU25 80 E3
Bridgeman Dr WDSR SL4 12 C7
Bridgemead FRIM GU16 94 D6
Bridge Rd ASC SL5 78 D2
BAGS GU19 89 L2
CBLY GU15 94 B3
CHERT KT16 82 B4
MDHD SL6 5 K4
UX/CGN UB8 31 L3
WEY KT13 82 F8
Bridges Cl WWKG RG41 14 A4
The Bridges THLE RG7 143 L9
Bridgestone Dr BNEND SL8 20 D3
Bridge St CAV/SC RG4 8 E1
DTCH/LGLY SL3 40 F7
MDHD SL6 5 J4
NWBY RG14 6 E4
READ RG1 8 F7
WOT/HER KT12 83 M4
Bridge Vw ASC SL5 79 H4
Bridge Wk YTLY GU46 86 D7
Bridgewater Cl
RDGW/BURGH RG30 44 C5
Bridgewater Ct DTCH/LGLY SL3 40 C4
Bridgewater Ter WDSR SL4 13 J4
Bridgewater Wy WDSR SL4 13 J5
Bridge Whf CHERT KT16 82 C5
Bridle Cl MDHD SL6 4 E1
Bridle Pth GOR/PANG RG8 113 J10
Bridlepath Wy
EBED/NFELT TW14 57 L6
Bridle Rd GOR/PANG RG8 125 J4
MDHD SL6 4 E1
Bridlington Sp SL SL1 38 D3
Bridport Cl EARL RG6 60 D4
Bridport Wy SLN SL2 28 D5
Bridus Md DID OX11 110 D1
Brierley Pl TILE/CALC RG31 125 N10
Briff La THLE RG7 134 D12
Brigham Rd READ RG1 8 F3
Brighton Rd ADL/WDHM KT15 82 C8
EARL RG6 46 A8
Brighton Sp SLN SL2 28 D5
Brightside Av STA TW18 70 C5
Brill Cl CAV/SC RG4 45 G2
MDHD SL6 35 M2
MLW SL7 18 E4
Brimblecombe Cl WWKG RG41 62 A5
Brimpton La THLE RG7 103 H1
Brimpton Rd
RDGW/BURGH RG30 58 B2
TADY RG26 103 L4
THLE RG7 99 G5
Brimshot La CHOB/PIR GU24 91 L4
Brinds Cl CAV/SC RG4 126 F5
Brinn's La BLKW GU17 93 J1
Brisbane Rd
RDGW/BURGH RG30 44 B6
Bristol Cl STWL/WRAY TW19 56 E5
Bristol Wy SL SL1 10 F4
Bristol & West Ar READ RG1 9 G5
Bristow Rd CBLY GU15 94 B3
Britannia Wy STWL/WRAY TW19 56 D6
Britten Rd WHIT RG2 59 H2
Britwell Rd SL SL1 27 L4
Brixham Rd WHIT RG2 59 H4
Broadacre STA TW18 70 A3
Broadcommon La
WAR/TWY RG10 48 B7
Broadcommon Rd
WAR/TWY RG10 48 A6
Broadford La CHOB/PIR GU24 91 L7
Broadhalfpenny La
TADY RG26 148 E2
Broad Hinton WAR/TWY RG10 47 L4
Broadlands FRIM GU16 94 F6
Broadlands Av SHPTN TW17 83 J3
Broadlands Cl TILE/CALC RG31 137 P5
Broadlands Dr ASC SL5 78 C4
Broad La BRAK RG12 3 H7
FLKWH/TG HP10 21 G4
NTHA RG18 134 B10
THLE RG7 134 D12
Broadley Gn BFOR GU20 90 D3
Broadmark Rd SLN SL2 11 L3
Broadmeadow End NTHA RG18 98 B3
Broadmoor La CAV/SC RG4 46 E2
Broadmoor Rd WAR/TWY RG10 34 D8
Broad Oak SLN SL2 28 E5
SUN TW16 71 M4
Broadoak TADY RG26 148 F2
Broad Oak Ct SLN SL2 28 E5
Broad Platts DTCH/LGLY SL3 39 M3
Broadpool Cots ASC SL5 66 A4
Broadrick Heath BRAK RG12 3 K1
Broad St CHOB/PIR GU24 90 D7
EWKG RG40 15 G6
KSCL RG20 109 L11
READ RG1 9 G6
Broad Wk FRIM GU16 94 E4
HEST TW5 43 M8
Broadwater La WAR/TWY RG10 47 L5
Broadwater Pk MDHD SL6 37 G5
Broadwater Rd WAR/TWY RG10 47 L3
Broad Wy THLE RG7 144 H11
Broadway BRAK RG12 2 F4
MDHD SL6 5 H5
STA TW18 * 70 B3
STHA RG19 97 M3
WDSR SL4 52 B7
Broadway Pde HYS/HAR UB3 * 43 H2
WDR/YW UB7 * 42 A2
Broadway Rd LTWR GU18 90 C5
The Broadway HUNG RG17 117 K3
SHST GU47 87 H7
STA TW18 70 C8
Brocas Rd THLE RG7 143 P5
Brocas St WDSR SL4 13 J3
Brocas Ter WDSR SL4 13 J3
Brock Cl FRIM GU16 95 K6
Brockenhurst Dr YTLY GU46 92 D1
Brockenhurst Rd ASC SL5 78 B2
BRAK RG12 64 F8
Brock Gdns
RDGW/BURGH RG30 44 C6
Brocklands YTLY GU46 92 B2
Brock La MDHD SL6 5 H5
Brockley Cl
RDGW/BURGH RG30 44 A6
Brocksett Cl
RDGW/BURGH RG30 44 D7
Brocks La NTHA RG18 134 D5
Brocks Wy HEN RG9 32 C3
Brockton Ct MDHD SL6 5 G7
Brock Wy VW GU25 80 C2
Broken Furlong WDSR SL4 38 E5
Broken Wy KSCL RG20 100 D4
Bromelia Cl TADY RG26 149 R6
Brompton Cl EARL RG6 60 D5
Brompton Dr MDHD SL6 25 L5
Bromycroft Rd SLN SL2 28 C4
Bronte Ri NWBY RG14 96 D6
Brookbank FLKWH/TG HP10 20 E3
Brook Cl SHST GU47 87 L5
STWL/WRAY TW19 56 F6
WWKG RG41 14 C2
Brook Crs SL SL1 28 A7
Brookdene Cl MDHD SL6 26 B4
Brook Dr BRAK RG12 3 M9
WHIT RG2 58 E6
Brooke Furmston Pl MLW SL7 * 19 G3
Brooke Pl BNFD RG42 63 K3
Brookers Cnr CWTH RG45 87 J1
Brooker's Hl WHIT RG2 59 K8
Brookers Rw CWTH RG45 75 J8
Brookfield Rd FLKWH/TG HP10 20 F3
Brook Gn BNFD RG42 2 B3
TADY RG26 148 F2
Brookhouse Dr BNEND SL8 20 E3
Brooklands Cl SUN TW16 71 L6
Brook La CHOB/PIR GU24 91 K6
WAR/TWY RG10 48 F4
Brook Lea CAV/SC RG4 9 K2
Brookleys CHOB/PIR GU24 91 M5
Brooklyn Dr CAV/SC RG4 126 H11
Brooklyn Wy WDR/YW UB7 41 M3
The Brookmill READ RG1 58 E2
Brook Pth SL SL1 28 A7
Brook Rd BAGS GU19 89 L4
CBLY GU15 94 B2
Brooksby Cl BLKW GU17 93 H1
Brooksby Rd TILE/CALC RG31 125 P12
Brookside CHERT KT16 81 L4
DTCH/LGLY SL3 40 E7
SHST GU47 87 J7
WGFD OX10 111 P1
WWKG RG41 14 B4
Brookside Av ASHF TW15 70 C3
STWL/WRAY TW19 54 D2
Brookside Cl EARL RG6 60 D3
Brookside Pk FARN GU14 * 94 A5
Brookside Wk TADY RG26 148 E2
Brooks Rd NTHA RG18 98 A2
Brook St WAR/TWY RG10 47 K2
WDSR SL4 13 K7
Brook St West READ RG1 8 E8
Brookway NWBY RG14 97 G3
Broom Acres SHST GU47 87 H5
Broom Cl TILE/CALC RG31 137 N5
Broome Cl YTLY GU46 86 C7
Broome Ct BRAK RG12 2 E7
Broomfield BNFD RG42 63 K6
Broom Fld LTWR GU18 90 A7
Broomfield Cl ASC SL5 79 H4
Broomfield Ga SLN SL2 28 D5
Broomfield Pk ASC SL5 79 H3
Broomfield Rd
RDGW/BURGH RG30 137 R2
Broom Gv WWKG RG41 73 K2
Broomhall La ASC SL5 78 F3
Broom Hl MDHD SL6 20 A8
SLN SL2 29 J1
Broomhill THLE RG7 * 142 C3
Broom La CHOB/PIR GU24 91 L4
Broomsquires Rd BAGS GU19 89 L4
Broom Wy BLKW GU17 93 K2
WEY KT13 83 K8
Broughton Cl
RDGW/BURGH RG30 44 C5
Broughton Ms FRIM GU16 94 F5
Brownfield Gdns MDHD SL6 4 E8
Browngraves Rd HYS/HAR UB3 42 E7
Browning Cl CBLY GU15 95 J2
NTHA RG18 97 L2
Browning Wy HEST TW5 43 M8
Brownlow Dr BNFD RG42 64 C5
Brownlow Rd READ RG1 8 B7
Brownrigg Crs BRAK RG12 3 M3
Brownrigg Rd ASHF TW15 71 G2
Browns Cl TADY RG26 149 Q6
Brownsfield Rd NTHA RG18 97 L3
Bruan Rd NWBY RG14 96 B6
Bruce Av SHPTN TW17 83 J3
Bruce Cl SL SL1 38 C1
Bruce Rd WODY RG5 46 D7
Brudenell WDSR SL4 52 F2
Brummell Rd NWBY RG14 6 A1
Brunel Ar READ RG1 * 9 G4
Brunel Cl HEST TW5 43 K7
MDHD SL6 4 E8
Brunel Dr CWTH RG45 75 J6
WODY RG5 46 F5
Brunel Rd MDHD SL6 4 C8
RDGW/BURGH RG30 58 A2
THLE RG7 137 J8
Brunel Wy SL SL1 11 G5
Brunswick BRAK RG12 76 A4
Brunswick Hl READ RG1 8 A7
Brunswick Rd FRIM GU16 95 J8
Brunswick St READ RG1 8 B8
Bruton Wy BRAK RG12 76 E4
Bryant Av SLN SL2 28 F6
Bryant Pl GOR/PANG RG8 125 M9
Bryants La NTHA RG18 134 G1
Brybur Cl WHIT RG2 59 K6
Bryer Pl WDSR SL4 52 D2
The Bryher MDHD SL6 25 H7
Buccaneer Cl WODY RG5 47 H6
Buccleuch Rd DTCH/LGLY SL3 39 J7
Buchanan Dr EWKG RG40 73 L7
Buchan Cl UX/CGN UB8 31 L4
The Buchan CBLY GU15 89 G6
Buckden Cl WODY RG5 47 G8
Buckham Hl HUNG RG17 118 G8
Buckhurst Gv EWKG RG40 74 F1
Buckhurst Hl BRAK RG12 76 F1
Buckhurst La ASC SL5 66 F8
Buckhurst Rd ASC SL5 66 F7
FRIM GU16 94 F8
Buckhurst Wy EARL RG6 60 A3
Buckingham Av SL SL1 28 A7
Buckingham Av East SL SL1 10 A1
Buckingham Dr CAV/SC RG4 45 H1
Buckingham Gdns SL SL1 11 G7
Buckingham Ga CAV/SC RG4 45 H2
MLW SL7 17 M7
Buckingham Rd NWBY RG14 6 B7
Buckingham Wy FRIM GU16 94 F6
Buckland Av DTCH/LGLY SL3 11 L9
Buckland Cl FARN GU14 94 C7
Buckland Crs WDSR SL4 12 B5
Buckland Ga DTCH/LGLY SL3 29 K4
Buckland Rd WHIT RG2 59 H3
Bucklebury BRAK RG12 76 A4
Bucklebury Cl MDHD SL6 36 E6
Buckle La BNFD RG42 50 B8
Bucknell Av GOR/PANG RG8 125 J9
Bucknell Cl TILE/CALC RG31 137 R6
Buckner Croke Wy STHA RG19 101 H1
Bucks Copse WWKG RG41 14 D7
Buck Side CAV/SC RG4 8 E1
Buckthorn Cl EWKG RG40 15 L3
Buckthorn La WGFD OX10 111 P1
Buckthorns BNFD RG42 63 L5
Budebury Rd STA TW18 69 M3
Budge's Gdns EWKG RG40 15 K3
Budge's Rd EWKG RG40 15 K3
Budham Wy BRAK RG12 76 B3
Buffins MDHD SL6 27 G4
Bugkingham Wy FRIM GU16 94 F5
Bulkeley Av WDSR SL4 12 F9
Bulkeley Cl EGH TW20 68 C3
Bullbrook Dr BRAK RG12 3 L3
Bullbrook Rw BRAK RG12 3 L4
Bullfinch Cl SHST GU47 87 L6
Bull La BNFD RG42 2 F2
HTWY RG27 145 L12
The Bull Meadow
GOR/PANG RG8 111 P12
Bullrush Gv UX/CGN UB8 31 L5
Bull's Br NWDGN UB2 43 J3
Bulls Bridge Rd NWDGN UB2 43 K3
Bullsbrook Rd YEAD UB4 43 L1
Bulls Down Cl HTWY RG27 150 C9
Bulmershe Ct EARL RG6 46 B8
Bulmershe Rd READ RG1 45 L8
Bulpit La HUNG RG17 138 H2
Bulpits Hl RAND SP11 146 A12
Bunby Rd SLN SL2 29 H1
Bunces Cl WDSR SL4 38 D5
Bunces La THLE RG7 143 Q4
Bundys Wy STA TW18 69 M4
Bungalow Dr
TILE/CALC RG31 * 137 P2
Bungler's Hl THLE RG7 72 B8
Bunkers Hl NWBY RG14 141 Q9
Bunten Meade SL SL1 38 D1
Burbage Gn BRAK RG12 76 F2
Burbidge Cl TILE/CALC RG31 137 R7
Burbidge Rd SHPTN TW17 83 G1
Burbury Woods CBLY GU15 88 E8
Burchell Rd NWBY RG14 96 A1
Burchett Coppice EWKG RG40 73 M6
Burchetts Green La MDHD SL6 24 E8
Burchett's Green Rd
MDHD SL6 34 C1
Burchetts Wy SHPTN TW17 83 H3
Burcombe Wy CAV/SC RG4 45 J2
Burcot Gdns MDHD SL6 26 A3
Burdens Heath THLE RG7 134 C11
Burdett Ct WHIT RG2 59 K3
Burdock Cl LTWR GU18 90 B6
THLE RG7 143 R4
Burfield Rd WDSR SL4 54 A5
Burford Cl MLW SL7 18 E1
Burford Ct EWKG RG40 15 L8
Burford Gdns SL SL1 27 L6
Burford Rd CBLY GU15 94 B2
Burford's HUNG RG17 118 A8
Burges Rd STA TW18 70 A4
Burgess Cl WODY RG5 60 D1
Burgess La KSCL RG20 140 C9
Burges Wy STA TW18 70 A3
Burgett Rd SL SL1 38 D3
Burghead Cl SHST GU47 87 K7
Burghfield Rd
RDGW/BURGH RG30 137 R9
Burgoyne Rd CBLY GU15 89 G8
SUN TW16 71 M4
Burleigh Gdns ASHF TW15 71 J3
Burleigh La ASC SL5 65 L6
Burleigh Ms CAV/SC RG4 127 J12
Burleigh Rd ADL/WDHM KT15 82 B8
ASC SL5 65 L7
FRIM GU16 94 D6
Burley Wy BLKW GU17 87 J8
Burlingham Cl WHIT RG2 59 J8
The Burlings ASC SL5 65 L7
Burlington Av SL SL1 10 E6
Burlington Cl
EBED/NFELT TW14 57 K6
Burlington Ct BLKW GU17 93 J3
SL SL1 10 F6
Burlington Rd
RDGW/BURGH RG30 137 P3
SL SL1 10 F6
SL SL1 27 K6
Burlsdon Wy BRAK RG12 3 L3
Burma Rd CHERT KT16 79 M6
Burn Cl ADL/WDHM KT15 82 D8
Burne-Jones Dr SHST GU47 87 K8
Burness Cl UX/CGN UB8 31 M3
Burnet Cl CHOB/PIR GU24 90 E8
Burnetts Rd WDSR SL4 38 A8
Burney Bit TADY RG26 148 G2
Burnham Cl BNEND SL8 20 C2
WDSR SL4 52 D1
Burnham Gdns HSLWW TW4 43 K8
HYS/HAR UB3 42 F3
Burnham Gv BNFD RG42 3 G1
Burnham La SL SL1 27 M6
Burnham Ri CAV/SC RG4 127 J11
Burnham Rd TADY RG26 142 B12
Burniston Cl EARL RG6 60 E4
Burnley Cl TADY RG26 148 D3
Burn Moor Cha BRAK RG12 76 E4
Burnmoor Meadow
EWKG RG40 85 L4
Burnsall Cl FARN GU14 94 B8
Burns Cl FARN GU14 93 M8
WODY RG5 60 E2
Burns Wy HEST TW5 43 M8
Burnthouse Br THLE RG7 144 E1
Burnthouse Gdns BNFD RG42 3 M1
Burnthouse La
RDGW/BURGH RG30 58 B7
Burnt Oak EWKG RG40 73 M6
MDHD SL6 20 B7
Burnt Pollard La LTWR GU18 90 E5
Burrcroft Rd
RDGW/BURGH RG30 58 A1
Burrell Rd FRIM GU16 94 C6
KSCL RG20 122 A2
Burr Hill La CHOB/PIR GU24 91 L4
Burr La MARL SN8 138 C12
Burroughs Crs BNEND SL8 20 C2
Burroway Rd DTCH/LGLY SL3 40 D3
Burrow Hill Gn CHOB/PIR GU24 91 K4
Burrows Hill Cl
STWL/WRAY TW19 56 B3
The Burrows TADY RG26 148 C1
Burton Cl WAR/TWY RG10 47 L4
Burtons Hl HUNG RG17 140 B4
Burton Wy WDSR SL4 52 E2
Burway Crs CHERT KT16 82 A1
Burwell Cl EARL RG6 60 C5
Bury's Bank Rd STHA RG19 96 F7
Busgrove La HEN RG9 113 R7
Bushell Wy WHIT RG2 72 E6
Bushey Rd HYS/HAR UB3 43 G4
Bush Rd SHPTN TW17 82 F2
Butchers La MDHD SL6 34 E5
Butchers Rw WAR/TWY RG10 * 47 K2
Bute St RDGW/BURGH RG30 58 B1
Butler Rd BAGS GU19 89 M4
CWTH RG45 75 H8
Butlers Cl WDSR SL4 52 D1
Butlers Orch CAV/SC RG4 126 D7
Butlers Pond GOR/PANG RG8 124 H4
Butlers Yd HEN RG9 126 F4
Butson Cl NWBY RG14 6 A4
Buttenshaw Av WHIT RG2 72 F6
Buttenshaw Cl WHIT RG2 73 G6
Buttercup Cl EWKG RG40 62 F8
Buttercup Pl NTHA RG18 97 M2
Buttercup Sq
STWL/WRAY TW19 * 56 D7
Butterfield CBLY GU15 94 B2
FLKWH/TG HP10 20 F2
Butter Market READ RG1 9 G6
Buttermere Av SL SL1 27 L6
Buttermere Cl
EBED/NFELT TW14 57 M7
Buttermere Dr CBLY GU15 95 K1
Buttermere Gdns BRAK RG12 3 H6
Buttermere Wy EGH TW20 69 H5
Buttersteep Ri ASC SL5 77 J5
Buttsfield Rd KSCL RG20 119 J5
Butts Furlong KSCL RG20 119 P3
Butts Hill Rd WODY RG5 46 E5
Butts Lake THLE RG7 * 142 D4
The Butts THLE RG7 149 K2
Buxton Av CAV/SC RG4 44 F2
Buxton Rd ASHF TW15 70 D3
Bybend Cl SLN SL2 28 D2
Byefield Rd
RDGW/BURGH RG30 58 A2
Byes La THLE RG7 149 K3
Byland Dr MDHD SL6 36 D5
Byreton Cl EARL RG6 60 B4
Byron Av CBLY GU15 95 H3
Byron Cl MLW SL7 19 H3
NWBY RG14 96 B7
YTLY GU46 92 B2
Byron Ct WDSR SL4 53 G2
Byron Dr CWTH RG45 87 G2
Byron Rd ADL/WDHM KT15 82 D8
EARL RG6 46 A7
WAR/TWY RG10 47 L2
Byron Wy WDR/YW UB7 42 B4
Bythorn Cl EARL RG6 60 E4
Byways SL SL1 27 J6
YTLY GU46 92 B1
Bywood BRAK RG12 76 A4
Byworth Cl WHIT RG2 59 H6

C

Cabbage Hill La BNFD RG42 63 L2
Cabbell Pl ADL/WDHM KT15 82 C8
Cabin Moss BRAK RG12 76 E4
Cabrera Av VW GU25 80 D2
Cabrera Cl VW GU25 80 C3
Cadbury Cl SUN TW16 71 L5
Cadbury Rd SUN TW16 71 L5
Caddy Cl EGH TW20 69 G3
Cadogan Cl CAV/SC RG4 45 L2
MDHD SL6 36 C6
RDGW/BURGH RG30 137 Q3
Cadugan Pl READ RG1 59 K1
Cadwell Dr MDHD SL6 35 M3
Caernarvon FRIM GU16 94 F6
Caesar's Camp Rd CBLY GU15 89 G6
Caesar's Cl CBLY GU15 89 G6
Caesars Ga BNFD RG42 3 M1
Caesar's Wy SHPTN TW17 83 K3
Cain Rd BNFD RG42 63 K7
BRAK RG12 63 L7
Cain's La EBED/NFELT TW14 57 K4
Cairn Cl CBLY GU15 95 H3
Cairngorm Pl FARN GU14 93 L7
Cairngorm Rd STHA RG19 97 M4
Caistor Cl TILE/CALC RG31 137 M6
Calard Dr NTHA RG18 97 J1
Calbourne Dr TILE/CALC RG31 137 P6
Calbroke Rd SLN SL2 28 B5
Calcot Pl TILE/CALC RG31 * 137 R6
Calcot Place Dr
TILE/CALC RG31 137 Q6
Calcott Pk YTLY GU46 86 C8
Caldbeck Dr WODY RG5 46 F8
Calder Cl MDHD SL6 4 E1
RDGW/BURGH RG30 137 R2
Calder Ct DTCH/LGLY SL3 40 B5
MDHD SL6 4 D1
Calder Wy DTCH/LGLY SL3 55 L2
Caldwell Rd BFOR GU20 90 D1
Caledonia Rd
STWL/WRAY TW19 56 E7
Caleta Cl CAV/SC RG4 45 K4
Calfridus Wy BRAK RG12 3 L7
Callington Rd WHIT RG2 59 H5
Callin's La WAR/TWY RG10 49 H3
Callis Farm Cl
STWL/WRAY TW19 56 E5
Callow Hl VW GU25 68 C7
Calshot Pl TILE/CALC RG31 137 P6
Calshot Rd HTHAIR TW6 57 H1
Calshot Wy FRIM GU16 95 G7
HTHAIR TW6 57 G1
Calvin Cl CBLY GU15 95 H2
Camberley Rd HTHAIR TW6 57 G2
Camborne Cl HTHAIR TW6 57 G2
Camborne Crs HTHAIR TW6 57 G2
Camborne Wy HTHAIR TW6 57 G2
Cambria Gdns
STWL/WRAY TW19 56 E6
Cambrian Cl CBLY GU15 94 B1
Cambrian Rd FARN GU14 93 K7
Cambrian Wy EWKG RG40 74 A6
TILE/CALC RG31 137 P6
Cambridge Av SL SL1 27 K3
SL SL1 28 C7
Cambridge Cl WDR/YW UB7 41 M6
Cambridge Rd ASHF TW15 71 J5
CWTH RG45 87 J2
MLW SL7 18 F4
SHST GU47 87 L5
Cambridgeshire Cl BNFD RG42 64 F5
WWKG RG41 * 61 L8
Cambridge St READ RG1 8 B5
Camden Pl BNEND SL8 20 C3
TILE/CALC RG31 137 M6
Camden Rd MDHD SL6 25 M5
Camelford Cl WHIT RG2 59 H5
Camellia Ct CHOB/PIR GU24 90 F8
Camellia Wy WWKG RG41 61 K7
Camilla Cl SUN TW16 * 71 M4
Camley Gdns MDHD SL6 25 J6
Camley Park Dr MDHD SL6 25 H6
Camm Av WDSR SL4 52 E2
Campbell Cl YTLY GU46 86 F8
Campbell Ct TADY RG26 150 B8
Campbell Pl FRIM GU16 94 F3
Campbell Rd TADY RG26 150 B8
WODY RG5 60 D
Camperdown MDHD SL6 5 M
Campion Cl BLKW GU17 93 M3
Campion Wy EWKG RG40 15 L3
Camp Rd THLE RG7 143 L3
Canada Rd FRIM GU16 95 K6
SL SL1 11 L6
Canal Est DTCH/LGLY SL3 * 40 C2
Canal Side HUNG RG17 * 129 M12
Canal View Rd NWBY RG14 7 M4
Canal Wk HUNG RG17 129 M12
NWBY RG14 6 E4
Canal Wy READ RG1 9 L6
Canal Whf DTCH/LGLY SL3 40 C2
Canal Yd NWDGN UB2 * 43 K4
Canberra Cl YTLY GU46 86 A7
Canberra Rd HTHAIR TW6 57 G2
Candleford Cl BRAK RG12 3 H
Candover Cl TADY RG26 148 D3
WDR/YW UB7 41 M7
Canford Dr ADL/WDHM KT15 82 B6
Canhurst La WAR/TWY RG10 33 M3
Cannock Cl MDHD SL6 5 L
Cannock Wy EARL RG6 60 C5
Cannon Cl SHST GU47 87 M6
Cannon Court Rd MDHD SL6 25 M3
Cannon Crs CHOB/PIR GU24 91 L6
Cannondown Rd MDHD SL6 26 A
Cannon Ga SLN SL2 29 L
Cannon Hl BRAK RG12 76 C
Cannon Hill Cl MDHD SL6 36 E4
Cannon La MDHD SL6 35 H
Cannon St READ RG1 8 B6
Canon Hill Dr MDHD SL6 36 D3
Canon Hill Wy MDHD SL6 36 D
Canopus Wy STWL/WRAY TW19 56 E6
Cansfield End NWBY RG14 6 D
Canterbury Av SLN SL2 28 E
Canterbury Ms WDSR SL4 12 E
Canterbury Rd WHIT RG2 59 H3
Cantley EWKG RG40 14 F
Cantley Crs WWKG RG41 14 D
Cape Farewell
WAR/TWY RG10 * 32 D
Capper Rd CBLY GU15 88 A
Captains Gorse
GOR/PANG RG8 123 P
Caraway Rd EARL RG6 60 A
Carbery La ASC SL5 66 B
Carbinswood La THLE RG7 99 M
Cardiff Ms READ RG1 * 8 D
Cardiff Rd READ RG1 8 B
Cardigan Cl SL SL1 28 B
Cardigan Rd READ RG1 45 L
Cardinal Cl CAV/SC RG4 9 G
The Cardinals BRAK RG12 * 3 K
Cardinals Wk MDHD SL6 27 L
SUN TW16 71 L

Cardwell Crs ASC SL5 78 C2
Carew Cl TILE/CALC RG31 125 M10
Carew Rd ASHF TW15 71 J4
Carey Cl WDSR SL4 53 H2
Carey Rd EWKG RG40 15 G8
Carey St READ RG1 8 D7
Carfax Rd HYS/HAR UB3 43 J5
Caribou Cl WODY RG5 46 E5
Carisbrooke FRIM GU16 94 F6
Carisbrooke Cl CAV/SC RG4 127 J12
MDHD SL6 4 A8
Carisbrooke Ct SL SL1 11 H3
Carland Cl EARL RG6 60 A5
Carlesgill Pl HEN RG9 127 R3
Carlile Gdns WAR/TWY RG10 32 F7
Carling Rd CAV/SC RG4 126 E4
Carlin Pl CBLY GU15 94 C2
Carlinwark Dr CBLY GU15 88 F7
Carlisle Rd SL SL1 10 C2
TILE/CALC RG31 125 Q11
Carlton Av HYS/HAR UB3 43 G4
Carlton Cl CBLY GU15 95 H3
WODY RG5 46 E8
Carlton Pl WEY KT13 * 83 H8
Carlton Rd CAV/SC RG4 44 D1
SLN SL2 11 M3
SUN TW16 71 M5
Carlyle Rd STA TW18 69 M5
Carmarthen Cl FARN GU14 93 M7
Carmarthen Rd SL SL1 10 E3
Carmelite Dr
RDGW/BURGH RG30 44 D8
Carnarvon Dr HYS/HAR UB3 42 E3
Carnarvon Rd READ RG1 45 L7
Carnation Cl EWKG RG40 75 H6
Carnation Dr BNFD RG42 65 G4
Carnegie Rd NWBY RG14 6 F5
Carnoustie BRAK RG12 75 L4
Carnoustie Ct READ RG1 * 9 M7
Carolina Pl EWKG RG40 73 L7
Caroline Cl WDR/YW UB7 41 M2
Caroline Ct ASHF TW15 71 H4
MLW SL7 19 G3
Caroline Dr WWKG RG41 14 C4
Caroline Pl HYS/HAR UB3 43 G7
Caroline St READ RG1 8 D5
Caroline Wy FRIM GU16 94 F5
Carousel Ct WHIT RG2 59 J4
Carpenter Ms BNFD RG42 63 K3
Carpenters Cl HTWY RG27 150 D9
WODY RG5 60 F1
Carrick Gdns WODY RG5 46 C7
Carrick La YTLY GU46 86 E8
Carrington Crs TADY RG26 148 D2
Carrington Rd SL SL1 10 F2
Carroll Crs ASC SL5 77 M1
Carron Cl RDGW/BURGH RG30 44 A7
Carsdale Cl READ RG1 58 F1
Carshalton Rd CBLY GU15 89 G5
Carshalton Wy EARL RG6 60 C4
Carston Gv TILE/CALC RG31 137 R6
Carter Cl WDSR SL4 12 C7
Carters Hl BNFD RG42 63 H1
EWKG RG40 63 H2
Carters Ri TILE/CALC RG31 137 Q7
Cartmel Dr WODY RG5 46 D8
Carvers Hl MARL SN8 138 B12
Cary Cl NWBY RG14 141 R8
Casey Ct THLE RG7 135 M7
Cassia Dr EARL RG6 59 M5
Cassiobury Av
EBED/NFELT TW14 57 M6
Castle Av DTCH/LGLY SL3 39 J6
Castle Cl CBLY GU15 94 E1
SUN TW16 71 L5
Castle Ct MDHD SL6 4 D4
Castlecraig Ct SHST GU47 * 87 K7
Castle Crs READ RG1 8 D8
Castle Dr MDHD SL6 4 D4
Castle End Rd WAR/TWY RG10 33 H8
Castle Gn WEY KT13 83 L7
Castle Gv NWBY RG14 96 B1
Castle Grove Rd
CHOB/PIR GU24 91 L7
Castle Hl MDHD SL6 4 E5
READ RG1 8 D8
THLE RG7 72 C7
WDSR SL4 13 K5
Castle Hill Rd EGH TW20 68 B2
Castle Hill Ter MDHD SL6 4 E5
Castle La NWBY RG14 132 E12
Castle Ms MDHD SL6 4 E5
WEY KT13 83 K7
Castle Rd CBLY GU15 94 E2
WEY KT13 83 L7
Castle St READ RG1 8 E7
SL SL1 11 H9
Castleview Rd DTCH/LGLY SL3 39 L4
WEY KT13 83 H8
Castor Ct YTLY GU46 86 B7
Caswall Cl BNFD RG42 63 J4
Caswall Ride YTLY GU46 92 E1
Caswell Cl FARN GU14 93 M8
Catalina Cl WODY RG5 47 H7
Catalina Rd HTHAIR TW6 57 H2
Catcliffe Wy EARL RG6 59 M6
Catena Ri LTWR GU18 90 A5
Catesby Gdns YTLY GU46 92 A1
Catherine Dr SUN TW16 71 M5
Catherine Howard Ct
WEY KT13 * 83 H7
Catherine Rd NWBY RG14 6 E6
Catherines Cl WDR/YW UB7 * 41 M2
Catherine St
RDGW/BURGH RG30 8 A5
Catlin Crs SHPTN TW17 83 K2
Catmore Rd KSCL RG20 108 C11
Catslip HEN RG9 114 F4
Caunter Rd NWBY RG14 141 R2
The Causeway CAV/SC RG4 9 L2
HTWY RG27 151 N3
MDHD SL6 36 E2
MLW SL7 19 G5
STA TW18 69 J2
Causmans Wy TILE/CALC RG31 137 N1
Cavalier Cl NWBY RG14 96 E1
THLE RG7 136 H7
Cavalry Crs WDSR SL4 53 H2
Cavelry Cl STHA RG19 98 A5
Cavendish Cl MDHD SL6 27 J7
SUN TW16 71 M4
Cavendish Ct BLKW GU17 93 K3
NWBY RG14 97 G1
SUN TW16 71 M4
Cavendish Gdns WWKG RG41 61 G3
Cavendish Meads ASC SL5 78 D3
Cavendish Rd CAV/SC RG4 127 J12
SUN TW16 71 M4
Caversham Br READ RG1 8 E1
Caversham Park Dr
CAV/SC RG4 45 J1
Caversham Park Rd
CAV/SC RG4 127 K12
Caversham Rd READ RG1 8 E2
Caversham Whf READ RG1 * 8 E2
Caves Farm Cl SHST GU47 87 G6
Cawcott Dr WDSR SL4 38 A8
Cawsam Gdns CAV/SC RG4 45 J2
Caxton Cl RDGW/BURGH RG30 44 C5
Caxton Dr UX/CGN UB8 31 L3
Caxton Rd NWDGN UB2 43 M3
Cecil Aldin Dr TILE/CALC RG31 125 M10
Cecil Cl ASHF TW15 71 J4
Cecil Rd ASHF TW15 71 J5
IVER SL0 31 G7
Cecil Wy SLN SL2 28 B5
Cedar Av BLKW GU17 93 K1
WDR/YW UB7 * 42 B1
Cedar Cha MDHD SL6 26 F5
Cedar Cl BAGS GU19 89 L3
EWKG RG40 15 G5
IVER SL0 30 E2
STA TW18 70 C7
TADY RG26 148 F4
Cedar Ct EGH TW20 69 G2
Cedar Dr ASC SL5 79 G4
BNFD RG42 3 G1
GOR/PANG RG8 124 G10
MDHD SL6 20 B8
Cedar Gv STHA RG19 97 L3
WEY KT13 83 J8
Cedar Mt NWBY RG14 96 B6
Cedar Ri STHA RG19 102 D1
Cedar Rd EBED/NFELT TW14 57 K7
WEY KT13 83 G7
WHIT RG2 59 L5
Cedars Cl SHST GU47 86 F6
Cedars Rd MDHD SL6 5 K5
The Cedars NWBY RG14 96 E7
SLN SL2 28 B4
TILE/CALC RG31 125 P12
Cedar Wy DTCH/LGLY SL3 40 A4
SUN TW16 71 L5
Cedar Wood Crs CAV/SC RG4 45 H2
Celandine Cl CWTH RG45 75 J8
Celandine Ct YTLY GU46 86 A7
Celandine Gv NTHA RG18 98 B3
Celia Crs ASHF TW15 70 D4
Cell Farm Av WDSR SL4 54 B4
Celsea Pl WGFD OX10 111 Q1
Cemetery La SHPTN TW17 83 H4
Centennial Ct BRAK RG12 * 3 G3
Central Ar ASHF TW15 * 70 F2
Central Av HYS/HAR UB3 43 H1
Central Dr SL SL1 28 B8
Central La WDSR SL4 52 B7
Central Wk EWKG RG40 15 G6
Central Wy WDSR SL4 52 A7
Centre Rd WDSR SL4 * 37 L7
Centurion Cl READ RG1 * 8 F8
SHST GU47 87 K6
Century Cha WAR/TWY RG10 * 34 A3
Century Dr THLE RG7 145 N5
Century Rd EGH TW20 69 J3
Cerotus Pl CHERT KT16 81 M4
Chackfield Dr WWKG RG41 61 K6
Chaffinch Cl SHST GU47 87 L6
TILE/CALC RG31 137 M3
WWKG RG41 14 A8
Chagford Rd WHIT RG2 59 H5
Chailey Cl HEST TW5 43 M8
Chainhill Rd WANT OX12 107 K2
WANT OX12 107 N8
Chain St READ RG1 8 F6
Chalcraft Cl HEN RG9 127 Q2
Chalfont Cl EARL RG6 60 A5
Chalfont Ct EARL RG6 * 60 A5
Chalfont Rd HYS/HAR UB3 43 J2
Chalfont Wy EARL RG6 60 A5
Chalford Rd NWBY RG14 6 A5
Chalgrove Cl MDHD SL6 5 L7
Chalgrove Wy CAV/SC RG4 126 H12
Chalk Hl DID OX11 110 H3
HEN RG9 127 Q5
Chalkhouse Green La
CAV/SC RG4 126 G9
Chalkhouse Green Rd
CAV/SC RG4 126 D7
Chalklands BNEND SL8 20 C2
Chalkpit La MLW SL7 18 D3
Chalk Pit La SL SL1 27 K2
Challenge Rd ASHF TW15 71 J1
Challenor Cl EWKG RG40 73 M7
Challis Pl BNFD RG42 63 L6
Challow Ct MDHD SL6 4 D1
Chalmers Rd ASHF TW15 71 H2
Chalmers Rd East ASHF TW15 71 H2
Chalvey Gdns SL SL1 10 E7
Chalvey Gv SL SL1 38 D3
Chalvey Pk SL SL1 10 F7
Chalvey Rd East SL SL1 10 E7
Chalvey Rd West SL SL1 10 D7
Chamberhouse Mill Rd
STHA RG19 98 B5
Chamberlain's Gdns WHIT RG2 72 E4
Chamberlains Meadow
HTWY RG27 151 N4
The Chambers READ RG1 * 9 H7
Champion Rd CAV/SC RG4 9 J2
Champney Cl DTCH/LGLY SL3 55 G2
The Chancellor's Wy WHIT RG2 59 K2
Chanctonbury Dr ASC SL5 78 E4
Chandlers Cl EBED/NFELT TW14 57 M6
Chandlers La YTLY GU46 86 C7
Chandos Rd NWBY RG14 96 B6
STA TW18 69 K3
Chantry Cl WDR/YW UB7 31 M8
WDSR SL4 12 D5
Chantry Md HUNG RG17 138 G1
Chantry Rd BAGS GU19 89 K4
CHERT KT16 82 B5
Chapel Av ADL/WDHM KT15 82 B8
Chapel Cl GOR/PANG RG8 112 A7
Chapel Ct HUNG RG17 129 M12
MDHD SL6 35 M2
NTHA RG18 98 A2
Chapel Gv ADL/WDHM KT15 82 B8
Chapel Hl TILE/CALC RG31 137 M2
Chapel La BAGS GU19 89 K4
BNFD RG42 63 J5
DID OX11 110 C2
FARN GU14 93 M6
GOR/PANG RG8 123 J8
HEN RG9 114 E8
HUNG RG17 117 K4
NTHA RG18 133 L6
NTHA RG18 133 Q2
NTHA RG18 134 G1
SLN SL2 29 K1
STHA RG19 103 H5
TADY RG26 148 A3
THLE RG7 134 F6
THLE RG7 142 H9
THLE RG7 145 L4
THLE RG7 145 N11
Chapel Md HTWY RG27 85 L6
Chapel Park Rd
ADL/WDHM KT15 82 B8
Chapel Rd CBLY GU15 94 B1
KSCL RG20 131 Q12
THLE RG7 143 L9
Chapels Cl SL SL1 38 A1
Chapel Sq CBLY GU15 87 M8
VW GU25 68 E8
Chapel St FARN GU14 94 D8
MLW SL7 18 F4
NTHA RG18 98 A3
SL SL1 11 G7
Chaplain's Hl CWTH RG45 87 K2
Chaplin Crs SUN TW16 71 L4
Chapman Cl WDR/YW UB7 42 B3
Chapman La BNEND SL8 20 C1
Chapter Ms WDSR SL4 13 K4
Chard Cl WODY RG5 46 E8
Chariotts Pl WDSR SL4 13 J6
Charlbury Cl BRAK RG12 76 F1
Charles Evans Wy CAV/SC RG4 45 K4
Charles Gdns SLN SL2 11 L1
Charles Rd STA TW18 70 D4
WGFD OX10 111 Q2
Charles Sq BRAK RG12 3 G4
Charles St CBLY GU15 88 C8
CHERT KT16 81 M5
NWBY RG14 141 R8
READ RG1 8 C5
WDSR SL4 13 H6
Charlock Cl NTHA RG18 98 A1
Charlotte Av SLN SL2 11 G2
Charlotte Cl NTHA RG18 133 N4
Charlottown NWBY RG14 7 K8
Charlton WDSR SL4 52 C1
Charlton Cl EWKG RG40 73 M6
SL SL1 38 D2
Charlton Ct SHST GU47 87 K5
Charlton Kings WEY KT13 83 L8
Charlton La SHPTN TW17 71 J8
THLE RG7 145 N9
Charlton Pl NWBY RG14 6 F2
Charlton Rd SHPTN TW17 71 J7
Charlville Dr TILE/CALC RG31 * 137 M6
Charmwood Cl NWBY RG14 96 B1
Charndon Cl READ RG1 59 H1
Charnham La HUNG RG17 129 M12
Charnham Pk HUNG RG17 129 M11
Charnham St HUNG RG17 129 L12
Charnwood ASC SL5 78 F3
Charrington Rd
TILE/CALC RG31 137 M6
Charta Rd EGH TW20 69 J3
Charter Cl SL SL1 * 11 H8
Charterhouse Cl BRAK RG12 76 E2
Charter Pl STA TW18 70 A4
UX/CGN UB8 31 M2
Charter Rd NWBY RG14 96 B6
SL SL1 28 A8
Charters La ASC SL5 78 D2
Charters Rd ASC SL5 78 F4
Charters Wy ASC SL5 78 F4
Charvil House Rd
WAR/TWY RG10 47 G1
Charvil La CAV/SC RG4 46 E2
Charvil Meadow Rd
WAR/TWY RG10 47 H1
Charwood Rd EWKG RG40 15 M5
Chase Gdns BNFD RG42 63 J3
Chaseside Av WAR/TWY RG10 32 F8
Chaseside Gdns CHERT KT16 82 B4
The Chase ASC SL5 66 A5
CWTH RG45 75 G8
FARN GU14 94 D8
MDHD SL6 25 M4
MLW SL7 19 J3
NWBY RG14 132 F11
TILE/CALC RG31 137 P6
Chatfield SLN SL2 28 C6
Chatham St READ RG1 8 D5
Chatsworth Av WWKG RG41 61 G4
Chatsworth Cl CAV/SC RG4 127 J12
MDHD SL6 4 A8
Chatsworth Hts CBLY GU15 89 G7
Chatteris Wy EARL RG6 60 C5
Chattern Hl ASHF TW15 71 H2
Chattern Rd ASHF TW15 71 J2
The Chatters THLE RG7 72 C7
Chatton Cl EARL RG6 60 A6
Chaucer Cl CAV/SC RG4 45 G1
EWKG RG40 15 M4
WDSR SL4 13 J9
Chaucer Crs NWBY RG14 96 A1
Chaucer Gv CBLY GU15 94 D1
Chaucer Rd ASHF TW15 70 E2
CWTH RG45 87 H2
FARN GU14 93 M8
Chaucer Wy SL SL1 11 G4
WWKG RG41 73 L1
Chauntry Cl MDHD SL6 26 E8
Chauntry Ms MDHD SL6 * 5 M6
Chauntry Rd MDHD SL6 5 L6
Chavey Down Rd BNFD RG42 65 H3
Chawridge La WDSR SL4 51 J7
Chazey Cl CAV/SC RG4 126 C10
Chazey Rd CAV/SC RG4 44 D2
Cheam Cl BRAK RG12 76 D2
Cheapside READ RG1 8 E5
Cheapside Rd ASC SL5 66 C8
Cheap St KSCL RG20 122 A1
NWBY RG14 6 E4
Cheddington Cl
RDGW/BURGH RG30 137 R4
Cheeseman Cl EWKG RG40 15 J3
Chelsea Cl RDGW/BURGH RG30 137 R1
Chelwood Dr SHST GU47 86 F5
Chelwood Rd EARL RG6 60 B4
Cheney Cl BNFD RG42 63 K4
Cheniston Gv MDHD SL6 25 H7
Chepstow Rd TILE/CALC RG31 125 N12
Chequer La THLE RG7 145 J12
Chequers La HTWY RG27 85 L7
Chequers Orch IVER SL0 31 H7
Chequers Wy WODY RG5 46 C7
Cherbury Cl BRAK RG12 3 L7
Cherington Ga MDHD SL6 25 K5
Cherington Wy ASC SL5 * 65 L7
Cheriton Av WAR/TWY RG10 32 F8
Cheriton Cl NWBY RG14 7 G8
TADY RG26 148 D3
Cheriton Ct READ RG1 8 E8
Cheriton Pl CAV/SC RG4 126 F5
Cheriton Wy BLKW GU17 93 K1
The Cherries SLN SL2 11 M1
Cherry Av DTCH/LGLY SL3 39 M2
STHL UB1 43 M1
Cherry Cl CAV/SC RG4 127 J10
NWBY RG14 6 D1
Cherrydale Rd CBLY GU15 95 K1
Cherry Garden La MDHD SL6 35 G3
Cherry Gv HUNG RG17 138 G1
HYS/HAR UB3 43 K1
WHIT RG2 59 L4
Cherry La WDR/YW UB7 42 B4
Cherry Orch HUNG RG17 118 F10
SLN SL2 29 K1
STA TW18 70 A3
WDR/YW UB7 42 A2
Cherry Tree Av STA TW18 70 B4
Cherry Tree Cl HEN RG9 114 A9
KSCL RG20 121 J10
SHST GU47 87 K5
Cherry Tree Dr BRAK RG12 3 J7
Cherry Tree Gv WWKG RG41 73 K2
Cherrytree La IVER SL0 31 J2
Cherry Tree Rd SLN SL2 28 D1
Cherry Wy DTCH/LGLY SL3 55 J2
SHPTN TW17 83 K1
Cherrywood Av EGH TW20 68 B4
Cherrywood Rd FARN GU14 94 A7
Chertsey Bridge Rd
CHERT KT16 82 D4
Chertsey La STA TW18 69 L3
Chertsey Rd ADL/WDHM KT15 82 B6
ASHF TW15 71 K5
BFOR GU20 90 E2
CHOB/PIR GU24 79 H8
FELT TW13 71 M1
SHPTN TW17 82 E4
SUN TW16 71 L4
Chertsey Wk CHERT KT16 * 82 A4
Chervil Wy THLE RG7 143 R4
Cherwell Cl DTCH/LGLY SL3 40 D6
MDHD SL6 5 J3
Cherwell Crs READ RG1 * 8 D6
Cherwell Rd BNEND SL8 20 D2
CAV/SC RG4 126 G12
Cheseridge Rd KSCL RG20 121 P4
Cheshire Pk BNFD RG42 64 E4
Chesnut Cha BNFD RG42 65 G5
Chessholme Rd ASHF TW15 71 J4
Chesterblade La BRAK RG12 76 D4
Chester Cl ASHF TW15 71 K3
NWBY RG14 7 K9
Chesterfield Rd ASHF TW15 70 E3
NWBY RG14 6 E7
Chesterfield Wy
HYS/HAR UB3 * 43 J2
Chesterman St READ RG1 9 G9
Chesterment Wy EARL RG6 60 D5
Chester Rd HTHAIR TW6 57 G2
SL SL1 28 F7
Chesters Rd CBLY GU15 95 H1
Chester St CAV/SC RG4 45 G4
RDGW/BURGH RG30 44 D6
Chesterton Dr
STWL/WRAY TW19 56 F7
Chesterton Rd NTHA RG18 97 L1
Chestnut Av CAV/SC RG4 45 L2
CBLY GU15 89 G8
DTCH/LGLY SL3 40 A2
VW GU25 79 M1
WWKG RG41 61 J8
Chestnut Cl ASHF TW15 71 H2
BLKW GU17 * 93 L1
EGH TW20 68 B4
HEN RG9 115 M6
HYS/HAR UB3 42 D7
MDHD SL6 26 D5
MLW SL7 17 M7
SUN TW16 71 M4
THLE RG7 137 J6
Chestnut Crs NWBY RG14 6 E1
WHIT RG2 145 Q2
Chestnut Dr EGH TW20 68 D4
RDGW/BURGH RG30 143 R2
WDSR SL4 52 E3
Chestnut Gv GOR/PANG RG8 125 P9
STA TW18 70 C4
Chestnut La CHOB/PIR GU24 91 J2
HUNG RG17 117 N2
Chestnut Manor Cl STA TW18 70 B3
Chestnut Rd ASHF TW15 71 G2
The Chestnuts HEN RG9 32 C3
Chestnut Wk HUNG RG17 138 H2
SHPTN TW17 83 L2
Chetwode Cl EWKG RG40 15 L6
Cheveley Gdns SL SL1 27 L3
Cheviot Cl CBLY GU15 95 J2
FARN GU14 93 L7
HYS/HAR UB3 42 F7
MDHD SL6 5 L7
NWBY RG14 141 Q9
Cheviot Dr WAR/TWY RG10 47 H2
Cheviot Rd DTCH/LGLY SL3 40 C5
SHST GU47 86 F5
Chewter La BFOR GU20 78 B8
Cheylesmore Dr FRIM GU16 95 K3
Cheyne Rd ASHF TW15 71 K4
Cheyne Wy FARN GU14 93 M7
Chichester Ct SL SL1 11 L8
Chichester Rd
RDGW/BURGH RG30 137 Q2
Chicory Cl EARL RG6 59 M5
Chieveley Cl TILE/CALC RG31 137 N2
Chilcombe Wy EARL RG6 60 D4
Child Cl EWKG RG40 15 K4
Childrey Wy TILE/CALC RG31 137 M2
Child St HUNG RG17 117 J3
Chilham Ct FRIM GU16 94 F6
Chillingham Wy CBLY GU15 94 C2
Chilsey Green Rd CHERT KT16 81 L5
Chiltern Cl HEN RG9 127 P2
NWBY RG14 141 Q9
STA TW18 70 A3
Chiltern Ct CAV/SC RG4 126 H12
Chiltern Crs EARL RG6 46 A7
Chiltern Dr WAR/TWY RG10 47 H2
Chiltern Hts CAV/SC RG4 * 45 J4
Chiltern Rd CAV/SC RG4 45 J2
HEN RG9 126 E3
MDHD SL6 5 L7
MLW SL7 18 E4
SHST GU47 86 F5
SL SL1 27 K6
Chilterns Pk BNEND SL8 20 D1
Chiltern Vw GOR/PANG RG8 125 P9
Chiltern View Rd UX/CGN UB8 31 L3
Chilton Wy HUNG RG17 138 G1
Chilwick Rd SLN SL2 28 B5
Chippendale Cl TADY RG26 148 A1
Chippendale Waye
UX/CGN UB8 31 M1
Chippenham Cl EARL RG6 59 M6
Chipstead Rd HTHAIR TW6 57 G2
Chisbury Cl BRAK RG12 76 E3
Chislett Gdns SHST GU47 86 F6
Chitterfield Ga WDR/YW UB7 42 C7
Chittering Cl EARL RG6 60 C5
Chive Rd EARL RG6 60 A5
Chivers Dr EWKG RG40 73 L7
Chives Pl BNFD RG42 64 D5
Chobham La CHERT KT16 80 A6
Chobham Rd ASC SL5 79 J6
FRIM GU16 94 E4
Choke La MDHD SL6 25 J2
Cholmeley Pl READ RG1 45 L7
Cholmeley Rd READ RG1 45 L6
Cholmeley Ter READ RG1 45 L7
Cholsey Rd STHA RG19 98 B3
Choseley Cl WAR/TWY RG10 34 A2
Choseley Rd WAR/TWY RG10 34 A2
Chrislaine Cl STWL/WRAY TW19 56 D5
Christchurch Ct WHIT RG2 59 J1
Christchurch Dr BLKW GU17 87 J8
Christchurch Gdns WHIT RG2 59 J1
Christchurch Rd VW GU25 68 A8
WHIT RG2 59 J1
Christian Sq WDSR SL4 13 H6
Christie Cl LTWR GU18 90 B5
Christie Hts NWBY RG14 96 D6
Christie Wk YTLY GU46 92 C2
Christopher Ct NWBY RG14 7 H6
Christopher Rd NWDGN UB2 43 K4
Christy Ct TADY RG26 148 E3
Chrysanthemum Dr WHIT RG2 59 L8
Chudleigh Gdns WHIT RG2 59 H4
Chuff Cnr BNFD RG42 64 D4
Church Ap EGH TW20 69 J8
Church Brook TADY RG26 148 C4
Church Cl ADL/WDHM KT15 82 B8
HEN RG9 127 K3
HUNG RG17 117 K3
KSCL RG20 141 L8
MDHD SL6 4 C6
STA TW18 70 C8
STHA RG19 97 M3
UX/CGN UB8 31 K3
WDR/YW UB7 42 A3
WDSR SL4 13 J2
WWKG RG41 61 J4
Church Dr MDHD SL6 36 E2
Church End DID OX11 110 C1
Church End La
RDGW/BURGH RG30 137 R3
Church Farm Barns THLE RG7 144 B9
Churchfield Ms SLN SL2 29 K7
Churchfield Rd WEY KT13 83 G8
Churchfields Av WEY KT13 83 H8
Church Ga STHA RG19 97 M3
Church Gv DTCH/LGLY SL3 29 L6
Church Hams EWKG RG40 73 K8
Church Hl BNFD RG42 63 J1
CBLY GU15 94 E1
DID OX11 109 K2
HUNG RG17 130 G8
KSCL RG20 109 L12
THLE RG7 99 G4
WAR/TWY RG10 47 L7
Churchill Cl EBED/NFELT TW14 57 M7
TADY RG26 148 F3
WHIT RG2 * 59 H4
Churchill Crs CAV/SC RG4 126 F4
FARN GU14 94 B6
Churchill Dr MLW SL7 19 H2
WEY KT13 83 J7
WWKG RG41 61 H4
Churchill Rd ASC SL5 65 M7
DTCH/LGLY SL3 40 B4
Church Lands TADY RG26 149 P7
Church La ASC SL5 67 G8
ASC SL5 78 D1
ASC SL5 79 H2
BNFD RG42 63 K1
BNFD RG42 64 D1
CAV/SC RG4 127 L11
DTCH/LGLY SL3 29 K5
EWKG RG40 73 J5
EWKG RG40 85 L2
GOR/PANG RG8 123 J8
HEN RG9 32 B5
HEN RG9 126 F2
HTWY RG27 151 N4
HUNG RG17 129 M12
HUNG RG17 146 F4
KSCL RG20 100 C7
KSCL RG20 132 G1
KSCL RG20 141 L8
MARL SN8 146 A4
MDHD SL6 36 E2
MLW SL7 18 F7
NTHA RG18 134 G1
NWBY RG14 141 R2
RDGW/BURGH RG30 137 Q12
READ RG1 9 G8
SLN SL2 29 H4
STHA RG19 97 M3
THLE RG7 72 D8
THLE RG7 99 H8
THLE RG7 143 K2
THLE RG7 145 M2
THLE RG7 149 N1
WAR/TWY RG10 47 M1
WDSR SL4 13 K5
WEY KT13 83 G8
WGFD OX10 112 B1
WHIT RG2 72 C2
Church Ms ADL/WDHM KT15 82 C8
GOR/PANG RG8 125 P9
WODY RG5 46 F6
Church Pde ASHF TW15 * 70 F2
Church Rd ASC SL5 65 H6
ASC SL5 78 A1
ASC SL5 79 G3
ASHF TW15 70 F2
BAGS GU19 89 K3
BFOR GU20 90 B2
BRAK RG12 3 G5
CBLY GU15 87 M7
CHOB/PIR GU24 90 F7
DID OX11 110 C2
EARL RG6 46 B7
EGH TW20 69 G3
FRIM GU16 94 F6
HEST TW5 43 K5
HYS/HAR UB3 43 H1
IVER SL0 30 E3
KSCL RG20 141 L1
MARL SN8 128 C12
MARL SN8 138 F12
MDHD SL6 5 M9
MDHD SL6 19 K8
MLW SL7 19 L1
NWBY RG14 96 C1
SHPTN TW17 83 H4
SHST GU47 86 F5
SHST GU47 87 K5
SLN SL2 28 E4
TADY RG26 148 D4
TADY RG26 148 G1
THLE RG7 142 C7
THLE RG7 143 L9
UX/CGN UB8 31 M5
WDR/YW UB7 41 M2
WDSR SL4 51 H8
WDSR SL4 54 B4
WODY RG5 46 F6
Church Rd East CWTH RG45 87 H1
Church Rd West CWTH RG45 87 H2
Church Sq SHPTN TW17 83 H4
Church St CAV/SC RG4 45 G4
CWTH RG45 87 H1
HEN RG9 127 R1
HUNG RG17 118 E11
HUNG RG17 129 M12
HUNG RG17 140 A4
NTHA RG18 122 B9
READ RG1 9 G7
SL SL1 10 C7
SL SL1 11 G8
SL SL1 27 L5
STA TW18 69 K2
THLE RG7 136 H7
WAR/TWY RG10 32 E4
WAR/TWY RG10 47 K2
WDSR SL4 13 H5
WEY KT13 83 G8
Church Ter READ RG1 8 E9
WDSR SL4 52 E1
Church Vw HEN RG9 113 R5
MDHD SL6 35 G6
THLE RG7 135 Q12
YTLY GU46 86 D7
Church Views MDHD SL6 5 G3
Church Wk WEY KT13 83 G7
Church Wy HUNG RG17 138 G1
Churchway KSCL RG20 108 G9
Churn Rd KSCL RG20 109 Q11
Chute Cl TADY RG26 149 R6
Cinnamon Cl EARL RG6 59 M5
WDSR SL4 12 A6
Cintra Av WHIT RG2 59 J2
Cintra Cl WHIT RG2 59 K1
Cippenham Cl SL SL1 28 B8
Cippenham La SL SL1 10 A6
Circle Hill Rd CWTH RG45 87 J1
Circuit La RDGW/BURGH RG30 58 C1
Circus Dr WHIT RG2 59 L7
City Rd TILE/CALC RG31 137 M4

Clacy Gn BNFD RG42 2 D1
Clairmore Gdns
TILE/CALC RG31 125 N10
Clairvale Rd HEST TW5 43 M8
Clammas Wy UX/CGN UB8 31 L6
Clandon Av EGH TW20 69 J5
Clanfield Crs TILE/CALC RG31 125 N12
Clanfield Ride BLKW GU17 93 K1
Clappers Farm Rd THLE RG7 149 P1
Clappers La CHOB/PIR GU24 91 J6
Clappers Meadow MDHD SL6 26 D5
Clapps Gate Rd TADY RG26 148 G1
Clare Av EWKG RG40 15 G4
Clare Ct EWKG RG40 15 G4
Clarefield Cl MDHD SL6 25 J5
Clarefield Dr MDHD SL6 25 J5
Clarefield Rd MDHD SL6 25 K5
Clare Gdns EGH TW20 69 G3
Claremont Av CBLY GU15 94 F1
Claremont Crs NWBY RG14 7 L2
Claremont Dr SHPTN TW17 83 H3
Claremont Gdns MLW SL7 19 G4
Claremont Rd MLW SL7 19 G4
STA TW18 69 K3
WDSR SL4 13 G7
Clarence Crs WDSR SL4 13 H6
Clarence Dr CBLY GU15 89 H7
EGH TW20 68 C2
Clarence Rd HEN RG9 115 R12
WDSR SL4 12 D7
Clarence St EGH TW20 68 F4
NWDGN UB2 43 M3
STA TW18 69 L2
Clarence Wy TILE/CALC RG31 137 M6
Clarendon Cl WWKG RG41 61 K4
Clarendon Copse MDHD SL6 4 D7
Clarendon Ct BLKW GU17 93 K3
SLN SL2 * 11 M2
Clarendon Gdns NWBY RG14 6 F2
Clarendon Ri TILE/CALC RG31 125 M10
Clarendon Rd ASHF TW15 70 F2
EARL RG6 46 A8
HYS/HAR UB3 43 H2
Clare Rd MDHD SL6 4 E7
MDHD SL6 27 L7
STWL/WRAY TW19 56 D7
Clares Green Rd THLE RG7 145 M3
Clarewood Dr CBLY GU15 88 E8
Clarke Crs SHST GU47 87 L7
Clark's Gdns HUNG RG17 138 H2
Clark Wy HEST TW5 43 M7
The Classics HUNG RG17 117 K5
Classon Cl WDR/YW UB7 42 A2
Claverdon BRAK RG12 76 A4
Clay Cl TILE/CALC RG31 137 M1
Clay Cnr CHERT KT16 82 B5
Claydon Ct CAV/SC RG4 8 F2
Claydon Gdns BLKW GU17 94 A5
Clayhall La WDSR SL4 53 M4
Clayhill Cl BRAK RG12 64 F8
Clay Hill Crs NWBY RG14 96 F1
Clayhill Rd
RDGW/BURGH RG30 143 R1
THLE RG7 143 P3
Clay La EWKG RG40 62 F8
STWL/WRAY TW19 56 F6
THLE RG7 135 P12
Clayton Gv BRAK RG12 3 L3
Clayton Pde DTCH/LGLY SL3 * 40 C3
Clayton Rd FARN GU14 93 M5
HYS/HAR UB3 43 G2
Claytons Meadow BNEND SL8 20 D4
Clayton Wk WHIT RG2 59 J2
Clayton Wy UX/CGN UB8 31 M5
Cleares Pasture SL SL1 27 K4
Clearsprings LTWR GU18 89 M6
Cleave Av HYS/HAR UB3 43 G4
Cleeve Ct EBED/NFELT TW14 57 L7
Cleeve Down GOR/PANG RG8 112 B11
Cleeve Rd GOR/PANG RG8 111 R11
Clement Gdns HYS/HAR UB3 43 G4
Clements Cl SL SL1 11 L7
THLE RG7 145 L5
Clements Md TILE/CALC RG31 137 M2
Clements Rd HEN RG9 115 Q11
Clent Rd WHIT RG2 59 H2
Cleopatra Pl BNFD RG42 3 L1
Clerewater Pl STHA RG19 97 H3
Clevedon Ct FRIM GU16 95 G6
Clevedon Dr EARL RG6 60 A4
Clevedon Gdns HYS/HAR UB3 42 F3
Clevedon Rd TILE/CALC RG31 125 Q11
Cleveland WAR/TWY RG10 47 H2
Cleveland Cl MDHD SL6 5 M7
Cleveland Dr STA TW18 70 B7
Cleveland Gv NWBY RG14 6 C3
Cleveland Rd UX/CGN UB8 31 M4
Clevemede GOR/PANG RG8 112 A11
Cleves Ct WDSR SL4 12 B9
Cleves Wy SUN TW16 71 M4
Cleves Wd WEY KT13 83 L7
Clewborough Dr CBLY GU15 89 H8
Clewer Av WDSR SL4 12 D7
Clewer Court Rd WDSR SL4 12 E4
Clewer Flds WDSR SL4 13 G5
Clewer Hill Rd WDSR SL4 52 E1
Clewer New Town WDSR SL4 12 D7
Clewer Pk WDSR SL4 12 D3
Clifford Gdns HYS/HAR UB3 42 F4
Clifford Gv ASHF TW15 71 G2
Cliffords Wy BNEND SL8 20 C1
The Cliffs HUNG RG17 * 140 B3
Clifton Cl ADL/WDHM KT15 82 B6
MDHD SL6 36 B2
Clifton Gdns FRIM GU16 94 F8
Clifton Park Rd CAV/SC RG4 44 F3
Clifton Pl BNEND SL8 * 20 E3
Clifton Ri WAR/TWY RG10 33 G5
WDSR SL4 37 M8
Clifton Rd HTHAIR TW6 57 H2
NWBY RG14 6 A5
SL SL1 11 L7
WWKG RG41 14 C2
Clifton St READ RG1 8 C7
Clinton Cl WEY KT13 83 H7
Clintons Gn BNFD RG42 2 D3
Clitheroe Rd BLKW GU17 92 F5
Clive Ct SL SL1 10 C7
Clivedale Rd WODY RG5 60 E2
Cliveden Md MDHD SL6 26 E4
Cliveden Pl SHPTN TW17 83 H3
Cliveden Rd MDHD SL6 26 F4
Clive Gn BRAK RG12 76 B2
Clivemont Rd MDHD SL6 4 F1
Clivesdale Dr HYS/HAR UB3 43 J1
Clockhouse La ASHF TW15 71 G2
EBED/NFELT TW14 71 H1
Clockhouse La East EGH TW20 69 H5
Clockhouse La West EGH TW20 69 G5
Cloister Ms THLE RG7 137 J7
The Cloisters CAV/SC RG4 45 G3
FRIM GU16 94 D5
Clonmel Cl CAV/SC RG4 9 L1
Clonmel Wy SL SL1 27 K4
Close End HUNG RG17 117 K4
The Close ASC SL5 65 K7
FRIM GU16 94 C6
GOR/PANG RG8 113 K10
HEN RG9 127 R2
HUNG RG17 118 E11
IVER SL0 30 E4
LTWR GU18 90 A5
NTHA RG18 97 K2
NTHA RG18 122 B9
SHST GU47 87 L6
SL SL1 27 M8
TADY RG26 148 F12
THLE RG7 143 Q3
VW GU25 80 D2
WODY RG5 60 E1
Clough Dr NTHA RG18 133 M4
Clove Cl EARL RG6 59 M5
Clover Cl EWKG RG40 15 M3
Clover La YTLY GU46 86 A8
Cloves Farm Wd BNFD RG42 * 63 K7
Club La CWTH RG45 87 K1
The Clumps ASHF TW15 71 K2
Clyde Rd STWL/WRAY TW19 56 D7
Clyve Wy STA TW18 69 L6
Coach House Cl FRIM GU16 94 E3
Coachman's Ct NWBY RG14 96 D1
Coach Ride MLW SL7 18 F2
Coach Rd ASC SL5 65 K5
Coalmans Wy SL SL1 27 J7
Coalport Wy
RDGW/BURGH RG30 137 Q1
Cobb Cl DTCH/LGLY SL3 39 M8
Cobbett's La BLKW GU17 92 F2
YTLY GU46 92 F1
Cobblers Cl SLN SL2 28 D3
Cobden Cl UX/CGN UB8 31 L2
Cobham Cl SL SL1 38 B1
Cobham Rd HEST TW5 43 L7
WODY RG5 46 F7
Cochrane Cl STHA RG19 98 A3
Cochrane Pl BFOR GU20 90 D1
Cock-a-Dobby SHST GU47 87 G5
Cockett Rd DTCH/LGLY SL3 40 A3
Cock La THLE RG7 135 M8
Cockney Hl
RDGW/BURGH RG30 137 R4
Cock's La BNFD RG42 51 G8
Cody Cl WODY RG5 47 H6
Coe Sp SL SL1 38 D2
Coftards SLN SL2 29 L7
Colbrook Av HYS/HAR UB3 42 F3
Colbrook Cl HYS/HAR UB3 42 F3
Colby Gdns MDHD SL6 5 G2
Cold Ash Hl NTHA RG18 133 Q10
Cold Harbour GOR/PANG RG8 124 G2
Coldharbour Cl EGH TW20 69 J8
HEN RG9 127 Q2
Cold Harbour La FARN GU14 93 L6
Coldharbour La
CHOB/PIR GU24 90 F6
EGH TW20 69 J8
HYS/HAR UB3 43 H2
Coldharbour Rd HUNG RG17 138 H2
WANT OX12 107 R2
Coldicutt St CAV/SC RG4 9 J2
Coldmoorholme La BNEND SL8 20 A2
Cole Gdns HEST TW5 43 J7
Colemans Moor La WODY RG5 46 F8
Colemans Moor Rd WODY RG5 60 F1
Colenorton Crs WDSR SL4 38 A4
Coleridge Av YTLY GU46 92 E1
Coleridge Cl CWTH RG45 87 J2
WAR/TWY RG10 47 L3
Coleridge Crs DTCH/LGLY SL3 41 G8
Coleridge La GOR/PANG RG8 124 B10
Coleridge Rd ASHF TW15 70 E2
Coleridge Wy WDR/YW UB7 42 A4
Coley Av READ RG1 8 C9
Coley Hl READ RG1 8 D8
Coley Park Rd READ RG1 8 D8
Coley Pl READ RG1 8 E8
Colham Av WDR/YW UB7 42 A1
Colham Mill Rd WDR/YW UB7 41 M1
Colin Wy SL SL1 38 D3
Collaroy Gln NTHA RG18 133 R10
Collaroy Rd NTHA RG18 133 Q11
College Av EGH TW20 69 H4
MDHD SL6 4 E4
SL SL1 10 E8
College Cl ADL/WDHM KT15 82 D7
CBLY GU15 88 D6
WGFD OX10 111 P1
College Crs SHST GU47 87 L6
WDSR SL4 13 G8
College Gln MDHD SL6 4 D4
College Piece THLE RG7 143 P8
College Ride BAGS GU19 89 J3
CBLY GU15 88 D7
College Ri MDHD SL6 4 D4
College Rd EARL RG6 45 M8
MDHD SL6 4 D3
SHST GU47 87 L7
SL SL1 38 B1
College Wy ASHF TW15 70 F2
HUNG RG17 118 B8
Colleton Dr WAR/TWY RG10 47 L3
Collier Cl MDHD SL6 5 G1
Colliers La HEN RG9 126 E2
Colliers Wy RDGW/BURGH RG30 44 B7
Collingsbourne
ADL/WDHM KT15 * 82 B8
Collingwood Grange Cl
CBLY GU15 89 H6
Collingwood Ri CBLY GU15 89 G7
Collins Cl NWBY RG14 7 J1
Collins Dr NTHA RG18 133 M4
Collins End GOR/PANG RG8 125 L4
Collis St WHIT RG2 59 H1
Colmore La HEN RG9 114 D10
Colmworth Cl EARL RG6 60 A6
Colnbrook By-Pass
DTCH/LGLY SL3 40 D6
WDR/YW UB7 41 K7
Coln Ct MDHD SL6 5 H3
Colndale Rd DTCH/LGLY SL3 55 L1
Colne Av WDR/YW UB7 41 L2
Colne Bank DTCH/LGLY SL3 55 K2
Colne Orch IVER SL0 31 H7
Colne Valley Wy DTCH/LGLY SL3 55 H1
IVER SL0 31 J7
STWL/WRAY TW19 55 L7
WDR/YW UB7 41 J3
Colne Wy STWL/WRAY TW19 69 H1
Colonel's La CHERT KT16 82 A3
Colonial Rd EBED/NFELT TW14 57 L6
SL SL1 11 K6
The Colonnade
TILE/CALC RG31 * 125 N12
Colston Cl TILE/CALC RG31 137 P6
Colthrop La STHA RG19 98 D4
Colthrop Wy STHA RG19 98 D4
Coltsfoot Cl THLE RG7 143 R3
Columbia Ct EWKG RG40 73 L7
Colville Gdns LTWR GU18 90 B6
Colwyn Cl YTLY GU46 86 B8
Colyer Cl NTHA RG18 133 Q2
Colyton Wy GOR/PANG RG8 125 N9
Combe La FARN GU14 94 A8
Combermere Cl WDSR SL4 12 E8
Combe Rd
RDGW/BURGH RG30 137 R3
Combe Vw HUNG RG17 138 H2
Comet Rd STWL/WRAY TW19 56 D6
Comet Wy WODY RG5 47 G7
Comfrey Cl EWKG RG40 15 M2
Commerce Pk THLE RG7 * 136 F11
Commercial Rd STA TW18 70 A4
WHIT RG2 59 G5
Commonfield La EWKG RG40 73 H6
Commonfields CHOB/PIR GU24 90 F8
Common Hl THLE RG7 136 D7
Common La KSCL RG20 119 P1
SL SL1 21 M5
WDSR SL4 38 E5
Common Rd DTCH/LGLY SL3 40 C4
STHA RG19 102 A6
WDSR SL4 37 M4
Commons Rd WWKG RG41 61 M5
The Common NWDGN UB2 43 M4
TADY RG26 148 B9
WDR/YW UB7 41 L5
Communications Rd
STHA RG19 101 H1
Community Cl HEST TW5 43 K8
Compass Cl ASHF TW15 71 J5
Compton Av TILE/CALC RG31 137 M3
Compton Cl BRAK RG12 75 L3
EARL RG6 60 C2
SHST GU47 87 J5
Compton Dr MDHD SL6 25 J6
Comsaye Wk BRAK RG12 76 C2
Concorde Ct WDSR SL4 12 D7
Concorde Rd MDHD SL6 35 M2
Concorde Wy SL SL1 10 A7
WODY RG5 47 G7
Condor Cl TILE/CALC RG31 125 N11
Condor Rd STA TW18 70 C8
Conduit La DTCH/LGLY SL3 40 A5
Conegar Ct SL SL1 10 E5
Coney Gra BNFD RG42 64 B4
Congreve Cl THLE RG7 142 B7
Conifer Cl TADY RG26 142 A12
Conifer Crest NWBY RG14 141 Q10
Conifer Dr CBLY GU15 89 G8
TILE/CALC RG31 125 M12
Conifer La EGH TW20 69 J3
Conifers WEY KT13 83 L8
The Conifers CWTH RG45 75 G7
MDHD SL6 25 J6
Conifer Wk WDSR SL4 * 37 L7
Coningham Rd WHIT RG2 59 J8
Coningsby BRAK RG12 3 G8
Coningsby Cl MDHD SL6 35 M3
Coningsby La MDHD SL6 36 E8
Conisboro Av CAV/SC RG4 44 E1
Conisboro Wy CAV/SC RG4 44 E1
Coniston Cl CBLY GU15 95 J3
STHA RG19 97 J3
WODY RG5 60 E1
Coniston Ct LTWR GU18 90 B5
Coniston Crs SL SL1 27 L6
Coniston Dr
RDGW/BURGH RG30 125 R12
Coniston Wy EGH TW20 69 H5
Connaught Av ASHF TW15 70 E2
Connaught Cl CWTH RG45 86 F3
MDHD SL6 26 A5
RDGW/BURGH RG30 44 D7
YTLY GU46 86 B8
Connaught Gdns STHA RG19 98 A4
Connaught Rd BAGS GU19 89 J5
CBLY GU15 94 F1
NWBY RG14 7 G4
RDGW/BURGH RG30 44 D7
SL SL1 11 L6
The Connection NWBY RG14 132 G12
Conniston Cl MLW SL7 18 D4
Connop Wy FRIM GU16 94 F3
Consort Dr CBLY GU15 89 J7
Constable Cl WODY RG5 47 H6
Constable Wy SHST GU47 87 L8
Constitution Rd
RDGW/BURGH RG30 44 B6
Consul Cl WODY RG5 61 G1
Control Tower Rd HTHAIR TW6 57 G2
Convent Rd ASHF TW15 71 H3
WDSR SL4 12 C8
Convent Wy NWDGN UB2 43 L4
Conway Dr ASHF TW15 71 J4
HYS/HAR UB3 42 E3
NTHA RG18 97 K1
Conway Rd MDHD SL6 27 K7
TILE/CALC RG31 137 N5
Conygree Cl EARL RG6 60 B5
Cooke Ri BNFD RG42 64 B4
Cookham Cl SHST GU47 87 J5
Cookham Dean Bottom
MDHD SL6 19 L6
Cookham Rd BRAK RG12 63 L7
MDHD SL6 5 G2
Cook La WGFD OX10 112 C1
Coolarne Ri CBLY GU15 89 G8
Coolgardie Rd ASHF TW15 71 J3
Coombe Cl FRIM GU16 94 D6
Coombe Ct STHA RG19 98 A3
Coombe Hill Ct WDSR SL4 52 D3
Coombe Pine BRAK RG12 76 D3
Coombe Rd KSCL RG20 122 B4
YTLY GU46 86 B7
Coombesbury La KSCL RG20 131 N9
Coombes La WWKG RG41 73 J2
Coombe Sq STHA RG19 98 A3
The Coombe GOR/PANG RG8 111 P12
Cooper Cl WHIT RG2 59 J7
Cooper Rd BFOR GU20 90 D2
HEN RG9 115 R11
Coopers Cl STA TW18 69 L3
Coopers Ct TADY RG26 149 R7
Coopers Crs NTHA RG18 97 L2
Cooper's Hill La EGH TW20 68 C1
Coopers La TADY RG26 149 Q7
Coopers Pightle CAV/SC RG4 126 D7
Coopers Rw IVER SL0 30 E5
Cooper Wy SL SL1 38 D3
Coote Cl BNFD RG42 63 J3
Cope Ct MDHD SL6 4 A4
Cope Hall La NWBY RG14 141 P7
Copelands Cl CBLY GU15 95 K2
Copenhagen Cl WHIT RG2 59 J7
Copes La HTWY RG27 84 A7
Copped Hall Dr CBLY GU15 89 J8
Copped Hall Wy CBLY GU15 89 J8
Copperage Rd WANT OX12 107 Q9
Copper Beech BNFD RG42 65 G5
Copper Beech Cl WDSR SL4 37 M8
Copperdale Cl WHIT RG2 59 L3
Copperdale Rd HYS/HAR UB3 43 J2
Copperfield Av SHST GU47 87 L4
Copperfields CAV/SC RG4 44 F3
SUN TW16 * 71 M4
Coppermill Rd
STWL/WRAY TW19 55 H5
Coppice Cl NWBY RG14 7 G9
TADY RG26 103 M6
Coppice Dr STWL/WRAY TW19 54 D6
Coppice Gdns CWTH RG45 86 E2
YTLY GU46 92 C1
Coppice Gn BNFD RG42 2 B1
Coppice Rd WODY RG5 60 E2
The Coppice ASHF TW15 71 H4
Coppid Hl WWKG RG41 * 73 J3
Coppins La IVER SL0 31 H6
Copse Av CAV/SC RG4 45 K3
Copse Cl CBLY GU15 95 G1
SL SL1 38 B1
TILE/CALC RG31 125 P11
WDR/YW UB7 41 M3
Copse Dr WWKG RG41 14 C3
Copse End CBLY GU15 88 F8
Copse Md WODY RG5 46 F5
The Copse TADY RG26 148 C2
WAR/TWY RG10 33 G3
WDSR SL4 * 52 B7
Copse Wy EWKG RG40 73 L7
Copse Wd IVER SL0 30 F2
Copthorn Cl MDHD SL6 35 J2
Copthorne Cl SHPTN TW17 83 J3
Copthorne Dr LTWR GU18 90 B5
Copthorne Ms HYS/HAR UB3 43 G4
Corbett Dr LTWR GU18 89 M7
Corbett Gdns WODY RG5 46 E7
Corbridge Rd WHIT RG2 59 J3
Corby Cl EGH TW20 68 C4
WODY RG5 47 G5
Corby Dr EGH TW20 68 C4
Cordelia Cft BNFD RG42 3 M2
Cordelia Gdns
STWL/WRAY TW19 56 E6
Cordelia Rd STWL/WRAY TW19 56 E6
Corderoy Cl STHA RG19 98 B4
Corderoy Pl CHERT KT16 81 L3
Cordwalles Rd CBLY GU15 88 F6
Cordwallis Rd MDHD SL6 4 F3
Cordwallis St MDHD SL6 4 F2
Cores End Rd BNEND SL8 20 C3
Corfe Gdns FRIM GU16 94 F5
SL SL1 28 C8
Corfe Ms CAV/SC RG4 45 L2
Corfe Pl MDHD SL6 4 A4
Corfield Cl EWKG RG40 85 L3
Corfield Gn WWKG RG41 14 A1
Coriander Wy EARL RG6 59 M5
Corinne Cl WHIT RG2 59 H5
Cormorant Pl SHST GU47 87 L6
Cormorant Wd NWBY RG14 7 K8
Cornbunting Cl SHST GU47 87 K7
Corn Cft BNFD RG42 3 K1
Corner Md NTHA RG18 133 Q11
Cornerside ASHF TW15 71 J5
Cornfield Cl UX/CGN UB8 31 M3
Cornfield Rd WODY RG5 47 G6
Cornfields YTLY GU46 92 B2
Cornflower Cl WWKG RG41 61 K7
Cornhill Cl ADL/WDHM KT15 82 B6
Cornwall Av SLN SL2 28 E5
Cornwall Cl BNFD RG42 64 F4
CBLY GU15 88 F7
MDHD SL6 26 A4
TILE/CALC RG31 125 M10
WDSR SL4 38 A5
WWKG RG41 61 K8
Cornwall Wy STA TW18 69 L4
Cornwell Rd WDSR SL4 54 A5
Cornwood Gdns WHIT RG2 59 J3
Coronation Av DTCH/LGLY SL3 30 A7
WDSR SL4 53 M1
Coronation Cl KSCL RG20 100 B7
Coronation Rd ASC SL5 78 A5
HYS/HAR UB3 43 H4
MDHD SL6 34 D1
YTLY GU46 86 D7
Coronation Sq EWKG RG40 15 J5
RDGW/BURGH RG30 58 B2
Corrie Gdns VW GU25 80 C4
Corrie Rd ADL/WDHM KT15 82 D8
Corsair Cl STWL/WRAY TW19 56 D6
Corsair Rd STWL/WRAY TW19 56 E6
Corsham Rd TILE/CALC RG31 137 R7
Corsham Wy CWTH RG45 75 H8
Corwen Rd
RDGW/BURGH RG30 137 P2
Coster Cl NWBY RG14 141 R1
Cotmans Cl HYS/HAR UB3 43 J1
Cotswold Cl FARN GU14 93 L7
MDHD SL6 5 L7
SL SL1 38 D3
STA TW18 70 A3
UX/CGN UB8 31 L2
Cotswold Rd SHST GU47 86 F5
Cotswold Wy TILE/CALC RG31 125 N12
Cottage Farm Wy EGH TW20 * 69 J8
Cotterell Cl BNFD RG42 2 E1
Cotterell Gdns WAR/TWY RG10 47 M3
Cottesbrooke Cl DTCH/LGLY SL3 40 F8
Cottesmore BRAK RG12 76 A4
Cottesmore Rd WODY RG5 46 D8
Cottrell Cl HUNG RG17 129 N12
Coulson Wy SL SL1 27 K6
County La BNFD RG42 64 E4
Courage Ct RDGW/BURGH RG30 58 B1
Courland Rd ADL/WDHM KT15 82 B7
Course Rd ASC SL5 66 A8
Court Cl MDHD SL6 36 E4
Court Crs SL SL1 28 F7
Court Dr MDHD SL6 26 E3
Courtenay Dr CAV/SC RG4 126 H11
Court Farm Cl SL SL1 38 D1
Courtfield Dr MDHD SL6 4 A6
Courtfield Rd ASHF TW15 71 H4
Court Gdns CBLY GU15 94 D1
Court Hill Rd WANT OX12 106 E1
Courthouse Rd MDHD SL6 4 A5
Courtlands MDHD SL6 5 G7
Courtlands Av DTCH/LGLY SL3 39 M4
Courtlands Hl GOR/PANG RG8 124 G10
Courtlands Rd NWBY RG14 7 G8
Court La IVER SL0 41 J1
SL SL1 27 M4
WDSR SL4 37 J3
Courtney Pl BNFD RG42 * 63 J4
Courtney Rd HTHAIR TW6 57 G2
Courtney Wy HTHAIR TW6 57 G2
Court Rd MDHD SL6 26 E4
Courts Rd EARL RG6 60 B2
The Court Yd STHA RG19 * 97 M3
The Courtyard THLE RG7 137 J7
Coventry Rd READ RG1 45 L7
Coverdale Wy SLN SL2 28 A5
The Coverts TADY RG26 148 D3
The Covert ASC SL5 78 B4
FARN GU14 93 L6
Coves Farm Wd BNFD RG42 63 K7
Covey Cl FARN GU14 94 A6
Cowfold La HTWY RG27 151 N12
Cow La KSCL RG20 109 L11
READ RG1 8 B1
WGFD OX10 111 P7
Cowley Av CHERT KT16 81 M4
Cowley Crs UX/CGN UB8 31 L6
Cowley La CHERT KT16 81 M4
Cowley Mill Rd UX/CGN UB8 31 K3
Cowley Rd UX/CGN UB8 * 31 L3
Coworth Cl ASC SL5 79 H2
Coworth Pk ASC SL5 * 67 J8
Coworth Rd ASC SL5 79 G2
Cowper Cl CHERT KT16 81 M3
Cowper Rd SLN SL2 28 C5
Cowper Wy
RDGW/BURGH RG30 58 D2
Cowslade NWBY RG14 141 R1
Cowslip Crs NTHA RG18 97 M1
Coxborrow Cl MDHD SL6 20 A7
Coxes Av SHPTN TW17 * 71 L8
Coxeter Rd NWBY RG14 6 A1
Coxgreen SHST GU47 87 K8
Cox Green La MDHD SL6 35 K3
Cox Green Rd MDHD SL6 35 L2
Cox's La HEN RG9 113 R5
MARL SN8 138 D11
THLE RG7 98 F3
Crabtree Cl NTHA RG18 133 M4
Crabtree Cnr WGFD OX10 112 H2
Crabtree La NTHA RG18 133 M4
Crabtree Rd CBLY GU15 94 B4
EGH TW20 69 J7
Cradock Rd WHIT RG2 59 G2
Crafts End DID OX11 109 L2
Craig Av RDGW/BURGH RG30 44 B6
Craigwell Cl STA TW18 69 L6
Crail Cl WWKG RG41 74 A3
Crake Pl SHST GU47 87 K6
Cramond Ct EBED/NFELT TW14 57 L7
Cranbourne Av
TILE/CALC RG31 137 N6
WDSR SL4 12 A8
Cranbourne Cl SL SL1 10 A5
Cranbourne Gdns
RDGW/BURGH RG30 125 R12
Cranbourne Rd SL SL1 10 A5
Cranbrook Dr MDHD SL6 25 K5
Cranbury Rd
RDGW/BURGH RG30 44 D7
Crane Ct SHST GU47 87 K6
Crane Gdns HYS/HAR UB3 43 H4
Crane Lodge Rd HEST TW5 43 K6
Crane Rd STWL/WRAY TW19 57 G5
Craneswater HYS/HAR UB3 43 H7
Crane Whf READ RG1 9 H6
Cranford Av STWL/WRAY TW19 56 E6
Cranford Cl STWL/WRAY TW19 56 E6
Cranford Dr HYS/HAR UB3 43 H4
WAR/TWY RG10 47 M6
Cranford La HEST TW5 43 L7
HTHAIR TW6 57 M2
HYS/HAR UB3 42 F6
Cranford Ms READ RG1 * 8 E9
Cranford Park Dr YTLY GU46 86 D8
Cranford Park Rd
HYS/HAR UB3 43 H4
Cranleigh Rd FELT TW13 71 M2
Cranmer Cl TILE/CALC RG31 125 M11
Cranwell Gv LTWR GU18 89 M6
SHPTN TW17 82 F1
Craufurd Ri MDHD SL6 4 F3
Craven Cl HUNG RG17 140 B5
Craven Dene NWBY RG14 7 H2
Craven Rd HUNG RG17 139 M8
NWBY RG14 6 C5
READ RG1 9 L8
Craven Wy HUNG RG17 140 B4
Crawford Cl EARL RG6 60 B3
Crawford Gdns CBLY GU15 94 B1
Crawford Pl NWBY RG14 6 D3
Crawley Cha BNFD RG42 65 H4
Crawley Dr CBLY GU15 88 F8
Crawley Hl CBLY GU15 94 F1
Crawley Rdg CBLY GU15 88 F7
Crawley Wood Cl CBLY GU15 94 F1
Crawshay Dr CAV/SC RG4 126 H11
Crayle St SLN SL2 28 C4
Crayonne Cl SUN TW16 71 L6
Craysleaze CAV/SC RG4 126 D7
Cray's Pond Cl GOR/PANG RG8 112 H12
Crecy Cl WWKG RG41 61 L8
Creden Cl MDHD SL6 4 D2
Crediton Cl WODY RG5 47 G8
Cree's Meadow BFOR GU20 * 90 D3
Cremyll Rd READ RG1 8 C2
Crendon Ct CAV/SC RG4 8 F1
Crescent Dl MDHD SL6 * 5 G7
Crescent Dr MDHD SL6 4 F3
Crescent Rd EWKG RG40 15 H7
READ RG1 45 L8
SHPTN TW17 83 J2
TILE/CALC RG31 137 P1
The Crescent ASHF TW15 70 F3
CHERT KT16 70 A8
EARL RG6 60 C2
EGH TW20 68 F4
HEN RG9 32 D2
HUNG RG17 * 140 A4
HYS/HAR UB3 42 E7
MDHD SL6 4 F4
SHPTN TW17 83 M4
SL SL1 10 E7
THLE RG7 137 J6
THLE RG7 142 E2
THLE RG7 143 Q8
WAR/TWY RG10 23 J8
WEY KT13 83 G7
WHIT RG2 * 59 L4
YTLY GU46 86 D7
Crescent Wy WGFD OX10 111 P1
Cressex Cl BNFD RG42 63 J4
Cressida Cha BNFD RG42 3 M1
Cressingham Rd WHIT RG2 59 J4
Cressington Ct BNEND SL8 20 C2
Cressington Pl BNEND SL8 20 C2
Cress Rd SL SL1 38 D2
Cresswell Rd NWBY RG14 7 M1
Cresswells Md MDHD SL6 36 D5
Crest Cl WAR/TWY RG10 33 G8
The Crest CAV/SC RG4 45 J1
Creswell Cl WHIT RG2 59 H8
Crichton Ct THLE RG7 143 Q8
Cricketers KSCL RG20 131 Q12
Cricketers La BFOR GU20 90 D1
BNFD RG42 65 G3
Cricket Field Gv CWTH RG45 87 K2
Cricket Field Rd UX/CGN UB8 31 M2
Cricketfield Rd WDR/YW UB7 41 L4
Cricket Hl EWKG RG40 85 M3
Cricket Hill La BLKW GU17 92 D3
Cricket Wy WEY KT13 83 L6
Crimea Rd FRIM GU16 95 K6
Crimp Hl EGH TW20 54 A8
WDSR SL4 53 M6
Cripley Rd FARN GU14 93 K8
Crisp Gdns BNFD RG42 63 L5
Crispin Cl CAV/SC RG4 44 D1
Crisp Rd HEN RG9 115 Q11
Crocker Cl ASC SL5 65 M6
Crockers Md KSCL RG20 140 H11
Crockford Cl ADL/WDHM KT15 82 C8
Crockford Pl BNFD RG42 2 A1
Crockhamwell Rd WODY RG5 46 E7
Crocus Md NTHA RG18 98 A2
Crocus Wy WWKG RG41 61 K7
Croft Cl HYS/HAR UB3 42 E7
WWKG RG41 74 A4
Crofters WDSR SL4 54 A5
Crofters Cl FRIM GU16 95 K5
Crofter's Cl SHST GU47 87 G6
The Crofters WDSR SL4 * 54 A5
Crofthill Rd SLN SL2 28 D5
Croft La NWBY RG14 6 B2
YTLY GU46 86 C7
Crofton Cl BRAK RG12 76 E2
Croft Rd EWKG RG40 74 A5
GOR/PANG RG8 112 A12
HUNG RG17 129 M12
NWBY RG14 6 D9
THLE RG7 143 P8
WHIT RG2 145 N4
The Crofts SHPTN TW17 83 L1
The Croft BNFD RG42 2 F1
DID OX11 110 H1
HUNG RG17 140 A4
MDHD SL6 4 B9
MLW SL7 19 J3

Croft Wy FRIM GU16 94 F5
GOR/PANG RG8 113 K10
Cromer Cl TILE/CALC RG31 137 N1
Cromer Rd HTHAIR TW6 57 G2
Cromer Rd West HTHAIR TW6 57 G2
Cromwell Cl HEN RG9 127 R2
Cromwell Dr SL SL1 29 G7
Cromwell Gdns MLW SL7 19 G4
Cromwell Pl NWBY RG14 6 D3
Cromwell Rd ASC SL5 78 B1
CAV/SC RG4 45 H4
CBLY GU15 88 D7
HEN RG9 22 A6
MDHD SL6 4 C4
MLW SL7 19 G4
NWBY RG14 96 E1
Cromwell Ter NWBY RG14 * 141 R1
Cromwell Wy FARN GU14 94 B7
Crondall Ct CBLY GU15 94 B2
Crondall End YTLY GU46 86 C7
Crookham Cl TADY RG26 148 D4
Crookham Common Rd
STHA RG19 98 B8
THLE RG7 99 G8
Crookham Hl STHA RG19 98 A6
Cropper Cl STHA RG19 98 C3
Crosby Gdns YTLY GU46 86 A7
Crosby Hill Dr CBLY GU15 88 F7
Crosfields Cl WHIT RG2 59 L6
Cross Fell BRAK RG12 2 C9
Cross Gdns FRIM GU16 94 F8
Cross Gates Cl BRAK RG12 64 F6
Cross Keys Rd GOR/PANG RG8 112 A7
Crossland Rd READ RG1 9 G7
Crosslands CHERT KT16 81 L7
Cross La FRIM GU16 94 F8
THLE RG7 144 E6
Cross Oak WDSR SL4 12 C7
Cross Rd ASC SL5 78 E5
WEY KT13 * 83 K7
Cross St EWKG RG40 15 H5
READ RG1 9 G6
UX/CGN UB8 31 L1
Crossway BRAK RG12 3 G4
Cross Wy HYS/HAR UB3 43 J2
Crossways EGH TW20 69 K4
SUN TW16 71 M6
Crosswell Cl SHPTN TW17 71 J7
Crosthwaite Wy SL SL1 27 M6
Crouch La WDSR SL4 51 L7
Crouch Oak La
ADL/WDHM KT15 82 C8
Crowfield Dr STHA RG19 97 K3
Crowland Av HYS/HAR UB3 43 G4
Crowle Rd HUNG RG17 117 J4
Crown Acre Cl STHA RG19 97 L3
Crown Cl DTCH/LGLY SL3 40 E7
HYS/HAR UB3 43 H2
Crown Colonnade READ RG1 * 45 L7
Crown Hill Ct ASC SL5 78 B2
Crown La MDHD SL6 5 J4
SLN SL2 28 D1
THLE RG7 137 J7
VW GU25 80 D3
Crown Md NTHA RG18 * 97 L3
Crown Meadow DTCH/LGLY SL3 40 D7
Crown Pl READ RG1 9 J8
SHST GU47 87 L5
Crown Ri CHERT KT16 81 M5
Crown Rd MLW SL7 18 F4
VW GU25 80 C3
Crown Rw BRAK RG12 76 D3
Crown Sq MDHD SL6 * 5 L4
Crown St EGH TW20 69 G3
READ RG1 9 G8
Crown Wy WDR/YW UB7 42 B1
Crown Yd STHA RG19 * 98 B5
Crow Piece La SLN SL2 28 B1
Crowsley Rd HEN RG9 32 C2
Crowsley Wy CAV/SC RG4 126 E5
Crowthorne Rd BRAK RG12 2 D8
BRAK RG12 75 M5
SHST GU47 87 H6
Crowthorne Rd North
BRAK RG12 2 F7
Croxley Ri MDHD SL6 4 C7
Croyde Av HYS/HAR UB3 43 G4
Croyde Cl FARN GU14 94 A8
Cruch La BNFD RG42 50 E5
Cruikshank Lea SHST GU47 87 L8
Crummock Cl SL SL1 27 L7
Crutchley Rd EWKG RG40 15 J3
Cuckoo La CHOB/PIR GU24 90 D8
Cuckoo V CHOB/PIR GU24 90 D8
Cuddesdon Cl GOR/PANG RG8 113 K10
Cufaude La TADY RG26 149 R12
Culford Cl EARL RG6 60 D4
Culham Dr MDHD SL6 26 A4
Cullen Cl YTLY GU46 92 C1
Cullen's Pas MDHD SL6 5 H5
Culley Wy MDHD SL6 35 J2
Culloden Wy WWKG RG41 61 L8
Culver Cft BNFD RG42 63 L5
Culverden Ter WEY KT13 * 83 K7
Culver La EARL RG6 46 A8
Culver Rd EARL RG6 45 M8
NWBY RG14 96 B6
SHST GU47 87 K5
Culvert La UX/CGN UB8 31 K3
Cumberland Av SLN SL2 28 E5
Cumberland Dr BRAK RG12 3 K3
Cumberland Rd ASHF TW15 70 D1
CBLY GU15 95 J2
READ RG1 9 M6
Cumberland St STA TW18 69 K3
Cumberland Wy WWKG RG41 61 K8
Cumbernauld Gdns SUN TW16 71 M3
Cumbrae Cl SLN SL2 11 K4
Cumbria Cl MDHD SL6 35 L2
Cumbrian Wy UX/CGN UB8 31 M2
Cumnor Wy BRAK RG12 3 M8
Cunworth Ct BRAK RG12 75 L3
Curfew Bell Rd CHERT KT16 81 M4
Curfew Yd WDSR SL4 * 13 J5
Curlew Cl STHA RG19 97 L3
Curlew Dr TILE/CALC RG31 137 N4
Curley Hill Rd LTWR GU18 89 L7
Curling Wy NWBY RG14 7 K1
Curls La MDHD SL6 36 A2
Curls Rd MDHD SL6 35 M2
Curl Wy WWKG RG41 14 C7
Curly Bridge Cl FARN GU14 93 M6
Curly's Wy THLE RG7 145 P8
Curnock Ct NWBY RG14 * 6 B7
Curran Cl UX/CGN UB8 31 L5
Curridge Gn NTHA RG18 133 L6
Curridge Rd NTHA RG18 133 J7
Curriers La SL SL1 21 M7
Curtis Cl CBLY GU15 89 J7
Curtis Rd TILE/CALC RG31 137 M5
Curzon Cl WEY KT13 83 G8
Curzon Rd WEY KT13 83 G8
Curzon St RDGW/BURGH RG30 44 D6
Cutbush Cl EARL RG6 60 B6
Cutbush Ct EARL RG6 60 A6
Cutbush La WHIT RG2 59 L8
Cutting Hl MARL SN8 138 E10
The Cuttings NTHA RG18 122 B9
Cwmcarn CAV/SC RG4 126 F12
Cygnet Cl STHA RG19 97 K3
The Cygnets STA TW18 69 M3
Cygnet Wy HUNG RG17 129 M11
Cypress Cl EWKG RG40 74 A6
Cypress Ct VW GU25 80 F1
Cypress Hill Ct FARN GU14 93 M5
Cypress Rd WODY RG5 47 G8
Cypress Wk EGH TW20 68 B4
Cyprus Rd FRIM GU16 95 K6
Cyril Vokins Rd NWBY RG14 97 G4

D

Dacre Av CAV/SC RG4 45 L2
Dagmar Rd WDSR SL4 13 J7
Dagnall Crs UX/CGN UB8 31 L6
Dairy Ct MDHD SL6 36 C7
Dairy La HEN RG9 16 D5
Daisy Meadow EGH TW20 69 G3
Dalby Cl WAR/TWY RG10 47 M6
Dalby Crs NWBY RG14 7 H9
Dalby Gdns MDHD SL6 5 G1
Dalcross BRAK RG12 76 E3
Dale Cl ASC SL5 79 G2
Dale Gdns SHST GU47 87 G6
Daleham Av EGH TW20 69 G4
Dale Lodge Rd ASC SL5 79 G2
Dale Rd SUN TW16 * 71 M5
WHIT RG2 59 H1
WOT/HER KT12 83 M4
Dallas Ter HYS/HAR UB3 43 H3
Dalley Ct SHST GU47 87 K7
Dalston Cl CBLY GU15 95 K3
Dalton Cl RDGW/BURGH RG30 137 Q2
Dalton Gn DTCH/LGLY SL3 40 B5
Damask Cl CHOB/PIR GU24 90 E8
Damer Gdns HEN RG9 22 A6
Damson Gv SL SL1 10 B7
Dandridge Cl DTCH/LGLY SL3 39 L3
Dandridge Dr BNEND SL8 20 E3
Danehill EARL RG6 60 B6
Danehurst Cl EGH TW20 68 E4
Dane Rd ASHF TW15 71 J4
Danes Gdns MDHD SL6 20 B8
Danvers Cl STHA RG19 97 M4
Danywern Dr WWKG RG41 61 J4
Darby Green La BLKW GU17 93 C1
Darby Green Rd BLKW GU17 93 C1
Darby La GOR/PANG RG8 123 R9
Darby V BNFD RG42 64 B4
Darell Rd CAV/SC RG4 44 F3
Dark La GOR/PANG RG8 136 C1
HUNG RG17 129 Q12
THLE RG7 136 A3
TILE/CALC RG31 125 M12
WAR/TWY RG10 32 F4
Darleydale Cl SHST GU47 87 K4
Darley Dene Ct
ADL/WDHM KT15 * 82 C8
Darling's La MDHD SL6 25 G6
Darnley Pk WEY KT13 83 H7
Darracott Cl CBLY GU15 89 H7
Darrell Cl DTCH/LGLY SL3 40 B4
Dart Cl DTCH/LGLY SL3 40 D6
EWKG RG40 73 M7
NTHA RG18 97 K1
Dartington Av WODY RG5 60 D2
Dartmouth Cl BRAK RG12 3 M6
Dartmouth Ter READ RG1 * 9 J8
Dart Rd FARN GU14 93 K8
Darvill's La SL SL1 10 D7
Darvills La WAR/TWY RG10 48 F5
Darwall Dr ASC SL5 65 K7
Darwin Cl WHIT RG2 59 G5
Darwin Pl BRAK RG12 3 H8
Darwin Rd DTCH/LGLY SL3 40 B2
Dashwood Cl BRAK RG12 3 J3
DTCH/LGLY SL3 39 L4
Dashwood Lang Rd
ADL/WDHM KT15 82 E8
Datchet Pl DTCH/LGLY SL3 39 K8
Datchet Rd DTCH/LGLY SL3 39 J4
DTCH/LGLY SL3 54 F2
WDSR SL4 13 K4
WDSR SL4 54 A3
Dauntless Rd THLE RG7 143 R2
Davenport Rd BRAK RG12 3 L5
Daventry Cl DTCH/LGLY SL3 41 H8
Daventry Ct BNFD RG42 2 E3
David Cl HYS/HAR UB3 42 F7
David Rd DTCH/LGLY SL3 55 M1
Davidson Rd DTCH/LGLY SL3 40 B5
Davis Cl MLW SL7 19 G5
Davis Gdns SHST GU47 87 L7
Davis St WAR/TWY RG10 61 K2
Davis Wy WAR/TWY RG10 61 K2
Davy Cl EWKG RG40 15 G8
Dawes East Rd SL SL1 27 L5
Dawes Moor Cl SLN SL2 29 L7
Dawley Ride DTCH/LGLY SL3 41 G8
Dawley Rd HYS/HAR UB3 42 F2
Dawlish Rd WHIT RG2 59 J4
Dawnay Cl ASC SL5 65 M6
Dawnay Rd CBLY GU15 88 F8
Dawn Redwood Cl
DTCH/LGLY SL3 55 G2
Dawsmere Cl CBLY GU15 95 J1
Dawson Cl WDSR SL4 12 C7
Daytona Dr STHA RG19 98 D4
Deacon Cl EWKG RG40 15 G2
Deacon Fld GOR/PANG RG8 112 A7
Deacons La NTHA RG18 133 Q3
Deacon Wy
RDGW/BURGH RG30 44 A4
Deadman's La GOR/PANG RG8 125 M3
Deadmans La STHA RG19 96 D8
Deadman's La THLE RG7 136 G6
Deadmoor La KSCL RG20 100 A4
Deal Av SL SL1 28 B7
Dean Cl WDSR SL4 52 D2
Deanfield Av HEN RG9 127 R1
Deanfield Cl MLW SL7 18 F3
Deanfield Rd HEN RG9 127 Q1
Dean Gv EWKG RG40 15 H3
Dean La MDHD SL6 19 K6
Dean Pde CBLY GU15 * 88 F6
Deans Cl SLN SL2 29 K2
Deans Copse Rd
RDGW/BURGH RG30 137 Q10
THLE RG7 137 K10
Deans Ct BFOR GU20 90 D3
Deans Farm CAV/SC RG4 9 L2
Deansfield Cl MDHD SL6 25 L4
Deansgate BRAK RG12 76 A4
Deansgate Rd READ RG1 9 G8
Deanside CBLY GU15 88 F6
Dean St MLW SL7 18 F4
Deanswood Rd TADY RG26 148 C2
Dean Vw MDHD SL6 20 A8
Deanwood Cl GOR/PANG RG8 113 J9
Deardon Wy WHIT RG2 145 P1
De Beauvoir Rd READ RG1 45 L7
Decies Wy SLN SL2 29 J2
Dedmere Ct MLW SL7 19 H4
Dedmere Ri MLW SL7 19 G4
Dedmere Rd MLW SL7 19 H4
Dedworth Dr WDSR SL4 38 A8
Dedworth Rd WDSR SL4 12 A7
Deena Cl SL SL1 28 A8
Deepcut Bridge Rd FRIM GU16 95 J7
Deepdale BRAK RG12 2 C8
Deepdene Cl READ RG1 8 B7
Deep Fld DTCH/LGLY SL3 39 K7
Deepfield Rd BRAK RG12 3 J4
Deep Well Dr CBLY GU15 94 E1
Deerfield Cl TADY RG26 150 B8
Deerhurst Av WWKG RG41 61 J4
Deer Leap LTWR GU18 90 A6
Dee Rd RDGW/BURGH RG30 44 A7
WDSR SL4 * 37 L7
Deer Rock Hl BRAK RG12 76 C3
Deer Rock Rd CBLY GU15 88 F7
Deer's La GOR/PANG RG8 113 N8
Deerswood MDHD SL6 5 K1
Defence Cl STHA RG19 98 A5
Defford Cl WWKG RG41 61 M5
De Havilland Rd HEST TW5 43 L7
De Havilland Wy
STWL/WRAY TW19 56 D5
Delafield Dr TILE/CALC RG31 137 N6
Delaford Cl IVER SL0 * 31 H7
Delamere Rd EARL RG6 46 B6
Delane Dr WWKG RG41 61 H4
Delaney Cl
RDGW/BURGH RG30 137 R2
Delft Cl RDGW/BURGH RG30 137 R2
Dell Campus BNFD RG42 * 2 C4
BRAK RG12 * 63 L7
Deller St BNFD RG42 2 A1
Dellfield Crs UX/CGN UB8 31 L5
Dellfield Pde UX/CGN UB8 * 31 L5
Dell Gv FRIM GU16 94 F4
Dell Rd EWKG RG40 86 A3
TILE/CALC RG31 125 N12
WDR/YW UB7 42 B3
The Dell MDHD SL6 * 20 A8
MDHD SL6 35 H3
RAND SP11 146 A12
READ RG1 9 J8
YTLY GU46 92 C1
The Delph EARL RG6 60 D4
Delta Cl CHOB/PIR GU24 91 M5
Delta Rd CHOB/PIR GU24 91 M5
Delta Wy EGH TW20 69 J6
De Montfort Gv HUNG RG17 138 G2
De Montfort Rd NWBY RG14 141 R1
READ RG1 8 F3
Denbeigh Pl READ RG1 8 D2
Denbigh Dr HYS/HAR UB3 42 E2
Denbury Gdns WHIT RG2 59 J6
Denby Wy
RDGW/BURGH RG30 137 R1
Dencliffe ASHF TW15 * 71 G3
Dene Cl BRAK RG12 3 H2
CBLY GU15 89 G6
EARL RG6 60 A3
Denefield Gdns
TILE/CALC RG31 125 M12
Dene Hollow DID OX11 109 L2
Dene Wy NWBY RG14 96 B1
Denford La HUNG RG17 130 A10
Denham Cl MDHD SL6 4 A6
Denham Dr YTLY GU46 92 D1
Denham Gv BRAK RG12 * 76 C3
Denham Rd EGH TW20 69 G2
IVER SL0 30 F2
Denison Rd FELT TW13 71 M2
Denly Wy LTWR GU18 90 C5
Denman Dr ASHF TW15 71 H4
Denmark Av WODY RG5 47 G5
Denmark Rd NWBY RG14 7 G4
READ RG1 9 L7
Denmark St EWKG RG40 15 G7
MDHD SL6 4 F2
Denmead Ct BRAK RG12 76 E3
Denmead Rd TADY RG26 148 D2
Dennis Cl ASHF TW15 71 K5
Dennisford Rd KSCL RG20 109 N12
Dennistoun Cl CBLY GU15 94 D1
Dennis Wy SL SL1 27 M8
Dennose Cl EARL RG6 60 A5
Denny Rd DTCH/LGLY SL3 * 40 B4
Denton Cl STHA RG19 97 L4
Denton Rd EWKG RG40 15 H7
Denton Wy FRIM GU16 94 D4
Derby Cl HUNG RG17 117 J4
Derby Rd CAV/SC RG4 45 H3
NWBY RG14 6 D7
UX/CGN UB8 31 L3
Derbyshire Gn BNFD RG42 64 F5
Derby St READ RG1 8 C5
Derek Rd MDHD SL6 26 E6
Deri Dene Cl
STWL/WRAY TW19 * 56 E5
Derley Rd NWDGN UB2 43 L5
De Ros Pl EGH TW20 69 G4
Derrick Cl TILE/CALC RG31 137 N6
Derry Rd FARN GU14 93 M5
Derwent Cl EBED/NFELT TW14 57 M7
WWKG RG41 61 L8
Derwent Dr MDHD SL6 4 C1
SL SL1 27 L6
Derwent Rd EGH TW20 69 H4
LTWR GU18 90 B6
STHA RG19 97 J3
Desborough Cl NWBY RG14 96 F1
SHPTN TW17 83 G4
Desborough Crs MDHD SL6 4 B9
Deseronto Est DTCH/LGLY SL3 * 40 A2
Desford Wy ASHF TW15 56 F8
Dettingen Crs FRIM GU16 95 K6
Dettingen Rd FRIM GU16 95 L6
Devenish La ASC SL5 78 D5
Devenish Rd ASC SL5 78 D3
Devereux Rd WDSR SL4 13 J7
Deverills Wy DTCH/LGLY SL3 40 E4
Deveron Dr
RDGW/BURGH RG30 44 A6
The Devil's Hwy CWTH RG45 86 E1
Devil's Hl HEN RG9 127 K4
Devil's La EGH TW20 69 J4
De-Vitre Gn EWKG RG40 62 F7
Devitt Cl WHIT RG2 59 L5
Devon Av SL SL1 28 E7
Devon Cha BNFD RG42 64 E4
Devon Cl SHST GU47 87 K7
WWKG RG41 61 L8
Devon Dr CAV/SC RG4 45 L2
Devonshire Dr CBLY GU15 88 F7
Devonshire Gdns
TILE/CALC RG31 125 M11
Devonshire Gn SLN SL2 28 D3
Devonshire Pk WHIT RG2 59 L4
Devonshire Rd WEY KT13 * 83 G8
Dewar Sp DTCH/LGLY SL3 40 B6
Dewberry Down NTHA RG18 98 B2
Dewe La RDGW/BURGH RG30 137 Q8
Dexter Wy WWKG RG41 61 G4
Dhoon Ri MDHD SL6 5 H7
Diamedes Av STWL/WRAY TW19 56 D6
Diamond Hl CBLY GU15 88 E7
Diamond Rdg CBLY GU15 88 D7
Diamond Rd SL SL1 11 K6
Diamond Wy WWKG RG41 61 L7
Diana Cl DTCH/LGLY SL3 30 A7
THLE RG7 145 L5
Dianthus Cl CHERT KT16 81 L4
Dianthus Pl BNFD RG42 65 H4
Dibleys DID OX11 110 C2
Dickens Cl CAV/SC RG4 9 L1
HYS/HAR UB3 43 G4
Dickens Pl DTCH/LGLY SL3 41 G8
Dickens Wk NWBY RG14 96 C6
Dickens Wy YTLY GU46 92 C1
Dick Turpin Wy
EBED/NFELT TW14 57 M3
Dido Rd DID OX11 108 F2
Dieppe Cl WWKG RG41 61 L8
Digberry La HEN RG9 114 B1
Digby Rd NWBY RG14 6 B1
Dines Wy NTHA RG18 133 P3
Dingle Rd ASHF TW15 71 H3
Discovery Pk BRAK RG12 * 76 D5
Disraeli Ct DTCH/LGLY SL3 40 D6
Ditchfield La EWKG RG40 73 L6
Ditchling BRAK RG12 76 A4
Dittany Gdns NTHA RG18 97 M1
Ditton Maze MDHD SL6 25 J5
Ditton Park Rd DTCH/LGLY SL3 40 A6
Ditton Rd DTCH/LGLY SL3 39 M8
The Dittons EWKG RG40 73 L8
Dixon Rd TADY RG26 150 B10
Dobsons La HEN RG9 115 Q5
Dockett Eddy La SHPTN TW17 82 F4
Dockett Moorings
CHERT KT16 * 82 F5
Doctors La NTHA RG18 133 N4
Doddington Cl EARL RG6 60 C5
Doddsfield Rd SLN SL2 28 C4
Dodsells Well EWKG RG40 73 M6
Doghurst Av WDR/YW UB7 42 D7
Doghurst Dr WDR/YW UB7 42 D7
Dogkennel La WANT OX12 106 G12
Dog La GOR/PANG RG8 123 J8
HEN RG9 126 G2
Doles Hl WWKG RG41 73 K3
Doles La WWKG RG41 73 L3
Dollis Gn TADY RG26 149 R7
Dolman Rd NWBY RG14 6 E1
Dolphin Cl WWKG RG41 61 J5
Dolphin Ct SL SL1 11 M7
STA TW18 70 A1
Dolphin Ct North STA TW18 * 70 A1
Dolphin Est SUN TW16 * 71 L6
Dolphin Rd SL SL1 11 M6
SUN TW16 71 L6
Dolphin Rd North SUN TW16 71 K6
Dolphin Rd South SUN TW16 71 K6
Dolphin Rd West SUN TW16 71 L6
Doman Rd CBLY GU15 94 A2
Domoney Cl STHA RG19 98 A3
Donaldson Wy WODY RG5 47 G6
Doncastle Rd BRAK RG12 2 A7
Don Cl RDGW/BURGH RG30 44 A6
Donegal Cl CAV/SC RG4 45 J3
Donkey La BNEND SL8 20 C3
WDR/YW UB7 41 L4
Donkin Hl CAV/SC RG4 45 J3
Donnington Cl CBLY GU15 94 B2
THLE RG7 135 L10
Donnington Gdns MDHD SL6 5 C1
READ RG1 9 M8
Donnington Pk NWBY RG14 132 F12
Donnington Pl WWKG RG41 61 K4
Donnington Rd READ RG1 9 M7
Donnington Sq NWBY RG14 96 B1
Donnybrook BRAK RG12 76 A4
Dorcas Ct CBLY GU15 94 B3
Dorchester Cl MDHD SL6 25 K5
Dorchester Ct EWKG RG40 * 62 F8
RDGW/BURGH RG30 44 C8
Dorchester Dr
EBED/NFELT TW14 57 L5
Dorchester Rd WEY KT13 83 H7
Doreen Cl FARN GU14 93 K6
Dorian Dr ASC SL5 66 E6
Doris Rd ASHF TW15 71 K4
Dorking Wy TILE/CALC RG31 137 L6
Dorly Cl SHPTN TW17 83 L1
Dormer Cl CWTH RG45 87 G1
NWBY RG14 96 A8
Dornels SLN SL2 29 L7
Dorney Gv WEY KT13 83 H6
Dorney Reach Rd MDHD SL6 37 H3
Dorney Wood Rd SL SL1 21 L5
Dorneywood Wy NWBY RG14 7 L2
Dorothy St READ RG1 9 G8
Dorset Rd ASHF TW15 70 D1
WDSR SL4 13 H7
Dorset St RDGW/BURGH RG30 44 C6
Dorset V BNFD RG42 64 E4
Dorset Wy WWKG RG41 73 L1
Doublet Cl STHA RG19 97 J3
Douglas Gra WAR/TWY RG10 61 K2
Douglas La STWL/WRAY TW19 54 F4
Douglas Rd ADL/WDHM KT15 82 B7
SLN SL2 28 F6
STWL/WRAY TW19 56 D5
The Doultons STA TW18 * 70 A4
Dove Cl EARL RG6 59 M6
Dovecote Cl WEY KT13 83 H7
Dovecote Rd WHIT RG2 59 H7
Dovedale Cl CAV/SC RG4 44 F3
SHST GU47 87 K4
Dove House Crs SLN SL2 28 A4
Dovehouse Gn WEY KT13 83 K8
Dove La HEN RG9 126 D2
Dover Rd SL SL1 28 B7
Dover St READ RG1 8 E8
Doveton Wy NWBY RG14 7 H1
Dowding Cl WODY RG5 * 47 G7
Dowding Ct CWTH RG45 75 J8
Dower Pk WDSR SL4 52 E3
Dowles Gn EWKG RG40 15 L2
Downend La KSCL RG20 120 H11
Downfield La WAR/TWY RG10 49 H2
Downfield Rd WAR/TWY RG10 49 G2
Downing Rd TILE/CALC RG31 137 N2
Downlands HUNG RG17 118 A8
Downmill Rd BRAK RG12 2 A5
Down Pl WDSR SL4 37 J6
Downs Cl FARN GU14 93 L7
HUNG RG17 117 P7
Downshire Cl HUNG RG17 118 F10
Downshire Sq READ RG1 8 B8
Downshire Wy BNFD RG42 2 D3
BRAK RG12 2 D4
Downside CHERT KT16 * 81 M5
DID OX11 109 J1
Downs Rd DTCH/LGLY SL3 39 M2
KSCL RG20 122 C2
Downs Wy DID OX11 108 F2
TILE/CALC RG31 125 N12
Doyle Gdns YTLY GU46 * 92 C1
Dragon Hill Rd FGDN SN7 104 C1
Drain Hl HUNG RG17 117 J2
Drake Av DTCH/LGLY SL3 39 M4
STA TW18 69 M3
Drake Cl BRAK RG12 76 B2
EWKG RG40 73 L7
Draper Cl STHA RG19 97 M4
Draycott BRAK RG12 76 E2
Drayhorse Dr BAGS GU19 89 L4
Dray's La HEN RG9 126 G2
Drayton Cl BRAK RG12 3 J5
Drayton Ct WDR/YW UB7 * 42 B4
Drayton Gdns WDR/YW UB7 41 M2
Drayton Rd
RDGW/BURGH RG30 44 B6
Draytons Vw STHA RG19 96 E7
Dresden Wy
RDGW/BURGH RG30 137 R1
Drewett Cl WHIT RG2 59 J8
Drifters Dr FRIM GU16 95 K5
Drift Rd MDHD SL6 50 B3
WDSR SL4 51 G3
Drift Wy DTCH/LGLY SL3 40 E8
Driftway Cl EARL RG6 60 C5
Drill Hall Rd CHERT KT16 82 A4
The Drive ASHF TW15 71 K5
BNEND SL8 20 B2
DTCH/LGLY SL3 39 K8
DTCH/LGLY SL3 40 A2
EARL RG6 46 A7
MDHD SL6 * 5 L4
NWBY RG14 6 B9
STWL/WRAY TW19 54 D4
VW GU25 80 F2
Droitwich Cl BRAK RG12 3 K6
Drome Pth WWKG RG41 61 G3
Dropmore Pk SL SL1 * 21 K5
Dropmore Rd SL SL1 21 L7
Drove La NTHA RG18 133 P8
Drovers Wy BRAK RG12 64 F8
WODY RG5 60 E1
Droveside WGFD OX10 111 P1
Droxford Crs TADY RG26 148 C3
Druce Wy STHA RG19 97 M3
Druce Wd ASC SL5 65 L6
Drummond Cl BRAK RG12 64 F6
Drury La THLE RG7 143 R10
Dry Arch Rd ASC SL5 78 F4
Dryden BRAK RG12 76 A4
Dryden Cl NTHA RG18 97 L1
Dryden Rd FARN GU14 93 M8
Drynham Pk WEY KT13 83 L7
Duchess Cl CWTH RG45 75 H7
Duchess Ct WEY KT13 83 K7
Duchess St SL SL1 38 A1
Dudley Cl ADL/WDHM KT15 82 B7
TILE/CALC RG31 137 Q1
Dudley Ms TILE/CALC RG31 125 Q12
Dudley Pl HYS/HAR UB3 42 F4
Dudley Rd ASHF TW15 70 F3
EBED/NFELT TW14 57 K7
NWDGN UB2 43 M2
Dudley Whf IVER SL0 * 40 E1
Dudset La HEST TW5 43 J8
Duffield La SLN SL2 29 H1
Duffield Pk SLN SL2 29 H4
Duffield Rd WODY RG5 46 F5
Duke of Cornwall Av
CBLY GU15 88 D5
Dukes Cl ASHF TW15 71 J2
Dukes Covert BAGS GU19 77 L8
Dukes Hl BAGS GU19 89 L1
Dukeshill Rd BNFD RG42 2 E2
Duke's La ASC SL5 67 G5
WDSR SL4 67 J2
Dukes Meadow BNEND SL8 * 20 D3
Dukes Pl MLW SL7 18 F4
Duke's Ride CWTH RG45 86 F2
Dukes Ride THLE RG7 149 J2
Duke St HEN RG9 22 A4
READ RG1 9 G6
WDSR SL4 12 F4
Dukes Wy UX/CGN UB8 31 K2
Dukes Wd CWTH RG45 87 H1
Dulnan Cl RDGW/BURGH RG30 44 A6
Dulverton Gdns WHIT RG2 59 J4
Dumas Cl YTLY GU46 92 C1
Dumbarton Wy CAV/SC RG4 45 L1
Dunally Pk SHPTN TW17 83 K4
Dunaways Cl EARL RG6 60 D3
Dunbar Cl SLN SL2 11 J2
Dunbar Dr WODY RG5 47 G8
Dunbar Rd FRIM GU16 94 F7
Dunboe Pl SHPTN TW17 83 J4
Duncan Dr EWKG RG40 15 K8
Duncan Gdns GOR/PANG RG8 125 N10
STA TW18 70 A4
Duncannon Crs WDSR SL4 52 D2
Duncan Rd WODY RG5 46 E8
Duncroft WDSR SL4 52 F2
Dundaff Cl CBLY GU15 95 G1
Dundas Cl BRAK RG12 2 E8
Dundee Rd SL SL1 28 B6
Dundela Cl WODY RG5 46 E8
Dunford Pl BNFD RG42 63 L5
Dungells Farm Cl YTLY GU46 92 D2
Dungells La YTLY GU46 92 C1
Dungrove Hill La MDHD SL6 24 E3
Dunholme Cl EARL RG6 60 E3
Dunholme End MDHD SL6 35 M3
Dunkirk Cl WWKG RG41 61 L8
Dunluce Gdns GOR/PANG RG8 125 J9
Dunn Crs HUNG RG17 140 B5
Dunnock Wy WAR/TWY RG10 33 G3
Dunoon Cl TILE/CALC RG31 137 Q6
Dunsfold Rd
RDGW/BURGH RG30 137 R3
Dunsmore Gdns YTLY GU46 92 A1
Dunstall Cl TILE/CALC RG31 137 P2
Dunstall Pk FARN GU14 94 A7
Dunstan Rd NTHA RG18 98 A2
Dunstans Dr WWKG RG41 61 H4
Dunster Cl CAV/SC RG4 127 J12
Dunster Gdns SL SL1 28 C8
Dunt Av WAR/TWY RG10 61 L2
Dunt La WAR/TWY RG10 61 L1
Duouro Cl TADY RG26 103 M6
Duppas Cl SHPTN TW17 83 K2
Dupre Cl SL SL1 38 A2
Durand Rd EARL RG6 60 A5
Durant Wy TILE/CALC RG31 125 P11
Durbidges STHA RG19 102 A6
Durham Av SL SL1 28 C7
Durham Cl WHIT RG2 59 J6
Durham Dr FRIM GU16 95 K5
Durham Rd SHST GU47 87 L4
Durley Md BRAK RG12 76 F2
Durrell Wy SHPTN TW17 83 K3
Dutch Barn Cl
STWL/WRAY TW19 56 D5
Dutton Wy IVER SL0 31 G7
Duval Pl BAGS GU19 89 L3
Dwyer Rd RDGW/BURGH RG30 137 R6
Dyer Rd EWKG RG40 15 M4
Dyer Straits DID OX11 108 F2
Dyson Cl WDSR SL4 12 F9
Dysons Cl NWBY RG14 6 B4
Dysonswood La CAV/SC RG4 126 E10

E

Eagle Cl CWTH RG45 75 G7
Eagle Rd HTHAIR TW6 57 M2
KSCL RG20 101 J4
Eagles Nest SHST GU47 87 G5
Earle Cft BNFD RG42 64 C5
Earleydene ASC SL5 78 B5
Earley Hill Rd EARL RG6 60 A1
Earley Pl READ RG1 9 G6
Earl of Chester Dr FRIM GU16 95 K6
Earlsfield MDHD SL6 36 E4
Earlsfield Cl CAV/SC RG4 45 L2
Earls Gv CBLY GU15 88 E8
Earls La SL SL1 38 A1
Earlswood BRAK RG12 76 B4
Early Ga EARL RG6 * 60 A2
Early Lands THLE RG7 149 J2
Easby Wy EARL RG6 60 D5

Easington Dr EARL RG6 60 E4
East Av HYS/HAR UB3 43 H2
Eastbourne Rd SL SL1 28 C7
Eastbridge SLN SL2 * 11 M5
East Burnham La SLN SL2 28 C2
Eastbury Av TILE/CALC RG31 137 M2
Eastbury Ct BNFD RG42 2 B1
Eastbury Pk WWKG RG41 61 K4
Eastbury Shute HUNG RG17 117 N12
Eastchurch Rd HTHAIR TW6 57 L1
Eastcourt Av EARL RG6 46 A8
East Crs WDSR SL4 12 B6
Eastcroft SLN SL2 28 D5
East Dr SLN SL2 29 G4
TILE/CALC RG31 137 Q5
VW GU25 80 B3
Eastern Av CHERT KT16 70 A8
READ RG1 45 L7
Eastern Dr BNEND SL8 20 E3
Eastern La CWTH RG45 87 M2
Eastern Perimeter Rd
HTHAIR TW6 57 L1
Eastern Rd BRAK RG12 3 K5
Eastfield DID OX11 110 C2
Eastfield Cl SL SL1 * 11 J8
Eastfield La GOR/PANG RG8 113 J12
GOR/PANG RG8 124 H7
Eastfield Rd SL SL1 27 J6
East Gn BLKW GU17 93 J2
Easthampstead Rd BNFD RG42 2 C4
EWKG RG40 15 J6
EWKG RG40 74 F3
Eastheath Av WWKG RG41 74 A2
Eastheath Gdns WWKG RG41 74 B3
Eastholme HYS/HAR UB3 43 J1
East La KSCL RG20 132 H1
Eastlyn Rd TADY RG26 148 G1
Easton Hl KSCL RG20 131 M5
East Paddock MDHD SL6 19 H8
East Park Farm Dr
WAR/TWY RG10 47 H2
East Rp HTHAIR TW6 42 D8
East Rdg BNEND SL8 20 D2
East Rd EBED/NFELT TW14 57 K6
MDHD SL6 4 F5
WDR/YW UB7 42 B4
East Stratton Cl BRAK RG12 76 F2
East St READ RG1 9 H7
East View Cl WAR/TWY RG10 33 G4
East View Rd WAR/TWY RG10 33 G4
East Wk HYS/HAR UB3 43 J2
East Wy HYS/HAR UB3 43 J1
Eastwood Rd WDR/YW UB7 42 C2
WODY RG5 60 E2
Eastworth Rd CHERT KT16 81 M5
Eaton Pl READ RG1 8 D6
Eaton Rd CBLY GU15 94 B2
Ebborn Sq EARL RG6 60 C6
Ebsworth Cl MDHD SL6 26 E3
Eccles Cl CAV/SC RG4 45 J4
Echelforde Dr ASHF TW15 71 G2
Ecton Rd ADL/WDHM KT15 82 B8
Eddington Hl HUNG RG17 129 N11
Eddington Rd BRAK RG12 75 L3
Eden Cl DTCH/LGLY SL3 40 C5
Edenhall Cl TILE/CALC RG31 125 P11
Edenham Cl EARL RG6 60 E4
Edenham Crs READ RG1 58 E1
Eden Wy WWKG RG41 61 H5
Edgar Milward Cl
RDGW/BURGH RG30 44 A5
Edgar Wallace Pl BNEND SL8 20 D1
Edgbarrow Ct CWTH RG45 * 87 G3
Edgbarrowhill Star CWTH RG45 87 G3
Edgbarrow Ri SHST GU47 87 G4
Edgcumbe Park Dr CWTH RG45 87 G1
Edgecombe La NWBY RG14 96 E1
Edgedale Cl CWTH RG45 87 H2
Edgehill Cl NWBY RG14 96 F1
Edgehill St READ RG1 59 H1
Edgell Cl VW GU25 68 F8
Edgell Rd STA TW18 69 M4
Edgemoor Rd FRIM GU16 95 J3
Edgewood Cl CWTH RG45 75 G7
Edinburgh Av SL SL1 28 C7
Edinburgh Dr STA TW18 70 D4
Edinburgh Gdns WDSR SL4 13 K8
Edinburgh Rd MDHD SL6 26 A5
MLW SL7 19 G3
RDGW/BURGH RG30 8 A6
Edison Cl WDR/YW UB7 42 B2
Edith Rd MDHD SL6 25 J7
Edmonds Ct BRAK RG12 3 H2
Edmunds Wy SLN SL2 29 K6
Edney's Hl WWKG RG41 73 K4
Edward Av CBLY GU15 94 A1
Edward Ct STA TW18 70 C4
Edward Rd BFOR GU20 90 D2
EBED/NFELT TW14 57 K4
WAR/TWY RG10 47 H1
Edwards Ct SL SL1 10 E7
Edwards Hl HUNG RG17 117 K4
Edward Wy ASHF TW15 56 F8
Edwin Cl STHA RG19 98 B3
Eeklo Pl NWBY RG14 6 F7
Egerton Rd CBLY GU15 87 M8
SHST GU47 87 L8
SLN SL2 28 A5
WHIT RG2 59 L5
Egerton Wy HYS/HAR UB3 42 D7
Egham By-Pass EGH TW20 68 F2
Egham Hl EGH TW20 68 D4
Eghams Gn BNEND SL8 20 D3
Egremont Dr EARL RG6 60 C3
Egremont Gdns SL SL1 28 C8
Eight Acres SL SL1 27 K5
Eight Av TILE/CALC RG31 137 M4
Eighth Av HYS/HAR UB3 43 J1
TILE/CALC RG31 * 137 M4
Eisenhower Av KSCL RG20 119 L10
Elan Cl RDGW/BURGH RG30 137 R3
Elbow Meadow
DTCH/LGLY SL3 * 41 H8
Eldart Cl RDGW/BURGH RG30 44 B7
Elderberry Wy EARL RG6 60 D5
Elder Cl TILE/CALC RG31 137 N1
Elderfield Crs DID OX11 109 K2
Elder Wy DTCH/LGLY SL3 * 40 B2
Eldon Pl READ RG1 9 K7
Eldon Rd READ RG1 9 K7
Eldon Sq READ RG1 9 K7
Eldon St READ RG1 9 L7
Eldon Ter READ RG1 9 L7
Electra Av HTHAIR TW6 57 M2
Elers Rd HYS/HAR UB3 42 E4
Elford Cl EARL RG6 60 C5
Elford Ct BNFD RG42 63 K3
Elgar Av CWTH RG45 75 H8
Elgar Est WHIT RG2 * 59 H1
Elgar Rd South WHIT RG2 59 H2
Elgarth Dr EWKG RG40 73 M6
Elgin Av ASHF TW15 71 J4
Elgin Crs HTHAIR TW6 57 L1
Elgin Rd BLKW GU17 92 E5
Elgin Wy FRIM GU16 94 F7
Eliot Cl CAV/SC RG4 45 G2
CBLY GU15 89 H7
NTHA RG18 97 L1
Elizabethan Wy
STWL/WRAY TW19 56 D6
Elizabeth Av BAGS GU19 89 M4
NWBY RG14 141 R7
STA TW18 70 C4
Elizabeth Cl BRAK RG12 3 H9
HEN RG9 127 N1
Elizabeth Ct TILE/CALC RG31 * 137 P2
Elizabeth Gdns ASC SL5 78 B2
Elizabeth Rd EWKG RG40 15 J5
HEN RG9 127 P2
MLW SL7 19 G3
Elizabeth Rout Cl THLE RG7 145 N4
Elizabeth Wk WHIT RG2 * 59 H1
Elizabeth Wy SLN SL2 29 H2
Elkington Cl KSCL RG20 100 C7
Ellenborough Cl BRAK RG12 3 J3
Ellen Gdns TADY RG26 149 Q7
Ellerton Cl THLE RG7 137 J6
Ellesfield Av BRAK RG12 75 L1
Ellesmere Cl CAV/SC RG4 45 H3
DTCH/LGLY SL3 39 J6
Ellies Ms ASHF TW15 56 E8
Elliman Av SLN SL2 10 F2
Ellington Ct MDHD SL6 26 E7
Ellington Gdns MDHD SL6 26 E7
Ellington Pk MDHD SL6 4 F1
Ellington Rd FELT TW13 71 M2
MDHD SL6 26 E7
Elliot Dr MLW SL7 19 H2
Elliots Wy CAV/SC RG4 9 G1
Elliott Gdns SHPTN TW17 83 G1
Elliott Ri ASC SL5 65 K7
Ellis Av SL SL1 10 E6
Ellison Cl WDSR SL4 52 F2
Ellison Wy EWKG RG40 14 F6
Ellis Rd CWTH RG45 75 H8
Ellis's Hl WHIT RG2 72 F2
Elmar Gn SLN SL2 28 C4
Elm Bank CHOB/PIR GU24 * 91 L6
YTLY GU46 86 C7
Elmbank Av EGH TW20 68 B4
Elm Cl STWL/WRAY TW19 56 D7
Elm Ct CAV/SC RG4 126 F6
HEN RG9 * 127 R3
Elm Cft DTCH/LGLY SL3 39 L8
Elmcroft GOR/PANG RG8 124 A1
Elmcroft Cl EBED/NFELT TW14 57 M5
FRIM GU16 94 F7
Elmcroft Dr ASHF TW15 * 71 G3
Elmdon Rd HTHAIR TW6 57 M2
Elm Dr CHOB/PIR GU24 91 M5
RDGW/BURGH RG30 143 R1
WDSR SL4 52 B7
Elmfield Gdns NWBY RG14 6 A2
Elm Gv MDHD SL6 4 F4
NTHA RG18 97 K1
Elmgrove Rd WEY KT13 83 G8
Elmhurst TADY RG26 148 D3
Elmhurst Rd DTCH/LGLY SL3 40 C3
GOR/PANG RG8 112 A11
NTHA RG18 97 J1
WHIT RG2 59 K1
Elm La BNEND SL8 20 B1
EARL RG6 59 M4
Elmleigh Ct CAV/SC RG4 45 J4
Elmleigh Cl WWKG RG41 61 M5
Elm Lodge Av
RDGW/BURGH RG30 44 D6
Elm Pk ASC SL5 78 E1
RDGW/BURGH RG30 44 C7
Elm Park Ct
RDGW/BURGH RG30 44 D7
Elm Park Rd
RDGW/BURGH RG30 44 D6
Elm Pl ASHF TW15 71 G3
Elm Rd CAV/SC RG4 126 D11
EARL RG6 59 M4
EBED/NFELT TW14 57 K7
WDSR SL4 52 E1
Elms Av STHA RG19 98 A3
Elms Dr BNEND SL8 20 E3
Elmshott La SL SL1 28 A8
Elmside HTWY RG27 * 150 D9
Elmsleigh Rd STA TW18 69 M3
Elms Rd EWKG RG40 14 F7
The Elms BLKW GU17 * 93 K2
Elmstone Dr TILE/CALC RG31 137 N1
Elmsway ASHF TW15 71 H2
Elms Wy HEN RG9 114 D3
Elm Tree Cl ASHF TW15 71 H3
CHERT KT16 81 L6
Elmwood MDHD SL6 26 D2
Elmwood Cl WODY RG5 46 D6
Elmwood Rd SLN SL2 11 M3
Elruge Cl WDR/YW UB7 41 M3
Elsenwood Crs CBLY GU15 89 G8
Elsenwood Dr CBLY GU15 89 G7
Elsinore Av STWL/WRAY TW19 * 56 E6
Elsley Cl FRIM GU16 94 F8
Elsley Rd TILE/CALC RG31 125 P11
Elstow Av CAV/SC RG4 127 J12
Elstree Cl TILE/CALC RG31 125 P12
Elsworth Cl EBED/NFELT TW14 57 K7
Eltham Av CAV/SC RG4 45 L1
SL SL1 38 A1
Elthorne Rd UX/CGN UB8 31 M3
Elton Dr MDHD SL6 4 D2
Elvaston Wy
RDGW/BURGH RG30 137 R3
Elveden Cl EARL RG6 60 E4
Elvedon Rd FELT TW13 71 M1
Elvendon La GOR/PANG RG8 112 G11
Elvendon Rd GOR/PANG RG8 112 B11
Elwell Cl EGH TW20 69 G4
Ely Av SL SL1 28 E6
Ely Cl FRIM GU16 95 G7
Ely Gv NWBY RG14 97 G1
Elyham GOR/PANG RG8 125 M9
Ely Rd HTHAIR TW6 57 M1
THLE RG7 137 K7
The Embankment
STWL/WRAY TW19 54 C6
Ember Rd DTCH/LGLY SL3 40 D3
Emblen Crs WHIT RG2 72 E4
Embrook Wy TILE/CALC RG31 137 L6
Emden Cl WDR/YW UB7 42 C2
Emerald Cl WWKG RG41 61 L7
Emerald Ct SL SL1 10 F7
Emerald Sq NWDGN UB2 43 M3
Emery Acres GOR/PANG RG8 123 Q8
Emery Down Cl BRAK RG12 65 G8
Emilia Cl MDHD SL6 5 G1
Emley Rd ADL/WDHM KT15 82 A7
Emma La WAR/TWY RG10 33 G4
Emmbrook Ct EARL RG6 59 L4
Emmbrook Ga WWKG RG41 14 B1
Emmbrook Rd WWKG RG41 14 A2
Emmbrook V WWKG RG41 62 A5
Emm Cl WWKG RG41 14 B2
Emmens Cl GOR/PANG RG8 113 P7
Emmens La GOR/PANG RG8 113 Q8
Emmer Green Ct CAV/SC RG4 45 J1
Emmets Nest BNFD RG42 63 J4
Emmets Pk BNFD RG42 63 J4
Emmview Cl WWKG RG41 14 B4
Empress Rd TILE/CALC RG31 137 N5
Enborne Cl TILE/CALC RG31 137 N2
Enborne Ct NWBY RG14 * 141 R5
Enborne Gdns BRAK RG12 3 J1
Enborne Ga NWBY RG14 141 R5
Enborne Gv NWBY RG14 6 B6
Enborne Lodge La
NWBY RG14 141 Q8
Enborne Pl NWBY RG14 6 B6
Enborne Rd KSCL RG20 141 Q5
NWBY RG14 6 A7
Enborne St KSCL RG20 141 N10
NWBY RG14 141 Q9
Enborne Wy THLE RG7 99 H8
Endfield Pl MDHD SL6 25 J8
Enfield Cl UX/CGN UB8 31 M3
Enfield Rd HTHAIR TW6 57 L1
Engineer's Rd STHA RG19 101 J1
Englefield Cl EGH TW20 68 C4
Englefield Rd THLE RG7 136 H6
Engleheart Dr
EBED/NFELT TW14 57 M5
Englehurst EGH TW20 68 C4
Englemere Pk ASC SL5 77 K1
Englemere Rd BNFD RG42 2 B1
Englesfield CBLY GU15 95 J1
English Gdns STWL/WRAY TW19 54 D3
English La HEN RG9 113 Q1
Ennerdale BRAK RG12 2 C8
Ennerdale Cl EBED/NFELT TW14 57 L7
Ennerdale Crs SL SL1 27 L6
Ennerdale Rd WHIT RG2 59 K3
Ennerdale Wy STHA RG19 97 J3
Ensign Cl STWL/WRAY TW19 56 D7
Ensign Wy STWL/WRAY TW19 56 D7
Enstone Rd WODY RG5 47 G6
Enterprise Wy STHA RG19 98 C4
Epping Cl READ RG1 8 D7
Epping Wy BRAK RG12 76 F1
Epsom Cl CBLY GU15 88 C6
Epsom Ct READ RG1 8 C9
Epsom Crs NWBY RG14 7 H8
Equine Wy NWBY RG14 96 D7
Erica Cl CHOB/PIR GU24 90 E8
SL SL1 28 A8
Erica Dr EWKG RG40 15 J8
Eric Av CAV/SC RG4 126 G12
Eriswell Cl EARL RG6 60 E4
Eriswell Rd WOT/HER KT12 83 M8
Erkenwald Cl CHERT KT16 81 L3
Erleigh Court Dr EARL RG6 46 A7
Erleigh Court Gdns EARL RG6 46 A7
Erleigh Dene NWBY RG14 6 C8
Erleigh Rd READ RG1 9 L8
Ermin Cl MARL SN8 116 A6
Ermin St HUNG RG17 116 F9
HUNG RG17 129 P1
KSCL RG20 131 Q12
Errington Dr WDSR SL4 12 D5
Erskine Cl TADY RG26 148 H1
Escot Rd SUN TW16 71 L5
Esher Crs HTHAIR TW6 57 M1
Esher Rd CBLY GU15 89 G5
Eskdale Gdns MDHD SL6 36 D5
Eskdale Rd UX/CGN UB8 31 K3
WWKG RG41 61 G2
Eskdale Wy CBLY GU15 95 J2
Eskin Cl RDGW/BURGH RG30 44 A7
Essame Cl EWKG RG40 15 J5
Essex Av SLN SL2 28 E6
Essex Cl ADL/WDHM KT15 82 C8
FRIM GU16 95 G7
Essex Pl HUNG RG17 117 K3
NWBY RG14 * 141 R1
Essex Ri BNFD RG42 64 F5
Essex St NWBY RG14 141 R7
WHIT RG2 59 H1
Essex Wy CAV/SC RG4 126 G7
Esther Carling La HEN RG9 126 D2
Ethel Rd ASHF TW15 70 E3
Eton Cl DTCH/LGLY SL3 39 J6
Eton Ct STA TW18 69 M3
WDSR SL4 13 J3
Eton Pl MLW SL7 18 F4
Eton Rd DTCH/LGLY SL3 39 J6
HYS/HAR UB3 43 H7
Eton Sq WDSR SL4 13 J3
Eton Wick Rd WDSR SL4 38 A4
Europa Cl TADY RG26 149 R7
Eustace Crs EWKG RG40 15 K2
Evedon BRAK RG12 76 B4
Evelyn Ct WODY RG5 60 F1
Evelyn Crs SUN TW16 71 M6
Evelyn Wy SUN TW16 71 M6
Evendon's Cl WWKG RG41 74 A3
Evendon's La WWKG RG41 73 K3
Evenlode MDHD SL6 5 H3
Evenlode Rd BNEND SL8 20 D2
Evenlode Wy SHST GU47 87 J6
Everard Av SL SL1 10 E6
Everest Rd CBLY GU15 88 D6
CWTH RG45 75 H8
STWL/WRAY TW19 56 D6
Evergreen Ct
STWL/WRAY TW19 * 56 D6
Evergreen Dr TILE/CALC RG31 137 R6
Evergreen Oak Av WDSR SL4 54 A2
Evergreen Rd FRIM GU16 94 F4
Evergreen Wy
STWL/WRAY TW19 56 D6
WWKG RG41 14 B8
Everington La NTHA RG18 134 C1
Everland Rd HUNG RG17 129 M12
Eversley Rd HTWY RG27 85 M6
WHIT RG2 72 E4
Eversley St HTWY RG27 85 G5
Eversley Wy EGH TW20 69 J7
Evesham Pl WWKG RG41 61 L6
Evesham Rd CAV/SC RG4 45 H1
Evesham Wk SHST GU47 87 J5
Evreham Rd IVER SL0 31 G7
Evreux Cl STHA RG19 * 98 B4
Ewhurst Rd TADY RG26 148 A11
Exbourne Rd WHIT RG2 59 J6
Exchange Rd ASC SL5 78 C2
Exeforde Av ASHF TW15 71 G2
Exeter Ct WHIT RG2 59 H6
Exeter Gdns YTLY GU46 86 B7
Exeter Rd HTHAIR TW6 57 L2
Exeter Wy HTHAIR TW6 57 L1
THLE RG7 137 K7
Exmoor Rd STHA RG19 98 B3
Explorer Av STWL/WRAY TW19 56 E7
Express Wy NWBY RG14 97 G4
Eynsford Cl CAV/SC RG4 45 L1
Eynsham Cl WODY RG5 46 E6

F

Faggs Rd EBED/NFELT TW14 57 M3
Fairacre MDHD SL6 4 B6
Fair Cl NWBY RG14 * 6 E6
Faircroft SLN SL2 28 D5
Faircross BRAK RG12 2 F6
NTHA RG18 133 M4
Faircross Rd
RDGW/BURGH RG30 58 C1
Fairdale Gdns HYS/HAR UB3 43 J2
Fairey Av HYS/HAR UB3 43 H3
Fairfax BNFD RG42 2 D3
Fairfax Cl CAV/SC RG4 45 H4
Fairfax Pl NWBY RG14 97 G1
Fairfax Rd FARN GU14 94 B7
Fairfield KSCL RG20 121 R2
WGFD OX10 111 N1
Fairfield Ap STWL/WRAY TW19 54 D5
Fairfield Av DTCH/LGLY SL3 39 L7
STA TW18 69 M2
Fairfield Cl BNEND SL8 20 B1
Fairfield Dr FRIM GU16 94 E3
Fairfield La CHOB/PIR GU24 90 F7
SLN SL2 28 D3
Fairfield Pk THLE RG7 * 143 P9
Fairfield Rd GOR/PANG RG8 112 B11
SL SL1 27 L4
STWL/WRAY TW19 54 D5
WDR/YW UB7 42 A1
Fairfields CHERT KT16 82 A5
HUNG RG17 138 H1
Fairford Rd MDHD SL6 4 F3
TILE/CALC RG31 125 N12
Fairhaven EGH TW20 68 F3
Fairholme EBED/NFELT TW14 57 K6
Fairholme Rd ASHF TW15 70 E3
Fair Lawn Gn WHIT RG2 59 M5
Fairlawn Pk WDSR SL4 52 E3
Fairlawn Rd TADY RG26 148 F3
Fairlawns Cl STA TW18 70 B4
Fairlea MDHD SL6 35 J2
Fairlie Rd SL SL1 28 C7
Fairlight Av WDSR SL4 13 J8
Fairlop Cl TILE/CALC RG31 137 P6
Fairmead Cl HEST TW5 43 M7
SHST GU47 87 L7
Fairmead Ct CBLY GU15 94 C2
Fairmead Rd WHIT RG2 145 Q1
Fair Mile HEN RG9 115 P9
Fair Oak La THLE RG7 150 C3
Fairoak Wy TADY RG26 103 M5
Fairsted Cl RDGW/BURGH RG30 44 A6
Fairview Av EARL RG6 46 B8
Fairview Dr SHPTN TW17 82 F2
Fairview Rd EWKG RG40 15 G8
HUNG RG17 138 H1
MDHD SL6 27 J7
SLN SL2 28 B5
Fairwater Dr WODY RG5 46 D8
Fairway CHERT KT16 82 B5
Fairway Av
RDGW/BURGH RG30 137 P4
WDR/YW UB7 41 L1
Fairway Dr WAR/TWY RG10 * 47 G1
Fairway Hts CBLY GU15 89 H8
Fairways ASHF TW15 71 G4
The Fairway CBLY GU15 95 G3
MDHD SL6 35 K3
SL SL1 27 L4
Faithfull Cl BNFD RG42 64 B4
Fakenham Cl EARL RG6 60 A6
Fakenham Wy SHST GU47 87 K5
Falaise EGH TW20 68 E3
Falcon Av WHIT RG2 59 M5
Falcon Cl LTWR GU18 89 M6
Falcon Dr STWL/WRAY TW19 56 D5
Falcon Flds TADY RG26 142 D12
Falcon Wy SUN TW16 71 L7
WWKG RG41 14 A6
YTLY GU46 * 86 B8
Falconwood EGH TW20 68 E3
Falkland Dr NWBY RG14 6 C9
Falkland Garth NWBY RG14 141 R7
Falkland Rd CAV/SC RG4 45 H4
NWBY RG14 141 R8
Fallowfield YTLY GU46 86 B7
Fallowfield Cl CAV/SC RG4 45 H2
The Fallows MDHD SL6 * 5 K1
Falmouth Cl CBLY GU15 95 G2
Falmouth Rd SL SL1 28 C7
WHIT RG2 59 J7
Falmouth Wy STHA RG19 98 B3
Falstaff Av EARL RG6 59 M4
Fanes Cl BNFD RG42 2 B3
Fane Wy MDHD SL6 4 D9
Fannys La THLE RG7 134 D9
Faraday Cl SLN SL2 * 28 D6
WHIT RG2 72 E7
Faraday Rd FARN GU14 94 C8
NWBY RG14 7 G3
SLN SL2 28 D6
Faraday Wy WHIT RG2 73 G6
Farcrosse Cl SHST GU47 87 J6
Fareham Dr YTLY GU46 86 B7
Faringdon Cl SHST GU47 87 J5
Faringdon Dr BRAK RG12 76 D2
Farleigh Ms CAV/SC RG4 45 L1
Farley Castle THLE RG7 * 72 C7
Farley Copse BNFD RG42 63 L6
Farman Cl WODY RG5 47 H6
Farm Cl ASC SL5 78 C2
BNFD RG42 2 A1
CAV/SC RG4 126 E5
CHERT KT16 81 G3
CWTH RG45 75 J7
GOR/PANG RG8 125 N9
MDHD SL6 25 J7
MDHD SL6 36 E5
SHPTN TW17 83 G4
STA TW18 69 L3
YTLY GU46 92 D1
Farm Ct FRIM GU16 * 94 F4
Farm Crs SLN SL2 29 K6
Farm Dr TILE/CALC RG31 137 M4
WDSR SL4 54 B5
Farmers Cl MDHD SL6 35 J2
WHIT RG2 59 H8
Farmers End WAR/TWY RG10 47 H2
Farmer's Rd STA TW18 69 L3
Farmers Wy MDHD SL6 35 J1
Farmhouse Ms NTHA RG18 98 A1
Farmiloe Cl GOR/PANG RG8 125 N10
Farm Rd BNEND SL8 20 B2
FRIM GU16 94 E4
GOR/PANG RG8 112 A12
HEN RG9 22 B6
MDHD SL6 25 J7
MDHD SL6 27 J8
STA TW18 70 B4
Farm Vw YTLY GU46 92 D1
Farm Wy STWL/WRAY TW19 55 M5
Farm Yd WDSR SL4 13 K4
Farnborough Ga FARN GU14 * 94 C7
Farnborough Rd FARN GU14 94 C7
Farnburn Av SL SL1 28 D6
Farnell Ms WEY KT13 83 H7
Farnell Rd STA TW18 70 A1
Farnesdown Dr WWKG RG41 14 A2
Farnham Cl BRAK RG12 3 J5
Farnham Dr CAV/SC RG4 45 L2
Farnham La SLN SL2 28 B3
Farnham Park La SLN SL2 28 E2
Farnham Rd SL SL1 10 A1
SL SL1 28 E6
SLN SL2 28 D4
Farningham BRAK RG12 76 E3
Farnsfield Cl EARL RG6 60 A6
Farrell Cl CBLY GU15 94 B3
Farriers Cl TADY RG26 149 R7
WODY RG5 46 E7
Farriers La KSCL RG20 109 L11
Farringdon Ct READ RG1 45 L8
Farringdon Wy TADY RG26 148 D3
Farrington Acres WEY KT13 * 83 K7
Farrowdene Rd WHIT RG2 59 J6
The Farthingales MDHD SL6 5 L5
Farthing Green La SLN SL2 29 J3
Fatherson Rd READ RG1 9 L7
Faulkner Pl BAGS GU19 89 L2
Faulkner Sq HUNG RG17 * 129 N12
Faversham Rd SHST GU47 87 K5
Fawcett Crs WODY RG5 46 D8
Fawcett Rd WDSR SL4 12 F6
Fawler Md BRAK RG12 76 F1
Fawley Bottom La HEN RG9 115 N6
Fawley Cl MDHD SL6 25 M4
Fawley Rd RDGW/BURGH RG30 58 C1
Fawns Manor Rd
EBED/NFELT TW14 57 K7
Fawsley Cl DTCH/LGLY SL3 41 G7
Faygate Wy EARL RG6 60 B5
Feathers La STWL/WRAY TW19 55 G8
Felbridge Cl FRIM GU16 94 F4
Felix La SHPTN TW17 83 L3
Felixstowe Cl EARL RG6 60 D4
Fellow Gn CHOB/PIR GU24 90 F8
Fellow Green Rd
CHOB/PIR GU24 90 F8
The Fells TILE/CALC RG31 137 L4
Felstead Cl EARL RG6 59 M4
Feltham Hill Rd ASHF TW15 71 G3
Feltham Rd ASHF TW15 71 G3
Felthorpe Cl EARL RG6 60 A6
Felton Wy TILE/CALC RG31 137 N2
Fencote BRAK RG12 76 D4
Fennel Cl ASC SL5 78 A1
EARL RG6 59 M5
NWBY RG14 96 F1
Fennscombe Ct
CHOB/PIR GU24 90 E8
Fenns La CHOB/PIR GU24 90 E8
Fenton Av STA TW18 70 C4
Fermi Av DID OX11 108 G1
Fernbank EWKG RG40 73 K8
Fernbank Crs ASC SL5 65 K6
Fernbank Pl ASC SL5 65 J6
Fernbank Rd ASC SL5 65 K7
Fernbrook Rd CAV/SC RG4 44 D1
Fern Cl CWTH RG45 75 H7
FRIM GU16 95 J3
TILE/CALC RG31 * 137 N5
Ferndale Av CHERT KT16 81 L7
RDGW/BURGH RG30 137 R6
Ferndale Cl TILE/CALC RG31 125 Q11
Ferndale Ct STHA RG19 97 M3
Ferndale Crs UX/CGN UB8 31 L4
WWKG RG41 14 A2
Ferndale Pk MDHD SL6 * 37 G6
Ferndale Rd ASHF TW15 70 D3
Fern Dr MDHD SL6 27 K7
Ferne Cl GOR/PANG RG8 112 A11
The Fernery STA TW18 69 L3
Fernes Cl UX/CGN UB8 31 L7
Fern Gln TILE/CALC RG31 137 N1
Fernhill Cl BLKW GU17 93 L5
BNFD RG42 2 A1
Fernhill La BLKW GU17 93 M5
Fernhill Rd BLKW GU17 93 L4
FARN GU14 93 L7
FARN GU14 93 L8
Fernhill Wk BLKW GU17 93 M5
Fernhurst Rd ASHF TW15 71 J2
TILE/CALC RG31 137 N6
Ferniehurst CBLY GU15 94 F2
Fernlands Cl CHERT KT16 81 L7
Fern La MLW SL7 20 A1
Fernleigh MDHD SL6 * 20 A8
Fernleigh Ri FRIM GU16 95 J7
Fernley Ct MDHD SL6 4 D1
Fern Wk ASHF TW15 70 D3
Ferrard Cl ASC SL5 65 K6
Ferrers Av WDR/YW UB7 41 M2
Ferrers Cl SL SL1 38 A1
Ferrier Gv NWBY RG14 7 G9
Ferry Av STA TW18 69 L5
Ferry End MDHD SL6 * 36 E2
Ferry La BNEND SL8 20 D5
CHERT KT16 82 A3
GOR/PANG RG8 111 R12
GOR/PANG RG8 111 R6
HEN RG9 16 F8
MDHD SL6 20 D7
MLW SL7 23 K1
SHPTN TW17 83 G5
STA TW18 70 C8
STWL/WRAY TW19 55 H8
WAR/TWY RG10 32 E4
WGFD OX10 111 Q6
Ferry Rd GOR/PANG RG8 112 A6
MDHD SL6 36 E2
Ferryside MDHD SL6 * 36 E2
Ferry Sq SHPTN TW17 83 H4
Ferry Wy WGFD OX10 111 Q2
Fettiplace HUNG RG17 118 F11
Fetty Pl MDHD SL6 35 M2
Fidler's La KSCL RG20 109 L11
Fidlers Wk WAR/TWY RG10 33 G4
Field Cl HSLWW TW4 43 K8
HYS/HAR UB3 42 E7
THLE RG7 143 R4
Field End CHOB/PIR GU24 90 F8
Fielden Pl BRAK RG12 3 K4
The Fielders HTWY RG27 85 L6
Fieldfare Av YTLY GU46 86 A8
Fieldfare Dr BRAK RG12 75 K1
Fieldhead Gdns BNEND SL8 20 C3
Field House Cl ASC SL5 78 A5
Fieldhouse La MLW SL7 19 H4
Fieldhouse Wy MLW SL7 19 H4
Field Hurst DTCH/LGLY SL3 40 B4
Fielding Gdns CWTH RG45 87 H2
DTCH/LGLY SL3 39 L2
Fielding Rd MDHD SL6 25 K7
SHST GU47 87 L8
The Fieldings MDHD SL6 36 B7
Field La FRIM GU16 94 E5
Field Pk BRAK RG12 3 K2
Fieldridge NWBY RG14 96 E1
Field Rd FARN GU14 93 M5
KSCL RG20 120 D6
READ RG1 8 D8
Field Vw CAV/SC RG4 45 H3
EGH TW20 69 J3
FELT TW13 71 K2
Field Wy UX/CGN UB8 31 M5
Fieldway WWKG RG41 61 K4
Fifehead Cl ASHF TW15 70 E4
Fifield La WDSR SL4 51 K2
Fifield Rd MDHD SL6 36 F8
Fifth Av HYS/HAR UB3 43 H1
TILE/CALC RG31 137 M4
Fifth Rd NWBY RG14 6 A8
Fifth St STHA RG19 101 H1
Filbert Dr TILE/CALC RG31 137 N2
Filey Rd READ RG1 45 L7
Filey Sp SL SL1 38 D3
Filmer Rd WDSR SL4 52 D1
Finbeck Wy EARL RG6 59 M6
Fincham End Dr CWTH RG45 86 F2
Finchampstead Rd EWKG RG40 14 F8
EWKG RG40 85 L1
Finch Cl TADY RG26 148 E3
Finch Ct MDHD SL6 4 D9
Finches La MARL SN8 116 A5
Finch Rd EARL RG6 60 C2
Finch Wy THLE RG7 143 R3
Findhorn Cl SHST GU47 87 K7
The Findings FARN GU14 93 L6
Finlay Dr HEN RG9 22 A4
Finlay Gdns ADL/WDHM KT15 82 C8
Finmere BRAK RG12 76 C3

nart Cl WEY KT13 83 J8
nney Dr BFOR GU20 90 D2
nstock Cl EARL RG6 60 D5
nstock Gn BRAK RG12 76 F1
ntry Pl FARN GU14 93 L7
rbank Pl EGH TW20 68 B4
r Cl STHA RG19 102 D1
WGFD OX10 112 H3
r Cottage Rd EWKG RG40 73 L6
rcroft Cl TILE/CALC RG31 137 N1
rcroft Rd EGH TW20 68 C5
r Dr BLKW GU17 93 K3
reball Hl ASC SL5 78 D4
rfield Rd ADL/WDHM KT15 82 A8
rglen Dr YTLY GU46 86 D7
rgrove Rd HTWY RG27 86 A8
YTLY GU46 86 B8
rlands BRAK RG12 76 C2
rlands Av CBLY GU15 94 D1
rmstone Cl EARL RG6 60 C5
rs Av WDSR SL4 12 B9
rs Cl EWKG RG40 73 M7
IVER SL0 30 E1
rs Dr DTCH/LGLY SL3 40 A1
HEST TW5 43 K7
r's End THLE RG7 143 Q4
r's La MDHD SL6 35 H2
RDGW/BURGH RG30 58 D1
r's Rd TILE/CALC RG31 137 N4
rst Av HYS/HAR UB3 43 H1
MLW SL7 19 J4
THLE RG7 142 E12
TILE/CALC RG31 137 M4
rst Crs SL SL1 28 E6
e Firs EBED/NFELT TW14 * 57 L5
HUNG RG17 139 Q9
NTHA RG18 97 K2
READ RG1 * 8 C8
rst St STHA RG19 101 J1
rst St East STHA RG19 101 J1
rth Cl THLE RG7 149 K2
r Tree Av SLN SL2 29 H5
WDR/YW UB7 42 C3
r Tree Cl ASC SL5 78 A4
rtree Cl SHST GU47 86 F6
r Tree Cnr TADY RG26 142 A12
r Tree La NWBY RG14 97 G2
r Tree Paddock KSCL RG20 108 G8
r Tree Pl ASHF TW15 * 71 G2
rview Cl MLW SL7 19 H5
rwood Dr CBLY GU15 94 C1
rwood Rd VW GU25 79 L3
sher Gn BNFD RG42 64 D3
sherman's La THLE RG7 142 C7
shermans Retreat MLW SL7 19 G5
sherman's Wy BNEND SL8 20 D4
shers Ct CAV/SC RG4 127 J12
sher's La NTHA RG18 133 N9
shers Wd ASC SL5 79 J5
shery Rd MDHD SL6 36 E1
shguard Sp SL SL1 11 M7
shponds Cl WWKG RG41 14 D9
shponds Est WWKG RG41 * 14 D9
shponds Rd WWKG RG41 14 D9
sk Cl SUN TW16 71 M4
tzrobert Pl EGH TW20 69 G4
tzroy Cl BRAK RG12 76 A3
tzroy Crs WODY RG5 47 G8
ve Acre TILE/CALC RG31 137 M1
agstaff Sq STHA RG19 98 A4
ambards CAV/SC RG4 45 J4
amborough Cl EARL RG6 60 E4
amborough Sp SL SL1 38 C2
amingo Cl WWKG RG41 73 L1
e Flats BLKW GU17 93 H2
axman Cl EARL RG6 59 M4
ecker Cl NTHA RG18 97 L1
eet Cl WWKG RG41 61 L8
eetham Gdns EARL RG6 60 B5
eet Hl EWKG RG40 85 J4
eet La EWKG RG40 85 H4
eetway EGH TW20 69 J8
eetwood Cl NWBY RG14 96 F1
eetwood Rd SLN SL2 11 H4
eming Cl FARN GU14 94 D8
WHIT RG2 72 E7
eming Rd NWBY RG14 7 G3
emish Flds CHERT KT16 81 M5
emish Pl BNFD RG42 64 D5
etcher Gdns BNFD RG42 63 K6
exford Gn BRAK RG12 75 L3
ntgrove BRAK RG12 3 J2
ntjack Pl HUNG RG17 117 J4
ntlock Cl STWL/WRAY TW19 56 A3
odden Dr TILE/CALC RG31 137 P6
oral Ct WAR/TWY RG10 * 33 G8
oral Wy NTHA RG18 97 M1
oreat Gdns NWBY RG14 6 A7
orence Av MDHD SL6 5 J2
orence Cl YTLY GU46 86 C8
orence Gdns NTHA RG18 97 J1
STA TW18 70 B5
orence Rd NWDGN UB2 43 M4
SHST GU47 87 L7
orence Wk READ RG1 9 M6
orence Wy UX/CGN UB8 31 L1
orian Gdns
RDGW/BURGH RG30 58 B1
ower's Hl GOR/PANG RG8 124 G10
owers Piece GOR/PANG RG8 123 K8
bney St READ RG1 8 F7
kerham Rd STHA RG19 98 B4
lder's La BNFD RG42 3 G1
liejohn Wy MDHD SL6 35 H4
lkestone Ct DTCH/LGLY SL3 40 C5
llet Cl WDSR SL4 54 B5
lly Gn GOR/PANG RG8 113 J10
lly La TADY RG26 150 B6
THLE RG7 143 P1
THLE RG7 150 B5
lly Orchard Rd
GOR/PANG RG8 113 J9
lly Rd HUNG RG17 116 G4
HUNG RG17 139 N8
e Folly LTWR GU18 * 90 B7
NWBY RG14 7 G8
ntmell Cl ASHF TW15 71 G3
ntmell Pk ASHF TW15 70 F3
ntwell Cl MDHD SL6 25 H6
ntwell Dr
RDGW/BURGH RG30 137 R5
ntwell Rd NWBY RG14 7 H8
rbes Cha SHST GU47 87 K7
rbury La HUNG RG17 140 B7
rbury Rd READ RG1 9 G5
rbury Sq READ RG1 9 G5
e Forbury READ RG1 9 H5
rdbridge Cl CHERT KT16 82 B5
rdbridge Rd ASHF TW15 70 E4
SUN TW16 83 L3
rd Cl ASHF TW15 70 E4
SHPTN TW17 83 G2
rdham Wy EARL RG6 60 C5
rdingbridge Cl CHERT KT16 * 82 B5
rd La HTWY RG27 84 A2
IVER SL0 31 J7
rd Rd ASHF TW15 70 F2
CHERT KT16 82 B5
CHOB/PIR GU24 91 J5
rdwater Rd CHERT KT16 82 B5
rdwells Dr BRAK RG12 76 F1

The Forehead THLE RG7 144 D10
Forest Cl ASC SL5 65 J8
TADY RG26 142 A12
Forest Ct WWKG RG41 74 A2
Forest Dean WHIT RG2 59 J7
Forest Dr SUN TW16 71 M5
Forest End Rd SHST GU47 86 F5
Foresters Sq BRAK RG12 3 M7
Foresters Wy CWTH RG45 75 M7
EWKG RG40 75 L6
Forest Gn MDHD SL6 36 B8
Forest Green Rd MDHD SL6 51 J1
Forest Hl RDGW/BURGH RG30 125 R12
Forest Hills CBLY GU15 94 B2
Forest La TADY RG26 148 F4
Forest Pk WDSR SL4 52 E5
Forest Rd ASC SL5 65 K4
BNFD RG42 64 A3
CWTH RG45 87 J1
EWKG RG40 62 A4
WDSR SL4 52 D1
WWKG RG41 61 M5
Forge Cl CAV/SC RG4 9 K2
HUNG RG17 140 A4
TADY RG26 150 A8
Forge Hl NTHA RG18 122 C9
The Forge HUNG RG17 129 M12
Forlease Cl MDHD SL6 5 K6
Forlease Dr MDHD SL6 5 K6
Forlease Rd MDHD SL6 5 J5
Formby Cl DTCH/LGLY SL3 40 E4
EARL RG6 60 E3
Forndon Cl EARL RG6 60 E4
Forris Av HYS/HAR UB3 43 H1
Forsete Pl READ RG1 45 L8
Forsters La WANT OX12 106 C4
The Forsters THLE RG7 * 142 B7
Fortescue Rd WEY KT13 82 F8
Forth Cl FARN GU14 93 K8
Fortrose Cl SHST GU47 87 K7
Forty Green Dr MLW SL7 18 D4
Forum THLE RG7 * 137 J8
Fosseway CWTH RG45 86 F1
Fossewood Dr CBLY GU15 88 D6
Foster Av WDSR SL4 52 E2
Fosters Gv BFOR GU20 78 B8
Fosters La WODY RG5 46 E8
Fosters Pth SLN SL2 28 B5
Fotherby Ct MDHD SL6 5 J5
Fotheringay Gdns SL SL1 28 C8
Foundry Ct CHERT KT16 82 A4
Foundry La DTCH/LGLY SL3 55 H2
Foundry Pl READ RG1 8 F8
Fountain Gdns WDSR SL4 13 K9
Fountains Garth BRAK RG12 2 C7
Fourth Av HYS/HAR UB3 43 H1
MLW SL7 19 J4
TILE/CALC RG31 137 M4
Fourth St STHA RG19 101 H1
Fowler Cl EARL RG6 60 A3
Fowlers La BNFD RG42 2 E3
Fowlers Md CHOB/PIR GU24 91 L4
Foxborough THLE RG7 145 P8
Foxborough Cl DTCH/LGLY SL3 40 C5
Foxborough Ct MDHD SL6 36 A2
Foxbury HUNG RG17 117 K4
Fox Cl THLE RG7 143 Q3
Foxcombe Dr TILE/CALC RG31 137 N3
Foxcote EWKG RG40 74 A7
Fox Covert LTWR GU18 90 A6
Fox Covert Cl ASC SL5 78 C2
Foxdown Cl CBLY GU15 94 C1
Fox Dr YTLY GU46 86 D7
Foxes Piece MLW SL7 19 G4
Foxes Wk WAR/TWY RG10 47 G3
Foxglove Cl BNFD RG42 65 G4
STWL/WRAY TW19 56 D7
WWKG RG41 61 K7
Foxglove Gdns READ RG1 8 B5
Foxglove Wy NTHA RG18 97 M1
Foxhays Rd WHIT RG2 59 K6
Foxherne DTCH/LGLY SL3 39 L2
Foxhill Cl CAV/SC RG4 46 A1
Foxhill Crs CBLY GU15 89 H6
Foxhill La CAV/SC RG4 127 K11
Foxhill Ms CHERT KT16 81 H7
Foxhill Rd READ RG1 45 L8
Foxhunter Wy STHA RG19 97 H3
Foxhunt Gv TILE/CALC RG31 137 R6
Fox La HTWY RG27 85 M6
Fox La North CHERT KT16 81 M5
Fox La South CHERT KT16 * 81 M5
Foxley Cl BLKW GU17 93 J1
Foxley La BNFD RG42 63 H4
Fox Rd DTCH/LGLY SL3 39 M4
Framewood Rd SLN SL2 29 L1
Framlingham Dr CAV/SC RG4 45 L1
Frampton Cl WODY RG5 46 E5
France Hill Dr CBLY GU15 94 C1
Frances Av MDHD SL6 26 E5
Frances Rd WDSR SL4 13 H9
The Frances NTHA RG18 97 M2
Francis Chichester Cl ASC SL5 78 B2
Francis Cl SHPTN TW17 83 G1
Francis Gdns BNFD RG42 64 D4
Francis St READ RG1 9 G9
Francis Wy SL SL1 27 M8
Francomes Fld HUNG RG17 117 L5
Franklin Av SLN SL2 28 D6
TADY RG26 148 B1
Franklin St READ RG1 8 C7
Frank Lunnon Cl BNEND SL8 20 E3
Franklyn Crs WDSR SL4 52 D2
Frank Sutton Wy SL SL1 10 C3
The Frantons MDHD SL6 25 H7
Frascati Wy MDHD SL6 5 G5
Fraser Av CAV/SC RG4 127 J12
Fraser Md SHST GU47 87 L8
Fraser Rd BNFD RG42 2 E2
Frays Av WDR/YW UB7 41 M2
Frays Cl WDR/YW UB7 41 M3
Frayslea UX/CGN UB8 31 L3
Fray's Waye UX/CGN UB8 31 L2
Frederick Pl WWKG RG41 14 D6
Freeborn Wy BRAK RG12 3 M4
Freeman Cl SHPTN TW17 83 L1
Freemantle Rd BAGS GU19 89 M3
Free Prae Rd CHERT KT16 82 A5
Freesia Cl WWKG RG41 61 K7
Freestone Yd DTCH/LGLY SL3 * 40 F7
French Gdns BLKW GU17 93 K2
Frenchum Gdns SL SL1 38 A1
Frensham BRAK RG12 76 D3
Frensham Cl YTLY GU46 86 B8
Frensham Gn WHIT RG2 59 M5
Frensham Rd CWTH RG45 75 H7
Freshfield Cl EARL RG6 60 E3
Freshfields La KSCL RG20 120 G12
Freshwater Rd READ RG1 45 L6
Freshwood Dr YTLY GU46 92 C2
Fresian Wy WWKG RG41 61 G4
Friars Keep BRAK RG12 2 F8
Friars Rd NWBY RG14 6 E9
VW GU25 80 D1
Friar St READ RG1 8 E5
Friars Wk READ RG1 8 F5
Friars Wy CHERT KT16 82 A3
Friary Island STWL/WRAY TW19 54 C5
Friary Rd ASC SL5 78 B3
STWL/WRAY TW19 54 C5
The Friary WDSR SL4 54 C5

Friday St HEN RG9 22 A5
Friendship Wy BRAK RG12 2 F7
Frieth Cl EARL RG6 60 A4
Frilsham Rd
RDGW/BURGH RG30 58 B2
Frimley Cl WODY RG5 * 46 D6
Frimley Green Rd FRIM GU16 94 E6
Frimley Grove Gdns FRIM GU16 94 D5
Frimley Hall Dr CBLY GU15 88 F8
Frimley High St FRIM GU16 94 C6
Frimley Rd CBLY GU15 94 B2
Frimley Sq FRIM GU16 94 E5
Fringford Cl EARL RG6 60 C5
The Frithe SLN SL2 11 M2
Frith Hill Rd FRIM GU16 95 C5
Frithwald Rd CHERT KT16 81 M4
Frobisher BRAK RG12 76 C4
Frobisher Crs
STWL/WRAY TW19 56 E6
Frodsham Wy SHST GU47 87 L4
Frog Hall Dr EWKG RG40 15 M6
Frog La BRAK RG12 2 D6
HTWY RG27 151 K11
TADY RG26 149 K5
Frogmill MDHD SL6 23 L2
Frogmill Ct MDHD SL6 * 23 L3
Frogmill Spinney MDHD SL6 23 M2
Frogmore Cl SL SL1 38 C2
Frogmore Dr WDSR SL4 13 L5
Frogmore Gv BLKW GU17 93 J2
Frogmore Park Dr BLKW GU17 93 K2
Frogmore Rd BLKW GU17 93 H1
Frogmore Wy
RDGW/BURGH RG30 58 B1
Frome Cl FARN GU14 93 K8
Frome Rd DID OX11 109 J1
Fromer Rd FLKWH/TG HP10 20 F2
Fromont Dr STHA RG19 97 M3
Fromow Gdns BFOR GU20 90 D2
Front St HUNG RG17 118 A8
Frouds La THLE RG7 142 B4
Froxfield Av READ RG1 58 E1
Froxfield Down BRAK RG12 76 F2
Fruen Rd EBED/NFELT TW14 57 M6
Frymley Vw WDSR SL4 37 M8
Frys Island READ RG1 * 8 F2
Fry's La BAGS GU19 89 K4
YTLY GU46 86 E7
Fuchsia Cl TILE/CALC RG31 137 N5
Fuchsia Wy CHOB/PIR GU24 90 E8
Fullbrook Cl MDHD SL6 5 J2
WWKG RG41 62 A5
Fullbrook Crs TILE/CALC RG31 125 P11
Fuller Cl STHA RG19 98 B4
Fullers La KSCL RG20 147 R3
Fuller's La THLE RG7 144 F2
Fullers Rd DID OX11 110 G1
Fullerton Wy TADY RG26 148 E3
Fuller Wy HYS/HAR UB3 43 H5
Fulmead Rd
RDGW/BURGH RG30 44 C6
Fulmer Cl EARL RG6 60 A4
Furlong Cl BNEND SL8 20 D3
Furlong Rd BNEND SL8 20 D3
Furness WDSR SL4 52 C1
Furnival Av SLN SL2 28 D6
Furnival Cl VW GU25 80 D3
Furrow Wy MDHD SL6 35 J2
Furse Cl CBLY GU15 95 H2
Furzebank ASC SL5 78 D1
Furzedown Cl EGH TW20 68 E4
Furzeground Wy STKPK UB11 42 E1
Furzeham Rd WDR/YW UB7 42 A2
Furze Hill Crs CWTH RG45 87 J2
Furzemoors BRAK RG12 76 B2
Furzen Cl SLN SL2 28 C4
Furze Platt Rd MDHD SL6 25 J4
Furze Rd MDHD SL6 25 M5
TADY RG26 142 B12
Fushsia Gv WHIT RG2 59 L8
Fuzzens Wk WDSR SL4 52 E1
Fydlers Cl WDSR SL4 66 B4
Fyfield Cl BLKW GU17 93 K1
Fyfield Rd STHA RG19 97 M4
Fylingdales STHA RG19 97 L4

G

Gables Av ASHF TW15 70 F3
Gables Cl DTCH/LGLY SL3 39 J6
MDHD SL6 5 M2
Gables Wy STHA RG19 98 D4
Gabriel Dr CBLY GU15 95 H2
The Gabriels NWBY RG14 141 R8
Gadd Cl EWKG RG40 62 F7
Gade Cl HYS/HAR UB3 43 K1
Gage Cl MDHD SL6 36 A2
Gainsborough BRAK RG12 76 C3
MDHD SL6 26 B1
Gainsborough Av HUNG RG17 140 B4
Gainsborough Cl CBLY GU15 88 F7
WODY RG5 47 G8
Gainsborough Crs HEN RG9 127 Q2
Gainsborough Dr ASC SL5 65 K8
MDHD SL6 35 M3
Gainsborough Hl HEN RG9 127 R2
Gainsborough Rd HEN RG9 127 Q2
RDGW/BURGH RG30 58 B1
Gairn Cl RDGW/BURGH RG30 44 A7
Galahad Cl SL SL1 38 C2
Gale Dr LTWR GU18 90 A5
Galleons La DTCH/LGLY SL3 29 M4
Galley La STHA RG19 101 M5
Galleymead Rd DTCH/LGLY SL3 41 H8
The Gallops KSCL RG20 109 L12
The Gallop YTLY GU46 86 D7
Galloway Cha SLN SL2 11 J3
Gallys Rd WDSR SL4 37 M8
Galsworthy Dr CAV/SC RG4 45 K1
Galsworthy Dr CHERT KT16 82 A4
Galton Rd ASC SL5 78 F3
Galvin Rd SL SL1 10 A4
Galway Rd YTLY GU46 92 C2
Gap Wy GOR/PANG RG8 113 K10
Garden Cl ADL/WDHM KT15 82 D8
ASHF TW15 71 J4
MDHD SL6 35 J1
Garden Close La NWBY RG14 141 R10
Gardeners La GOR/PANG RG8 124 A10
Gardenia Ct CHOB/PIR GU24 90 F8
The Gardens EBED/NFELT TW14 57 K5
GOR/PANG RG8 112 A7
Garde Rd CAV/SC RG4 46 E3
Gardner House MDHD SL6 * 26 A5
Gardner Rd MDHD SL6 25 M4
Gardners Rd BNFD RG42 65 G4
Garfield Pl WDSR SL4 13 J7
Garfield Rd ADL/WDHM KT15 * 82 C8
CBLY GU15 94 C1
Garford Crs NWBY RG14 141 R6
Garlands Cl THLE RG7 143 P4
Garnet Cl SL SL1 38 C2
Garnet Ct MLW SL7 18 E5
Garnet Fld YTLY GU46 92 A1
Garnet Hl READ RG1 8 D8
Garnet St READ RG1 8 E8
Garrard Rd SLN SL2 28 A5
Garrard St READ RG1 8 F5
Garrett Rd EWKG RG40 73 L6

Garretts La MDHD SL6 26 B4
Garrick Cl STA TW18 70 A5
Garrick Wy FRIM GU16 94 E8
Garson La STWL/WRAY TW19 54 D6
Garson's La BNFD RG42 51 G8
Garsons La WGFD OX10 112 H4
Garston Cl RDGW/BURGH RG30 58 A2
Garston Crs TILE/CALC RG31 137 M5
Garston Gv EWKG RG40 73 L5
Garswood BRAK RG12 76 D3
Garth Cl WWKG RG41 61 J4
Garthlands MDHD SL6 25 M4
Garth Rd THLE RG7 143 Q9
Garth Sq BNFD RG42 64 B5
Gascoigne Rd WEY KT13 83 H7
Gascon's Gv SLN SL2 28 D5
Gashes La GOR/PANG RG8 125 J3
Gaskell Ms NWBY RG14 7 G9
Gaskells End CAV/SC RG4 126 D10
Gas La MDHD SL6 36 C3
WAR/TWY RG10 47 K2
Gaston Bridge Rd SHPTN TW17 83 K2
Gaston Wy SHPTN TW17 83 K2
Gas Works Rd READ RG1 9 K6
Gatcombe Cl TILE/CALC RG31 137 N6
Gatcombe Crs ASC SL5 65 M6
Gatehampton Rd
GOR/PANG RG8 112 A12
Gatehouse Cl WDSR SL4 53 H2
Gatewick Cl SL SL1 10 E5
Gatward Av MDHD SL6 35 J3
Gaveston Rd SLN SL2 28 B4
Gayhurst Cl CAV/SC RG4 127 K12
Gaywood Dr NWBY RG14 7 L1
Gazelle Cl WWKG RG41 61 G3
Geffers Ride ASC SL5 65 L8
Gelder Cl EARL RG6 60 D5
Genesis Cl STWL/WRAY TW19 56 F7
Geneva Cl SHPTN TW17 71 L7
Geoffreyson Rd CAV/SC RG4 44 D1
George Cl CAV/SC RG4 45 J3
MLW SL7 19 H2
George Green Dr
DTCH/LGLY SL3 30 B7
George Green Rd
DTCH/LGLY SL3 30 A7
Georgeham Rd SHST GU47 87 K4
George St READ RG1 8 C5
READ RG1 9 H3
STA TW18 69 M2
UX/CGN UB8 31 M1
Georgian Cl CBLY GU15 88 E7
STA TW18 70 B2
Georgian Hts BNEND SL8 20 D1
Georgina Gdns TADY RG26 148 F2
Geranium Cl CWTH RG45 75 H6
German Rd TADY RG26 150 A8
Gerring Rd WHIT RG2 72 E7
Gervaise Cl SL SL1 38 B1
Gibbet La CBLY GU15 89 G7
Gibbins La BNFD RG42 64 D3
Gibbons Cl SHST GU47 87 J7
Gibbs Cl EWKG RG40 73 L8
Gibbs Wy YTLY GU46 92 B2
Gibraltar La MDHD SL6 19 K5
Gibson Ct DTCH/LGLY SL3 40 B5
Gibson Pl STWL/WRAY TW19 56 C5
Gidley La KSCL RG20 120 E12
Giffard Dr FARN GU14 93 M8
Gifford Cl CAV/SC RG4 45 L1
Gilbert Rd FRIM GU16 94 C5
Gilbert Wy EWKG RG40 73 L6
Gilchrist Wy MDHD SL6 34 D1
Giles Cl NWBY RG14 * 6 B5
Giles Ct TADY RG26 148 E2
Giles Rd TADY RG26 148 E2
Giles Travers Cl EGH TW20 69 J8
Gillette Wy WHIT RG2 59 H3
Gilliat Rd SL SL1 10 F3
Gilliatt Cl IVER SL0 31 G7
Gillotts Cl HEN RG9 127 P3
Gillott's La HEN RG9 127 P3
Gill Ri BNFD RG42 64 C4
Gilman Crs WDSR SL4 52 D2
Gilmore Cl DTCH/LGLY SL3 39 L2
Gilmore Crs ASHF TW15 71 G3
Gilpin Wy HYS/HAR UB3 42 F7
Gilroy Cl NWBY RG14 141 Q8
Gilson Ct WDSR SL4 54 C6
Gingells Farm Rd
WAR/TWY RG10 47 H1
Gipsy La BRAK RG12 3 J5
EARL RG6 60 C5
EWKG RG40 15 G8
HUNG RG17 129 N10
RDGW/BURGH RG30 137 Q1
WWKG RG41 60 F7
Girton Cl SHST GU47 87 L5
Glade Rd MLW SL7 19 G4
The Glade ASC SL5 78 C2
GOR/PANG RG8 125 N10
NWBY RG14 96 B7
STA TW18 70 B5
Gladridge Cl EARL RG6 60 B2
Gladstone Cl HUNG RG17 140 B4
Gladstone La NTHA RG18 133 Q10
Gladstone Wy SL SL1 38 C2
Glaisdale STHA RG19 97 L4
Glaisyer Wy IVER SL0 30 E3
Glamis Cl FRIM GU16 94 F7
Glamis Crs HYS/HAR UB3 42 E3
Glamis Wy TILE/CALC RG31 137 M6
Glanmor Rd SLN SL2 11 M3
The Glanty EGH TW20 69 J2
Glasgow Rd SL SL1 28 C7
Glaston Hill Rd HTWY RG27 85 G7
Glebe Cl LTWR GU18 90 C5
MDHD SL6 37 H2
TADY RG26 148 E3
WGFD OX10 111 P5
Glebe Flds KSCL RG20 119 L7
Glebefields NWBY RG14 96 D1
Glebeland Gdns SHPTN TW17 83 J3
Glebeland Rd CBLY GU15 93 M2
Glebelands STHA RG19 97 L3
Glebelands Rd EWKG RG40 15 G4
Glebe La CAV/SC RG4 46 E3
KSCL RG20 141 L1
Glebe Pl HUNG RG17 129 J8
Glebe Ride GOR/PANG RG8 111 R12
Glebe Rd EGH TW20 69 J4
GOR/PANG RG8 125 M9
MDHD SL6 5 M8
STA TW18 70 B3
UX/CGN UB8 31 L3
WDSR SL4 54 B4
WHIT RG2 59 J1
The Glebe BLKW GU17 93 L2
GOR/PANG RG8 122 H3
HEN RG9 114 E9
WDR/YW UB7 42 A4
Glebewood BRAK RG12 76 C2
Gleeson Ms ADL/WDHM KT15 82 C8
Glen Av ASHF TW15 71 G2
Glenavon Gdns DTCH/LGLY SL3 39 L3
YTLY GU46 92 D2
Glenbeigh Ter READ RG1 8 A8
Glen Cl SHPTN TW17 83 G1
Glencoe Cl FRIM GU16 94 F6
Glencoe Rd WEY KT13 83 G7
Glendale Av NWBY RG14 141 Q9

Glendale Rd TADY RG26 148 C1
Glendevon Rd WODY RG5 46 F6
Gleneagles Cl
STWL/WRAY TW19 56 C5
Gleneagles Ct READ RG1 * 9 M7
Glenfield Rd ASHF TW15 71 H4
Glenhurst BFOR GU20 78 A8
Glenhurst Cl BLKW GU17 93 L2
Glen Innes SHST GU47 87 M5
Glenmore Cl ADL/WDHM KT15 82 B7
STHA RG19 * 97 M4
Glenn Miller Cl KSCL RG20 119 L9
Glennon Cl RDGW/BURGH RG30 58 C2
Glenrhondda CAV/SC RG4 44 F1
Glenrosa Rd
RDGW/BURGH RG30 137 R2
The Glen ASC SL5 * 78 D1
DTCH/LGLY SL3 39 L4
MDHD SL6 * 20 A8
TADY RG26 148 G1
Glentworth Pl SL SL1 10 B5
Glenwood BRAK RG12 3 K9
Glenwood Dr TILE/CALC RG31 137 N3
Globe Farm La BLKW GU17 93 H1
Gloucester Av SL SL1 28 E6
WHIT RG2 145 Q1
Gloucester Cl FRIM GU16 94 E8
Gloucester Ct
RDGW/BURGH RG30 * 44 D7
Gloucester Crs STA TW18 70 D4
Gloucester Dr STA TW18 69 J1
Gloucester Lea BNFD RG42 64 F5
Gloucester Pde HYS/HAR UB3 * 42 E3
Gloucester Pl BNFD RG42 64 F5
WDSR SL4 13 K8
Gloucester Rd BAGS GU19 89 L3
MDHD SL6 26 A4
NWBY RG14 6 B5
RDGW/BURGH RG30 44 D7
Glyncastle CAV/SC RG4 44 F1
Glynswood CBLY GU15 94 F3
Goaters Rd ASC SL5 65 J7
Goddard Cl SHPTN TW17 70 F8
WHIT RG2 145 Q1
Goddard Ct WWKG RG41 61 H5
Goddard Dr THLE RG7 99 H3
Goddards Cl HTWY RG27 150 D10
Goddards La CBLY GU15 94 B3
Goddard Wy BNFD RG42 64 D4
Goddington Rd BNEND SL8 20 C1
Godfrey Cl SHST GU47 87 K7
Godolphin Rd SL SL1 10 C2
Godstow Cl WODY RG5 46 E6
Goffs Rd ASHF TW15 71 K4
Gogmore Farm Cl CHERT KT16 81 L4
Gogmore La CHERT KT16 82 A4
Goldcrest Cl YTLY GU46 86 B8
Goldcrest Wy TILE/CALC RG31 137 M4
Gold Cup La ASC SL5 65 K6
Golden Ball La MDHD SL6 25 H3
Golden Crs HYS/HAR UB3 43 G1
Golden Orb Wd BNFD RG42 63 K6
Golding Cl STHA RG19 98 B3
Goldney Rd CBLY GU15 95 H2
Goldsmid Rd READ RG1 8 C7
Goldsmith Cl EWKG RG40 * 73 L5
NTHA RG18 97 L1
Goldsmith Wy CWTH RG45 87 H2
Goldsworthy Wy SL SL1 27 L7
Goldthorpe Gdns EARL RG6 59 M6
Goldwell Dr NWBY RG14 6 C2
Golf Dr CBLY GU15 94 F2
Gooch Cl WAR/TWY RG10 47 M3
Goodall Cl HEN RG9 127 R1
Goodboy's La THLE RG7 144 E5
Goodchild Rd EWKG RG40 15 J6
Goodings La HUNG RG17 129 Q1
Goodliffe Gdns
TILE/CALC RG31 125 N10
Goodman Pk SLN SL2 39 L1
Goodman Pl STA TW18 * 69 M2
Goodrich Cl CAV/SC RG4 45 L1
Goodways Dr BRAK RG12 3 H5
Goodwin Cl TILE/CALC RG31 137 Q6
Goodwin Rd SLN SL2 28 B4
Goodwood Cl CBLY GU15 88 C6
THLE RG7 143 P4
Goodwood Wy NWBY RG14 7 K8
Goose Cnr BNFD RG42 * 64 F3
Goosecroft La GOR/PANG RG8 125 M9
Goose Gn HUNG RG17 117 K3
SLN SL2 28 D3
Goose Green Wy STHA RG19 98 A3
Goose La KSCL RG20 119 Q9
Gordon Av CBLY GU15 94 B2
Gordon Cl CHERT KT16 81 L7
STA TW18 70 B4
Gordon Crs CBLY GU15 94 C2
HYS/HAR UB3 43 J4
KSCL RG20 121 R2
Gordon Dr CHERT KT16 81 L7
SHPTN TW17 83 K3
Gordon Palmer Cl THLE RG7 144 B9
Gordon Pl RDGW/BURGH RG30 44 C6
Gordon Rd ASHF TW15 70 E1
CBLY GU15 94 C2
CWTH RG45 87 K3
MDHD SL6 4 C4
NTHA RG18 97 J1
NWBY RG14 7 C5
SHPTN TW17 83 K3
STA TW18 69 J2
WDSR SL4 12 B8
Gordon Wk YTLY GU46 92 E1
Gore End Rd KSCL RG20 140 H11
Gore Rd SL SL1 27 K4
Goring La THLE RG7 143 P5
Goring Rd GOR/PANG RG8 112 H11
STA TW18 69 K3
Gorrick Sq WWKG RG41 74 B3
Gorse Bank LTWR GU18 * 90 A6
Gorse Cottage Dr NTHA RG18 133 P9
Gorse Dr WODY RG5 47 G6
Gorse Hill La VW GU25 80 D1
Gorse Hill Rd VW GU25 68 D8
Gorselands CAV/SC RG4 126 G12
NWBY RG14 141 R9
TADY RG26 148 D1
Gorse La CHOB/PIR GU24 91 L3
Gorse Meade SL SL1 38 D1
Gorse Pl BNFD RG42 * 65 H5
Gorse Ride North EWKG RG40 73 L7
Gorse Ride South EWKG RG40 73 L7
Gorse Rd FRIM GU16 94 E4
MDHD SL6 20 A8
Gosbrook Rd CAV/SC RG4 9 G1
Gosden Rd CHOB/PIR GU24 90 F8
Gosforth Cl EARL RG6 60 D4
Goslar Wy WDSR SL4 12 F7
Gosling Gn DTCH/LGLY SL3 40 A3
Gosling Rd DTCH/LGLY SL3 40 A3
Gosnell Cl FRIM GU16 95 K3
Gossmore Cl MLW SL7 19 H5
Gossmore La MLW SL7 19 H5
Gossmore Wk MLW SL7 19 H5
Goswell Rd WDSR SL4 13 J5
Gothic Ct HYS/HAR UB3 42 F6
Gough's Barn La BNFD RG42 50 A6
Gough's La BRAK RG12 3 J1
Gough's Meadow SHST GU47 87 H7
Gould Cl NWBY RG14 7 H4

Gould Rd EBED/NFELT TW14 57 L6
Governors Rd CBLY GU15 87 M8
Govett Av SHPTN TW17 * 83 J2
Govett Gv BFOR GU20 90 D1
Gower Pk SHST GU47 87 K7
Gower St READ RG1 8 B6
The Gower EGH TW20 69 H8
Gowings Gn SL SL1 38 A2
Grace Bennett Cl FARN GU14 * 94 A7
Grace Ct SL SL1 10 B4
Graces La KSCL RG20 132 H2
Gracious Pond Rd
CHOB/PIR GU24 91 M3
Graffham Cl EARL RG6 60 B6
Grafton Cl DTCH/LGLY SL3 30 A7
MDHD SL6 26 A4
Grafton Ct EBED/NFELT TW14 57 K7
Grafton Rd
RDGW/BURGH RG30 137 P3
Graham Cl DID OX11 110 B2
MDHD SL6 4 A9
TILE/CALC RG31 137 Q6
Grahame Av GOR/PANG RG8 124 H9
Graham Rd BFOR GU20 90 C2
MDHD SL6 20 A8
Grampian Cl HYS/HAR UB3 42 F7
Grampian Rd SHST GU47 86 F4
Grampian Wy DTCH/LGLY SL3 40 C5
Gramp's Hl WANT OX12 106 B6
The Granary NWBY RG14 * 6 D4
Granby Ct READ RG1 45 L7
Granby End THLE RG7 143 R3
Granby Gdns READ RG1 45 L7
Grand Av CBLY GU15 88 C8
Grand Union Canal Wk
DTCH/LGLY SL3 39 M1
HYS/HAR UB3 43 J3
IVER SL0 40 E1
NWDGN UB2 43 K3
SLN SL2 11 J3
UX/CGN UB8 31 K3
UX/CGN UB8 31 L8
WDR/YW UB7 42 D2
Grange Av CWTH RG45 75 H8
EARL RG6 45 M8
HEN RG9 126 G2
Grange Cl GOR/PANG RG8 123 R1
STWL/WRAY TW19 54 E5
Grange Ct EGH TW20 * 68 F3
Grange Dr FLKWH/TG HP10 20 F3
Grange La MDHD SL6 20 B6
Grangely Cl TILE/CALC RG31 137 P6
Grange Ms FELT TW13 * 71 K1
Grange Pl STA TW18 70 C7
Grange Rd BRAK RG12 3 H3
CBLY GU15 94 E1
EGH TW20 68 F3
FARN GU14 94 B7
HEN RG9 22 A5
MDHD SL6 20 B7
The Grange CHOB/PIR GU24 91 L5
NWBY RG14 141 Q9
SL SL1 * 27 L4
WDSR SL4 54 B4
Grange Wy IVER SL0 31 H7
Grangewood DTCH/LGLY SL3 29 L6
Grant Av SL SL1 10 F1
Grant Cl SHPTN TW17 83 H3
Grantham Cl SHST GU47 87 L5
Grantham Rd
RDGW/BURGH RG30 137 R6
The Granthams HUNG RG17 117 K3
Grant Rd CWTH RG45 87 J2
Grant Wk ASC SL5 78 E5
Granville Av SLN SL2 28 F6
Granville Rd HYS/HAR UB3 43 H4
RDGW/BURGH RG30 58 B1
Grasholm Wy DTCH/LGLY SL3 40 E4
Grasmere Av
RDGW/BURGH RG30 125 R12
SLN SL2 11 J3
Grasmere Cl EBED/NFELT TW14 57 M7
EGH TW20 69 H5
WWKG RG41 61 H5
Grasmere Pde SLN SL2 * 11 L2
Grasmere Rd LTWR GU18 90 B5
Grass Hl CAV/SC RG4 44 E3
Grassington Pl STHA RG19 97 M4
Grassmead STHA RG19 98 B4
Grassy La MDHD SL6 4 E4
Gratton Dr WDSR SL4 52 E3
Gratton Rd WHIT RG2 59 J6
Gratwicke Rd
RDGW/BURGH RG30 137 Q2
Gravel Hl CAV/SC RG4 126 E12
HEN RG9 126 F4
KSCL RG20 141 L1
Gravel Hill Crs HEN RG9 126 F4
Gravelly Cl KSCL RG20 140 G11
TADY RG26 148 E4
Gravel Rd HEN RG9 127 M9
Graveney Dr CAV/SC RG4 44 E3
Gravett Cl HEN RG9 127 Q2
Grayling Cl MLW SL7 18 E6
Grays Crs WODY RG5 46 C6
Grayshot Dr BLKW GU17 93 J1
Grays La ASHF TW15 71 H2
Grays Park Rd SLN SL2 29 J3
Grays Pl SLN SL2 11 H4
Grays Rd SL SL1 11 G4
Grazeley Green Rd THLE RG7 144 F3
Grazeley Rd THLE RG7 145 L2
Great Benty WDR/YW UB7 42 A4
Greatfield Cl FARN GU14 94 B6
Greatfield Rd FARN GU14 94 A6
Great Hill Crs MDHD SL6 35 K1
Great Hollands Rd BRAK RG12 75 M3
Great Hollands Sq BRAK RG12 75 M2
Great Knollys St READ RG1 8 C5
Great Lea THLE RG7 145 L1
Great Severals HUNG RG17 140 A4
Great South-West Rd
EBED/NFELT TW14 57 J6
Greenacre WDSR SL4 52 E1
Greenacre Ct EGH TW20 * 68 C4
Green Acre Mt
RDGW/BURGH RG30 137 P2
Greenacres Av WWKG RG41 61 G4
Greenacres La WWKG RG41 61 G3
Green Cl MDHD SL6 5 H1
MDHD SL6 27 J7
Green Common La BEAC HP9 21 M2
Green Cft EWKG RG40 15 L1
Greendale Ms SLN SL2 11 J3
Green Dean Hl CAV/SC RG4 126 B8
Green Dr EWKG RG40 15 K9
Greene Fielde End STA TW18 70 D5
Green End YTLY GU46 86 D7
Green End Cl THLE RG7 * 145 M4
Green Farm Rd BAGS GU19 89 M3
Greenfern Av SL SL1 27 L7
Greenfields MDHD SL6 5 J7
Greenfields Rd WHIT RG2 59 H6
Greenfield Wy CWTH RG45 75 G7
Green Finch Cl CWTH RG45 * 74 F8
Greenfinch Cl TILE/CALC RG31 137 M4
Greenfinch Dr WAR/TWY RG10 47 K1
Greenham Cl STHA RG19 96 F6
WODY RG5 47 G8
Greenham Rd NWBY RG14 6 F6
Greenham Wd BRAK RG12 76 C4
Greenhaven YTLY GU46 92 B1
Green Hill Cl CBLY GU15 89 J8
Green Hill Rd CBLY GU15 89 J8
Greenholme CBLY GU15 95 K1
Greenhow BRAK RG12 2 C7
Greenidge Cl READ RG1 58 E1
Greenlake Ter STA TW18 * 70 A5
Greenland Crs NWDGN UB2 43 L3
Greenlands CHERT KT16 81 J7
Greenlands Rd CBLY GU15 94 B5
NWBY RG14 7 G8
STA TW18 70 A2
WEY KT13 83 H7
Green La ADL/WDHM KT15 82 B7
ASC SL5 66 E6
BAGS GU19 89 M4
BLKW GU17 93 H2
CAV/SC RG4 126 F5
CHERT KT16 81 L6
CHOB/PIR GU24 91 M5
DTCH/LGLY SL3 39 K8
EGH TW20 69 H2
EGH TW20 69 J7
EWKG RG40 63 G4
GOR/PANG RG8 113 K11
GOR/PANG RG8 124 G9
HEN RG9 127 N9
HEN RG9 127 R2
KSCL RG20 132 H2
MDHD SL6 5 K8
MDHD SL6 34 D1
MDHD SL6 36 D2
MDHD SL6 36 E8
MDHD SL6 50 A1
NTHA RG18 97 L3
NWBY RG14 6 B5
RDGW/BURGH RG30 58 A4
SHPTN TW17 83 J2
SHST GU47 87 J6
SL SL1 27 L4
STA TW18 69 L6
SUN TW16 71 M5
TADY RG26 148 G6
THLE RG7 135 P7
THLE RG7 143 L4
THLE RG7 150 D2
WAR/TWY RG10 61 L3
WDSR SL4 12 E7
WWKG RG41 61 K5
YTLY GU46 86 B7
Green Lane Cl CBLY GU15 88 C7
CHERT KT16 81 L6
Green Lane Ct SL SL1 27 L4
Greenleaf Ct DTCH/LGLY SL3 39 J6
Greenleas FRIM GU16 94 E4
Green Leas SUN TW16 71 M5
Greenleas Av CAV/SC RG4 126 H11
Green Leas Cl SUN TW16 71 M4
Greenleas Cl YTLY GU46 86 C7
Greenleaves Ct ASHF TW15 * 71 H4
Green Leys MDHD SL6 26 B4
Greenmoor GOR/PANG RG8 113 K10
Green Oaks NWDGN UB2 * 43 M3
Greenock Rd SL SL1 28 C7
Greeno Crs SHPTN TW17 83 G2
Green Pk STA TW18 69 L1
Green Rd EARL RG6 59 M1
EGH TW20 81 G1
Greenside BNEND SL8 20 C1
CWTH RG45 86 F1
SLN SL2 28 C6
Greensward La WHIT RG2 72 C3
The Green ASHF TW15 * 70 D3
BRAK RG12 2 E9
DID OX11 109 L2
EGH TW20 68 C2
FLKWH/TG HP10 21 G1
FRIM GU16 94 F8
HEN RG9 114 E4
HUNG RG17 140 B5
KSCL RG20 132 H1
SL SL1 10 C7
STWL/WRAY TW19 54 E5
TADY RG26 148 E4
THLE RG7 136 G8
WDR/YW UB7 41 M3
WWKG RG41 61 L7
Green Trees HEN RG9 126 F3
Green Verges MLW SL7 19 G3
Greenway HTWY RG27 150 D10
SL SL1 27 K3
Greenway Dr STA TW18 70 C6
Greenways EGH TW20 68 E4
HUNG RG17 117 K4
SHST GU47 87 H5
Greenways Dr ASC SL5 78 B5
MDHD SL6 25 J6
The Greenway SL SL1 37 M1
UX/CGN UB8 31 M3
Greenwich Rd EARL RG6 59 L7
Green Wd ASC SL5 65 J6
Greenwood Cots ASC SL5 79 J3
Greenwood Gv WWKG RG41 61 K3
Greenwood Rd CWTH RG45 75 G8
RDGW/BURGH RG30 137 R5
Gregory Cl EARL RG6 60 C6
Gregory Dr WDSR SL4 54 B5
Grenfell Av MDHD SL6 5 G6
Grenfell Pl MDHD SL6 5 G6
Grenfell Rd MDHD SL6 4 E5
Grensell Cl HTWY RG27 85 L6
Grenside Rd WEY KT13 83 H7
Grenville Cl SL SL1 27 K3
Grenville Gdns FRIM GU16 94 E8
Grenville Pl BRAK RG12 3 H4
Grenville Sq BRAK RG12 3 H4
Gresham Rd SL SL1 28 C7
STA TW18 69 M3
Gresham Wy FRIM GU16 94 E8
RDGW/BURGH RG30 44 A4
Greyberry Copse Rd STHA RG19 96 F6
Greyfriars Dr ASC SL5 78 B3
Greyfriars Rd READ RG1 8 F5
Greys Ct READ RG1 9 J7
Greys Hl HEN RG9 127 R1
Greys Rd HEN RG9 127 N2
Greystock Rd BNFD RG42 64 D4
Greystoke Ct CWTH RG45 87 G2
Greystoke Rd CAV/SC RG4 45 J2
SLN SL2 28 B6
Greywell Cl TADY RG26 148 C2
Griffin Cl MDHD SL6 4 E9
SL SL1 10 A7
Griffiths Cl STHA RG19 98 B4
Grimmer Wy GOR/PANG RG8 113 K10
Grindle Cl NTHA RG18 97 L1
Gringer Hl MDHD SL6 4 E2
Grosvenor Ct BLKW GU17 93 K3
Grosvenor Lawn NWBY RG14 * 6 A5
Grosvenor Pl WEY KT13 83 K7
Grosvenor Rd CAV/SC RG4 45 J3
CHOB/PIR GU24 91 K8
STA TW18 70 A5
Grotto Rd WEY KT13 83 H7
Grove Cl EWKG RG40 74 E7
SL SL1 11 H8
WDSR SL4 54 B6
Grove Ct EGH TW20 69 G3
Grove Cross Rd FRIM GU16 94 D5
Grove End BAGS GU19 89 M2
Grovefields Av FRIM GU16 94 D5
Grove Hl CAV/SC RG4 45 G2
Groveland Pl
RDGW/BURGH RG30 44 B6
Groveland Rd NWBY RG14 141 R1
Grovelands Av WWKG RG41 61 K4
Grovelands Cl WWKG RG41 61 K3
Grovelands Pk WWKG RG41 * 61 K4
Grovelands Rd
RDGW/BURGH RG30 44 B6
THLE RG7 145 N4
Grove La BNFD RG42 65 H3
Groveley Rd SUN TW16 71 M3
Grove Ms CAV/SC RG4 45 H1
Grove Rd CAV/SC RG4 45 G1
CAV/SC RG4 126 F5
CBLY GU15 94 E1
CHERT KT16 81 M3
HEN RG9 22 A5
MDHD SL6 5 H5
NWBY RG14 141 R1
SHPTN TW17 83 J3
SL SL1 28 A1
UX/CGN UB8 31 M1
WDSR SL4 13 J7
Groves Cl BNEND SL8 20 E3
Groves Lea THLE RG7 143 P8
Grovestile Waye
EBED/NFELT TW14 57 K6
Groves Wy MDHD SL6 20 A8
The Grove ASC SL5 65 J6
EGH TW20 69 G3
FRIM GU16 94 D5
NTHA RG18 97 M2
READ RG1 9 J7
SL SL1 11 J7
WAR/TWY RG10 47 K1
Grove Wy UX/CGN UB8 31 M1
Grubwood La MDHD SL6 19 J7
Guards Club Rd MDHD SL6 26 E7
Guards Ct ASC SL5 79 H4
Guards Rd WDSR SL4 52 C1
Guerdon Pl BRAK RG12 76 D4
Guernsey Wy WWKG RG41 61 G5
Guildford Av FELT TW13 57 M8
Guildford Rd BAGS GU19 89 L3
CHERT KT16 81 K7
CHOB/PIR GU24 90 E7
CHOB/PIR GU24 91 K8
Guildford St CHERT KT16 81 M4
STA TW18 70 A4
Guinness Cl HYS/HAR UB3 42 F3
Gullane Ct READ RG1 * 9 M7
Gun St READ RG1 8 F6
Gunthorpe Rd MLW SL7 19 H3
Gurnard Cl WDR/YW UB7 31 M8
Gurney Cl CAV/SC RG4 44 D1
Gurney Dr CAV/SC RG4 44 D2
Guttridge La TADY RG26 148 C2
Gwendale MDHD SL6 25 L5
Gwent Cl MDHD SL6 35 K2
Gwyn Cl NWBY RG14 96 B6
Gwynne Cl TILE/CALC RG31 125 P11
WDSR SL4 38 A8
Gwyns Piece HUNG RG17 117 K3
Gypsy La MLW SL7 19 G2

H

Habershon Dr FRIM GU16 95 K4
Haddon Cl WEY KT13 83 L7
Haddon Dr WODY RG5 46 E6
Hadfield Rd STWL/WRAY TW19 56 D5
Hadleigh Gdns FRIM GU16 94 E8
Hadleigh Ri CAV/SC RG4 45 L1
Hadlow Ct SL SL1 10 A4
Hadrian Cl STWL/WRAY TW19 56 E6
Hadrian Wk East WHIT RG2 59 J2
Hadrian Wk West WHIT RG2 59 J2
Hadrian Wy STWL/WRAY TW19 56 D6
Hafod CAV/SC RG4 126 F12
Hagbourne Cl GOR/PANG RG8 113 K10
Hag Hill La MDHD SL6 27 J7
Hag Hill Ri MDHD SL6 27 J7
Hagley Rd WHIT RG2 59 H2
Haig Dr SL SL1 38 D2
Haig Rd CBLY GU15 87 M8
Hailey La KSCL RG20 120 D6
Hailsham Cl SHST GU47 87 K5
Halcyon Ter
RDGW/BURGH RG30 137 Q2
Haldane Rd CAV/SC RG4 44 E1
Halebourne La CHOB/PIR GU24 91 G5
Hale End BRAK RG12 76 F1
Hale St STA TW18 69 L2
Hale Wy FRIM GU16 94 D5
Halewood BRAK RG12 75 M3
Halfacre Cl THLE RG7 145 M3
Half Mile Rd HUNG RG17 129 J1
Halfpenny La ASC SL5 79 G4
WGFD OX10 111 N5
Halfway La MARL SN8 128 A6
Halifax Cl MDHD SL6 25 J6
Halifax Pl NTHA RG18 97 L2
Halifax Rd BRAK RG12 3 H7
MDHD SL6 25 J6
Halifax Wy MDHD SL6 25 J6
Halkingcroft DTCH/LGLY SL3 39 L2
Hallbrooke Gdns BNFD RG42 63 L5
Hall Cl CBLY GU15 88 E8
Hall Ct DTCH/LGLY SL3 39 K7
Halldore Hl MDHD SL6 20 A7
Halley Dr ASC SL5 65 K7
Hall Farm Crs YTLY GU46 92 C1
Hallgrove Bottom BAGS GU19 89 M1
Halliford Cl SHPTN TW17 71 L8
Halliford Rd SHPTN TW17 83 L2
Hall La HYS/HAR UB3 42 F7
YTLY GU46 92 C1
Hallmark Cl SHST GU47 87 L6
Hall Meadow SL SL1 27 K1
Hallows Gv SUN TW16 71 M3
Hall Place La MDHD SL6 24 D6
Halls La WAR/TWY RG10 34 C8
WHIT RG2 59 L5
Halls Rd RDGW/BURGH RG30 137 N4
Hall's Wy HTWY RG27 86 A6
Halpin Cl TILE/CALC RG31 137 N6
Halsend HYS/HAR UB3 * 43 K1
Halstead Cl WODY RG5 46 E7
Halsway HYS/HAR UB3 43 J1
The Halters NWBY RG14 96 D6
Hamble Av BLKW GU17 93 K1
Hambledon Cl EARL RG6 60 E5
Hamble Dr TADY RG26 148 F2
Hambleton WDSR SL4 * 54 C7
Hambleton Cl FRIM GU16 95 H3
Hamblin Meadow HUNG RG17 129 N11
Ham Br NWBY RG14 97 G3
NWBY RG14 7 M4
Hambridge La NWBY RG14 97 G4
Hambridge Rd NWBY RG14 7 J5
Hamilton Av HEN RG9 22 A5
Hamilton Cl BAGS GU19 89 L3
CHERT KT16 81 K5
FELT TW13 71 M3
Hamilton Ct NWBY RG14 6 F9
Hamilton Dr ASC SL5 78 E4
Hamilton Gdns SL SL1 27 K4
Hamilton Ms WEY KT13 * 83 G8
Hamilton Pk MDHD SL6 25 J8
Hamilton Rd FELT TW13 71 M2
READ RG1 45 L8
SL SL1 28 C7
UX/CGN UB8 31 M5
WAR/TWY RG10 33 G4
Ham La EGH TW20 68 B2
TADY RG26 103 K8
WDSR SL4 54 C3
Hamlet St BNFD RG42 3 L2
The Hamlet CAV/SC RG4 126 B5
Hamm Ct WEY KT13 82 F7
Hamm Court Est WEY KT13 82 F6
Ham Ml NWBY RG14 * 7 L3
Hammond Cl STHA RG19 98 A4
Hammonds End
GOR/PANG RG8 * 113 M6
Hammonds Heath THLE RG7 143 R8
Hammond Wy LTWR GU18 90 B5
Hampden Cl SLN SL2 29 J4
Hampden Rd CAV/SC RG4 45 H4
DTCH/LGLY SL3 40 B3
MDHD SL6 25 K6
The Hampdens NWBY RG14 141 Q8
Hampshire Av SL SL1 28 E6
Hampshire Ri BNFD RG42 64 F4
Hampshire Rd CBLY GU15 88 F6
Hampshire Wy WWKG RG41 61 K8
Hampstead Hl HEN RG9 127 Q10
Hampstead Norreys Rd
NTHA RG18 133 P3
Hampton Rd NWBY RG14 6 D7
Ham Rd MARL SN8 138 E11
Hanbury Cl SL SL1 27 J6
Hanbury Dr TILE/CALC RG31 137 P6
Hanbury Wy CBLY GU15 94 C3
Hancocks Mt ASC SL5 78 D3
Hancombe Rd SHST GU47 87 G4
Handford La YTLY GU46 92 D1
Hangerfield Cl YTLY GU46 92 C1
Hanger Rd TADY RG26 148 B1
THLE RG7 137 K9
Hangman's Stone La
KSCL RG20 119 K9
Hanley Cl WDSR SL4 37 M8
Hannibal Rd STWL/WRAY TW19 56 E6
Hannington Wy THLE RG7 144 A3
Hanover Cl EGH TW20 68 B4
FRIM GU16 94 E5
SL SL1 11 K8
WDSR SL4 12 A6
YTLY GU46 86 D7
Hanover Ct CAV/SC RG4 * 127 J12
Hanover Gdns BRAK RG12 75 M4
FARN GU14 93 L8
WAR/TWY RG10 33 H3
Hanover Ga SL SL1 38 B1
Hanover Md MDHD SL6 36 E3
NWBY RG14 141 R8
Hanover Wk WEY KT13 83 K7
Hanover Wy WDSR SL4 12 A6
Hanson Cl CBLY GU15 89 H7
WDR/YW UB7 42 B3
Hanwood Cl WODY RG5 46 C6
Hanworth Cl BRAK RG12 76 C3
Hanworth La CHERT KT16 81 M5
Hanworth Rd BRAK RG12 76 A4
Harbour Cl FARN GU14 94 A6
Harbury Ct NWBY RG14 6 F6
Harcourt STWL/WRAY TW19 54 E5
Harcourt Cl EGH TW20 69 J4
HEN RG9 127 Q1
MDHD SL6 37 H3
Harcourt Dr EARL RG6 59 M4
Harcourt Gdns MLW SL7 * 19 G4
Harcourt Rd BRAK RG12 76 B3
CBLY GU15 94 B1
MDHD SL6 37 H3
WDSR SL4 38 A8
Hardell Cl EGH TW20 69 G3
Harding Pl EWKG RG40 15 G5
Harding Rd WODY RG5 46 C6
Harding Sp DTCH/LGLY SL3 40 B5
Hardings Rw IVER SL0 30 E4
Hardwell Wy BRAK RG12 3 M8
Hardwick Cl MDHD SL6 25 H6
Hardwick Est GOR/PANG RG8 * 125 N4
Hardwick La CHERT KT16 81 J4
Hardwick Rd GOR/PANG RG8 124 H7
RDGW/BURGH RG30 137 R3
Hardy Av YTLY GU46 92 C2
Hardy Cl CAV/SC RG4 9 J1
NTHA RG18 97 L1
SL SL1 38 C1
Hardy Gn CWTH RG45 87 H2
Harebell Dr NTHA RG18 98 A2
Harefield Cl WWKG RG41 61 J4
Harefield Rd MDHD SL6 25 J7
Hare Shoots MDHD SL6 4 E9
Harewood Dr NTHA RG18 133 Q10
Harewood Pl SL SL1 11 K8
Hargrave Rd MDHD SL6 4 D2
Harkness Rd SL SL1 27 K6
Harlech Av CAV/SC RG4 45 L1
Harlech Gdns HEST TW5 43 L6
Harlech Rd BLKW GU17 93 K2
Harleyford MLW SL7 * 18 B8
Harleyford La MLW SL7 18 C7
Harley Rd CAV/SC RG4 9 G1
Harlington Cl HYS/HAR UB3 42 E7
Harlton Cl EARL RG6 60 C6
Harman Ct WWKG RG41 61 H4
Harmans Water Rd BRAK RG12 76 D2
Harmar Cl EWKG RG40 15 M6
Harmondsworth La
WDR/YW UB7 42 A6
Harmondsworth Rd
WDR/YW UB7 42 A3
Harmsworth Rd TADY RG26 148 D2
Harness Cl WHIT RG2 59 H8
Harold Av HYS/HAR UB3 43 H3
Harold Rd HUNG RG17 140 B3
Harpdon Pde YTLY GU46 86 D7
Harpesford Av VW GU25 80 C2
Harpsden Rd HEN RG9 22 A6
Harpsden Wy HEN RG9 22 A7
Harpton Cl YTLY GU46 86 D7
Harrier Cl WODY RG5 47 G8
Harrier Wy BRAK RG12 75 K1
Harrington Cl EARL RG6 60 C4
NWBY RG14 96 F1
WDSR SL4 52 F3
Harris Ar READ RG1 9 G5
Harris Cl HUNG RG17 117 K3
WODY RG5 47 H6
Harris Gdns SL SL1 10 B6
Harrison Cl WAR/TWY RG10 47 M3
Harrison Ct SHPTN TW17 * 83 H2
Harrison Wy SHPTN TW17 83 H2
SL SL1 37 M1
Harris Wy SUN TW16 71 L6
Harrogate Ct DTCH/LGLY SL3 40 C5
Harrogate Rd CAV/SC RG4 44 E2
Harrow Bottom Rd VW GU25 80 F3
Harrow Cl ADL/WDHM KT15 82 B6
MDHD SL6 26 A5
Harrow Ct READ RG1 8 C8
Harrow La MDHD SL6 4 D1
Harrow Rd DTCH/LGLY SL3 40 B3
EBED/NFELT TW14 57 G7
Harrow Wy SHPTN TW17 71 J7
WWKG RG41 61
Hart Cl BNFD RG42 2
FARN GU14 93
Hart Dene Ct BAGS GU19 89
Hart Dyke Cl WWKG RG41 74
Hartford Ri CBLY GU15 88
Hartigan Pl WODY RG5 47
Hartland Cl SL SL1 10
Hartland Pl FARN GU14 94
Hartland Rd WHIT RG2 59
The Hartlands HEST TW5 43
Hartley Cl BLKW GU17 93
SLN SL2 29
Hartley Copse WDSR SL4 54
Hartley Court Rd THLE RG7 58
Hartley Gdns TADY RG26 148
Hartley La HTWY RG27 150
Hartleys THLE RG7 149
Hartmead Rd STHA RG19 98
Hartsbourne Rd EARL RG6 60
Harts Cl WHIT RG2 72
Harts Hill Rd NTHA RG18 98
Hartshill Rd TADY RG26 148
Harts La KSCL RG20 100
Hart's La THLE RG7 143
Harts Leap Cl SHST GU47 87
Harts Leap Rd SHST GU47 87
Hartslock Bridleway
GOR/PANG RG8 124
Hartslock Ct GOR/PANG RG8 124
Hartslock Vw GOR/PANG RG8 124
Hartslock Wy TILE/CALC RG31 125
Hart St HEN RG9 22
READ RG1 8
Harvard Cl WODY RG5 47
Harvard Rd SHST GU47 87
Harvest Cl TILE/CALC RG31 137
YTLY GU46 92
Harvest Dr WWKG RG41 61
Harvest Gn NWBY RG14 6
Harvest Hl BNEND SL8 20
Harvest Hill Rd MDHD SL6 36
Harvest Lea BNFD RG42 65
Harvest Pl WAR/TWY RG10 33
Harvest Ride BNFD RG42 3
Harvest Rd EGH TW20 68
Harwich Cl EARL RG6 60
Harwich Rd SL SL1 28
Harwood Gdns WDSR SL4 54
Harwood Ri KSCL RG20 141
Harwood Rd MLW SL7 18
Haslemere Cl FRIM GU16 95
Haslemere Rd WDSR SL4 12
Haslett Rd SHPTN TW17 71
Hasting Cl MDHD SL6 36
Hastings Cl FRIM GU16 95
RDGW/BURGH RG30 58
Hastings Meadow SLN SL2 * 29
Hatchbury La RAND SP11 146
Hatch Cl ADL/WDHM KT15 82
THLE RG7 135
Hatch End BFOR GU20 90
The Hatches FRIM GU16 94
Hatchet La ASC SL5 66
WDSR SL4 66
Hatchets La NTHA RG18 134
Hatchett Rd EBED/NFELT TW14 57
Hatchgate Cl NTHA RG18 133
Hatchgate Copse BRAK RG12 75
Hatchgate Gdns SL SL1 27
Hatch Gate La WAR/TWY RG10 23
Hatch La RDGW/BURGH RG30 137
THLE RG7 135
WDR/YW UB7 41
WDSR SL4 12
Hatch Ride CWTH RG45 75
EWKG RG40 74
The Hatch WDSR SL4 37
Hatfield Cl MDHD SL6 4
Hatfield Ct CBLY GU15 94
TILE/CALC RG31 137
Hatfield Rd SL SL1 11
Hatford Rd RDGW/BURGH RG30 58
Hatherley Rd READ RG1 45
Hatherwood YTLY GU46 * 92
Hatton Av SLN SL2 28
Hatton Ct WDSR SL4 13
Hatton Cross Est HTHAIR TW6 * 57
Hatton Gv WDR/YW UB7 * 41
Hatton Hl BFOR GU20 90
GOR/PANG RG8 123
Hatton Rd EBED/NFELT TW14 57
HTHAIR TW6 57
Haughurst Hl TADY RG26 103
Havelock Crs MDHD SL6 25
Havelock Rd MDHD SL6 25
WWKG RG41 14
Havelock St WWKG RG41 14
Haven Ct READ RG1 9
Haven Rd ASHF TW15 71
The Haven HUNG RG17 140
Haversham Dr BRAK RG12 76
Hawkchurch Rd WHIT RG2 59
Hawkedon Wy EARL RG6 60
Hawker Wy WODY RG5 47
Hawkesbury Dr
TILE/CALC RG31 137
Hawkes Cl DTCH/LGLY SL3 40
WWKG RG41 14
Hawkes Leap BFOR GU20 78
Hawkesworth Dr BAGS GU19 89
Hawkins Cl BRAK RG12 65
Hawkins Wy EWKG RG40 15
Hawk La BRAK RG12 3
Hawkley Dr TADY RG26 148
Hawks Hl BNEND SL8 20
Hawkshill Rd SLN SL2 28
Hawksway STA TW18 69
Hawkswood Av FRIM GU16 94
Hawksworth Rd THLE RG7 143
Haw La NTHA RG18 122
Hawley Cl TILE/CALC RG31 137
Hawley Ct FARN GU14 93
Hawley Gn BLKW GU17 93
Hawley Gv BLKW GU17 93
Hawley La FARN GU14 94
Hawley Rd BLKW GU17 93
Hawley Wy ASHF TW15 71
Hawthorn Cl BNFD RG42 2
HEST TW5 43
IVER SL0 30
Hawthorn Ct ASHF TW15 71
Hawthorn Dr HEN RG9 126
Hawthorne Av WDSR SL4 52
Hawthorne Cl MLW SL7 19
NTHA RG18 97
Hawthorne Ct
STWL/WRAY TW19 * 56
Hawthorne Crs BLKW GU17 93
SL SL1 10
WDR/YW UB7 42
Hawthorne Dr WDSR SL4 * 52
Hawthorne Rd CAV/SC RG4 45
STA TW18 69
Hawthornes TILE/CALC RG31 125
Hawthorne Wy HUNG RG17 118
STWL/WRAY TW19 56
WDSR SL4 52
Hawthorn Gdns MDHD SL6 4
WHIT RG2 59
Hawthorn La BNFD RG42 50

'LN SL2 28 B1
wthorn Rd FRIM GU16 94 F4
JWBY RG14 6 E1
Hawthorns DTCH/LGLY SL3 41 H8
ADY RG26 148 A2
WAR/TWY RG10 47 C3
wthorn Wy CAV/SC RG4 46 E4
HPTN TW17 83 K1
wtrey Cl SL SL1 11 M7
wtrey Rd WDSR SL4 13 G7
den La HEN RG9 114 A4
don La KSCL RG20 109 L11
es La WWKG RG41 73 J2
es Rd NWDGN UB2 43 K4
field Cl TILE/CALC RG31 137 N2
ley Gn BNFD RG42 64 F3
mill Rd SL SL1 27 M5
'LN SL2 27 M5
nes Cl DTCH/LGLY SL3 40 B5
Rd READ RG1 58 F1
se Hl WDSR SL4 37 M8
soms Dr STHA RG19 96 D7
wards Cl HEN RG9 127 Q1
wards Md WDSR SL4 38 B5
Haywards NTHA RG18 97 M2
wood BRAK RG12 76 C4
wood Ct READ RG1 45 M7
wood Wy
DGW/BURGH RG30 137 R5
el Av WDR/YW UB7 42 C3
elbank EWKG RG40 73 K8
elbank Rd CHERT KT16 82 C4
el Cl EGH TW20 68 B4
DGW/BURGH RG30 143 R1
WWKG RG41 14 A8
el Crs WHIT RG2 59 L4
eldene KSCL RG20 132 H1
el Dr WODY RG5 60 C1
el Gdns CAV/SC RG4 126 F5
el Gn TADY RG26 103 M5
el Gv HEN RG9 114 B12
THA RG18 97 M1
TA TW18 70 B4
elhurst Rd SL SL1 27 L3
ell Cl MDHD SL6 5 H2
ell Hl BRAK RG12 3 G7
elmere Cl
BED/NFELT TW14 57 K5
elmoor La CAV/SC RG4 126 C6
el Rd GOR/PANG RG8 125 N10
els Paddock NTHA RG18 133 Q10
elwood Cl TILE/CALC RG31 137 N1
elwood La BNFD RG42 63 M3
lemere Rd SLN SL2 11 M4
cham Cl EARL RG6 60 A6
dington Cl EWKG RG40 15 H2
DHD SL6 25 J7
dington Dr EWKG RG40 15 J2
dington Rd MDHD SL6 25 J6
dley Cl WODY RG5 47 G6
dley Rd WODY RG5 46 E7
dley Rd East WODY RG5 46 F7
ds La HUNG RG17 140 A9
rdman Cl STHA RG19 98 B4
rmon Cl YTLY GU46 86 D8
rne Dr MDHD SL6 36 C6
rn Rd WODY RG5 60 E1
rns La CAV/SC RG4 126 C5
rn Wk BRAK RG12 3 L3
rsey Gdns BLKW GU17 87 H8
th Cl HYS/HAR UB3 42 F7
TWL/WRAY TW19 56 C5
W GU25 80 D1
WWKG RG41 74 B2
th Cnr CBLY GU15 95 G3
thcote MDHD SL6 36 D4
thcote Rd CBLY GU15 94 D1
thcote Wy WDR/YW UB7 41 M1
thcourt TADY RG26 148 A1
thcroft Av SUN TW16 71 M5
th Dr HEN RG9 127 N9
th End Farm TADY RG26 148 A1
th End Rd TADY RG26 142 A12
ther Cl CAV/SC RG4 126 F5
WKG RG40 73 L7
therdale Rd CBLY GU15 94 C2
therden Cl WHIT RG2 59 J7
therdene Av CWTH RG45 86 E2
therden Gn IVER SL0 30 E2
ther Dr ASC SL5 79 H4
THA RG18 97 M1
ADY RG26 142 B12
ther Gdns NWBY RG14 96 A7
therley Cl CBLY GU15 94 B1
therley Rd CBLY GU15 94 B1
ther Md FRIM GU16 94 F4
thermount Dr CWTH RG45 74 F8
therside Dr VW GU25 80 A3
Heathers
TWL/WRAY TW19 56 F6
ther Wy CHOB/PIR GU24 91 L3
therway CWTH RG45 87 G1
thfield Av ASC SL5 78 E2
EN RG9 127 P8
DGW/BURGH RG30 137 P3
thfield Cl HEN RG9 127 P8
thfield Rd MDHD SL6 21 H6
thfields KSCL RG20 132 G2
ADY RG26 148 A1
th Gv SUN TW16 71 M5
th Hill Rd North
WTH RG45 87 H1
th Hill Rd South
WTH RG45 87 H1
thlands Dr MDHD SL6 25 J8
thlands Rd EWKG RG40 74 E4
th La NTHA RG18 97 L1
thmoors BRAK RG12 76 C2
thpark Dr BFOR GU20 90 E2
th Pl BAGS GU19 * 89 L3
th Ride CWTH RG45 86 D2
WKG RG40 74 A8
th Ri CBLY GU15 94 D1
W GU25 80 D1
th Rd BAGS GU19 89 L3
ARL RG6 60 A1
ADY RG26 148 G1
HLE RG7 135 Q8
throw Cl WDR/YW UB7 41 K8
throw Copse TADY RG26 103 M6
hside Pk CBLY GU15 89 J7
h Wy IVER SL0 30 F3
chway ASC SL5 65 L6
BLY GU15 94 D1
WDGN UB2 * 43 M4
LE/CALC RG31 137 N2
hway Cl CBLY GU15 94 D1
hwood Cl YTLY GU46 86 D7
vens Lea BNEND SL8 20 E4
becastle Down BNFD RG42 64 C4
den Cl STHA RG19 97 L5
don Wk FARN GU14 94 A7
gecroft YTLY GU46 * 86 B8
geway NWBY RG14 7 K1
ingham Ms MDHD SL6 * 4 C5
sor Hl BNEND SL8 20 F5
sor La FLKWH/TG HP10 21 H4
sor Rd BNEND SL8 20 D4
as Rd WWKG RG41 14 C6
nan Cl FRIM GU16 94 E7
ena Rd WDSR SL4 13 J7
Helgiford Gdns SUN TW16 71 L5
Helksham Cl SHST GU47 87 K5
Hellyer Wy BNEND SL8 20 E3
Helmsdale BRAK RG12 76 E2
Helmsdale Cl
RDGW/BURGH RG30 44 B6
Helston Gdns WHIT RG2 59 H5
Helston La WDSR SL4 12 E6
Helvellyn Cl EGH TW20 69 H5
Hemdean Hl CAV/SC RG4 45 G3
Hemdean Ri CAV/SC RG4 45 G3
Hemdean Rd CAV/SC RG4 45 G2
Hemming Wy SLN SL2 28 D4
Hemmyng Cnr BNFD RG42 64 C4
Hempson Av DTCH/LGLY SL3 39 L3
Hemsdale MDHD SL6 25 K5
Hemwood Rd WDSR SL4 52 D2
Hencroft St North SL SL1 11 H7
Hencroft St South SL SL1 11 H8
Hendons Wy MDHD SL6 36 D5
Hendon Ter ASHF TW15 * 71 K4
Hendon Wy STWL/WRAY TW19 56 D4
Hengrave Cl EARL RG6 60 E4
Hengrove Crs ASHF TW15 70 D1
Henley Cl FARN GU14 93 L6
Henley Dr FRIM GU16 94 E7
Henley Gdns YTLY GU46 92 D1
Henley Rd CAV/SC RG4 45 H3
CAV/SC RG4 45 L2
MDHD SL6 23 K4
MLW SL7 18 D6
SL SL1 28 A7
Henley Wood Rd EARL RG6 60 D2
Henry Rd SL SL1 10 D6
The Henrys NTHA RG18 97 M2
Henry St READ RG1 9 G8
Henshaw Crs NWBY RG14 141 R6
Hensworth Rd ASHF TW15 70 D4
Henwick Cl NTHA RG18 133 N12
Henwick La NTHA RG18 97 J2
Henwood Copse
GOR/PANG RG8 123 Q8
Hepplewhite Cl TADY RG26 148 A1
Hepworth Cft SHST GU47 87 L8
Hepworth Wy WOT/HER KT12 83 M5
Herald Wy WODY RG5 47 G8
Herbert Cl BRAK RG12 76 B2
Hereford Cl STA TW18 70 B6
Herewood Cl NWBY RG14 6 C1
Heriot Rd CHERT KT16 82 A4
Heritage Cl UX/CGN UB8 31 L5
Heritage Ct EGH TW20 68 F3
Hermes Cl WWKG RG41 61 H7
Hermitage Cl DTCH/LGLY SL3 39 L3
FRIM GU16 94 F5
SHPTN TW17 83 G1
Hermitage Dr ASC SL5 65 L7
WAR/TWY RG10 47 K1
Hermitage Gn NTHA RG18 133 N4
Hermitage La WDSR SL4 53 G2
Hermitage Pde ASC SL5 * 66 A8
Hermitage Rd NTHA RG18 133 P8
The Hermitage BNFD RG42 * 64 D3
FELT TW13 * 71 M1
Hermits Cl THLE RG7 143 R3
Hermon Gv HYS/HAR UB3 43 J1
Herndon Cl EGH TW20 69 G2
Heroes Wk WHIT RG2 59 H7
Heron Cl ASC SL5 65 K6
Herondale BRAK RG12 76 C4
Heron Dr DTCH/LGLY SL3 40 D4
WAR/TWY RG10 33 G7
Heronfield EGH TW20 68 B4
Herongate HUNG RG17 129 M11
Heron Island CAV/SC RG4 9 J2
Heron Rd WWKG RG41 61 L8
Heronscourt LTWR GU18 90 C6
Heron Shaw GOR/PANG RG8 112 A11
Heron's Wy EWKG RG40 15 K4
Heron Wy READ RG1 58 E2
STHA RG19 97 K3
THLE RG7 142 D3
Herriard Wy TADY RG26 148 D3
Herrick Cl FRIM GU16 95 J3
Herridge Cl TADY RG26 150 B8
Herrings La BFOR GU20 90 D1
CHERT KT16 82 A3
Herriot Ct YTLY GU46 92 C1
Herschel Gra BNFD RG42 64 D3
Herschel Park Dr SL SL1 11 J8
Herschel St SL SL1 11 G7
Hertford Cl CAV/SC RG4 127 K12
WWKG RG41 73 L1
Hetherington Cl SLN SL2 28 B4
Hetherington Rd SHPTN TW17 71 J7
Hever Cl MDHD SL6 4 A6
Hewett Av CAV/SC RG4 44 D2
Hewett Cl CAV/SC RG4 44 D2
Hewlett Pl BAGS GU19 89 L3
Hexham Cl SHST GU47 87 K4
Hexham Rd WHIT RG2 59 J3
Heynes Gn MDHD SL6 35 K3
Heywood Av MDHD SL6 35 J5
Heywood Court Cl MDHD SL6 35 J5
Heywood Dr BAGS GU19 89 J4
Heywood Gdns MDHD SL6 35 J5
Hibbert Rd MDHD SL6 36 D2
Hicks Cl TADY RG26 148 E2
Hicks La BLKW GU17 93 H1
Hieatt Cl READ RG1 9 H9
Higgs La BAGS GU19 89 K3
Highams La CHOB/PIR GU24 91 G2
High Beech BRAK RG12 76 F1
High Beeches FRIM GU16 94 D4
Highbridge Cl CAV/SC RG4 45 L1
Highbridge Whf READ RG1 9 H6
Highbury Crs CBLY GU15 89 G7
Highbury Rd TILE/CALC RG31 137 L3
Highclere ASC SL5 78 D2
Highclere Cl BRAK RG12 3 L4
Highclere Dr CBLY GU15 89 G7
Highcliffe Cl WODY RG5 46 F5
High Cl EWKG RG40 * 15 H4
Highdown Av CAV/SC RG4 126 C12
Highdown Hill Rd CAV/SC RG4 126 C11
Higher Alham BRAK RG12 76 E4
Highfield BRAK RG12 75 M3
EARL RG6 60 B4
Highfield Av NWBY RG14 6 E5
Highfield Cl EWKG RG40 14 F5
Highfield Ct EGH TW20 68 C4
Highfield La MDHD SL6 35 J2
Highfield Pk MLW SL7 18 D5
WAR/TWY RG10 33 H4
Highfield Rd BNEND SL8 20 D3
CHERT KT16 82 A5
EGH TW20 68 D4
MDHD SL6 25 K7
NWBY RG14 6 D9
SUN TW16 83 M1
TILE/CALC RG31 125 M10
WDSR SL4 12 A9
High Flds ASC SL5 78 F2
Highgate Rd WODY RG5 60 D1
Highgrove FARN GU14 94 B7
Highgrove Av ASC SL5 65 M6
Highgrove Pk MDHD SL6 4 E2
Highgrove Pl WAR/TWY RG10 47 L1
Highgrove St READ RG1 59 J1
Highgrove Ter READ RG1 9 H9
Highland Pk FELT TW13 71 M2
Highland Rd CBLY GU15 88 E6
Highlands Av WWKG RG41 73 J1
Highlands La HEN RG9 127 N3
Highmead Cl WHIT RG2 59 L4
High Meadow CAV/SC RG4 44 D3
High Meadow Pl CHERT KT16 81 M3
High Meadow Rd CAV/SC RG4 45 F3
High Rd MDHD SL6 20 A7
UX/CGN UB8 31 L6
High St IVER SL0 31 H7
ADL/WDHM KT15 82 B8
ASC SL5 65 M8
ASC SL5 78 D2
ASC SL5 79 G2
BAGS GU19 89 L3
BRAK RG12 2 F4
CAV/SC RG4 46 D2
CBLY GU15 88 D8
CHOB/PIR GU24 90 E7
CHOB/PIR GU24 91 L6
CWTH RG45 87 G1
DTCH/LGLY SL3 39 K8
DTCH/LGLY SL3 40 C3
DTCH/LGLY SL3 40 E7
EGH TW20 68 F3
FELT TW13 71 M1
GOR/PANG RG8 111 Q12
GOR/PANG RG8 124 H7
HEN RG9 114 D4
HEST TW5 43 K6
HUNG RG17 116 F1
HUNG RG17 117 K4
HUNG RG17 138 H1
HUNG RG17 140 A4
HYS/HAR UB3 42 F6
IVER SL0 31 G7
KSCL RG20 109 L12
KSCL RG20 121 R2
KSCL RG20 131 L9
KSCL RG20 131 N7
KSCL RG20 132 H1
MDHD SL6 5 G5
MDHD SL6 20 C7
MDHD SL6 27 G6
MDHD SL6 36 E2
MLW SL7 18 F5
READ RG1 9 G6
SHPTN TW17 83 H3
SHST GU47 86 F6
SL SL1 10 C8
SL SL1 11 H6
SL SL1 27 L4
STA TW18 69 M2
STHA RG19 97 M3
STWL/WRAY TW19 54 E5
STWL/WRAY TW19 56 D5
THLE RG7 137 J7
UX/CGN UB8 31 L1
UX/CGN UB8 31 L5
WAR/TWY RG10 32 F5
WAR/TWY RG10 47 K1
WDR/YW UB7 41 M6
WDR/YW UB7 42 A1
WDSR SL4 13 J1
WDSR SL4 13 K5
WEY KT13 83 G8
High St Harlington
HYS/HAR UB3 42 F6
High Town Rd MDHD SL6 4 F6
High Tree Dr EARL RG6 46 B8
Highview TILE/CALC RG31 137 M5
Highview Crs CBLY GU15 88 F5
High View Rd LTWR GU18 89 L6
Highway CWTH RG45 87 G1
Highway Av MDHD SL6 25 J7
Highwayman's Rdg BFOR GU20 78 B8
Highway Rd MDHD SL6 25 K8
Highwood Cl NWBY RG14 132 H12
YTLY GU46 92 C2
Highworth Wy
TILE/CALC RG31 125 M12
Hilary Cl WHIT RG2 59 J7
Hilborn Wy WHIT RG2 73 G5
Hilbury Rd EARL RG6 60 A3
Hilcot Rd RDGW/BURGH RG30 44 D6
Hildens Dr TILE/CALC RG31 137 N3
Hilfield YTLY GU46 92 F1
Hillary Dr CWTH RG45 75 H8
Hillary Rd DTCH/LGLY SL3 40 A3
Hillberry BRAK RG12 76 C4
Hillborne Cl HYS/HAR UB3 43 J5
Hill Bottom Cl GOR/PANG RG8 125 J3
Hillbrow WHIT RG2 59 L5
Hill Cl NWBY RG14 141 R7
Hill Copse Vw BRAK RG12 3 L3
Hill Crs THLE RG7 * 99 L4
Hillcrest WEY KT13 83 H8
Hillcrest Av CHERT KT16 81 L7
MDHD SL6 26 A1
Hillcrest La HEN RG9 126 F3
Hillcrest Rd CBLY GU15 89 H7
Hilldrop La HUNG RG17 116 H10
Hillersdon SLN SL2 29 K6
Hill Farm Rd MDHD SL6 27 G4
Hill Gdns GOR/PANG RG8 111 P12
Hillgreen La KSCL RG20 120 C7
Hillhampton ASC SL5 78 F4
Hillhouse La STHA RG19 102 B7
Hilliards Rd UX/CGN UB8 31 M7
Hillingdon Av
STWL/WRAY TW19 56 E7
Hillingdon Rd UX/CGN UB8 31 L2
Hillingdon Trail
HYS/HAR UB3 43 J5
Hill Lands WAR/TWY RG10 32 F4
Hillmead Ct MDHD SL6 27 H6
Hill Piece DID OX11 109 L3
Hill Pl SLN SL2 28 D1
Hillrise DTCH/LGLY SL3 40 C6
Hill Rd NWBY RG14 6 A2
WHIT RG2 72 F5
Hillsborough Ct FARN GU14 93 L8
Hillsborough Pk CBLY GU15 95 J1
Hill Side MDHD SL6 * 20 B7
Hillside ASC SL5 * 78 C2
CBLY GU15 87 M7
GOR/PANG RG8 124 H6
MDHD SL6 4 D9
READ RG1 * 59 J1
SL SL1 10 E6
THLE RG7 144 A3
VW GU25 80 C3
Hillside Crs FRIM GU16 94 F7
Hillside Dr BNFD RG42 63 J4
Hillside Pk ASC SL5 78 F5
WHIT RG2 59 M5
Hillside Rd EARL RG6 60 D3
HUNG RG17 138 H2
MLW SL7 19 G2
Hills La MDHD SL6 19 L7
Hill St READ RG1 9 G9
Hillswood Dr CHERT KT16 81 J8
Hilltop Cl ASC SL5 66 E7
Hill Top Dr MLW SL7 18 D4
Hilltop Rd CAV/SC RG4 44 D1
EARL RG6 46 B6
WAR/TWY RG10 33 G7
Hilltop Vw YTLY GU46 92 B1
Hill Vw CHOB/PIR GU24 * 79 J8
THLE RG7 145 L5
Hillview Cl TILE/CALC RG31 125 M12
Hill View Ms
RDGW/BURGH RG30 * 137 Q2
Hill View Rd STWL/WRAY TW19 54 D5
Hilmanton EARL RG6 59 M6
Hilperton Rd SL SL1 10 E6
Hilton Cl UX/CGN UB8 31 K3
Hindell Cl FARN GU14 94 A6
Hindhay La MDHD SL6 25 K3
Hindhead Rd EARL RG6 60 A3
Hinksey Cl DTCH/LGLY SL3 40 D3
Hinton Cl CWTH RG45 75 H7
TADY RG26 148 D3
Hinton Dr CWTH RG45 75 H7
Hinton Rd SL SL1 28 A8
UX/CGN UB8 31 L2
WAR/TWY RG10 47 M6
Hirstwood
RDGW/BURGH RG30 137 Q1
Hirtes Av WHIT RG2 145 Q1
Hitcham La SL SL1 27 J4
Hitcham Rd SL SL1 27 J5
Hitchcock Cl SHPTN TW17 70 F8
Hitherbroom Rd HYS/HAR UB3 43 J1
Hitherhooks Hl BNFD RG42 63 L6
Hithermoor Rd
STWL/WRAY TW19 55 M5
Hobbis Dr MDHD SL6 25 J8
Hobbs End HEN RG9 127 P2
Hockett La MDHD SL6 19 H8
Hocketts Cl GOR/PANG RG8 125 J3
Hockford La THLE RG7 103 J3
Hockham Rd KSCL RG20 121 R1
Hockley La SLN SL2 29 K1
Hodgedale La WAR/TWY RG10 23 M8
Hodge La WDSR SL4 * 53 J3
WDSR SL4 66 A3
Hodges Cl BAGS GU19 89 K5
Hodsoll Rd READ RG1 8 C4
Hoe Benham La KSCL RG20 131 K12
Hoffman Cl BNFD RG42 64 D4
Hogarth Av ASHF TW15 71 J4
RDGW/BURGH RG30 137 R5
Hogarth Cl SHST GU47 87 L8
SL SL1 28 A8
UX/CGN UB8 31 L4
Hogfair La SL SL1 27 L5
Hogmoor La WAR/TWY RG10 47 M5
Hogoak La BNFD RG42 51 G6
WDSR SL4 51 G3
Hogwood La EWKG RG40 73 G8
Holbeche Cl YTLY GU46 92 A1
Holbeck BRAK RG12 75 M3
Holberton Rd WHIT RG2 59 K6
Holborne Cl NWBY RG14 141 Q9
Holborn Hl WANT OX12 106 B3
Holbrook Meadow EGH TW20 69 J4
Holder Cl WHIT RG2 145 P1
Holford Cl TILE/CALC RG31 137 N2
Holkham Cl
RDGW/BURGH RG30 137 R1
Holland Gdns EGH TW20 69 M7
Holland Pines BRAK RG12 75 M4
Holland Rd MLW SL7 19 H4
RDGW/BURGH RG30 137 P3
The Hollands STHA RG19 98 A3
Hollicombe Cl
RDGW/BURGH RG30 137 Q3
The Hollies BLKW GU17 * 93 M5
NWBY RG14 141 R9
Hollington Pl STHA RG19 * 97 L3
Hollins Wk RDGW/BURGH RG30 44 C8
Holloway Cl WDR/YW UB7 42 A5
Holloway Dr VW GU25 80 E1
Holloway Hl CHERT KT16 81 J7
Holloway La WDR/YW UB7 42 B5
Hollow Hill La DTCH/LGLY SL3 40 E2
IVER SL0 30 D8
Hollow La VW GU25 68 C8
WHIT RG2 145 Q1
Hollow Wy DID OX11 109 N4
Holly Av FRIM GU16 95 H3
Hollybank CHOB/PIR GU24 90 F8
Hollybush Hl SLN SL2 29 K1
Hollybush La HTWY RG27 85 L6
IVER SL0 30 D7
MDHD SL6 19 K8
TADY RG26 148 B8
THLE RG7 143 P4
Hollybush Ride EWKG RG40 86 C1
Hollybush Tr BFOR GU20 77 M8
Holly Cl CHERT KT16 80 A7
EGH TW20 68 B4
HEN RG9 114 E9
STHA RG19 102 D1
TADY RG26 150 A8
Hollycombe EGH TW20 68 C2
Holly Ct CWTH RG45 * 86 F1
Holly Crs WDSR SL4 52 D1
Hollycroft STHA RG19 103 G5
Hollycroft Cl WDR/YW UB7 42 C6
Hollycroft Gdns WDR/YW UB7 42 C6
Hollydale Cl WHIT RG2 59 K5
Holly Dr MDHD SL6 5 H2
WDSR SL4 53 L4
Hollyfields Cl CBLY GU15 94 B1
Holly Gdns WDR/YW UB7 42 B4
Holly Gn WEY KT13 83 K8
Holly Hedge Cl FRIM GU16 94 E4
Holly Hedge Rd FRIM GU16 94 E4
Holly La GOR/PANG RG8 123 K8
NTHA RG18 134 D7
THLE RG7 149 K2
Hollym Cl EARL RG6 60 E4
Holly Orch WWKG RG41 14 A8
Holly Rd WODY RG5 47 G8
Holly Spring La BRAK RG12 3 J2
Hollytree Gdns FRIM GU16 94 D6
Holly Wk WDSR SL4 66 E2
Holly Wy BLKW GU17 93 K2
Holman Cl TADY RG26 150 B8
Holmanleaze MDHD SL6 5 J4
Holmbank Dr SHPTN TW17 83 L1
Holmbury Av CWTH RG45 75 G7
Holmbury Gdns HYS/HAR UB3 43 H1
Holmdene THLE RG7 143 R3
Holme Cl CWTH RG45 75 G7
Holmedale SLN SL2 29 L8
Holme Gra EWKG RG40 * 74 F3
Holme Gn EWKG RG40 * 74 E2
Holmemoor Dr CAV/SC RG4 46 D4
Holme Park Farm La
CAV/SC RG4 46 C4
Holmes Cl ASC SL5 78 C3
WWKG RG41 14 B9
Holmes Crs WWKG RG41 14 C9
Holmes Rd EARL RG6 60 A1
Holmewood Cl WWKG RG41 74 A4
Holmlea Rd DTCH/LGLY SL3 39 M8
GOR/PANG RG8 124 A1
Holmlea Wk DTCH/LGLY SL3 39 L8
Holmsdale Cl IVER SL0 31 H7
Holmwood Av
RDGW/BURGH RG30 137 R5
Holmwood Cl MDHD SL6 35 K1
Holstein Av WEY KT13 83 G8
Holsworthy Cl EARL RG6 60 E3
Holt Cl FARN GU14 94 C7
Holt Cots STHA RG19 103 H6
Holt La KSCL RG20 119 P4
WWKG RG41 14 E4
Holton Heath BRAK RG12 76 F1
Holt Rd HUNG RG17 140 B4
The Holt GOR/PANG RG8 125 P10
Holtwood Rd KSCL RG20 140 H8
Holybrook Crs
RDGW/BURGH RG30 58 A2
Holybrook Rd READ RG1 58 F1
Holyhook Cl CWTH RG45 75 G8
Holyport Rd MDHD SL6 36 D6
Holyport St MDHD SL6 36 C6
Holyrood Cl CAV/SC RG4 127 K12
Holywell Cl FARN GU14 94 A7
STWL/WRAY TW19 56 E7
Holywell Ct STHA RG19 97 M3
Holywell Wy STWL/WRAY TW19 56 E7
Hombrook Dr BNFD RG42 63 L6
Home Cl VW GU25 80 D3
Home Cft TILE/CALC RG31 137 M1
Home Farm Cl FARN GU14 94 D8
SHPTN TW17 83 L1
WHIT RG2 59 H2
Home Farm Wy DTCH/LGLY SL3 29 L2
Homefield Wy HUNG RG17 138 G1
Homelands Wy HEN RG9 127 R1
Homelea Cl FARN GU14 94 B6
Home Mead Cl NWBY RG14 96 A6
Home Meadow SLN SL2 28 E3
Home Park Rd YTLY GU46 86 C8
Homers Rd WDSR SL4 37 M8
Homeside Cl MDHD SL6 26 A4
Homestead Rd MDHD SL6 35 M2
STA TW18 70 B4
Homewaters Av SUN TW16 71 M6
Homewood DTCH/LGLY SL3 29 M7
Hone Hl SHST GU47 87 H6
Honesty Bottom KSCL RG20 119 P4
Honeybottom Rd TADY RG26 148 D1
Honey End La
RDGW/BURGH RG30 44 A8
Honeyfields HUNG RG17 138 H1
Honey Hl EWKG RG40 74 F4
HUNG RG17 117 K3
Honeyhill Rd BNFD RG42 2 C3
Honey La MDHD SL6 24 A4
WGFD OX10 111 P1
Honey Meadow Cl CAV/SC RG4 45 L4
Honeysuckle Cl CWTH RG45 75 G7
IVER SL0 30 E7
YTLY GU46 86 A8
Honiton Rd WHIT RG2 59 J4
Honnor Rd STA TW18 70 D5
Hook Cl STHA RG19 96 D7
Hookend La GOR/PANG RG8 113 P9
Hook End La GOR/PANG RG8 123 P7
GOR/PANG RG8 124 A3
Hook La CHOB/PIR GU24 90 C8
TADY RG26 103 K8
Hook Mill La LTWR GU18 90 D4
Hookstone La CHOB/PIR GU24 90 F6
Hoops Wy WHIT RG2 58 F6
Hope Av BRAK RG12 76 E4
Hope Fountain CBLY GU15 94 F2
Hopeman Cl SHST GU47 87 K7
Hop Gdns HEN RG9 115 R12
NWBY RG14 * 96 D1
Hopper V BRAK RG12 76 A3
Hopwood Cl NWBY RG14 7 L1
Horatio Av BNFD RG42 3 M2
Horewood Rd BRAK RG12 76 B3
Hormer Cl SHST GU47 87 K5
Hornbeam Cl GOR/PANG RG8 * 125 N9
SHST GU47 87 K5
WWKG RG41 73 K3
Hornbeam Copse BNFD RG42 65 G6
Hornbeam Dr EARL RG6 60 D5
Hornbeam Gdns
DTCH/LGLY SL3 11 J9
Hornbeam Pightle THLE RG7 143 R3
Hornbeams THLE RG7 145 N7
Hornbill Cl UX/CGN UB8 31 M7
Hornby Av BRAK RG12 76 D4
Horncastle Dr
RDGW/BURGH RG30 * 137 R5
Horndean Rd BRAK RG12 76 F3
Horne Rd SHPTN TW17 82 F1
STHA RG19 98 A4
Hornsea Cl
RDGW/BURGH RG30 137 Q1
Horn St KSCL RG20 122 A1
Horsebrass Dr BAGS GU19 89 L4
The Horse Cl CAV/SC RG4 45 J2
Horsecroft Wy
ILE/CALC RG31 125 M10
Horse Gate Ride ASC SL5 78 A3
Horseguards Dr MDHD SL6 5 M5
Horsell Ct CHERT KT16 82 B4
Horsemoor Cl DTCH/LGLY SL3 40 C4
Horsepond Rd CAV/SC RG4 126 B5
CAV/SC RG4 126 C4
Horseshoe Cl CBLY GU15 88 F6
Horseshoe Crs CBLY GU15 88 F6
THLE RG7 143 Q3
Horseshoe End NWBY RG14 96 D6
Horseshoe Hl SL SL1 21 L6
Horseshoe Pk GOR/PANG RG8 124 H9
Horseshoe Rd GOR/PANG RG8 124 H9
Horsham Rd EBED/NFELT TW14 57 J5
SHST GU47 87 K5
Horsnape Gdns BNFD RG42 63 H4
Horsneile La BNFD RG42 2 E2
Horton Bridge Rd
WDR/YW UB7 42 B1
Horton Cl MDHD SL6 26 E5
WDR/YW UB7 42 B1
Horton Gdns DTCH/LGLY SL3 * 54 F2
Horton Pde WDR/YW UB7 * 42 A1
Horton Rd DTCH/LGLY SL3 39 L8
DTCH/LGLY SL3 55 L2
WDR/YW UB7 42 A1
Horvath Cl WEY KT13 83 K8
Hose Hl THLE RG7 137 L11
Hosier St READ RG1 8 F6
Hoskins Cl HYS/HAR UB3 43 H5
Houlton Ct BAGS GU19 89 L4
Hound Green Cl HTWY RG27 151 P7
Houseman Rd FARN GU14 93 M8
Houston Wy CWTH RG45 86 D1
Howard Av SLN SL2 28 F6
Howard Cl BRAK RG12 76 A2
SUN TW16 71 M4
Howard Ct BNEND SL8 20 C3
Howard Rd EWKG RG40 15 H7
NWBY RG14 6 E7
Howard St READ RG1 8 D6
Howarth Rd MDHD SL6 5 K6
Howe La BNFD RG42 49 L6
MDHD SL6 50 A2
Howell Cl BNFD RG42 64 C4
WHIT RG2 72 E6
How's Rd UX/CGN UB8 31 L2
Howth Dr WODY RG5 46 D7
Hubbard Cl WAR/TWY RG10 47 M3
Hubberholme BRAK RG12 2 D6
Hubert Rd DTCH/LGLY SL3 39 M3
Huckleberry Cl GOR/PANG RG8 125 N10
Huddington Gld YTLY GU46 92 A1
Hudson Pl DTCH/LGLY SL3 40 B5
Hudson Rd HYS/HAR UB3 42 F6
WODY RG5 60 F1
Hudsons Meadow HTWY RG27 151 P7
Hughenden Cl MDHD SL6 4 A7
Hughenden Rd SL SL1 10 D1

Hughes Rd *ASHF* TW15 ... 71 J5
EWKG RG40 ... 15 K4
Hugh Fraser Dr
TILE/CALC RG31 ... 137 N4
Hull Cl *SL* SL1 ... 10 A6
Humber Cl *NTHA* RG18 ... 97 K1
WDR/YW UB7 ... 41 M1
WWKG RG41 ... 14 A4
Humber Wy *DTCH/LGLY* SL3 ... 40 C4
SHST GU47 ... 87 K6
Hummer Rd *EGH* TW20 ... 69 G2
Humphrey's La *HUNG* RG17 ... 118 A8
Hungerford Av *SLN* SL2 ... 29 G6
Hungerford Cl *SHST* GU47 ... 87 J6
Hungerford Dr *MDHD* SL6 ... 26 A3
READ RG1 ... 58 E1
Hungerford Hl *HUNG* RG17 ... 117 J5
HUNG RG17 ... 130 C1
Hungerford La *THLE* RG7 ... 135 N8
WAR/TWY RG10 ... 48 C4
Hungerford Rd *HUNG* RG17 ... 139 M2
Hungerford Sq *WEY* KT13 ... 83 K8
Hunstanton Cl *DTCH/LGLY* SL3 ... 40 E7
Huntercombe Cl *MDHD* SL6 ... 27 K7
Huntercombe End La
HEN RG9 ... 114 A2
Huntercombe La North *SL* SL1 ... 27 L6
Huntercombe La South
MDHD SL6 ... 37 K1
Hunters Cha *CAV/SC* RG4 ... 44 F1
Hunters Gv *HYS/HAR* UB3 ... 43 J1
Hunter's Hl *THLE* RG7 ... 143 P3
Hunters Meadow *HUNG* RG17 ... 118 E11
Hunters Wy *SL* SL1 ... 38 A1
THLE RG7 ... 145 L5
Huntingdon Cl *EARL* RG6 ... 60 E4
Huntingfield Wy *EGH* TW20 ... 69 K5
Huntington Gdns *NWBY* RG14 ... 97 G1
Huntington Pl *DTCH/LGLY* SL3 ... 40 D3
Huntley Cl *STWL/WRAY* TW19 ... 56 E6
Huntsgreen Ct *BRAK* RG12 ... 3 H6
Hunt's La *MDHD* SL6 ... 27 G3
Huntsmans Meadow *ASC* SL5 ... 65 M6
Huntsmoor Rd *TADY* RG26 ... 148 B2
Huntswood La *MDHD* SL6 ... 27 H1
Hurford Dr *STHA* RG19 ... 98 B3
Hurley High St *MDHD* SL6 ... 24 B2
Hurley La *MDHD* SL6 ... 24 D3
Hurricane Wy *DTCH/LGLY* SL3 ... 40 D5
WODY RG5 ... 47 G7
Hursley Cl *RDGW/BURGH* RG30 ... 137 Q3
Hurst Cl *BRAK* RG12 * ... 3 J9
BRAK RG12 * ... 76 A2
Hurstdene Av *STA* TW18 ... 70 B4
Hurstfield Dr *MDHD* SL6 ... 27 K7
Hurst Gv *WOT/HER* KT12 ... 83 M5
Hurst La *EGH* TW20 ... 68 F8
Hurst Park Rd *WAR/TWY* RG10 ... 47 L4
Hurst Rd *FARN* GU14 ... 94 B6
SL SL1 ... 27 M6
WAR/TWY RG10 ... 47 L3
Hurst Wy *WHIT* RG2 ... 58 F6
Hurstwood *ASC* SL5 ... 78 A3
Hurworth Av *DTCH/LGLY* SL3 ... 39 L3
Huscarle Wy *TILE/CALC* RG31 ... 125 N10
Huson Rd *BNFD* RG42 ... 64 C5
Hutsons Cl *EWKG* RG40 ... 15 K2
Hutton Cl *BFOR* GU20 ... 90 D3
EARL RG6 ... 60 A4
NWBY RG14 ... 7 G1
Huxley Cl *SLN* SL2 ... 29 K5
Huxtable Gdns *MDHD* SL6 ... 36 F6
Hyde End La *THLE* RG7 ... 102 F1
THLE RG7 ... 145 N2
Hyde End Rd *THLE* RG7 ... 145 M4
Hyde Gn *MLW* SL7 ... 19 H5
Hyde La *KSCL* RG20 ... 101 J5
Hydes Platt *THLE* RG7 ... 149 K2
The Hydes *TILE/CALC* RG31 ... 125 N10
Hyde Ter *ASHF* TW15 ... 71 L4
The Hyde *MDHD* SL6 * ... 5 H2
Hyde Wy *HYS/HAR* UB3 ... 43 H4
Hylle Cl *WDSR* SL4 ... 38 A8
Hylton Ct *TADY* RG26 ... 148 E2
Hyperion Wy *WHIT* RG2 ... 59 H3
Hythe Cl *BRAK* RG12 ... 76 E2
TADY RG26 ... 148 D3
Hythe End Rd
STWL/WRAY TW19 ... 55 G8
Hythe Field Av *EGH* TW20 ... 69 K4
Hythe Park Rd *EGH* TW20 ... 69 J3
Hythe Rd *STA* TW18 ... 69 K3
The Hythe *STA* TW18 ... 69 L3

I

Ian Mikardo Wy *CAV/SC* RG4 ... 9 M1
Iberian Wy *CBLY* GU15 ... 89 H8
Ibstock Cl *RDGW/BURGH* RG30 ... 44 B7
Ibstone Av *CAV/SC* RG4 ... 45 L1
Icknield Pl *GOR/PANG* RG8 ... 112 B10
Icknield Rd *GOR/PANG* RG8 ... 112 B10
Iden Ct *NWBY* RG14 ... 7 H2
Iffley Cl *UX/CGN* UB8 ... 31 M1
Ilbury Cl *WHIT* RG2 ... 145 Q1
Ilchester Cl *MDHD* SL6 ... 4 B8
Ilchester Ms *CAV/SC* RG4 ... 127 L12
Ilex Cl *CAV/SC* RG4 ... 126 F6
EGH TW20 ... 68 B5
TADY RG26 ... 148 C1
YTLY GU46 ... 86 B8
Ilfracombe Wy *EARL* RG6 ... 60 E3
Ilkley Rd *CAV/SC* RG4 ... 44 E3
Ilkley Wy *STHA* RG19 ... 97 L4
Illiffe Cl *READ* RG1 ... 9 H9
Illingworth *WDSR* SL4 ... 52 E2
Illingworth Av *CAV/SC* RG4 ... 127 L12
Illingworth Cl *TADY* RG26 ... 150 B8
Illingworth Gv *BRAK* RG12 ... 64 F6
Ilsley Cl *CAV/SC* RG4 ... 126 F5
Ilsley Gdns *KSCL* RG20 * ... 121 R2
Ilsley Rd *KSCL* RG20 ... 109 P12
Imperial Ct *HEN* RG9 * ... 22 B5
WDSR SL4 ... 53 G2
Imperial Rd *EBED/NFELT* TW14 ... 57 L6
WDSR SL4 ... 12 D9
Imperial Wy *STHA* RG19 ... 98 A4
WHIT RG2 ... 59 G7
Impstone Rd *TADY* RG26 ... 148 H1
Inchwood *BRAK* RG12 ... 76 C5
India Rd *SL* SL1 ... 11 L6
Indrapura *EWKG* RG40 * ... 63 G1
Infantry Dr *STHA* RG19 ... 98 A5
Ingle Dell *CBLY* GU15 ... 94 D2
Ingle Gln *EWKG* RG40 * ... 74 A7
Ingles Edge *HUNG* RG17 ... 139 P10
Ingleside *DTCH/LGLY* SL3 ... 41 G8
Ingleton *BRAK* RG12 ... 2 D7
Inglewood *CHERT* KT16 ... 81 M7
Inglewood Av *CBLY* GU15 ... 95 J2
Inglewood Cl *CAV/SC* RG4 ... 126 F5
Inglewood Ct
RDGW/BURGH RG30 ... 44 C8
Inglewood Rd *HUNG* RG17 ... 139 L5
Ingress V *BNFD* RG42 * ... 2 E1
Inhams Wy *THLE* RG7 ... 149 J2
Inhurst La *TADY* RG26 ... 103 L5
Inhurst Wy *TADY* RG26 ... 148 B1
Inkerman Rd *WDSR* SL4 ... 38 B4
Inkpen Cl *RDGW/BURGH* RG30 ... 58 A2
Inkpen Rd *HUNG* RG17 ... 139 J3
HUNG RG17 ... 140 A4
Inner Ring East *HTHAIR* TW6 ... 57 H2
Innings La *BNFD* RG42 ... 3 K2
MDHD SL6 ... 34 F7
Institute Rd *MDHD* SL6 ... 27 H7
MLW SL7 ... 19 G5
Instow Gdns *FARN* GU14 ... 94 A7
Instow Rd *EARL* RG6 ... 60 B4
International Av *HEST* TW5 ... 43 L5
International Wy *SUN* TW16 ... 71 L6
In The Ray *MDHD* SL6 ... 5 M2
Invergordon Cl
TILE/CALC RG31 ... 137 Q6
Inverness Wy *SHST* GU47 ... 87 K7
Invicta Cl *EBED/NFELT* TW14 ... 57 M7
Inwood Cl *MDHD* SL6 ... 19 K8
Iona Crs *SL* SL1 ... 28 A7
Ipswich Rd *SL* SL1 ... 28 B7
Ireton Av *WOT/HER* KT12 ... 83 M6
Irish Hill Rd *HUNG* RG17 ... 140 B4
Iron Bridge Rd *STKPK* UB11 * ... 42 D1
Iron Bridge Rd North
STKPK UB11 ... 42 C1
Iron Bridge Rd South
WDR/YW UB7 ... 42 C2
Irvine Dr *FARN* GU14 ... 93 L6
Irvine Pl *VW* GU25 ... 80 E2
Irvine Wy *EARL* RG6 ... 60 C6
Isaac Newton Rd *EWKG* RG40 ... 72 F5
Isis Cl *WWKG* RG41 ... 61 H5
Isis Ct *READ* RG1 ... 8 F3
Isis Wy *BNEND* SL8 ... 20 D2
SHST GU47 ... 87 K6
Island Cl *STA* TW18 ... 69 L2
Island Farm Rd *THLE* RG7 ... 143 N5
Island Rd *WHIT* RG2 ... 58 F3
Islandstone La *WAR/TWY* RG10 ... 48 A8
Islet Pk *MDHD* SL6 ... 26 E3
Islet Park Dr *MDHD* SL6 ... 26 E3
Islet Rd *MDHD* SL6 ... 26 D3
Ismay Cl *SLN* SL2 * ... 10 F1
Ivanhoe Cl *UX/CGN* UB8 ... 31 M6
Ivanhoe Rd *EWKG* RG40 ... 73 G8
Iverdale Cl *IVER* SL0 ... 30 E8
Iver La *IVER* SL0 ... 31 K6
Iver Ldg *IVER* SL0 ... 31 H6
Iverna Gdns *EBED/NFELT* TW14 ... 57 K4
Ives Cl *YTLY* GU46 ... 86 B7
Ives Rd *DTCH/LGLY* SL3 ... 40 Q3
Ivybank *TILE/CALC* RG31 ... 137 N1
Ivy Cl *MDHD* SL6 ... 36 C7
Ivy Crs *SL* SL1 ... 28 B8
Ivydene Rd *RDGW/BURGH* RG30 ... 44 C5
Ivy Dr *LTWR* GU18 ... 90 A7

J

Jackson Cl *BRAK* RG12 ... 76 B2
Jacksons La *CAV/SC* RG4 ... 44 A1
Jacob Cl *BNFD* RG42 ... 63 K7
WDSR SL4 ... 38 A8
Jacob Rd *CBLY* GU15 ... 88 A7
Jago Ct *NWBY* RG14 ... 96 C6
James Butcher Dr *THLE* RG7 ... 137 J7
James Cl *MLW* SL7 ... 19 H2
James Meadow *DTCH/LGLY* SL3 ... 40 B6
James Pl *TADY* RG26 ... 148 E2
James Rd *CBLY* GU15 ... 94 B4
James's La
RDGW/BURGH RG30 ... 144 B2
THLE RG7 ... 144 D3
James St *READ* RG1 ... 8 C6
WDSR SL4 ... 13 J6
Jameston *BRAK* RG12 ... 76 C5
James Watt Rd *WHIT* RG2 ... 72 F8
James Wy *CBLY* GU15 ... 94 B4
Jamnagar Cl *STA* TW18 ... 69 M4
Janson Ct *READ* RG1 ... 8 C8
Japonica Cl *WWKG* RG41 ... 73 K2
Jaques's La *THLE* RG7 ... 137 K12
Jarvis Cl *HTWY* RG27 ... 85 L6
Jarvis Dr *WAR/TWY* RG10 ... 32 F8
Jasmine Cl *WWKG* RG41 ... 61 K7
Jasmine Ter *WDR/YW* UB7 ... 42 C2
Jasmine Wy *STHA* RG19 ... 102 D1
Jay Av *ADL/WDHM* KT15 * ... 82 E7
Jay Cl *EARL* RG6 ... 60 B5
Jays Nest Cl *BLKW* GU17 ... 93 K2
Jedburgh Cl *STHA* RG19 ... 98 B3
Jefferson Cl *CAV/SC* RG4 ... 127 J11
DTCH/LGLY SL3 ... 40 C4
Jeffries Ct *BNEND* SL8 ... 20 C4
Jellicoe Cl *SL* SL1 ... 38 D2
Jenkins Cl *RDGW/BURGH* RG30 ... 44 C8
Jenkins' Hill London Rd
BAGS GU19 ... 89 J5
Jenner Dr *CHOB/PIR* GU24 ... 91 G8
Jenner Wk *TILE/CALC* RG31 ... 137 L3
Jennery La *SL* SL1 ... 27 L4
Jennetts Cl *THLE* RG7 ... 135 N7
Jenny's Wk *YTLY* GU46 ... 86 E8
Jerome Cl *MLW* SL7 ... 19 H2
Jerome Cnr *CWTH* RG45 ... 87 J3
Jerome Rd *WODY* RG5 ... 46 D8
Jerrymoor Hl *EWKG* RG40 ... 73 M6
Jersey Cl *CHERT* KT16 ... 81 M7
Jersey Dr *WWKG* RG41 ... 61 G4
Jersey Pl *ASC* SL5 ... 78 D3
Jesmond Dene *NWBY* RG14 ... 6 C2
Jessamy Rd *WEY* KT13 ... 83 G6
Jesse Cl *YTLY* GU46 ... 92 F1
Jesse Ter *READ* RG1 ... 8 D7
Jessiman Ter *SHPTN* TW17 ... 83 G2
Jevington *BRAK* RG12 ... 76 C4
Jibbs Meadow *TADY* RG26 ... 149 R7
Jig's La North *BNFD* RG42 ... 64 E4
Jig's La South *BNFD* RG42 ... 3 L1
Job's La *MDHD* SL6 ... 19 K6
Jock's La *BNFD* RG42 ... 2 B1
Joel Cl *EARL* RG6 ... 60 A3
John Childs Cl *NWBY* RG14 ... 6 E7
John Hunt Cl *STHA* RG19 ... 98 A4
John Nike Wy *BRAK* RG12 ... 63 J7
John Pl *BNFD* RG42 ... 64 E5
John's Cl *ASHF* TW15 ... 71 J2
Johnson Dr *EWKG* RG40 ... 74 B7
Johnson Rd *HEST* TW5 ... 43 L7
Johnson St *NWDGN* UB2 ... 43 L3
John Taylor Ct *SL* SL1 ... 10 B5
Joinville Pl *ADL/WDHM* KT15 ... 82 D8
Jonathan Hl *KSCL* RG20 ... 100 D3
Jones Cnr *ASC* SL5 ... 65 L6
Jordan Cl *CAV/SC* RG4 ... 45 L1
THLE RG7 ... 145 P5
Jordans Cl *STWL/WRAY* TW19 ... 56 C6
Jordan's La *THLE* RG7 ... 143 P4
Joseph Ct *BNFD* RG42 * ... 64 E4
Josephine Ct
RDGW/BURGH RG30 ... 44 D8
Josey Cl *CAV/SC* RG4 * ... 126 F4
Jouldings La *THLE* RG7 ... 84 D2
Journeys End *SLN* SL2 ... 29 G6
Jubilee Arch *WDSR* SL4 ... 13 J5
Jubilee Av *ASC* SL5 ... 65 L6
WWKG RG41 ... 14 D3
Jubilee Cl *ASC* SL5 ... 65 L6
STWL/WRAY TW19 ... 56 C6
TADY RG26 ... 148 G1
WODY RG5 ... 46 E8
Jubilee Rd *EARL* RG6 ... 46 A8
EWKG RG40 ... 85 M1
MDHD SL6 ... 35 D2
NWBY RG14 ... 7 G6
Jubilee Sq *READ* RG1 ... 9 H8
Jubilee Wy *DTCH/LGLY* SL3 ... 39 L7
Judges Rd *GOR/PANG* RG8 ... 113 Q7
Juliet Gdns *BNFD* RG42 ... 64 F5
Julius Hl *BNFD* RG42 ... 64 F6
Julkes La *WHIT* RG2 ... 60 E7
Junction Rd *ASHF* TW15 ... 71 J3
LTWR GU18 ... 90 B5
READ RG1 ... 45 L8
Junction Ter *NWBY* RG14 ... 7 J5
Juniper *BRAK* RG12 ... 76 C5
Juniper Ct *SL* SL1 ... 11 K7
Juniper Dr *MDHD* SL6 ... 5 L3
Juniper Gdns *SUN* TW16 ... 71 M4
Juniper Pl *STHA* RG19 ... 98 C8
Juniper Rd *MLW* SL7 ... 18 F1
The Junipers *WWKG* RG41 ... 73 K2
Juniper Wy *TILE/CALC* RG31 ... 125 P12
Jupiter Wy *WWKG* RG41 ... 14 A6
Justice Cl *STHA* RG19 ... 98 B4
Jutland Cl *WWKG* RG41 ... 61 L8
Jutland Pl *EGH* TW20 ... 69 J3

K

Katesgrove La *READ* RG1 ... 8 F8
Kathleen Sanders Ct
THLE RG7 ... 137 J6
Kay Av *ADL/WDHM* KT15 ... 82 E7
Kaynes Pk *ASC* SL5 ... 65 L6
Kaywood Cl *DTCH/LGLY* SL3 ... 39 L3
Keane Cl *WODY* RG5 ... 46 E6
Kearsley Rd
RDGW/BURGH RG30 ... 44 C8
Keates Gn *BNFD* RG42 ... 2 F2
Keats Cl *WODY* RG5 ... 60 E1
Keats La *WDSR* SL4 ... 13 H2
Keats Rd *WODY* RG5 ... 60 E2
Keats Wy *CWTH* RG45 ... 75 H7
WDR/YW UB7 ... 42 B4
YTLY GU46 ... 92 B2
Keble Rd *MDHD* SL6 ... 4 D3
Keble Wy *SHST* GU47 ... 87 L4
Keel Dr *SL* SL1 ... 10 A7
Keeler Cl *WDSR* SL4 ... 52 E2
Keensacre *IVER* SL0 ... 30 F3
Keepers Combe *BRAK* RG12 ... 76 D3
Keepers Farm Cl *WDSR* SL4 ... 52 E1
Keepers Wk *VW* GU25 ... 80 D2
Keephatch Rd *EWKG* RG40 ... 15 L2
Keighley Cl *STHA* RG19 ... 97 L4
Keith Rd *HYS/HAR* UB3 ... 43 G3
Kelburne Cl *WWKG* RG41 ... 61 J3
Keldholme *BRAK* RG12 ... 2 D7
Kelly Cl *SHPTN* TW17 ... 71 L7
Kelmscott Cl *CAV/SC* RG4 ... 44 E3
Kelpatrick Rd *SL* SL1 ... 27 M7
Kelsey Av *EWKG* RG40 ... 73 L8
Kelsey Cl *MDHD* SL6 ... 35 M3
Kelsey Gv *YTLY* GU46 ... 92 E1
Kelton Cl *EARL* RG6 ... 60 E4
Kelvedon Wy *CAV/SC* RG4 ... 44 E1
Kelvin Cl *WHIT* RG2 ... 72 E7
Kelvin Rd *NWBY* RG14 ... 7 G2
Kemble Cl *WEY* KT13 ... 83 K8
Kemble Ct *TILE/CALC* RG31 ... 137 P6
Kemerton Cl *TILE/CALC* RG31 ... 137 P6
Kemp Ct *BAGS* GU19 ... 89 M4
Kempe Cl *DTCH/LGLY* SL3 ... 40 E4
Kempton Cl *NWBY* RG14 ... 7 K8
Kemsley Cha *SLN* SL2 ... 28 E2
Kenavon Dr *READ* RG1 ... 9 J5
Kendal Av *CAV/SC* RG4 ... 45 K1
WHIT RG2 ... 59 L8
Kendal Cl *EBED/NFELT* TW14 ... 57 M7
NTHA RG18 ... 97 L2
SLN SL2 ... 11 J3
Kendal Dr *SLN* SL2 ... 11 J3
Kendal Gv *CBLY* GU15 ... 95 K2
Kendall Pl *MDHD* SL6 ... 35 L2
Kendal Ms *UX/CGN* UB8 ... 31 L2
Kendrick Cl *EWKG* RG40 ... 14 F8
Kendrick Rd *DTCH/LGLY* SL3 ... 11 M9
NWBY RG14 ... 141 R9
READ RG1 ... 9 J8
Kenilworth Av *BRAK* RG12 ... 3 H2
RDGW/BURGH RG30 ... 58 D1
Kenilworth Cl *SL* SL1 ... 11 H9
Kenilworth Gdns *STA* TW18 ... 70 C3
Kenilworth Rd *ASHF* TW15 ... 70 D1
Kenmore Cl *FRIM* GU16 ... 94 D6
Kenneally *WDSR* SL4 ... 52 C1
Kennedy Cl *MDHD* SL6 ... 4 A7
MLW SL7 ... 19 G3
NWBY RG14 ... 141 R8
Kennedy Crs *WGFD* OX10 ... 111 P1
Kennedy Dr *GOR/PANG* RG8 ... 124 H9
Kennedy Gdns *EARL* RG6 ... 60 B3
Kennedy Meadow *HUNG* RG17 ... 138 G2
Kennel Av *ASC* SL5 ... 65 M6
Kennel Cl *ASC* SL5 ... 65 M4
Kennel Gn *ASC* SL5 ... 65 L6
Kennel La *BFOR* GU20 ... 90 C1
BNFD RG42 ... 2 E1
Kennel Ride *ASC* SL5 ... 65 M5
Kennel Wd *ASC* SL5 ... 65 M6
Kennet Cl *FARN* GU14 ... 93 K8
STHA RG19 ... 98 A3
Kennet Ct *WWKG* RG41 ... 14 A5
Kennet Pl *THLE* RG7 ... 143 R3
Kennet Rd *BNEND* SL8 ... 20 C2
DID OX11 ... 109 J1
MDHD SL6 ... 5 H3
NWBY RG14 ... 6 D5
Kennet Side *NWBY* RG14 ... 7 J4
READ RG1 ... 9 J6
Kennet St *READ* RG1 ... 9 J6
Kennett Pl *NWBY* RG14 ... 7 G2
Kennett Rd *DTCH/LGLY* SL3 ... 40 D3
Kennet Wk *READ* RG1 ... 9 L5
Kennet Wy *HUNG* RG17 ... 129 M11
Kennylands Rd *CAV/SC* RG4 ... 126 F6
Kensington Cl *EARL* RG6 ... 60 B5
Kensington Rd
RDGW/BURGH RG30 ... 44 D7
Kent Av *SL* SL1 ... 28 E6
Kent Cl *STA* TW18 ... 70 D4
WWKG RG41 ... 73 K1
Kent Folly *BNFD* RG42 ... 64 F4
Kentigern Dr *CWTH* RG45 ... 87 L1
Kenton Cl *BRAK* RG12 ... 3 J5
FRIM GU16 ... 94 F4
MLW SL7 ... 19 G4
Kenton Rd *EARL* RG6 ... 60 C2
Kenton's La *WAR/TWY* RG10 ... 22 E8
Kentons La *WDSR* SL4 ... 52 E1
Kent Rd *BFOR* GU20 ... 90 D1
RDGW/BURGH RG30 ... 44 D7
Kent Wy *MDHD* SL6 ... 26 A5
Kentwood Cl
RDGW/BURGH RG30 ... 137 Q1
WGFD OX10 ... 111 P1
Kentwood Hl *TILE/CALC* RG31 ... 125 Q12
Kenwood Cl *MDHD* SL6 ... 25 J7
WDR/YW UB7 ... 42 C6
Kenworth Gv *LTWR* GU18 ... 89 M5
Keppel Sp *WDSR* SL4 ... 54 B6
Keppel St *WDSR* SL4 ... 13 K7
Kepple Pl *BAGS* GU19 ... 89 L3
Kernham Dr *TILE/CALC* RG31 ... 125 M12
Kerria Wy *CHOB/PIR* GU24 ... 90 E8
Kerris Wy *EARL* RG6 ... 60 A5
Kersey Crs *NWBY* RG14 ... 96 A1
Kersten Cl *NWBY* RG14 ... 7 K9
Kesteven Wy *WWKG* RG41 ... 61 L8
Keston Cl *CAV/SC* RG4 ... 45 J3
Kestrel Av *STA* TW18 ... 69 M1
Kestrel Cl *STHA* RG19 ... 97 K3
Kestrels Md *TADY* RG26 ... 142 D12
Kestrel Wy *HYS/HAR* UB3 ... 42 F2
RDGW/BURGH RG30 ... 58 A2
THLE RG7 ... 143 R3
WWKG RG41 ... 14 A6
Keswick Cl *CBLY* GU15 ... 95 J2
RDGW/BURGH RG30 ... 137 P3
Keswick Ct *SLN* SL2 ... 11 H3
Keswick Dr *LTWR* GU18 ... 90 B6
Keswick Gdns *WODY* RG5 ... 60 E1
Keswick Rd *EGH* TW20 ... 69 H5
Ketcher Gn *BNFD* RG42 ... 63 J2
Kettering Cl *TILE/CALC* RG31 ... 137 Q6
Kevins Dr *YTLY* GU46 ... 86 E7
Kew Cl *UX/CGN* UB8 ... 31 L3
Keynsham Wy *SHST* GU47 ... 87 K4
Keysham Av *HEST* TW5 ... 43 J8
Keys Pl *MDHD* SL6 ... 5 G6
Kibble Gn *BRAK* RG12 ... 76 C3
Kibblewhite Crs
WAR/TWY RG10 ... 32 F8
Kidderminster Rd *SLN* SL2 ... 28 C4
Kidmore End Rd *CAV/SC* RG4 ... 126 G10
Kidmore La *CAV/SC* RG4 ... 126 D7
Kidmore Rd *CAV/SC* RG4 ... 126 E12
Kidwells Cl *MDHD* SL6 ... 5 H3
Kidwells Park Dr *MDHD* SL6 ... 5 H4
Kier Pk *ASC* SL5 ... 66 C8
Kilburn Cl *TILE/CALC* RG31 ... 137 P6
Kildare Gdns *CAV/SC* RG4 ... 45 J3
Killarney Dr *MDHD* SL6 ... 4 F4
Kilmartin Gdns *FRIM* GU16 ... 94 F5
Kilmington Cl *BRAK* RG12 ... 76 E4
Kilmiston Av *SHPTN* TW17 ... 83 J3
Kilmore Dr *CBLY* GU15 ... 95 H2
Kilmuir Cl *SHST* GU47 ... 87 K7
Kiln Cl *HYS/HAR* UB3 ... 42 F6
NTHA RG18 ... 133 P3
Kiln Croft Cl *MLW* SL7 ... 19 J3
Kiln Dr *NTHA* RG18 ... 133 L5
Kiln Flds *MDHD* SL6 ... 21 G5
Kiln Hl *THLE* RG7 ... 72 B7
Kiln La *ASC* SL5 ... 79 G2
BRAK RG12 ... 2 C5
FLKWH/TG HP10 ... 21 G3
HEN RG9 ... 127 P8
THLE RG7 ... 144 A9
TILE/CALC RG31 ... 137 L2
WDSR SL4 ... 66 B4
Kiln Pl *MDHD* SL6 ... 25 J3
Kiln Ride *EWKG* RG40 ... 74 A6
GOR/PANG RG8 ... 123 P9
Kiln Ride Extension
EWKG RG40 ... 74 A8
Kiln Rd *CAV/SC* RG4 ... 127 J11
NWBY RG14 ... 96 E1
Kilnsea Dr *EARL* RG6 ... 60 D4
Kiln Ter *NTHA* RG18 * ... 133 L5
Kiln View Rd *WHIT* RG2 ... 59 K4
Kilowna Cl *WAR/TWY* RG10 ... 47 G2
Kilross Rd *EBED/NFELT* TW14 ... 57 K7
Kilrue La *WOT/HER* KT12 ... 83 M8
Kimber Cl *WDSR* SL4 ... 53 G2
Kimberley *BRAK* RG12 ... 76 C5
Kimberley Cl *DTCH/LGLY* SL3 ... 40 B4
READ RG1 ... 58 E1
Kimbers Cl *NWBY* RG14 ... 6 D4
Kimbers Dr *NWBY* RG14 ... 141 Q1
SL SL1 ... 27 M4
Kimber's La *MDHD* SL6 ... 36 A3
Kimbers La *TADY* RG26 ... 148 F5
Kimmeridge *BRAK* RG12 ... 76 E3
Kimpton Cl *WHIT* RG2 ... 59 L6
Kinburn Dr *EGH* TW20 ... 68 E3
King Edwards Cl *ASC* SL5 * ... 65 L6
King Edwards Ri *ASC* SL5 ... 65 L6
King Edwards Rd *ASC* SL5 ... 65 L6
King Edward St *SL* SL1 ... 10 D7
King Edward VII Av *WDSR* SL4 ... 13 L3
Kingfisher Cl *FARN* GU14 ... 93 J8
THLE RG7 ... 142 E3
Kingfisher Ct *NWBY* RG14 ... 7 L4
WAR/TWY RG10 ... 47 L3
Kingfisher Dr *STA* TW18 ... 69 M2
WODY RG5 ... 46 C8
YTLY GU46 ... 86 B8
Kingfisher Gv *THLE* RG7 ... 145 K2
Kingfisher Pl *READ* RG1 ... 9 H4
King George Cl *SUN* TW16 ... 71 L3
Kinghorn La *MDHD* SL6 ... 25 M3
Kinghorn Pk *MDHD* SL6 ... 25 M3
King James Wy *HEN* RG9 ... 127 Q2
King John's Cl
STWL/WRAY TW19 ... 54 C5
Kings Apartments *CBLY* GU15 ... 94 C2
King's Av *SUN* TW16 ... 71 M3
Kingsbridge Hl *THLE* RG7 ... 145 L8
Kingsbridge Rd *NWBY* RG14 ... 6 A7
WHIT RG2 ... 59 H4
Kingsbury Crs *STA* TW18 ... 69 K2
Kingsbury Dr *WDSR* SL4 ... 54 A6
Kingsclear Pk *CBLY* GU15 ... 94 D2
King's Cl *STA* TW18 ... 70 D5
Kings Common Cl *HEN* RG9 ... 127 P9
King's Crs *CBLY* GU15 ... 88 C6
Kingscroft La *BNFD* RG42 ... 50 F8
Kingsdown Cl *EARL* RG6 ... 60 B4
Kings Farm La *HEN* RG9 ... 127 K4
Kingsfield *WDSR* SL4 ... 37 M8
Kingsford Cl *WODY* RG5 ... 61 G1
Kings Gdns *WAR/TWY* RG10 ... 32 F8
Kingsgate Pl *READ* RG1 ... 9 M6
Kingsgate St *READ* RG1 ... 9 M7
Kings Gld *YTLY* GU46 ... 86 F8
Kings Gv *MDHD* SL6 ... 4 E6
King's Keep *SHST* GU47 ... 87 H5
Kingsland Gra *NWBY* RG14 ... 96 A6
Kings La *BFOR* GU20 ... 90 E1
EGH TW20 ... 68 A3
MDHD SL6 ... 19 K6
Kingsley Av *CBLY* GU15 ... 94 C2
EGH TW20 ... 68 B4
Kingsley Cl *CWTH* RG45 ... 87 H3
NWBY RG14 ... 132 H12
WAR/TWY RG10 ... 47 G1
WHIT RG2 ... 59 H7
Kingsley Rd *FARN* GU14 ... 93 M8
HTWY RG27 ... 85 J6
Kingsmead *FRIM* GU16 ... 94 E7
King's Meadow Rd *READ* RG1 ... 9 H4
Kingsmere Rd *BNFD* RG42 ... 2 A2
Kings Ms *FRIM* GU16 ... 94 F8
Kings Reach *READ* RG1 ... 9 K4
King's Ride *ASC* SL5 ... 77 J1
CBLY GU15 ... 88 D5
King's Rd *ASC* SL5 ... 78 D2
CAV/SC RG4 ... 9
CWTH RG45 ... 87
EGH TW20 ... 69
Kings Rd *HEN* RG9 ... 115
King's Rd *HEN* RG9 ... 115
Kings Rd *NWBY* RG14 ... 6
King's Rd *READ* RG1 ... 9
SL SL1 ... 10
Kings Rd *THLE* RG7 ... 149
King's Rd *UX/CGN* UB8 ... 31
Kings Rd *WDR/YW* UB7 ... 42
WDSR SL4 ... 13
Kings Road West *NWBY* RG14 ... 6
King Stable St *WDSR* SL4 ... 13
Kingston Av *EBED/NFELT* TW14 ... 57
Kingston Crs *ASHF* TW15 ... 70
Kingston Gdns *WHIT* RG2 ... 59
Kingston La *THLE* RG7 ... 136
WDR/YW UB7 ... 42
Kingston Rd *ASHF* TW15 ... 70
CBLY GU15 ... 89
MARL SN8 ... 138
STA TW18 ... 70
King St *CHERT* KT16 ... 82
MDHD SL6 ... 5
READ RG1 ... 9
THLE RG7 ... 143
King Street La *WWKG* RG41 ... 61
King's Wk *CBLY* GU15 ... 87
Kings Wk *READ* RG1 ... 9
Kingsway *BLKW* GU17 ... 93
CAV/SC RG4 ... 127
STWL/WRAY TW19 ... 56
Kingswick Cl *ASC* SL5 ... 78
Kingswick Dr *ASC* SL5 ... 78
Kings Wd *MLW* SL7 ... 17
Kingswood Cl *ASHF* TW15 ... 71
CBLY GU15 ... 89
EGH TW20 ... 68
Kingswood Ct *MDHD* SL6 ... 36
RDGW/BURGH RG30 ... 44
Kingswood Creek
STWL/WRAY TW19 ... 54
Kingswood Ri *EGH* TW20 ... 68
Kings Yd *ASC* SL5 * ... 77
Kinnaird Cl *SL* SL1 ... 27
Kinross Av *ASC* SL5 ... 77
Kinross Cl *SUN* TW16 ... 71
Kinross Ct *ASC* SL5 ... 77
Kinross Dr *SUN* TW16 ... 71
Kinson Rd *RDGW/BURGH* RG30 ... 44
Kintbury Cross Ways
HUNG RG17 ... 140
Kintbury Rd *HUNG* RG17 ... 139
Kintbury Sq *HUNG* RG17 ... 140
Kinver Wk *WHIT* RG2 * ... 59
Kipling Cl *NTHA* RG18 ... 97
YTLY GU46 ... 92
Kirby Est *WDR/YW* UB7 * ... 31
Kirkby Ct *FRIM* GU16 ... 94
Kirkfell Cl *TILE/CALC* RG31 ... 125
Kirkham Cl *CAV/SC* RG4 ... 127
SHST GU47 ... 87
Kirkstall Ct *TILE/CALC* RG31 * ... 137
Kirkstone Cl *CBLY* GU15 ... 95
Kirkwall Sp *SL* SL1 ... 29
Kirkwood Crs *THLE* RG7 ... 143
Kirton Cl *RDGW/BURGH* RG30 ... 44
Kirtons Farm Rd
RDGW/BURGH RG30 ... 58
Kit La *HEN* RG9 ... 113
WGFD OX10 ... 113
Kitsmead La *CHERT* KT16 ... 80
VW GU25 ... 80
Kittiwake Cl *WODY* RG5 ... 47
Kitwood Dr *EARL* RG6 ... 60
Klondyke *MLW* SL7 ... 18
Knappe Cl *HEN* RG9 ... 127
Knapp La *TADY* RG26 ... 148
Knapp Rd *ASHF* TW15 ... 70
Knappswood Cl
GOR/PANG RG8 ... 124
The Knapp *EARL* RG6 ... 60
Knighton Cl *CAV/SC* RG4 ... 45
Knightsbridge Crs *STA* TW18 ... 70
Knightsbridge Dr *STHA* RG19 ... 101
Knightsbridge Rd *CBLY* GU15 ... 88
Knights Cl *EGH* TW20 * ... 69
WDSR SL4 ... 37
Knights La *KSCL* RG20 ... 141
Knights Lea *KSCL* RG20 ... 140
Knights Pl *WDSR* SL4 ... 13
Knights Wy *CAV/SC* RG4 ... 45
CBLY GU15 ... 95
Knightswood *BRAK* RG12 ... 76
Knole Wd *ASC* SL5 * ... 78
Knoll Cl *WANT* OX12 ... 106
Knoll Gdns *KSCL* RG20 ... 141
Knoll Park Rd *CHERT* KT16 ... 81
Knoll Rd *CBLY* GU15 ... 88
The Knoll *CHERT* KT16 ... 81
TILE/CALC RG31 ... 125
Knollys Rd *TADY* RG26 ... 148
Knolton Wy *SLN* SL2 ... 29
The Knook *SHST* GU47 * ... 87
Knossington Cl *EARL* RG6 ... 60
Knott La *THLE* RG7 ... 142
Knowle Cl *CAV/SC* RG4 ... 44
Knowle Gn *STA* TW18 ... 70
Knowle Gv *VW* GU25 ... 80
Knowle Grove Cl *VW* GU25 ... 80
Knowle Hl *VW* GU25 ... 80
Knowle Park Av *STA* TW18 ... 70
Knowle Rd *WODY* RG5 ... 60
Knowles Av *CWTH* RG45 ... 86
Knowles Cl *WDR/YW* UB7 ... 42
Knowl Hill Common
WAR/TWY RG10 ... 34
Knowsley Cl *MDHD* SL6 ... 25
Knowsley Rd
TILE/CALC RG31 ... 125
Knox Gn *BNFD* RG42 ... 63
Korda Cl *SHPTN* TW17 ... 70
Krooner Rd *CBLY* GU15 ... 94
Kybes La *THLE* RG7 ... 144
Kyle Cl *BRAK* RG12 ... 2

L

Laburnham Rd *MDHD* SL6 ... 4
Laburnum Cl *MLW* SL7 ... 19
Laburnum Gdns *WHIT* RG2 ... 59
Laburnum Gv *DTCH/LGLY* SL3 ... 40
NWBY RG14 ... 6
Laburnum Pl *EGH* TW20 ... 68
Laburnum Rd *CHERT* KT16 ... 82
HYS/HAR UB3 ... 43
WWKG RG41 ... 61
Laburnums *HTWY* RG27 * ... 150
The Laburnums *BLKW* GU17 ... 93
Laburnum Wy
STWL/WRAY TW19 ... 56
Lacey Cl *EGH* TW20 ... 69
Lackmore Gdns
GOR/PANG RG8 ... 113
Ladbroke Cl *WODY* RG5 ... 46
Ladbrooke Rd *SL* SL1 ... 10
Ladwell Cl *NWBY* RG14 ... 141
Ladybank *BRAK* RG12 ... 76

dyday Pl SL SL1 10 A5
dy Jane Ct CAV/SC RG4 45 H3
dy Margaret Rd ASC SL5 78 F5
dymask Cl TILE/CALC RG31 137 R6
dythorpe Cl
ADL/WDHM KT15 82 B8
e Laffords THLE RG7 135 Q8
ggan Rd MDHD SL6 26 B4
ggan Sq MDHD SL6 26 B5
ird Ct BAGS GU19 89 L5
ke Av SL SL1 10 C3
ke Ct TADY RG26 148 F2
ke End Ct MDHD SL6 * 27 K7
ke End Rd MDHD SL6 27 K8
WDSR SL4 37 K2
ke End Wy CWTH RG45 87 G2
keland Dr FRIM GU16 94 E5
ke Rd FRIM GU16 95 G8
VW GU25 80 B1
keside BNFD RG42 3 G1
EARL RG6 60 B3
MDHD SL6 26 D4
WEY KT13 83 L6
keside Dr SLN SL2 29 G2
keside Gdns FARN GU14 93 K7
keside Gra WEY KT13 83 J7
keside Rd DTCH/LGLY SL3 41 H7
e Lake Side BLKW GU17 93 K2
ke Vw MDHD SL6 26 C5
lande Cl WWKG RG41 61 L8
leham Abbey STA TW18 * 82 C1
leham Cl STA TW18 70 B6
leham Reach CHERT KT16 70 B7
leham Rd SHPTN TW17 82 E1
SHPTN TW17 83 G2
STA TW18 69 M4
mb Cl NTHA RG18 97 L1
mbdens Hl THLE RG7 136 B9
mbdens Wk TADY RG26 148 D2
mbert Av DTCH/LGLY SL3 40 A3
mbert Crs BLKW GU17 93 J2
mbert Dr NWBY RG14 97 G1
mbeth Ct
RDGW/BURGH RG30 137 R3
mbfields THLE RG7 * 136 H7
mbly Hl VW GU25 68 E8
mborne Cl SHST GU47 87 G5
mbourn Ct HUNG RG17 * 117 J4
mbourne Cl TILE/CALC RG31 137 P2
mbourne Ct UX/CGN UB8 31 K2
mbourne Dr BAGS GU19 89 K4
MDHD SL6 35 L3
mbourne Gdns EARL RG6 60 D2
mbourne Rd CAV/SC RG4 126 E5
mbourn Pl HUNG RG17 117 K3
mbourn Rd KSCL RG20 132 C12
mbourn Valley Wy
FGDN SN7 104 C1
HUNG RG17 104 G8
HUNG RG17 117 Q7
HUNG RG17 118 G12
KSCL RG20 131 J3
KSCL RG20 132 B10
NWBY RG14 6 B4
WANT OX12 104 E3
mbridge La HEN RG9 115 P11
mbridge Wood Rd HEN RG9 115 P10
mbs La THLE RG7 145 L6
mden Wy THLE RG7 143 R3
merton Rd WHIT RG2 59 H5
mmas Cl STA TW18 69 L1
mmas Ct WDSR SL4 13 H8
mmas Dr STA TW18 69 K2
mmas Md BNFD RG42 63 L5
mmas Rd SL SL1 27 M6
mora Crs TILE/CALC RG31 137 N1
mp Acres NWBY RG14 96 D1
mpards Cl HTWY RG27 151 M12
mtarra Wy NWBY RG14 7 K9
nark Cl FRIM GU16 94 E4
WODY RG5 47 G8
ncashire Hl BNFD RG42 64 F4
ncaster Av SLN SL2 28 E5
ncaster Cl ASHF TW15 70 E2
EGH TW20 68 D3
HUNG RG17 138 G2
NTHA RG18 97 K2
READ RG1 59 J1
STWL/WRAY TW19 56 E5
ncaster Dr CBLY GU15 88 D8
ncaster Gdns EARL RG6 60 B3
ncaster Rd MDHD SL6 26 B6
ncaster Sq HUNG RG17 138 H2
ncaster Wy FARN GU14 94 C7
ncastria Ms MDHD SL6 4 D5
ncelot Cl SL SL1 38 C2
ncers Dr STHA RG19 98 A4
nchester Dr CWTH RG45 75 J6
ncing Cl RDGW/BURGH RG30 44 D7
ncing Rd FELT TW13 57 M8
nden Ct EWKG RG40 14 F9
nden Gv WWKG RG41 61 L6
ndon Wy ASHF TW15 * 71 H4
ndrake Crs WHIT RG2 59 J5
ndseer Cl SHST GU47 87 L8
ndsend La WAR/TWY RG10 47 H4
ne End TADY RG26 149 R8
ne End Cl WHIT RG2 59 L8
ne End Vls WHIT RG2 * 59 L8
neswood THLE RG7 143 N9
e Lane CHERT KT16 70 A8
DID OX11 109 L2
TADY RG26 148 D2
VW GU25 68 E8
ngborough Rd EWKG RG40 15 G7
ngdale Cl MDHD SL6 5 K5
ngdale Dr ASC SL5 65 L7
ngdale Gdns EARL RG6 59 M4
ngdon Cl CBLY GU15 95 J2
ngford Cl CAV/SC RG4 45 J1
ngham Pl EGH TW20 68 F3
nghams Wy WAR/TWY RG10 32 F4
ngley Broom DTCH/LGLY SL3 40 B5
ngley Common Rd WHIT RG2 75 F5
ngley Crs HYS/HAR UB3 43 H7
ngley Dr CBLY GU15 88 D8
ngley Hl TILE/CALC RG31 137 N5
ngley Hill Cl
RDGW/BURGH RG30 137 N4
ngley Pk DTCH/LGLY SL3 * 30 C6
ngley Park Rd
DTCH/LGLY SL3 40 C1
IVER SL0 30 D8
ngley Quay DTCH/LGLY SL3 * 40 C2
ngley Rd DTCH/LGLY SL3 39 L2
STA TW18 69 M4
ngley Wy MLW SL7 18 D4
ngton Cl ADL/WDHM KT15 82 B7
MDHD SL6 4 C2
SL SL1 37 M1
ngton Wy EGH TW20 69 J4
ngworthy End MDHD SL6 36 D6
ngworthy La MDHD SL6 36 C6
niver Cl EARL RG6 60 B5
nnock Rd HYS/HAR UB3 43 H1
nsdowne Av SL SL1 10 E5
nsdowne Ct SL SL1 10 F5
nsdowne Gdns THLE RG7 145 N5
nsdowne Rd FRIM GU16 95 G6
RDGW/BURGH RG30 137 P3
STA TW18 70 B5
Lansdowne Ter
WAR/TWY RG10 * 47 K1
Lantern Wk MDHD SL6 5 M5
Lantern Wy WDR/YW UB7 42 A2
Lapwing Cl TILE/CALC RG31 137 M4
Lapwing La WGFD OX10 111 Q1
Larch Av ASC SL5 78 E2
WWKG RG41 14 D3
Larch Cl CBLY GU15 88 E5
NWBY RG14 141 R1
RDGW/BURGH RG30 143 R2
SLN SL2 28 D6
Larch Dr STHA RG19 98 D8
WODY RG5 60 D1
Larchfield Rd MDHD SL6 4 D9
Larchside Cl THLE RG7 145 M4
Larchwood Dr EGH TW20 68 A4
Larchwood Gld CBLY GU15 89 G7
Larges Bridge Dr BRAK RG12 3 H6
Larges La BRAK RG12 3 H5
Larissa Cl TILE/CALC RG31 137 Q1
Lark Av STA TW18 69 M1
Larkes-Meade EARL RG6 60 A5
Larkfield WGFD OX10 111 P1
Larkham Cl FELT TW13 71 L1
Larkings La SLN SL2 29 K2
Larksfield EGH TW20 68 B5
Larkspur Cl WWKG RG41 61 K7
Larkspur Gdns NTHA RG18 98 B2
Larkswood Cl SHST GU47 87 G5
TILE/CALC RG31 * 125 P12
Larkswood Dr CWTH RG45 87 H1
La Roche Cl DTCH/LGLY SL3 39 L3
Lascelles Rd DTCH/LGLY SL3 11 L9
Lashbrook Rd HEN RG9 32 D2
Lassell Gdns MDHD SL6 5 M4
Lasswade Rd CHERT KT16 81 M4
Latham Av FRIM GU16 94 E4
Latimer BRAK RG12 76 B5
Latimer Dr TILE/CALC RG31 137 N6
Latimer Rd WWKG RG41 14 E7
Latton Cl DID OX11 109 L2
Latymer Cl WEY KT13 83 J8
Laud Cl NWBY RG14 96 F1
READ RG1 8 F9
Lauder Cl FRIM GU16 94 E4
Laud's Cl HEN RG9 127 Q1
Laud Wy EWKG RG40 15 M5
Launceston Av CAV/SC RG4 127 L12
Launcestone Cl EARL RG6 60 B4
Laundry La HTWY RG27 151 P5
SHST GU47 93 L1
Lauradale BRAK RG12 2 D8
Laurel Av DTCH/LGLY SL3 40 A2
EGH TW20 68 B3
STHA RG19 102 C1
Laurel Bank CHOB/PIR GU24 * 91 L6
Laurel Cl CBLY GU15 94 D2
DTCH/LGLY SL3 41 G7
WWKG RG41 14 B7
Laurel Ct IVER SL0 * 30 F1
Laurel Dr TILE/CALC RG31 137 M2
Laurel La WDR/YW UB7 42 A4
Laurels Rd IVER SL0 30 F3
The Laurels GOR/PANG RG8 124 H9
NTHA RG18 * 97 L1
WODY RG5 46 E5
Lauser Rd STWL/WRAY TW19 56 C6
Lautree Gdns MDHD SL6 20 A7
Lavell's La THLE RG7 150 A2
Lavender Ri WDR/YW UB7 42 C2
Lavenham Dr WODY RG5 46 F6
Lawford Crs YTLY GU46 86 D8
Lawkland SLN SL2 28 E4
Lawn Av WDR/YW UB7 41 L2
Lawn Cl DTCH/LGLY SL3 39 L7
Lawn Rd UX/CGN UB8 31 L1
The Lawns DTCH/LGLY SL3 * 41 G8
WHIT RG2 * 59 K3
The Lawn DTCH/LGLY SL3 * 39 L8
Lawrence Cl EWKG RG40 15 J5
Lawrence Crs BFOR GU20 90 D2
Lawrence Gv BNFD RG42 63 K6
Lawrence Md HUNG RG17 140 A4
Lawrence Pl NWBY RG14 96 E1
Lawrence Rd
RDGW/BURGH RG30 44 A6
Lawrences La NTHA RG18 133 R12
Lawrence Wy CBLY GU15 93 M2
SL SL1 27 L6
Lawson Dr CAV/SC RG4 44 E1
Lawson La DID OX11 109 K2
Lawson Rd HEN RG9 22 B7
Lawson Wy ASC SL5 79 H3
Laxton Gn MDHD SL6 35 J4
Layburn Crs DTCH/LGLY SL3 40 D6
Layland's Gn HUNG RG17 140 B5
Layleys Gn NTHA RG18 133 M6
Laytom Ri TILE/CALC RG31 125 N11
Layton Ct WEY KT13 83 H8
Layton's La SUN TW16 71 M7
Lea Cl RDGW/BURGH RG30 58 A3
Lea Cl CWTH RG45 75 H8
Leacroft ASC SL5 79 G2
STA TW18 70 B3
Leacroft Cl STA TW18 70 B2
Leacroft Rd IVER SL0 30 F8
Leafield Copse BRAK RG12 76 F1
Lea Heath Wy WAR/TWY RG10 61 K1
Leaholme Gdns SL SL1 27 H6
Leamington Rd NWDGN UB2 43 M4
Lea Rd CAV/SC RG4 126 F6
CBLY GU15 94 B4
Leas Dr IVER SL0 31 G7
The Leas STA TW18 * 70 A2
The Lea EGH TW20 69 H5
EWKG RG40 73 M6
Leaver Rd HEN RG9 127 Q1
Leaves Gn BRAK RG12 76 D3
Lea Vw NTHA RG18 * 133 Q2
Ledbury Cl RDGW/BURGH RG30 44 B5
Ledbury Dr TILE/CALC RG31 137 P6
Ledger La MDHD SL6 36 F8
Ledger's Rd SL SL1 10 A7
Ledran Cl EARL RG6 60 C5
Leeds Rd SL SL1 10 E2
Lee La MDHD SL6 25 G3
Lees Cl MDHD SL6 35 K1
Lees Gdns MDHD SL6 35 K1
Leeson Gdns WDSR SL4 38 A4
Leicester BRAK RG12 76 D4
Leicester Cl HEN RG9 115 R11
Leigh Fld THLE RG7 143 P8
Leigh Pk DTCH/LGLY SL3 * 39 L7
Leigh Rd SL SL1 28 D8
Leigh Sq WDSR SL4 52 D1
Leighton Gdns MDHD SL6 5 M1
Leiston Cl EARL RG6 60 D5
Leiston Sp SL SL1 29 G7
Leith Cl CWTH RG45 75 G7
SL SL1 11 J5
Le Marchant Rd FRIM GU16 94 F3
Lemart Cl TILE/CALC RG31 137 Q2
Lemington Gv BRAK RG12 76 B3
Lendore Rd FRIM GU16 94 D6
Leney Cl EWKG RG40 15 J1
Lenham Cl WWKG RG41 61 K5
Lennox Cl TILE/CALC RG31 137 M6
Lennox Rd EARL RG6 60 A1
Lent Green La SL SL1 27 K5
Lent Rise Rd MDHD SL6 27 K7
SL SL1 27 K6
Leonard Cl FRIM GU16 94 D6
Leonard Rd NWDGN UB2 43 M3
Leonardslee Crs NWBY RG14 7 L2
Leopold Wk READ RG1 9 M6
Leppington BRAK RG12 76 B5
Lerwick Dr SL SL1 29 G6
Lesford Rd READ RG1 58 E2
Leslie Rd CHOB/PIR GU24 91 K5
Leslie Southern Ct NWBY RG14 7 G2
Lesters Rd MDHD SL6 19 M8
Letchworth Av
EBED/NFELT TW14 57 M6
Letcombe Sq BRAK RG12 76 F1
Letcombe St READ RG1 9 G7
Letts Cl WODY RG5 60 F1
Leverkusen Rd BRAK RG12 2 F7
Leverton La HUNG RG17 129 J9
Lewendon Rd NWBY RG14 96 A1
Lewes Ct SL SL1 10 A7
Lewington Ms HUNG RG17 138 H1
Lewins Wy SL SL1 28 B8
Lewin Ter EBED/NFELT TW14 57 K6
Lewis Cl ADL/WDHM KT15 82 C8
Lewisham Wy SHST GU47 87 K5
Lexington Av MDHD SL6 4 C8
Lexington Gv WHIT RG2 59 J8
Leyburn Cl WODY RG5 47 G6
Leycester Cl BFOR GU20 78 B8
Leyland Gdns WHIT RG2 145 Q1
Leylands La STWL/WRAY TW19 55 M3
Ley Rd FARN GU14 94 A6
Leys Gdns NWBY RG14 6 D2
Leyside CWTH RG45 87 G1
Library Pde WODY RG5 * 46 E7
Lichfield Cl EARL RG6 60 C5
Lichfields BRAK RG12 3 M4
Liddall Wy WDR/YW UB7 42 B1
Liddell WDSR SL4 52 C2
Liddell Cl EWKG RG40 85 L3
Liddell Wy ASC SL5 77 M2
Lido Rd DID OX11 108 F2
Lidstone Cl EARL RG6 60 D5
Liebenrood Rd
RDGW/BURGH RG30 44 C8
Lightlands La MDHD SL6 26 B1
Lightwater Meadow
LTWR GU18 90 B6
Lightwater Rd LTWR GU18 90 B6
Lightwood BRAK RG12 76 D3
Lilac Cl GOR/PANG RG8 125 N9
The Lilacs WWKG RG41 73 J3
Lilac Wk STHA RG19 102 D1
Lilley Wy SL SL1 38 A1
Lillibrooke Crs MDHD SL6 35 J3
Lillyfee Farm La
FLKWH/TG HP10 21 J2
Lily Dr WDR/YW UB7 41 M4
Lily Hill Dr BRAK RG12 3 M5
Lily Hill Rd BRAK RG12 3 M4
Lima Ct READ RG1 8 C8
Lime Av CBLY GU15 89 G8
HEN RG9 126 A1
WDSR SL4 39 H7
WDSR SL4 66 F1
Lime Cl NWBY RG14 7 M2
STHA RG19 102 C1
WWKG RG41 14 A7
Limecroft YTLY GU46 92 C1
Limefield Cl EARL RG6 60 E3
Lime Gv ADL/WDHM KT15 82 A8
Limerick Cl BNFD RG42 2 C2
Limes Av KSCL RG20 100 C7
Limes Cl ASHF TW15 71 G3
Limes Rd EGH TW20 68 F3
WEY KT13 83 G8
The Limes BNFD RG42 64 F3
TADY RG26 150 B8
WDSR SL4 52 C1
Lime Tree Copse BNFD RG42 65 G5
Limetree Rd GOR/PANG RG8 111 R12
Limetrees DID OX11 109 L1
Lime Tree Wk VW GU25 80 E1
Lime Wk BRAK RG12 3 G8
MDHD SL6 25 J5
Limmer Cl WWKG RG41 73 J2
Limmerhill Rd WWKG RG41 73 L1
Linchfield Rd DTCH/LGLY SL3 39 L8
Lincoln Cl CBLY GU15 95 H2
WWKG RG41 61 G4
Lincoln Ct NWBY RG14 6 C5
Lincoln Gdns WAR/TWY RG10 47 K1
Lincoln Hatch La SL SL1 27 L5
Lincoln Rd MDHD SL6 25 K6
WHIT RG2 59 J2
Lincolnshire Gdns BNFD RG42 64 E5
Lincoln Wy SL SL1 27 M8
SUN TW16 71 L6
Lindale Cl VW GU25 79 M1
Lindberg Wy WODY RG5 47 H5
Lind Cl EARL RG6 60 B4
Linden Av MDHD SL6 4 C1
Linden Cl NWBY RG14 6 C1
WWKG RG41 14 A9
Linden Ct CBLY GU15 88 F7
EGH TW20 68 B4
Linden Dr SLN SL2 28 E2
Linden Gv WOT/HER KT12 83 M6
Linden Hill La WAR/TWY RG10 33 L4
Lindenhill Rd BNFD RG42 2 A3
Lindenmuth Wy STHA RG19 101 H1
Linden Rd WHIT RG2 59 L4
WODY RG5 60 D2
Linden Ter UX/CGN UB8 * 31 M7
Linden Wy SHPTN TW17 83 J2
Lindores Rd MDHD SL6 36 D6
Lindsay Cl STWL/WRAY TW19 56 D4
Lindsay Dr SHPTN TW17 83 K3
Lindsey Cl WWKG RG41 61 L8
Lindsey Gdns
EBED/NFELT TW14 * 57 K6
Lines Rd WAR/TWY RG10 47 L8
Ling Dr LTWR GU18 89 M7
Lingfield Rd NWBY RG14 7 J9
Lingholm Cl MDHD SL6 4 B7
RDGW/BURGH RG30 137 R5
Lingwood BRAK RG12 76 C3
Link Rd ADL/WDHM KT15 82 E8
DTCH/LGLY SL3 39 L7
EBED/NFELT TW14 57 M6
NWBY RG14 6 E6
Linkscroft Av ASHF TW15 71 H4
Links Dr RDGW/BURGH RG30 44 A6
Links Rd ASHF TW15 70 E3
The Links ASC SL5 65 L7
Linkswood Rd SL SL1 27 L3
The Link SLN SL2 29 K7
YTLY GU46 86 C7
Link Vw NWBY RG14 * 132 F11
Linkway CBLY GU15 94 C2
CWTH RG45 86 F1
Link Wy NTHA RG18 97 K2
STA TW18 70 B4
WHIT RG2 72 E4
Linnet Cl TILE/CALC RG31 137 M4
Linstead Rd FARN GU14 93 L6
Linton Cl TADY RG26 148 E3
Lintott Ct STWL/WRAY TW19 56 D5
Lion Cl SHPTN TW17 70 E8
Lion Meadow HEN RG9 114 D4
Lion Ms HUNG RG17 * 117 K4
Lip La KSCL RG20 130 H10
Lipscomb Cl NTHA RG18 133 P4
Lipscombe Cl NWBY RG14 6 A5
Liscombe BRAK RG12 76 B4
Liskeard Dr FARN GU14 94 A8
Lisle Cl NWBY RG14 96 B1
Lismore Cl WODY RG5 60 E2
Lismore Pk SLN SL2 11 G1
Lister Cl GOR/PANG RG8 125 N9
Liston Rd MLW SL7 18 F4
Litcham Sp SL SL1 10 D1
Lithgow's Rd HTHAIR TW6 57 L3
Littington Cl EARL RG6 60 C6
Little Aldershot La THLE RG7 103 L4
Little Benty WDR/YW UB7 41 M5
Little Bowden La
GOR/PANG RG8 124 D9
Littlebrook Av SLN SL2 28 A6
Little Buntings WDSR SL4 12 B9
Little Copse YTLY GU46 86 C7
Littlecote Dr READ RG1 8 B9
Littlecroft Rd EGH TW20 68 F3
Little Croft Rd GOR/PANG RG8 124 A1
Littledale Cl BRAK RG12 3 L6
Littledown Rd SL SL1 11 G4
Little Elms HYS/HAR UB3 42 F7
Littlefield Gn MDHD SL6 35 H8
Little Foxes EWKG RG40 74 A7
Little Fryth EWKG RG40 74 C8
Little Glebe CAV/SC RG4 46 E3
Little Green La CHERT KT16 81 L7
Little Heath Rd CHOB/PIR GU24 91 L4
TILE/CALC RG31 137 L3
Little Hill Rd WAR/TWY RG10 61 K2
Little Horse Cl EARL RG6 60 E2
Little John's La
RDGW/BURGH RG30 44 C6
Littlejohn's La
RDGW/BURGH RG30 44 D5
Little La THLE RG7 134 E12
Little London Rd THLE RG7 149 J4
Little Marlow Rd MLW SL7 19 G3
Little Md MARL SN8 138 D12
Little Moor SHST GU47 87 J5
Little Oak Cl SHPTN TW17 82 F1
Little Oaks Dr TILE/CALC RG31 137 N2
Little Paddock CBLY GU15 89 G6
Littleport Sp SL SL1 10 E1
Little Ringdale BRAK RG12 3 M9
Little Rd HYS/HAR UB3 43 H2
SL SL1 21 L5
Littlestead Cl CAV/SC RG4 127 L12
Little St READ RG1 8 B5
Little Sutton La DTCH/LGLY SL3 40 D6
Littleton La SHPTN TW17 82 E2
Littleton Rd ASHF TW15 71 J5
Little Vigo YTLY GU46 92 B2
Little Woodlands WDSR SL4 12 B9
Litton Rd WHIT RG2 59 K4
Liverpool Rd READ RG1 45 L6
SL SL1 28 D7
Livery Cl READ RG1 9 H7
Livingstone Gdns WODY RG5 60 E1
Livingstone Rd NWBY RG14 7 G5
Llangar Gv CWTH RG45 87 G1
Llanvair Cl ASC SL5 78 A3
Llanvair Dr ASC SL5 77 M4
Llewellyn Pk WAR/TWY RG10 32 E8
Lochinvar Cl SL SL1 38 D2
Lochinver BRAK RG12 76 B4
Lock Av MDHD SL6 26 E4
Lockbridge Ct MDHD SL6 26 E6
Lock Bridge Rd BNEND SL8 20 C2
Locke Gdns DTCH/LGLY SL3 39 L2
Lockets Cl WDSR SL4 37 M8
Lock Island MLW SL7 * 19 H5
Lock La MDHD SL6 35 L2
Lock Md MDHD SL6 26 E4
Lock Pth WDSR SL4 37 M6
Lock Pl READ RG1 9 L6
Lockram La THLE RG7 144 A5
Lock Rd MLW SL7 19 G5
Locksbridge La TADY RG26 149 P8
Lockside Ct THLE RG7 142 E3
Locksley Gdns WWKG RG41 61 K3
Locks Ride ASC SL5 65 J5
Lockstile Md GOR/PANG RG8 112 A11
Lockstile Wy GOR/PANG RG8 112 A12
Lockton Cha ASC SL5 65 K8
Lockwood Cl FARN GU14 93 L6
Lockyer Cl WWKG RG41 61 G4
Loddon Br WWKG RG41 60 F3
Loddon Bridge Rd EARL RG6 60 F2
WODY RG5 46 F8
Loddon Cl CBLY GU15 89 G8
Loddon Dr MDHD SL6 4 C2
WAR/TWY RG10 32 D4
Loddon Hall Rd WAR/TWY RG10 47 K1
Loddon Rd BNEND SL8 20 C2
FARN GU14 93 K8
Loddon Sp SL SL1 10 E2
Loddon Vw WAR/TWY RG10 * 47 L3
Lodge Cl EGH TW20 68 D3
MLW SL7 19 G5
SL SL1 10 A6
UX/CGN UB8 31 L5
WAR/TWY RG10 * 48 A6
Lodge Gv YTLY GU46 86 F8
Lodge Rd WAR/TWY RG10 47 L6
Lodge Wy ASHF TW15 56 E8
SHPTN TW17 71 J7
WDSR SL4 52 E2
Logan Cl RDGW/BURGH RG30 137 R3
Lois Dr SHPTN TW17 83 H2
Lomond Av CAV/SC RG4 45 L1
London Rd ASC SL5 66 C8
ASHF TW15 56 F8
BFOR GU20 78 C7
BLKW GU17 93 L2
BNFD RG42 63 K6
BRAK RG12 3 J4
CBLY GU15 93 M1
DID OX11 109 R1
DTCH/LGLY SL3 39 K7
DTCH/LGLY SL3 39 L3
EARL RG6 45 M7
EGH TW20 68 C5
EWKG RG40 15 K5
EWKG RG40 63 H7
NTHA RG18 98 A3
NWBY RG14 6 E2
NWBY RG14 7 G2
READ RG1 9 J8
STA TW18 69 M2
VW GU25 79 L1
WAR/TWY RG10 33 G8
London St CHERT KT16 82 A4
READ RG1 9 H6
Loneacre BFOR GU20 * 90 E2
Longacre NWBY RG14 141 R6
Long Barn La WHIT RG2 59 H3
Longbourn WDSR SL4 12 C9
Longbourne Wy CHERT KT16 81 M3
Longbridge Cl HTWY RG27 150 E9
Longbridge Rd TADY RG26 149 R7
Longbridge Wy UX/CGN UB8 31 K3
Long Cl HUNG RG17 140 B4
SLN SL2 28 D1
Longcroft Rd STHA RG19 98 A4
Longcross Rd CHERT KT16 80 B7
Longdon Rd WWKG RG41 61 J5
Longdown Rd SHST GU47 87 G5
Long Dr SL SL1 27 L4
WDR/YW UB7 * 42 A2
Longfield Cl FARN GU14 94 A6
Longfield Rd WAR/TWY RG10 32 F8
Longford Av EBED/NFELT TW14 57 L5
STWL/WRAY TW19 56 E7
Longford Cl CBLY GU15 94 D2
Longford Wy STWL/WRAY TW19 56 E7
Long Furlong Dr SLN SL2 28 A5
Long Gv TADY RG26 103 M4
THLE RG7 98 D1
Long Half Acre MDHD SL6 34 D2
Long Hedge HUNG RG17 117 M5
Long Hill Rd ASC SL5 65 H6
BRAK RG12 65 G7
Longhurst Cl CAV/SC RG4 45 J3
Long La KSCL RG20 119 P3
MDHD SL6 25 L1
MDHD SL6 50 D2
NTHA RG18 133 M8
NWBY RG14 133 J11
STWL/WRAY TW19 56 F6
TILE/CALC RG31 137 L1
Longleat Dr TILE/CALC RG31 125 M11
Longleat Gdns MDHD SL6 4 C7
Longleat Wy EBED/NFELT TW14 57 J6
Longmead WDSR SL4 38 A8
Longmead La SL SL1 27 M1
Longmeadow FRIM GU16 94 F3
Long Meadow GOR/PANG RG8 123 R1
Long Mickle SHST GU47 87 G5
The Long Mile WAR/TWY RG10 48 D6
Longmoor Cl EWKG RG40 73 L8
Longmoor La THLE RG7 143 Q7
Longmoors BNFD RG42 63 L6
Longmore Rd WHIT RG2 59 K8
Long Readings La SLN SL2 28 D4
Longridge Cl
RDGW/BURGH RG30 44 B7
Longshot La BRAK RG12 63 L7
Longside Cl EGH TW20 69 J6
Longstone Rd IVER SL0 30 E3
Long's Wy EWKG RG40 15 L4
Long Toll GOR/PANG RG8 125 L1
Long Wk HUNG RG17 138 B5
WDSR SL4 * 53 K4
Longwalk Rd STKPK UB11 42 D1
The Long Wk WDSR SL4 13 L6
Longwater Av
RDGW/BURGH RG30 58 E5
Longwater La EWKG RG40 85 L4
Longwater Rd BRAK RG12 76 C3
EWKG RG40 85 M4
HTWY RG27 85 M6
Longwood Av DTCH/LGLY SL3 40 D5
Longworth Av TILE/CALC RG31 137 M3
Longworth Dr MDHD SL6 26 E5
The Long Yd HUNG RG17 * 130 E3
Lonsdale Cl MDHD SL6 26 C5
Lonsdale Rd NWDGN UB2 43 M3
Lonsdale Wy MDHD SL6 36 E5
Loosen Dr MDHD SL6 35 J3
Lord Knyvett Cl
STWL/WRAY TW19 56 D5
Lord Knyvetts Ct
STWL/WRAY TW19 * 56 E5
Lordswood THLE RG7 149 J2
Loring Rd WDSR SL4 12 A6
Lorne Cl SL SL1 38 D3
Lorne Pl READ RG1 8 B6
Lorne St READ RG1 8 B6
Lorraine Rd CBLY GU15 88 F7
Lory Rdg BAGS GU19 89 L2
Losfield Rd WDSR SL4 38 A8
Lossie Dr IVER SL0 30 D8
Loughborough BRAK RG12 76 E3
Loundyes Cl NTHA RG18 97 K2
Lovatt Cl TILE/CALC RG31 137 M3
Lovedean Ct BRAK RG12 76 E3
Love Green La IVER SL0 30 F6
Lovegrove Dr SLN SL2 28 B5
Lovegrove's La
GOR/PANG RG8 113 N6
Love Hill La DTCH/LGLY SL3 30 C8
Lovejoy La WDSR SL4 52 D1
Lovelace Cl MDHD SL6 24 B1
Lovelace Rd BRAK RG12 75 L1
Lovelands La CHOB/PIR GU24 91 J8
Love La IVER SL0 30 F7
NWBY RG14 132 F12
Lovel Hl WDSR SL4 * 66 B3
Lovel La WDSR SL4 66 B3
Lovell Cl HEN RG9 127 Q2
Lovells Cl LTWR GU18 90 B5
Lovel Rd WDSR SL4 65 M2
Loverock Rd
RDGW/BURGH RG30 8 A3
Love's Cl THLE RG7 143 P3
Loves Wd THLE RG7 143 P9
Lovett Gdns MDHD SL6 26 E3
Lovett Rd STA TW18 69 H2
Lowbrook Dr MDHD SL6 35 J3
Lowbury BRAK RG12 3 M8
Lower Armour Rd
TILE/CALC RG31 137 P1
Lower Boyndon Rd MDHD SL6 4 D6
Lower Britwell Rd SLN SL2 27 M5
Lower Broadmoor Rd
CWTH RG45 87 J2
Lower Brook St READ RG1 8 F8
Lower Canes YTLY GU46 86 A8
Lower Church Rd SHST GU47 86 E5
Lower Cippenham La SL SL1 38 B1
Lower Common HTWY RG27 84 E5
Lower Cookham Rd MDHD SL6 26 E3
Lower Earley Wy EARL RG6 60 C6
Lower Earley Wy (North)
EARL RG6 60 F4
Lower Earley Wy (West)
EARL RG6 59 M7
Lower Elmstone Dr
TILE/CALC RG31 137 N1
Lower Farm Ct NWBY RG14 97 H5
Lower Field Rd READ RG1 8 E9
Lower Henley Rd CAV/SC RG4 45 J4
Lower Lees Rd SLN SL2 28 C4
Lower Md IVER SL0 30 F4
Lower Meadow Rd WHIT RG2 59 K4
Lower Mill Fld BAGS GU19 89 K4
Lower Moor YTLY GU46 92 D1
Lower Mt READ RG1 59 J1
Lower Nursery ASC SL5 79 G2
Lower Pound La MLW SL7 18 E7
Lower Rdg BNEND SL8 20 D2
Lower Rd DID OX11 109 K2
MDHD SL6 20 A7
Lower Sandhurst Rd
EWKG RG40 86 A4
SHST GU47 86 D4
Lower Ter WWKG RG41 * 61 H6
Lower Village Rd ASC SL5 78 C2
Lower Wy STHA RG19 97 H3
Lower Wokingham Rd
EWKG RG40 74 D8
Lowes Cl HEN RG9 32 D2
Lowestoft Dr SL SL1 27 L7
Lowfield Cl LTWR GU18 90 A6
Lowfield Gn CAV/SC RG4 45 L2
Lowfield Rd CAV/SC RG4 45 K1
Lowlands Dr STWL/WRAY TW19 56 D4

166 Low - Mil

Lowlands Rd BLKW GU17 93 J2
Lowry Cl SHST GU47 87 K8
Lowther Cl WWKG RG41 14 A1
Lowther Rd WWKG RG41 14 A1
Loxwood EARL RG6 60 C4
Loxwood Cl EBED/NFELT TW14 57 K7
THLE RG7 145 L2
Lucan Dr STA TW18 70 D5
Lucas Cl YTLY GU46 92 D1
Lucas Green Rd
CHOB/PIR GU24 90 F8
Lucey Cl TILE/CALC RG31 125 M11
Lucie Av ASHF TW15 71 H4
Luckley Pth EWKG RG40 15 H6
Luckley Rd WWKG RG41 74 B3
Luckley Wd WWKG RG41 74 B3
Luckmore Dr EARL RG6 60 A3
Luddington Av VW GU25 68 F7
Ludlow BRAK RG12 76 B4
Ludlow Cl FRIM GU16 95 G7
NWBY RG14 97 G2
Ludlow Pl TADY RG26 148 E2
Ludlow Rd MDHD SL6 4 F8
Luff Cl WDSR SL4 52 E2
Luker Av HEN RG9 115 Q11
Lulworth Cl FARN GU14 94 A7
Lulworth Rd WHIT RG2 59 J6
Lunds Farm Rd WODY RG5 47 G6
Lundy Dr HYS/HAR UB3 43 G4
Lundy La RDGW/BURGH RG30 44 C7
Lupin Cl BAGS GU19 89 J5
WDR/YW UB7 41 M5
Lupin Ride CWTH RG45 75 H6
Luscina Vw READ RG1 9 K4
Luscombe Cl CAV/SC RG4 45 K4
Lutman's Hvn WAR/TWY RG10 34 A1
Lutterworth Cl BNFD RG42 64 C5
Lutton Cl EARL RG6 59 M6
Lych Gate Cl SHST GU47 86 F6
Lycroft Cl GOR/PANG RG8 112 A11
Lydbury BRAK RG12 64 F8
Lydford Av SLN SL2 28 F6
Lydford Cl FARN GU14 * 94 A7
FRIM GU16 95 G7
Lydford Rd READ RG1 59 L1
Lydney BRAK RG12 76 B4
Lydsey Cl SLN SL2 28 C4
Lye Copse Av FARN GU14 94 B6
Lyefield Ct CAV/SC RG4 126 H12
Lyell Rd WDSR SL4 52 C2
Lyme Gv TILE/CALC RG31 137 P1
Lymington Av YTLY GU46 92 C1
Lymington Ga CAV/SC RG4 44 E1
Lynch Cl UX/CGN UB8 31 L1
Lynchen Cl HEST TW5 43 J8
Lynch Hill La SLN SL2 28 A5
Lynch La HUNG RG17 117 K3
The Lynch MARL SN8 138 D12
UX/CGN UB8 31 L1
Lynden Cl MDHD SL6 36 D6
Lyndhurst Av BLKW GU17 87 J8
MDHD SL6 * 20 A8
Lyndhurst Cl BRAK RG12 65 G8
Lyndhurst Rd ASC SL5 77 M1
GOR/PANG RG8 112 A12
RDGW/BURGH RG30 137 R1
Lyndhurst Wy CHERT KT16 81 L7
Lyndwood Dr WDSR SL4 54 A5
Lyndwood Pde WDSR SL4 * 54 A5
Lyne Cl VW GU25 80 F3
Lyne Crossing Rd CHERT KT16 81 H3
VW GU25 81 G3
Lynegrove Av ASHF TW15 71 J3
Lyneham Gdns MDHD SL6 25 K5
Lyneham Rd CWTH RG45 87 H1
Lyne La CHERT KT16 81 G5
EGH TW20 81 G2
VW GU25 81 G3
Lyne Rd VW GU25 80 D3
Lynmouth Gdns HEST TW5 43 M8
Lynmouth Rd READ RG1 8 F3
Lynn Cl ASHF TW15 71 K3
Lynn Wy FARN GU14 93 M7
Lynton Cl WODY RG5 60 C1
Lynton Gn MDHD SL6 4 E4
Lynwood Av DTCH/LGLY SL3 39 M3
EGH TW20 68 E4
Lynwood Cha BRAK RG12 3 H1
Lynwood Crs ASC SL5 78 E3
Lyon Cl STHA RG19 98 B4
Lyon Oaks BNFD RG42 64 B4
Lyon Rd CWTH RG45 75 J8
Lyon Sq RDGW/BURGH RG30 44 A6
Lyon Wy FRIM GU16 94 C5
Lysander Cl WODY RG5 47 G6
Lysander Dr BRAK RG12 3 H8
Lytchet Minster Cl BRAK RG12 76 F2
Lytham BRAK RG12 75 L3
Lytham Cl RDGW/BURGH RG30 58 C2
Lytham End TILE/CALC RG31 125 M11
Lytham Rd WODY RG5 46 E7

M

Mabett Cl WHIT RG2 72 E6
Macadam Av CWTH RG45 75 J7
Macbeth Ct BNFD RG42 3 L2
Macdonald Rd LTWR GU18 89 M6
Mace Cl EARL RG6 60 A5
Mackay Cl TILE/CALC RG31 137 Q7
Mackenzie St SL SL1 11 G6
Macklin Cl HUNG RG17 138 H1
Maclaren Dr BNFD RG42 64 F6
Macmahon Cl CHOB/PIR GU24 91 L5
Macnaghten Woods CBLY GU15 88 E8
Macphail Cl EWKG RG40 15 L2
Macrae Rd YTLY GU46 86 C8
Maddle Rd HUNG RG17 104 F11
Maddock Cl WHIT RG2 145 P2
Madeira Pl NWBY RG14 6 E6
Madeira Wk WDSR SL4 13 K6
Madingley BRAK RG12 76 B5
Madox Brown End SHST GU47 87 L8
Mafeking Rd STWL/WRAY TW19 55 H8
Magdalene Rd SHPTN TW17 82 F1
SHST GU47 87 M4
Magill Cl THLE RG7 145 M4
Magna Carta La
STWL/WRAY TW19 54 D7
Magna Rd EGH TW20 68 B4
Magnolia Cl BNFD RG42 65 G6
SHST GU47 87 K5
Magnolia Ct STHA RG19 102 D1
Magnolia Gdns DTCH/LGLY SL3 11 M8
Magnolia St WDR/YW UB7 41 M4
Magnolia Wy WWKG RG41 14 A8
Magpie Cl STHA RG19 97 K3
Magpie Wy TILE/CALC RG31 137 M4
Maguire Dr FRIM GU16 95 J3
Mahonia Cl CHOB/PIR GU24 * 90 F8
Maiden Erlegh Dr EARL RG6 60 B2
Maidenhead Court Pk
MDHD SL6 26 D2
Maidenhead Rd BNFD RG42 50 B7
EWKG RG40 62 E3
MDHD SL6 26 A2
WDSR SL4 12 C4
WDSR SL4 37 L7
Maiden Hythe Pl MDHD SL6 4 D4
Maiden Pl EARL RG6 60 D4
Maidensfield WWKG RG41 61 K4
Maiden's Gn BNFD RG42 51 H8
Main Av TILE/CALC RG31 137 M4
Main Dr ASC SL5 65 H5
DTCH/LGLY SL3 41 G3
Mainprize Rd BRAK RG12 3 L3
Main Rd TADY RG26 148 F4
WDSR SL4 * 38 C7
Mainstone Cl FRIM GU16 95 J7
Main St ADL/WDHM KT15 82 E7
DID OX11 109 K2
KSCL RG20 108 G8
KSCL RG20 119 M7
STHA RG19 101 H1
Maise Webster Cl
STWL/WRAY TW19 * 56 D6
Maitland Rd READ RG1 8 B7
Maiwand Gdns
RDGW/BURGH RG30 137 P3
Maize La BNFD RG42 64 D4
Majendie Cl NWBY RG14 141 R1
Major's Farm Rd
DTCH/LGLY SL3 39 M7
Makepiece Rd BNFD RG42 64 B5
Maker Cl RDGW/BURGH RG30 58 B1
Makins Rd HEN RG9 127 Q2
Malders La MDHD SL6 25 K3
Maldon Cl RDGW/BURGH RG30 44 D8
Malet Cl EGH TW20 * 69 K4
Malham Fell BRAK RG12 2 D8
Malham Rd STHA RG19 97 L3
Mallard Cl EARL RG6 60 A3
WAR/TWY RG10 47 L3
Mallard Ct NWBY RG14 6 C4
Mallard Dr SL SL1 28 A8
Mallard Pl FARN GU14 94 A6
Mallard Rw READ RG1 8 F8
Mallard's Reach WEY KT13 83 K6
The Mallards FRIM GU16 94 F4
HUNG RG17 118 E11
STA TW18 70 B7
Mallards Wy LTWR GU18 90 A6
Mallard Wy THLE RG7 142 D3
YTLY GU46 * 86 B8
Mallory Av CAV/SC RG4 127 J12
Mallowdale Rd BRAK RG12 76 E4
Mallow Gdns NTHA RG18 97 M1
Mallow Pk MDHD SL6 4 A1
Malone Rd WODY RG5 46 D8
Malpas Rd SLN SL2 11 L3
Malta Rd FRIM GU16 95 K6
Maltby Wy EARL RG6 59 M6
Malt Hl BNFD RG42 64 E1
EGH TW20 68 E3
Malt House Cl WDSR SL4 54 B6
Malthouse Ct CHOB/PIR GU24 * 90 F7
Malthouse La CHOB/PIR GU24 90 F7
READ RG1 8 D5
TADY RG26 148 F4
Malthouse Wy MLW SL7 18 F5
Maltings Pl READ RG1 8 F7
The Maltings KSCL RG20 108 G8
NWBY RG14 6 D5
STA TW18 69 L2
TADY RG26 149 R8
Malton Av SL SL1 28 D7
Malt Shovel La HUNG RG17 116 H2
Malvern Cl WODY RG5 46 F8
Malvern Ct NWBY RG14 6 D7
READ RG1 9 M9
Malvern Rd BLKW GU17 92 F5
FARN GU14 93 K7
HYS/HAR UB3 43 G7
MDHD SL6 25 M5
Malvern Wy WAR/TWY RG10 32 F7
Malyns Wy TILE/CALC RG31 125 M10
The Malyons SHPTN TW17 * 83 K3
Managua Cl CAV/SC RG4 45 K4
Manchester Rd READ RG1 45 L6
Mandarin Ct NWBY RG14 * 7 J5
Mandarin Dr NWBY RG14 7 J7
Mandela Ct READ RG1 9 K6
Mandeville Cl
RDGW/BURGH RG30 137 R5
Mandeville Rd SHPTN TW17 83 G2
Manea Cl EARL RG6 60 C6
Manfield Cl SLN SL2 28 C4
Manners Rd WODY RG5 46 D7
Mannock Wy WODY RG5 47 H6
Manor Cl BNFD RG42 64 A5
DID OX11 109 L1
Manor Ct MLW SL7 18 E3
SL SL1 38 B1
WEY KT13 83 H8
Manor Crs KSCL RG20 121 R2
Manorcrofts Rd EGH TW20 69 G4
Manor Farm Av SHPTN TW17 83 H3
Manor Farm Cl WDSR SL4 12 A9
Manor Farm Cots WDSR SL4 54 A4
Manor Farm Ct EGH TW20 * 69 G3
Manor Farm La EGH TW20 69 G3
GOR/PANG RG8 124 G12
Manor Farm Rd WHIT RG2 59 H4
Manor Gdns FLKWH/TG HP10 21 G1
Manor Gv MDHD SL6 36 F8
Manor House Ct SHPTN TW17 83 H4
Manor House Dr ASC SL5 66 A5
Manor House La
DTCH/LGLY SL3 39 K8
Manor La HYS/HAR UB3 42 F6
KSCL RG20 119 R9
KSCL RG20 132 G1
MARL SN8 116 A6
MDHD SL6 36 A2
NTHA RG18 133 P1
NWBY RG14 97 G2
THLE RG7 98 F7
Manor Leaze EGH TW20 69 H3
Manor Pk STA TW18 69 K1
Manor Park Cl
RDGW/BURGH RG30 137 N4
Manor Park Dr EWKG RG40 73 K8
YTLY GU46 92 D1
Manor Pl NWBY RG14 141 R1
STA TW18 70 B3
Manor Rd ASHF TW15 70 F3
GOR/PANG RG8 111 R12
GOR/PANG RG8 124 G7
HEN RG9 127 R2
MDHD SL6 36 A2
WANT OX12 106 H2
WDSR SL4 52 E1
WOT/HER KT12 83 M4
WWKG RG41 74 A4
Manor Stables
WAR/TWY RG10 * 32 F4
The Manor WHIT RG2 145 Q1
Manor Vw THLE RG7 * 99 H7
Manor Wy BAGS GU19 89 L4
EGH TW20 68 F4
MDHD SL6 36 C6
NWDGN UB2 43 M4
Manor Waye UX/CGN UB8 31 M2
Manor Wood Ga HEN RG9 32 C2
Manse Cl HYS/HAR UB3 42 F6
Manse La TADY RG26 148 F4
Mansel Cl SLN SL2 29 K6
Mansell Cl WDSR SL4 52 E1
Mansell Ct WHIT RG2 59 L4
Mansell Dr NWBY RG14 141 Q9
Mansfield Cl ASC SL5 65 K7
Mansfield Crs BRAK RG12 76 B3
Mansfield Pl ASC SL5 65 K7
Mansfield Rd READ RG1 8 D9
WWKG RG41 14 B7
Man's Hl THLE RG7 144 A3
Mansion House St NWBY RG14 * 6 D4
Mansion La IVER SL0 40 E1
Manston Dr BRAK RG12 76 B3
Mant Cl KSCL RG20 130 H6
Manton Ter ADL/WDHM KT15 * 82 C8
Manygate La SHPTN TW17 83 J3
Maple Cl BLKW GU17 93 J1
CAV/SC RG4 126 G6
MDHD SL6 4 B8
SHST GU47 86 F5
WWKG RG41 61 K3
Maple Ct ASHF TW15 71 K4
EGH TW20 68 B4
GOR/PANG RG8 111 R12
Maple Crs NWBY RG14 6 E1
SLN SL2 11 M3
Mapledene CAV/SC RG4 44 E3
Maple Dr CWTH RG45 75 J7
LTWR GU18 89 M6
Mapledurham Dr
GOR/PANG RG8 125 N9
Mapledurham Vw
TILE/CALC RG31 125 P12
Maple Gdns ASHF TW15 56 E8
WHIT RG2 59 L4
YTLY GU46 92 D1
Maple Gv TADY RG26 148 D2
WODY RG5 46 E5
Maple La GOR/PANG RG8 123 R9
Maple Pl WDR/YW UB7 42 A1
Maple Ri MLW SL7 19 G3
Maplespeen Ct NWBY RG14 6 D2
The Maples BNEND SL8 * 20 D3
Maplin Pk DTCH/LGLY SL3 40 D2
Marathon Cl WODY RG5 47 H6
Marbeck Cl WDSR SL4 37 M8
Marbull Wy BNFD RG42 64 B4
Marchant Cl STHA RG19 96 F7
Marcheria Cl BRAK RG12 76 B3
Marchside Cl HEST TW5 43 M8
Marchwood Av CAV/SC RG4 127 J10
Marcia Ct SL SL1 38 B1
Marconi Rd NWBY RG14 7 G2
Mardale CBLY GU15 95 J2
Mardy CAV/SC RG4 126 E12
Marefield EARL RG6 60 C4
Marefield Rd MLW SL7 18 F4
Mare La WAR/TWY RG10 49 L3
Marescroft Rd SLN SL2 28 A5
Mareshall Av BNFD RG42 64 B4
Marfleet Cl EARL RG6 * 60 E4
Margaret Cl STA TW18 70 D5
WHIT RG2 59 J7
Marguerite Cl TADY RG26 149 R7
Marigold Cl CWTH RG45 74 F7
Marina Cl CHERT KT16 82 B5
Marina Pde STA TW18 * 70 B6
Marina Wy IVER SL0 31 H8
SL SL1 27 M8
Mariners Cl TADY RG26 148 F4
Mariners Dr FARN GU14 94 C7
Mariners La THLE RG7 135 Q7
Marino Wy EWKG RG40 73 G8
Marion Av SHPTN TW17 83 H2
Marish Whf DTCH/LGLY SL3 * 40 A2
Markby Wy EARL RG6 60 E4
Market La DTCH/LGLY SL3 40 E3
Market Pl BRAK RG12 2 F4
DTCH/LGLY SL3 * 40 E7
EWKG RG40 15 G6
HEN RG9 115 R12
NWBY RG14 6 E4
READ RG1 9 G5
Market Sq EWKG RG40 15 G6
Market St BRAK RG12 2 F4
MDHD SL6 5 H5
NWBY RG14 6 E5
WDSR SL4 13 K5
Market Wy READ RG1 9 G5
Markham Ct CBLY GU15 88 D8
Marks Rd WWKG RG41 14 C2
Marlborough Av READ RG1 59 K1
Marlborough Ct READ RG1 8 C9
Marlborough Crs HYS/HAR UB3 42 F7
Marlborough Dr WEY KT13 83 J7
Marlborough Ri CBLY GU15 88 E8
Marlborough Rd ASHF TW15 70 E3
DTCH/LGLY SL3 39 M4
MDHD SL6 25 J8
NWDGN UB2 43 L3
Marlborough Wy
TILE/CALC RG31 137 M6
Marlin Cl SUN TW16 71 L4
Marlin Ct MLW SL7 18 F5
Marling Cl TILE/CALC RG31 125 N12
Marlow Bottom MLW SL7 18 F1
Marlow Bridge La MLW SL7 19 G6
Marlow Common MLW SL7 18 B4
Marlow Ct CAV/SC RG4 45 K3
The Marlowes NWBY RG14 96 B6
Marlow Gdns HYS/HAR UB3 42 F3
Marlow Mi MLW SL7 * 19 G5
Marlow Rd BNEND SL8 20 B1
HEN RG9 22 A3
MDHD SL6 4 F4
MDHD SL6 25 G1
MLW SL7 18 F7
MLW SL7 19 L1
Marlston Rd NTHA RG18 133 Q5
Marmion Rd HEN RG9 22 A6
Marnham Pl ADL/WDHM KT15 82 C8
Marriott Cl EBED/NFELT TW14 57 K5
Marriott Lodge Cl
ADL/WDHM KT15 82 C7
Marrowells WEY KT13 83 L7
Marsack St CAV/SC RG4 45 J4
Marshall Cl FARN GU14 93 M7
FRIM GU16 95 K4
GOR/PANG RG8 125 P10
Marshall Rd SHST GU47 87 K7
Marshalls Ct NWBY RG14 141 R1
Marshfield DTCH/LGLY SL3 39 L8
Marshland Sq CAV/SC RG4 45 H1
Marsh La ADL/WDHM KT15 82 B8
HTWY RG27 85 M7
HUNG RG17 138 F1
MDHD SL6 37 H2
NTHA RG18 133 K6
NWBY RG14 6 E3
Marsh Rd NTHA RG18 98 A2
The Marsh HUNG RG17 * 129 J12
Marshwood Rd LTWR GU18 90 D6
Marston Dr FARN GU14 94 B7
Marston Wy ASC SL5 * 96 F1
NWBY RG14 65 L7
Martel Cl CBLY GU15 89 J7
Marten Pl TILE/CALC RG31 125 M11
Martin Cl WDSR SL4 37 L8
WODY RG5 46 E8
Martindale IVER SL0 30 E5
Martindale Av CBLY GU15 95 J3
Martineau La WAR/TWY RG10 47 L7
Martingale Cha NWBY RG14 7 J2
Martin Rd MDHD SL6 5 G2
SL SL1 10 E8
Martins Cl BLKW GU17 93 K2
Martins Dr WWKG RG41 14 E2
Martins La BRAK RG12 3 L6
Martins Pk FARN GU14 * 93 K7
Martin's Pln SLN SL2 29 H4
The Martins STHA RG19 98 B4
Martin Wy FRIM GU16 94 E5
Marunden Gn SLN SL2 28 B4
Maryland EWKG RG40 73 K7
Mary Md BNFD RG42 64 D4
Maryside DTCH/LGLY SL3 40 A2
Masdar Gdns EWKG RG40 73 L8
Masefield Gdns CWTH RG45 87 H3
Masefield Rd NTHA RG18 97 L2
Masefield Wy
STWL/WRAY TW19 56 F7
Mason Cl YTLY GU46 * 92 E1
Masonic Hall Rd CHERT KT16 81 M3
Mason Pl SHST GU47 86 F6
Mason Rd FARN GU14 93 L8
Masons Rd SL SL1 28 A8
Mason St READ RG1 8 B5
Master Cl WODY RG5 47 H6
Matchlock Ms NWBY RG14 * 96 E1
Mathisen Wy DTCH/LGLY SL3 41 G8
Matlock Rd CAV/SC RG4 44 E2
Matson Dr HEN RG9 22 B4
Matthew Arnold Cl STA TW18 70 C4
Matthews Cha BNFD RG42 63 M5
Matthews Cl STHA RG19 97 K3
Matthews Ct ASC SL5 78 D1
Matthewsgreen Rd
WWKG RG41 14 C1
Matthews La STA TW18 69 M2
Matthews Rd CBLY GU15 88 C6
Maultway Cl CBLY GU15 89 H6
Maultway Crs CBLY GU15 89 H6
Maultway North CBLY GU15 89 H5
The Maultway CBLY GU15 89 H6
Mawbray Cl EARL RG6 60 C3
Maxine Cl SHST GU47 87 H5
Maxwell Cl WODY RG5 46 E6
Maxwell Rd ASHF TW15 71 J4
WDR/YW UB7 42 A4
Maybrick Cl SHST GU47 86 F5
Maybury Cl FRIM GU16 94 D6
SL SL1 27 M6
May Cl SHST GU47 87 K6
Mayfair RDGW/BURGH RG30 137 P3
Mayfair Dr NWBY RG14 6 A7
Mayfield Av TILE/CALC RG31 137 M6
Mayfield Cl ASHF TW15 71 H4
Mayfield Dr CAV/SC RG4 45 K3
WDSR SL4 53 G2
Mayfield Gdns STA TW18 69 M5
Mayfield Rd CBLY GU15 * 94 B5
FARN GU14 93 M7
May Flds WWKG RG41 61 G5
Mayflower Dr YTLY GU46 86 A7
Maygoods Cl UX/CGN UB8 31 M6
Maygoods Gn UX/CGN UB8 31 M6
Maygoods La UX/CGN UB8 31 M6
Maygoods Vw UX/CGN UB8 * 31 L6
The Maying WHIT RG2 59 H8
Maynard Cl NTHA RG18 97 L1
Mayors La NWBY RG14 6 E5
Mayow Cl STHA RG19 98 B4
May Pk TILE/CALC RG31 137 Q6
Maypole Rd MDHD SL6 27 J6
Mays Cl EARL RG6 60 B1
Mays Cft BRAK RG12 * 3 H7
Mays La EARL RG6 60 B1
May's La THLE RG7 143 J7
Mays Rd EWKG RG40 15 M5
Maywood Dr CBLY GU15 89 H7
Mc Ardle Wy DTCH/LGLY SL3 40 F7
Mc Carthy Wy EWKG RG40 73 M6
Mc Crae's Wk WAR/TWY RG10 32 F4
McNair Cl EARL RG6 * 60 A5
Mead Av DTCH/LGLY SL3 40 D2
Mead Cl DTCH/LGLY SL3 40 D2
EGH TW20 69 H4
MLW SL7 19 H3
TILE/CALC RG31 137 M4
Mead Ct EGH TW20 69 J4
Meade Pk CAV/SC RG4 * 46 C4
Meadfield Av DTCH/LGLY SL3 40 C3
Meadfield Rd DTCH/LGLY SL3 40 C3
Meadhurst Pk SUN TW16 71 L4
Meadhurst Rd CHERT KT16 * 82 B5
Mead La CHERT KT16 82 C5
GOR/PANG RG8 124 A8
Meadowbank Gdns HEST TW5 43 J8
Meadowbank Rd LTWR GU18 90 C5
Meadowbrook Cl
DTCH/LGLY SL3 55 L1
Meadow Cl BLKW GU17 93 K2
GOR/PANG RG8 112 A12
KSCL RG20 122 A1
MLW SL7 19 H5
STHA RG19 97 L3
WDSR SL4 54 B4
WGFD OX10 111 P6
Meadow Ct STA TW18 69 L1
Meadowcroft Rd WHIT RG2 59 H6
Meadow Gdns STA TW18 69 K3
Meadow La WDSR SL4 12 E1
Meadowlea Cl WDR/YW UB7 41 M6
Meadow Rd ASHF TW15 71 K3
DTCH/LGLY SL3 40 A3
EARL RG6 60 D3
FARN GU14 94 B7
HEN RG9 22 A5
NWBY RG14 6 D9
READ RG1 8 D3
VW GU25 79 L2
WWKG RG41 14 C7
Meadowside TILE/CALC RG31 137 M1
Meadowside Rd
GOR/PANG RG8 124 H9
Meadows Leigh Cl WEY KT13 83 J7
The Meadows HTWY RG27 150 D9
Meadowsweet Cl NTHA RG18 98 A2
Meadow Vw CHERT KT16 82 C5
STWL/WRAY TW19 55 M4
UX/CGN UB8 * 31 L6
WWKG RG41 61 K3
Meadowview La MDHD SL6 36 A6
Meadow Wk BNEND SL8 20 C1
WWKG RG41 14 C6
Meadow Wy ADL/WDHM KT15 82 B8
BLKW GU17 93 J1
BNFD RG42 2 C1
CHOB/PIR GU24 90 F8
MDHD SL6 36 F8
MDHD SL6 37 H2
THLE RG7 136 H7
WDSR SL4 54 B5
WWKG RG41 14 C7
Meads Cl KSCL RG20 120 D7
The Mead HUNG RG17 118 F11
Mead Wk DTCH/LGLY SL3 40 D2
Meadway ASHF TW15 71 G2
FRIM GU16 94 F4
Mead Wy SL SL1 27 M6
Meadway STA TW18 70 A5
Meadway Cl STA TW18 69 M5
The Meadway
RDGW/BURGH RG30 137 Q3
The Mearings
RDGW/BURGH RG30 144 C2
Measham Wy EARL RG6 60
Meashill Wy DID OX11 108
Meavy Gdns WHIT RG2 59
Medallion Pl MDHD SL6 5
Mede Cl STWL/WRAY TW19 54
Medhurst Cl CHOB/PIR GU24 91
Medill Cl GOR/PANG RG8 113
Medina Cl WWKG RG41 61
Medlake Rd EGH TW20 69
Medlar Dr BLKW GU17 93
Medman Cl UX/CGN UB8 31
Medway Cl NTHA RG18 97
WWKG RG41 14
Medway Dr FARN GU14 93
Meitner Cl TADY RG26 149
Melbourne Av SL SL1 28
WWKG RG41 61
Melbury Cl CHERT KT16 82
Meldreth Wy EARL RG6 60
Meldrum Cl NWBY RG14 141
Melford Gn CAV/SC RG4 127
Melksham Cl EARL RG6 59
Melling Cl EARL RG6 60
Mellor Wk WDSR SL4 13
WHIT RG2 * 59
Melody Cl WWKG RG41 61
Melrose BRAK RG12 76
Melrose Av EARL RG6 60
Melrose Gdns WHIT RG2 72
Melton Ct MDHD SL6 5
Melville Av FRIM GU16 94
Membury Cl FRIM GU16 95
Membury Wk BRAK RG12 3
Memorial Av HEN RG9 32
Mendip Cl DTCH/LGLY SL3 40
HYS/HAR UB3 42
WAR/TWY RG10 47
Mendip Dr TILE/CALC RG31 * 137
Mendip Rd BRAK RG12 76
FARN GU14 93
Menpes Rd TILE/CALC RG31 125
Meon Cl FARN GU14 93
TADY RG26 148
Merchants Pl READ RG1 8
Mercian Wy SL SL1 37
Mercia Rd MDHD SL6 35
Mercury Av WWKG RG41 61
Mercury House HYS/HAR UB3 * 43
Mereoak La THLE RG7 145
Mere Pk MLW SL7 * 19
Mere Rd SHPTN TW17 * 83
SL SL1 11
WEY KT13 83
Mereside Pk ASHF TW15 * 71
Merivale Gdns WHIT RG2 * 59
Merlewood BRAK RG12 76
Merlin Cl DTCH/LGLY SL3 * 40
Merlin Clove BNFD RG42 65
Mermaid Cl WWKG RG41 61
Merrivale Gdns WHIT RG2 59
Merrivale Ms WDR/YW UB7 * 41
Merron Cl YTLY GU46 92
Merryfields UX/CGN UB8 31
Merryhill Green La WWKG RG41 61
Merryhill Rd BNFD RG42 2
Merrylands CHERT KT16 81
Merryman Dr CWTH RG45 74
Merryweather Cl EWKG RG40 73
Merrywood Pk CBLY GU15 94
Mersey Wy NTHA RG18 97
Merthyr V CAV/SC RG4 126
Merton Cl MDHD SL6 35
SHST GU47 87
Merton Ford EWKG RG40 * 15
Merton Rd SL SL1 11
Merton Rd North WHIT RG2 59
Merton Rd South WHIT RG2 59
Mervyn Rd SHPTN TW17 83
Merwin Wy WDSR SL4 * 52
Metcalf Rd ASHF TW15 71
Meteor Cl WODY RG5 47
The Mews READ RG1 45
TADY RG26 150
Meyrick Dr NWBY RG14 141
Michaelmas Cl YTLY GU46 92
Micheldever Wy BRAK RG12 76
Michelet Cl LTWR GU18 90
Micklands Rd CAV/SC RG4 45
Mickle Hl SHST GU47 87
Midcroft SLN SL2 28
Middle Cl CBLY GU15 89
NWBY RG14 141
Middle Culham HEN RG9 * 22
Middlefarm Cl KSCL RG20 120
Middlefields WAR/TWY RG10 33
Middle Gordon Rd CBLY GU15 94
Middle Gn DTCH/LGLY SL3 30
Middlegreen Rd DTCH/LGLY SL3 39
Middle Hl EGH TW20 68
Middlemoor Rd FRIM GU16 94
Middle Springs
GOR/PANG RG8 112
Middleton Ct NWBY RG14 97
Middleton Gdns FARN GU14 93
Middleton Rd CBLY GU15 88
Middletons Cl HUNG RG17 129
Middle Wk SL SL1 27
Midsummer Meadow
CAV/SC RG4 126
Midway Av CHERT KT16 70
EGH TW20 69
Midway Cl STA TW18 70
Midwinter Cl
RDGW/BURGH RG30 137
Milam Cl WHIT RG2 72
Milbanke Ct BNFD RG42 2
BRAK RG12 2
Milbanke Wy BRAK RG12 2
Milden Cl FRIM GU16 95
Milden Gdns FRIM GU16 95
Mildenhall Rd SL SL1 29
Mildred Av HYS/HAR UB3 42
Mile Elm MLW SL7 19
Miles Pl LTWR GU18 89
Milestone Av WAR/TWY RG10 32
Milestone Crs WAR/TWY RG10 47
Miles Wy WODY RG5 47
Milford Ct SL SL1 * 11
Milford Rd READ RG1 8
Military Dr STHA RG19 98
Milkhouse Rd KSCL RG20 131
Mill Av UX/CGN UB8 31
Mill Bank HUNG RG17 140
Millbank MLW SL7 * 19
Millbank Crs WODY RG5 46
Millboard Rd BNEND SL8 20
Mill Bridge Pl UX/CGN UB8 31
Millbridge Rd YTLY GU46 86
Millbrook WEY KT13 83
Millbrook Cl DID OX11 110
Millbrook Wy DTCH/LGLY SL3 55
Mill Cl BAGS GU19 89
HEN RG9 115
WDR/YW UB7 41
WWKG RG41 14
Mill Ct WDR/YW UB7 41
Milldown Av GOR/PANG RG8 112
Milldown Rd GOR/PANG RG8 112
Millennium Cl UX/CGN UB8 31
Millennium Wy BNFD RG42 2
Millers Cl GOR/PANG RG8 111

STA TW18 70 B3
iller's Fld HUNG RG17 118 E11
illers Gv TILE/CALC RG31 137 Q6
illers Rd TADY RG26 148 D2
illey La WAR/TWY RG10 33 K6
illey Rd WAR/TWY RG10 33 M7
ill Farm Av SUN TW16 71 L5
ill Fld BAGS GU19 89 K3
illfield HUNG RG17 117 K3
SUN TW16 71 K6
illgate Ct WAR/TWY RG10 47 L1
ill Gn BNFD RG42 63 L5
CAV/SC RG4 9 J2
illgreen La STHA RG19 102 B4
ill House La EGH TW20 81 H1
illington Cl WHIT RG2 59 K3
illington Rd HYS/HAR UB3 43 G3
illins Cl SHST GU47 87 K5
ill La ASC SL5 67 H7
BRAK RG12 2 B8
CAV/SC RG4 126 C9
DTCH/LGLY SL3 55 H2
EARL RG6 60 E3
EGH TW20 81 J1
HEN RG9 22 B6
HEN RG9 32 C4
HTWY RG27 150 C7
HTWY RG27 150 H10
HUNG RG17 117 L4
MARL SN8 138 D10
MDHD SL6 20 D7
MDHD SL6 24 B2
MDHD SL6 26 E6
NWBY RG14 6 F4
READ RG1 9 G7
STHA RG19 98 D4
THLE RG7 142 E3
THLE RG7 150 C5
TILE/CALC RG31 137 Q6
WDSR SL4 12 D4
WWKG RG41 60 F5
YTLY GU46 94 E4
ill Md STA TW18 69 M2
illmead WWKG RG41 14 C3
illmere YTLY GU46 86 D7
ill Pl DTCH/LGLY SL3 54 D1
ill Pond Rd BFOR GU20 78 B8
ill Reef Cl STHA RG19 97 H3
ill Ride ASC SL5 65 K6
ill Rd CAV/SC RG4 9 J2
GOR/PANG RG8 112 A11
HEN RG9 32 D3
HEN RG9 114 E3
MLW SL7 19 G5
RDGW/BURGH RG30 137 Q8
WDR/YW UB7 41 M3
illside BNEND SL8 20 E3
illside Pk WDSR SL4 * 52 D1
ills Sp WDSR SL4 54 B4
illstream La SL SL1 38 A1
ill St DTCH/LGLY SL3 40 F7
SLN SL2 11 H4
illworth La WHIT RG2 145 Q2
ilman Cl BRAK RG12 64 F7
ilman Rd WHIT RG2 59 H1
ilner Rd SL SL1 27 J6
ilsom Cl WHIT RG2 145 Q1
ilton Cl BRAK RG12 76 A3
DTCH/LGLY SL3 55 G2
HEN RG9 115 R12
ilton Ct EWKG RG40 14 F4
ilton Dr EWKG RG40 14 F4
SHPTN TW17 82 E1
ilton Gdns EWKG RG40 14 F5
STWL/WRAY TW19 56 F7
ilton Pk EGH TW20 * 69 G5
ilton Rd EARL RG6 46 A7
EGH TW20 68 F3
EWKG RG40 14 F4
SLN SL2 28 F5
WWKG RG41 14 F3
ilton Wy WAR/TWY RG10 47 L1
WDR/YW UB7 42 B4
ilverton Cl MDHD SL6 35 K3
ilward Gdns BRAK RG12 63 J7
imosa Dr WHIT RG2 59 L8
ina Av DTCH/LGLY SL3 39 M2
inchens La TADY RG26 149 Q5
inchin Gn BNFD RG42 63 J3
incing La CHOB/PIR GU24 91 M4
inden Cl WWKG RG41 61 L8
inerva Cl STWL/WRAY TW19 * 56 A4
inet Dr HYS/HAR UB3 43 J1
inet Gdns HYS/HAR UB3 43 K1
inistry Rd STHA RG19 101 J1
inley Rd BLKW GU17 92 E5
inniecroft Rd SL SL1 27 K4
inorca Av FRIM GU16 95 L4
inorca Rd FRIM GU16 95 L5
WEY KT13 83 G8
instead Cl BRAK RG12 64 F8
TADY RG26 148 D4
instead Dr YTLY GU46 92 C1
inster Ct CBLY GU15 * 93 M2
insterley Av SHPTN TW17 83 L1
inster St READ RG1 8 F6
inster Wy DTCH/LGLY SL3 40 B2
int Cl EARL RG6 59 M5
inton Cl RDGW/BURGH RG30 137 Q2
inton Ri MDHD SL6 27 K7
irador Crs SLN SL2 11 M2
ire La WAR/TWY RG10 48 D2
issenden Cl
EBED/NFELT TW14 57 M7
issenden Gdns SL SL1 27 K7
istletoe Rd YTLY GU46 92 D2
itcham Cl WHIT RG2 59 H1
itcham Ct CBLY GU15 89 G5
itcham Rd CBLY GU15 89 G5
itchell Cl SL SL1 38 C2
itchell Wy WODY RG5 47 G7
itford Cl WHIT RG2 59 K6
itre Cl SHPTN TW17 83 K3
ixnams La CHERT KT16 70 A8
oat Cl TADY RG26 149 Q6
oat Dr SLN SL2 29 L6
odbury Gdns WHIT RG2 59 J4
offatts Cl SHST GU47 87 G6
offy Hl MDHD SL6 26 A4
ohawk Wy WODY RG5 47 H6
ole Cl FARN GU14 93 K8
ole Rd WHIT RG2 72 F1
WWKG RG41 61 G6
oles Cl EWKG RG40 15 J7
ollison Cl WODY RG5 47 H6
olly Millar Br WWKG RG41 14 E9
olly Millars Cl WWKG RG41 14 E9
olly Millar's La WWKG RG41 14 C8
olyneux Rd BFOR GU20 90 C2
WEY KT13 83 G8
olyns Ms SL SL1 38 A1
onarch Cl EBED/NFELT TW14 57 L6
onarch Dr WHIT RG2 59 L8
onastery Gdns
DTCH/LGLY SL3 * 54 B2
onck Ct RDGW/BURGH RG30 44 D8
ondial Wy HYS/HAR UB3 42 E7
oney La WDR/YW UB7 41 M3
oneyrow Gn MDHD SL6 36 C7
onkey Island La MDHD SL6 36 F3
onksbarn WHIT RG2 59 K4
Monks Cl ASC SL5 78 B3
Monks Dr ASC SL5 78 B3
Monksfield Wy SLN SL2 28 C5
Monk Sherborne Rd
TADY RG26 148 B11
Monks Hollow MLW SL7 19 G1
Monkshood Cl EWKG RG40 15 L3
Monks La NWBY RG14 96 A7
Monks Rd VW GU25 80 D1
WDSR SL4 52 D1
Monks Wk ASC SL5 78 B3
Monks Wy
RDGW/BURGH RG30 58 D1
STA TW18 70 D5
Monkswood Cl NWBY RG14 141 R7
Monks Wood Crs TADY RG26 148 D3
Monktons La THLE RG7 144 A9
Monmouth Rd HYS/HAR UB3 43 G4
Mons Cl WWKG RG41 61 L8
Mons Wk EGH TW20 69 J3
Montacute Dr STHA RG19 98 B4
Montague Cl CBLY GU15 94 B1
EWKG RG40 15 M3
LTWR GU18 90 A5
Montague Rd SL SL1 11 G2
UX/CGN UB8 31 M1
Montague St CAV/SC RG4 9 J1
READ RG1 9 L7
Montague Ter NWBY RG14 6 E9
Montagu Rd DTCH/LGLY SL3 39 K8
Monteagle La YTLY GU46 86 A8
Montem La SL SL1 10 C6
Montgomery Cl SHST GU47 87 H6
Montgomery Dr THLE RG7 145 M4
Montgomery Pl SLN SL2 29 L7
Montgomery Rd NWBY RG14 6 A9
Montpelier Dr CAV/SC RG4 45 K1
Montpellier Ct WDSR SL4 13 H8
Montrose Av DTCH/LGLY SL3 39 L7
SL SL1 28 D7
Montrose Cl ASHF TW15 71 J4
FRIM GU16 94 E4
Montrose Dr MDHD SL6 25 J8
Montrose Rd
EBED/NFELT TW14 57 K5
Montrose Wk WEY KT13 83 H7
Montrose Wy DTCH/LGLY SL3 39 M8
Monument Cl NWBY RG14 141 R7
Monument Hl WEY KT13 83 H8
Monument Rd WEY KT13 83 H8
Monycrower Dr MDHD SL6 4 E5
Moorbridge Rd MDHD SL6 5 K4
Moor Cl EWKG RG40 73 L7
SHST GU47 87 L5
Moor Copse Cl EARL RG6 60 B3
Moordale Av BNFD RG42 2 B1
Moore Cl SL SL1 38 D2
Moore Grove Crs EGH TW20 68 E5
Moor End MDHD SL6 36 E5
Moores Gn EWKG RG40 15 L2
Moores La WDSR SL4 38 B4
Moore's Pl HUNG RG17 138 G1
Moorfield Rd UX/CGN UB8 31 M7
Moorfields Cl STA TW18 69 L6
Moorfield Ter MDHD SL6 5 K4
Moor Furlong SL SL1 38 A1
Moorhayes Dr STA TW18 70 C8
Moorhen Dr EARL RG6 60 B5
The Moorings WDSR SL4 12 D3
WDSR SL4 * 37 M7
WDSR SL4 54 C6
Moorland Rd WDR/YW UB7 41 L7
Moorlands Dr MDHD SL6 25 H6
Moorlands Rd CBLY GU15 94 E5
Moor La BRAK RG12 63 J8
MDHD SL6 26 B5
NWBY RG14 6 B3
STA TW18 69 L1
STWL/WRAY TW19 55 J7
WDR/YW UB7 41 L6
Moormede Crs STA TW18 69 M2
Moor Pl BFOR GU20 90 B1
Moor Rd FARN GU14 94 A6
FRIM GU16 94 F6
Moorside Cl FARN GU14 94 A5
MDHD SL6 26 B5
The Moors GOR/PANG RG8 124 H9
NTHA RG18 97 M3
STHA RG19 97 L4
Moorstown Ct SL SL1 10 F7
The Moor MLW SL7 19 L2
Moray Av HYS/HAR UB3 43 H1
SHST GU47 87 K7
Moray Dr SLN SL2 11 K1
SLN SL2 11 L1
Mordaunt Dr CWTH RG45 87 H3
Morden Cl BRAK RG12 76 F1
Morecambe Av CAV/SC RG4 44 E1
Moreland Cl DTCH/LGLY SL3 40 E7
Moreleigh Cl WHIT RG2 59 H6
Morella Cl VW GU25 80 C1
Morello Dr DTCH/LGLY SL3 40 B1
Moretaine Rd ASHF TW15 70 D1
Moreton Wy SL SL1 37 M1
Morgan Rd READ RG1 59 J1
Morgaston Rd TADY RG26 149 K11
Moriston Cl
RDGW/BURGH RG30 44 B6
Morlais CAV/SC RG4 44 F1
Morlands Av
RDGW/BURGH RG30 58 A1
Morley Cl DTCH/LGLY SL3 40 B2
YTLY GU46 92 B1
Morley Pl HUNG RG17 138 H1
Mornington Av EWKG RG40 73 M6
Mornington Cl TADY RG26 103 M5
Mornington Crs HEST TW5 43 K8
Mornington Rd ASHF TW15 71 J3
Morpeth Cl WHIT RG2 59 J3
Morrice Cl DTCH/LGLY SL3 40 B4
Morrison Cl GOR/PANG RG8 124 B10
Morris Pl MLW SL7 * 18 F4
Mortimer Cl WHIT RG2 59 J7
Mortimer Gdns TADY RG26 148 E3
Mortimer La THLE RG7 144 C11
THLE RG7 150 B2
Mortimer Rd DTCH/LGLY SL3 39 M3
THLE RG7 144 F7
Morton Cl FRIM GU16 94 F7
Morton Pl THLE RG7 137 J6
Mortons La THLE RG7 134 E12
Morval Rd BLKW GU17 92 F5
Moss Cl CAV/SC RG4 45 J1
Mossy V MDHD SL6 25 M5
Moston Cl HYS/HAR UB3 43 H5
Mothes House TADY RG26 148 E3
Mothes Houses TADY RG26 * 148 E3
Moulsham Copse La
YTLY GU46 86 B7
Moulsham La YTLY GU46 86 B7
Mountbatten Cl NWBY RG14 96 E1
SL SL1 11 J8
Mountbatten Ri SHST GU47 86 F5
Mountbatten Sq WDSR SL4 13 H5
Mount Cl NWBY RG14 6 E8
The Mount Cl VW GU25 80 D3
Mount Felix WOT/HER KT12 83 M5
Mountfield GOR/PANG RG8 112 A11
Mount La BRAK RG12 3 G6
KSCL RG20 119 K6
Mount Lee EGH TW20 68 E3
Mount Pleasant BNFD RG42 * 65 G1
BRAK RG12 3 H6
READ RG1 9 H9
SHST GU47 87 G5
TADY RG26 148 C2
WEY KT13 83 G7
WWKG RG41 14 D5
Mount Pleasant Cl LTWR GU18 90 A5
Mount Pleasant Cots
EGH TW20 * 68 D4
Mount Pleasant Gv READ RG1 9 H9
Mount Rd HYS/HAR UB3 43 J2
NTHA RG18 97 M2
Mountsfield Cl
STWL/WRAY TW19 56 A4
Mounts Hl WDSR SL4 66 B4
Mount St READ RG1 59 H1
WHIT RG2 59 H1
The Mount CAV/SC RG4 44 F3
NWBY RG14 * 6 E9
READ RG1 59 K1
VW GU25 80 D3
WEY KT13 83 L6
Mount Vw HEN RG9 115 R12
NWDGN UB2 * 43 M4
Mowbray Crs EGH TW20 69 G3
Mowbray Dr
RDGW/BURGH RG30 44 A6
Mower Cl EWKG RG40 62 F7
Mowforth Cl GOR/PANG RG8 113 J9
Moyleen Ri MLW SL7 18 E5
Muckhatch La EGH TW20 69 H8
Mud La HTWY RG27 84 F5
KSCL RG20 120 D8
Muirfield Cl READ RG1 9 L7
Mulberry Av STWL/WRAY TW19 56 E7
WDSR SL4 53 M2
Mulberry Cl CWTH RG45 87 J2
SHST GU47 87 K6
WEY KT13 83 H7
WODY RG5 46 E8
Mulberry Crs WDR/YW UB7 42 C2
Mulberry Dr DTCH/LGLY SL3 40 A5
Mulberry Pde WDR/YW UB7 42 C3
Mulberry Trees SHPTN TW17 83 K4
Mulberry Wk MDHD SL6 4 A2
Mulberry Wy THLE RG7 137 J8
Mulfords Hl TADY RG26 148 D1
Mulgrave Rd FRIM GU16 94 F4
Mullens Rd EGH TW20 69 J3
Mulroy Dr CBLY GU15 89 G8
Mumberry Hl WAR/TWY RG10 * 33 H6
Mumbery Hl WAR/TWY RG10 33 G5
Muncaster Cl ASHF TW15 71 G2
Muncaster Rd ASHF TW15 71 H3
Munday Ct BNFD RG42 63 L5
Mundaydean La MLW SL7 18 B1
Mundesley Sp SL SL1 10 E1
Mundesley St READ RG1 9 G8
Munkle Marsh STHA RG19 * 98 C3
Munnings Dr SHST GU47 87 K8
Munro Av WODY RG5 60 F2
Murdoch Cl STA TW18 70 A3
Murdoch Rd EWKG RG40 15 H8
Murray Ct ASC SL5 78 C3
Murray Rd WWKG RG41 14 C6
Murrellhill La BNFD RG42 63 J5
Murrells La CBLY GU15 94 B3
Murrin Rd MDHD SL6 4 A3
Mushroom Castle BNFD RG42 65 H4
Mustard La CAV/SC RG4 46 E5
Mustard Mill Rd STA TW18 69 L2
Muswell Cl THLE RG7 137 J7
Mutton Oaks BRAK RG12 63 K6
Myddleton Rd UX/CGN UB8 31 L2
Myers Wy FRIM GU16 95 K4
Mylne Sq EWKG RG40 15 K5
Mylum Cl WHIT RG2 59 J8
The Myrke DTCH/LGLY SL3 39 H4
Myrtle Av EBED/NFELT TW14 57 L3
Myrtle Cl DTCH/LGLY SL3 41 G8
LTWR GU18 90 B6
THLE RG7 143 R3
TILE/CALC RG31 125 N11
WDR/YW UB7 42 B4
Myrtle Crs SLN SL2 11 H2
Myrtle Dr BLKW GU17 93 K2
Myton Wk THLE RG7 137 J7

N

Nabbs Hill Cl TILE/CALC RG31 137 N5
Nairn Cl FRIM GU16 94 E4
Nalderhill Rd KSCL RG20 131 M11
Napier Cl CWTH RG45 87 J2
WDR/YW UB7 42 B3
Napier Ct READ RG1 * 9 H4
Napier Dr CBLY GU15 89 G7
Napier Rd ASHF TW15 71 K5
CWTH RG45 87 J2
MDHD SL6 25 K8
READ RG1 9 H4
Napier Wk ASHF TW15 71 K5
Napoleon Av FARN GU14 94 B8
Napper Cl ASC SL5 65 J7
Narromine Dr TILE/CALC RG31 137 R6
Naseby BRAK RG12 76 B5
Naseby Ri NWBY RG14 96 F1
Nash Cl EARL RG6 60 A3
Nashdom La SL SL1 27 J1
Nash Gdns ASC SL5 65 K7
Nash Grove La EWKG RG40 73 L4
Nash Pk BNFD RG42 63 H4
Nash Rd DTCH/LGLY SL3 40 B5
Natalie Cl EBED/NFELT TW14 57 K6
The Naylors THLE RG7 145 P8
Neals La CAV/SC RG4 114 B12
Neath Gdns
RDGW/BURGH RG30 137 R3
Needham Cl WDSR SL4 38 A8
Neil Cl ASHF TW15 71 J3
Nell Gwynn Av SHPTN TW17 83 K3
Nell Gwynne Av ASC SL5 78 D1
Nelson Cl BRAK RG12 3 M4
DTCH/LGLY SL3 39 M4
EBED/NFELT TW14 * 57 M7
Nelson Rd ASHF TW15 70 E3
CAV/SC RG4 9 J1
HTHAIR TW6 42 B8
WDSR SL4 12 B9
Nelson's La WAR/TWY RG10 48 A8
Nelson Ter READ RG1 * 9 H8
Nelson Wy CBLY GU15 93 M2
Nene Rd HTHAIR TW6 42 D8
Neptune Cl WWKG RG41 61 L8
Neptune Rd HTHAIR TW6 * 42 E8
Nestle's Av HYS/HAR UB3 43 H3
Netherton BRAK RG12 2 D8
Netley Cl CAV/SC RG4 127 L12
Nettlecombe BRAK RG12 76 D2
Nettleton Rd HTHAIR TW6 42 D8
Neuman Crs BRAK RG12 76 A3
Nevelle Cl BNFD RG42 63 K6
Neville Cl WAR/TWY RG10 34 B8
Neville Dr STHA RG19 98 A3
Neville Duke Rd FARN GU14 93 M6
Nevis Rd TILE/CALC RG31 125 P11
New Acres EWKG RG40 * 74 E7
Newall Rd HTHAIR TW6 42 E8
Newalls Ri WAR/TWY RG10 33 G4
New Ar UX/CGN UB8 * 31 M2
Newark Rd BFOR GU20 78 B8
BLKW GU17 92 E5
Newark St READ RG1 9 H8
New Bath Rd WAR/TWY RG10 47 G2
Newberry Crs WDSR SL4 37 L8
Newbery Cl TILE/CALC RG31 137 P1
Newbery Wy SL SL1 10 C7
Newbold Rd NWBY RG14 141 R1
Newbolt Cl NTHA RG18 97 L1
New Bright St READ RG1 8 F8
Newbury Cl WAR/TWY RG10 47 H2
Newbury Dr MDHD SL6 5 L6
Newbury Hl NTHA RG18 122 B9
Newbury La KSCL RG20 121 R2
Newbury Rd DID OX11 109 J1
HTHAIR TW6 42 A8
HUNG RG17 117 L4
HUNG RG17 118 F12
NTHA RG18 133 N4
Newbury St HUNG RG17 117 K4
HUNG RG17 140 B4
Newcastle Rd WHIT RG2 59 J2
Newchurch Rd SLN SL2 28 B6
TADY RG26 148 C1
New Ct MLW SL7 18 F4
Newcourt UX/CGN UB8 31 L6
Newell Gn BNFD RG42 64 C3
Newell's La CAV/SC RG4 126 B11
New Farm Cl STA TW18 70 C6
Newfield Av FARN GU14 93 L8
Newfield Gdns MLW SL7 19 H3
Newfield Rd CAV/SC RG4 126 F4
MLW SL7 19 H4
Newfield Wy MLW SL7 19 G4
New Forest Ride BRAK RG12 76 E4
Newfoundland Rd FRIM GU16 95 K6
New Garden Dr WDR/YW UB7 42 A2
Newhaven Cl HYS/HAR UB3 43 H4
Newhaven Crs ASHF TW15 71 K3
Newhaven Sp SLN SL2 * 28 D5
New Hl GOR/PANG RG8 125 N9
Newhurst Gdns BNFD RG42 64 D3
Newlands Av CAV/SC RG4 45 H3
Newlands Cl YTLY GU46 92 D1
Newlands Dr DTCH/LGLY SL3 55 L2
MDHD SL6 25 J7
Newlands La HEN RG9 114 A9
Newlands Rd CBLY GU15 94 B5
New Lane Hl
RDGW/BURGH RG30 137 Q4
Newlyn Gdns WHIT RG2 59 H5
Newmans Pl ASC SL5 79 H4
Newmarket Cl EARL RG6 60 D4
New Meadow ASC SL5 65 K6
New Mile Rd ASC SL5 66 B7
New Mill La HTWY RG27 84 E4
New Mill Rd HTWY RG27 84 E4
Newnhamhill Bottom
HEN RG9 114 B8
New North Dr HTWY RG27 150 E11
New Pde ASHF TW15 * 70 F2
WDR/YW UB7 * 42 A1
New Park Rd ASHF TW15 71 J3
New Peachey La UX/CGN UB8 31 M7
New Pl ASC SL5 * 78 E6
Newport Cl NWBY RG14 7 H2
Newport Dr BNFD RG42 64 B4
Newport Rd HTHAIR TW6 42 C8
NWBY RG14 7 H1
READ RG1 8 E2
SLN SL2 28 A5
New Rd ASC SL5 65 M4
BAGS GU19 89 M3
BLKW GU17 93 L2
BNEND SL8 20 D2
BRAK RG12 3 K4
CWTH RG45 87 J1
DTCH/LGLY SL3 39 M8
DTCH/LGLY SL3 40 C3
EBED/NFELT TW14 57 K5
HEN RG9 32 C3
HEN RG9 127 P8
HTWY RG27 85 L7
HYS/HAR UB3 42 E7
MDHD SL6 20 A7
MDHD SL6 24 B3
MDHD SL6 36 D6
NWBY RG14 7 J8
READ RG1 59 K1
SHPTN TW17 71 G8
SHST GU47 87 G6
STA TW18 69 J3
STHA RG19 96 F7
TADY RG26 148 C3
TADY RG26 148 G7
THLE RG7 144 B6
WAR/TWY RG10 32 F7
WWKG RG41 61 G6
New Road Hl THLE RG7 99 K3
New Site ADL/WDHM KT15 * 82 E8
New Sq EBED/NFELT TW14 57 J7
SL SL1 11 G6
Newstead Ri WHIT RG2 59 L5
New St HEN RG9 22 A4
STA TW18 70 A2
THLE RG7 150 E2
Newton Av CAV/SC RG4 45 K1
Newton Cl DTCH/LGLY SL3 40 B2
Newton Ct WDSR SL4 54 A5
Newton La WDSR SL4 54 B5
Newton Rd FARN GU14 94 D8
Newtonside Orch WDSR SL4 * 54 A5
Newtown TADY RG26 148 C1
Newtown Gdns HEN RG9 22 A6
Newtown Rd HEN RG9 22 B6
MARL SN8 128 A6
MLW SL7 19 H3
NWBY RG14 6 E8
SHST GU47 87 H6
STHA RG19 96 C8
New Vls KSCL RG20 * 140 H11
New Wy THLE RG7 135 Q8
New Wickham La EGH TW20 69 G5
New Wokingham Rd
CWTH RG45 75 G7
New Zealand Av
WOT/HER KT12 83 M5
Niagara Rd HEN RG9 22 A6
Nicholas Gdns SL SL1 38 A1
Nicholas Rd HEN RG9 127 P2
Nicholls WDSR SL4 52 C2
Nicholson Ms EGH TW20 * 69 G3
Nicholsons La MDHD SL6 5 G5
Nicholson Wk EGH TW20 69 G3
Nideggan Cl STHA RG19 97 M3
Nield Rd HYS/HAR UB3 43 H2
Nightingale Av FARN GU14 93 J8
Nightingale Ct SL SL1 11 J8
Nightingale Crs BRAK RG12 76 C2
Nightingale Gdns SHST GU47 87 H6
Nightingale La MDHD SL6 25 M3
THLE RG7 144 B8
Nightingale Pk SLN SL2 28 B1
Nightingale Pl MDHD SL6 * 20 B8
Nightingale Rd WODY RG5 60 D2
Nightingale Shott EGH TW20 68 F4
The Nightingales NWBY RG14 6 F9
STWL/WRAY TW19 56 F7
Nightingale Wk WDSR SL4 53 J2
Night Owls STHA RG19 96 E7
Nimms Meadow HUNG RG17 * 118 E11
Nimrod Cl WODY RG5 47 G7
Nimrod Wy WHIT RG2 59 H1
Nine Acres SL SL1 38 B1
Nine Elms Av UX/CGN UB8 31 M6
Nine Elms Cl EBED/NFELT TW14 57 M7
UX/CGN UB8 31 M6
Nine Mile Ride BRAK RG12 76 A5
EWKG RG40 73 J8
EWKG RG40 75 L5
Ninth Av TILE/CALC RG31 137 M4
Nire Rd CAV/SC RG4 45 L3
Nixey Cl SL SL1 11 K7
Noakes Hl GOR/PANG RG8 123 K7
Nobel Dr HYS/HAR UB3 43 G7
Noble Rd HEN RG9 22 B6
Nobles Wy EGH TW20 68 E5
Norbury Rd FELT TW13 71 M1
Norcot Rd
RDGW/BURGH RG30 137 Q2
Norden Cl MDHD SL6 35 L2
Norden Mdw MDHD SL6 4 A8
Norden Rd MDHD SL6 4 B9
Norelands Dr SL SL1 27 L3
Nores Rd WHIT RG2 59 K7
Norfolk Av SL SL1 28 E6
Norfolk Cha BNFD RG42 64 F5
Norfolk Cl WWKG RG41 61 L8
Norfolk Park Cots MDHD SL6 5 G2
Norfolk Rd MDHD SL6 4 F3
RDGW/BURGH RG30 44 C7
Norlands NTHA RG18 97 L1
Norlands La EGH TW20 69 L7
Norman Av HEN RG9 22 A5
Norman Crs HEST TW5 43 M7
Normandy Cl FRIM GU16 95 L6
Normandy Wk EGH TW20 * 69 J3
Norman Keep BNFD RG42 64 F6
Norman Pl READ RG1 9 G3
Norman Rd ASHF TW15 71 K4
CAV/SC RG4 45 J2
Normanstead HEN RG9 127 R1
Normanstead Rd
TILE/CALC RG31 137 N2
The Normans SLN SL2 29 K7
Normay Ri NWBY RG14 141 Q9
Normoor Rd THLE RG7 143 P5
Norreys Av EWKG RG40 15 J4
Norreys Dr MDHD SL6 35 L2
Norris Fld KSCL RG20 119 M6
Norris La KSCL RG20 119 M6
Norris Pl FLKWH/TG HP10 * 21 J2
Norris Rd EARL RG6 45 M8
STA TW18 69 M2
Northam Cl EARL RG6 60 E3
Northampton Av SL SL1 10 B1
Northampton Cl BRAK RG12 3 K7
Northborough Rd SLN SL2 28 C5
Northbourne Cl EARL RG6 60 B5
Northbrook Copse BRAK RG12 76 F3
Northbrook Rd CAV/SC RG4 45 K1
Northbrook St NWBY RG14 6 E3
North Burnham Cl SL SL1 27 K3
Northbury Av WAR/TWY RG10 47 L1
Northbury La WAR/TWY RG10 33 G8
North Cl EBED/NFELT TW14 57 K5
FARN GU14 94 A6
MLW SL7 17 M7
WDSR SL4 12 A5
North Common WEY KT13 * 83 J8
Northcote ADL/WDHM KT15 82 D8
Northcote Rd FARN GU14 93 L8
Northcott BRAK RG12 76 A5
Northcourt Av WHIT RG2 59 K2
Northcroft SLN SL2 28 D5
Northcroft Cl EGH TW20 68 B3
Northcroft Gdns EGH TW20 68 B3
Northcroft La NWBY RG14 6 C3
Northcroft Rd EGH TW20 68 B3
Northcroft Ter NWBY RG14 6 D4
Northcroft Vls EGH TW20 68 B3
North Dean MDHD SL6 5 H1
North Dr THLE RG7 136 H11
VW GU25 79 L2
North End La ASC SL5 79 G4
Northern Av NWBY RG14 96 C1
Northern Hts BNEND SL8 20 D1
Northern Perimeter Rd
HTHAIR TW6 42 E8
Northern Perimeter Rd (West)
HTHAIR TW6 42 A8
WDR/YW UB7 41 L8
Northern Rd SLN SL2 28 F5
Northern Wy WHIT RG2 58 F5
North Farm Cl HUNG RG17 117 L3
North Farm Rd FARN GU14 93 L6
Northfield LTWR GU18 90 B6
Northfield Av HEN RG9 32 C2
Northfield Cl HYS/HAR UB3 43 H3
Northfield Ct STA TW18 70 B6
Northfield End HEN RG9 115 R11
Northfield Pde HYS/HAR UB3 * 43 H3
Northfield Pk HYS/HAR UB3 43 G3
Northfield Rd HEN RG9 32 D2
HEST TW5 43 M6
HTWY RG27 150 D9
MDHD SL6 26 B5
NTHA RG18 97 K2
READ RG1 8 E3
STA TW18 70 B6
WDSR SL4 38 B4
Northfields HUNG RG17 117 K3
KSCL RG20 120 G10
Northfields Ter HUNG RG17 * 117 L3
North Fryerne YTLY GU46 86 D6
Northgate Dr CBLY GU15 89 G7
North Gn BRAK RG12 3 K3
MDHD SL6 5 H1
SL SL1 10 F3
North Gv CHERT KT16 81 M3
North Hyde Gdns HYS/HAR UB3 43 J3
NWDGN UB2 43 K3
North Hyde Rd HYS/HAR UB3 43 G3
North Hyde Whf NWDGN UB2 * 43 L4
Northington Cl BRAK RG12 76 F3
North Ldg THLE RG7 * 144 E7
North Lodge Dr ASC SL5 65 J7
North Lodge Ms READ RG1 8 D1
Northmead Rd SLN SL2 28 B5
Northolt Rd HTHAIR TW6 41 M8
North Pk DTCH/LGLY SL3 40 F3
North Rd ASC SL5 65 H6
EBED/NFELT TW14 57 K5
HEST TW5 43 L6
MDHD SL6 4 F5
WDR/YW UB7 42 B3
WGFD OX10 111 P6
Northrop Rd HTHAIR TW6 43 G8
North Standen Rd
HUNG RG17 138 E2
North Star La MDHD SL6 4 B7
North St CAV/SC RG4 45 H4
EGH TW20 68 F3
READ RG1 8 D5
WDSR SL4 65 M1
North Town Cl MDHD SL6 5 H1
North Town Md MDHD SL6 5 H1
North Town Moor MDHD SL6 26 B4

North Town Rd MDHD SL6 5 H1
Northumberland Av WHIT RG2 59 J3
Northumberland Cl BNFD RG42 64 F5
STWL/WRAY TW19 56 E5
Northumberland Crs
EBED/NFELT TW14 57 L5
Northumbria Rd MDHD SL6 35 K2
North Vw BRAK RG12 63 J8
Northview HUNG RG17 138 H1
North View Rd TADY RG26 148 F3
North Wk THLE RG7 137 J6
Northway NTHA RG18 97 L1
NWBY RG14 7 G6
WWKG RG41 61 K7
Northwick HTWY RG27 85 L7
Northwood Dr NWBY RG14 7 J1
Northwood Rd HTHAIR TW6 41 M8
Norton Cl NWBY RG14 141 Q8
Norton Pk ASC SL5 78 C2
Norton Rd CBLY GU15 95 J2
EWKG RG40 15 G7
READ RG1 45 L7
THLE RG7 145 N12
UX/CGN UB8 31 M4
WODY RG5 60 F1
Norway Dr SLN SL2 29 K6
Norwich Av CBLY GU15 94 E3
Norwich Dr WODY RG5 46 C6
Norwood La IVER SL0 30 F5
Norwood Rd READ RG1 9 M6
Notley End EGH TW20 * 68 C5
Notley Pl CAV/SC RG4 45 H2
Nottingham Fee DID OX11 110 C2
Notton Wy EARL RG6 59 M6
Nottwood La HEN RG9 114 A9
Nuffield Dr SHST GU47 87 M5
Nuffield Rd WHIT RG2 72 F7
Nugee Ct CWTH RG45 87 H1
Nuneaton BRAK RG12 76 E3
Nunhide La GOR/PANG RG8 137 K1
TILE/CALC RG31 137 K5
Nun's Acre GOR/PANG RG8 111 R11
Nuns Wk VW GU25 80 D2
Nuptown La BNFD RG42 50 F7
Nursery Cl FRIM GU16 94 F7
HEN RG9 32 C2
WAR/TWY RG10 47 L6
Nursery Gdns GOR/PANG RG8 125 M9
STA TW18 70 B5
SUN TW16 71 M7
Nursery La ASC SL5 65 L6
DTCH/LGLY SL3 39 L1
Nursery Pl WDSR SL4 54 B5
Nursery Rd MDHD SL6 27 K7
SUN TW16 71 L7
Nursery Wy STWL/WRAY TW19 54 D5
Nursery Waye UX/CGN UB8 31 M2
Nutbean La THLE RG7 145 R9
Nuthatch Cl STWL/WRAY TW19 56 F7
Nuthatch Dr EARL RG6 60 B2
Nuthurst BRAK RG12 76 E2
Nut La WAR/TWY RG10 34 A8
Nutley BRAK RG12 76 A5
Nutley Cl YTLY GU46 92 D1
Nutmeg Cl EARL RG6 59 M5
Nutter's La WHIT RG2 72 A5
Nutty La SHPTN TW17 83 J1

O

Oak Av EGH TW20 69 J5
HEST TW5 43 M7
SHST GU47 87 K5
WDR/YW UB7 42 C3
Oak Cl TADY RG26 103 M6
Oakdale BRAK RG12 76 D3
Oakdale Cl TILE/CALC RG31 137 N2
Oakdale Rd WEY KT13 83 G7
Oakdene ASC SL5 78 F3
CHOB/PIR GU24 91 M5
GOR/PANG RG8 113 K11
THLE RG7 143 Q3
Oakdown Cl GOR/PANG RG8 125 J3
Oak Dr NWBY RG14 6 C6
THLE RG7 143 P4
WODY RG5 47 G8
Oaken Copse CBLY GU15 89 J7
Oaken Copse Crs FARN GU14 94 B7
Oak End Dr IVER SL0 30 E3
Oak End Wy THLE RG7 142 E2
Oakengates BRAK RG12 76 A5
Oaken Gv MDHD SL6 4 A1
NWBY RG14 141 R6
Oakes Ct HUNG RG17 138 H1
Oakey Dr EWKG RG40 14 F8
Oak Farm Cl BLKW GU17 93 J1
Oakfield Av SL SL1 38 D1
Oakfield Cl WEY KT13 83 J8
Oakfield Ct WWKG RG41 14 C8
Oakfield Gld WEY KT13 83 J8
Oakfield Rd ASHF TW15 71 H2
BLKW GU17 93 L2
BNEND SL8 20 C3
TADY RG26 148 G1
Oakfields CBLY GU15 * 94 B1
Oak Grove Crs CBLY GU15 87 M8
Oakhall Dr SUN TW16 71 M3
Oakham Cl TILE/CALC RG31 125 P12
Oakhill Gdns WEY KT13 83 L6
Oakhurst CHOB/PIR GU24 91 L4
MDHD SL6 26 D2
Oakington Av HYS/HAR UB3 42 F4
Oaklands NTHA RG18 133 J7
YTLY GU46 86 D8
Oaklands Cl ASC SL5 65 M5
Oaklands Ct ADL/WDHM KT15 82 B7
Oaklands Dr ASC SL5 66 A5
WWKG RG41 14 B9
Oaklands La CWTH RG45 75 G8
Oaklands Pk WWKG RG41 74 A2
Oak La EGH TW20 68 C1
WDSR SL4 12 C6
Oaklea Dr HTWY RG27 84 E4
Oaklea Gdns TADY RG26 150 B8
Oakley Cl ADL/WDHM KT15 82 D8
Oakley Crs SL SL1 10 E2
Oakley Green Rd WDSR SL4 51 M1
Oakley Rd CAV/SC RG4 44 F2
CBLY GU15 94 B2
NWBY RG14 7 L1
Oakmead TADY RG26 149 Q6
Oakridge CHOB/PIR GU24 90 F8
Oak Ridge Cl NWBY RG14 96 A6
Oakside Wy WHIT RG2 59 L6
Oaks Rd HEN RG9 32 C2
STWL/WRAY TW19 56 D4
The Oaks BRAK RG12 3 J4
NWBY RG14 96 C7
STA TW18 * 69 M2
TADY RG26 148 C2
YTLY GU46 92 D1
Oak Stubbs La MDHD SL6 37 H2
Oak Tree Av MLW SL7 18 F3
Oaktree Av STHA RG19 102 D1
Oak Tree Cl MLW SL7 18 F3
TADY RG26 148 D1
VW GU25 80 D3
Oak Tree Copse
TILE/CALC RG31 125 Q11
Oak Tree Dr DTCH/LGLY SL3 40 D5
EGH TW20 68 C3
Oak Tree Rd MLW SL7 18 F2
STHA RG19 98 A4
TILE/CALC RG31 125 P12
Oak Tree Wk GOR/PANG RG8 125 P9
Oaktree Wy SHST GU47 87 G5
Oak Vw EWKG RG40 * 14 F9
TILE/CALC RG31 137 N2
Oakview Gdns DTCH/LGLY SL3 40 B4
Oak Wy EBED/NFELT TW14 57 L7
WODY RG5 60 D2
Oakway Dr FRIM GU16 94 E5
Oakwood Rd BFOR GU20 90 E2
BRAK RG12 3 M4
VW GU25 80 C2
Oareborough BRAK RG12 3 M9
Oareborough La NTHA RG18 121 N12
Oare Vw NTHA RG18 * 133 Q2
Oast House Cl
STWL/WRAY TW19 54 E6
Oatlands Av WEY KT13 83 L6
Oatlands Cha WEY KT13 83 L7
Oatlands Cl WEY KT13 83 J8
Oatlands Dr SL SL1 10 D1
WEY KT13 83 H8
Oatlands Gn WEY KT13 83 K7
Oatlands Mere WEY KT13 83 K7
Oatlands Rd WHIT RG2 59 M8
Oban Ct SL SL1 10 D6
Oban Gdns WODY RG5 60 E2
O'Bee Gdns TADY RG26 148 A1
Obelisk Wy CBLY GU15 88 C8
Oberon Wy SHPTN TW17 70 E8
The Observatory SL SL1 * 11 J6
Observer Dr STHA RG19 98 A4
Ockwells Rd MDHD SL6 35 K3
Octavia BRAK RG12 76 A5
Octavia Wy STA TW18 70 A4
Oddfellows Rd NWBY RG14 6 D5
Odds Farm Est
FLKWH/TG HP10 * 21 K2
Odell Cl EARL RG6 60 B6
Odencroft Rd SLN SL2 28 C4
Odette Gdns TADY RG26 148 D1
Odiham Av CAV/SC RG4 45 L1
Odiham Rd THLE RG7 145 N11
Odney La MDHD SL6 20 D7
Officers Rw TADY RG26 150 B8
Offlands Ct WGFD OX10 111 P4
Ogden Pk BRAK RG12 3 L6
Ogmore Cl
RDGW/BURGH RG30 137 Q3
Okingham Cl SHST GU47 87 K5
Oldacre CHOB/PIR GU24 90 F7
Old Acre La WAR/TWY RG10 47 H1
Oldacres MDHD SL6 5 M5
Old Acres La WAR/TWY RG10 47 H1
Old Anvilles HUNG RG17 139 J5
The Old Apple Yd WWKG RG41 61 G3
Old Barn Cl CAV/SC RG4 126 G12
Old Bath Rd CAV/SC RG4 46 C5
NWBY RG14 6 B1
WAR/TWY RG10 47 G2
Old Bisley Rd FRIM GU16 95 G4
Old Bix Rd HEN RG9 115 M7
Old Bothampstead Rd
KSCL RG20 121 K8
Old Bracknell Cl BRAK RG12 2 E6
Old Bracknell La East BRAK RG12 2 E6
Old Bracknell La West
BRAK RG12 2 D6
Oldbury BRAK RG12 2 B6
Oldbury Cl FRIM GU16 94 F6
Oldbury Rd CHERT KT16 81 L4
Old Charlton Rd SHPTN TW17 83 J2
Old Coach Works HUNG RG17 117 J4
Old College Rd NWBY RG14 6 C1
Old Copse Gdns CAV/SC RG4 126 F4
Oldcorne Hollow YTLY GU46 92 A1
Old Court Cl MDHD SL6 35 K3
Old Crown SL SL1 * 11 G6
Old Dean Rd CBLY GU15 88 D7
Oldean Cl TILE/CALC RG31 137 N1
Olde Farm Dr BLKW GU17 93 H1
Old Elm Dr
RDGW/BURGH RG30 137 P3
Oldershaw Ms MDHD SL6 25 K6
Old Farm Crs TILE/CALC RG31 125 N12
Old Farm Dr BRAK RG12 64 C5
Old Farm Rd WDR/YW UB7 41 M2
Old Ferry Dr STWL/WRAY TW19 54 C5
Oldfield Cl EARL RG6 46 B7
Oldfield Rd MDHD SL6 5 L6
Oldfield Vw MDHD SL6 * 36 E2
Old Fives Ct SL SL1 27 K4
Old Forest Rd EWKG RG40 62 A4
WWKG RG41 61 L6
Old Forge Cl MDHD SL6 * 36 C3
Old Forge Crs SHPTN TW17 83 H3
Old Forge End SHST GU47 87 H7
Old Green La CBLY GU15 88 C7
Old Hayward La HUNG RG17 129 M8
Old House Ct DTCH/LGLY SL3 * 29 M7
Old House La BFOR GU20 90 B3
Oldhouse La BFOR GU20 90 C4
The Old Kiln HEN RG9 114 E4
Old Lands Hl BRAK RG12 3 J2
Old La KSCL RG20 140 E5
STHA RG19 103 G5
The Old La READ RG1 58 F1
Old Manor Rd NWDGN UB2 43 M4
Old Marsh La MDHD SL6 37 H2
Old Mill Ct WAR/TWY RG10 47 K1
Old Mill La MDHD SL6 36 E2
UX/CGN UB8 31 K6
Old Mill Pl STWL/WRAY TW19 55 H5
Old Newtown Rd NWBY RG14 6 D7
Old Nursery Pl ASHF TW15 71 H3
The Old Nursery NTHA RG18 133 N3
Old Orch IVER SL0 31 H7
The Old Orch TILE/CALC RG31 137 Q6
Old Palace Rd WEY KT13 83 H7
Old Pasture Rd FRIM GU16 94 F3
Old Pharmacy Ct CWTH RG45 * 87 J2
Old Pond Cl CBLY GU15 94 B5
Old Portsmouth Rd CBLY GU15 95 G2
Old Post Office La MDHD SL6 5 H5
Old Priory La BNFD RG42 64 D3
Old Sawmill La CWTH RG45 75 J8
The Old Sawmills HUNG RG17 139 Q8
Old School Ct
STWL/WRAY TW19 54 A5
Old School La YTLY GU46 86 C8
Old School Ms WEY KT13 83 K8
The Old School
FLKWH/TG HP10 * 20 F2
Old Slade La DTCH/LGLY SL3 41 H4
Old Stables Yd WANT OX12 106 E1
Old Stanmore Rd KSCL RG20 109 L11
Old Station La
STWL/WRAY TW19 54 F5
Old Station Rd HYS/HAR UB3 43 H3
Old Station Wy
FLKWH/TG HP10 21 G1
The Old Station Yd
HUNG RG17 117 K4
Oldstead BRAK RG12 76 D2
Old Stocks Ct GOR/PANG RG8 123 P9
Old St KSCL RG20 121 J9
NTHA RG18 133 L3
Old Thornford Rd STHA RG19 101 M1
Old Vicarage Wy
FLKWH/TG HP10 20 F2
Old Vyne La TADY RG26 148 B9
Oldway La SL SL1 27 L8
Old Welmore YTLY GU46 92 E1
Old Wharf Wy WEY KT13 82 F8
Old Whitley Wood La WHIT RG2 59 J8
Old Wokingham Rd CWTH RG45 75 J7
EWKG RG40 75 H4
Old Woosehill La WWKG RG41 14 A4
Oleander Cl CWTH RG45 74 F7
Oliver Cl ADL/WDHM KT15 82 B8
Oliver Dr TILE/CALC RG31 137 M5
Oliver Rd ASC SL5 78 A1
Olivers Cl TADY RG26 150 A8
Oliver's La TADY RG26 150 A6
Oliver's Paddock MLW SL7 18 F1
Olivia Dr DTCH/LGLY SL3 40 B5
Ollerton BRAK RG12 76 A5
Omega Wy EGH TW20 69 J6
Omer's Ri THLE RG7 143 P3
Onslow Dr ASC SL5 66 A5
Onslow Gdns CAV/SC RG4 45 J3
Onslow Ms CHERT KT16 81 M3
Onslow Rd ASC SL5 79 H4
Opal Ct DTCH/LGLY SL3 29 L5
READ RG1 * 8 D9
Opal Wy WWKG RG41 61 L7
Opecks Cl SLN SL2 29 K5
Opendale Rd SL SL1 27 K6
Opladen Wy BRAK RG12 76 C2
Oracle Pkwy EARL RG6 45 M6
Oram Ct MLW SL7 18 F4
Orbit Cl EWKG RG40 73 L8
Orchard Av ASHF TW15 71 J4
CAV/SC RG4 126 E5
EBED/NFELT TW14 57 K4
SL SL1 27 M6
WDSR SL4 12 D6
Orchard Cha WAR/TWY RG10 47 M7
Orchard Cl ASHF TW15 71 J4
BLKW GU17 93 M5
CHOB/PIR GU24 90 D8
EGH TW20 69 H3
EWKG RG40 15 K6
HEN RG9 22 A5
HEN RG9 32 A4
MDHD SL6 36 C3
NTHA RG18 133 Q2
NWBY RG14 96 E1
THLE RG7 99 L4
THLE RG7 145 M4
TILE/CALC RG31 125 M10
Orchard Coombe
GOR/PANG RG8 124 H3
Orchard Cots HYS/HAR UB3 * 43 G2
Orchard Ct BRAK RG12 3 H5
Orchard Dene Dr THLE RG7 142 E4
Orchard Dr FLKWH/TG HP10 20 F2
UX/CGN UB8 31 M5
Orchard End WEY KT13 83 L6
Orchardene NWBY RG14 7 H2
Orchard Est WAR/TWY RG10 47 L1
Orchard Fld CAV/SC RG4 126 C5
Orchard Ga SHST GU47 87 H6
Orchard Gv CAV/SC RG4 45 L2
MDHD SL6 4 B5
Orchard Hl BFOR GU20 90 D3
The Orchard Lake Vw
WDSR SL4 * 51 M7
Orchard Lea KSCL RG20 109 L11
Orchard Mi BNEND SL8 20 D5
Orchard Park Cl HUNG RG17 138 H2
Orchard Pl EWKG RG40 15 G5
UX/CGN UB8 * 31 L6
Orchard Rd THLE RG7 143 R9
WAR/TWY RG10 47 M7
WDSR SL4 54 B6
Orchard St READ RG1 8 F8
The Orchard EARL RG6 * 60 D3
LTWR GU18 90 B6
MLW SL7 19 G3
STHA RG19 * 97 H3
TADY RG26 148 F2
THLE RG7 137 J6
VW GU25 80 E2
WEY KT13 83 H8
Orchard Vw CHERT KT16 82 A3
Orchardville SL SL1 27 K5
Orchard Wy ASHF TW15 56 F8
CBLY GU15 94 B4
DTCH/LGLY SL3 40 A1
Orchard Waye UX/CGN UB8 31 M3
Orchid Ct EGH TW20 69 H2
The Orchids DID OX11 109 K3
Oregon Av TILE/CALC RG31 125 N11
Oregon Wk EWKG RG40 73 K7
Oriel Hl CBLY GU15 94 D2
Oriental Rd ASC SL5 78 D1
Orion BRAK RG12 76 A5
Orkney Cl TILE/CALC RG31 137 Q6
Ormathwaites Cnr BNFD RG42 64 E5
Ormonde Gdns NWBY RG14 6 D1
Ormonde Rd WWKG RG41 14 D7
Ormsby St READ RG1 8 B6
Orpington Cl WAR/TWY RG10 47 K2
Orrin Cl RDGW/BURGH RG30 44 A6
Orts Rd READ RG1 9 K6
Orville Cl WODY RG5 47 G7
Orwell Cl CAV/SC RG4 44 F2
FARN GU14 93 L7
WDSR SL4 53 K2
Osborne Av STWL/WRAY TW19 56 E7
Osborne Ct WDSR SL4 13 G8
Osborne Dr LTWR GU18 90 A6
Osborne La BNFD RG42 64 C3
Osborne Ms WDSR SL4 13 G8
Osborne Rd EGH TW20 68 F4
EWKG RG40 15 H5
RDGW/BURGH RG30 44 B6
WDSR SL4 13 G8
Osborne St SL SL1 11 H7
Osborn Rd UX/CGN UB8 * 31 L1
Osier Pl EGH TW20 69 J4
Osler Ct TADY RG26 149 R7
Osman's Cl BNFD RG42 65 H5
Osnaburgh Hl CBLY GU15 94 B1
Osney Rd MDHD SL6 26 A4
Osprey Cl WDR/YW UB7 41 M2
Osterley Cl EWKG RG40 * 74 F1
Osterley Dr CAV/SC RG4 127 L12
Ostler Ga MDHD SL6 4 A1
Ostlers Dr ASHF TW15 71 J3
Oswald Cl BNFD RG42 64 D5
Otterbourne Crs TADY RG26 148 D4
Otter Cl CWTH RG45 75 G7
Otter Ct WHIT RG2 59 H7
Ouseley Rd STWL/WRAY TW19 54 C6
WDSR SL4 54 C6
Overbecks NWBY RG14 7 L2
Overbridge Sq NWBY RG14 97 G3
Overdale Ri FRIM GU16 94 E3
Overdown Rd TILE/CALC RG31 125 N12
Overlanders End
TILE/CALC RG31 125 Q11
Overlord Cl CBLY GU15 88 C6
Owen Cl DTCH/LGLY SL3 40 B5
Owen Rd BFOR GU20 90 D1
NWBY RG14 132 H12
Owl Cl WWKG RG41 73 L1
Owletts Gv NWBY RG14 7 L2
Owlsmoor Rd SHST GU47 87 K6
Owston EARL RG6 60 C4
Oxenhope BRAK RG12 2 C9
Oxford Av HYS/HAR UB3 43 H7
SL SL1 27 J3
SL SL1 28 B6
Oxford Cl ASHF TW15 71 J5
Oxford Rd GOR/PANG RG8 125 N9
KSCL RG20 133 J1
MLW SL7 18 E4
NWBY RG14 6 D1
RDGW/BURGH RG30 44 B6
READ RG1 8 C6
SHST GU47 87 L4
TILE/CALC RG31 125 P10
WDSR SL4 12 F5
WWKG RG41 14 C4
Oxford Rd East WDSR SL4 * 13 H6
Oxfordshire Pl BNFD RG42 64 F5
Oxfordshire Wy HEN RG9 115 J2
Oxford St CAV/SC RG4 45 G4
HUNG RG17 117 K4
HUNG RG17 129 N11
NWBY RG14 6 D2

P

Pacific Cl EBED/NFELT TW14 57 M7
Pack And Prime La HEN RG9 127 Q1
Packet Boat La IVER SL0 31 K7
UX/CGN UB8 31 L7
Packman Dr WAR/TWY RG10 32 F8
Padbury Cl EBED/NFELT TW14 57 K7
Padcroft Rd WDR/YW UB7 41 M1
Paddick Cl CAV/SC RG4 46 E3
Paddick Dr EARL RG6 60 D5
Paddison Ct STHA RG19 98 A4
Paddock Cl CBLY GU15 89 G8
Paddock Hts WAR/TWY RG10 47 L2
The Paddock Lake Vw
WDSR SL4 * 51 L6
Paddock Rd CAV/SC RG4 9 L2
NWBY RG14 6 D8
The Paddocks MLW SL7 * 19 H4
WEY KT13 83 L7
Paddocks Wy CHERT KT16 82 B5
The Paddock CWTH RG45 75 G8
DID OX11 109 K2
DTCH/LGLY SL3 39 K8
MDHD SL6 25 L4
NWBY RG14 7 K5
VW GU25 * 80 E3
WDSR SL4 * 37 L7
WDSR SL4 * 52 B7
Paddock Vw WAR/TWY RG10 * 34 C8
Padstow Cl DTCH/LGLY SL3 * 40 A3
Padstow Gdns WHIT RG2 59 H5
Padstow Wk EBED/NFELT TW14 57 M7
FELT TW13 57 M8
Padworth La THLE RG7 142 G3
Padworth Rd THLE RG7 143 N5
Page Rd EBED/NFELT TW14 57 K5
Page's Cft EWKG RG40 15 K7
Pages Orch CAV/SC RG4 126 E5
Pages Whf MDHD SL6 * 26 E7
Paget Cl CBLY GU15 89 H7
MLW SL7 19 H2
Paget Dr MDHD SL6 35 J2
Paget Rd DTCH/LGLY SL3 40 B4
The Pagoda MDHD SL6 26 D5
Paice Gn EWKG RG40 15 J3
Paices Hl THLE RG7 142 C10
Painesfield Dr CHERT KT16 82 A6
Pakenham Rd BRAK RG12 76 D4
Palace Cl SL SL1 38 B1
Palace Dr WEY KT13 83 H7
Palace Yd CAV/SC RG4 * 46 D2
Paley St MDHD SL6 35 K8
Palmera Av TILE/CALC RG31 137 N6
Palmer Cl EWKG RG40 75 G6
KSCL RG20 120 D7
Palmer Park Av EARL RG6 45 M8
Palmer School Rd EWKG RG40 15 H5
Palmers Cl MDHD SL6 35 J3
Palmer's Hl GOR/PANG RG8 123 L9
Palmer's La THLE RG7 143 Q4
THLE RG7 144 E3
Palmer's Moor La IVER SL0 31 J5
Palmerston Av DTCH/LGLY SL3 11 M8
Palmerstone Rd EARL RG6 46 A7
Palmers Yd KSCL RG20 101 J8
Pamber Heath Rd TADY RG26 148 F2
Pamber Rd THLE RG7 149 J1
Pamela Rw MDHD SL6 * 36 C6
Pangbourne Hl
GOR/PANG RG8 124 G9
Pangbourne Pl
GOR/PANG RG8 124 H8
Pangbourne Rd
GOR/PANG RG8 124 A10
Pangbourne St
RDGW/BURGH RG30 44 B6
Pankhurst Dr BRAK RG12 76 D2
Pannells Cl CHERT KT16 81 M5
Pan's Gdns CBLY GU15 94 F2
Panters Rd WGFD OX10 111 Q1
Pantile Rd WEY KT13 83 K8
Pantile Rw DTCH/LGLY SL3 40 C4
The Pantiles
RDGW/BURGH RG30 137 R4
Papist Wy WGFD OX10 111 P1
Paprika Cl EARL RG6 59 M5
Parade Ct BNEND SL8 * 20 C2
The Parade BNEND SL8 20 C2
EARL RG6 * 60 B3
FRIM GU16 * 94 D6
STA TW18 * 69 K3
SUN TW16 71 M5
TADY RG26 * 148 D1
UX/CGN UB8 * 31 L6
VW GU25 * 80 D3
WODY RG5 46 F6
Paradise Rd HEN RG9 127 Q1
Paradise Wy THLE RG7 135 L11
Park Av CBLY GU15 94 C2
EGH TW20 69 J5
EWKG RG40 14 F6
NTHA RG18 97 M2
STA TW18 69 M4
STWL/WRAY TW19 54 D4
Park Cl CAV/SC RG4 126 G4
EGH TW20 * 67 M3
WDSR SL4 13 K7
WOT/HER KT12 83 M6
Park Cnr MDHD SL6 * 25 H3
WDSR SL4 12 A9
Parkcorner La WHIT RG2 60 F8
Park Crs ASC SL5 78 F2
RDGW/BURGH RG30 44 B8
Park Dr ASC SL5 78 F3
Park End NWBY RG14 6 F2
Parkers Ct BAGS GU19 89 L3
Parker's La BNFD RG42 65 H1
Parkfields YTLY GU46 92 D1
Parkgate SL SL1 27 L5
Parkhill Cl BLKW GU17 93 K2
Parkhill Dr TILE/CALC RG31 125 P12
Parkhill Rd BLKW GU17 93 K2
Parkhouse La
RDGW/BURGH RG30 44
Parkland Av DTCH/LGLY SL3 39
Parkland Dr BRAK RG12 3
Parkland Gv ASHF TW15 71
Parkland Rd ASHF TW15 71
Park La BRAK RG12 63
CBLY GU15 * 94
DTCH/LGLY SL3 11
DTCH/LGLY SL3 55
EWKG RG40 85
GOR/PANG RG8 113
HEST TW5 43
KSCL RG20 140
NTHA RG18 97
NWBY RG14 * 7
THLE RG7 144
THLE RG7 144
TILE/CALC RG31 137
WAR/TWY RG10 47
WDSR SL4 52
Park Lawn Rd WEY KT13 83
Park Ms STWL/WRAY TW19 56
Park Pl BLKW GU17 93
Park Rd ASHF TW15 71
BRAK RG12 3
CBLY GU15 94
EGH TW20 69
EWKG RG40 14
HEN RG9 22
SHPTN TW17 83
SHST GU47 87
SLN SL2 28
STWL/WRAY TW19 56
UX/CGN UB8 31
Park Rd East HGDN/ICK UB10 31
Parkside HEN RG9 115
MDHD SL6 4
Parkside Pl STA TW18 70
Parkside Rd ASC SL5 79
NTHA RG18 97
RDGW/BURGH RG30 44
Parkside Wk SL SL1 11
Park Sq WDSR SL4 * 52
Parkstone Dr CBLY GU15 94
Park St BAGS GU19 89
CBLY GU15 88
DTCH/LGLY SL3 40
HUNG RG17 139
MDHD SL6 5
NWBY RG14 6
SL SL1 11
WDSR SL4 13
Park Ter NWBY RG14 6
The Park HUNG RG17 117
Park Vw BAGS GU19 89
MDHD SL6 5
THLE RG7 143
WHIT RG2 59
Parkview Cha SL SL1 28
Park View Dr North
WAR/TWY RG10 32
Park View Dr South
WAR/TWY RG10 47
Park Wk GOR/PANG RG8 125
Park Wall La GOR/PANG RG8 123
Park Wy HUNG RG17 138
NWBY RG14 6
Parkway CBLY GU15 94
CWTH RG45 87
MLW SL7 19
WEY KT13 83
Parkway Dr CAV/SC RG4 46
The Parkway HEST TW5 43
IVER SL0 30
NWDGN UB2 43
Parlaunt Rd DTCH/LGLY SL3 40
Parliament La SL SL1 27
Parnham Av LTWR GU18 90
Parry Gn North DTCH/LGLY SL3 40
Parry Gn South DTCH/LGLY SL3 40
Parsley Cl EARL RG6 59
Parsonage Gdns MLW SL7 19
Parsonage La HUNG RG17 117
HUNG RG17 129
SLN SL2 28
WDSR SL4 12
Parsonage Pl HUNG RG17 117
Parsonage Rd EGH TW20 68
Parsonage Wy FRIM GU16 94
Parsons Cl NWBY RG14 6
WHIT RG2 73
Parsons Fld SHST GU47 87
Parsons Rd DTCH/LGLY SL3 40
Parson's Wood La SLN SL2 28
Parthia Cl READ RG1 8
Part La THLE RG7 145
Partridge Av YTLY GU46 86
Partridge Cl BRAK RG12 75
FRIM GU16 94
Partridge Dr TILE/CALC RG31 137
Partridge Md MDHD SL6 26
Pasadena Cl HYS/HAR UB3 43
Paschal Rd CBLY GU15 88
Pasture Cl EARL RG6 60
Patches Fld MLW SL7 19
Paternoster La WGFD OX10 111
Paterson Cl FRIM GU16 95
Pates Manor Dr
EBED/NFELT TW14 57
Patricia Cl SL SL1 28
Patrick Gdns BNFD RG42 3
Patrick Rd CAV/SC RG4 9
Patrington Cl UX/CGN UB8 31
Patriot Pl READ RG1 9
Patten Ash Dr EWKG RG40 15
Patten Av YTLY GU46 92
Pattinson Rd WHIT RG2 59
Paul's Fld HTWY RG27 85
Pavenham Cl EARL RG6 60
Pavilion Gdns STA TW18 70
The Pavilions End CBLY GU15 94
The Pavilions WAR/TWY RG10 * 47
Pavy Cl STHA RG19 98
Paxton Av SL SL1 10
Payley Dr EWKG RG40 15
Paynes Cl STHA RG19 102
Paynesdown Rd STHA RG19 97
Peace La MDHD SL6 20
Peace Rd DTCH/LGLY SL3 30
IVER SL0 30
Peachey Cl UX/CGN UB8 31
Peachey Dr STHA RG19 98
Peachey La UX/CGN UB8 31
Peach St EWKG RG40 15
Peach Tree Cl FARN GU14 94
Peacock Av EBED/NFELT TW14 57
Peacock La BRAK RG12 75
Peacock Rd MLW SL7 19
Pearce Cl MDHD SL6 26
Pearce Dr MDHD SL6 20
Pearce Rd MDHD SL6 26
Pearces Meadow HEN RG9 114
Pearce's Meadow HEN RG9 115
Pearl Gdns SL SL1 38
Pearmain Cl SHPTN TW17 83
Pears Av SHPTN TW17 * 71
Pearson Rd CAV/SC RG4 46
Pearson Wy WODY RG5 60
Peartree Cl SL SL1 38
Pear Tree La NWBY RG14 96

ear Tree Rd ASHF TW15 71 J3
ne Pear Trees WDR/YW UB7 * 31 M8
eascod St WDSR SL4 13 J6
ease HI THLE RG7 134 H10
easemore HI KSCL RG20 120 A5
ebble HI HUNG RG17 140 B7
eckmoor Dr NWBY RG14 96 E7
eddlars Gv YTLY GU46 86 B8
eel Av FRIM GU16 95 G7
eel Cl CAV/SC RG4 45 K4
WDSR SL4 12 E9
eel Ct SL SL1 28 D6
egasus Cl STHA RG19 97 J2
egasus Ct TILE/CALC RG31 137 N3
egasus Rd FARN GU14 * 93 M7
eggotty Pl SHST GU47 87 K4
egg Rd HEST TW5 43 M7
eg's Gn RDGW/BURGH RG30 44 B8
eket Cl STA TW18 69 L7
elican La NWBY RG14 6 D2
elican Rd TADY RG26 142 G12
elling HI WDSR SL4 54 B6
ell St READ RG1 9 G9
emberton Gdns
TILE/CALC RG31 137 P6
emberton Rd SLN SL2 28 A5
embroke BRAK RG12 75 M4
embroke Broadway
CBLY GU15 94 C1
embroke Cl ASC SL5 78 D2
THLE RG7 144 A3
embroke Pl CAV/SC RG4 45 J3
embroke Rd NWBY RG14 6 D3
embury Ct HYS/HAR UB3 42 F6
emerich Cl HYS/HAR UB3 * 43 H5
endals Cl NTHA RG18 122 B9
endell Av HYS/HAR UB3 43 H7
endennis Av CAV/SC RG4 127 L12
endine Pl BRAK RG12 76 B2
endlebury BRAK RG12 76 A4
endragon Wy CBLY GU15 95 K2
endred Rd WHIT RG2 59 K8
endry's La BNFD RG42 50 A5
enfurzen La BNFD RG42 50 D6
eninsular Cl CBLY GU15 89 H7
EBED/NFELT TW14 57 K5
enling Cl MDHD SL6 20 A8
enn Cl CAV/SC RG4 126 G12
UX/CGN UB8 31 M5
ennfields WAR/TWY RG10 33 G8
ennine Cl TILE/CALC RG31 137 M4
ennine Rd SLN SL2 28 C6
ennine Wy FARN GU14 93 L7
HYS/HAR UB3 42 F7
WAR/TWY RG10 47 H2
ennington Dr WEY KT13 83 L7
enn Meadow SLN SL2 29 H2
enn Rd DTCH/LGLY SL3 39 M8
NWBY RG14 141 R1
SLN SL2 28 F5
enny La SHPTN TW17 83 L4
ennylets Gn SLN SL2 29 H1
enny Piece GOR/PANG RG8 112 A11
ennypot La CHOB/PIR GU24 91 H8
ennyroyal Ct READ RG1 8 E9
enroath Av
RDGW/BURGH RG30 44 C8
enrose Av WODY RG5 46 E8
enrose Cl NWBY RG14 96 B1
enrose Ct EGH TW20 68 C4
ensford Cl CWTH RG45 75 H7
enshurst Ri FRIM GU16 94 F6
enshurst Rd MDHD SL6 4 C8
entland Av SHPTN TW17 83 K2
entland Cl
RDGW/BURGH RG30 137 R5
entland Rd SLN SL2 28 C6
he Pentlands HUNG RG17 140 C4
enton Av STA TW18 69 M5
enton Hall Dr STA TW18 70 A6
enton Rd STA TW18 69 M5
enwood Ct MDHD SL6 25 K7
enwood Gdns BRAK RG12 75 K3
enwood La MLW SL7 18 E5
enwood Rd KSCL RG20 141 Q11
enyston Rd MDHD SL6 4 B5
enzance Sp SLN SL2 28 D5
epler Wy SL SL1 27 K4
eplow Cl WDR/YW UB7 41 M1
eppard HI HEN RG9 126 F2
eppard La HEN RG9 127 R3
eppard Rd CAV/SC RG4 45 H3
CAV/SC RG4 126 G5
epper La WHIT RG2 59 L2
epys Cl DTCH/LGLY SL3 40 D6
erch Cl MLW SL7 18 E6
ercival Rd FELT TW13 57 M8
ercy Av ASHF TW15 71 G3
ercy Bryant Rd SUN TW16 71 L5
ercy Bush Rd WDR/YW UB7 42 B3
ercy Pl DTCH/LGLY SL3 39 K8
eregrine Cl BRAK RG12 76 B2
eregrine Rd SUN TW16 71 L7
eriam Cl HEN RG9 127 Q2
erimeter Rd DID OX11 109 J1
erkins Wy WWKG RG41 14 C7
erpetual Park Dr HEN RG9 22 B6
errin Cl ASHF TW15 70 F3
erring Av FARN GU14 93 L6
errycroft WDSR SL4 52 F2
erryfields Wy SL SL1 27 K5
erryhill Dr SHST GU47 86 F5
erryman Wy SLN SL2 28 B4
erry Oaks BRAK RG12 3 L5
erry Wy BRAK RG12 3 M4
LTWR GU18 89 M7
erseverance HI HEN RG9 127 N5
erth Av SL SL1 28 D7
erth Cl WODY RG5 47 G5
etherhead Ms DTCH/LGLY SL3 40 C5
eterhouse Cl SHST GU47 87 M4
etersfield Av SLN SL2 11 J4
STA TW18 70 C3
etersfield Rd STA TW18 70 C3
eters La MDHD SL6 25 J2
etrel Cl WWKG RG41 73 L1
etts La SHPTN TW17 83 G1
etty Cross SL SL1 27 M7
etworth Av
RDGW/BURGH RG30 137 R6
etworth Cl FRIM GU16 94 F6
evensey Av CAV/SC RG4 45 L1
evensey Rd SLN SL2 28 C6
evensey Wy FRIM GU16 95 G6
ewsey V BRAK RG12 76 F2
heaben's Fld TADY RG26 149 Q7
heasant Cl WWKG RG41 61 J5
heasants Cft MDHD SL6 35 J2
heasant Vw BRAK RG12 75 K1
helps Wy HYS/HAR UB3 43 H4
hilbye Ms SL SL1 38 B2
hilip Rd STA TW18 70 D4
hillimore Rd CAV/SC RG4 127 J10
hillips Cl WODY RG5 47 H5
hilpots Cl WDR/YW UB7 31 M8
hipps Cl MDHD SL6 35 J4
hipps Rd SL SL1 27 M6
hoebe Ct READ RG1 8 F9
hoenix Cl WWKG RG41 14 A6
hoenix Wy HEST TW5 43 M6
hyllis Court Dr HEN RG9 22 A3
Pickering BRAK RG12 2 D9
Picket Post Cl BRAK RG12 64 F8
Picketts La GOR/PANG RG8 124 C10
Pickford Dr DTCH/LGLY SL3 40 A1
Pickfords Gdns SL SL1 10 E4
Pickins Piece DTCH/LGLY SL3 55 G1
Pickwell Cl EARL RG6 60 C4
Pickwick Gdns CBLY GU15 95 H2
Picton Cl CBLY GU15 89 J7
Picton Wy CAV/SC RG4 45 H2
Piercefield TILE/CALC RG31 137 M6
Pierce's HI TILE/CALC RG31 137 N1
Pierson Rd WDSR SL4 52 D1
Pigeon Cl TADY RG26 150 A8
Pigeonhouse La WDSR SL4 65 L1
Pigeons Farm Rd STHA RG19 96 F7
Piggott's Rd CAV/SC RG4 9 K2
The Pightle KSCL RG20 120 D7
THLE RG7 144 D3
Pigott Rd EWKG RG40 15 K1
Pike Cl MLW SL7 18 E6
Pikeshaw Wy
TILE/CALC RG31 * 137 N1
Pike St NWBY RG14 7 H1
Pilgrims Pl ASHF TW15 * 70 F2
The Pilgrim's Wy DID OX11 110 C3
Pimento Dr EARL RG6 59 M5
Pimpernel Pl NTHA RG18 98 B2
Pincents La TILE/CALC RG31 137 L5
Pinchcut THLE RG7 143 Q3
Pinchington La NWBY RG14 96 C7
STHA RG19 96 D7
Pindar Pl NWBY RG14 97 G1
Pine Av CBLY GU15 94 D2
Pine Cl CBLY GU15 87 L7
MDHD SL6 25 K7
Pinecote Dr ASC SL5 78 A8
Pinecroft MLW SL7 18 E3
Pine Croft Rd WWKG RG41 74 A4
Pine Dr BLKW GU17 93 L3
EWKG RG40 74 A7
THLE RG7 143 P8
Pinefields ADL/WDHM KT15 * 82 B8
Pinefields Cl CWTH RG45 87 H1
Pine Gv BFOR GU20 90 D2
WAR/TWY RG10 47 K1
Pinehill Ri SHST GU47 87 H6
Pinehill Rd CWTH RG45 87 H2
Pinehurst ASC SL5 78 D3
TADY RG26 148 D3
Pinel Cl VW GU25 80 E1
Pine Mount Rd CBLY GU15 94 D2
Pine Rdg NWBY RG14 96 E1
Pineridge Cl WEY KT13 83 L8
Pine Ridge Rd THLE RG7 143 Q3
The Pines CBLY GU15 88 F7
WAR/TWY RG10 33 G7
Pine Tree Cl HEST TW5 43 M8
Pinetree Ct CAV/SC RG4 45 G1
Pine Trees STA TW18 * 69 L3
Pine Wy EGH TW20 68 B4
Pinewood Av CWTH RG45 75 H8
Pinewood Cl IVER SL0 30 E1
SHST GU47 86 F6
TADY RG26 103 M5
Pinewood Dr CAV/SC RG4 44 E1
KSCL RG20 100 C4
STA TW18 * 70 A4
Pinewood Gdns BAGS GU19 89 J3
Pinewood Gn IVER SL0 30 E1
Pinewood Ms
STWL/WRAY TW19 56 D5
Pinewood Pk FARN GU14 93 J7
Pinewood Rd IVER SL0 30 D2
VW GU25 79 M1
Pingewood Cl
RDGW/BURGH RG30 137 R9
Pingewood Rd North
RDGW/BURGH RG30 58 A4
Pingewood Rd South
RDGW/BURGH RG30 58 B7
Pinglestone Cl WDR/YW UB7 42 A7
Pink La SL SL1 27 K3
Pinkneys Dr MDHD SL6 25 H6
Pinkneys Rd MDHD SL6 25 J6
Pinks La TADY RG26 148 A1
Pinkwell Av HYS/HAR UB3 42 F4
Pinkwell La HYS/HAR UB3 42 F4
Pinn Cl UX/CGN UB8 31 M7
Pipers Cl SL SL1 27 L4
Pipers Ct STHA RG19 * 98 C4
Piper's End VW GU25 68 D8
Pipers Island CAV/SC RG4 * 8 E1
Pipers La STHA RG19 98 B5
Pipers Wy STHA RG19 98 B5
Pipistrelle Wy WAR/TWY RG10 47 G2
Pipit Cl STHA RG19 97 K3
Pippins Cl WDR/YW UB7 41 M3
Pippins Ct ASHF TW15 71 H4
The Pippins DTCH/LGLY SL3 40 B1
Pipsons Cl YTLY GU46 86 D8
Pitch Pl BNFD RG42 63 K3
Pitcroft Av EARL RG6 46 A8
Pitfield La THLE RG7 143 Q12
Pitford Rd WODY RG5 46 F6
Pitson Cl ADL/WDHM KT15 82 B8
Pitts Cl BNFD RG42 63 J4
Pitt's La EARL RG6 46 F3
Pitts Rd SL SL1 10 A4
Plackett Wy SL SL1 37 M1
Plaines Cl SL SL1 38 B1
The Planes CHERT KT16 82 C4
Plantagenet Pk BNFD RG42 64 F6
Plantation Cl NTHA RG18 133 M5
Plantation Rd DID OX11 108 F2
TADY RG26 142 B12
Plantation Rw CBLY GU15 94 B1
Platt Ct HUNG RG17 139 J3
Platt La HUNG RG17 116 E8
Players Gn WODY RG5 * 60 E1
Playhatch Rd CAV/SC RG4 46 A1
Play Platt THLE RG7 136 H6
Pleasant HI TADY RG26 148 D2
Ploughlands BNFD RG42 2 A2
Plough La EWKG RG40 62 F7
HEN RG9 32 A5
SLN SL2 29 K2
Ploughlees La SL SL1 10 F3
Plough Rd YTLY GU46 86 F7
Plover Cl STA TW18 69 M1
Plowden Wy HEN RG9 32 A5
The Plummery READ RG1 9 J6
Plumpton Rd NWBY RG14 7 J8
Plumtrees EARL RG6 60 B6
Pluto Rd DID OX11 108 F2
Plymouth Av WODY RG5 60 C1
Plymouth Rd SL SL1 28 A7
Plympton Cl EARL RG6 60 E3
Pocket Cl BRAK RG12 * 63 K7
Pocket Pl EARL RG6 60 B2
Pocock Av WDR/YW UB7 42 B3
Pococks La WDSR SL4 39 G5
Poffley Pl STHA RG19 98 C4
Pointers Cl KSCL RG20 120 H12
The Points MDHD SL6 35 K3
Poldark Pl WHIT RG2 59 H7
Polden Cl FARN GU14 93 L7
Polehampton Cl
WAR/TWY RG10 47 K2
Pollard Cl WDSR SL4 54 B4
Pollard Gv CBLY GU15 95 J2
Pollardrow Av BNFD RG42 2 A3
Pollards Wy TILE/CALC RG31 137 N6
Polsted Rd TILE/CALC RG31 137 P1
Polyanthus Wy CWTH RG45 75 H6
Pond Cl NWBY RG14 141 R7
WANT OX12 107 Q9
Pond Cft YTLY GU46 86 E8
Pond End Rd CAV/SC RG4 126 G4
Pond Head La EARL RG6 60 D2
Pond La CAV/SC RG4 125 R7
NTHA RG18 133 Q3
Pond Moor Rd BRAK RG12 76 B2
Pond Rd EGH TW20 69 J4
TADY RG26 150 A8
Pondside Cl HYS/HAR UB3 42 F7
Poneys Cl BRAK RG12 * 3 L7
Poole Cl RDGW/BURGH RG30 137 R3
Pool End Cl SHPTN TW17 83 G2
Pooley Av EGH TW20 69 H3
Pooley Green Rd EGH TW20 69 H3
Pool La SL SL1 10 E3
WAR/TWY RG10 49 G1
Poolmans Rd WDSR SL4 52 D2
Pope Cl EBED/NFELT TW14 57 M7
Poperinghe Wy WHIT RG2 72 D6
Popes Cl DTCH/LGLY SL3 40 E7
Popes La MDHD SL6 19 L7
Popeswood Rd BNFD RG42 63 K6
Popham Cl BRAK RG12 76 F3
Poplar Av BFOR GU20 78 A8
RDGW/BURGH RG30 137 R5
Poplar Cl BRAK RG12 3 K6
DTCH/LGLY SL3 41 G8
HTWY RG27 150 D9
STHA RG19 98 C8
TADY RG26 103 M6
Poplar Gdns WHIT RG2 59 L5
Poplar La WAR/TWY RG10 47 M5
WWKG RG41 61 K3
Poplar Pl HYS/HAR UB3 43 J1
NWBY RG14 96 C1
Poplar Rd ASHF TW15 71 J3
Poplars Gv MDHD SL6 26 D4
The Poplars ASC SL5 78 A2
Poppy Dr NTHA RG18 98 B2
Poppyhills Rd CBLY GU15 88 F6
Poppy Pl EWKG RG40 14 F5
Poppy Wy TILE/CALC RG31 137 N5
Porchester ASC SL5 78 A1
Porchester Rd NWBY RG14 6 E8
Porchfield Cl EARL RG6 60 A5
Porlock Cl STHA RG19 * 97 M4
Porlock Pl TILE/CALC RG31 * 137 N6
Port Down HUNG RG17 139 J1
Porter Cl EARL RG6 60 C6
Porter End NWBY RG14 7 H9
Porters Wy WDR/YW UB7 42 B3
Portesbery Hill Dr CBLY GU15 88 D7
Portesbery Rd CBLY GU15 88 D8
Port HI HEN RG9 114 B4
Portia Gv BNFD RG42 3 M2
Portiswood Cl TADY RG26 148 F2
Portland Cl SLN SL2 27 M5
Portland Crs FELT TW13 71 K2
Portland Gdns MLW SL7 18 F5
RDGW/BURGH RG30 137 N3
Portland Rd ASHF TW15 70 E1
Portlock Rd MDHD SL6 4 A5
Portman Cl BNFD RG42 2 C3
Portman Rd
RDGW/BURGH RG30 44 B5
Portmeirion Gdns
RDGW/BURGH RG30 137 R1
Portmore Park Rd WEY KT13 83 G7
Portmore Quays WEY KT13 82 F8
Portmore Wy WEY KT13 * 83 G7
Portnall Dr VW GU25 79 L3
Portnall Ri VW GU25 79 M2
Portnall Rd VW GU25 79 M2
Portrush Cl WODY RG5 46 D8
Portsmouth Rd FRIM GU16 94 E3
Portway TADY RG26 103 M5
THLE RG7 145 N12
Portway Cl READ RG1 8 B9
Post Horn Pl TILE/CALC RG31 137 R6
Posting House Ms NWBY RG14 6 B1
Post Meadow IVER SL0 30 F4
Post Office La DTCH/LGLY SL3 29 M7
RDGW/BURGH RG30 144 A1
WANT OX12 106 E1
Post Office Rd HUNG RG17 139 Q9
Potkiln La GOR/PANG RG8 113 J12
Potley Hill Rd YTLY GU46 92 F1
The Potteries FARN GU14 93 K8
Potters Cross IVER SL0 31 G4
Potters La HTWY RG27 150 F7
Pottery Cl WDSR SL4 66 B4
Pottery Flds HEN RG9 114 E4
Pottery La HUNG RG17 139 P9
Pottery Rd
RDGW/BURGH RG30 137 Q1
Potts Pl MLW SL7 * 18 F4
Poulcott STWL/WRAY TW19 54 E5
Pound Cl TADY RG26 149 Q7
Pound Crs MLW SL7 18 E5
Poundfield La MDHD SL6 20 B7
Poundfield Wy
WAR/TWY RG10 47 M3
Pound La BFOR GU20 90 C2
CAV/SC RG4 46 D3
KSCL RG20 100 A8
MLW SL7 18 E5
MLW SL7 19 K2
NWBY RG14 141 R2
STHA RG19 97 J3
WAR/TWY RG10 62 B1
Pound Meadow HTWY RG27 150 E10
Pound Pl BNFD RG42 63 J3
Pound Rd CHERT KT16 82 B4
Pound St NWBY RG14 6 D6
The Pound MDHD SL6 20 B7
Powis Cl MDHD SL6 35 K2
Powney Rd MDHD SL6 4 B5
Poyle Gdns BRAK RG12 3 J2
Poyle La SL SL1 27 K2
Poyle Pk DTCH/LGLY SL3 * 55 L2
Poyle Rd DTCH/LGLY SL3 55 K2
The Poynings DTCH/LGLY SL3 41 H4
Prairie Cl ADL/WDHM KT15 82 B7
Prairie Rd ADL/WDHM KT15 82 B7
Prancing Horse Cl STHA RG19 98 A3
The Precincts SL SL1 27 K5
The Precinct EGH TW20 * 69 G3
Prentice Cl FARN GU14 94 B6
Prescott BRAK RG12 75 M4
Prescott Rd DTCH/LGLY SL3 55 L1
Press Rd UX/CGN UB8 31 M1
Preston Pl NWBY RG14 96 F1
Preston Rd SHPTN TW17 83 G2
SLN SL2 29 L8
WHIT RG2 59 H1
Prestwick Ct READ RG1 * 9 M7
Prestwood SLN SL2 11 L1
Pretoria Rd CHERT KT16 81 M5
Price Gdns BNFD RG42 64 B4
Prides Crossing ASC SL5 66 A5
Priest Av EWKG RG40 74 F1
Priest Cl HEN RG9 114 D3
Priest HI CAV/SC RG4 45 G3
WDSR SL4 54 C8
Priestwood Av BNFD RG42 2 A2
Priestwood Court Rd
BNFD RG42 2 B2
Priestwood Sq BNFD RG42 2 B2
Priestwood Ter BRAK RG12 * 3 H1
Primrose Cl GOR/PANG RG8 125 N9
Primrose Dr WDR/YW UB7 41 M4
Primrose La MDHD SL6 36 C8
WWKG RG41 61 J3
Primrose Lea MLW SL7 18 F3
Primrose Wk BRAK RG12 76 C2
Primrose Wy SHST GU47 87 H5
Prince Albert Dr ASC SL5 77 K1
Prince Andrew Cl MDHD SL6 5 L1
Prince Andrew Rd MDHD SL6 5 L1
Prince Andrew Wy ASC SL5 65 K7
Prince Charles Crs FARN GU14 94 B6
Prince Consort Cots WDSR SL4 13 J8
Prince Consort Dr ASC SL5 77 K1
Prince Consort's Dr WDSR SL4 52 F5
WDSR SL4 53 G8
Prince Dr SHST GU47 87 G5
Prince Hold Rd STHA RG19 97 J3
Prince of Wales Av
RDGW/BURGH RG30 44 D7
Princes Cl BAGS GU19 89 L5
WDSR SL4 38 B5
Prince's La KSCL RG20 120 C8
Princes Rd ASHF TW15 70 F3
BNEND SL8 20 E3
EGH TW20 68 F4
FELT TW13 71 M1
Princess Av WDSR SL4 53 H2
Princess Marina Dr
EWKG RG40 73 G5
WHIT RG2 72 F6
Princess Mary's Rd
ADL/WDHM KT15 82 C8
Princess St MDHD SL6 5 G6
Princes St READ RG1 9 K7
SL SL1 11 L6
Princess Wy CBLY GU15 94 C1
Prince William Dr
TILE/CALC RG31 137 N1
Printinghouse La HYS/HAR UB3 43 G2
Prior Croft Cl CBLY GU15 95 G2
Prior End CBLY GU15 95 G1
Prior Rd CBLY GU15 95 G1
Priors Cl FARN GU14 94 B6
MDHD SL6 36 D4
SL SL1 11 J8
Prior's Ct READ RG1 9 G8
Priors Court Rd NTHA RG18 133 J2
NTHA RG18 133 N4
Priors Farm EWKG RG40 * 75 H4
Prior's La BLKW GU17 93 G1
Priors Rd TADY RG26 148 C1
WDSR SL4 52 D2
Priors Wy MDHD SL6 36 D4
Priors Wd CWTH RG45 86 D2
Priory Av CAV/SC RG4 45 G4
HUNG RG17 138 H2
Priory Cl ASC SL5 79 G4
HUNG RG17 138 H2
Priory Ct CBLY GU15 * 93 M1
WWKG RG41 61 J3
Priory Gdns ASHF TW15 71 K3
Priory Gn STA TW18 70 B3
Priory La BNFD RG42 64 C5
Priory Ms STA TW18 70 B3
Priory Pl HUNG RG17 138 H1
STHA RG19 96 D8
Priory Rd ASC SL5 65 H6
ASC SL5 79 G4
HUNG RG17 138 H1
NWBY RG14 6 E8
SL SL1 27 L6
The Priory WWKG RG41 61 J3
Priory Wk BRAK RG12 76 F1
Priory Wy DTCH/LGLY SL3 39 K7
NWDGN UB2 43 M3
WDR/YW UB7 42 A6
Pritchard Cl STHA RG19 96 F7
Privet Cl EARL RG6 60 B5
Proctors Rd EWKG RG40 62 F8
Promenade Rd CAV/SC RG4 8 E1
Prospect Av FARN GU14 94 B8
Prospect La EGH TW20 68 A3
Prospect Ms READ RG1 * 8 C6
Prospect Pk
RDGW/BURGH RG30 * 44 B8
Prospect Pl MDHD SL6 24 B3
NWBY RG14 6 E7
STA TW18 69 M3
Prospect Rd HUNG RG17 138 H1
MLW SL7 18 E4
Prospect St CAV/SC RG4 45 G4
READ RG1 8 B7
Providence La HYS/HAR UB3 42 F7
Providence Pl MDHD SL6 5 H4
Providence Rd WDR/YW UB7 42 A1
Prune HI EGH TW20 68 D5
Prunus Cl CHOB/PIR GU24 90 E8
Pryor Cl TILE/CALC RG31 125 M10
Ptarmigan Hts EWKG RG40 75 K1
Pudding HI WAR/TWY RG10 23 M8
Pudding La KSCL RG20 119 Q5
Pudseys Cl MDHD SL6 19 K8
Puffers Wy NWBY RG14 6 A5
Pulleyn Pk WHIT RG2 * 59 G1
Pullmans Pl STA TW18 70 A3
Pump La ASC SL5 66 E6
HYS/HAR UB3 43 J2
THLE RG7 144 G4
Pump La South MLW SL7 19 J1
Purbrook Ct BRAK RG12 76 E3
Purbrook Rd TADY RG26 148 C2
Purcell Rd CWTH RG45 75 H7
Purfield Dr WAR/TWY RG10 33 G3
Purley La GOR/PANG RG8 125 N9
Purley Ri GOR/PANG RG8 125 K9
Purley Village
GOR/PANG RG8 125 N9
Purley Wy FRIM GU16 94 E6
GOR/PANG RG8 125 J9
Pursers Ct SLN SL2 10 F2
Pursers Farm THLE RG7 145 M3
Purslane EWKG RG40 15 J8
Pursell Cl MDHD SL6 35 J3
Purton Ct SLN SL2 28 E1
Purton La SLN SL2 28 E1
Pyegrove Cha BRAK RG12 76 E4
Pyke Cl EWKG RG40 15 K5
Pyke's HI GOR/PANG RG8 123 M10
Pyle HI NWBY RG14 7 H8
Pyrcroft Rd CHERT KT16 81 L4

Q

The Quadrangle FRIM GU16 * 94 C6
Quadrant Ct BRAK RG12 3 L6
Quadrant Wy WEY KT13 83 G8
Qualitas BRAK RG12 75 M5
Quantock Av CAV/SC RG4 45 K1
Quantock Cl DTCH/LGLY SL3 40 C5
HYS/HAR UB3 42 F7
WAR/TWY RG10 47 H2
The Quantocks STHA RG19 97 M4
Quarrington Cl STHA RG19 98 A4
Quarry Bank LTWR GU18 89 M6
Quarrydale Dr MLW SL7 19 H4
Quarry La HEN RG9 32 C2
YTLY GU46 92 E1
Quarry Wood Rd MLW SL7 19 G6
Quartz Cl WWKG RG41 61 K7
Quaves Rd DTCH/LGLY SL3 11 M8
Quebec Gdns BLKW GU17 93 K2
Quebec Rd HEN RG9 22 A6
Queen Anne's Cl WDSR SL4 67 H1
Queen Annes Ga CAV/SC RG4 45 J3
Queen Annes Ride WDSR SL4 * 67 H1
Queen Anne's Ride WDSR SL4 53 J6
Queen Anne's Rd WDSR SL4 53 J3
Queen Cl HEN RG9 22 A5
Queen Elizabeth Rd CBLY GU15 88 D5
Queen Elizabeth's Wk WDSR SL4 13 M7
Queen Mary Av CBLY GU15 94 A1
Queen Mary Rd SHPTN TW17 71 J7
Queens Acre WDSR SL4 53 K3
Queensborough Dr CAV/SC RG4 44 E1
Queensbury Pl BLKW GU17 93 J3
Queen's Cl WDSR SL4 54 A4
Queen's Cots READ RG1 9 H6
Queens Ct SL SL1 * 11 H3
Queen's Dr DTCH/LGLY SL3 30 B2
The Queen's Dr WHIT RG2 59 K2
Queenshill Ldg ASC SL5 66 B8
Queens Hill Ri ASC SL5 66 C8
Queens La MDHD SL6 5 H5
Queensmead DTCH/LGLY SL3 39 K8
Queensmere SL SL1 11 H6
Queensmere Rd SL SL1 11 H6
Queens Park Gdns FELT TW13 * 71 M1
Queens Pine BRAK RG12 76 E3
Queen's Pl ASC SL5 66 A8
Queens Ride CWTH RG45 75 G7
Queens Ride CWTH RG45 75 G7
Queen's Rd ASC SL5 78 D2
CAV/SC RG4 9 H2
Queens Rd CBLY GU15 94 B2
Queen's Rd DTCH/LGLY SL3 39 K8
EGH TW20 68 F4
MLW SL7 18 E4
NWBY RG14 7 G6
NWDGN UB2 43 M2
READ RG1 9 H6
Queens Rd SL SL1 11 G3
Queen's Rd UX/CGN UB8 31 L4
Queens Rd WDR/YW UB7 42 B2
WDSR SL4 13 G8
WDSR SL4 38 A5
WGFD OX10 111 P1
Queen St CAV/SC RG4 45 G3
CHERT KT16 82 A5
HEN RG9 22 A5
MDHD SL6 5 H6
Queen Street Ms HEN RG9 22 A5
Queens Wk ASHF TW15 70 D2
READ RG1 8 E6
Queens Wy HUNG RG17 140 B4
Queensway CAV/SC RG4 127 K12
FRIM GU16 95 G7
MDHD SL6 26 A4
Queen Victoria St READ RG1 9 G5
Queen Victoria's Wk WDSR SL4 13 M5
Quentin Rd WODY RG5 46 D8
Quentin Wy VW GU25 80 B1
Quiet Cl ADL/WDHM KT15 82 A8
Quinbrookes SLN SL2 29 L7
Quince Cl ASC SL5 78 D1
Quincy Rd EGH TW20 69 G3
Quintilis BRAK RG12 75 M5
Quinton Cl HEST TW5 43 K7
Quoitings Dr MLW SL7 18 E4
Quoiting Sq MLW SL7 * 18 F5

R

Racecourse Rd NWBY RG14 7 G7
Rachaels Lake Vw BNFD RG42 3 M1
Rackstraw Rd SHST GU47 87 K4
Radbourne Rd TILE/CALC RG31 137 P6
Radcliffe Cl FRIM GU16 94 F7
Radcliffe Wy BNFD RG42 63 L6
Radcot Av DTCH/LGLY SL3 40 D3
Radcot Cl MDHD SL6 26 A3
WODY RG5 46 E5
Radical Ride EWKG RG40 73 M7
Radius Pk EBED/NFELT TW14 * 57 M3
Radley Bottom HUNG RG17 130 A7
Radley Cl EBED/NFELT TW14 57 M7
Radnor Cl HEN RG9 22 A4
Radnor Rd BRAK RG12 64 F8
EARL RG6 60 C3
WEY KT13 83 G7
Radnor Wy DTCH/LGLY SL3 40 A4
Radstock La EARL RG6 60 A4
Radstock Rd READ RG1 45 M7
Raeburn Wy SHST GU47 87 K8
Ragdale THLE RG7 143 Q3
Raggleswood Cl EARL RG6 60 C3
Raghill THLE RG7 142 F8
Raglan Cl FRIM GU16 94 F6
Raglan Gdns CAV/SC RG4 45 J2
Ragley Ms CAV/SC RG4 127 K12
Ragstone Rd SL SL1 10 E8
Railside THLE RG7 142 B4
Railton Cl WHIT RG2 59 K7
Railway Ap CHERT KT16 * 81 M5
Railway Rd NWBY RG14 7 G5
Railway Ter SLN SL2 11 G4
STA TW18 69 K3
Railway Vw DTCH/LGLY SL3 * 54 F2
Rainbow Pk WWKG RG41 61 H4
Rainforest Wk BRAK RG12 76 B2
Rainsborough Cha MDHD SL6 35 K3
Rainworth Cl EARL RG6 60 A6
Raleigh Cl SL SL1 38 C1
WODY RG5 60 E1
Raleigh Ct STA TW18 70 A2
Raleigh Rd FELT TW13 57 M8
Raleigh Wy FRIM GU16 94 F3
Ralphs Ride BRAK RG12 3 L6
Ram Aly STHA RG19 102 E6
Rambler Cl MDHD SL6 27 K7
Rambler La DTCH/LGLY SL3 39 L3
Ramptons La THLE RG7 143 K8
Rampton's Meadow
TADY RG26 148 F3
Ramsay Cl CBLY GU15 89 H6
Ramsay Rd BFOR GU20 90 E1
Ramsbury Cl BRAK RG12 75 L3
Ramsbury Dr EARL RG6 60 A2
HUNG RG17 139 J1
Ramsbury Ter HUNG RG17 139 J1
Ramsdell Cl TADY RG26 148 D3
Ramsdell Rd TADY RG26 148 F9
Ramsey Cl EARL RG6 60 E4
Ramsey Ct SLN SL2 27 M5
Rances La EWKG RG40 15 L7
Randall Cl DTCH/LGLY SL3 40 B5
Randall Md BNFD RG42 63 H4
Randell Cl BLKW GU17 93 L5
Randolph Gdns THLE RG7 * 142 F2
Randolph Rd DTCH/LGLY SL3 40 A4
READ RG1 8 E2
Ranelagh WDSR SL4 * 52 B7
Ranelagh Crs ASC SL5 65 J6
Ranelagh Dr BRAK RG12 3 H6

Ranelagh Rd STHL UB1 43 M1
Range Ride CBLY GU15 87 M7
Range Rd EWKG RG40 74 B7
Range Vw SHST GU47 87 L6
Range Wy SHPTN TW17 83 G4
Rangewood Av
RDGW/BURGH RG30 137 R7
Rapley Cl CBLY GU15 88 F6
Rapley Gn BRAK RG12 76 C3
Ratby Cl EARL RG6 60 C4
Ratcliffe Cl UX/CGN UB8 31 M4
Ratcliffe Rd FARN GU14 93 M6
Raven Cl YTLY GU46 86 B8
Ravendale Rd SUN TW16 71 M7
Ravenglass Cl EARL RG6 60 C4
Ravensbourne Av
STWL/WRAY TW19 56 E7
Ravensbourne Dr WODY RG5 46 E6
Ravenscourt SUN TW16 71 M6
Ravenscroft Rd HEN RG9 115 R12
Ravensdale Rd ASC SL5 78 A2
Ravens Fld DTCH/LGLY SL3 39 M2
Ravensfield EGH TW20 68 B4
Ravenshoe Cl BNEND SL8 20 C3
Ravenstone Rd CBLY GU15 95 K1
Ravenswood Av CWTH RG45 86 E1
Ravenswood Dr CBLY GU15 95 G1
Ravensworth Rd SLN SL2 28 C4
THLE RG7 143 N8
Rawlinson Rd CBLY GU15 87 M8
Ray Dr MDHD SL6 5 M4
Ray Lea Cl MDHD SL6 5 L2
Ray Lea Rd MDHD SL6 5 L2
Ray Lodge Ms MDHD SL6 5 M3
Ray Mead Ct MDHD SL6 26 E5
Ray Meadow MDHD SL6 5 K1
Ray Mead Rd MDHD SL6 26 E6
Ray Mill Rd East MDHD SL6 5 K1
Ray Mill Rd West MDHD SL6 5 H2
Raymond Cl DTCH/LGLY SL3 41 G8
Raymond Rd DTCH/LGLY SL3 40 C4
MDHD SL6 4 D4
Rayner Dr WHIT RG2 72 E6
Rayners Cl DTCH/LGLY SL3 40 E7
Ray Park Av MDHD SL6 5 M1
Ray Park La MDHD SL6 5 L3
Ray Park Rd MDHD SL6 5 L3
Rays Av WDSR SL4 12 A4
Rays Cl TADY RG26 148 E2
Ray St MDHD SL6 5 L4
Raywood Cl HYS/HAR UB3 42 E7
Reades La CAV/SC RG4 126 A6
Reade's La CAV/SC RG4 126 C5
Reading Br READ RG1 9 H3
Reading Rd BLKW GU17 93 H2
CAV/SC RG4 125 R3
EWKG RG40 84 F2
GOR/PANG RG8 111 Q12
GOR/PANG RG8 113 K9
GOR/PANG RG8 123 H3
GOR/PANG RG8 124 H9
HEN RG9 22 A6
HTWY RG27 85 K6
HTWY RG27 150 D10
HTWY RG27 151 Q10
RDGW/BURGH RG30 144 B1
THLE RG7 142 H9
THLE RG7 143 P6
THLE RG7 143 Q4
WGFD OX10 111 Q3
WHIT RG2 72 C2
WODY RG5 46 D6
WWKG RG41 14 C4
YTLY GU46 86 B7
Recreation Cl FARN GU14 93 M5
Recreation La THLE RG7 145 M4
Recreation Rd BNEND SL8 20 C3
RDGW/BURGH RG30 137 Q2
THLE RG7 143 Q4
WAR/TWY RG10 33 G4
Rectory Cl BRAK RG12 3 G8
EWKG RG40 15 G5
NWBY RG14 6 C6
SHPTN TW17 83 F6
SHST GU47 86 F6
SLN SL2 28 E4
TADY RG26 148 E4
WDSR SL4 12 D6
Rectory Gdns HTWY RG27 150 E10
Rectory La BFOR GU20 90 C3
BRAK RG12 2 F9
DID OX11 110 H1
HEN RG9 115 K7
WANT OX12 106 C3
Rectory Rd CAV/SC RG4 45 G4
EWKG RG40 15 H4
GOR/PANG RG8 111 L11
MDHD SL6 26 F5
THLE RG7 142 H7
Rectory Rw BRAK RG12 2 E9
Redberry Cl CAV/SC RG4 45 K1
Red Cottage Dr
TILE/CALC RG31 137 N6
Red Cottage Ms
DTCH/LGLY SL3 39 L3
Red Ct SL SL1 10 E5
Redcrest Gdns CBLY GU15 94 F1
Red Cross Rd GOR/PANG RG8 112 A12
Reddington Dr DTCH/LGLY SL3 40 B4
Redditch BRAK RG12 76 D4
Rede Ct WEY KT13 83 H7
Redfern Cl UX/CGN UB8 31 L2
Redfield Ct NWBY RG14 7 M2
Redford Cl FELT TW13 57 M8
Redford Rd WDSR SL4 37 M8
Redford Wy UX/CGN UB8 31 L1
Redgauntlet EWKG RG40 73 L8
Redgrave Pl MLW SL7 19 H3
Redhatch Dr EARL RG6 59 M4
Red Hl HEN RG9 127 M5
Red House Cl EARL RG6 60 B6
Red House Dr CAV/SC RG4 126 F5
Redlake La EWKG RG40 74 F4
Redlands Pl WWKG RG41 73 M4
Redlands Rd READ RG1 59 K1
Red La GOR/PANG RG8 113 J8
THLE RG7 142 F9
WGFD OX10 112 G6
Redlane Ct READ RG1 59 K1
Redlane Hl THLE RG7 142 E8
Redlane Rd KSCL RG20 120 F2
Redleaves Av ASHF TW15 71 H4
Red Lion La CHOB/PIR GU24 91 L4
Red Lion Rd CHOB/PIR GU24 91 L4
Redmayne CBLY GU15 95 J2
Redmead Rd HYS/HAR UB3 43 G4
Redriff Cl MDHD SL6 4 D7
Red Rd LTWR GU18 90 A7
Red Rose BNFD RG42 63 J3
Redruth Gdns WHIT RG2 59 H5
Redshank Ct STHA RG19 97 J3
Redshots Cl MLW SL7 19 G2
Red Shute Hl NTHA RG18 133 N6
Redvers Rd BRAK RG12 76 B2
Redwood EGH TW20 69 L7
SL SL1 27 J3
Redwood Av WODY RG5 61 G1
Redwood Dr ASC SL5 79 H3
CBLY GU15 95 K2
Redwood Gdns SL SL1 10 C8
Redwood Ms ASHF TW15 * 71 K5
The Redwoods WDSR SL4 53 K2
Redwood Wy TILE/CALC RG31 125 P11
Reed Cl IVER SL0 31 G7
Reed Pl SHPTN TW17 82 F5
Reeds Av EARL RG6 59 M3
Reedsfield Cl ASHF TW15 71 H1
Reedsfield Rd ASHF TW15 71 G2
Reed's Hl BRAK RG12 76 B2
Reed Wk NWBY RG14 7 J1
Reeve Rd MDHD SL6 36 C4
Reeves Wy WWKG RG41 74 A2
Reform Rd MDHD SL6 5 L5
Regal Ct MDHD SL6 36 D4
Regatta Pl BNEND SL8 * 20 C2
Regency Ct ADL/WDHM KT15 * 82 D8
Regency Hts CAV/SC RG4 44 E2
Regent Cl EARL RG6 60 C5
HSLWW TW4 43 K8
HUNG RG17 138 G1
Regent Ct BAGS GU19 89 M4
MDHD SL6 * 5 G5
READ RG1 8 E4
SL SL1 10 E1
Regents Ct NWBY RG14 6 D3
Regents Pl SHST GU47 87 J6
Regent St READ RG1 45 L7
Regents Wk ASC SL5 78 C3
Regent Wy FRIM GU16 94 F5
Regis Cl WHIT RG2 59 K7
Regnum Dr NWBY RG14 96 D1
Reid Av MDHD SL6 4 D9
Rembrandt Cl WWKG RG41 61 K8
Rembrandt Wy READ RG1 58 E1
Remembrance Rd NWBY RG14 6 A6
Remenham Church La
HEN RG9 22 C2
Remenham La HEN RG9 22 B4
Remenham Rw HEN RG9 22 A5
Remenham Ter HEN RG9 * 22 E4
Renault Rd WODY RG5 47 G8
Renfree Wy SHPTN TW17 83 G4
Rennie Cl ASHF TW15 70 D1
Repton Av HYS/HAR UB3 42 F4
Repton Cl MDHD SL6 35 L3
Repton Rd EARL RG6 60 C3
Resham Cl NWDGN UB2 43 L3
Restwold Cl
RDGW/BURGH RG30 58 C2
Retford Cl WODY RG5 46 F5
The Retreat EGH TW20 68 D4
MDHD SL6 36 F7
Reuben's Crs TADY RG26 148 D3
Revelstoke Av FARN GU14 94 B8
Revesby Cl CHOB/PIR GU24 90 D8
MDHD SL6 35 M3
Rex Av ASHF TW15 71 G4
Reynards Cl TADY RG26 148 D2
WWKG RG41 61 J4
Reynolds Gn SHST GU47 87 K8
Rhigos CAV/SC RG4 126 F12
Rhine Cl CAV/SC RG4 45 K4
Rhodes Cl EARL RG6 60 E3
EGH TW20 69 J3
Rhodes Ct EGH TW20 * 69 J3
Rhododendron Cl ASC SL5 65 L5
Rhododendron Ride EGH TW20 67 M3
Rhododendron Rd FRIM GU16 95 H6
Rhododendron Wk ASC SL5 65 L5
Ribble Pl FARN GU14 93 L8
Ribbleton Cl EARL RG6 60 E3
Ribstone Rd MDHD SL6 35 K3
Ricardo Rd WDSR SL4 54 B5
Richards Cl HYS/HAR UB3 42 F6
Richardson Cl TADY RG26 149 R7
Richards Wy SL SL1 38 B1
Richborough Cl EARL RG6 60 B4
Richfield Av READ RG1 8 B2
Richings Pl DTCH/LGLY SL3 41 G3
Richings Wy DTCH/LGLY SL3 41 H3
Richmond Av
EBED/NFELT TW14 57 L5
STHA RG19 97 J3
Richmond Cl FRIM GU16 94 F5
Richmond Crs SL SL1 11 J5
STA TW18 * 69 M3
Richmond Dr SHPTN TW17 83 J3
Richmond Ri WWKG RG41 61 L7
Richmond Rd CAV/SC RG4 44 E2
RDGW/BURGH RG30 44 C6
SHST GU47 87 L6
STA TW18 69 M3
Richmond Wd ASC SL5 79 H5
Rickard Cl WDR/YW UB7 41 M3
Rickman Cl BRAK RG12 76 C3
WHIT RG2 72 E5
WODY RG5 60 D1
Rickman Crs ADL/WDHM KT15 82 B7
Riddings La STHA RG19 102 E1
Rider's La THLE RG7 144 E2
Rideway Cl CBLY GU15 94 B2
Ridgebank SL SL1 28 B8
Ridge Hall Cl CAV/SC RG4 44 E3
Ridgemead Rd EGH TW20 68 B1
Ridgemount WEY KT13 83 L6
Ridgemount Cl
TILE/CALC RG31 125 M12
Ridge Mount Rd ASC SL5 79 G5
The Ridge ASC SL5 * 79 G4
GOR/PANG RG8 124 D6
NTHA RG18 133 Q9
Ridge Wy IVER SL0 31 G8
VW GU25 80 E2
WAR/TWY RG10 32 F4
Ridgeway CKL/HW SN6 104 B2
DID OX11 108 E4
FGDN SN7 104 E1
GOR/PANG RG8 112 A8
KSCL RG20 110 C10
WANT OX12 105 P4
WANT OX12 107 M5
WGFD OX10 111 Q5
WOT/HER KT12 83 M5
Ridgeway Cl LTWR GU18 90 A6
NTHA RG18 133 P3
The Ridgeway BRAK RG12 3 G7
CAV/SC RG4 45 G3
HEN RG9 114 D4
LTWR GU18 90 B5
MLW SL7 19 G2
WANT OX12 107 J5
WANT OX12 108 C3
WODY RG5 60 F1
Ridgewood Dr FRIM GU16 95 K3
Riding Court Rd DTCH/LGLY SL3 39 L6
The Ridings CAV/SC RG4 127 J10
DTCH/LGLY SL3 41 H4
FRIM GU16 95 H3
MDHD SL6 25 H7
WDSR SL4 * 37 L7
Riding Wy WWKG RG41 61 K8
Ridlington Cl EARL RG6 60 E4
Rigby La HYS/HAR UB3 42 E3
Righton Cl WAR/TWY RG10 47 H3
Riley Rd MLW SL7 18 F4
RDGW/BURGH RG30 137 R2
Rimes's La TADY RG26 148 B4
Ringmead BRAK RG12 75 L2
Ringshall Gdns TADY RG26 149 Q7
The Ring BRAK RG12 2 C5
BRAK RG12 2 F4
Ringway NWDGN UB2 43 M5
Ringwood BRAK RG12 75 M4
Ringwood Cl ASC SL5 78 A1
Ringwood Rd BLKW GU17 87 J8
FARN GU14 94 C7
RDGW/BURGH RG30 137 R1
Ripley Av EGH TW20 68 E4
Ripley Cl DTCH/LGLY SL3 40 A4
Ripley Rd RDGW/BURGH RG30 44 A5
Ripon Cl CBLY GU15 95 K3
Ripon Rd BLKW GU17 92 F5
Ripplesmere BRAK RG12 76 D2
Ripplesmore Cl SHST GU47 87 H6
Ripston Rd ASHF TW15 71 K3
Risborough Rd MDHD SL6 4 F2
Riseley Rd MDHD SL6 4 C5
Rise Rd ASC SL5 78 E3
The Rise CAV/SC RG4 45 H2
CWTH RG45 86 F1
EWKG RG40 85 G4
NTHA RG18 133 Q10
THLE RG7 * 144 A9
WWKG RG41 14 C3
Rissington Cl TILE/CALC RG31 125 Q11
Rivacres GOR/PANG RG8 125 J3
Rivar Rd MARL SN8 138 C12
The Riverbank WDSR SL4 12 E4
River Ct MDHD SL6 26 E7
Riverdene Dr WWKG RG41 60 F3
Riverfield Rd STA TW18 69 M4
River Gdns GOR/PANG RG8 125 P9
MDHD SL6 36 F2
Rivermead Ct MLW SL7 19 G6
Rivermead Rd CBLY GU15 94 B4
WODY RG5 60 F1
River Mt WOT/HER KT12 83 M4
River Pk NWBY RG14 7 H3
River Park Av STA TW18 69 K2
Riverpark Dr MLW SL7 19 H5
River Rd CAV/SC RG4 44 D3
MDHD SL6 26 E7
READ RG1 8 F9
STA TW18 69 M6
WDSR SL4 * 37 L7
YTLY GU46 86 B7
Riversdale BNEND SL8 20 D5
Riversdale Ct READ RG1 45 L6
Riversdell Cl CHERT KT16 81 M4
Riverside BNEND SL8 * 20 E3
CHERT KT16 * 70 A7
MDHD SL6 * 36 E2
SHPTN TW17 83 L4
STWL/WRAY TW19 54 C6
Riverside Av LTWR GU18 90 C6
Riverside Cl STA TW18 69 M5
Riverside Ct CAV/SC RG4 8 E1
Riverside Dr STA TW18 69 L3
Riverside Level READ RG1 * 9 G7
Riverside Pk
RDGW/BURGH RG30 * 44 B4
Riverside Pl STWL/WRAY TW19 56 D5
Riverside Rd STA TW18 69 M5
STWL/WRAY TW19 56 D4
Riverside Wk WDSR SL4 13 K4
Riverside Wy CBLY GU15 94 A3
UX/CGN UB8 31 K2
River St WDSR SL4 13 J4
Riverview Rd GOR/PANG RG8 124 G8
River Wk NWBY RG14 7 J1
Riverway HUNG RG17 118 E11
STA TW18 70 B6
Riverwood Av MLW SL7 19 J5
Riverwoods Dr MLW SL7 19 J5
Rixman Cl MDHD SL6 4 C9
Rixon Cl DTCH/LGLY SL3 30 A7
Road Eight DID OX11 108 G2
Road Eighteen DID OX11 108 H1
Road Eleven DID OX11 108 G1
Road Fifteen DID OX11 108 G1
Road Five DID OX11 108 H1
Road Four DID OX11 108 H1
Road One DID OX11 108 G1
Road Six DID OX11 108 H1
Road Thirteen DID OX11 108 H1
Road Twelve DID OX11 108 G1
Road Two DID OX11 108 G1
Roakes Av ADL/WDHM KT15 82 B6
Roberts Cl STWL/WRAY TW19 56 C5
WDR/YW UB7 42 A1
Robertsfield STHA RG19 97 H3
Roberts Gv WWKG RG41 73 M3
Robertson Cl NWBY RG14 96 D6
Roberts Rd CBLY GU15 88 A8
Roberts Wy EGH TW20 68 C5
Robin Cl THLE RG7 * 143 R3
Robindale Av EARL RG6 60 D3
Robin Hill Dr CBLY GU15 95 G3
Robin Hood Cl FARN GU14 94 A7
SL SL1 38 A1
Robinhood La WWKG RG41 61 J4
Robin Hood Wy WWKG RG41 61 J3
Robin La SHST GU47 87 J6
Robins Cl NWBY RG14 96 B7
UX/CGN UB8 31 L6
Robins Grove Crs YTLY GU46 86 B8
Robinson Cl DID OX11 110 C2
Robinson Ct EARL RG6 60 A5
Robin Wy STA TW18 69 M1
TILE/CALC RG31 137 M4
Robin Willis Wy WDSR SL4 54 A5
Roby Dr BRAK RG12 76 D4
Rochester Av FELT TW13 57 M8
WODY RG5 46 E5
Rochester Rd EGH TW20 69 K3
Rochfords Gdns SLN SL2 29 L8
Rochford Wy MDHD SL6 27 J8
Rockall Ct DTCH/LGLY SL3 40 D3
Rockbourne Gdns
RDGW/BURGH RG30 44 A5
Rockfel Rd HUNG RG17 117 J4
Rockfield Wy SHST GU47 * 87 K6
Rockingham Cl UX/CGN UB8 * 31 L2
Rockingham Pde UX/CGN UB8 31 L1
Rockingham Rd NWBY RG14 6 A5
UX/CGN UB8 31 K2
Rockmoor La RAND SP11 146 B8
Rocky La HEN RG9 114 F10
Roden Down Ms KSCL RG20 122 A1
Rodney Wy DTCH/LGLY SL3 41 G8
Rodway Rd
RDGW/BURGH RG30 125 Q12
Roebuck Est BNFD RG42 63 J5
Roebuck Gn SL SL1 38 A1
Roebuck Ri TILE/CALC RG31 125 P11
Roebuts Cl NWBY RG14 6 C9
Rogers La SLN SL2 29 H2
Rogers's La HUNG RG17 118 A8
Rokeby Cl BRAK RG12 3 J4
NWBY RG14 96 C7
Rokeby Dr CAV/SC RG4 126 D10
Rokesby Rd SLN SL2 28 B4
Rokes Pl YTLY GU46 86 A8
Rolls La MDHD SL6 36 A6
Romana Ct STA TW18 * 70 A2
Roman Lea MDHD SL6 20 B7
Roman Ride CWTH RG45 86 D1
Romans Fld THLE RG7 149 K2
Romans Ga TADY RG26 148 H1
Roman Wy BNEND SL8 20 C2
BNFD RG42 64 F6
EARL RG6 60 D3
NTHA RG18 97 J2
Romany Cl RDGW/BURGH RG30 44 A5
Romany La RDGW/BURGH RG30 44 A5
Romeo Hl BNFD RG42 64 F6
Romney Cl ASHF TW15 71 J3
Romney Lock Rd WDSR SL4 13 K3
Romsey Cl BLKW GU17 87 J8
DTCH/LGLY SL3 40 B3
Romsey Rd RDGW/BURGH RG30 44 A5
Rona Ct RDGW/BURGH RG30 44 B6
Ronaldsay Sp SL SL1 29 G6
Ronneby Cl WEY KT13 83 L7
Rood Hl KSCL RG20 131 M5
Rook Cl WWKG RG41 73 L1
Rookery Ct MLW SL7 18 F4
Rookery Rd STA TW18 70 B3
The Rookery KSCL RG20 120 D7
Rooke's Wy NTHA RG18 97 G2
Rook Rd FLKWH/TG HP10 20 F2
Rooksfield KSCL RG20 101 J4
Rooksmead Rd SUN TW16 71 M7
Rooksnest La HUNG RG17 140 A9
Rooks Ter WDR/YW UB7 * 42 A2
Rookswood BNFD RG42 64 B5
KSCL RG20 131 R12
Rookwood Av SHST GU47 87 L5
Rope Wk STHA RG19 97 L3
Ropley Cl TADY RG26 148 C3
Rosa Av ASHF TW15 71 G2
Rosary Gdns ASHF TW15 71 H2
YTLY GU46 * 86 D8
Roseacre Cl SHPTN TW17 83 G2
Roseary Cl WDR/YW UB7 41 M4
Rosebank Cl MDHD SL6 20 A7
TADY RG26 148 D2
Rosebay EWKG RG40 15 M2
Rosebery Rd CAV/SC RG4 126 D11
Rose Cl WODY RG5 47 H7
Rose Ct EWKG RG40 15 H5
Rosecroft Wy WHIT RG2 145 Q1
Rosedale BNFD RG42 63 J3
Rosedale Crs EARL RG6 46 A6
Rosedale Gdns BRAK RG12 76 A2
STHA RG19 97 L4
Rosedene La SHST GU47 87 K7
Rosefield Rd STA TW18 70 A2
Rose Gdns STWL/WRAY TW19 56 D6
Rose Hl BNFD RG42 63 J3
SL SL1 27 J1
Rosehill Pk CAV/SC RG4 127 J11
Rose Kiln La READ RG1 59 G1
WHIT RG2 59 G2
Rose La HEN RG9 23 K5
WAR/TWY RG10 23 J6
Roseleigh Cl MDHD SL6 25 J7
Rosemary Av EARL RG6 59 M5
Rosemary Dr TADY RG26 148 D4
Rosemary Gdns BLKW GU17 93 J1
NTHA RG18 98 A2
Rosemary La BLKW GU17 87 J8
EGH TW20 69 H8
Rosemead CHERT KT16 82 B4
Rosemead Av FELT TW13 57 M8
TILE/CALC RG31 125 M11
Rose Meadow CHOB/PIR GU24 91 G8
Rosemoor Gdns NWBY RG14 7 K1
The Rosery BNEND SL8 20 C3
Roses La WDSR SL4 52 D1
Rose St EWKG RG40 15 G6
Rosevale Dr WAR/TWY RG10 47 M6
Roseville Rd HYS/HAR UB3 43 J5
Rose Wk READ RG1 8 F7
SLN SL2 28 D6
Rosewood WODY RG5 60 D2
Rosewood Dr SHPTN TW17 82 F2
Rosewood Wy CHOB/PIR GU24 90 E8
Rosier Cl STHA RG19 98 B4
Rosken Gv SLN SL2 28 D3
Roslyn Rd WODY RG5 46 D8
Rossby WHIT RG2 59 L7
Ross Cl HYS/HAR UB3 42 F4
Rossendale Rd CAV/SC RG4 45 K3
Rosset Cl BRAK RG12 2 E9
Rossington Pl WHIT RG2 59 J6
Rossiter Cl DTCH/LGLY SL3 40 A3
Rosslea BFOR GU20 78 A8
Rosslyn Cl SUN TW16 71 L4
Rosslyn Pk WEY KT13 83 K8
Ross Rd MDHD SL6 4 D9
READ RG1 8 D3
Rostrever Gdns HYS/HAR UB3 43 G1
Rostrevor Gdns IVER SL0 30 F3
Rotary Wy STHA RG19 97 M5
Rother Cl SHST GU47 87 J6
Rotherfield Av WWKG RG41 14 C3
Rotherfield Cl THLE RG7 137 K6
Rotherfield Rd HEN RG9 127 R3
Rotherfield Wy CAV/SC RG4 45 G2
Rother Rd FARN GU14 93 L8
Rotherwick La HTWY RG27 150 H10
Rotherwick Rd TADY RG26 148 D3
Rothwell Gdns WODY RG5 46 F5
Rothwell Wk CAV/SC RG4 9 L1
Rotten Green Rd HTWY RG27 92 A8
Rotten Row Hl THLE RG7 135 P7
Roughgrove Copse BNFD RG42 63 H4
Rounce La CHOB/PIR GU24 90 D8
Roundabouts La WWKG RG41 61 K6
Round Cl YTLY GU46 92 F1
Round End NWBY RG14 141 R9
Roundfield THLE RG7 134 D12
Roundhead Rd THLE RG7 136 H7
Round Oak Rd WEY KT13 82 F8
Roundshead Dr BNFD RG42 3 K1
Rounds Hl BNFD RG42 * 2 E1
Roundway CBLY GU15 89 J8
EGH TW20 69 J3
Roundway Cl CBLY GU15 89 J8
Roundwood Av STKPK UB11 42 E1
Routh Ct EBED/NFELT TW14 57 K7
Routh La RDGW/BURGH RG30 137 Q4
Rowallan Cl CAV/SC RG4 127 K12
Rowan Av EGH TW20 69 J3
Rowan Cl CAV/SC RG4 126 F6
CBLY GU15 88 F6
WWKG RG41 14 A8
Rowan Dr CWTH RG45 75 J7
NWBY RG14 96 C1
WODY RG5 46 E6
Rowan Gdns IVER SL0 30 E3
Rowan Rd TADY RG26 148 E3
WDR/YW UB7 41 M4
Rowans Cl FARN GU14 93 L5
The Rowans SUN TW16 71 M3
Rowan Wy
RDGW/BURGH RG30 143 R2
SLN SL2 28 D6
Rowcroft Rd WHIT RG2 72 F7
Rowdell Dr WHIT RG2 59 K5
Rowe Ct RDGW/BURGH RG30 44 B6
Rowland Cl WDSR SL4 52 D2
Rowland Rd WGFD OX10 111 Q1
Rowland's Cl THLE RG7 143 L9
Rowland Wy ASHF TW15 71 J5
EARL RG6 59 M4
Row La CAV/SC RG4 127 L10
Rowley Cl BRAK RG12 3 M6
Rowley La DTCH/LGLY SL3 30 A3
Rowley Rd WHIT RG2 59 H2
Rowlheys Pl WDR/YW UB7 42 A3
Roxborough Wy MDHD SL6 35 H3
Roxburgh Cl CBLY GU15 95 J2
Roxford Cl SHPTN TW17 83
Roxwell Cl SL SL1 38
Royal Av TILE/CALC RG31 137
Royal Ct READ RG1 * 9
Royal Oak Cl YTLY GU46 86
Royal Oak Dr CWTH RG45 75
The Royal FRIM GU16 95
Royal Victoria Gdns ASC SL5 78
Royal Wy WHIT RG2 58
Roy Cl NTHA RG18 133
Roycroft La EWKG RG40 73
Royston Cl HEST TW5 43
RDGW/BURGH RG30 137
Royston Wy SL SL1 27
Rubastic Rd NWDGN UB2 43
Rubus Cl CHOB/PIR GU24 90
Ruby Cl SL SL1 38
WWKG RG41 61
Ruby Ct READ RG1 * 8
Rudd Hall Ri CBLY GU15 94
Ruddlesway WDSR SL4 37
Rudland Cl STHA RG19 97
Rudsworth Cl DTCH/LGLY SL3 40
Ruffle Cl WDR/YW UB7 42
Rufus Isaacs Rd CAV/SC RG4 45
Rugby Cl SHST GU47 87
Ruggles-Brise Rd ASHF TW15 70
Rugosa Rd CHOB/PIR GU24 90
Runnemede Rd EGH TW20 68
Runnymede Ct EGH TW20 69
Rupert Cl HEN RG9 22
Rupert Rd NWBY RG14 96
Rupert's La HEN RG9 22
Rupert Sq READ RG1 9
Rupert St READ RG1 9
Rupert Wk READ RG1 9
Ruscombe Gdns DTCH/LGLY SL3 39
Ruscombe La WAR/TWY RG10 47
Ruscombe Pk WAR/TWY RG10 47
Ruscombe Wy
EBED/NFELT TW14 57
Rushall Cl EARL RG6 59
Rusham Park Av EGH TW20 68
Rusham Rd EGH TW20 68
Rushbrook WODY RG5 46
Rushbrook Rd WODY RG5 46
Rushden Dr WHIT RG2 59
Rushes Md UX/CGN UB8 31
The Rushes MDHD SL6 5
MLW SL7 18
Rushey Wy EARL RG6 59
Rushington Av MDHD SL6 5
Rushmere Pl EGH TW20 68
Rushmoor Gdns
TILE/CALC RG31 137
Ruskin CAV/SC RG4 45
Ruskin Av EBED/NFELT TW14 57
Ruskin Ct CWTH RG45 * 86
Ruskin Rd STA TW18 69
Ruskin Wy WWKG RG41 61
Russell Cl BRAK RG12 76
Russell Ct BLKW GU17 93
MDHD SL6 5
Russell Dr STWL/WRAY TW19 56
Russell Gdns WDR/YW UB7 42
Russell Rd CAV/SC RG4 126
NWBY RG14 6
SHPTN TW17 83
Russell St READ RG1 8
WDSR SL4 13
Russell Wy WWKG RG41 61
Russet Cl CAV/SC RG4 126
STWL/WRAY TW19 55
Russet Gdns CBLY GU15 94
Russet Gld CAV/SC RG4 127
THLE RG7 143
Russet Rd MDHD SL6 35
Russett Gdns WAR/TWY RG10 33
Russet Wy KSCL RG20 121
Russington Rd SHPTN TW17 83
Russley Gn EWKG RG40 74
Rustington Cl EARL RG6 60
Ruston Wy ASC SL5 65
Rutherford Cl WDSR SL4 12
Rutherwyk Rd CHERT KT16 81
Rutland Av SL SL1 28
Rutland Ga MDHD SL6 4
Rutland Pl MDHD SL6 4
Rutland Rd HYS/HAR UB3 42
MDHD SL6 4
RDGW/BURGH RG30 * 44
Rutters Cl WDR/YW UB7 42
Ruxbury Rd CHERT KT16 81
Ryan Mt SHST GU47 87
Ryans Mt MLW SL7 18
Rycroft WDSR SL4 52
Rydal Av RDGW/BURGH RG30 125
Rydal Cl CBLY GU15 95
Rydal Dr NTHA RG18 97
Rydal Pl LTWR GU18 90
Rydal Wy EGH TW20 69
The Ryde STA TW18 70
Rydings WDSR SL4 52
Rye Cl BRAK RG12 3
FARN GU14 93
MDHD SL6 35
Rye Ct SL SL1 * 11
Ryecroft Cl WAR/TWY RG10 33
WODY RG5 46
Ryecroft Gdns BLKW GU17 93
Rye Gv BFOR GU20 90
LTWR GU18 90
Ryehurst La BNFD RG42 63
Ryeish La THLE RG7 145
Ryelands Pl WEY KT13 83
Ryemead La WDSR SL4 65
Ryhill Wy EARL RG6 59
Ryland Cl FELT TW13 71
Rylstone Cl MDHD SL6 35
Rylstone Rd
RDGW/BURGH RG30 44
Ryvers End DTCH/LGLY SL3 40
Ryvers Rd DTCH/LGLY SL3 40
Ryves Av YTLY GU46 92

S

Sackville St READ RG1 8
Saddleback Rd CBLY GU15 88
Saddlebrook Pk SUN TW16 71
Saddler Cnr SHST GU47 87
Saddlewood CBLY GU15 94
Sadlers Ct WWKG RG41 61
Sadlers End WWKG RG41 61
Sadler's La WWKG RG41 61
Sadlers Ms MDHD SL6 5
Sadlers Rd HUNG RG17 139
The Sadlers TILE/CALC RG31 137
Saffron Cl DTCH/LGLY SL3 39
EARL RG6 60
NWBY RG14 6
Saffron Rd BRAK RG12 2
Sage Cl EARL RG6 60
Sagecroft Rd NTHA RG18 97
Sage Rd TILE/CALC RG31 125
Sage Wk BNFD RG42 3
Sailing Club Rd BNEND SL8 20
St Adrian's Cl MDHD SL6 35
St Albans Av WEY KT13 83

Albans Cl *WDSR* SL4 13 K5
Alban's St *WDSR* SL4 13 K5
Andrews *BRAK* RG12 75 L3
Andrew's Av *WDSR* SL4 12 B8
Andrews Cl *CWTH* RG45 74 F8
Andrew's Cl *SHPTN* TW17 83 K1
STWL/WRAY TW19 54 E5
WDSR SL4 54 A5
Andrews Ct *READ* RG1 * 9 M7
Andrew's Crs *WDSR* SL4 12 A8
Andrew's Rd *CAV/SC* RG4 44 F2
HEN RG9 127 R2
Andrew's Wy *FRIM* GU16 94 F7
SL SL1 27 M8
Anne's Av *STWL/WRAY* TW19 56 D6
Anne's Cl *HEN* RG9 127 R1
Annes Dr *EWKG* RG40 63 G8
Annes Gld *BAGS* GU19 89 K3
Anne's Rd *CAV/SC* RG4 45 G4
Ann's Cl *CHERT* KT16 81 M2
Ann's Hill Rd *CHERT* KT16 81 J3
Ann's Rd *CHERT* KT16 81 L3
Anselms Rd *HYS/HAR* UB3 43 H2
Anthonys Cl *BNFD* RG42 2 D2
Anthony's Wy
EBED/NFELT TW14 57 M3
Barbara's Cl *TADY* RG26 150 B8
Barnabas Rd *CAV/SC* RG4 126 G12
WHIT RG2 59 M5
Bartholomews Rd *READ* RG1 45 M7
Benets Wy *CAV/SC* RG4 127 J12
Bernards Rd *DTCH/LGLY* SL3 39 L3
Birinus Rd *TILE/CALC* RG31 137 N5
Catherines *WEY* KT13 * 83 H7
Catherine's Cl *WWKG* RG41 61 G5
Catherine's Hl *THLE* RG7 143 N9
Catherines Rd *FRIM* GU16 95 G5
Catherines Wd *CBLY* GU15 94 C2
Chad's Rd *MDHD* SL6 35 K2
Christopher Rd *UX/CGN* UB8 31 M7
Christophers Gdns *ASC* SL5 65 K6
Clement Cl *UX/CGN* UB8 31 M7
Clements Cl *EARL* RG6 * 60 C5
aint-Cloud Wy *MDHD* SL6 5 H4
Columba's Cl *MDHD* SL6 35 K2
Cross Rd *FRIM* GU16 95 G7
Cuthbert's Cl *EGH* TW20 68 D4
David Cl *UX/CGN* UB8 31 M6
David's Cl *CAV/SC* RG4 44 F1
FARN GU14 93 M6
IVER SL0 30 F2
MDHD SL6 35 J2
David's Dr *EGH* TW20 68 C5
David's Rd *NWBY* RG14 6 C5
Dominic Cl *FARN* GU14 94 A6
Donats Pl *NWBY* RG14 6 E6
Dunstans Cl *HYS/HAR* UB3 43 H4
Dunstan's Rd *FELT* TW13 71 M1
Edwards Rd *EARL* RG6 * 46 A8
Edward's Rd *EARL* RG6 46 A8
Elizabeth Cl *WHIT* RG2 59 H7
Elmo Cl *SLN* SL2 28 F5
Elmo Crs *SLN* SL2 28 F5
George's Av *NWBY* RG14 6 B6
George's Cl *WDSR* SL4 38 A8
George's Crs *SL* SL1 27 M8
George's La *ASC* SL5 66 B8
Georges Rd *ADL/WDHM* KT15 82 C8
George's Rd *CBLY* GU15 88 D8
RDGW/BURGH RG30 44 B6
George's Ter
RDGW/BURGH RG30 44 B6
Giles Cl *READ* RG1 9 G8
Giles Ct *READ* RG1 9 G8
Helen Cl *UX/CGN* UB8 31 M7
Helens Crs *SHST* GU47 87 H6
Helier Cl *WWKG* RG41 74 B3
Hilda's Av *ASHF* TW15 70 E3
Ives Cl *THLE* RG7 136 H7
Ives Rd *MDHD* SL6 5 J5
James Cl *GOR/PANG* RG8 124 G8
TADY RG26 150 B9
WAR/TWY RG10 47 L1
James Ctyd *MLW* SL7 * 19 G6
James Ga *ASC* SL5 78 F4
James Ms *WEY* KT13 83 H8
James Pl *SL* SL1 * 27 L7
James Rd *EWKG* RG40 73 L6
James Wk *DTCH/LGLY* SL3 41 G2
John Cl *TADY* RG26 150 A8
John's Cl *UX/CGN* UB8 * 31 K2
Johns Cl *WODY* RG5 46 F6
Johns Ct *EGH* TW20 69 G3
Johns Dr *WDSR* SL4 12 B7
Johns Hl *READ* RG1 * 9 K7
John's Hl *READ* RG1 9 K7
John's Rd *ASC* SL5 65 M5
CAV/SC RG4 9 J1
NWBY RG14 6 E7
Johns Rd *READ* RG1 * 9 K7
John's Rd *READ* RG1 9 K7
SHST GU47 87 H7
Johns Rd *SLN* SL2 11 J3
John's Rd *STHA* RG19 97 L3
THLE RG7 143 Q9
UX/CGN UB8 31 K3
Johns Rd *WDSR* SL4 12 D7
Johns St *READ* RG1 * 9 K7
John's St *READ* RG1 9 K6
John's Wy *CHERT* KT16 82 A5
Jude's Cl *EGH* TW20 68 C3
Jude's Rd *EGH* TW20 68 C2
Katherine's Rd *HEN* RG9 127 R3
Laurence Cl *UX/CGN* UB8 31 L6
Laurence Wy *SL* SL1 11 J8
Lawrence Sq *HUNG* RG17 138 H1
Leger Ct *NWBY* RG14 6 B1
Leonard's Av *WDSR* SL4 13 H7
Leonard's Hl *WDSR* SL4 52 D3
Leonard's Rd *WDSR* SL4 13 H8
WDSR SL4 52 C5
Leonards Wk *DTCH/LGLY* SL3 41 H3
Luke Cl *UX/CGN* UB8 31 M7
Luke's Rd *MDHD* SL6 5 G4
WDSR SL4 54 A5
Lukes Wy *CAV/SC* RG4 45 H2
Margarets Av *ASHF* TW15 71 H2
Margaret's Cl *IVER* SL0 30 F3
Margaret's Rd *MDHD* SL6 25 J7
Marks Cl *STHA* RG19 97 L3
TADY RG26 150 A8
Mark's Crs *MDHD* SL6 25 K7
Mark's Pl *WDSR* SL4 13 H7
Mark's Rd *BNFD* RG42 63 J5
HEN RG9 127 R2
MDHD SL6 4 D4
WDSR SL4 13 G7
Martin Cl *UX/CGN* UB8 31 M7
Martins Cl *EARL* RG6 60 C5
Martin's Cl *WDR/YW* UB7 41 L3
Martin's Ct *ASHF* TW15 70 C3
Marys *WEY* KT13 * 83 K7
Mary's Av *GOR/PANG* RG8 125 N9
STWL/WRAY TW19 56 D6
TADY RG26 150 B8
Mary's Butts *READ* RG1 8 F6
Mary's Cl *HEN* RG9 127 N2
MDHD SL6 5 J4
Marys Cl *SHST* GU47 87 J6
Mary's Ct *TADY* RG26 150 B8
Mary's Crs *STWL/WRAY* TW19 56 D6
St Mary's Dr *EBED/NFELT* TW14 57 J6
St Mary's Gdns *BAGS* GU19 89 L3
St Marys Hl *ASC* SL5 78 C2
St Marys La *WDSR* SL4 65 K1
St Marys Paddock
NTHA RG18 * 133 Q9
St Mary's Pl *NWBY* RG14 6 F2
St Mary's Rd *ASC* SL5 78 B3
CBLY GU15 88 C8
DTCH/LGLY SL3 40 A2
NWBY RG14 6 F2
THLE RG7 143 Q8
WEY KT13 83 K8
WWKG RG41 61 H5
St Marys Wk *MDHD* SL6 5 H4
St Mary's Wy *THLE* RG7 143 R3
St Matthew Cl *UX/CGN* UB8 31 M7
St Michael's Cl *HUNG* RG17 117 J4
St Michael's Ct *SLN* SL2 27 M5
St Michaels Ct *WAR/TWY* RG10 33 G8
St Michaels La *THLE* RG7 143 M1
St Michaels Rd *ASHF* TW15 71 G3
CBLY GU15 * 94 B1
St Michael's Rd *FARN* GU14 94 B8
NWBY RG14 6 C6
RDGW/BURGH RG30 137 P2
SHST GU47 86 F6
St Nazaire Cl *EGH* TW20 * 69 J3
St Neot's Rd *HTWY* RG27 84 F7
St Nicholas Cl *UX/CGN* UB8 31 M7
St Nicholas Dr *SHPTN* TW17 83 G4
St Nicholas' Rd *NWBY* RG14 6 D5
St Olave's Cl *STA* TW18 69 M5
St Patrick's Av *WAR/TWY* RG10 47 G1
St Patrick's Br *WAR/TWY* RG10 32 B8
St Patrick's Cl *MDHD* SL6 35 J2
St Paul Cl *UX/CGN* UB8 31 M6
St Pauls Av *SLN* SL2 11 J3
St Paul's Cl *ADL/WDHM* KT15 82 A8
ASHF TW15 71 J3
St Pauls Cl *HYS/HAR* UB3 42 F5
St Paul's Ct *READ* RG1 8 E9
St Paul's Ga *WWKG* RG41 14 D4
St Pauls Ms *WHIT* RG2 * 59 H6
St Paul's Rd *STA* TW18 69 K3
St Peters *CHERT* KT16 * 81 J7
St Peter's Av *CAV/SC* RG4 44 E2
St Peter's Cl *SL* SL1 27 K5
STA TW18 69 M4
St Peters Cl *STHA* RG19 101 M4
St Peter's Cl *WDSR* SL4 54 A4
St Peter's Gdns *YTLY* GU46 86 D8
St Peter's Hl *CAV/SC* RG4 44 F3
St Peter's Rd *EARL* RG6 46 A8
MDHD SL6 25 M4
UX/CGN UB8 31 M6
St Peter St *MLW* SL7 19 G5
St Peter's Wy *ADL/WDHM* KT15 82 A7
CHERT KT16 81 L8
FRIM GU16 94 F7
St Peters Wy *HYS/HAR* UB3 42 F5
St Pinnock Av *STA* TW18 70 A6
St Richards Rd *NWBY* RG14 7 H1
St Ronans Rd
RDGW/BURGH RG30 44 B6
St Saviour's Rd *READ* RG1 58 F1
St Saviours Ter *READ* RG1 8 D9
St Sebastian's Cl *EWKG* RG40 74 E6
St Stephens Cl *CAV/SC* RG4 8 F1
St Stephens Ct *READ* RG1 * 9 M6
St Stephen's Rd *WDR/YW* UB7 41 M1
St Swithins Cl *KSCL* RG20 130 H6
St Theresa's Rd
EBED/NFELT TW14 57 M3
St Thomas Wk *DTCH/LGLY* SL3 40 F7
Salamanca *CWTH* RG45 86 E1
Salcombe Dr *EARL* RG6 60 B2
Salcombe Rd *ASHF* TW15 70 E2
NWBY RG14 6 A7
WHIT RG2 59 K3
Saleby Cl *EARL* RG6 60 E4
Sale Garden Cots *EWKG* RG40 15 G7
Salford Cl *WHIT* RG2 59 J7
Salisbury Av *SLN* SL2 28 E5
Salisbury Cl *WWKG* RG41 74 A4
Salisbury Rd *BLKW* GU17 93 J1
HUNG RG17 138 G2
MARL SN8 138 B11
RDGW/BURGH RG30 8 A4
UX/CGN UB8 31 K3
Salix Gdns *WAR/TWY* RG10 32 F8
Salmon Cl *THLE* RG7 145 M4
Salmond Rd *WHIT* RG2 59 J8
Salters Cl *MDHD* SL6 5 K4
Saltersgate Cl *EARL* RG6 60 D4
Salters Heath Rd *TADY* RG26 148 F12
Salters' Rd *MDHD* SL6 5 K4
Salters Rw *FLKWH/TG* HP10 * 21 J2
Salt Hill Av *SL* SL1 10 B4
Salt Hill Dr *SL* SL1 10 B4
Salt Hill Wy *SL* SL1 10 B4
Saltire Gdns *BNFD* RG42 2 C2
Salwey Cl *BRAK* RG12 76 B3
Samarkand Cl *CBLY* GU15 95 H2
Samian Pl *BNFD* RG42 63 L5
Sampage Cl *WHIT* RG2 59 J8
Sampson Pk *BNFD* RG42 63 K6
Sampsons Gn *SLN* SL2 28 B4
Sanctuary Cl
RDGW/BURGH RG30 137 Q2
Sanctuary Rd *HTHAIR* TW6 57 G5
Sandalwood Av *CHERT* KT16 81 K7
Sandcroft Rd *CAV/SC* RG4 126 E12
Sandell's Av *ASHF* TW15 71 J2
Sanden Cl *HUNG* RG17 138 G1
Sandford Cl *GOR/PANG* RG8 113 K10
Sandford Down *BRAK* RG12 76 F2
Sandford Dr *WODY* RG5 46 F5
Sandford La *WAR/TWY* RG10 47 J8
WODY RG5 47 H7
Sandford Rd *TADY* RG26 148 C2
Sandgate Av
RDGW/BURGH RG30 125 R12
Sand Hl *FARN* GU14 94 B7
Sandhills *WAR/TWY* RG10 33 M3
Sandhills Ct *VW* GU25 80 E2
Sandhills La *VW* GU25 80 E2
Sandhurst La *BLKW* GU17 87 H8
Sandhurst Rd *CWTH* RG45 87 H3
EWKG RG40 74 B6
YTLY GU46 86 E8
Sandisplatt Rd *MDHD* SL6 25 J8
Sandleford Cl *WHIT* RG2 59 J8
Sandleford La *STHA* RG19 96 D8
Sandleford Lodge Pk
STHA RG19 96 D8
Sandleford Pde *NWBY* RG14 * 96 C7
Sandlers End *SLN* SL2 28 D5
Sandow Crs *HYS/HAR* UB3 43 H3
Sandown Av *TILE/CALC* RG31 137 M6
Sandown Cl *BLKW* GU17 93 K1
HEST TW5 43 J8
Sandown Dr *FRIM* GU16 94 D4
Sandown Rd *SLN* SL2 28 B6
Sandown Wy *NWBY* RG14 7 J8
Sandpipers Pl *MDHD* SL6 20 A8
Sandpit Hl *KSCL* RG20 141 Q11
Sandpit La *CAV/SC* RG4 127 L10
THLE RG7 84 B1
Sandringham Ct *SL* SL1 27 M7
Sandringham Dr *ASHF* TW15 70 D2
Sandringham Gdns *HEST* TW5 43 J8
Sandringham Rd *HTHAIR* TW6 56 E4
MDHD SL6 26 A4
Sandringham Wy *FRIM* GU16 94 F6
TILE/CALC RG31 137 M6
Sands Farm Dr *SL* SL1 27 L5
Sandstone Cl *WWKG* RG41 61 J5
Sandy Cl *NTHA* RG18 133 M6
Sandy Dr *EBED/NFELT* TW14 57 L7
Sandygate Cl *MLW* SL7 18 F3
Sandygate Rd *MLW* SL7 18 F3
Sandy La *ASC* SL5 65 J6
ASC SL5 79 G2
BNFD RG42 3 G1
BRAK RG12 3 G2
CBLY GU15 88 E8
CHOB/PIR GU24 91 L4
FARN GU14 93 J8
NTHA RG18 133 M6
SHST GU47 86 F5
TADY RG26 148 F2
VW GU25 80 E2
WGFD OX10 111 N1
WWKG RG41 73 J2
Sandy Md *MDHD* SL6 36 E5
Sandy Wy *WOT/HER* KT12 83 M5
Sargeant Cl *UX/CGN* UB8 31 M4
Sargood Cl *STHA* RG19 98 A4
Sarisbury Cl *TADY* RG26 148 C2
Sarsby Dr *STWL/WRAY* TW19 55 G8
Sarum *BRAK* RG12 75 L5
Sarum Complex *UX/CGN* UB8 * 31 K3
Sarum Crs *EWKG* RG40 15 H3
Sarum Gn *WEY* KT13 83 L7
Sarum Rd *TADY* RG26 148 C1
Saturn Cl *WWKG* RG41 61 L8
Saturn Cft *BNFD* RG42 65 H4
Satwell Cl *HEN* RG9 114 G11
Saunders Cl *WAR/TWY* RG10 47 M4
Saunders Ct *GOR/PANG* RG8 * 125 N9
Saunders Gdn *TADY* RG26 148 D2
Saunton Av *HYS/HAR* UB3 43 H7
Saunton Gdns *FARN* GU14 94 A8
Savera Cl *NWDGN* UB2 43 L3
Savernake Cl
RDGW/BURGH RG30 137 R3
Savernake Wy *BRAK* RG12 76 F2
Saville Crs *ASHF* TW15 71 K4
Saville Gdns *CBLY* GU15 95 H1
Savill Ms *EGH* TW20 68 D4
Savill Wy *MLW* SL7 19 H4
Savory Wk *BNFD* RG42 63 J4
Savoy Av *HYS/HAR* UB3 43 G5
Savoy Ct *MDHD* SL6 26 B5
Savoy Gv *BLKW* GU17 93 K3
Sawmill Rd *NTHA* RG18 133 N6
Sawpit Rd *WAR/TWY* RG10 47 L7
Sawtry Cl *EARL* RG6 60 E4
Sawyers Cl *MDHD* SL6 35 J4
Sawyer's Cl *WDSR* SL4 12 A4
Sawyers Crs *MDHD* SL6 35 H4
Sawyers Ley *THLE* RG7 144 B6
Saxby Cl *THLE* RG7 143 R3
Saxon Cl *DTCH/LGLY* SL3 40 B2
Saxon Ct *STHA* RG19 97 J3
Saxon Dr *BNFD* RG42 64 F6
Saxon Gdns *MDHD* SL6 26 F6
Saxon Pl *GOR/PANG* RG8 124 H8
Saxon Rd *ASHF* TW15 71 K4
Saxons Acre *KSCL* RG20 119 P3
Saxon Wy *WDR/YW* UB7 41 L6
WDSR SL4 54 B5
Saxony Wy *YTLY* GU46 92 C2
Sayers Cl *FRIM* GU16 94 E7
NWBY RG14 96 D6
Scafell Cl *TILE/CALC* RG31 125 M12
Scafell Rd *SLN* SL2 28 B6
Scampton Rd
STWL/WRAY TW19 56 F5
Scania Wk *BNFD* RG42 65 H4
Scarborough Rd *HTHAIR* TW6 57 J5
Scarborough Wy *SL* SL1 38 D2
Scarlet Oaks *CBLY* GU15 94 E3
Scarletts La *WAR/TWY* RG10 33 K6
Scholars Cl *CAV/SC* RG4 44 F4
HUNG RG17 118 E11
Scholars Wk *DTCH/LGLY* SL3 40 C2
School Hl *CWTH* RG45 87 K2
SHST GU47 87 G5
THLE RG7 99 H3
WAR/TWY RG10 32 F5
School La *ADL/WDHM* KT15 82 A8
ASC SL5 65 K6
BAGS GU19 89 K4
BFOR GU20 90 D2
CAV/SC RG4 8 F1
CAV/SC RG4 45 H1
EGH TW20 69 G3
HEN RG9 113 R6
HUNG RG17 118 B8
KSCL RG20 131 P6
MDHD SL6 19 K7
MDHD SL6 20 C7
MDHD SL6 26 A5
MDHD SL6 34 D2
MLW SL7 17 K8
MLW SL7 19 L1
SHPTN TW17 83 H3
SLN SL2 11 G2
SLN SL2 29 K1
THLE RG7 143 P4
THLE RG7 145 Q11
THLE RG7 149 K1
WAR/TWY RG10 32 F4
YTLY GU46 86 B8
School Rd *ASC* SL5 78 D2
ASHF TW15 71 H4
BFOR GU20 78 A8
EWKG RG40 15 J6
KSCL RG20 122 A2
KSCL RG20 132 F1
RDGW/BURGH RG30 137 N12
THLE RG7 142 H5
THLE RG7 145 Q10
TILE/CALC RG31 137 P2
WAR/TWY RG10 47 M7
WAR/TWY RG10 47 F3
WDR/YW UB7 41 M6
WWKG RG41 72 F4
School Ter *READ* RG1 9 M5
Schroder Ct *EGH* TW20 68 B3
Scobell Cl *WHIT* RG2 145 P1
Scotland Hl *SHST* GU47 87 G6
Scotlands Dr *SLN* SL2 28 D1
Scots Cl *STWL/WRAY* TW19 56 D7
Scots Dr *WWKG* RG41 61 L6
Scottalls La *NTHA* RG18 122 B9
Scott Cl *CAV/SC* RG4 45 G1
WDR/YW UB7 42 B4
WODY RG5 47 G7
Scott Gdns *HEST* TW5 43 M7
Scotts Av *SUN* TW16 71 L5
Scott's Ct *FARN* GU14 94 B7
Scott's Grove Cl
CHOB/PIR GU24 91 K8
Scotts Grove Rd
CHOB/PIR GU24 91 K8
Scotts Ms *ASC* SL5 65 H6
Scotts Rd *NWDGN* UB2 43 L3
Scotts Wy *SUN* TW16 71 L5
Scott Ter *BRAK* RG12 3 M2
Scours La *RDGW/BURGH* RG30 44 B5
Scratchface La *THLE* RG7 135 M3
Scrivens Md *STHA* RG19 98 B3
Scutley La *BFOR* GU20 90 E3
Scylla Crs *HTHAIR* TW6 57 H6
Scylla Rd *HTHAIR* TW6 57 H5
Seacourt Rd *DTCH/LGLY* SL3 40 D4
Seaford Gdns *WODY* RG5 46 E8
Seaford Rd *EWKG* RG40 15 J6
HTHAIR TW6 56 D4
Sealand Rd *HTHAIR* TW6 57 G5
Searing Wy *TADY* RG26 148 C1
Searles Farm La
RDGW/BURGH RG30 58 B5
Seaton Dr *ASHF* TW15 56 E8
Seaton Gdns *WHIT* RG2 59 J4
Seaton Rd *CBLY* GU15 94 B1
HYS/HAR UB3 42 F4
Second Av *HYS/HAR* UB3 43 H1
THLE RG7 142 E12
TILE/CALC RG31 137 M4
Second Crs *SL* SL1 28 E6
Second St East *STHA* RG19 101 J1
Second St West *KSCL* RG20 101 G2
STHA RG19 101 J2
Seddon Hl *BNFD* RG42 64 B5
Sedgefield Cl *CAV/SC* RG4 126 F4
Sedgefield Rd *NWBY* RG14 7 J9
Sedge Gv *NTHA* RG18 98 A2
Sedgemoor *FARN* GU14 94 B7
Sedgewell Rd *CAV/SC* RG4 126 F5
Seebys Oak *SHST* GU47 87 K8
Sefton Cl *CHOB/PIR* GU24 90 F8
SLN SL2 29 H2
Sefton Paddock *SLN* SL2 29 J1
Sefton Pk *SLN* SL2 * 29 J1
Sefton Wy *UX/CGN* UB8 31 L7
Segsbury Gv *BRAK* RG12 3 M8
Selborne Cl *BLKW* GU17 87 J8
Selborne Ct *READ* RG1 9 J6
Selborne Gdns
RDGW/BURGH RG30 44 A5
Selby Rd *ASHF* TW15 71 J4
Selcourt Cl *WODY* RG5 46 D6
Sellafield Wy *EARL* RG6 60 C4
Selsdon Av *WODY* RG5 46 F6
Selsey Wy *EARL* RG6 60 B6
Selva Ct *READ* RG1 9 J9
Selwood Cl *STWL/WRAY* TW19 * 56 C5
Selwood Gdns
STWL/WRAY TW19 56 C5
Selwyn Cl *WDSR* SL4 52 D1
Selwyn Dr *YTLY* GU46 86 B8
Sen Cl *BNFD* RG42 64 C4
Send Rd *CAV/SC* RG4 9 K1
Setley Wy *BRAK* RG12 64 F8
Seton Dr *TILE/CALC* RG31 137 R5
Setter Combe *BNFD* RG42 64 D4
The Sett *YTLY* GU46 92 B1
Sevenoaks Dr *THLE* RG7 145 L3
Sevenoaks Rd *EARL* RG6 60 B3
Seventh Av *HYS/HAR* UB3 43 J1
TILE/CALC RG31 * 137 M4
Seventh St *STHA* RG19 101 H1
Severn Cl *NTHA* RG18 97 K1
SHST GU47 87 J6
Severn Crs *DTCH/LGLY* SL3 40 D5
Severn Rd *DID* OX11 108 H1
FARN GU14 93 L8
Severn Wy
RDGW/BURGH RG30 137 R4
Sewell Av *WWKG* RG41 14 C1
Sewell Cl *NTHA* RG18 133 Q9
Seymour Av *WHIT* RG2 145 Q1
Seymour Cl *MDHD* SL6 35 K3
Seymour Court La *MLW* SL7 18 D1
Seymour Court Rd *MLW* SL7 18 E2
Seymour Dr *CBLY* GU15 89 H6
Seymour Park Rd *MLW* SL7 18 F3
Seymour Pln *MLW* SL7 18 E1
Seymour Rd *SL* SL1 10 C6
Seymour Wy *SUN* TW16 71 L4
Shackleton Rd *SL* SL1 11 G3
Shackleton Wy *WODY* RG5 47 G7
Shaftesbury Cl *BRAK* RG12 76 D2
Shaftesbury Ct *EWKG* RG40 15 J3
Shaftesbury Crs *STA* TW18 70 D5
Shaftesbury Mt *BLKW* GU17 93 J3
Shaftesbury Rd
RDGW/BURGH RG30 44 B6
Shaggy Calf La *SLN* SL2 11 H2
Shakespeare Cl *CAV/SC* RG4 45 K1
Shakespeare Rd
ADL/WDHM KT15 82 D8
NTHA RG18 97 L2
Shakespeare Wy *BNFD* RG42 3 M2
Shalbourne Cl *HUNG* RG17 138 F1
Shalbourne Ri *CBLY* GU15 94 D1
Shamrock Cl *FRIM* GU16 94 D6
Shannon Cl *NWDGN* UB2 43 M5
Sharman Rw *DTCH/LGLY* SL3 40 B5
Sharney Av *DTCH/LGLY* SL3 40 D3
Sharnwood Dr
TILE/CALC RG31 137 R5
Sharpethorpe Cl *EARL* RG6 60 B5
Shaw Br *NWBY* RG14 * 96 D1
Shaw Farm Rd *NWBY* RG14 96 D1
Shaw Gdns *DTCH/LGLY* SL3 40 B5
Shaw Hl *NWBY* RG14 96 D1
Shaw La *TADY* RG26 148 B4
Shaw Pk *CWTH* RG45 87 H3
Shaw Rd *NWBY* RG14 7 G1
READ RG1 8 D9
The Shaw *MDHD* SL6 26 A1
Sheehy Wy *SLN* SL2 11 M2
Sheepcote Cl *HEST* TW5 43 J7
Sheepcote La *MDHD* SL6 50 C2
SL SL1 21 H5
Sheepcote Rd *WDSR* SL4 38 C5
WDSR SL4 52 E1
Sheepdown *KSCL* RG20 109 L11
Sheepdrove Rd *HUNG* RG17 117 L3
Sheep Fair Wy *HUNG* RG17 117 K4
Sheephouse Rd *MDHD* SL6 26 D3
Sheephouse Wy *KSCL* RG20 119 L8
Sheep Leaze La *KSCL* RG20 120 B3
Sheep Wk *CAV/SC* RG4 45 H2
Sheepwalk *SHPTN* TW17 82 F3
Sheepwash La *KSCL* RG20 100 C4
TADY RG26 148 B12
Sheepways La *CAV/SC* RG4 126 B10
Sheerlands Rd *EWKG* RG40 72 E8
WHIT RG2 72 F6
Sheet St *WDSR* SL4 13 K6
Sheet Street Rd *WDSR* SL4 66 E1
Sheffield Rd *HTHAIR* TW6 57 J5
SL SL1 28 E7
Sheffield Wy *HTHAIR* TW6 57 K4
Shefford Crs *EWKG* RG40 15 J2
Shelgate Wk *WODY* RG5 46 C7
Shelley Av *BRAK* RG12 3 M4
Shelley Cl *DTCH/LGLY* SL3 40 C5
MLW SL7 17 M7
WODY RG5 * 60 E2
Shelley Ct *CBLY* GU15 94 C1
Shelley Crs *HEST* TW5 43 M8
Shelley Rd *MLW* SL7 19 H3
NTHA RG18 97 L2
Shelley Wk *YTLY* GU46 92 B1
Shellfield Cl *STWL/WRAY* TW19 56 A4
Shelly Ri *FARN* GU14 93 M8
Shelson Av *FELT* TW13 71 M1
Shelson Pde *FELT* TW13 * 71 M1
Shenstone Cl *EWKG* RG40 74 A6
Shenstone Dr *SL* SL1 27 M5
Shenstone Pk *ASC* SL5 78 E1
Shenstone Rd *WHIT* RG2 59 H2
Shepherds Av *EARL* RG6 46 B6
Shepherds Cha *BAGS* GU19 89 L4
Shepherds Cl *MDHD* SL6 24 B3
SHPTN TW17 83 H3
UX/CGN UB8 * 31 L5
Shepherd's Gn *HEN* RG9 114 G11
Shepherds Hl *BRAK* RG12 3 H2
EARL RG6 46 B6
KSCL RG20 122 A3
Shepherd's House La
EARL RG6 46 A6
Shepherds La *BFOR* GU20 91 G1
BNFD RG42 2 E1
CAV/SC RG4 126 D12
MDHD SL6 23 M2
Shepherds Mt *KSCL* RG20 122 A3
Shepherds Ri *KSCL* RG20 122 A2
Shepherds Wk *FARN* GU14 93 L7
Shepherds Wy *CWTH* RG45 86 E2
Shepiston La *HYS/HAR* UB3 42 D4
Shepley Dr *ASC* SL5 79 K3
RDGW/BURGH RG30 58 C2
Shepley End *ASC* SL5 79 J2
Shepperton Court Dr
SHPTN TW17 83 H2
Shepperton Marina
SHPTN TW17 * 83 L3
Shepperton Rd *STA* TW18 82 D1
Shepperton Studios
SHPTN TW17 * 70 F8
Sheraton Cl *BLKW* GU17 93 L2
Sheraton Dr *TILE/CALC* RG31 137 M1
Sherborne Cl *DTCH/LGLY* SL3 41 G8
Sherborne Rd
EBED/NFELT TW14 57 K6
Sherbourne Dr *ASC* SL5 79 K2
MDHD SL6 35 L3
WDSR SL4 52 F3
WODY RG5 46 F6
Sherbourne Gdns *SHPTN* TW17 83 L4
Sherfield Cl *WHIT* RG2 59 K2
Sherfield Dr *WHIT* RG2 59 K2
Sherfield Rd *TADY* RG26 149 R7
Shergold Wy *MDHD* SL6 20 B8
Sheridan Av *CAV/SC* RG4 44 F2
Sheridan Crs *TADY* RG26 148 A1
Sheridan Gra *ASC* SL5 79 G3
Sheridan Rd *FRIM* GU16 94 D6
Sheridan Wy *WWKG* RG41 73 L1
Sherington Cl *FARN* GU14 94 B8
Sherlock Lea *HTWY* RG27 85 L7
Sherman Pl *READ* RG1 9 G8
Sherman Rd *READ* RG1 9 G8
SL SL1 29 G6
Sherrardmead *NWBY* RG14 96 D1
Sherring Cl *BNFD* RG42 64 C5
Sherwin Crs *FARN* GU14 94 B6
Sherwood Cl *BRAK* RG12 65 G7
DTCH/LGLY SL3 40 A3
Sherwood Dr *MDHD* SL6 25 J8
Sherwood Gdns *HEN* RG9 127 Q2
Sherwood Ri *GOR/PANG* RG8 125 M10
Sherwood Rd *WWKG* RG41 61 J4
Sherwood St
RDGW/BURGH RG30 44 C6
Shewens Rd *WEY* KT13 83 K8
Shield Rd *ASHF* TW15 71 J2
Shifford Crs *MDHD* SL6 26 A4
Shildon Cl *CBLY* GU15 95 K3
Shilling Cl *RDGW/BURGH* RG30 44 A8
Shillingridge Pk *MLW* SL7 18 A1
Shinfield Pk *WHIT* RG2 * 59 L7
Shinfield Ri *WHIT* RG2 59 L5
Shinfield Rd *WHIT* RG2 59 L2
Ship Aly *FARN* GU14 94 C8
Shiplake Bottom *HEN* RG9 126 E3
Ship La *FARN* GU14 94 C8
Shipley Cl *WODY* RG5 47 G5
Shipton Cl *TILE/CALC* RG31 125 N12
Ship Yd *WEY* KT13 83 G7
Shire Cl *BAGS* GU19 89 L4
Shire's Head Cl
RDGW/BURGH RG30 44 D8
The Shires *WWKG* RG41 73 K2
Shires Wy *YTLY* GU46 86 D6
Shirley Av *WDSR* SL4 12 B6
WHIT RG2 59 J7
Shirley Rd *MDHD* SL6 4 A9
Shirville Hl *GOR/PANG* RG8 112 H11
Shoesmith Ct *READ* RG1 8 F5
Shooter's Hl *GOR/PANG* RG8 124 D6
Shooters Wy *WHIT* RG2 58 F6
Shop La *KSCL* RG20 119 R10
NWBY RG14 132 F12
Shoppenhanger's Rd *MDHD* SL6 4 F8
Shop Rd *WDSR* SL4 * 37 L7
Shoreham Ri *SLN* SL2 27 M5
Shoreham Rd (East)
HTHAIR TW6 56 E4
Shoreham Rd (West)
HTHAIR TW6 56 E4
Shorland Oaks *BNFD* RG42 64 C4
Shortfern *SLN* SL2 29 L7
Shortheath La *THLE* RG7 143 M3
Shortlands *HYS/HAR* UB3 42 F6
Shortlands Hl *WGFD* OX10 111 L6
Short La *STWL/WRAY* TW19 56 F6
Short Rd *HTHAIR* TW6 56 E5
Short St *CAV/SC* RG4 45 H4
GOR/PANG RG8 124 H9
READ RG1 9 H9
The Short *GOR/PANG* RG8 125 P9
Shortwood Av *STA* TW18 70 B1
Shottesbrooke Pk *MDHD* SL6 * 34 E8
Showers Wy *HYS/HAR* UB3 43 J1
Shrewsbury Rd *HTHAIR* TW6 57 J5
Shrewsbury Ter *NWBY* RG14 * 6 B7
Shrivenham Cl *SHST* GU47 87 K6
Shropshire Gdns *BNFD* RG42 64 F5
Shrubbs Hl *CHOB/PIR* GU24 91 J4
Shrubbs Hill La *ASC* SL5 79 J3
Shrubland Dr
RDGW/BURGH RG30 58 A2
Shrublands Dr *LTWR* GU18 90 B6
Shute End *EWKG* RG40 14 F6
Shyshack La *TADY* RG26 148 A1
Sibley Park Rd *EARL* RG6 60 A4
Sibson *EARL* RG6 60 C4
Sidbury Cl *ASC* SL5 79 G2
Sidestrand Rd *NWBY* RG14 141 R6
The Sidings *STA* TW18 70 B2
Sidlaws Rd *FARN* GU14 93 K7
Sidmouth Ct *READ* RG1 9 J7
Sidmouth Grange Cl *EARL* RG6 46 B7
Sidmouth Grange Rd *EARL* RG6 46 B7
Sidmouth St *READ* RG1 9 J6
Sidney Cl *UX/CGN* UB8 31 L1
Sidney Rd *STA* TW18 70 A2
WDSR SL4 52 C2
Silbury Cl *TILE/CALC* RG31 137 M6
Silchester Pl *THLE* RG7 145 L1
Silchester Rd
RDGW/BURGH RG30 58 C2
TADY RG26 148 D1
TADY RG26 149 J5

THLE RG7 142 H12
Silco Dr MDHD SL6 4 F7
Silverbeck Wy
STWL/WRAY TW19 56 A4
Silver Birches WWKG RG41 73 J3
Silver Cl MDHD SL6 35 J1
Silverdale Av WOT/HER KT12 83 M6
Silverdale Ct STA TW18 * 70 B3
Silverdale Gdns HYS/HAR UB3 43 J2
Silverdale Rd EARL RG6 60 B3
HYS/HAR UB3 43 J2
TADY RG26 148 D1
WAR/TWY RG10 32 F5
Silver Dr FRIM GU16 95 J3
Silver Fox Crs WODY RG5 46 D8
Silverglades YTLY GU46 92 C2
Silver Hl SHST GU47 87 L6
Silverlands Cl CHERT KT16 * 81 K7
Silver La THLE RG7 143 J6
Silver St READ RG1 9 H8
Silverthorne Dr CAV/SC RG4 126 D12
Silvertrees Dr MDHD SL6 35 J1
Silverwood Dr CBLY GU15 89 G7
Silwood BRAK RG12 75 L5
Silwood Cl ASC SL5 66 D7
Silwood Pk ASC SL5 * 66 D7
Silwood Rd ASC SL5 78 F1
Simkins Cl BNFD RG42 65 H4
Simmonds Cl BNFD RG42 63 L6
Simmonds St READ RG1 8 F7
Simmons Cl DTCH/LGLY SL3 * 40 C4
Simmons Fld NTHA RG18 98 B2
Simmons Flds WAR/TWY RG10 47 H3
Simmons Pl STA TW18 69 L3
Simmons Rd HEN RG9 115 R11
Simms Farm La THLE RG7 143 P9
Simons Cl TILE/CALC RG31 125 N10
Simon's La WWKG RG41 61 K6
Simons Wk EGH TW20 68 C5
Simplemarsh Rd
ADL/WDHM KT15 82 A8
Simpson Cl MDHD SL6 5 L3
Simpsons Wy SL SL1 10 E4
Sims Cl TADY RG26 150 B8
Sinclair Rd WDSR SL4 13 H9
Sindle Cl WWKG RG41 61 H4
Sindlesham Rd WHIT RG2 72 E3
Sine Cl FARN GU14 94 B6
Singers Cl HEN RG9 22 A6
Singers La HEN RG9 22 A5
Singret Pl UX/CGN UB8 * 31 L5
Sinhurst Rd CBLY GU15 94 B2
Sipson Cl WDR/YW UB7 42 C6
Sipson La HYS/HAR UB3 42 E6
WDR/YW UB7 42 D6
Sipson Rd WDR/YW UB7 42 B3
Sipson Wy WDR/YW UB7 42 C7
Sirius Cl WWKG RG41 14 A5
WWKG RG41 14 A5
Sir Robert Ms DTCH/LGLY SL3 40 C5
Six Acre La HUNG RG17 138 D8
Sixth Av HYS/HAR UB3 43 H1
TILE/CALC RG31 137 M4
Sixth St STHA RG19 101 H1
Skarries Vw CAV/SC RG4 126 D10
Skates La TADY RG26 148 F5
Skeffling Cl EARL RG6 60 E4
Skelmerdale Wy EARL RG6 60 E3
Skelton Flds BNFD RG42 64 C5
Skerritt Wy GOR/PANG RG8 125 P10
Skillman Dr STHA RG19 98 B3
Skilton Rd TILE/CALC RG31 125 N11
Skimpedhill La BRAK RG12 2 D5
Skinner's Green La KSCL RG20 141 K8
KSCL RG20 141 P5
Skippons Cl NWBY RG14 141 Q8
Skipton Dr HYS/HAR UB3 42 E3
Skye Cl TILE/CALC RG31 * 137 Q6
Skylark Wy WHIT RG2 145 Q1
Skylings NWBY RG14 7 J2
Skyport Dr WDR/YW UB7 41 M7
Slaidburn Gn BRAK RG12 76 E4
Slanting Hl NTHA RG18 133 P5
Sledmere Ct EBED/NFELT TW14 57 L7
Slim Rd CBLY GU15 88 B7
The Slipway WDSR SL4 * 51 M7
Sloane Cl GOR/PANG RG8 112 A12
The Slopes CAV/SC RG4 45 K4
Slough Rd IVER SL0 30 E4
SL SL1 10 F9
WDSR SL4 38 F5
Smaldon Cl WDR/YW UB7 42 C3
Smalley Cl WWKG RG41 73 L2
Smallmead Rd
RDGW/BURGH RG30 58 D5
WHIT RG2 58 F5
Smallridge KSCL RG20 141 Q10
Smewins Rd MDHD SL6 34 F8
Smitham Bridge Rd
HUNG RG17 138 G1
Smith Cl CAV/SC RG4 126 F5
Smithfield Cl MDHD SL6 35 H3
Smithfield Rd MDHD SL6 35 J3
Smith's Hl WANT OX12 106 C5
Smiths La WDSR SL4 52 E1
Smith Sq BRAK RG12 3 J4
Smithy's Gn BFOR GU20 90 D2
The Smithy TADY RG26 149 R7
Snake La KSCL RG20 132 A12
Snape Sp SL SL1 29 G7
Snowball Hl MDHD SL6 35 K5
Snowberry Cl WWKG RG41 14 B7
Snowcrete DTCH/LGLY SL3 * 29 L3
Snowden Cl WDSR SL4 52 D3
Snowden Dr TILE/CALC RG31 137 L4
Snowdon Cl STHA RG19 97 M4
Snowdon Crs HYS/HAR UB3 42 E3
Snowdon Rd FARN GU14 93 L7
HTHAIR TW6 57 J5
Snowdrop Copse NTHA RG18 98 B2
Snowdrop Gv WWKG RG41 61 J3
Snows Paddock BFOR GU20 78 B7
Snows Ride BFOR GU20 78 B8
Soane End CAV/SC RG4 126 G12
Soham Cl EARL RG6 60 C6
Soho Crs FLKWH/TG HP10 20 F2
Soke Rd THLE RG7 142 G10
Soldiers Ri EWKG RG40 74 D7
Somerford Cl MDHD SL6 5 M3
Somersby Crs MDHD SL6 35 M3
Somerset Cl HUNG RG17 138 G1
WWKG RG41 61 K8
Somerset Gv BNFD RG42 64 F5
Somerset Wy WDR/YW UB7 41 H2
Somerstown Ct READ RG1 8 C7
Somerton Gdns EARL RG6 60 A4
Somerton Gv STHA RG19 97 L4
Somerville Cl WWKG RG41 73 K2
Somerville Crs YTLY GU46 86 E8
Somerville Ri BRAK RG12 76 B2
Somerville Rd WDSR SL4 38 E5
Songbird Cl WHIT RG2 145 Q1
Sonninge Cl SHST GU47 87 K6
Sonning La CAV/SC RG4 46 D4
Sonning Mdw CAV/SC RG4 46 C5
Sopwith Cl WODY RG5 * 47 G7
Sopwith Rd HEST TW5 43 L7
Sorrel Cl EWKG RG40 15 L2
NWBY RG14 96 F1
THLE RG7 143 R3
Sorrel Dr LTWR GU18 89 M7
Sospel Ct SLN SL2 28 E3
Southall La HEST TW5 43 K5
Southampton Cl BLKW GU17 87 J8
Southampton Rd HTHAIR TW6 56 F5
Southampton St READ RG1 9 G8
South Av EGH TW20 69 J4
HEN RG9 22 A6
Southbank Gdns HUNG RG17 117 L4
Southbourne Dr BNEND SL8 20 C3
Southbury La WAR/TWY RG10 47 M1
South Cl EWKG RG40 15 H8
MLW SL7 17 M7
SL SL1 27 M8
WDR/YW UB7 42 B3
Southcote Av FELT TW13 57 M8
Southcote Dr CBLY GU15 95 G1
Southcote Farm La
RDGW/BURGH RG30 58 D1
Southcote La
RDGW/BURGH RG30 58 A2
Southcote Pde
RDGW/BURGH RG30 58 D2
Southcote Rd
RDGW/BURGH RG30 44 D8
Southcroft EGH TW20 68 B3
SLN SL2 28 D5
Southdown Rd CAV/SC RG4 45 H1
STHA RG19 97 H3
TADY RG26 148 C1
South Dr CAV/SC RG4 46 C5
EARL RG6 59 M4
EWKG RG40 15 H8
HTWY RG27 150 D11
THLE RG7 136 H11
VW GU25 80 A4
Southend NTHA RG18 133 Q12
South End Rd THLE RG7 135 N9
Southerland Cl WEY KT13 83 J8
Southern Ct READ RG1 * 9 J7
Southerndene Cl
TILE/CALC RG31 125 N12
Southern Hl READ RG1 59 K1
Southern Perimeter Rd
STWL/WRAY TW19 56 C4
South Farm La BAGS GU19 90 A4
South Field Cl WDSR SL4 37 L3
Southfield Gdns SL SL1 27 K6
Southfields Av ASHF TW15 71 H4
South Gate Av FELT TW13 71 K2
Southglade WHIT RG2 59 K6
South Gn SL SL1 10 F3
South Gv CHERT KT16 81 M3
South Hill Rd BRAK RG12 76 A3
South Lake Crs WODY RG5 60 E1
South Lake Pde WODY RG5 * 60 D1
Southlands Cl EWKG RG40 15 K9
Southlands Rd EWKG RG40 15 K9
Southlea Rd DTCH/LGLY SL3 39 K8
WDSR SL4 54 A2
South Lynn Crs BRAK RG12 76 B2
South Meadow CWTH RG45 87 K3
South Meadow La WDSR SL4 13 G2
South Oak Wy WHIT RG2 58 E7
South Pl MLW SL7 19 G5
South Rd BRAK RG12 75 K4
CWTH RG45 87 L3
EGH TW20 68 C4
EWKG RG40 75 L5
HEST TW5 43 L6
MDHD SL6 4 F6
WDR/YW UB7 42 C3
South Rw DID OX11 109 K2
Southside CHERT KT16 70 A8
South Stoke Rd
GOR/PANG RG8 112 E7
South St CAV/SC RG4 45 H4
DID OX11 110 C2
READ RG1 9 H7
STA TW18 69 M3
WANT OX12 106 E1
South Vw BRAK RG12 63 K8
HUNG RG17 138 H1
WDSR SL4 * 38 E5
South View Av CAV/SC RG4 45 H4
Southview Cl WAR/TWY RG10 33 G8
South View Gdns NWBY RG14 7 G2
South View Pk CAV/SC RG4 45 J4
Southview Rd MLW SL7 19 G2
Southville Cl EBED/NFELT TW14 57 L6
Southville Crs
EBED/NFELT TW14 57 L7
Southville Rd
EBED/NFELT TW14 57 L7
Southwark Cl YTLY GU46 86 C8
Southway CBLY GU15 94 B2
Southwell Park Rd CBLY GU15 94 B1
Southwick BAGS GU19 89 L5
Southwick Ct BRAK RG12 76 E3
Southwold BRAK RG12 75 L5
Southwold Cl EARL RG6 60 D4
Southwold Sp DTCH/LGLY SL3 40 E2
Southwood EWKG RG40 75 H3
Southwood Gdns MDHD SL6 26 A1
THLE RG7 143 Q3
Southwood Rd BLKW GU17 92 E5
MDHD SL6 26 A1
Sovereign Dr CBLY GU15 89 H7
Sovereign Hts DTCH/LGLY SL3 40 C6
Sovereign Wy TILE/CALC RG31 137 N5
Sowbury Pk KSCL RG20 132 G2
Spackman Cl STHA RG19 97 M4
Spackmans Wy SL SL1 10 B9
Spade Oak Meadow
BNEND SL8 20 A2
Spa Meadow Cl STHA RG19 96 E6
Span Hl CAV/SC RG4 127 P11
Sparrowbill KSCL RG20 119 Q4
Sparrow Cl WWKG RG41 73 L1
Sparrow Rw CHOB/PIR GU24 91 H2
Sparvells HTWY RG27 85 L6
Speedbird Wy WDR/YW UB7 41 K7
Speedwell Wy NTHA RG18 98 B2
Speen Hill Cl NWBY RG14 6 A1
Speen La NWBY RG14 6 A2
Speen Lodge Ct NWBY RG14 6 A2
Speen Pl NWBY RG14 6 A1
Spelthorne Gv SUN TW16 71 M5
Spelthorne La ASHF TW15 71 J5
Spencer Cl FRIM GU16 94 E8
TADY RG26 148 G1
UX/CGN UB8 31 L4
WWKG RG41 61 K8
Spencer Gdns EGH TW20 68 D3
Spencer Rd BNFD RG42 2 B3
DTCH/LGLY SL3 40 B3
NWBY RG14 141 R8
WHIT RG2 59 H7
Spencers Cl MDHD SL6 4 B3
Spencers La MDHD SL6 20 A8
Spencers Rd MDHD SL6 4 B3
Spencer St NWDGN UB2 43 M3
The Spens MDHD SL6 * 5 H3
Sperling Rd MDHD SL6 26 B5
Spey Rd RDGW/BURGH RG30 44 A6
Spiers Cl TADY RG26 148 F2
Spinfield La MLW SL7 18 D5
Spinfield La West MLW SL7 18 E5
Spinfield Mt MLW SL7 18 D5
Spinfield Pk MLW SL7 18 E5
Spinis BRAK RG12 75 L5
Spinner Gn BRAK RG12 76 A2
Spinners Wk MLW SL7 18 F5
WDSR SL4 13 H6
Spinney SL SL1 38 D1
Spinney Cl CAV/SC RG4 126 H11
Spinney Dr EBED/NFELT TW14 57 J6
Spinney La WDSR SL4 52 B7
The Spinney ASC SL5 78 E2
CBLY GU15 89 J8
EWKG RG40 73 M6
TILE/CALC RG31 * 137 P5
YTLY GU46 86 C7
Spinningwheel La BNFD RG42 49 J6
Spitfire Cl DTCH/LGLY SL3 40 C5
Spitfire Est HEST TW5 * 43 L5
Spitfire Wy HEST TW5 43 L5
WODY RG5 47 G7
Spittal St MLW SL7 18 F4
The Splash BNFD RG42 64 B4
Spode Cl RDGW/BURGH RG30 137 Q2
Spout La STWL/WRAY TW19 56 A4
Spout La North
STWL/WRAY TW19 56 B3
Spray La KSCL RG20 119 N5
Spray Rd MARL SN8 139 J11
Spriggs Cl STHA RG19 97 M4
Springate Fld DTCH/LGLY SL3 40 A2
Spring Av EGH TW20 68 E4
Spring Cl GOR/PANG RG8 124 B9
MDHD SL6 26 B4
Springcross Av BLKW GU17 93 K3
Springdale EARL RG6 60 B4
EWKG RG40 73 L6
Springfield LTWR GU18 90 C6
Springfield Cl WDSR SL4 12 F8
Springfield End
GOR/PANG RG8 112 A11
Springfield Gv SUN TW16 * 71 M6
Springfield La NWBY RG14 96 C6
WEY KT13 83 H8
Springfield Mdw WEY KT13 83 H8
Springfield Pk MDHD SL6 36 D5
WAR/TWY RG10 47 L2
Springfield Rd ASHF TW15 70 F3
BRAK RG12 63 J7
CBLY GU15 95 G1
DTCH/LGLY SL3 40 D7
TADY RG26 148 G1
WDSR SL4 12 F8
YEAD UB4 43 L1
Springfields Cl CHERT KT16 82 B5
Spring Gdns ASC SL5 78 B1
CBLY GU15 95 G1
EWKG RG40 * 85 M1
FARN GU14 94 A7
KSCL RG20 141 P11
MLW SL7 18 F3
THLE RG7 145 M5
BNEND SL8 20 C2
Spring Gv READ RG1 9 H9
Spring Hl MDHD SL6 36 A3
Springhill Rd GOR/PANG RG8 112 A10
Springhurst NWBY RG14 * 96 D6
Spring La CAV/SC RG4 127 P12
DID OX11 110 G2
KSCL RG20 100 B8
MDHD SL6 19 K8
NTHA RG18 133 Q10
SL SL1 38 B1
SLN SL2 28 D1
THLE RG7 142 E8
THLE RG7 143 Q7
THLE RG7 145 L11
Spring Meadow BRAK RG12 3 K2
Spring Mdw HUNG RG17 118 F10
Spring Ri EGH TW20 68 E4
Spring Rd FELT TW13 71 M1
The Springs THLE RG7 150 B2
Spring Ter HEN RG9 * 127 N10
WHIT RG2 * 59 H1
Spring Wk WAR/TWY RG10 32 F4
Springwell Rd HEST TW5 43 M8
Springwood La HEN RG9 126 F2
Spring Wood La THLE RG7 143 Q4
Spring Woods SHST GU47 87 J5
VW GU25 80 B1
Spruce Dr LTWR GU18 90 A7
Spruce Rd WODY RG5 47 G8
Spurcroft Rd STHA RG19 97 M4
The Spur SL SL1 27 M6
WAR/TWY RG10 33 G3
The Square BAGS GU19 89 L3
BRAK RG12 3 M9
STHA RG19 101 J2
STKPK UB11 42 F1
THLE RG7 145 M4
WDR/YW UB7 41 K8
Squire's Bridge Rd SHPTN TW17 82 F1
Squire's Rd SHPTN TW17 82 F1
Squires Wk ASHF TW15 71 K5
Squirrel Cl SHST GU47 87 H6
Squirrel Dr WDSR SL4 52 B8
Squirrel La WDSR SL4 52 B7
Squirrels Drey CWTH RG45 86 F1
Squirrels Wy EARL RG6 60 B4
Squirrel Wk WWKG RG41 14 A3
Stable Cl THLE RG7 143 Q3
Stable Ct NWBY RG14 96 D1
Stable Cft BAGS GU19 89 K4
Stables Ct MLW SL7 18 D5
Stable Vw YTLY GU46 86 D7
Stable Yd GOR/PANG RG8 * 136 A1
Staddlestone Cl
TILE/CALC RG31 125 N12
Stadium Wy
RDGW/BURGH RG30 44 B5
Staff College Rd CBLY GU15 88 B8
Stafferton Wy MDHD SL6 5 J7
Stafford Av SLN SL2 28 E5
Stafford Cl MDHD SL6 27 K7
WODY RG5 46 F7
Staffordshire Cl
RDGW/BURGH RG30 137 R2
Staffordshire Cft BNFD RG42 64 F4
Stag Hl HUNG RG17 129 J6
Stag Pl FLKWH/TG HP10 * 20 F2
Stainash Crs STA TW18 70 B3
Stainash Pde STA TW18 * 70 B3
Stainby Cl WDR/YW UB7 42 A3
Staines By-Pass STA TW18 69 L1
Staines La CHERT KT16 81 M3
Staines Lane Cl CHERT KT16 81 M2
Staines Rd CHERT KT16 81 L3
EBED/NFELT TW14 57 H7
STA TW18 69 M7
STWL/WRAY TW19 54 E6
Staines Rd West ASHF TW15 71 J5
SUN TW16 71 M5
Stainford Cl ASHF TW15 71 K3
Stamford Av FRIM GU16 94 F5
Stamford Rd MDHD SL6 4 B7
Stanbrook Cl THLE RG7 135 Q9
Stanfield TADY RG26 148 D2
Stanham Rd
RDGW/BURGH RG30 137 R2
Stanhope Heath
STWL/WRAY TW19 56 C5
Stanhope Rd CBLY GU15 93 M2
SL SL1 27 M7
WHIT RG2 59 K3
Stanhope Wy
STWL/WRAY TW19 56 C5
Stanlake La WAR/TWY RG10 47 M2
Stanley Cl MLW SL7 19 H3
UX/CGN UB8 31 M3
Stanley Cots SLN SL2 11 G4
Stanley Gn East DTCH/LGLY SL3 40 B4
Stanley Gn West
DTCH/LGLY SL3 40 B4
Stanley Gv READ RG1 8 B5
Stanley Rd ASHF TW15 70 E3
EWKG RG40 15 L6
NWBY RG14 7 G6
Stanley St READ RG1 8 C5
Stanley Wk BRAK RG12 3 G5
Stanmore Cl ASC SL5 78 A1
Stanmore Gdns THLE RG7 143 P9
Stanmore Rd KSCL RG20 120 H4
Stanshawe Rd READ RG1 8 E4
Stansted Rd HTHAIR TW6 56 F5
Stanton Cl EARL RG6 60 C2
Stanton Wy DTCH/LGLY SL3 40 A4
Stanway Cots CHERT KT16 * 82 A4
Stanwell Cl STWL/WRAY TW19 56 D5
Stanwell Gdns
STWL/WRAY TW19 56 D5
Stanwell Moor Rd STA TW18 56 B8
STWL/WRAY TW19 56 B1
WDR/YW UB7 41 K8
Stanwell New Rd STA TW18 70 B2
Stanwell Pl STWL/WRAY TW19 * 56 C5
Stanwell Rd ASHF TW15 70 E1
DTCH/LGLY SL3 55 H2
EBED/NFELT TW14 57 J6
HTHAIR TW6 57 H6
Stapleford Rd
RDGW/BURGH RG30 58 C2
Staple Hl CHERT KT16 79 M8
CHOB/PIR GU24 91 K2
Staplehurst BRAK RG12 75 L4
Stapleton Cl MLW SL7 19 H2
NWBY RG14 141 Q8
Star La WAR/TWY RG10 23 L8
Starling Cl WWKG RG41 14 A7
Starlings Dr TILE/CALC RG31 137 M4
Starmead Dr EWKG RG40 15 K8
Star Post Rd CBLY GU15 88 E6
Star Rd CAV/SC RG4 9 K1
Starting Gates NWBY RG14 7 J8
The Starting Ga NWBY RG14 7 J7
Startins La MDHD SL6 19 L6
Starveall Cl WDR/YW UB7 42 B3
Starveall Rd GOR/PANG RG8 110 F12
Starwood Ct DTCH/LGLY SL3 39 L3
Statham Ct BNFD RG42 63 L6
Station Ap BLKW GU17 93 L2
HYS/HAR UB3 43 H3
MDHD SL6 5 G6
MLW SL7 19 G4
NWBY RG14 6 E5
READ RG1 8 F4
SHPTN TW17 * 83 J3
STA TW18 70 A3
VW GU25 80 D1
WDR/YW UB7 42 A1
Station Crs ASHF TW15 70 D2
Station Hl ASC SL5 66 A8
MDHD SL6 20 B7
NTHA RG18 122 B8
READ RG1 8 F4
Station Pde MDHD SL6 * 20 B7
VW GU25 80 D1
Station Ri MLW SL7 19 G4
Station Rd ADL/WDHM KT15 82 C8
ASC SL5 79 G3
ASHF TW15 70 F2
BAGS GU19 89 L2
BNEND SL8 20 C3
BRAK RG12 2 F5
CHERT KT16 81 M5
CHOB/PIR GU24 91 M7
DTCH/LGLY SL3 40 C2
EARL RG6 60 C2
EGH TW20 69 G3
EWKG RG40 14 E6
FRIM GU16 94 C5
GOR/PANG RG8 112 A12
HEN RG9 22 A5
HEN RG9 32 C2
HUNG RG17 117 K4
HUNG RG17 118 A8
HUNG RG17 118 E11
HUNG RG17 130 E10
HYS/HAR UB3 43 G4
KSCL RG20 141 M12
MDHD SL6 20 B7
MDHD SL6 27 H7
MLW SL7 19 G5
NWBY RG14 6 E6
NWBY RG14 141 R1
READ RG1 9 G5
SHPTN TW17 83 J2
SL SL1 28 A7
STHA RG19 97 M3
STHA RG19 98 A4
STWL/WRAY TW19 54 F5
THLE RG7 99 L4
THLE RG7 137 J7
THLE RG7 137 J8
THLE RG7 144 C9
UX/CGN UB8 31 L5
WAR/TWY RG10 32 E5
WAR/TWY RG10 47 K2
WDR/YW UB7 42 A2
WGFD OX10 111 P1
Station Wy BRAK RG12 3 G5
Station Yd ASHF TW15 * 70 F2
Staunton Rd SLN SL2 28 F6
Staveley Rd ASHF TW15 71 K4
Staverton Cl BNFD RG42 64 B5
EWKG RG40 62 F8
Staverton Rd WHIT RG2 59 J3
Stayne End VW GU25 80 A1
Steam Farm La
EBED/NFELT TW14 57 M3
Steep Hl CHOB/PIR GU24 91 J3
Steeple Point ASC SL5 66 B8
Steeple Wk EARL RG6 59 M6
Steerforth Copse SHST GU47 87 L4
Steggles Cl WODY RG5 46 D6
Stepgates CHERT KT16 82 B4
Stepgates Cl CHERT KT16 * 82 B4
Stephanie Chase Ct EWKG RG40 15 J4
Stephen Cl EGH TW20 69 J4
WAR/TWY RG10 47 M3
Stephen's Cl THLE RG7 143 P8
Stephens Firs THLE RG7 143 N8
Stephenson Cl NTHA RG18 97 M2
Stephenson Ct NWBY RG14 6 D1
SL SL1 * 11 H7
Stephenson Dr WDSR SL4 12 E4
Stephenson Rd WHIT RG2 73 G7
Stephens Rd TADY RG26 148 E2
Stephen's Rd THLE RG7 143 P8
Sterling Centre BRAK RG12 3 K5
Sterling Gdns SHST GU47 87 L6
Sterling Pl WEY KT13 83 L8
Sterling Wy
RDGW/BURGH RG30 44 A5
Stevens Hl YTLY GU46 92 E1
Stevens La HEN RG9 126 D2
Stevenson Dr BNFD RG42 63 J3
Stewart Av SHPTN TW17 71 G8
SL SL1 29
Stewart Cl MDHD SL6 36
Stewart Quay HYS/HAR UB3 43
Stickle Down FRIM GU16 95
Stile Rd DTCH/LGLY SL3 39 N
Stilton Cl EARL RG6 60
Stilwell Cl YTLY GU46 86
Stirling Av SHPTN TW17 * 71
Stirling Cl CAV/SC RG4 127 K
FRIM GU16 94
UX/CGN UB8 31
WDSR SL4 52
Stirling Gv MDHD SL6 25
Stirling Rd SL SL1 28
Stirling Wy NTHA RG18 97
Stirrup Cl NWBY RG14 96
Stockbridge Wy YTLY GU46 92
Stockbury Cl EARL RG6 60
Stockdales Rd WDSR SL4 38
Stockley Cl WDR/YW UB7 42
Stockley Farm Rd
WDR/YW UB7 42
Stockley Rd WDR/YW UB7 42
Stockton Rd WHIT RG2 59
Stockwells MDHD SL6 26
Stockwood Ri CBLY GU15 94
Stoke Court Dr SLN SL2 29
Stokeford Cl BRAK RG12 76
Stoke Gdns SL SL1 10
Stoke Gn SLN SL2 29
Stoke Park Av SLN SL2 28
Stoke Poges La SL SL1 10
Stoke Rd SLN SL2 11
Stoke Row Rd HEN RG9 114 A
Stokesay SLN SL2 11
Stokes La TADY RG26 103
Stokes Vw GOR/PANG RG8 124
Stompits Rd MDHD SL6 36
Stomp Rd SL SL1 27
Stonea Cl EARL RG6 60
Stonebridge Fld WDSR SL4 38
Stone Cl WDR/YW UB7 42
Stone Copse NTHA RG18 133 L
Stone Crs EBED/NFELT TW14 57
Stonecroft Av IVER SL0 31
Stonefield Pk MDHD SL6 4
Stonegate CBLY GU15 89
Stoneham Cl
RDGW/BURGH RG30 44
Stonehaven Dr WODY RG5 47
Stonehill Ga ASC SL5 * 78
Stonehill Rd CHERT KT16 81
LTWR GU18 90
Stone House La MDHD SL6 19
Stonehouse Ri FRIM GU16 94
Stoneleigh Ct FRIM GU16 94
Stone St RDGW/BURGH RG30 44
Stoney Cl YTLY GU46 92
Stoneyfield THLE RG7 135 Q
Stoneyland Ct EGH TW20 68
Stoneylands Rd EGH TW20 68
Stoney La NTHA RG18 133 K
SLN SL2 28
STHA RG19 98
Stoney Meade SL SL1 38
Stoney Rd BNFD RG42 2
Stoney Ware MLW SL7 18
Stoney Ware Cl MLW SL7 18
Stony La HUNG RG17 117 L
Stookes Wy YTLY GU46 92
Stork House Dr HUNG RG17 117
Stormount Dr HYS/HAR UB3 42
Stornaway Rd DTCH/LGLY SL3 40
Stour Cl RDGW/BURGH RG30 44
SL SL1 38
Stovell Rd WDSR SL4 12
Stowe Rd SL SL1 28
Strachey Cl GOR/PANG RG8 124 G
Straight La HUNG RG17 117 N
The Straight Mile
WAR/TWY RG10 48
Straight Rd WDSR SL4 54
The Straight NWDGN UB2 43 M
Strand La MDHD SL6 26
Strand View Wk MDHD SL6 26
Strand Wy EARL RG6 60
Stranraer Gdns SL SL1 10
Stratfield BRAK RG12 75
Stratfield Av TADY RG26 148
Stratfield Rd SL SL1 11
Stratfield Saye Rd TADY RG26 150
Stratford Cl SLN SL2 27 M
Stratford Dr FLKWH/TG HP10 20
Stratford Gdns MDHD SL6 35
Stratford Rd HTHAIR TW6 57
Stratford Wy TILE/CALC RG31 137
Strathearn Av HYS/HAR UB3 43
Stratheden Pl READ RG1 8
Strathmore Dr WAR/TWY RG10 47
Strathy Cl RDGW/BURGH RG30 44
Stratton Gdns WHIT RG2 59
Stratton Rd SUN TW16 71 M
Stratton Wk FARN GU14 94
Strawberry Ct FRIM GU16 95
Strawberry Flds TADY RG26 149
THLE RG7 143
Strawberry Hl BNFD RG42 64
NWBY RG14 6
Streamside SL SL1 38
Streatley Hl GOR/PANG RG8 111 N
Streets Heath CHOB/PIR GU24 90
The Street GOR/PANG RG8 111
TADY RG26 149
THLE RG7 136
THLE RG7 142
THLE RG7 143
THLE RG7 145
WAR/TWY RG10 34
WGFD OX10 111
WGFD OX10 112
WGFD OX10 112
Stretton Cl THLE RG7 135
Strodes College La EGH TW20 68
Strode's Crs STA TW18 70
Strode St EGH TW20 69
Stroma Ct SL SL1 27 M
Strongrove Hl HUNG RG17 129 K
Strood La WDSR SL4 66
Stroud Cl TADY RG26 148
WDSR SL4 52
Stroude Rd VW GU25 80
Stroud Farm Rd MDHD SL6 36
Stroud Gn NWBY RG14 7
Stroud La BLKW GU17 93
Strouds Meadow NTHA RG18 133 Q
The Strouds THLE RG7 135 P
Stroud Wy ASHF TW15 71
Stuart Cl CAV/SC RG4 45
WDSR SL4 12
Stuart Rd NWBY RG14 141
Stuart Wy STA TW18 70
VW GU25 80
WDSR SL4 12
Stubbles La MDHD SL6 19
Stubbs Folly SHST GU47 87
Studios Rd SHPTN TW17 70
Studland Cl WHIT RG2 59
Sturbridge Cl EARL RG6 60
Sturdee Cl FRIM GU16 94
Sturges Rd EWKG RG40 15
Sturt Gn MDHD SL6 36

Styventon Pl CHERT KT16 81 M4
Suck's La GOR/PANG RG8 123 M12
Suffolk Cl BAGS GU19 89 L4
SL SL1 28 A7
WWKG RG41 61 K8
Suffolk Combe BNFD RG42 64 F5
Suffolk Ct FRIM GU16 95 K6
Suffolk Rd MDHD SL6 4 D9
RDGW/BURGH RG30 44 D7
Sulham La GOR/PANG RG8 125 J10
Sulhamstead Hl THLE RG7 136 E11
Sulhamstead Rd
RDGW/BURGH RG30 143 R1
THLE RG7 136 G12
Sullivan Rd CBLY GU15 94 A1
Sullivans Reach
WOT/HER KT12 83 M4
Sumburgh Wy SL SL1 29 G6
Summerfield Cl WWKG RG41 61 M5
Summerfield Ri
GOR/PANG RG8 112 B11
Summer Gdns CBLY GU15 95 J1
Summerhouse La
WDR/YW UB7 41 M6
Summerlea SL SL1 38 D1
Summerleaze Rd MDHD SL6 26 C5
Summerplug THLE RG7 143 Q9
Summers Rd SL SL1 27 L4
Summit Cl EWKG RG40 73 M8
Sunbury Ct WDSR SL4 13 J2
Sunbury Rd FELT TW13 71 M1
WDSR SL4 13 J2
Sun Cl WDSR SL4 13 J2
Sunderland Cl WODY RG5 47 H6
Sunderland Gdns NWBY RG14 141 R4
Sunderland Pl NTHA RG18 97 L2
Sunderland Rd MDHD SL6 25 K6
Sundew Cl EWKG RG40 15 L3
LTWR GU18 90 D6
Sundial Cl RDGW/BURGH RG30 137 R4
Sundon Crs VW GU25 80 B2
Sundown Rd ASHF TW15 71 J3
Sun Gdns THLE RG7 143 Q5
Sun La MDHD SL6 5 G4
THLE RG7 145 M12
Sunley Cl NWBY RG14 141 R8
Sunning Av ASC SL5 78 E4
Sunningdale Pk ASC SL5 * 78 F2
Sunninghill Cl ASC SL5 78 D1
Sunninghill Pk ASC SL5 * 66 D7
ASC SL5 * 66 E4
Sunninghill Rd ASC SL5 66 F5
ASC SL5 78 D2
BFOR GU20 78 A7
WDSR SL4 66 D3
Sunnybank ASC SL5 78 A1
MLW SL7 18 E2
Sunnybank Rd FARN GU14 93 K8
Sunray Av WDR/YW UB7 41 M2
Sun Ray Est SHST GU47 86 F6
Sun St READ RG1 9 M6
Surbiton Rd CBLY GU15 89 G5
Surley Rw CAV/SC RG4 45 G1
Surly Hall Wk WDSR SL4 12 A6
Surrey Av CBLY GU15 94 A2
SLN SL2 28 E6
Surrey Ct BNFD RG42 64 F5
Surrey Rd WHIT RG2 59 H2
Surridge Ct BAGS GU19 89 L4
Sussex Cl SL SL1 11 L8
Sussex Gdns WODY RG5 46 E7
Sussex Keep SL SL1 * 11 L7
Sussex La THLE RG7 145 N5
Sussex Pl SL SL1 11 K7
Sussex Rd NWDGN UB2 43 M3
Sutcliffe Av EARL RG6 60 D3
Sutherland Av HYS/HAR UB3 43 J4
SUN TW16 71 M7
Sutherland Cha ASC SL5 65 L7
Sutherland Gdns SUN TW16 71 M7
Sutherland Gv TILE/CALC RG31 137 Q6
Sutherlands NWBY RG14 96 A7
Sutherlands Av WHIT RG2 59 J1
Sutton Av DTCH/LGLY SL3 39 L2
Sutton Cl MDHD SL6 4 B8
MDHD SL6 20 D8
Sutton La DTCH/LGLY SL3 40 D6
Sutton Pl DTCH/LGLY SL3 40 D6
Sutton Rd CBLY GU15 89 G5
MDHD SL6 20 D8
NWBY RG14 141 R1
Suttons Park Av EARL RG6 45 L6
Sutton Wk READ RG1 59 J1
Swabey Rd DTCH/LGLY SL3 40 C4
Swains Cl TADY RG26 148 D2
WDR/YW UB7 42 A2
Swains Rd TADY RG26 148 D2
Swainstone Rd WHIT RG2 59 H1
Swaledale BRAK RG12 76 A2
Swale Rd FARN GU14 93 K8
Swallow Cl STA TW18 69 M2
TILE/CALC RG31 137 N4
YTLY GU46 86 B8
Swallowdale IVER SL0 30 F4
Swallowfield EGH TW20 68 B4
Swallowfield Dr WHIT RG2 59 H8
Swallow Field Gdns THLE RG7 137 J6
Swallowfield Rd THLE RG7 72 A8
Swallowfield Wy HYS/HAR UB3 42 F2
Swallows Cft READ RG1 58 E1
Swallow St IVER SL0 30 F4
Swallow Wy WWKG RG41 73 L1
Swancote Gn BRAK RG12 76 B2
Swan Ct NWBY RG14 6 D4
Swan Dr THLE RG7 142 D3
Swangate HUNG RG17 129 M11
Swan La SHST GU47 87 H8
Swanmore Cl EARL RG6 60 E5
Swan Pl READ RG1 8 F7
Swan Rd IVER SL0 31 H6
WDR/YW UB7 41 M2
Swans Ct WAR/TWY RG10 * 47 J3
Swansea Rd HTHAIR TW6 57 J5
READ RG1 8 E3
Swansea Ter TILE/CALC RG31 137 P1
Swanston Fld GOR/PANG RG8 124 H7
Swan's Wy WGFD OX10 112 E4
The Swansway WEY KT13 * 83 G7
Swan Wk SHPTN TW17 83 L4
Swanwick Wk TADY RG26 148 D2
Swedish Houses TADY RG26 148 E3
Sweeps Ditch Cl STA TW18 70 A6
Sweeps La EGH TW20 68 F3
Sweetbriar CWTH RG45 * 75 G7
Sweet Briar Dr
TILE/CALC RG31 137 N6
Sweetzer's Piece THLE RG7 143 N8
Swepstone Cl EARL RG6 60 C4
Swift Cl WWKG RG41 61 L8
Swift La BAGS GU19 89 M3
Swinbrook Cl TILE/CALC RG31 125 P11
Swindon Rd HTHAIR TW6 57 J4
Swinley Rd ASC SL5 77 J1
Swiss Cottage Cl
TILE/CALC RG31 137 N2
Switchback Cl MDHD SL6 25 M4
Switchback Rd North
MDHD SL6 26 A3
Switchback Rd South
MDHD SL6 25 M4
The Switchback MDHD SL6 * 25 M4
Swithin Cha BNFD RG42 64 E5
Swordsman's Rd FRIM GU16 95 K5
Sycamore Cl BNEND SL8 20 D3
FRIM GU16 94 E5
MDHD SL6 35 L3
RDGW/BURGH RG30 143 R1
SHST GU47 87 H7
WODY RG5 60 C1
Sycamore Ct WEY KT13 83 M7
Sycamore Dr FRIM GU16 94 E4
MLW SL7 18 F1
WAR/TWY RG10 47 K1
Sycamore Ri BRAK RG12 3 K6
NWBY RG14 133 J12
Sycamore Rd WHIT RG2 59 L4
The Sycamores BLKW GU17 93 H1
Sycamore Wk DTCH/LGLY SL3 30 A7
EGH TW20 68 B4
The Sydings NWBY RG14 141 R1
Sydney Cl CWTH RG45 75 J7
STHA RG19 * 98 A3
Sydney Crs ASHF TW15 71 H4
Sydney Gv SL SL1 28 E7
Sydney Loader Pl BLKW GU17 87 G8
Syke Cluan DTCH/LGLY SL3 41 G2
Syke Ings DTCH/LGLY SL3 41 G3
Sykes Dr STA TW18 70 B3
Sykes Rd SL SL1 28 D7
Sylvan Rdg SHST GU47 87 G5
Sylvanus BRAK RG12 75 M4
Sylverns Ct BNFD RG42 64 D5
Sylvester Cl NWBY RG14 96 A1
WWKG RG41 61 K3
Sylvester Rd MDHD SL6 26 A4
Symondson Ms BNFD RG42 63 J2
Sympson Rd TADY RG26 148 F1

T

Tachbrook Rd
EBED/NFELT TW14 57 M6
NWDGN UB2 43 M4
UX/CGN UB8 31 L3
Tadham Pl STHA RG19 97 L4
Tadley Common Rd
TADY RG26 148 E1
Tadley Hl TADY RG26 148 E2
Tadmor Cl SUN TW16 83 M1
Taff Wy RDGW/BURGH RG30 44 A7
Tag La WAR/TWY RG10 33 J5
Talavera Cl CWTH RG45 86 E2
Talbot Av DTCH/LGLY SL3 40 B3
Talbot Cl CAV/SC RG4 9 L1
NWBY RG14 96 A1
Talbot Ct READ RG1 8 E7
Talbot Pl BAGS GU19 89 L3
DTCH/LGLY SL3 39 L8
Talbot Rd ASHF TW15 70 D3
Talbots Dr MDHD SL6 25 J8
Talbot Wy TILE/CALC RG31 125 N11
Talfourd Av EARL RG6 60 A1
Talisman Cl CWTH RG45 86 D1
Tallis La RDGW/BURGH RG30 58 D2
Tall Trees DTCH/LGLY SL3 41 G8
Tamar Gdns WHIT RG2 59 J3
Tamarind Wy EARL RG6 59 M5
Tamarisk Av WHIT RG2 59 L5
Tamarisk Ct NTHA RG18 98 B2
Tamarisk Ri EWKG RG40 15 G3
Tamarisk Wy SL SL1 38 D2
Tamar Wy DTCH/LGLY SL3 40 D5
WWKG RG41 14 A4
Tamesis Pl CAV/SC RG4 9 G2
Tamworth BRAK RG12 76 D4
Tamworth Cl EARL RG6 60 C5
Tangier La WDSR SL4 13 J2
Tanglewood EWKG RG40 74 A7
Tanglewood Cl CHERT KT16 80 B7
Tanglewood Ride
CHOB/PIR GU24 90 D7
Tangley Dr WWKG RG41 74 B2
Tanglyn Av SHPTN TW17 83 G2
Tanhouse La WWKG RG41 14 D7
Tank Rd CBLY GU15 93 M1
Tanners Cl THLE RG7 143 P5
Tanners La CAV/SC RG4 126 F10
Tanners Rw WWKG RG41 74 A3
Tanners Yd BAGS GU19 * 89 L3
Tape La WAR/TWY RG10 47 M6
Taplow Common Rd MDHD SL6 21 H8
SL SL1 27 J3
Taplow Rd MDHD SL6 27 J7
Tarbat Ct SHST GU47 87 K6
Tarbay La WDSR SL4 52 B1
Target Cl EBED/NFELT TW14 57 L5
Target Hl BNFD RG42 64 D5
Targett Ct WWKG RG41 * 61 H4
Tarlton Ct RDGW/BURGH RG30 137 Q4
Tarmac Wy WDR/YW UB7 41 K7
Tarnbrook Wy BRAK RG12 76 E4
Tarn Howes Cl STHA RG19 97 J3
Tarn La NWBY RG14 6 C9
Tarragon Cl BRAK RG12 3 K1
EARL RG6 59 M5
Tarragon Wy THLE RG7 143 R3
Tarrant Gn BNFD RG42 64 C5
Tarrant's Hl HUNG RG17 138 H1
Tasker Cl HYS/HAR UB3 42 E7
Tatchbrook Cl MDHD SL6 5 J2
Tattersall Cl EWKG RG40 15 M7
Tavistock Cl MDHD SL6 25 J7
STA TW18 70 D5
Tavistock Gdns FARN GU14 94 B7
Tavistock Rd WDR/YW UB7 41 M1
WHIT RG2 59 H3
Tawfield BRAK RG12 75 L4
Tawny Rw SHST GU47 * 87 K6
Tayberry Gv THLE RG7 143 R8
Tay Cl FARN GU14 93 L8
Taylor Dr TADY RG26 150 A8
Taylors Cl MLW SL7 19 H4
Taylors Ct MDHD SL6 25 K6
Taynton Wk READ RG1 * 59 H1
Tay Rd RDGW/BURGH RG30 44 A6
Tazewell Ct READ RG1 8 B9
Tealgate HUNG RG17 129 M11
Teal Gv WHIT RG2 145 Q2
Tebbit Cl BRAK RG12 3 J5
Tees Cl FARN GU14 93 L8
Teesdale Rd SLN SL2 28 B6
Tekels Av CBLY GU15 94 D1
Tekels Wy CBLY GU15 94 E3
Telford Av CWTH RG45 75 J6
Telford Ct NWBY RG14 6 D1
Telford Crs WODY RG5 46 F5
Telford Dr SL SL1 38 C1
Telston Cl BNEND SL8 20 C1
Tempest Rd EGH TW20 69 J4
Templar Cl SHST GU47 87 G6
Templedene Av STA TW18 70 B5
Temple Gdns STA TW18 69 M6
Temple La MLW SL7 18 F8
Temple Ms WODY RG5 46 F7
Temple Mill Island MLW SL7 24 E1
Temple Pk MDHD SL6 24 B3
Temple Pl READ RG1 8 F8
Temple Rd WDSR SL4 13 H7
Templeton Gdns WHIT RG2 59 J5
Temple Wy BNFD RG42 63 L5
Ten Acre La EGH TW20 69 J7
Tenaplas Dr GOR/PANG RG8 123 P9
Tenby Av CAV/SC RG4 45 K1
Tenby Dr ASC SL5 78 D2
Tenby Rd FRIM GU16 95 G6
Tennyson Rd ADL/WDHM KT15 82 E8
ASHF TW15 70 E3
NTHA RG18 97 L2
WODY RG5 60 E2
Tennyson Wy SLN SL2 28 A5
Tenth Av TILE/CALC RG31 137 M4
Teresa V BNFD RG42 64 E4
Tern Cl RDGW/BURGH RG30 44 A7
Terrace Rd North BNFD RG42 63 J2
Terrace Rd South BNFD RG42 63 J4
The Terrace ASC SL5 78 D2
CBLY GU15 93 M1
CWTH RG45 87 K1
EWKG RG40 14 F5
Terrington Hl MLW SL7 18 D4
Terry Pl UX/CGN UB8 * 31 L6
Terry's La MDHD SL6 20 D4
Tesimond Dr YTLY GU46 92 A1
Tessa Rd READ RG1 8 C2
Test Cl RDGW/BURGH RG30 44 A6
Test Wy HUNG RG17 146 E1
RAND SP11 146 C6
RAND SP11 146 E11
Testwood Rd WDSR SL4 37 M8
Teviot Rd RDGW/BURGH RG30 137 Q3
The Thakerays STHA RG19 97 M4
Thames Av CHERT KT16 70 A8
GOR/PANG RG8 124 H8
READ RG1 8 F2
WDSR SL4 13 J4
Thamesbourne Ms
BNEND SL8 * 20 C3
Thames Cl BNEND SL8 20 C2
CHERT KT16 82 B4
FARN GU14 93 L8
Thames Crs MDHD SL6 26 D5
Thames Dr WAR/TWY RG10 32 B8
Thamesfield Gdns MLW SL7 19 G5
Thamesfield Ms SHPTN TW17 83 J4
Thamesgate STA TW18 70 B7
Thames Lock WEY KT13 * 83 G6
Thames Md WDSR SL4 38 A8
Thames Meadow SHPTN TW17 83 K5
Thames Pth BNEND SL8 20 C4
CAV/SC RG4 9 K3
CAV/SC RG4 44 D4
CAV/SC RG4 46 C3
CHERT KT16 82 D5
DTCH/LGLY SL3 54 B1
EARL RG6 45 M5
EGH TW20 69 G1
GOR/PANG RG8 112 A10
GOR/PANG RG8 125 N7
HEN RG9 22 A3
HEN RG9 22 D8
HEN RG9 22 F1
HEN RG9 32 B6
MDHD SL6 19 L4
MDHD SL6 20 F8
MDHD SL6 23 L2
MDHD SL6 36 E1
MLW SL7 18 F7
MLW SL7 23 J3
READ RG1 9 G3
SHPTN TW17 83 H4
STA TW18 69 M6
TILE/CALC RG31 125 R11
WAR/TWY RG10 32 A8
WDSR SL4 12 B1
WDSR SL4 54 B3
WEY KT13 83 H6
WGFD OX10 111 P5
Thames Reach GOR/PANG RG8 125 P10
MLW SL7 17 M8
Thames Rd DTCH/LGLY SL3 40 D4
GOR/PANG RG8 111 R12
NTHA RG18 97 L2
WDSR SL4 * 37 L7
Thames Side HEN RG9 22 C4
READ RG1 9 H3
STA TW18 70 A6
WDSR SL4 13 K4
Thames Side Prom READ RG1 8 D1
Thames St CAV/SC RG4 46 D2
STA TW18 69 M3
WDSR SL4 13 J4
WEY KT13 83 H6
WOT/HER KT12 83 M4
Thames Valley Park Dr
EARL RG6 45 M5
Thanington Wy EARL RG6 60 B4
Thatcher Cl WDR/YW UB7 42 A4
Thatchers Dr MDHD SL6 35 J1
Theal Cl SHST GU47 87 K6
Theale Rd RDGW/BURGH RG30 137 M12
Theobald Dr TILE/CALC RG31 125 P10
Theobalds Wy FRIM GU16 95 J3
Thetford Ms CAV/SC RG4 127 K12
Thetford Rd ASHF TW15 70 E2
Thibet Rd SHST GU47 87 J6
Thicket Gv MDHD SL6 25 H7
Thicket Rd
RDGW/BURGH RG30 137 Q2
Thickthorne La STA TW18 70 C5
Third Av HYS/HAR UB3 43 H1
MLW SL7 19 H4
TILE/CALC RG31 137 M4
Third Crs SL SL1 28 E6
Third St East STHA RG19 101 J1
Thirkleby Cl SL SL1 10 A4
Thirlmere Av
RDGW/BURGH RG30 137 R1
SL SL1 27 L6
Thirlmere Cl EGH TW20 69 H5
Thirtover NTHA RG18 133 P9
Thistledown TILE/CALC RG31 137 N1
Thistleton Wy EARL RG6 60 E4
Thomas Ct MDHD SL6 35 J4
Thomas Dr BNFD RG42 3 L1
Thomas La EWKG RG40 73 L6
Thomas Merriman Ct
NWBY RG14 * 6 E5
Thomas Rd FLKWH/TG HP10 20 F2
Thompkins La SLN SL2 28 B1
Thompson Cl DTCH/LGLY SL3 40 C4
NTHA RG18 133 M4
Thompson Dr STHA RG19 98 A4
Thompson's La
CHOB/PIR GU24 91 K4
Thomson Wk TILE/CALC RG31 137 Q6
Thorburn Cha SHST GU47 87 L8
Thornbers Wy WAR/TWY RG10 47 H1
Thornbridge Rd IVER SL0 30 E2
WHIT RG2 59 H6
Thornbury Cl CWTH RG45 87 H1
Thornbury Gn WAR/TWY RG10 47 K1
Thorn Cl WWKG RG41 73 K3
Thorncroft EGH TW20 68 C5
Thorndike SLN SL2 28 C6
Thorndown La BFOR GU20 90 D3
Thorn Dr DTCH/LGLY SL3 30 A7
Thorne Cl ASHF TW15 71 J5
CWTH RG45 75 G7
HEN RG9 127 P3
Thorney Cl EARL RG6 60 E4
Thorney La North IVER SL0 31 H7
Thorney La South
WDR/YW UB7 41 H2
Thorney Mill Rd WDR/YW UB7 41 J3
Thornfield STHA RG19 101 M3
Thornfield Gn BLKW GU17 93 M3
Thornford Rd STHA RG19 101 K2
STHA RG19 101 M4
Thornhill BRAK RG12 3 L9
Thornhill Wy SHPTN TW17 83 G2
Thorningdown DID OX11 109 K2
Thorn La READ RG1 9 G6
Thorn St READ RG1 8 E6
Thornton Av WDR/YW UB7 42 B3
Thornton Cl TADY RG26 150 B8
WDR/YW UB7 42 B3
Thornton Ms
RDGW/BURGH RG30 44 C6
Thornycroft Cl NWBY RG14 7 H4
Thorp Cl BNFD RG42 63 J3
Thorpe By-Pass EGH TW20 69 H8
Thorpe Cl WWKG RG41 74 A3
Thorpe Lea Rd EGH TW20 69 H5
Thorpe Pk CHERT KT16 * 69 M8
Thorpe Rd CHERT KT16 69 K3
STA TW18 69 K3
Thorpeside Cl STA TW18 69 L7
Thorpe St DID OX11 110 G1
Thrale Ms RDGW/BURGH RG30 44 B6
Three Acre Rd NWBY RG14 96 B6
Three Castles Pth ASC SL5 77 H2
BRAK RG12 76 C6
BRAK RG12 76 F3
CWTH RG45 87 H4
EWKG RG40 86 C5
HTWY RG27 85 K7
SHST GU47 86 F4
WDSR SL4 13 L8
WDSR SL4 53 K4
WDSR SL4 67 J2
Three Firs Wy THLE RG7 143 N5
Three Gables La
GOR/PANG RG8 111 Q11
Three Post La HUNG RG17 117 K3
Threshfield BRAK RG12 76 A2
Thrift La MDHD SL6 35 M4
Throgmorton Rd YTLY GU46 92 A1
Thrush Cl THLE RG7 143 R3
Thurlby Wy MDHD SL6 35 M3
Thurlestone Cl SHPTN TW17 * 83 J3
Thurlestone Gdns WHIT RG2 59 J4
Thurlestone Pde SHPTN TW17 * 83 J3
Thurnscoe Cl EARL RG6 59 M6
Thurso Cl RDGW/BURGH RG30 44 A6
Thurston Rd SL SL1 28 F7
Thyme Cl EARL RG6 59 M5
Tichborne Cl BLKW GU17 93 K1
Tichbourne Cl FRIM GU16 94 F3
Tickenor Dr EWKG RG40 73 M7
Tickhill Cl EARL RG6 59 M7
Tickleback Rw BNFD RG42 50 B8
Tidmarsh La GOR/PANG RG8 124 E12
Tidmarsh Rd GOR/PANG RG8 124 G10
Tidmarsh St
RDGW/BURGH RG30 44 B6
Tidmore La GOR/PANG RG8 113 K9
Tidwells Lea BNFD RG42 3 L1
Tiffany Cl WWKG RG41 61 K8
Tiger Cl WODY RG5 47 H7
Tigerseye Cl WWKG RG41 61 K7
Tiggell Cl EARL RG6 60 D2
Tilbury Cl CAV/SC RG4 45 J3
Tilbury Wk DTCH/LGLY SL3 40 D3
Tile Barn Cl FARN GU14 94 A8
Tilebarn Cl HEN RG9 127 Q1
Tilebarn La HEN RG9 127 P2
Tilecotes Cl MLW SL7 18 F4
Tilehurst La BNFD RG42 63 K3
Tilehurst Rd
RDGW/BURGH RG30 44 B6
READ RG1 8 B7
Tilling Cl TILE/CALC RG31 125 M12
Tilly's La STA TW18 69 L2
Tilney Rd NWDGN UB2 43 L4
Tilney Wy EARL RG6 59 M6
Tilstone Av WDSR SL4 38 A5
Tilstone Cl WDSR SL4 38 A4
Timberley Pl CWTH RG45 86 E2
Timbers Wk MDHD SL6 35 K1
Time Sq BRAK RG12 2 F5
Timline Gn BRAK RG12 64 F7
Timsway STA TW18 69 M3
Tindal Cl YTLY GU46 86 D8
Tinkers La WDSR SL4 52 D1
Tinsey Cl EGH TW20 69 H3
Tinsley Cl EARL RG6 59 M6
Tintagel Dr FRIM GU16 94 F5
Tintagel Farm Cl EWKG RG40 74 B6
Tintagel Rd EWKG RG40 74 A6
Tintern Cl SL SL1 10 A8
Tintern Crs READ RG1 58 F1
Tinwell Cl EARL RG6 60 E4
Tippett Ri WHIT RG2 59 H2
Tippings La WODY RG5 47 G5
Tippits Md BNFD RG42 63 K7
Tiptree Cl EARL RG6 59 M6
Titchfield Cl TADY RG26 148 E3
Titcombe Wy HUNG RG17 140 A4
Tite Hl EGH TW20 68 D3
Tithe Barn Dr MDHD SL6 36 F5
Tithebarn Gv TILE/CALC RG31 137 Q5
Tithe Cl MDHD SL6 36 E5
VW GU25 80 D3
Tithe Ct DTCH/LGLY SL3 40 C4
Tithe La STWL/WRAY TW19 54 F5
Titlarks Hill Rd ASC SL5 79 H5
Titness Pk ASC SL5 * 67 G8
Tiverton Cl WODY RG5 46 E5
Toad La BLKW GU17 93 L2
Tobermory Cl DTCH/LGLY SL3 40 A4
Tocker Gdns BNFD RG42 64 B4
Tockley Rd SL SL1 27 K4
Tofrek Ter RDGW/BURGH RG30 44 C7
Tokers Green La CAV/SC RG4 126 D8
Toll Gdns BRAK RG12 64 F8
Tollgate MDHD SL6 25 G8
Tolpuddle Wy YTLY GU46 92 F1
Tomlin Cl STHA RG19 98 A4
Tomlin Rd SLN SL2 28 A5
Tomlins Av FRIM GU16 94 F4
Tomlins Cl TADY RG26 148 D3
Tomlinscote Wy FRIM GU16 95 G4
Tomlinson Dr EWKG RG40 74 A8
Toogood Pl BNFD RG42 64 D3
Toomers Whf NWBY RG14 * 6 E4
Toonagh WDSR SL4 * 51 J8
Topaz Cl SL SL1 38 D1
WWKG RG41 61 L7
Top Common BNFD RG42 3 J1
Tope Rd WHIT RG2 72 F6
Topping La UX/CGN UB8 31 M4
Torcross Gv TILE/CALC RG31 137 M6
Torin Ct EGH TW20 68 C3
Torquay Sp SLN SL2 28 D4
Torridge Rd DTCH/LGLY SL3 40 D6
Torrington Rd WHIT RG2 59 J4
Toseland Wy EARL RG6 60 E3
Totale Ri BNFD RG42 64 B4
Totland Cl FARN GU14 94 A8
Totnes Rd WHIT RG2 59 J4
Tottenham Cl TADY RG26 149 R6
Tottenham Wk SHST GU47 87 K5
Totterdown THLE RG7 143 P5
Toutley Cl WWKG RG41 61 L5
Toutley Rd WWKG RG41 62 A5
Tower Cl CAV/SC RG4 127 J11
Tower Gv WEY KT13 83 L6
Tower Hl KSCL RG20 119 L6
Towers Dr CWTH RG45 87 H2
Town Farm Wy
STWL/WRAY TW19 * 56 D6
Townfield Rd HYS/HAR UB3 43 H1
Townfield Sq HYS/HAR UB3 43 H1
Town La FLKWH/TG HP10 20 F2
STWL/WRAY TW19 56 D5
Town Mills NWBY RG14 * 6 E4
Town Pl READ RG1 * 9 L7
Town Quay STA TW18 * 70 C8
Townsend DID OX11 109 K1
Townsend Cl BRAK RG12 76 E2
Townsend Rd ASHF TW15 70 E3
GOR/PANG RG8 111 Q11
GOR/PANG RG8 122 G3
Townside Pl CBLY GU15 88 D8
Town Sq BRAK RG12 3 G4
Town Tree Rd ASHF TW15 71 G3
Towpath SHPTN TW17 82 F5
Tracy Av DTCH/LGLY SL3 40 B5
Trafalgar Cl WWKG RG41 61 L8
Trafalgar Ct
RDGW/BURGH RG30 44 D8
THLE RG7 * 136 H6
Trafalgar Wy CBLY GU15 93 M2
Trafford Rd FRIM GU16 94 D6
READ RG1 8 B3
Travellers Cnr THLE RG7 * 143 N9
Travic Rd SLN SL2 28 B4
Travis Ct SLN SL2 28 D4
Travis La SHST GU47 87 J7
Tredegar Rd CAV/SC RG4 44 F1
Tree Cl RDGW/BURGH RG30 137 P2
Treeside Cl WDR/YW UB7 41 M4
Treesmill Dr MDHD SL6 35 K3
Trees Rd BNEND SL8 20 D3
Treeton Cl EARL RG6 59 M6
Tree Tops Av CBLY GU15 89 G6
Trefoil Cl EWKG RG40 15 M3
Trefoil Dro NTHA RG18 98 B2
Treforgan CAV/SC RG4 44 F1
Trelawney Av DTCH/LGLY SL3 40 A3
Trelawney Dr TILE/CALC RG31 137 M1
Trelleck Rd READ RG1 58 F1
Tremayne Wk CBLY GU15 95 J2
Trenchard Rd MDHD SL6 36 D6
Trenches La DTCH/LGLY SL3 40 C1
Trent Cl FARN GU14 93 L8
WWKG RG41 61 L7
Trent Crs NTHA RG18 97 K1
Trenthams Cl GOR/PANG RG8 125 M9
Trenton Cl FRIM GU16 95 G4
Trent Rd DTCH/LGLY SL3 40 D6
Tresham Crs YTLY GU46 86 A8
The Tressell MDHD SL6 4 C7
Trevelyan BRAK RG12 75 L4
Trevelyan Ct WDSR SL4 12 E7
Trevithick Cl EBED/NFELT TW14 57 M7
Trevor Rd HYS/HAR UB3 43 G2
Trewarden Av IVER SL0 30 F3
The Triangle NWBY RG14 96 D7
Trident Wy NWDGN UB2 43 K3
Trindledown BNFD RG42 64 A5
Tring Rd TILE/CALC RG31 125 N11
Trinity SHST GU47 87 L4
Trinity Av MLW SL7 18 F3
Trinity Cl STWL/WRAY TW19 56 C5
Trinity Ct BNFD RG42 * 2 F2
THLE RG7 136 H7
Trinity Crs ASC SL5 79 G2
Trinity Pl READ RG1 8 D6
WDSR SL4 13 H7
Trinity Rd MLW SL7 18 F4
Triumph Cl HYS/HAR UB3 42 E8
WODY RG5 60 F1
Troon Ct READ RG1 * 9 M7
Trotsford Meadow BLKW GU17 93 J2
Trotsworth Av VW GU25 80 D1
Trotwood Cl SHST GU47 87 L4
Troutbeck Cl SLN SL2 11 J3
WAR/TWY RG10 32 F8
Trout Cl EARL RG6 46 A6
MLW SL7 18 E6
Trout La WDR/YW UB7 31 L8
Trout Rd WDR/YW UB7 31 L8
Trowe's La THLE RG7 144 H12
THLE RG7 145 N9
Trumbull Rd BNFD RG42 64 A5
Trumper Wy SL SL1 38 B1
Trumps Green Av VW GU25 80 D3
Trumps Green Cl VW GU25 80 E2
Trumpsgreen Rd VW GU25 80 C5
Trumps Green Rd VW GU25 80 E2
Trumps Mill La VW GU25 80 F8
Truro Cl MDHD SL6 25 J7
Truss Hill Rd ASC SL5 78 C2
Trust Cnr HEN RG9 22 A6
Trusthorpe Cl EARL RG6 60 E4
Trys Hl CHERT KT16 80 F6
Tubbs Farm Cl HUNG RG17 117 K4
Tubb's La TADY RG26 148 E10
Tubwell Rd SLN SL2 29 K2
Tudor Av KSCL RG20 121 J10
Tudor Cl ASHF TW15 70 D2
EWKG RG40 74 F1
TADY RG26 149 N8
Tudor Ct MDHD SL6 26 E4
TADY RG26 148 D1
Tudor Dr YTLY GU46 * 92 D1
Tudor Gdns SL SL1 27 L6
Tudor La WDSR SL4 54 C6
Tudor Rd ASHF TW15 71 K4
NWBY RG14 6 F7
READ RG1 8 E4
Tudor Wk WEY KT13 83 H8
Tudor Wy WDSR SL4 38 A8
Tulip Wy WDR/YW UB7 41 M4
Tull Wy NTHA RG18 97 H2
Tunnel Link Rd HTHAIR TW6 57 G4
Tunnel Rd East WDR/YW UB7 42 D7
Tunnel Rd West WDR/YW UB7 42 C8
Tuns Hill Cots EARL RG6 60 A1
Tuns La HEN RG9 22 A4
SL SL1 10 A8
Tunworth Ct TADY RG26 148 E3
Tunworth Ms TADY RG26 148 E2
Tupsley Rd READ RG1 58 F1
Turbary Gdns TADY RG26 148 D1
Turf Hill Rd CBLY GU15 88 F6
Turfhouse La CHOB/PIR GU24 91 L4
Turing Dr BRAK RG12 76 A2
Turk's La THLE RG7 143 P10
Turmeric Cl EARL RG6 59 M5
Turnberry BRAK RG12 75 L3
Turnbridge Cl EARL RG6 60 B6
Turner Pl SHST GU47 87 K8
Turner Rd DTCH/LGLY SL3 39 L2
Turners Cl STA TW18 70 B3
Turners Dr STHA RG19 98 A3
The Turnery STHA RG19 97 L3
Turnfields STHA RG19 97 M3
Turnhams Green Pk
TILE/CALC RG31 * 137 L5
Turnoak Pk WDSR SL4 52 E3
Turnpike Rd BNFD RG42 63 K7

NTHA RG18 97 G2
NWBY RG14 7 M1
Turnstone Cl WWKG RG41 61 G3
Turnstone End YTLY GU46 86 B8
Turnville Cl LTWR GU18 90 A5
Turpin Rd EBED/NFELT TW14 57 M5
Turpins Gn MDHD SL6 * 35 J1
Turpins Ri BFOR GU20 78 B8
Turton Wy SL SL1 10 C8
Tuscan Cl RDGW/BURGH RG30 137 Q2
Tuscany Wy YTLY GU46 92 C2
Tuxford Ms RDGW/BURGH RG30 44 B7
Tweed Cl FARN GU14 93 L8
Tweed Ct RDGW/BURGH RG30 44 B7
Tweed Rd DTCH/LGLY SL3 40 D6
Twinches La SL SL1 38 D1
Twin Oaks CAV/SC RG4 126 H12
Twinwoods KSCL RG20 119 L10
Two Mile Dr SL SL1 38 A2
Two Rivers Wy NWBY RG14 7 M3
Two Tree Hl HEN RG9 127 P2
Twycross Rd EWKG RG40 15 M4
Twyford Orch WAR/TWY RG10 * 33 H7
Twyford Rd BNFD RG42 49 J6
EWKG RG40 14 E1
WAR/TWY RG10 34 A8
Twynersh Av CHERT KT16 81 M3
Twynham Rd MDHD SL6 25 K7
Tyberton Pl READ RG1 58 F1
Tydehams NWBY RG14 96 A7
Tyle Pl WDSR SL4 54 A4
Tyler Cl CAV/SC RG4 44 E1
Tyler Dr WHIT RG2 72 E7
Tyler Gdns ADL/WDHM KT15 82 C8
Tyle Rd RDGW/BURGH RG30 137 P2
Tyler's La THLE RG7 134 D8
Tylers Pl RDGW/BURGH RG30 137 R2
Tyler Wk DTCH/LGLY SL3 40 B5
Tylorstown CAV/SC RG4 44 F1
Tymawr CAV/SC RG4 44 F1
Tyndale Ms SL SL1 38 D2
Tyne Cl FARN GU14 93 L8
Tyne Wy NTHA RG18 97 K1
Tyrell Gdns WDSR SL4 12 A9
Tytherton BRAK RG12 3 H5

U

Uffcott Cl EARL RG6 59 M6
Uffington Cl TILE/CALC RG31 137 N2
Uffington Dr BRAK RG12 3 M8
Ufton Br THLE RG7 136 D12
Ufton La THLE RG7 136 C12
Ullswater BRAK RG12 75 L4
Ullswater Cl LTWR GU18 90 B5
SL SL1 27 L6
STHA RG19 97 J3
Ullswater Dr TILE/CALC RG31 125 P11
Ullswater Rd LTWR GU18 90 B5
Ulster Cl CAV/SC RG4 45 K1
Umberstone VW GU25 80 D3
Umberville Wy SLN SL2 28 B5
Underhill WGFD OX10 111 P6
Underhill Cl MDHD SL6 4 E6
Underwood BRAK RG12 75 L3
Underwood Rd
RDGW/BURGH RG30 137 R6
Union Cl SHST GU47 87 L4
Union Rd FRIM GU16 95 K6
THLE RG7 136 A7
Union St READ RG1 8 F5
Unity Cl CAV/SC RG4 126 H12
Unwin Av EBED/NFELT TW14 57 K4
Upavon Dr READ RG1 58 E1
Upavon Gdns BRAK RG12 76 F2
Upcroft WDSR SL4 12 E9
Updown Hl BFOR GU20 90 D2
Up Gn HTWY RG27 85 M8
Upland Rd CBLY GU15 88 D7
Uplands HUNG RG17 138 G1
Uplands Cl SHST GU47 87 H6
Uplands Rd CAV/SC RG4 44 E1
Upper Bray Rd MDHD SL6 36 E4
Upper Broadmoor Rd
CWTH RG45 87 J1
Upper Chobham Rd CBLY GU15 95 G3
Upper College Ride CBLY GU15 88 E6
Upper Crown St READ RG1 9 H8
Upper Eddington HUNG RG17 129 N10
Upper End KSCL RG20 119 L6
Upper Gordon Rd CBLY GU15 94 D1
Upper Ground Level READ RG1 * 9 H8
Upper Halliford Rd
SHPTN TW17 71 L7
Upper Lambourn Rd
HUNG RG17 117 J3
Upper Lees Rd SLN SL2 28 C4
Upper Meadow Rd WHIT RG2 * 59 K4
Upper Nursery ASC SL5 79 G2
Upper Park Rd CBLY GU15 94 D1
Upper Red Cross Rd
GOR/PANG RG8 112 A11
Upper Redlands Rd READ RG1 59 K1
Upper Thames Wy BNEND SL8 20 A2
Upper Verran Rd CBLY GU15 94 D3
Upper Village Rd ASC SL5 78 C2
Upper Wk VW GU25 80 E1
Upper Warren Av CAV/SC RG4 44 C3
Upper Woodcote Rd
CAV/SC RG4 44 D1
Uppingham Dr WODY RG5 46 F5
Uppingham Gdns CAV/SC RG4 127 K12
Upshire Gdns BRAK RG12 76 F1
Upton Cl HEN RG9 22 A5
SL SL1 11 H8
Upton Court Rd DTCH/LGLY SL3 11 J9
Upton Lea Pde SLN SL2 * 11 L2
Upton Pk SL SL1 10 F8
Upton Park Cl SL SL1 11 G9
Upton Rd RDGW/BURGH RG30 44 A7
SL SL1 11 J9
Urquhart La WGFD OX10 113 L3
Urquhart Rd STHA RG19 98 A5
Usk Rd RDGW/BURGH RG30 137 R4
Uxbridge Rd DTCH/LGLY SL3 30 A6
SL SL1 11 K7
SLN SL2 29 L8
Uxmore Rd GOR/PANG RG8 113 P7

V

Vachel Rd READ RG1 8 E5
Vaillant Rd WEY KT13 83 J8
Vale Cl WEY KT13 83 K7
Vale Ct WEY KT13 83 K7
Vale Crs RDGW/BURGH RG30 137 Q1
Vale Gv SL SL1 10 F9
Valentia Cl RDGW/BURGH RG30 44 D6
Valentia Rd
RDGW/BURGH RG30 44 D6
Valentine Cl WHIT RG2 59 L5
Valentine Crs CAV/SC RG4 45 J2
Vale Rd CBLY GU15 94 A2
WDSR SL4 12 B4
WEY KT13 83 K7
Vale Vw WAR/TWY RG10 47 H2
Vale View Dr THLE RG7 144 H9
Valley Cl CAV/SC RG4 45 G2
GOR/PANG RG8 112 A12
Valley Crs WWKG RG41 14 C2
Valley End DTCH/LGLY SL3 29 L5
Valley End Rd CHOB/PIR GU24 91 H2
Valley Rd FRIM GU16 95 H6
HEN RG9 127 P2
NWBY RG14 6 A9
THLE RG7 143 Q3
Valley Vw SHST GU47 87 G7
Valley Wy TADY RG26 148 G1
Valon Rd WHIT RG2 72 E5
Valpy St READ RG1 9 G5
Valroy Cl CBLY GU15 88 D8
Vandyke BRAK RG12 75 L3
Vanguard Wy HTHAIR TW6 57 L1
Vanlore Wy TILE/CALC RG31 137 N6
Vanners La KSCL RG20 141 K9
Vansittart Est WDSR SL4 13 G5
Vansittart Rd MLW SL7 19 G7
WDSR SL4 12 F5
Vanwall Rd MDHD SL6 35 K2
Vastern Ct READ RG1 * 8 F3
Vastern Rd READ RG1 8 F3
Vaughan Gdns WDSR SL4 38 B4
Vaughan Wy SLN SL2 28 A5
Vauxhall Dr WODY RG5 46 F8
Vegal Crs EGH TW20 68 C3
Veitch Cl EBED/NFELT TW14 57 M6
Venetia Cl CAV/SC RG4 127 J11
Venning Rd WHIT RG2 72 F6
Ventnor Rd TILE/CALC RG31 137 P1
Venus Cl SLN SL2 28 B5
Verbena Cl WWKG RG41 61 G3
Verey Cl WAR/TWY RG10 47 M3
Verica Gdns TADY RG26 142 G12
Vermont Rd SLN SL2 28 A5
Vermont Woods EWKG RG40 73 L7
Verney Cl MLW SL7 18 F4
Verney Ms RDGW/BURGH RG30 44 C7
Verney Rd DTCH/LGLY SL3 40 C4
Vernon Cl STWL/WRAY TW19 56 E7
Vernon Crs WHIT RG2 59 H7
Vernon Dr ASC SL5 65 K7
Vernon Rd FELT TW13 57 M8
Verona Cl UX/CGN UB8 31 L7
Verran Rd CBLY GU15 94 D3
Vibia Cl STWL/WRAY TW19 56 D6
Viburnum Ct CHOB/PIR GU24 90 E8
Vicarage Av EGH TW20 69 H4
Vicarage Cl EWKG RG40 73 M8
MDHD SL6 20 C7
Vicarage Ct EGH TW20 69 H4
WHIT RG2 * 145 P1
Vicarage Crs EGH TW20 69 H3
Vicarage Dr MDHD SL6 36 E2
Vicarage Gdns ASC SL5 78 A2
MDHD SL6 35 G6
Vicarage La HTWY RG27 151 M9
NTHA RG18 133 Q10
STA TW18 70 B8
STWL/WRAY TW19 54 E7
YTLY GU46 86 C7
Vicarage Rd BAGS GU19 89 J3
BLKW GU17 93 L2
EGH TW20 69 H3
HEN RG9 22 A6
MDHD SL6 5 G3
STA TW18 69 L1
SUN TW16 71 M3
WHIT RG2 59 J1
YTLY GU46 86 C7
Vicarage Wk MDHD SL6 36 E2
Vicarage Wy DTCH/LGLY SL3 40 F7
Vicarage Wood Wy
TILE/CALC RG31 137 M1
Vickers Cl WHIT RG2 145 Q2
Victor Cl MDHD SL6 25 K6
Victoria Av CBLY GU15 94 A1
Victoria Cl WEY KT13 83 K7
Victoria Ct BAGS GU19 89 L5
Victoria Crs IVER SL0 31 J8
Victoria Dr BLKW GU17 93 J2
Victoria Gdns EWKG RG40 15 M1
MLW SL7 19 G4
NWBY RG14 6 F2
Victoria Gv NWBY RG14 7 G6
Victoria La HYS/HAR UB3 42 F5
Victoria Pl BNFD RG42 * 63 J3
Victoria Rd ADL/WDHM KT15 82 D8
ASC SL5 78 A2
CAV/SC RG4 45 G3
MLW SL7 19 G4
SHST GU47 87 L5
SLN SL2 11 M5
STA TW18 69 L1
THLE RG7 143 P8
TILE/CALC RG31 137 P2
UX/CGN UB8 31 L1
WAR/TWY RG10 33 G4
WDSR SL4 38 B5
WEY KT13 83 K7
Victoria St EGH TW20 68 C4
READ RG1 9 L7
SL SL1 11 H7
WDSR SL4 13 J6
Victoria Wy READ RG1 9 M6
WEY KT13 83 K7
Victor Pl THLE RG7 99 L4
Victor Rd STHA RG19 98 A3
WDSR SL4 53 J2
Victor Wy WODY RG5 47 G7
Victory Cl STWL/WRAY TW19 56 E7
Victory Park Rd
ADL/WDHM KT15 82 C7
Victory Rd CHERT KT16 82 A5
Victory Wy HEST TW5 43 L5
Vigo La YTLY GU46 92 C1
Viking BRAK RG12 75 L2
Village Cl WEY KT13 83 K7
WHIT RG2 59 H8
Village Ms ASC SL5 78 C1
Village Rd EGH TW20 69 J8
WDSR SL4 37 K3
The Village EWKG RG40 85 L3
WDSR SL4 * 53 H8
Village Wy ASHF TW15 70 F2
YTLY GU46 86 D7
Villiers Md WWKG RG41 14 C5
Villiers Rd SLN SL2 28 F6
Villier St UX/CGN UB8 31 M4
Villiers Wy NWBY RG14 141 Q8
Vincent Cl CHERT KT16 81 L4
WDR/YW UB7 42 C6
WODY RG5 46 F8
Vincent Dr SHPTN TW17 71 L8
Vincent Ri BRAK RG12 3 L6
Vincent Rd CHERT KT16 81 L4
NTHA RG18 98 A2
Vine Cl STWL/WRAY TW19 56 A4
WDR/YW UB7 42 C4
Vine Crs RDGW/BURGH RG30 58 A2
Vineries Cl WDR/YW UB7 42 C6
The Vines WWKG RG41 73 J3
Vine St UX/CGN UB8 31 M2
Vine Tree Cl TADY RG26 148 F3
Vineyard Dr BNEND SL8 20 B1
Viola Av STWL/WRAY TW19 56 E7
Viola Cft BNFD RG42 64 F6
Violet Gv NTHA RG18 98 A1
Violet La TADY RG26 103 L8
Virginia Av VW GU25 80 C2
Virginia Cl STA TW18 70 C8
Virginia Dr VW GU25 80 C1
Virginia Pk VW GU25 * 80 E1
Virginia Wy
RDGW/BURGH RG30 58 B1
Viscount Rd STWL/WRAY TW19 56 D6
Viscount Wy HTHAIR TW6 57 L3
WODY RG5 46 F7
Viveash Cl HYS/HAR UB3 43 H3
Vivien Cl MDHD SL6 20 B8
Voller Dr TILE/CALC RG31 137 N4
Volunteer Rd THLE RG7 136 H7
Vulcan Cl WODY RG5 47 H5
Vulcan Wy SHST GU47 87 G7
Vyne Rd TADY RG26 149 N10

W

Waborne Rd BNEND SL8 20 D2
Wade Dr SL SL1 38 C1
Wadham SHST GU47 87 M5
Wadham Cl SHPTN TW17 83 J4
Wagbullock Ri BRAK RG12 76 C3
Waggoners Hollow BAGS GU19 89 L4
Wagner Cl MDHD SL6 35 H3
Wagtail Cl WAR/TWY RG10 47 L2
Waingels Rd WAR/TWY RG10 47 G4
Wainwright Cl EWKG RG40 63 G8
Wakefield Crs SLN SL2 29 H1
Wakeford Cl TADY RG26 148 G1
Wakeford Ct TADY RG26 142 G12
Wakelins End MDHD SL6 20 A7
Wakeman Rd BNEND SL8 20 C3
Wakemans GOR/PANG RG8 124 B10
Walbury BRAK RG12 3 M9
Waldeck Rd MDHD SL6 5 K5
Waldeck St READ RG1 59 H1
Waldegrave Pl NWBY RG14 * 6 E4
Walden Av WHIT RG2 72 C3
Waldens Cl BNEND SL8 20 C3
Waldorf Hts BLKW GU17 93 J3
Waldron Hl BRAK RG12 64 F6
The Waldrons HUNG RG17 118 A8
Walford Rd UX/CGN UB8 31 L3
Walgrove Gdns MDHD SL6 35 G8
Walker Cl EBED/NFELT TW14 57 M6
GOR/PANG RG8 113 J9
Walker Crs DTCH/LGLY SL3 40 B5
Walker Rd MDHD SL6 36 C2
Walker's La HUNG RG17 117 K3
Walkers Pl RDGW/BURGH RG30 44 C7
Walker's Rdg CBLY GU15 94 E1
The Walk WDSR SL4 38 C5
Wallace Cl MLW SL7 19 H2
SHPTN TW17 83 K1
WODY RG5 60 D1
Wallace Gv THLE RG7 145 L2
Wallace Wk ADL/WDHM KT15 82 C8
WDSR SL4 39 H5
Wallcroft Cl BNFD RG42 63 L5
The Walled Gdn
WAR/TWY RG10 32 F4
Waller Ct CAV/SC RG4 45 H4
Waller Dr NWBY RG14 97 G1
Wallingford Cl BRAK RG12 3 M9
Wallingford Rd
GOR/PANG RG8 111 Q10
KSCL RG20 122 A1
UX/CGN UB8 31 K3
WGFD OX10 112 C2
Wallington Rd CBLY GU15 89 G5
Wallingtons Rd HUNG RG17 139 R4
Wallis Dr TADY RG26 150 B8
Wall La THLE RG7 143 L12
Wallner Wy EWKG RG40 15 K7
Walmer Cl CWTH RG45 87 J1
FRIM GU16 94 F7
RDGW/BURGH RG30 44 A8
Walmer Rd WODY RG5 46 F5
Walnut Av WDR/YW UB7 42 C3
Walnut Cl CAV/SC RG4 126 B5
WWKG RG41 14 A7
YTLY GU46 92 D2
Walnut Tree Cl BNEND SL8 20 D4
WAR/TWY RG10 33 G8
Walnut Tree Ct
GOR/PANG RG8 112 A12
Walnut Tree Rd SHPTN TW17 71 J7
Walnut Wy BNEND SL8 20 D4
RDGW/BURGH RG30 137 P2
Walpole Rd SL SL1 27 M7
WDSR SL4 54 B6
Walronds Cl MARL SN8 116 A6
Walrus Cl WODY RG5 47 H7
Walsh Av BNFD RG42 3 M1
Walter Rd WWKG RG41 61 L6
Walters Cl HYS/HAR UB3 43 H2
NTHA RG18 133 Q10
Waltham Av HYS/HAR UB3 42 E3
Waltham Cl MDHD SL6 35 H4
SHST GU47 87 K5
Waltham Rd MDHD SL6 35 G7
WAR/TWY RG10 47 K2
Walton Av HEN RG9 22 A6
Walton Bridge Rd SHPTN TW17 83 L4
Walton Cl WODY RG5 46 C7
Walton Dr ASC SL5 65 M6
Walton Gdns FELT TW13 71 M2
Walton La SHPTN TW17 83 M4
SLN SL2 28 B3
WEY KT13 83 J6
WOT/HER KT12 83 J5
Walton Wy NWBY RG14 7 J1
Wanbourne La HEN RG9 114 D4
Wandhope Wy
TILE/CALC RG31 125 N12
Wandsdyke Cl FRIM GU16 94 F6
Wansey Gdns NWBY RG14 96 F1
Wanstraw Gv BRAK RG12 76 E4
Wantage Cl BRAK RG12 76 E2
Wantage Rd GOR/PANG RG8 111 P9
HUNG RG17 117 L1
HUNG RG17 118 G8
RDGW/BURGH RG30 44 C7
SHST GU47 87 K6
Wapshott Rd STA TW18 69 L4
Waram Cl HUNG RG17 129 N11
Warbler Cl TILE/CALC RG31 137 M4
Warbler Dr EARL RG6 60 B5
Warblington Cl TADY RG26 148 E3
Warborough Av
TILE/CALC RG31 137 M3
Warborough Rd WANT OX12 106 E2
Warbreck Dr TILE/CALC RG31 125 M11
Warbrook La HTWY RG27 85 G6
Ward Cl EWKG RG40 15 J2
IVER SL0 31 H8
Ward Gdns SL SL1 28 A8
Wardle Av TILE/CALC RG31 137 P1
Wardle Cl BAGS GU19 89 L3
Ward Royal WDSR SL4 13 H5
Ward Royal Pde WDSR SL4 * 13 H5
Wards Pl EGH TW20 69 J4
Wards Stone Pk BRAK RG12 76 E4
Wareham Rd BRAK RG12 76 F2
Warehouse Rd STHA RG19 101 H1
Warfield Rd BNFD RG42 3 H1
EBED/NFELT TW14 57 L6
Warfield St BNFD RG42 64 C3
Wargrave Hl WAR/TWY RG10 32 F4
Wargrave Rd HEN RG9 22 C6
WAR/TWY RG10 22 E8
WAR/TWY RG10 32 E7
Wargrove Dr SHST GU47 87 K6
Waring Cl EARL RG6 60 C6
The Warings THLE RG7 135 Q11
Warley Ri TILE/CALC RG31 125 M10
War Memorial Pl HEN RG9 22 A7
Warner Cl HYS/HAR UB3 42 F7
SL SL1 38 A1
Warners Hl MDHD SL6 19 L7
Warnford Rd
RDGW/BURGH RG30 137 R3
Warnham La KSCL RG20 121 P4
Warnsham Cl EARL RG6 60 B5
Warren Cl DTCH/LGLY SL3 40 A3
SHST GU47 87 G6
THLE RG7 143 Q4
Warren Down BNFD RG42 63 L6
Warren Fld IVER SL0 30 E3
Warren House Rd EWKG RG40 15 H2
Warren La EWKG RG40 85 L1
Warren Pde SLN SL2 * 39 L1
Warren Ri FRIM GU16 94 E3
Warren Rd ASHF TW15 71 L5
NWBY RG14 141 R8
WODY RG5 46 D5
Warren Rw ASC SL5 65 K7
Warren Row Rd
WAR/TWY RG10 23 H7
The Warren BRAK RG12 * 76 F1
CAV/SC RG4 44 C3
TADY RG26 148 C2
Warren Vw MDHD SL6 * 36 C6
Warrington Av SL SL1 28 E7
Warrington Sp WDSR SL4 54 B6
Warwick BRAK RG12 76 E4
Warwick Av EGH TW20 69 J6
SLN SL2 28 E5
STA TW18 70 C4
Warwick Cl CBLY GU15 95 H3
MDHD SL6 35 K2
Warwick Dr NWBY RG14 7 H8
Warwick Pl UX/CGN UB8 31 L1
Warwick Rd ASHF TW15 70 E3
WDR/YW UB7 42 A1
WHIT RG2 59 J2
Warwick Vls EGH TW20 * 69 J6
Wasdale Cl SHST GU47 87 K4
Wash Hl FLKWH/TG HP10 21 G3
Wash Hill Lea FLKWH/TG HP10 20 F2
Washington Dr SL SL1 27 M8
WDSR SL4 52 E2
Washington Rd CAV/SC RG4 45 H4
Wash Water KSCL RG20 141 P11
Wasing La THLE RG7 99 M8
Watchetts Dr CBLY GU15 94 C4
Watchetts Lake Cl CBLY GU15 94 D3
Watchetts Rd CBLY GU15 94 B3
Watchmoor Point CBLY GU15 * 94 B2
Watchmoor Rd CBLY GU15 94 A3
Waterbeach Cl SL SL1 28 F7
Waterbeach Rd SL SL1 28 F7
Waterfall Cl VW GU25 67 M8
Waterford Wy EWKG RG40 15 G6
Waterham Rd BRAK RG12 76 B3
Waterhouse Md SHST GU47 87 K7
Water La FARN GU14 94 A7
STHA RG19 96 E6
Waterloo Cl CBLY GU15 89 H7
EBED/NFELT TW14 57 M7
WGFD OX10 111 Q3
Waterloo Crs EWKG RG40 15 L8
Waterloo Pl CWTH RG45 * 87 H2
Waterloo Ri WHIT RG2 59 H2
Waterloo Rd CWTH RG45 87 G2
EWKG RG40 15 L8
UX/CGN UB8 31 L2
WHIT RG2 59 H1
Waterloo Ter WEY KT13 * 83 G8
Waterman Ct SL SL1 38 A1
Waterman Pl READ RG1 8 F2
Waterman's Rd HEN RG9 22 A6
Watermans Wy WAR/TWY RG10 32 E5
Watermead EBED/NFELT TW14 57 L7
Watermill Ct THLE RG7 * 99 M4
Waterperry La CHOB/PIR GU24 91 M5
Water Reach MDHD SL6 5 J1
Water Rd RDGW/BURGH RG30 44 B7
Waters Dr STA TW18 69 M2
Watersfield Cl EARL RG6 60 B5
Waterside UX/CGN UB8 31 L6
Waterside Dr DTCH/LGLY SL3 40 B2
GOR/PANG RG8 125 P9
THLE RG7 137 K7
Waterside Gdns READ RG1 8 F7
Water Splash La ASC SL5 66 E6
Watersplash La BNFD RG42 64 B4
HEST TW5 43 K5
HYS/HAR UB3 43 J4
Watersplash Rd SHPTN TW17 83 G1
Water St NTHA RG18 122 B8
Watery La CHERT KT16 81 K4
CHOB/PIR GU24 91 K5
HYS/HAR UB3 42 F5
KSCL RG20 140 F9
Watlington St READ RG1 9 J6
Watmore La WWKG RG41 61 K3
Watson Cl THLE RG7 142 E3
Watt's La DID OX11 110 C2
Wavell Cl WHIT RG2 59 M5
Wavell Gdns SLN SL2 28 B4
Wavell Rd MDHD SL6 25 K8
Wavendene Av EGH TW20 69 J5
Waverley BRAK RG12 75 L2
Waverley Cl CBLY GU15 94 F2
HYS/HAR UB3 42 F4
Waverley Dr CBLY GU15 94 E1
CHERT KT16 81 K7
VW GU25 80 A1
Waverley Rd BAGS GU19 89 L3
RDGW/BURGH RG30 44 B7
SLN SL2 28 E6
The Waverleys NTHA RG18 97 M2
Waverley Wy EWKG RG40 73 L5
Waybrook Crs READ RG1 45 L8
Waye Av HEST TW5 43 J8
Wayfarer's Wk HUNG RG17 147 K3
KSCL RG20 147 P6
Wayland Cl BRAK RG12 76 F1
Wayland Crs DID OX11 109 J1
Waylands STWL/WRAY TW19 54 E5
Waylands Cl THLE RG7 136 A6
Waylen St READ RG1 8 D6
Wayman Rd FARN GU14 93 L6
Ways End CBLY GU15 94 E2
Wayside Gn GOR/PANG RG8 112 H9
Wayside Ms MDHD SL6 5 H2
Wealden Wy
RDGW/BURGH RG30 137 Q2
Weald Ri RDGW/BURGH RG30 125 R12
Weardale Cl WHIT RG2 59 K2
Weather Wy BRAK RG12 3 H4
Weaver Moss SHST GU47 87 H7
Weavers Wk NWBY RG14 * 6 E3
Weavers Wy WAR/TWY RG10 47 K2
Webb Cl BAGS GU19 89 L5
BNFD RG42 63 L5
DTCH/LGLY SL3 39 M4
Webb Ct EWKG RG40 15 M2
Webbs Acre STHA RG19 98 B4
Webbs Cl READ RG1 * 8 D9
Webbs La THLE RG7 135 R11
Webster Cl MDHD SL6 35 J1
Wedderburn Cl WWKG RG41 61 K4
Wedgewood Wy
RDGW/BURGH RG30 137 R1
Wedman's La HTWY RG27 151 M11
Weedon Cl WGFD OX10 111 Q2
Weekes Dr SL SL1 38 D1
Weighbridge Rw READ RG1 8 D3
Weir Cl TILE/CALC RG31 137 R6
Weir Pl STA TW18 69 L6
Weir Rd CHERT KT16 82 B4
Weirside Ct READ RG1 9 L6
Weirside Gdns WDR/YW UB7 41 M1
Welbeck BRAK RG12 75 L2
Welbeck Rd MDHD SL6 4 C8
Welby Cl MDHD SL6 35 J2
Welby Crs WWKG RG41 61 H5
Weldale St READ RG1 8 D5
Welden SLN SL2 29 L7
Welford Rd KSCL RG20 130 H6
WODY RG5 47 G6
Welland Cl DTCH/LGLY SL3 40 C6
TILE/CALC RG31 137 N1
Wellbank MDHD SL6 27 G5
Wellburn Cl SHST GU47 87 H7
Well Cl CBLY GU15 94 B2
Wellcroft Rd SL SL1 38 D1
Weller Dr CBLY GU15 94 C3
EWKG RG40 73 G8
Weller's La BNFD RG42 64 C1
Wellesley Av DTCH/LGLY SL3 41 H3
Wellesley Cl BAGS GU19 89 J3
Wellesley Dr CWTH RG45 86 E1
Wellesley Pth SL SL1 11 J6
Wellesley Rd SL SL1 11 J6
Welley Av STWL/WRAY TW19 54 E3
Welley Rd STWL/WRAY TW19 54 E3
Wellfield Cl TILE/CALC RG31 137 N3
Wellhill Rd WANT OX12 118 G1
Well House La HTWY RG27 84 B5
Wellhouse La NTHA RG18 133 R4
Wellhouse Rd MDHD SL6 26 A4
Wellington Av VW GU25 80 B3
WHIT RG2 59 K2
Wellington Cl MDHD SL6 25 K6
NWBY RG14 96 E1
SHST GU47 87 J6
WOT/HER KT12 83 M5
Wellington Crs TADY RG26 103 M5
Wellington Dr BRAK RG12 76 D2
Wellington Gdns THLE RG7 135 P9
Wellingtonia Av EWKG RG40 86 B2
Wellington Rd ASHF TW15 70 E3
CWTH RG45 87 J2
EBED/NFELT TW14 57 L4
EWKG RG40 14 E7
MDHD SL6 4 C4
SHST GU47 87 H6
UX/CGN UB8 31 L2
Wellington St SL SL1 11 H6
Wellington Ter SHST GU47 87 J6
Well Meadow NWBY RG14 96 D1
Wells Cl WDSR SL4 12 D4
Wells La ASC SL5 66 B8
Well St KSCL RG20 100 C8
Well Vw HEN RG9 113 R6
Wellwood ASC SL5 66 B8
Welsh La THLE RG7 145 L12
Welshman's Rd THLE RG7 143 K9
Welwick Cl EARL RG6 * 60 E4
Welwyn Av EBED/NFELT TW14 57 M5
Wendan Rd NWBY RG14 6 D9
Wendover Dr FRIM GU16 95 J3
Wendover Pl STA TW18 69 K3
Wendover Rd BNEND SL8 20 C2
SL SL1 27 K6
STA TW18 69 K3
Wendover Wy
RDGW/BURGH RG30 137 P3
Wenlock Edge WAR/TWY RG10 47 H2
Wenlock Wy STHA RG19 97 M4
Wensley Cl WAR/TWY RG10 47 K1
Wensleydale Dr CBLY GU15 95 K1
Wensley Rd READ RG1 58 D2
Wentworth Av ASC SL5 65 J7
SLN SL2 28 C4
WHIT RG2 59 K6
Wentworth Cl ASHF TW15 71 H2
CWTH RG45 74 F8
YTLY GU46 92 D1
Wentworth Ct NWBY RG14 7 G7
Wentworth Crs HYS/HAR UB3 42 F3
MDHD SL6 4 A7
Wentworth Dr VW GU25 79 M1
Wentworth Rd NWDGN UB2 43 L4
Wentworth Wy ASC SL5 65 J7
Wescott Rd EWKG RG40 15 J6
Wescott Wy UX/CGN UB8 31 L3
Wesley Dr EGH TW20 69 G4
Wesley Ga READ RG1 * 9 J7
Wesley Pl WDSR SL4 * 52 B8
Wessex Cl HUNG RG17 138 G1
Wessex Gdns WAR/TWY RG10 47 L3
Wessex Rd BNEND SL8 20 D4
Wessex Wy MDHD SL6 35 K2
Westacott Wy MDHD SL6 34 F1
Westborough Ct MDHD SL6 4 B7
Westborough Rd MDHD SL6 4 B6
Westbourne Rd FELT TW13 71 M1
SHST GU47 87 L7
STA TW18 70 B5
Westbourne Ter NWBY RG14 6 D1
RDGW/BURGH RG30 44 C7
Westbrook MDHD SL6 37 G5
Westbrook Cl HUNG RG17 138 G1
Westbrook Ct WWKG RG41 61 H4
Westbrook Gdns BRAK RG12 3 H3
Westbrook Gn DID OX11 110 B2
Westbrook Rd
RDGW/BURGH RG30 44 C5
STA TW18 69 M3
Westbrook St DID OX11 110 B2
Westbury Cl CWTH RG45 75 H8
SHPTN TW17 * 83 H3
Westbury La GOR/PANG RG8 125 L8
West Chiltern GOR/PANG RG8 113 J10
West Cl ASHF TW15 70 E2
MLW SL7 17 M7
Westcombe Cl BRAK RG12 76 D4
Westcote Rd
RDGW/BURGH RG30 44 D8
Westcotts Gn BNFD RG42 64 D5
West Ct CAV/SC RG4 45 E4
West Crs WDSR SL4 12 B6
Westcroft SLN SL2 28 D5
West Dean MDHD SL6 5 H2
Westdene Crs CAV/SC RG4 44 E2
Westdene Wy WEY KT13 83 L7
West Drayton Park Av
WDR/YW UB7 42 A3
West Dr ASC SL5 79 K2
CAV/SC RG4 46 D5
TILE/CALC RG31 137 Q5
VW GU25 79 L4
West End WGFD OX10 111 N1
West End La BNFD RG42 64 B3
HYS/HAR UB3 42 E7

SLN SL2 29 G2
West End Rd THLE RG7 143 N9
Westerdale STHA RG19 97 L3
Westerdale Dr FRIM GU16 95 H3
Westerham Wk WHIT RG2 * 59 H1
Western Av CHERT KT16 70 A8
EGH TW20 69 H8
HEN RG9 22 A6
NWBY RG14 6 B1
NWBY RG14 6 E1
WODY RG5 46 D6
Western Cl CHERT KT16 70 A8
HEN RG9 * 22 A6
Western Dr FLKWH/TG HP10 21 G1
SHPTN TW17 83 K2
Western Elms Av
RDGW/BURGH RG30 8 A7
Western End NWBY RG14 6 A6
Western Oaks TILE/CALC RG31 125 Q12
Western Perimeter Rd
HTHAIR TW6 56 B2
WDR/YW UB7 56 B1
Western Rd BNFD RG42 2 C4
BRAK RG12 2 A4
HEN RG9 22 A6
NWDGN UB2 43 L4
READ RG1 8 A8
Western Vw HYS/HAR UB3 43 H2
West Field Cl TADY RG26 148 F2
Westfield Crs HEN RG9 32 D3
NTHA RG18 97 K2
Westfield Rd CAV/SC RG4 9 G1
CBLY GU15 94 B4
MDHD SL6 25 K8
NTHA RG18 97 J1
SLN SL2 28 D5
WGFD OX10 111 M4
WWKG RG41 61 H4
Westfields KSCL RG20 121 R2
Westfield Wy NWBY RG14 6 A6
West Fryerne YTLY GU46 86 D7
Westgate Crs SL SL1 28 B8
Westgate Est
EBED/NFELT TW14 * 57 H7
Westgate Rd NWBY RG14 6 A6
West Gn YTLY GU46 86 B7
Westhatch La BNFD RG42 64 C2
West Hl READ RG1 9 G9
Westhorpe Pk MLW SL7 * 19 K3
Westhorpe Rd MLW SL7 19 K3
Westland NTHA RG18 97 K2
Westland Cl
STWL/WRAY TW19 * 56 E5
Westlands Av SL SL1 27 L7
WHIT RG2 59 L5
Westlands Cl HYS/HAR UB3 43 J4
SL SL1 27 L7
Westlands Rd NWBY RG14 6 F9
West La HEN RG9 115 R12
Westleigh Dr CAV/SC RG4 126 G6
Westley Mi BNFD RG42 49 L6
Westlyn Rd TADY RG26 148 G1
Westmacott Dr
EBED/NFELT TW14 57 M6
West Md MDHD SL6 26 B4
Westmead WDSR SL4 12 E9
Westmead Dr NWBY RG14 96 B6
West Mills NWBY RG14 6 D4
West Mills Yd NWBY RG14 * 6 D4
Westminster Wy EARL RG6 60 C5
Westmorland Cl WWKG RG41 61 K8
Westmorland Dr BNFD RG42 64 F4
CBLY GU15 95 H3
Westmorland Rd MDHD SL6 4 D5
Weston Av ADL/WDHM KT15 82 A8
Westonbirt Dr CAV/SC RG4 44 E3
Weston Gv BAGS GU19 89 M4
Weston Rd SL SL1 28 B6
Weston's KSCL RG20 121 K6
West Palace Gdns WEY KT13 83 H7
West Point SL SL1 37 M1
West Rp HTHAIR TW6 42 C8
West Rdg BNEND SL8 20 D2
Westridge Av GOR/PANG RG8 125 N9
Westridge Gn
GOR/PANG RG8 * 123 J2
West Rd CBLY GU15 94 D1
EBED/NFELT TW14 57 K6
EWKG RG40 75 J4
FARN GU14 94 A6
MDHD SL6 4 F5
WDR/YW UB7 42 B3
Westside Ct CHOB/PIR GU24 * 90 E8
West Spur Rd UX/CGN UB8 31 M4
West St HEN RG9 115 R12
MDHD SL6 5 G5
MLW SL7 18 E5
NWBY RG14 6 D3
READ RG1 8 F5
TADY RG26 148 E2
West Street Cl TADY RG26 148 E2
West Vw EBED/NFELT TW14 57 J7
KSCL RG20 120 C7
Westview Dr WAR/TWY RG10 32 F8
West Wk HYS/HAR UB3 43 J1
Westward Rd WWKG RG41 14 A3
West Wy GOR/PANG RG8 112 A10
SHPTN TW17 83 K3
Westwood Gln
TILE/CALC RG31 137 N2
Westwood Gn MDHD SL6 20 B8
Westwood Ho HTWY RG27 85 K6
Westwood Rd BFOR GU20 90 D1
MLW SL7 18 E5
NWBY RG14 7 H9
TILE/CALC RG31 137 P1
Westwood Rw
TILE/CALC RG31 125 N12
Wetherby Cl CAV/SC RG4 127 J12
Wethered Pk MLW SL7 18 F5
Wethered Rd MLW SL7 18 F4
SL SL1 27 K7
Wetton Pl EGH TW20 68 F3
Wexham Park La
DTCH/LGLY SL3 29 L5
Wexham Rd SL SL1 11 K6
SLN SL2 11 L1
Wexham St DTCH/LGLY SL3 29 K3
SLN SL2 29 K4
Wexham Woods
DTCH/LGLY SL3 29 L6
Wey Av CHERT KT16 70 A8
Weybridge Md YTLY GU46 86 E7
Weybridge Rd
ADL/WDHM KT15 82 E8
Wey Cl CBLY GU15 94 B1
Weycrofts BNFD RG42 2 B1
Weyhill Cl TADY RG26 148 D3
Weymead Cl CHERT KT16 82 C5
Wey Rd WEY KT13 82 F7
Whaley Rd EWKG RG40 15 K2
Wharfedale Rd WWKG RG41 60 F2
Wharfe La HEN RG9 22 A4
Wharfenden Wy FRIM GU16 94 F8
Wharf La BNEND SL8 20 C3
Wharf Rd FRIM GU16 94 F8
NWBY RG14 6 E3
STWL/WRAY TW19 54 C6
Wharfside THLE RG7 142 E3
Wharf St NWBY RG14 6 E4
The Wharf NWBY RG14 * 6 F4
Wharf Wy FRIM GU16 94 F8
Whatley Gn BRAK RG12 * 76 B3
Whatmore Cl
STWL/WRAY TW19 56 A5
Wheatash Rd ADL/WDHM KT15 82 B6
The Wheatbutts WDSR SL4 38 B5
Wheatfield Cl MDHD SL6 35 J2
Wheatfields Rd WHIT RG2 145 Q1
Wheatlands Cl TILE/CALC RG31 137 Q6
Wheatlands La NWBY RG14 141 P8
Wheatlands Rd DTCH/LGLY SL3 11 M9
Wheatley BRAK RG12 75 L2
Wheatley Cl WHIT RG2 59 L5
Wheatsheaf La NWBY RG14 7 H1
STA TW18 69 M5
Wheatsheaf Pde WDSR SL4 * 54 A4
Wheatstone Cl DTCH/LGLY SL3 11 J9
Wheble Dr WODY RG5 46 D6
Wheeler Cl THLE RG7 143 R3
Wheeler Ct TILE/CALC RG31 137 Q1
Wheelers Green Wy STHA RG19 98 A4
Wheelton Cl EARL RG6 60 E3
Wheelwrights Pl
DTCH/LGLY SL3 * 40 E7
Whins Cl CBLY GU15 94 B2
Whins Dr CBLY GU15 94 B2
Whinshill Ct ASC SL5 79 G5
Whistler Gv SHST GU47 87 K8
Whistlers La THLE RG7 149 K1
Whistley Cl BRAK RG12 3 L7
Whitakers Ct NTHA RG18 97 K2
Whitamore Rw HEN RG9 22 A6
Whitby Dr READ RG1 59 J1
Whitby Gn CAV/SC RG4 127 K12
Whitby Rd SL SL1 10 B2
Whitchurch Cl MDHD SL6 26 A3
Whitchurch Rd
GOR/PANG RG8 124 H8
Whitebeam Cl WWKG RG41 73 K3
White Bridge Cl
EBED/NFELT TW14 57 M5
Whitebrooke Pk MDHD SL6 26 E2
Whitebrook Pk MDHD SL6 * 26 E2
White City CWTH RG45 87 K1
White Cl NTHA RG18 133 M4
SL SL1 10 C4
Whitedown Rd TADY RG26 148 B2
White Farm La MARL SN8 146 A4
Whiteford Rd SLN SL2 29 G6
Whitegates La EARL RG6 46 A7
Whitehall Dr WHIT RG2 72 E6
Whitehall Farm La VW GU25 68 E8
Whitehall La EGH TW20 68 F5
GOR/PANG RG8 113 P7
STWL/WRAY TW19 55 G5
VW GU25 68 F6
Whitehall Rd UX/CGN UB8 31 M2
Whitehart Cl THLE RG7 137 J6
White Hart La TADY RG26 148 C10
White Hart Rd MDHD SL6 5 H5
SL SL1 10 C9
White Hart Rw CHERT KT16 * 82 A4
Whitehaven SL SL1 11 H2
White Hermitage WDSR SL4 * 54 C4
White Hl BFOR GU20 78 B8
GOR/PANG RG8 123 M8
HEN RG9 22 A4
HEN RG9 127 N5
Whitehill Cl CBLY GU15 88 D7
Whitehill Pl VW GU25 80 E2
Whitehills Gn GOR/PANG RG8 112 A12
Whitehorn Pl WDR/YW UB7 42 B1
White Horse La EWKG RG40 85 J1
White Horse Rd WDSR SL4 52 D1
Whitehouse Cl FARN GU14 94 B8
White House Gdns YTLY GU46 86 C7
White House La THLE RG7 145 K6
Whitehouse Rd
GOR/PANG RG8 113 J10
WGFD OX10 112 D1
Whitehouse Wy DTCH/LGLY SL3 39 M3
IVER SL0 30 F4
Whiteknights Rd EARL RG6 59 M1
Whitelands Dr ASC SL5 65 K6
Whitelands Rd NTHA RG18 97 L2
White La HEN RG9 115 L7
Whiteley WDSR SL4 38 A7
White Lilies Island WDSR SL4 12 E3
White Lion Wy YTLY GU46 86 D7
Whitelocks Piece HUNG RG17 129 J8
White Lodge Cl
TILE/CALC RG31 125 M11
Whitemoor La GOR/PANG RG8 123 N9
White Paddock MDHD SL6 35 J4
White Rd CBLY GU15 87 M8
DID OX11 109 K2
White's Hl THLE RG7 143 N2
White Shoot DID OX11 110 C4
Whites La DTCH/LGLY SL3 39 K6
White's La THLE RG7 135 R10
Whitestone Cl EARL RG6 60 E3
White St STHL UB1 43 M2
Whitewalls Cl KSCL RG20 121 R1
Whitewell Cl WHIT RG2 72 E4
Whitley Cl STWL/WRAY TW19 56 E5
Whitley Park La WHIT RG2 59 K2
Whitley Rd YTLY GU46 92 D2
Whitley St WHIT RG2 59 H1
Whitley Wood La WHIT RG2 59 H6
Whitley Wood Rd WHIT RG2 59 H8
Whitmoor Rd BAGS GU19 89 L4
Whitmore Cl SHST GU47 87 K6
Whitmore La ASC SL5 79 G2
Whitstone Gdns WHIT RG2 59 J5
Whittaker Rd SL SL1 28 A5
Whittenham Cl SLN SL2 11 J5
Whittle Cl EWKG RG40 73 L7
SHST GU47 87 G5
Whittle Crs FARN GU14 93 M7
Whittle Pkwy SL SL1 27 M7
Whittle Rd HEST TW5 43 L7
Whitton Cl EARL RG6 60 D4
Whittonditch Rd MARL SN8 128 A6
Whitton Rd BRAK RG12 64 F8
Whitworth Rd EWKG RG40 73 G7
Whurley Wy MDHD SL6 26 A4
Whynstones Rd ASC SL5 78 A2
Whytecroft HEST TW5 43 M7
Whyteladyes La MDHD SL6 20 A8
The Wickets ASHF TW15 70 E2
MDHD SL6 4 A5
Wickford Wy EARL RG6 59 M6
Wickham Cl TADY RG26 148 D2
Wickham La EGH TW20 69 G5
Wickham Rd CBLY GU15 88 E6
EARL RG6 60 E5
Wickham V BRAK RG12 75 L3
Wick Hl La EWKG RG40 74 A8
Wick La EGH TW20 68 A2
Wick Rd EGH TW20 68 B5
Wick's Gn BNFD RG42 63 H3
Wicks La WAR/TWY RG10 48 E4
Widbrook Rd MDHD SL6 26 D3
Widecroft Rd IVER SL0 31 G7
Widmore La CAV/SC RG4 126 G4
Wield Ct EARL RG6 * 60 E5
Wiggett Gv BNFD RG42 63 J4
Wigmore La
RDGW/BURGH RG30 44 B5
THLE RG7 136 G8
Wigmore Rd TADY RG26 148 B1
Wilberforce Ms MDHD SL6 5 G4
Wilberforce Wy BRAK RG12 76 D2
Wilcox Gdns SHPTN TW17 70 E8
Wild Briar EWKG RG40 73 M7
Wild Cl EARL RG6 60 C6
Wildcroft Dr EWKG RG40 74 A5
Wilder Av GOR/PANG RG8 125 J9
Wilderness Ct EARL RG6 60 A3
Wilderness Rd EARL RG6 59 M3
FRIM GU16 94 E4
Wilders Cl BNFD RG42 2 C1
FRIM GU16 94 D3
Wildgreen North
DTCH/LGLY SL3 40 C4
Wildgreen South
DTCH/LGLY SL3 40 C4
Wildmoor La HTWY RG27 150 C12
Wildridings Rd BRAK RG12 2 B8
Wild Ridings Sq BRAK RG12 2 C8
Wildwood Dr TADY RG26 103 M5
Wildwood Gdns YTLY GU46 92 C2
Wilford Rd DTCH/LGLY SL3 40 A4
Wilfred Wy STHA RG19 98 B3
Wilkins Cl HYS/HAR UB3 43 H5
Willant Cl MDHD SL6 35 H4
Willats Cl CHERT KT16 * 81 M3
William Cl STHA RG19 97 M4
William Ellis Cl WDSR SL4 54 A4
William Hartley Yd
DTCH/LGLY SL3 * 29 K5
Williams Ct HUNG RG17 129 M12
William Sim Wd BNFD RG42 65 H4
Williamson Cl WWKG RG41 61 H3
William St READ RG1 8 C5
SL SL1 11 G5
WDSR SL4 13 J6
Willington Cl CBLY GU15 88 B8
Willis Cl NTHA RG18 133 P7
Willoners SLN SL2 28 C6
Willoughby Rd BRAK RG12 2 A7
DTCH/LGLY SL3 40 D3
Willow Bank MLW SL7 18 F1
Willowbrook WDSR SL4 38 F4
Willowbrook Rd
STWL/WRAY TW19 56 E7
Willow Cl DTCH/LGLY SL3 40 E7
MDHD SL6 25 M5
NWBY RG14 6 D8
RDGW/BURGH RG30 143 R1
Willow Ct FRIM GU16 94 D5
GOR/PANG RG8 * 124 G8
Willow Court La WGFD OX10 111 P5
Willow Crs FARN GU14 94 B7
Willowdale EWKG RG40 73 M6
Willow Dr BRAK RG12 3 H3
MDHD SL6 36 D4
WAR/TWY RG10 32 F8
Willowford YTLY GU46 86 D8
Willow Gdns TILE/CALC RG31 125 M12
WHIT RG2 59 K5
Willow Gn CHOB/PIR GU24 91 G8
Willowherb Cl EWKG RG40 15 L4
Willow La BLKW GU17 93 K2
WAR/TWY RG10 32 E2
Willowmead STA TW18 70 B6
Willowmead Cl MLW SL7 19 H3
NWBY RG14 141 Q9
Willowmead Gdns MLW SL7 19 H3
Willowmead Rd MLW SL7 19 H3
Willowmead Sq MLW SL7 19 H3
Willow Pk SLN SL2 29 J1
Willow Pl WDSR SL4 13 G1
Willow Rd DTCH/LGLY SL3 55 L1
KSCL RG20 101 H4
TADY RG26 148 D2
Willows End SHST GU47 87 H6
Willowside WODY RG5 46 E5
Willows Rd BNEND SL8 20 D3
The Willows BNEND SL8 * 20 D3
CAV/SC RG4 8 F1
LTWR GU18 90 C6
WEY KT13 83 G7
Willow St READ RG1 8 E8
Willow Tree Gld
TILE/CALC RG31 137 N6
Willow Wk EGH TW20 68 C3
Willow Wy HTWY RG27 150 D9
SHST GU47 86 F5
Willow Wood Cl SL SL1 27 K3
Willow Wren Whf
NWDGN UB2 * 43 K4
Willson Rd EGH TW20 68 B3
Wilmar Cl UX/CGN UB8 31 M1
Wilmington Cl WODY RG5 46 E6
Wilmot Cl BNFD RG42 63 J5
Wilmot Rd SL SL1 27 K4
Wilmot Wy CBLY GU15 94 F3
Wilsford Cl EARL RG6 59 L7
Wilson Av HEN RG9 22 A6
Wilson Cl KSCL RG20 122 A2
Wilson Ct WWKG RG41 61 H5
Wilson Rd RDGW/BURGH RG30 44 C7
Wilstrode Av BNFD RG42 63 M5
Wilton Cl WDR/YW UB7 41 M6
Wilton Crs WDSR SL4 52 D3
Wilton Rd CBLY GU15 94 B3
RDGW/BURGH RG30 44 C6
Wiltshire Av CWTH RG45 75 H8
SLN SL2 28 E5
Wiltshire Dr EWKG RG40 15 J4
Wiltshire Gv BNFD RG42 64 F4
Wiltshire Rd EWKG RG40 15 H2
MLW SL7 19 H1
Wilwood Rd BNFD RG42 63 L6
Wilwyne Cl CAV/SC RG4 45 J2
Wimbledon Cl CBLY GU15 88 F5
Wimbledon Rd CBLY GU15 88 F5
Wimblington Dr EARL RG6 60 B6
Wimborne Gdns
RDGW/BURGH RG30 44 A5
Wimbushes EWKG RG40 73 K8
Wimpole Rd WDR/YW UB7 41 M1
Winbury Ct MDHD SL6 4 F5
Wincanton Rd WHIT RG2 59 J6
Winch Cl BNFD RG42 63 J3
Winchcombe Rd NWBY RG14 6 F5
WAR/TWY RG10 47 L3
Winchester Cl DTCH/LGLY SL3 41 G8
Winchester Dr MDHD SL6 35 K3
Winchester Rd HYS/HAR UB3 43 G7
WHIT RG2 59 H2
Winchester Wy BLKW GU17 87 J8
Winchfield Gdns TADY RG26 148 D3
Winchgrove Rd BNFD RG42 2 D1
Winchstone Cl SHPTN TW17 82 F1
Wincroft Rd CAV/SC RG4 44 E1
Windermere Cl
EBED/NFELT TW14 57 L7
EGH TW20 69 H5
STWL/WRAY TW19 56 D8
WWKG RG41 61 J3
Windermere Rd LTWR GU18 90 B5
WHIT RG2 59 K3
Windermere Wy SL SL1 27 L6
STHA RG19 97 J3
WDR/YW UB7 42 A1
Winding Wood Dr CBLY GU15 95 H2
Windle Cl BFOR GU20 90 D2
Windlesham Ct BFOR GU20 78 C8
Windlesham Rd BNFD RG42 2 B2
CHOB/PIR GU24 90 E6
Windmill Av WWKG RG41 61 L6
Windmill Cl SUN TW16 71 L5
WDSR SL4 12 E7
WWKG RG41 61 L6
Windmill Cnr THLE RG7 143 Q8
Windmill Fld BFOR GU20 90 D2
Windmill La THLE RG7 99 J1
Windmill Rd BNFD RG42 2 B2
MDHD SL6 20 A8
SL SL1 10 C5
SUN TW16 71 L6
THLE RG7 143 Q8
Windmill Rd West SUN TW16 71 L6
Windmill Shott EGH TW20 68 F4
Windmill Ter SHPTN TW17 * 83 L4
Windrush Av DTCH/LGLY SL3 40 D3
Windrush Hts SHST GU47 87 H6
Windrush Wy MDHD SL6 5 H3
RDGW/BURGH RG30 44 B7
Windsor Br WDSR SL4 13 J4
Windsor Cl SL SL1 * 27 L5
Windsor Ct NWBY RG14 7 G4
Windsor Court Rd
CHOB/PIR GU24 91 L4
Windsor Dr ASHF TW15 70 D2
Windsor Gdns HYS/HAR UB3 42 F3
Windsor Great Pk ASC SL5 * 66 F5
Windsor Hl FLKWH/TG HP10 21 G1
Windsor La SL SL1 27 L5
Windsor Park Rd HYS/HAR UB3 43 H7
Windsor Pl CHERT KT16 * 82 A3
Windsor Ride ASC SL5 77 H2
BRAK RG12 76 E5
CBLY GU15 88 A6
EWKG RG40 74 A7
Windsor Ri NWBY RG14 7 J9
Windsor Rd ASC SL5 65 M7
CHOB/PIR GU24 91 L4
DTCH/LGLY SL3 39 J7
MDHD SL6 36 D4
SL SL1 10 F7
STWL/WRAY TW19 54 E5
WDSR SL4 54 D7
WDSR SL4 66 C3
Windsor Sq READ RG1 * 9 H9
Windsor St CHERT KT16 82 A3
UX/CGN UB8 31 L2
Windsor Wy FRIM GU16 94 F6
TILE/CALC RG31 137 M6
Wingate Rd WODY RG5 46 E8
Wing Cl MLW SL7 18 E5
Wingfield Gdns FRIM GU16 95 K3
Wingrove Rd
RDGW/BURGH RG30 44 C8
Winkfield Cl WWKG RG41 74 B3
Winkfield La WDSR SL4 51 H8
Winkfield Pln WDSR SL4 52 B6
Winkfield Rd ASC SL5 66 A4
WDSR SL4 52 C6
Winkfield Rw BNFD RG42 65 H3
Winkfield St WDSR SL4 51 J8
Winkworth La THLE RG7 142 E12
Winnersh Ga WWKG RG41 61 K4
Winnersh Gv WWKG RG41 61 J5
Winnock Rd WDR/YW UB7 41 M1
Winscombe BRAK RG12 75 L2
Winser Dr RDGW/BURGH RG30 58 D2
Winslet Pl
RDGW/BURGH RG30 * 44 B5
Winston Av TADY RG26 148 F3
Winston Cl FRIM GU16 94 F8
THLE RG7 145 P4
Winston Ct MDHD SL6 25 K6
Winston Wy STHA RG19 97 H2
Winterberry Wy CAV/SC RG4 126 E12
Winterbourne Rd KSCL RG20 131 Q6
Winter Hl MDHD SL6 19 K6
Winter Hill Rd MDHD SL6 25 J4
Winterton Dr NWBY RG14 141 R1
Winton Crs YTLY GU46 92 D1
Winton Rd WHIT RG2 59 K6
Wintringham Wy
GOR/PANG RG8 125 P9
Winvale SL SL1 10 F9
Winwood SLN SL2 29 L7
Wise La WDR/YW UB7 41 M4
Wise's Firs THLE RG7 143 M3
Wishmoor Cl CBLY GU15 88 E6
Wishmoor Rd CBLY GU15 88 E6
Wispington Cl EARL RG6 60 D4
Wistaria La YTLY GU46 92 C1
Wisteria Cl WWKG RG41 14 B8
Wiston Ter READ RG1 9 G5
Witcham Cl EARL RG6 60 D6
Withey Cl WDSR SL4 38 A8
Witheygate Av STA TW18 70 B4
Withybed La HUNG RG17 139 Q4
Withybed Wy NTHA RG18 98 A1
Withy Cl LTWR GU18 90 C5
TILE/CALC RG31 137 N5
Withycroft DTCH/LGLY SL3 30 A7
The Withys NTHA RG18 134 G1
Wittenham Av TILE/CALC RG31 137 M2
Wittenham Cl GOR/PANG RG8 113 K10
Wittenham Rd BRAK RG12 64 F6
Wittington Gn MLW SL7 * 17 M8
Woburn Cl CAV/SC RG4 44 E2
FRIM GU16 95 G5
Woburn Hl ADL/WDHM KT15 82 C6
Woburn Pk ADL/WDHM KT15 * 82 D6
Wokefield Rw THLE RG7 144 B6
Wokingham Rd BNFD RG42 2 A3
CWTH RG45 86 E3
EARL RG6 60 A1
READ RG1 45 L7
WAR/TWY RG10 47 M6
Wolf La WDSR SL4 52 D2
Wolseley St READ RG1 8 E8
Wolsey Rd ASHF TW15 70 E2
CAV/SC RG4 8 F1
SUN TW16 71 M5
Wolsingham Wy STHA RG19 97 M4
Wolverton Rd TADY RG26 103 L7
Wondesford Dl BNFD RG42 63 J2
Wooburn Common Rd SL SL1 21 K4
Wooburn Gra FLKWH/TG HP10 20 F3
Wooburn Manor Pk
FLKWH/TG HP10 21 G1
Wooburn Md FLKWH/TG HP10 21 G1
Wooburn Town
FLKWH/TG HP10 20 F2
Woodavon Gdns NTHA RG18 97 M1
Woodberry Cl CAV/SC RG4 45 G2
Woodbine Cl EARL RG6 * 60 C5
SHST GU47 87 J7
Woodbine La KSCL RG20 100 B5
Woodbourne Cl YTLY GU46 86 D8
Woodbridge Dr CBLY GU15 88 D7
Woodbridge Rd BLKW GU17 93 H1
TILE/CALC RG31 137 M4
Woodbury HUNG RG17 117 L4
Woodby Dr ASC SL5 78 F4
Wood Cl WDSR SL4 53 J3
Woodcock Ct THLE RG7 145 L2
Woodcock Dr CHOB/PIR GU24 91 J3
Woodcock La CHOB/PIR GU24 91 H3
Woodcote MDHD SL6 4 D6
Woodcote Pl ASC SL5 65 M6
Woodcote Rd CAV/SC RG4 44 E2
GOR/PANG RG8 112 B6
Woodcote Wy CAV/SC RG4 44 D1
Wood End CWTH RG45 86 F2
Woodend Dr ASC SL5 78 B2
Woodend Rd FRIM GU16 95 J7
Woodenhill BRAK RG12 75 L4
Woodfield Dr MDHD SL6 25 J8
Woodfield Wy THLE RG7 137 J6
Woodford Cl CAV/SC RG4 44 E2
Woodford Gn BRAK RG12 76 F1
Woodford Wy SLN SL2 28 C4
Wood Gn GOR/PANG RG8 113 J10
Wood Green Cl
RDGW/BURGH RG30 8 A7
Woodhall La ASC SL5 78 E6
Woodhaw EGH TW20 69 H2
Woodhouse Cl HYS/HAR UB3 43 G3
Woodhouse La STHA RG19 103 G3
Woodhouse St BNFD RG42 * 63 L6
Woodhurst La WWKG RG41 14 B1
Woodhurst North MDHD SL6 * 26 E5
Woodhurst Rd MDHD SL6 5 M1
Woodhurst South MDHD SL6 * 26 E5
Woodies Cl BNFD RG42 63 J5
Woodland Av SL SL1 10 C2
WDSR SL4 52 F3
Woodland Cl MLW SL7 18 F2
WEY KT13 * 83 K8
Woodland Crs BNFD RG42 3 G1
FARN GU14 94 C8
Woodland Dr
RDGW/BURGH RG30 137 P3
TADY RG26 150 B8
Woodland Gld CBLY GU15 88 D7
Woodland Gra DTCH/LGLY SL3 41 G3
Woodland Gv WEY KT13 83 K8
Woodlands ADL/WDHM KT15 82 E7
YTLY GU46 92 D3
Woodlands Av THLE RG7 143 Q3
WODY RG5 46 D7
WWKG RG41 61 K6
Woodlands Cl ASC SL5 77 M3
BLKW GU17 93 L5
NTHA RG18 133 K5
Woodlands Ct SHST GU47 87 M5
Woodlands Gv CAV/SC RG4 45 K2
Woodlands La BFOR GU20 90 F3
Woodlands Pde ASHF TW15 71 J4
Woodlands Park Av MDHD SL6 35 J4
Woodlands Park Rd MDHD SL6 35 J4
Woodlands Ride ASC SL5 77 M3
Woodlands Rd CAV/SC RG4 126 E4
CBLY GU15 94 B1
FARN GU14 93 K8
HEN RG9 22 A8
STHL UB1 43 M1
TADY RG26 103 M5
VW GU25 80 C1
Woodlands Rd East VW GU25 80 C1
Woodlands Rd West VW GU25 68 C8
The Woodlands WWKG RG41 73 K2
Woodlands Wk BLKW GU17 93 L5
Woodland Wy MLW SL7 19 G2
Wood La BNFD RG42 63 K4
CAV/SC RG4 126 B6
GOR/PANG RG8 112 H10
IVER SL0 30 D4
SL SL1 38 B3
THLE RG7 144 H8
WWKG RG41 72 F4
Wood Lane Cl CAV/SC RG4 126 F5
Woodlee Cl VW GU25 68 C7
Woodley Gn WODY RG5 46 F6
Woodman Cl WHIT RG2 59 H8
Woodmancott Cl BRAK RG12 76 F2
Woodman's La THLE RG7 143 P3
Woodmere BRAK RG12 3 L9
Woodmere Cl EARL RG6 60 B4
Wood Moor EWKG RG40 85 M4
Woodmoor End MDHD SL6 20 D7
Woodpecker Cl WAR/TWY RG10 47 L3
Wood Rdg NWBY RG14 141 R7
Woodridge Cl BRAK RG12 3 G7
Wood Rd CBLY GU15 94 B5
SHPTN TW17 83 G1
Woodrow Ct CAV/SC RG4 * 44 F3
Woodrow Dr EWKG RG40 15 M5
Woodsend Cl EARL RG6 59 L6
Woodshore Cl VW GU25 80 B3
Woodside BLKW GU17 93 J3
CBLY GU15 87 M7
NTHA RG18 133 Q9
NWBY RG14 141 R7
Woodside Cl EWKG RG40 73 L6
THLE RG7 98 E1
THLE RG7 143 Q8
Woodside Dr NTHA RG18 133 P4
Woodside La CAV/SC RG4 126 C5
WDSR SL4 66 C2
Woodside Rd WDSR SL4 66 B3
Woodside Wy VW GU25 68 B8
WHIT RG2 59 K7
Woods Rd CAV/SC RG4 45 K2
Woodstock Av DTCH/LGLY SL3 39 M4
Woodstock Cl MDHD SL6 26 B5
Woodstocks FARN GU14 94 C8
Woodstock St READ RG1 9 M6
Woodthorne Cl
TILE/CALC RG31 125 M10
Woodthorpe Rd ASHF TW15 70 D3
Woodview SLN SL2 * 28 B1
Woodview Rd GOR/PANG RG8 124 H9
Woodville Cl BLKW GU17 93 H1
Woodward Cl WWKG RG41 61 K4
Woodway CBLY GU15 94 B1
Woodwaye WODY RG5 46 D7
Woodway Rd DID OX11 110 C4
Woodyer Cl WODY RG5 60 E1
Woolacombe Dr WHIT RG2 59 L4
Woolacombe Wy HYS/HAR UB3 43 G4
Woolf Dr EWKG RG40 14 F3
Woolford Cl BNFD RG42 65 H5
Woolhampton Hl THLE RG7 99 L4
Woolhampton Wy BRAK RG12 76 D2
Woolley Firs MDHD SL6 35 G1
Woolridge Cl EBED/NFELT TW14 57 J7
Woolton Lodge Gdns
KSCL RG20 141 M12
Woosehill WWKG RG41 14 A5
Woosehill La WWKG RG41 14 B6
Wootton Cl TILE/CALC RG31 137 N2
Wootton Rd HEN RG9 127 Q2
Wootton Wy MDHD SL6 4 A7
Worcester Cl FARN GU14 94 B7
MDHD SL6 35 L3
RDGW/BURGH RG30 58 A1
Worcester Dr ASHF TW15 71 H4
Worcester Gdns SL SL1 10 D7
Worcester Rd UX/CGN UB8 31 L6
Worcestershire Lea BNFD RG42 64 F5
Wordsworth BRAK RG12 75 M2
Wordsworth Av YTLY GU46 92 B2
Wordsworth Rd
ADL/WDHM KT15 82 D8
NTHA RG18 97 L2
SLN SL2 27 M5
Wordsworth Wy WDR/YW UB7 42 A4
Worlds End Hl BRAK RG12 76 F3
Wormersley Rd STHA RG19 96 F6
Worple Av STA TW18 70 B4
Worple Rd STA TW18 70 B5
The Worple STWL/WRAY TW19 54 F5
Worrall Wy EARL RG6 59 M6

Worsley Pl THLE RG7 137 J7
Worsley Rd FRIM GU16 94 E7
Worster Rd MDHD SL6 20 A8
Worton Dr WHIT RG2 59 G6
Wrabness Wy STA TW18 70 B6
Wraysbury Dr WDR/YW UB7 31 M8
Wraysbury Gdns STA TW18 69 L2
Wraysbury Rd STA TW18 69 J1
STWL/WRAY TW19 55 H8
Wren Cl THLE RG7 143 R3
WWKG RG41 73 L1
YTLY GU46 * 86 B8
Wren Dr WDR/YW UB7 41 M2
Wrenfield Dr CAV/SC RG4 44 F1
Wren's Av ASHF TW15 71 J3
Wrensfield MLW SL7 18 E5
Wrenswood Cl WHIT RG2 59 H8
Wren Wy FARN GU14 93 M7
Wright WDSR SL4 52 C2
Wright Gdns SHPTN TW17 83 G2
Wright Rd HEST TW5 43 L7
Wroxham BRAK RG12 75 M2
Wroxham Rd WODY RG5 46 D6
Wulwyn Side CWTH RG45 * 87 G1
Wyatt Rd STA TW18 70 A3
WDSR SL4 52 D2
Wychcotes CAV/SC RG4 44 F4
Wychelm Rd LTWR GU18 90 C6
WHIT RG2 145 Q1
Wychwood Av BRAK RG12 76 F1
Wychwood Cl EARL RG6 59 M4
Wychwood Crs EARL RG6 59 M3
Wychwood Pl CBLY GU15 89 H5
Wycombe Rd MLW SL7 19 G1
Wye Cl ASHF TW15 71 H2
RDGW/BURGH RG30 137 R4
Wyfold La CAV/SC RG4 126 A3
HEN RG9 126 D2
Wykeham Cl WDR/YW UB7 42 C6
Wykeham Rd EARL RG6 46 A8
Wylam BRAK RG12 75 M2
Wylands Rd DTCH/LGLY SL3 40 C5
Wyld Court Hl NTHA RG18 122 D9
Wyldewood ASC SL5 78 D3
Wymers Cl SL SL1 27 K3
Wymers Wood Rd SL SL1 27 J2
Wyncote Cl WHIT RG2 59 M5
Wyndale Cl HEN RG9 22 A5
Wyndham Cl YTLY GU46 86 D7
Wyndham Crs SL SL1 27 K3
WODY RG5 46 D5
Wyndham Rd NWBY RG14 96 F1
Wynford Cl RDGW/BURGH RG30 58 C2
Wynnstay Gdns MLW SL7 19 G1
Wynsham Wy BFOR GU20 90 B1
Wyre Ct TILE/CALC RG31 125 N11
Wyre Gv HYS/HAR UB3 43 J4
Wyresdale BRAK RG12 76 E4
Wythemede BNFD RG42 63 H4
Wyvern Cl BRAK RG12 2 D8
Wyvern Pl ADL/WDHM KT15 * 82 B8
Wyvern Wy UX/CGN UB8 31 K2

Y

Yale Cl SHST GU47 87 M4
Yardley BRAK RG12 75 M2
Yard Md EGH TW20 69 G1
Yarmouth Rd SL SL1 10 A1
Yarnold Cl EWKG RG40 62 F7
Yarnton Cl CAV/SC RG4 127 J12
Yarrow Cl NTHA RG18 97 M1
Yateley Rd YTLY GU46 86 F7
Yates Copse NWBY RG14 97 G1
Yattendon La GOR/PANG RG8 123 N11
NTHA RG18 122 E11
Yattendon Rd
GOR/PANG RG8 * 124 C10
NTHA RG18 133 Q3
Yaverland Dr BAGS GU19 89 K4
Yelverton Rd WHIT RG2 59 J3
Ye Meads MDHD SL6 37 H1
Yeoman Dr STWL/WRAY TW19 56 E7
Yeoman Pl WODY RG5 46 C7
Yeomanry Cl STHA RG19 98 A4
Yeomans HTWY RG27 85 L7
Yeomans La KSCL RG20 100 C5
Yeomans Wy CBLY GU15 94 E1
Yeoveney Cl STWL/WRAY TW19 55 K8
Yeovil Rd SHST GU47 87 L5
SL SL1 28 A6
Yew Cl BNFD RG42 65 G5
WWKG RG41 14 A7
Yew Cnr BRAK RG12 3 H6
Yew Ga NWBY RG14 132 F12
Yewhurst Cl WAR/TWY RG10 32 E8
Yew La READ RG1 58 F2
Yew Pl WEY KT13 * 83 M7
The Yews ASHF TW15 * 71 H2
Yew Tree Cl MDHD SL6 4 F3
TADY RG26 150 A8
Yew Tree Ct GOR/PANG RG8 112 A12
Yew Tree La THLE RG7 145 K6
Yew Tree Ri TILE/CALC RG31 137 N5
Yew Tree Rd SL SL1 11 J9
Yewtrees EGH TW20 69 J8
Yew Trees SHPTN TW17 82 F1
Yew Tree Stables KSCL RG20 122 A2
Yew Tree Wk FRIM GU16 94 E5
Yield Hall La READ RG1 9 G6
Yield Hall Pl READ RG1 9 G6
Yockley Cl CBLY GU15 95 K3
Yoreham Cl EARL RG6 60 E5
York Av SL SL1 10 C1
WDSR SL4 12 F8
York Cl NWBY RG14 7 G6
York Pl CBLY GU15 88 D7
York Rd BNFD RG42 63 K3
CBLY GU15 88 D7
HEN RG9 115 R12
HUNG RG17 138 H2
MDHD SL6 5 H6
MLW SL7 18 F4
NWBY RG14 7 G6
READ RG1 8 E3
UX/CGN UB8 31 M1
WDSR SL4 12 F8
Yorkshire Pl BNFD RG42 64 E5
York Terrace La CBLY GU15 * 94 A1
Yorktown Rd SHST GU47 87 H7
York Wy SHST GU47 87 G6
Youlden Cl CBLY GU15 95 G1
Youlden Dr CBLY GU15 95 G1
Young Crs STHA RG19 7 M9

Z

Zealand Av WDR/YW UB7 41 M7
Zinnia Cl WWKG RG41 61 K7
Zinzan St READ RG1 8 D6

Index - featured places

21 South Street Arts Centre
READ RG1 9 H7
Abbey Gate
READ RG1 9 H5
The Abbey Junior School
WHIT RG2 59 J1
The Abbey School
READ RG1 9 J9
Aberglen Industrial Estate
HYS/HAR UB3 42 F2
Acre Business Park
WHIT RG2 59 H6
ACS Egham International School
EGH TW20 68 C6
Addington Special School
WODY RG5 46 F8
Addlestone Cemetery
ADL/WDHM KT15 82 A6
Adler Industrial Estate
HYS/HAR UB3 42 F2
Adult Education Centre
CBLY GU15 94 B1
Aerial Business Park
HUNG RG17 116 G10
AFC Newbury
NWBY RG14 7 G3
Airbus Coach Station
HTHAIR TW6 56 F2
Airlinks Golf Club
NWDGN UB2 43 L4
Air Links Industrial Estate
HEST TW5 43 L5
Airport Gate Business Centre
WDR/YW UB7 42 B7
Albany Park Industrial Estate
FRIM GU16 94 B5
Alderbridge School
THLE RG7 142 E4
Aldermaston CE Primary School
THLE RG7 142 B7
Alexander First School
WDSR SL4 52 C2
Alfred Sutton Primary School
READ RG1 45 M8
All Saints CE Controlled Junior School
MDHD SL6 4 A7
All Saints CE Infant School
READ RG1 8 B7
All Saints Cemetery
MDHD SL6 4 B3
Altwood CE School
MDHD SL6 35 K1
Alwyn Infant School
MDHD SL6 4 A2
Amen Corner Business Park
BRAK RG12 63 K7
Animal Care College
ASC SL5 66 A8
Annie Lawson School
NWBY RG14 6 B6
Arborfield CE Junior School
WHIT RG2 72 E3
Arbour Vale Special School Sports College
SLN SL2 29 J7
Arena Leisure Centre
CBLY GU15 88 C8
Argent Centre Industrial Estate
HYS/HAR UB3 43 J2
The Argyle Clinic
READ RG1 8 B6
The Ark School
THLE RG7 142 H5
Arlington Business Park
BRAK RG12 2 D4
Arts Link Theatre Cinema
CBLY GU15 88 D8
Ascot Heath Infant School
ASC SL5 65 L5
Ascot Racecourse
ASC SL5 65 M8
Ashdown House (NT)
HUNG RG17 104 A9
Ashfields Farm Industrial Estate
NTHA RG18 133 P1
Ashford Cemetery
STWL/WRAY TW19 56 F8
Ashford CE Primary School
ASHF TW15 71 H4
Ashford Clinic
ASHF TW15 70 E1
Ashford Hill Primary School
STHA RG19 103 G5
Ashford Hospital
STWL/WRAY TW19 56 E8
Ashford Industrial Estate
ASHF TW15 71 J2
Ashford Manor Golf Club
ASHF TW15 70 F4
Ashford Park Primary School
ASHF TW15 70 C2
Ashford Sports Club
ASHF TW15 70 D2
STWL/WRAY TW19 56 F7
Aspect Park Golf Centre
HEN RG9 22 F5
The Atrium
CBLY GU15 94 C1
Avenue Medical Centre
SLN SL2 28 C4
The Avenue Special School
WHIT RG2 59 J2
Aysgarth Medical Centre
IVER SL0 30 F3
BAA Heathrow Visitor Centre
HTHAIR TW6 42 D8
Badgemore Park Golf Club
HEN RG9 115 P11
Badgemore Primary School
HEN RG9 115 Q12
Bagshot School
BAGS GU19 89 L3
Balfour Business Centre
NWDGN UB2 43 M3
Barrow Hills Golf Club
CHERT KT16 80 C6
Basildon CE Primary School
GOR/PANG RG8 123 R8
Basildon House (NT)
GOR/PANG RG8 124 C5
Basildon Park (NT)
GOR/PANG RG8 124 B6
Battle Farm Trading Estate
RDGW/BURGH RG30 44 D5
Battle Primary School
RDGW/BURGH RG30 44 D7
Battlesite 1643
NWBY RG14 141 R7
Battlesite 1644
NWBY RG14 96 A1
Baydon St Nicholas CE Primary School
MARL SN8 116 A5
Baylis Business Centre
SL SL1 10 D2
Baylis Court School
SL SL1 28 F6
Beale Park
GOR/PANG RG8 124 D5
Bearwood College
WWKG RG41 61 H7
Bearwood Golf Club
WWKG RG41 60 F7
Bearwood Primary School
WWKG RG41 61 H6
Bedfont Cemetery
EBED/NFELT TW14 57 J7
Bedfont Health Clinic
EBED/NFELT TW14 57 L6
Bedfont Industrial Park
ASHF TW15 71 K1
Bedfont J & I School
EBED/NFELT TW14 57 L5
Bedfont Lakes Country Park
EBED/NFELT TW14 57 J8
Bedfont Lakes Office Park
EBED/NFELT TW14 57 J7
Beechwood Primary School
WODY RG5 46 E7
Beechwood School
SLN SL2 28 D4
Beedon CE Primary School
KSCL RG20 121 K6
Bell Business Centre
MDHD SL6 5 H6
Belmont Medical Centre
UX/CGN UB8 31 M1
Benham Park
KSCL RG20 141 N2
Berkeley Business Park
WWKG RG41 73 J3
Berkeley Primary School
HEST TW5 43 M6
Berkshire Business Centre
NTHA RG19 98 C4
The Berkshire Golf Club
ASC SL5 77 J6
Berkshire Independent Hospital
READ RG1 58 E1
Best Western Calcot Hotel
TILE/CALC RG31 137 N6
Best Western Moat House Hotel
WWKG RG41 60 F5
Best Western West Grange Hotel
THLE RG7 98 E3
The Bharani Medical Centre
SL SL1 27 M7
Bilton Industrial Estate
BRAK RG12 75 L1
Binfield CE Primary School
BNFD RG42 63 J4
Birch Copse Primary School
TILE/CALC RG31 137 N2
Birch Hill Medical Centre
BRAK RG12 76 B4
Birch Hill Primary School
BRAK RG12 76 C5
Bird Hills Golf Club
MDHD SL6 50 C4
Bird in Hand Country Inn Hotel
WAR/TWY RG10 33 M3
Bisham Abbey National Sports Centre
MLW SL7 18 F7
Bisham CE Primary School
MLW SL7 18 F7
Bishopsgate School
EGH TW20 68 A1
Bishops Green Farm Camp Site
KSCL RG20 101 J4
Bishopswood Golf Club
TADY RG26 148 B3
Bishopswood J & I Schools
TADY RG26 148 D3
Bishopswood School
CAV/SC RG4 126 F5
Bishop Wand CE Secondary School
SUN TW16 71 M7
Blackburn Trading Estate
STWL/WRAY TW19 56 F5
Blackbushe Airport
BLKW GU17 92 A4
Blackbushe Business Park
YTLY GU46 92 C2
Blackdown Barracks
FRIM GU16 95 K8
Black Park Country Park
IVER SL0 30 C3
Blackwater & Hawley Leisure Centre
BLKW GU17 93 K3
Blackwater Industrial Estate
BLKW GU17 93 L1
Blair Peach Primary School
STHL UB1 43 M1
Blessed Hugh Faringdon Catholic School
RDGW/BURGH RG30 58 C1
Blewbury Endowed CE Primary School
DID OX11 110 B1
Blue Mountain Golf Club & Conference Centre
BNFD RG42 63 K4
Bone Lane Industrial Area
NWBY RG14 7 K3
Botwell RC Primary School
HYS/HAR UB3 43 H2
Bourne Business Park
ADL/WDHM KT15 82 C6
Bourne End Business Centre
BNEND SL8 20 D3
Boyne Hill CE Infants School
MDHD SL6 4 C7
Boyn Valley Industrial Estate
MDHD SL6 4 F7
Bracknell Business Centre
BRAK RG12 2 B5
Bracknell Ice Rink
BRAK RG12 63 J7
Bracknell RFC
BRAK RG12 3 M5
Bracknell Ski & Snowboard Centre
BNFD RG42 63 J7
Bracknell Sports Centre
BRAK RG12 76 C2
Bracknell Town FC
BRAK RG12 3 H5
Bracknell & Wokingham College
BNFD RG42 3 G2
BRAK RG12 3 H5
EARL RG6 46 A8
Bradfield CE Primary School
THLE RG7 135 Q8
Bradfield College
THLE RG7 136 A4
Brakenhale School
BRAK RG12 2 F9
Bramley CE J & I School
TADY RG26 149 R6
Braywick Cemetery
MDHD SL6 36 C2
Braywick Sports Centre
MDHD SL6 5 J8
Braywood CE First School
WDSR SL4 51 M1
Brent Park Industrial Estate
NWDGN UB2 43 K3
Brickfields Industrial Park
BRAK RG12 2 C5
Brick Kiln Industrial Estate
TADY RG26 148 E1
Bridge Retail Park
EWKG RG40 14 F8
Bridges Hall
EARL RG6 59 M1
Brightwalton CE Primary School
KSCL RG20 119 P3
The Brigidine School
WDSR SL4 53 K2
Brimpton CE Primary School
THLE RG7 99 H8
Bristow Infant School
CBLY GU15 94 B4
Britannia Industrial Estate
DTCH/LGLY SL3 55 L1
Britwell Health Clinic
SLN SL2 28 C4
Broadmoor CP School
CWTH RG45 87 K2
Broadmoor Hospital
CWTH RG45 87 L1
Broad Street Mall Shopping Centre
READ RG1 8 E6
Brockenhurst Hotel
ASC SL5 78 B3
Brockhurst & Marlston House School
NTHA RG18 134 C6
Brook Business Centre
IVER SL0 31 J3
Brookfields Special School
TILE/CALC RG31 125 N11
Brook Industrial Estate
YEAD UB4 43 M1
Brookside Business Centre
THLE RG7 145 P8
Brooksland College
ASHF TW15 70 F2
Brookway Industrial Estate
NWBY RG14 7 M5
Brunel Bus Station
SL SL1 11 G5
Brunel Retail Park
WHIT RG2 59 G3
Brunel University (Runnymede Campus)
EGH TW20 68 D1
Buckland Primary School
STA TW18 70 C5
Bucklebury CE Primary School
THLE RG7 134 E12
Bullsbridge Industrial Estate
NWDGN UB2 43 K4
The Bulmershe School
WODY RG5 46 C7
Burchetts Green CE Infant School
MDHD SL6 24 D7
Burford School
MLW SL7 18 E1
Burghclere Primary School
KSCL RG20 100 C8
Burghfield Aqua Sports Club
RDGW/BURGH RG30 58 A5
Burghfield Health Centre
THLE RG7 143 R3
Burghfield St Marys Primary School
RDGW/BURGH RG30 137 N12
Burnham Abbey
MDHD SL6 37 K1
Burnham Beeches Golf Club
SL SL1 27 M2
Burnham Beeches Hotel
SL SL1 27 M3
Burnham Copse J & I Schools
TADY RG26 148 C1
Burnham FC
SL SL1 27 K4
Burnham Grammar School
SL SL1 27 M5
Burnham Health Centre
SL SL1 27 K4
Burnham Upper School
SL SL1 27 K5
The Business Centre
THLE RG7 99 H8
WWKG RG41 14 E9
The Business Village
SLN SL2 11 L4
Calcot J & I School
TILE/CALC RG31 137 M6
Calcot Park Golf Club
TILE/CALC RG31 137 Q5
Caldicott School
SLN SL2 28 D1
California Chalet & Touring Park
EWKG RG40 73 K7
California Country Park
EWKG RG40 73 J7
Calleva Atrebatum Roman Town
THLE RG7 143 N12
Calleva Business Park
THLE RG7 142 A12
Camberley CC
CBLY GU15 94 D3
Camberley County Infant School
CBLY GU15 94 B1
Camberley Health Centre
CBLY GU15 94 B3
Camberley Heath Golf Club
CBLY GU15 95 G2
Camberley Magistrates Court
CBLY GU15 88 D8
Camberley RFC
CBLY GU15 94 C3
Camberley Town FC
CBLY GU15 94 B3
Campbell Court Industrial Estate
TADY RG26 150 A8
Cannons Health Club
NWBY RG14 7 M6
WHIT RG2 58 F6
Carlyle Business Centre
CHERT KT16 81 M4
Carnival Pool
EWKG RG40 14 F8
Carwarden House School
CBLY GU15 95 G3
Casa dei Cesari Hotel
YTLY GU46 92 E2
Castle Hill Clinic
READ RG1 8 C7
Castle Industrial Park
NWBY RG14 96 E1
The Castle School
NWBY RG14 132 F12
Castleview Combined School
DTCH/LGLY SL3 39 M4
Caversham Park Primary School
CAV/SC RG4 127 L12
Caversham Primary School
CAV/SC RG4 45 G3
Caxton Trading Estate
HYS/HAR UB3 43 G2
Cedar Park School
WAR/TWY RG10 47 J1
The Cedars Primary School
HEST TW5 43 J7
Cedars School
THLE RG7 142 C7
Centenary Business Park
HEN RG9 22 B5
Central Swimming Pool
READ RG1 8 C5
Chailey Industrial Estate
HYS/HAR UB3 43 J2
Chambers Business Park
WDR/YW UB7 42 C6
Charles Kingsleys CE Primary School
HTWY RG27 85 J6
Charter Court
SL SL1 10 F7
Charters School
ASC SL5 78 D4
Cheam School
STHA RG19 101 M6
Cheapside CE Primary School
ASC SL5 66 E6
Checkendon CE Primary School
GOR/PANG RG8 113 N7
Chequers Inn
BNEND SL8 20 F4
Cherry Lane Primary School
WDR/YW UB7 42 B4
Cherry Wood Primary School
FARN GU14 94 A8
Chertsey Business Centre
CHERT KT16 82 A4
Chertsey C & CC Site
CHERT KT16 82 C4
Chertsey Cemetery
CHERT KT16 82 A5
Chertsey Hall
CHERT KT16 82 A4
Chertsey Museum
CHERT KT16 82 A3
Chertsey Recreation Centre
CHERT KT16 81 L5
Chertsey Town FC
CHERT KT16 81 M3
Chieveley Primary School
KSCL RG20 132 G2
Childs Hall
READ RG1 59 M1
Chiltern Business Village
UX/CGN UB8 31 K3
Chiltern College School
CAV/SC RG4 45 H3
Chiltern Edge School
CAV/SC RG4 126 E6
Chiltern Enterprise Centre
THLE RG7 137 J7
Chilton Foliat CE Primary School
HUNG RG17 128 H8
Chilton Primary School
DID OX11 109 J2
The Chimes Shopping Centre
UX/CGN UB8 31 M1
Chobham Common National Nature Reserve
CHOB/PIR GU24 79 J7
Chobham FC
CHOB/PIR GU24 91 M7
Chobham RFC
CHOB/PIR GU24 91 L5
Chobham St Lawrence CE Primary School
CHOB/PIR GU24 91 L6
Christchurch CE Infant School
VW GU25 68 A8
Christopher Hotel
WDSR SL4 13 J3
Christ the King RC Primary School
WHIT RG2 59 J6
Churchend Primary School
RDGW/BURGH RG30 137 Q4
Church Hill House Hospital
BRAK RG12 76 A2
Churchmead School Church of England (VA) School
DTCH/LGLY SL3 39 K7
Cineworld
SL SL1 11 H6
Cippenham Infants School
SL SL1 27 M8
Cippenham Junior School
SL SL1 27 M8
Cippenham Medical Centre
SL SL1 38 C1
Civil Service College
ASC SL5 78 F2
Claires Court School
MDHD SL6 4 E4
MDHD SL6 5 M1
MDHD SL6 35 G1
Clarendon Primary School
ASHF TW15 70 F1
Claycots Primary School
SLN SL2 28 C5
Claytons Combined School
BNEND SL8 20 C1
Cleves Junior School
WEY KT13 83 M8
Clewer Green CE First School
WDSR SL4 12 B9
Cliveden Hotel
MDHD SL6 21 G7
Cliveden (NT)
MDHD SL6 21 G8

Clockhouse Industrial Estate
EBED/NFELT TW14 ....57 H7
The Club at Mapledurham
CAV/SC RG4 ....126 D11
Coach Museum
WDSR SL4 ....13 K6
Cold Ash St Marks CE
Primary School
NTHA RG18 ....133 P9
Coley Park CP School
READ RG1 ....58 F1
Coley Primary School
READ RG1 ....8 E8
Coliseum Business Centre
CBLY GU15 ....94 A3
College Town J & I School
SHST GU47 ....87 L6
The Colleton Primary School
WAR/TWY RG10 ....47 L3
Collingwood College
CBLY GU15 ....89 G6
Colnbrook CE Primary School
DTCH/LGLY SL3 ....40 F8
Colnbrook Sports Club
DTCH/LGLY SL3 ....41 H8
Coln Industrial Estate
DTCH/LGLY SL3 ....41 H7
Colthrop Business Park
NTHA RG19 ....98 A3
Combe Gibbet
HUNG RG17 ....146 F1
Combermere Barracks
WDSR SL4 ....12 F9
Comfort Inn
HYS/HAR UB3 ....43 G5
Commonwealth War Graves
Commission
MDHD SL6 ....5 G4
Compleat Angler Hotel
MLW SL7 ....19 G5
Compton CE Primary School
KSCL RG20 ....122 A2
Compton Place Business Centre
CBLY GU15 ....94 A2
Connaught County Junior School
BAGS GU19 ....89 L4
Convent of St John the Baptist
WDSR SL4 ....12 C8
Cookham Dean CE
Primary School
MDHD SL6 ....19 K7
Cookham Reach Sailing Club
MDHD SL6 ....20 C6
Cookham Rise Primary School
MDHD SL6 ....20 A8
The Coombes Infant School
WHIT RG2 ....72 F3
Coppid Beech Hotel
BNFD RG42 ....63 J7
Copthorne Hotel
RDGW/BURGH RG30 ....58 C6
SL SL1 ....10 B7
Cordwalles Junior School
CBLY GU15 ....88 F6
Corn Exchange
NWBY RG14 ....6 E4
Country Gardens Estate
BFOR GU20 ....78 C6
Court Farm Industrial Estate
STWL/WRAY TW19 ....56 F5
Court Garden Leisure Centre
MLW SL7 ....18 F5
Courthouse Junior School
MDHD SL6 ....25 K6
Courtyard by Marriott
SL SL1 ....10 B7
THLE RG7 ....142 F2
Cove Infant School
FARN GU14 ....93 L8
Cowley Business Park
UX/CGN UB8 ....31 L4
Cowley Mill Industrial Estate
IVER SL0 ....31 J3
Cowley St Laurence CE
Primary School
UX/CGN UB8 ....31 L6
Coworth Flexlands School
CHOB/PIR GU24 ....91 M6
Cox Green School
MDHD SL6 ....35 J2
Cranbourne Primary School
WDSR SL4 ....66 A2
Cranford Community College
HEST TW5 ....43 K6
Cranford House School
WGFD OX10 ....111 P5
Cranford Park Junior School
HYS/HAR UB3 ....43 H4
Cranford Park Primary School
HYS/HAR UB3 ....43 H4
Crawley Ridge Infant School
CBLY GU15 ....88 F7
Crazies Hill CE Primary School
WAR/TWY RG10 ....23 H8
Croft Hall
HUNG RG17 ....129 M12
Crosfields School
WHIT RG2 ....59 L6
Cross Farm Infant School
FRIM GU16 ....94 E8
Crown Business Centre
WDR/YW UB7 ....42 B1
Crown Trading Centre
HYS/HAR UB3 ....43 G2
Crown Wood Primary School
BRAK RG12 ....76 D3
Crowthorne Business Centre
CWTH RG45 ....87 J7
Crowthorne CE Primary School
CWTH RG45 ....87 H1
Curridge Primary School
NTHA RG18 ....133 K6
Dair House School
SLN SL2 ....28 D2
D'Albiac House
HTHAIR TW6 ....57 G1
Danesfield House Hotel
MLW SL7 ....23 M1
Danesfield School
MLW SL7 ....18 A7
Daneshill House School
HTWY RG27 ....151 K6
Datchet Golf Club
DTCH/LGLY SL3 ....39 J7
Datchet St Marys
Primary School
DTCH/LGLY SL3 ....39 K7
Datchet Sports Club
DTCH/LGLY SL3 ....39 K7
David Lloyd Sports Centre
EARL RG6 ....46 A5
Days Inn
HUNG RG17 ....116 F9
Dedworth Clinic
WDSR SL4 ....38 A8
Dedworth County Middle School
WDSR SL4 ....38 A8
Dedworth Green First School
WDSR SL4 ....52 E1
Delwood Hospital
RDGW/BURGH RG30 ....44 C8

Denefield School
TILE/CALC RG31 ....125 M11
Dene House Hospital
WDSR SL4 ....13 H9
Denvale Trading Park
NWBY RG14 ....7 L5
Desborough School
MDHD SL6 ....4 F8
Dinton Pastures
WAR/TWY RG10 ....61 J1
The Dolphin School
WAR/TWY RG10 ....48 A4
Donnington Castle
NWBY RG14 ....132 E11
Donnington Valley Hotel
NWBY RG14 ....132 F10
Dorney County
Combined School
WDSR SL4 ....37 H2
Dorney Court
WDSR SL4 ....37 K3
Downe House School
NTHA RG18 ....133 N7
Downlands Sports Centre
KSCL RG20 ....121 K2
Downshire Golf Complex
EWKG RG40 ....75 K4
The Downs School
NTHA RG18 ....121 J9
Downsway Primary School
TILE/CALC RG31 ....125 N11
Dropmore Infant School
SL SL1 ....21 L5
Dryleas Sports Ground
HEN RG9 ....115 R11
Dunedin Hospital
READ RG1 ....8 C8
Eagle House School
SHST GU47 ....87 G4
East Berkshire College
(Maidenhead Campus)
MDHD SL6 ....4 C6
East Berkshire College
(Windsor Campus)
WDSR SL4 ....13 H7
East Berkshire Golf Club
CWTH RG45 ....86 E1
Eastern Business Centre
BRAK RG12 ....3 K5
Eastern Business Park
HTHAIR TW6 ....57 M1
Easthampstead Park
Crematorium
EWKG RG40 ....75 K5
Easthampstead Park School
EWKG RG40 ....75 K5
Ebony Health Centre
WAR/TWY RG10 ....47 K1
Echelford Primary School
ASHF TW15 ....71 H3
Edgebarrow School
CWTH RG45 ....87 H3
Edgebarrow Sports Centre
CWTH RG45 ....87 H3
Edward Pauling School
FELT TW13 ....57 L8
Egham Business Village
EGH TW20 ....69 J7
Egham CC
EGH TW20 ....69 H4
Egham Sports Centre
EGH TW20 ....69 H4
Egham Town FC
EGH TW20 ....69 J4
Elers Clinic
HYS/HAR UB3 ....42 F4
Ellington Primary School
MDHD SL6 ....5 G1
Elmbridge Museum
WEY KT13 ....83 G8
The Elmsleigh Centre
Shopping Precinct
STA TW18 ....69 M2
Elstree School
THLE RG7 ....99 M3
Elva Lodge Hotel
MDHD SL6 ....4 E5
The Elvian School
RDGW/BURGH RG30 ....58 D1
Emmbrook Junior School
WWKG RG41 ....61 M5
The Emmbrook School
WWKG RG41 ....14 B1
Emmer Green Primary School
CAV/SC RG4 ....126 H12
Enborne CE Primary School
KSCL RG20 ....141 L8
Englefield CE Primary School
THLE RG7 ....136 F5
Englefield Estate Yard
THLE RG7 ....136 F5
Englefield Green Infant School
EGH TW20 ....68 C3
English Martyrs Catholic
Primary School
RDGW/BURGH RG30 ....44 A7
EP Collier Primary School
READ RG1 ....8 E5
Eton College
WDSR SL4 ....13 J1
Eton College Rowing Lake
WDSR SL4 ....37 L6
Eton End PNEU School
DTCH/LGLY SL3 ....39 J6
Eton Porny CE First School
WDSR SL4 ....13 J2
Eton Wick CE First School
WDSR SL4 ....38 C5
Eton Wick FC
WDSR SL4 ....38 B5
European Language School
WDSR SL4 ....12 F3
Eurospeak Language School
WWKG RG41 ....14 B1
Eversley CC
HTWY RG27 ....85 M6
Fairacres Industrial Estate
WDSR SL4 ....52 C1
Fairholme Primary School
EBED/NFELT TW14 ....57 K7
Fairview Industrial Estate
HYS/HAR UB3 ....43 H2
Fairview Trading Estate
HEN RG9 ....22 B6
Falcon Business Park
EWKG RG40 ....73 G8
Falkland Memorial
NWBY RG14 ....141 R8
Falkland Primary School
NWBY RG14 ....141 R8
Falkland St Gabriels School
KSCL RG20 ....100 D1
Farley Hill Primary School
THLE RG7 ....84 C1
Farnborough Gate Retail Park
FARN GU14 ....94 C7
Farnborough Grange
Infant School
FARN GU14 ....94 A6
Farnborough Hill School
FARN GU14 ....94 C8

Farnborough RFC
FARN GU14 ....94 A8
Farnborough Town FC
FARN GU14 ....94 A6
Farnham Park Golf Club
SLN SL2 ....29 G2
Farnham Royal CE
Combined School
SLN SL2 ....28 A3
Farnham Royal CC
SLN SL2 ....28 A3
Featherstone Primary School
NWDGN UB2 ....43 M4
Feltham Cemetery
FELT TW13 ....71 J4
Feltham Hill Infant School
FELT TW13 ....71 M1
Feltham Hill Junior School
FELT TW13 ....71 M1
Fernhill Primary School
FARN GU14 ....93 M5
Fernhill School
FARN GU14 ....93 M5
Film Theatre Cinema
READ RG1 ....59 M2
Finchampstead CE
Primary School
EWKG RG40 ....85 L3
Finchampstead Sports Club
EWKG RG40 ....85 L3
Fir Tree Primary School
NWBY RG14 ....97 G2
Forbury Retail Park
READ RG1 ....9 J3
Fordbridge Medical Centre
ASHF TW15 ....70 F2
Fordwater Trading Estate
CHERT KT16 ....82 C5
Forest Boys School
WWKG RG41 ....61 J4
Forest End Medical Centre
BRAK RG12 ....76 B3
Foundation Park
MDHD SL6 ....35 H2
Foxes Piece Combined School
MLW SL7 ....19 G3
Fox Hill Primary School
BRAK RG12 ....76 B2
Foxhills Club & Resort
CHERT KT16 ....80 F8
Francis Baily Primary School
NTHA RG18 ....98 A3
Fredrick's Hotel
MDHD SL6 ....4 F3
Freemantles School
CHERT KT16 ....81 L4
The French Horn Hotel
CAV/SC RG4 ....46 C2
Frimley Business Park
FARN GU14 ....94 B6
Frimley CE Junior School
FRIM GU16 ....94 E7
Frimley Green Medical Centre
FRIM GU16 ....94 E7
Frimley Park Hospital
CBLY GU15 ....94 D4
Frogmore Community School
YTLY GU46 ....92 F1
Frogmore County Infant School
BLKW GU17 ....93 H2
Frogmore House
WDSR SL4 ....53 M2
Frogmore Industrial Estate
HYS/HAR UB3 ....43 G2
Frogmore Junior School
BLKW GU17 ....93 H1
Furze Platt Junior School
MDHD SL6 ....25 L5
Furze Platt Senior School
MDHD SL6 ....25 L5
Garland Junior School
THLE RG7 ....143 Q3
Garth Hill College
BNFD RG42 ....3 G2
Geoffrey Field J & I School
WHIT RG2 ....59 J6
George Palmer Primary School
WHIT RG2 ....59 J2
Gillotts School
HEN RG9 ....127 P3
Gladstone Industrial Estate
MDHD SL6 ....4 F2
Globeside Business Park
MLW SL7 ....19 H4
Godolphin Infant School
SL SL1 ....28 E6
Godolphin Junior School
SL SL1 ....28 E6
Gordons School
CHOB/PIR GU24 ....90 E7
Goring CE Primary School
GOR/PANG RG8 ....112 A11
Goring & Streatley Golf Club
GOR/PANG RG8 ....111 N11
Gorse Ride Infant School
EWKG RG40 ....73 J7
Gorse Ride Junior School
EWKG RG40 ....73 J8
Grange Community
Junior School
NWBY RG14 ....93 M6
The Grange Hotel
BRAK RG12 ....3 G4
Grazeley Parochial
Primary School
THLE RG7 ....145 J4
Great Hollands Health Centre
BRAK RG12 ....75 M3
Great Hollands Primary School
BRAK RG12 ....75 L2
Great Hollands
Recreation Centre
EWKG RG40 ....75 L5
Great Marlow School
MLW SL7 ....19 H2
Green Business Centre
EGH TW20 ....69 J2
Greenham Court Primary School
NWBY RG14 ....96 D6
Greenham Road Retail Park
NWBY RG5 ....6 F6
Green Park Business Area
WHIT RG2 ....58 C5
Grenadier Tennis Club
WDSR SL4 ....12 C5
Gresham Way Industrial Estate
RDGW/BURGH RG30 ....44 A4
Greys Court (NT)
HEN RG9 ....115 J11
Grimsbury Castle
NTHA RG18 ....133 Q5
Grovefield Hotel
SL SL1 ....27 J3
Grove Park Industrial Estate
MDHD SL6 ....35 G6
Grove Village Medical Centre
EBED/NFELT TW14 ....57 L7
Guards Polo Club
EGH TW20 ....67 K6

Guillemont County Junior School
BLKW GU17 ....93 J8
Guru Nanak Medical Centre
STHL UB1 ....43 M1
Guru Nanak Sikh Primary School
YEAD UB4 ....43 L1
Guru Nanak Sikh
Secondary School
YEAD UB4 ....43 L1
Hall Grove Farm Industrial Estate
BAGS GU19 ....89 M1
Hall Grove School
BAGS GU19 ....90 A1
Halliford Health Clinic
SHPTN TW17 ....83 L1
Halliford School
SHPTN TW17 ....83 J4
Halls Business Centre
HYS/HAR UB3 ....43 J3
Hammond Junior School
LTWR GU18 ....90 A5
Hampstead Norreys CE
Primary School
NTHA RG18 ....122 B9
Hanworth Business Park
CHERT KT16 ....81 M5
Harleyford Golf Club
MLW SL7 ....18 A8
Harlington Community School
HYS/HAR UB3 ....42 F1
Harmans Water J & I School
BRAK RG12 ....76 E2
Hatch Ride Primary School
CWTH RG45 ....87 H7
Hawkedale GM School
SUN TW16 ....71 M8
Hawkedon Primary School
EARL RG6 ....60 E4
Hawley CP School
BLKW GU17 ....93 L3
Hawley Lane Industrial Estate
FARN GU14 ....94 B6
Hawley Place School
BLKW GU17 ....93 L5
Hawthorns Primary School
WWKG RG41 ....61 L7
Hayes Pool
HYS/HAR UB3 ....43 H1
Headley Park Industrial Estate
WODY RG5 ....47 G6
Heathermount
The Learning Centre
ASC SL5 ....78 D3
Heather Ridge County
Infant School
CBLY GU15 ....95 K2
Heatherwood Hospital
ASC SL5 ....65 L8
Heathfield St Marys School
ASC SL5 ....65 H7
Heathlands Cemetery
YTLY GU46 ....92 E2
Heathpark Golf Club
WDR/YW UB7 ....42 C3
Heathrow Airport
(Terminals 1,2 & 3)
HTHAIR TW6 ....57 H1
Heathrow Airport (Terminal 4)
HTHAIR TW6 ....57 H4
Heathrow Airport (Terminal 5)
HTHAIR TW6 ....56 C2
Heathrow Airport
Central Bus & Coach Station
HTHAIR TW6 ....57 G2
Heathrow Medical Centre
HYS/HAR UB3 ....42 F5
Heathrow Primary School
WDR/YW UB7 ....42 B6
Heathrow World Cargo Centre
HTHAIR TW6 ....56 F4
Hedsor School
BNEND SL8 ....20 F4
Helix Business Park
CBLY GU15 ....94 B3
Hemdean House School
CAV/SC RG4 ....45 G3
The Henley College
HEN RG9 ....127 Q1
Henley & District
Indoor Sports Centre
HEN RG9 ....127 P3
Henley Golf Club
HEN RG9 ....127 R4
Henley Management College
HEN RG9 ....16 C7
Henley Road Municipal
Cemetery
CAV/SC RG4 ....45 K2
Henley Town FC
HEN RG9 ....22 B6
Hennerton Golf Club
WAR/TWY RG10 ....32 F1
Henry Tyndale School
FARN GU14 ....94 C8
The Herb Farm
CAV/SC RG4 ....126 G7
Hermitage Primary School
NTHA RG18 ....133 P2
UX/CGN UB8 ....31 M1
Hernes Estate
HEN RG9 ....127 M2
Heron Industrial Estate
THLE RG7 ....145 L6
Herries School
MDHD SL6 ....19 K6
Herschel Grammar School
SL SL1 ....10 B1
The Hexagon
READ RG1 ....8 E6
Highclere Hotel
ASC SL5 ....78 D2
High Close School
EWKG RG40 ....15 H4
Highdown School
CAV/SC RG4 ....45 G1
Highdown Sports Centre
CAV/SC RG4 ....45 G1
Highfield PNEU School
MDHD SL6 ....4 F5
Highwood Primary School
WODY RG5 ....46 C8
The Hill Cemetery
GOR/PANG RG8 ....124 F9
The Hill Primary School
CAV/SC RG4 ....45 J1
Hillside Primary School
EARL RG6 ....59 M6
Hill Top First School
EARL RG6 ....52 E2
HM Customs
HTHAIR TW6 ....42 D8
HM Prison
READ RG1 ....9 J5
HM Young Offender Institution
FELT TW13 ....71 H1
Hogwood Industrial Park
EWKG RG40 ....73 G8
Holiday Inn
SHPTN TW17 ....83 M3
Holly Spring Infant School
BRAK RG12 ....3 L4

Hollywood Bowl
BRAK RG12 ....2 F4
Holme Grange School
EWKG RG40 ....74 F3
The Holt School
WWKG RG41 ....14 E4
The Holybrook School
RDGW/BURGH RG30 ....58 A2
Holy Family Catholic School
DTCH/LGLY SL3 ....40 B5
Holyport CE Primary School
MDHD SL6 ....36 D6
Holyport Manor School
MDHD SL6 ....36 A8
Holy Trinity CE (A) School
MLW SL7 ....18 F3
Holy Trinity CE Primary School
ASC SL5 ....79 G3
CHOB/PIR GU24 ....91 G7
MDHD SL6 ....20 C7
Home Farm School
THLE RG7 ....99 M3
Homers First School
WDSR SL4 ....37 M8
Horizon West Industrial Estate
NWBY RG14 ....7 M4
Horris Hill School
KSCL RG20 ....100 A3
Horton Industrial Park
WDR/YW UB7 ....42 B1
Horton Trading Estate
DTCH/LGLY SL3 ....55 H2
Hoskins Place Industrial Estate
CBLY GU15 ....94 B3
Hotel du Vin
HEN RG9 ....22 A4
Household Cavalry Museum
WDSR SL4 ....13 G9
Houston Business Centre
YEAD UB4 ....43 L1
Humphries Industrial Estate
BRAK RG12 ....3 G9
Hungerford Community
Health Clinic
HUNG RG17 ....129 L12
Hungerford Leisure Centre
HUNG RG17 ....138 H2
Hungerford Primary School
HUNG RG17 ....138 H2
Hungerford Town FC
HUNG RG17 ....138 H1
Hungerford Trading Estate
HUNG RG17 ....138 F1
Huntercombe Manor Hospital
MDHD SL6 ....27 L8
Hurley Riverside Park
MDHD SL6 ....24 B2
The Hurst Community College
TADY RG26 ....103 M4
Hurst Leisure Centre
TADY RG26 ....103 M5
Hurst Lodge School
ASC SL5 ....78 B5
Hythe First & Middle School
STA TW18 ....69 K3
Ibis Hotel
HYS/HAR UB3 ....57 H1
READ RG1 ....8 F5
Ibis Sports Club
RDGW/BURGH RG30 ....44 B4
The Isleys Primary School
KSCL RG20 ....109 L12
Imperial College Athletic Ground
HYS/HAR UB3 ....42 E6
Imperial College of Science
Technology & Medicine
ASC SL5 ....66 F8
Independent Industrial Estate
WDR/YW UB7 ....42 B1
Industrial Health Clinic
UX/CGN UB8 ....31 K4
Inkpen Common
Nature Reserve
HUNG RG17 ....140 A9
Inkpen Primary School
HUNG RG17 ....139 P9
Innkeeper's Lodge
CBLY GU15 ....94 E3
DTCH/LGLY SL3 ....40 B5
WDSR SL4 ....54 A4
WEY KT13 ....83 L7
International Trading Estate
NWDGN UB2 ....43 K3
Iver Golf & Leisure Centre
IVER SL0 ....40 D1
Iver Heath Health Centre
IVER SL0 ....30 F3
Iver Heath Infant School
IVER SL0 ....30 F4
Iver Heath Primary School
IVER SL0 ....30 F3
Iver Village Infant School
IVER SL0 ....31 H7
Iver Village Junior School
IVER SL0 ....31 G7
Ivyleaf Working Mens Club
MDHD SL6 ....5 J4
Jackson Industrial Estate
BNEND SL8 ....20 D3
James Elliman School
SLN SL2 ....10 C3
John Nike Athletics Stadium
BRAK RG12 ....76 C2
John O'Gaunt School
HUNG RG17 ....138 H3
John Rankin Infant School
NWBY RG14 ....141 R6
John Rankin Junior School
NWBY RG14 ....141 R6
Johnsons Industrial Estate
HYS/HAR UB3 ....43 J3
The Junior School
GOR/PANG RG8 ....124 D9
Jurys Inn Hotel
HTHAIR TW6 ....57 M2
Katesgrove Primary School
READ RG1 ....8 F8
Keep Hatch Primary School
EWKG RG40 ....15 K3
Kendall Court Business Park
CBLY GU15 ....93 M2
Kendrick School
READ RG1 ....9 H8
Kennel Lane Special School
BNFD RG42 ....64 A4
Kennet Leisure Centre
NTHA RG19 ....98 A3
Kennet School
NTHA RG19 ....98 A3
Kennet Shopping Centre
NWBY RG14 ....6 E4
Kennet Valley Primary School
TILE/CALC RG31 ....137 R6
Kenton Theatre
HEN RG9 ....22 A4
Kidmore End CE Primary School
CAV/SC RG4 ....126 D7
King Edward Court
WDSR SL4 ....13 H5
King Edward VII Hospital
WDSR SL4 ....13 H9

Kingfisher Court
  Industrial Estate
  NWBY RG14 ......7 L4
Kings Court First School
  WDSR SL4 ......54 A6
Kingscroft School
  STA TW18 ......70 A4
Kings Grove Industrial Estate
  MDHD SL6 ......4 F6
Kings International College
  CBLY GU15 ......94 C4
Kingsland Centre
  NTHA RG19 ......97 M3
Kintbury St Marys CE
  Primary School
  HUNG RG17 ......140 B4
Knowle Park Infant School
  STA TW18 ......70 A3
Knowl Hill CE Primary School
  WAR/TWY RG10 ......34 B2
Laffords Industrial Estate
  THLE RG7 ......137 L8
Lakeside Business Park
  SHST GU47 ......87 G7
Lakeside Country Club
  FRIM GU16 ......95 G8
Lakeside Industrial Estate
  DTCH/LGLY SL3 ......41 J6
Lakeside International Hotel
  FRIM GU16 ......95 G8
Lakeside Primary School
  FRIM GU16 ......94 F7
Laleham CE Primary School
  STA TW18 ......70 C4
Laleham Golf Club
  CHERT KT16 ......82 B1
Lambourn CE Primary School
  HUNG RG17 ......117 K5
Lambourne Golf Club
  SL SL1 ......21 K8
The Lambourn Sports Club
  HUNG RG17 ......117 K4
Lambrook Haileybury School
  BNFD RG42 ......65 G3
Lambs Farm Business Park
  THLE RG7 ......145 L6
Lambs Lane Primary School
  THLE RG7 ......145 L6
Lambwood Industrial Estate
  THLE RG7 ......144 C5
Langley Business Centre
  DTCH/LGLY SL3 ......40 C2
Langley Business Court
  KSCL RG20 ......121 J9
Langley Business Park
  DTCH/LGLY SL3 ......40 B2
Langley Grammar School
  DTCH/LGLY SL3 ......40 B2
Langley Health Centre
  DTCH/LGLY SL3 ......40 C5
Langley Manor School
  DTCH/LGLY SL3 ......40 A1
Langley Park Country Park
  DTCH/LGLY SL3 ......30 C5
Langleywood School
  DTCH/LGLY SL3 ......40 A3
Langtree School
  GOR/PANG RG8 ......113 K10
Larchfield Primary School
  MDHD SL6 ......36 A2
Larges Lane Cemetery
  BRAK RG12 ......3 J5
Larchfield Primary School
  MDHD SL6 ......36 A2
Lavender Park Golf Club
  ASC SL5 ......65 J8
Lea Infant School
  SLN SL2 ......11 L3
Lea Junior School
  SLN SL2 ......11 K3
Legoland Windsor
  WDSR SL4 ......52 D4
Leighton Park School
  WHIT RG2 ......59 L2
  WHIT RG2 ......59 L4
Lent Rise Combined School
  SL SL1 ......27 K6
Lewis Industrial Court
  HUNG RG17 ......118 E11
The Licensed Victuallers
  School
  ASC SL5 ......65 J7
Light Industrial Estate
  WDSR SL4 ......52 B8
Lightwater Country Park
  LTWR GU18 ......89 M5
Lightwater Leisure Centre
  LTWR GU18 ......89 M5
Lightwater Village School
  LTWR GU18 ......90 A5
Linden Medical Centre
  MDHD SL6 ......4 C1
Littlecote
  HUNG RG17 ......128 F9
Littledown Special School
  SL SL1 ......11 G3
Little Marlow CE Infant School
  MLW SL7 ......19 M1
Little Marlow Cemetery
  MLW SL7 ......20 A1
Littleton CE Infant School
  SHPTN TW17 ......71 G8
The Living Rainforest
  NTHA RG18 ......122 E9
The Loddon Infant School
  EARL RG6 ......60 D3
The Loddon Junior School
  EARL RG6 ......60 D3
Loddon Valley Leisure Centre
  EARL RG6 ......60 A5
London Area
  Terminal Control Centre
  WDR/YW UB7 ......42 B2
London Irish RFC
  WHIT RG2 ......58 F6
London Road Industrial Estate
  NWBY RG14 ......7 G3
Long Close School
  DTCH/LGLY SL3 ......39 J4
Longford Community School
  EBED/NFELT TW14 ......57 M6
Long Lane Primary School
  GOR/PANG RG8 ......125 M10
Longmead Business Park
  WDR/YW UB7 ......41 M4
Longshot Industrial Estate
  BRAK RG12 ......63 L8
Longwood Business Park
  SUN TW16 ......83 M2
The Look Out Discovery Centre
  BRAK RG12 ......76 D5
Lorraine Infant School
  CBLY GU15 ......89 G5
Lowbrook Primary School
  MDHD SL6 ......35 J3
Luckley Oakfield School
  EWKG RG40 ......74 B3
Lynch Hill School
  SLN SL2 ......28 B4
Lyndhurst School
  CBLY GU15 ......94 B1

Lyne & Longcross CE
  Infant School
  CHERT KT16 ......81 H6
Lyons Industrial Estate
  UX/CGN UB8 ......31 L9
Lyon Way Industrial Estate
  FRIM GU16 ......94 C5
Macdonald Berystede Hotel
  ASC SL5 ......78 C3
Macdonald Castle Hotel
  WDSR SL4 ......13 J5
Macdonald Frimley Hall
  Hotel & Spa
  CBLY GU15 ......88 F7
The Magna Carta School
  STA TW18 ......69 K4
The Magnet Leisure Centre
  MDHD SL6 ......5 H3
Maharajah's Well
  HEN RG9 ......113 M5
Maiden Erlegh School
  EARL RG6 ......60 B2
Maidenhead Clinic
  MDHD SL6 ......5 H5
Maidenhead Golf Club
  MDHD SL6 ......5 G5
Maidenhead Retail Park
  MDHD SL6 ......5 J7
Maidenhead RFC
  MDHD SL6 ......5 J9
Maidenhead Rowing Club
  MDHD SL6 ......26 E7
Maidenhead Sailing Club
  MDHD SL6 ......26 C4
Maidenhead Superbowl
  MDHD SL6 ......5 H3
Maidenhead United FC
  MDHD SL6 ......5 H6
Main Square Shopping Centre
  CBLY GU15 ......88 C8
Manby Lodge Infant School
  WEY KT13 ......83 H8
Manorcroft Primary School
  EGH TW20 ......69 C4
Manor Infant School
  FARN GU14 ......93 M8
Manor Mead School
  SHPTN TW17 ......83 H2
Manor Park Medical Centre
  SLN SL2 ......28 D7
Mansbridge House School
  EARL RG6 ......45 M8
Mansfield Hall
  (Witan International College)
  READ RG1 ......9 H8
Mapledurham House
  CAV/SC RG4 ......125 Q8
Mapledurham Watermill
  GOR/PANG RG8 ......125 P8
Marish Infant School
  DTCH/LGLY SL3 ......40 B3
The Marist Preparatory School
  ASC SL5 ......78 D2
Marist Senior School
  ASC SL5 ......78 D1
The Marjory Kinnon School
  EBED/NFELT TW14 ......57 L4
Market Trading Estate
  NWDGN UB2 ......43 K4
Marlow CE Infants School
  MLW SL7 ......18 F3
Marlow Cemetery
  MLW SL7 ......18 F3
Marlow Community Hospital
  MLW SL7 ......19 G4
Marlow FC
  MLW SL7 ......19 G3
Marlow RFC
  MLW SL7 ......19 J5
Marlow Rowing Club
  MLW SL7 ......19 G5
Marlow Sports Club
  Pavilion Ground
  MLW SL7 ......18 F6
Marriott Hotel
  DTCH/LGLY SL3 ......40 B5
  HYS/HAR UB3 ......42 F7
Mary Hare Primary School
  NTHA RG19 ......97 C6
Mary Hare School for the Deaf
  NWBY RG14 ......132 F7
The Matthew Arnold School
  STA TW18 ......70 C4
McKay Trading Estate
  DTCH/LGLY SL3 ......55 L7
Meadowbrook Montessori
  Farm School
  BNFD RG42 ......64 E1
Meadowcroft County
  Infant School
  CHERT KT16 ......81 M7
The Meadows
  SHST GU47 ......93 L1
Meadow Vale Primary School
  BNFD RG42 ......2 A2
Meadowview Squash Club
  HUNG RG17 ......129 N11
Meadway Comprehensive
  School
  RDGW/BURGH RG30 ......137 R3
Meadway Sports Centre
  RDGW/BURGH RG30 ......137 R4
Megabowl
  TILE/CALC RG31 ......137 K6
Membury Airfield
  Industrial Estate
  HUNG RG17 ......116 F10
Membury Business Park
  HUNG RG17 ......116 G10
Mercure Thames Lodge
  STA TW18 ......69 L3
Micklands Primary School
  CAV/SC RG4 ......45 K2
The Microcentre
  WHIT RG2 ......59 G3
Midas Industrial Estate
  UX/CGN UB8 ......31 K3
Middlegreen Trading Estate
  DTCH/LGLY SL3 ......39 M2
Millars Business Centre
  WWKG RG41 ......14 B7
The Mill at Sonning
  CAV/SC RG4 ......46 C2
Millennium Madejski Hotel
  WHIT RG2 ......58 F6
The Mill House Hotel
  THLE RG7 ......145 M4
Mill Ride Golf Club
  ASC SL5 ......65 K6
Milman Road Health Centre
  WHIT RG2 ......59 H1
Minet Clinic
  HYS/HAR UB3 ......43 J1
Minet J & I Schools
  HYS/HAR UB3 ......43 K1
Monkey Island Hotel
  MDHD SL6 ......37 G3
Montem Primary School
  SLN SL1 ......38 D2
Montem Sports Centre
  SLN SL1 ......10 C6

Moorlands Primary School
  RDGW/BURGH RG30 ......137 Q3
Mortimer St John's
  Infant School
  THLE RG7 ......143 Q9
Mortimer St Marys CE
  Junior School
  THLE RG7 ......144 B9
Moulsford Preparatory School
  WGFD OX10 ......111 Q4
Mrs Blands Infant School
  THLE RG7 ......143 P4
Mulberry Business Park
  WWKG RG41 ......14 D9
The Museum of
  Berkshire Aviation
  WODY RG5 ......47 H8
Museum of English Rural Life
  READ RG1 ......9 K9
Nettlebed Community School
  HEN RG9 ......114 D4
Newbold College
  BNFD RG42 ......63 K5
Newbold School
  BNFD RG42 ......63 K5
Newbury Business Park
  NWBY RG14 ......7 J2
Newbury Bus Station
  NWBY RG14 ......6 E5
Newbury College
  NWBY RG14 ......96 C7
Newbury & Crookham Golf Club
  NTHA RG19 ......97 G7
Newbury Hockey & CC
  NWBY RG14 ......6 C3
Newbury Manor Hotel
  NWBY RG14 ......7 M3
Newbury Racecourse
  NWBY RG14 ......7 K6
Newbury Retail Park
  NWBY RG14 ......96 D7
Newbury RFC
  NWBY RG14 ......96 B8
Newbury Showground
  NWBY RG14 ......133 J3
New Christ Church CE
  Primary School
  WHIT RG2 ......59 H1
The New College
  WDSR SL4 ......13 J3
New Greenham Park
  Leisure Centre
  NTHA RG19 ......101 J1
Newlands CP School
  YTLY GU46 ......92 C1
Newlands Girls School
  MDHD SL6 ......25 J7
New Regal Cinema
  HEN RG9 ......115 R12
New Scotland Hill
  Primary School
  SHST GU47 ......87 G4
New Town Primary School
  READ RG1 ......9 M5
Nicholsons Shopping Centre
  MDHD SL6 ......5 G5
Nimrod Industrial Estate
  READ RG1 ......59 G1
Northcroft Leisure Centre
  NWBY RG14 ......6 B3
Northfield Farm
  Industrial Estate
  HUNG RG17 ......118 F8
North Maidenhead CC
  MDHD SL6 ......26 C4
Novello Theatre
  ASC SL5 ......78 D2
Novotel
  READ RG1 ......8 F5
  WDR/YW UB7 ......42 C4
Oak Farm Community School
  FARN GU14 ......94 A8
Oakfield First School
  WDSR SL4 ......12 E8
Oaklands Business Centre
  WWKG RG41 ......74 A3
Oaklands Junior School
  CWTH RG45 ......75 G8
Oakley Court Hotel
  WDSR SL4 ......37 J6
Oast House Centre
  STA TW18 ......69 M2
Oatlands Park Hotel
  WEY KT13 ......83 J7
Oatlands School
  WEY KT13 ......83 K8
The Observatory
  Shopping Centre
  SLN SL1 ......11 J6
Odds Farm Rare Breeds Centre
  FLKWH/TG HP10 ......21 K2
Odeon Cinema
  UX/CGN UB8 ......31 M2
Oldfield Primary School
  MDHD SL6 ......5 M7
Old Kiln Industrial Estate
  MDHD SL6 ......25 J3
Old Station Business Park
  READ RG1 ......122 A2
Old Town Hall
  CHERT KT16 ......82 A4
Oracle Shopping &
  Leisure Centre
  READ RG1 ......9 G6
The Oratory Preparatory School
  GOR/PANG RG8 ......124 H2
The Oratory School
  GOR/PANG RG8 ......113 L10
Our Lady of Peace
  Infant School
  SL SL1 ......27 L6
Our Lady of Peace
  Junior School
  SL SL1 ......27 L6
Our Lady of the Rosary RC
  Primary School
  STA TW18 ......70 A4
Our Ladys Preparatory School
  CWTH RG45 ......87 G1
Owlsmoor Primary School
  SHST GU47 ......87 L5
Oxford Road Community School
  READ RG1 ......8 B6
Paddock Road Industrial Estate
  CAV/SC RG4 ......9 L1
Padworth College
  THLE RG7 ......142 C5
The Palmer CE Junior School
  EWKG RG40 ......15 J3
Palmer Park Sports Stadium
  EARL RG6 ......45 M7
Pangbourne College
  GOR/PANG RG8 ......124 D11
Pangbourne Medical Centre
  GOR/PANG RG8 ......124 G8
Pangbourne Primary School
  GOR/PANG RG8 ......125 J9
Papplewick School
  ASC SL5 ......65 M6
Park Farm Industrial Estate
  FRIM GU16 ......94 C5

Park House School
  NWBY RG14 ......96 A8
Park Lane Primary School
  TILE/CALC RG31 ......137 N2
Parkside Business Park
  WODY RG5 ......46 E6
Parkway Trading Estate
  HEST TW5 ......43 L6
Parlaunt Park Combined School
  DTCH/LGLY SL3 ......40 D3
Parsons Down Infant School
  NTHA RG19 ......97 K3
Parsons Down Junior School
  NTHA RG19 ......97 J3
Pavilions Shopping Centre
  UX/CGN UB8 ......31 L1
The Peel Centre
  BRAK RG12 ......2 E5
Penn Wood School
  SLN SL2 ......28 F5
Pennyhill Park Hotel & The Spa
  BAGS GU19 ......89 H4
Peppard CE Primary School
  HEN RG9 ......126 C2
Perborough Castle
  NTHA RG18 ......122 A6
Perth Trading Estate
  SLN SL1 ......28 D6
Peter James Business Centre
  HYS/HAR UB3 ......43 J2
Phoenix Business Park
  BRAK RG12 ......63 J7
Phoenix College
  WHIT RG2 ......59 K1
Phoenix Plaza Bowling Alley
  EWKG RG40 ......14 E7
The Piggott School
  WAR/TWY RG10 ......32 E7
Pincents Kiln Industrial Park
  TILE/CALC RG31 ......137 L6
Pine Ridge Golf Club
  FRIM GU16 ......95 K4
Pine Ridge Infant School
  CBLY GU15 ......89 C5
The Pines Primary School
  BRAK RG12 ......76 A4
Pine Trees Business Park
  STA TW18 ......69 L3
Pinewood Film Studios
  IVER SL0 ......30 D1
The Pinewood Hotel
  DTCH/LGLY SL3 ......30 A6
Pinewood Infant School
  FARN GU14 ......93 K7
Pinewood Leisure Centre
  EWKG RG40 ......75 H6
Pinkwell Primary School
  HYS/HAR UB3 ......42 C4
Pipers Industrial Estate
  NTHA RG19 ......98 B5
Pippins School
  ASHF TW15 ......70 F2
  DTCH/LGLY SL3 ......41 H8
PMS Health Centre
  READ RG1 ......9 J9
The Point
  BRAK RG12 ......2 F4
Polehampton Infant School
  WAR/TWY RG10 ......47 K1
Polehampton Junior School
  WAR/TWY RG10 ......32 F8
Polygon Business Centre
  DTCH/LGLY SL3 ......55 M1
Portesbery School
  CBLY GU15 ......88 D8
Portland Business Centre
  DTCH/LGLY SL3 ......39 K8
Potley Hill Primary School
  YTLY GU46 ......93 G1
Premier Inn
  BAGS GU19 ......89 L1
  BRAK RG12 ......2 E4
  SHST GU47 ......87 K7
  SL SL1 ......16 L6
  THLE RG7 ......98 F4
  THLE RG7 ......144 E3
Princess Margaret Hospital
  WDSR SL4 ......13 J8
Princess Marina College
  WHIT RG2 ......72 F5
The Princess Royal Barracks
  FRIM GU16 ......95 K7
Princess Square
  Shopping Centre
  BRAK RG12 ......2 F4
Prior Heath Infant School
  CBLY GU15 ......95 G1
Priors Way Industrial Estate
  MDHD SL6 ......36 D4
The Priory Primary School
  TADY RG26 ......148 F9
Priory School
  SL SL1 ......27 M6
Progress Business Centre
  SL SL1 ......27 M7
Progress Theatre
  READ RG1 ......59 J1
Prospect Technology College
  RDGW/BURGH RG30 ......58 A1
Providence Road School
  WDR/YW UB7 ......42 A1
Provident Industrial Estate
  HYS/HAR UB3 ......43 J2
Pump Lane Industrial Estate
  HYS/HAR UB3 ......43 K2
Purley CE Infant School
  GOR/PANG RG8 ......125 N9
Pyrcroft Primary School
  CHERT KT16 ......81 L3
Quality Hotel
  DTCH/LGLY SL3 ......40 D6
  RDGW/BURGH RG30 ......44 C6
The Queen Anne Royal Free
  CE First School
  WDSR SL4 ......13 K9
Queen Annes School
  CAV/SC RG4 ......45 H3
Queen's Building
  HTHAIR TW6 ......57 H2
Queensmere Shopping Centre
  SL SL1 ......11 H6
Queens Schools
  WDSR SL4 ......13 J1
Rabbsfarm Primary School
  WDR/YW UB7 ......31 M7
Racecourse Yacht Basin
  WDSR SL4 ......12 B3
Raceview Business Centre
  NWBY RG14 ......7 H5
Radisson Edwardian Hotel
  HYS/HAR UB3 ......42 E7
Radstock Primary School
  EARL RG6 ......60 A4
Rainbow Industrial Estate
  WDR/YW UB7 ......31 M8
Ramada Hotel
  KSCL RG20 ......130 H11
Randolph Medical Centre
  DTCH/LGLY SL3 ......39 K7
Ranelagh School
  BRAK RG12 ......3 G6

Ranikhet Primary School
  RDGW/BURGH RG30 ......44 A5
Reading Abbey Ruins
  READ RG1 ......9 H1
Reading Adult & Community
  College
  CAV/SC RG4 ......8 F7
Reading Auction Market
  READ RG1 ......8 D7
Reading Blue Coat School
  CAV/SC RG4 ......46 C3
Reading Clinic
  READ RG1 ......9 K1
Reading County Court
  READ RG1 ......9 G4
Reading Crematorium
  CAV/SC RG4 ......45 K4
Reading Crown Court
  READ RG1 ......9 H1
Reading Family Planning Clinic
  READ RG1 ......9 L8
Reading FC (Madejski Stadium)
  WHIT RG2 ......58 F7
Reading Gate Retail Park
  WHIT RG2 ......58 F7
Reading Girls School
  WHIT RG2 ......59 J3
Reading Golf Club
  CAV/SC RG4 ......126 H1
Reading Link Retail Park
  READ RG1 ......59 G
Reading Retail Park
  RDGW/BURGH RG30 ......44 B8
Reading School
  READ RG1 ......9 M
Reading University
  EARL RG6 ......60 A1
Rebellion Brewery
  MLW SL7 ......19 G
Redingensians RFC
  CAV/SC RG4 ......46 E
Redlands Primary School
  READ RG1 ......59 L
Red Shute Hill Industrial Estate
  NTHA RG18 ......133 N
Reed Place Business Park
  SHPTN TW17 ......82 F
Regency Park Hotel
  NTHA RG18 ......133 P12
Regent Business Centre
  HYS/HAR UB3 ......43 K
REME Museum of Technology
  WHIT RG2 ......73 G
Renaissance Hotel
  READ RG1 ......8 E
The Renaissance Hotel
  HTHAIR TW6 ......42 E
Research Centre
  (University of Reading)
  EARL RG6 ......59 M
Richings Park Golf Club
  DTCH/LGLY SL3 ......40 F
Richings Park Sports Club
  WDR/YW UB7 ......41 H
Riders Country House Hotel
  MDHD SL6 ......34 D
Ridge House
  Pre-Preparatory School
  NTHA RG18 ......133 R1
The Ridgeway Primary School
  WHIT RG2 ......59 K
Rivermead Industrial Estate
  NTHA RG19 ......98 B5
Rivermead Leisure Centre
  READ RG1 ......8 C
Rivermead Primary School
  WODY RG5 ......46 F
Riverpark Industrial Estate
  READ RG1 ......7 J
River & Rowing Museum at
  Henley & Wind in the Willows
  HEN RG9 ......22 B
Robert Cort Industrial Estate
  WHIT RG2 ......59 H
The Robert Piggott CE
  Infant School
  WAR/TWY RG10 ......33 G2
The Robert Piggott CE
  Junior School
  WAR/TWY RG10 ......32 F
Robert Sandilands Primary School
  NWBY RG14 ......6 B
Rodd Estate
  SHPTN TW17 ......83 J
Romans Country House Hotel
  THLE RG7 ......149 K
Rosedale Clinic
  MLW SL7 ......19 G
Rose Industrial Estate
  MLW SL7 ......18 F
Rose Kiln Trading Estate
  WHIT RG2 ......59 G
Ross Road Medical Centre
  MDHD SL6 ......36 A
Royal Adelaide Hotel
  WDSR SL4 ......13 K
Royal Ascot Golf Club
  ASC SL5 ......66 A
Royal Berkshire & Battle
  Hospital
  RDGW/BURGH RG30 ......44 D
Royal Berkshire Hospital
  READ RG1 ......9 K
The Royal Berkshire
  Ramada Plaza Hotel
  ASC SL5 ......67 G
The Royal First School
  (Crown Aided)
  WDSR SL4 ......67 J
Royal Holloway
  University of London
  EGH TW20 ......68 D
Royal Holloway University of
  London (Hall of Residence)
  EGH TW20 ......68 A
Royal Logistic Corps Museum
  FRIM GU16 ......95 K
Royal Mews
  WDSR SL4 ......13 L
Royal Military Academy
  CBLY GU15 ......88 A
Royal Oak Hotel
  NTHA RG18 ......122 G1
Royal Windsor Racecourse
  WDSR SL4 ......12 C
Runnymede (NT)
  EGH TW20 ......68 E
Runnymede Hospital
  CHERT KT16 ......81 K
Runnymede Hotel & Spa
  EGH TW20 ......69 H
Rupert House School
  HEN RG9 ......22 A
Ruscombe Business Park
  WAR/TWY RG10 ......47 L
Ryeish Green School
  THLE RG7 ......145 N
Ryvers School
  DTCH/LGLY SL3 ......39 M
Sacred Heart RC Primary School
  HEN RG9 ......127 N

St Andrews CE J & I School UX/CGN UB8 31 M2
St Andrews CE Primary School KSCL RG20 119 M7
St Andrews School GOR/PANG RG8 136 A1
St Annes Catholic Primary School CHERT KT16 82 A5
St Annes CP School STWL/WRAY TW19 56 E6
St Annes RC Primary School CAV/SC RG4 45 H4
St Anns Heath Junior School VW GU25 80 F2
St Anthonys RC Primary School SLN SL2 28 E4
St Augustines Primary School FRIM GU16 94 F4
St Bartholomews School NWBY RG14 6 B7
NWBY RG14 6 C8
St Bernards Preparatory School SL SL1 11 M6
St Catherines RC J & I School WDR/YW UB7 41 M2
St Charles Borromeo RCP School WEY KT13 83 G7
St Crispins School EWKG RG40 15 L6
St Crispins Sports Centre EWKG RG40 15 L6
St Cuthberts CE Primary School EGH TW20 68 C5
St David's Hall (Witan International College) READ RG1 9 J8
St Davids Health Centre STWL/WRAY TW19 56 D6
St Davids School ASHF TW15 70 F1
St Dominic Savio Catholic Primary School WODY RG5 46 D6
St Edmund Campion RC Primary School MDHD SL6 25 K8
St Edwards Catholic First School WDSR SL4 12 D5
St Edwards Royal Free Ecumenical Middle School WDSR SL4 12 C5
St Edwards School RDGW/BURGH RG30 8 A7
St Ethelberts Catholic Primary School SLN SL2 29 J7
St Finians RC Primary School NTHA RG18 133 R10
St Francis RC Primary School ASC SL5 78 A3
St George's Chapel WDSR SL4 13 K4
St Georges College ADL/WDHM KT15 82 D7
St George's College Track ADL/WDHM KT15 82 D6
St George's Hall READ RG1 59 K1
St Georges Industrial Estate CBLY GU15 94 B3
St Georges Pre-Preparatory School WDSR SL4 13 K4
St Georges School ASC SL5 78 B1
St James CE Primary School WEY KT13 83 J7
St Johns Beaumont School WDSR SL4 54 B8
St John the Evangelist Infant School NWBY RG14 6 D8
St Joseph RC Primary School NWBY RG14 7 H1
St Josephs Catholic High School SLN SL2 11 J1
St Josephs RC Primary School BRAK RG12 3 J5
St Judes CE Junior School EGH TW20 68 C4
St Lukes CE Primary School MDHD SL6 5 H2
St Margaret Clitherow RC Primary School BRAK RG12 75 M4
St Marks Hospital MDHD SL6 4 A4
St Martins East Woodhay CE Primary School KSCL RG20 147 Q3
St Martins RC Primary School CAV/SC RG4 127 L12
St Marys & All Saints CE Primary School READ RG1 58 E2
St Marys CE Junior School STWL/WRAY TW19 56 E5
St Marys CE Primary School BNFD RG42 65 H3
SL SL1 11 J8
St Marys RC Primary School UX/CGN UB8 31 L2
St Marys School HEN RG9 22 A6
St Marys School Ascot ASC SL5 78 B4
St Matthews CE Primary School WDR/YW UB7 42 A1
St Michaels CE Primary School ASC SL5 78 D2
BRAK RG12 76 A2
SHST GU47 86 E6
St Michaels Primary School RDGW/BURGH RG30 44 A8
St Michaels RC School ASHF TW15 71 G3
St Michaels School KSCL RG20 100 B8
St Neots School HTWY RG27 84 F6
St Nicholas CE Combined School MDHD SL6 26 F5
St Nicholas CE Primary School SHPTN TW17 83 H3
WAR/TWY RG10 47 M6
St Nicolas CE Junior School NWBY RG14 6 D6
St Patricks Hall WHIT RG2 59 J2
St Pauls Catholic Primary School TILE/CALC RG31 137 N3
St Pauls CE Combined School FLKWH/TG HP10 20 F2
St Pauls CE Junior School WWKG RG41 14 C5
St Pauls CE Primary School ADL/WDHM KT15 82 A8
St Peters Catholic School MLW SL7 18 E3
St Peters CE Combined School SL SL1 27 K4
St Peters CE Junior School YTLY GU46 86 D8
St Peters CE Middle School WDSR SL4 53 M5
St Peters CE Primary School EARL RG6 60 B1
St Peters Hospital CHERT KT16 81 K7
St Pirans School MDHD SL6 4 E1
St Sebastians CE Primary School EWKG RG40 74 E6
St Teresas Catholic Primary School EWKG RG40 15 J7
Salesian College CHERT KT16 82 A5
Salesian RC School CHERT KT16 81 L6
Sampson Business Park CBLY GU15 94 B3
Sandham Memorial Chapel (NT) KSCL RG20 100 A8
Sandhurst School SHST GU47 87 K5
Sandhurst Sports Centre SHST GU47 87 K6
Sandhurst Sports Club SHST GU47 87 J7
Sand Martins Golf Club EWKG RG40 73 M5
Sandringham Infant School FRIM GU16 94 F7
Sandy Lane Primary School BNFD RG42 3 G1
Savill Garden (Windsor Great Park) EGH TW20 67 L4
Saxon CP School SHPTN TW17 82 F2
Sefton Park School SLN SL2 29 K1
Shalbourne CE Primary School MARL SN8 138 C11
Shaw cum Donnington Primary School NWBY RG14 132 G12
Sheeji Medical Centre SL SL1 10 D2
Shefford CE Primary School HUNG RG17 118 F10
Shepperton Business Park SHPTN TW17 83 J2
Shepperton Health Centre SHPTN TW17 83 H2
Shepperton Studios SHPTN TW17 70 F8
Sheraton Skyline Hotel HYS/HAR UB3 42 F7
Sherfield Hall WHIT RG2 59 J2
Sherfield on Loddon CC HTWY RG27 150 D10
Sherfield School HTWY RG27 150 E11
Shinfield Infant School WHIT RG2 145 Q2
Shinfield Players Theatre WHIT RG2 59 K7
Shinfield St Marys CE Junior School WHIT RG2 145 R2
The Ship Hotel WEY KT13 83 H7
Shiplake CE Primary School HEN RG9 32 A4
Shiplake College HEN RG9 32 B5
Shortwood Infant School STA TW18 70 B1
Showcase Cinemas Reading WWKG RG41 60 F3
Sibly Hall EARL RG6 60 A4
Silchester CE Primary School THLE RG7 149 K1
Silchester Manor School MDHD SL6 26 E7
Silverdale Industrial Estate HYS/HAR UB3 43 J1
Sir Christopher Wren's House Hotel WDSR SL4 13 J4
Sir William Borlases Grammar School MLW SL7 18 E5
Sir William Perkins School CHERT KT16 81 L5
The Sixth Form Academy at Reading College READ RG1 45 M8
The Sixth Form College FARN GU14 94 B7
Skimped Hill Health Centre BRAK RG12 2 F4
Sky Business Park EGH TW20 69 J7
Slough Cemetery SL SL1 29 H7
Slough Community Mental Health Centre DTCH/LGLY SL3 40 C4
Slough Crematorium SLN SL2 29 H7
Slough & Eton CE School SL SL1 10 D8
Slough Grammar School SL SL1 11 L8
Slough Ice Arena SL SL1 10 C6
Slough Indoor Tennis Centre SL SL1 10 C5
Slough Museum SL SL1 11 J7
Slough RFC DTCH/LGLY SL3 39 K5
Slough Sports Club SL SL1 10 E8
Slough Town FC SLN SL2 29 J6
Slough Trading Estate SL SL1 10 A3
SL SL1 28 C6
The SMAE Institute MDHD SL6 25 K8
Smallmead Stadium WHIT RG2 58 F5
Snelsmore Common Country Park KSCL RG20 132 D8
Soho Mills Industrial Estate FLKWH/TG HP10 20 F2
Sonning CE Primary School CAV/SC RG4 46 D3
Sonning Common Health Centre CAV/SC RG4 126 F5
Sonning Common Primary School CAV/SC RG4 126 F5
Sonning Golf Club CAV/SC RG4 46 E4
Southcote Clinic RDGW/BURGH RG30 58 B2
Southcote Primary School RDGW/BURGH RG30 58 C2
Southfield School EWKG RG40 15 J8
South Hill Park Arts Centre BRAK RG12 76 B4
South Lake Primary School WODY RG5 60 D1
South Reading Leisure Centre WHIT RG2 59 J5
South Stoke Primary School GOR/PANG RG8 111 R6
Southville Infant School EBED/NFELT TW14 57 M7
Speedw ay Industrial Estate HYS/HAR UB3 42 F2
Speenhamland Primary School NWBY RG14 6 D1
Spelthorne Clinic ASHF TW15 71 K4
Spelthorne Infant School ASHF TW15 71 K4
Spelthorne Leisure Centre STA TW18 70 A3
Spelthorne Sports Club ASHF TW15 71 K5
Spinfield School MLW SL7 18 D4
Springfield Primary School SUN TW16 71 L6
TILE/CALC RG31 137 M3
Spring Meadows Business Centre WAR/TWY RG10 33 H1
The Springs Hotel & Golf Club WGFD OX10 112 C1
Spurcroft Primary School NTHA RG19 97 M4
Squirrels Trading Estate HYS/HAR UB3 43 H3
Stadium Industrial Estate RDGW/BURGH RG30 44 B5
Staines Cemetery STA TW18 70 C1
Staines County Court STA TW18 70 A3
Staines Preparatory School STA TW18 70 A3
Staines Town FC STA TW18 70 A5
Stanwell Burial Ground STWL/WRAY TW19 56 C6
Station Industrial Estate WWKG RG41 14 E5
Station Road Industrial Estate NTHA RG19 98 B5
Station Yard Industrial Estate HUNG RG17 139 J1
Stepgates Community School CHERT KT16 82 B4
Sterling Industrial Estate NWBY RG14 7 G5
Stirrups Country House Hotel BNFD RG42 65 H1
Stockcross Primary School KSCL RG20 131 Q12
Stockley Park Business Centre STKPK UB11 42 E1
Stoke Green CC SLN SL2 29 K5
Stoke Park Golf Club SLN SL2 28 F4
Stoke Poges School SLN SL2 29 H1
Streatley CE Primary School GOR/PANG RG8 111 P12
Strodes College EGH TW20 68 F3
Studholme Medical Centre ASHF TW15 70 F2
Studland Industrial Estate KSCL RG20 140 H10
Sulhamstead & Ufton Nervet Primary School THLE RG7 143 L2
Sunbury Business Centre SUN TW16 71 L6
Sunbury Golf Centre SHPTN TW17 83 J1
Sunbury Leisure Centre SUN TW16 71 M6
Sunbury Manor School SUN TW16 71 M6
Sunningdale Golf Club ASC SL5 79 G5
Sunningdale Ladies Golf Club ASC SL5 78 F5
Sunningdale School ASC SL5 78 E3
Surrey Heath Museum CBLY GU15 88 D8
Suttons Business Park EARL RG6 45 M6
Swallowfield Park THLE RG7 145 Q6
The Swan Hotel GOR/PANG RG8 111 R12
Swan Wharf Business Centre UX/CGN UB8 31 L3
Swinley CP School ASC SL5 78 A2
Swinley Forest Golf Club ASC SL5 77 M4
Swiss Farm International Camping HEN RG9 115 R10
The Symonds Medical Centre MDHD SL6 4 C5
TA Centre CHERT KT16 82 A4
Tadley Community Primary School TADY RG26 148 E4
Tadley Learning Centre TADY RG26 148 D1
Tadley Swimming Pool TADY RG26 148 E3
Tapling Trading Estate WDR/YW UB7 31 M8
Taplow Health Centre MDHD SL6 27 K7
Taplow House Hotel MDHD SL6 26 F6
Tasis the American School in England EGH TW20 69 J8
Tavistock Industrial Estate WAR/TWY RG10 47 M1
Teikyo School SLN SL2 29 M1
Temple Golf Club MDHD SL6 24 D4
Thamesbridge College WHIT RG2 59 J5
Thameside Primary School CAV/SC RG4 9 G1
Thames Industrial Estate MLW SL7 19 H4
Thamesmead School SHPTN TW17 83 K3
Thames Riviera Hotel MDHD SL6 26 E7
Thames Valley Athletics Centre WDSR SL4 39 G5
Thames Valley Business Park EARL RG6 46 A5
Thames Valley Community Infant School SL SL1 10 B7
Thames Valley Cultural Centre WDSR SL4 13 K6
The Thames Valley Nuffield Hospital DTCH/LGLY SL3 29 L2
Thames Valley University READ RG1 9 M6
SL SL1 10 F5
Thatcham Bowling Club NTHA RG18 97 M2
Thatcham Business Village NTHA RG19 98 D4
Thatcham Park CE Primary School NTHA RG18 97 M1
Thatcham Town FC NTHA RG19 98 B5
Theale CE Primary School THLE RG7 136 H7
Theale Commercial Estate THLE RG7 137 K7
Theale Golf Club THLE RG7 137 J6
Theale Green Community School THLE RG7 136 H7
Theale Medical Centre THLE RG7 136 H7
Theale Sailing Club THLE RG7 137 L9
Theatre Royal WDSR SL4 13 K4
Thistle Hotel WDR/YW UB7 41 L8
Thomas Knyvett College ASHF TW15 70 E1
Thorney Park Golf Club WDR/YW UB7 41 K2
Thornford Park Track NTHA RG19 98 A8
Thorpe CE Infant School EGH TW20 69 J8
Thorpe Cemetery EGH TW20 69 J7
Thorpe CC EGH TW20 80 F1
Thorpe Industrial Park EGH TW20 69 K6
Thorpe Lea Primary School EGH TW20 69 K4
Thorpe Park CHERT KT16 81 M1
Three Swans Hotel HUNG RG17 138 H1
Tilehurst Medical Centre RDGW/BURGH RG30 137 Q2
Tomlinscote School & Sixth Form College FRIM GU16 94 F4
Tomo Industrial Estate UX/CGN UB8 31 L7
Toutley Industrial Estate WWKG RG41 61 M4
Town Farm Primary School STWL/WRAY TW19 56 D6
Town Hall & Museum READ RG1 9 G5
Townlands Hospital HEN RG9 115 R12
Travelodge BRAK RG12 63 K6
CBLY GU15 93 M1
HEST TW5 43 L6
NTHA RG18 133 J4
RDGW/BURGH RG30 137 Q9
READ RG1 8 E6
SL SL1 11 G6
STA TW18 69 L2
WHIT RG2 59 H4
Trevelyan Middle School WDSR SL4 53 J3
Trident Industrial Estate DTCH/LGLY SL3 55 L2
Trilakes Country Park SHST GU47 86 F7
Trinity CE Primary School HEN RG9 22 A5
Trinity St Stephen CE First School WDSR SL4 13 G5
Trinity School & Performing Arts College NWBY RG14 96 D1
Trinity Trading Estate HYS/HAR UB3 43 J3
Trumps Green Infant School VW GU25 80 D3
Turnpike Industrial Estate NWBY RG14 7 L1
Two Rivers Retail Park STA TW18 69 L2
Twyford Business Park WAR/TWY RG10 47 K2
Twyford Health Centre WAR/TWY RG10 47 L1
UCI Cinema BRAK RG12 2 F4
MDHD SL6 5 G6
Uffington Castle, White Horse & Dragon Hill FGDN SN7 104 D1
Underwood Shopping Centre TILE/CALC RG31 137 R6
Union Business Park UX/CGN UB8 31 L1
University of Reading READ RG1 45 L6
WHIT RG2 59 K2
University of Reading (Bulmershe Court Campus) EARL RG6 46 B8
University of Reading (St Davids Campus) READ RG1 9 J8
University of Reading (Wightknights Campus) EARL RG6 59 M2
University Vandals RFC SHPTN TW17 83 J4
Upcroft Primary School RDGW/BURGH RG30 137 R2
Uplands CP School SHST GU47 87 H6
Upton Hospital SL SL1 11 G8
Upton House School WDSR SL4 13 H8
Uxbridge Health Centre UX/CGN UB8 31 M1
Uxbridge High School UX/CGN UB8 31 M3
Uxbridge Industrial Estate UX/CGN UB8 31 K3
Valley End CE Infant School CHOB/PIR GU24 91 G2
Valley End CC CHOB/PIR GU24 91 G3
The Valley Gardens EGH TW20 67 M7
Valley Road Primary School HEN RG9 127 Q2
Van Alloys Industrial Estate HEN RG9 114 A10
Vanwall Business Park MDHD SL6 4 B9
Vastern Court Retail Park READ RG1 8 F3
Victoria Barracks WDSR SL4 13 J6
The Village Medical Centre SL SL1 37 M1
Village Shopping Centre SL SL1 11 G6
The Vineyard Hotel KSCL RG20 141 N1
Viscount Industrial Estate DTCH/LGLY SL3 55 L2
Vue Cinema READ RG1 9 G7
STA TW18 69 L2
The Vyne (NT) CHIN RG24 149 M12
Waingels College WODY RG5 47 G4
Walbury Hill HUNG RG17 146 G2
Walter Infant School WWKG RG41 14 D5
Waltham St Lawrence Primary School WAR/TWY RG10 48 F3
Walton Leigh School WOT/HER KT12 83 L8
Walton-on-Thames CC WOT/HER KT12 83 M5
Wantage Hall READ RG1 59 K1
Warfield Primary School BNFD RG42 64 E5
Warnford Industrial Estate HYS/HAR UB3 43 G2
Waste Disposal & Recycling Centre MDHD SL6 5 K8
The Watchetts Junior School CBLY GU15 94 C4
The Waterloo Hotel CWTH RG45 87 G1
Watermans Business Park STA TW18 69 L2
Watermill Theatre KSCL RG20 132 C11
Waterside Trading Estate ADL/WDHM KT15 82 E8
Waverley School EWKG RG40 73 M5
Waylands Smithy CKL/HW SN6 104 A3
The Wee Waif Hotel WAR/TWY RG10 47 G2
Welfare Clinic TILE/CALC RG31 137 P2
Welford & Wickham CE Primary School KSCL RG20 130 H6
Wellington Arms Hotel HTWY RG27 150 H5
Wellington Business Park CWTH RG45 86 E2
Wellington College CWTH RG45 87 G2
Wellington Country Park THLE RG7 145 P12
Wellingtonia Avenue (Arboretum) CWTH RG45 86 C2
Wellington Industrial Estate THLE RG7 145 L5
Wellington Monument HTWY RG27 151 M2
Wellington Sports Centre CWTH RG45 86 F2
Wellplace Zoo WGFD OX10 113 K3
Wells Hall READ RG1 59 K1
Wentworth Golf Club VW GU25 80 A2
Wescott Infant School EWKG RG40 15 J6
Wessex Downs Golf Club THLE RG7 142 A2
Wessex Hall EARL RG6 59 M1
Wessex Primary School MDHD SL6 35 K3
Wessex Road Industrial Estate BNEND SL8 20 D4
Westacott Business Centre MDHD SL6 35 G4
West Berks Golf Club KSCL RG20 119 K9
West Berkshire Community Hospital NTHA RG18 97 G2
West Berkshire Museum NWBY RG14 6 E4
West Drayton Cemetery WDR/YW UB7 42 A3
West Drayton CC WDR/YW UB7 41 L4
West Drayton Primary School WDR/YW UB7 42 A2
Westende Junior School EWKG RG40 15 K6
Western House Primary School SL SL1 28 B8
Western International Market NWDGN UB2 43 K4
Westfield School BNEND SL8 20 D2
Westfields Infant School YTLY GU46 92 B1
Westfields Junior School YTLY GU46 92 B1
Westgate Retail Park SL SL1 28 C8
Westgate School SL SL1 38 C1
Weston Farm Industrial Estate KSCL RG20 130 H2
West Ramp Coach Park HTHAIR TW6 42 C8
Westwood Farm Primary School TILE/CALC RG31 125 N11
Westwood Road Health Centre TILE/CALC RG31 137 P1

Wexham Court Primary School
SLN SL2 .... **29** L6
Wexham Park Golf Club
DTCH/LGLY SL3 .... **29** L3
Wexham Park Hospital
DTCH/LGLY SL3 .... **29** L5
Wexham School Sports College
SLN SL2 .... **29** K6
Weybridge Business Park
ADL/WDHM KT15 .... **82** E8
Weybridge CC
WEY KT13 .... **83** L6
Weybridge Hospital
WEY KT13 .... **83** G8
Wharf Business Centre
BNEND SL8 .... **20** C3
The Wheatsheaf Hotel
VW GU25 .... **67** M8
Whitchurch Primary School
GOR/PANG RG8 .... **125** J7
Whitegrove School
BNFD RG42 .... **64** F5
Whitehall Infant School
UX/CGN UB8 .... **31** L3
The White Hart Hotel
HEN RG9 .... **114** D4
White Hart Industrial Estate
BLKW GU17 .... **93** L1
Whiteknights Hall
READ RG1 .... **59** L1
Whiteknights Primary School
WHIT RG2 .... **59** M4
Whitelands Park Primary School
NTHA RG18 .... **97** L1
Whitelocke Infant School
EWKG RG40 .... **15** K4
White Lodge Centre
CHERT KT16 .... **81** K6
White Waltham Airfield
MDHD SL6 .... **35** G5
White Waltham CC
MDHD SL6 .... **34** F7
White Waltham CE Primary School
MDHD SL6 .... **34** F6
Whitley Park Infant School
WHIT RG2 .... **59** H4
Wilderness Medical Centre
MDHD SL6 .... **5** H4
Wildridings CP School
BRAK RG12 .... **2** C9
William Byrd School
HYS/HAR UB3 .... **42** E6
Willink Leisure Centre
THLE RG7 .... **143** P4
Willink School
THLE RG7 .... **143** P4
Willow Bank J & I School
WODY RG5 .... **46** F5
Wilson J & I School
RDGW/BURGH RG30 .... **44** C6
Winbury School
MDHD SL6 .... **36** C2
The Winchcombe School
NWBY RG14 .... **96** C1
Windlemere Golf Club
CHOB/PIR GU24 .... **90** E6
Windlesham Golf Club
BAGS GU19 .... **89** M2
Windlesham Village Infant School
BFOR GU20 .... **78** A8
Windmill Trading Estate
SUN TW16 .... **71** K6
Windsor Arts Centre
WDSR SL4 .... **13** H7
The Windsor Boys School Performing Arts College
WDSR SL4 .... **12** E5
Windsor Business Centre
WDSR SL4 .... **13** G4
Windsor Castle
WDSR SL4 .... **13** L4
Windsor Cemetery
WDSR SL4 .... **53** H2
Windsor Cricket, Hockey, Tennis & Rugby Clubs
WDSR SL4 .... **13** L2
Windsor English Language Centre
WDSR SL4 .... **13** H7
Windsor & Eton FC
WDSR SL4 .... **53** H3
Windsor Girls School
WDSR SL4 .... **12** C9
Windsor Hall
READ RG1 .... **59** L1
Windsor Leisure Centre
WDSR SL4 .... **12** F3
Windsor Royal Shopping
WDSR SL4 .... **13** J5
Winnersh Primary School
WWKG RG41 .... **61** K3
Winnersh Triangle Industrial Estate
WWKG RG41 .... **61** G2
Winterbourne House Clinic
RDGW/BURGH RG30 .... **8** A6
Winter Hill Golf Club
MDHD SL6 .... **20** B6
Wishmore Cross School
CHOB/PIR GU24 .... **91** L5
Witan International College
READ RG1 .... **9** K8
Wokefield Park Golf Club
THLE RG7 .... **144** C6
Wokingham Bowling Club
WWKG RG41 .... **14** E4
Wokingham Child Guidance Clinic
EWKG RG40 .... **14** E6
Wokingham CC
EWKG RG40 .... **14** E7
Wokingham Hospital
WWKG RG41 .... **14** D6
Wokingham Theatre
EWKG RG40 .... **14** E2
The Wolfenden Sports Centre
WHIT RG2 .... **59** K1
Woodcote House School
BFOR GU20 .... **90** B1
Woodcote Primary School
GOR/PANG RG8 .... **113** K9
Wooden Hill Primary School
BRAK RG12 .... **75** L4
Woodford Park Leisure Centre
WODY RG5 .... **46** D6
Woodlands Business Park
MDHD SL6 .... **35** J4
Woodlands Park CP School
MDHD SL6 .... **35** J5
Woodley CE Primary School
WODY RG5 .... **47** H6
Woodley Park Estate
WODY RG5 .... **46** D6
Woodside Business Park
WHIT RG2 .... **59** H7
Woolhampton CE Primary School
THLE RG7 .... **99** M2
World Business Centre Heathrow
HTHAIR TW6 .... **42** E8
Worton Grange Industrial Estate
WHIT RG2 .... **59** G6
Wraysbury Medical Centre
STWL/WRAY TW19 .... **54** F5
Wraysbury Primary School
STWL/WRAY TW19 .... **54** E5
The Wye Valley School
BNEND SL8 .... **20** D2
Yateley Common Country Park
YTLY GU46 .... **92** F3
Yateley Health Centre
YTLY GU46 .... **86** D8
Yateley Infant School
YTLY GU46 .... **86** D8
Yateley Manor School
YTLY GU46 .... **86** D7
Yateley School
YTLY GU46 .... **92** C1
Yattendon CE Primary School
NTHA RG18 .... **122** G12
Yeading FC
YEAD UB4 .... **43** L1
Yiewsley Health Centre
WDR/YW UB7 .... **42** A1
York Town Industrial Estate
CBLY GU15 .... **94** A1
Youngs Industrial Estate
THLE RG7 .... **142** B10

Acknowledgements

Schools address data provided by Education Direct.

Petrol station information supplied by Johnsons.

Garden centre information provided by:

Garden Centre Association Britains best garden centres

Wyevale Garden Centres

The statement on the front cover of this atlas is sourced, selected and quoted from a reader comment and feedback form received in 2004

Speed camera locations

Speed camera locations provided in association with RoadPilot Ltd

RoadPilot is the developer of one of the largest and most accurate databases of speed camera locations in the UK and Europe. It has provided the speed camera information in this atlas. RoadPilot is the UK's pioneer and market leader in GPS (Global Positioning System) road safety technologies.

microGo (pictured right) is RoadPilot's latest in-car speed camera location system. It improves road safety by alerting you to the location of accident black spots, fixed and mobile camera sites. RoadPilot's microGo does not jam police lasers and is therefore completely legal.

RoadPilot's database of fixed camera locations has been compiled with the full co-operation of regional police forces and the Safety Camera Partnerships.

For more information on RoadPilot's GPS road safety products, please visit **www.roadpilot.com** or telephone 0870 240 1701

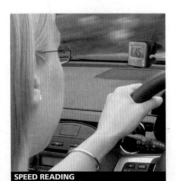

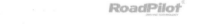

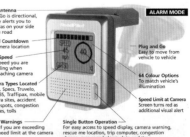